FAMILY LIFE NOW

Third Edition

Dave, my love for you is more than a memory. It's all of me.
The next time I hold you, I'm never letting go.

Sara Miller McCune founded SAGE Publishing in 1965 to support the dissemination of usable knowledge and educate a global community. SAGE publishes more than 1000 journals and over 600 new books each year, spanning a wide range of subject areas. Our growing selection of library products includes archives, data, case studies and video. SAGE remains majority owned by our founder and after her lifetime will become owned by a charitable trust that secures the company's continued independence.

Los Angeles | London | New Delhi | Singapore | Washington DC | Melbourne

FAMILY LIFE NOW

Third Edition

Kelly J. Welch
Kansas State University

Los Angeles | London | New Delhi
Singapore | Washington DC | Melbourne

FOR INFORMATION:

SAGE Publications, Inc.
2455 Teller Road
Thousand Oaks, California 91320
E-mail: order@sagepub.com

SAGE Publications Ltd.
1 Oliver's Yard
55 City Road
London EC1Y 1SP
United Kingdom

SAGE Publications India Pvt. Ltd.
B 1/I 1 Mohan Cooperative Industrial Area
Mathura Road, New Delhi 110 044
India

SAGE Publications Asia-Pacific Pte. Ltd.
18 Cross Street #10-10/11/12
China Square Central
Singapore 048423

Acquisitions Editor: Josh Perigo
Editorial Assistant: Lauren Younker
Content Development Editor: Alissa Nance
Production Editor: Rebecca Lee
Copy Editor: Diana Breti
Typesetter: C&M Digitals (P) Ltd.
Proofreader: Jeff Bryant
Indexer: Integra
Cover Designer: Janet Kiesel
Marketing Manager: Jennifer Jones

Printed in Canada

Library of Congress Cataloging-in-Publication Data

Names: Welch, Kelly, author.

Title: Family life now / Kelly J. Welch, Kansas State University.

Description: Third edition. | Los Angeles : SAGE, [2022] | Includes bibliographical references and index.

Identifiers: LCCN 2020040156 | ISBN 978-1-5443-7102-3 (paperback) | ISBN 978-1-5443-7103-0 | ISBN 978-1-5443-7104-7 (epub) | ISBN 978-1-5443-7105-4 (epub) | ISBN 978-1-5443-7106-1 (pdf)

Subjects: LCSH: Marriage. | Families. | Interpersonal relations.

Classification: LCC HQ734 .W43 2022 | DDC 306.85—dc23

LC record available at https://lccn.loc.gov/2020040156

This book is printed on acid-free paper.

21 22 23 24 25 10 9 8 7 6 5 4 3 2 1

/// BRIEF CONTENTS

/// DETAILED CONTENTS

FAMILY LIFE NOW: THE ENHANCED EXPERIENCE

Family Life Now provides students with a fresh, engaging, realistic, and academically informative introduction to the study of intimate relationships, marriages, and families. The third edition builds on the success of the first two editions and maintains its student-focused, conversational, down-to-earth tone. Comprehensive, contemporary, personally relevant, and relatable to today's diverse and complex individual, family, and societal issues, *Family Life Now* engages students through a balanced, integrated approach of the human development and family science disciplines. This text describes and promotes the ways in which those considering a helping profession career (such as social worker, therapist, psychologist, teacher, early childhood educator, child care provider, or health care provider) can employ strengths-oriented best practices to create and deliver effective, quality couple and family life education.

Family Life Now Is a Standout Experience

Traditionally, marriage and family books and courses adopt a sociological approach, a lens that emphasizes "the family" as a social institution and how this institution provides social stability. These books fall short of providing an in-depth understanding of individual development and how we develop our relational strengths and weaknesses within these systems. Traditional textbooks also often neglect the study of how development is influenced by the multiple processes that occur within the family system. By using a **family science** lens to understand today's couples and families, *Family Life Now* meets the needs of today's professionals by employing the scientific study of children, families, and close interpersonal relationships to gain a comprehensive understanding of the diversity of intimate partner and family living. In addition to social science research and theories, the third edition of *Family Life Now* implements the pillars of family science:

Relationship focused: An emphasis is placed on forming, strengthening, and maintaining healthy interpersonal relationships across the lifespan. Throughout the third edition, myriad couple and family experiences and processes are discussed at length.

Multi-disciplinary: There are many theoretical strengths and concepts found in other disciplines. All key aspects of the social sciences are drawn upon in a family science approach, and each chapter provides an exploration and investigation of major theoretical concepts.

Evidence based: When working with families and parents, family science professionals access research findings to develop and implement effective programs. This edition of *Family Life Now* provides substantially more attention to diversity, sexual orientation and identity experiences, and enhanced coverage of multicultural issues. Throughout the book, the research is significantly updated: Hundreds of current, relevant empirical studies and demographic trends are reported.

Strengths oriented: The core belief of family science is that all families have strengths. With this belief at the forefront, programs are designed and implemented that enable individuals and families to become self-sufficient. This book provides students with the understanding that *all* families have strengths, *all* families experience struggles, and that *all* families can learn to struggle well and to "do" relationships to their best capabilities.

Preventive: Rather than intervene after problems and difficulties crop up, the family science approach seeks to prevent problems through educational programs with individuals, couples, and families. Students are given an in-depth look at family science career opportunities, such as family life educator (FLE) and couple and family therapist (CFT). This book also provides a robust discussion about government policies that affect family living.

Applied: Professionals trained in the family science paradigm possess the knowledge and skills to apply research findings to effectively service all couples and families in today's diverse and global society. To this end, by synthesizing the chapter subject matter with family life educators' practice guidelines, each chapter concludes with a Family Life Education discussion that applies the content to the real world:

Chapter 1   Family Life Education: Strengthening Families

Chapter 2   Family Life Education: Creating, Implementing and Evaluating Effective Family Programming

Chapter 3   Family Life Education: Forging Family Strengths

Chapter 4   Family Life Education: Practicing With Sensitivity and Respecting Diversity

Chapter 5   Family Life Education: Valuing Diverse Couple Experiences

Chapter 6   Family Life Education: Relating to Others With Respect, Sincerity, and Responsibility

Chapter 7   Family Life Education: Using Reinforcing Strategies to Aid Couple Formation and Maintenance

Chapter 8   Family Life Education: Identifying Social and Cultural Influences Affecting the Marital Experience

Chapter 9   Family Life Education: Advancing Healthy Sexual Well-Being From a Value-Respectful Position

Chapter 10 Family Life Education: Fostering Healthy Family Formation

Chapter 11 Family Life Education: Guiding and Influencing a Child's Development

Chapter 12 Family Life Education: Understanding and Assisting Families' Decisions

Chapter 13 Family Life Education: Educating and Assisting Families Through Transition and Change

Chapter 14 Family Life Education: Protecting Children's and Adults' Well-Being

Chapter 15 Family Life Education: Providing Knowledge and Skills

Chapter 16 Family Life Education: Removing Barriers and Assisting in Transitions

GLOBAL FEATURES

Family Life Now is intentionally written in a compelling, first-person voice that draws students into the conversation. Perhaps one of its greatest distinguishing features is that it is written *to* students and *for* them—not *at* them. To provide a rich, minds-on, applied learning experience for students, each chapter begins with a **chapter opener:** stories from my experiences in couple and family living and real-life stories shared by college students. Discussions in each chapter also include the five pillars of family science, and chapters close with an application of the subject matter. Each chapter also includes sound pedagogy to engage students with the content and to enhance their learning experiences:

- **Learning Objectives:** Introducing each chapter, the learning objectives can be used as learning targets or they can be rephrased to be used as essential questions. These are a great tool for students to check their understanding of the chapter subject matter.
- **Family Life Now:** In this feature a contemporary issue is introduced, and each side of the matter is discussed with supporting research. Students are then asked to form their

own informed opinion. This can be used for debate topics in class or online. Students' responses are insightful and thought provoking, and they lead to discussions of other topics and issues.

- **Taking Sides:** A favorite of students, this feature describes, from both sides, a relationship dilemma that is commonly experienced by families and couples.
- **Summaries:** Each chapter concludes with a summary of the content, and these points are tied directly to the Learning Objectives introduced in the beginning.
- **Key Terms** and **Glossary:** Not only do the key terms in boldface and the glossary of key terms give students an accurate source for definitions, they are essential for helping students to acquire the vocabulary of the discipline.

WHAT'S NEW IN THE THIRD EDITION

One of the things that makes the study of couple and family living so challenging is the rapidly changing nature of these experiences and the diversity that accompanies them. The changes in the experiences of individuals, couples, and families in our culture are happening so swiftly that there is sometimes a lag between people's experiences and research. Every effort has been made to bring you the most relevant, current information, and I think that you will find that this book provides the most thorough, comprehensive, and racially/ethnically sensitive material available today. Global changes, enhancements, and additions include the following:

- All chapters have been substantially updated with the newest available research.
- Trends and demographics have been updated.
- Diversity coverage has been significantly expanded and updated, and the concept of **intersectionality** is woven throughout.
- Revised and enhanced coverage of racial and ethnic experiences are discussed in each chapter, including new discussions regarding **undocumented individuals** and their families.
- There is new material on **social networking** and its impact on mate selection, dating experiences, jealousy, and breaking up.
- Extensive sexual orientation and sexual identity coverage has been added, including expanded and updated discussions about **LGBTQ+ families of choice**, **lesbian co-mothering**, **transgenderism**, **androgyny**, **LGBTQ+ dating scripts**, and **gender-based violence**, including intimate partner and dating violence experienced by LGBTQ+ individuals.
- New content about **mixed-orientation** relationships and marriages has been added.
- A **nonheteronormative** approach to pregnancy and childbirth introduces the term **gestational parent.**
- Discussion regarding the **Equal Rights Amendment** and the **Violence Against Women Act** has been added.
- The **COVID-19 pandemic** and its resulting stressors, including unemployment and the severe economic downturn in the United States, are discussed.
- An expanded, enhanced discussion about the burden of **student loan debt** and the effects on individual, couple, and family experiences has been added.

DIGITAL RESOURCES

This text includes an array of instructor teaching materials designed to save you time and to help you keep students engaged. To learn more, visit **sagepub.com** or contact your SAGE representative at **sagepub.com/findmyrep.**

A NOTE TO STUDENTS

Often, students ask me what leads me to teach, research, and write about marriages, families, and intimate relationships—and it's always a tough question to answer because there are so many reasons! I suppose the short answer to "why" I do what I do is because, to me, our families and our intimate partners are our foundation: They are our source for being nurtured and loved, and they are of the utmost importance in our lives. While it is safe to say that all families are far from perfect and have room for improvement (mine included!), our families—whether they are families created by couples or they are families of choice—are usually there for us when the rest of the world is not. And, however each of us experiences family and intimate relationships, most of us want to be supportive, active participants.

But our families also serve as models for learning to love and to be intimate. In many, many ways, the family that a person is raised in sets the stage for a person's relational future. How *do* we learn to love? To communicate? To resolve conflict? To be sexual? And, if our family life isn't/wasn't healthy, are we doomed to failure in our future relationships? I am passionate about what I do because I want to empower and equip you to "do" family and intimate relationships to the best of your capabilities. I consider it an *honor* and a *privilege* to be able to help you learn about this important area of study—a subject that affects your everyday life.

There are so many issues that intimate partners and families face today. Before I began to write this third edition, I spent a lot of time talking to my students and reading their e-mails so I could get to the heart of what *students really want to know*. As I write this, our nation is in isolation, locked away from others because of the pandemic COVID-19 virus. The full impact of this virus won't be known for some time: How will the 33 million U.S. citizens who lost their jobs financially rebound? Will they? Did the incidents of domestic violence, intimate partner violence, and child abuse increase due to the stressors associated with being home? How many individuals returned to addictions to help them cope? What will be the impact of a lost semester of school? My students are concerned not only about their families (Will my parents have to file bankruptcy? Will we lose our home? Will my dad get his job back?), but also themselves (Will I be able to graduate on time? Will I be able to complete my internship? Will I be able to get a job after I graduate?). Add these worries to those that students had before the pandemic, such as wondering how to deal with past and/or present effects of intimate partner violence, and the questions they had about sex. *All* of these are very real concerns, and each has the potential to severely impact individual and family health and well-being.

In this edition, I have included a lot of personal stories and stories from students. I've worked really hard to listen to what *students* want to learn and know so that I can bring you the most current, up-to-date research to guide you through your exploration of intimate and family life. It is my sincerest hope that you see yourself somewhere among the pages of this book. I think you'll find that this textbook is just what you are looking for—it's *real*, it's *transparent*, and it's *relevant* to your life.

As you work your way through this text, you may have questions or opinions you'd like to share with me. Please feel free to e-mail me your thoughts at drkellywelch@gmail.com. I look forward to hearing from you!

Your professor, instructor, and I are partners. With this book and their guidance, instruction, and care, you are sure to come away with the knowledge that allows you to enjoy rich and satisfying intimate and family relationships. Now, let's roll up our sleeves and get busy!

A NOTE TO INSTRUCTORS

It's been said that if knowledge is power, then enthusiasm pulls the switch—and I bring this third edition of *Family Life Now* to you with much enthusiasm!

As I began to research and write this third edition, I spent a great deal of time talking with students, colleagues, and even friends, to try to get to the heart of what people *want* and what they *need* today in a book that addresses marriage, family, and intimate relationship experiences. But, as I was writing this revision, my life as I knew it was seemingly destroyed. My husband of 37 years went to run a quick errand—and that was the last time I saw him. He suffered from early onset dementia and didn't return from his errand. He was missing for 7 weeks. Gone. Just gone. There I was—suddenly finding myself navigating a horrific, terror-filled, unimaginable experience (a missing loved one), an experience for which there is no social template, no script about how to handle everything that accompanied the situation (Just who *does* pick up his dental records?). It felt as though I had lost everything that I read about, write about, and teach about for a living. I *knew* and *understood* the workings of a family crisis, but despite this knowledge I felt helpless and lost. I *knew* and *understood* the systems nature of family living, yet the instability in my family was so confusing. Too many times to count, it seemed as though I was making things up as I went. And somewhere along that turbulent path, I thought, "How do people with no knowledge of intimate and family relationships do this? I've got any number of colleagues I can turn to, *where do people go who don't have immediate access to helping professionals? How do people even know where to start?*" During that 7-week period and in the subsequent days, weeks, and months after he was found deceased, there were times his loss felt truly unsurvivable. It wasn't "How do I make it through this day?" It was "How do I make it through this minute?"

But as time passed, I was again reminded that what we do as family practitioners and educators *really is life changing*—and so greatly needed in our hectic, uncertain, stress-filled society today. As difficult as life has been since his death, and as difficult as it has been to rebuild a life without him, the experiences have deepened the passion I have to educate and to inform others about how to "do" family to the best of their capabilities. And I have brought this passion to this textbook.

Having taught more than 35,000 undergraduate students in human development, sexuality, marriage, and family classes, I know from personal experience that teaching is a demanding and often daunting task—especially more so now that we are doing our best to educate our students in the midst of the COVID-19 pandemic. Adding to this stress, in our field we are confronted with the difficulty that much of what we teach is value-laden and sometimes politically polarizing. From heterosexuality to LGBTQ, to sex inside and outside of marriage, to dating and cohabitation, to marriage and divorce, as instructors we are challenged to teach the material with balanced and equitable viewpoints so that we don't alienate any student and so they can come away with the "best of the best." Adding to this challenge, our students today must often at once cope with the demands of school and unprecedented stressors, such as experiencing the loss of a family home or the inability to get financial aid because of the recent economic downturn experienced in the Unites States. So, how do we best reach and teach them?

As you thumb through the pages of this book, I think you'll find a voice that is simultaneously informative and rigorous, humorous and entertaining, and always compassionate and heartfelt. I bring you and your students the most current, relevant information about the social and emotional aspects of relational and intimate living, and I present a candid, sensitive, inclusive, nonjudgmental balance of theory and "real life." The contemporary research in this book is accompanied by practical, minds-on, hearts-on activities that make your students feel comfortable and safe talking about everything from dating, to sex, to intimate partner violence. It is my hope that you find this to be a natural partner to your course and that your students discover a resource to help them make informed decisions about their personal and family relationships.

As students begin their process of discovery, they will notice a prominent theme woven throughout this text: We are all, as relational people, products of our intergenerational families of origin. Indeed, we do not develop our relationship capacities in isolation! From love, to intimacy, to communication, to our experiences of sexuality, even to the experiences of divorce, this text shows students how we affect and are affected by those in our environments—both at family and societal levels.

This book adopts the **Family Life Education** framework to examine marriages, families, and intimate relationships. Throughout the text, theories from the fields of sociology, family studies, psychology, lifespan human development, and other social sciences are integrated, making this text applicable to students' everyday lives. I am proud to deliver to you a textbook that provides to you and your students a relevant, realistic approach to understanding intimate and family life. *Thank you* for entrusting your students to me. I look forward to partnering with you to provide a life-changing course for them.

All my best to you,
Kelly

Years ago, I overheard one of my son's phone conversations with a friend. He had been asked by the friend if we could all go out to dinner, and I heard him reply, "No, we can't. We're writing my mom's book." *We're* writing—truer words have never been spoken because I certainly didn't accomplish this on my own! There are so very many people who deserve to be recognized—and praised!—for their roles in helping to launch this book. I am especially moved as I express my gratitude, because after the death of my husband I was paralyzed by change and uncertainty—I didn't think I'd ever be able to write or to teach again. But with the help of so many, you moved me from fear to confidence, from uncertainty to purpose, from hopelessness to gratitude. *Thank you* for your outpouring of care and concern and for working together to make this a superb third edition.

THIRD EDITION REVIEWERS

Often, reviewers are the last group to be thanked in the writing process. I acknowledge them first because *without them, this book would not exist.* Although I have never met them, I owe them a *tremendous* amount of gratitude and many, many thanks for the insight, direction, and suggestions they provided. Their comments gave me clear direction and focus and guided me in making sure that all students who hold this book in their hands see themselves and their experiences somewhere in the pages. I especially thank Tina Marie Johnson and her student at the University of Louisville for their suggestions regarding gender experiences in contemporary society. Thank you also to the following:

Angie Andrus, Fullerton College

Rachel Arocho, Utah Valley University

Rhonda R. Buckley, Texas Woman's University

Stacey L. Callaway, Rowan University

Ian H. Cameron, University of Maine

Gary Dick, University of Cincinnati

C. Ryan Dunn, Weber State University

Jacob A. Esplin, The University of Southern Mississippi

Jill Gomez, UC Clermont College

Victor William Harris, University of Florida

Kim A. Horejs, Truckee Meadows Community College.

Daniel Hubler, Weber State University

Mark O. Jarvis, Salt Lake Community College

Melanie Evans Keyes, Eastern Connecticut State University

Karl Morgan, Kansas State University

Lisa Moyer, Auburn University

Julie K. Nelson, Utah Valley University

Timothy Phoenix Oblad, Texas A&M University–Kingsville

COLLEAGUES MORE PRECIOUS THAN TREASURES

I first and foremost wish to thank Dr. Rick Scheidt, professor of Family Studies and Human Services, Kansas State University. Without his rock-solid friendship and presence in my life and his confidence in my ability to bounce back, I'm not certain where I would be in my rebuilding journey. Rick, thank you for helping me to confront the reality of my situation and for helping me to always see beyond "tomorrow." Friends such as you are truly one of this life's most precious treasures.

I'd also like to thank my colleague Dr. Vic Harris, associate professor in the Department of Family, Youth, and Community Sciences, University of Florida. You share my passion and commitment to families and their health and well-being, and I cannot wait to see where our teaming up takes us! It is a privilege to call you "friend." And Dr. Dan Hubler, associate professor in the Department of Child and Family Studies, Weber State University, although we have never met face to face, I so greatly appreciate your selfless sharing of ideas, guidance, and insight with this new edition. Your direction has been priceless. Thank you!

I am also very appreciative and grateful to my mentors at Kansas State University:

- Dr. Ginny Moxley, former dean of the College of Human Ecology
- Dr. Morey MacDonald, past chair, School of Family Studies & Human Services
- Dr. Pat Bosco, retired vice president for student life
- Nancy Forsyth, SVP Sales and Services Learning & Development, North American Higher Education at Pearson (you changed my life and the lives of my children . . . thank you!)
- Sharon Geary, who encouraged me very early on in my writing career to focus on the words, the meanings, the pedagogy, and the learning. Those words are framed and have a permanent place in my office.

Each of you walked me through some very, very difficult days. Without your support, guidance, flexibility, and frequent yes-you-can words of encouragement, I think a part of me would have died with my husband. But because of your belief in me, you refused to let that happen. *Thank you.* I love you.

THE FOLKS AT SAGE

I am so richly blessed to be able to work with this remarkable group of people! I don't know how to thank Joshua Perigo, acquisitions editor for Family Sciences. Josh, you shared my vision to create a powerful and relevant tool that not only educates students, but also gives them a realistic approach on ways to successfully navigate and tackle the "everythings" that come with intimate relationships. No matter the obstacle in this process, with your calm, steady, and unflappable demeanor, you kept this project (and me) on course. You are, and will always be, a friend. Thank you for not listening to my first round of "no's." Alissa Nance, associate content developmental editor, you shepherded this book from start to finish, and your expertise knows no bounds! You have a remarkable talent and ability to massage the text to ensure that I was conveying what I really wanted to say. Thank you for pushing back when needed and for stepping back and stepping up when needed. It was truly a pleasure to work with you, and I look forward to future projects. You. Are. Amazing. I am also grateful to Lauren Younker, editorial assistant, who worked so diligently in preparing the manuscript for production. Your attention to detail is second to none! Finally, I owe a world of gratitude to Jeff Lasser, publisher for sociology titles. Jeff, it was your belief in me nearly 20 years ago that set me on the path to developing and writing textbooks. I'll never understand what you saw in me, and as I sit here remembering that first conversation we had about your vision for a relationship book, I still shake my head in disbelief that your dream came to fruition and that I was a part of that dream—and that writing textbooks is a part of my life today. You are a true and cherished friend. Thank you for believing in me, then and now.

TO THOSE CLOSER TO HOME

First, I have to thank my students. *You* are the reason I do this every day. You breathe life and energy into me. You make me look forward to coming to campus every day. You laugh at my stupid jokes and encourage the frustrated comedian within me. You put up with my crazy schedule as I prepared this manuscript. You found a path around the piles of research papers on the floor around my desk. And always, always, you turn my day around when you smile and say, "Hey Dr. Dub, what's up?!" I hope you know how much I truly love you.

Finally, I could not have written this book without my family and friends. They alone know the countless sacrifices they made:

- My Guys and Gals: Eric and Gretchen, Shawn and Lindsey, Dan and Kateland, and Kyle and Laura. Educators. Mentors. Servants to those in despair. Missionaries. Entrepreneurs. Adventurers. One of the most awesome things about being a parent is learning things from your kids. Eric, you taught me that love endures all things. Shawn, you taught me that that gentleness and tenderness are compassionate lenses and this is the way to view others' limitations. Danny, you taught me that no matter what, *laughter and joy* will carry us through. Always! Kyle, you taught me that silence is strength. Guys and gals, only you know the pain and torment this family has endured. No matter what happened, though, we never stopped loving. And that is the greatest legacy your dad could have given you.

- My siblings and their spouses: Terri and Pete, Tim and Michele, and Dan and Roxanne. You loved me through my worst, and I love and cherish you all.

- BreAnn: I'm so proud of you. So. Very. Very. Proud. Of. You. (hearts and more hearts)

Again, I sincerely hope that you enjoy reading and teaching from this book. I've worked so diligently to try to incorporate everything on your wish lists, and I have given my best to ensure that issues facing us all today are included. At the end of the day, I hope that students are presented a realistic picture of intimate and family life today and that they hold in their hands a book that is relevant to their lives. My very best to you!

Kelly

Kelly J. Welch, PhD, CFLE, has vast experience as a human development and family science professor, author, researcher, program developer, and practitioner. An award-winning teaching professor, Dr. Welch's primary areas of research, writing, and practice include lifespan development, the formation and maintenance of interpersonal relationships, family processes across the lifespan, family crisis and change, and human sexuality across the life course. She has developed programming for individuals and families who are navigating medical crises, as well as programming for sexual and reproductive health. After 20+ years at Kansas State University as an associate professor of teaching in Human Development and Family Science, feeling a social responsibility to help empower and improve the lives of others, Dr. Welch recently transitioned to teaching Early Childhood Education courses in impoverished, diverse, at-risk public schools in Kansas; these schools often experience high rates of violent incidents and experience high teen pregnancy and sexually transmitted infection rates. Through creative, innovative programming, Dr. Welch seeks to bring parenting education to those who often need it the most but have little or no access to it. She hopes to begin to break intergenerational poverty in pockets of Kansas by equipping high school students, high school drop outs, and adult learners with the education needed to obtain the Child Development Associate certification through hands-on experiences in early childhood education centers, giving learners a solid footing to earn sustainable wages. Dr. Welch spends her summers volunteering in HIV clinics in the Caribbean, working with HIV+ mothers and their infants.

iStock.com/ kate_sept2004

1

FAMILY LIFE NOW

LEARNING OBJECTIVES

1.1 Examine the characteristics of marriage in a global society and how generational views differ regarding the function of marriages and families.

1.2 Describe the landscape and trends of various family structures in the U.S. today.

1.3 Summarize the similarities and differences between contemporary families.

1.4 Explain the ways in which societies and cultures influence the experiences of marriage and family life.

1.5 Assess the ways in which family practitioners and other helping professionals work to assist families to develop their full potential.

It has been nearly 39 years since my wedding day, and I remember it as if it happened yesterday—the dusting of snow on the ground, friends I knew I would never lose touch with, the tears in my mother's eyes, my husband-to-be's locked gaze on mine. And my father's words have stayed with me, spoken just seconds before we took that first step toward my chosen life mate: "When you take your first step down the aisle, you must do so as if the word 'divorce' does not exist—you must enter this marriage knowing that divorce is a possibility, but something that should be your very last resort. Because after today, I can guarantee you that along with the happiness and joy you are feeling at this very moment, marriage will bring with it sorrow. There will be heartbreak. There will be tragedy. There will be financial difficulties. Before I walk you down the aisle, you must know in your heart that marriage—and everything that comes with it—is truly what you want." I didn't fully understand then that marriage is beautiful and terrible things.

Characterizing couple relationships, marriage, and family life is a tall order. My youngest son once asked me, "Mom, why do you need to teach a class about families? Doesn't everyone have one?" He had no idea how complicated and lengthy my response would be! Intimate relationships, marriage, and family are a complex web of interwoven influences: intimacy, gender and gender roles, sex, childbearing and parenting, family conflict, divorce and remarriage, family stress, family distress, family communication patterns, dual careers, work/family conflicts, finances, and a wide array of realistic and not-so-realistic expectations. In addition to this potentially endless list of influences, we all experience family life from a different perspective: Each of us is an expert in our own interpretations and experiences of "family" and other intimate relationships. Because of these experiences, we often take our first steps into a serious intimate relationship thinking we *know* everything that comes with a commitment to a life partner.

But realistically speaking, none of us is equipped to tackle the "everything" that comes with coupling, marriage, and other intimate relationships. Parents may argue; they may experience financial hardship or the loss of a pregnancy; parents or children may become ill; sex may be less than ideal; and in-laws may be a point of contention. Couples may disagree about who should get the children off to school or daycare, or they may have difficulty getting used to each other's sometimes-annoying habits. In the course of a relationship, we may experience infidelity or family or partner violence. Events outside of our control, such as being deployed to a military zone overseas or falling victim to a national economic crisis, may forever shake our sense of reality. We change. Our partners change. Families change. We grow. Maybe together, maybe apart. And the "everything" we have in our relationships is different from what we expected.

WHAT IS MARRIAGE?

Our intimate relationships, marriages, families, and individual lives within the context of family are integral facets of who we are. Most of us don't need a course in family life to enable us to be active family members. Some students taking this course do so because they hope to pursue careers in family services or policy, family therapy, ministry, or family education. Other students take this course because they want to deepen their understanding of the workings of family so that they may someday enjoy fulfilling, gratifying, and rewarding relationships of their own. Is it really possible to prepare for relationship life and family life? Is it possible, for example, to "divorce-proof" a marriage, or to understand how and why people communicate the way they do? If it seems our parents' relationship is in a crisis, or if a sibling is causing parents undue stress, does our understanding of the science of family life make a difference?

Your instructor and I are privileged to help you gain an understanding of how you affect and are affected by the intimate relationships in your life and to help you better understand the dynamics of your family life. By pointing you toward a path along which you make your own discoveries, we are helping you to gain insight into the intricacies of family life and intimate life. We begin our intriguing study of contemporary family life and intimate relationships by first gaining an understanding of the different facets of marriage. This discussion is followed by an examination of the composition of today's families.

Marriage in a Global Society

Marriage includes religious, legal, and social aspects, and people worldwide experience marriage and family differently. To some, marriage is only a piece of paper that has no significance or importance to the relationship. To others, marriage is believed to be a social union, wherein the partners declare a commitment to one another. And to others, marriage is a religious, holy, consecrated act.

Understanding Marriage as a Social or Civil Union

A social union—often referred to as a civil union—is a legal term that speaks to the commitment, or the marriage contract, made by the partners. In the United States, marriage is a union that is legally allowed between heterosexual couples or homosexual couples. In 2004, one state had legalized same-sex marriage, but in June 2015, the United States Supreme Court struck down all state bans on same-sex marriage, legalizing it in all 50 states. The decision also required that all states honor out-of-state same-sex marriage licenses. This social/civil union carries with it binding, legal obligations. Although the term *civil union* was once more commonly associated with same-sex partners who desired to socially declare their commitment to one another, the term is still used worldwide to acknowledge the legal status of marriages.

Social union: a legal relationship between two people that provides legal protections to the couple at the state level.

Students often ask me why couples need a piece of paper (a marriage license) in order for their state to recognize their union. According to the U.S. Supreme Court (1888), American marriage is defined as a *legally* recognized social union—a *legal* and binding civil contract that is thought to be permanent—between adults who meet the specified *legal* age requirements, and who are otherwise not *legally* married to another individual. And a marriage is not considered *legal* unless the couple obtains a government-issued marriage license. Thus, couples need a marriage license because, within the United States, marriage is a *legal* commitment, not a private bond between people.

Marriage is also a legal contract between the couple and the state in which the couple resides. The instant the couple says "I do," and the wedding officiate pronounces them to be wed, their relationship acquires legal status. As the Supreme Court observed in 1888, "The relation once formed, the law steps in and holds the parties to various obligations and liabilities."

Many of you may someday choose a marriage partner based on love and intimacy, your shared values and principles, and a desire for a similar lifestyle. Or, perhaps after completion of your studies, you will return to your home country where your life mate will be (or has already been) chosen for you. As you begin your study of couples, marriage, and family

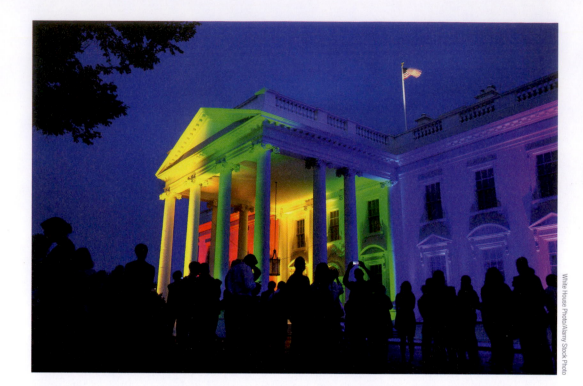

Marriage is a social or civil union, and it is a legal contract between spouses. In 2015, the U.S. Supreme Court legalized same-sex marriage in all 50 states. This ruling qualifies all married persons to receive the benefits of marriage, such as social security, tax, and veteran/military benefits.

life, it is important to keep in mind that marriages across cultures do not necessarily follow the Western process of selecting a life mate. In parts of the world today, for instance, child brides, charity marriages (*sadaqa*), and forced marriages are commonplace social unions (Saad, 2002).

Child marriage is not specific to any one religion, culture, or ethnicity, and it occurs in regions across the globe. South Asia and Sub-Saharan Africa have the highest rates of child marriage. In India, 15.5 million women aged 20 to 24 are married before the age of 18, making it the country with the highest number of child marriages (Ministry of Health and Family Welfare, 2016). Niger has the highest rate of child marriage, with 76% of girls married before their 18th birthday (Institut National de la Statistique, 2013). These marriages occur for a variety of reasons, including poverty, gender norms, and lack of education (Girls Not Brides, 2020). Girls may be married off to relative strangers or even to family members. For example, in Bedouin communities in Egypt, some girls are forced to marry their paternal cousins. The Amhara people of Ethiopia negotiate marriages between two families, with a civil ceremony following to seal the contract. In Somalia, a man becomes engaged to the woman before she is even born. He makes the marriage arrangements with the expectant parents, to whom gifts are given to seal the marital rights. And in the United States, people often chose their future mates based on love or other interpersonal attraction reasons, without necessarily seeking their parents' approval.

Understanding the Social and Economic Aspects of Marriage. Marriage is an important social institution, or structure, and serves society on several levels. The structure of the 17th-century American family in Colonial Williamsburg protected the aristocratic family's wealth and political power; at the same time, the common family structure provided efficient production units for lower-class families, such as planters (farmers) and shopkeepers. It was within the family that children were educated and received religious instruction. It was also within the family that the elderly and disabled were cared for. Thus, the family was *the* basic political, religious, social, and economic unit of colonial living. Even today in contemporary America, the family is foundational to many levels of society. David Popenoe and Barbara Dafoe Whitehead, co-founders of the National Marriage Project, maintain that the marital union is the "social glue," the "fundamental social institution that contributes to the physical, emotional, and economic health of men, women, and children—and thus to the nation as a whole" (2002, p. 4).

In addition to forming a social union, many couples form an economic partnership by sharing economic resources such as bank and investment accounts, property, and cars. Each time a marriage takes place—whether heterosexual or same-sex—the new social unit takes on certain financial responsibilities that are necessary for the society's survival, such as rearing and socializing children either born or brought into the relationship (such as by foster parenting or adoption). We explore the economics of marriage at length in Chapter 12.

Marriage as a Religious Act. In the Christian, Islamic, Hindu dharma, and Jewish religions, marriage is considered to be divinely ordained, a sacred, religious act not to be entered into lightly. In these religions, marriage is viewed as a lifelong commitment between a woman and a man. Within these religious communities, the sacrament or act of marriage is believed to be the strongest of all social bonds around which the rest of society is organized. This bond, in turn, "initiates the new generations into the culture and traditions and facilitates further evolution of their civilization. It is the link that joins the past with the present and with the future in such a way that social transition and change can take place through a healthy and stable process" (Saad, 2002, p. 13). In Chapter 8, we'll examine the aspects of marriage as a religious commitment and sacred act.

Across the world, marriage is experienced as a civil union, a sacred act, a legal partnership or a social and/or economic union. There are also variations in marital types, such as monogamy and polygamy.

Marital Types. Marriages across the world are typically classified as either monogamous or polygamous. **Monogamy**, the legal structure of marriage recognized in the United States and in other Western civilizations, is a dyadic (two-person) form of marriage that involves the practice of having only one sexual partner. The sex partner reciprocates this exclusivity to his or her marital partner. The word *monogamy* refers solely to sexual exclusivity to one partner, but in the context of marriage there is also an expectation of exclusivity of emotional fidelity and love. **Monogamism** is the belief that monogamy is the only true morally and socially appropriate type of marriage or love relationship.

In some non-Western cultures, exclusivity is not a right of marriage. Today, **polygamy**, the practice of having more than one marriage partner, is the more widely practiced form of marriage across the world, particularly in those regions where the Islamic faith dominates the culture. Generally, polygamy is a form of plural marriage wherein either multiple wives or multiple husbands exist. The practice is usually passed down from generation to generation, and has existed throughout the recordings of history. In the biblical Old Testament, for instance, Abraham, David, and Solomon (who had 700 wives and 300 concubines, or mistresses) practiced polygamy. Likewise, in the 1500s, Martin Luther tolerated polygamy in instances where he believed the practice would "ensure the success of the Reformation" (Stack, 1998, p. 2).

Polygyny is one form of polygamy or plural marriage, and involves the practice of a man having multiple wives at the same time. In the Islamic faith, polygyny is permitted by the Quran (Koran), and its practice is commonplace, with certain limitations. The popular television series *Sister Wives* depicts the daily lives of four women who are "married" to the same man. This family belongs to a nonconformist sect of Mormons. In a polygynous marriage, a woman is simultaneously the sister and co-wife of another. Along with small pockets of nonconformist Mormons who practice polygyny in the United States, many Native American tribes allow the practice of polygyny. In his essay on the practical aspects of polygamy, polygamist Samuel Chapman denotes the benefits of plural marriages for women, citing, among other things, the availability of built-in childcare, the lack of pressure that husbands may feel to commit adultery, and the availability of a female friend for life.

Monogamy:
a dyadic (two-person) form of marriage that involves the practice of having only one sexual partner.

Monogamism:
the belief that monogamy is the only true morally and socially appropriate type of marriage or love relationship.

Polygamy:
the practice of having more than one marriage partner.

Polygyny:
the practice of a man having multiple wives at the same time.

Although the practice of having more than one marriage partner was banned by the Mormon church in the late 1880s, today some nonconformist segments of the church still practice polygamy.

Why would a woman choose to live in a relationship with multiple wives? Why would a woman choose to emotionally, physically, and sexually share her husband with other women? Mary Ben David (2005) notes that many benefits of her polygamous marriage, particularly in the areas of shared housekeeping, cooking, and childcare. She furthers notes that with several women in her home, her identity "cannot be wrapped up in her husband's identity."

Polyandry:
the practice of a woman having multiple husbands at the same time.

Polyandry is another form of polygamy in which women have multiple husbands at the same time. Researchers have identified 53 societies that permit polyandrous unions, and they note that although polyandry is rare, it is common in egalitarian (classless) societies (Starkweather & Hames, 2012). These husbands are typically brothers. In polyandrous relationships, the woman mates with more than one male. This is a rare sexual mating system, even in the animal kingdom. Polyandry is a common practice among families in Tibet, where it is considered a wealth-conserving kinship mechanism (Goldstein, 1987/2002). According to anthropologist Melvin Goldstein, polyandry is practiced as a means of preventing or prohibiting the family's estate from being divided too many ways and thereby diminishing the family's overall wealth. When brothers share a wife, it is seen as the means by which the family's quality of life is sustained and the way to maximize economic advantage, generation to generation.

Cenogamy:
a form of marriage often referred to as "group marriage," in which every man and woman is married to each other at the same time.

Cenogamy is a form of marriage often referred to as "group marriage." In this type of marital community, every man and every woman is married to each other at the same time. This form of marriage allows casual, indiscriminate sexual activity among all its members. Today, the practice of cenogamy is most often found in communal living—when a group of people live together and share property and resources—such as in tribal cultures. This form of marriage is not legal in the United States.

Now that you have a good understanding of the historical and legal definitions of marriage and family, let's take a look at how people view couple relationships and marriage today.

Understanding Couple Relationships: Shifting Views

Our attitudes and beliefs about coupling, marriage, parenting, and family life are largely shaped by the society in which we live. Several distinct generations comprise the demographic fabric of the United States. Not surprisingly, each generation's attitudes, behaviors, and lifestyles form the underpinnings of their approaches to intimate and family relationships.

The Silent Generation. Born between 1928 and 1945, the silent generation is often referred to as "traditionalists." Many fought in the Korean and Vietnam wars in an era of conformity. Although this generation ushered in the Civil Rights movement in 1964 and brought to light issues of racism and other issues of inequality, by and large they conformed to the traditional views of marriage, family, and divorce. Commonly, divorce wasn't viewed as a realistic option (Goldberg Jones, 2018).

Baby Boomers. Boomers were born between 1946 and 1965. This rebellious drug, sex, and rock and roll generation welcomed resistance to the established values and norms in U.S. culture. Pushing the traditional boundaries of the silent generation, this "Me generation" caused great cultural change by putting individual needs ahead of marriage and family needs. Baby Boomers emphasized climbing the career ladder over the importance of family. Living together before marriage increased. Because couples devoted more time to career success than to marriage and family, divorce increased. Women poured into the workforce, creating an increase in dual-income households. Birth control options freed women to dictate their fertility and childbearing. Still today, Baby Boomers divorce more than any other age group (Goldberg Jones, 2018).

Generation X. Generation X, or Gen Exers, were born between 1965 and 1980. Because Boomers experienced such high divorce rates, Gen X was the first generation to have divorced parents as a common experience. They were also the first generation to commonly experience stepfamily living. Interestingly, Gen Exers reacted to their parents' divorces by staying married for much longer and at much higher rates than their parents (Goldberg Jones, 2018).

Millennials. Born between 1981 and 1996, Millennials are blamed for just about all of society's problems—from killing shopping malls and bars of soap to dinner dates and straws. But unlike the generations before them, Millennials not only put off marriage longer, they're opting to start families before marriage or forgo marriage all together. Their views on established gender roles are also impacting society's traditional views on the meaning of "male" and "female" (Goldberg Jones, 2018).

Generation Z. Generation Z, or the "iGeneration," are those born after 1997. It's still too early to know how Generation Z will shape our society's views on couple relationships, marriage, and family. But one thing is for certain: Given the sway of technology on how people communicate and relate to one another, it will be interesting to see how the "*i* everything" impacts intimate and marital relationships and parenting practices. Just as the television changed Boomers' connections to their world, so, too, will technology change lifestyles and relationships (Dimock, 2019).

Just as there are differences in how we can experience marriage, there are also differences in how each of us defines and experiences family.

WHAT IS FAMILY?

What is "family?" How do you define it? In all likelihood, your definition may be entirely different from the federal government's definition, or from mine. The reason for these differences is that my definition and your definition of family are based on our *unique experiences within our own families.* Throughout this book, I will be sharing some of my family life experiences with you as I ask you to explore aspects of your family life that have helped shape who you are. Your professor or instructor may also share stories of family life, as may your classmates. As you exchange stories, you might find that you share similar family experiences. Most likely, you will have some experiences that are vastly different from any you have heard or read about.

According to the United States Census Bureau (2019e), a **family** "is a group of two people or more (one of whom is the householder) related by birth, marriage, or adoption and residing together; all such people (including related subfamily members) are considered as members of one family." On the other hand, a **household** "consists of all the people who occupy a housing unit. A household includes the related family members and all the unrelated people, if any, such as lodgers, foster children, wards, or employees who share the housing unit. A person living alone in a housing unit, or a group of unrelated people sharing a housing unit such as partners or roomers, is also counted as a household." Thus, according to the federal government, a married couple and their children are considered to be a family, whereas intimate couples who live together who are not married make up a household. In nearly all societies the world over, the family is the social unit that is responsible for nurturing, protecting, educating, and socializing children (Barbour, Barbour, & Scully, 2005). Figure 1.1 illustrates for us the types of households in the United States (U.S. Census Bureau, 2019b). As you can see, nearly three-fourths (72 percent) of all households today are married-couple families, but there is great diversity in family forms (U.S. Census Bureau, 2019b). It's interesting to observe that nearly 13 percent of families today classify themselves as "other nonfamily households." A **nonfamily household** consists of a householder living alone, such as a widow, or a householder sharing the home with people to whom she/he is not related, such as a widow sharing her home with two friends. Not only has the distribution of households shifted over time, so too has the size of U.S. households. For example, in 1970 the average household size was 3.14, whereas today it is 2.53.

The question arises, then, whether it is possible to arrive at a one-size-fits-all definition of "family," as the U.S. Census Bureau describes. Probably not, for there exist as many definitions or descriptions of "family" as there are students who are reading this textbook, and more. The concept of family is, indeed, a subjective notion.

Figure 1.1 /// Types of Households in the United States

Today, there is no such thing as a "traditional" family form in the United States. There is great diversity in the configurations of households.

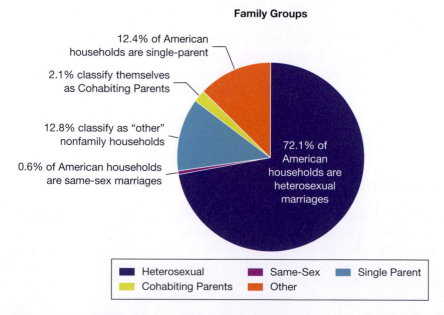

Family Groups

- 12.4% of American households are single-parent
- 2.1% classify themselves as Cohabiting Parents
- 12.8% classify as "other" nonfamily households
- 0.6% of American households are same-sex marriages
- 72.1% of American households are heterosexual marriages

Legend: Heterosexual · Same-Sex · Single Parent · Cohabiting Parents · Other

Source: United States Census Bureau (2019b), Table F3.

Each of us begins our relational journey in our family of origin or family of orientation. Our **family of origin** is the family into which we are born or brought by adoption. It is the family in which we are raised and socialized to adhere to the customs and norms of the culture in which we live. And, just as important, it is within the family of origin we learn how to love and to be intimate with others. The **family of procreation** is the family unit that is formed when we marry and produce children. As we explore the nature of today's families, we use statistics to help us identify current patterns and trends. Although it is sometimes tempting to skip over statistics when reading, numbers are necessary because they present overall trends and provide us with an instant snapshot—and understanding—of U.S. families.

Nuclear and Extended Families

Today, it is essential that students of intimate couple and family life know the differing arrangements of families because this understanding allows human service providers and other family professionals to more effectively support, value, and work with diverse families (Banks & McGee Banks, 2002).

In essence, **diversity** refers to the broad spectrum of demographic and philosophical differences among groups of people within a culture. When we talk about being **diverse**, or about diversity in the United States, we are referring to people's differences in age, gender, race, ethnicity, cultures, sexual orientation, sexual identity, and religion. When we talk about being diverse when studying families, we are referring to the varying ways in which people experience coupling and family life. When we study people from a diversity perspective, we not only broaden our knowledge base about the variances in marriage and family, but we value individuals and groups, free from bias and preconceptions. This, then, fosters a climate of equity and mutual respect. In the sections that follow, we'll first take a look at nuclear and extended family forms. We'll then examine the expanding family landscape in our culture today.

Nuclear Family

The **nuclear family** consists of a father, a mother, and their biological or adopted children. In the truest sense of the definition, nuclear families consist of first-time married parents, their biological or adopted children, and no other family members living in the home. In 2019, the "typical" nuclear family form was found in about 65 percent of family households (Pew Research Organization, 2018b). Figure 1.2 illustrates the family configurations in which children in the United States live today. Notice that although the majority of children live in nuclear families, other family forms show the complexity of contemporary family living. For example, among parents living with a child, a growing share of unmarried parents are cohabiting: In 2017, 35 percent of unmarried parents were cohabiting, in comparison to 13 percent in 1968 (Pew Research Organization, 2018b). We'll discuss cohabiting parents at length later in this chapter.

Often, the nuclear family is referred to as the *traditional* family. This term carries with it a conventional depiction of the family form and the accompanying family values and traditions. *Family values* is a term that is commonly used today by politicians and TV news reports, although it may mean different things to different people. Most often, **family values** refers to a society's paradigm or viewpoint that expects its members to adhere to perceived proper social roles, such as marrying and having children, remaining monogamous and faithful to the marriage partner, and opposing same-sex relationships, marriages, and parenting by gay or lesbian partners. The family values viewpoint also frowns on births to women outside of marriage. It evokes a certain set of ascribed gender roles; for example, the women fulfill homemaker and mothering responsibilities (the bread maker role), and the men fulfill the role of primary wage earner (the breadwinner role). This particular family form is also considered a patriarchy, wherein the male is dominant and is in charge of most decision making in the family.

Historian and author Peter McWilliams (1998) offers insight into the roots of the traditional family. He notes that the modern concept of two adults rearing their children under

Family of origin: the family into which we are born or brought by adoption.

Family of procreation: the family unit that is formed when we marry and produce children.

Diversity: the broad spectrum of demographic and philosophical differences among groups within a culture.

Diverse: people's differences in age, gender, race, ethnicity, cultures, sexual orientation, and religion.

Nuclear family: a father, a mother, and their biological or adopted children.

Family values: usually refers to a society's paradigm or viewpoint that expects its members to adhere to perceived proper social roles, such as marrying and having children, remaining monogamous and faithful to the marriage partner, and opposing same-sex relationships, marriages, and parenting by gay or lesbian partners.

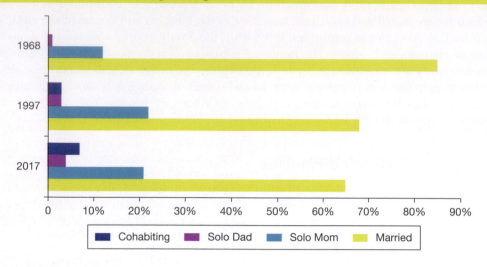

Figure 1.2 /// Parents' Living Arrangements Over Time

Legend: Cohabiting | Solo Dad | Solo Mom | Married

Source: Pew Research Center (2018).

---

a single roof grew out of necessity during the Middle Ages, when the minimum number of people required to own and maintain a plot of land was two. In order to multiply their wealth, they needed others to work the land; children were free labor. Thus, in order to have the free labor provided by children, it was economically necessary that one of the adults was a man and the other was a woman—and they were thus paired until death. According to McWilliams, love had nothing to do with the pairing. "Even if a husband and a wife hated each other, all they had to do was wait a little while—with disease, war, childbirth, and an average lifespan of about 25, most marriages lasted less than five years. The departed partner was immediately replaced, and the system continued." Men and older children worked the land and the women tended to the livestock, the crops near the home, and the younger children. Because the system worked so well, the church eventually got involved and, over time, the one-man/one-woman for life theology emerged.

Which child abuses substances? Which child has behavioral problems in school? Which child copes with mental health issues? Is this a nuclear family or a stepfamily? In the 1950s, we would never know because these real-life problems were never addressed. The television and media portrayed an idealized image of the American family: The breadwinning dad, the bread maker mom, and the practically perfect children who all live in their always-perfectly-kept home.

If we were to identify a specific period in American history that the traditional family form was in vogue, we would look at the period of the 1950s in the United States (McWilliams, 1998). The high postwar marriage and birth rates, coupled with a prosperous economy in which a single wage earner could support a family, led to a national perception of the period as a "golden era" for families (McWilliams, 1998).

Through the television and the media, families tuned in to watch the idealized image of the American family: the wise, reassuring father who came home from a hard day at the office; the apron-clad homemaker mother (wearing pearls and heels and lipstick) who offered comfort and support to her hardworking husband and perfect children; the

Gerlad Smith/NBCU Photo Bank/NBCUniversal via Getty Images

clutter-free, immaculate home; and the homogenous neighborhood. Notes McWilliams (1998), the family life portrayed in the 1950s media was wholesome: There were no single parents (unless the father was a widower, such as with the fathers in *My Three Sons, The Andy Griffith Show,* and *Bonanza*), no infidelities, no divorce, no abuse, no teen runaways, no financial problems, no stress, and no prior marriages or children from prior marriages. There was no discussion about religion. Politics. The economy. No one lost his job. There was no violence in the home or school or neighborhood. There was no drug usage. No racism. No homosexuality. And no babies born out of wedlock.

Despite TV Land's depiction of the American family during this era, like *Leave It to Beaver,* it is questionable whether this idealized image of family really ever existed. Author and professor of comparative family history Stephanie Coontz notes the discrepancies between the idealized 1950s "good old days" family form portrayed in the media and the reality of family living during the 1950s (Coontz, 1992, 1999):

- About one-quarter of the population lived below the poverty line.
- The number of pregnant brides more than doubled from the 1940s.
- From 1944 to 1955, the number of babies born outside of marriage and relinquished for adoption rose 80 percent.
- Juvenile delinquency was so prevalent that in 1955 Congress considered nearly 200 bills to address the social problem.

As Coontz notes, the 1950s were a dismal time for women, minorities, gays and lesbians, and any other social group that did not "fit in" with the images typified on the television screen.

The traditional nuclear family is no longer predominant in the United States. In the 21st century, 1950s television shows like *I Love Lucy* have been replaced by shows such as *Family Guy, Modern Family, Black-ish,* and *A Million Little Things,* which better reflect the diversity found in today's families.

Extended Family

The **extended family** is typically defined as a family unit in which two or more generations of close family relatives live together in one household. There are three common extended family configurations:

1. A mother and father with children (may be married or not), with one or more grandparents
2. A mother and father with children (may be married or not), with at least one unmarried sibling of the parents or another relative, such as a cousin
3. A divorced, separated, or never-married single parent with children, in addition to a grandparent, sibling, or other relative (Barbour et al., 2005)

This type of extended or multigenerational family structure was the basic element of slave life in the 19th century and remains today an integral part of the lives of many families, particularly families of color. For example, families with African roots often experience close-knit, multigenerational family groups—in addition to parents and children, family members may be grandparents, aunts, uncles, and cousins. Today, about 57 percent of African American/Black Caribbean children have lived in an extended family home, compared to 20 percent of white children (Banerjee, 2019). Similarly, about 35 percent of Hispanic children have lived in an extended family home. Overall, 17 percent of all children in the United States live in an extended family household (Banerjee, 2019). No data exist to determine how many extended family members live nearby (not necessarily with) other family members, but we know that multigenerational family members can provide much emotional and economic support, along with the richness of family legacy and heritage.

Extended family:
a family unit in which two or more generations of close family relatives live together in one household.

Is the American Family Deteriorating?

So prominent are the changes in the structures and experiences of the American family over the past 40 years that great debate erupted during many political campaigns in the 2018 election cycle about the "family values" of America. Is the American family deteriorating?

YES: Founder of the National Marriage Project, author David Popenoe asserts that the American family is in a state of deterioration. "It is well known that there has been a weakening of marriage and the nuclear family in advanced, industrialized societies, especially since the 1960s" (Popenoe & Whitehead, 2005). According to Dr. John DeFrain, professor of family studies for more than four decades, most families today in the U.S. are "doing well and are satisfied with their lives" (DeFrain, 2018). DeFrain does, however, point out that when looking at American families top down—from the *macro level*—there are difficulties families are facing; these difficulties, in turn, affect the form and functions of today's families:

- Increased number of couples opting to cohabit before marriage or instead of marriage
- Increased number of out-of-wedlock births
- Increased number of women in the workforce
- Increased number of children living in non-nuclear families
- Increased numbers of those living in poverty
- Increase in domestic and intimate partner violence
- Increase in alcohol-related problems
- Increase in substance use
- Decrease in marital satisfaction and happiness

Other research indicates that the changes in family structure significantly impact children's health and well-being (Anderson, 2014; Hadfield & Ungar, 2018). These findings align with what other family scientists were finding in 1996: That all of the trends seen in family structure—"the breakdown of family and the erosion of family values"—affect children significantly (National Issues Forum, 1996). These impacts are seen in the increased incidence of teen violence, teen pregnancy, and teen substance abuse (Hadfield & Ungar, 2018).

NO: Other scholars believe that the family is in a continuous state of change, as it always has been, in order to adapt to societal influences. For example, the first settlers in America experienced extended family forms in order to adjust to their harsh environmental conditions; as life improved, family structures reflected this change. A scientist for the Institute for Social and Behavioral Research, Rand Conger (Conger & Conger, 2002) studied today's emerging family systems and made these conclusions:

- The *quality* of parenting—not the experience of nuclear adult relationships—teaches children and adolescents how to behave in marital relationships.
- The *quality* of the parents' relationship did not directly influence how young adults experience their own adult relationships.
- The *quality* of parenting (nurturing and affectionate versus harsh and angry) influences whether children/adolescents use drugs, become teen parents, or engage in teen violence—not whether the child is reared in a single-parent home or stepfamily.

And some contend that the American family is not deteriorating but is adapting to the social changes brought by diversity of races, ethnicities, genders, and sexual orientations. Dr. John DeFrain (2018) echoes these findings. He asserts that if we examine families face-to-face—the *micro level*—we will see that families around the world are incredibly diverse and that *function* (not structure) is the most important aspect of family health and well-being. He rightly states, "Strong families tend to produce great kids" (p. 78).

What Do You Think?

1. Are the trends we see in today's families a result of change or deterioration?

2. Where do you see the American family in the year 2030? 2050?

Sources: National Issues Forum (1996); Popenoe and Whitehead (2005); Conger and Conger (2002).

THE EXPANDING FAMILY LANDSCAPE

In the United States today, there is no such thing as a "traditional" or "typical" family configuration. In order to better serve today's families and to help them reach their full potentials, we need to understand the changing compositions of contemporary families, as well as the racial and ethnic compositions of families.

Single-Parent Families

Today, one in four U.S. parents is unmarried (Cilluffo & Cohn, 2019). **Single-parent family** types can be the result of the choice of the parent or of circumstance; they can result from divorce, the death of a spouse, or unmarried parenthood. Trends indicate that single-parent households are on the increase in the American family: In the past 10 years, the number of children who live with two married parents has decreased from 68 to 65 percent (Institute of Family Studies, 2019). Table 1.1 illustrates children's living arrangements from 1970 to 2018. Although the percentage of children living with no parents has remained relatively stable over the past nearly 50 years, the percentage of children living with unmarried parents has increased, while those living with two parents has decreased. Understanding these trends in single-parenting experiences is important because as our study will show us in just a bit, single parents often live in poverty—which, in turn, affects their children's development.

Single-parent family: families with only one parent, as a result of the choice of the parent or of circumstance such as divorce, the death of a spouse, or unmarried parenthood.

Childless/Childfree Families

Couples may consider themselves **childless** if they are unable to conceive or bear children of their own or adopt children. Some couples today prefer to remain **childfree** as a conscious choice. And although they're waiting longer to have children, older women are more likely to have children today than a decade ago. Today, 86 percent of women aged 40 to 44 are mothers, in comparison to 80 percent in 2006 (Pew Research Center, 2018c). The U.S. Census Bureau measures the presence of children primarily by examining the **general fertility rate** (the ratio of the number of live births per 1,000 women of childbearing age). In 2018, there were 59 births for every 1,000 women aged 15 to 44; this is a decrease from 70 births for every 1,000 women aged 15 to 44 in 2010 (Pew Research Center, 2018c). The typical American family today has an average of 1.9 children under 18; this is a decrease from the average number of 2.44 children per family in 1970 (Pew Research Center, 2019).

It is important to note, however, that this is not the first generation of people who are deciding not to have children. Notes Philip Morgan, professor of sociology at Duke University, "Childlessness is not new, [but] in the past it was more closely connected with non-marriage than now. During the Depression, many Americans also chose not to have children because

Childless: couples may consider themselves childless if they are unable to conceive or bear children of their own or adopt children.

Childfree: people who deliberately choose not to have children.

General fertility rate: the ratio of the number of live births per 1,000 women of childbearing age.

Table 1.1 /// Children's Living Arrangements by Presence of Parents in the Home, 1970–2018						
Percentage of children who live with. . . .						
	1970	1980	1990	2000	2010	2018
2 Parents	85.2	76.7	72.5	69.1	69.4	68.9
Single Parents	11.9	19.7	24.7	26.7	26.6	27.0
No Parents	2.9	3.7	2.8	4.2	4.1	4.1

Source: Current Population Survey Annual Social and Economic Supplement (CPS-ASEC) 1970-2010 and CPS March, 2018. Retrieved April 10, 2019, from www.ifstudies.org.

they could not afford them. Childlessness levels no are not higher than those in the 1930s" (Taylor, 2005). Morgan adds that there are many factors involved in couples' decision to remain childfree today. We discuss the childless/childfree contemporary trends in depth in Chapter 10.

Stepfamilies

Stepfamily:

a family formed when, after death or divorce, a parent marries again. A stepfamily is also formed when a never-married person marries someone who has children.

A **stepfamily** (or reconstituted family) is formed when, after death or divorce, a parent marries again. A stepfamily is also formed when a never-married parent marries and children from different biological families end up living with the new married couple for part of the time. In short, the presence of a stepparent, stepsibling, or half sibling designates a family as a stepfamily (U.S. Census Bureau, 2019b).

The U.S. Census Bureau no longer provides data related to marriage, divorce, and remarriage, so it is difficult to obtain accurate statistics about stepfamilies. But census experts today estimate that one in three Americans—about 33 percent—is now either a stepparent, a stepchild, a stepsibling, or some other member of a stepfamily (Gaille, 2017). Although the popular 1970s television show *The Brady Bunch* portrayed stepfamily living as an emotionally cohesive, trouble-free, happily adjusted family, this idealized concept of the stepfamily form is simply not the norm. (Because of the complexities of stepfamily living, an entire segment is devoted to this family form in Chapter 14).

Cohabiting Families

Cohabiting:

unmarried partners who live together in a single household.

Unmarried partners who live together in a single household are referred to as **cohabiting** couples. Although once considered a scandalous, uncommon alternative lifestyle, cohabiting before marriage (or instead of marriage) is now the prevailing living arrangement of intimate partners—the next step following serious dating. The U.S. Census Bureau today estimates that 35 percent of couples in the United States are cohabiting (U.S. Census Bureau, 2019b). In 2018, cohabitation was a more common living arrangement of children than living with a single parent. For example, while 3.5 percent of children lived with an unmarried parent, 4.2 percent lived with a parent and the parent's unmarried partner (Institute of Family Studies, 2019). This is a significant increase from 2007, when the percentage of children living with unmarried single parents and cohabiting parents was nearly identical (2.6 percent and 2.9 percent, respectively). Today, an estimated 5.8 million American children live with cohabiting parents (Institute of Family Studies, 2019). In 2018, there were 8.5 million unmarried opposite-sex couples living together (U.S. Census Bureau, 2019b). Many of these couples have no plans for eventual marriage. Indeed, 51 percent of women's first marriages are preceded by cohabitation (Institute of Family Studies, 2019). The rates of cohabiting parents vary by race; these data are presented in Figure 1.3. We discuss the multifaceted aspects of cohabitation in Chapter 7.

Gay and Lesbian Families

Lesbian and gay families consist of same-sex partners who live together in the same household; they may include either natural-born or adopted children. In the United States today, there are 935,000 same-sex households, up from 780,000 same-sex households in 2011 (U.S. Census Bureau, 2019d). Census Bureau statisticians point out, however, that this increase reflects the fact that same-sex families were previously uncounted, undercounted, or underreported, and not that the numbers of gay or lesbian families have increased significantly (U.S. Census Bureau, 2019d). Same-sex family forms may or may not resemble traditional marriage roles, but they often do. Legally married today, they share property, expect sexual fidelity, and share joint responsibility in child rearing.

Chosen family:

a type of informal family structure that is common among LGBTQ+ communities and is based on nonbiological kinship bonds.

In the LGBTQ+ community, **chosen family**—nonbiological kinship bonds—replaces blood family and becomes the bedrock of trust, support, and love; sometimes, LGBTQ+ individuals live with their chosen family (Carlson & Dermer, 2017; Hull, 2018). Kathleen Hull (2018), professor of sociology and gender, women, and sexuality studies, notes that many LGBTQ+

Figure 1.3 /// Children's Living Arrangements by Race/Ethnicity

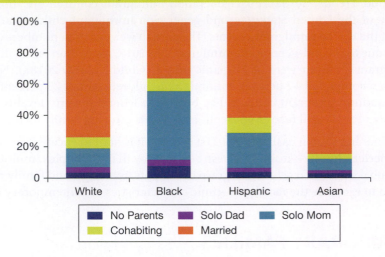

Source: Institute of Family Studies (2019). Cohabitation is pervasive. Retrieved May 10, 2019, from www.ifstudies.org/blog/cohabitation-is-pervasive.

individuals do not receive support and acceptance from their blood relatives, and because of this they have formed nonbiological families with people who do love and support them. Another social scientist observes, "Until the world is a more inclusive place, [chosen family] will continue to exist within the LGBT community" (Mitchell, 2008).

Immigrant Families With Children

Immigrants are people who reside permanently in the United States but were not U.S. citizens at birth. Immigrant families with children are families in which at least one parent was born outside of the United States. From 1994 to 2017, the population of immigrant children

Immigrants: foreign-born people who have been granted the right to permanently live and work in the United States.

ZUMA Press Inc/Alamy Stock Photo

Today, there are nearly 1 million same-sex households in the United States, and nearly 200,000 children live with their same-sex parents.

in the U.S. grew by 51 percent, to 19.6 million. This number represents one-fourth of all U.S. children (Child Trends, 2018a). First-generation immigrant children are those who were born outside of the United States; second-generation immigrant children are those who were born in the U.S. to immigrant parents. The growth we've seen in numbers of immigrant children are due to second-generation immigrants. In 2017, more than one-half (54 percent) of all immigrant children were of Hispanic origin (Child Trends, 2018a). Non-Hispanic Asian children comprised 17 percent of immigrant children. About 25 percent of first- and second-generation immigrant children live below the federal poverty level (Child Trends, 2018a). In Chapter 10 we'll take an in-depth look at this growing family form.

Our study so far has shown us that in the 21st century, it is hard to encapsulate or sum up the "typical" American family—it simply doesn't exist today in our complex, multifaceted, ever-changing, global society. To get the full grasp of intimate, marriage, and family relationships, we now need to examine the racial and ethnic characteristics of contemporary families.

CONTEMPORARY FAMILIES

Is the American family in a state of decline, or is it in a state of change? As we have seen so far, the "traditional" family form is no longer the norm in American culture, and today's intimate relationships and families are experiencing a number of changes. The family structures, values, and attitudes we observe today are a result of changes that have evolved over the past five or six decades.

As the United States moved into the second half of the 20th century, a number of social, cultural, economic, and political changes occurred that continue to have an impact on today's 21st-century families and family living: Social and cultural changes include lower birth rates and an increase in nonmarital cohabitation; economic factors include the influx of women into the workforce; and political factors include legalized abortion in 1973 and the Civil Rights legislation of 1965, which bans racial, ethnic, sexual, and sexual orientation discrimination.

All of these factors worked in tandem to change the traditional family in this century. Experts in the field of marriage and family living, however, view the changes occurring during the last half of the 20th century differently. Those with more conventional, conservative, or religious outlooks are concerned about what they perceive to be a moral decline in family life—that is, the increase in nonmarital cohabitation and same-sex relationships and in the number of births outside of marriage. These groups prescribe a return to more conventional, long-held family values as a way to reverse the trends (Popenoe & Whitehead, 2005). Those with a more contemporary outlook hold that these trends represent both flexibility and adaptability in today's families and in the society at large (Solot & Miller, 2004). In spite of increasing relational and economic stresses faced by today's families, marriage represents the most frequently chosen family form, with approximately 93 percent of the population choosing marriage at least once (U.S. Census Bureau, 2019e).

In the United States, there is more diversity now than ever before. Families today are complex and diverse, ranging from traditional two-biological-parent family structures, to single-parent homes, to extended family forms, to married gay or lesbian couples. There is also greater diversity of racial, ethnic, economic, and religious composition, and so social workers, family life educators, psychologists, sociologists, and health and mental health professionals must be aware of the full range of diversity in families today (see Figure 1.4).

Knowing the racial and ethnic composition of U.S. families is important because it aids in our understanding of the complex, changing nature of family living. Here, we briefly examine the racial and ethnic compositions of families so that you have a firm understanding of the diversity within the United States.

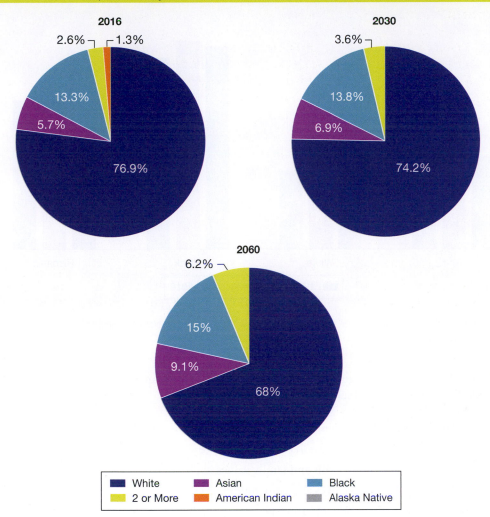

Figure 1.4 /// Racial and Ethnic Composition of American Families: Projected Population by Race, 2016–2060

2016
2.6% ⌐ ⌐1.3%
13.3%
5.7%
76.9%

2030
3.6% ⌐
13.8%
6.9%
74.2%

2060
6.2% ⌐
15%
9.1%
68%

Legend:
■ White ■ Asian ■ Black
■ 2 or More ■ American Indian ■ Alaska Native

Source: Vespa, Jonathan, David M. Armstrong, and Lauren Medina, Demographic Turning Points for the United States: Population Projections for 2020 to 2060, Current Population Reports, P25-1144, U.S. Census Bureau, Washington, DC, 2018.

African American/Black Caribbean Families

Historically, African American/Black Caribbean families assumed the traditional married-couple family structure, with children born inside the marital union. Today, it is common for Black children to be born to a single mother. As Figure 1.5 illustrates, nearly 70 percent of the births to Black women of all ages are to unmarried women (Child Trends, 2018b). In comparison to white families, where nearly one-fourth (24 percent) live in a single-parent home (Kids Count Data Center, 2019a), 65 percent of Black children live in a single-parent home (Kids Count Data Center, 2019b). Eventually, 37 percent of Black children reside in two-parent homes, but many of these families are formed with a child who was born outside of marriage (Kids Count Data Center, 2019b).

Multigenerational, extended family ties are common among Black families. Census bureau data estimate that about 26 percent of African American/Black Caribbean children live in some type of extended family (Pew Research Center, 2018a). According to a study by

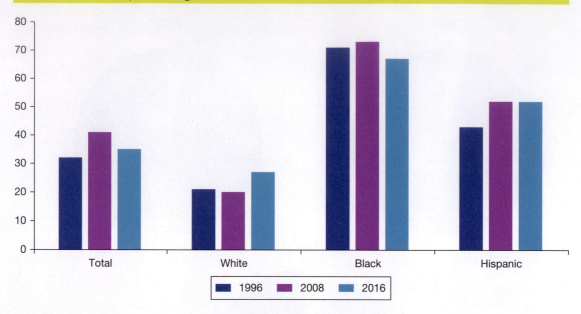

Figure 1.5 /// Percentage of All Births That Were to Unmarried Women, by Race and Hispanic Origin

Source: Child Trends. (2018a). Births to Unmarried Women. Retrieved from https://www.childtrends.org/indicators/births-to-unmarried-women.

Noelle St. Vil and her colleagues (2018), characteristics of African American/Black Caribbean extended family networks include the following:

- Strong commitment to family and family obligation
- Availability of and willingness to provide childcare
- Reinforcement of social skills and family values in children
- Willingness to allow relatives and close nonrelatives to move into the family home
- Strong network of emotional support
- Strengthen marriages by protecting against the inability to meet responsibilities of multiple roles
- Close system of mutual aid and support

Because of the large numbers of female-headed households among African American/Black Caribbeans, some research suggests that the childrearing and economic support of extended kin is necessary; it is within the extended family networks of grandmothers, grandfathers, aunts, uncles, and cousins that children are cared for, socialized, educated, and have their emotional needs met (Taylor, 2000). Of all racial and ethnic groups in the United States, African American/Black Caribbean families suffer some of the highest levels of unemployment and poverty and the lowest median family income—slightly more than $40,000 annually (U.S. Census Bureau, 2018a).

Latinx Families

Latinx:

people of Latin American origin or descent. The term is used as a gender-neutral alternative to Latino or Latina.

Latinx are people of Latin American origin or descent. This term is used as a gender-neutral alternative to Latino or Latina. Today, Latinx Americans account for slightly more than 18 percent of the total U.S. population; this figure does not include the 3 million residents of the U.S. territory Puerto Rico (U.S. Census Bureau, 2018b). This population trace their roots to Spain, Mexico, and the Spanish-speaking nations of Central America, South America, and

Latinx families enjoy the rich, multigenerational relationships of extended family members and nonrelated kin who become as close as blood relatives. Latinx families embrace familism: The best interests of the family are placed ahead of the interests of the individual family member.

iStock.com/ aldomurillo

the Caribbean. The fastest-growing population in the United States because of the large proportion of Latinx women of childbearing age, the Hispanic population of the United States is nearly 59 million, making people of Hispanic origin the nation's largest ethnic or racial minority (U.S. Census Bureau, 2018b).

Latinx place a high value on familialism, which emphasizes the importance of family life, and close, interdependent relationships among the person, the family, and the community (among many, Constante, Marchand, Cross, & Rivas-Drake, 2019; Stein, Cavanaugh, Castro-Schilo, Mejia, & Plunkett, 2019). Typically, familialism also stresses the importance of extended family; thus, Latinx families are also composed of extended kinship networks (grandparents, aunts, uncles, and cousins). Within this family dynamic, family members are provided clothing, shelter, food, education, and emotional support. People of Hispanic origin further extend family relationships to **fictive kin** (nonrelated members), such as godparents and close friends. Within Latinx communities, the well-being of the family takes precedence over the well-being of the individual.

Fictive kin: people who are not biologically related but who fulfill a family role.

As you saw earlier in this chapter, Latinx children often have families in which at least one parent is an immigrant—foreign born—or are themselves foreign born. Today, one out of four U.S. children is living in an immigrant family (Zong, Batalova, & Burrows, 2019). Latinx immigrants and their children commonly live within extended family forms during the first 10 years following immigration (Carranza, Gouveia, Cogua, & Ondracek-Sayers, 2002). Even as immigrants establish their own households, they do so nearby their families' homes. Second- and third-generation Hispanic Americans have even larger extended kin networks than do immigrants (Carranza et al., 2002).

About 76 percent of Latinx children live in two-parent families (U.S. Census Bureau, 2019f). Similar to the experiences of African American/Black Caribbean women, births to unmarried Latinx women have increased since the 1970s. Nearly 40 percent of all Hispanic origin births are to unmarried women (Child Trends, 2018a). Currently, nearly 20 percent of Latinx children live in a household with their mothers and have no father

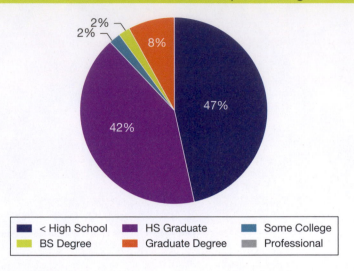

Legend:
- < High School
- HS Graduate
- Some College
- BS Degree
- Graduate Degree
- Professional

Pie chart values: 47%, 42%, 8%, 2%, 2%

Source: United States Census Bureau (2019f).

present; 27 percent live in an extended, multigenerational family household with grandparents, and one-fourth live with their grandparents (Pew Research Center, 2018a; U.S. Census Bureau, 2019f).

Educational attainment varies among this population, as Figure 1.6 illustrates. In the United States today, Latinx families earn, on average, about $50,000 per year (U.S. Census Bureau, 2019f). It's important to keep in mind that many Hispanic immigrants may have had successful businesses in other countries or professional degrees from other countries, but because of the language barrier when they arrive in the United States, they are unable to secure high-paying jobs.

Asian American Families

Asian American families come to the United States from countries including Korea, Japan, China, Taiwan, Vietnam, Cambodia, Sri Lanka, and Indonesia. Each Asian country has a unique culture, which accounts for the vast cultural and ethnic differences within this racial group. Like Latinx families, Asian American families place great emphasis on extended kinship ties and the needs of the entire family, rather than on the needs of the individual. About 61 percent of all Asian American children live with both biological parents; only 9 percent live in mother-only families, and about 4 percent live in father-only families (U.S. Census Bureau, 2019c). Today, about 13 percent of Asian women give birth outside of marriage (Child Trends, 2018b). With an annual income of more than $80,000 per year, Asian American families have the highest median household income of all racial groups in the United States (U.S. Census Bureau, 2019c). This is perhaps because Asian Americans have the highest educational attainment and qualifications of all ethnic groups in the United States—nearly 54 percent have earned at least a bachelor's degree (U.S. Census Bureau, 2019c).

Asian American families are child-centric. Within the Asian family structure a greater emphasis is placed on the parent–child relationship than on the husband–wife relationship. In exchange for the undivided loyalty and for sacrifices parents make for their children, Asian American parents expect respect and obedience from their children (Fong, 2002).

Native American/Alaska Native Families

The terms *Native American, American Indian, Alaska Native,* and *Indian* are often used interchangeably. Here, we use the term **Native American/Alaska Native** to refer to aboriginal peoples of the United States and their descendants who maintain tribal affiliation or community attachment. Today, about 2 percent of the total U.S. population reports that they are Native American or Alaska Native (U.S. Census Bureau, 2019a). About one-third of the population is under the age of 18, making this a young ethnic group (U.S. Census Bureau, 2019a). As with other racial and ethnic groups in the United States, Native American or Alaska Native communities are culturally diverse, with 561 federally recognized Native entities and an additional 365 state-recognized American Indian tribes (U.S. Census Bureau, 2019a). Native Americans prefer to be identified by tribal names, such as Wampanoag, Lakota, and Kickapoo (Fleming, 2007); our discussion here is generalized.

In order for us to accurately understand Native American marriage and family experiences, we must be aware of the unique qualities associated with this race. Unfortunately, comparatively little research has been conducted on Native American family life, and especially on Native American marriage. Despite this gap in the empirical literature, however, the census data do give us insight into some characteristics of Natives. For instance, nearly 67 percent of all Native American households are married couple households. Interestingly, more than one-third of households are nonfamily households; this means that a significant number of Native American families are headed by someone other than a parent, such as a grandparent, or even by nonfictive kin. Nearly 52 percent of Native grandparents assume responsibility for their grandchildren (U.S. Census Bureau, 2019a). Although nearly 80 percent of this population has at least a high school diploma, the median household income of single-race American Indian and Alaska Native households is slightly more than $39,000. This compares with $58,000 for the nation as a whole.

The predominance of extended family/nonfictive kin households among NA/AN is a reflection of the cultural roots of this racial group. Native Americans/Alaska Natives embrace a social identity that stresses the importance of family ties. For example, when Native Americans

Native American/Alaska Native: the aboriginal peoples of the United States and their descendants, who maintain tribal affiliation or community attachment.

iStock.com/FatCamera

Native Americans/Alaska Natives embrace rich cultural heritages and an identity that stresses the importance of intergenerational family ties. Native spiritual and religious beliefs are numerous and diverse, and the beliefs often shape their attitudes toward marriage and family life.

introduce themselves to other Natives, they do so by telling them their maternal heritage, clans, and homelands (Makes Marks, 2007). In contrast to societies in which kinship is determined along patrilineal lines (the father's heritage), the roots of Native social and clan relationships are by and large matrilineal; that is to say, these societies trace their heritage from a female ancestor to a descendent of either sex. This is also referred to as a *uterine descent*. Within these societies, women are not given power per se because they are women—they are given power because of their status of mother, the power of female as mother.

Native Americans' spiritual traditions and religious beliefs are also numerous and diverse, and as such, the depth and dynamics of their religious experiences are difficult to categorize or classify. Even so, there is an underlying or essential principal belief that informs most Natives' spiritual practices: the belief in the existence of unseen powers, that something exists beyond them that is sacred and mysterious (Makes Marks, 2007). Within this belief are embedded tradition, respect, and reverence. But how these religious beliefs shape marital and family attitudes, norms, and behaviors is unknown, because Native Americans are among the most misunderstood and understudied ethnic group in our culture; this is because they are commonly culturally isolated (Hellerstedt, Peterson-Hickey, Rhodes, & Garwick, 2006).

Muslim/Arab Americans

Very little empirical information exists about Muslim American families, although their population is increasing in the United States. Coming from countries such as Afghanistan, Israel, Iran, Iraq, Kuwait, Palestine, Saudi Arabia, Syria, and Turkey, the term *Arab American* does not refer necessarily to a racial group as much as it does geographic location and religion, which among Middle Eastern families is very diverse. There are no U.S. government demographics on the number of Muslim Americans because the U.S. Census Bureau does not track information and trends on the religious practices of those who reside in the United States. According to Pew Research Center (2017a), there are 3.45 million Muslims living in the United States; they account for about 1 percent of the total U.S. population. The fastest growing immigrant population today, 3 in 10 have immigrated to the United States since 2010 (Pew Research Center, 2017a). Nearly 42 percent of Muslim/Arab Americans are American citizens. Of those who were foreign born, nearly 70 percent have become naturalized U.S. citizens (Pew Research Center, 2017a).

The most common living situation among Muslim Americans is a multigenerational household; 57 percent live in this type of home configuration (Pew Research Center, 2017a). Nearly 20 percent live in a home with non-Muslims (such as a spouse). The Islamic faith is a sex-positive religion, wherein sex and sexuality are viewed as gifts from Allah (God); sexuality is thought to be the right of every person (Boellstorff, 2005). Marriage, then, is the social institution that organizes and controls sexuality. Further, within the Islamic faith anything that "violates the order of the world"—in this instance, marriage as an organizer of sexuality—is considered to be a source of evil and anarchy (Bouhdiba, 2001, p. 30). As a result of these tenets of the Muslim faith, heterosexual marriages and nuclear families are expected of devout Muslims (Boellstorff, 2005). Table 1.2 denotes the living arrangements of Muslim Americans today in the United States.

Table 1.2 /// Household Configurations of Muslim Americans		
	% All U.S. Muslims	% Foreign Born
One-person household	23	22
Multiple-person household	75	75
Households with children	50	55
No children	46	43

Source: Pew Research Center (2017a).

It's very important to understand that Arab Americans differ widely in their religious beliefs and practices of religion (Arab American Institute, 2019). This is essential to know because cultural stereotypes of Muslim/Arab American women tend to lump religion (Muslim) and ethnicity (Arab) into one-and-the-same components of culture, portraying them as veiled Islamic traditionalists who are submissive, secluded in the home, and uneducated (Zahedi, 2007).

But, as sociology professor and researcher Jen'nan Ghazel Read of the University of California points out, understanding Muslim/Arab American culture is complicated (2003). On the one hand, as a group, Arab Americans are more highly educated and are more likely to earn $100,000 or more per year than any other ethnic or racial group in the United States (Arab American Institute, 2019; Pew Research Center, 2017b). On the other hand, Arab religious and cultural customs and rituals reinforce traditional gender roles wherein women raise and nurture the children and men protect and provide for the family. As a result, many Arab Americans' marital and family experiences are strongly shaped by traditional Arab views of honor, modesty, and gender, as well as by the historical values of Islam (Davis & Davis, 1993; Arab American Institute, 2019). A good example of the complexities of Arab American culture is Ilhan Abdullahi Omar, a Somali-American politician who was elected to serve in the U.S. House of Representatives in 2019; she and Rashida Tlaib are the first two Muslim American women to serve in Congress. Although in the U.S. it is commonplace for women to hold political office, only within the last decade have women in Arab countries made political inroads.

Without a doubt, there is great variation and diversity in our upbringing and our individual experiences with family and family living. It is virtually impossible in contemporary society to rely on the U.S. Census Bureau's rigid definition of *family* consisting of "two or more persons living together and related by blood, marriage, and adoption."

Talking With Children About Diversity

Because we live in a world that is not free from bias and discrimination, as parents, guardians, and teachers we impart to our children that *everyone* has the right to feel included. It is important to teach children that hate hurts and leaves emotional scars that can affect not only a person's self-worth but also every aspect of a person's life. Because a child develops his or her self-concept and beliefs about others well before entering kindergarten, anti-bias and antidiscrimination education must begin early in the home and in school. Parents, guardians, and teachers need to model attitudes and behaviors that help young children appreciate and value the differences in others. To avoid prejudice and discrimination, we must

- Model the values, attitudes, and behaviors we want our children to develop. This requires being aware of our own conscious and unconscious stereotypes and behaviors.
- Expose children to people and experiences from other cultures and belief systems.
- Encourage children to see that relationships with people who are different from themselves can be rich and rewarding experiences.
- Talk with children about the similarities and differences between themselves and others. Help them to see that being "different" from someone does not mean the person is "worse" than someone else.
- Integrate diversity information and communication into conversations and activities.
- Teach children to be sensitive, critical thinkers, so that through examining and questioning they can better understand any issue.
- Adopt a "zero tolerance" policy about racism, prejudice, bias, and discrimination. Teach them that words *do hurt.*

Despite the fact that today's families are diverse in structure, income level, and racial and ethnic composition, and despite the fact that today's families experience family living in diverse ways, one particular theorist has been able to organize the different cultural contexts of family life so we can see the level of influence each context has on us. With this in mind, in the section that follows we'll take a look at Bronfenbrenner's Ecological Model, a model noted for grouping the various contexts that surround us and influence our individual and family development.

FAMILIES IN CULTURAL CONTEXTS

John Donne, in his *Meditation*, reminds us that who we are is influenced by factors outside of ourselves and beyond our control. He says, *"No man is an island entire of itself; every man is a piece of the continent, a part of the main."* Each of us has needs for sustenance, clothing, shelter, security, intimacy, and emotional support. Because of these needs, we find ourselves interacting with others in some capacity throughout our lives.

As we begin our study of marriage, family, and intimate relationships, it is necessary to understand and embrace the idea that we do not develop in isolation. Who we are as human beings—every emotion, fear, thought, and behavior—is somehow linked to the family in which we were raised, both genetically and environmentally. It is also important to understand that there are many areas of family life that are affected and influenced by the broader culture in which we live, by the many facets of society that surround us. Often these influences are overlooked in the study of both individual development and the processes associated with family life.

Social Identity: All for One and One for All?

How individuals understand and practice their intimate and family relationships is influenced by the culture in which they live. It is important to understand that family life experiences are determined in large part by how a culture defines its **social identity**, or whether societal goals emphasize the advancement of the group's interest or individual interests. Particularly important is whether the culture defines itself as a *collectivist* culture or an *individualistic* culture because culturally approved beliefs influence our expectations, experiences, attitudes, and behaviors (Neto, 2007). It profoundly affects the ways we behave and respond to the world.

Collectivist Cultures

In **collectivist cultures**, individuals define their identity in terms of the relationships they hold with others. For instance, if asked, "Who are you?" a collectivist is likely to respond by giving the family's name or the region from which he or she originates (Triandis & Suh, 2002). The goals of the collective—the whole society—are given priority over individual needs, and group membership is important (Myers, 2008). In these cultures, members strive to be equal, contributing, beneficial members of the society, and their personal behavior is driven by a feeling of obligation and duty to the society (Triandis & Suh, 2002; Johnson, Kulesa, Cho, & Shavitt, 2005). Collectivist cultures promote the well-being and goals of the collective *group*, rather than the well-being and goals of the *individual*. Because of the desire to maintain harmony within the group, collectivist cultures stress harmony, cooperation, and promoting feelings of closeness (Kupperbusch et al., 1999).

Latinx, for example, value strong interdependent relationships with their families and they value the opinions of close friends (who, in many cases, are treated as family members); this, in turn, influences how they select mates and display and experience emotions, such as love and intimacy (Castañeda, 1993; Fernandez-Dols, 1999). Asians, too, accentuate the importance of the collective whole and they therefore emphasize family bonds in their experiences of love, including extended family members. People's self-concepts, personal goals, mate selection, sexual attitudes, expectations of family members, family experiences, and the larger society are inseparable in collective societies (Johnson et al., 2005).

Social identity:
whether the goals of a society/culture emphasize the advancement of the group's interests or individual interests.

Collectivist cultures:
cultures that define their identity in terms of the relationships individuals hold with others, which takes priority over individual needs; group membership is important.

How couples and families experience their relationships is largely dependent on whether their culture adopts a *collectivist* or an *individualist* identity.

iStock.com / Rawpixel

Individualistic Cultures

In **individualistic cultures**, individual goals are promoted over group goals, and people define their identity or sense of self in terms of personal attributes, such as wealth, social status, education level, and marital status (Myers, 2008). Unlike collectivists, individualists view themselves as truly independent entities from the society in which they live, and their personal needs and rights guide their behavior, rather than the needs of the society (Johnson et al., 2005). Individualistic cultures, such as those of the United States and some countries in western Europe, promote the idea of autonomy and individuation from the family; in turn, this autonomy promotes the practice of people selecting partners based on individual reasons (such as attraction, love, sex, money, security), rather than collective reasons (such as prearranged marriages in China and India) that might benefit the culture as a whole. Along these lines, when cultures promote the autonomy and independence of individuals (as seen in much of Western civilization), this autonomy, in turn, affects relationship satisfaction, the ease with which intimacy is established, and "love" as a basis for marriage (Dion & Dion, 1993). Relationship partners are free, by society's standards, to choose a partner that best suits their needs; it is thought that this freedom of choice enhances relationship satisfaction and the experiences of love, intimacy, and sex.

As you saw earlier in this chapter, a culture's social identity shapes and directs the attitudes, norms, and behaviors of its members, such as how extended family members are important to Latinx and Asian families—these behaviors are the result of how collectivist ideals shape families. But there are other cultural factors that significantly influence and shape intimate and family life experience. The **social ecology** perspective recognizes that individual family members' experiences, along with outside social factors and policies, significantly affect the quality and the nature of their relationships (Alberts, 2002). In the section that follows, we examine the ways in which families are affected by the variety of contexts that surround them as we study the Ecological Model and the various contexts within that model: the microsystem, mesosystem, exosystem, macrosystem, and chronosystem.

Individualistic cultures: culture in which individual goals are more important than the goals of the group. Individuals define their identity or sense of self by way of personal attributes (wealth, social status, education level, marital status, etc.).

Social ecology: the perspective that recognizes that individual family members' experiences, as well as outside social factors and policies, significantly affect the quality and the nature of their relationships.

The Ecological Model: Culturally Specific Influences That Affect Family Life

Ecological Model:
a theory developed by Russian-born Uri Bronfenbrenner that explains the multiple influences that affect individuals' and families' development over their lifetimes. The central concept is that people develop in a variety of interacting contexts.

Contexts:
areas of individual and family development that play a role in the relationship between people and their environments. These multiple environments surround individuals from birth; a person is in constant interaction with these different contexts.

To understand the multiple areas of individual and family development, we turn our attention to the **Ecological Model** developed by Uri Bronfenbrenner (1979). Central to this model is the concept that people develop in a variety of interacting contexts. **Contexts** are the areas of individual and family development that play a role in the relationship between people and their environments. These multiple environments surround individuals from birth and play a significant interactive role in development. In order to truly understand individual relationship behaviors (such as communication) and the development of family life, we must first understand the interactive relationships between and among the different factors within the various contexts of development (Huitt, 2003). For example, if we want to study the effects of divorce on a child's development, we can study the child separately, but we can also introduce or take away various factors within a certain context to better determine which has the greatest impact on a child's development. Similarly, if we want to better understand a couple's difficulty with sexual arousal and response, we can look at contextual factors, such as the stressors associated with employment, to see if they are exerting negative influences on the couple.

Figure 1.7 presents the Ecological Model. Notice that the person is located in the center of five concentric, nested circles that expand outward, similar to ripples on the surface of water.

Figure 1.7 /// Bronfenbrenner's Ecological Model

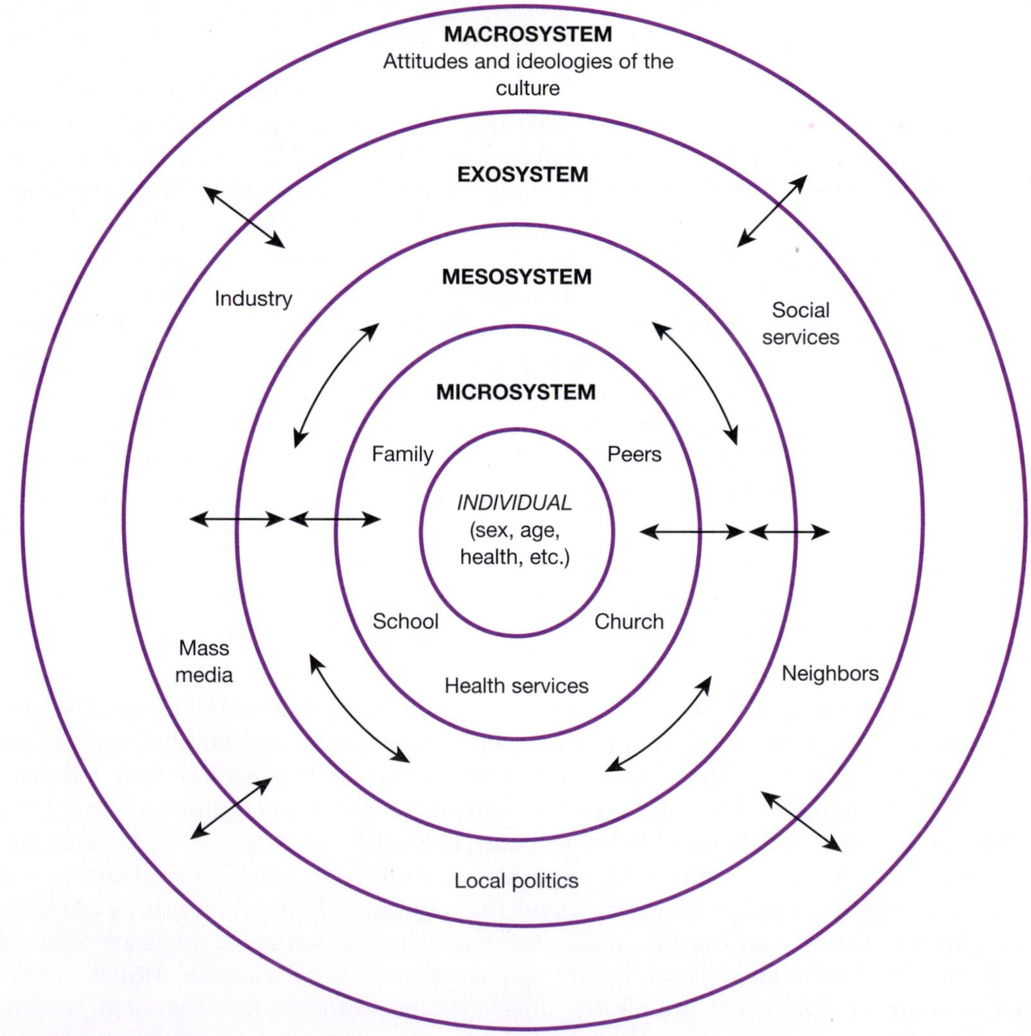

Source: Hchokr at English Q52/CC BY-SA (https://creativecommons.org/licenses/by-sa/3.0)/Wikimedia Commons.

Each of those circles represents a different layer of societal interactions and influences external to the individual, which affects his or her development. The circles nearest the individual have more immediate impacts on us, and those farther out have less impact. Perhaps what makes this model so useful is that Bronfenbrenner recognized that the impact on relationships is *bi-directional*. Not only does the environment influence the individual but the individual influences the environment. For example, a new baby in a family has an impact on the parents just as much as the parents have an impact on the baby. When a couple goes through a divorce, both spouses are affected, but their children and other extended family members and friends are also affected. And, even though the individual or the family may not directly interact with various levels of society (such as the different levels of government), as you will see later in our study this term, these social influences have an impact on family functioning and health.

As we examine each context in the model, it is important to bear in mind the positioning of the context to better understand the degree of influence on the individual. To help guide this process, we will discuss each context, or **ecosystem**, within the Ecological Model. Those contexts nearest the individual carry the greatest influence on her or his development.

The Person

At the center of this model is the person. Bronfenbrenner recognized that a person's development is not simply a matter of biology, cognition, or social interaction. Development is, instead, an intricate intertwining of *all three* of these components. Individual influences include race, ethnicity, genetics, health, nutrition, and physiological abilities or disabilities. The contexts that surround us can affect, for example, our overall health.

The Microsystem

The **microsystem** is the developmental context nearest the individual and represents those interactions in which people are directly involved. The elements that make up this ecosystem are the individuals, groups, and agencies that have the earliest and most immediate influences on the individual, such as the following:

- *The family of origin.* The family in which we are raised is the most influential on our development. The family structure (single-parent or two-parent family), socioeconomic status (wealthy, middle class, or low income), race and ethnicity (strong influences on family educational and income levels), parenting styles (Are the parents warm and supportive? Do they abuse or use substances?), and parental involvement all play important roles in who children become.

- *Daycare/schools.* Because children spend an average 7 hours a day in daycare or in a classroom, Bronfenbrenner believed them to be a key influence on development. For example, the location of the school is important; students in small or rural communities or small suburbs tend to score higher on standardized tests than children from larger schools (Huitt, 2003).

- *The community.* Many of us have heard the saying, "It takes a village to raise a child." Neighbors, neighborhoods, peer groups, and workplaces make up a community. The greater the community's involvement in the child's life, the greater the child's success and achievement throughout life (Niemiec, Sikorski, & Walberg, 1999). Community involvement may include literacy programs, nutritional programs, recreational opportunities, or teen mentoring programs.

- *The church, synagogue, or mosque.* Religious institutions influence the development of a person's character and ethical and moral development (Nord & Haynes, 1998).

We individuals also have an impact on our environment: As we comply or rebel, agree or disagree, or express our views, hopes, and ambitions, we exert influence on the elements with which we interact.

Ecosystem: areas of individual and family development that play a role in the relationship between people and their environments.

Microsystem: the developmental context nearest the individual and representing those interactions to which people are directly exposed. The elements composing this ecosystem are the individuals, groups, and agencies that have the earliest and most immediate influences on the individual.

FatCamera/Getty Images

The microsystem is the developmental context nearest the individual, and its components exert the most influence on a person's development, such as the influence of a child's school and teachers.

The Mesosystem

Mesosystem: the ecosystem that shares all of the elements that are present in the microsystem but focuses on the interaction between the various elements rather than on the individual.

In the **mesosystem,** Bronfenbrenner retains all of the elements that are present in the microsystem, but now focuses on the interaction *between* the various elements rather than on the individual. For instance, how does the school affect the family? How does the church or temple affect the family? In what ways does the school impact the neighborhood? Consider a school district that tries to establish a sex education program that offers free condom distribution and referrals to health clinics for abortion in a community that has a strong fundamental religious belief system. Is it likely that a conservative community would endorse these practices? Likewise, consider the influence of a neighborhood organization that creates an after-school athletic and academic program for children located in a neighborhood that has a large gang presence, or a neighborhood watch organization that creates a network of "safe" houses that children can run to if a stranger attempts to approach them on the way home from school. These scenarios illustrate how elements within the microsystem interact with each other rather than directly with an individual and his or her family.

The Exosystem

Exosystem: the fabrics of society in which policies are made and influenced that ultimately have an impact on the elements of the microsystem and the individual.

The **exosystem** consists of the fabrics of society in which policies are made and influenced that ultimately have an impact on the elements of the microsystem and the individual. Social policies are beneficial to families when they foster and support the major functions of a family, such as childrearing, economic support, and caring for family members (Alberts, 2002). As Figure 1.7 shows us, the exosystem serves as an umbrella for all of the "systems" in a society.

Consider the state board of education, which establishes policies and selects curricula that are used in each of the local school districts. At the same time, the hierarchies of various religious denominations determine the central tenets of their faith, which include and determine what behaviors are deemed to be appropriate or inappropriate according to those tenets. In turn, those religious beliefs, in large part, determine what is taught in the public schools. As a result of this influence, a public school education may be vastly different in one state compared to another, depending on the components of the exosystem. In Kansas public schools, for example, teachers are permitted to teach the tenets of evolution, but they are also required to teach "creation by intelligent design." The theory of intelligent design maintains that the universe is best explained by creation by an intelligent cause, rather than by evolution of species. Further, in 2016, battles raged in the Kansas legislature over a bill under consideration in the House that would prevent school boards from using the national sexual education curriculum to give more control to local educators. Also up for debate was whether Kansas schools should continue to provide sex education in public schools. These issues remain undecided. The broader point here is that because Kansas is in the center of the "Bible belt" in the United States, many curricula decisions are centered on the religious hierarchy of the state.

The media are another element within the exosystem. Some news outlets are thought to have either liberal or conservative bias in the way that they report information, consequently influencing how certain policies and perspectives are viewed. In movies and through television programming, we also see changes in how families and family life are portrayed. Whether these changes are simply representations of historical changes in families over time or are attempts to change perceptions about what family life should be is not always clear. How these movies and TV shows are perceived may depend, to some extent, on a person's life experiences and the influences that have shaped their development to this point.

The Macrosystem

The **macrosystem** represents the next layer in Bronfenbrenner's model. It recognizes that a society has a set of overarching cultural values and beliefs that affects individual development by establishing either implicit or explicit rules about what is or is not acceptable behavior. In a population as diverse as that of the United States, there are hundreds of different religious, racial, and ethnic groups. Each may have specific cultural norms that do not conform to a broader set of values. Additionally, not all groups that fall within a general ethnic category will be the same. For instance, not all Hispanics share the same belief system. Mexican Americans may have cultural values and expectations different from those of Cuban Americans. Jews have different values than do Muslims or Buddhists. And liberals have different values than do conservatives. The cultural values of parents who are first-generation immigrants to the United States may be vastly different from those of their children who have been acculturated in American values through their interactions with peers at school and the media.

Macrosystem: the set of overarching cultural values and beliefs that affect individual development by establishing either implicit or explicit rules about what is or is not acceptable behavior in a society.

The Chronosystem

The **chronosystem,** the next, and outermost layer, reflects changes that happen over time. It accounts for the collective historical precursors of current social debates over, for example, social and economic discrimination, women's rights to reproductive choice, and the long-held definition of marriage, such as who can marry whom (Dutton, 1998).

Chronosystem: the changes that happen over time, accounting for the collective historical precursors of current social attitudes (discrimination, definition of marriage, etc.).

Bronfenbrenner's (1979) framework allows us to both grasp the nature of the main interacting influences on our lives and to examine the role that each plays. With the Ecological Model we can explore and better understand marriage, intimate relationships, and family life in various contexts. Throughout our study together, we'll explore certain areas of Bronfenbrenner's model, such as the economic, religious, and government contexts, and how they shape and affect the experiences of intimate partners and families today.

Up to this point, our study has highlighted the fact that the United States is a blend of races, ethnicities, and religions from all over the world. Often, though, we tend to focus on our own families, failing to realize the vastness of the human race. Many of us fall into the trap of thinking that how *we* experience family and intimate relationships is the *only* way to experience these aspects of life. After all, we are each experts in our individual understandings. In order to gain a truer insight into the workings of family, intimate relations, and marriage, we must step back from our cultural norms and stereotypes and enlarge our scope, so that we may see and take in more—and so far, our study has given us this opportunity.

But this wonderful medley of race, ethnicity, culture, and ways of life is not embraced by all. With this in mind, Dorian Solot and Marshall Miller (2004), founders and directors of the Alternatives to Marriage Project, put forth the following affirmation of family diversity:

We believe that all families should be valued, that the well-being of children is critical to our nation's future, and that people who care for one another should be supported in their efforts to build happy, healthy relationships. One of America's strengths is its diversity, which includes not only a wide range of races, ethnicities, creeds, abilities, genders, and sexual orientations, but also a range of family forms.

Now that you have a knowledge base in the forms and functions of marriages and families, before we conclude this chapter let's take a brief look at one of the central ways in which we'll explore family life throughout our course of study: the family life education perspective.

FAMILY LIFE EDUCATION: THE STUDY OF FAMILIES THROUGH A FAMILY LENS

Family life education:
borrowing and adapting theoretical frameworks from the fields of sociology and psychology, this perspective provides organized, programmatic education to help families cope with change.

The central concept of this book is to examine family and intimate relations using a family life education approach as a central theme. Borrowing and adapting theoretical frameworks from the fields of sociology and psychology, the family life education perspective unveils the inadequacies families feel when they are faced with change and then provides organized, programmatic education to help strengthen families. Some approaches (such as family therapy) first look to intervention instead of education; however, this text's approach acknowledges that intervention often comes too late to be effective in fully developing the potential of individuals and families. Family life education is a tool used to explore family and intimate relationships, but it is not a "theory." Instead, it is a lens through which we can study and understand family and couple relationships.

Understanding Families' Needs and Developing their Potentials

Dealing-with-problems focus:
education for family living that focused on problems of sexuality, gender roles, marriage, and other social issues.

As early as the 1960s, when U.S. culture experienced much social upheaval, people who had concerns for the "staggering list of social ills" that had an impact on family life began to conceive and organize education for family living (Smith, 1968). With young adults' newfound emphasis on sex, drugs, and rock and roll, the country was ripe for a family education concept. These early efforts to educate families centered on a **dealing-with-problems focus** (Arcus, Schvaneveldt, & Moss, 1993). Society was rapidly changing. The Vietnam War provoked cries from young adults against the "establishment"—those who promoted long-held, established societal beliefs and norms about marriage, sexuality, gender roles, childbearing, childrearing, and politics.

Preventing-the-problems focus:
family life educator Richard Kerckhoff maintained that families faced with radical societal changes only need to be shown how to do the correct things to prevent family problems.

A concept that went hand in hand with the dealing-with-problems focus to educate families was the **preventing-the-problems focus**. Family life education professor and parent educator Richard Kerckhoff (1964) maintained that families faced with radical societal changes only needed to be shown how to do the correct things. According to Kerckhoff, if families could somehow be pointed in the right direction, then "the divorce rate would drop, children would be reared properly, and the institution of family would be save" (p. 898). Problem prevention remains a prevalent theme in family life education today. As renowned family life educator and professor of human sciences Carol Darling (1987, p. 816) noted, efforts to educate families in family living is "the foremost preventive measure for the avoidance of family problems." The **developing-family-potentials focus** also arose out of the societal turmoil of the 1960s. Promoting goals ranging from building on family strengths to developing healthy, fulfilling, and responsible interpersonal relationships, family life education efforts were—and still are today—intended to build on positive aspects of family life and bring about human capabilities that improve and enhance personal life and family living (Arcus, Schvaneveldt, & Moss, 1993).

Developing-family-potentials focus:
family life education that aims to build on positive aspects of family life and the family's potential to enhance personal life and family living by promoting goals ranging from building on family strengths to developing healthy, fulfilling, and responsible interpersonal relationships.

The definitions of family life education have changed and progressed over time, as the timeline in Figure 1.8 shows us. But what has remained consistent over the decades is that the family life education perspective takes into consideration individual development and life-course experiences and how our interpersonal relationship skills and interaction patterns

Figure 1.8 /// Timeline of Family Life Education

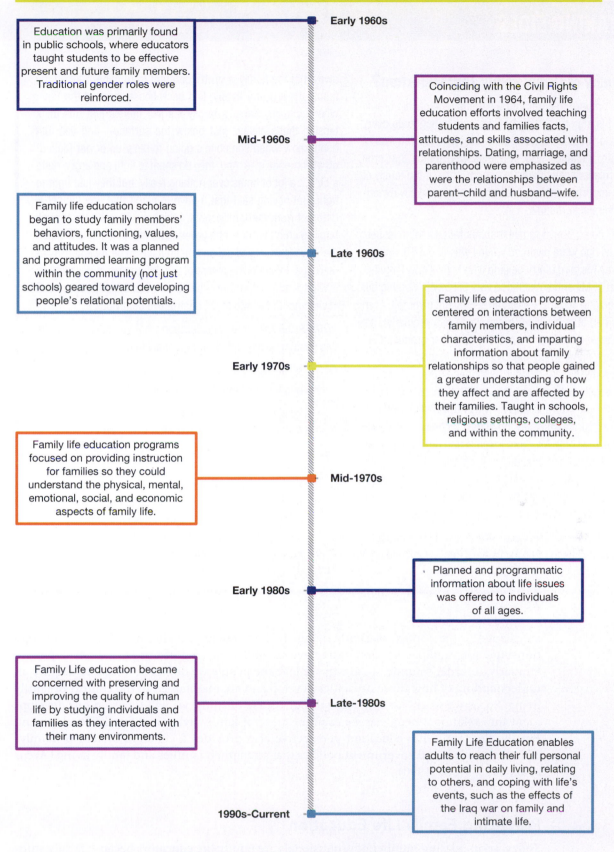

Early 1960s

Education was primarily found in public schools, where educators taught students to be effective present and future family members. Traditional gender roles were reinforced.

Mid-1960s

Coinciding with the Civil Rights Movement in 1964, family life education efforts involved teaching students and families facts, attitudes, and skills associated with relationships. Dating, marriage, and parenthood were emphasized as were the relationships between parent–child and husband–wife.

Late 1960s

Family life education scholars began to study family members' behaviors, functioning, values, and attitudes. It was a planned and programmed learning program within the community (not just schools) geared toward developing people's relational potentials.

Early 1970s

Family life education programs centered on interactions between family members, individual characteristics, and imparting information about family relationships so that people gained a greater understanding of how they affect and are affected by their families. Taught in schools, religious settings, colleges, and within the community.

Mid-1970s

Family life education programs focused on providing instruction for families so they could understand the physical, mental, emotional, social, and economic aspects of family life.

Early 1980s

Planned and programmatic information about life issues was offered to individuals of all ages.

Late-1980s

Family Life education became concerned with preserving and improving the quality of human life by studying individuals and families as they interacted with their many environments.

1990s-Current

Family Life Education enables adults to reach their full personal potential in daily living, relating to others, and coping with life's events, such as the effects of the Iraq war on family and intimate life.

Source: Handbook of Family Life Education by Margaret E. Arcus. Copyright 1993 by SAGE Publications Inc Books.

Is the Family of Origin Really That Important?

As couples prepare to enter into a serious relationship or into marriage, it is important that they are able to negotiate every kind of issue. But their past experiences in their families of origin greatly influence how they deal with things that crop up in their relational life. Given the importance of the family of origin, is it important that couples share similar family experiences in their background?

ONE SIDE: I come from a family that has faced a lot of issues. My mom and dad were divorced when I was about 10, and my dad is now on his third marriage (and who knows how long that one will last?). My entire childhood was filled with nothing but my mom and dad arguing—even after they got divorced. Even though my dad is in my life (I mean, I see him regularly), it's not like he's ever lived up to anything he's ever promised . . . he didn't even come to my high school graduation. So I don't know. I love my fiancé, but our experiences are just so different, especially with my parents and their marriage. I only know certain ways to act, certain ways to handle conflict (I tend to clam up and not say anything, whereas my fiancé wants to talk it all out). My mom is remarried now, but it's like she can't fully trust him because in the back of her mind she thinks he'll leave her like my dad did. So when you talk about family of origin, I have to question whether it's wise to marry someone with vastly different experiences from mine.

THE OTHER SIDE: I've given our differences a lot of thought. On my first trip home to meet my fiancé's family, I noticed right away that the family is pretty different from mine. Like, in my family it's a pretty happy, laid back house most of the time, whereas in my fiancé's family it's like there's just this thick tension that's always just below the surface—and you just don't know when someone's going to blow up or get [ticked] off at someone else. And, they do seem to fight and argue quite a bit . . . a lot of times over nothing really, but they just fight to fight. But having said that, I have to admit that [my fiancé] *is* different from the family roots. I think my fiancé sees that all families aren't fighters and yellers, and that just because that's the way life was lived doesn't mean it has to be *repeated* in our marriage. I think being aware of the differences in our families is what is most important—being aware of the differences and vowing not to fall into those destructive behaviors.

YOUR SIDE: Take into consideration what you have learned in this chapter, along with your personal life experiences.

1. Do you believe couples who have opposing families of origin should marry? Why or why not?

2. What potential difficulties do you foresee in this couple's marital future? In what ways can their discrepant backgrounds strengthen their marital relationship?

3. Before you read the information about the influences the family of origin exerts in our future relationships, had you given much thought to this area of family living? Why or why not? Is similar family background an important mate selection factor for you?

are shaped in the context of family living. To understand sexuality in the context of relationships, for example, we first must have an understanding of our sexual development. Similarly, in order to understand why we love the people we do, we first have to acquire an understanding of how those capacities develop and are maintained in the context of family living. So, as we work our way through our course of study, we will focus on our development into relational people as we examine areas of family living and family development. Finally, the family life education perspective also provides a coherent system of family-oriented services and government policies that strengthen families and family living (Arcus et al., 1993; Weiss, 1990).

Practicing Family Life Education

Today, an increasing number of professionals are family life educators because family studies is multidisciplinary. For example, psychologists, sociologists, and social workers may

Table 1.3 /// Key Content Areas in Family Life Education

- **Families in Society** includes varying family forms; cross-cultural and diverse families and family values; and social and cultural variations (ethnicity, rage, religion).

- **Family Dynamics** focuses on family communication patterns, conflict resolution, coping strategies, families in crisis/stress and distress and families with special needs (military, step-foster, adoptive families, etc.).

- **Human Growth and Development** explores human development across our lifespan.

- **Human Sexuality** presents sexual anatomy and physiology, reproduction, the emotional aspects of sexuality, sexual response and dysfunction, and our sexual values.

- **Interpersonal Relationships** focuses on love, human intimacy, and relational skills, such as communication.

- **Family Resource Management** focuses on family financial goals and planning and money decisions.

- **Parent Education** looks at the choice and challenges of parenthood, including the rights and responsibilities of parents, parental roles, and variations in parenting practices and styles.

- **Family Law and Public Policy** focuses on laws relating to marriage, divorce, cohabitation, child custody, child protection and the rights of children, and public policy (civil rights, social security) as it affects the family.

- **Ethics** concerns the diversity of human values and the complexity of how values are shaped in contemporary society.

Source: *HANDBOOK OF FAMILY LIFE EDUCATION* by S.R. Czaplewski and S.R. Jorgensen, Copyright 1993 by SAGE Publications Inc Books.

---

also simultaneously practice as family life educators. A **Certified Family Life Educator (CFLE)** is someone who has demonstrated knowledge (gained through work experience and college coursework) in the content areas displayed in Table 1.3. As you can see, the family life education perspective addresses every area of couple, intimate, marital, and family living, including diversity and family policy. Family life education is also multiprofessional in its scope—pastors, rabbis, priests, health professionals, social workers, mental health professionals, and researchers may be family life educators.

Today, the National Council on Family Relations (NCFR) sponsors the only international program that certifies family life educators; such certification recognizes a professional's proven background, understanding, and knowledge of the content areas. And although a CFLE may concentrate his or her expertise in one discipline, such as sexuality education, competencies in the multiple areas reflect the understanding that today's families face a wide range of issues that affect their ability to "do" family well. Thus, the awareness of and knowledge in the content areas also enables CFLEs to be more effective in their educational work with individuals and families (NCFR, 2019).

Now, armed with an understanding of the many aspects of family life education, as well as the diversity in families today, it's time to roll up our sleeves and begin our exploration of contemporary family life. The next step is to help you gain an appreciation of how you affect and are affected by the intimate relationships in your life. Although each of us accomplishes many milestones in our individual lifespan development, we do so within the context of family living. Every phase of our individual development across our human life cycle intersects with the development of the family throughout its developmental cycle, ultimately shaping who we are as relational people. In the next chapter, we'll examine how people's family of origin shapes their individual development and, in turn, shapes their capacity to love and to be loved later in life.

Certified Family Life Educator (CFLE): a person who has demonstrated knowledge (gained through work experience and college coursework) in the following content areas: families in society, family dynamics, human growth and development, human sexuality, interpersonal relationships, family resource management, parent education, family law and public policy, and ethics.

FAMILY LIFE EDUCATION: STRENGTHENING FAMILIES

All of the diversity seen today in the United States contributes to a unique, distinct social fabric that adds a deep richness to our culture. But along with diversity comes substantial differences in family structure, family living, and family experiences. Although the "traditional" family has long been held as the "ideal" standard in childrearing and family life, we are no longer a society composed primarily of married couples raising their biological or adopted children. Today, there really is no such thing as a homogenized American family composed of a breadwinning male who provides for all of the family's needs and a bread-making female who tends to the family's needs. While some family practitioners maintain that the changes we see in family structures today is a negative experience, others argue that the changes simply reflect more acceptance of diversity in our culture. You may also have a strong feeling or opinion about the changes seen in today's families; throughout our course of study together, you will gain not only a deeper understanding of family life today but also a deeper appreciation for these differences.

As diverse and distinct as U.S. families are today, though, they are all a part of the whole. We do not develop in isolation! Just as important, we do not experience family living and family life separately from our surrounding environments—and we do not experience family life in isolation from other families, no matter how different they may be from our own.

Because "family" and intimate relationships transcend race, religion, ethnicity, sexual orientation, and sexual identity, you will see yourself somewhere among the pages of this book. *Together*—you the student, your classmates, I the author/teacher, and your professor/instructor—using this text as our guide, we will examine and understand the complexities and intricacies of family life. I hope that this book will help you gain a solid, practical understanding of family and intimate relationships and equip you and empower you with the education to help you develop your full potential in your professional, personal, and family life. In this pursuit, I hope to engage your entire essence—your intellect, your emotions, and your heart.

/// SUMMARY

What Is Marriage?

- There are differing cultural, religious, legal, and social aspects of marriage worldwide. To some, marriage is a social union; to others, it is a religious act and a strong social bond around which the rest of society is organized.

- Marriage is an important social structure that serves society on political, religious, social, and economic levels.

- Marriages across the world are typically classified as either monogamous or polygamous. Monogamy is the legal structure of marriage recognized in the United States and in other Western civilizations. Polygamy is the more widely practiced form of marriage across the world.

What Is Family?

- The concept of family is a subjective experience, and "real-world" definitions are infinitely varied. Your family of origin (or family of orientation) is the family into which you were born or brought into by adoption and where you learn cultural norms. The family of procreation is the family unit that is formed when you marry and produce children. Sociocultural, economic, and political changes in the United States have influenced the family form and family life, giving way to a more complex and diverse definition of family.

- To help families reach their full potential, those who study family life education attempt to understand the changing compositions of contemporary families by using statistics to help them identify current patterns and trends. Students of family life understand that the new family landscape includes a wide array of family forms: nuclear, extended, single-parent, childless/childfree, stepfamily, cohabiting family, gay/lesbian families, and immigrant families.

Contemporary Families

- Students of family life understand that contemporary families are racially, ethnically, religiously, economically, and sexually diverse. They study the ever-changing composition of U.S. families to further their understanding of the complex, changing nature of family health and family living.

Families in Cultural Contexts

- No human being develops in isolation—every emotion, every fear, every thought, and every behavior is linked to the family in which we were raised, either by genetics or by the family environment. In addition, many areas of family life are influenced by the economic, religious, and political systems that make up the broader culture in which we live.

- Family experiences are largely shaped by the culture's social identity—whether it adopts a collectivist or individualist identity. Collectivists work together for the good of the group, while individualists do what they believe to be in their best personal interests.

- In his Ecological Model, Uri Bronfenbrenner theorized that people develop within development contexts, with the individual at the center of five ecosystems, or outside influences on the individual or family. The individual is influenced by the environment and also influences the environment.

  - *Microsystem:* This is the developmental context nearest to the individual and includes environments to which people are directly exposed, such as the family of origin, schools, the community, and religious affiliation.

  - *Mesosystem:* This describes the interaction between the various elements (e.g., How does the school have impact on the family? How does the religious institution?).

  - *Exosystem:* This is the context in which policies are made and influenced that ultimately have an impact on the elements of the microsystem and the individual. This context of development can be seen as an umbrella for all of the systems in a society (educational, religious, economic, etc.).

  - *Macrosystem:* The recognition that a society has a set of overarching cultural values and beliefs that also affects development by giving its members either implicit or explicit rules about what is or is not acceptable behavior.

  - *Chronosystem:* This system reflects the changes that happen over time.

Family Life Education: The Study of Families Through a Family Lens

- Borrowing and adapting theoretical frameworks from the fields of sociology, psychology, and other theories, the family life education perspective unveils the inadequacies families feel when they are faced with change and then provides organized programmatic education to help strengthen families. These theories, as well as statistics, help us understand and recognize family trends and experiences, but a student of couple relationships, marriage, and family life should look beyond the numbers to see what they are really telling us.

- Family life education is multidisciplinary and multiprofessional in its scope, examining theories and frameworks that are foundational to the understanding of human behavior and couple/family relationship patterns. Family life education is a lens through which we can study family processes.

/// KEY TERMS

Cenogamy   6

Certified Family Life
   Educator (CFLE)   33

Childfree   13

Childless   13

Chosen family   14

Chronosystem   29

Civil union   3

Cohabiting   14

Collectivist cultures   24

Contexts   26

Dealing-with-problems focus   30

Developing-family-potentials
   focus   30

Diverse   9

Diversity   9

Ecological model   26

Ecosystem   27

Exosystem   28

Extended family   11

Family   8

Family life education   30

Family of origin   9

Family of procreation   9

Family values   9

Fictive kin   19

General fertility rate   13

CHAPTER **2**

UNDERSTANDING FAMILIES THROUGH RESEARCH AND THEORY

LEARNING OBJECTIVES

2.1 Explain the research method from start to finish.

2.2 Evaluate the essential components of empirical research.

2.3 Describe several family theories that enhance our understanding of family processes and promote the development of effective family programs.

2.4 Defend the idea that we do not develop in isolation using the concepts of the human life cycle and the family life cycle.

Consider the experiences of this 21-year-old college student:

> Like many newlyweds, I couldn't wait to set up our first home. Everything was perfectly planned. Our five-year goals were in place: He would join the Army, I would finish my degree, he would finish his four-year stint in the service, finish his degree, and we would then begin to start our family. Because of his service in the military, our student loans would be minimal, and we would be in a position to buy our first home. It was a perfect plan.
>
> I have been married for nine months, and nothing has gone like we thought it would. Two weeks before our wedding, my husband was called up to serve in the war in Iraq. Our wedding went off without a hitch, but we had to cut our honeymoon short because of his deployment to the war. We were transferred to a military base in the Midwest! I didn't know anyone, I had no family, no friends. I felt like I was dropped off alongside the highway and expected to make the best of it. But we survived his first tour of duty. I thought to myself, "Finally, we can start our marriage." We both felt that if we could survive the separation so early in our marriage, we could survive anything. He was home for about three months and everything changed again—he was deployed again to Iraq.
>
> To be honest, I'm scared. I'm scared every day that he won't come back to me, that something will happen to him. I feel so cheated—I didn't bargain for this! I have to wonder, what will happen to our marriage? Can we make it through these separations? How many more separations will there be over the next three years? How do couples get through this?

Science is humankind's exploration of how the world works. Religion, philosophy, art, mythology, and literature have also historically attempted to quench the insatiable thirst of human inquiry, but science is distinguished from these other modes of exploration—and explanation—by the methods used to discover and to know (Babbie, 2016; Pedhazur & Schmelkin, 1991; Kidder, 1981). The exploration to discover and understand often begins with a simple inquiry, such as the question posed by the newlywed: How are marriages and families affected when a loved one serves his or her country overseas for extended periods of time? Will their marriage survive? When examining social and individual processes by engaging in and using methods beyond logic, common sense, intuition, or reason alone, we engage in scientific inquiry—in the practice of social science research.

The research method allows family scientists to explore intimate couple and family relationships. The results of the research enable family practitioners to create programs that enhance couples' relationships and family living.

iStock.com/PeopleImages

UNDERSTANDING FAMILIES THROUGH RESEARCH

Many students feel alienated from and intimidated by the research process. They have a hard time understanding how facts and figures help us understand the "big picture." This alienation, in fact, has been an obstacle for many would-be social science practitioners over the years. A colleague of mine, for example, told me that for as long as she could remember, she had wanted to be a psychologist. She majored in psychology as an undergraduate—that is, until it was time to begin coursework in research methods and statistics. Because she had a fear of and an aversion to statistics, her advisor suggested that she change her major to English. I must confess I had a similar fear of the research process. I remember thinking, "But I'm not a statistician— that's why I'm studying the family, not numbers!" As it happened, I was luckier than my colleague. Because of a dynamic research methods professor who was able to show the relevance and importance of theories and research, I was able to replace my fear with excitement about the research process. And it was while I was taking that course that the research bug bit me.

The research process is an integral and critical part of your study of marriage and family. Research is important because it enables social scientists, family practitioners, psychologists, and sociologists to develop family theories and family education programs, create family policies that strengthen and serve today's families, and better understand societal trends, such as the demographic trends of contemporary families, as you saw earlier. Indeed, research is neither boring nor insignificant because it has an impact on the daily lives of today's couples and families. It is through research and these theories that we come to a deeper understanding of family functioning and family process.

Social Science Research

The term **research** means to study thoroughly using the process of scholarly or scientific inquiry. **Social science research** is the scholarly discipline used to examine human society and relationships. When conducting research in the social sciences, researchers examine behaviors, emotions, and relationships—all of which cannot be easily quantified or examined within neat, tidy categories. I like to refer to social science research as "the other side of the microscope"—in other words, social scientists are not concerned with what the results

Research:
to study the family thoroughly using the process of scholarly or scientific inquiry.

Social science research:
the scholarly discipline used to examine human society and relationships.

are under the microscope as are biologists; instead, they are concerned with factors that cannot be seen microscopically; they are concerned with *people*. The *whole person.*

Researching couple relationships and family life allows us to explore intimate relationships within the context of partnerships, marriage, and family. Family research provides information that enables family practitioners—such as family life educators, social workers, teachers, members of the clergy, therapists, and psychologists—to develop, implement, and evaluate programs that may enhance family life and family growth. Understanding the problems that face today's family and finding explanations and answers to those problems would not be possible without the practice of social science inquiry through research.

As 19th-century American humorist Artemus Ward once noted, "It ain't the things we don't know that gets us in trouble. It's the things we know that ain't so" (Kidder, 1981). This tongue-in-cheek statement has an element of truth. We often believe we "know" something to be true or factual because it seems to be the logical, commonsense conclusion. Take, for example, the following statements:

- Children reared by same-sex parents experience negative outcomes.
- A couple who cohabits before marriage increases their chances that their marriage will last because they will work out all of their difficulties before going down the aisle.
- Married couples who frequently argue have lower levels of marital satisfaction than couples who experience few conflicts.

What is your logical, commonsense response to these statements?

Relying on logic or common sense frequently "limits us to the familiar" (Kidder, 1981, p. 4). If you agree or disagree with the previous statements, you are using your intuition or existing beliefs, your life experiences, and your expectations to draw those conclusions. You are reasoning about what might be a plausible or the most likely outcome and drawing your conclusions based on your interpretation of circumstances. Are your conclusions accurate?

The problem with using our common sense and logic is that everyone sees things differently based on different value systems, political beliefs, religious beliefs—the very values and beliefs that provide the lens through which we view our social environments. Because of our differences in values and beliefs, how can we "know" that, for example, children reared by same-sex couples really do (or really do not) experience negative developmental outcomes? What aspects of our belief system would lead us to believe that couples who live together before marriage have a higher (or lower) success rate than couples who do not? How can we "know" how marital separation, such as in the opening vignette, impacts marital happiness or satisfaction? We "know" when we conduct research that supports or does not support our suppositions. We look at the numbers, we draw conclusions, and we apply theories, all of which gives us insight and helps us know and understand the truth.

The Research Method: Start to Finish

In his 1911 work, *The Grammar of Science,* statistician Karl Pearson maintained, "There is no shortcut to truth, no way to gain a knowledge of the universe except through the gateway of scientific method" (p. 17). The **scientific method** is a process by which social science researchers formulate questions concerning social and individual phenomena and seek out answers. Using the scientific method, researchers design a process from start to finish that details the sequential, interrelated investigative steps the researcher will follow. Much like building a house, a solid investigative design plan moves researchers systematically through each step as they look for answers to their initial questions.

Scientific method:
the process by which researchers formulate questions concerning social and individual phenomena and seek out answers.

From Start to Finish

If you have a well-conceived research design and a sound, logical plan, your plan is more likely to yield valuable results. Figure 2.1 illustrates the starting point of a research design, either through interest in a topic, an idea, or a desire to explore a theory. This design can be used

Figure 2.1 /// The Research Process from Start to Finish

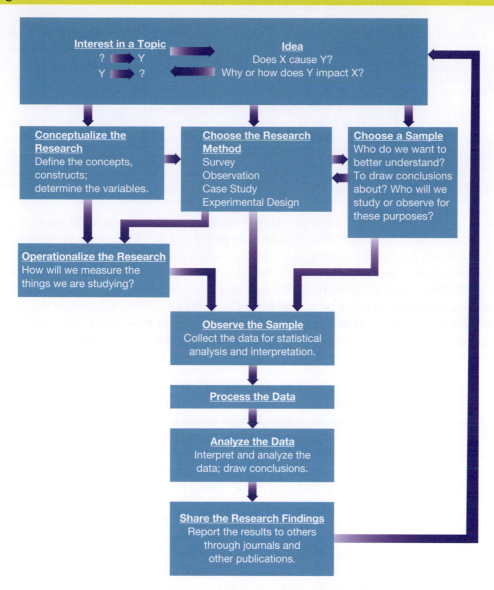

Interest in a Topic
? ➡ Y
Y ➡ ?

Idea
Does X cause Y?
Why or how does Y impact X?

Conceptualize the Research
Define the concepts, constructs; determine the variables.

Choose the Research Method
Survey
Observation
Case Study
Experimental Design

Choose a Sample
Who do we want to better understand? To draw conclusions about? Who will we study or observe for these purposes?

Operationalize the Research
How will we measure the things we are studying?

Observe the Sample
Collect the data for statistical analysis and interpretation.

Process the Data

Analyze the Data
Interpret and analyze the data; draw conclusions.

Share the Research Findings
Report the results to others through journals and other publications.

Source: From BABBIE. *The Practice of Social Research* (with CD-ROM and Info Trac) 11th edition, © 2016 Wadsworth, a part of Cengage Learning, Inc. Reproduced by permission, www.cengage.com/permissions.

Quantitative research:
a form of research that uses statistical methods to count and measure outcomes from a study.

Qualitative research:
a form of research that involves detailed verbal or written descriptions of characteristics under investigation.

for both quantitative research and qualitative research. **Quantitative research** uses statistical methods to count and measure outcomes from a study; it is a systematic attempt to define, measure, and report on the relationships between elements that are being studied. **Qualitative research** involves detailed verbal or written descriptions of characteristics under investigation; this research typically involves observation and interviews to collect data. To aid in your understanding of the research process, we'll follow a research design plan that examined marital satisfaction among deployed members of the U.S. Army (Schumm, Bell, & Gade, 2000).

Step 1. Choosing the Research Topic. Intimacy, jealousy, the effects of divorce on children, sexuality, gender identity and gender roles, family communication and conflict—the number of potential research topics is virtually limitless, and investigators choose to examine topics for a variety of reasons. Some may select a research topic because of a concern with a social issue or problem, such as the effects of peacetime and war deployment on military families, as illustrated in the opening vignette; some may have a great interest in a particular area of behavior; others may choose to examine the validity of a certain theory; still others may select a topic because of financial or professional incentives to do so (Kidder, 1981).

Once a research topic is chosen, the investigator needs to determine which variables to study. A **variable** is a characteristic that is measured in a study. It is called a variable because the value or degree of the characteristic *varies* among the people or group of people being studied.

In the military study, for example, the examiners wanted to assess changes in marital satisfaction over time among soldiers who were on a peacekeeping mission overseas. They wanted to better understand whether long-term separation reduced marital satisfaction and to see whether satisfaction became elevated once the soldiers returned home (Schumm et al., 2000). The variables for this investigation included soldiers' assessments of their marital satisfaction pre-deployment, mid-deployment, and post-deployment. Another variable was marital stability, or how stable the soldiers' marriages were before, during, and after deployment.

Step 2. Creating the Research Question. At the core of any valid research is the **research question**, or the research hypothesis. Before researchers pose a research question or hypothesis, they must first have a clear understanding of the problem and a clear vision of their objective. In the military study, the research question was *What impact do long overseas deployments have on the families of soldiers?* Because initial research hypotheses may involve many unknowns at the outset, researchers often need to refine their investigation by doing an exhaustive search of the existing research studies related to their topic of inquiry. This is referred to as a **literature review**. This process allows researchers to get a better grasp on the scope of the problem and all aspects related to the research topic.

After the researcher has a solid understanding of the problem he or she wants to investigate, a research hypothesis is formed. A **hypothesis** is a speculative statement about a variable or the relationship between variables in a study. In a sense, hypotheses are predictions about the variables that will be measured in the study (Agresti & Finlay, 2008). In the sequential research process, statistical **hypotheses testing** takes place at a later point in the investigation. A hypothesis is never accepted or confirmed; based on the evidence gathered, a researcher can either *reject* a hypothesis or *fail to reject* a hypothesis.

Step 3. Conceptualizing the Research. Once a researcher has generated an idea or interest in a topic area, has formulated a research question, and has selected the variables to be studied, the next step in planning the design of the research study is conceptualization. **Conceptualization** is the process by which the researcher specifically denotes or indicates all of the concepts—or constructs—under investigation. A concept, or **construct**, refers to intangibles. For example, if I asked you to define *marital satisfaction,* we would soon discover that definitions for these terms are as numerous as the number of students reading this textbook. As research methodologists Elazur Pedhazur and Liora Schmelkin put it, "Even for people who speak the same language, words have different meanings, depending on, among other things, who speaks, to whom, in what context, at what time, and with what purpose. Words . . . are loaded with connotations" (1991, p. 164). Thus, a construct is a "mental creation" (Babbie, 2016) that enables individuals to communicate in concrete terms about abstract ideas that have no single, unwavering meaning—such as "love." If we pause just a moment to think about Earl Babbie's description of a construct, then we quickly come to the conclusion that just about everything examined in the social sciences is a construct!

Step 4. Using Operational/Empirical Definitions. Because constructs are mental creations and words may have different connotations, it is important that researchers come to a workable definition for the constructs under investigation. For example, how can I be sure that when you are reading my research you, in your mental creation, are referring to "marital satisfaction" in the same capacity that I am? In the past, marital satisfaction has been operationally defined by some researchers as a set of desirable characteristics of the ideal marriage, such as maintaining feelings of mutual love and respect, equitable sharing of duties and responsibilities, making decisions together, mutual sharing of interests, and mutual agreement on important issues (Fowers &

Variable:
a characteristic that is measured in a study. The value of the characteristic varies among the people or group being studied, hence the name.

Research question:
the research question, or research hypothesis, is the core of any valid project and takes into account a clear understanding of the problem to be addressed and a clear vision of the objective. With these addressed, the answer to this question is presented clearly and concisely.

Literature review:
a comprehensive search of existing research studies related to a particular topic of inquiry.

Hypothesis:
a speculative statement about a variable or the relationship between variables in a study.

Hypotheses testing:
based on evidence gathered, a researcher can either reject a hypothesis or fail to reject a hypothesis.

Conceptualization:
the process by which the researcher specifically denotes or indicates all of the concepts—or constructs—under investigation.

Construct:
a concept referring to intangibles in the inquiry.

Olson, 1993). Today, other researchers define marital satisfaction by using global evaluations of a couple's behaviors and feelings, such as the amount of conflict between the couple or whether the individual would marry his or her spouse again if he or she had it to do over (Kamp, Dush, Taylor, & Kroeger, 2008). So you see, the definition of a construct can change depending on who the researcher is and the purpose of the study.

To avoid confusion, *at the outset of the research,* researchers create **operational definitions** that describe or characterize the constructs (concepts) that are being studied. As the research progresses, the empirical (scientific) definitions may need to be refined. Whether a consumer of the research agrees with empirically defined terms is not important.

Operational definitions: created by researchers at the outset of research to describe or characterize the constructs (concepts) that are being studied.

Step 5. Choosing the Research Method. The next step in the research process involves selecting which research method (or combination of research methods) to use when pursuing the investigation. In order to represent in a statistical format human behaviors and patterns of behavior, empirical data must be gathered. The best method for studying couples, the family, marriage, and other interpersonal relationships largely depends on the purpose of the research—whether it is exploration, description, or explanation. To study families, family scientists typically use four primary research methods to collect data: the survey, observational research, the case study, and experimental design.

Surveys. For three decades, influential social and economics science researcher Don Dillman has helped social scientists effectively plan and conduct survey research with his landmark book, *Mail and Internet Surveys: The Tailored Design Method* (1978). The **survey** research method, a structured questionnaire, is the most popular technique for gathering data when studying families and interpersonal relationships (Dillman, 1999). Standardized questionnaires are an excellent method for determining trends and behavioral patterns and for gathering original data about a certain population. By collecting survey responses from a group of people, a **sample**, researchers can sometimes infer conclusions based on survey data and extend them to the larger population.

Survey: a structured questionnaire comprising a list of questions.

Sample: a group of people from whom researchers collect survey responses.

We will discuss methods of sampling later in this chapter. For now, understand that in order for a questionnaire or survey to yield valuable information that reflects the characteristics

Sparky/Getty Images

A structured questionnaire, or a survey instrument, is the most popular way in which family scientists gather data and information.

of the population being studied, it must be well constructed and well designed. According to Don Dillman (1999), a well-constructed survey is unbiased and easily understood by study respondents. The questions in a good survey should also be carefully worded and nonobjectionable.

There are many different types of surveys and questionnaires. Some are mailed or e-mailed to potential respondents, some are Web based, and others are carried out by telephone or face-to-face interviews. Whatever the method, each has its strengths and weaknesses. And the success of any survey research is measured by the response rate of the study subjects.

Response rate:
the percentage of study subjects who respond to the survey.

Response rate. The **response rate** is the percentage of the study subjects who respond to the survey. Perhaps one of the most questionable response rates was obtained by Shere Hite, author of the well-known human sexuality study, *The Hite Report*. Hite indicated she sent out 100,000 sexuality questionnaires to women, but only about 4,500 women responded to the survey, or a 4.5 percent response rate. This low response rate was a red flag for social scientists. Because the response rate to a survey or questionnaire indicates how representative the study sample is (to what extent it accurately reflects the characteristics) of the larger population, very low response rates such as Hite's show that those who *did not* respond to the survey differed from those who *did* respond. How high a response rate is high enough? Universally, a response rate of 50 percent is considered to be adequate for analyzing data; 60 percent is good; and a 70 percent response rate is very good (Babbie, 2016).

Survey drawbacks. Despite the fact that surveys and questionnaires are the most common means of obtaining social science data, there are some inherent problems with their use. In the physical sciences, the units of measurement are very precise, but in social science research, we must depend on human beings to provide information—which is subjective—on their feelings and behaviors.

Take the example of a teenage male filling out a survey that assesses how sexually active he is—while sitting beside his very sexually experienced buddy. To impress his friend, the adolescent may overreport his sexual encounters. Conversely, if his friend is an active member of a church youth group that frowns on premarital sex, it is possible the teen male might underreport his sexual activity. Because survey research is dependent on human beings providing human responses about their past and current experiences, there is an inherent risk of overreporting or underreporting certain behaviors. This is referred to as **response bias**, a flaw that may occur when researchers rely on individuals' self-reports.

Response bias:
when using human beings as subjects, this is the risk whereby subjects' past and current experiences may affect their responses. This is a flaw that may occur when researchers rely on individuals' self-reports.

Another area of concern is whether surveys reliably assess human behavior, attitudes, and experiences. These may be difficult to assess by rigid, standardized questions. For example, how can research measure "commitment" or "love"? It is quite possible that when responding to a survey, the respondents may want to delve deeper into their responses—which would provide much greater insight into their behavior and feelings—but there is no provision on the survey or questionnaire to do so. Thus, researchers are left with an incomplete understanding of the context of the respondent's life situation.

Validity:
the extent to which a researcher is able to provide an empirical definition that reflects the true meaning of the construct being considered.

As we discussed earlier, much of what researchers examine in social science inquiry are constructs. For this reason, researchers must take care when empirically defining these concepts to ensure that responses are valid. **Validity** speaks to the extent that a researcher is able to provide an empirical definition that reflects the true meaning of what is being studied. For example, if we want to study marital satisfaction, do we want to study the amount of conflict in the couple's relationship or do we want to study the couple's mutual love and respect for each other? We have to make sure that our measurements accurately assess what we want them to assess.

The validity of survey research is often criticized because the questions may not really measure what the researchers claim they are measuring. In a sense, what happens is the researcher strains to provide an empirical definition that (ideally) accurately represents a construct, and then the research participant is asked to fit that behavior or emotion to a predetermined scale that may or may not reflect how the respondent wants to answer. In Babbie's (2016) view, very seldom do our opinions neatly fall into categories of "always," "sometimes," "never," "strongly agree," "somewhat agree," and the like. When people are asked to approximate their behavior to fit within a standardized scale, validity is put in jeopardy.

Observational Research. Our observations help us understand and make sense of our world. Each of us continuously observes the behavior of others, whether we are craning our necks to see who is going into whose dorm room, or whether we're driving slowly by a vehicle accident. Our media-savvy society allows us to peer into the lives of bachelors and bachelorettes seeking "true love" through reality TV programming. The problem with reality TV, however, is that it is part reality and part entertainment, and what we ultimately observe is not "real" at all. Social science inquiry requires a much more systematic method of observation.

The **observational research method** is a systematic process in that (1) the observation is systematically planned, (2) the data are gathered and recorded in a systematic format, and (3) systematic checks and balances assess the reliability and validity of the observations (Kidder, 1981). Observational research can take place either in a laboratory-like setting, such as a married couple in a counseling session being observed behind a one-way glass, or the more natural setting that we call **field research**. In both cases, investigators want to objectively record and describe the behavior that is being observed.

Researcher Kidder (1981) described three purposes of using observational research:

1. *Observational research may be performed for purposes of description,* such as describing how children respond immediately after viewing a violent video clip or how infants respond when their parents leave them unattended.

2. *This research method is used when the subject matter does not lend itself to other methods.* For example, in 2019, hundreds of immigrant children were separated from their parents at the United States southern border and detained in prison-like facilities. If researchers were present at these detainment sites, they could more accurately record the immediate reactions and responses of the children, directly assess the impact of the separation trauma for these children, and ultimately implement immediate interventions and create counseling programs that truly meet and reflect the needs of the children to move forward in healthy ways.

3. *Observational research is appropriate when other research methods are inaccurate.* When trying, for example, to ascertain information about behaviors, experiences, and attitudes, observational research may enable researchers to observe and record accurate descriptions of behavior that other methods would not permit. The results of such studies may, in some cases, be representative of the larger population and not just relevant to the sample studied. For instance, if we wanted to better understand the effects of the long-term displacement of immigrant families and parents being separated from their children, observing their behaviors and experiences would yield much more valuable information than a survey, which might not be able to fully capture the feelings and attitudes of the victims. These observational experiences could then be used to formulate policies and educational programs that promote family health, home relocation/replacement, and family reunification following immigration.

Case Study. The **case study** methodology involves study of either a single person or a small group of people. Case studies are often used to obtain an in-depth understanding of emotional and/or behavioral patterns by providing detailed descriptions of either an individual case or a group of case studies related to one another. When a comprehensive (almost biographical) description is needed or desired, researchers turn to case studies. Sometimes an

Observational research method:

a type of research method wherein an observation is systematically planned and data are gathered and recorded systematically.

Field research:

observational research taking place in a natural setting, such as at the family's own home or a playground, instead of at a clinic.

Case study:

the study of either a single person or a small group of people.

area of interest is so new that one-by-one case studies are the means by which the data are gathered and new theories are subsequently generated; other times the area under investigation is an uncommon or rare occurrence, such as our examples of immigrant children being separated from their families and detained.

Aside from the drawback of being time consuming for the researcher, case study methodology findings may be limited in that they are not typically *generalizable*—applicable—to the larger population. For example, although the case studies of the migrant children provide very valuable information about the effects of family separation and trauma on children, researchers cannot assume that these effects could be generalized to children in war-torn Iraq. Case studies do not allow us to see cause-and-effect relationships.

Experimental Design. **Experimental design** is used to determine causal relationships among variables. Conducting experimental design research requires researchers to control the experimental procedure—controlling or holding constant the variables being studied in order to determine which variable is, indeed, effecting the change in the other variable.

An experimental design consists of two groups: the **experimental group** is the group that is exposed to the independent variables under question; the **control group** is treated exactly the same as the experimental group, except they are not exposed to the independent variable (see Figure 2.2).

A limitation of experimental research is that the laboratory is an artificial environment in which to study human response. Consider, for example, the reality TV show *The Bachelorette*. When Jed headed to Los Angeles to woo Bachelorette Hannah in front of millions of viewers, was their relationship and their emotions authentic? For instance, what if the producers of the television show omitted the fact that Jed had a girlfriend back home, and the only reason he appeared on *The Bachelorette* was to further his music career? Would these people be acting the way they act or saying what they do if the cameras were not on them? The answer is no. In other words, we have to consider how much the presence of the camera is influencing their behavior. In this same vein, how much does the knowledge of an experiment alter an individual's behavior?

Step 6. Selecting a Population and Sampling. After a researcher has conceptualized the research, empirically defined all constructs/concepts under investigation, and chosen the type of research method to be used, the next step in the research process involves selecting a population or sample to be studied. In the military research, the examiners wanted to study the effect of separation on marital satisfaction among service members. The researcher could not possibly locate all the service men and women in that **population** (the entire group of people who shared this experience); to overcome this, a researcher selects a sample from the population under investigation.

Experimental design:

used to determine causal relationships among variables. In this mode, researchers control or hold constant certain variables being studied in order to determine which variable is effecting the change in the other variable.

Experimental group:

in an experiment, the subjects in this group are exposed to the independent variable.

Control group:

in an experiment, the subjects in this group are treated exactly the same as those in the experimental group, except they are not exposed to the independent variable.

Population:

the entire group of people who share a common experience or characteristic under academic examination.

Figure 2.2 /// The Experimental Design Research Method

Population (N = Sample Size)	Groups (R = Random Selection)	Pre-Test	Experimental Treatment (X)	Post-Test	Differences
N (number in sample)	R—Experimental Group	The group's characteristics before the treatment or program.	X—One group gets the treatment or program.	The group's characteristics after the treatment or program.	Change?
N (number in sample)	R—Control Group	The group's characteristics at the start of the study.	No treatment or program.	The group's characteristics at the end of the study.	Change?

One of the most important steps in the research method is selecting a population or a sample to be examined. Researchers can use either a probability (random) sample or a nonprobability (not random) sample.

In the social sciences, our investigation of people's behavior and emotional states must take into account people's differences. For this reason, we have to be very precise and deliberate in our selection of whom we study via sampling. There are two types of sampling: probability sampling and nonprobability sampling (see Figure 2.3).

Figure 2.3 /// Research Samples

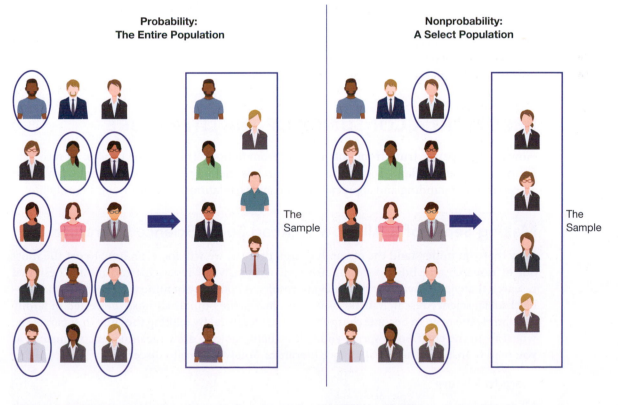

**Probability:
The Entire Population**

The Sample

**Nonprobability:
A Select Population**

The Sample

Source: iStock.com/yuoak

Probability sampling is necessary because not every person in every population shares exact characteristics. In a **probability** (random) **sample**, each person has the same likelihood (probability) of being selected for the study. In probability sampling, the notion of **representativeness**, or the degree to which the characteristics of the population are represented by the sample, is key. The **sample size** also affects the degree to which the sample is considered to be representative. Statistics gathered based on probability samples are used to draw conclusions about the sample because researchers can reasonably assess the amount of sampling error that is expected to occur.

Nonprobability samples are not selected randomly but are used when the use of probability samples is impossible. For example, when the investigators decided to study U.S. service members, it was not feasible for the researcher to select a probability sample from the population at large (what would their chances be that their sample would include people who had served overseas?); they instead used a nonprobability sample.

Step 7. Collecting, Processing, and Analyzing Data. Only after careful methodological planning of the total research design is the social scientist ready to collect, process, and analyze the data. These processes are beyond the scope of our discussion here, but it is vitally important for novice researchers to understand the relevance and necessity of each step in the design process. Although inexperienced researchers may be eager to collect data in an area that is of great interest to them, and even though it might be tempting for experienced researchers to become lax and complacent in research design, less-than-desirable results are almost assured. Remember, these steps are not necessarily sequential; the overlap among the design elements is continuous throughout the entire investigative procedure. *A poor research design almost always produces poor research results.*

Step 8. Applying Research Findings. Once a researcher collects, processes, and analyzes the data generated from the research, the findings of the study are usually presented in some type of format (such as a journal or professional conference) for scholars, researchers, policy makers, or other users to employ. Some may choose to use their findings to support and bring about societal change through the creation of family policy. Other researchers may elect to have their study reviewed by colleagues and then publish the research process and findings in a journal devoted to a given area of study, such as the *Journal of Marriage and Family,* the *Journal of Sex Research,* the *Journal of Men's Studies,* and *Family Relations,* to name a few. Still other researchers may use their research findings and research skills to design, implement, and evaluate family life education programs that promote the health and functioning of today's families.

BECOMING A CONSUMER OF THE LITERATURE

How do we separate truth from untruth, fact from fiction? Through the process of research. Despite its inherent flaws, social science research is the only method by which we can gain a deeper understanding and appreciation of couples, relationships, family, and family life.

Making Sense of It All: How to Read Social Science Literature

Now that you understand the research design process, we will focus on how to get the most out of research and how to distinguish well-written, valid research from poorly designed research that yields invalid or insignificant results. A colleague of mine who teaches graduate-level social science research methods courses makes the point that those interested in family and family life need to become *consumers* of the literature. By making the time to separate the wheat from the chaff, so to speak, you will be better able to draw meaningful conclusions as you read (consume) the social science literature. You will learn to discern.

Learn to Discern

Many readers in search of information tend to skip over the results section of a research article and jump directly to the more engaging, accessible discussion section where authors take the liberty to interpret the results of their study. Most authors include within the discussion a section devoted to the limitations of the current study. Many novice consumers of the literature, however, are also novices when it comes to interpreting what they are reading, and they mistakenly assume the discussion section portrays a precise interpretation of the results section. Unfortunately, this is not always the case.

Throughout this book, you will notice numerous research citations that substantiate the information that is conveyed. These citations or references refer to research or findings presented by an author or several authors. As you read research, consider the following questions to ensure that it is valid and reliable.

Are the Purposes of the Research and/or the Hypotheses Clearly Stated?

Be wary of research that does not specifically state the intended purpose of the research or present a clearly stated research hypothesis at the outset. There is an expression, "Anyone can make any research say anything." Although educated consumers of the literature will avoid this pitfall, to a certain extent this statement is true. **Data churning**, or "fishing," refers to the practice of devising the purposes of the research or formulating a research hypothesis *after* the data are gathered and analyzed. Data churning reduces the value of statistical findings because, sooner or later, something that appears to be statistically significant will turn out that way simply because of random chance.

Data churning: also known as "fishing," this refers to the practice of devising the purposes of the research or formulating a research hypothesis after the data are gathered and analyzed.

What Is the Method by Which the Data Are Collected?

Researchers obtain data by asking carefully constructed questions or through the direct observation of behavior. Because surveys and questionnaires are the means by which the majority of social science information is gathered, it is important to examine the survey instrument (a questionnaire, for example) and the survey process.

The content of surveys and/or questionnaires largely depends on the purpose of the study (exploration, description, or explanation) and the type of information the researcher is hoping to gather. Types of question content areas may include the following:

1. Content aimed at ascertaining facts
2. Content aimed at ascertaining beliefs about the facts
3. Content aimed at ascertaining feelings
4. Content aimed at discovering standards of action
5. Content aimed at past or present behavior
6. Content designed to discover beliefs, feelings, and behavior (Kidder, 1981)

When scrutinizing surveys, look at how demanding the questions are. Are they asking people to articulate, recall, and express detailed information? Are the questions written in a biased format to elicit desired statements, or are they unbiased and open? For instance, if a survey posed the question, "Why did President Trump make the wrong decision in deciding to detain children of immigrants?" it would be asking a biased question because the way this question is constructed presupposes a value on his decision (the word *wrong).* As a careful reader, consider what questions skew the results of the study. Are the questions too vague? Too precise? Has the researcher assumed too much about the respondents' behavior? Has the researcher assumed too much about the respondents' knowledge base?

How Was the Study Sample Selected? Is the Sample Representative?

What constitutes a "good" study sample? In order for a study sample to represent a desired population under investigation, a probability sample is the research method of choice. By employing randomization—a sample that ensures everyone has an equal chance of being selected—the researcher minimizes the possibility of misleading results. Does the study sample have enough participants from the population under inquiry so that statistical approximations can

Convenience sample:

a sample whose elements are selected based on convenience.

be made? Or is the sample, instead, a convenience sample or a volunteer sample? A sample that is not scientifically selected calls even the most well-intended research into question.

What Is the Response Rate?

In order to fully interpret the meaning of statistical data, it is imperative that consumers of the literature understand the composition of the study participants. To determine the applicability of survey findings, the response rate must be sizable. Recall from our earlier discussion that in social science research, a response rate of 50 percent is considered a "good" response rate. Why is this an important measure? The response rate is an indicator of how representative the survey or questionnaire is; the higher the response rate, the more likely it is that the survey responses reflect the population under investigation. For example, in the military group under study, of the 200 married service personnel, 113 responded to the survey— or about 57 percent of the population under investigation. Of these 113 soldiers, 70 percent provided data throughout the length of the study.

Investigators must also understand the makeup of the population. Are the respondents' characteristics more heavily concentrated in one area than another? (This may or may not pose a problem, depending on the intended purpose of the research.) Equally important is the consideration of who *did not* respond.

What Is the Weight of the Evidence for Conclusions?

Always be wary of claims that cite "most" or "many" or "several," if the sample size is not known. Ask yourself, "Most, many, or several of what number?" When viewing data that are represented by percentages, immediately ask, "X percentage of how many?" In other words, is the percentage reported 33.3 percent of a sample of *three,* or of *three hundred thousand?* Whether data are presented in graphic form, such as a bar graph, or in tables that present percentages, keep the percentages in perspective. Always know the sample size and response rate before trusting the percentages.

Do Confounding (Rival) Factors Exist?

Confounding (or rival) variables:

variables that are unrelated, unconnected, or not pertinent to the variables under investigation that can skew or affect the results of the study.

Confounding (or rival) variables are variables that are unrelated, unconnected, or not pertinent to the variables under investigation, which can skew or affect the results of the study. Results are often influenced by these extraneous factors. My college statistics professor gave an example of confounding variables in a study that sought to determine who had the greater incidence of cancer, individuals who ate oatmeal or individuals who consumed Kellogg's Frosted Flakes. The researchers found that individuals who ate oatmeal had higher rates of cancer than those who ate Frosted Flakes. The confounding variable? Those who ate oatmeal were older than those who ate Frosted Flakes—*age* was the contributing factor to incidence of cancer, not what was consumed for breakfast!

Whether you are preparing to become a social worker, an educator, a family life educator, a member of the clergy, a child life specialist, or any type of human services provider, the very nature of your profession calls on you to make judgments and assessments about the reliability and validity of research results.

It is the researcher's ethical responsibility to present information in a forthright and honest manner, but it is also the consumer's responsibility to determine the sufficiency of the research process and the dependability of the results. It is together in the researcher/consumer enterprise that reliable, repeatable, useful information is obtained through social science investigation.

Research Ethics and Integrity

The practice of social science research is an endeavor that requires responsible conduct on the part of the researcher, particularly in light of the fact that human subjects are the object of study. The federal government sets procedural guidelines to ensure that researchers conduct their research ethically and with integrity.

In general, **ethics** refers to the principals or standards of people's conduct or the principals of right and good. In the realm of social science research, ethics refers to the rules and standards that govern researchers' conduct as they examine human behaviors, feelings, and attitudes (National Academy of Sciences, 1995). Following research procedural guidelines set forth by the federal government, and to ensure the ethical treatment of research subjects, academic institutions and other research institutions have established research review committees, or **Institutional Review Boards (IRB)**. Often, IRBs are referred to as *human subjects committees.* Before pursuing a research plan, scientists must first gain the approval of their institution's IRB. These committees are concerned with the study participants' safety and well-being, ensuring that all participants have been fully informed of the true nature of the research and have been assured of privacy and confidentiality.

Scientific endeavors are based on trust: IRBs trust researchers to abide by the ethical guidelines that are set in place to ensure the protection of research subjects; study subjects trust researchers to treat them with care and concern; academic and medical communities trust that the results reported by researchers are accurate and valid; and society trusts that research results are accurate and not biased (National Academy of Sciences, 1995).

Whereas research ethics is concerned with the relationship between the researcher and the research subjects, **research integrity** is concerned with the relationship between researchers and the truth in reporting their findings (Pimple, 2001). In other words, is it good, reliable science? Research integrity requires

- A competent research design plan
- No manipulation of the data to construe the results one way or another
- Sound statistical methods
- No falsification of the results
- No fabrication of the results
- Sharing the results with the academic and/or medical world
- Giving credit where credit is due (citing research sources used in the gathering and publishing of research findings)

As you can see, the process of social science research is a carefully crafted balance of research design, research ethics, and research integrity. Discovering ways through research to strengthen families and the quality of family life is a tedious yet exhilarating experience. Within the social sciences, it is especially rewarding to know that our research efforts have direct impact on the populations we care deeply and passionately about. It is through research that family practitioners and social scientists create educational programs and family polices that serve humankind. Research also promotes the creation of family theories.

UNDERSTANDING FAMILIES THROUGH THEORY

Because we all consider ourselves knowledgeable about family life, it can be quite tempting to make assertions about a form of family behavior we consider to be "right" or "wrong" based on our personal experience. But "family life" extends well beyond our personal worlds. One way to understand and envision "family" beyond our own worlds is to expand our knowledge through theories.

Strongly held beliefs about what constitutes "family" have molded, and at times dominated, services available to families and family policy. Yet, in order to move beyond these commonly held assumptions and common beliefs about family, family scientists and theorists cannot rely on widely held suppositions about family; rather, they must study the family empirically.

A solid, foundational knowledge base in family theory is essential for students of and professionals interested in the fields of couple and family life. Throughout our study, we will examine several theories and frameworks that are fundamental to the understanding of

Ethics:
in social science research, the rules and standards that govern researchers' conduct as they examine human behaviors, feelings, and attitudes.

Institutional Review Boards (IRBs):
research review committees established by academic and other research institutions that review and approve research plans for scholars and researchers and ensure the ethical treatment of research subjects.

Research integrity:
the relationship between researchers and the truth in reporting their findings.

Theory:

a general principle that is used to understand or to explain certain events or family experiences.

Framework:

a systematic structure for classifying families, their behaviors, or their experiences.

human behavior and family relationship patterns. In the family sciences, a **theory** is a general principle that is used to understand or to explain certain events or family experiences, such as family communication or family crisis. A **framework** is a systematic structure for classifying families, their behaviors, or their experiences. Theories profoundly affect what we know about families because they provide structure for how we think about families, what we observe, how we interpret what we observe, and how we use this information to create programs and introduce policies that affect and enhance family life (Smith, 1995). In short, a theory allows us to move beyond our everyday, common beliefs about family and move toward an objective, scientific understanding of family and family processes.

An Introduction to Family Theories

We do not develop in a vacuum. The most significant influence on both our individual development and our ability to relate to others, by far, is our *family of origin*. Our family is the base from which we venture out and learn to share ourselves in close and intimate relationships. The ability to share ourselves is a complicated, elaborate mixture of our own individual development and our family experiences (whatever they might be). Our family history also plays a significant role, as generations before produced our grandparents and parents—those who have influenced us the most.

Today, many theories exist that attempt to explain the workings of family, and each has made numerous contributions to the field of family studies. James White, David Klein, and Todd Martin, authors of *Family Theories: An Introduction* (2014), describe today's prevailing family theories.

1. *Ecological theory* is concerned with the many social and cultural contexts that affect family living. As you learned in Chapter 1, these contexts include factors that exert immediate influences on the family, such as schools, churches or temples, and neighborhoods. Other contexts include the government, educational systems, the political system, and the overarching value system of a given society.

2. *Family Development theory* divides the experiences of family into phases, or stages, of normative changes associated with family growth and development, such as the birth of children and the launching of these children into early adulthood. This theory is concerned with understanding the changes in family structures and the roles of family members across each stage of family development. According to this theory, healthy families are able to adapt to these changes across time.

3. *Conflict theory* maintains that society shapes individual and family behavior. At the core of this theory is the notion that conflict is normal and expected in families and in society. Thus, to understand families, Conflict theory maintains that we need to understand the sources of conflict and the sources of power.

4. *Family Systems theory* concentrates on the interactions between family members, and it views the family as an interconnected group of individual members whose behaviors affect and are affected by other family members' behaviors. What happens to one family member, such as an illness or a loss of a job, affects every family member. (Chapter 3 provides an in-depth discussion about Family Systems theory.)

5. *Symbolic Interaction theory* concerns itself with how people form and share meanings in their communication efforts. Its primary focus is the use of symbols to convey meaning through verbal and nonverbal communication. (We examine this theory at length in Chapter 3.)

6. *Social Exchange theory* (discussed in Chapter 7) focuses on the costs and rewards associated with our human behaviors. In short, this theory maintains that people weigh costs and rewards before they decide to act—we engage in behavior that brings us maximum rewards and minimum costs. According to this theory, we form relationships with other people if we expect that the relationship will be rewarding. It is human nature to avoid relationships that we perceive will be costly to us.

Do Fathers Matter?

Are children reared by lesbian mothers as well adjusted as children who are raised in families with a mother and a father? This is a question that social and family scientists have sought to answer for nearly four decades. As you become a consumer of the empirical research and literature, it's important to understand that in most instances, bodies of research often support one side of the argument or the other—rarely today is there a clear-cut, definitive answer to what can be, at times, polarizing questions. To provide you an example of this, let's look at a research question that still today poses heated debate among some group: Do fathers matter in the lives of children?

YES: According to one substantial body of research, fathers positively influence children's development in four areas of well-being:

- Behavior: Children with involved fathers exhibit less aggression and have fewer incidents of delinquency.
- Emotional/psychological: When fathers are engaged in their children's lives, children are better able to self-regulate their emotions; they experience anxiety and depression less frequently than children who do not have involved fathers.
- Cognitive/academic: Children with engaged fathers have more success in school.
- Social: As children get older, those who have fathers actively involved in their lives are more likely to have stronger social connections with their peers. (Behson, Holmes, Hill, & Robbins, 2018)

Another study found that fathers' behaviors and interactions with their children both directly (as noted above) and indirectly positively influence children's development (Cabrera, Volling, & Barr, 2018). For example, the quality of children's home experiences is increased with the presence of a father. The relationship with the children's mother, whether it is in the marital home or coparental interactions, also increases the emotional well-being of children.

Sources: Behson, S. and others (2018); Gartrell and others, (2012); The Williams Institute (2020).

NO: Today, same-sex couples are four times more likely than opposite-sex couples to raise adopted children and six times more likely to foster children (Williams Institute, 2018). There is sound evidence that children who are raised by same-sex parents are happy and well adjusted (for a complete review, see Williams Institute, 2018; Gartrell, Bos, Peyser, Deck, & Rodas, 2012):

- Adolescents raised by lesbian mothers indicate that their overall quality of life is equal to or higher than their peers raised by heterosexual parents.
- The stress children and adolescents experience is related to the quality of a couple's relationship, not the sexual orientation of the parents or the presence of a father in the home.
- Teens with lesbian mothers are academically successful and are more likely to attend college upon high school graduation.
- Children and teens of lesbian mothers report that their mothers are good role models.
- Adolescents indicate that they have strong peer relationships who are predominantly heterosexual.

According to the findings of several researchers, the involvement of fathers in lesbian couple parenting experiences isn't important—rather, the quality of family relationships is more important than the sexual orientation of parents.

What Do You Think?

1. Are children's outcomes related to the sex of the parent, or are they a reflection of good or highly motivated parenting?
2. What are some potential limitations for each research position? For example, what conclusions can be drawn without knowing the sample size and who was actually being studied?
3. In what ways does this help you to become a better consumer of research studies?

Because of the family life education approach of this textbook, and because of this book's topical nature, as we work our way through our study we will focus on the foundations of various family theories and how they help us understand the intricacies of our interpersonal relationships. We will examine the theories throughout the coming chapters as they relate

Structural-Functionalist theory:

this theory, introduced by Talcott Parsons, maintains that gender-based role specialization is a necessary function in order to promote family (and, hence, societal) equilibrium.

Instrumental roles:

an element of Parsons's Structural-Functionalist theory, instrumental roles were assigned to the male husband-father who, as the task-oriented mate, was assigned responsibility for being primary breadwinner and protector against imbalance or disequilibrium in the family.

Expressive roles:

these roles, described by Talcott Parsons, were given to the female as a compliment to the male. The wife-mother was the people-oriented mate responsible for enhancing emotional relationships among members of the family.

to certain topics. We begin by looking at what is recognized by many family specialists and sociologists as the "grandfather of family theory": Structural Functionalism.

Structural Functionalism

Perhaps the most influential contributor to the study of family and family life is Talcott Parsons (1902–1979). Out of his passion to investigate the wide range of problems concerning American values, social structure, social problems, and patterns of institutional change, Parsons devised the Structural-Functionalist theory of the family (Fox, Lidz, & Bershady, 2005). This theory has continued to influence family theory for 30 years.

Parsons's functionalist view of the family maintained that gender-based role specialization was necessary in order to promote family (and, hence, societal) equilibrium. Instrumental roles were assigned to the husband-father, who, as the task-oriented mate, was assigned responsibility for being the primary breadwinner and protector against imbalance or disequilibrium. To complement the male, the wife-mother was assigned expressive roles, the people-oriented mate responsible for enhancing emotional relationships among the members of the family (Boss, Doherty, LaRossa, Schumm, & Steinmetz, 1993). According to Parsons, then, the 1950s heterosexual, nuclear breadwinner-homemaker family represented the most functional of all family forms (Parsons, 1951). To be sure, Parsonian thought heralded the belief that if men and women abided by their gender-specific roles, not only would the family unit be ensured stability and solidity, but society at large would similarly benefit.

Although some of the original ideas of this theory have been discarded because of their patriarchal nature (such as the belief that the "correct" family form is that of a man, woman, and child), many of the theory's assumptions are still in use today. Much of what you will see in other family theories in this text are clear descendants of functionalism.

Key Concepts of Structural Functionalism

At the heart of Structural Functionalism rests the notion that society is considered to be a whole that is made up of separate, interconnected parts, and that this whole (social system) seeks maintenance and stability in order for it to persist and endure. Functionalism also holds that each subsystem (or social unit) seeks balance or homeostasis; a change in one

According to Structural-Functionalist theory, males adopt instrumental roles such as providing for the family, while females adopt expressive roles, such as keeping the home and nurturing the husband and children.

iStock.com/ grinvalds

unit effects a change in the other units in order for balance to be maintained. The core of Structural Functionalism is that each member of the social system conforms to a certain set of clearly defined rules or beliefs that exist for the sole purpose of advancing the greater good and continued existence of the society to which the individual belongs. In other words, the whole social system must survive, and it cannot survive without individual members working together toward its continued existence by way of certain functional requirements (Boss et al., 1993, p. 196), such as sexual reproduction, economic reproduction, education, and religion (Bernardes, 2000). This theory derives its name in part because of the function of each subsystem—the contribution—to the survival of the whole societal system. A subsystem's function can contribute either in a positive fashion (functional) or a negative fashion (dysfunctional) to the society.

In order for functions to contribute to the overall good of the society, they must adhere to **structures**, or patterns of role arrangement. For example, the family is thought to be a key subsystem because it promotes the survival of the societal system by providing new members through procreation and by socializing children to conform to societal beliefs, norms, and ways of life (Boss et al., 1993). According to structural functionalists, the traditional nuclear family has historically been thought to best promote the needs of the larger society. A *nuclear family* is defined as the "socially sanctioned cohabitation [marriage] of a man and a woman who have preferential or exclusive enjoyment of economic and sexual rights over one another and are committed to raise the children brought to life by the woman" (Pitts, 1964). This definition clearly delineates social organization and properties of the family system, as the following conditions illustrate:

Structures: patterns of role arrangement within a society.

1. The marital couple assumes the responsibility of childrearing, and such specialized roles increase the functionality of the system.

2. The man and the woman have exclusive economic and sexual rights over one another. According to Boss and colleagues, such clearly outlined marital roles establish well-defined rights and obligations to one another—and thus, to the society at large.

3. With the clearly specified roles that foster exclusive economic and sexual rights over one another, in addition to bearing and rearing children within the socially sanctioned form of cohabitation, these types of role specialization underscore the most significant property of a system—its ability to maintain homeostasis or balance. When family balance is enhanced, the overall equilibrium of the society is reinforced, as well. (Boss et al., 1993)

Structural Functionalism dominated sociological theory from the early 1940s through the 1960s, then fell out of the theoretical limelight; however, despite being considered obsolete by some scholars, particularly feminist scholars, other academics believe that Structural Functionalism still governs much study of family sociology and family life (Boss et al., 1993; Smith, 1995).

Structural Functionalism and the Family

Structural Functionalism emphasizes the traditional, heterosexual nuclear family and highlights two primary functions of the family in society: the socialization of children to society's culture and norms and the stabilization of adult personalities. This view revolves around the idea that the family is organized and governed by unchangeable, fixed, irreversible role configurations—and that these gender-specific family functions operate in order to benefit the family itself as well as to promote the greater good of the society. With these functions and family structures in mind, let's take a look at research that addresses the increasing occurrence of same-sex couples bearing or adopting children.

In 2002, the American Academy of Pediatrics supported legislation permitting lesbian partners to co-parent children born to one partner or adopted by the couple. The Academy maintained that children reared in lesbian families "can have the same advantages and the same expectations . . . for adjustment, and development" as those children reared in heterosexual families (p. 339). And, as you will see in our study together throughout this course (see Chapters 10, 11, and 12), a number of contemporary research findings suggest that no substantial differences exist between lesbian and heterosexual parents in affective development or areas of self-concept, happiness, and overall adjustment. Dr. Susan Golombok (1983, 1999), founder of the Family and Child Psychology Research Centre at City University, London, further maintains that children of lesbian mother families do not appear to demonstrate greater instances of psychological disorders, difficulties in peer relationships, or atypical gender development. As for sexual orientation, Golombok notes that most children reared in lesbian families identified with heterosexuality.

If we were to apply Parsons's Structural-Functionalist theoretical framework to this research, the *male* husband-(always)father and the *female* wife-(always)mother, we see the theory calls into question the function of same-sex couples. Recall, too, that these specialized gender roles allow the family to successfully carry out its chief function of socializing the children to the predominant beliefs and norms of the culture.

If we compare Parsons's assigned roles to roles depicted in contemporary research on lesbian parenting, where there exist two family members—*both female* wife-mothers—what happens to family stability? When two women rear children and do not abide by clearly outlined, specialized gender roles, what happens to the family structure? By Parsonian assumption, the lesbian parenting family form deviates from the ideal family form, and as such should turn out children who are nonconforming to societal norms. But is this what studies of lesbian parenting suggest? On the contrary, the studies indicate that children born into and/or reared by lesbian parents show no significant negative or harmful effects in the children's emotional development, self-concepts, or overall adjustment (Baiocco et al., 2015; Baiocco, Carone, Ioverno, Lingiardi, 2019; Bos, Know, van Rijn-van Gelderen, & Gartrell, 2016; Farr, 2017). In fact, there appear to be no differences between children of lesbian parents and children of heterosexual parents. According to current research, then, the gender of the parents doesn't affect children's sexual orientation. The only parenting factor that is important is that the children are being cared for in a nurturing environment. One could perhaps argue, however, that one lesbian parent assumed the instrumental role and the other assumed the expressive role and that as long as both roles were filled, one's gender doesn't matter.

Structural Functionalism may be considered the grandfather of family theories, but many more theories have been created to shed new perspectives on intimate and family life today.

Conflict Theory

Conflict theory:

similar to Structural Functionalism, Conflict theory concentrates primarily on social structures and their interrelationships. Like the functionalist view, this theory supports the notion that society has some bearing on and to some degree shapes individual behavior. It differs in its basic theme that human beings are prone to conflict.

Similar to Structural Functionalism, **Conflict theory** concentrates primarily on social structures and their interrelationships. Like Structural Functionalism, Conflict theory supports the notion that society has some bearing on and to some degree shapes individual behavior. This paradigm differs, however, in its basic theme that human beings are prone to conflict—that conflict between members of the human race is expected, natural, and inevitable.

Why is there conflict? According to the conflict perspective, inequality is a defining trait built into any society or culture. Dominant and subordinate groups and classes within society are always in competition for the society's limited resources and for whatever the society deems important. It is the competition for resources—with the "haves" competing to keep what they possess and the "have nots" trying to gain what they do not have—that produces conflict. For example, there is economic inequality in nearly every society. Some society members will always have more economic resources than others, while some will always have less.

Because of these inequalities, some society members inherently have more power and control than others. According to Conflict theory, then, friction, discord, disputes, tensions, and antagonism are normal and natural societal experiences.

The big question in Conflict theory is, Who benefits at whose expense? Nineteenth-century social theorist and political activist Karl Marx sought to answer this question.

Karl Marx and Class Struggles

Karl Marx (1818–1883) was a German economist who viewed the world through the perspective that every aspect of human life is based on economics and economic relationships. Indeed, Marx believed that the economic system was the driving force, the real foundation, of any society. His viewpoint revolutionized the ways in which people think about social arrangements and human society.

Marx observed that during the Industrial Revolution (the late 18th and early 19th centuries) in Europe, there appeared to be two fundamental, distinct classes of people. The owners or ruling class—the capitalists—possessed the land, businesses, and factories. The working class—the proletariat—was subordinate to the demands of the ruling class. Their value was based on how much they could produce as a result of their labor. Class was determined by means of one's production and one's productivity. Marx was outraged at the cruel and vicious treatment that factory workers and their families endured at the hands of the ruling class and concluded that owners exploited workers by paying them far less than their work was worth, in order to gain economic (and hence, societal) power. The economic exploitation of the working class led to oppression. Further, Marx believed that the ruling class used its economic power to gain more control of the society, such as using police power to protect its property. Marxian theory supports the notion that the function of every social institution (such as the educational system, religious institutions, and even marriage and the family) is to support the society's class structure.

This exploitative economic composition of capitalism—the class struggle—is the root of all conflict because the two classes have opposing interests and unequal balance of power. And it is because of this unequal balance of power that conflict is an inherent part of human existence and human relationships. Who benefits at whose expense? The capitalists can only pursue their individual needs, goals, and resources at the expense of the proletariat. Thus, Marxian theory holds that because of the inequality of power, the working class would organize and begin a revolution to establish a classless society wherein the society's wealth, resources, and power would be evenly distributed among the members. But what does social inequality have to do with marriage and the family?

Conflict Theory and the Family

Conflict theorists view the family as a social institution composed of varying relationships. These relationships benefit some family members more than others. Throughout history, women and children were considered to be the property of men. Consequently, in relationships between men and women, one class (men) exploited and oppressed the other class (women) in order to gain resources and power. In fact, according to conflict theorists, the entire reason marriage evolved as a legal contract was to protect the property of men.

As Marxian theory illustrates, property owners wielded power. In most societies, the power possessed by men is endorsed by social norms. In other words, because society approves of men attaining higher educational levels and employment opportunities or capitalist endeavors than women, men are able to pursue particular self-interests that afford them more power than the women who are relegated to the home to provide unpaid labor and childcare. Conflict theory suggests that men do not do housework (Doan & Quadlin, 2018) despite the fact that 57 percent of today's workforce is composed of women (U.S. Bureau of Labor Statistics, 2019) because it is not profitable for them to do so. Thus, the family as a social structure perpetuates or maintains the inequalities and imbalance of power in male-female relationships. This inequality is reinforced as children are socialized according to the same male-dominant paradigm. This, then, perpetuates social norms that contribute to the class system.

Throughout your course of study, you will see discussed at length in subsequent chapters a number of social conflicts that some sociologists and family scientists would argue are a

Feminist movements and organizations, such as the National Organization of Women (NOW), focus their efforts on experiences that are unique to women, such as reproductive rights and violence that is perpetrated against women.

direct result of the inequalities of power in family structures: family violence, the feminization of poverty, divorce, single motherhood, and violence against the elderly. Although Conflict theory is not frequently used in family studies to shed light on marriage and family life, its application is of great value when examining the inequalities in human relationships and factors such as gender, ethnicity, race, and socioeconomic class. Conflict theory survives today in its contemporary form—Feminist theory.

Women's Studies: Feminist Theory

Feminist theory embraces the conflict approach to understanding and analyzing the roles of marriage and family in perpetuating inequalities in male-female relationships. Because most societies the world over promote male domination in the home and in the workplace, feminism, or Feminist theory, focuses on the plight of women.

Feminist theory:

a theory that embraces the conflict approach to understanding and analyzing the roles of women in terms of marriage and family in perpetuating inequalities in male/female relationships.

There is no single Feminist theory; rather, there are a number of feminist perspectives that apply to sociological and family studies that help us better understand human behavior. A theory is deemed Feminist theory if it (1) centers on the experiences specific to women, (2) views experiences from a woman's vantage point, and (3) advocates on behalf of women (Lengermann & Brantley, 1988). Types of Feminist theory, outlined by authors MaryAnn Schwartz and Barbara Scott (2003), include the following:

- *Marxist Feminist theory,* similar to Marx's theory, maintains that the inequality and oppression that women experience is a result of women's subordinate class position.

- *Radical Feminist theory* states that the universal oppression that women experience is a result of patriarchy (male-dominated society). Violence against women is another consequence of patriarchy.

- *Liberal Feminist theory* views the inequality and oppression of women as a result of sexism—the belief that men are superior and women are inferior. Liberal feminists focus their efforts on issues of equal opportunity, such as in the workplace and in education.

- *Lesbian Feminist theory* focuses primarily on the predominance of heterosexuality in patriarchal (male-dominated) societies. Adherents to this theory believe that in order to fully understand women's inequality, attention must be given to the oppression of lesbians.
- *Women-of-Color Feminist theory,* along with sexism and classism, focuses its attention on forms of racism—the belief that women of color are inferior to white men and women. According to this perspective, women do not share common experiences; instead, they are thought to be molded by their unique experiences of race, class, and societal and cultural influences.

These different types of feminist theory indicate there are a number of ways in which the feminist perspective can be applied to the study of family and intimate relationships. Many researchers use these theories to acknowledge that there is great diversity not just between men and women, but among women. These perspectives help them explain individual experiences within the contexts these theories provide.

Do men and women engage in power struggles in today's marriages? If so, what is it about contemporary society that accounts for this conflict in marriages (Guvensel, Dixon, Chang, & Dew, 2017)? Do gender differences affect the day-to-day lives of today's families (Young & Schieman, 2017)? If so, what generates or perpetuates these gender differences and how are they expressed? Are gender differences necessarily a bad thing—or a good thing (Maney, 2016)?

For Feminist theorists, the aim of family research is to determine why and how gender inequality and power differences develop and are sustained and maintained in family life. Feminist theorists may question, for example, whether women's oppression is inherent because of the predominance of the patriarchal family structure seen throughout the world. Or instead, they may question whether these differences, perpetuated through the processes of marriage and family living, affect the way children are socialized. Are these behaviors and interaction patterns then repeated when these children mature, marry, and start families of their own? Throughout this course of study, you will see how much of what we learn as infants and children through our family of origin is reinforced in subsequent interpersonal relationships throughout our lives.

Men's Studies

We've just discussed how male–female inequality causes conflict, antagonism, and tension. In this section, we will view gender differences from another perspective: that of "being male." Women's studies courses and degree programs have been offered at U.S. universities and colleges for the past 30 years, but men's studies have not.

Sam McCready is the co-director of the Center for Young Men's Studies at the University of Ulster, Northern Ireland. He and his colleagues maintain that with the ushering in of the feminist movement and the influence of feminist studies, and because of the significant cultural changes seen in the past three decades with the dawn of women's studies (and the resultant changes in roles and responsibilities for men), the study of men with a particular lens is necessary (McCready, Harland, & Beattie, 2006). Since the 1990s, organizations that examine issues specific to men's lives have emerged, such as the American Men's Studies Association (AMSA) and the National Coalition of Free Men. Empirical journals and print media, such as the *Journal of Men's Studies* and *Men's Lives,* devote their scholarship to important areas of men's lives, such as defining gender roles and exploring shifting definitions of masculinity. The primary objective in men's studies has been to encourage scholarship in an effort to generate theory specific to the study of masculinity, as well as to shun all forms of oppression—sexism, racism, homophobia, and classism. To be clear, men's studies is not a negative reaction to feminism, but instead is a useful area of study that helps to promote gender equality.

Today, scholars pay increasing attention to the socialization and cultural expectations of men, such as how their roles are changing to include the nurturing and care of children.

iStock.com/PeopleImages

Empirical research in men's lives has been prompted by the fact that, as one professor of a university men's studies program observes, men are victims of sexism and sexist norms in society; men, similar to women, also exist under oppression because of their social conditioning (Laughlin, 2005; Davis, 2018; Emmons & Mocarski, 2014). In other words, because of their social learning and conditioning, men are limited in their emotional capacities and in how they can express their personalities. This social conditioning may, in fact, limit men's career choices. As a result of these socially imposed limitations, men may feel oppressed. It is the basic assumption of men's studies, then, that sexism and gender affect men's lives as significantly as they do the lives of women (Coston & Kimmel, 2012; McCready et al., 2006; Manzi, 2019).

Men's studies:

research and study of male/female inequality (conflict, antagonism, and tension) from the male perspective.

Like women's and feminist studies, **men's studies** investigate the multiple social and cultural forces and issues that affect men. It is an interdisciplinary academic field devoted to topics concerning men, such as sex, gender, politics, and sexuality. Men's studies academically explore what it means to be a "man" in contemporary society (American Men's Studies Association, 2020). It is an umbrella term that encompasses a number of issues specific to men's lives, such as men's and father's rights, family violence, sexuality, and war and trauma.

Men's studies is not to be confused with the pop culture concept of meninist or meninism. In the early 2000s, males used the term *meninist* to describe themselves as male feminists who support women's rights for equality. However, in the 2010s the term morphed into a cause that is often in direct opposition to feminism. In short, meninism is a movement that focuses on a man's side of gender equality, or "men's rights," and is in direct opposition to feminism (Marthouse, 2015).

Men's studies is not to be confused with the number of men's movements seen in the 1980s and 1990s, such as Promise Keepers, National Center for Fathers, and the Alliance for Non-custodial Parents. It is instead a specific area of academic study that looks at the ways in which men are oppressed by their socialization and societal or cultural expectations. John Laughlin (2005), professor of men's studies at Akamai University, Hilo, Hawaii, suggests that men's studies programs are designed to equip students with "the capabilities needed to effectively manage the resulting changes in men's roles and responsibilities." Men's studies combine theory and practice to effect social policy and to build a broad knowledge base in the study and research of both genders. In this manner, both women's and men's studies seek to better understand the ways in which gender affects both men's and women's individual and family experiences. Having a parallel body of academic work that examines issues specific to men affirms the idea that social, cultural, political, economic, educational, and family structures are equally important to both genders.

Today, no single portrait portrays the essence of "manhood" or "fatherhood," because men and their roles in society and the family are multifaceted, complex, and ever-changing. Because of the cultural evolution taking place in Western society, social and family scientists are now shifting their focus to men's roles. Of particular interest to social science researchers and family practitioners is the role of fatherhood.

In the 1980s, research began to focus on the fact that men were playing more active roles in childrearing, as demonstrated by their ability, and willingness, to change their babies' diapers. Since that time, empirical study in the roles and lives of fathers has been gaining momentum. For instance, contemporary studies are seeking to better understand the unique characteristics of fathers of various cultural and religious heritages. They are also investigating different fathering styles in the wide array of family arrangements, such as single-parent fathers, fathers in two-parent homes, fathers who are men of color, and fathers who are gay. Subsequent chapters in this textbook present information about social trends that affect the lives of men, such as questions pertaining to how much time fathers devote to their role as caregivers in these various family forms.

Researchers are also looking at how involved fathers are in the lives of their children. They are looking at whether the father's role today is still utilitarian (useful, practical), or whether men are adopting women's emotional/expressive roles to better accommodate the multiple roles of the working woman. How do factors such as age, occupation, education, and sexual orientation affect the experiences of fathering? Of what significance is grandfathering in an individual's lifespan? And a question that remains unanswered in empirical study today is: How does the experience of fathering affect and influence the lives of men?

Now that you have a knowledge base in the forms and functions of marriage and family and the basic concepts of family theory, it is necessary that you understand how you affect and are affected by the intimate relationships in your life. Next, we build on our knowledge base as we explore individual and family development.

FAMILY INTERACTIONS AND YOU

Each of us accomplishes many developmental milestones in our individual lifespan development, and we do so within the context of family living. Every phase of our individual development across our human life cycle intersects with the development of the family throughout its developmental cycle, ultimately shaping who we are as relational people. In this section, we take a close look at the human life cycle and the family life cycle.

The Human Life Cycle

All human development is a complex, dynamic, and multifaceted process. As we grow and change, we accomplish what developmentalists, psychologists, and therapists term **developmental tasks.** These entail achieving certain biological, physical, cognitive/intellectual, social, emotional, and spiritual tasks across the lifecourse (see Figure 2.4). It is important to be aware of these developmental milestones because every point in our life cycle interconnects with the developmental stages of the family (Carter & McGoldrick, 2005). A son who becomes chronically ill during his college experience, for example, may disrupt a parent's plans to retire early because of the added health expenses. Conversely, a dying parent might delay a student's college experience because she feels she needs to be with her family through her parent's illness.

Developmental tasks: developmental tasks entail achieving certain biological, physical, cognitive/intellectual, social, emotional, and spiritual tasks across the lifecourse.

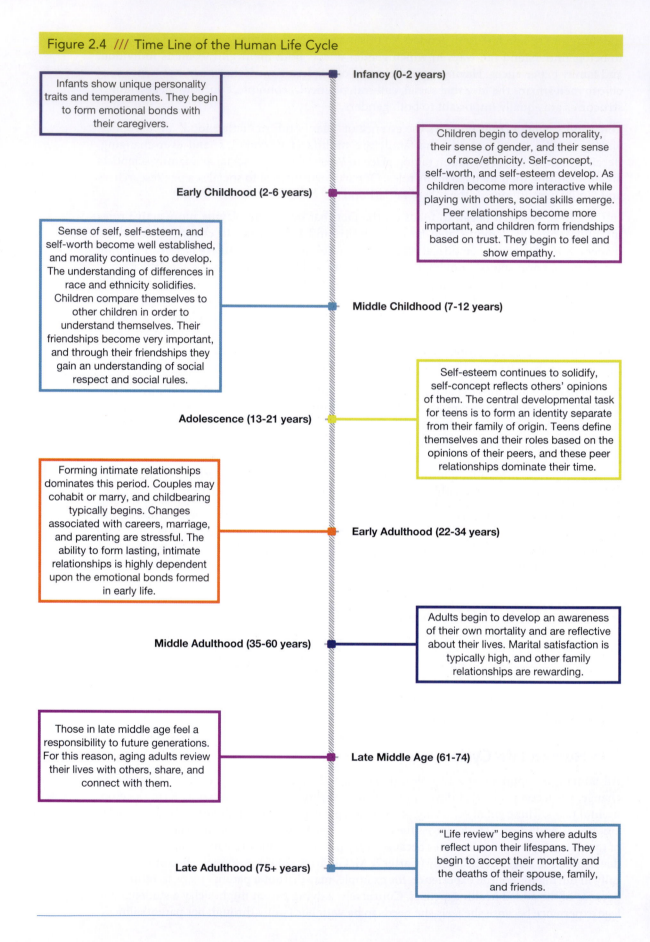

Figure 2.4 /// Time Line of the Human Life Cycle

Infancy (0-2 years)

Infants show unique personality traits and temperaments. They begin to form emotional bonds with their caregivers.

Early Childhood (2-6 years)

Children begin to develop morality, their sense of gender, and their sense of race/ethnicity. Self-concept, self-worth, and self-esteem develop. As children become more interactive while playing with others, social skills emerge. Peer relationships become more important, and children form friendships based on trust. They begin to feel and show empathy.

Middle Childhood (7-12 years)

Sense of self, self-esteem, and self-worth become well established, and morality continues to develop. The understanding of differences in race and ethnicity solidifies. Children compare themselves to other children in order to understand themselves. Their friendships become very important, and through their friendships they gain an understanding of social respect and social rules.

Adolescence (13-21 years)

Self-esteem continues to solidify, self-concept reflects others' opinions of them. The central developmental task for teens is to form an identity separate from their family of origin. Teens define themselves and their roles based on the opinions of their peers, and these peer relationships dominate their time.

Early Adulthood (22-34 years)

Forming intimate relationships dominates this period. Couples may cohabit or marry, and childbearing typically begins. Changes associated with careers, marriage, and parenting are stressful. The ability to form lasting, intimate relationships is highly dependent upon the emotional bonds formed in early life.

Middle Adulthood (35-60 years)

Adults begin to develop an awareness of their own mortality and are reflective about their lives. Marital satisfaction is typically high, and other family relationships are rewarding.

Late Middle Age (61-74)

Those in late middle age feel a responsibility to future generations. For this reason, aging adults review their lives with others, share, and connect with them.

Late Adulthood (75+ years)

"Life review" begins where adults reflect upon their lifespans. They begin to accept their mortality and the deaths of their spouse, family, and friends.

The developmental tasks that most of us experience are considered to be **normative life events**—they come at relatively predictable points in our lives and are generally expected. These events are often referred to as **on-time events** because of their relative predictability across the lifespan. For example, we expect an adolescent to undergo physical changes somewhere between 10 and 16 years of age. Along with these physical changes, we expect them to begin to desire more and more independence and freedom from their family of origin. Even though certain developmental tasks may be normative, they may nevertheless cause disruptions in the family's interactions. Additionally, sometimes events occur at atypical points in the lifespan, such as when a young adolescent gives birth. This is referred to as an **off-time event** because it does not take place at the more typical point in the person's life.

Non-normative life events are those that we do not anticipate, and that we cannot predict, but that do have an impact on our developmental lifecourse. It is not expected that both parents who are in the military will be called to serve in a war oceans away, for example, leaving the children to be reared by grandparents, aunts, uncles, or friends. We don't anticipate or expect that our son or daughter will have a severe reading disability. Nor do we expect that a parent will lose his or her job or that a natural disaster such as fire or floods will destroy our homes. Whatever the situation or circumstance, the nuances of our individual development affect the family and its development.

Although human development is complex, it is important to gain a fundamental understanding of what developmental tasks take place over the lifecourse. This allows us to grasp the significance of how the members of our family affect us and each other through each stage of our development. For our purposes of more fully understanding the intricacies of human relationships, our discussion focuses on the **psychosocial** (social and emotional) aspects of development. What follows is a brief synopsis, adapted in part from renowned and influential family life educators Betty Carter and Monica McGoldrick (2005).

Infancy (0–2 years). From infancy to about 2 years of age, babies learn to walk, talk, and trust their caregivers. Every time a baby cries, the baby is sending out a signal of distress or need. Every time a caregiver responds to the baby's signals of distress or need and meets those needs with comfort and love, the baby learns that the world is a secure place and begins to form the foundation of trust that will be central—in fact crucial—to his or her future intimate relations.

Early Childhood: The Play Years (2–6 years). During this period of growth, children are eager and able to learn new skills—including social and emotional skills. In this phase, children begin to learn empathy and show concern for others' feelings; they will comfort someone who appears to be sad or in need. Children of this age begin to form relationships with peers, learn to obey rules, control their emotions, and delay the need for immediate gratification—all essential stepping stones to future, "grown-up" relationships.

Middle Childhood: The School Years (7–12 years). This phase of development brings with it a growth in moral development and what is termed by some researchers as *heart logic* (Carter & McGoldrick, 2005). As friendships become increasingly important, so does the importance of being able to express feelings and emotions in an appropriate fashion and of being able to respect the rights and needs of others. As children's capacity for empathy and understanding develops, so too does their tolerance for diversity, such as differences in gender, race, and ethnicity, unless parents and those in authority over them instruct them differently. During the school years, a child's sexual development and sexual identity also begin to intensify. All of these developmental leaps add to "who" the child will be someday in her or his intimate partnerships.

Adolescence (13–21 years). With rapid body changes also comes an increase in the adolescent's capacity for moral understanding; an increase in the understanding of self in relation to peers, family, and the community; and an increased awareness of his or her sexual identity

Normative life events:
life events that are relatively predictable across the lifespan.

Non-normative life events:
life events not occurring at the typical, more common points in a person's lifespan. For example, a pregnancy is considered non-normative if it occurs during adolescence.

Psychosocial:
the social and emotional aspects of development.

(Carter & McGoldrick, 2005). As their ability to understand the world and relationships increases, adolescents become better equipped to tackle intimate social relationships.

Early Adulthood (22–34 years). As young adults, men and women during this developmental phase develop the ability—based on the relational foundations laid throughout all of infancy and childhood—to form and engage in emotionally mature intimate relationships. Throughout this phase of life they continue to master their abilities to negotiate the complexities of marriage, family, and intimate relationships. At this phase, they learn to steer the course in interdependence, mutuality, and reciprocity in relationships and open themselves up to those they trust (see more about this in Chapter 5). At this juncture, they seek someone to share their lives with.

Middle Adulthood (35–60 years). Adults in their middle adulthood years are typically actively involved in raising and caring for their children. Adults look beyond themselves and focus their energies and attentions on the next generation and on others, such as their aging parents.

Late Middle Age (60–74 years). Although adults at this age deal with and manage declines in their physical and intellectual abilities, they begin to take steps to "pass the torch" to the next generation (Carter & McGoldrick, 2005). They feel a responsibility to future generations and will reach out in an attempt to make connections with them. My father, for example, a veteran of the Vietnam war, faced and endured such difficulties during his year in combat that he never shared them with his family. As he nears the end of his own lifecourse, he is beginning to share his experiences with his children and grandchildren; in doing so, he is connecting us to his past.

Late Adulthood (75 and older). Grief, loss, retrospection, and growth are the benchmarks of this developmental phase (Carter & McGoldrick, 2005). As adults age and start to think about the end of life, they begin to reflect on their lives and come to grips with the legacy they will leave to future generations. At the same time, they must accept the deaths of family and friends and their spouse or life partner—and they must accept the inevitability of their own mortality and death's eventuality. Not only do they need to accept death and dying but they must also accept the life that they lived.

As you can see, our early life experiences—from the moment of birth—have an impact on our development of our relational skills and abilities.

The Family Life Cycle

What perhaps best distinguishes a family life education approach in the study of marriage, family, and intimate relations from other disciplines is the focus on and application of the family life cycle. Although some fields such as psychology, sociology, and feminist studies might disagree with the tenets of the family life cycle, Carter and McGoldrick perhaps best sum up the efficacy of its inclusion in the examination of family when they note, "We strongly believe that individual development takes place only in the context of significant emotional relationships and that most significant emotional relationships are family relationships, whether by blood, adoption, marriage, or commitment" (1999, p. 5).

There are experiences throughout our lives that establish a foundation for our ability to love and relate to others. Integral to these experiences is our family of origin. As you have learned throughout our study so far, we do not develop in isolation! Every phase of our development is affected by, intersected by, and overlapped with the developmental cycle of our family, and our family development is influenced by the multiple cultural contexts that surround it, as Bronfenbrenner's model illustrated for us in Chapter 1. The **family life cycle** consists of multiple entrances and exits from the family of origin. For example, a young adult leaving for college is an exit, whereas the formation of a new family of origin as children marry is an entry. Families with young children experience multiple entries with their new family members, but families in later life experience multiple exits, such as when family members die.

Family life cycle:
the life cycle consisting of multiple entrances and exits from the family of origin.

Along with the changes in the structure of the family come certain emotional transitions and related changes in the family status that are needed to move on developmentally.

This cycle of family growth and transition is depicted for us in Table 2.1, As you can see, in each stage there are challenges in family life that cause us to develop or gain certain relational skills. Developing these skills helps us work through the changes associated with family life; at the same time, we develop relational skills we will someday carry into our own intimate relationships. Of course, few make these transitions seamlessly; sometimes families' relationships are painfully stretched as they experience job loss or financial problems, severe illness, or the death of a loved one.

Throughout our study, we will examine a number of family processes (such as communication, gender roles, love, intimacy, and sexuality) and how they are developed over time within the family of origin. You will come to see that family development is, certainly, a multifaceted molding process as change occurs both inside and between family members. Whether you are a parent or child, brother or sister, bonded by blood or love, your experiences through the family life cycle affect who you are and who you become.

It is important to note, however, that there are criticisms of the family life cycle. Specifically, the family life cycle has been criticized because it ignores the varying family constellations we discussed in Chapter 1 (such as families of color, gay/lesbian families, or intergenerational/extended families). In short, any deviations or differences from a "traditional"

Table 2.1 /// The Family Life Cycle: Phases, Tasks, and Issues

Phase	Task	Issue
Pairing/Marriage	Fusion as couple	Leaving family of origin Readiness for intimacy Establishing goals, roles, values as new couple
Childbearing	Creation	Sharing each other with children Role ambiguity—wife, woman, mother?
School-age children	Nurturing	Providing security (emotional and environmental) Learning how to parent Simultaneously spouse and parent Increasing parenting demands Increasing work demands
Family with adolescent children	Boundary testing	Control versus freedom Power struggle and rebellion Separation from family of origin Social and sexual exploration
Family as "launching ground"	Leaving/letting go	Changing roles of children still at home The empty nest—loss or opportunity? Parents rediscover each other Latent marital conflict may surface
Middle years	Reviewing/reappraising	Mid-life crisis? Fulfilment/disappointment Accepting limitations Changing self-image Death of parents Anticipating retirement
Aging	Facing mortality	Aging, illness, death Religion and philosophy Isolation/dependency Bereavement

Source: Adapted from Neighbour, R. H. The Family Life Cycle. *Journal of the Royal Society of Medicine*, (1985); 78(Suppl 8): 11–15. Reproduced by permission of the Royal Society of Medicine Press.

family is ignored by the family life cycle. It also assumes that *all* families of origin share a common group identity, ignoring the fact that many today have departed from the previously common progression of family life. Finally, the model has been criticized because it is child-centric—it assumes that all families have children.

Prominent family life educators Betty Carter and Monica McGoldrick address these inadequacies of the family life cycle in their book, *The Expanded Family Life Cycle* (2005). They note that today students of family and intimate life need to think about human development and the life cycle in a way that reflects society's shifts to a more diverse and inclusive definition of the family. Without question, as Chapter 1 showed us, today there is no prototype of an American family.

FAMILY LIFE EDUCATION: CREATING, IMPLEMENTING, AND EVALUATING EFFECTIVE FAMILY PROGRAMMING

Although we are a diverse people, we all have in common that we were born into or brought into a family, and each of us has experienced some degree of family life. But because of the enormous differences that exist in families today (Single-parent or two-parent? Absent father or present father? Divorced or married? Single-earner couple or dual-earner couple? Children or no children? Cohabiting or married? Same-sex partners/parents or heterosexual partners/parents?), the study of family presents difficult challenges to sociologists, family life practitioners, and researchers.

As a practicing family professional or family life educator, it is vitally important to be an effective consumer of the family studies literature: As you've seen in this chapter, knowing how to discern what we're reading helps us to better provide for those individuals and families who seek our services because it removes us from our opinions and preconceived ideas to openly embrace differences and experiences not our own. Not only does understanding empirical research help us to be sensitive to varying diversity and community values and beliefs, it also helps us to employ a wide range of strategies to meet these unique needs (National Council on Family Relationships [NCFR], 2020). Particularly, family life educators are better equipped to create, implement, and evaluate effective, culturally competent, evidence-based programming.

The study of marriage, family, and intimate relationships is fascinating. By using a solid research methodology that provides researchers and consumers with reliable scholarship, we can look beyond our own family experiences, intuition, logic, and instinct to examine and understand the impact of our family members on our lives. By using the many theoretical frameworks provided by sociological and family studies, we have a lens through which we can view and better understand marriage and family relationships. By employing the practice of social science research and theoretical frameworks, we can explore, explain, and develop a far deeper understanding of family. In essence, we can "know" family and family life.

/// SUMMARY

Understanding Families Through Research

- Social science research uses the tools of scientific inquiry to examine human society and relationships (logic or common sense is not effective because everyone sees things differently based on different value systems, political beliefs, religious beliefs, etc.). Family research provides information that allows professionals to develop, implement, and evaluate programs that seek to enhance family life and family growth. Understanding the problems that face today's family and finding explanations and answers to those problems would not be possible without the practice of social science inquiry through research.

- The scientific method is a process by which social science researchers formulate questions concerning social and individual phenomena and seek out answers. Using the scientific method, researchers design a process from start to finish that details the sequential, interrelated investigative steps the researcher will follow. These steps include choosing the research topic; creating the research question and hypothesis; conceptualizing the research; using operational/empirical definitions; choosing a research method; selecting a population and sampling; collecting, processing, and analyzing the data; and, finally, applying research findings.

Becoming a Consumer of the Literature

- In order to get the most out of research and learn how to distinguish well-written, valid research from poorly designed research that yields invalid or insignificant results, those interested in family and family life need to become consumers of social science literature by asking demanding questions of the literature.

- Because human subjects are the object of study, the practice of social science research is an endeavor that requires responsible conduct on the part of the researcher. To ensure the ethical treatment of research subjects, academic institutions and other research institutions establish research review committees, or Institutional Review Boards (IRBs).

Understanding Families Through Theory

- Family theories allow us to move beyond our everyday, common beliefs about family and move toward an objective, scientific understanding of family and family process. Today, many theories exist that attempt to explain the workings of family, and each has made numerous contributions to the field of family studies, among them Ecological theory, Family Development theory, Conflict theory, Family Systems theory, Symbolic Interaction theory, and Social Exchange theory.

- Considered the "grandfather of family theory," Structural Functionalism (Talcott Parsons) maintains that gender-based role specialization is a necessary function in order to promote family (and hence, societal) equilibrium. Instrumental roles are assigned to the husband-father, and the wife-mother is assigned expressive roles.

- Structural Functionalism revolves around the idea that the family is organized and governed by unchangeable, fixed, irreversible role configurations. These gender-specific family functions operate in order to benefit the family itself as well as to promote the greater good of the society. Research suggests, however, that no substantial differences exist between lesbian and heterosexual parents in affective development or in areas of self-concept, happiness, and overall adjustment.

- Conflict theory states that competition for resources is built into every society and that the struggle for these resources leads to inequality and conflict. Because of these inequalities, some society members inherently have more power and control than others.

- Feminist theory centers on the experiences specific to women, views experiences from a woman's vantage point, and advocates on behalf of women in an effort to understand and analyze the roles of marriage and family in perpetuating inequalities in the male-female relationships. Although there is no one feminist theory, there are a number of feminist perspectives that apply to sociological and family studies that help us better understand human behavior.

- The influence of feminist studies and significant cultural changes in the past three decades (and the resultant changes in roles and responsibilities for men) has created a need for specialized men's studies. Men's studies explore important areas of men's lives, such as defining gender roles and shifting definitions of masculinity. Men's studies also strive to generate theory specific to the study of masculinity, as well as to shun all forms of oppression—sexism, racism, homophobia, and classism.

Family Interactions and You

- All human development is a complex, dynamic, and multifaceted process. During our lifecourse, we accomplish developmental tasks, which include biological, physical, intellectual, social, emotional, and spiritual growth.

- Most developmental tasks we experience are normative— coming at relatively predictable points in our lives. Non-normative life events are unanticipated and also affect our development.

- Understanding what psychosocial (social and emotional) developmental tasks take place over the lifecourse allows family life educators to understand how members of a family affect each other through each stage of development.

- Because every phase of our development is integrated with the developmental cycle of our family, family practitioners use the family life cycle to study marriage, family, and intimate relationships.

/// KEY TERMS

Case study   45

Conceptualization   42

Conflict theory   56

Confounding (or rival) variables   50

Construct   42

Control group   46

Convenience sample   50

Data churning   49

Developmental tasks   61

Ethics   51

Experimental design   46

Experimental group   46

Expressive roles   54

Family life cycle   64

Feminist theory   58

Field research   45

Framework   52

Hypotheses testing   42

Hypothesis   42

Institutional Review Boards (IRB)   51

Instrumental roles   54

Literature review   42

Men's studies   60

Non-normative life events   63

Nonprobability samples   48

Normative life events   63

Observational research method   45

Off-time event   63

On-time events   63

Operational definitions   43

Population   46

Probability Sample   48

Psychosocial   63

Qualitative research   41

Quantitative research   41

Representativeness   48

Research   39

Research integrity   51

Research question   42

Response bias   44

Response rate   44

Sample   43

Sample size   48

Scientific method   40

Social science research   39

Structural-Functionalist perspective   54

Structures   55

Survey   43

Theory   52

Validity   44

Variable   42

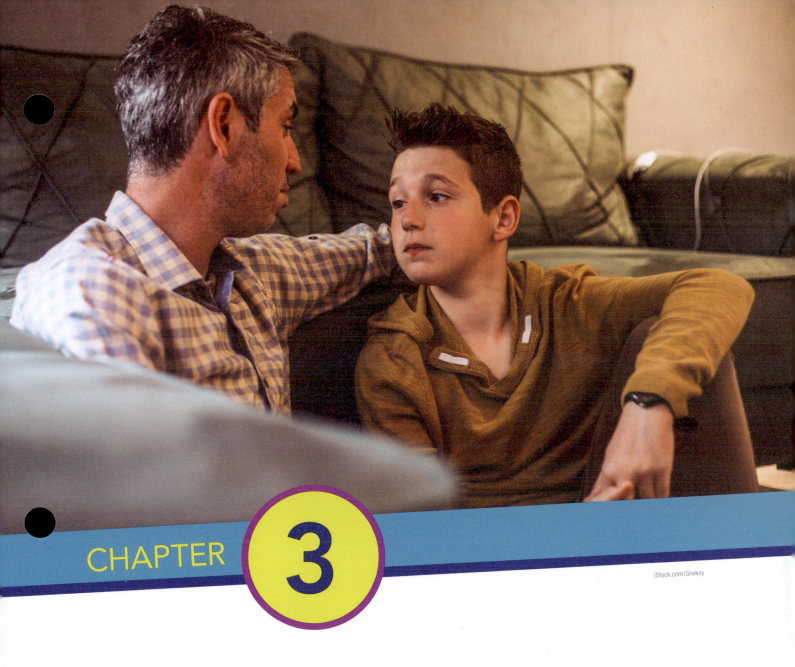
iStock.com/Sneksy

CHAPTER 3

FAMILY COMMUNICATION, CONFLICT, AND FORGIVENESS

LEARNING OBJECTIVES

3.1 Contrast the key concepts of Family Systems theory and Symbolic Interaction theory.

3.2 Characterize the differences between how men and women communicate.

3.3 Summarize the characteristics of verbal and nonverbal communication.

3.4 List the cornerstones of communication.

3.5 Describe the sources of conflict in relationships and the difference between constructive and destructive conflict.

3.6 Discuss the role forgiveness plays in strengthening and maintaining healthy couple and family relationships.

My mother's sister was only in her 30s when she learned that her cancer had metastasized to her rib cage. Her condition was considered terminal, and other than medical treatment to ease her pain, there was nothing that could be done. Although we lived in the Midwest and she and her family lived in California, my mom and my aunt talked almost daily until about two or three days before Aunt Jean died. My aunt was honest with my mother about her illness, and my parents were, in turn, honest with my siblings and me. We knew our aunt was dying. We began our mourning and began to say our goodbyes to this person who would be so greatly missed.

But there was a secret: Aunt Jean's children did not know she was ill. They did not know that she had had surgery for her cancer about four years earlier. They did not know she was dying. Her children, aged 12 and 15, were not told of their mother's imminent death. They were brought to the hospital only as she approached the last hours of her life, and only then were they able to express their love and say goodbye.

Although I was only in the eighth grade when these events unfolded, I couldn't believe how unfair it was to the children that they did not know their mother was dying. How could anyone keep this devastating and life-altering news from someone they loved? Why all the secrecy?

In my frustration with the situation I yelled at my parents, *"Who makes up these rules about when we can say things in our families and when we can't?"*

At one time or another in our families we have probably either said or heard,

"That's not what I said!"

"You never listen to me!"

"That's not what I mean."

"Let me finish!"

Not too much time elapsed in my relationship with my husband before I realized that there were potentially rough seas ahead as we moved in and through the uncharted waters of inter-personal communication. With differing views of "too much" (such as, "It costs too much"), "not enough" (such as, "Not enough sex each week"), or "a few" of anything ("I'll be home in a few minutes," "Let's just spend a few days with my parents"), we quickly discovered that although we *thought* we were communicating, we were far from it.

Our parents or guardians spend the first 2 years of our lives teaching us to walk and to talk— and the next 16 years teaching us to sit down and be quiet. We all have been "communicating" in one form or another since the moment of birth and have been using words to convey our needs, wants, hopes, and feelings since about the first year of life, so why is it that so many of us have such difficulty conveying what we *mean?* Why is it that our mate or other family members have such difficulty in *accurately receiving* the messages we send? And who *does* make up the rules for when and what we can or cannot say in our families?

THE COMMUNICATION PROCESS

Communication is best thought of as a process. Process implies progression, development, and change over time. All interpersonal relationships involve change, and communication is no exception. As our intimate relationships grow, change, and develop over time, so too do our communication patterns and behaviors. The communication process is such a critical aspect of our lives that it shapes the family and gives it its distinct identity (Galvin, Braithwaite, Schrodt, & Bylund, 2019).

When we communicate, whether in interpersonal or social interactions, we have a joint or reciprocal impact on each other in our exchanges. This dynamic is a **transactional** process in which we simultaneously affect and are affected by our intimate relations. When we discuss communication in this context, the focus of the interaction is not on the *words* individual family members speak, but instead on the *interconnectedness* of the relationship. To fully understand the communication process, we first need to explore two theoretical frameworks that are a foundation of family studies: the Family Systems theory and the Symbolic Interaction theory.

Family Systems Theory: The Family as an Interconnected System

The family as a system of interrelated components is a contemporary framework for examining family interactions. Developed by psychiatrist and theorist Murray Bowen (1913–1990), the **Family Systems theory (FST)** views families as a whole entity made up of interconnected parts that seek to maintain balance. In recent years, this theoretical approach has become so popular among family researchers and family practitioners that an expanding array of family topics have been examined through this lens, including youth suicide, cancer treatments, family grief, and spiritual development. The popularity of its use is due, in part, to a central concept that all of us maintain interdependent relationships with others on a day-to-day basis. Within family life, FST acknowledges that the family is made of interconnected parts that affect each other.

The Family as a System

Encompassing areas of study from economics to biology to the intricacies of family life, **General Systems theory (GST)** is a world view or a paradigm that puts forth the notion that objects do not exist in isolation, but instead are interconnected to parts of a larger whole (Boss, Doherty, LaRossa, Schumm, & Steinmetz, 1993). The term **system** means "to place together" or to connect one entity to another (Rosenblatt, 1994).

Consider the human body—as a whole, living, breathing, ever-changing organism. As a system, it consists of numerous interdependent yet separate entities, such as the nervous system, the circulatory system, the digestive system, the reproductive system, and so forth. In short, the human body is a complex network of many subsystems that are organized into a single whole. Just as the human body illustrates how a system works, a **family system** is also a living, ever-changing, dynamic entity that consists of various individuals and their interconnected, intergenerational patterns of interactions. In this context, a system's primary function is to bring together and arrange the various interrelated parts into a whole, organized entity (Rosenblatt, 1994).

The Family Systems theory provides a framework for those who work with families and allows them to gain insight into the relational patterns and interactions among the separate individuals, or **subsystems**. Prior to the 1950s, the treatment of psychological and behavioral problems and emotional distress focused on the internal world—the internal dysfunction—of the individual patient. However, that treatment model failed to take into consideration the

Transactional:
the dynamic process whereby our exchanges with others simultaneously affect and are affected by our intimate relations.

Family Systems theory (FST):
developed by Murray Bowen, this theory views a family as a whole entity consisting of interconnected parts seeking to maintain balance.

General System theory (GST):
encompassing areas of study from economics to biology to the intricacies of family life, this theory constitutes a world view or a paradigm that keeps at the forefront the notion that objects do not exist in isolation, but instead are interconnected to parts of a larger whole.

System:
according to Rosenblatt, it means to "piece together" or to connect one entity to another.

Family system:
the family is a living, ever-changing, dynamic system that consists of various individuals and their interconnected, intergenerational patterns of interactions. In this context a system's primary function is to bring together and arrange the various interrelated parts into a whole, organized entity.

Subsystems:
the relational patterns and interactions among the separate individuals within a family.

All communication is multigenerational and cultural. When we communicate with others, we draw on the ways we have learned to speak. We rely on verbal communication—our languages we speak—and our nonverbal communication.

iStock.com/filadendron

reciprocal, interactive nature of interpersonal relationships (Nichols & Schwartz, 2009). As the concepts of the General Systems theory gained widespread acceptance across disciplines, family practitioners, social workers, and family therapists began to view and understand individual psychological problems in a new way—that these problems *were developed and maintained within the context of the family.*

Key Concepts: Applying the Systems Framework to the Family

There are several key concepts and metaphors used to convey the thoughts and ideas central to Family Systems theory. The core assumptions of this family framework hold that every part of the system is interconnected and that we can understand only by viewing the whole (White, Klein, & Martin, 2014).

Interconnecting. To get a better handle on these assumptions, let's return to the example of the human body. Suppose that through laboratory diagnosis you are found to have diabetes; if left untreated, will the disease remain in its initial state or will it eventually spread to and affect other systems in the body? You probably assumed correctly that, indeed, if left untreated, the diabetes would eventually spread throughout the multiple body systems, causing blindness and even loss of a limb because of the interrelated, interdependent relationship between the various body systems.

The family as a system of interconnected subsystems is no different. Family members affect and are affected by each other—what happens to one family member eventually affects (or happens to) others within the family unit. Thus, the Family Systems theory is concerned with the *interactions* and *interrelations* between the various pieces of the whole and their effect on each other.

Consider what happens to a mobile or wind chime when anything disrupts it or causes it to move. What disrupts one piece of the mobile, for example, disrupts and affects all of the other pieces on the mobile. The same holds true in family life (see Figure 3.1). Expected or not, joyous or tragic, such events impact and have an effect on every family member (subsystem) within the family system.

Looking at the Whole. A second key assumption of Family Systems theory is the idea that the only way we can understand an individual family member's behavior and communication patterns is by looking not just at the individual member, but by *looking at the whole,* the entire family system. Because we affect and are affected by each member in our families, it is impossible for us

Figure 3.1 /// Virginia Satir's Concept of the Family as a Mobile

Source: iStock.com/ArtParnyuk

to understand each other's behavior and communication patterns without knowing more about the families in which we were reared—our family of origin.

In your family, have you ever been able to finish another family member's sentence? Have you ever been able to predict, almost to the minute, how long your parents' argument will last, and what it is about? Most of us know what behavior or communication pattern will elicit certain responses from our siblings or parents in many situations. Similarly, we recognize patterns in our family members such as what might lead to an argument or praise. The communication patterns that exist in our families come about as a result of this concept of wholeness. As interconnected pieces, we create our family's own reality, and that reality is distinct and separate from any other family (Galvin et al., 2019).

Establishing Boundaries. Every system, whether it is an educational system, political system, or family system, has some type of border or **boundary** between it and its environment. In a family—and particularly in a discussion about family communication—boundaries serve the purpose of affecting the flow of information within the system. Boundaries are essential because they are what separate and make us distinct from our environment or from other family members.

Boundaries fall along a continuum. On one end are **closed boundaries**, where no information comes in or goes out; on the other end, there are **open boundaries** where the transfer of information is so unobstructed that family members within the systems lose their identity. A family system's health is categorized by the degree to which the boundaries are permeable (White et al., 2014). In Figure 3.2, note how in the closed boundary system the borders are so tightly closed that little or no information is allowed in or out of the family system. This type

Boundary:

every system has some type of border, or boundary, between it and its environment. In a family, boundaries serve the purpose of affecting the flow of information within the system. They are essential because they are what separate us from our environment or from other family members.

Closed boundaries:

forming one end of the boundary spectrum, closed boundaries prevent information from coming in or going out.

Open boundaries:

boundaries where the transfer of information is so unobstructed that family members within the systems lose their identities.

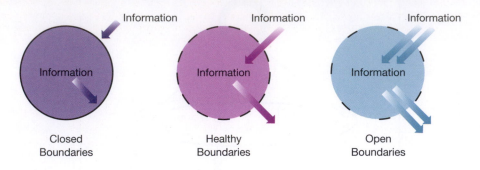

Figure 3.2 /// Types of Boundaries

Boundaries affect the flow of information within a family system and make us distinct from other family members. A family's health and well-being is categorized by how open or closed the boundaries are.

Information   Information   Information

Information   Information   Information

Closed   Healthy   Open
Boundaries   Boundaries   Boundaries

of a closed boundary is often seen in families where abuse occurs. The amount of information that leaves the family system is quite limited (such as family members not discussing publicly what takes place privately in the home). In the same way, information or interference from outside of the family system is limited or prohibited (such as the abusive partner dictating who can visit or phone family members).

Conversely, notice in open systems that information is allowed to freely come in and exit the family system. A certain level of open boundaries is necessary for the health and well-being of families. However, when boundaries are too open—when too much information flows between the subsystems—members in the family system lose their distinct identity. For example, if parents continually share pieces of their parental subsystem with their children (such as their marital problems, their financial problems, or their work-related problems), the boundaries become blurred and the children lose their distinct identity as children.

Maintaining Balance. When an infection enters your body, various systems work together to bring your body back into balance, or **homeostasis**. According to Family Systems theory, every family has the same goal, which is to maintain its balance or homeostasis when it experiences any departure from its usual state of balance (the family's state of "normal"). Regardless of the system type, it will act to reduce any source of disruption or disturbance (Boss et al., 1993). The disruption can be of internal origin, such as a teenager who suffers from an eating disorder, or it can be of external origin, such as a parent who loses his or her job. Whether from within the family or outside the family, the system will do whatever it takes to bring it back to balance—and this includes arguing, disagreeing, and family conflict.

To restore equilibrium in a family system, we most often use established, habitual communication interactions and behaviors. Sometimes our communication strategies are healthy and adaptive; sometimes they are dysfunctional, unhealthy, and maladaptive. The Circumplex Model is a tool family therapists and family practitioners use to understand the boundaries of families and hence to better understand families' health and level of functioning.

The Circumplex Model. Those who study and work with family systems are particularly interested in what constitutes behavioral, relational, and communication interaction patterns. In an effort to provide a means by which to assess a family's level of functioning and health, the **Circumplex Model of Marital and Family Systems** was created to address family cohesion, adaptability, and communication (Olson, Sprenkel, & Russeli, 1979).

David Olson, an influential family scientist, family therapist, and professor, posited that families whose cohesion, adaptability, and communication patterns place them more toward the center of the model exhibit balance, as illustrated in Figure 3.3. Consequently, these families function more sufficiently and effectively over time than do families whose interaction

Homeostasis:

when an infection enters the body, various systems work together to bring it back into balance or homeostasis. The same holds true for a family system when it experiences any departure from its usual state of balance (normal).

Circumplex Model of Marital and Family Systems:

this model was created to address family cohesion, adaptability, and communication, providing the means to assess a family's level of functioning and health. According to David Olson's model, families who exhibit balance function more sufficiently and effectively over time than families who are more out of balance.

Figure 3.3 /// Olson's Circumplex Model of Family Functioning

The Circumplex Model focuses on two primary dimensions necessary for family health: cohesion and flexibility. Families that are balanced (toward the center) tend to be more functional than unbalanced families (toward the edge). *Cohesion* refers to the family's emotional bonding. This ranges from *disengaged* (very low) to *connected* (moderate) to *enmeshed* (very high). *Flexibility* refers to how families balance change in roles and relationships. This ranges from *rigid* (very low) to *structured* (moderate) to *chaotic* (very high).

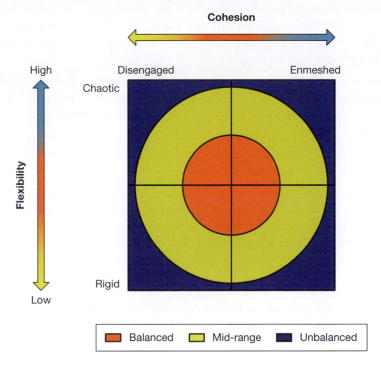

Source: Olson, Sprenkil, & Russell (1979).

patterns place them on the outer edges of the model. A family's position on the model on the outer edges rather than toward the center does not necessarily indicate a level of dysfunction; this placement may just reflect current circumstances. For example, a family in the midst of crisis or stress may exhibit lower than usual levels of cohesion, adaptability, and communication. Additionally, although some families may fall on the extreme outer levels on the model, satisfactory levels of family function may still exist if those levels represent usual, normative family members' expectations (Boss et al., 1993).

Creating Rules. This chapter's opening vignette reminds us that some families have secrets. These secrets may range anywhere from a college student's substance abuse to Aunt Betty's eating disorder to child maltreatment or financial difficulties. In many cases, families with secrets appear fully functional, cohesive, and adaptable, but perhaps within these families, the family members recognize that this is far from the truth. All families have rules for how they communicate with each other and how and what information is shared (or not shared) with those outside of the family system. There are **communication rules** that govern what family members can and cannot discuss or share and how they are to interact with their own family members.

Who *does* make the rules concerning what family members can and cannot say within their families, and how do these rules come about? The family of origin—with its cultural, ethnic, and multigenerational influences—creates an individual family's rules of communication. For example, you may have only been "shssshʼd" once or twice before you learned that it was not okay to talk with your friends or other relatives about how your parents seem to constantly argue about money. You may have discovered after an attempt or two or three that your parents were not comfortable talking about sex with you. Through repeated interactions such as these, over time you learned what is acceptable to talk about, either within or outside of the home.

Communication rules: rules that govern what family members can and cannot discuss or share and how they are to interact with their own family members.

Professor of communication studies Kathleen Galvin and her colleagues (2019) provide some categories of rules for communication:

What we can and cannot talk about. Every family has different values and contexts that dictate how they communicate about sex, health issues, salaries, bills, or a family member who is deceased.

Feelings that are allowed to be shared. In some family cultures, feelings are masked by accepted behaviors. In other family settings, expressing anger, fear, sadness, and rage is encouraged. Culture, ethnicity, values, and family history come into play when establishing rules for dealing with feelings and emotions.

Decision making. Each family has its own set of rules for decision making. Are decision-making responsibilities shared? Divided? Dictated by the head of household? Can decisions be challenged? Families may run the gamut on how decisions are made.

How we can talk about it. Can you talk about a situation openly, or do you have to somehow dance around the real issue? Is Mom really just "under the weather" with a cold or the flu, or does she have a more serious illness?

Communication strategy. Each family has rules that govern its communication strategies. Do you talk about a situation only when everyone has calmed down? For example, in some families there is the timing-is-everything strategy. Family members learn *when* they can approach a parent for advice or ask for something special. Some families also strategize *with whom* they can share certain information (such as, Don't tell Dad, he'll get upset!).

Such communication rules are not easily broken. Even if we know that our family's communication rules do not work or are not effective, we tend to remain loyal to them (Kellogg, 1990). We are less likely to try to challenge or change the rules if our family is not flexible or adaptable to change. Well-adjusted families allow some rules to be renegotiated as the family passes through the various developmental stages in the family's life cycle (Galvin et al., 2019).

Putting Family Systems Theory Into Action: Family Wholeness and Interconnection

To continue our examination of the interconnectedness of families and the concept of wholeness in family communication, let's take a look at a hypothetical family situation (Natenshon, 1999).

It was quite obvious to Amybeth's parents that some sort of medical intervention was needed for their daughter. She was becoming dangerously thinner, and her eating disorder was now all consuming. But Amybeth wasn't the only one suffering—everyone in the family home was suffering along with her.

Because Amybeth only picked at her food, family meals had become a battleground with tempers flaring and emotions running high. Her brother often retreated to his bedroom in the heat of the arguments. Her mother, Terri, usually ended up in tears, and her father, Peter, usually ended up yelling at no one in particular. Even though her parents did not feel that they were the cause of their daughter's disordered eating, they did experience feelings of confusion, inadequacy, and overwhelming guilt—and they transferred their feelings to everyone in the family. They knew their reactions to Amybeth's disordered eating were contributing to the deterioration of the family.

Peter explored the treatment options for Amybeth by speaking with their family doctor and by searching the Internet. He found that most eating disorder treatment plans excluded the parents and siblings, relying instead on psychoanalysis for the individual patient. This puzzled him because not only was it obvious that the entire family was affected by Amybeth's illness, but the entire family would also be instrumental in her recovery process. The family doctor referred him to a licensed family therapist who specialized in the treatment of eating disorders in children and adolescents.

What affects one family member affects the entire family, as is the case when a teen girl deals with an eating disorder. Have you ever experienced a situation in your personal life that affected your whole family? Has someone in your family experienced a situation that affected or impacted you?

iStock.com/KatarzynaBialasiewicz

During the initial consultation with Amybeth and her parents, the therapist noted that family therapy would be a very effective way to treat not just Amybeth's individual needs but also to treat every family member's needs. The therapist outlined a treatment program of facilitated changes that would aid her recovery. The treatment plan also allowed the family to make its own parallel changes that would accommodate Amybeth's changing needs, as well as the needs of their family system.

In our hypothetical example, Amybeth's parents came to understand through family therapy their daughter's patterns of disordered eating and learned how to help her. They also understood that they must lead a joint effort between the various components of the family system so the family could work together to help Amybeth—and in doing so, help the entire family. The family-centered therapeutic treatment they selected recognized and respected the power of the family system to help eradicate the disease Amybeth was fighting (Natenshon, 1999). The family system had the potential to either bring about a positive, healing change or continue family behaviors and communication/interaction patterns that sustained Amybeth's eating disorder.

Unlike conventional psychological theories (such as psychoanalysis) that focus on the individual person and his or her behavioral problems or emotional distress, Family Systems theory encourages the examination and the inclusion of the entire family system in the medical or psychological treatment of one family member. Understanding the interconnection of family members is important because it is within the family system that communication patterns *and* behaviors are acquired (from the family of origin), and it is within the family system that *every* family member plays a part in the family's health and functioning.

And herein lies the dilemma that each new couple faces: Each partner brings to the relationship the established and familiar boundary types, balance, and rules from his or her own family of origin. Each member of the couple acts on his or her own subjective meanings of what family life is and what it is not. In our everyday interactions with one another, then, how do we communicate these meanings? How do we understand one another? What determines whether our communication efforts are successful? Symbolic Interaction theory, a foundation of family studies, seeks to answer these questions.

Meanings: The Symbolic Interaction Framework

We all have probably viewed a play or movie when we had to stifle laughter because the acting was so awful. And we all have been brought to sobs and tears or side-splitting laughter because the actors on stage were *so* believable, so realistic, and authentic in their character portrayal. Why is it that some actors are able to convey their meanings and their messages—their *roles*— so skillfully and credibly that we are drawn into the very center of their agony or humor, whereas others clearly didn't pay attention in acting class? The ability to effectively communicate meanings between actors is essential not just in the theater but in family life, too.

In our daily interactions, most of us have said, often in frustration, "That's not what I mean!" The **Symbolic Interaction theory** revolves around the notion that human behavior is a continuous dialogue in which people watch the behaviors of other people and then react to those behaviors. All human behavior is social behavior in which there is an exchange of messages and symbolic meanings between actors. This is much more complex than it appears at first glance because in order to understand the exchange of these messages/meanings, we also have to gain an understanding of *how* we acquire the meaning in the first place.

Key Concepts: Conveyors and Interpreters of Meaning

Fundamental to Symbolic Interaction theory is that people react based on the meanings they find in any situation. According to Symbolic Interaction theory, the goal of human interaction is to create shared meanings and to understand the meanings that are communicated between people.

Symbols: In an attempt to share meanings, each culture uses **symbols**, or codes. Some symbols are universal behaviors, such as the kiss, which represents affection, love, or a greeting. All cultures use language as a means to anchor meanings to each symbol.

We live in a world that is full of symbols, and knowingly or not, we communicate using these shared codes or shared meanings. From the moment a newborn baby takes its first breath, communication between the baby and its caregivers is based on the sharing of symbols; from birth and throughout life, we attach meanings to symbols, define symbols, and interpret symbols in our individual environments. For example, a smile can be a symbol of reassurance, compassion, understanding, or greeting. Or it can be a symbol of contempt or condescension.

Our socialization within our culture and how we socially interact aid in our acquisition and interpretation of the meanings of symbols. For example, children in the United States are taught to maintain eye contact with adults while they are spoken to, but children from Hispanic and Asian cultures avoid eye contact with authority figures as a symbol of respect (Akechi et al., 2013; Adetunji & Sze, 2012). Similarly, Native American children are taught that direct eye contact with a teacher is "showing off" (Richardson, 2012; Adetunji & Sze, 2012).

Culture also affects attitudes about symbols of affection, such as a hug or a handshake. In European and Asian cultures, hand-holding or casual embraces by members of the same sex is culturally acceptable (Sorokowska et al., 2017). Americans, however, may not share these symbols of friendship and may feel uncomfortable with this display (Sorokowska et al., 2017). Physical distance during a conversation is a symbol of respect in some cultures. For instance, in the Middle East and South America, people stand closely while conversing, whereas European Americans and African Americans prefer more distance. Being sensitive to cultural communication practices enhances our communication skills (Sorokowska et al., 2017).

Cultural competence refers to accepting and respecting cultural differences, being aware of the dynamics of these differences, and continually expanding cultural knowledge (Torres, 1993). Being sensitive to cultural beliefs and practices not only conveys respect for the diverse people in contemporary U.S. society, but it also minimizes cultural stereotyping. It's important to note, however, that while it's our responsibility as helping professionals to understand

Symbolic Interaction theory: this approach to examining family life and family communication assumes that human behavior is a continuous dialogue in which people watch the behaviors of other people and then react to these behaviors.

Symbols: in an attempt to share meanings, each culture uses symbols, or codes. Some symbols are universal behaviors, such as the kiss, which represents affection, love, or a greeting.

cultural differences, it is equally as important that we not adopt a one-size-fits-all view of each people group. As one group of researchers observe, cultural competency requires ongoing education: "Cultural competence is about continually developing and refining a skill set and worldview that are useful across different situations, not about acquiring discrete bits of knowledge that are results of overgeneralization" (Povenmire-Kirk, Bethune, Alverson, & Guttman Kahn, 2015).

There are guidelines to consider when communicating among diverse cultures (Torres, 1993):

1. *Cultural awareness* refers to the process of becoming sensitive to another culture's beliefs, practices, and lifestyles. It also includes appreciating our own culture and becoming aware of biases or prejudices we may hold toward others.

2. *Cultural knowledge* refers to understanding the worldviews from which others operate.

3. *Cultural skill* involves being able to accurately interpret others' cultural ways of interacting.

4. *Cultural encounter* refers to directly engaging in cross-cultural interactions in order to gain a culture-specific understanding of someone.

Although we spend a lifetime sharing and interpreting symbols, we run into difficulty in our interpersonal and family relationships when we operate on the assumption that we all are on "the same page," that we all share the exact, precise meanings of symbols.

As an example of this, when walking across campus one day with an emeritus professor much older than I am, a student passed by and called out, "Hey, Dr. Dawg, wassup?" Knowing the student, I stopped and engaged in conversation for a moment or two. As the professor and I continued our walk, she was visibly shaken and upset, "Dog? What does he mean, *dog*? Dog? Students are now calling professors *dog*?" I spent several minutes trying to convince her that when the student used the term, it really was a term of endearment and affection. This example illustrates that all social and intimate relationships depend on our ability to nurture a culture of shared **meanings** (White et al., 2014). We must, as individual actors, ensure that we are on common ground—or be able to recognize when we are not on common ground—and share the same connotation in our communication efforts.

Meanings: in the context of family communication, the definition we assign to verbal and nonverbal interactions.

Roles: Another key concept in Symbolic Interaction theory is the idea of **role**, which Boss and colleagues (1993) call a "system of meanings" (p. 147). We all have different roles in our families and in our circles outside our families. Sometimes one role takes priority over another, but that does not negate or minimize the other roles we have either taken on or have been assigned. For example, I simultaneously have the roles of wife, mother, mother-in-law, grandmother, sister, aunt, friend, professor, volunteer, researcher, patient, and author. In each of my roles, I take on the role of actor and I follow the rules—the *expectations*—assigned to that role (like it or not). As audience members during a play or a movie, we have certain expectations of the actors on stage or on screen. This is different from being a theatrical actor; taking on or being assigned a role carries with it certain expectations, not just from oneself but from others as well (Mead, 1934). These role expectations enable us to anticipate the behavior of others (Boss et al., 1993). When a person takes on or is assigned too many roles, role strain and role conflict may result. Role strain occurs when there are competing demands from multiple roles. Role conflict is the psychological stress and tension that result when people undertake multiple roles that are incompatible. (See Chapter 4 for an in-depth discussion about role conflict and role strain.)

Role: a key concept in Symbolic Interaction theory is that of role, or a "system of meanings." A woman may simultaneously have the role of wife, mother, sister, daughter, aunt, and so forth. She will take on the role of actor and follow the rules—the expectations—assigned to that role.

The Symbolic Interaction framework has been used to examine a number of family issues. These issues include father involvement following divorce, the study of the cultural influences of ethnicity, shared grief work following the death of a loved one, the shared meanings associated with sexuality, and gender role attitudes between mothers and daughters. Family and interpersonal communication interactions lend themselves to the use of Symbolic

The Symbolic Interaction theory holds that all of human behavior is social behavior in which there is an exchange of messages and symbolic meanings between actors. Knowingly or unknowingly, we are continuously conveying messages to others.

Interaction theory because the central themes of this theory are concerned with how meanings are formed, assessed, sustained, and transformed through culturally and socially defined processes (Blumer, 1969). When thinking about the central themes of Symbolic Interaction theory and the theory's significance of understanding meanings, how does the use of technology and social media impact interpersonal communication?

Makers of Meanings: Adolescent and Parent Views About Social Media

There's no doubt about it: The ways in which individuals, couples, families, and peers communicate today has changed significantly, even within the last 10 years (Procentese, Gatti, & Di Napoli, 2019). For example, in early 2020, many of you had your college or high school experiences come to an abrupt halt due to the novel Coronavirus, COVID-19—you were learning in a traditional brick-and-mortar setting, and within a matter of hours your learning was transitioned to online formats. So, although digital technology can serve a society very well, such as when it was needed to bridge the gap in teaching and learning, not everyone shares the same meanings about it and social media. There is a particular difference of meaning between adolescents and their parents.

One researcher accurately describes what the day looks like for most of us:

> Every morning, almost every individual's first instinct is to reach for their phone and check through their notifications and social media accounts. They wake up scrolling through them, liking pictures, commenting, sharing, tweeting, etcetera. There is never a moment where an individual is not connected through a social media platform somehow. Social media has become a big part of our lives, and most of us cannot live without it. We spend every waking second engaging with it, learning and receiving new information, ideas, and concepts through it. This has shaped our culture, our society, and, perhaps, even our general view of life. And in the moments where we are not attached to it, we react in ways that are similar to the symptoms of withdrawal. People hardly consider or ponder about why we feel that way, and how heavily social media impacts us as a society. (Phoon, 2017, p. 1)

In the United States, over three-fourths (77 percent) of adults aged 18 and over own a cell phone (Ictech, 2018). Given that 88 percent of U.S. teens have either a desktop or laptop computer at home, and 95 percent have a smartphone (Pew Research Center, 2018), just how often are today's youth and teens connected to their friends through texting and/or social media? On average, teens (ages 13 to 17) send 67 texts per day (Pew Research Center, 2016). Another study found that nearly one-fourth (22 percent) of teenagers log on to a social media site at least 10 times per day, and more than 50 percent log on to social media at least once per day (O'Keeffe & Clark-Pearson, 2011). Teens in the United States say they use the following platforms (Pew Research Center, 2018):

- YouTube   85 percent
- Instagram   75 percent
- Snapchat   69 percent
- Facebook   51 percent
- Twitter   32 percent
- Tumblr   9 percent
- Reddit   7 percent
- None   3 percent

There's no question about it: Smartphones and social media impact our daily lives. But is this impact negative or positive? What *meanings* do teens assign to the use of technology to communicate with others—is it a positive experience or a negative experience? Among those teens surveyed, 45 percent stated that technology had neither a positive or negative impact on their lives. The survey also found

Positive: About one-third (31 percent) of teens say that social media and texting have mostly a positive effect on their lives. Those surveyed reported that technology helps them to connect with family and friends; meet others with the same interests; helps them to get support from others; and helps with their self-expression.

Negative: Nearly one-fourth (24 percent) of teens report that technology has mostly a negative effect on their lives. The main reasons teens say it has a negative impact on their lives are bullying; rumor spreading; lack of in-person contact; harms relationships; peer pressure. (Pew Research Center, 2018)

Overall, the teens' meanings assigned to digital technology and social media are mixed. But how do their parents feel? As you have seen in our study of couples and families so far in this chapter, the effectiveness of families relies on how families handle daily interactions and communication within the family system (Procentese et al., 2019). In a study of 227 parents and their teens (ages 13 to 18), the researchers wanted to determine the parents' positive and negative interpretations of their teens' use of cell phones and social media:

Positive: Parents said that technology improves healthy family communication and cohesion; it helps in bringing different generations together (i.e., teens, parents, grandparents); it helps families to navigate developmental transitions; digital technology strengthens family resilience—the ability to positively face difficulties.

Negative: Parents said that cell phones and social media interfere with family rules and boundaries; they expose families to privacy risks; they risk deteriorating family intimacy (i.e., the emotional connections between family members); they make the relationships within the family more vulnerable. (Procentese et al., 2019)

The researchers conclude their work with this impactful insight: "It is not the real impact of social media on family systems that matters, but it is how family members *perceive it*"—it is the meaning they assign to its use (Procentese et al., 2019).

Should Children Be Used as Language Brokers?

In the United States, 22 percent of the children—slightly more than 12 million—speak a non-English language at home; in California, that percentage is as high as 44 percent (Kids Count, 2018). Because many of the adults in these families do not speak the English language, their children are called on to be mediators and to speak or read for the adults, since in most cases the children are the first to acquire competence in a new language. This mediating activity is called child language brokering.

Child language brokering is typically an informal social interaction in which children are asked to act as the go-between for their parents or other family members and an English-speaking person, such as a teacher, a postal worker, or a store clerk. Child language brokers fulfil an important role in their families. But does child language brokering positively contribute to the child's development?

YES: According to language broker researcher Linda Halgunseth (as presented in Coleman & Ganong, 2003), the experiences of the child language broker positively shape the child's development in the following areas:

- Cognitively. Because child language brokers are called on to mediate communication between parents and various members of the community, these children acquire vocabularies and word lists that enhance their school performance.

- Interpersonally. Language brokering develops children's communication and social skills because children learn to adapt them to the situation. According to Halgunseth, these skills help children develop strong feelings of self-worth, value, and usefulness.

- Emotionally. Enhanced self-esteem, feelings of independence and autonomy, confidence, and

Sources: Crawford (2005), Halgunseth (2003), Umaña-Taylor & Fine (2003).

feelings of maturity and importance result when children feel they fulfill the important function of communicator in their families.

NO: Child language brokering does not necessarily positively shape the development of children. It can instead be a stressful experience for immigrant children in the following areas (Umaña-Taylor. as presented in Coleman & Ganong, 2003):

- Role reversals. Child language brokering almost always involves a bilingual child who is under the authority of the beneficiary. Because of this, unequal power exists, and parents become dependent on their children.

- Increased anxiety. During the brokering process, children often learn or are asked to convey confidential information about their parents. Because situations such as these are typically not developmentally appropriate for children, it may be stressful for them.

- Inhibited identity formation. A central developmental task of all children as they mature is to establish an identity that is separate and distinct from that of their parents. Child language brokers are continually called on by their parents to fulfill adult tasks, and this in turn limits their opportunities to explore their own identity.

What Do You Think?

1. Is child language brokering a positive or a negative life experience for bilingual children?

2. Have you acted in the capacity of a language broker for your family? If so, were you embarrassed to share private health or financial information? If you have not acted as a child language broker, would you have felt comfortable performing this role for your family?

One of the central themes of Symbolic Interaction theory is that meanings are changed through culturally and socially defined processes (Blumer, 1969), and we can see from our own daily lives and our dependence on our devices how culture has influenced/is influencing our interpersonal interactions. Given this, helping professionals, such as Certified Family Life Educators, are in a unique position to educate families about the ways in which digital technology can be both a positive and a negative influence on relationships (O'Keeffe & Clarke-Pearson, 2011). As helpers, we can educate and advise families, schools, and communities about healthy online use, as well as those things that may have adverse effects on individuals.

This lack of shared meanings and inaccurate interpretations cause frustrations and misunderstandings in all forms of human interactions—especially in family and intimate relationships. Some researchers argue that these frustrations would be greatly minimized if we understood the differences between how men and women acquire and share language meanings.

COMMUNICATION BETWEEN MEN AND WOMEN

I admit it—I am technology challenged! I was quite proud of myself when I recently learned how to create graphs and bar charts in PowerPoint, and I was even prouder of myself when I figured out how to text message *with my thumbs*. Consider this phone conversation I had with my son, a computer engineer.

Me:	"Help!"
Son:	"What's wrong *this* time?"
Me:	"I think I killed my laptop!"
Son:	"Did you plug it in to recharge the battery?"
	I begin to explain the problem as I see it ("stupid computer," or words to that effect).
Son (politely interrupting me):	"Well, what you need to do is [technical term], [very technical term], and [even more very technical term]. And that will fix the problem."
Me:	"What??"
Son:	"It's really simple, Mom. Put Dad on the phone and I'll explain it to him."

I thought about this conversation for quite a while. Did I really have that much trouble following my son's instructions to fix my computer? Were we just not on the same page because I'm not familiar with technology lingo? Or was there a fundamental gender difference in how we communicate? Would a woman have differently explained how to fix the computer?

The study of gender differences in interpersonal communication is a topic that generated great interest in the 1990s. In her best-selling book, *You Just Don't Understand: Women and Men in Conversation,* professor of linguistics Deborah Tannen proposed a framework that maintains that men and women interpret communication messages in fundamentally different ways (Tannen, 1990).

We will explore gender at length in the next chapter, but for now it's necessary to understand that as we grow up, we are taught how to be a "boy" or a "girl" or a "man" or a "woman" in a number of different ways. We receive countless messages from society on a daily basis that reinforce these gender cues. It's no different with communication: We are taught, by examples in our environment, how to communicate as a boy and how to communicate as a girl. And as we have seen so far in this chapter, we then carry these patterns of communicating and relating into our future relationships.

According to Tannen (1990), boys and girls grow up and learn entirely different—yet equally valid—communication meanings and symbols. She asserts that men and women are so different in how they communicate and interpret relational messages, and in what they focus on while communicating, that their communication is, in essence, akin to differences we might expect to see between people from different cultures. Tannen thus refers to the man-woman communication differences as *genderlects,* or *cross-sex* communication styles (p. 42).

iStock.com/PeopleImages

Although there are gender differences in how men and women communicate, understanding communication isn't as simple as asserting that males communicate one way while females communicate another way. *All* communication is dependent on the context in which it is taking place and how we were socialized to interact with others.

She proposed that these gender differences can lead to problems, misunderstandings, and tensions in all kinds of communication between men and women.

In the sections that follow, we'll briefly examine what the empirical evidence has to say about how men and women communicate; we'll pay particular attention to Tannen's (1990) difference framework of gender communication.

Men's Communication: Offering Advice

Message:
the obvious meaning of a communication.

Meta message:
the underlying context in which a communication takes place.

In all human behavior and communication, there are two levels of meaning that are conveyed. First there is the **message**, which is the obvious meaning of the communication. If we return to the example of my son assisting me with my computer problems, the clearcut message was that I was helpless to fix the problem. The second level of meaning is what Tannen (1990) refers to as the metamessage. A **metamessage** is the underlying context in which the communication takes place—it is the information about the relationship between the parties communicating (in this case, mother and son) and their attitudes toward each other. Tannen's gender difference linguistic research shows that men attune to the metamessage of *helping* and *fixing problems.* That is to say, the underlying context of men's communication is to be a problem solver and an advice giver (Tannen, 1990; Merchant, 2012). In the case of my computer woes, this is precisely what took place: I had a problem, and my son immediately jumped to the solution, rather than listen to me describe the problem in detail. Tannen asserted that men's communication behaviors are focused on control and dominance, and that is why men are problem solvers in dialogues with women.

Trouble talk:
talking about emotional and relationship problems.

Tannen (1990) also suggested that when men are confronted with **trouble talk**, or talking about emotional and relationship problems, they are much more likely than women to give advice, tell jokes, change the subject, or remain silent (to avoid emotional expression). Thus, Tannen asserts that when men engage in trouble talk and women offer sympathy to them, men feel that they are being looked down on, put in a lower status, or being condescended to (Michaud & Warner, 1997; Merchant, 2012).

Women's Communication: Connecting With Others

Let's suppose that I had a daughter who was a computer engineer, and she answered the phone when I had difficulties with my computer:

Me:	"Help!"
Daughter:	"What's wrong *this* time, Mom?"
Me:	"I think I killed it!"
Daughter:	"Oh, I'm so sorry you're having so many troubles. I know how busy you are. Don't worry; we'll figure this out."
	I begin to explain the problem as I see it ("stupid computer," or words to that effect).
Daughter (who politely lets me describe the problem):	"Well, what you need to do is—okay, do you see that little slot on the back? Okay, now twist that to the left and that will pop out your battery. Okay, now put the battery back and try to turn it on."
Me:	"It's working! Thanks!" And we continue our conversation—that has nothing to do with the computer.

According to Tannen's research, women attune to the metamessage of *empathy* and *understanding*. In trouble talk, then, women tend to openly express sympathy for and care about the situation; this shows that they align with or show solidarity with the other person. The hypothetical situation with my "daughter" handling the computer problem illustrates Tannen's assertions that when women communicate, they desire to connect with others, to build relationships, give support, and show cooperation (Tannen, 1990; Merchant, 2012).

And Herein Lies the Problem

When we communicate, there are a number of possible emotional responses to receiving messages, and we often expect the same emotional response that we would give in a similar situation (Michaud & Warner, 1997; Merchant, 2012). For instance, when a woman conveys sympathy in trouble talk, she anticipates that she will receive sympathy in response to her trouble talk (Michaud & Warner, 1997; Edwards & Hamilton, 2004). When a man gives advice or suggestions for solving a problem, he expects that he will receive advice in response to his trouble talk. But when he offers *advice* when she is expecting *sympathy*, she feels that her feelings are invalidated or that her problems are being trivialized. When she offers *sympathy* when he needs or wants *advice*, he feels that she is putting him down (Michaud & Warner, 1997). She may feel that his joke-telling is making fun of her situation; he may feel that her comforting is treating him like a child. Thus, it is not the *words* that are the underlying source of communication differences between men and women; it is the tendency for women and men to *interpret messages in systematically different ways* that is at issue (Edwards & Hamilton, 2004).

Tannen (1990) puts forth the idea that if men and women stop blaming one another for their communication difficulties, differences, and frustrations, and instead begin to communicate across gender cultures, then marriages and other intimate relationships would become strengthened. When men and women enhance their understanding of gender differences in communication, they are less likely to say to their intimate partner, "You don't understand!"

It's Really Not That Simple

Although there has been widespread acceptance of different communication cultures both in academics and in popular culture, it is important to point out that recent studies do not support Tannen's gender differences framework. For instance, one study showed that there was no evidence that men were more unresponsive than women when talking to friends about problems; in fact, they did not differ in their expressions of sympathy or minimize the other's problem (MacGeorge, Graves, Feng, & Gillihan, 2004). Another study found that the use of humor by men is a means of support for distressed friends—not a *lack* of support as Tannen asserted (Bippus, 2000), Indeed, as one study concluded, "Both men and women view the provision of support as a central element of close personal relationships; both value the supportive communication skills of their friends, lovers, and family members; both make similar judgments about what counts as sensitive, helpful support; and both respond quite similarly to various support efforts" (MacGeorge et al., 2004, p. 172).

Other bodies of science assert that although at face value it seems that gender differences in communication, or genderlect, is evident, it's not as simple as males-communicate-this-way-females-communicate-that-way. For example, one researcher maintains that gender *by itself* isn't the determinant of how people communicate with others (Hall & Matsumoto, 2004). If we consider this statement with what we've learned about individual development so far—that we do not develop in isolation, and that we are each a part of an interconnected whole that shapes us—then clearly, biological sex alone cannot account for differences in communication styles. As one recent study accurately points out, "Communication is a complex, context-dependent phenomenon in which numerous interrelated variables operate simultaneously" (Hidalgo Tenorio, 2016).

Family Diversity and Communication

Because our first experiences with interpersonal relationships occur within our families of origin, our understanding of how families communicate and of family life is often narrow (Turner & West, 2006), so we need to widen our knowledge of communication behaviors within a broad range of family types. Do family structures differ in the issues that challenge them?

Communication Within Nuclear Families: Issues important in today's contemporary families center on communicating about the division of household chores, the effects of work life on family life, and the involvement of men in their children's lives. Men in contemporary nuclear families have increased the amount of time they spend with their children as well as doing household chores. But spillover—when the stresses associated with work affect home life—tends to increase levels of conflict at home.

Communication in Gay and Lesbian Families: Gay and lesbian partners and parents struggle with relationship issues (such as conflict) and parenting issues (such as child care) just as heterosexual parents do. But gay fathers tend to receive more support from their families of origin than do lesbian mothers, although self-disclosure of their sexual identity is a difficult communication subject for many.

Communication Within Stepfamilies: Family communication within stepfamily structures most often centers on negotiating roles, communication rules, and the unique family subsystems that are formed when two families merge to form a stepfamily. Families who understand that it takes time for families to "blend" see less family conflict than those families who challenge or resist the process of merging the two families.

Communication Within Single-Parent Families: As discussed in Chapter 1, American culture promotes autonomy and independence, making the U.S. a predominantly individualistic country. In families that embrace this culture, the family of origin may communicate blame and guilt to single parents. However, it should be noted that certain racial and ethnic groups in the U.S. endorse collectivism. This is common among African Americans and Hispanic or Mexican Americans. In these families, single parents receive a great deal of support, protection, and emotional reinforcement.

Communication Within Heterosexual Cohabiting Families: Unique to cohabiting couples is a lack of communication role models for this specific family configuration. Cohabiting couples face greater demands in the areas of roles and support of their family structure.

Now that you have a firm understanding of communication as a transactional process, a knowledge base about how we acquire/share meanings, and the significance of these meanings in gendered and family form communication, it is time to explore two more fundamental topics of communication: verbal and nonverbal communication.

TYPES OF COMMUNICATION

Any interpersonal or social interaction provides us with a wealth of information. But why is it that today's divorce courts commonly hear that husbands and wives are "failing" to communicate (Gottman, 1999; Gottman, Ryan, Carrere, & Erlye, 2002; Stanley, 2017)?

How we communicate in our families influences the quality and the content of our relationships. Because we develop all of our interpersonal (social and relational) communication skills within our family of origin, this is where we build our foundation (whether in healthy ways or unhealthy ways) for communicating to resolve conflict; share intimacy; and express our needs, wants, fears, hopes, frustrations, anger, or desires. When we discuss marital and family communication, we are referring not just to the talk that takes place among couples, but also to the entire array of communication transactions.

Broadly stated, **communication** is the process of making and sharing meanings. Professors and researchers of communication studies Richard West and Lynn Turner (2018) summarize the general concepts of communication that we have learned so far:

Communication:
the process of making and sharing meanings.

Communication is a transaction. Communication is a transactional process in which parties act simultaneously as senders or receivers of messages. All human behavior is a continuous dialogue.

Communication is a process. Communication is dynamic and ever-changing. Viewed in this way, emphasis is placed on the *process* of meaning-making, rather than on the *outcome* of the exchanges. Each family undertakes the process of meaning-making differently; culture and ethnicity are key in the process of meaning-making.

Communication involves co-construction of meanings. Each person in a relationship speaks a unique language that was acquired from his or her family of origin. The process of communication thus consists of learning the meaning of things—*constructing definitions*—between family members.

Communication involves symbols. In order to construct meanings or definitions of things, people rely on *symbols* or *codes*. Across cultures, the codes that are used for communication are *verbal* and *nonverbal*. These two broad categories are used to describe how we convey meanings to one another, both in our interpersonal and social relationships.

Verbal Communication

The role of communication receives a lot of attention when talking about marriage and intimate relationships, and for good reason: The presence of or absence of effective communication skills plays a key part in whether a marriage succeeds or fails (Gottman, 1999). Our ability to effectively send and receive messages to a large extent predicts, or is associated with, marital satisfaction in couples (Markman, 1984; Gottman, 1999; Gottman et al., 2002).

Verbal communication refers to exchanges of thoughts, messages, or information through the spoken word. It includes the content and substance of the words being spoken, the tone and the expression, as well as the structure and organization of the words. All verbal communication takes place within the context of a specific environment. It is the language we speak. Despite the information communicators exchange, though, exclamations of "You don't understand!" and "That's not what I mean!" echo throughout the hallways of our homes.

Verbal communication:
refers to exchanges of thoughts, messages, or information through the spoken word.

In the 20th century, empirical marital and family communication studies were conducted to examine the significance of effective verbal communication skills and how these skills affect overall marital satisfaction. For example, one study looked at couples whose marriages were not in distress, couples who were in marital therapy, and couples in the process of divorce (Christensen & Shenk, 1991). The researchers found that couples who were not in distress showed more effective verbal communication styles in their day-to-day communication efforts than did the couples engaged in marital therapy and the couples divorcing. In addition, the couples in therapy and the divorcing couples exhibited lower levels of verbal communication skills than the nondistressed couples did.

Barbara Okun (2002), a professor of counseling psychology, also examined verbal communication skills as they relate to marital satisfaction. She notes that the majority of the problems found in marriages and families stem from ineffective communication. When role expectations and desires are not fulfilled, frustration and anger result. Okun further adds that couples who seek professional help with their verbal communication inadequacies consistently have trouble recognizing and communicating their problems or concerns to the spousal partner. Training couples in the area of verbal communication skills is becoming an increasingly popular and important component in approaches to marital counseling (O'Donohue & Crouch, 1996). Psychologist William Shadish (1993) and his colleagues maintain that the reason troubled couples rarely have positive outcomes is because each member of the couple lacks effective communication skills.

There are four fundamental verbal communication processes or skills that Brant Burleson (1992), professor of communication studies at Purdue University, lists that affect how we send and receive messages:

- **Communication effectiveness.** This skill requires us to convey messages accurately; it is the ability to send messages with the intended meaning. This is a fundamental skill in communication.

- **Perceptual accuracy.** Being able to deliver messages so they are received in the manner we *intend* is another critical skill.

- **Predictive accuracy.** This skill requires us to be able to accurately anticipate how our words will affect the other person. Usually when we speak, we know before the words leave our mouths what impact those words will have on the person we are speaking to.

- **Interpersonal cognitive complexity.** This area of communication skills deals more with our ability to process social information we receive from our environments than from person-to-person communication. Burleson and Denton (1997) refer to this skill as a *social perception* skill.

As you can see, these skills range from accurately conveying our messages, to accurately anticipating how our words will affect the other person, to how we process social information we receive from our environment. But conveying meanings through the spoken word is not the only means of communication. When people communicate, they use symbols and behaviors other than words to express and exchange their thoughts, feelings, and information. This is referred to as *nonverbal communication*.

Nonverbal Communication

Our emotions are almost always accompanied by overt physical displays. **Nonverbal communication** occurs with or without the spoken word. It includes facial expressions, motions of the body, eye contact, patterns of touch, expressive movements, hand gestures, the spatial arrangements in the physical environment, and displayed emotions. Emotions provide invaluable information as we attempt to interpret the messages conveyed by the sender. The physical gestures and movements that convey our emotions are most often referred to as

Nonverbal communication: communication via facial expressions, motions of the body, eye contact, patterns of touch, expressive movements, hand gestures, the spatial arrangements in the physical environment, and emotions that occurs with or without the spoken word.

iStock.com/FluxFactory

nonverbal communication or **emotional communication** (Senecal, Murad, & Hess, 2003). Although we all may have difficulty accurately interpreting the meaning of words that we hear, interpreting nonverbal/emotional communication can present an even greater challenge. Emotional communication is conveyed and interpreted in a number of different ways.

Emotional communication: the physical gestures and movements that convey our emotions.

Relational and Nonrelational Messages

Of particular interest to communication studies researchers Ascan Koerner and Mary Anne Fitzpatrick (2002a) is the idea that **relational messages**, which are messages that have something to do with the partner or the relationship, differ from **nonrelational messages**, or those issues or topics that have to do with things outside of the relationship. Specifically, the researchers hold that most often, relational information is not communicated with words; instead, when we wish to discuss something that concerns our partner or the state of the relationship, these relational messages are almost always communicated using nonverbal or emotional behaviors. For example, if a partner feels insecure or rejected by the other partner, rather than say the words, "I feel really insecure and rejected when you have long phone conversations with your ex," a person may instead pout, pull away from a hug or a touch, or give glaring, dirty looks. And herein lies a secret to effective, well-adjusted marital, family, and couple relationships—a secret about how to successfully navigate relational communication: Increase your ability to accurately decode your partner's emotional communication.

Relational messages: messages that have something to do with the partner or relationship.

Nonrelational messages: issues or topics concerning things outside of the relationship.

Decoding

How we **decode** or interpret the unspoken exchanges that take place in the many nuances of "couple talk" greatly affects marital adjustment and marital satisfaction (Tannen, 1990). In fact, research since the 1970s consistently indicates that couples who are well adjusted relationally decode the emotional/nonverbal communication of their mates better than those couples who are less well adjusted (Carton, Kessler, & Pape, 1999; Lindlof & Taylor, 2002; Koerner & Fitzpatrick, 2002a; Noller, 1993). In other words, couples who have stronger marriages are better able to read their partner's nonverbal behaviors than are those couples who are relationally not as strong.

Decode: to interpret unspoken exchanges.

In a study that investigated how married couples decode messages and the impact this has on marital satisfaction, Koerner and Fitzpatrick (2002b) describe their findings in terms of three specific emotional messages as they relate to nonverbal communication: *Positive emotional messages* are experienced as love, pleasure, and affection. *Negative emotional messages* are experienced in the form of anger and irritation and are often the result of being injured, harmed, or mistreated in interpersonal interactions. *Neutral emotional messages* are often hard to interpret because the person delivering the message either gives no specific cues or gives ambiguous cues. This type of nonspecific emotional communication, unfortunately, leads to many misunderstandings (and hurt feelings).

Koerner and Fitzpatrick (2002a) maintain that being able to recognize or decode messages so we can recognize whether emotional communication is due to relational or nonrelational factors is crucial for overall relationship satisfaction. The danger lies in how we decode messages. There are times we may *think* a partner's behavior concerns the relationship, when, in fact, it does not. For example, there may be a situation in which a partner seldom comes home from work in time for dinner. At the same time, perhaps a partner always comes home to a messy house. If we decode the nonverbal information as something that pertains to the relationship—if we *personalize* it—when it does not, these misinterpretations over time can lead to the dissolution of the marriage or the couple.

Private Couple Meanings

Couples represent special, unique pairs of interaction and have specific rules of communication. In their effort to study partners' predictions and judgments about each other's emotional communication behaviors, nonverbal communication researcher Sacha Senecal and colleagues (2003) discovered that married couples in particular are quite astute at predicting their partner's reaction to certain situations. These researchers attribute this ability to the fact that couples generally have a lot of information about each other that no one else has. This, in turn, influences the dynamics of interpersonal interactions.

For example, if college student Molly is going back and forth to her home to help care for an ill parent or assist her family during a difficult time, her partner will take this information into consideration if she snaps at him or is unusually quiet. But a clerk at a store or a waiter who does not know Molly's contextual information might assume that she is being rude or impolite in a social interaction. Because of this additional "inside" knowledge, couples develop private communication systems (Gottman, Markham, & Notarius, 1977; Gottman & Porterfield, 1981) that allow them to form couple-specific interpretations of verbal and nonverbal information (Senecal et al., 2003).

CORNERSTONES OF COMMUNICATION

Functional communication: communication that addresses only the ins and outs of daily life, leaving one feeling as though something is lacking in one's family connections.

Nurturing communication: interactions that convey intimacy, caring, recognition, and validation of family members.

Why is it that some couples have such deep trust and intimacy in their relationships while others find it difficult to discuss even day-to-day issues such as bill paying, childrearing, or grocery shopping? Why is it that some families stay tightly knit across multiple generations and others are emotionally distant or torn apart? Maybe in your family of origin the sole form of communication is **functional communication**—the type that addresses only the ins and outs of daily life—which leaves you feeling as though something is lacking in your family connections. Or, conversely, perhaps your family experiences deeper levels of **nurturing communication**, which translates into interactions that convey intimacy, caring, recognition, and validation of family members (Galvin et al., 2019).

To better understand nurturing communication in marital and family settings, it helps to know what forms the basis for effective communication patterns and behaviors. Kathleen Galvin and her colleagues (2019) offer insight into concepts that provide families with rewarding and satisfying communication across the developmental life of the family; from their research they outline the key concepts of family-strengthening communication.

Develop Relational Cultures

Intimacy is the foundation of every aspect of satisfying, successful interpersonal relationships, whether they are friendships, romantic relationships, or family. Communication that takes place in intimate relationships can be thought of as a relational culture. **Relational culture** refers to a framework of understandings—a private, unique, distinct language—that couples construct in private. These understandings serve to coordinate the attitudes, actions, and identities of the couple and of the family members. Relational cultures among couples and families are important examples of communication dynamics, for interpersonal relationships "are created out of communication, maintained and altered in communication, and dissolved through communication" (Galvin et al., 2019).

As newly formed couples attempt to share and interpret the meanings of their private language, most will struggle to coordinate these meanings as they transfer them from each of their families of origin to their new relationship. It is not uncommon for newlyweds or those couples newly cohabiting to discover that they argue and disagree much, much more than they did before they lived together. Misunderstandings, arguments, disagreements, and hurt feelings are common (and perhaps even necessary) as couples form their own, unique relational culture and shared meanings.

Relational culture:
a framework of understandings—a private, unique, distinct language—that couples construct in private.

Use Confirming Messages and Responses

Confirming messages or responses validate those with whom we are communicating. These types of communication are characterized by recognition of the other person, relevant dialogue, and acceptance; all of these show a willingness to be involved in the relationship (Sieburg, 1973). When we use confirming messages and responses, not only do we acknowledge the other person's presence but we also suggest we are willing to become involved with that person.

There are two key aspects of confirming messages or responses: recognition and acceptance. Recognition essentially consists of confirming or acknowledging—either verbally or nonverbally—another's presence and validates the person as a significant, contributing member of the relationship. Such confirmation is an absolute must for intimate marital and family relationships. Confirming messages such as "It was so sweet of you to run that errand for me today—it really freed up my afternoon," or "Thank you so much for unplugging the phone so I could sleep in this morning!" imply acceptance of the other. On the other hand, rejecting responses such as "You're so stupid," or "Oh shut up, you don't know what you're talking about!" serve only to invalidate or reject the family member or mate (Canary, Cody, & Manusov, 2000). Over time, the individual feels rejected and that he or she is of little importance to the family system.

Confirming messages or responses:
types of communication characterized by recognition of the other person, relevant dialogue, and acceptance; all of these show a willingness to be involved in the relationship.

Acceptance simply means that every family member has the sense that they are "all right" (Galvin et al., 2019). On the surface, this seems reasonable and easy to achieve. But ethnic and cultural differences affect how we react and respond to those with whom we are communicating. In some cultures, families talk openly and are affectionate, but in other cultures, family members are reserved and formal. To illustrate, I was reared in a very warm, affectionate southern family; my husband was reared in a family where affection was not displayed physically or verbally. When I first ventured to say "I love you" to him and he replied, "Thanks," I interpreted his reply as rejection. At the time, I didn't recognize how he had been raised. Only as we became a couple, then a family, did our communication intimacy grow deeper. As our relationship grew, only then did we each feel the other's acceptance and recognition. Our experiences are not unique. For everyone, the growth of interpersonal relationships depends on messages that reflect each person's investment in the relationship (Galvin et al., 2019). To communicate in confirming and meaningful ways, it is necessary to self-disclose.

Self-Disclose

Self-disclosure is voluntarily sharing something personal or private with someone else. This is a *two-way* process because it means that when we send a message, we take a risk that the

Self-disclosure:
voluntarily sharing things with someone else that are personal or private to us.

iStock.com/South_agency

When we share our deepest thoughts, fears, hopes, dreams, and goals with our partner, we are increasing our relational intimacy. Do you struggle with self-disclosure, or does it come easily to you? Why do you think this is?

Emotional safety: the high degree of trust required to self-disclose.

person receiving the message will accept what we are sharing. Self-disclosure requires a high degree of trust, which Galvin and associates (2019) refer to as **emotional safety**; in general, self-disclosure

- Increases as relational intimacy increases
- Tends to be reciprocal (mutual)
- Increases relational satisfaction (relational satisfaction appears to be greatest when moderate levels of disclosure take place)

Disclosure is also affected by gender and socialization; it is particularly related to family of origin, cultural, and ethnic backgrounds. Empirical study, for example, found that married men self-disclose less frequently to their male friends than married women do to their female friends (Omarzu, 2000; Tschann, 1988). The broader point here is that each couple and each family has its own unique opportunities for sell-disclosure, yet this can only take place if family members take advantage of these opportunities and communicate often.

Communicate Often

Students in my family relationships and gender roles class hear me state repeatedly throughout the semester, "A hectic, chaotic lifestyle supports a hectic, chaotic relationship." Family and marital intimacy can either be enhanced or hindered by the time devoted to—committed to—nurturing the process of communication. According to the Pew Research Center (2019), more than one-half of the dads surveyed and 60 percent of the moms surveyed indicated that a lack of time with family was a greater family problem than a lack of money. Simply stated, if you are not ever together as a couple, then precious little time exists to nurture the relationship, and this includes the fundamental element of family: communication. It helps if couples and families periodically take an inventory of what is happening in each other's lives and open the lines of communication when taking stock of communication patterns and behaviors. **Family meetings** or weekly family discussions (whether they are formal or informal) provide structure and organization to the family system and allow for meaningful

Family meetings: formal or informal regular family discussions that provide structure and organization to the family system and allow for meaningful conversation.

conversation. It is up to the parents to ensure that a safe, trusting atmosphere exists within the home to foster an environment that encourages open, honest communication between parents and the children.

Listen Actively

Communication is most effective when **active listening** takes place. When we actively listen, we *hear* what the other person is saying. We are interacting with someone who is important to us. This process is considered an art that connects us to another so we understand not only what others are saying but what they are feeling, too (Lindgren, 1998). When active listening does not take place, the effects of poor listening can be quite detrimental to a family's communication patterns. Family scientist Herbert Lindgren (1998) describes several styles of poor listening in Table 3.1. Notice that the primary reasons behind poor listening styles tend to be *self*-centered rather than *other*-centered. And herein lies a basic skill in effective, meaningful communication: accurately hearing and receiving the words, meanings, attitudes, feelings, and emotions of the person sending the messages.

Another form of attentive listening is **reflective listening**, when we pay close attention to a person's verbal and emotional (nonverbal) messages and respectfully acknowledge their perspective. During the course of the communication exchange, we should occasionally seek clarification from family members by saying things such as, "When you said _____, did you mean _____? I want to make sure I understand," or "Am I understanding you correctly when you say _____?" By taking time to *repeat in our own words* what we think the message is, we are both clarifying and validating the message we are receiving. Although reflective listening

Active listening: when we actively listen, we become connected to another person so we not only hear what they are saying but understand what they are feeling.

Reflective listening: a form of active listening in which we pay close attention to a person's verbal and emotional messages and respectfully acknowledge their perspective.

Table 3.1 /// Poor Listening Styles

To truly listen to others involves the art of connecting in such a way that you fully understand not only what they are saying but also what they are feeling. Indeed, active listening is a vital, essential skill that is needed in marriages, families, and intimate relationships. Family scientist and practitioner Herbert Lindgren notes that ineffective or poor listening often is the result of bad listening habits or styles:

- **The Faker.** Fakers pretend to listen but don't. Their minds wander in and out of the conversation, but they may nod their head or smile as if they are listening.

- **The Interrupter.** Interrupters are more concerned about their own thoughts and feelings than they are with those of others. They seldom allow the other person to finish, or they immediately respond without pausing for much reflection or consideration of what the other has said. They seldom offer an understanding ear.

- **The Intellectual Listener.** Rather than listen relationally, intellectual listeners attend only to the actual spoken words. They ignore nonverbal communication cues and approach the conversation in a rational, logical way, rather than relying on their feelings or emotions.

- **The Self-Conscious Listener.** These listeners are more concerned with their own status and impressing someone than they are with the thoughts, ideas, or feelings of the other. Because they are trying to impress people with whom they are communicating, they do not listen with understanding. Instead, while the other is talking, the self-conscious listener is already forming his or her reply.

- **The Judge and Jury Listener.** These listeners judge the ideas and behaviors of others, letting others know how wrong or incorrect their thoughts and feelings are. In doing so, they do not hear what the other is saying.

Communication is a two-way, transactional process. Both the listener and the speaker have responsibility to make sure the message is understood.

Source: Lindgren (1998).

exchanges such as these will sometimes result in a family member saying, "You're still not listening; that is not what I mean!" we need to keep in mind that reflective listening is not necessarily aimed at reaching an agreement as much as it is aimed at trying to come to understanding the message.

Reframe:
to view the issue from
another perspective.

Another effective strategy in resolving conflict is to **reframe** an issue, which means looking at the issue from another perspective. Reframing allows you to see the issue while standing in the shoes of another. Reflective listening and reframing together foster an open, trusting, and caring communication environment.

Use Humor: A Little Laugh Goes a Long Way

When I was seriously ill battling breast cancer, my husband and I found ourselves talking about those things we hoped we would not have to address at such an early point in our marriage—what would happen if I died. It was a tough conversation, and there came the time when we began to discuss funeral arrangements. In the midst of this emotion-packed conversation, I quickly added, "I know what I want on my tombstone; I want it to say *I told you I was sick!*" It took several minutes for our laughter to subside, and at that point my husband indicated that he, too, knew what he wanted inscribed on his tombstone: *She told me she was fine!* It was at that moment that we both knew that no matter the outcome of my illness, everything would eventually be okay.

There are several reasons why humor and laughter aid family communication and contribute to overall marital and family satisfaction. First of all, when we laugh our bodies produce endorphins, a feel-good, natural pain reliever. These chemicals are released not only while we are laughing but also after exercise, after sexual encounters, after eating, while holding a baby—all of those things relax and calm us. When our bodies are flooded with endorphins, they lower the level of cortisol that our body produces when under stress (Lindgren, 1998). Humor also brings people together and helps to keep things in perspective, sometimes protecting us from focusing too intently on what is immediately before us.

Despite our blue-ribbon efforts, however, sometimes our communication efforts are ineffective or they fail. When this happens, couples and families experience conflict or instances of stress or disagreements (Anderson & Sabatelli, 2011). Sometimes the conflict is chronic or ongoing.

CONFLICT IN RELATIONSHIPS

Every couple fights. Every family fights. Due to the complex, interrelated nature of interpersonal relationships, conflict is inevitable. In all facets of intimacy, love, sexual encounters, parenting, childrearing, communication, and communication patterns, there are opportunities for quarrels and differences of opinion that may lead to arguments, conflict, and all-out shouting matches. Because of the interactive, systemic nature of family and intimate relationships, conflict can quickly spill into every area of family life. When this occurs, strained relationships lead to a stressful living environment.

Although the experience of conflict is unique to each family, when looking at empirical studies that examine conflict there appear to be common themes of marital and family conflict. Family interaction authors Stephen Anderson and Robert Sabatelli (2011) provide an overview of the current scientific studies as they relate to these areas of marital conflict:

- *Money matters.* Who makes it? Who spends it and how? Who manages the family finances?
- *Division of household labor.* Who does what and when and how often? Is there role equity within the home? Is equality important in this context? Who decides?
- *Sex.* How frequently does each partner want to have sex? How long should it last? Who does what and when? What are each partner's sexual scripts and are these scripts flexible enough to accommodate the partner's desires?

- *"Tremendous trifles."* This category is a catch-all for a wide array of disputes that emerge over personal habits such as snoring, not picking up after oneself, and consistently being late; personal preferences, such as preferring to watch television reruns and figure skating competitions over golf, baseball, and action adventure movies; and day-to-day living, such as who picks up the kids from school, who takes the kids to soccer, who picks up the dry cleaning, and who does the grocery shopping.

The issue at hand, then, is not whether conflict will erupt—it will. The question is what kind of conflict will it be? Just because conflict exists does not mean that there is a problem with the relationship. John Gottman (1994b), the most influential researcher in the areas of marital happiness/marital satisfaction and conflict management, points out that the basic difference between functional and dysfunctional families is the way in which families process—or *use*—conflict.

Next, we will have a look at the process of conflict and the factors associated with family conflict, as well as the nuances of destructive, constructive, and unresolved conflict.

What's All The Fuss? The Sources of Conflict

Conflict typically occurs when family members believe that their desires and goals are not compatible with those of one or more members in the family (Galvin et al., 2019). Many newly formed couples or families try to avoid conflict, but if they manage it properly, conflict can actually be quite beneficial to the relationship and foster growth within the family system. As with any other aspect of marriage and family life, learning about the sources of conflict allows us to better navigate our personal relationships and helps us help others to use conflict to foster stronger relationships.

There are so many things we can argue about when it comes to family living: where to go to eat, whether a once-used towel is clean or not and needs to be thrown into the laundry hamper, what time the children should be home—the list is virtually endless! Anderson and Sabatelli (2011) provide a comprehensive discussion concerning marital and family conflict and the underlying sources of conflict in marriage: conflicting role expectations, conflicting needs for connection and autonomy, and conflicts in fairness and equity.

When Role Expectations Conflict

We establish relationships, and when we marry or partner with someone we bring with us a ready set of expectations based on how each of us has been socialized. When our expectations are not met, conflict results. For example, women who have been socialized to accept more traditional gender roles may expect to be the primary caretakers and disciplinarians for the children. They may also expect to be primarily responsible for household tasks and expect their husbands to manage the household finances. These women may also expect their husbands to initiate sexual activities. Conversely, men who have been reared according to more contemporary gender roles may expect to be equal partners and have equal say in how the children are reared. They may also assume that household tasks and household finances will be divided equally between the spouses. They may expect sex to be initiated by either partner. When expectations such as those just described are not fulfilled, conflict erupts.

Anderson and Sabatelli (2011) note an impressive body of research that speaks to role conflict and differences in role expectations as major sources of marital strain, friction, opposition, and hostility (among others, Bagarozzi & Anderson, 1989; Sabatelli, 1988). When spouses have opposing expectations, and when couples do not discuss their expectations or periodically align them, fertile ground exists for discontent to take root.

When Connection and Autonomy Conflict

The interdependent nature of marital and family relationships essentially guarantees that conflict is inevitable due to a human need to be intimately connected and yet separate (autonomous) at the same time. According to Anderson and Sabatelli (2011), as long as one partner's needs do not conflict with the other's, the couple peacefully coexists. But when one partner's need to be alone competes with the other partner's need to be together, the potential for conflict arises.

When Fairness and Equity Are in Question

When we enter into a marital partnership, we do so with our own unique perceptions of what constitutes a fair and equitable relationship. For instance, many people enter into committed partnerships and marital relationships expecting that the relationship will always be 50/50. Perhaps the relationship would remain relatively conflict-free if these expectations were consistently met. But how realistic are these expectations? Anderson and Sabatelli (2011) point out that any infringement, breach, or abuse of these norms—our perceptions—becomes the underlying source of conflict in our interpersonal relationships.

As you will see in Chapter 7, intimate relationships can be viewed in terms of cost versus benefit. In assessing the concepts of equity and fairness, we tend to believe that the relationship is fair if the benefits we receive are comparative to the costs. In other words, if we get as much out of the relationship as we put into it, then it is fair. An equitable relationship exists when each partner gains similar benefits for being in the relationship. When there is perceived unfairness or perceived inequity, conflict results (Anderson & Sabatelli, 2011). When couples work at resolving the conflict, the result is a change in how the couple interacts.

Types of Conflict

Relationship conflict usually occurs because of miscommunication, poor communication, or misperception. Sometimes it is the result of negative behaviors. We generally think of conflict as something we need to avoid because the term implies that conflict is harmful to a relationship. But conflict can be beneficial and strengthen the relationship and initiate growth if dealt with properly. Conflict can be either constructive or destructive to the marital relationship. Additionally, couples vary in their conflict styles.

Not all conflict in a relationship is bad. Constructive conflict can help deepen a couple's intimacy and commitment. The key is to make sure that there are more positive exchanges than negative exchanges. Do you shy away from conflict? Or do you confront it and deal with it? Why do you think you respond to conflict the way you do?

iStock.com/diego_cervo

Constructive Conflict

While in the midst of a heated argument it might be difficult to think that any good can come out of it; however, constructive conflict serves to build relationships and foster loyalty, commitment, and intimacy.

John Gottman has consistently found that the manner in which couples handle conflict ultimately determines whether they divorce. In a study that sought to determine the differences in communication patterns of those couples who sought marital counseling and those who did not, Gottman and his colleagues (1977) found that the more happily married couples avoided negative comments (such as hurling insults at one another during a disagreement or a heated battle) and instead affirmed the value and worth of the other partner, in spite of their disagreements.

In a landmark empirical study, Gottman (1994b) found that how couples communicated about their differences determined marital longevity: Even though some of the arguments the couples experienced were all-out shouting matches or openly verbally combative, couples with high marital satisfaction maintained a ratio of *five* positive comments to every *one* negative comment. In his work *Why Marriages Succeed or Fail* (1994b), Gottman explored his idea that conflict management styles distinguish troubled from nontroubled couples. Through his study, he found there are two specific marriage types: regulated and nonregulated.

Regulated couples use communication patterns and interpersonal behaviors that promote closeness and intimacy, such as using more positive comments than negative comments during times of tension. According to Gottman (1994b), there are three types of regulated couples: the validating couple, the volatile couple, and the conflict-minimizing couple.

> *The validating couple.* This type of couple uses a constructive conflict management style. They tend to be empathic and supportive of one another and try to gauge each other's emotions. These couples listen actively and respectfully and validate that what their partner is feeling is important. Validating couples seldom express negative emotions toward one another. They tend to be happy but not necessarily passionate.
>
> *The volatile couple.* Unlike the validating couple, the volatile couple type is charged with intense emotion, passion, and romance, and it is this emotion and passion that spills over into every area of marital and family life, including conflict. But despite the intense, emotional disputes, fights, and shouting matches that take place, these couples remain genuinely and intimately connected to one another.
>
> *The conflict-minimizing couple.* These couples ignore or avoid conflict or minimize the significance of the trouble, Despite the fact that the conflict-minimizing couple reduces or lessens the conflict that exists—and hence, lives with unresolved issues just below the surface— these couples manage to keep the discontentment and unresolved problems from spilling over into other areas of their relationship, According to Gottman (1994b), they still manage to use positive language rather than negative, distancing language, which ultimately promotes a deeper level of intimacy.

How can a volatile couple with explosive emotions or a couple who totally ignores or avoids the conflict be considered constructive in their conflict management? When Gottman proposed that successful, satisfied married couples maintain a five-to-one ratio of positive comments to negative comments, he illustrated the importance of balance and affirmation. When couples are able to balance positives and negatives constructively, the end result is an effective relationship that withstands and grows from conflict.

Destructive Conflict

We have all had our share of disputes and arguments with family members. The dispute or conflict may have been successfully resolved so that the relationship was able to change,

Constructive conflict: conflict that serves to build relationships and to foster loyalty, commitment, and intimacy.

Regulated couples: regulated couples use communication patterns and interpersonal behaviors that promote closeness and intimacy, such as using more positive comments than negative comments during times of tension.

adjust to the stress, and subsequently deepen loyalty, commitment, and intimacy levels. At other times, however, many of us have experienced conflict that resulted in greater hurt, anger, confusion, and pain. **Destructive conflict** can be either overt, which refers to obvious conflict, or covert, which is subtler but nonetheless hurtful. Whether it is overt or covert, destructive conflict is unhelpful, and at its very worst, deadly (as in the case of physical violence that escalates).

According to Galvin and her colleagues (2019), covert destructive conflict falls within five specific categories:

1. *Denial* is exhibited when a person's words do not align with his or her nonverbal behavior, for example, when someone shouts, "Nothing is wrong!" as he storms out the room.

2. *Disqualification* occurs when a person attempts to cover up an expressed emotion; for example, she might say, "I'm sorry I'm so upset with you, but it's been a horrible day at work."

3. *Displacement* refers to a situation in which someone takes out his or her frustration on someone who is not the original object of anger. An example of this displacement is **scapegoating**, which occurs when anger and hostility are directed at one family member in particular, who always bears the brunt of everyone's frustration. A child who is always blamed for instigating trouble in the family, for example, is known as the family's scapegoat.

4. *Disengaged* couples or family members have little or no emotional closeness. These family members act out their anger or hostility through their lack of interaction with one another.

5. *Pseudomutuality* refers to pseudo (fake or false) mutuality (getting along). Pseudomutual families may appear to be close with no indication that conflict exists, yet anger and hostility are always just beneath the surface.

Overt destructive conflict is often verbal and is characterized by the use of negative, hurtful language, such as "idiot," "stupid," or "jerk." Verbal assaults may or may not involve screaming or yelling (Galvin et al., 2019). When couples and families engage in this type of destructive conflict, they often resort to language that will inflict the most harm possible.

Another type of verbal conflict is **gunnysacking**, which is also destructive. This describes when a spouse or a family member holds in resentment, hurt, anger, frustration, and bitter feelings until that "last straw," finally unloading all of the pent-up feelings in the midst of an argument.

According to Gottman (1994b), **nonregulated couples** are those who have a difficult time bouncing back from arguments and disputes because the way they handle the conflict only compounds the issues at hand, so even day-to-day disagreements erupt into full-fledged arguments. Nonregulated couples are distinguished from regulated couples in that their interactions tend to be far more negative than regulated couples, and they have a substantially lower ratio of positive-to-negative exchanges. According to Gottman, there are four ways in which nonregulated couples handle conflict. He characterized these as the "Four Horsemen of the Apocalypse":

1. *Criticism.* Criticism almost always involves the word *you. You* never . . . *You* always . . . *You* are so . . . *You* are such a . . . Almost without exception, criticism involves an attack on the *person,* rather than a complaint against the family member's *behavior.* In other words, the comments are meant to hurt, and usually they do.

2. *Defensiveness.* It is human nature to defend ourselves if we perceive that we are being attacked, be it physically, verbally, or emotionally. Recall from our previous

Destructive conflict:

destructive conflict can be either overt, which refers to obvious conflict, or covert, which is more subtle, but nonetheless hurtful. Whether it is overt or covert, destructive conflict is unhelpful and, at its very worst, deadly (as in the case of physical violence that escalates).

Scapegoating:

an example of displacement, scapegoating occurs when anger and hostility are directed at one family member in particular who always bears the brunt of everyone's frustration.

Gunnysacking:

this refers to a spouse or a family member who holds in resentment, hurt, anger, frustration, and bitter feelings until that "last straw," when the spouse or family member unloads all of the pent-up feelings in the midst of an argument.

Nonregulated couples:

couples who have a difficult time bouncing back from arguments and disputes because the manner in which they handle the conflict only compounds the issues at hand.

discussion that often the way we perceive a message is not the way that the sender intended it to be received; however, often someone speaks words deliberately aimed to hurt. The criticism/defense/criticism/defense interaction pattern becomes a vicious cycle of negativity.

3. *Contempt.* Contempt can be characterized as disrespect, scorn, or all-out hatred for one another, and it is most often the result of constant critical interactions. This pattern of criticisms and defensiveness breeds deeper levels of disdain in a marriage. Over time, the mutual contempt becomes so pervasive and all-encompassing that it erodes all other areas of the marriage to the point where the couple eventually focuses only on the negative behaviors of the other spouse.

4. *Stonewalling.* According to Gottman (1994a), **stonewalling** lakes place when communication between marital partners completely shuts down. In these instances, either one or both spouses distance themselves by refusing to communicate, ignoring and becoming remote from the other. Marital separation or dissolution is a likely outcome when this negativity process becomes the standard.

Stonewalling:

takes place when communication between marital partners completely shuts down. Either one or both spouses distance themselves by refusing to communicate, ignoring each other, and becoming remote.

Nonregulated couples' inability to constructively manage their conflict ultimately causes a downward spiral in the marriage. As the negativity increases and intensifies, over time nonregulated couples eventually reframe their perception of their marriage and *focus only on the negative aspects of one another's behavior and the relationship.*

Anger: Are You Controlling It or Is It Controlling You?

The innate, natural way to respond to anger is through aggression because anger is the body's way of responding to something that we perceive to be threatening. Some people exhibit more anger than others, perhaps because they are genetically wired to be irritable. Others learn from their families of origin to have a low tolerance for frustration and don't take things in stride. Often these individuals come from family backgrounds that are

iStock.com/Takassu

It is a common experience in couple and family life to experience unresolved conflict or conflict that causes even greater hurt, anger, and confusion. Destructive conflict results in antagonism, not resolution.

disruptive and chaotic and from families with low verbal and nonverbal communication skills. There are three primary ways in which people deal with their anger (American Psychological Association, 2005):

1. **Expressing angry feelings.** Expressing feelings of anger in assertive or firm ways—without aggression—is the healthiest way. Being assertive means to be able to convey to others in a confident, self-assured manner what your needs are without hurting the other person. Assertive expression of anger does not mean being demanding or difficult.

2. **Suppressing angry feelings.** People who suppress their anger often try to think of a more positive thought in an attempt to keep the angry feelings at bay or convert the anger into more positive feelings. Although this anger management technique is acceptable for mild frustrations, it is not healthy over the long run. Some people who consistently suppress their anger redirect it to other people, becoming cynical or hostile.

3. **Calming angry feelings.** Try to calm the feelings that anger arouses. Not only does this mean calming and controlling external behaviors such as yelling but also internal responses, such as breathing slower to control the heart rate and blood pressure. Some people use self-talk techniques to calm themselves, such as, "He's not late on purpose just to ruin my day. Traffic jams happen."

For healthy selves and healthy families, keep anger at bay by learning those things that trigger anger among family members. Also, develop coping strategies, such as the following:

- **Relaxing.** Take a moment to step back, to take a few deep breaths, or to count to 10. Discuss the situation only after the immediate tensions and sensations subside.
- **Reframing/restructuring.** Change the way you think about the situation. Logic defeats anger because it prevents us from becoming irrational when we are upset and keeps a balanced perspective.
- **Planning.** Not all problems have a solution, but planning ahead or anticipating that anger will crop up in family relationships provides families with proactive coping techniques.
- **Listening.** When a family member is upset or angry, it helps to listen to the emotions behind the words. For example, he might be angry because she did not call to say she was going to be home late from work, but in actuality he is angry because he is afraid something happened to her on her way home. (American Psychological Association, 2005)

Conflict in family and marital life is normal and is to be expected. Marital partners and families who deal with conflict in constructive, positive ways and avoid negative interactions with their mates further increase their intimacy, loyalty, and commitment. On the other hand, spouses and family members who engage in destructive communication and experience frequent negative interactions increase the likelihood of relationship deterioration and divorce.

THE ROLE OF FORGIVENESS IN FAMILY AND INTIMATE RELATIONSHIPS

Betrayal. Aggression. Just plain insensitivity. People can, and do, hurt us in countless ways, whether it's being cut off in traffic, being backstabbed by a co-worker, or being yelled at by a loved one.

When someone—a family member, a friend, or a dating partner—hurts you or offends you, do you let the hurtful comments or actions go and get back to the business of the relationship, or do you tend to hold a grudge and silently vow to "get even" somehow? Although the concept of forgiveness has received a lot of attention from philosophers, theologians, and

Biblical scholars for decades, only as recently as the past decade has forgiveness as a family process emerged as an area of interest in the social sciences (Rusbult, 2002). For instance, what motivates someone to forgive? Or not to forgive and hold the trespass against someone? And why is it so hard to forgive, even if we want to?

What Is Forgiveness?

A number of researchers have undertaken studies to deepen our understanding of forgiveness and how reconciliation takes place (among many, Fincham & May, 2019; Hook, Davis, Owen, Worthington, & Utsey, 2013; Worthington & Scherer, 2004). They seek to answer questions such as, How does forgiveness improve the human condition? How do we choose to forgive? What are the effects of holding grudges and seeking revenge? In the social science literature, **forgiveness** is described as a deliberate process that transforms a strong desire for revenge into a positive response (Maio, Thomas, Fincham, & Carnelley, 2008). In other words, forgiveness is a process in which the forgiver intentionally moves from negative thoughts, feelings, and behaviors associated with the event to more positive ones (Maio et al., 2008). It is not condoning, excusing, or forgetting what happened. Forgiveness occurs at two different levels: at an individual level and at a relationship level (Thompson et al., 2005).

Forgiveness: a deliberate process that transforms a strong desire for revenge into a positive response.

Forgiving: The Individual Level

All too frequently, the people we love the most are the people who we hurt and are hurt by (Fincham, Beach, & Davila, 2004). But how can we move past this inevitable hurt? What motivates us to forgive someone? Why do some people put more effort into forgiveness than others?

When discussing forgiveness at the individual, or intrapersonal, level, we first need to recognize that the concept of forgiveness is an internal process; it is primarily for the individual who was hurt, not for the offender. When we forgive someone, we free ourselves from the control of the person who hurt us.

We also need to understand that forgiveness is subjective. As our study in this chapter has shown us, each of us comes into our intimate relationships with different beliefs and family experiences—and forgiveness is no exception. We are each taught in our families of origin what behaviors demonstrate or convey forgiveness and unforgiveness; the concept of forgiveness is defined in each home to serve the needs of those particular family members. For example, each semester I pose this question to my class: If your partner had sex with

Many relationships can survive even the deepest of emotional hurt, such as infidelity. There is no question that forgiveness aids in the longevity and health of family and intimate relationships. It is one of the most underutilized tools we have to strengthen the relationship with those we love and care about.

another person while committed to you, would you leave that partner and end the relationship? Overwhelmingly, the class responds that yes, they would leave their partner. But every now and then a student will indicate that one of their parents had been cheated on, yet chose to stay in the marriage and work things out. By their example, the couple taught their children that forgiveness is an option in this situation.

Certainly, subjective notions of forgiveness vary from person to person and from culture to culture. In fact, this has been one of the looming hurdles for investigators who desire to examine the application of forgiveness to certain relationship problems (Silberman, 1995). In addition to the intrapersonal level, forgiveness can be applied differently to situations within the same relationship.

Forgiving: The Relationship Level

The reality of intimate relationships is that everyone fights! In order for a relationship to succeed, then, it is important for us to grasp the concept that forgiveness is essential in our relational lives because it can break patterns that would otherwise interfere with—or even destroy—the relationship. When we discuss forgiveness at the relationship level, we are referring to the interpersonal level.

Forgiving spouses report more positive outcomes in their relationships because forgiveness is linked to tendencies to behave more positively in the marriage (Fincham et al., 2004; Fincham, Hall, & Beach, 2006). For example,

- Forgiveness is the cornerstone of a successful marriage (Fincham et al., 2006; Hook, Worthington, & Utsey, 2009).
- Forgiveness cultivates positive moods, feelings, and behaviors and builds strong connections between the couple (Worthington, Witvliet, Pietrini, & Miller, 2007; David & Stafford, 2015).
- Being able to forgive enables couples to resolve marriage challenges and keep marital stability intact (Entezar, Othman, Kosnin, & Panah, 2011; Braithwait, Mitchell, Selby, & Fincham, 2016; Kato, 2016).
- Couples who forgive are less negative with each other (such as bickering, arguing, stonewalling; McNulty, 2008).

There is no question about it: Those couples who choose forgiveness are happier in their marriages and couple relationships than those who do not report high levels of forgiveness (He et al., 2018).

Other scholarship suggests that there are a number of factors associated with the interpersonal level of forgiveness. These include conflict resolution skills and the willingness to forgive, overall relationship satisfaction, and the commitment to the relationship (Fincham et al., 2004; Kachadourian, Fincham, & Davila, 2004; Younger, Piferi, Jobe, & Lawler, 2004). The rapidly expanding body of forgiveness research shows us that people forgive others both at the intrapersonal and interpersonal levels. But we still must determine *how* people forgive.

Communicating Forgiveness: A Family Process

Forgiveness is an essential family process that is necessary to help family members deal with and heal from the inevitable offenses, hurts, or traumas that take place in relationships (Wade, Bailey, & Schaffer, 2005). If we don't forgive, emotional and relational wounds fester and cause anger, fear, and rage to develop—just as our earlier exploration of Gottman's research showed us. But how do families and individuals develop the capacity to forgive?

There are many different pathways to forgiveness, and researchers have begun to better understand models of relational forgiveness. For example, Dr. Fred Luskin, a researcher from Stanford University, put forth a model of forgiveness in which people pinpoint their rage, realize that harboring anger is unhealthy, and look at their situation differently so it's not

Table 3.2 /// Rank Ordering of the Forgiveness Process by Study Participants

1. I admitted to myself that the person hurt me.
2. I became aware of my anger.
3. I admitted to myself that I felt shamed or humiliated by what the person did.
4. I lost my energy by staying resentful.
5. I thought over and over about what happened.
6. I compared my unfortunate state with my offender's more fortunate state.
7. I realized that I may have been permanently changed by the offense.
8. I began to think that people in general—not just my offender—were bad and selfish.
9. I realized that my ways of handling the problem were not working.
10. I was willing to consider forgiveness as an option.
11. I committed to forgive the person who hurt me.
12. I thought of the person who offended me in broader and more positive terms.
13. The anger left me.

Source: Knutson, Enright, & Garbers (2008).

as problematic as they first thought (Luskin, 2003). One study found that people contemplate their situation and go through a series of thoughts before considering forgiveness as an option (Knutson, Enright, & Garbers, 2008). Table 3.2 presents the 82 study participants' responses, in order of importance. As you can see, forgiveness is a process that begins with admitting to ourselves that someone hurt us. As we move through the process, we acknowledge that our resentment is consuming us and changing us and that we have to consider forgiving the offender before the anger can leave us.

Other contemporary research reveals that there are three ways in which we communicate forgiveness: directly, indirectly, and conditionally (Kelley, 1998).

- *Direct forgiveness.* With **direct forgiveness**, family members or intimate partners clearly, plainly, and directly tell the offender that she or he is forgiven. Forgivers use statements such as, "We talked about the situation and I told her she was forgiven," and "I let him know that by saying I forgave him so he has no doubts about it" (Merolla, 2008). When using direct forgiveness, people typically use strategies that include discussing the offense and the issues surrounding it and the forgiver telling the person that he or she understands (Kelley, 1998).

- *Indirect forgiveness.* Family members or intimate partners communicate **indirect forgiveness** by nonverbal displays (such as a hug, a smile, or eye contact) and by acting as though the transgression never happened—by getting back to normal (Kelley, 1998). Forgivers indicate, "I forgave him by acting the way we did before the event took place" (Merolla, 2008).

- *Conditional forgiveness.* The third way people forgive is with conditions attached to the forgiveness, which is why it's referred to as **conditional forgiveness**. This type of forgiveness is used when people want relational repair, but they want to make it very clear that repeating certain behaviors will not be tolerated (Merolla, 2008). For instance, a forgiver might say, "I'll forgive you, but you have to stay off the booze," or "If you promise never to do it again, I'll forgive you" (Merolla, 2008).

Clearly, forgiveness is not a process in which the forgiver condones, excuses, or forgets what happened to him or her (Knutson et al., 2008). For example, it is certainly possible to forgive

Direct forgiveness: family members or intimate partners clearly, plainly, and directly tell the offender that she or he is forgiven.

Indirect forgiveness: family members or intimate partners communicate this type of forgiveness by nonverbal displays (such as a hug, a smile, or eye contact) and by acting as though the transgression never happened,

Conditional forgiveness: the type of forgiveness used when people want relational repair, but they want to make it very clear that repeating certain behaviors will not be tolerated.

an absent father, an abuser, or a cheating partner without reconciling with the person. As one group of researchers observes, "When forgiveness is properly understood, it occurs from a position of strength, not weakness, because the forgiver recognizes the injustice and labels it for what it is" (Knutson et al., 2008, p. 193).

Finally, forgiveness needs to be understood just as any other process in family living. That is to say, the traits associated with forgiveness change as individuals progress through their lifespans and as families progress through the family life cycle (Maio et al., 2008).

Barriers and Benefits

The most common roadblocks to forgiveness in intimate relationships center on pride (Baumeister, 2002). First, those people who believe that they are entitled to, or deserve, only the good things in life view forgiveness as too risky and unfair to them (Baumeister, 2002). These people are referred to as having a strong sense of **narcissistic entitlement**. This is an important finding because as another researcher notes, if someone possesses a sense of entitlement and thus believes that she or he is above forgiving or asking for forgiveness, how can a relationship survive? (Exline, Baumeister, Bushman, Campbell, & Finkel, 2004). As Gottman's research showed us, unresolved conflict eventually leads to a breakdown in the relationship.

Another pride-related barrier to forgiveness is **self-righteousness**, when a person can't see his or her own potential for doing wrong or hurting another person. Roy Baumeister (2002), a researcher with Florida State University, found in a series of studies that when people have a sense of self-righteousness, they tend to be less willing to forgive others and are harsher in their judgments of others. Baumeister observed that following the national tragedy of September 11, 2001, people reported they had less vengeful, unforgiving feelings if they believed the United States had committed similar serious acts in other countries in the past. In other words, low levels of self-righteousness allow people to see that they themselves are capable of committing such acts; as such, they are quicker to forgive or ask for forgiveness.

Finally, some people are afraid to forgive because they think it opens them up to or sets them up for being hurt again (Baumeister, 2002). Although researchers have found very little evidence that forgiving someone increases the chance of being hurt again by the same person, Baumeister's findings suggest that people still worry about the possibility.

Forgiveness is one of the most underutilized family processes that people can use to maintain healthy intimate and family relationships and friendships. Outside of love, forgiveness is perhaps the most important tool available for the longevity of relationships.

FAMILY LIFE EDUCATION: FORGING FAMILY STRENGTHS

One of the key responsibilities of Certified Family Life Educators (CFLEs) and other helping professionals is to help couples and families establish and maintain strong, healthy, well-functioning interpersonal relationships and to improve how they relate to one another (NCFR, 2019). To this end, CFLEs are required to gain a knowledge and an understanding of how couples and families communicate (patterns seen in the couple's relationship, as well as in parent-child relationships), as well as the sources of conflict and how they manage it. CFLEs are skilled professionals who can assess these internal family processes from a family systems perspective.

If we reflect on the opening story of this chapter, we can begin to recognize the destructive and potentially damaging long-term effects certain communication patterns can have on us. When my family members involved in keeping "the secret" were doing what they felt was best, they did not anticipate that eventually this very secret would significantly damage people's abilities to trust, self-disclose, and form their own relational cultures. The story should remind us that although we all need to communicate—to give or receive information—the communication process involves much more than the sharing or withholding of information.

Narcissistic entitlement: a sense of being entitled to, or deserving, only the good things in life; a pride-related barrier to forgiveness.

Self-righteousness: the inability to see one's own potential for doing wrong or hurting another person; a pride-related barrier to forgiveness.

Why Are Men So Analytical? Why Do Women Talk So Much?

There have been many attempts over the years to determine and explain the differences in communication between men and women. Geneticist Anne Moir and coauthor David Jessel (1991) contend that the areas of the brain that are essential to communication are programmed in the early stages of pregnancy by the presence or the absence of testosterone. According to their work, male and female brains are structured differently—wired differently—and thus they process information differently. This accounts for the differences in communication. Moir and Jessel claim the innate, biological differences appear to be the following:

High-Testosterone People (Male Brains) Prefer	Low-Testosterone People (Female Brains) Prefer
facts, logic	feelings, senses
power/status	relationships
winning	sharing
analyzing	"knowing"
intellectual understanding	empathizing
sex	intimacy
thinking	feeling
reports/information	rapport/bonding

Source: A. Moir & Jessel (1991).

Whether communication differences between the genders are due to genetics or environmental influences, these contrasting language practices can create discord and become fertile ground for conflict.

Her Side: Sometimes he seems so distant, so insensitive. He doesn't want to talk about real things, like how he's feeling about something or what he thinks about a certain topic. If I share a problem with him, he immediately has a solution for the problem or has a suggestion about how to "fix" it. He doesn't try to understand my *feelings*. When I ask him about how his day went, he gives me an item-by-item report. I don't want to hear a list of facts—I want him to talk to me.

His Side: She talks all the time! *Everything* is an important topic to her, and she shares every detail. And to top it off, she always wants to talk about our relationship. I think our relationship is fine. If I don't want to talk about it, she gets offended and will say something like, "You see, our relationship is in trouble!" It's very confusing and frustrating to me.

Your Side: In your opinion, do you think there are gender differences in men's and women's communication styles? Consider the following questions:

1. Do you agree or disagree with the "male brain" list and the "female brain" list the researchers compiled? What leads you to your conclusion?

2. In your opinion, are the differences in communication between the genders determined genetically or are they due to the influences of socialization?

With divorce courts backed up with marriages that failed because couples believe they are not communicating, communication is not, in fact, the reason for the dissolution of the marriages. Couples *are* communicating—by every spoken word, every form of nonverbal or emotional behavior. The trouble is that they are not communicating effectively. As we discussed, effective, healthy communication means listening and hearing *beyond the words*. Sometimes it means hearing with our hearts—listening compassionately—and not with our ears. Productive and healthy communication also involves a basic understanding that everything we say or do in a family affects us, as we simultaneously affect others. And sometimes it means forgiving someone who has offended us or deeply wounded us, even though it can be a challenge—and a lot of individual and relational work—to do so.

Who makes the rules about what we can or cannot say in a family? *We* make the communication rules. *We* enforce these communication rules over time, through repeated interactions, even if they prove to be ineffective or destructive. To create a relational culture that is rich and rewarding to each family member, confirming your family members and/or your partners by recognizing and accepting their messages is essential. One of the greatest gifts a couple can give their children is to create an environment where each child is valued as a contributing member to the family system, as a contributor to family communication, an environment where communication aids in self-disclosure and the creation of intimacy, where family members communicate often. Active, reflective listening, too, fosters self-disclosure and intimacy. Finally, remember that humor goes a long way to bring family and partners together.

/// SUMMARY

The Communication Process

- Communication is a transactional process in which we affect and are affected by our intimate relations. When we discuss communication in this context, the focus of the interaction is not on the words individual family members speak, but on the interconnectedness of the relationship.

- Family Systems theory (FST) is a General Systems theory (GST) that sees the family as an interconnected system—a whole entity composed of interconnected parts that seek balance.

- Family Systems theory concerns *interactions* and *interrelations.* This includes study of both normative (expected) and nonnormative (not expected) life events that affect all members within the family unit.

- We can understand an individual family member's behavior and communication patterns only by looking at the entire family system and a person's family of origin.

- Every family system has some type of border or boundary, from closed to open, between it and its environment that affects the flow of information within the system and separates us from our environment or from other family members. Boundaries fall along a continuum that ranges from closed (no information comes in or goes out) to open (the transfer of information is so unobstructed that family members within the systems lose their identity). A family system's health is categorized by the degree to which the boundaries are permeable.

- According to Family Systems theory, every family's goal is to maintain its balance when confronted with any departure from the family's usual state of "normal." To restore equilibrium, families most often use established, habitual communication interactions and behaviors, which may be healthy or unhealthy.

- Olson's Circumplex Model is a tool that was created to address family cohesion, adaptability, and communication and to assess a family's level of functioning and health.

- The family of origin creates an individual family's rules of communication. They include what things may be talked about and how.

- Symbolic Interaction theory proposes that all human behavior is a continuous dialogue in which there is an exchange of messages and symbolic meanings. People assign learned symbolic meanings to others' behavior.

- To share meanings, each culture uses symbols (codes) and uses language to anchor meanings to each symbol. These meanings are indicated by communication symbols acquired and developed throughout life, and, knowingly or not, we communicate using these *shared codes* or *shared meanings.*

- All people are assigned or take on roles (systems of meanings) within their families and society, and these roles carry with them certain expectations. When a person takes on or is assigned too many roles, role strain and role conflict may result.

Communication Between Men and Women

- As we are growing up, we are bombarded with cultural messages about what it is to be a "boy" or a "girl" in our society. These messages are referred to as *gender cues.*

- Linguist researcher Deborah Tannen discovered that in all human communication, there are two levels of meaning: the message and the metamessage.

- Men are attuned to the metamessages of helping and fixing problems. The underlying context of men's communication is to be a problem solver and an advice giver.

- Women are attuned to the metamessages of empathy and understanding. The underlying context of women's communication is to show sympathy and empathy for the situation.

- When men and women communicate, they need to be aware that genders may convey and interpret messages in systematically different ways.

Types of Communication

- Communication is the process of making and sharing meanings. The process is a dynamic transaction involving shared definitions of symbols or codes.

- Verbal forms of communication refer to exchanges of thoughts, messages, or information through the spoken word. They include the content and substance of the words being spoken, the tone and the expression, as well as the structure and organization of the words. All verbal communication takes place within the context of a specific environment.

- Nonverbal communication occurs with or without the spoken word and includes facial expressions, motions of the body, eye contact, patterns of touch, expressive movements, hand gestures, the spatial arrangements in the physical environment, and emotions.

- Relational messages refer to those messages that have something to do with the partner or the relationship. Nonrelational messages refer to issues outside of the relationship. Relational messages are almost always communicated by nonverbal or emotional behaviors. A couple's skill in decoding, or interpreting, unspoken exchanges greatly affects marital adjustment and satisfaction.

- Armed with "inside" knowledge about each partner that no one else has, many couples can predict their partners' reactions to certain situations and develop private communication systems and private couple meanings.

Cornerstones of Communication

- Couples and families that communicate effectively learn to send verbal and emotional messages more clearly and also how to interpret received messages. They are able to move beyond mere functional communication toward nurturing communication.

Conflict in Relationships

- Conflict normally occurs in family life, typically when family members believe that their desires and goals are not compatible with one or more members in the family. Typical sources of conflict include conflicting role expectations, degrees of independence, and issues of fairness and equity.

- Constructive conflict builds relationships and is typical of regulated couples who use communication patterns and interpersonal behaviors that promote closeness and intimacy. Nonregulated couples have difficulty recovering from arguments because their interactions tend to be far more negative, compounding the issues at hand.

- Destructive conflict—conflict that results in greater hurt, anger, confusion, and pain—can be either overt (obvious) or covert (subtler). Destructive conflict is typically manifested through "gunnysacking," denial, disqualification, displacement, disengagement, or pseudomutuality.

The Role of Forgiveness in Family and Intimate Relationships

- Forgiveness is a deliberate intrapersonal process that transforms a person's strong desire for revenge into positive thoughts, feelings, and behaviors toward the offender. Forgiveness is for the person who was hurt, not for the person who hurts.

- Forgiveness first occurs at the individual, or intrapersonal, level. There are a number of variables linked to whether we forgive someone, such as level of empathy, high levels of emotional stability, how agreeable a person is, and how able someone is to forgive herself or himself,

- Forgiveness also occurs at the relationship, or interpersonal, level. People who forgive their spouses report more positive outcomes in their marriages than those who do not. Factors associated with interpersonal forgiveness include conflict resolution skills, overall relationship satisfaction, and commitment to the relationship.

- Forgiveness is a family process that undergoes change over time. There are three types of forgiveness: direct, indirect, and conditional.

- There are a number of barriers and benefits to forgiveness. Ultimately, forgiveness aids in the longevity of family and intimate relationships by opening doors for emotional and psychological healing. There are also physical benefits to forgiveness.

/// KEY TERMS

Active listening   93

Boundary   73

Circumplex Model of Marital and
  Family Systems   74

Closed boundaries   73

Communication   87

Communication rules   75

CHAPTER 4

GENDER IN TODAY'S SOCIETY

LEARNING OBJECTIVES

4.1 Describe the ways in which gender is influenced by biology.

4.2 Explain how culture influences our understanding of gender roles.

4.3 Recognize how gender polarization shapes the experiences of women and men.

4.4 Summarize three fundamental theories that explain gender development.

4.5 Characterize the primary cultural agents of gender socialization.

4.6 List contemporary policy issues related to gender.

There's really not a typical [transgender] story. A lot of people will say that they have always felt they were trapped in the wrong body, that their body was wrong, or that their gender identity was at odds with what their genitals said they should be. [I was born a male] . . . when I look back, I think I remember that I wouldn't have minded being a girl . . . but in my early 20s it became clearer to me that I wanted to express my gender differently from how I was expressing it [as a male]. While I was expressing it in the "traditional" way at the time, I wished I could express more femininity . . . I knew all along I ideally wanted to express myself differently, but at the time there wasn't much [information] about being transgender.

I thought of myself as being in the middle [somewhere between "male" and "female"] for quite a while, and that's where I identified. I think maybe that was just safer for me. Then I began to make tiny, tiny little changes over time . . . I had both ears pierced . . . I let my hair grow out . . . I'd wear the tiniest hints of mascara and sometimes eyeliner . . . I used a lot of tinted lip balm. Then one day I wore a skirt in public. Being a man is complicated and multidimensional. Being a woman is complicated and multidimensional. When I began experimenting with clothing and hair, I finally thought, "I can feel comfortable here." I wasn't sure I wanted to do the physical changes. It took a few years for me to want to undergo surgery . . . I think I finally just threw in the towel on trying to be intergender, in-between . . . it just didn't feel OK. And I'd spent my whole life not feeling OK.

But now, being transgender is a hard place to be. I mean, unlike 10 years ago, I can look around and see other people like me. But even today people just don't get it. They don't get us. Gender is a social construction, and people respond to us differently . . . despite the fact that we're doing a gender and we present to others that this is our gender, and that we convey to others this is our identity . . . but what do they give us? It leaves you in this super weird space because no one can make sense of you. No one can figure you out.. Unless my body looks "this way," people won't get me . . . But I've told myself that I would do this for myself . . . I'm experiencing gender my own way, on my own terms . . . internally and externally . . . I think I will always be "male" in some sense—and maybe that's OK? Given the choices [between male or female], I'm different and that's OK.

Can we as a culture learn to respond to other gender cues? . . . I don't know, but we should give it a try . . . I don't want to keep waiting for society to change . . . Whether a person is transgender or not, we're all just trying to find comfort being who we are.

—Amber

Abraham Lincoln once posed the following question to a group of intellectuals: "If you call the tail of a donkey a leg, how many legs does the donkey then have?" The group replied, "Well, Sir, of course it would have five legs." Lincoln replied, "No, Gentlemen. Simply calling it a leg does not make it a leg." Could the same hold true in a discussion about gender? In other words, does the presence of certain anatomy make someone a "male" or the absence of certain anatomy make someone a "female"?

Scientific literature strives to understand the processes by which we "become" male or female and how the varying roles associated with "male" and "female" evolve and help society achieve its goals. With this in mind, it is not surprising that the study of gender has typically been, and still is, interdisciplinary and multidisciplinary in its scope, composed of socio-logical, anthropological, political, and relational inquiry (Muehlenhard, Peterson, Karwoski, Bryan, & Lee, 2003). To more fully understand the intricacies involved in human relation-ships, this chapter examines the **nature** influences of gender (the influences of biology) and the **nurture** influences of gender (environmental influences).

Nature:
the influences of biology.

Nurture:
environmental influences.

Before we begin our discussion, it is important to revisit what we discussed in Chapter 2 regarding the ways in which researchers choose their topics of study. In many cases, research-ers choose to examine a topic or life experience because they themselves have personal expe-riences with that area. Although this almost always produces informative, insightful results that help to guide professionals in their careers and working with others, it also sometimes creates "gaps" in the research and areas that need to be studied or more fully studied. Such is the case in the study of gender: The changes in the experiences and expressions of gender in our culture are happening so swiftly that there is a lag between people's experiences and research that helps us to better understand these experiences. Every effort has been made to bring you the most relevant, current information to help you to better understand "gender."

IT MATTERS: THE BIOLOGY OF GENDER

When I had my four children in the 1980s, the now routine prenatal ultrasound examina-tions that are used today to determine the age, sex, and health of the developing fetus were not commonly performed unless a problem arose during pregnancy. As each of my children inched his way into the world, intense anticipation filled my heart as I waited to discover the sex of my baby. When my husband and I were minutes away from the delivery of our fourth child—*a fourth son?*—my obstetrician quipped, "Boy, girl, what does it matter?"

Sex Is Not Gender

We begin our study of gender and gendered behavior here, because the world over, biology is the basis of all social and cultural influences that ultimately have impact on our gender roles and gender identity—and subsequently our experiences in and with interpersonal relation-ships. There has been much debate over the years about which comes first: Do boys act "boy-ish" (active, aggressive) and do girls act "girly" (cuddly, early to jabber) because of innate drives to do so, because of "boy" or "girl" inborn personality traits? Or does the presence or absence of a penis at birth carry with it certain parental and societal expectations and thus reinforce-ment of certain socially created, expected—maybe even anticipated—gender behaviors?

Sex:
biological traits that distinguish males from females, such as the internal and external reproductive anatomy, chromosomes, hormones, and other physiological characteristics.

Gender:
encompasses characteristics such as gender role, gender identity, gender presentation, and gender stereotypes.

XX sex chromosome:
this chromosome combination results in a "female" genetic blueprint for the developing embryo.

XY sex chromosome:
this chromosome combination results in a "male" genetic blueprint for the developing embryo.

Sexual differentiation:
the prenatal physiological and anatomical differentiation into male and female.

Sex hormones:
hormones that direct sexual differentiation in the womb and continue to influence sexual maturation through puberty.

Sex and *gender* are two distinct terms, although in our culture the words are used interchangeably. **Sex** refers to biological traits that distinguish males from females, such as the internal and external reproductive anatomy, chromosomes, hormones, and other physiological characteristics. Sex, then describes *biologically* determined characteristics—the *nature* side of the debate about what creates a boy or a girl. Without complicated surgical procedures and artificial hormone supplements, sex cannot be changed. Gender is more than a social label ascribed to us on our birth certificates. In essence, **gender** can be thought of as the sum of our developmental and lifecourse experiences and it encompasses a number of characteristics, which we will explore at length throughout this chapter.

Biological Sex: The Foundations of Gender

A person's biological sex is determined the moment the sperm and ovum fuse together in the process of fertilization. The developing person receives either two X sex chromosomes (one from the mother and one from the father) or one X and one Y sex chromosome (an X from the mother and a Y from the father). The **XX sex chromosome** combination results in a "female" genetic blueprint for the developing embryo, and the **XY sex chromosome** combination results in a "male" genetic blueprint. It is the coupling of the XX or XY chromosomes, then, that determines a fetus's sex characteristics (Ovaries or testes? Clitoris or penis?), both internally and externally.

John Bancroft, MD (2009) is one of the world's leading authorities on human sexuality and has been involved in various aspects of sex research for the past 30 years. He provides a comprehensive review of the key concepts relative to understanding the role of biology—XX or XY—in shaping gender experiences.

- **Sexual differentiation** refers to the prenatal physiological and anatomical differentiation into male and female. Throughout the prenatal period of human development, certain hormones are produced in the developing baby, which direct the development of the reproductive organs, as well as the central nervous system.

- **Sex hormones** not only direct sexual differentiation in the womb, but they also continue to influence sexual maturation through puberty. Sex hormones also play key roles in sexual response and the experiences of sexual pleasure, pregnancy, childbirth, breastfeeding, and sexuality through the aging process.

- **Sexual orientation** refers to whether a person expresses a heterosexual, gay, lesbian, bisexual, or asexual desire toward another person. There are multiple biological elements to sexual orientation including genetics, prenatal hormonal influences and brain differentiation, and hormonal levels after birth.

- **Gender identity** is a person's innermost concept of self as male, female, a blend of both, or neither—how people perceive themselves and what they call themselves. Gender identity can be the same or different from a person's sex assigned at fertilization.

Male and Female

When a Y sex chromosome is present, tissue begins to develop into the testes in the male. The testes then begin to produce **androgens** (testosterone), the masculinizing sex hormones. These increasing levels of testosterone then direct the development of the internal male reproductive organs, which include the seminal vesicles, vas deferens, and testes. Sometime during the third month of pregnancy, the external male genitalia, the penis and scrotum, form under the direction of the androgens, primarily **testosterone**.

It was once believed that, without hormonal influences, the overall pattern for prenatal sexual development is female (Pinel, 1997). Today, we know that when a Y sex chromosome is not present and thus testosterone is not produced, the tissue continues to develop into internal reproductive organs, which include the ovaries, uterus, Fallopian tubes, and vagina. So, it is not the *presence* of **estrogen**, the feminizing sex hormone, that produces the biological sex, female—it is the *absence of testosterone* that ultimately results in the creation of a female. By around the third month of prenatal development, the external female genitalia begin to develop. As you can see from Figure 4.1, females and males are more biologically similar than many people think. Many of the sex parts of males and females are *homologous*, or corresponding. Shown in Figure 4.1, note that the clitoris of the female corresponds with the glans (head) of the penis in the male, and so on.

Somewhere Between "Male" and "Female"

At the moment of birth we are branded, or labeled, to be *one* genetic sex *or* the other; we are then raised in this gender brand of our assigned sex. **Gender binary** (also known as gender *binarism, binarism,* or *genderism*) is the classification of gender into two distinct, opposite, and disconnected forms of masculine and feminine, whether by social system or cultural belief.

For 98 percent of babies born in in the United States, this binary, either/or sex assignment accurately describes their biological sex (Intersex Campaign for Equality, 2019). That is to say, the outward appearance (the genitals) match up with the sex-linked brand of "male" or "female." But what happens when the genetic sex of a child is just not that clear? Is that child "male" or "female"—or somewhere between? And, just as important, does it matter?

Intersex

An **intersex** person is someone who is anatomically somewhere along the continuum between binary male and female. Today, these anatomical variances are known as **disorders of sex development** or **DSD** (Lundberg, Donasen, Hegarty, & Roen, 2019; Danon, 2018). Although there are different types of intersex conditions, the root is always genetic. These genetic anomalies or irregularities can occur due to a person acquiring both male and female anatomical structures and/or sex chromosomes, to varying degrees, or because of ambiguous (not easily distinguishable as male or female) genitalia. It is currently estimated that as many as 2 percent—about 2 births out of every 100 live births—of the total U.S. population is affected by an intersex condition (Intersex Society of North America, 2019). Being intersex is about as common as having red hair.

Sexual orientation:
the focus of a person's erotic desires or fantasies, or a person's affectionate or romantic feelings toward a particular gender.

Gender identity:
our intuitive sense of our gender.

Androgens:
the group of masculinizing sex hormones.

Testosterone:
the masculinizing hormone produced by the testicles.

Estrogen:
the feminizing hormone.

Gender binary:
the classification of gender into two distinct, opposite, and disconnected forms of masculine and feminine, whether by social system or cultural belief.

Intersex:
an individual whose genitalia are ambiguous or indistinguishable.

Disorders of sex development (DSD):
a mismatch between a person's genetic sex and the appearance of their genitals.

Figure 4.1 /// Sex Differentiation of Males and Females

Males and females are more biologically similar than most people think. Notice the similarity of the undifferentiated tissue.

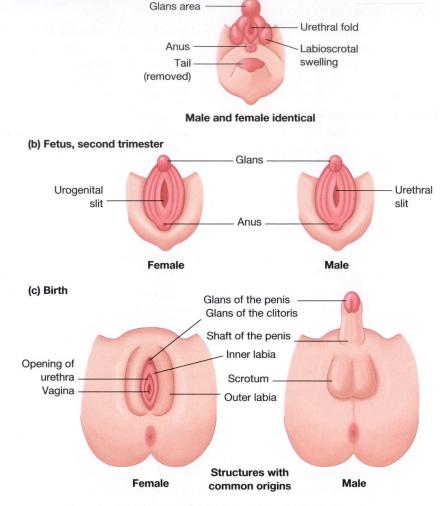

(a) Embryo, 6 weeks

Glans area — Urethral fold

Anus — Labioscrotal swelling

Tail (removed)

Male and female identical

(b) Fetus, second trimester

Glans

Urogenital slit — Urethral slit

Anus

Female   **Male**

(c) Birth

Glans of the penis
Glans of the clitoris
Shaft of the penis
Inner labia
Opening of urethra
Scrotum
Vagina
Outer labia

Female   **Structures with common origins**   **Male**

Source: Garrett, Bob. *Brain & Behavior: An Introduction to Biological Psychology*, 4e. SAGE Publishing, 2015. Pp. 189.

There are a number of other genetic anomalies or irregularities that can occur, resulting in other types of intersex conditions. Although a detailed discussion of these syndromes is beyond the scope of our discussion here, a basic understanding of them is necessary because they are not necessarily rare occurrences: You, your partner, or your child may be affected by one of these types of intersex syndromes. Table 4.1 describes intersex conditions and their associated characteristics.

Although intersex conditions are not medical emergencies that threaten a child's overall health, infants are often seen as "social emergencies" in need of "fixing" in some way. This implies that since intersexual children do not fit neatly into the binary "male" or "female" brand, there is the general social perception that something must be done to "fix" them.

Management: One Body, One Gender?

As commonly as some of the chromosomal irregularities and prenatal hormonal imbalances occurs, why have the majority of cultures the world over settled into an either/or categorization of male/female? What do we—a two-sex-categories-only culture—do when a child is born with ambiguous, indistinguishable genitalia; when a child is born intersex; or when a child is born with other chromosomal anomalies that make it difficult to determine the "sex"?

Table 4.1 /// Types and Characteristics of Intersex Conditions

Condition	Characteristics
Turner Syndrome (affects 1 in 2,000 live births) Turner's Syndrome Society (2019)	affects females only; occurs when one of two X chromosomes is completely or partially absent
	the dropped chromosome results in the failure of the developing fetus to develop ovaries, rendering her infertile
	affected females are often short in stature; have mental or learning delays; and have heart, kidney, and thyroid problems
Klinefelter Syndrome (affects 1 in 500 live male births) National Institutes of Health (2019)	affects males only; a genetic disorder in which an extra X chromosome is present, resulting in an XXY chromosomal pattern
	75 percent of those affected are never diagnosed
	characterized by smaller-than-normal testes that produce no sperm
	affected males often have a round body type, height greater than brother or father, enlarged breasts, and little facial or body hair
Androgen Insensitivity Syndrome (AIS) (affects 1 in 100 live births) National Institutes of Health (2019)	characterized by an abnormality of the X sex chromosome
	the gonads within the abdomen may be male, but the baby is born with feminized external genitalia

The typical medical treatment of intersex infants and infants with ambiguous genitalia throughout the 20th century was to "match" their socialization to the outward signs of "gender." In the 1950s, John Money, an American psychologist and sexologist who focused his research on sexual identity and the biology of gender, established the dominant protocol of treating intersex infants and children; this protocol remained in effect until 2006 (Danon, 2018). The prevailing method of treatment was early genital surgeries followed by long-term psychiatric treatment to help children establish their gender identities (Danon, 2018).

If surgery was required to "fix" genitalia to appear more "normalized," then surgery was performed very early in the infant's life (as early as within a month after birth, but typically before age 18 months); supplemental hormones later in child and adolescent development sustained the surgically assigned "gender." But since the formation in 1993 of the Intersex Society of North America and the testimony of adults who underwent sex reassignment surgery since the 1970s, earlier medical practices are now being criticized. Today, the medical field understands more and more the complexities and intricacies in the formation of gender and understands that it takes more than external genitalia alone to constitute gender. An extensive review of the literature, however, reveals that despite this knowledge base about the development of gender, the standard of care is slow to change (see Danon, 2018). Starting in about 2006, the rights of intersex individuals and those with ambiguous genitalia were taken up by human rights activist groups, in hopes of raising awareness about the demedicalization of intersex/DSD and to help those affected and their families to make informed decisions (Lundberg et al., 2019; Danon, 2018).

But there's more to becoming a male or a female than the development of the sex organs. Crucial to our experiences of male or female is the sex differentiation that occurs in the prenatal brain—specifically, the influences of sex hormones on the developing embryo's brain.

Sex Differentiation in the Prenatal Brain

There is a great deal that can be discussed about the differences between the male and female brains; let's focus primarily on the factors that masculinize and feminize the human brain. The central nervous system and primitive brain development begin during the third week of prenatal development. Brain development becomes quite rapid from the ninth week of pregnancy until birth, generating as many as 250,000 brain cells per minute! The prenatal brain is significantly influenced in structure and function by the exposure to sex hormones during pregnancy (Swaab, Gooren, & Hofman, 1995).

During prenatal development, a male (XY) fetus produces large amounts of testosterone in his testicles. This is quickly converted in the male brain to an estrogen hormone called *estradiol*, which masculinizes and defeminizes the male brain. On the other hand, while a female (XX) fetus produces estrogen in her ovaries, a specific protein binds the estrogen and prohibits it from reaching the brain. Because of this, the female brain gets less estrogen than male brains and the brain is feminized. The absence of heightened estrogen allows the female brain to develop attributes different from male brains.

Understanding how sex differentiation of the brain develops is important to our study of gender for several reasons:

- Masculinized/feminized differentiation sets the stage for secretion of certain hormones in the brain that regulate puberty in adolescence, as well as the lifelong cyclical production of testosterone in males and estrogen in females.
- Brain sex differentiation is responsible for sex-specific gendered behaviors, such as the male-typical behaviors of aggression and a high sex drive.
- Prenatal brain sex differentiation may be responsible for determining a person's sexual orientation.
- Prenatal brain sex differentiation may be responsible for a person's transgender experiences.

In short, studying how sex differentiation develops in the brain provides more opportunities to learn how the functions and mechanisms of the brain operate more clearly. Table 4.2 shows us the relationship between biological influences and gender.

Gender Identity and Gender Expression

Gender roles have more to do with what society expects of its males and females; gender identity refers to our intuitive sense of our gender (White, 2003)—our internal feelings of our gender. Gender identity speaks to how a person settles in to society's assigned gender roles. In other words, it is a *subjective*, continuous, persistent sense of who we are.

Table 4.2 /// Biological Sex and the Experiences of "Gender"	
Biological Sex	Biological sex may involve genetic factors in the early uterine environment. These factors, which may be related to the development of your sexual orientation, include genes, prenatal hormones, and brain structure.
Gender Identity	Gender identity is our intuitive sense of our gender. It doesn't define gender but rather how we experience gender.
Gender Expression	Gender expression includes the ways we express our masculinity or femininity through our behaviors, demeanors, and actions. For some, however, how we behave, what we wear, and how we speak each day doesn't match our biological sex.
Sexual Orientation	Your sexual orientation determines who you are attracted to and influences your sexuality experiences. Categories of sexual orientation include having an attraction to members of your own sex, members of the opposite sex, and members of both sexes.

iStock.com/FotografiaBasica

When a person's sense of identity and their birth sex are in alignment, they are said to be **cisgender** (pronounced "sis"-gender). In our culture, we tend to recognize only two genders—male and female. This is referred to as binary gender, meaning "having two parts" (National Center for Transgender Equality, 2018). **Nonbinary (NB)** is a term used to describe persons who don't fall into the either/or categories of male/female. Today, nonbinary individuals use varying terms to describe themselves, such as genderqueer, agender, and bigender (National Center for Transgender Equality, 2018). **Gender nonconforming** and **gender fluid** are umbrella terms that define people who have a gender expression that doesn't conform to a society's traditional gender norms. In the United States, 40 percent of Americans believe that there is a range of many possible gender identities (Public Religion Research Institute [PRRI], 2019).

When we have discussions in class about gender identity, there are inevitably a lot of questions. The most common question I hear is, "How do I know how to refer to someone without offending them?" I like this question because it points to the direction our society is going: a society of caring responsiveness to differences and to inclusiveness. There are a number of ways that culture can be respectful and supportive of nonbinary persons (National Center for Transgender Equality, 2018):

- Don't make assumptions about a person's gender based on their appearance.
- Use the name a person asks you to use.
- Use the appropriate pronouns—if you're not sure, *ask*. Although it may feel uncomfortable to ask someone, it is respectful to do so.
- Respect a person's right to use the restroom of their choice.

Of course, the best way to learn about who they are is to talk to them, engage in conversations with them, get to know them, and listen to their stories (their truths; National Center for Transgender Equality, 2018).

It is important to point out that gender identity is not the same as sexual orientation.

Sexual orientation refers to the focus of a person's erotic desires or fantasies, or a person's affectionate or romantic feelings toward a particular gender. This is the term most often used

Cisgender:
a person whose gender identity and birth sex are in alignment.

Nonbinary (NB):
a term used to describe persons who don't fall into either/or categories of male/female.

Gender nonconforming:
umbrella term that describes people who have gender expressions that don't conform to a society's traditional gender norms.

by family practitioners, therapists, and the medical community because the word *orientation* implies that a persons' gender preference is biologically predetermined. Those who believe that sexuality is fluid and more a matter of choice than biology use the alternative term, sexual preference. A combination of genetic, hormonal, and social factors determines sexual orientation. As such, sexual orientation refers to whether a person expresses a heterosexual, gay, lesbian, bisexual, or asexual desire toward another person.

Gender identity and sexual orientation are often confused. In an exploratory study of early childhood teachers' attitudes toward gender roles, for example, the researchers observed that the preschool teachers had a difficult time differentiating gender identity from sexual orientation. The researchers note, "When a child's behaviour (such as a boy wanting to play with dolls or who easily cries; a girl who is rough-and-tumble) calls into question [masculinity and femininity], the issue of the child's *sexual* identity was raised" (Cahill & Adams, 1997, p. 518). Cahill and Adams comment that because of this assumed relationship between gender identity and sexual orientation in young children, parents, teachers, and society at large have a fear of allowing greater gender latitude, for fear of "making" a child become a homosexual. Their research concludes that when preschool teachers limit gender expression to society's expectations, "it is related to homophobia" (p. 528).

Our gender expression is an external extension of our gender identity. It includes the ways in which we express our masculinity or femininity. How we behave, what we wear, and how we speak each day can express our gender. Although, for some, their expression of gender doesn't match their biological sex. Transgender is an umbrella term for people who have a gender identity or gender expression that differs from their assigned sex. The term, coined by gender activist Virginia Prince in the 1970s, refers to people who feel that their biologically assigned gender is a false or incomplete description of themselves (Greenberg, Najle, Jackson, Bola, & Jones, 2019). It's very important to understand that being trans does not carry with it any specific sexual orientation. Trans individuals may identify as straight, gay, lesbian, bisexual, queer, etc. Trans persons may express themselves through their appearance, behaviors, or other factors that differ from what society typically associates with the sex they were assigned at birth (Greenberg et al., 2019).

What is support like for trans persons in the United States? Today, more than three-fourths (79 percent) of Americans say that trans people live with stigma in their communities;

PRAKASH SINGH/AP via Getty Images

74 percent believe that gays and lesbians face stigma (PRRI, 2019). Encouragingly, 63 percent of Americans surveyed said they are comfortable having a close friend tell them that they are trans, and more than half (56 percent) report they would be comfortable with having a trans person teach in the local elementary school; nearly one-half (48 percent) say they would be comfortable having their own child tell them they're trans (PRRI, 2019).

There are several ways transgender people may refer to themselves using a range of descriptive terms (e.g., trans, transgender, etc.):

- FTM (female to male) are people who were born female but see themselves as partly to fully masculine; also referred to as *transman*
- MTF (male to female) are people who were born male but see themselves as partly to fully feminine; also referred to as *transwoman* (Landén, Wålinder, Hambert, & Lundström, 1998)

Some people use the terms *transgender* and *transsexual* interchangeably, but many transgender people do not identify as transsexual. **Transsexual** is an older term for someone who has permanently changed or seeks to change their body through medical interventions because their identity is opposite to the sex they were assigned at birth. A stereotypical description of a transsexual is a woman feeling that she is "trapped inside a man's body," or vice versa. Most transsexuals report that this intense longing to be a different sex begins early in life and intensifies over time.

Transsexual: an older term for someone who has permanently changed or seeks to change their body through medical interventions because their identity is opposite to the sex they were assigned at birth.

Although the medical science community today still does not understand the precise reasons behind such feelings, it does recognize that some people experience a gender identity disorder, in particular, **gender dysphoria**. Not surprisingly, those individuals with gender dysphoria experience significant emotional and physical distress when their genetic sex is not the same as the one with which they identify. Gender dysphoria is a mental health classification that describes this longing to live as and be accepted as the opposite sex.

Gender dysphoria: the distress a person feels because their sex assigned at birth is in conflict with the gender with which they identify.

Transsexual men and women work toward transition from the gender of their birth to a permanent identity of the opposite gender through a complex process called **gender reassignment**. In most cases, gender reassignment involves psychological counseling, hormonal supplements, and **sex reassignment surgery (SRS)** or, as is preferred today, **sex confirmation surgery (SCS)**. Most people considering SRS/SCS are required to make a gradual transition to their preferred gender over a period of several months.

Sex confirmation surgery (SCS): the surgical alteration to the body that transforms a person's gender from male to female or female to male.

At the core, each of us experiences gender differently. From the moment of conception, our gender begins to form as our DNA and hormones work to establish the anatomy of each male and female. After birth, our sex hormones continue to influence us through puberty, ultimately guiding us through our sexuality experiences. Earlier I posed the question, Does labeling someone as "male" or "female" make him or her so? As you have seen in our study of gender so far, the presence or absence of a penis does not necessarily make someone a boy or a girl. Gender is much more complex than that because it is an intricate interaction of *both* biology (physiological characteristics) and environment. In the case of gender, it's not nature *or* nurture; it's nature *and* nurture. Indeed, gender is as much a social and cultural process as it is a biological process.

IT MATTERS: THE CULTURE OF GENDER

The concept of gender is significantly more complex than biological attributes alone. Those who study social interactions have, in a number of different ways, defined gender as

- "the socially constructed roles associated with each sex" (Rosenblum & Travis, 2003, p. 23)
- "what culture makes out of the 'raw material' of biological sex" (Crawford & Unger, 2000, p. 21)
- "the culturally and historically specific acting out of 'masculinity' and 'femininity'" (Rosenblum & Travis, 2003, p. 23)

From these varying definitions one central theme emerges. "Sex" refers to the biological attributes of male and female, but "gender" refers to the *socially* or *culturally* determined traits, characteristics, and expectations of male and female—it is a social conceptualization, culturally specific, experienced differently in different cultures.

Gender Roles: The Making of Male or Female, Masculine or Feminine

Gender is multidimensional and it is *created* by people's culture. It includes the following characteristics (Human Rights Campaign, 2019):

- *Gender role* refers to behaviors, attitudes, beliefs, and values that culture deems appropriate for males and females.

- *Gender identity* refers to how a person accepts the culture's prescribed gender roles; how an individual adapts the expected gender role to his or her identity. Gender identity is subjective to the individual; it can be the same or different from their sex assigned at fertilization.

- *Gender expression/presentation* refers to how an individual externally presents his or her gender identity through personality, habits, and behaviors, such as clothing, haircut, or voice. These may or may not conform to socially defined traits and characteristics commonly associated with being male or female.

Each individual society orchestrates, directs, and dictates its expected gender roles, gender expressions/presentations, and gender stereotypes of male and female. From these, gender identity is shaped. In essence, we *learn* what it means to be male and female, masculine and feminine, from cultural cues. Societal roles are therefore *gendered*, meaning that differences are assigned to each biological sex. However, rather than emphasize the similarities between men and women, cultural viewpoints almost always emphasize the difference between men and women. This "opposite" model is referred to as **gender polarization** or **bipolar gender** (Liben & Bigler, 2017). Table 4.3 shows us common viewpoints of gender polarization.

Gender polarization: a model in which cultural viewpoints almost always emphasize the differences between men and women.

Table 4.3 /// Typically Associated Gender Characteristics	
Many problems crop up when cultures use the either/or, polarized gender descriptions. If a person deviates from a society's gender norms then that person is seen as belonging in the "other" category.	
Male	Female
aggressive	passive
competitive	polite
independent	relationship-oriented
dominating	submissive
hides emotions	talkative
confident	empathetic
protective	nurturing
risk-taker	risk-avoider
one-track mind	multitasker
rational	emotional
secret-keeper	gossiper
disorganized	responsible
leader	follower

Source: Liben, L. S., & Bigler, R. S. (2015). Understanding and undermining the development of gender dichotomies: The legacy of Sandra Lipsitz Bem. *Sex Roles*, 1–12.

From the moment of birth (or a prenatal diagnostic test that reveals the sex of a baby), we are repeatedly exposed to culturally driven beliefs, ideas, perceptions, and opinions about the differences between genders. Because this continuous flow of cultural information informs us of what is "appropriate" behavior and what is "inappropriate" behavior, we eventually internalize (make part of ourselves) these prototypes for behavior and adopt them. We are taught from our culture how to be "male" or "female" (Bem, 1981; Bussey & Bandura, 1999; Martin & Ruble, 2013; Saewyc, 2017). We then use these models to organize and categorize all social information—including all of the various types of relationships in which we engage. **Gender socialization** refers to the specific messages and practices we received from our culture, concerning the nature of being a male or a female, of being feminine or masculine (Martin & Ruble, 2013)—and these messages significantly impact our couple and family experiences. As we progress through our study of couples and families, we'll see how gender and gender roles influence experiences such as intimacy, emotional bonding between partners, and friendships (Chapter 5), dating/romantic attraction (Chapter 7), parenting (Chapter 10), and work life (Chapter 12).

Societal expectations establish certain criteria to which its members are to adhere to ensure the longevity and the continuation of that society. From industrialized societies such as the United States, Canada, and Europe, to the most remote tribal cultures such as the Honeymen, the southern Ethiopian tribes, these social expectations are broken down along gender lines. **Gender roles** are the cultural norms for male and female attitudes and behaviors; these roles delineate what is considered to be appropriate for people of a particular sex.

These gender roles, then, are the explicitly expressed and implied behaviors, feelings, attributes, and traits that society expects of the male or the female (Saewyc, 2017). Women are typically thought to possess more nurturing tendencies than males (Mmari et al., 2017). Because of this gender-ascribed *characteristic,* the gender *role* of childcare responsibilities typically fall to the women. Similarly, because men are thought to be stronger and possess more protective capabilities than women, the primary gender role of responsibility and provision for the family unit typically falls to the male (Mmari et al., 2017). Essentially, gender roles are referred to as either masculine or feminine. When we refer to *masculinity* or *femininity,* we are talking about the configurations of how we practice our biological sex.

Masculinity: "Doing" Male

The term *male* can be used to describe the genetic sex of any species, but **masculinity** is a socially/culturally constructed set of beliefs, values, and opinions that shape manly character or manliness—it prescribes and defines how men should act and feel. Every culture also has an ideal, dominant standard of masculinity for which men are to aim. This is referred to as **hegemonic** (pronounced heh-jeh-MON-ick) **masculinity** (Connell, 1987). Although hegemonic masculinity isn't necessarily the most prevalent form of manliness found in a culture, it is the most socially endorsed and desired; this standard changes over time. For example, in the 1950s and 1960s, the normative, desired way of being masculine was represented in movies by the actors John Wayne and Elvis Presley. Today in the United States, images of hegemonic masculinity abound in popular culture media representations, such as *WWE Wrestling* and Lucas Till, the actor who plays the do-it-yourself persona of MacGyver in the television sitcom. These presentations of masculinity are consistent with an earlier landmark study that described seven areas of masculinity that are commonly found in most Western societies (Chafetz, 1975). This study found that "ideal" men are physically strong, sexually aggressive and experienced, and dominating leaders.

Throughout their lives, boys learn and acquire these masculine characteristics and traits through language, the toys they play with, certain behaviors that are rewarded or discouraged, and occupations they are encouraged to pursue (Jandt & Hundley, 2007). By age 3, for example, boys engage in more competitive games, wrestling, play fighting, and rough-and-tumble play than girls do, and fathers encourage these types of behaviors in their sons (Geary, 1998; Jhally, 2002). We'll look at the various gender socializing agents at length later in this chapter.

Gender socialization: the specific messages and practices we receive from our culture concerning the nature of being a male or a female, of being feminine or masculine.

Gender roles: the explicitly expressed and implicitly implied behaviors, feelings, attributes, and traits that society expects of the male or the female.

Masculinity: a socially/culturally constructed set of beliefs, values, and opinions that shape manly character or manliness.

Hegemonic masculinity: each culture's ideal, dominant standard of masculinity for which men are to aim.

Each society determines its conception of what a "male" is supposed to look like and how he is supposed to act. Hegemonic masculinity is the culture's ideal, dominant standard of masculinity. In what ways do you think this image is an accurate portrayal of masculinity in our society? Inaccurate? In what ways does hegemonic masculinity affect a person's development?

Black Masculinities

Of course, one problem with this characterization of masculinity is that it most often describes *white*, middle-class conceptions of what a "man" is supposed to act or look like. Most of the existing empirical science tends to overlook men of color and their construction of masculinity (Alexander, 2006; Harris, Palmer, & Struve, 2011; McCune, 2014; Wester, Vogel, Wei, & McLain, 2006).

Euro-American masculinity stresses *individual* success and economic achievement, often excluding collaborative or group efforts (Alexander, 2006; Harris et al., 2011; McCune, 2014; Wester et al., 2006). Conversely, within traditional Black cultures, cooperation and the promotion of the collective good are promoted, as is *group* success. Because of these conflicting masculine gender expectations, many men of color in the United States have had to adopt the Euro-American ideal of "success through competition" while at the same time expressing their Black cultural beliefs that highlight support, community, and the importance of interpersonal relationships (Alexander, 2006; McCune, 2014; Wester et al., 2006). This blending of two cultural masculinities among African Americans and Afro-Caribbeans has resulted in a new, exaggerated version of masculinity for them. Referred to as "cool pose," Black masculinity "presents a powerful face to the world" while at the same time entails the expected cooperative behaviors of Black culture (Alexander, 2006; see Canales, 2000; Harris et al., 2011; McCune, 2014; Wester et al., 2006). Cool pose is intended to depict control and a way to show masculinity as a source of dignity and worth (Alexander, 2006; McCune, 2014).

Intercultural Masculinities

Because of the global nature of our society today, researchers have begun to argue that there is an increasing need to recognize the integral role of culture in shaping masculinity beliefs (Yim & Mahalingam, 2006). Prior studies, for example, have identified features of masculinity across cultures; these include sexual prowess, the ability to protect women and one's family, and the ability to provide for family (Gilmore, 1990; Malhotra, 2002). Societies that emphasize hegemonic masculinity (such as the United States, Australia, Japan, and Latin American cultures) are characterized by high degrees of male dominance, independence, aggression, achievement, and endurance (Albrecht, 2016; Williams & Best, 1990). These types of cultures are referred to as *masculine cultures* (Albrecht, 2016).

There is perhaps no better example of masculine cultures than Latin America, such as Mexico, Central and South America, Puerto Rico, and the Caribbean, which are collectivist societies. Embedded within these cultures are deeply held traditions that influence gender behaviors and attitudes. One such attitude is that of machismo.

Machismo refers to the idea that men are superior to women and that men are socially and physically dominant. The adjective *machista* is a derivative of the word *machismo,* and it means "sexist." Machismo is not necessarily an act per se; it is more of an attitude that can range from a sense of sexual power, to masculinity, to male superiority. This machismo cultural attitude translates to many areas of interpersonal relationships, including choosing whom to date and to marry and the power to decide birth control and/or contraceptive behaviors during sex (Afable-Munsuz & Brindis, 2006; Villarruel & Rodriguez, 2003). In just a bit we'll look at the opposite of machismo in Latin America, the female culture of *marianismo.*

Another example of masculine cultures is that of India. In India, honor, or *izzat,* is the dominant masculinity theme that governs the lives of men (Chowdhury & Baset, 2018; Dasgupta & Gokulsing, 2013). Within this culture, a man's primary duty is to be a defender of women's purity, his family, and his family's position in the society (Chowdhury & Baset, 2018). Thus, much value is placed on a man's ability to protect (Chowdhury & Baset, 2018; Dasgupta & Gokulsing, 2013; Gilmore, 1990). Asian American men tend to adopt gender roles such as a strong obligation to family, the authority figure in the home, and restricting displays of emotions (Nguyen, 2014; Sue & Sue, 2003).

Psychologists and other social scientist have been interested in whether there are negative outcomes associated with masculine gender roles. They are particularly interested in determining whether masculinity is associated with additional stressors.

Pressures Associated With Masculinity

Since the 1970s, women have broadened and overlapped their roles with men's roles. For example, women today are free to enter into occupations traditionally held by males, such as airline pilots, firefighting, architecture, and engineering. To be sure, women even serve as military personnel on the front lines in military service today. But while women's gender roles have expanded, men have not been given the same freedom to take on roles that have traditionally been held by women, such as childcare providers and maternity nurses (McCreary, Newcomb, & Sadava, 1998). Men have also been prohibited by cultures to adopt certain characteristics associated with femininity, such as being emotionally expressive (Yim & Mahalingam, 2006). This rigid confinement to traditional gender roles, sometimes referred to as "the hazards of being male," is associated with increased pressures and stress (Goldberg, 1976; Gallagher & Parrott, 2011; Swartout, Parrott, Cohn, Hagman, & Gallagher, 2015).

Masculine Gender Roles Stress theory (MGRS) maintains that there are stressors that may result from a man's fear that he is not measuring up to or meeting societal expectations for masculinity (Eisler & Skidmore, 1987). Using a survey that researchers administered to 1,729 male college students to assess masculine gender role stress, researchers found four general areas and 15 specific stressors that speak to the stress men feel regarding gender roles today (Swartout et al., 2015). This information is presented in Table 4.4. As you can see, the researchers found that being in situations that required emotional expression and feeling physically inadequate are stressful and pressure inducing. Previous research found that men scored higher than women on MGRS measure such as anxiety, depression, and hostility (McCreary et al., 1998):

> All of these findings speak to the importance of realizing that today, masculine gender role socialization is not always compatible with situational demands. In other words, today's concept of "masculinity" often conflicts with nontraditional behaviors, such as striking a balance between the demands of work with the responsibilities of parenting or being a loving, supportive spouse. (Wester et al., 2006)

Machismo:

the attitude, common in Latin American cultures, that men are superior to women and that men are socially and physically dominant.

Masculine Gender Roles Stress theory (MGRS):

this theory maintains that there are stressors that may result from a man's fear that he is not measuring up to or meeting societal expectations for masculinity.

Table 4.4 /// Masculine Gender Role Stressors

Subordination to Women:

Being outperformed at work by a woman
Letting a woman control the situation
Being married to someone who makes more money than you
Being with a woman who is more successful than you
Being outperformed in a game by a woman

Physical Inadequacy

Being perceived by someone as "gay"
Losing a sports competition
Appearing less athletic than a friend
Being perceived as having feminine traits

Intellectual Inferiority

Having people say that you are indecisive
Having others say that you are too emotional

Emotional Inexpressiveness

Admitting that you are afraid of something
Having children see you cry

Performance Failure

Getting passed over for a promotion

Source: Swartout and others, 2016.

Femininity: "Doing" Female

Femininity:
the qualities, behaviors, and attitudes that are deemed by a particular culture to be ideally appropriate for girls and women; most often associated with nurturing and life-giving attributes such as kindness, gentleness, and patience.

Distinct from the biological sex classification of *female,* **femininity** refers to qualities, behaviors, and attitudes that are deemed by a particular culture to be ideally appropriate for girls and women. Femininity, or womanliness, is most often associated with nurturing, life-giving attributes such as kindness, gentleness, and patience.

For the past decade, social and family scientists have attempted to design survey instruments to measure the degree to which study participants agree with or adhere to "traditional" femininity values, ideas, and opinions—how women *should* act and feel. The Femininity Ideology Scale (FIS) survey contains 45 statements with which research participants indicate their agreement or disagreement (Levant, Richmond, Cook, House, & Aupont, 2007). With statements such as, "Women should have soft voices," "A woman's natural role should be the caregiver of the family," and "Women discuss their feelings with others," researchers attempted to identify five categories of femininity attributes: (1) Images and Activities, (2) Dependence/Deference, (3) Purity, (4) Caretaking, and (5) Emotionality (Levant et al., 2007).

Overall, the participants did not agree with the traditional beliefs and attitudes associated with the five areas of femininity under investigation, and the women indicated they held less traditional views than the men did. However, both women and men strongly endorsed *Caretaking* as a feminine characteristic or attribute (such as women should try to soothe hurt feelings of others; women should be gentle; women should be the caretaker of the family; women are responsible for making/organizing family plans; Levant et al., 2007). The same researchers continued their study of the FIS, and in 2015 found that because of contemporary notions of femininity, analysis supported a four-factor model rather than the five-factor model mentioned above. This new study resulted in the researchers eliminating the Dependency/Deference factor (Richmond, Levant, Smalley, & Cook, 2015). Although items that relate to Dependence/Deference are no longer supported by research, as you can see in Table 4.5, commonly held traditional beliefs still hold.

iStock.com/Kebal Aleksandra

How attainable is the thin, athletic, muscular "ideal" female body? Scientists have discovered that for women, exposure to unattainable images in the media contributes to female body dissatisfaction and lower self-esteem. This can lead to unhealthy lifestyles, such as bingeing/purging or excessive exercise.

Table 4.5 /// Femininity Ideology Scale

Selected Feminine Characteristics by Category

Appearance/Attractiveness

A women should wear attractive clothing, shoes, lingerie, and bathing suits, even if they are not comfortable.
A woman should have a petite body frame.
Women should have large breasts.

Purity

A woman should feel guilty after an abortion.
A woman should not curse.
A woman should not read or engage with pornography.
Women should not masturbate.

Caretaking

Nursing is an appropriate female occupation.
A woman should know how others are feeling.
It is a woman's responsibility to make and organize family plans.

Emotionality

Women in leadership roles are not taken seriously.
A single woman is less fulfilled than a married woman.
Women who relinquish custody of their children are not respected.

Source: Adapted in part from Richmond, K.A., Levant, R.F., & Cook, S.L. (2015)

Intercultural Femininities

Just as with men, there are racial and ethnic differences in how cultures define and social-ize "femininity." In Hispanic cultures, for example, the female equivalent of machismo is marianismo, the essence of Latina femininity. Based on the Catholic religion's belief that Mary gave birth to Jesus and is thus the mother of God, **marianismo** teaches that women

Marianismo:

the belief among Latin American cultures that women are semi-divine and are morally superior to and spiritually stronger than men.

are semi-divine and are morally superior to and spiritually stronger than men (Faulkner, 2003; Noland, 2006). The Latino male thus wants a "Maria" (Mary) for a wife—a wife who is observant of religious laws and who is emotional, kind, instinctive, passive, compliant, and unassertive.

In white, Westernized cultures, gender roles are largely delineated by divisions of labor based on a person's biological sex—there are separate spheres of labor for men (protection and provision) and women (nurturing and caregiving). However, for more than 200 years, Black women functioned in similar capacities to their male counterparts (Buckley & Carter, 2005). That is to say, as a necessary means of survival, Black women traditionally had to adopt *both* masculine and feminine gender roles, such as hard work, self-reliance, resistance, and perseverance (masculine) and care and nurturance (feminine; Collins, 2004). Today, Black men and women still tend to adopt more flexible and less restrictive gender roles (Hall & Pichon, 2014). For example, one study found that Black adolescent girls take on both masculine and feminine gender roles in that they assume roles of worker, independence, and assertiveness, as well as that of mother and caregiver (Buckley & Carter, 2005). Contemporary research holds that today, African American mothers have simultaneous public and private gender roles: "African American mothers are faced with performing *motherwork* [italics added] responsibilities in addition to the public sphere of providing for their family economically" (Jardine & Dallafar, 2012, p. 23). The authors note that this simultaneous carrying out of roles challenges eras-old social constructions of work and family as separate entities. These findings support prior research that revealed that adolescent girls today continue to adopt these both/and gender roles because the roles—and the characteristics associated with them—are consistent with their cultural histories and teachings (Buckley & Carter, 2005).

In many Far East Asian countries (such as China, Japan, Korea, Taiwan, Thailand, and Vietnam), Confucian philosophy dominates, influences, and shapes societal attitudes regarding relationships and gender (Oldstone-Moore, 2002). Confucius believed that the society—which is *the family*—is based on unequal, hierarchical relationships, and that each individual has his or her responsibility to carry out certain functions within these relationships (Phuong-Mai, Terlouw, & Pilot, 2005; Hsin, 2018). To be masculine is to be an active, dominant provider who continues his ancestors' traditions and behaves appropriately according to cultural expectations. Conversely, to be feminine is to be a passive, subordinate, submissive, obedient, nurturing caretaker who models these behaviors to her subordinate, submissive children (Bi & D'Agostino, 2004; Hsin, 2018; Suarez-Orozco and Qin, 2006). In Chinese culture, the *yin-yang* comparison is used to describe the hierarchical nature of gender (see Figure 4.2)—one is different from the other, but one gender cannot live without the other.

Examining the role of gender in the study of intimate, marital, and family relationships is important because gender carries with it socially sanctioned, approved, and endorsed prescribed *life roles* (housewife or provider?), *occupations* (flight attendant or pilot?), *relationships* (heterosexual or homosexual marriage?), and *abilities* (verbal or mathematical?; Bussey & Bandura, 1999; Howard & Hollander, 1997). It is these commonly held beliefs that lead to gender stereotypes or long-held assumptions or labels about male and female capabilities and limitations. When we or society pigeonhole gender characteristics and gender roles, it is very difficult to move toward change.

Being a Girl or a Woman: Does It Mean a Lower Status?

In her work that examined the difficult for societies to make the transition away from traditional gender stereotypes and gender roles, gender activist Joyce Banda (2004) holds that throughout the world, life opportunities are gender based. She notes specifically, "Nearly every society throughout history has traditionally ascribed a lower status for women, and therefore, ascribed to control the lives of women in society" (p. 1).

The status of women in Afghanistan during the rule of the Taliban provides an example that substantiates Banda's perspective. The Taliban is a political and military movement that ruled Afghanistan for a five-year period from about 1996 to 2001; today, the Taliban is a threat to

Figure 4.2 /// Yin-Yang of Relationships

Yin and Yang is a common symbol that comes from ancient Chinese philosophy. When referring to gender, yin/yang means that men and women are interconnected yet independent, complete opposites within a greater whole.

Yin
moon, female, wife, passive, nature, shady

Yang
sun, male, husband, active, human, sunny

Source: iStock/vitalik19111992

more than 70 percent of Afghanistan (Sharifi & Adamou, 2018). Historically, the fundamentalist Islamist sect sharply restricted the daily lives of women, including prohibiting them from working and receiving medical care. And, although Article 43 of the Afghan constitution guarantees a woman's right to access education, girls today are still banned from going to school under threat of death (Haymon, 2018). To make sure girls do not attend schools, a number of schools have been destroyed: More than a dozen girls' schools have been either destroyed or closed since 2014 (Haymon, 2018). During past Taliban rule, women were required to wear a long veil that fully covered their faces and bodies. So restricted were the lives of women that former President Bill Clinton called Afghanistan "perhaps the most difficult place in the world for women."

Banda's (2004) work concludes with comments about the ongoing, tremendous gender-related changes that are taking place across the world, and she notes than in order for the advancement and progress to continue in countries where women are undervalued, "it is necessary to incorporate the interests of *both* men and women effectively within society's vision for progress" (p. 2).

This discussion leads us to another concept about masculinity and femininity that we haven't yet looked at: gender polarization.

GENDER POLARIZATION: COMPLEMENTARY OPPOSITES—OR INEQUALITY?

Rather than emphasize the similarities between men and women, cultural viewpoints almost always emphasize the *differences* between men and women. This "opposite" model is referred to as gender polarization or bipolar gender (Bem, 1993).

Many problems crop up when cultures polarize gender. For instance, when we emphasize masculine/feminine differences and categorize them as total opposites, if a person deviates from the "typical" cultural characteristics, she or he is then seen as belonging to the *other* category (Bem, 1993). If a man freely expresses his emotions, for instance, he is not only seen as less masculine but also more feminine. Similarly, if a woman shows aggression, she is seen as less feminine and more masculine.

Gender polarization is also problematic because there are individuals who are somewhere "in between" on this continuum, as Amber's story in the opening vignette showed us. This view also poses difficulties because traditional views of masculinity and femininity as opposites can cause a number of different types of inequality or gaps, such as inequality in societal status (such as what happened to women and education in Afghanistan), wages, education, employment opportunities and advancement, and social and intimate relationships.

Society's division of gender into either/or categories leads to **gender inequality**, which can be obvious or hidden disparities or discrimination in opportunities or advancements among individuals; these differences are based solely on a person's gender. Inequality between the sexes is often referred to as *sexism*. **Sexism** is defined in a number of different ways:

- A prejudice or discrimination based on biological sex
- A belief system that assumes a hierarchy of human worth based on the social construction of the differences between the sexes
- An ideology of male supremacy, superiority, authority, and beliefs/behaviors that support and sustain this ideology

Sexism, then, supports the belief that people of one sex (typically, males) are inherently superior to people of the other sex. These attitudes and beliefs lead to the unfair treatment or discrimination of the "weaker" sex (typically, females)—the cultural dominance of one sex over the other leads to disadvantages and/or unequal opportunities. In short, people are treated differently because of their biological sex. For example, during a political campaign, a female candidate was photographed through her legs, from behind. Would this same photo have been taken of her rival, a male? If so, would the photos have elicited the same response? Further, the female candidate's wardrobe and the cost of her wardrobe were discussed extensively by the media. However, the media failed to mention the cost of the male candidate's tailor-made suits. This type of treatment is referred to as sexist because the female candidate was treated differently because of her sex.

These types of inequalities and differences in how a person is treated can be manifest in a number of dimensions in a person's daily life, but today in the United States it is still seen particularly in the work and education arenas.

The Glass Ceiling

The term **glass ceiling** refers to situations where the advancement of a qualified person within the hierarchy of an organization is stopped at a lower level due to some form of discrimination, such as sexism (Hesse-Biber & Carter, 2005). The glass ceiling is often associated with women and their ability to advance in their careers. The term *ceiling* is used because it represents her block to upward advancement; the term *glass* is used because limitations to advancement aren't apparent—often, these limitations are "unofficial, unspoken policy" (Hesse-Biber & Carter, 2005).

A good example of the effects of the glass ceiling was played out in front of American voters in the 2016 presidential election. Many sociologists, political authorities, and critics believed that Hillary Clinton, the presidential nominee for the Democratic party, faced a glass ceiling throughout her campaign. Not only did they believe that she was a victim of sexism (such as, she couldn't be "aggressive" in political debates because she would appear to be "unfeminine" and "demeaning") but they also believed that there are still invisible gender barriers in the United States that impeded her success. Indeed, while campaigning Clinton herself noted numerous times that the presidency is the "highest glass ceiling in America." In fact, had

Gender inequality:
the obvious or hidden disparities or discrimination in opportunities or advancements among individuals, based solely on a person's gender.

Sexism:
a prejudice or discrimination based on biological sex; a belief system that assumes a hierarchy of human worth based on the social construction of the differences between the sexes; an ideology of male supremacy, superiority, authority, and beliefs/behaviors that support and sustain this ideology.

Glass ceiling:
refers to discrimination against women in the workplace, specifically in situations where advancement in an organization is stopped because of occupational sexism.

Referring to the presidency as the highest glass ceiling in America, Democratic primary candidate Hillary Clinton said in 2008, "Although we weren't able to shatter that highest, hardest class ceiling, it's got about 18 million cracks [votes] in it." Although Clinton did not win the presidency in 2016, she was the first female presidential nominee of a major U.S. political party, and she was the first woman to lead a major political party presidential ticket.

she won the election, her victory speech would have been held in a convention center with a glass ceiling. As of 2017, of the 146 nations in the world, 56 have been led by a female head of government (Pew Research Center, 2017). Many sociologists and social scientists believe that there are still prevailing gender attitudes in the United States that aren't compatible with having a woman as the president of the United States.

The Wage Gap

The United States also still struggles with equality in the workforce, particularly in wages. This inequality in wages is referred to as the **wage gap**. On average, a woman today earns about 80 percent of what a man earns (Hegewisch, 2018). This means a gender wage gap of 20 percent: Men's median full-time annual income is $52,000, but women's median full-time annual income is about $42,000 (Hegewisch, 2018). Although the wage gap has closed considerably since 1960 (when it was 60.7 percent), according to Ariane Hegewisch, a demographer for the Institute for Women's Policy Research, it will take another 41 years—until 2059—for men and women to reach equality in pay. In other words, since the passing of the Equal Pay Act in 1963, it will have taken nearly *100 years* for the United States to abolish wage disparity based on sex.

Wage gap: the inequality between men's and women's wages in the United States.

The reasons for this discrepancy in income are difficult to determine. For instance, is it because girls are socialized to nurture others, and because of this they choose "helping" careers (such as teacher or therapist), which typically pay less than professional careers (such as engineering or architecture)? Or is it because throughout elementary school and high school they came to believe that they didn't have the abilities to success in professional careers?

The Confidence Gap

Linda J. Sax (2008), a professor of education at the University of California at Los Angeles, believes it's time to get a better understanding of the gender issues facing men and women on college campuses. Using data gathered from millions of college students nationwide in a freshman survey, Sax found that men and women have different confidence levels in their academic abilities. In every area other than writing ability, freshmen women have less confidence than men do. These are very interesting findings because women's self-ratings aren't consistent with data that show that they actually do better academically than men do. So, it's not that men *perform* better than women do in these areas—they don't. Instead, it's that men have *much more confidence* than women do. Sax refers to this phenomenon as the **confidence gap**. Of particular concern to Sax is that women have difficulty believing that they are "as competent as their performance would suggest." Unfortunately, the confidence gap appears to grow and widen throughout college. More recent research analyzed survey data from more than 985,000 men and women from 48 countries (Bleidorn et al., 2016). In her study of self-esteem across the lifespan, Bleidorn and her colleagues found that worldwide, from adolescence to adulthood, men at every age report higher levels of self-esteem than women.

Because of this universal finding, we need to ask ourselves what cultural influences guide the development of self-esteem—and confidence—in men and women? How does it form? What reinforces it? Why is it so prevalent? Do lower confidence and self-esteem levels influence the college majors/career choices of women? Much more research needs to be conducted in this area so that we have a more complete understanding of the issues that may create and perpetuate the glass ceiling and the wage gap.

Intersectionality: When Gender and Race Overlap

When discussing the glass ceiling and the wage gap, it is important to introduce the concept of intersectionality. **Intersectionality** refers to the interconnected nature of social categorizations—such as race, social economic class, and gender—regarded as creating overlapping and interdependent systems of discrimination or disadvantage (Oxford Learner's Dictionary, 2019). Put another way, intersectionality is a theoretical perspective that helps to explain the complex and cumulative ways in which the effects of multiple types of discrimination combine or overlap: They *intersect*.

Conceptualized by Kimberlé Crenshaw, law professor and social theorist, the basic premise of intersectionality maintains that people are often disadvantaged in multiple ways by multiple sources of oppression. Identity markers, such as race, SES, gender, gender identity, and religion, do not exist independently of each other. Indeed, each informs and impacts the other, which in turn affect the others; this creates a complex coming together, merging, of oppression. Figure 4.3 presents not only the wage inequalities between men and women by racial groups, but also wage disparities between all racial groups.

Confidence gap: the phenomenon in which men and women have different confidence levels in their academic abilities—men tend to have more confidence in their academic abilities than women.

Intersectionality: the interconnected nature of social categorizations—such as race, class, and gender—regarded as creating overlapping and interdependent systems of discrimination or disadvantage.

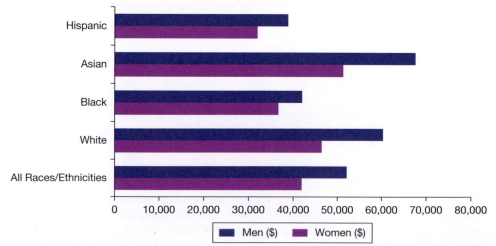

Figure 4.3 /// The Gender Wage Gap: 2017 Earnings Differences by Gender, Race, and Ethnicity

Source: Hegewisch, A. (2018).

Do Men Experience Sexism?

Historically, gender-based discrimination has interfered with women's academic, professional, and economic success, and there is no question that it has thwarted gender equality (Manzi, 2019). The question arises, then: Do men experience sexism?

Very little data or empirical science exists that addresses men's experiences with sexism. According to the Pew Research Center (2017), men report that they *do* believe they have experienced sexism in the workplace; however, the percentage of men who report sexism is far less than women who say they have experienced it (22 percent vs. 42 percent). Some studies indicate that men believe that discrimination against men is increasing in our society (Bosson, Vandello, Michniewicz, & Lenes, 2012; Kehn & Ruthing, 2012, as cited in Manzi, 2019). This then raises another question: If men are discriminated against because of their gender, if they do experience sexism, does it have as many consequences as it does for women? Francesca Manzi (2019), a professor of psychology at New York University, observes, "Because of their social standing, men are less threatened than women by gender-based bias because gender discrimination does not impede men's upward mobility."

Gender Schemas: Perceiving Male or Female, Masculine or Feminine

The ways we internalize and incorporate specific gendered behaviors and expectations are called **gender schemas**. A *schema* is a mental representation or a set of specific symbols or images we hold about something. These cognitive frameworks organize and guide an individual's perception about what it is to be male or female, masculine or feminine (Bem, 1981). These self-schemas allow us to organize and categorize social information and to "organize the way individuals think about themselves in social interactions" (Belansky & Boggiano, 1994, p. 647).

Gender schemas: the ways in which we internalize and incorporate specific gendered behaviors and expectations.

Perhaps some of the earliest research designed to distinguish between masculine and feminine characteristics and traits is attributed to Gough's Masculinity-Femininity Scale (1957). Sandy Bem's (1974) later work—considered to be one of the primary works concerning gender schemas—was based on her assumption that there appear to be characteristics that are more socially desirable for men than for women and characteristics that are more socially desirable for women than for men. Because of the implied cultural mandate to adhere to specifically assigned gender roles, Bem suggests that individuals will suppress "any behavior that might be considered undesirable or inappropriate for his sex" (p. 155). She notes that a person who has "internalized"—made a mental schema of—"desirable" behavior for men and women is *sex-typed*.

Instrumental and Expressive Schemas

Instrumental schemas are associated with masculinity and focus on task-orientated behaviors and "getting the job done" (Bem, 1974, p. 156). According to Bem, masculine behavior is thought to be task-oriented and includes traits such as ambition, competitiveness, and acting as a leader. **Expressive schemas** are associated with femininity and have an interpersonal or relational orientation. As Bem notes, those with an expressive schema are concerned for the welfare of other people and include such traits as being gentle and loyal.

Instrumental schemas: patterns associated with masculinity that focus on task-oriented behaviors and "getting the job done."

Expressive schemas: patterns of behavior associated with femininity that have an interpersonal or relational orientation.

The lists in Table 4.6 drive home an important point. Are any changes noted since 1974 in how males in our culture are socialized to become "male"? Still today, men in Western civilization are socialized—taught—to be independent, strong, assertive, aggressive, responsible leaders. Take a look at the list of expressive traits thought to characterize women. Are any changes noted in how females in our culture are socialized to be "female"? Despite the efforts of the feminist movement in the 20th century, it appears that women are still being socialized to be relationally oriented—to be affectionate, nurturing, empathic, sensitive, compassionate, and dependent.

Table 4.6 /// Instrumental and Expressive Schemas

Instrumental Schemas (Masculinity)	Expressive Schemas (Femininity)
Acting as a leader	Affection
Aggression	Compassion
Ambition	Gentleness
Assertiveness	Loyalty
Competitiveness	Understanding
Dominance	Sensitivity
Independence	Sympathy
Self-reliance	
Willingness to take risks	

Source: Bem (1974).

The experience of maleness or femaleness is socially and culturally driven. What happens in the instances where a person displays *both* male and female traits?

Androgyny: A Spectrum of Expression

Androgyny:
without assigned gender value; when a person possesses traits, behaviors, or characteristics typically associated with the opposite gender.

When referring to the concept of **androgyny**, we mean that something either has no gender value assigned to it or that a person possesses traits, behaviors, or characteristics that are typically associated with the opposite gender. It occurs as a result of the two primary concepts associated with gender: the biological influences of gender and the social influences of gender.

There are three types of androgyny. The first is *physiological androgyny,* which deals with physical or biological traits, such as occurs in the cases of intersex individuals. The second

The Hijras in India, Pakistan, and Bangladesh are often described as "neither male or female." Feared and revered in Hindu society, Hijras perform rituals for religious ceremonies.

is *behavioral androgyny,* which involves the blending of masculine and feminine traits; an androgynous person might display traits and behaviors that are typically associated with male and female—not one or the other. The third type of androgyny is *psychological androgyny,* which involves the individual's gender identity.

Some cultures are androgynous. This means that there are no rigid gender roles guiding men's and women's behaviors. The Hijras of India, Pakistan, and Bangladesh are often described, for example, as "neither male nor female." In her book, *Neither Man nor Woman,* Serena Nanda (1990) discusses the fascinating lives of the Hijras. Raised as boys, the ritualistic removal of the genitals takes place between the ages of 10 and 15. The Hijras have a separate social category—they are not male; they are not female. The social role of Hijras is to dress and act as women and perform at weddings and religious ceremonies after the birth of a boy. Hijras are feared and revered in Hindu society, as they are thought to ward off both impotence and infertility.

About her friendship with a Hijra, British photographer Dayanita Singh (2001) writes, "When I once asked her about her [anatomy], she told me, 'You really don't understand. I am the third sex, not a man trying to be a woman. It is your society's problem that you only recognize two sexes.'" So commonplace are Hijras in Indian society that in 2005, Indian passport application forms were updated and now include three gender options: M (male), F (female), and E (eunuch).

As we have discussed throughout this chapter, gender is not a case of either/or. As the National Transgender Advocacy Coalition (NTAC, 2019) notes, ultimately "gender is a mix-and-match mode of self-expression . . . it is best to think of [gender roles, gender behavior, and] gender identity as varying along a *continuous spectrum of self-expression* [italics added], rather than in just one of two or three ways." When we think of gender as a continuum of self-expression, then we can see how this conceptualization of gender best explains the contemporary expressions of androgyny seen in our culture today: Not adhering to established, expected gender roles. For some today, an androgynous identity may include aspects of both "masculine" and "feminine" characteristics, such as in the choice of clothing. For example, some biological males may choose to wear a dress and make-up while simultaneously sporting a beard. The important thing to remember is that how a person dresses or speaks or acts may not necessarily have anything to do with their sexuality—it could just be how they desire to express themselves and present themselves to the world.

There is no question—"gender" is as much a social and intrapersonal construction as it is a biological construction. But another important question remains to be answered: By what processes do we "become" male or female, androgynous or transgender?

THE THEORIES OF GENDER DEVELOPMENT

A student of mine, Sarah, once shared with me an interesting story involving her 3-year-old son, Ethan. As a never-married single mom, Sarah's life revolved around her full-time college student status and the two jobs she worked in order to support and provide for her son, leaving little time for dating or much else. Because there was no male influence in her son's life, Sarah was concerned that Ethan would not "learn" how to be a "boy." But an all-too-infrequent trip to the city park one Saturday afternoon seemed to calm her anxieties.

As they were making their third lap around the park, the young boy noticed that a man-hole cover near the curb of the street was missing. Seemingly out of nowhere Ethan remarked, "Mommy, look at that big hole." "Umhm," replied his mom. "That is very dangerous, Ethan. Don't ever go near things like that."

The precocious 3-year-old responded, "Mommy, a big, strong man needs to come here and lift that and put that back on the hole to make it safe again." Sarah was stunned. "Ethan, can't Mommy fix that?" He retorted, "No, Mommy! Only someone big and strong can fix that and mommies aren't big and strong."

She later asked me, "Where did he learn that from? Where did he pick up that only a big, strong, man could fix the problem to make things safe again?" Perhaps he was influenced by books, television, Disney movies, or billboards. Gender influences are found everywhere.

"If there was no such thing as gender, if we had no expectations of children biased by their sexual label, would gender-specific behavior disappear?" asks researcher J. Bland (1998, p. 2). In other words, if there were no such thing as gender, what expectations would Sarah have of Ethan? In order to answer Bland's question, we need to consider some theories that attempt to explain the process by which we are socialized to adhere to gender-specific behaviors.

Learning Theory

Psychologists David Perry and Kay Bussey (1984) define gender role development as "the process whereby children come to acquire the behaviors, attitudes, interests, and emotional reactions that are culturally defined as appropriate for members of their sex" p. 262). Implicit in this definition, then, is the notion that we are not *born* with gendered behaviors, attitudes, interests, and the like, but take them on through the daily stream of incoming information from our environment. Such is the nature of Learning theory: Traits and behaviors are not inborn—we learn them.

Early behaviorists such as B. F. Skinner, Ivan Pavlov, and John Watson attempted to explain all human behaviors through learning theories, with the notion that all behaviors are learned. The basic learning theories were predicated on the belief that we are born as "blank slates" waiting to be filled by the social instruction of our parents, teachers, the media, and society. Strict behaviorists maintained that a given stimulus (**S**) would produce a given response (**R**). Schematically, the theory would look something like this:

$$S \rightarrow R$$

By applying the concepts of reward and punishment, behaviorists contend that all behaviors—including gendered behaviors—are *learned responses*. If, for example, a little girl in a party dress is rewarded for sitting daintily in a chair with her ankles crossed, she is likely to repeat that behavior. And if the girl is punished for sitting or acting not so ladylike or acting tomboyish, she is less likely to repeat that behavior. Similarly, if a little boy desires to play with a Barbie doll and is punished, he is more likely to choose his fire truck out of the toybox the next time. By repeated "rewards" and "punishments" throughout infancy, early childhood, childhood, adolescence, and adulthood, specific gender behaviors are either *reinforced* (and thus, more likely to occur again and again) or *extinguished* (less likely to occur).

Social Learning Theory

Social Learning theory (SLT) is an offshoot of traditional Behaviorism theory. Although SLT does address the roles of reward and punishment, it goes a step further to include an individual's realm of *cognition*—the role of observation—in the process of learning. Schematically, SLT would look something like this

$$S \rightarrow C \rightarrow R$$

Children make countless day-to-day observations that ultimately shape their gender-related thinking, understanding, and behavior. These daily social and environmental cues are quite specific to males and females. Albert Bandura is an academic psychologist who has made an enormous impact on personality theory and therapy techniques. He placed an emphasis on observational learning and is the theorist most associated with SLT. Bandura (1977) maintained that individuals learn behaviors via observation in three different ways:

- *By imitating observed behaviors in their environment.* Children learn gendered behaviors by observing and then imitating the behavior of a model, someone who demonstrates a particular behavior.

- *By observing the punishments or rewards based on others' behaviors.* Bandura did not believe that a person had to actually experience the rewards and punishments themselves. Simply watching the consequences of others is enough to "teach"—we learn by watching what happens to others. Because the learning doesn't necessarily have to happen directly to us, Bandura thought that much of learning was vicarious.

- *By exposure to another's thinking.* Exposure to many different models is particularly useful in changing traditional stereotypes (Rutledge, 2000). For example, exposing someone to an intersexual or transgender child might serve to break down long-held beliefs.

Indeed, Bandura's research highlighted the role of cognition or observational learning in the acquisition of gender. He maintained that there are three reciprocal, interacting components in acquiring any human behavior:

- You, the **P**erson—your genetics, race, ethnicity, age, biological sex

- Your **B**ehavior—the choices and decisions you make, your responses and reactions to the incoming information in your daily life

- Your **E**nvironment—your parents, school, peers, neighborhood, the media, the religious hierarchy, and the political structure of the culture in which you live (similar to Bronfenbrenner's Ecological Model, discussed in Chapter 1).

These three interwoven components—**P, B, E**—are dynamic, in a continuous state of change. Rather than the seemingly straightforward approach to learning represented as **S→R** put forth by earlier learning theorists, Bandura added the element of cognition (thought) and advanced the notion that cognition then acts as a *filter* of sorts between the stimulus and the response. As the **P**erson, **B**ehavior, and **E**nvironment all interact, countless messages, cues, and forces (stimuli) from the social environment are filtered through the process of cognition (observation); ultimately, certain behaviors are accepted and thus acted out, and certain behaviors are rejected (response). A schematic drawing of Bandura's Social Learning theory would look something like Figure 4.4.

Bandura's (1986) work also addresses the many social factors that contribute to gendered behavior. In particular, he paid attention to the influences of media in the shaping, molding, and directing of gendered behaviors. Bandura best sums up the impact of social and cultural influences on gender development when he comments that from the moment of birth, we are continuously exposed to clear-cut environmental and social cues that dictate our gender behaviors. Specifically, Bandura notes that these gender cues are experienced "in the home, in school, in readers and storybooks, and in representations of society on the television screens of every household" (p. 93). Indeed, the environmental cues are many and they are what ultimately transform the basic fundamental biological attributes of sex into a socially and culturally determined "gender."

Cognitive Development Theory

As a developmental psychologist and professor for many years at Harvard University, Lawrence Kohlberg popularized his theory of moral development through research studies at Harvard's Center for Moral Education. In 1966, Kohlberg proposed the **Cognitive Development theory** of gender, which holds that children could not be influenced by outside experiences until they developed cognitively. In other words, the Cognitive Development theory maintains that before social and environmental forces can influence a child's concept of gender (as believed by behaviorists and Social Learning theory, for example), the child must first gain a certain awareness or understanding about gender (Helwig, 1998). Ultimately, though,

Cognitive Development theory:

this theory holds that before social and environmental forces can influence a child's concept of gender, the child must first gain a certain awareness or understanding about gender.

Figure 4.4 /// The Social Cognitive Filter

As the person, behavior, and environment interact, innumerable messages, cues, and stimuli from the environment are filtered through a social cognitive filter. An individual may choose to accept certain messages and act on them, or reject them entirely.

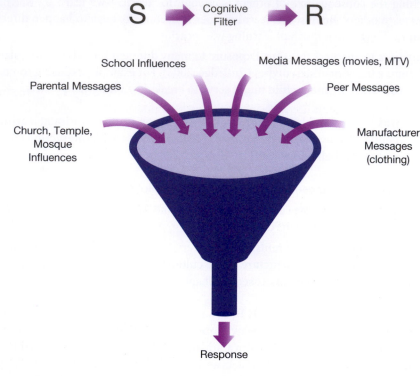

Source: iStock.com/MD Badsha Meah

Kohlberg held that children develop stereotypes of gender based on what surrounds them in their social worlds. To this end, Kohlberg suggested that children's conception of gender changes as their cognitive development progresses. He thus delineated three phases of gender understanding:

- *Gender identity.* Around the age of 3, children become keenly aware that they biologically are male or female. Around the same age, they are able to label others as "girls" or "boys" or "mommies" or "daddies."

- *Gender stability.* Sometime between the ages of 4 and 6, children reach the realization that their gender will always be the same—that they were a boy or a girl as a baby and will be a boy or a girl when they grow up. This is referred to as **gender stability**.

- *Gender constancy.* Sometime around the age of 6, children reach the understanding that no matter what they might change in how they dress or how they play or what they play with, they are still a boy or a girl. It is only after children consistently think of themselves as an unchangeable boy or girl that they begin to take on both family and socially expected gendered behaviors.

Kohlberg believed that **gender constancy** is achieved when children cognitively reach the understanding that biological "sex is a permanent attribute" (Bussey & Bandura, 1999, p. 4) that is associated with certain anatomical characteristics that cannot be changed. This understanding ultimately leads to what Kohlberg defined as a *stable gender identity.* In short, children come to realize that their gender is constant across age and time.

Gender stability: between the ages of 4 and 6, children reach the realization that their gender will always be the same—that they were a boy or a girl as a baby and will be a boy or a girl when they grow up.

Gender constancy: between kindergarten and about second grade, children understand that acting like a girl if you are a boy doesn't make you a girl, and acting like a boy if you are a girl doesn't make you a boy. Children realize that sex is a permanent attribute.

Kohlberg's research has come under fire and been hotly debated in the past several decades, particularly by Carol Gilligan (1982), a gender studies professor at Harvard University. Gilligan was a former student of Kohlberg, but she believed that Kohlberg's concepts of moral development and gender identity development are biased against women because women develop their moral codes differently than men. Other empirical studies have also found limited support for Kohlberg's theory as well (among many, many others, Bussey & Bandura, 1984; O'Keefe & Hyde, 1983; Franken, 1983; Huston, 1983; Nelson, 1978).

Gender identity is a lifelong process and involves a delicate, complicated interaction between biological and cultural forces. As these gender theories help us to understand, gender, gender behavior, and gender thinking are constantly influenced by the environment in which we live. In the following section, we take a deeper look at the different socializing agents in our contemporary culture: the influence of parents, peers, and the media.

IT MATTERS: THE AGENTS OF SOCIALIZATION

As we have discovered throughout this chapter, gender and gender roles—and, to a large extent, perhaps even gender identity—are learned from exposure to a number of sources across an individual's lifespan, from parents and other family members, to the schoolroom, from sports icons to toys, from peers to books.

Learning Gender From Parents

Because of the immediate and consistent influences of the newborn's family, it is not surprising that parents infuse gender messages into their children, knowingly or unknowingly. Think about it—from encouraging certain behaviors and discouraging other behaviors (Big boys don't cry), to parents exhibiting certain overt gender behaviors (Boys take out the trash; girls don't) and making covert suggestions (Is that any way to act like a lady?), to the activities and opportunities that parents expose their children to, children are in a constant state of being gender socialized (Witt, 1997).

iStock.com/Romrodinka

In our daily lives, we are exposed to countless gender messages, messages that tell us what duties boys are supposed to perform and what duties girls are supposed to perform. If you have children, will you socialize them to adhere to traditional gender roles? Why or why not?

The various theories of gender socialization show us that because children are exposed to culturally specific expectations of gender and culturally defined gender roles, they internalize, and ultimately act out, what is expected and what is appropriate for each biological sex—boys act and think one way, girls act and think in different ways. Parents socialize children through a number of ways, but most especially through modeling particular gendered behaviors, such as mothers assuming the lion's share of nurturing the children and housekeeping tasks, and fathers assuming the physical tasks, such as home repair and maintenance and protection/provider for the family (Boyd & Bee, 2015).

Play and Gender Messages

Parents also send gender messages by the ways in which they encourage their children to play. A number of empirical studies have found that parents encourage their children to engage in certain sex-typed activities, such as encouraging their daughters to play with dolls instead of trucks and to take ballet lessons instead of playing football (among many others, Campenni, 1999). Not surprisingly, other research has discovered that the toys children prefer to play with are related to how parents sex-typed their children (Wood, Desmarais, & Gugula, 2002). All of these messages with play and toys send clear-cut messages to children that girls are to play and to assume future roles that are nurturing and geared toward childrearing and housekeeping, while boys are taught to play and to assume future roles that are more along the lines of providing and protecting (Campenni, 1999). However, these studies all examined children who were reared by heterosexual parents. Do children who are reared by gay or lesbian parents assume traditional gender roles?

Learning Gender From Gay or Lesbian Parents

Although it should not be expected that children growing up in lesbian-mother households or gay-father households would fare worse than children who are raised by heterosexual parents with similar parenting styles (such as warm, responsive, communicative parenting), some segments of American society and other cultures expect that children who are raised in same-sex parenting families will have psychological or gender role identity problems—in particular, there is a prevalent belief that children of gay or lesbian parents will have difficulty constructing "appropriate" gender schemas and gender roles (Stacey & Biblarz, 2001; Golombok et al., 2003). To date, emerging social science research has failed to bear out these concerns (among many others, Goldberg, Kashy, & Smith, 2012). To the contrary, current research suggests that gendered behavior, gender roles, and gender identity develop in similar ways among all children, whether they are raised by heterosexual parents or same-sex parents (Patterson, 2004).

There are research efforts that focus on outcomes for children growing up in nontraditional family forms (see, for example, Goldberg et al., 2012; Golombok et al., 2003). In one study that sought to understand the quality of parent–child relationships and gender development of children with lesbian parents, the investigators found no significant differences in the ways in which children in lesbian-mother families, single-mother families, and two-parent heterosexual families were raised (Golombok et al., 2003). There were no differences in the ways children draw/write/read, the shows they watched on television, or their rough-and-tumble play. In short, boys and girls raised in lesbian-mother families did not differ from those children raised in heterosexual families in their gender-typed behavior—sexual orientation of mothers was not a major or significant influence on children's gender development.

A more recent study in 2012 that included gay male couples, lesbian female couples, and heterosexual couples examined gender-typed play behavior in these couples' preschool-age children (Goldberg et al., 2012). The researchers discovered that play behaviors of boys and girls in same-sex couple households were less gender stereotyped than the play behaviors of boys and girls in heterosexual-parent families. This study revealed, for example, that sons of lesbian mothers were less masculine in their play behaviors than sons of gay fathers and sons of heterosexual parents.

Of course, we don't learn gender experiences just from our families of origin. Throughout our lives we receive numerous other gender cues from our environments, particularly from our friends.

Learning Gender From Peers

As children enter into social settings in the early years, and subsequently throughout the rest of childhood during their school years, a child's gender identity is further reinforced through play and within the classroom setting.

Children exhibit a preference for same-sex playmates, referred to as **homosocial play**, from about the age of 3 until about the age of early adolescence (age 11 or 12; Boyd & Bee, 2015). As children interact with their same-sex peers, established gender roles continue to be reinforced. As an example, boys prefer to engage in rough and aggressive types of play, and girls prefer to engage in fantasy, imaginary, and relational play (Boyd & Bee, 2015). Because of these differing play styles, children often choose playmates of their same sex because they, too, enjoy that particular brand of play. While engaging in play, the gender differences are made more concrete.

In recent years, significant strides have been made in both policy and practice in early childhood programs. In efforts to value the importance of children as active participants in their own gender development, early childhood educators are attempting to de-feminize the preschool culture. In general, early childhood centers (and, to a large extent, school settings in general) are feminized cultures; that is, the staff is predominately females who nurture and provide care in stereotypical gendered fashion (Skelton & Hall, 2011). Essentially, there is no presence of men within early childhood centers, which can potentially transmit the message that only women are capable of caring for young children.

Christine Skelton and Elaine Hall (2001), early childhood education professors in the United Kingdom, were commissioned by the Equal Opportunities Commission to investigate the development of gender in young children. Their two-pronged purpose was to recreate early childhood programs that would challenge stereotypes and encourage diversity and to create guidance materials for instructors that encouraged examples of how to achieve gender equity. To achieve these ends, Skelton and Hall suggest that early childhood educators should

- Be aware of and understand their own subconscious gender stereotypings, such as, *Do I expect children to act differently because they are boys or girls? Do I have different expectations for a child's performance based on whether the child is a boy or a girl?*
- Be aware of what images of "male" and "female" children bring with them into the classroom setting, such as, *What are children's favorite games, toys, and books? What do these tell children about the "correct" way of being a boy or a girl?*
- Pay attention to the messages given to children in day-to-day routines, such as, *Am I aware that "girls" and "boys" are not always homogenous groups—that sometimes girls will act aggressively and boys will play cooperatively?*

In sum, Skelton and Hall (2001) put forth the notion that teachers should provide children in their care with a nonsexist, nontraditional, nonstereotypical environment. An interesting question is brought to the surface here: Given all that you have learned so far in your study of the construction of gender, do you believe it is really possible (or necessary?) to socialize children to behave in gender neutral ways? Talking at glance at "Family Life Now" may help you to better decide.

As children move through their middle childhood and adolescent years, peers become increasingly important. This change in peer involvement brings with it increasing pressure for children to feel that they "fit in" (Carver, Yunger, & Perry, 2003). Gender identity has as much to do

Homosocial play:
children's preference for same-sex playmates; occurs from age 3 to age 11 or 12.

Is It Possible to Raise Gender-Neutral Children?

Although most people adhere to the socially and culturally determined gender roles ascribed to them, today more and more individuals are filling nontraditional gender roles. This flexibility and fluidity between the genders has some researchers questioning whether it is possible to raise gender-neutral children in contemporary society. Is it possible to raise children with no clear-cut lines between "male" and "female"?

YES: Psychologist and researcher Sandra Lipsitz Bem contends that is it possible to raise gender-neutral children, and she uses her own children as examples in her scholarly writings. Bem and her husband sought to retard the stereotypical gender messages in their children's environments.

Intent on exposing their children to nontraditional gender roles, Bem and her husband did all they could to eliminate the common correlations between a person's biological sex and day-to-day tasks. For example, the Bems took turns doing certain household tasks, caring for the children, and driving the car. They went out of their way to show their children men and women engaging in nontraditional occupations, such as driving by a construction site every day so their children would see the female construction workers. So gender neutral were they in their parenting that their son referred to individuals as "heorshe," implying there were not two genders, but one.

Throughout childhood and adolescence, the Bems

- encouraged their children to be skeptical of conventional cultural messages about gender by emphasizing diversity;
- provided their children with nongendered ways of observing traditional messages about gender (by saying such things as, "Yes, boys like to play baseball, but so do girls"); and
- helped them understand that all gender messages are created by culture and society.

NO: Sociologists Denise Segura and Jennifer Pierce (1993) maintain that gender identity and gender roles are very closely tied to family and cultural expectations; because of this, they contend that gender-specific role fulfillment is critically vital to certain cultures. To support their claim, they examine the Chicana/o culture of Mexico, in which the role of women as mothers is central to both gender identity formation and group or ethnic identity formation.

Central to the development of gendered personality of the Chicana/o are the family and cultural influences; of particular interest is the unique constellation of features that define these families. The constellation of Latinx family types include *familism* (where a strong value is placed on family unity and the presence of multigenerational ties), *compadrazgo* (a high level of interaction with close nonfamily), and *nonexclusive mothering* (mothering by other trusted individuals through extensive family networks, such as grandmothers and aunts).

All of these features of the Hispanic family types have significant implications in the development of masculine or feminine personalities because gender identities in this culture are closely blended or intertwined with community and society. Unlike European American mothers, Chicana mothers rear their children to act communally, or to think and acts in ways that benefit the family and the community. Sons and daughters in Hispanic cultures are raised to believe that they are extensions not of their parents but of their culture. Consider how females are reared in this culture:

- With multiple mother figures, daughters' gender identification centers on Hispanic cultural practices and beliefs, such as appropriate mother roles; knowledge of cultural traditions, behaviors, and values; and honoring other kin ties. The Chicano believe that these roles compliment the role of men, which is to be the provider for the family.

Consider how males are reared in Hispanic cultures:

- Because of the presence of several female role models in the sons' lives, the transmission of culture and gender expectations is accomplished by a process known as "becoming masculine." Chicana women repeat the centuries-old Mexican saying, "*feo, fuerte y formal.*" Roughly translated, the young boy is to be rugged and strong, to be a man who is steadfast and responsible, and to be a good provider for his family. Young Chicano boys learn how to be a male by *not* being a female.

In Hispanic cultures, the role of women is emphasized, yet it is these unique family constellation features that ultimately contribute to the acquisition of gender identity—a gender identity that is nearly inseparable from group, ethnic, and cultural identity.

Sources: Bem (1998); Segura & Pierce (1993).

What Do You Think?

1. Is it possible to raise gender-neutral children in societies where gender messages abound?

2. Is it necessary to raise gender-neutral children?

3. What are the advantages of a gender-neutral society? What are the disadvantages?

with people's perceptions of how they fit in as it does with how they feel about their biological gender assignment and their ascribed gender roles. Carver and her colleagues found that during the preadolescent years of human development, feelings of gender typicality and gender contentedness increase with age; feelings of intergroup bias and gender conformity decrease with age. In other words, as children move toward adolescence, feeling the need to conform to gender stereotypes decreases and contentedness with their assigned biological sex increases, thus allowing children to "be" who they are, male or female, or who they desire to be.

Gender, gender roles, and gender identity are learned from exposure to a number of sources across an individual's lifespan. Still, we need to examine one more influence on gender development and gender behavior in contemporary society: the role of the media.

Learning Gender From the Media

When examining the influences of popular culture and the media on gender, a decades-old debate emerges: Does the media influence social patterns? Or is the media merely a reflection of the existing cultural values and norms? The question has perplexed communication experts, social science researchers, and social analysts for decades. That gender roles and stereotypes are *determined* and *formed* by the media would be a difficult case to make. But it is clear that gender roles are *supported* and *reinforced* by media. To better understand how the media reinforces gender and gender behaviors, here we examine the portrayal of gender in television, film, and advertising.

Television and Film

Children's conceptions of gender are based primarily on what they see and hear (Bussey & Bandura, 1999). Television cartoons and movies play a powerful role in gender stereotyping, in part because they are so popular among children of all ages. Beginning in early childhood, movie viewers are exposed to numerous images of masculine and feminine "ideals." Consider the Walt Disney compilation of the ideal woman:

Snow White possesses fair, flawless skin and dark hair; she is shapely, pleasant, and patient; she has a soprano singing voice. She is waiting for her prince to bring her to life.

Cinderella possess fair, flawless skin and blonde hair; she is shapely, pleasant, and patient (even in the most degrading situations); she has a soprano singing voice. She is waiting for her prince to save her.

Belle *(Beauty and the Beast)* has fair skin, has flowing brown hair, and is shapely. She has a lilting soprano voice and falls in love with a wolfish-looking beast—who turns out to be a prince.

Children's perceptions of "male" and "female" are the result of what they see and hear. In what ways does Disney typecast and socialize "ideal" images of boys and girls?

Even as the cultural form of Disney's heroine has evolved, certain physiological and behavioral traits continue to linger. Consider the Native American motif of Pocahontas. Although her skin tones are darker, the thin, shapely body and soprano singing voice are still present. Films with characters such as these reinforce the socially and culturally driven concept of the "ideal" woman: She is thin; has curves in all the right places; is pretty; has long, flowing, luxurious hair; is pleasant and cheery, in even the most horrible of circumstances; has a sing-song voice; and is very dependent on the strong handsome prince (who, some would argue, is prone to wearing puffy sleeves).

Once a person outgrows Disney movies and turns his or her attention to other forms of media, the gender stereotypes are still present; societal expectations still prevail, and women are rewarded for their nurturing abilities and beauty and men for their strength and intellect. Media trends tracked by women's groups such as the National Organization for Women (NOW) indicate that women in the media are commonly portrayed as young, attractive, nurturing, married (or romantically involved), and employed in traditional female occupations, such as teaching or nursing. Conversely, men are portrayed as heads of government, as lead criminal investigators and crime specialists, and in dominant positions in hospitals.

Media Watch, a volunteer feminist organization, was established in 1981 in an effort to change the media's portrayal and treatment of women. At that time, their analysis of prime-time television found more than 140 female television stars who were look-alikes: They were thin, white, and beautiful. They were not women of color, lesbian, overweight, single (for long), or impoverished (Media Watch, 2008). On the other hand (and similar to real life), men in television typically held positions of power—and it didn't necessarily matter if they possessed drop-dead good looks (Media Watch, 2008). More recent research confirms Media Watch's prior analysis: Today, the most common themes in television shows in the United States are boys who prize girls for their physical appearance and attributes and girls who self-objectify and stroke boys' egos (Murnen, Greenfield, Younger, & Hope, 2016).

Additional research found two common themes in contemporary television (Coyne, Ward, Kroff, & Davis, 2019):

1. Men are depicted as heterosexual, dominant, aggressive, and sex-driven. "In mainstream media, male sexuality is often portrayed as active, powerful, and persistent." (p. 431)

2. Women are portrayed as objects whose value is dependent upon their physical appearance and sexual appeal. Female characters are depicted as passive, appearance-based, and partner-pleasing.

The authors note that these common depictions of men and women in television are similar to society's traditional, accepted heterosexual dating and partnering scripts (see Chapter 7 for an in-depth discussion about dating scripts). Coyne and her colleagues (2019) aptly summarize, "Because this script posits an adversarial relationship between the sexes, one in which women are sexually objectified (and therefore dehumanized) and male pleasure is prioritized, the concern is that these dynamics could help legitimize sexual violence against women" (p. 431).

Media Watch (2008) has identified the pervasive gender trends in film and television media, and recent studies confirm their findings (Kirsch & Murnen, 2015; Dinella, Claps, & Lewandowski, 2017; Trekels & Eggermont, 2018; Coyne et al., 2019):

- *Irrelevant sexualization* uses women's bodies in sexual ways in an attempt to attract attention or to use a woman's or man's sexuality to sell products.

- *Infantilization* presents women as childish, coy, silly, passive, or vulnerable. This is in contrast to men who are commonly portrayed as strong, confident, assertive, and serious.

- *Domestication* defines women in relationship to their husbands, boyfriends, or the man to whom they are attracted. Even if the female TV character works outside of the home, she is typically shown interacting in her home relationship.

- *Victimization* portrays women as victims of violent acts or as victims of female and male brutality.

Shari Graydon (2003), educator, past president of Media Watch, and a columnist for the *Vancouver Sun,* maintains that distorted imagery of women in the media worsens or aggravates sexist attitudes, discriminatory conditions, and behaviors. Graydon notes that teenagers are especially vulnerable to the effects of these media messages because they are at a particularly vulnerable stage in their developmental process. This vulnerability makes them more sensitive to "impossible-to-attain" messages about the feminine ideal, expected sexual availability, and limited career opportunities for women.

Advertising

Television shows and movies aren't the only ways boys and girls are socialized by the media today. They are also exposed to advertising. For example, the typical North American child views some 40,000 each year, and companies spend $17 billion annually marketing to children—compared to the $100 million spent in 1983 (Campaign for a Commercial-Free Childhood [CCFC], 2019). The messages they receive are clear: Men are dominant and strong. Women are submissive and weak. Men are aggressive and intelligent. Women are passive and intuitive. These are the traits deemed appropriate by society, and advertising in the media does much to strengthen them (Macdonald, 2003). Typically, men are featured in autonomous settings displaying numerous occupations and skills. Women in advertisements usually are in a domestic setting, most often portraying girlfriends and wives, homemakers and mothers (Macdonald, 2003). The commercial voiceover—the "expert" of the ad, the "trusted" person—is most often male. In fact, some advertising experts estimate that men appear in ads four times more often than women, and 94 percent use a male voiceover (Chandler, 2005; Monllos, 2017).

As little girls and little boys develop into adolescents, and then into women and men, they are continuously exposed to countless hours of media influences. For instance, teenagers today drive the consumption and development of new video platforms, such as playing videos on their iPhones and iPads and accessing streaming video on the Internet with YouTube, Netflix, and Hulu, among others (Nielsen Media, 2019). With children spending an average of four hours a day in front of a television screen (Boyse, 2008), gender representation in media will certainly play a profound role in shaping the ideals of gender and gender identity.

As we have discussed throughout this chapter, we all have different conceptions of what it is to be a man or a woman in contemporary society, and we came to these understandings through multiple biological, cultural, and psychosocial forces that are continuously at work in our lives. Whether on a big screen, the television screen, in magazines, in music, or on the Internet, the representation of gender roles in media are clearly reinforcing cultural understandings of manhood and womanhood.

IT MATTERS: GENDER AND CONTEMPORARY ISSUES

Professors of law Catherine Mackinnon (2001) and William Eskridge and Nan Hunter (1997) compiled a comprehensive, extensive review of case law as it applies to gender and sexuality. The equal protection doctrine (part of the Fourteenth Amendment to the United States Constitution) provides that "no state shall . . . deny to any person . . . the equal protection of its laws." In essence, this clause of the Constitution addresses the proposition that "all men are created equal" and should be treated as such. As the law professors suggest, a broad survey of gender as it relates to the law is an important area of study because the equal protection doctrine is shaped by gender issues in our daily lives. In today's political, economic, and home environments, issues of gender are front and center, with concerns such as women in combat and the adoption of children by gays and lesbians.

Even though the Fourteenth Amendment to the U.S. Constitution was passed in 1868 in an effort to "eliminate legalized racism" (Mackinnon, 2001, p. 13), some 100 years later racial equality was far from realized in the United States. The Civil Rights Act of 1964 was passed by Congress to prohibit discrimination in the workplace on the basis of race, color, religion, sex, or national origin. But as Mackinnon notes, "Equality in human societies is commonly affirmed, but rarely practiced. Few lives are lived in equality, even in democracies. As a fact, social equality is hard to find anywhere" (p. 2). Beyond a form of justice to ensure the rights of all U.S. citizens, the Civil Rights Act has changed and still contributes to the changing experiences of the American family and family life.

Equal Protection for All?

Interestingly, although the Fourteenth Amendment is known as the "protection clause" in the U.S. Constitution, it does not expressly prohibit discrimination against women. To remedy this, the **Equal Rights Amendment (ERA)** was first introduced to the U.S. Congress in 1923 and was brought about because the rights affirmed in the U.S. Constitution applied only to white males—the rights of women as equals to men were not guaranteed, and thus there was no legal remedy to protect women against sex discrimination (Alice Paul Institute, 2018). Nearly 100 years later, the ERA has still not been added to the U.S. Constitution. The amendment was passed by Congress in 1972, but as of 2020, only 38 states had ratified the ERA.

When we discuss the ERA in class, I commonly hear such statements as, "I thought women already had equal rights protection under the law. Why is there a need for an equal rights amendment?" This is a common misconception: According to a 2016 poll by the ERA Coalition, 80 percent of those polled believed that women are already guaranteed equal protection (ERA Coalition, 2016). In fact, the U.S. Constitution does not prohibit sex discrimination. The ratification of the ERA would assure every American citizen that they have the federal, legal right to be free from any and all discrimination on the basis of sex (ERA Coalition, 2016). Today, 90 percent of men and 90 percent of women on both sides of the political aisles support the ratification of the Equal Rights Amendment (Hager & Jenkins, 2016).

Equal Rights Amendment (ERA): proposed amendment to the U.S. Constitution to prohibit sex discrimination. The amendment was passed by Congress in 1972, but as of 2020, only 38 states had ratified the ERA.

Protection Against Violence

Another piece of legislation that would significantly impact women's well-being is the **Violence Against Women Act of 1994 (VAWA)**. This federal law, signed by President Bill Clinton in 1994, provided more than $1.6 billion to enable legal recourse by and financial restitution to women who were victims of violent crimes (Violence Against Women Reauthorization Act of 2019). In 2000, however, the U.S. Supreme Court struck down the provision that permitted women to sue their attackers. In 2012, the VAWA suffered another blow: Conservative lawmakers objected to extending protections to same-sex couples and to undocumented immigrants (Violence Against Women Reauthorization Act of 2019). The Act was reauthorized in 2013, but expired again in 2019. As of 2020, although it was passed in the House of Representatives, the VAWA is stalled by the U.S. Senate. What's the hold up? There are two primary issues (Belanger, 2020):

- *The "Boyfriend" Loophole:* As the law exists today, perpetrators who abuse current or former dating partners are not prohibited from owning firearms. The version of VAWA passed by the House closes this loophole. As you will learn in Chapter 15, more than one-half of all intimate partner homicides are committed by current and ex dating partners.
- *The "Stalker" Loophole:* Currently, only those convicted of felony stalking are prohibited from owning and/or accessing guns. Those perpetrators convicted of misdemeanor stalking are still allowed to own firearms. The version of VAWA passed by the House closes this loophole as well.

Advocates of the legislation that closes these loopholes contend that as long as perpetrators have access to firearms, women are not protected (Belanger, 2020).

Sexual harassment is any unwelcome sexual or physical conduct by either gender. The Equal Employment Opportunity Commission (2004) states that "unwelcome sexual advances, requests for sexual favors, and other verbal or physical conduct of a sexual nature constitutes sexual harassment when submission to or rejection of this conduct explicitly or implicitly affects an individual's employment, unreasonably interferes with an individual's work performance, or creates an intimidating, hostile, or offensive work environment." Sexual harassment is an issue wherein gender and authority are the central components. It involves the unfair use of power that one person exerts over another. It can occur in a work setting such as when a boss holds a good performance evaluation over the head of an employee by requesting sexual favors. It can also occur in academic setting, as in the following examples:

- A university freshman seeks help from his female teaching assistant. After going over the coursework, she suggests they go out to grab a bite to eat, indicating his grades might improve if he got to know her better.
- A female worker having a bad day at work is told by her male co-worker that maybe she is in a bad mood because she just needs to have more sex.

In some of the situations the harassment is obvious; in other cases it is subtler. Many people, *regardless of their gender,* who experience unwanted sexual comments or advances report feeling powerless to stop a situation. Many fear retaliation if the incidents are reported (such as receiving a lower grade or consequences at work), and as a result they may feel the need to change their major or drop a course, or they begin to have physical symptoms of stress. Mental health experts advise victims of sexual harassment not to ignore the behavior. College campuses and workplaces alike have an Affirmative Action office where the victim can file a complaint. Universities and colleges also have student counseling services. They emphasize that the victim hasn't done anything wrong and that the offending behavior was not just a joke. Such behavior is not a "guy/gal kind of thing." Sexual harassment has nothing to do with the intent of the offender ("I didn't mean it, it was only a joke!")—it has everything to do with its effect on the victim. *If the behavior is unwanted, it is sexual harassment.*

Violence Against Women Act of 1994 (VAWA):
federal law signed by President Bill Clinton in 1994 to provided more than $1.6 billion for financial restitution to women who were victims of violent crimes. The Act expired in 2019. As of 2020, although it was passed in the House of Representatives, the VAWA is stalled by the U.S. Senate.

Sexual harassment:
any unwelcome sexual or physical conduct by a person of either gender, directed to a person of either gender.

Taking Sides

Should Boys Play With Dolls? Should Girls Be Allowed to Play in Male-Dominated Sports, Such as Football?

Meredith is a 14-year-old freshman in high school. A gifted, talented athlete, she excels in every sport she plays, from volleyball to softball, from soccer to track, and from basketball to football. She began playing football in elementary school and played on the flag football teams for a number of years. She played football in junior high. Now that Meredith is in high school, she wants to continue playing football. This issue has started a heated battle between her parents.

Mom's Side: We have always taught Meredith that she can do anything she puts her mind to, whether it is in sport, in academics, or in her career someday. I think it's fine for Meredith to continue to play football. She is extremely talented in sports, and football is no exception to that. She excels in the sport and even has aspirations of playing Division 1 college football someday. No, we don't see female running backs in collegiate football. Who's to say Meredith won't be the one to change that some day? I fully embrace her decision to play high school football.

Dad's Side: I was okay when Meredith wanted to play football in elementary school and junior high school, but I cannot

endorse her decision to play high school football or college football. In the lower grades, Mere's physical stature was similar to boys'—one gender was not necessarily more muscular or taller than the other. But in high school those same boys are now becoming men. It is not about "gender" to me—it is about her getting hurt. Some of those young men will weigh over 300 pounds; Meredith barely weighs 130 pounds. I played high school football; I know where people get hit and I know how hard those hits are. Can a developing woman's body take those kinds of impacts? I don't know.

Your Side: If you were Meredith's parents, would you allow her to play high school football? In your decision-making process, consider the following questions:

1. Can young women physically compete against young men?

2. Is football socially constructed? In other words, has society defined the roles of the actors in football—that women are to be on the sidelines as cheerleaders or dancers and men are to be on the field as coaches, players, and referees?

3. Do existing beliefs about gender differences affect your decision? If so, how?

FAMILY LIFE EDUCATION: PRACTICING WITH SENSITIVITY AND RESPECTING DIVERSITY

In the words of my obstetrician, "Boy, girl, what does it matter?" As the opening story demonstrates, the issue of gender does matter to those individuals who feel they don't conform to society's gender expectations.

Even though we are early in our study of couples and families, you are already beginning to see that professionals who work with individuals and families must do so with sensitivity, respecting the diversity of the people they serve. You have already learned that family life educators and other helping professionals communicate through their beliefs, their values, and their work that "all families" and "all couples" includes LGBTQ+ persons and their families (Powers-Barker, 2020). When serving families, it is incumbent upon helpers and educators to know and understand the characteristics of couples and families so that we are better able to provide relevant, accurate, beneficial content and programming (Powers-Barker, 2020). When we do, we create a safe space for all.

The simple truth is: Gender matters! It matters in our examination of marital, family, and intimate relationships because the socially sanctioned, approved, and endorsed gendered behaviors affect life roles, occupations, and every aspect of our interpersonal relationships. It matters in some parts of the world where adherence to gender roles and behaviors literally means life or death. It matters because of the countless social and environmental gender cues that surround us from the moment we are born. It matters because sometimes "boy" or "girl" isn't always a clear-cut determination. It matters because sometimes the outward signs of the biological sex are not congruent with how someone feels internally about his or her gender, as Amber's experiences show us. It matters because sometimes being a particular gender does not grant permission to those of the opposite gender to behave in a sexually offensive manner or perpetrate crimes against them. It matters because many gender-centered legal battles have shaped and continue to shape the fabric of the American family. It matters.

/// SUMMARY

The Biology of Gender

- Because men and women constitute the social, economic, and political reality of every society, it's important to understand both the nature influences of gender (the influences of biology) and the nurture influences of gender (environmental influences).

- Sex and gender are not interchangeable terms. *Sex* describes biologically determined characteristics, anatomical, hormonal, physiological. *Gender* encompasses society's expectations, such as how we behave and how we present ourselves.

- During fertilization, XX or XY chromosome pairs (inherited from the sperm and ovum) determine a person's sex

characteristics. The XX sex chromosome combination results in a "female" genetic blueprint, and the XY sex chromosome combination results in a "male" genetic blueprint.

- Rare cases of genetic anomalies can result in an intersexed condition such as hermaphroditism or Androgen Insensitivity Syndrome or other genetic conditions like Turner's Syndrome or Klinefelter's Syndrome. Genetic irregularities have presented tremendous medical management challenges, and although advances have been made, the standard of care for intersex persons is slow to change.

- A transgender person is someone whose gender identity does not line up with his or her biological sex.

The Culture of Gender

- Sociocultural gender assumptions assign prototypical male and female behaviors and traits.

- *Gender roles* are the explicitly expressed and implicitly implied behaviors, feelings, attributes, and traits and society expects of the male or the female.

- *Masculinity* and *femininity* are defined differently within cultures.

Gender Polarization: Complementary Opposites—Or Inequality?

- *Gender polarization* refers to the concept that masculinity and femininity are on opposites and ends of a continuum. Inherent to gender polarization is the emphasis of the differences between the genders. This emphasis leads to inequality, particularly in women's career advancements, earnings, and education.

- *Intersectionality* refers to the cultural patterns of oppression that are bound together in a society, such as race, gender, socioeconomic class, and ethnicity.

- *Gender stereotypes* are long-held assumptions about gender capabilities.

- *Gender schemas* are mental constructs of how a person internalizes specific gendered behaviors and expectations. Three such schemas are the *instrumental* schema ("getting the job done"), the *expressive* schema (relation oriented), and the concept of *androgyny,* where an individual can be both (or neither) masculine and feminine, but not one or the other.

The Theories of Gender Development

- Children learn to "do" masculine or feminine from their parents (heterosexual or homosexual), children's first and primary agents of socialization. They also learn what is appropriate for their gender through play.

- Peers reinforce stereotypical gender roles that children learn at home.

- Children's conceptions of gender are based primarily on what they see and hear, and beginning in early childhood, move and television viewers are exposed to numerous images of masculine and feminine "ideals." The social impact of distorted portrayals of women and men exacerbate and reinforce existing gender attitudes.

Gender and Contemporary Issues

- Gender issues play a significant role in legal and public policy.

- Nearly 100 years ago, the **Equal Rights Amendment (ERA)** was first introduced to the U.S. Congress in an effort to extend equal rights to women and to protect them from discrimination. To date, only 38 states have ratified the ERA.

- The **Violence Against Women Act of 1994 (VAWA)** is a federal law that enabled legal recourse and financial restitution to women who were victims of violent crimes. However, to date the U.S. Senate has held up the legislation because it does not prohibit perpetrators from owning firearms.

/// KEY TERMS

Androgens   113

Androgyny   132

Bipolar gender   120

Cisgender   117

Cognitive Development theory   135

Confidence gap   130

Disorders of sex development or DSD   113

Equal Rights Amendment (ERA)   144

Estrogen   113

Expressive schemas   131

Femininity   124

Gender   112

Gender binary   113

Gender constancy   136

Gender dysphoria   119

Gender expression   118

Gender fluid   117

Gender inequality   128

Gender nonconforming   117

Gender polarization   120

Gender role development   134

Gender roles   121

Gender schemas   131

Gender socialization   121

Gender stability   136

Glass ceiling   128

Hegemonic masculinity   121

Homosocial play   139

Instrumental schemas   131

Intersectionality   130

Intersex   113

Learning theory   134

Machismo   123

Marianismo   125

Masculine Gender Roles Stress theory (MGRS)   123

Masculinity   121

Nature   111

Nonbinary (NB)   117

Nurture   111

Sex confirmation surgery (SCS)   119

Sex reassignment surgery (SRS)   119

Sexism   128

Sexual harassment   145

Sexual preference   118

Sex   112

Sex hormones   112

sexual differentiation   112

sexual orientation   113

Social Learning theory (SLT)   134

Testosterone   113

Transgender   118

Transsexual   119

Violence Against Women Act of 1994 (VAWA)   145

Wage gap   129

XX sex chromosome   112

XY sex chromosome   112

Klaus Vedfelt/Getty Images

CHAPTER 5

INTIMACY: DEVELOPING AND EXPERIENCING AFFECTIONATE BONDS

LEARNING OBJECTIVES

5.1 Explain the role of intimacy in relationships.

5.2 Identify the components and characteristics of intimacy.

5.3 Summarize the stages of psychosocial development in children.

5.4 Summarize the stages of psychosocial development in adolescents.

5.5 Understand the barriers to developing, establishing, and maintaining intimacy.

....

At his zenith of fame and popularity, Academy Award winner Brad Pitt sat down for an interview with *Rolling Stone* magazine (Heath, 1999). In this interview, Pitt noted, "I know all these things are supposed to seem important to us—the car, the condo, our version of success—but if that's the case, why is the general feeling out there reflecting more impotence and isolation and desperation and loneliness?" He refers to the society-wide chase for success and wealth as a "numbing of the soul."

Although Brad Pitt possesses great looks, has enjoyed a successful acting career, and has achieved what many would consider tremendous success, the "guy who has everything" recognizes that great fame and wealth beyond what you and I can probably comprehend are not what brings happiness and contentment, not what brings a sense of richness and satisfaction in life. In his interview with *Rolling Stone* magazine, this popular, American cultural icon identified what he believes is perhaps an atrophy, a wasting away of a basic, necessary human need in our society—intimacy.

Much of what you learn throughout this academic term in your study of marriage and the family is interconnected. You will notice as you make your way through your course, for example, that sex and intimacy are as much interrelated as are intimacy and love, love and family communication, and family communication and parenting, circling back to parenting and intimacy, and so on. In fact, it is difficult to disentangle or separate one aspect of coupling, marriage, and family from another. This is the complex task of yesterday's and today's family scientists and family practitioners.

As we begin our in-depth examination of marital, family, and intimate relationships, it is important for you to keep in mind that I have broken the topics down into chapters for ease of study and discussion, but this in no way implies that they are separate areas of study. Remember, each and every chapter you read ties into and relates to the other chapters. As you read the chapters that follow this one, you may find yourself thinking, "Wait a minute . . . this sounds a lot like what we were studying in the love chapter," or "This area is very similar to the communication chapter." When you find yourself synthesizing and weaving together the material from one chapter to the next, then you will know that learning is taking place.

To understand the nature of intimate relationships among those people who are close to us, we must have a solid understanding of why we need to relate to others, how intimacy develops, and what happens to relationships when there are obstacles to the development of intimacy.

INTIMACY: DO WE HAVE A NEED TO RELATE TO OTHERS?

Man is by nature a social animal . . . anyone who either cannot lead the common life or is so self-sufficient as to not need to, and therefore does not partake of society, is either a beast or a god. (Aristotle, 384–322 B.C.E.)

iStock.com/Pekic

Human nature requires that each of us desires to be emotionally close to another person.

Aristotle penned these words centuries ago. Although our cultural experiences of intimate, marriage, and family life have changed since then, human nature has remained the same. As Aristotle recognized, the human race is a social people. We are *relational creatures* who seek—either by design or evolutionary drives—to be with another or to be with others. That's human nature.

We all want to belong to someone, to share with someone, to be intimate with someone. To be human carries with it almost a requirement of sorts that we relate to or relate with another human being, that we share intimacy with someone. Derived from the Latin word *intimus*, intimacy means inner or internal, or to come from within the individual. In personal relationships, intimacy is often conceptualized as a reciprocal trust between the partners, emotional closeness, and comfortable levels of self-disclosure in which partners can openly share their thoughts and feelings (Timmerman, 1991). It is a process of relating that promotes closeness, bondedness, and connectedness (Heller & Wood, 2000). Intimacy is thought to also include **responsiveness**, which is the verbal and/or nonverbal behavior that conveys support and affection to a partner (Miller, Berg, & Archer, 1983). Recall also from Chapter 3 that the multiple processes in interpersonal relationships are *transactional* and *interconnected,* which means that we simultaneously affect and are affected by our interpersonal relationships. So, if we weave together these concepts, we see that **intimacy** is the feelings of closeness that result from a transactional process between partners' self-disclosures and responsiveness (Marshall, 2008). In other words, as we self-disclose and share, and as our partner responds to these disclosures, our emotional bond to one another is strengthened and deepened. One researcher defines intimacy as "individuals' subjective experiences of closeness and connectedness with their romantic partners, which emerge from couple relationship processes that involve self-disclosure, mutual trust and validation, empathy, and acceptance (Yoo, Bartle-Haring, Day, & Gangamma, 2013, p. 1). Although the meaning of intimacy varies from relationship to relationship, physical closeness is not necessarily a component of intimacy. To be sure, relationship satisfaction is rooted in intimacy (Ubando, 2016).

Some sociologists and anthropologists believe that intimacy is the **need for affiliation**, or the need to have relationships in our lives, and that this is a universal, innate drive. They believe

Responsiveness: the verbal and/or nonverbal behavior that conveys support and affection to a partner.

Intimacy: loving relationships characterized by feelings of closeness, connectedness, and bondedness.

Need for affiliation: the universal and innate drive to have relationships in our lives.

that this may explain why intimate, interpersonal bonds are found the world over, across all ethnic and cultural boundaries (Erber & Erber, 2001). This drive for interpersonal relations is thought to fulfill important psychological needs. *Need fulfillment* was at one time considered to be perhaps *the* primary purpose and function of intimacy in marriage and family relationships (Clinebell & Clinebell, 1970).

Fulfilling Psychological Needs

Empirical investigation in the 1970s, 1980s, and much of the 1990s virtually ignored the concept of relationship intimacy as a contributor to psychological need fulfillment. Karen Prager, one of the definitive researchers in the area of marital and relational intimacy, and her colleague Duane Buhrmester (1998) sought to determine whether the presumed links between need fulfillment and intimacy would promote a better understanding of the link between couple intimacy and individual well-being. The primary goals of this study were to see if and in what ways intimate couple communication and various intimacy components contributed to the overall well-being of the individuals and how these also contributed to need fulfillment. Prager and Buhrmester's work concluded that relational intimacy, measured by a couple's daily interactions, positively correlates with individual need fulfillment. They found that through frequent, intimate communication in which partners' communications consist of a positive tone, daily personal sharing with the partner, listening, and understanding, *individual* psychological needs are met by way of the *couple*. Other bodies of research substantiate that high levels of intimacy in relationships enhance the psychological, physical, and relational well-being of each partner, as well as lower the risk of divorce (Aykutoğlu & Uysal, 2017; Triscoli, Croy, Olausson, & Sailer, 2017; Hassebrauck & Fehr, 2002; Firestone & Firestone, 2004; Schneller & Arditti, 2004; van Lankveld, Jacobs, Thewissen, Dewitte, & Verboon, 2018).

The universality of human relationships and the global drive of humans to connect to others can be explained by the survival needs that are met, such as safety, shelter, and provisional needs. But psychological needs must also be met. Sociologist Robert Weiss's (1969) discussion of sociability or friendliness suggests that when people form close interpersonal relationships, five essential psychological needs are met that cannot be met by other forms of impersonal human contact:

1. *Intimacy* is a basic, universal psychological need that drives us to share our innermost feelings with another or others.

2. *Social integration* is the innate need to belong to a social group. These needs propel us to vent our worries, fears, and anxieties with others.

3. We all have an internal desire to *nurture and to be nurtured,* to care for another and be taken care of.

4. At times we need *assistance* from others. Interpersonal relationships provide this.

5. *Reassurance* that we have worth and that we are wanted, needed, and loved comes from intimacy with another person.

Through our intimate relationships, our basic psychological needs and our basic relationship needs are met. These healthy intimate relationships, in turn, contribute to the overall well-being of each partner (Aykutoğlu & Uysal, 2017; Triscoli et al., 2017; Kirby, Baucom, & Peterman, 2005; van Lankveld et al., 2018).

The Role of Intimacy In Relationships

Intimacy is experienced differently from relationship to relationship. Its meaning varies not only from couple to couple but over time as well. For some couples, the experience of intimacy has to do with sharing moments of emotional closeness. For other couples, intimacy

For many couples, expressing affection and feelings of commitment and emotional closeness are important aspects of the intimacy they share.

is linked with sex or physical closeness. For still others, intimacy is a spiritual or religious experience. However couples define and experience intimacy, it is necessary to meaningful relationships, Multifaceted and multidimensional, intimacy's components vary from culture to culture, ethnicity to ethnicity, and person to person.

Intimacy Is Multicontextual

As Prager (1999) notes, each couple experiences intimacy and intimate relating in unique ways because of the many contextual factors that influence, impinge on, and nurture the couple's relationship. Figure 5.1 illustrates the multicontextual factors of intimacy.

According to Prager (1999), there are five different levels of intimacy contexts, which are shown in Figure 5.1. At the very center, the **immediate context** refers to factors that influence the couple's interaction, such as the physical setting (is it quiet, relatively free of interruptions, private?), the couple's mood during the intimate interaction, and the couple's reason for talking,

The **personal context** includes factors specific to each person, such as personality traits, attitudes and beliefs about the overall status of the relationship; emotional reactions to intimacy; willingness to self-disclose; and each partner's intimacy needs, goals, and motives. The level of a partner's individual development of intimacy influences how we experience intimacy; it will be different at different stages of our relationship development.

The **relational context** refers to characteristics of the relationship and how the couple defines it. Factors such as companionship, trust, level of commitment, each partner's intimacy needs, and the presence of or type of conflict are all part of the relational context. For example, if a couple has underlying conflict in their relationship, such as unresolved problems with the in-laws, this conflict is always in the background of the couple's relationship. Much like background noise that can interrupt or interfere with our concentration when reading, unresolved conflict can ultimately interfere with how each partner experiences elements associated with intimacy, such as trust and/or commitment.

The **group context** is the couple's social network, including each partner's family, peer relationships, neighborhood, and the community in which the couple lives. As Prager (1999)

Immediate context: factors influencing a couple's interaction, such as the physical setting, the couple's mood, and the couple's reason for talking.

Personal context: factors specific to each member of the couple, such as personality traits and the attitudes and beliefs about the overall status of the relationship; emotional reactions to intimacy; willingness to self-disclose; and each partner's intimacy needs, goals, and motives.

Relational context: characteristics of the relationship and how the couple defines it. Factors such as companionship, trust, commitment level, intimacy needs, and type of conflict.

Group context: the couple's social network of family, peers, and community.

Figure 5.1 /// The Many Contexts of Intimacy

According to Karen Prager (1999), there are five different levels of intimacy contexts. Intimate interactions can occur *between* aspects of each context as well as *among* all other contexts.

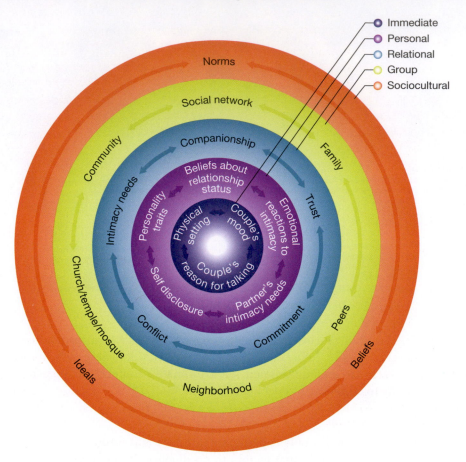

Source: 1999 from *The Intimate Couple* by J. Carlson and L Sperry (Eds.). Adapted by permission of Routledge/Taylor & Francis Group. LLC

reminds us, social networks are important because they provide couples with instrumental support, such as advice, assistance with needs, guidance, and emotional support. This support, in turn, supports intimacy levels within the couple's relationship. (In Chapter 14, when we turn our attention to family crisis, you will see how these group context resources aid families in navigating the difficult twists and turns of family life.)

Sociocultural context:

the norms, beliefs, and ideals of the culture and subcultures in which couples live and relate.

The **sociocultural context** is the overarching umbrella that contains such factors as the norms, beliefs, and ideals of the culture and subcultures in which couples live and relate. This context shapes each person's expectations about intimacy in her or his interpersonal relationships. Prager (1999) points out that it is society and culture that determine, or *prescribe,* how we are to intimately relate to another. In large part, it is the culture's social identity that emphasizes either the group's interests or the individual's interests. Particularly important is whether the culture defines itself as a collectivist culture or an individualistic culture. Recall from Chapter 1 that in collectivist cultures, individuals define their identity in terms of the relationships they hold with others, and because of this they give priority to the needs of the whole society, the collective. On the other hand, in individualistic cultures, personal needs guide behavior, rather than the needs of the society.

Social identity is important because it directly influences how we experience intimacy. For example, within individualistic (Western) cultures, *both* self-disclosure and responsiveness are important to the experience of a couple's intimacy, which ultimately determines to a large extent overall relationship satisfaction (Laurenceau, Barrett, & Rovine, 2005). But does this hold true for other cultures? In East Asian cultures, such as China, some research has discovered that *responsiveness* is a very necessary component of intimacy and that it heightens relationship satisfaction (Heine, 2001). Other research has shown that *self-disclosure* is less significant (Chen, 1995). In other words, in some collectivist cultures both components are not necessary for the experience of intimacy—only responsiveness is.

There is also evidence that gender roles are significantly influenced and shaped by the culture's social identity and that these gender roles then influence the experiences of intimacy. In China, for instance, traditional gender roles are emphasized. In these roles, wives are subordinate to husbands and are more likely to assume household and mothering roles, while their husbands are more likely to work (Marshall, 2008). Gender role traditionalism is associated with lower levels of self-disclosure in relationships because, as you saw in the previous chapter, men are not encouraged to reveal their feelings. Today, there is evidence that some Chinese men influence the levels of intimacy experienced within the relationship because of gender role traditionalism that inhibits self-disclosure (Marshall, 2008). Due to the transactional nature of intimacy, as Chinese men restrain self-disclosure, Chinese women reciprocate these low disclosures by lower levels of responsiveness, resulting in low levels of intimacy. This isn't to say, however, that there are lower levels of relationship satisfaction. Because the culture is a collectivist one and doesn't emphasize personal needs and wants, the lower levels of intimacy may not result in relationship dissatisfaction, as it would in individualistic cultures. The broader point to consider here is that cultural groups outside of the United States define and experience intimacy differently and that lower levels of intimacy may not be a negative influence on relationships.

Prager's (1999) multitiered model of the many contexts of intimacy is important in our discussion of intimacy because it provides a visual reference for the factors that influence how intimacy is shaped, expressed, and experienced. In Figure 5.1, note the interactions that occur *between* aspects of each distinct context; note the interactions that occur *among* each of the different contexts. Without question, these many contexts of intimacy determine and drive the extent to which intimacy is enhanced or hindered in our personal lives.

Intimacy Is an Emotional Attachment

Although the aspects of intimacy may vary from one person to another, intimacy in committed relationships can best be thought of as an emotional attachment to another person (Openshaw, 2004). **Emotional attachment** is at the core of all love relationships, and it is characterized by feelings that promote a sense of closeness, bonding with one another, and connection (Heller & Wood, 1998). These feelings of closeness and bonding promote the well-being of another. According to Prager (1999), intimacy can be thought of as a three-pronged process that involves (1) disclosing things that are personal and private to ourselves, (2) experiencing positive feelings about ourselves and the other person(s) involved in the relationship, and (3) having interpersonal interactions that serve to advance or reflect partners' understanding of each other. For instance, as a couple shares, over time, private things about themselves with one another, they negotiate the differences in the way they think, feel, and behave. This sharing leads to the couple's "speaking the same language," which, in turn, strengthens the couple's common bond and their emotional attachment to one another (Heller & Wood, 2000). It is this emotional attachment that distinguishes their relationship from any other couple relationship.

Emotional attachment: feelings that promote a sense of closeness, bonding with one another, and connection.

Intimacy Is a Process

Developing intimacy is a process, as it is dynamic and ever-changing. The term *process* implies *change* and *progression* over time. Just as we grow, change, and develop over time, so too do the contexts of our relational experiences. Intimacy is not a static or unchanging aspect of a relationship. The intimacy we share with our partners and family today will not be the same intimacy levels we share with them 5, 10, or even 20 years from now. As we get to know another person and as we begin to self-disclose our thoughts and feelings, personal sharing often leads to deepened levels of trust. This trust, in turn, facilitates greater self-disclosure and greater sharing of personal vulnerabilities, which even further deepens the level of trust (Heller & Wood, 1998). Over time, these interactions strengthen the intimate bonds couples and families share.

WHAT DO INTIMATE RELATIONSHIPS LOOK LIKE?

The exact experiences of intimacy are unique to each of us because as you're learning in our study of coupling and relationships, we each bring our own one-of-a-kind experiences to a relationship—and because of this uniqueness in experiences, the meaning of and degree to which we experience intimacy varies between relationships and even within the same relationship.

Components of Intimacy

What constitutes intimate relationships? Family researchers have attempted to answer this question through empirical study. From his research of intimacy among married couples, marriage therapist Edward Waring (1984) describes eight components of intimacy:

1. *Conflict resolution.* This component addresses how couples manage the inevitable conflict that occurs within the relationship and how they resolve differences of opinion. Effectively managing conflict optimizes high levels of intimacy.

2. *Affection.* How partners express affection and show feelings of emotional closeness are important aspects of intimacy and affect the degree to which partners self-disclose and the degree to which each reciprocates by sharing feelings and emotions.

3. *Cohesion.* This component looks at the degree to which the marriage relationship is valued—not only the level of commitment to the marriage but also each partner's sense of the other's level of commitment. A cohesive relationship fosters trust.

4. *Sexuality.* Not only is it important that each partner is able to communicate sexual needs, wants, and desires, but it is also important that each partner's sexual needs, wants, and desires are fulfilled by the marriage. This aspect of intimacy is considered the most intense togetherness a couple can experience.

5. *Identity.* Maintaining partners' individual identities is another aspect of intimacy that is important in order for both partners to be self-confident and have a high level of self-esteem. It is important that each partner's *individual* identity is not lost in the identity of the couple.

6. *Compatibility.* This component speaks to how partners relate to each other, work together, and play together. When intimacy exists, couples have a sense of comfort when they are together; they mutually fulfill the other's needs.

7. *Expressiveness.* The degree to which partners allow each other to know their most personal thoughts, beliefs, and feelings are strong indicators of intimacy.

8. *Autonomy.* Independence from a person's family of origin provides the emotional freedom a person needs to develop, nurture, and sustain intimacy with a partner.

Psychologist Bernard Schulman and his colleague have also determined, through scientific study, the relational components of intimacy (Peven & Shulman, 1999). Their work resulted in similar findings to Waring's. They, too, found that couples' ability to express themselves sexually, to resolve conflict, and to trust their partners influence and enhance marital intimacy. The researchers also found respect and the management of anger and warfare (times of conflict) to be components of intimacy. Social workers Mackey, Diemer, and O'Brien (2000) list personal disclosure, companionship, mutual appreciation, nonverbal communication, equity (mutuality in decision making), physical closeness (both sexual and nonsexual contact), and warmth as components of intimacy. And still other theorists have determined that love, affection, trust, and personal validation are components of intimacy (Berscheid, 1985; Hatfield & Rapson, 1993). There is no doubt that "intimacy" is a concept that means different things to different people.

Finally, other researchers have found spirituality and shared religious faith to be the foundation of all other components of intimacy. For example, shared religious and ethnic heritages provide couples with a useful resource and a strong foundation from which they can navigate and negotiate their differences (Heller & Wood, 2000). The shared religious beliefs provide common ground (the "glue") for the marital couple. Others also found spirituality and faith to be a foundation for marital intimacy. They note that sharing and self-disclosing of a person's spiritual life and self-disclosing through moments of shared prayer are "probably the strongest knot that binds a couple" (Morgan & Kuykendall, 2000, p. 60). Through the sharing of faith and religious customs such as prayer, maintain both Heller and Wood (2000) and Morgan and Kuykendall (2000), intimacy is intensified.

There are also gendered differences in how people define and experience intimacy. For example, earlier studies suggested that women initiate *verbal* intimacy with their husbands more than their husbands do with them, and they tend to define intimacy as "being" together with someone (Tannen, 1990). This finding shows us that, in general, women try to get closer to people by engaging in discussions with them; they also express more concern in their relationships than men do. Conversely, men have what is referred to as a "doing" orientation. That is to say, men prefer to engage in activities with their partners to show togetherness, rather than just "being" together. According to this body of research, then, women define and experience intimacy as "being," whereas men express "doing" characteristics of intimacy (Tannen, 1990).

In another body of research, investigators examined the attitudes and beliefs of nearly 400 undergraduate college students and found that there are sex differences in the experiences of intimacy (Hook, Gerstein, Detterich, & Gridley, 2003). In this study, women scored higher than men on the intimacy factors of love and affection and personal validation. These findings suggest that women place more emphasis on love, affection, emotional sharing, and the expression of tenderness (such as warm feelings) than men do. A surprising finding was that women and men did not significantly differ in their responses about trust as it relates to intimacy; both men and women expressed that they were comfortable with giving and receiving emotional support in relationships.

More recent research investigated relationship satisfaction, intimacy, and emotional expressivity in college students aged 18 to 24 (Ubando, 2016). Similar to studies in the past, this study revealed that both intimacy and emotional expressivity are tied to relationship satisfaction for both men and women. Similar to research in the 1990s, though, women indicated that they self-disclosed and shared more personal information with their male partners than men; they also reported feeling less trusting of and comfortable with their male partners than males reported with their female partners. Interestingly, males in this study perceived their intimacy to be high, even more so than women did.

Certainly, it is difficult to assess and define intimacy because of its multidimensional components and characteristics, but an understanding of this relationship process as a separate experience from love is important: If any component (however a couple defines it) is missing, relationship satisfaction will be negatively impacted (Hook et al., 2003). On the other hand, if couples work to discover—at the outset of their relationships—what factors of intimacy are important to them and in what ways they experience intimacy differently, then the gendered experiences and expressions of intimacy would no longer be an obstacle to relationship satisfaction (Hook et al., 2003).

Types of Intimates

Not only have family researchers over the years attempted to identify those components that make up intimacy, researchers and family practitioners have also attempted to define the different types of intimates. These typologies are categorized according to attributes that reflect an individual's capacity for intimacy.

Basing their work on Erikson's (1963) classic theory of intimacy development in young adulthood (which we will explore in depth a bit later in this chapter), psychologist Jacob Orlofsky and his colleagues (1973) developed specific types of intimates. Using a framework that has as its foundation *commitment,* the degree to which each partner in the couple is dedicated to the relationship, and *depth,* the closeness and involvement in the relationship, Orlofsky, Marcia, and Lesser (1973) identified **intimacy status**:

- The first intimacy status is the **intimate**. The intimate is capable of experiencing closeness, forming an emotional attachment to another, and is committed to depth in a relationship, which fosters long-term, enduring relationships. Intimates can be any age, and this intimacy status can be found in many types of relationships, such as marriage, same-sex partnerships, and even friendships. The distinguishing characteristic of intimates is that they possess the capacity to express their innermost feelings and thoughts with another person—this leads to deeper levels of commitment and closeness.

- A **pseudointimate** appears to be intimate on the surface but lacks depth. Pseudointimate relationships may never progress beyond friendship, or the pseudointimate may experience only superficial levels of emotional closeness in a dating, cohabiting, or marital relationship. Some pseudointimates bounce from one seemingly intimate relationship to another, but because of their inability to develop emotional closeness—and thus, their inability to fully commit to another person—these relationships are doomed from the outset.

- **Preintimates** are capable of intimacy, and may even desire it, but they lack the ability to make the commitment necessary to sustain long-term, or perhaps long-distance, relationships. For instance, education or career demands or a military deployment may impede someone from being able to fully commit to his or her partner until the individual's circumstances change. Some clergy, such as nuns and priests, may also be considered to be preintimates because their statuses preclude them from being able to share commitment and depth in a couple relationship.

- **Stereotyped relationships** are those in which an individual has any number of casual relationships; however, these relationships are devoid of depth and commitment. Unlike pseudointimates, where there is a superficial appearance that relationships are intimate even though they are not, in stereotyped relationships there is no representation of commitment or depth.

- **Isolates** are people who are socially withdrawn and have no apparent need for either social or close interpersonal interactions. For example, Ted Kaczynski is the infamous "Unibomber," a domestic terrorist in the United States from the 1970s through much of the 1990s. Until he was captured in 1996, Kaczynski lived in isolation and seclusion, away from human contact, for nearly 20 years.

Other intimacy researchers expanded the intimacy statuses developed by Orlofsky and colleagues to include the **merger status** (Whitbourne & Weinstock, 1979). These researchers contend that the intimate status requires partners in a relationship to experience an equal balance of power, or equity. When there is an imbalance of power, with one partner dominating, the partner being dominated feels a subsequent loss of autonomy and sense of individual identity. Because of this imbalance of power, a relationship may appear to have depth and commitment, yet it cannot reach the full status of intimate.

THE PSYCHOSOCIAL DEVELOPMENT OF CHILDREN

Although we are just at the start of our study of coupling, marriage, family, and intimate relationships, you have already discovered that much of our ability to relate to others in a meaningful way takes place during the very early years of life. Although each of us develops

Intimacy status: the commitment to and depth of a relationship.

Intimate: a person capable of experiencing closeness and forming a deep and enduring emotional attachment to another.

Pseudointimate: a person or relationship that appears to be intimate but lacks depth.

Preintimates: individuals who are capable of intimacy, and may even desire it, but lack the ability to make the commitment necessary to sustain long-term relationships.

Stereotyped relationships: relationships in which an individual has a number of casual relationships that are devoid of commitment.

Isolates: people who are socially withdrawn with no apparent need for social or close personal interactions.

Merger status: when intimate partners in a relationship experience an equal balance of power or merger.

iStock.com/RyanJLane

Although some parents may be concerned that picking up a baby when he or she is crying may spoil the child, researchers have discovered that doing so establishes a sense of trust in the infant. This trust is the foundation on which all other forms of intimacy are built throughout life.

the capacity to love and be intimate with others throughout infancy, childhood, adolescence, and early adulthood, it is the very early stages of life that establish the foundation of the ability to love and share intimacy. In a very real sense, the relationships experienced from the moment of birth help shape and mold a person's "intimate" self because each relationship formed during the first 20 years or so serves as a first-of-a-kind interaction upon which later interpersonal interactions and intimate relationships are built.

Recall from Chapter 1 that we do not develop in isolation; rather, our individual development takes place in the context of significant emotional relationships, particularly in our family of origin. This is true of the development of intimacy as well. The moment a baby is born, a mutual, interdependent relationship exists between the newborn and his or her caregivers. It is within the family context, in combination with the environment and other outside factors, that intimacy develops—in essence, we learn to be intimate (Cardillo, 2005). We have already established that intimacy is a universal human need. If this is the case, then do we really need to *learn* to be intimate, as Cardillo suggests? Erik Erikson's (1902–1994) theory of social and emotional development provides insight into this question. In the section that follows, we'll take a brief look at Erikson's theory because it allows us to see how our capacity to be intimate with another person develops over our lifespan.

Erikson's Theory of Psychosocial Development

Similar to the foundation of a house that is built, floor by floor, so too is the foundation of our ability to be intimate with another built, developmental stage by developmental stage. In the 1950s, psychologist Erik Erikson provided a lifespan approach to **psychosocial development**, which is the social and emotional development of an individual. Essentially, Erikson's **Eight Stages of Man** were formulated to put forth the notion that our social and emotional development is a lifelong process; that what happens or does not happen at one stage will eventually affect our psychosocial development during later stages of life. Table 5.1 outlines Erikson's eight developmental stages, which encompass what developmentalists refer to as a *cradle-to-grave* approach to understanding individual psychosocial development. We begin our study of intimacy formation by examining the early experiences in life, from infancy through the school years.

Psychosocial development: the social and emotional development of an individual.

Eight Stages of Man: Erik Erikson's theory that social and emotional development is a lifelong process that takes place in eight stages.

Table 5.1 /// Erikson's Developmental Stages

Influential psychologist Erik Erikson formulated the Eight Stages of Man developmental theory. According to Erikson, a person is in a continuous state of development from the cradle to the grave.

Erikson's Theory of Psychosocial Development

Stage	Age	Developmental Task
Trust vs. Mistrust	Infancy, 0–24 months	Child develops a belief that his or her caregivers will provide a secure and trustful environment
Autonomy vs. Shame and Doubt	Toddlerhood, 2–4 years	Child develops a sense of independence and free will; feels shame if he or she doesn't use the free will appropriately
Initiative vs. Guilt	Early Childhood, 4–6 years	"The Age of Acquiring": Child learns to explore his or her environment and acquires a newfound set of skills; feels a newfound sense of initiative and accomplishment
Industry vs. Inferiority	Middle Childhood, 7–12 years	"The Age of Mastery": Child masters the skills acquired during early childhood
Identity vs. Role Confusion	Adolescence, 13–21 years	Teen develops a sense of who he or she is in comparison to others (sense of "self"); develops a keen sense of role expectations
Intimacy vs. Isolation	Young Adult. 22–35 years	Develops ability to give and receive love; begins to consider long-term relationships, marriage, and parenting as realistic options
Generativity vs. Stagnation	Middle Adulthood, 36–65 years	Develops interest in giving of himself or herself to younger generations by helping them lead meaningful lives and by caring for them
Integrity vs. Despair	Older Adulthood, 65+ years	Desires to find meaningful and personal gratification with the life he or she has lived

Learning to Trust

The fundamental developmental task of infancy (0 to 2 years) is learning to *trust* our primary caregivers. During this time, if the child is nurtured, loved, and receives affection, he or she will develop a sense of trust and security. Every time a parent or caregiver responds to a baby's cries of distress or needs for attention, the adult sends resounding signals to the baby that the world is a safe place to be in. If, on the other hand, a parent or primary caregiver does not respond to the needs of the baby, or if the baby's distress signals are ignored or neglected, the baby will become insecure and mistrustful of others. It is during this time the child's initial capacity for intimate and loving relationships begins to take shape—and the foundation for *current and future intimacy* and loving relationships is laid.

Consider the following scenario. When my sons were younger, I took them to the city swimming pool one afternoon. While there, I saw a friend who had recently adopted a son. The child was about 3 years old at the time of his adoption; he had been removed from his birth mother's home because of neglect and physical abuse. The adoptive father and I engaged in conversation while his son played in the "kiddie" pool. He relayed to me how the child appeared to be withdrawn. He explained that his son would not snuggle or cuddle with them and would not respond to any displays of affection. A woman approached us and said, "Excuse me, but is that your little boy?" My friend looked up to see that his child had fallen and seriously cut his forehead. We might expect a 3-year-old who has banged his head to scream and cry or run over to a parent for emotional and physical comfort, but this little boy, cut and bleeding, did not cry. He did not come to his father for help. Instead, he got out of the swimming pool, lay down on the concrete, and put his head in his arms. Quiet. Not seeking help.

This story illustrates the significance of early relationships and their impact on relational intimacy in later life stages. Because this child received little or no nurturing and affection from his first intimate relationship—the mother-child relationship—he did not develop a sense of trust in his caregivers, as most children do. And because of this lack of trust, he did not turn to his father when he was hurt. Without a doubt, having security and comfort needs met in the early years of life plays a significant role in shaping intimate relationships (McAdams, 1989). In a very real sense, early intimate relationships provide a "crystal ball" that allows us to look into the future of a child's relational and intimacy abilities. This child's early experiences don't necessarily spell relational doom for him, however; there are many opportunities for him to form healthy attachments during his lifespan. (In Chapter 6 we more closely examine the development of trust and emotional attachment.)

Developing Independence

Through early childhood (age 2 through about 6) children develop independence, or *autonomy*, in their social and emotional capacities. This is important to the foundation of intimacy because it is this capacity that allows children to explore their environments with confidence and surety. This, in turn, helps children learn to get along and cooperate with others, as well as learn to relate to other family members and peers—all necessary components in the giving and receiving of intimacy later in life.

As children's sense of autonomy heightens during the preschool years, this drive for independence affects their relationships with peers. Their relationship with peers, however, is influenced by and embedded in their intimate relationships with their parents or primary caregivers. Research also indicates that children in this early stage of life are capable of expressing sensitivity and empathy in peer interactions; these abilities are key elements in intimate relationships when we are older (Prager, 1999; Prager & Buhrmester, 1998; Cardillo, 2005).

Childhood and adolescent friendships provide children with companionship and support for their emerging self-concepts and sense of identity. Think back to your childhood chumships. In what ways did these friendships promote your intimacy capacities? In what ways did these friendships hinder your intimacy capacities?

Consider the interaction and relational patterns between you and your parent(s) or primary caregiver. Did these experiences allow you to feel that you were worthy of affection and love? Or instead, did your early parent–child experiences cause you to feel shame, guilt, and doubt, resulting in fear of intimacy, fear of abandonment, betrayal, and rejection in your adult relationships?

Developing and Mastering Friendships

The elementary school years present a tremendous opportunity for social and emotional growth. For children in about first grade through sixth grade, the initiation and formation of peer groups increases, as does the significance of these relationships to the child's developing sense of self. As children move through elementary school, more and more of their time is spent interacting with same-sex peers. Be it a whispered secret during recess, a quick pickup game of basketball after school, or helping with the drudgeries of long division in a school hallway, childhood friendships provide children with great companionship and an opportunity to disclose their innermost secrets, wishes, and fears. In addition, childhood peer relationships afford children a "safely net" that allows them to practice and rehearse their new relational roles.

The formation of peer groups is a multistep process. An academic who studied the formation of friendships, D. C. Dunphy (1963) in a classic study examined adolescent friendship development in urban areas. The earlier stages of friendship development described by Dunphy are found during the school years:

Pre-crowd stage:
from about kindergarten through fifth grade, isolated same-sex peer groups exist in the form of cliques, or small groups, of four to nine members. Spontaneous shared activities provide the opportunity to relate personally.

- **Stage One: Pre-Crowd Stage.** From about kindergarten through fifth grade, during this stage of friendship development, isolated unisex peer groups exist in the form of *cliques*, small groups of four to nine members. Spontaneous, shared activities provide the opportunity to relate personally. Boys tend to join larger groups and enjoy doing activities together, whereas girls tend to join smaller, more intimate groups. These peer group types dominate the school years. It is not uncommon to see these types of peer groups on a school playground, where boys are excluding girls from their pickup football game at recess, or where girls forbid boys to listen in on their "girl talk." Members are attracted to one another on the basis of similar interests, neighborhoods, schools, or religions. Boys' groups are often larger and more stable than girls' groups (Atwater, 1992).

Beginning of the crowd:
still same-sex in nature, peer groups toward the end of sixth grade/ beginning of seventh grade begin to shift to crowds that consist of 10 or more core members. Crowd activities (dances, ball games, etc.) provide preadolescents the chance to "practice" interacting with the opposite sex.

- **Stage Two: Beginning of the Crowd.** Still same-sex in nature, peer groups toward the end of sixth grade or beginning of seventh grade begin to shift to *crowds,* which consist of 10 or more members. Crowds are essentially a collection of cliques—membership in cliques is required to belong to the crowd (Atwater, 1992). Crowd activities such as after-school dances and sporting events provide preadolescents the chance to "practice" interacting with the opposite sex, alleviating the uneasiness that often comes with opposite-sex relationships. For instance, Katie may have a crush on Danny, yet she flirts with all the other boys in her friendship crowd. In this way, she practices her newfound intimacy skills on others, without the risk of being rejected by Danny if she flirts with only him.

Crowd in transition:
during the end of junior high and throughout high school, peer groups are seen as in transition. Smaller cliques are formed within the larger crowd.

- **Stage Three: Crowd in Transition.** During the end of junior high (eighth or ninth grade) and throughout high school, peer groups are seen as in transition. During this time, smaller cliques are formed within the larger crowd. The pairing off of male and female couples, typically seen sooner in early maturing boys and girls, drives the crowd into transition. While the crowd may still hang out together for certain events, such as going to a movie or to a school basketball game, they more frequently begin to prefer to interact with the smaller group of friends and begin to exclude others from the emerging smaller clique.

Fully developed crowd:
a group of opposite-sex cliques; the same-sex friendship affiliations from elementary school and early years of junior high are no longer dominant.

- **Stage Four: Fully Developed Crowd.** The fully developed crowd is composed entirely of opposite-sex cliques; no longer are the same-sex friendship affiliations dominant as they were throughout elementary school and the early years of junior high. Peer groups during this stage exist only long enough for members to learn or to be socialized into those characteristics needed for adult relationships, such as sharing intimate thoughts and feelings and interdependence.

- **Stage Five:** Crowd Disintegration. As adolescents mature into adulthood and take on adult responsibilities, such as a job or pursuing a college degree, and as they become involved in serious intimate relationships, crowd-type friendship groups begin to disintegrate. Often the support of friends is replaced by an intimate partner with whom young adults now share and disclose, and with whom they are perhaps sexually involved. Friendship groups consequently become more loosely associated. Over time, many find their spouse or life mate to be their "best" friend, although they still hold on to one or two close friends.

Other researchers have since found peer group formation to be similar to Dunphy's original 1960s study of peer group formation (Atwater, 1992; Paul & White, 1990).

What is it that makes friendship so special or so different from other kinds of relationships in our lives? Research has shown that friendships, unlike family relationships, provide us more feelings of freedom, closeness, and pleasure; we are also able to experience higher levels of self-disclosure with our friends than we do with our families (Mendelson & Kay, 2003; Rybak & McAndrew, 2006). Furthermore, friendships are often quite emotionally rewarding because the sharing that takes place between friends fosters the growth and development of empathy. Empathy is the capacity to understand another's circumstances or situation and the ability to feel or express emotional concern for another person. It is believed that the experiences of empathy are what lead to a greater sensitivity—and emotional bond—to each other, both in friendships and any other intimate relationship (Rybak & McAndrew, 2006).

As you can see from Dunphy's (1963) study, as children grow through childhood and enter adolescence, their dependence on their parents for intimacy lessens and they turn to "chumships" for support. It is also interesting to note how the changes in friendships are associated with life transitions. Some researchers have discovered that maintaining and adapting friendships throughout these life changes helps buffer the stress associated with major transitions, such as going away to college or getting married (Brooks, 2002; Oswald & Clark, 2003). It is important to understand these developmental changes in peer groups structures and the significance of friendships because each type of friendship group (intimate relationships) throughout life affects a person's psychosocial development in all subsequent stages of life. During adolescence, intimate friendships contribute to adolescents' identity formation and the establishment of their autonomy, intimacy, and sexuality.

ADOLESCENTS' AND YOUNG ADULTS' PSYCHOSOCIAL DEVELOPMENT

The adolescent period of human growth and development is a time of many transitions for the teen. According to adolescent intimacy researcher D. Kim Openshaw (1999), the biological, cognitive, and psychosocial changes that occur during adolescence trigger a change in teens' *need* for intimacy. These changes, in turn, create a change in teens' *capacity to experience* intimate relationships and the extent to which and the way in which intimacy is expressed.

Along with the physical changes that take place during puberty come changes in teens' cognitive capabilities, as well as growth and change in the social and emotional areas. Family practitioner and professor of child development Angela Huebner (2000) provides a thorough discussion of these psychosocial changes. The following key points highlight her findings.

Establishing an Identity, Autonomy, and Intimacy

In order to experience healthy intimate relationships in later stages of adult development, an individual must first have a strong sense of identity, or the sense of "who" he or she is

Crowd disintegration: as adolescents mature into adulthood and take on adult responsibilities, such as a job, and as they become involved in serious intimate relationships, crowd-type friendship groups begin to disintegrate. Often the support of friends is replaced by an intimate partner with whom young adults now share and disclose.

Empathy: the capacity to understand another's circumstances or situation and the ability to feel or express emotional concern for another person.

Identity: an individual's sense of who she or he is.

(Erikson, 1963). Friendships play a key role in the adolescent's social, emotional, and relational development.

The questions "Who am I?" and "Why am I on Earth?" occupy an adolescent's thoughts, and over the course of the adolescent developmental period, teens incorporate their beliefs, values, and opinions of influential others (parents, peers, teachers) into their own identity. At the same time, adolescents begin the process of **individuation**—that is, forming an identity that is separate from that of their family of origin.

This developmental process of individuation affects the development of intimacy because as teens open up and disclose to their peers, it helps them clarify their own thoughts and emotions and thus helps them better define their own uniqueness (German, 2002). As teens share with their peers and the significant others in their lives, they develop a deeper understanding of not only themselves but also of others. Intimate friendships are more common during adolescence because teens feel that it's safer to reveal their thoughts and feelings to friends rather than to family (Berndt & Savin-Williams, 1990). In essence, teens feel that because others their same age are going through similar experiences, they are better able to relate. The outcome of this process is that as adolescents approach the transition to early adulthood, they have a clearer sense of their values, beliefs, and relationship expectations. This enhanced sense of identity promotes intimacy.

Teens must also develop **autonomy**, which refers to not only establishing a sense of independence but also becoming a self-governing person within the context of relationships. Adolescents must begin to take responsibility for their actions and decisions that affect themselves and, in many cases, those around them. For instance, if an adolescent chooses to have unprotected sex, he or she must realize that this decision may carry associated risks, such as acquiring a sexually transmitted infection or resulting in an unwanted pregnancy, and that these risks don't just affect them but their partner and families, as well.

As we discussed earlier in this chapter, the capacity for intimacy is acquired from the moment of birth, from our very first intimate relationship with our parent(s) or primary caregiver. As we develop throughout our early childhood and our school years, our peers become increasingly important to us, and also to the formation of our capacity for intimacy. Perhaps more than at any other time in our lifecourse development, it is during adolescence that friends are most significant. Through friendships we learn to be open and honest, to self-disclose, to share empathy, and to trust. These are the foundations of intimacy.

During adolescence, friends provide advice, counsel, comfort, ego strokes, and a sense of belonging. As we progress through adolescence and approach early adulthood, our friendships move from same-sex group interaction, to mixed-sex interactions, to coupling or pairing off, to eventually having only a select, few friends.

Establishing Comfort With Sexuality

We are all sexual beings. Our capacity to engage with another person on a sexually intimate level is a process that begins during the prenatal period. The discovery process begins for adolescents, however, as they experience the biological, cognitive, and psychosocial changes that we have just discussed. These changes lead adolescents to explore who they are sexually, perpetuating the desire to become sexually intimate with another.

As the adolescent experiences the changes in cognition and thought processes, his or her need for intimacy changes—there is much to make sense of in this world, and reaching out to another who is experiencing the world as an adolescent helps teens navigate these changes. As adolescents individuate, find their own identity, and are given more freedom, their capacity to have intimate relationships changes. This, too, is seen in the formation and maintenance of peer relationships. As adolescents undergo the physiological changes associated with puberty, they have a new way in which to be intimate with others—sexual intimacy is now possible. Of course, there is much, much more to being sexually intimate than the sex

Individuation:
the process of forming an identity separate from one's family of origin.

Autonomy:
one's desire to self-rule, or one's will.

act itself (such as being comfortable with our sexual skin or being comfortable expressing our sexuality). We will examine sexual intimacy in great detail in the sexuality chapter later in this text.

It is important to note that there are differences between male intimacy experiences and female intimacy experiences. There are also cultural differences.

Experiencing Gender Differences in Friendships

How do male friendships differ from female friendships? As you saw from Dunphy's (1963) study, as children mature, their peer groups shift in gender preference. As the shifts in gender preference occur, other discrepancies between males and females emerge:

- Females attach more emotional importance to their friends than do males (Lempers & Clark-Lempers, 1993).
- Men are less expressive and supportive toward friends than women are (Bank & Hansford, 2000; Burleson, 2003).
- Men are less likely to turn to their friends in time of trouble than women are (Rubin, 1986).
- Females more strongly emphasize mutual understanding, security, and mutual exploration of interests than do males (Kuttler, LaGreca, & Prinstein, 1999).
- More so than males, females discuss family problems and activities, personal dreams, fears, personal problems, and secrets (Johnson & Airies, 1983).
- Males emphasize activity and achievement in their group friendships; they show less interest in reciprocity/mutuality and support/caring than do girls (Thorne, 1986).
- Males discuss sports and hobbies more than females do (Johnson & Airies, 1983).

Researchers believe that the differences found between male and female friendship experiences are due to socialization patterns, or **gender typing** (Johnson & Aries, 1983; Kuttler et al., 1999). As you learned in Chapter 4, male socialization tends to emphasize the establishment and maintenance of achievement, whereas female socialization tends to emphasize the importance

Gender typing: the process of developing the behaviors, thoughts, and emotions associated with a particular gender.

iStock.com/SolStock

Research has found that commonly, male friendships emphasize participating together in activities, and that men are less likely to turn to their friends in times of trouble than women are. In what ways do you agree or disagree with these research findings? Do you think that gender differences in friendships are changing along with society's understanding of "gender"? If so, in what ways?

of the establishment and maintenance of interpersonal relationships. Recent empirical study has revealed that gender typing affects the type of communication between friends (Basow & Rubenfeld, 2003). For example, women are more likely to try to resolve a problem, offer sympathy, and share a similar story as a response to a friend with a problem, whereas men are more likely to try to resolve the problem, tell the friend not to worry, or change the subject in a similar circumstance (Basow & Rubenfeld, 2003). There are also gender differences in feelings and emotions in response to being given advice from a friend—women are more likely to feel comforted and grateful when advice is offered by a friend, whereas men are more likely to feel angry and hurt.

Some research suggests that there is still much to learn about friendships, particularly in the area of cross-sex friendships. **Cross-sex friendships (CSFs)** are friendships between different-sex peers. For many decades, CSFs were viewed by researchers as potential romantic attractions between partners, and not as friendships (Bleske-Rechek & Buss, 2001). Today, however, empirical study is beginning to view CSFs as qualitatively different from both romantic relationships and friendships in four distinct areas: defining the relationship, managing sexual attraction, establishing equality, and managing the interference of other friends and family (such as pushing the cross-sex friends to pursue dating; Lenton & Webber, 2006).

A number of other studies show us that

- Men have more CSFs than women do (Reeder, 2003). This may be because men view the friendship as a potential gateway to sexual interaction; it may also be because men are more comfortable sharing their thoughts and feelings with a woman rather than a man.
- Men may gain intimacy from their female friends (West, Anderson, & Duck, 1996).
- Women may gain protection from their male friends (Bleske-Rechek & Buss, 2000).
- Cross-sex friendships may be a mate acquisition strategy for women (Bleske-Rechek & Buss, 2001).
- Some men and women may use CSF as a way to become exposed to more opposite-sex people, thus increasing their chances of meeting a romantic partner (Monsour, 2002).
- More single people have CSFs than married people (Lenton & Webber, 2006).
- "Feminine" people (both men and women) report having more female than male friends; "masculine" people (both men and women) report having more male friends (Reeder, 2003).

The research about core qualities of face-to-face friendships is robust. But given that many of us—regardless of our age—connect with friends online, it's important to understand in what ways technology impacts friendships. Connecting online may be commonplace today, but still little empirical evidence exists that helps us to see if there are any differences between traditional friendship formation/maintenance and those friendships that are essentially maintained online. One body of research set out to determine if the quality of offline friendships is present in digital interactions (Yau & Reich, 2018). The researchers looked at six key areas of friendship: self-disclosure, validation, companionship, instrumental support, conflict, and conflict resolution. They found that it didn't matter whether the friends were interacting in person or via technology—the six core qualities of friendship persist.

All of these recent findings are interesting because they point to potential societal changes in how and why we select the friends that we do and to changes in how we select potential mates. Much more study needs to be done to understand the multiple factors associated with CSFs and to understand the benefits of these relationships to the development of intimacy.

So far we have discovered that there are differences between male intimacy experiences and female intimacy experiences. Considering the intrinsic diversity within contemporary society, another question remains to be answered: How do cultural differences influence adolescent friendships and intimacy?

Cross-sex friendships (CSFs):

friendships between different-sex peers.

LGBTQ+ Friendship Experiences

Even though the importance of friendships to children's, adolescents', and young adults' mental health and well-being is firmly established, scant literature exists that speaks to the friendship experiences of LGBTQ+ individuals. As you have seen so far, friendships—and the intimacy they provide—positively impact development because of the social and emotional benefits they offer. But given that friendships also help people to learn more about themselves and to develop their unique identities, how do sexual orientation and sexual identity affect friendship experiences? What do we know about friendship experiences of LGBTQ+ young adults?

Up to this point, LGBTQ+ friendship research has put its attention to better understanding how friendships form between LGBTQ+ individuals (Galupo et al., 2014). According to psychologist M. Paz Galupo of Townson University, Maryland, friendships are critically important for gays, lesbians, bisexual, and transgender individuals because these friendships "function as families of choice, and serve to buffer gender and sexual minorities from social isolation or rejection associated with homophobia and transphobia" (Galupo et al., 2014, p. 2). Groundbreaking bodies of science further helps to inform our understanding and importance of LGBTQ+ friendships:

- Friendships within the LGBTQ+ community provide emotional support (Hines, 2007).
- Friendships provide opportunities to gain comfort in sharing experiences with coming out (Hines, 2007).
- These friendships provide opportunities for transgender people to share their knowledge and decision-making process about transitioning with others (Galupo, 2007, 2009).
- LGBTQ+ friendships provide the unique benefit of helping one another to emotionally process their orientation and identity minority statuses (Galupo, 2007, 2009).
- LGBTQ+ friendships are seen as providing "needed counseling that [is] unavailable from the traditional healthcare system" (Galupo et al., 2014, p. 2).
- Friendships fill in the gaps of support in society—vitally necessary in a society where LGBTQ+ identities are at odds with established social norms (Galupo et al., 2014).

Galupo et al. (2014) studied 536 gender-variant individuals. Their results provide us a deeper understanding of the benefits and barriers across gender identity and sexual orientation of a friend. The results are presented in Table 5.2. As you can see, there are specific pros and cons in friendship experiences.

Table 5.2 /// Friendship Benefits Across Gender Identity and Sexual Orientation of a Friend
Benefits of Friendships With Transgender People and Sexual Minorities
Understanding sexual minority and transgender experiences
Knowledgeable on issues of gender, sex, and privilege
Shared experiences
Can talk about transgender issues
Offers support via mentoring and shared resources
Comfortable being myself
Shared community: "Family" and belonging
Non-judgmental/open-minded
Accepting
Affirmative use of language in reference to identity
Opportunity for dating/sexual partners

(Continued)

Table 5.2 /// (Continued)

Benefits of Friendships With Cisgender and Heterosexuals

Helps me feel "normal"
Transgender/sexuality issues don't dominate the conversation and friendship
Validation more powerful from someone with normative identity
More opportunity for friendships due to larger population
Helps me present as identified gender ("Pass")
Accepting
Affirmative use of language in reference to identity
Offers more diverse perspectives and interactions

Barriers of Friendships With Transgender People and Sexual Minorities

Invalidating gender identity and personal experience
Transgender issues dominate conversation and friendships
Negative emotions, drama, and emotional instability
Fear of being "outed" by association or disclosure

Barriers of Friendships With Cisgender and Heterosexuals

Not knowledgeable on issues of gender, sex, and privilege
Insensitive use of language in reference to identity
Difficult to talk about transgender/sexuality issues
Fosters feelings of discomfort
Not understanding non-normative experience
Fewer shared experiences

Culture/Ethnicity and Friendship

Despite the fact that the United States is rich in cultural diversity, scant research exists that examines the influences of culture and/or ethnicity on friendship formation.

In a study of the formation of adolescent friendships, researcher Caryn Dolich (2005) examined three cultures in an attempt to determine whether cultural differences affect males' and females'

Research shows that interracial friendships provide richness to college students' university experiences.

iStock.com/FatCamera

Should Parents Put Themselves and Their Desires Ahead of Their Children?

In 2014, when the *New York Times* covered a story about the parents of 1-year-old and 3-year-old children who decided to sail 3,000 miles on the open sea from San Diego, California, to New Zealand—with the tots on board the sailing vessel—little did they know that their news report would open up a colossal debate on social media about whether or not parents should put their lifestyle desires ahead of their children. When the 36-foot sailboat became disabled, the Kauman family was stranded 900 miles off the coast of Mexico—away from urgent medical care needed for their ill 1-year-old infant. Their choice to sail with toddlers spurred great debate in the United States, and people were infuriated that parents would endanger their children's lives. As one commenter said, "This is tantamount to child abuse." Others referred to the parents as neglectful. The most common thread of the comments, though, was that the parents were selfish for putting their dream of sailing from the U.S. to New Zealand ahead of their children's well-being. "Why have kids if you think they interfere with your life so much?" wrote one observer. Another commented, "It's not selfish for parents to want to go on an adventure. It crosses over to selfish when they choose to endanger the lives of their children."

As you've seen in our study in this chapter, intimacy is especially important for successful couple relationships and marital satisfaction and happiness. Should parents put themselves and their desires ahead of their children?

YES: Couple and family therapists Linda and Charlie Bloom (2011) note that there are negative outcomes when one or both parents give a higher priority to children than to their marriage. By making the needs of the children more important than the needs of the couple, parents

- neglect the needs of the marriage, which leads to resentment, resignation, and alienation in themselves and/or each other
- erode the quality of their emotional and physical connections

Sources: Bloom and Bloom (2011); Ashton-James et al. (2013).

- send a message to the children that marriage makes people unhappy

The bottom line? Devoted parents do not produce happy children (Code, 2009). David Code, family coach and minister, believes that parents today are essentially having affairs with their children: Many couples today go too far, letting their entire worlds revolved around their children.

NO: A common feature of modern parenting is "child-centrism," meaning parents put their children's needs above their own (Ashton-James, Kushlev, & Dunn, 2013). Although many family scientists and therapists believe that putting the kids first almost always undermines the couple's relationship, this isn't necessarily so, according to one body of research:

- parents who put their kids first report getting much happiness and meaning from their parenthood experiences
- greater child-centrism is associated with more positive emotions for parents, fewer negative emotions, and greater meaning in life
- personal well-being is associated with investing in others rather than oneself (Ashton-James et al., 2013)

What Do You Think?

1. Do you positively or negatively assess the parents' decision to take their children on a lengthy sailboat trip? What is your reasoning?

2. What do you think the benefits are for parents who continue to fulfill their personal desires after becoming parents? What are some potential drawbacks for parents who choose to be child-centric and lessen the priority of their own needs and wants?

3. Are parents who put their own needs first selfish? Are parents who put their children's needs ahead of their own having "affairs" with their children? If you choose to become a parent, which camp do you think you'll be in? Why?

friendships. She compared the differences in aspects of friendship among Moroccan, European, and American adolescents. Dolich found that within all of the cultures, females reported higher ratings of the importance of intimacy and companionship than did males. In addition, she found that among the cultures, females discussed personal and daily events/trivial issues more frequently than males did. Consistent with prior research (such as Johnson & Airies, 1983), females among the three cultures in Dolich's study developed more intimate and personal relationships than males did. However, unlike the results found in previous research, the males in Dolich's study did report that they discuss with some frequency such things as intimacy, family relationships, dating, and sex with opposite-sex friends. Dolich's study did not determine whether culture ultimately influences the experience of friendship during adolescence.

Contact hypothesis:
the idea that negative stereotypes (prejudices) about other groups exist because of the lack of contact and interaction between groups.

The **contact hypothesis** maintains that negative stereotypes (prejudices) about other groups exist because of the lack of contact and interaction between racial groups (Allport, 1958). Given that college and university campuses are often the most racially and ethnically diverse environments that most students have experienced, does this mean that the college environment translates into a more diverse friendship network? Some studies have shown that greater diversity in junior high and high school does foster the development of relationships across racial and ethnic lines and that intergroup contact leads to improved racial attitudes (Duncan, Boisjoly, Levy, Kremer, & Eccles, 2003; Quillian & Campbell, 2003; Sacerdote & Marmaros, 2005). This intergroup contact, in turn, leads to fewer negative stereotypes (Pettigrew & Tropp, 2006). Unfortunately, to date little research exists about interracial/ethnic friendships in college, but one recent study gives us insight into these friendship experiences.

In a study of nearly 4,000 white, Black, Hispanic, and Asian first-time college students in the United States, the investigator sought to determine friendship diversity on college campuses (Fischer, 2008). White and Black students reported that most of their friends belong to the same racial/ethnic group as they do; there are few cross-group friendships. Asian and Hispanic students reported fewer same-group friendships. Furthermore, students who had more diverse friendship networks in high school were more likely to report having cross-group friends in college. These findings about diversity in friendships are important because past research has shown that interracial friendships are rewarding experiences.

In the United States, 60 percent of teens say they have a close friend who is of a different race or ethnicity (Pew Research Center, 2018). While in the past interracial friendships were largely the result of demographic characteristics, such as living in the same neighborhood, today this isn't necessarily so. Today, white, African American, and Hispanic teens are likely to say they have a racially or ethnically diverse friend, regardless of living in proximity to their friends (Pew Research Center, 2018). Technology may play a part in these friendship formations. For example, as Figure 5.2 shows us, online forums appear to play a significant role in exposing teens to new types of people (particularly among Black teens) and making them feel more accepted.

Figure 5.2 /// Why Teens Spend Time in Online Forums

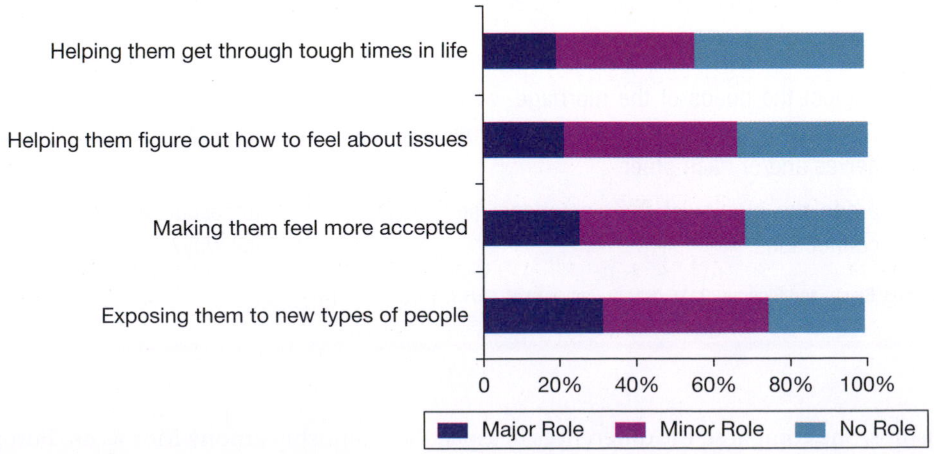

Source: Pew Research Center (2018).

As you can see from our discussion, there are differences in how each gender experiences intimate relationships with others. Cultural and ethnic differences also appear to enrich the adolescent and young adult developmental periods. Within these friendships, adolescents establish their unique identities and intimacy.

Forming Deeper Bonds

Each time I attend a high school graduation ceremony, I can't help but smile as graduate after graduate crosses the platform. As the adolescent crosses the platform to receive the high school diploma and tries to remember which hand to shake with, so much more is taking place than is visible to the casual observer. This ceremony represents a bridge between adolescence and early adulthood, taking most adolescents from total dependence on their family of origin to more independent emotional, moral, and financial responsibility. The platform on which the diploma is received seems to be launching the adolescent into a new phase of development. So it seems appropriate that early adulthood is often referred to as the *bridge years*.

During the years between adolescence and middle adulthood, young men and women find themselves accepting both the rewards and challenges of independence and the responsibility that accompanies autonomy. Along with this independence, young adults begin examining the qualities they find desirable in a life partner or spouse and begin to contemplate the commitment of marital and life-partnering relationships. The notion of bearing children also becomes more appealing and more realistic.

Social and emotional development during early adulthood is marked with the formation of deeper intimacy in interpersonal relationships. These intimate relations differ from childhood and adolescent friendships in that they involve a greater level of mutuality, respect, reciprocity, and self-sacrifice. Erikson (1986) suggested that these intimate relationships are essential to healthy development and without such, developing adults are at risk for an isolation-filled life. More attention will be given to adult (early, middle, and late) development throughout this textbook.

We saw earlier how the process of intimacy development unfolds from the moment of our birth, as we experience our first intimate relationship with our parents or primary caregiver, and continues throughout infancy, early childhood, childhood, the teen years, and early adulthood. Our intimacy capacity does not develop in one isolated period in our lifespan; rather, it is a *continuous* process that is built on as we make our way through the lifecourse. It is the relationships that we are born into, are surrounded by, and surround ourselves with that ultimately shape our intimate selves. The Miller Social Intimacy Scale (MSIS) helps people assess their levels of intimacy (see Table 5.3).

OBSTACLES TO INTIMACY

Because we each have different needs and capacities for intimacy, we may find that our need for intimacy is not the same as that of our partner or significant other. Similarly, we may find that the needs of our family members may be different from our own. Thus, we can think of intimacy as a continuum; at one end is total isolation with no need for intimacy, and at the other end there exists total enmeshment, where partner or family intimacy needs so overlap that it is difficult to distinguish whose need is whose. Neither extreme is healthy. Such differences may lead to significant levels of relationship discord.

Barriers to Developing Intimacy

Intimacy is achieved as we build trust with another person and as we disclose our innermost feelings and thoughts. There are many reasons why some relationships experience poor levels of intimacy, including lack of communication, work-related pressures, and financial

Table 5.3 /// Miller Social Intimacy Scale (MSIS)

The Miller Social Intimacy Scale was developed to assess people's levels of intimacy. The 17-item scale requires participants to assess, among other things, their displays of affection and their levels of self-disclosure in close relationships. Scores can range from 17 (the lowest level of intimacy) to 85 (the highest level of intimacy). The scale is used by social and family scientists to examine couple and family intimacy, but it is also used by some social workers and other mental health professionals to assess intimacy levels of those who commit crimes such as child molestation.

	Very Rarely		Some of the Time		Almost Always
1. When you have leisure time, how often do you choose to spend it with him/her alone?	1	2	3	4	5
2. How often do you keep very personal information to yourself and do not share it with him/her?	1	2	3	4	5
3. How often do you show him/her affection?	1	2	3	4	5
4. How often do you confide very personal information to him/her?	1	2	3	4	5
5. How often are you able to understand his/her feelings?	1	2	3	4	5
6. How often do you feel close to him/her?	1	2	3	4	5
7. How much do you like to spend time alone with him/her?		2	3	4	5
8. How much do you feel like being encouraging and supportive to him/her when he/she is unhappy?	1	2	3	4	5
9. How close do you feel to him/her most of the time?	1	2	3	4	5
10. How important is it to you to listen to his/her personal disclosures?	1	2	3	4	5
11. How affectionate do you feel toward him/her?	1	2	3	4	5
12. How important is it to you that he/she understands your feelings?	1	2	3	4	5
13. How much damage is caused by a typical disagreement in your relationship with him/her?	1	2	3	4	5
14. How important is it to you that he/she be encouraging and supportive to you when you are unhappy?	1	2	3	4	5
15. How important is it to you that he/she shows you affection?	1	2	3	4	5
16. How important is your relationship with him/her in your life?	1	2	3	4	5
17. How satisfying is your relationship with him/her?	1	2	3	4	5

Total Score: _____

Source: Adapted from Miller and Lefcourt (1982).

difficulties. Every close relationship experiences lapses in intimacy from time to time; however, researchers have found the family environment and the family's past experiences to be essential components in establishing intimacy.

Our Family Environment

Family environment is a key player in people's capacity to experience and express intimacy. As you saw in Chapter 3, different families and different cultures relate and communicate in different ways. For example, each culture has its own standards about nonverbal communication, such as how much distance between the communicators is acceptable or how much eye contact can be made. Each culture also has its own rules about emotional expression or the expression of intimacy, such as what kind and how much. In Asian cultures, for instance, emotional reserve is not only expected, it is cherished (Prince & Hoppe, 2000). On the other hand, in Italian and Greek cultures, feelings are freely expressed, often loudly (Prince & Hoppe, 2000).

Just as culture influences our experiences and expressions of intimacy, past family experiences are very much a part of present relationships. Family scientist Danielle Sjoberg (2002) sought to understand parent–adolescent relationships and how they relate to intimacy formation. She examined the ways in which having close relationships with a parent or parents impacts intimacy formation in later life.

The relationships adolescent boys have with their fathers, for example, has more impact on intimacy formation than does their relationship with their mothers. Good communication with fathers was linked to close, personal relationships in adolescent boys. These boys had more close friends, longer friendships, and higher self-esteem. The significance of the boys' relationships with their fathers cuts across ethnic and racial differences. Sjoberg's findings indicate that meaningful relationships with fathers helps adolescent males achieve close, personal, and enjoyable relationships with their peers.

In contrast, Sjoberg's review of studies indicates that adolescent girls from single-parent homes headed by mothers are more likely to become teen single mothers, engage in high levels of sexual activity, and experience poorer interpersonal relationships with the opposite sex. Father-absent females tend to experience less intimacy in their marriages than father present females.

In her review, Sjoberg notes that children raised in same-sex parent households experience little or no differences in the kinds and levels of intimacy compared to those children reared in opposite-sex parent homes. Sjoberg concludes that it is not the family structure, per se, that influences the development of a healthy sense of intimacy but whether the adolescent feels closeness and trust with influential adult figures.

Consider your own family. If your family of origin encouraged you and your siblings to express feelings for one another, it is likely that you will enjoy emotional closeness with another (or others) when you establish friendships and a family of your own someday. It is also likely that you will not have difficulty in experiencing and expressing intimacy. But sometimes a family can be too emotionally close—too intimate—when no boundaries exist between family members. Then intimacy can be smothering and intrusive. When children from this kind of family engage in new relationships, they may be wary if their partner is too emotionally demanding. They may push the other away by causing an argument or trying to create distance in some other way (Maleki, 2000). Conversely, some family environments do not encourage the expression of intimacy or emotions. Children whose parents are ill at ease expressing their feelings may require excessive attention when starting new relationships. They may seem overly demanding in having their intimacy needs met (Maleki, 2000).

Past Families and Past Experiences

Researchers have found some evidence that indicates the experience and expression of intimacy are influenced not just by our immediate family of origin but by multigenerational

Intergenerational Family theory suggests that the ways we experience and express intimacy are influenced by our family of origin and by multigenerational influences. As you intimately relate to your friends and family members, do you find yourself repeating the relational patterns of your parents? Which intimacy patterns from your family of origin do you desire to keep? To change?

Intergenerational Family theory:

the theory that patterns of relational functioning (including intimacy) are passed down from generation to generation.

influences as well (Lawson & Brossart, 2001). **Intergenerational Family theory** suggests that patterns of relational functioning (including intimacy) are passed down from generation to generation. The theory's basic premise is that our parents acquired their family relational patterns from their parents, who acquired them from their parents, and so on. Consequently, the way we relate to and interact with others is a product of not just our parents' influence on our lives but also the relational patterns that were passed down to them. In turn, our intimacy patterns with our parents (and their parents) are replicated some day with our own spouses, children, friends, and significant others.

To illustrate this concept, consider the following example. As a child, Molly was brought up in a family where her mother and father's relationship was more platonic than romantic. It was companionable, friendly, and nonphysical. Soon, though, the friendship faded and they eventually divorced. As Molly looked back into her mother's childhood, she learned that her mother was reared in a physically abusive, secret-filled home. Rather than risk more hurt, her mother closed herself off emotionally to others—including her husband and her children. Her mother then carried her fear of intimacy to her marriage and to her parenting. Molly recently found herself repeating the relational patterns of her parents (particularly those of her mother). After dating someone for nearly a year and a half, she felt that the relationship was not progressing beyond the friendship stage, even though on the surface it seemed that both partners desired the relationship to deepen. She realized that she was replicating her parents' relationship, platonic and devoid of intimacy. In an attempt to break an unhealthy relational cycle she saw in her family and in herself, she entered into therapy to better recognize and correct the destructive relationship patterns passed down to her.

Sometimes trusting others and revealing ourselves to others is difficult—maybe even impossible because of some trauma we suffered and endured during the early years of our development. If we have been hurt, violated, attacked, bullied, or relentlessly teased, it can be difficult to allow ourselves to open up to another, as this could leave us vulnerable. Individuals who have been sexually abused often find it difficult to trust others and may have difficulty making a commitment. They may also expect that their intimate partner will leave them, and therefore they won't allow their partner to become too emotionally close (Burney, 2002). We'll examine the effects of sexual trauma and other forms of violence on interpersonal relationships later in this text. For now, it's important to understand that the family environment and family experiences help shape our capacity to be intimate. The past is very much a part of our present relationships.

Barriers to Establishing and Maintaining Intimacy

Some people put up barriers to establishing intimacy. There are many reasons for this, such as jealousy and deception (Galvin, Braithwaite, & Bylund, 2014). However, the fear of intimacy is often a primary barrier to establishing a relational environment that allows couples to share their vulnerabilities, a wide range of feelings, and their hurts and fears.

Fear of Intimacy

"Our fear of intimacy . . . inspires ingenious ways of avoiding it" (Barbor, 2001, p. 1). Because intimacy with another requires that we unmask ourselves and thus become vulnerable in doing so, many people have a fear of intimacy. Many of these people may not even be aware that they possess these fears. People afraid to establish and maintain intimate relationships put up walls, or form barriers, that prevent anyone from getting in; this, in turn, prevents them from getting hurt. For example, some people may form many friendships rather than one close, intimate relationship; others may become overly involved in work or volunteer activities to avoid interacting more personally with others; others shut themselves off from others completely, becoming isolated.

Fear of intimacy comes in many forms and may manifest itself in any of the following ways, according to intimacy researchers Robert Firestone and Joyce Catlett (2000):

- A fear of *failure*—What if this relationship doesn't work out?
- A fear of being *vulnerable*—Is it worth subjecting myself to hurt and emotional pain?
- A fear of *rejection*—Should I risk opening myself up without knowing if the other person will reciprocate?
- A fear of being *smothered* in a relationship—What if I lose my identity?
- A fear *of sex*—What if we end up having sex and he/she doesn't really love me? What if he/she disapproves of my body?
- A fear of *losing someone we love*—What happens if I fall in love or become intimate and this person breaks up with me or dies? How will I ever recover from the loss?
- A fear to take a *risk*—I can only go with the "sure thing" in my life. I don't have time to invest in someone if it isn't going to work out.
- A fear to *accept the responsibility* of an intimate relationship—Relationships are hard work; I just don't have the time or desire to invest that kind of energy.
- A fear of experiencing *anger* or *hostility* in the relationship—My father (or mother) is a very angry person. I just can't risk being immersed in all of that hostility again.
- A fear *of abandonment*—What if she/he leaves me?
- A fear of being *"found out"*—What if someone finds out who I "really am"?

The Glendon Association (2005), a teaching and research organization dedicated to enhancing mental health, notes that fear in personal relationships sets up barriers to becoming truly intimate with another person. The organization notes that most of what goes wrong in an intimate relationship comes from fear; because we bring these fears into our relationships from our family experiences, we become guarded so as not to become hurt. In turn, we stop disclosing, confiding, and trusting in our significant other—and subsequently we set up walls to guard our emotions.

Can a Relationship Work When There Are Differing Intimacy Needs?

How do couples sustain pleasure, contentment, and happiness in intimate relationships when there are differing intimacy needs? In many relationships, one person needs more or less intimacy than the other. This can be frustrating and upsetting when one person desires or needs more intimacy than the other person is willing to give or is capable of providing. Most of the time, for the person whose intimacy needs are not met, hurt and feelings of neglect mount. In the following case, what can be done so that each partner enjoys a satisfactory and comfortable level of intimacy?

One Side: He knows that I love him, but why can't he just give me some space? I feel like when I allow him into my personal thoughts more, when I share more, or when I open up more, he just wants more of me—no matter how much I share, it's not enough. When he's like this, I feel totally smothered and I pull away. Sometimes I start an argument on purpose just so he will back off a little bit. Why can't he understand that sometimes I just need a little distance? It doesn't mean I don't love him anymore—it just means that I feel like I'm losing who I am when he gets too close. I try to tell him how I feel, but he just doesn't seem to understand. I know he wants to understand.

The Other Side: From our first date, I have always felt like the pursuer in the relationship. I feel like I'm the only one who wants this relationship, the one who is chasing. This is crazy—we're living together, and I feel like I still have to chase her to keep her! The closer I move to her, the more distance she seems to create. I'm the pursuer; she's the distance. Sometimes we'll have very close periods of intimacy, and then just as suddenly, she'll pull away again. This you-can-have-me-but-only-at-a-distance relationship has to end. I love her, but it hurts too much. One of these days she is going to push me away and it will be the last time. The last time.

Your Side: Each partner in this relationship expects the other to show her or his intimacy in a way that is different from the current pattern. What can be done so that each partner enjoys a satisfactory and comfortable level of intimacy? Consider:

1. Is a change in the way the couple expresses and shares intimacy a realistic expectation? Is it possible?

2. How can this couple build the intimacy in their relationship?

3. Does either partner have fears about intimacy? What can be done when a partner or a friend has intimacy fears?

Source: Although the case scenario is hypothetical, information about intimacy pursuers was adapted for use from Gordon (2001).

Communication

According to the American Psychological Association (2005), an ideal intimate relationship is one in which openness, honesty, respect, and integrity exist. To foster the growth of intimacy, and to maintain intimacy, meaningful communication is essential. So crucial is the communication process of personal sharing to intimate relationships that marital and familial intimacy is not possible without effective communication strategies in place. It is difficult to examine intimacy without taking into account communication, and it is difficult to examine communication without taking into account intimacy.

Recall from Chapter 3 that there is an interconnectedness of the family. This family systems framework provides an understanding of the boundaries we establish and maintain in our family, verbal and nonverbal communication skills, decoding our partner's messages, and self-disclosure. Marital/partner and family intimacy requires communication that promotes acceptance and worth of the individuals in the family. It also requires private, personal self-disclosure that promotes a reciprocal, mutual sharing on a number of levels (emotional, intellectual, spiritual, physical). The capacity to experience intimacy within a marriage or life partnership and within family requires effective, meaningful communication. Healthy communication thus serves to encourage and promote intimacy within the marriage and the family.

FAMILY LIFE EDUCATION: VALUING DIVERSE COUPLE EXPERIENCES

Central to the Family Life Education framework is understanding the development and maintenance of intimacy in relationships (National Council on Family Relations, 2020). Not only is it essential that family scientists and practitioners recognize the ways in which relationships develop and are maintained, it's also vitally important that family professionals appreciate the different theoretical perspectives that inform our understanding of intimacy experiences across the lifespan. With this knowledge of intimacy, family life educators and other family practitioners are better equipped to develop and deliver healthy relationship strategies to couples and their families.

Whether intimacy is an innate, driving force that binds together social, relational beings or whether being intimate with another fulfills our basic, individual psychological needs, this family process is necessary for healthy, happy, fulfilling, and satisfying relationships. Not only is it a critical component in our lives; our intimate relationships establish interaction patterns for generations that follow.

Some of you may experience intimacy on a cognitive or intellectual level where you share ideas and thoughts and enjoy expressing your differences of opinions. Some of you may enjoy a type of experiential closeness where you actively involve yourselves with each other whenever you are together. Although you might not share many of your innermost thoughts and feelings, you take pleasure in mutual activities. And some of you may experience an emotional bond whereby you comfortably share your feelings and are aware of your partner's emotional needs. This type of intimate relationship often leads to physical or sexual intimacy.

As you have discovered, intimacy is many things to many different people—and it is different things to the same people at different times. Each relationship you have, from your first intimate relationship with your parent(s) or primary caregiver through old age, will build on the previous relationships. Each of these relationships creates who you are as an intimate. Your culture, ethnicity, family environment, intergenerational experiences, and the multicontextual aspects of intimacy all play an important role in how you experience it.

Intimacy does not always come easily to everyone. In fact, most of the time establishing and maintaining a close personal relationship with another requires hard work because it is a process that unfolds and changes over time. With this in mind, it is important to remember that if you find yourself having to work at your relationship, it does not necessarily mean that something is wrong or that your partner is the wrong partner. If you desire someone to openly, honestly, and completely share with you, you must be willing to be open and honest about your needs and desires. And you must also be willing to reciprocate the personal sharing and empathy shown by your partner. Only then will the seeds of intimacy have a chance to flourish and thrive.

And maybe this kind of intimacy is what Brad Pitt was referring to in his interview with *Rolling Stone* magazine. Knowingly or unknowingly, Pitt is speaking to a perpetual sense of meaninglessness in our success/consumer/power-driven society—to the notion that our relationships today are less and less grounded in purpose and in meaning.

In the drive for "the car, the condo, and our version of success," we are what the actor calls a society of desperate and lonely people. As you turn your attention back to the opening vignette in this chapter, you see that Pitt refers to this feeling of meaninglessness as a sense of impotence in our society—a sense of weakness, inability, or an incapacity. An incapacity for what? Relating? Belonging? Human connection?

As you take that step that brings you to reveal, share, and disclose your innermost personal thoughts and feelings, as you lower the barriers and allow another person to really know you, you begin the process of intimacy. As your partner reciprocates, this mutual sharing, co-created process unfolds. Thus, intimacy not only allows you to know and understand your partner but it also helps you to be known and to be understood by your partner. And it is this process of mutuality and reciprocating in human interactions that not only fulfills our psychological needs, but helps us to successfully navigate expected and unexpected family experiences.

Even the Lone Ranger wasn't alone!

/// SUMMARY

Intimacy: Do We Have a Need to Relate to Others?

- Humans are relational creatures who seek—either by design or evolutionary drives—to be with another or to be with others.

- Intimacy is the need for affiliation and refers to reciprocity of trust between the partners, emotional (not just physical) closeness, and comfortable levels of self-disclosure.

- The drive for interpersonal relations is thought to fulfill important psychological needs, or need fulfillment.

- Researchers Prager and Buhrmester (1998) found that through frequent, intimate, and positive communication, individual psychological needs are met by the couple.

- The global drive of humans to connect to others is motivated not only by survival needs, such as safety, shelter, and sustenance, but also by the psychological need for intimacy, social integration, nurture and nurturing, assistance, and reassurance.

- Intimacy is experienced differently from relationship to relationship. Although its meaning may vary, intimacy is a necessary component in meaningful relationships.

- Each couple's experience of intimacy is unique because of the many factors that influence, impinge on, and nurture the couple's relationship. There are five different levels of intimacy contexts: the immediate, the personal, the relational, the group, and the sociocultural.

- In collectivist cultures, the goals of the entire society are important, and this is reflected in experiences of intimacy.

- In individualistic cultures, the goals of the individual are emphasized, causing people to strive for higher levels of intimacy,

- Emotional attachment is at the core of all love relationships and is characterized by feelings that promote a sense of closeness, bonding, and connection that promote the well-being of another.

- Intimacy can be thought of as a three-pronged process that involves (1) disclosing things that are personal and private to ourselves, (2) experiencing positive feelings about ourselves and the other person(s) involved in the relationship, and (3) having interpersonal interactions that serve to advance or reflect partners' understanding of each other.

- Researchers describe eight components of intimate relationships: conflict resolution, affection, cohesion, sexuality, identity, compatibility, expressiveness, and autonomy. Researchers have also found that respect and the management of anger, self-disclosure, companionship, mutual appreciation, nonverbal communication, equity in decision making, physical closeness (both sexual and nonsexual contact), warmth and spirituality, and shared religious faith are significant components of intimacy.

- With a foundation of commitment and depth, Orlofsky and colleagues (1973) identified five intimacy statuses: the intimate, the pseudointimate, the preintimate, stereotyped relationships, and isolates.

Developing Intimacy

- While each of us develops the capacity to love and be intimate with others throughout infancy, childhood, adolescence, and early adulthood, it is the very early stages of life that establish the foundation of the ability to love and to share intimacy.

- Psychosocial development is the social and emotional development of an individual over his or her life span.

- Erikson's Eight Stages of Man were formulated to assert that our social and emotional development is a lifelong process.

- Development of need and capacity for intimacy revolves around biological, cognitive, and psychosocial changes that occur throughout adolescence.

- Adolescence marks the processes of individuation and the establishment of autonomy, of intimacy, and the exploration of sexuality.

- We learn the foundations of intimacy through adolescent friendships. There are significant differences between male intimacy experiences and female intimacy experiences, as well as cultural differences.

- In early adulthood—the bridge years—young adults contemplate deeper intimacy in interpersonal relationships. These intimate relationships are essential to healthy development; without such, developing adults are at risk for an isolation-filled life.

Obstacles to Intimacy

- Researchers have found the family environment and the family's past experiences are essential to establishing intimacy. Intergenerational Family theory suggests that patterns of relational functioning (including intimacy) are passed down from generation to generation.

- Because intimacy with another requires that we unmask ourselves and thus become vulnerable, many people fear intimacy. The fear may manifest itself in any number of ways.

- Intimacy found in the friendships of LGBTQ+ persons is critically important to help buffer gender and sexual minorities from social isolation or rejection associated with homophobia and transphobia.

- Marital and familial intimacy is not possible without effective communication strategies. Marital/partner and family intimacy not only requires communication that promotes acceptance and worth of the individuals in the family but also self-disclosure that promotes mutual sharing, on emotional, intellectual, spiritual, and physical levels.

/// KEY TERMS

Autonomy   164

Beginning of the crowd   162

Contact hypothesis   170

Cross-sex friendships (CSFs)   166

Crowd in transition   162

Crowd disintegration   163

Eight Stages of Man   159

Emotional attachment   155

Empathy   163

Fully developed crowd   162

Gender typing   165

Group context   153

Identity   163

Immediate context   153

Individuation   164

Intergenerational Family theory   174

Intimacy   151

Intimacy status   158

Intimate   158

Isolates   158

Merger status   158

Need for affiliation   151

Personal context   153

Preintimates   158

pre-crowd stage   162

Pseudointimate   158

Psychosocial development   159

Relational context   153

Responsiveness   151

Sociocultural context   154

Stereotyped relationships   158

iStock.com/svetikd

LOVE AND LOVING

LEARNING OBJECTIVES

6.1 Summarize the cultural and historical experiences of love and romance.

6.2 Explain the similarities and differences between infatuation and passionate love.

6.3 Describe the traits that characterize love as a commitment.

6.4 Identify the ways in which love develops across the lifespan.

6.5 Distinguish between the theories of love and loving.

I stand by the postoperative bed of my partner of four years and soon-to-be-wife. It's been a rough four years . . . although our parents and families know that we're gay, I think in the backs of their minds they didn't think we'd actually marry and desire to have children together. Together, we've overcome so many obstacles. And now this. We're only 27. A tumor had been embedded in her cheek, and in order to remove the growth, the surgeon had to severe a tiny twig of my partner's facial nerve. Her mouth is now twisted, giving her face a clownish appearance. I step back. I was told beforehand by her physician that my love's appearance would be different. But I wasn't at all prepared for what I saw.

My fiancée speaks, mumbling. It's difficult to understand what she's saying, so I lean in closer to her. She looks so fragile. Breakable. I'm terrified that she can see the shock on my face.

She asks, "Will my mouth always be like this?"

"Yes," I say, "it will. When removing the tumor, the doctor had to cut a nerve near your mouth."

She nods and is silent. She turns away from me. I lean in closer and smile. "I like it," I say. "It's pretty cute." Unmindful, I bend to kiss her crooked mouth, twisting my own lips to accommodate her now forever mouth and face. I show her that no matter what, our kiss still works (adapted from Selzer, 1978).

Love is a tough subject to tackle in one chapter, but it is a necessary discussion as we consider intimate relationships among friends, lovers, and family. But what is *love*? Even among researchers in the social and family sciences, "love" has been a difficult concept to define because different people experience it in ways that are unique to them. Depending on whom they are "loving" and their past experiences of love, no two people experience or express their love in precisely the same way because the concept of love has such a vast, diverse, tremendous range in its meaning. Is it a fiancée's unconditional acceptance of her chosen life mate with permanent twisted and crooked facial features who conforms her own lips to hers, to assure her the "kiss still works"? Is it the scrawling, scribbling handwriting of a kindergartner in permanent red ink? Is it a pounding heart and a nervous stomach every time a certain person is near? Is it a sense of calm and comfort—or anger, hurt, and jealousy?

LOVE IS A CULTURAL AND HISTORICAL EXPERIENCE

Several researchers have studied love as it is defined among different cultures of the world. Social psychologists Anne Beall and Robert Sternberg's (1995) research concludes that the experience and definition of love are culturally determined. Psychologists and researchers Elaine Hatfield and Richard Rapson's (1993) work appears to support the notion that "love" and "loving" experiences are driven by the culture in which we live. Their particular body of research found, for instance, that culture plays a key role in how individuals display emotions as well as how they react to the emotions and feelings of others. Is the culture in which a person lives a culture that accepts public demonstrations of affection toward another (such as in Italy), or is the culture more reserved in the display of affection (such as in England)?

It is important to understand that "love" and "loving" are determined in large part by how a culture defines its social identity. As you saw in the previous chapter in our discussion about intimacy, when examining various processes found in interpersonal relationships, it is particularly useful to understand whether a culture defines itself as a collectivist culture or an individualistic culture.

Love in Collectivist and Individualistic Cultures

Recall from Chapter 1 that in collectivist cultures the goals of the collective, or the whole society, are emphasized over a person's individual needs or wants, which are emphasized in individualistic cultures. Because of this desire to promote harmony within the cultural group, collectivists approach love differently than individualistic cultures do.

In the United States, Canada, and Europe, the idea of autonomy and individuation from the family is promoted; in turn, this autonomy encourages the practice of people selecting partners based on *individual* reasons (such as attraction, love, money, security, and so on), rather than *collective* reasons (such as arranged marriages in China) that might benefit the culture as a whole. Individualistic cultures also promote strong levels of desire for romantic relationships compared with collectivist cultures (Medora, Larson, Hortacsu, & Dave, 2002). Furthermore, the importance of love for choosing a marriage mate is much more prevalent in individualistic cultures than in collectivist cultures such as Japan and India.

When cultures promote the autonomy and independence of individuals (as seen in much of Western civilization), this autonomy then affects relationship satisfaction, the ease with which intimacy is established, and "love" as a basis for marriage (Dion & Dion, 1993). Relationship partners are free, by society's standards, to choose a partner that best suits their needs and with whom they are "in love"; it is thought that this freedom of choice enhances relationship satisfaction and the experiences of love and intimacy. One study helps to explain how and why relationship satisfaction is enhanced. In a study that examined emotional closeness and loneliness in 271 American and Korean college students, the researchers found that American students have a greater degree of closeness in their romantic relationships than Korean students do because of two interacting reasons: (1) They have an individualistic cultural desire to have a romantic relationship and therefore invest more in their love relationships, and (2) they have idealized romantic notions that magnify the feelings found in romantic relationships (Seepersad, Choi, & Shin, 2008). The researchers also discovered that Korean students do not necessarily identify their feelings as "loneliness" or a lack of emotional closeness because they don't view romantic relationships with the same degree of importance as a source of love and psychological intimacy as American students do.

Most of us are familiar with the societal expectations of love and loving in our individualistic culture in the United States, but we often have questions about love in other cultures. For example, is love as important a family process in collectivist cultures, such as Pakistan, as it is in U.S. culture?

In Muslim societies, romantic love is the source of much discussion today, particularly because love experiences in collectivist cultures have been seldom documented in the scholarly literature (Marsden, 2007). Among these people groups, "love" means many things—there is a clear distinction in love between family, friends, romantic partners, and physical

In collectivist cultures such as in India, marriages are typically arranged by the parents of the bride and groom. Parents believe that joining certain blood lines through marriage is beneficial to society, or to the collective. Today, though, more and more couples are eloping in secret marriages, marrying someone they love.

Elopement:

secret marriages between love partners that take place without parental approval and/or knowledge.

attraction, and different words are used to describe these various experiences. More recently, however, researchers are examining the various experiences of love and loving in these societies, particularly among Muslims in South Asia, because individualistic, Western attitudes of romantic love are making inroads into Muslim societies.

Although traditionally many marriages are arranged in these South Asian collectivist societies, a contemporary sweeping trend is **elopement**, or secret marriages between love partners that take place without parental approval and/or knowledge. In some villages in Pakistan, elopement marriages are viewed as an act of resistance against collectivist Muslim society traditionalism and as rebellion against arranged marriages (Marsden, 2007). This is an important trend to understand because it speaks to a gradual shift in this particular society's social identity—a potential shift away from collectivism and toward individualism. Young couples' relationships are becoming injected with a recognition that there are emotional and physical elements associated with love that are rewarding and pleasurable (Marsden, 2007).

The experience of love is driven by not only culture but by the period in history in which the relationship exists, as well (Beall & Sternberg, 1995). A glimpse of the past can help us understand how and why we view and experience love today and how our experiences of love have evolved over the centuries.

The History of Love and Romance

Throughout history, perhaps no topic has generated as much attention as the topic of love. Philosophers, poets, writers, scholars, and lyricists have all sought to provide an account of love and its mysteries. In keeping with the theme of this book, the study of marriage and family, our focus will be on various experiences of love as recorded throughout history. This journey into the past illustrates how the historical influences of love affect how we experience love in our contemporary society.

Love and Romance Throughout History

If you consider the biblical account of Adam and Eve, it might be said that they fell in love first. Although, some have commented that they probably didn't have much choice in the matter!

Fast-forward several thousand years: In the 1st century, love was thought of as a bittersweet emotion, an ambivalent feeling (Hunt, 1994); in the 3rd century, love was experienced as a somber, guilt-ridden experience intertwined with the act of sex (Hunt, 1994); by the 16th century, marriage was viewed as a physical and financial union—love was not the foundation, or even a significant part of the marriage (Hunt, 1994). But when the British came to New England during the 16th and 17th centuries, the Puritans and Pilgrims showed themselves to be romantically sentimental—and thoroughly enjoyed sex within the confines of marriage. As a result of this new relationship dynamic, romance and sex became hallmarks of love. But these love experiences were short-lived as 18th-century Puritanism gave way to the oppressive, stuffy formality of the 19th-century Victorians—in love, romance, and sexual practices.

Mexican Archival/Alamy Stock Photo

Our experiences of love are shaped not only by our culture, but by the period in history in which our relationship exists. Marrying for romantic love—which includes sexuality, affection, intimacy, and togetherness—did not become popular until early in the 20th century.

During the Victorian era (1837–1901), the virginal, shy, virtuous woman was the epitome of the attitude toward sexuality and the role of women. Although attitudes toward sexuality were prim and stuffy, the Victorian ideal of love, for the first time in history, perpetuated a sense of *couple togetherness*. When not at work, men during the Victorian era were expected to be at home, enjoying the company of their wives and family. Relative to the scope of love throughout history, the Victorian era was short-lived and quickly gave way to the emergence of the concept of romantic love in the early 20th century.

Romantic Love

The early decades of the 20th century saw rapid social changes: Family planning activist Margaret Sanger (1914) claimed that lovemaking and procreation were two entirely different experiences, and she gained national attention when she claimed that women had the right to control their own fertility. At the same time, the nation ushered in the emancipation of women and experienced the rise in capitalism and industrialization. And, for the first time in the annals of history, *both* men and women sought out romantic love relationships that combined sexuality, affection, intimacy, and togetherness—and discovered that all of these relational elements could be found in one relationship.

By the 1930s, romantic attraction to another became *the* acceptable form of choosing a life mate. The way many of us experience love today came into being within the past century. In a true sense, the concept of romantic love is in its infancy, a 20th-century phenomenon (Luhmann, 1986). Yet, this form of partnering based on love and affection, and tenderness and care, is still today a goal for many.

WHAT IS LOVE, ACTUALLY?

Today, *love* is perhaps the most overused four-letter word in the English language. I "love" buttered movie popcorn. I "love" the sound of a newborn baby's cry. I "love" spring. I "love" the prairie. I really "love" collegiate football. I "love" my children and my grandchildren and my

Family Life Now

Is Love the Basis for Marriage?

Is love a prerequisite for marital bliss and happiness? While people from collectivist cultures may marry someone based on what is considered to be good for the entire group, people from individualistic cultures, like the United States, typically marry someone who fulfills their personal, individual goals, such as being in love. Is love the basis for marriage?

YES: Marriage and family therapist Henry Grunebaum (2003) notes that "love" contains unique characteristics that are unlike any other emotion or feeling experienced by human beings and that true love rarely occurs. He believes people consider love to be a precious and enduring experience, and he claims the elements needed to foster an enduring relationship of any kind are needed to foster a strong, enduring love relationship: intimacy, communication, kindness, and an active interest in the other person. Grunebaum points out that loveless marriages are difficult to repair. In his clinical experience, "When romantic love is lost, it is almost always gone for good."

NO: Marriage and family therapist Joseph Silverman (2003) contends that the feelings associated with love are mainly nervousness associated with the excited feelings produced by the chemicals in the brain when we are attracted to another person. While in this excited state, couples make lifelong commitments to one another—and set themselves up for disappointment.

Sources: Grunebaum (2003) and Silverman (2003).

According to Silverman, there are problems with linking love as a basis for marriage:

- People overestimate the importance of love, and they feel deprived or empty if the excitement wanes. Other aspects of the relationship—such as compatibility, sharing experiences, or similar family goals—are equally important as feelings of love.

- There is no such thing as a "perfect partner"; anyone who is reasonably tolerant and flexible can successfully marry nearly anyone.

- The most important relationship in any person's life—marriage—cannot fulfill every desire of both partners.

In Silverman's (2003) view, "not every marriage has to be violins and roses." Marriages of convenience and marriages where love does not exist have a place.

What Do You Think?

1. Do you agree with Grunebaum's statement that romantic love occurs rarely? Why or why not?

2. Do you agree with Silverman's statement that a person can "successfully marry nearly anyone"? Why or why not?

3. Is love a prerequisite for marriage for you?

---

family and friends. I "love" teaching. This crazy little thing called love has been assigned more than 20 definitions in the dictionary as well as in the thesaurus, and includes such descriptions as

- feeling affection for
- adoration
- worship
- devotion
- fondness
- passion
- feeling a weakness for

A problem with the dictionary and thesaurus definitions still remains, though. As you can see, we can "have a weakness for" pizza; we can be "fond of" pizza; we may even be "devoted to" or "adore" pizza! In today's society, we tend to use the word *love* when we really mean we *prefer* something or *enjoy* something or *like* to be in someone's company.

Eros:
sensual or sexual love.

The ancient Greeks recognized this dilemma and distinguished between the different key qualities of or types of love. For example, the term **eros** was used to describe the sexual, physical components of love (this is the root word of the term *erotic*). **Philos**, or brotherly love, was used to describe the affectionate feelings shared between friends and family (hence the name Philadelphia, the "city of brotherly love"). **Agape** was thought to be a self-sacrificing, spiritual love that looked out for the interests and well-being of others. Today in North America, we still have only one word to express our love. One researcher, Beverley Fehr (1988), paid particular attention to how individuals assess or appraise the essential aspects of love, or what she termed *love prototypes*.

Love as a Prototype

Fehr (1988) decided to take a somewhat different approach to her scientific quest in an effort to understand the definitions people attach to the concept of love. Fehr started with the premise that each of us acquires a model in our own families of origin of what love is and what it is not. In her research, she asked her study sample to free write (unedited, uninhibited writing) various features or attributes they assigned to "love." The list the study sample provided was thought to be their **prototype** or model of love. A different sample group later ranked the features in order of importance. There are 12 central features of love identified by Fehr's research (1988):

1. Trust
2. Care
3. Honesty
4. Friendship
5. Respect
6. Desire to promote the well-being of the other
7. Loyalty
8. Commitment
9. Accepting the other without wanting to change the other
10. Support
11. A desire to be in the other's company
12. Consideration of and interest in the other

Does your love prototype list include attributes or characteristics of love that Fehr's list does not? If so, why do you think that is?

It is important to note that if any group of individuals, such as a group of students, were given the task of creating attributes they assigned to "love," each person would generate a love prototype list of attributes or characteristics that is unique to them. The list a person generates is important because it represents his or her own *definition of love*. As Fehr (1988) notes, the aspects a person lists are central to and ultimately *characterizes* his or her love relationships. If any of the key attributes of love is dishonored, violated, or lost at any time during the relationship, the love relationship is threatened and may end. It's interesting to note how many of the 12 central features of love identified in this study three decades ago still hold true today for many people.

Similar to Fehr's (1988) concept of love prototypes is world-famous sexologist John Money's (2003) concept of **love maps**. A love map is a mental blueprint of sorts that we carry internally. According to Money, love maps present an image of the "ideal" love relationship that is shaped by our experiences with love in infancy and early childhood. It is also informed by the attitudes of love and sexuality of our parents or primary caregivers.

Each of us has a love prototype or love map when we first begin to question whether we are "in love" with another person, but it is often difficult to determine whether our feelings are feelings of *infatuation* or whether they are feelings that will lead to an enduring, *committed* love relationship.

Philos:

brotherly love, used to describe the affectionate feelings shared between friends and family.

Agape:

self-sacrificing, spiritual love that looks out for the interests and well-being of others; a selfless, enduring, other-centered type of love that provides intrinsic satisfaction with no reciprocity expected or demanded.

Prototype:

a model. Researcher Beverly Fehr asked her study sample to free write various features or attributes they assigned to "love." The list provided a prototype of love.

Love maps:

a mental blueprint of the "ideal" love relationship, which is shaped by our experiences with love in infancy and early childhood and by our parents' and primary caregivers' attitudes toward love and sexuality.

Infatuation—often described as a "crush" or "puppy love"—is a common type of intense passion for someone who is usually unattainable, such as a pop idol.

Infatuation:

an intense, extravagant, and often short-lived passion for another person, often confused with love.

Simple infatuation:

physical attraction that is often accompanied by emotion-filled daydreams and fantasies about someone, perhaps an actor or actress, a pop star or singing idol, or even a teacher.

Romantic infatuation:

a type of infatuation that is often referred to as *romantic love.* Defined in the *American Heritage Dictionary* as "a foolish, unreasoning, or extravagant passion or attraction," and "an object of extravagant short-lived passion," romantic infatuation involves a complicated, often overpowering, blend of emotion and sexuality.

Passionate love:

a wildly powerful emotion experienced as intense longing for the selected love object, along with profound sexual arousal and confused feelings.

Passionate Love: Experiencing Love as Infatuation

Infatuation refers to an intense, extravagant, and often short-lived passion for another person, and many times these feelings are confused with love. Most of us have had a "crush" on someone or we have suffered through "puppy love" at some point in our early teens or younger. These crushes are referred to as **simple infatuation**, a physical attraction that is often accompanied by emotion-filled daydreams and fantasies about someone—perhaps an actor/actress, a pop star or singing idol, or even a teacher. In the 1970s, the object of my infatuation was Donny Osmond (my choices were slim—I had the options of Donny or Greg Brady of *The Brady Bunch).* Today, there is a seemingly endless array of people to become infatuated with, from pop stars, to actors in Netflix shows, to YouTube stars and influencers. Objects of infatuation can also be classmates and even teachers.

These and similar first love experiences, often during junior high school or the early high school years, are actually simple infatuation. Although parents, social workers, clergy, educators, and other providers of human services understand this love is not the "real," committed love that marriages are made of, it is important that they recognize that the feelings experienced are no less intense than those adults experience.

Infatuation as Romance

Romantic infatuation is often referred to as *romantic love.* Defined in the *American Heritage Dictionary* as "a foolish, unreasoning, or extravagant passion or attraction," and "an object of extravagant short-lived passion," romantic infatuation involves a complicated, often overpowering blend of emotion and sexuality.

Empirical studies appear to support the dictionary's definition. Notably, Elaine Hatfield and her colleagues (Hatfield, 1988, Hatfield, Brinton, & Cornelius, 1989, Hatfield & Rapson, 1998) distinguish between two different types of love: passionate and companionate (to be discussed later in this chapter). The researchers describe **passionate love** as a wildly powerful emotion that is experienced as intense longing for the selected love object, along with profound sexual arousal and confused feelings, Passionate love can either be a blissful experience, if the love is reciprocated, or a painful experience if the love is ignored. Other research shows that romantic love involves a mix of intense emotional and physical characteristics, such as a pounding heart, a choking sensation in the throat, sweating palms, and/or a constricting sensation in

Table 6.1 /// The Passionate Love Scale

Think of the person whom you love most passionately right now. If you are not in love, please think of the last person you loved. If you have never been in love, think of the person you came closest to caring for in that way. Try to describe the way you felt when your feelings were most intense. Answers range from (1) Not at all true to (9) Definitely true.

	Not at all true								Definitely true
I would feel deep despair if _____ left me.	1	2	3	4	5	6	7	8	9
Sometimes I feel I can't control my thoughts; they are obsessively on_____.	1	2	3	4	5	6	7	8	9
I feel happy when I'm doing something to make _____ happy.	1	2	3	4	5	6	7	8	9
I would rather be with _____ than anyone else.	1	2	3	4	5	6	7	8	9
I'd get jealous if I thought _____ was falling in love with someone else.	1	2	3	4	5	6	7	8	9
I yearn to know all about _____.	I	2	3	4	5	6	7	8	9
I have an endless appetite for affection from _____.	1	2	3	4	5	6	7	8	9
For me, _____ is the perfect romantic partner.	1	2	3	4	5	6	7	8	9
I sense my body responding when _____ touches me.	1	2	3	4	5	6	7	8	9
_____ always seems to be on my mind.	1	2	3	4	5	6	7	8	9
I want _____ to know me—my thoughts, fears, and my hopes.	1	2	3	4	5	6	7	8	9
I eagerly look for signs indicating _____'s desire for me.	1	2	3	4	5	6	7	8	9
I possess a powerful attraction for _____.	1	2	3	4	5	6	7	8	9
I get extremely depressed when things don't go right in my relationship with _____.	1	2	3	4	5	6	7	8	9

Passionate Love Scale Scores

Extremely passionate: 106–135 points *You are wildly and recklessly in love!*

Passionate: 86–105 points *You are passionate, but with less intensity.*

Average: 66–85 points *You have occasional bursts of passion.*

Cool: 45–65 points *Your passion is lukewarm and infrequent.*

Extremely cool: 15–44 points *Sorry baby, but the thrill is gone.*

Sources: Hatfield & Sprecher (1986); Fehr (1988); Hendrick & Hendrick (1989).

the chest (Rice, 1993). The emotional manifestations of romantic love include idealizing the romantic partner; intense sexual attraction; a surge of self-confidence; adoration of the love interest; and an all-consuming, selfless desire to promote the well-being of the partner (Rice, 1993). In short, it's the love-struck stuff that the relationships on reality TV dating shows *(The Bachelor, The Bachelorette)* are made of—but not what long lasting marriages are made of.

Are you in love with someone now, or have you been in love? The Passionate Love Scale was developed by Elaine Hatfield (Hatfield & Sprecher, 1986) to assess the cognitive, physiological, and behavioral indicants of passionate love. As you can see from Table 6.1, this scale measures attitudes associated with passionate love. To date, this scale has been translated into a number of languages, including Farsi, German, Indian, Indonesian, Korean, Peruvian, Spanish, and Swedish (Kim & Hatfield, 2004; Lundqvist, 2006). And today, a number of anthropologists believe that passionate love is a universal experience that transcends culture (Fisher, 2004).

Social psychologist Z. Rubin (1973) studied romantic love/infatuation and how the attachment to the love interest develops, both physically and psychologically. Akin to what happens on the reality TV dating shows, Rubin found that infatuation tends to start very quickly and often leads to what people think of as "love at first sight." Romantic infatuation occurs as the result of an attraction, probably to some physical trait, such as an appealing body part, her captivating smile, or his bedroom eyes. Physical attraction is an important element in emotionally mature love relationships, but it is not one of the *primary* factors in relationship satisfaction and longevity. With romantic love, however, there are relatively few factors beyond the physical traits that attract us to the other; thus, such attraction doesn't lead to loving someone else but only to loving or being attracted to a certain part of the person. It should come as no surprise that as the attraction to a particular trait begins to wane, so too does the "love." **Fatuous** (infatuation) relationships tend to end as quickly as they begin.

Fatuous:
a descriptive term referring to infatuation-based relationships.

Like Rice (1993), Rubin (1973) found that romantic infatuation carries with it an urge to assist or aid the lover in whatever capacity needed, to promote the lover's well-being. I often comment to my students that the popular *Judge Judy* courtroom television show would not exist if it were not for jilted, once-infatuated lovers attempting to reclaim property that they gave away during the course of a romantic infatuation relationship. Cries of "But your Honor, I *had* to pay his tuition or he couldn't finish school," or "But your Honor, she *needed* to use my cell phone so she could apply for a job," or "But your Honor, I *had* to buy him the car so he could get a job so we could afford rent so we could live together" flood the popular judge's courtroom.

Another characteristic of romantic infatuation relationships was documented by Elaine Hatfield (1988). She found that when couples are in relationships consumed by romantic infatuation, both partners become completely absorbed with each other and exclude friends and

Passionate love is often a wildly powerful emotion and driven by a sexually charged physical longing for one another.

iStock.com/PeopleImages

family. Family, friends, academics, sports, work, and anything else that was once important lose their priority in life. Because of the exclusive nature of the relationship, family and friends may disapprove of the relationship because they are being neglected and ignored by the couple. In fact, if parents, family, and friends voice concern about the exclusivity of the relationship, it is perhaps an indication that the relationship is not "real love."

Passionate Love: The Influences of Culture

As we saw earlier, whether a culture defines itself as collectivist or individualistic has a profound effect on how people experience and define "love." Given this, it stands to reason that social identity would also have an effect on how passionate love is experienced. Unexpectedly, though, passionate love is a more common global experience than researchers anticipated (Hatfield & Rapson, 2007). For example, in a study of 1,667 college-aged men and women from the United States, Russia, and Japan, the investigators found no evidence that the individualistic cultures (the United States and Russia) had more experiences of passionate love than those from the collectivist culture, Japan (Sprecher, Sullivan, & Hatfield, 1994). Another study using the Passionate Love Scale found that young adults from European, Filipino, and Japanese ethnicities appeared to love their partners as passionately as young adults from the United States do (Hatfield & Rapson, 1987).

Conversely, Dan Landis and William O'Shea (2000), researchers from the University of Mississippi, found that the experience of passionate love/infatuation is influenced by cultural attitudes and social identity. Landis and O'Shea's elaborate multicultural research concludes that the experience and expression of fatuous love is multifaceted and is "uniquely defined within each culture" (p. 752). Studying nearly 2,000 participants from the United States (consisting of Caucasians as well as Japanese Americans and Chinese Americans), Denmark, England, Canada, and Israel, Landis and O'Shea asked respondents to complete a sexual behavior and sexual attitudes questionnaire and to rate how strongly they agreed with statements such as

- Sometimes my body trembles with excitement at the sight of him/her.
- I want him/her physically, emotionally, mentally.
- I yearn to know all about him/her.
- No one else could ever love him/her like I do (would).
- Sometimes I feel I can't control my thoughts; they are obsessively on him/her.
- I would get jealous if I thought he/she were falling in love with someone else.

Each culture under investigation provided culture-specific responses. For example, Canadian males were characterized as more excited about their love object, whereas males from the United Kingdom were characterized as more melancholy on the same measures. The researchers found that, overall, those cultures that were characterized as relatively feminine (such as Denmark) showed differences in their passionate love experiences in terms of security and commitment; masculine cultures, such as Israel, appeared to foster more "self-centered" relationships.

The physical and emotional exhilaration, the fever-pitched excitement, and the sexually charged atmosphere that accompanies infatuation may be more the work of the not very romantic-sounding neurotransmitters and hormones than the work of rational decision making. These neurotransmitters and hormones may, in fact, be the primary influence on relationship junkies.

I Can't Help Falling in Love: The Neuroscience of Love

What is love, actually? What is the basis of the giddy, walking-on-air feelings we experience when we fall in love? Recent advances in science may reveal the answer. The initial feelings of love don't have much to do with romance, but instead have more to do with functions of the brain. Information between brain neurons is communicated by the movement of certain chemicals—neurotransmitters—across areas of the brain. When we begin to fall in love, the "high" we experience is the result of the release of these neurotransmitters (Aaron et al., 2005).

When two people are attracted to one another, the brain becomes flooded with a gush of neurotransmitters that mimic amphetamines (commonly referred to as "uppers"). The neurotransmitter culprits are dopamine, which make us feel good, norepinephrine, which causes pounding hearts and racing pulses, and PEA (phenylethylamine), which causes feelings of excitement and euphoria (Aaron et al., 2005). Because chocolate contains PEA, it has long been rumored to promote infatuation between lovers (however, it is probably more the result of the large amounts of caffeine and sugar found in chocolate).

The neurotransmitters then signal the pituitary gland (located in the region of the brain known as the hypothalamus) to release a multitude of hormones that rapidly flood the bloodstream (Aaron et al., 2005). The sex glands, in turn, release even more hormones into the bloodstream. It is the combination of the flood of neurotransmitters in the brain and the subsequent release of the hormones into the bloodstream that enables new lovers to make love all night or talk for hours on end. When these chemicals are produced over a period of time, people interpret the physical sensations as "falling in love." Love, actually, is a cocktail of neurochemicals.

Unfortunately, there is also a negative side of infatuation: stalking.

The Negative Sides of Love

In February 2007, NASA astronaut Lisa Nowak was arrested and charged with the attempted murder of the woman she believed was her romantic rival for a space shuttle pilot's affections. So obsessed was Nowak in finding her rival, she drove from Texas to Florida wearing adult diapers so she would not have to stop along the way. When arrested, Nowak noted that she was not stalking her victim and that she only wanted to scare her victim into talking with her. Prior to her arrest, Nowak had persistently harassed her victim, via cell phone and text messages, for more than two months. We discuss intimate partner violence at length in Chapter 15, but here it is necessary to understand that there is a negative side to passionate love and infatuation: stalking.

Stalking: An Obsessive Following

Stalking:

the obsessive following, observing, or contacting of another person, or the obsessive attempt to engage in any of these activities.

Cyber-stalking:

online stalking.

Stalking is the obsessive following, observing, or contacting of another person, or the obsessive attempt to engage in any of these activities. It can be done in person or online; online stalking is referred to as **cyber-stalking**. The U.S. Department of Justice (2018) provides us with some relevant statistics regarding stalking:

- Each year, 7.5 million people are stalked in the United States
- 1 in 6 women and 1 in 17 men will be stalked in their lifetime
- Most victims know their stalker: 76 percent of female victims and 44 percent of male victims are stalked by a current or former intimate partner
- 67 percent have also been physically assaulted by that partner
- 54 percent of murdered women reported stalking to police before they were killed by their stalkers

Stalking is also a problem on college campuses, with as many as 43 percent of women reporting being emotionally, psychologically, or physically harmed from being stalked (Wood & Stichman, 2018).

Stalking exists in many forms, and sometimes victims don't even realize that it is happening because it can be subtle. In general, there are five types of stalkers (Mullen, Pathe, & Purcell, 2000):

Rejected stalkers:

stalkers who want to reverse, correct, or avenge rejection of their affections, infatuation, or love.

1. **Rejected stalkers** want to reverse, correct, or avenge rejection of their affections, infatuation, or love. This type of stalking begins either as the perpetrator senses the relationship is about to end or after the couple has separated and/or terminated the relationship.

2. **Intimacy seekers** desire to establish an intimate, loving relationship with their victim. They believe that their victim is their one and only soul mate and that fate has brought them together.

3. **Incompetent suitors** commonly have poor social and emotional skills and have difficulty expressing themselves. They develop a fixation on someone they feel romantically attracted to. In most cases, however, the victim is already in a relationship with someone else.

4. **Resentful stalkers** are out for vengeance because they believe they were wronged by their victim. This type of stalking is motivated primarily by the desire to frighten the victim and cause her or him distress.

5. **Predatory stalkers** spy on the victim in order to plan a sexual attack.

Online and offline stalking are federal crimes under the laws of all 50 states. It is also considered to be a crime in Canada, Japan, and the United Kingdom. We'll explore the multiple mental, emotional, and physiological health effects of stalking later in this text. Stalking is a form of violence that must be taken seriously.

Jealousy: A Perceived Threat

"Heaven has no rage like love to hatred turned, Nor hell a fury like a woman scorned." These infamous words, penned by William Congreve in 1697, refer to a woman's jealousy in a love-gone-bad relationship. We don't know the relational experiences that led Congreve to write this passage, but we can come to a pretty quick conclusion that he experienced the wrath and anger of a jealous woman! A popular theme in movies such as *Closer* and *Unfaithful*, jealousy is a component of love for most of us.

Jealousy is an emotional reaction to the perception that a valued relationship is threatened because of a third party (Bevan, 2013; Knox, Breed, & Zusman, 2007). This perceived threat can be real or imaginary. Typically, jealousy is aroused when one person believes that someone is getting what the person wishes to have for himself or herself, such as attention, love, or affection. It is an emotion that can manifest in several ways, including anger, fear, hurt, betrayal, anxiety, sadness, paranoia, depression, feelings of powerlessness, or inadequacy

Intimacy seekers: stalkers who want to establish an intimate, loving relationship with their victim.

Incompetent suitors: stalkers who have poor social and emotional skills and have difficulty expressing themselves.

Resentful stalkers: stalkers who are out for vengeance because they believe they were wronged by their victim.

Predatory stalkers: stalkers who spy on the victim in order to plan a sexual attack.

Jealousy: an emotional reaction to the perception that a valued relationship is threatened because of a third party.

iStock.com/AntonioGuillem

Jealousy is a common emotional reaction to a perceived threat to a relationship. Almost always, jealousy is the result of an underlying fear that someone will take our love away.

(Brem, 1992). It can be experienced in a number of different relationships: Children can be jealous of siblings who get the attention of parents; friends can be jealous of other friends in the peer group; and workers can be jealous of co-workers (DeSteno, 2004). The central theme to jealousy is that a valued relationship is endangered and may be taken over by a rival (DeSteno, 2004).

Whatever we feel when we are jealous, the central emotion behind jealousy is *fear*—fear about change, fear about the future of the relationship, fear of abandonment, or fear of losing power in the relationship. At the very least, jealousy causes hurt feelings; at its worse, it can result in family violence (see Chapter 15) or lead to a murderous rage (White, 1981). "Enraged jealousy" was the motivation for murder suggested by the prosecution team during the O. J. Simpson trial; indeed, jealousy was a likely contributing factor in about 40 percent of female homicides in 2000 (Knox et al., 2007; U.S. Department of Justice, 2003).

Some theories, such as Social Learning theory and Evolutionary theory (see Chapter 7) maintain that jealousy serves a useful, adaptive function in relationships. We established in the previous chapter that we all have an innate, intrinsic drive to be involved in an intimate relationship with someone and that intimacy fulfills both psychological and physiological needs. To protect intimacy, theorists believe that a specific emotion designed to protect relationships—jealousy—has evolved over time (DeSteno, Valdesolo, & Bartlett, 2006). Given that jealousy is a global experience, found in cultures all over the world, it stands to reason that this emotion has evolved as an adaptive response, triggered by fear of rejection, to safeguard relationships. None of us is immune to the experiences and emotions associated with jealousy.

Research reveals there are four stages of jealousy (White, 1981):

1. *Suspecting the threat.* Some people look for signs of relationship deterioration or relationship threat where there are none, while others overlook obvious signals. In general, women are more likely to admit feeling jealous. Typically, women are jealous over a mate's emotional attachment to another person. Conversely, men are more likely to deny feelings of jealousy. Men typically become jealous of sex, and they accept the belief that "jealousy shows love" (Knox et al., 2007). Sadly, men are more likely to be abusive when they feel they can no longer control their partner's feelings for them (Sagarin, Becker, Guadango, Nicastle, & Millevoi, 2003).

2. *Emotionally reacting.* Emotional reactions to threats to our love relationships can range from clinging dependency (more often by women but by men as well), to violent rage (mostly by men), to depression with thoughts of suicide (mostly by women). Although men respond more intensely to jealousy, women take longer to get over it.

3. *Coping.* In general, when coping with jealousy, women often cry, plead, or blame themselves for the problems in the relationship. They also tend to eat to cope with their jealous feelings (Knox et al., 2007). They also confide more often in their friends about jealous feelings than men do. Men attempt to bolster their egos by becoming competitive (this may involve becoming sexually involved with a different, more attractive partner). They also tend to drink alcohol when they feel jealous (Knox et al., 2007). Women tend to delay entering into another relationship.

4. *Moving on.* If feelings of jealousy erupt, it is important to discuss these feelings of vulnerability openly with the partner and then find a creative way to deal with them. For example, some couples create a private code word to use in social gatherings to indicate that they are feeling insecure or jealous. Above all, it's important to validate and respect the partner's feelings.

Seeing Green: Recognizing and Managing Jealousy

Commonly referred to as the *green-eyed-monster,* feelings of jealousy are an indicator of underlying fear—we may feel insecure and threatened that someone or something will take our lover away from us. Although some jealousy can be unhealthy and dangerous, such as in the case of controlling and/or abusive partners or stalking, for the most part it is a common component of our love relationships. To overcome—or at least dilute it a bit—here are some suggestions (Sorgen, 2008):

- **Don't compare yourself to anyone else.** *Everyone* is unique and *everyone* has something to bring to a relationship. When you compare yourself to other people, you only sabotage your own uniqueness and individuality—and the relationship.
- **Know your own strengths.** What do you bring to the relationship? Just remember: You have the advantage because you are the one that is currently in the relationship—not your rival!
- **Use jealousy to your advantage.** Okay, so you're jealous of someone else's attributes. Use this energy as the fuel to help you accomplish your goals and to grow!
- **Affirm the other person.** Look at the rival for who he or she really is. What are his or her good qualities? Try to see the other person for who he or she really is, not just as a threat to your relationship.
- **Get rid of the toxicity.** If someone in your circle of friends is toxic to you and to your relationship, remove yourself from their presence. And, if necessary for your emotional well-being and health, remove yourself permanently.

Remember, there will always be someone who is more talented, more beautiful, more successful, and wealthier than you. So what?

Looking Back and Social Networking: Jealousy Directed at the Past

As we've seen so far, romantic relationships are typically characterized by mutual, ongoing interactions and often embody affection, closeness, and physical intimacy, and exclusivity is an expected romantic partner norm in the United States (Collins, Welsh, & Furman, 2009; Penke & Asendorph, 2008). But what happens when a relationship ends and a partner moves on to a new relationship? According to relationship researchers Jessica Frampton and Jesse Fox (2018), retroactive jealousy occurs when a romantic partner is bothered by their partner's past romantic or sexual relationships—even though the ex is not actively trying to interfere with the present relationship, the ex and the past relationship are perceived as a rival. The researchers sought to determine how contemporary social networking sites influence retroactive jealousy, and they found that past and current partners engage in two specific behaviors (Frampton & Fox, 2018):

Retroactive jealousy: a type of jealousy that occurs when a romantic partner is bothered by their partner's past romantic or sexual relationships.

Partner Monitoring: Social networking sites, such as Facebook, Twitter, Snapchat, and Instagram, provide ways for current and ex romantic/sexual partners to monitor their partner's interpersonal interactions with others. Pictures, links, audio or video clips, and screen shots of text messages are commonly posted, tagged, and shared on these sites—all of these provide a wealth of information regarding someone's current relationship(s). Because it's quite easy to access this information, a current partner typically has no idea that his/her love interest is creeping them on social media (Frampton & Fox, 2018).

Gathering Information: Partners also use social networking sites to gather information about what a partner has done in the past with other love or sexual interests. Because it's relatively easy to find historical profile information on social media, current partners can easily inspect the new romantic partner's past posts and interactions with others (Frampton & Fox, 2018). Today, it is common for ex partners to remain in contact on social media (Fox, Osborn, & Warber, 2014; Marshall, Bejanyan, Di Castro, & Lee, 2013; Tokunaga, 2011).

Both of these jealousy behaviors threaten the current relationship. As most of us can relate, people tend to post only the best photographic or video images of themselves. This tendency to selectively self-present our "best" promotes the notion that the couple and/or the relationship was far more ideal than it actually was (remember: the couple broke up for a reason). This "ideal" relationship presents a threat and, thus, triggers jealousy (Frampton & Fox, 2018; Dainton & Stokes, 2015).

Of course, there are a number of things that determine how we experience jealousy, such as family of origin experiences, past relationship experiences, sexual attitudes and beliefs (for instance, some people are more sexually permissive than others), and gender role attitudes (Russell & Harton, 2005). Jealousy is a complex emotion that has many sides to it, and because of this, it has been difficult for scientists to measure. But given its purposes of protecting intimate and family relationships, and given its consequences to our psychological and physical well-being, more research needs to be conducted so we can better understand its forms, functions, and outcomes.

So far, our study has shown us that love can be experienced as a romantic infatuation, which involves a complicated, overpowering blend of emotion and sex. There are also negative sides of romantic love, which include stalking and jealousy (although jealousy can be experienced in any type of relationship). But unlike passionate love, in which feelings may wax and wane, *companionate* love is characterized by deep, mature, affectionate attachment bonds.

COMPANIONATE LOVE: EXPERIENCING LOVE AS A COMMITMENT

There's love . . . and there's love that lasts. It is not uncommon for us to question whether our experiences with love are "real love" or "true love." With such a flood of biochemicals in the brain and the surge of hormones in the bloodstream when we become attracted to someone, it is little wonder that it is difficult to determine whether what we are feeling is the real, lasting thing or a fleeting fling. Unlike infatuation, *companionate love* leads to committed, perhaps even lifelong, love relationships.

Companionate Love

It is not uncommon for relationships to move from the have-to-be-intimate-24-hours-a-day phase (passionate love) to a phase of love that is less dominated by lust. Much in the same

Passionate love often gives way to companionate love over time. This type of love is characterized by deep, tender, and mature emotional bonds to one another.

iStock.com/MixMedia

way ravenous binge eating must eventually come to an end, so too must the ravenous passionate/infatuated love come to an end. (If the love remained at the sexually and emotionally charged level, we would be too worn out to accomplish much else!) If the romantic love experience is to endure, it must at some point be combined with or transition into a calmer, more tender, more affectionate type of love. While passionate/romantic love is a rapid-fire frenzy of emotion, sexual arousal, anxiousness, and life that revolves around the two-person world, companionate love is distinctly different. **Companionate love** refers to deep, tender, mature, affectionate attachment bonds shared between two people; companionate love may or may not include feelings of physical arousal.

Passionate love happens quickly; companionate love grows gradually over time. Contrary to "love at first sight" relationships or "love [hormone] connections" observed in passionate love relationships, companionate love develops between partners who have known each other long enough to have acknowledged and accepted all of the failings, faults, shortcomings, oddities, and quirks of each partner—and still *like* the partner.

Liking is a necessary ingredient in companionate love. It is impossible to arrive at companionate love without liking each other. Why? Liking develops as a result of consistent, repeated **rewards**, such as nurture, care, appreciation, trust, and making/seeing the other person happy. Essentially, whatever attributes people have on their love prototype list are their perceived rewards in the relationship. Building the rewards takes time and patience—both fundamental components of companionate love. Passionate love relationships typically do not want to devote the time necessary to build up rewards because the very nature of these relationships contradicts spending time on anything.

Expressions of Love

To further our understanding of the distinctions among the experiences of liking, infatuation, and committed love, Robert Sternberg (1986, 1988) developed his **Triangular Theory of Love**, which conceptualizes eight different types of love relationships. These relationships take into account that each individual will experience many types of love throughout life. Recognizing that love is a *process* that undergoes change, Sternberg proposed that love relationships consist of three interconnected components: intimacy, commitment, and passion. As you can see in Figure 6.1, each of these interlocking components corresponds to one side

Figure 6.1 /// Sternberg's Triangular Theory of Love

Robert Sternberg conceptualized love as a process that undergoes change throughout a person's life, with three interconnected components: intimacy, commitment, and passion. Because love is not a fixed experience, the three components are not always in perfect balance.

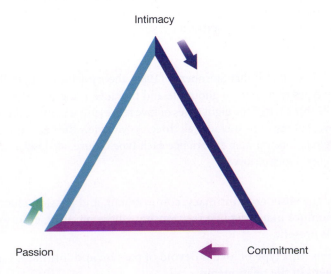

of the love triangle; because love is not a fixed or static experience, the three components of love will not always be in perfect balance. Indeed, all three components may not necessarily be present at the same time. For this reason, we may experience different types of loving, even within the same relationship, over a period of time.

Intimacy. According to Sternberg (1986), intimacy refers to loving relationships characterized by feelings of closeness, connectedness, and bondedness. Recall from Chapter 5 that intimacy involves an emotional attachment (we can think of intimacy as the *emotional component* in a love relationship) and includes many components such as self-disclosure of personal and private aspects of our lives, respect, trust, affection, warmth, mutuality, and spirituality. As with companionate love, intimacy builds slowly and gradually over time and is a prominent feature of a love relationship.

Commitment. Sternberg (1986) defines *commitment* as a decision to love someone else and as a decision to maintain that love over time. **Commitment** refers to loving another person as a conscious act of will—it is a deliberate choice. Commitment can thus be thought of as the *cognitive component* in a love relationship. It includes such things as being loyal to another person, being responsible and reliable, being trustworthy and trusting, and putting forth our best effort in a relationship (Fehr, 1988).

Sternberg (1986) observed that the process of commitment occurs gradually, with the levels of commitment to the partner increasing somewhat slowly at first. Commitment—just as in the instances of loving and liking—is possible only after several rewards are reciprocated between the partners. After commitment begins to increase in a relationship, these levels accelerate and then gradually find a leveling-off point. If at any time during the relationship any of the key attributes of commitment are dishonored, violated, or lost, the love relationship becomes threatened or may even end.

Passion. The passion element of Sternberg's (1986) triangle of love refers to many of the facets discussed earlier in our coverage of passionate/infatuation love relationships. **Passion**, in this instance, refers to the physical attraction and romantic feelings that initially draw us to another person. According to Sternberg, passion is the driving force of romance, physical attraction, and sexual consummation. It is important to note, however, that passion can still exist in a relationship whether sexual intercourse is a part of the relationship or not.

Of the three components of Sternberg's (1986) theory, passion is the most intense and immediate. Passion peaks quickly. Over time, however, the initial excitement levels of passion reduce to a stable level; at the same time, liking and intimacy levels continue to rise, giving way to companionate love. Although some couples fear that they have "fallen out of love" when the passion begins to fade, others become comfortable with the calm stabilization of their love relationship. Sternberg notes that if a relationship is ended, an individual may experience feelings of loss. If this occurs, a person's capacity for passion may be negative for a time until the sense of loss abates.

Sternberg's Love Types. Recall that Sternberg's (1986) theory acknowledges that each individual experiences many types of love throughout life and that love is a *process* that undergoes change. Notice in Figure 6.2 that each of the eight types of love represents a combination of any of the three components of love, but only one includes all three. As you view the varying types of love, keep in mind that a single relationship may experience each type of love, as described by Sternberg. The following are the eight types of love:

1. **Nonlove.** The absence of intimacy, commitment, and passion characterizes this type of love. Nonlove may exist in a relationship where physical, emotional, or sexual violence is present.

2. **Empty love.** This type of love is devoid of passion and intimacy. *Commitment* is the only element in the relationship.

Commitment:

refers to loving another person as a conscious act of will—it is a deliberate choice. Commitment can thus be thought of as the cognitive component in a love relationship.

Passion:

the physical attraction and romantic feelings that initially draw us to another person.

Nonlove:

the absence of intimacy, commitment, and passion. Nonlove may exist in a relationship where physical, emotional, or sexual violence is present.

3. **Liking.** *Intimacy* is the sole element in the relationship and is the stuff that great, long-lasting friendships are made of. There is typically no passion or commitment.

4. **Infatuated love.** This type of love consists of *passion* only; this is the stuff that television dating shows and "Hollywood" marriages are made of but not long-term marriages. Characterized by sudden and explosive physical feelings along with the idealizing of the love object, infatuated love relationships end as quickly as they begin.

5. *Companionate love.* This love type combines the elements of *intimacy* and *commitment*. Companionate love often starts as romantic love and is then transformed into companionate love as couples take time to build intimacy. Passionate love junkies probably will not give romantic relationships the time needed for companionate love to grow.

6. **Fatuous love.** Combining *passion* and *commitment*, fatuous love relationships result in a sprint toward a cohabiting partnership or down the marital aisle. But because the relationship lacks intimacy and the time necessary for intimacy to grow and develop, and because passion will fade sooner or later, the only element remaining is commitment. The commitment is not the type that has been nurtured through the ups and downs of relational life; the commitment thus fades in time.

7. **Romantic love.** *Intimacy* and *passion* are the elements that make up romantic love. Because of the physical and/or sexual attraction and arousal that accompanies romantic love, it is thought to be a more intense form of love than liking.

8. **Consummate love.** Sternberg considers consummate love to be total, whole, absolute, and all-inclusive. This type of love combines all three elements of love—*intimacy, commitment,* and *passion.* Some may attain this type of relationship, but not without nurturing and working to maintain the relationship.

DEVELOPING LOVE

The ability and capacity to love *are not totally inherited*—they are nurtured from our first experiences of love. The development of love is a complex interaction of heredity, such as personality traits; the environment in which we are reared; our family of origin; and the

Empty love:

this type of love is void of passion and intimacy. Commitment is the only element in the relationship.

Liking:

intimacy is the sole element in the relationship and is the stuff that great, long-lasting friendships are made of. There is typically no passion or commitment.

Infatuated love:

this type of love consists of passion only; "Hollywood" marriages are made of this, but not long-term marriages.

Fatuous love:

combining passion and commitment, fatuous love relationships result in a sprint toward cohabitation or marriage. Because the relationship lacks intimacy and the time necessary for intimacy to grow and develop, and because passion will fade sooner or later, the only element remaining is commitment.

Romantic love:

intimacy and passion comprise romantic love. Because of the accompanying physical and/or sexual attraction and arousal, it is a more intense form of love than liking.

Consummate love:

considered by Sternberg to be total, whole, absolute, and all-inclusive, consummate love combines all three elements of love—intimacy, commitment, and passion.

Figure 6.2 /// Sternberg's Love Types

Each of the eight types of love proposed by Sternberg represents a combination of the three components of love. As a relationship grows and changes, it may experience each type of love. The solid lines represent the components that are present in the different types of love. The dots represent the missing components (such as empty love has commitment but not intimacy or passion).

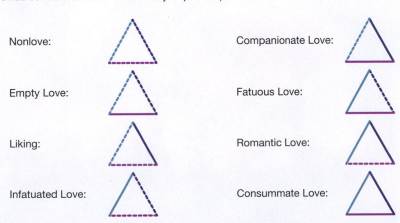

Nonlove:

Empty Love:

Liking:

Infatuated Love:

Companionate Love:

Fatuous Love:

Romantic Love:

Consummate Love:

myriad events, incidents, and situations we experience in family life. Interactions and love experiences we have with people across our lifespan, as well as our educational background, all contribute to how love develops in our lives.

First Experiences of Love

The first love relationship many of us experience is the parent–infant relationship. Thrust into an unfamiliar, foreign environment, we begin our relational lives as dependent creatures, fully reliant on our parents and caregivers for our most basic survival needs (nourishment, shelter, warmth, and touch). It is this very dependency on others that propels us to form emotional bonds in which we give and receive love. Likewise, it is from the experiences of the earliest of all love relationships that all of our later-in-life love relationships take shape.

The early love bond that parents form toward their child is **altruistic love**, an unselfish, giving kind of love in which they seek to provide for the needs of their child. Altruistic love promotes the well-being of another with no expectation of reciprocity or return, and it is difficult to specifically pinpoint the rewards or benefits such a love relationship provides. Indeed, the rewards of altruistic love are **intrinsic rewards** (such as joy, satisfaction, contentment, pleasure, gratification, etc.) derived from the relationships. Most of us do not feel the need for altruistic love to be reciprocated because the rewards obtained are pleasurable in and of themselves.

Perhaps the key concept that differentiates adult-infant love from adult-adult love is the concept of *reciprocity*. Certainly, parents and caregivers cannot realistically expect the return of love from a baby, but adults do expect their love to be reciprocated by their friends and love partners. The ability for people to be dependent and have someone depend on them is referred to as **interdependent love**. Unlike **dependent love** as seen in the adult-infant pair bond, where an adult immediately meets and gratifies the needs of an infant, interdependent love is expressed between emotionally mature adults who recognize that love is a give-and-take process. Adults recognize that there are times when one partner may have to give more than the other, such as in the case of illness or times of extreme stress or distress. Emotionally mature adults understand that interdependent love requires that, at times, some wants and needs may have to be delayed in order to promote the well-being of a partner or the couple.

Altruistic love:
an unselfish, giving kind of love. Most of us do not feel the need to reciprocate altruistic love because the rewards are intrinsic.

Intrinsic rewards:
rewards that are pleasurable in and of themselves, such as joy, satisfaction, contentment, pleasure, gratification.

Interdependent love:
the ability for people to be dependent and have someone depend on them. Interdependent love is expressed between emotionally mature adults who recognize that love is a give-and-take process.

Dependent love:
love between an adult and an infant or child, wherein the adult meets and gratifies the needs of the infant or child without expectation of anything in return.

Altruistic or unconditional love is expressed through freely given care, tenderness, affection, and acceptance. With this type of love, nothing is expected in return.

iStock.com/Mihailomilovanovic

Figure 6.3 /// Time Line of Love Experiences

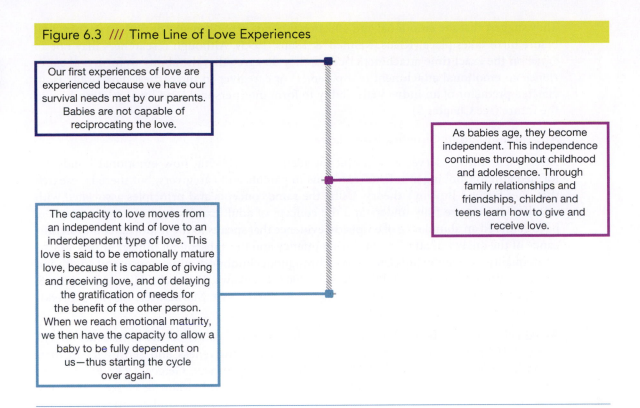

The growth from dependent love to interdependent love is a process that takes place over many developmental phases of life, from infancy, through childhood and adolescence, through the transition to early adulthood, to the end of life (see Figure 6.3). As in the case of intimacy, the capacity to love others develops throughout the lifespan. As you have learned, relationships we form during the early years of life serve as template interactions on which subsequent interpersonal intimate and love relationships are built.

The development of our capacity and ability to love takes place in the context of early emotional relationships, particularly within our family of origin. In the next section, we take a closer look at the emotional bond that significantly impacts our ability to give and receive love throughout our lives: attachment.

Attachment: An Emotional Bond

Attachment is best described as an emotional or affectional bond that ties or binds the child to the parent or primary caregiver (Bowlby, 1988). In order to describe enduring, lasting patterns of interpersonal relationships from the cradle to the grave, John Bowlby (1969–1980) developed the **Attachment theory** based on his observation of parent–child interactions. With the premise that all infants need nurturance in order to survive, Bowlby asserted that in the process of providing for these survival needs, newborns form a type of bond—an attachment—with their caregivers (typically the mother and/or father). Bowlby's Attachment theory posits that it is from this close affectional and emotional bond that children derive a sense of security, a trusting sense that the world, and the interpersonal relationships we encounter along the way, is a safe place to be.

Because of the importance of these early human relationships, Bowlby, along with prominent researcher Mary Ainsworth and her associates, asserted that the attachment behaviors that take place throughout infancy ultimately direct, shape, and mold our personality. Consequently, these behaviors significantly direct, shape, and mold the interpersonal attachment relationships we experience later on as children, adolescents, and adults (Ainsworth, Belhar, Waters, & Wall, 1978). Some researchers believe that attachment may begin even earlier.

Attachment:
an emotional or affectional bond that binds the child to a parent or primary caregiver.

Attachment theory:
John Bowlby's Attachment theory describes enduring patterns of interpersonal relationships from cradle to grave. With the premise that all newborns must be nurtured in order to survive, Bowlby observed that they form a type of bond—an attachment— with their caregivers. From this close affectional and emotional bond, children derive a sense of security, a trusting sense that the world is a safe place to be.

They suggest that the emotional and affectional bonds actually begin during pregnancy, well before birth takes place (Klaus, Kennell, & Klaus, 1995). Although researchers may not all agree on the exact time attachment occurs, they do agree that the ability to form and experience an emotional attachment to a parent(s) or caregiver in the earliest days of life is, in effect, a predictor of an individual's ability to form interpersonal (and love) relationships in the future (see Chapter 5).

Attachment and Its Significance to Love

Attachment theory serves as a useful foundation for viewing how emotional bonds are formed and for looking at infants' reactions to parents and caregivers, but there is research that goes beyond Bowlby's theory. Using the same concepts and principles associated with attachment to more fully understand the concept of adult experiences of love, researchers have gathered an abundance of empirical evidence that speaks to the importance and significance of the quality of attachment during infancy and the subsequent impact of this attachment quality to relationships later in life, throughout childhood, adolescence, and adulthood (such as Allen & Land, 1999; Elliot & Reis, 2003; Furukawa, Yokouchi, Hirai, Kitamura, & Takahashi, 1999; Howe, Brandon, Hinings, & Scofield, 1999; Markeiwicz, Doyle, & Brendgen, 2001; Seiffge-Krenke, 1993; Weiss, 1982).

An equally abundant body of research exists that examines adults' secure or insecure attachment to their own parents and their subsequent responsiveness and sensitivity in their parenting behaviors toward their own children (among others, Geiger, 1996; Field, 1996; Bartholomew, 1990; Crittenden, Partridge, & Claussen, 1991; Main & Hesse, 1990). For example, Marinus van Ijzendoorn (1995), a developmentalist who studies intergenerational aspects of childrearing and attachment, sought to understand the extent to which parents transmit their own attachment experiences to their children. He found in his study of 59 mother-infant pairs that about three-fourths of the pairs were identical in their attachment behaviors. There is even some evidence that attachment behaviors and patterns span multiple generations (Benoit & Parker, 1994). According to researchers Clyde Hendrick and Susan Hendrick (1992), attachment is a developmental phase that we never outgrow.

Attachment Types

One study in particular is quite helpful in our quest to gain insight into the development of our ability to love others. Based on Ainsworth and colleagues' (1978) descriptive categories of attachment styles observed in infants, psychologists Cindy Hazan and Phillip Shaver's (1987) research supports the notion that patterns of attachment early in life influence adult love relationships. In their examination of adult love relationships conceptualized as an attachment process, Hazan and Shaver classified adult love relationships in the following way.

- **Secure attachment types.** Secure adults, like securely attached infants, have little difficulty seeking or maintaining closeness (physical, emotional, affectional) with another. They don't fear being abandoned or losing their partner. Secure adults allow others to get close to them and depend on them. These adults report enduring, happy, warm, trusting relationships that promote self-esteem.

- **Avoidant attachment types.** Avoidant types report that they seldom find "real" love. Hazan and Shaver (1987) described these adults as being uncomfortable when too emotionally or physically close to another person. Avoidant attachment types show discomfort with intimacy and are hesitant to trust others (Feeney & Noller, 1991), They find it difficult to allow themselves to depend on others. Avoidant types commonly report that they experienced separation from their mothers (emotional and/or physical separation).

- **Anxious/ambivalent attachment types.** Insecurity is the hallmark of this adult attachment type. When an adult shows this type of attachment, it is not a matter of *if* a romantic partner leaves them, but *when*. With the constant fear or worry that the partner isn't really in love with them, anxious/ambivalent adults cling to their partner and push for commitment

Secure attachment types:

secure adults, like securely attached infants, have little difficulty seeking or maintaining closeness with another. They don't fear being abandoned or losing their partner.

Avoidant attachment types:

avoidant adults show discomfort with intimacy and are hesitant to trust others. Avoidant types report that they seldom find "real" love.

Anxious/ambivalent attachment types:

insecurity is the hallmark of this attachment type. Fearing for the partner's love, anxious/ambivalent adults cling to the partner and push for commitment—often pushing the partner away.

(Feeney & Noller, 1991)—and in doing so, often push the partner completely out of the picture. Poor attachment in adulthood can prohibit people from getting too emotionally close to attachment figures, causing them to withdraw and pull away before they get rejected (Pickover, 2002).

As a student told me,

> My experiences leave me very distrustful of others . . . although it has been very difficult to undergo counseling, I have become aware of the many areas in which I need to heal. I have to totally re-learn to relate to people. I am learning that I don't have to feel guilty when I am not punished for doing or saying the wrong thing . . . I am learning that I don't have to constantly apologize for things I have no control over . . . I don't have to earn people's kindness or love! I do still, though, feel extreme guilt in knowing I am— and might always be—an emotionally high-need person. Eventually I will have to take the risk of telling another person what happened to me and letting him decide if he is willing to deal with me while I deal with the past. (Author's files)

The empirical evidence is clear—our experiences with early attachment relationships to our parent(s) or primary caregiver become the foundation on which all future love relationships are built.

Love Stories: Shaped From Generation to Generation

As recipes and cooking may be passed down from generation to generation, so too are the origins of our capacity to love and to be loved. It is these family influences that ultimately shape our **love stories**—our unique, personal experiences with love. There is a story that surfaced several years ago about a newly married couple. It makes a strong point concerning the development of love within the family of origin.

Love stories: our unique, personal experiences with love.

In preparation for their first big dinner with both sets of parents and grandparents, the new husband was puzzled as he watched his new bride put the ham in the oven. He inquired of her, "Honey, why did you cut the ham in half and then put it in the pan?"

There's more to this intergenerational family than we can see at the surface. Each of us learns our relational behaviors—including how we give and receive love—from our parents, and they received those love models from their parents. How we love is an intergenerational experience!

She replied, "Oh, I don't know . . . I suppose because that's how Mom always did it. It must help it cook faster or something."

At dinner that evening the bride asked her mother, "Mom, why do you cut the ham in half before you bake it?"

The mother, baffled by her daughter's question, thoughtfully replied, "I suppose it's because that's how my mom always did it." All eyes in the room turned on the bride's grandmother. The grandmother, quite amused, chuckled and replied, "When I was first married I didn't have a pan large enough for the ham to fit in—so I always cut it into two halves and just kept doing it that way. I guess I just got accustomed to doing it that way."

As this story illustrates, so often we do things and interact in certain established ways because we have become accustomed to doing things in these ways. So it is with much of what makes up family life, including how we love others and how we allow others to love us. Thus far in your study of family and intimate relations you have come to understand the nature of family process. You have learned to recognize that our actions influence and are influenced by our family of origin.

Intergenerational approach to family therapy:

an approach seeking to understand the transmission of relational behaviors from one generation to the next.

Murray Bowen (1974), a central figure in an **intergenerational approach to family therapy**, sought to understand the transmission of relational behaviors from one generation to the next. Indeed, as marriage and family therapists Michael Nichols and Richard Schwartz (2004) point out, "The family remains with us wherever we go" (p. 119).

According to Nichols and Schwartz (2004), Bowen believed that when examining the family, it is not enough to say that past experiences influence present experiences; he also wanted to look at the relationships within the family and explore the path that guided the emotional processes from generation to generation. And it is from this theory the use of genograms was born.

Genogram:

a diagram with various figures that illustrate relationships between family members.

Bowen (1974) created **genograms**, which are diagrams with various figures that serve to illustrate relationships between family members. These relationships can be drawn to illustrate simply the immediate family, or, in greater detail, they may include extended family relationships and multigenerational relationships. Whether using a genogram to trace certain medical histories, such a cancer or heart disease; to create family trees; or to gain a clearer understanding of the family processes and emotional behaviors and patterns passed down through the generations, as Bowen did, genograms give us an instant snapshot of relationship history within a given family.

In Figure 6.4a, squares are used to represent males; females are represented by circles. Notice that each of the figures is assigned an age. A solid horizontal line indicates marriage and the marriage date, while the vertical lines link parents and children. To denote a family member who has died, an "·" is placed through the square or the circle. Figure 6.4b illustrates other symbols used to indicate relationship dynamics. These dynamics speak, in large part, to the emotional connection of the family members.

Genograms are most commonly used for therapeutic purposes. When an individual family member or a family seeks family therapy, the marriage and family therapist may use the genogram to map out family dynamics. So, one family's genogram may resemble something similar to Figure 6.4b. Notice how this illustration shows that the relationship between all of the siblings is either distant or estranged, as is the relationship between the husband and the wife. Only the mother and daughter appear to have emotional closeness. A therapist can use this information to help the family establish healthier boundaries and, thus, improve the family's health and functioning.

THEORIES OF LOVE AND LOVING

We have already taken a look at one prominent theory, Sternberg's Triangular Theory of Love, and we have devoted significant time to Attachment theory. Let me now turn your attention to other conceptualizations of love. Two additional theories, Lee's Six Types of

Figure 6.4a /// Basic Genogram Symbols

In family genograms, squares represent males and circles represent females. The solid horizontal line indicates marriage and the marriage date. The vertical lines link parents and children.

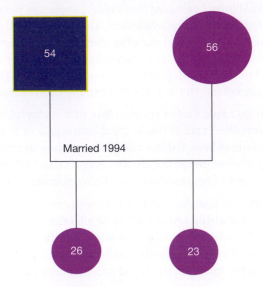

Figure 6.4b /// Genogram Symbols for Relationship Dynamics

Genograms are useful tools used by therapists to map out family dynamics, particularly the emotional connections between family members.

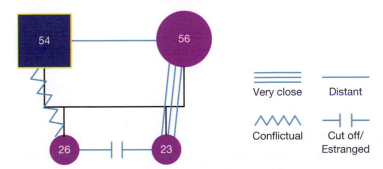

Love Styles and Reiss's Wheel Theory of Love, have received much attention and consideration. Further, today a new type of love relationship is gaining momentum in the United States, that of polyamory. Another theory, Love Economic Model, is just emerging on the social science scene.

Lee's Six Types of Love Styles

As noted earlier in this chapter, the Greeks solved the problem of using only one word—love—for perhaps the most complex emotion known to humankind. Canadian sociologist John Alan Lee (1973) conceptualized love in a manner similar to that of the Greeks in that he proposed six different love styles. Recognizing the theoretical richness and multidimensionality of Lee's work, Hendrick and Hendrick (1986) then built on Lee's work to create instruments with which to measure the varying types of love (Neto, 2001).

1. *Eros; Passionate and Tantalizing.* The Greeks used the term *eros* to refer to a type of sensual or sexual love. Lee noted that **erotic lovers** are passionate and romantic and seek out passionately expressive lovers. They thrive on the tantalizing nature of love and sex. They have an "ideal mate" in their mind's eye and believe there is only one "true love" in the world for them. Sexual activity usually occurs early on in the relationship, and the sex is hot, passionate, exciting, and insatiable all at once. Once sexual activity takes place, the eros lover is usually monogamous.

2. *Ludus: Flirtatious and Fun.* **Ludus** refers to love that is playful, flirtatious, carefree, and casual. **Ludic lovers** don't care as much about commitment as they do about playing the sport or the game of love. For the ludic lover, variety is truly the spice of life—the more partners, the better. Because ludic lovers don't share intimacy, love with a ludic person is fun and easygoing, nonchalant and unconcerned about tomorrow.

3. *Storge: Affectionate and Constant.* **Storge** (pronounced STOR-gay) love can best be conceptualized as friendship love, or a type of affectionate love between companions. **Storgic lovers** typically come to love each other over time, as opposed to the instantaneous type of love found with eros lovers. Neto (2001) notes that this type of love engenders shared interests, trust, and acceptance, all of which develop over time.

4. *Manic: Frenzied and Chaotic.* Jealousy, envy, protectiveness, and exclusivity are the hallmark traits of **manic lovers**. Manic love is frenzied, agitated, hectic, and chaotic all at the same time. The highs are very high, the lows are very low—making the relationship very much a roller coaster ride of emotions. When a love relationship ends, a manic lover has difficulty thinking of anyone or anything else except the lost love.

5. *Pragma: Practical and Careful.* Practicality and logic guide the pragmatic lover. With **pragma love**, the costs and benefits associated with love are carefully weighed and considered before entering into a relationship. If the "perfect mate" items on the pragmatic lover's list are fulfilled—suitability of education, family background, socioeconomic stains, religion, and so on—the love candidate has a good chance of becoming a mate or life partner.

6. *Agape: Selfless and Patient.* Lee describes **agape love** (pronounced uh-gah-PAY) as a selfless, enduring, other-centered type of love. Taken from the Latin word *caritas,* which means "charity," the Greeks used the term *agape* love to refer to unconditional, willful, "I-love-you-because-I-choose-to" kind of love. It is a love type that provides intrinsic (rewarding in and of itself) satisfaction, with no reciprocity expected or demanded. Inherent to agape love is patience, kindness, and permanence.

Felix Neto, from the University of Porto, Portugal, focused his research on the question of whether everyone experiences love, worldwide, in the same way (see Neto et al., 2000). His previous work (Neto, 1993, 1994) indicated that Lee's love styles, characteristic of American students, were also found to be relevant to students in Portugal. In Neto and his colleagues' more recent work (2000), the love typologies were found across multiple cultures, including Africa, Asia, South America, and Europe, although they did find some cross-cultural differences. Specifically, those love typologies that involved "strong emotional feelings," such as mania, eros, and agape, were nearly free of cultural influences—in other words, across cultures people tend to experience these love typologies in very similar ways. Those love typologies that involved "strict social rules," such as pragma, storge, and ludus, were quite dependent on cultural values.

According to Hendrick and Hendrick (1983), an individual's love style is not static and fixed, but can change over the course of a lifetime, or even during a relationship. Neto's (2001) work that investigated the love styles held by three generations of women (college students, their mothers, and their maternal grandmothers) seems to support this notion. The goal of Neto's study was to determine the similarities and differences in love styles among the three generations and to explore whether experiences of love styles change over time. Each of the 144 study participants from 48 families was given a questionnaire that assessed their love styles. Results of this study indicate that there was very little similarity in the experiences of love styles among the three generations of women. In fact, Neto found significant differences between the women in the eros, storge, pragma, and agape love styles.

Finally, one body of research suggests that some love styles are considered to be more socially desirable among men and some more socially desirable among women (Davies, 2001). Primarily, eros and ludus were found to be associated with social desirability in men but not in women. Agape love was found to be associated with social desirability in women, but not in men. As you learned in Chapter 4, many experiences in intimate and family relationships are influenced by how men and women are socialized. The experiences of love are no different; this research supports the notion that how a person is taught to be male or female helps determine love styles.

Polyamory: When Two Won't Do

As you learned in Chapter 1, in the United States the social norm for intimate couple and marital relationships is monogamy, which is the cultural practice of having only one romantic and/or sexual partner at a time. But today, non-monogamous relationships are on the uptick. These non-monogamous relationships are referred to using the umbrella term *polyamory*. **Polyamory** is the practice of intimate relationships with more than one partner. The term *polyamory* is derived from the Greek *poly*, which means many or several, and from the Latin *amor*, which means love. Polyamory, then, is an intimate relationship lifestyle wherein one or both partners engage in intimate, romantic, and/or sexual relationships with more than one partner (Sheff, 2016). It is the "practice . . . of having more than one sexual loving relationship at the same time, with the full knowledge and consent of all partners involved" (Oxford Dictionary, 2019). Polyamorous relationships are practiced by straight people, gays, lesbians, bisexuals, and transgender people (Shernoff, 2006).

Polyamory:
the practice of intimate relationships with more than one partner with all partners' consent.

RONALDO SCHEMIDT/AFP via Getty Images

Polyamory is often described as consensual, ethical, and responsible non-monogamy. It is the practice of having intimate relationships with more than one partner, and all of the partners consent to these relationships. Is polyamory right for you? Why or why not?

You may be asking yourself, how is this different from having an affair or cheating on a partner? The distinction between cheating and polyamory is simple: Cheating on a spouse involves deceit, dishonesty, and deception; polyamory has been described as "consensual, ethical, and responsible monogamy" (Klesse, 2011, 2016). People who practice polyamory reject the cultural norm that intimate and sexual relationships are to be exclusive; instead, they embrace the notion that long-term loving relationships can be established with more than one partner. It's important to note that the practice of polyamory values trust, love, intimacy, fidelity, loyalty, honesty, integrity, equality, communication, and commitment—and these values are what distinguish polyamory from cheating on a partner (Sheff, 2016).

By the Numbers

Polyamory is gaining popularity in the United States. Today, it is estimated that 4 to 5 percent of American couples practice consensual non-monogamy (CNM); it is believed that the numbers are even higher, but most who practice CNM are closeted (Sheff, 2016). In a random sample of nearly 1,000 adults in the United States, the researchers found that typical views of monogamy are eroding, although more than two-thirds of those Americans surveyed (68 percent) said they would not be okay with their romantic partner having sex with someone else, no matter what the circumstances (Ballard, 2020). Figure 6.5 shows us that attitudes about open relationships in the U.S. are opening up. While it's clear that, among those surveyed, most Americans would not be okay if their partner wanted to engage in sexual activities with another person, 78 percent of older adults (65+) were against it, compared to 56 percent of Gen Z'ers (ages 18 to 29, and 60 percent of Millennials (ages 30 to 44; Ballard, 2020). Of those surveyed, about 1 in 10 have had sexual contact with other people with the consent of their partner. It's interesting to note that the younger the age group, the more open the attitudes are.

Fulfilling Needs

Other common questions surrounding polyamory and polyamorous relationships are, Why is such a relationship necessary? Why would I need/want to turn to someone else other than my partner for sexual or intimacy needs? Psychologist Melissa Mitchell and her

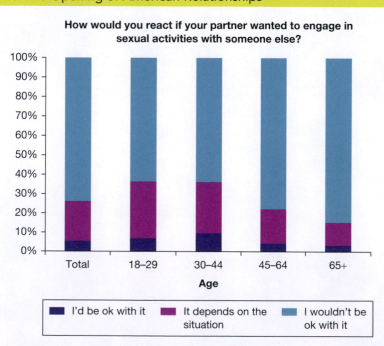

Figure 6.5 /// The Opening of American Relationships

How would you react if your partner wanted to engage in sexual activities with someone else?

Legend:
- I'd be ok with it
- It depends on the situation
- I wouldn't be ok with it

Age: Total, 18–29, 30–44, 45–64, 65+

Source: Sternberg (1986, 1988).

colleagues (2013) address these questions in their research of 1,093 polyamorous individuals. Their research investigated whether within polyamorous relationships, two relational components are met: need fulfillment and satisfaction.

In this study, the authors note that since the 1920s, the Western expectation in love and sexual relationships is that one partner meets all of their partner's needs, from emotional needs to psychological, spiritual, sexual, companionship, and physical needs (Mitchell et al., 2013). And, as you are coming to know in our study so far, when these needs are not met, relationship problems begin to crop up and relationship satisfaction begins to drop. But in polyamorous relationships, "relationship needs can be distributed across multiple partners, potentially lessening the expectation that one romantic partner should meet all or most of the relationship needs" (p. 2). The researchers found an interesting paradox: When needs were met in one relationship, it had an enhancing effect on the other relationship; when need fulfillment was not met in one relationship, however, it had a negative effect on the other relationship. Overall, the study results suggest that polyamorous couples were more fulfilled with their primary partners. The researchers note, "a second intimate relationship may only be threatening to another relationship if individuals feel that the latter relationship is not fulfilling their needs in some respects" (p. 8). The authors conclude that it is possible to have loving, committed relationships with more than one partner.

Drawbacks and Pitfalls

Even though poly relationships are gaining in practice and popularity in Western cultures, it's important to note that this relationship lifestyle isn't for everyone. Several researchers have noted drawbacks and pitfalls of polyamorous relationships:

- *Complexity:* Monogamous relationships are difficult enough to manage, so how do poly couples manage their time, emotions, and the intensities that relationships bring? According to Sheff (2015), many who engage in polyamorous relationships find it difficult to balance all of their relationships.

- *Jealousy:* Polys are human—and jealousy is a part of human nature. Jealousy does crop up in polyamorous relationships, but as all researchers point out, responsible polyamorous partners accept their partners' jealousy and work through it together. They note that some people are more prone to jealousy than others are, and for this reason, they should steer clear of the poly lifestyle.

- *Health risks:* Being with multiple partners, who themselves might have multiple partners, increases the risk of contracting a sexually transmitted infection.

- *Social ostracism:* Polyamorous relationships are not accepted by U.S. culture, and because of this, couples may experience prejudice, discrimination, and ostracism.

- *Lopsided power:* Perhaps one of the greatest strengths of the poly relationship is the equality it affords to each of the partners in the relationship. At times, however, there can be lopsided power dynamics. These power or equality differences make the relationship more beneficial to one partner than to the others. For example, some polyamorous relationships are formed under duress—this can be as overt as one partner physically or emotionally threatening his/her partner to accept the relationship, or it can be as subtle as agreeing to make the partner happy and to satisfy his/her needs, but internally resenting it. (Hawkins & VanDenBerghe, 2017; Keenan, 2013; Rubel & Bogaert, 2014; Masters, 2011; Sheff, 2015; Brunning, 2016)

As with all aspects of any other healthy love and intimate relationship, polyamorous relationships require that couples remain in open, honest, and trustworthy communication with each other.

Reiss's Wheel Theory of Love

Sociologist Ira Reiss (1960, 1971) described love as a developmental process, a process that unfolds over time. Reiss's Wheel Theory of Love (Figure 6.6) suggests four stages or processes of love: rapport, self-revelation, mutual dependency, and personality need fulfillment.

Reiss's Wheel Theory of Love: sociologist Ira Reiss described love as a developmental process that unfolds over time, with four stages: rapport, self-revelation, mutual dependency, and personality need fulfillment. Similar to a rolling wheel, these stages of love may be experienced many times and, in turn, deepen the love bonds between partners.

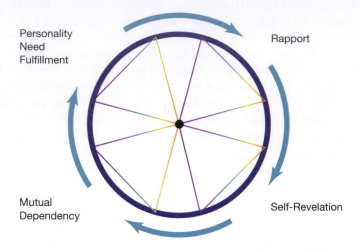

Figure 6.6 /// Reiss's Wheel Theory of Love

Sociologist Ira Reiss described love as a developmental process that unfolds over time, in four stages. Similar to a rolling wheel, these stages of love may be experienced many times within the same relationship, deepening the love bonds between partners. If the wheel stops turning, the love relationship may end.

Source: Reiss (1960, 1971).

Similar to a rolling wheel, these stages of love may be experienced many times and, in turn, deepen the love bonds between partners:

1. *Rapport.* **Rapport** refers to a connection or bond we feel with another person. Most often, we establish rapport with someone who is similar to us in our cultural background, social class, religious beliefs, educational background, or upbringing. According to Reiss, we are typically more comfortable with someone who is most like us. These similarities allow us to pursue our initial interests in another person.

2. *Self-revelation.* When we feel comfortable in another person's presence, we feel more comfortable self-disclosing our personal hopes, dreams, fears, and goals. **Self-revelation** refers to self-disclosure; as you learned in Chapter 5, self-disclosure deepens a couple's relationship.

3. *Mutual dependency.* As a couple self-discloses, the intimacy levels deepen in their relationship. The couple begins to spend more time together, and they enjoy sharing activities and pursing shared interests. **Mutual dependency** refers to the couple's reliance on one another for need fulfillment, such as social needs and sexual needs.

4. *Personality need fulfillment.* During the fourth and final stage, partners experience **personality need fulfillment**, which is an established pattern of mutual exchanges of support, sympathy, and decision making. Each person also satisfies their partner's deeper needs, such as emotional needs and sexual needs.

Reiss (1960, 1971) suggests that as long as the wheel continues to move forward, a deep and lasting relationship is formed and maintained. If, however, the wheel stops turning—if the processes diminish—the love relationship may come to an end.

The love theories we have explored so far have received much attention and consideration among family life educators, sociologists, psychologists, and family practitioners. A new theory of love is emerging on the social science scene: the Love Economic Model.

Rapport:

a connection or bond we feel with another person.

Self-revelation:

when we feel comfortable in another person's presence, we feel more comfortable self-disclosing our personal hopes, dreams, fears, and goals.

Mutual dependency:

a couple's reliance on one another for need fulfillment, such as socially and sexually.

Personality need fulfilment:

an established pattern of mutual exchanges of support, sympathy, and decision making. Each person also satisfies his or her partner's deeper emotional and sexual needs.

Love Economic Model

It was bound to happen sooner or later. With the premise that no one, single source answers eras-old questions such as "How do I find love?" "Why do I fall in love?" and "How do I get out of love?" researcher Chau Vuong (2003) conceptualized a theoretical framework in which he uses mathematical equations to examine "love." He contends that his mathematical, economic model of love provides a means to predict and explain all human behavior pertaining to love.

Vuong's **Love Economic Model** is based on the primary assumptions that people are rational decision makers who are able to tally up both the benefits and costs of falling in love and being in love. In addition, Vuong contends, "Sex and commitment are the only differences between friendship and love" (p. 12). The Love Economic Model is based on several core variables.

The Benefits of Love

The equation for the benefits of love looks like this:

Benefits of love = emotional needs + entertainment needs + materialistic needs

1. **Emotional needs** include esteem needs, social needs, spiritual needs, and safety needs. *Esteem needs* refer to obtaining those things that make us happy and content, such as a family. *Social needs* refer to the need for social acceptance, prestige, and access to certain people, events, and resources. *Spiritual needs* include feeling connected to a higher power than ourselves, and *safety needs* include the size and quality of and access to our support network of family and friends.

2. **Entertainment needs** are considered by Vuong to be, by and large, social aspects of day-to-day living and family life. Needs variables include hobbies, interests, and experiences that serve to provide automatic partners. By engaging in these activities, we are bound to meet potential love partners.

3. **Materialistic needs** refer to those primary needs required for survival and happiness, including food, water, shelter, and transportation. Vuong also considers sexual needs to be a materialistic need. *Materialistic desires* are those things not necessarily needed for survival or happiness, but that make life more enjoyable. Vuong terms these "the finer things in life," and contends that if a person cannot satisfy these materialistic desires personally, she or he will seek out someone who can and will.

The Costs of Love

The equation for the costs of love looks like this:

Costs of love = search cost (attractiveness + social networking skills + search time cost [free time · selectiveness] + financial cost [social network size · selectiveness]) + rejection costs + maintenance costs + breakup risk (lover's future net benefit with you + lover's net benefit with another love + lover's current breakup cost) + breakup costs (breakup emotional cost + breakup financial cost + replacement cost for another love + previous friendship loss)

Whew! Let's break it down:

1. **Search cost** includes our attractiveness, or our ability to attract potential partners, along with social networking skills. The author of the Love Economic Model posits "love is a numbers game" (Vuong, 2003, p. 22)—the more people we date, the

Love Economic model:
Chau Vuong's Love Economic model is based on the primary assumptions that people are rational decision makers and, as a result, are able to tally up both the benefits and costs of falling in love and being in love. Vuong further contends that "sex and commitment are the only differences between friendship and love."

Emotional needs:
self-esteem, social and spiritual needs, and safety.

Entertainment needs:
social aspects of day-to-day living and family life (hobbies, interests, etc.).

Materialistic needs:
the primary needs required for survival and happiness, including food, water, shelter, and transportation.

Search costs:
include our attractiveness, or our ability to attract potential partners, along with social networking skills.

Rejection costs:

include rejection sensitivity (anxiety, lowered self-esteem), immunity to rejection (frequency of past rejections), and the emotional cost of the rejection.

Maintenance costs:

emotional costs and time costs involved in finding the right person.

Breakup risk:

a relationship cost that includes determining the lover's future overall benefit with the individual, the lover's future net benefit with another lover, and the lover's current breakup costs. If these costs are considered high, the risk of being "dumped" is relatively low.

Breakup costs:

emotional and financial costs of a breakup, and the search cost necessary to find another love.

better our odds of finding someone to love. In what Vuong defines as the "soulmate criteria for a picky person," he calculates how many opposite-sexed people a finicky dater would have to meet in order to find a life mate: 2,604,167!

2. **Rejection costs** include, among other things, rejection sensitivity (anxiety, lowered self-esteem), immunity to rejection (frequency of past rejections), and the emotional cost of the rejection.

3. **Maintenance costs** are delineated as emotional costs and time costs involved in finding the right person. Consequently, those who have relatively little free time have no time for relationships and are less susceptible to falling in love. Financial costs are those costs associated with pursuing the relationship (for example, if he or she wants children, children cost money and the financial costs are elevated if the relationship is pursued).

4. **Breakup risk** is a relationship cost that includes determining the lover's future overall benefit with the individual, the lover's future net benefit with another lover, and the lover's current breakup cost. If these costs are considered high, the risk of being "dumped" is relatively low.

5. **Breakup costs** include emotional costs, financial costs, and the search cost necessary to find another love.

Table 6.2 depicts Vuong's (2003) conceptualization of "love economics" translations (p. 62). Vuong's framework is complex (and at times difficult to understand if a person is as mathematically challenged as I am!) but nonetheless intriguing. This is the first theoretical framework that examines love by the numbers.

FAMILY LIFE EDUCATION: RELATING TO OTHERS WITH RESPECT, SINCERITY, AND RESPONSIBILITY

Family practitioners understand how healthy relationships are formed, developed, and maintained over time. One of the primary responsibilities of family life educators, therapists, social workers, psychologists, clergy, and others who daily work with couples and families is to educate individuals how to communicate with and relate to others with respect, sincerity, and responsibility. In order for love to flourish and thrive, couples need healthy family process skills such as effective listening, empathy, and self-disclosure—key characteristics of a love relationship.

Love is perhaps the strongest emotion known to humankind and no two people experience it in the same way. It can keep us up all night because of a fiery-hot, erotic/ludic/manic attraction to another, or it can keep us up all night because of a child who is fiery-hot with fever.

Table 6.2 /// Love Economics Translations

According to Vuong's Love Economic Model, when a partner says one thing, it really translates into Love Economics.

English	Love Economics
You are funny.	You are fulfilling my entertainment needs.
I don't care about money.	I have already fulfilled my primary and materialistic needs.
You are picky.	Your selectiveness coefficient is very small.
I am falling for you.	Your net benefit is at sufficient levels for me to reciprocate my love.
We are in love.	Our net benefits exchange is at equilibrium.

Are There Gender Differences in Emotional and Affection Needs?

Love is a developmental process that unfolds overtime. After we establish rapport with someone we find similar to us, we begin to self-disclose our most personal hopes, dreams, fears, and ambitions. In doing so, the intimacy levels deepen within the relationship—so much so that over time, couples become mutually dependent and reliant on each other for the fulfillment of their intimacy and love needs. In the beginning stages of the love experience, couples are eager to care for one another; they are highly motivated to satisfy each other's emotional needs and to nurture one another's love needs. When emotional needs are met, a person feels happy and content. When these needs are not met, a person is left feeling frustrated, unsatisfied, and unfulfilled. Because men and women do not prioritize needs in the same manner, it is likely that at some point emotional needs will be unmet. Compounding this discrepancy, we tend to try to meet our partner's needs based on *our* needs—not what our *partner* needs. If left unattended, the relationship begins to suffer.

The question then arises: How do we know what our partner's love needs/emotional needs are? Are there gender differences in emotional and affection needs? Psychologist and marriage counselor Willard Harley (2001) denotes the 10 most commonly cited emotional needs of men and women:

1. Admiration
2. Affection
3. Conversation

Source: Harley (2001).

4. Sexual fulfillment
5. Family commitment
6. Honesty/openness
7. Physical attraction
8. Recreational companionship
9. Domestic support
10. Financial support

Her Side: In Harley's research and practice, he observes that women's top five emotional needs are affection, conversation, family commitment, domestic support, and honesty/openness.

His Side: Men's top five emotional needs are admiration, sexual fulfillment, physical attraction, recreational companionship, and honesty.

Your Side: Harley notes that everyone's emotional needs are different, and he also states that emotional needs change overtime. In considering his research and his findings from his marriage counseling practice,

1. Do you agree or disagree with Harley's categories of emotional needs?
2. To what extent do you believe these emotional needs, as suggested by Harley, are socialized (that is, shaped by our environment)? What led you to your conclusion?
3. In a love relationship, is it realistic to expect that your partner can meet *all* of your emotional needs?

The world over and across all racial, ethnic, and cultural lines, it can be experienced as a sudden romantic infatuation or an enduring, committed love.

Each of us carries with us an internal prototype of love, a "list" of those components of our unique definitions and characterizations of love. The way we love is indeed complex; it is a compilation of our family of origin and the multitude of events, incidents, and situations we experience in our family life, in tandem with the interpersonal interactions and love relationships we experience throughout our lifespan. But it is from the earliest of all relationships—our parent–infant relationship and the ensuing attachment that takes place—that our ability and capacity to love others (and allow others to love us) is shaped and molded.

And as any society evolves over time, so, too, do their concepts of love and loving. Today we are seeing increasing numbers of people who choose to romantically love more than one person at the same time. Although our culture may now frown upon this relationship choice, only time will tell whether these relationships have the right stuff to make them work and to meet the needs of the partners.

Inherent to any love relationship is the fact that sometimes unimaginable, unforeseeable things happen, things that will serve to rattle even the most solid of all relationships, as in the case of the young couple in the opening of this chapter. But as we look back to the opening story of the young woman, we see that the real-life story contains within it all the elements of an enduring, long-lasting love relationship that Sternberg (1986) described in his love types theory.

As we draw near to the postoperative bedside of the young woman, we envision the couple's situation. We picture her forever-deformed facial features and wonder what we might do in that situation—would our love really be strong enough to withstand this unexpected turn of events? Notice in the story the first element essential to love relationships, that of *passion*. Sternberg (1986) maintained that passion does not necessarily refer to sexual intercourse; rather, it refers to that drive, that physical attraction between lovers. Despite her now "clownish" appearance and twisted mouth, the fiancée went out of her way to assure her love that their kiss would always still work—that the passion would always remain.

The *intimacy* element of their relationship is demonstrated in the couple's closeness, connectedness, and bondedness they share as they dwell in each other's presence. To be sure, the type of intimacy that survives a tragic accident is the kind that develops slowly over time and is the bedrock of a long-lasting relationship.

Sternberg (1986) defined *commitment* as "the decision that one loves someone else . . . and the [decision] to maintain that love." In other words, *it's the commitment to the commitment,* a conscious act of our will to remain committed to our partner, regardless of life's circumstances. As the woman bent over to kiss her fiancée, she assured her that she would be there for the long haul.

True passion. True intimacy. True commitment. That's the stuff that lasting partnerships are made of—that's real love.

/// SUMMARY

Love Is a Cultural and Historical Experience

- "Love" and "loving" are determined largely by how a culture defines its social identity, whether as collectivist (society's goals take priority over individual needs) or individualistic (individual goals are promoted over group goals).

- The experience of "love" is also driven by the period in history in which the relationship exists. From "somber, joyless, guilt-ridden experience intertwined with the act of sex" to love relationships that combine sexuality, affection, and togetherness, each expression of love is as distinct as the society and time period in which it was formed.

What Is Love, Actually?

- An individual's love *prototype,* or model of love, will ultimately characterize an individual's love relationships. Similarly, *love maps,* or mental blueprints, shaped by our experiences with love in infancy and early childhood, present images of our "ideal" love relationship.

- *Infatuation,* an intense, extravagant, and often short-lived passion for another person, is often confused with love. *Romantic infatuation,* or *romantic love,* involves a complicated, often overpowering blend of emotion and sex. Couples in relationships consumed by romantic infatuation often become completely absorbed with each other to the exclusion of friends and family. The experience of passionate love/infatuation is multifaceted and culturally determined.

- *Stalking* and *jealousy* are negative components of love.

- *Jealousy* is common, but it can become unhealthy and dangerous.

- *Retroactive jealousy* happens when a partner is jealous of his/her partner's past romantic or sexual relationships. Today, social networking sites propel this type of jealousy.

- *Companionate love* refers to deep, tender, mature, affectionate attachment bonds shared between two people and may or may not include feelings of physical arousal. *Liking,* which develops over time as a result of consistent repeated rewards, is essential to companionate love.

Developing Love

- The ability and capacity to love *are not inherited*—they are nurtured. One's first experiences of love develop as a result of the interaction of heredity, environment, family of origin, educational background, and the interactions and love experience one has with people across his or her lifespan.

- The first love relationship many of us experience—the *dependent* parent–infant relationship—propels us to form emotional bonds in which we give and receive love. This relationship has additional importance in that it is from the experiences of the earliest of all love relationships that all of our later-in-life love relationships take shape. Parental love toward infants is typically altruistic love and reaps intrinsic rewards.

- The key difference between adult-infant love and adult-adult love is *reciprocity:* Adults experience *interdependent* love and expect their love to be reciprocated by their friends and love partners.

- *Attachment* is best described as an emotional or *affectional* bond that ties or binds the child to the parent or primary caregiver, *Attachment* theory asserts that newborns form an attachment with their caregivers and that it is from this close affectional bond that children derive a sense

Theories of Love and Loving

- Researchers continue to develop theories to explain the complex contexts of love. Drawing from the ancient Greek's multifaceted view of love, sociologist John Alan Lee developed six types of love styles: *eros, ludus, storge, manic, pragma,* and *agape.*

- Research shows that although Lee's love typologies are found across multiple cultures, there are cultural differences: All people tend to experience the love typologies of mania, eros, and agape, but the love typologies of pragma, storge, and ludus are quite dependent on culture. Additional research suggests that an individual's love style is not static and fixed and may change over the course of a lifetime (or even during a relationship). And the social desirability of some love styles may be different for women and men.

- Sociologist Ira Reiss's *Wheel Theory of Love* describes love as a four-staged developmental process: rapport,

- Robert Sternberg proposed that love relationships are expressed through three interconnected components—passion, intimacy, and commitment. His *Triangular Theory of Love* conceptualizes eight different types of love relationships that each individual may experience throughout his or her life.

- *Polyamory* is the practice of intimate relationships with more than one partner.

of security. The attachment behaviors that take place throughout infancy shape our personality and these behaviors in turn shape the interpersonal attachment relationships we experience later on as children, adolescents, and adults.

- The concept of attachment and Attachment theory is important to the study of love because research has shown that the quality of attachment during infancy significantly affects the quality of attachments (and love) throughout childhood, adolescence, and adulthood. Research has also shown a direct correlation between adults' secure or insecure attachment to their own parents and their subsequent responsiveness and sensitivity in their parenting behaviors toward their own children. Attachment behaviors and patterns may even span multiple generations. There are three attachment types in adult love relationships: secure attachment types, avoidant attachment types, and anxious/ambivalent attachment types.

- Family influences ultimately shape our personal experiences with love. *Genograms* can illustrate relationships between family members, providing family therapists with a snapshot of relationship history within a given family.

self-revelation, mutual dependency, and personality need fulfillment. Similar to a rolling wheel, these stages of love may be experienced many times; as long as the wheel continues to move forward, a deep and lasting relationship is formed and maintained. If, however, the wheel stops turning, the love relationship may come to an end.

- Today, more and more people are engaging in the practice of *polyamorous* love relationships. These relationships are ethical, consensual non-monogamous relationships, where partners are free to go outside the marriage to have a number of needs fulfilled.

- Vuong's *Love Economic Model* is an equation that attempts to calculate the benefits of love. Its basic assumption is that people are rational decision makers who are able to tally up both the benefits and costs of falling in love and being in love.

/// KEY TERMS

Agape   187

Agape love   206

Altruistic love   200

Anxious/ambivalent
attachment types   202

Attachment   201

Attachment theory   201

Avoidant attachment types   202

Breakup costs   212

Breakup risk   212

Commitment   198

Companionate love   197

Consummate love   199

Cyber-stalking   192

Dependent love   200

Elopement   184

Emotional needs   211

Empty love   199

Entertainment needs   211

Eros   186

Erotic lovers   206

Fatuous   190

Fatuous love   199

Genograms   204

Incompetent suitors   193

Infatuated love   199

Infatuation   188

Interdependent love   200

Intergenerational approach to family
therapy   204

Intimacy seekers   193

Intrinsic rewards   200

Jealousy   193

Liking   199

Love Economic Model   211

Love maps   187

Love stories   203

Ludic lovers   206

Ludus   206

Maintenance costs   212

Manic lovers   206

Materialistic needs   211

Mutual dependency   210

Nonlove   198

Passion   198

Passionate love   188

Personality need fulfillment   210

Philos   187

Polyamory   207

Pragma love   206

Predatory stalkers   193

Prototype   187

Rapport   210

Reiss's Wheel Theory of Love   209

Rejected stalkers   192

Rejection costs   212

Resentful stalkers   193

Retroactive jealousy   195

Rewards   197

Romantic infatuation   188

Romantic love   199

Search cost   211

Secure attachment types   202

Self-revelation   210

Simple infatuation   188

Stalking   192

Storge   206

Storgic lovers   206

Triangular Theory of Love   197

CHAPTER 7

THE PATH TO COMMITMENT: ATTRACTION, DATING, PARTNERING, AND COHABITATION

LEARNING OBJECTIVES

7.1 Summarize the three primary interpersonal attraction theories.

7.2 Characterize courtship, dating, and hooking up in the United States.

7.3 Describe the development of relationships and the processes of commitment and breaking up.

7.4 Analyze the multiple facets and experiences of nonmarital cohabitation.

....

We are an odd pair, my husband and me. He stands more than 6 feet tall; I am about 5 feet tall on a good day. I love opera; he prefers to listen to original heavy metal music by Led Zeppelin or Steppenwolf. Calm, cool, and collected, he seldom raises his voice; I have a fiery temper and occasionally enjoy a good argument. Skiing, mountains, and snow are his heaven on earth; beaches, ocean waves, and sand between my toes is mine. We are polar opposites in the truest sense. How, then, did we come together as partners in life? Why didn't these dissimilarities drive a wedge between us rather than pull us together?

The study of interpersonal attraction and the pathways to partnering are important in our examination of couple, intimate, and marital relationships because dating, courtship, and partnering practices map out different courses to marriage and other lifelong couple relationships, such as cohabitation between gays or lesbians who choose not to marry. In this chapter, we explore the theories and realities associated with interpersonal attraction, dating, and mate selection in contemporary society. When we use the term **interpersonal attraction**, we are referring to the attraction between people that leads to the development of platonic (friendly, nonsexual) or romantic (sexual) relationships. When we use the term to discuss intimate couple relationships, we are specifically looking at views of what is and what is not considered beautiful or attractive to each partner in the relationship.

Interpersonal attraction: the attraction between people that leads to the development of platonic (friendly, nonsexual) or romantic (sexual) relationships.

You may have asked yourself at one time or another, Why are we attracted to one person and not another? If we're straight, do we choose intimate partners differently than if we're gay or bisexual or transgender? We begin by examining the theories that address why we are attracted to certain people but not others. You will notice that some theories specifically address heterosexual attraction, while other theories are more general and thus account for heterosexual, homosexual, or bisexual attraction.

"FRISKY BUSINESS": INTERPERSONAL ATTRACTION THEORIES

Every society the world over has some type of socially approved union between couples (Erber & Erber, 2001). Whether we are referring to a technologically advanced society, such as the United States, or to a tribal culture, such as the Zoé in the state of Para, Northern Brazil, all societies have certain beliefs and expectations when it comes to selecting a mate. Since all societies place such emphasis and importance on the process of selecting a mate, it seems logical to assume that choosing the most suitable mate is essential to the longevity of a society or culture. For instance, if a person continually chooses an unsuitable mate, the consequences of such decisions would ultimately be the failure to reproduce; if poor mate selection continued, at some point the longevity of the society would be jeopardized. Perhaps the next logical assumption could then be that throughout history, mate selection has had an evolutionary purpose to ensure the continuation, longevity, and survival of a culture or society. Although we cannot answer here the age-old question, "How do I know if he (she) is the right one for me?" we can investigate how and why we have been socialized to think the way we do about certain physical characteristics and qualities in those to whom we are attracted as we take a look at three influential interpersonal attraction theories: Evolutionary theory, Social Exchange theory, and Filter theory.

Evolutionary Theory: The Evolution of Physical Attraction

I am a heterosexual female in the 21st century. I pride myself on the fact that I take people at more than face value, that I appreciate human beings for their character rather than their looks. Why do I find myself making conversations with physically attractive males while blowing off [others]? Why does my head whip around when I see a man in a Porsche? Why do my male friends all have the same prerequisites for the perfect female despite race and ethnicity [differences]: perky breasts, slim waist, and full hips? Despite most people's lofty notions of equality, and beauty being in the eye of the beholder, we are all susceptible to certain physical and material traits that make some human beings more "desirable" than others. (Fernandez, 2002)

British scientist and environmentalist Charles Darwin (1809–1882) became famous for his theories about evolution and **natural selection**, the process by which nature selects the best adapted varieties of species to survive and reproduce. Modern theory defines **sexual selection** as occurring in two ways (Janicke & Morrow, 2019). In the first, members of one sex compete among themselves for opportunities to mate—the pool of potential mating candidates is limited. The "winners" reproduce more than the other competitors and natural selection occurs. In the second type of sexual selection, a member of one sex chooses to mate with a specific person (or people)—some people are more preferable to mate with than others. Thus, the **Evolutionary theory** for mate selection purports that we choose mates for the sole purpose of maximizing and enhancing our reproductive efforts, to ensure reproductive success—and the success of the species and society (Dixson, 2009; Janicke & Morrow, 2019; Morrow, 2015; Singh, 2002, 2004).

Mate selection evolution-based theories, then, maintain that there are two specific biological goals—one for male sexual selection and one for female sexual selection—that must be achieved when selecting a mate.

What Men Want: Reproductive Promise

The primary biological goal of males in mate selection is the need to impregnate as many women as possible (Dixson, 2009; Needham, 1999). According to evolutionists, *men are concerned with quantity*—mating is a numbers game, and the more mates the better to ensure numerous offspring are produced. Interpersonal attraction empirical research findings conclude that this is perhaps why men engage in more casual sex than women do and why men have more sexual partners across their lifespan than do women (Schmitt & Buss, 2001; Schmitt, Shackelford, Duntley, Tooke, & Buss, 2001). When seeking mates, then, men will select women who possess certain **fertility cues**, such as youth and curves (full breasts, small waist, curvy hips), because men associate these traits with successful fertility (Dixson, 2009; Gilks, Abbot, & Morrow, 2014; Janicke & Morrow, 2019; Zuk, 2009).

What Women Want: Protectors and Providers

Charles Darwin (1871) reasoned that because childbearing (pregnancy, labor, birth, and breastfeeding) is riskier for women than for men, women are more selective when it comes to finding a mate. A man produces literally millions of sperm each day and therefore has seemingly limitless supplies of his genetic materials, but the female is very limited in her ability to reproduce. Thus, while men may be concerned with the *number* of children they produce, women are concerned with the *quality* of the children they produce. Consequently, they not only look for someone who can contribute positive genetic traits and characteristics but they also tend to seek out a mate who possesses **protector/provider cues**, such as intelligence, physical strength, industry (a hard worker), and ambition (Dixson, 2009; Janicke & Morrow, 2019; Morrow, 2015; Zuk, 2009).

Personality traits and behavior characteristics are important factors for women in choosing a marriage mate. Characteristics such as kindness, warmth, openness, and commitment are key influences in women's selection of a mate (among many others, Buss & Shackelford, 2008;

Natural selection: the process by which nature selects the best adapted varieties of species to survive and reproduce.

Sexual selection: a form of natural selection that happens in two ways: (1) Members of one sex compete among themselves for opportunities to mate, thereby "out-reproducing" other competitors; and (2) a sex chooses to mate with a specific, more preferable person.

Evolutionary theory: the theory that we choose mates for the sole purpose of ensuring reproductive success— and thus the success of the species and society.

Fertility cues: physical traits associated with fertility, such as youth and curves in women.

Protector/provider cues: the cues women tend to look for in a mate, such as intelligence, physical strength, and ambition.

Because childbearing is a risky experience for women, the Evolutionary theory proposes that women select men based on the quality of children they produce, and therefore they seek men who project protector/provider cues, such as wealth.

Edlund & Sagrain, 2010; Arnocky & Vaillancourt, 2017; Arnocky, Woodruff, & Schmitt, 2016). Other research indicates that women rate emotional stability and the commitment to marriage and family (family orientation) more highly than do men (Arnocky, Ribout, Mirza & Knack, 2014; Arnocky, Pearson, & Vaillancourt, 2015).

Now that you have an understanding of why men and women are attracted to certain physical traits and certain personality characteristics, we turn our attention to two other theoretical frameworks that seek to explain why we choose the marriage mate or lifelong partner that we do. Here we examine the Social Exchange theory and the Filter Theory of Mate Selection.

Social Exchange Theory: The Rewards and Costs of Attraction

Let's suppose you exchanged phone numbers with someone you met at a bar, and a few days later your cell phone rings—with that certain person's number showing on the caller ID. At the first ring, a scenario like the one that follows may play out in your mind (or even aloud!), and within a couple of ticks on the clock you have a certain conversation with yourself that goes something like this:

Phone:	Ping!
You:	Who could this possibly be? Don't they know I've got a huge Chem test in an hour?
Phone:	Ping!
***You** [glancing at your phone screen]:*	Wow! It's so-and-so from the bar! Do I answer the phone or not? Was I only interested in him/her because I had a few too many drinks? Or do I really want to invest the time in getting to know this person? (You weigh the rewards of answering the text. You weigh the costs. You perceive that responding to the text may result in greater benefits or rewards than not texting back. You decide that answering the text has more potential rewards than a good grade on your Chem test. You text back.)

This example illustrates the essence of the **Social Exchange theory**. Very broadly stated, the Social Exchange theory centers on the exchange of people's resources: the resources can be material or symbolic. This theory asserts that individuals act out of self-interest in ways to enlarge and make the most of the resources they possess. It also helps explain what *motivates* individuals to act (White & Klein, 2008).

Key Concepts of the Social Exchange Theory

Susan Sprecher (1998), a social psychologist who studies personal relationships, outlines the key concepts of the Social Exchange theory:

1. All social behavior is a series of varying exchanges.
2. Within these social exchanges, all individuals attempt to maximize their *rewards* (exchanged resources that are rewarding and satisfying) and minimize their *costs* (missed opportunities or exchanged resources that result in loss or punishment).
3. When rewards are received from others, the benefactor or the receiver feels obligated to reciprocate.
4. Reward minus cost equals the outcome of the impersonal exchange.

Rewards are the benefits (the payback, profits, or compensations) that are exchanged in a social relationship (Boss, Doherty, LaRossa, Schuram, & Steinmetz, 1993). Family theory authors James White and David Klein (2008) note that a reward is *anything* considered beneficial to an individual. The role of rewards in a relationship is the probability that a behavior will continue—as long as the perceived rewards are greater than the perceived costs of a given behavior, the behavior will continue. A cost increases the likelihood or probability that a person will *not* take part in a given behavior. Costs can be experienced as punishments (lost rewards) because individuals may engage in one behavior rather than another (Boss et al., 1993). For example, an unmarried woman may cohabit with her alcoholic, abusive partner. Although her partner gets drunk and physically abuses her (the *costs*), she may consider his paycheck, her home, and her financial security (the perceived *rewards*) to be greater than the costs of his drinking and abusive behavior. If there is no reward that results from a behavior, the individual will act in a way that will result in the least cost. For instance, although there may be no rewards in staying in the abusive relationship, if she tries to leave the relationship, he may harm her. She may therefore conclude that staying in the cohabiting relationship is the least costly to her.

The Social Exchange theory presents the notion that when you (Actor) are presented with a situation in your impersonal or family relationships, you sensibly and judiciously analyze the ratio of the rewards to the costs, and you then make a decision that results in the greatest rewards (White & Klein, 2008). Because of the assumption that all Actors are rational when making decisions, the theory presumes that Actors' behaviors in like situations are interchangeable. In other words, given the same situation with the same potential rewards and costs, *you* would make exactly the same decision that *I* would make.

Several examples illustrate this point. If I decided to seek a divorce because my husband and I drifted apart, I could assume that you would seek a divorce under like circumstances. I could assume that you would respond to a crisis by reaching out to others, as I would in a crisis. These comparisons may seem rational and logical, but they don't take into account individual differences.

You may think, "Wait a minute! How do you know what I consider to be rewarding or what I consider to be costly?" Precisely! Let's suppose that you are in a new relationship, and you view the increased time you spend together as a couple as rewarding. Your partner, on the other hand, may feel like he or she has less time, less freedom, and less independence because of the increased time spent together as a couple, and he or she sees the time commitment as a cost. Thus, when examining intimate and sexual relationships, we need to have an understanding of the significance or importance (the weight) that *each* person assigns to each reward and to each cost.

Social Exchange theory: this theory centers on the exchange of people's material or symbolic resources, asserting that individuals act out of self-interest to capitalize on the resources they possess.

Cost: a missed opportunity or exchanged resources that results in loss or punishment and increases the likelihood or probability that a person will *not* take part in a given behavior.

Just as the Social Exchange theory's name implies, human interaction of any kind has a built-in requirement of some type of reciprocity or exchange. Thibaut and Kelley (1959) were the first scholars to suggest that the behaviors of Actors in relationships are interdependent or reciprocal in nature. In a dating relationship, even though one partner (as an *individual* relationship member) seeks to make the most of personal rewards and minimize costs, that individual must also consider what rewards and costs will occur for the other partner. For example, one dating partner may be eager to propose marriage (reward) but may have to delay his or her proposal so the other dating partner can finish a college degree (potential cost if the degree is not completed). Even though a couple represents a collection of individuals (White & Klein, 2008) who are seeking to maximize their own rewards, Thibaut and Kelley (1959) held that they are *mutually reliant on one another* for rewarding results.

Putting Social Exchange Theory Into Action: Partner Selection

We can use the Social Exchange theory and apply it to interpersonal attraction and human sexuality. In an extensive, comprehensive research study that addresses the use of exchange theories in the understanding of human interpersonal and sexual interactions, Sprecher (1998) used the Social Exchange theory to better understand sexual and relational interactions with regard to partner selection, the negotiation of the onset of sex, the evaluation of sexual satisfaction, and the initiation and refusal of sex.

Sprecher (1998) found that most researchers who use the Social Exchange theory in their study of interpersonal attraction equate mate/partner selection to a competitive *marketplace* (such as a marketplace of available men and women) that has rewards and costs. The **matching hypothesis** refers to the fact that most of us want a "socially desirable person regardless of his or her own level of social desirability" (Sprecher, 1998, p. 35). To put it another way, people who possess socially desirable characteristics (such as beauty, wealth, status, and education) tend to partner with people who also possess these same desirable characteristics—their resources are equally matched. With regard to Social Exchange theory, when we select dating or sexual partners, we calculate and weigh the perceived rewards (partnering with someone who is socially desirable) against the perceived costs (partnering with someone who does not possess socially desirable characteristics).

As we examine the intricacies of relationship development and family life throughout this text, you will see time and again how relationships and family life take place in a series of interdependent relationships. White and Klein (2008) suggest that because the Social Exchange theory focuses on cost-benefit analysis, tenets of this framework are helpful in aiding those working with families and individual family members to employ intervention and prevention strategies that focus on increasing positive/rewarding behaviors and decreasing negative/costly behavioral interactions.

Filter Theory of Mate Selection

Earlier in the chapter I pondered how my husband and I came to be marriage partners, given the fact that our personality traits and physical characteristics are such polar opposites. The **Filter Theory of Mate Selection** may provide an explanation; it suggests that when looking for mates, we use a filtering mechanism that helps us sort out a potential mate from the vast **pool of candidates**, or eligible partners. Figure 7.1 illustrates how this theory draws on tenets from the evolutionary perspective as well as the Social Exchange theory. The variables we use to filter potential mates include propinquity, homogamy, heterogamy, physical attraction, and reciprocity.

You will more than likely marry someone who comes from the same geographic region as you. **Propinquity** refers to geographic closeness. Simply stated, you can't meet someone face-to-face if you are not in the same general location. Like their heterosexual counterparts, gay men and lesbians indicate that they meet their potential dates/mates/marriage partners in "conventional" ways, such as through friends, at work, at a bar, or at a social event (for a thorough review, see Umberson, Thomeer, Kroeger, Lodge, & Xu, 2015). In addition to

Matching hypothesis:
the premise that most of us want a socially desirable person regardless of our own degree of social desirability.

Filter Theory of Mate Selection:
this theory suggests that individuals use a filtering mechanism that helps them sort out a potential mate from the vast pool of candidates.

Pool of candidates:
eligible relationship partners.

Propinquity:
geographical closeness.

Figure 7.1 /// The Filter Theory of Mate Selection

According to the Filter theory, we narrow the pool of all eligible partner candidates to select someone who is most similar to us. Through our filter, we consider such things as geographic closeness, age, race, religious beliefs, physical attraction, and whether we think that person will reciprocate our feelings. From here, we eventually select the right partner.

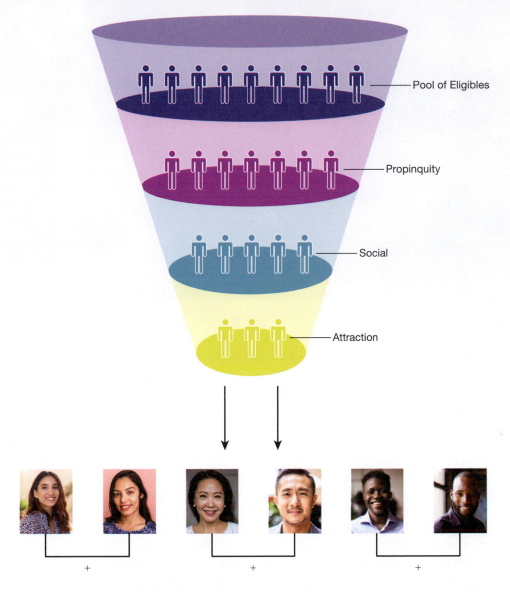

Source: istockphoto.com/Drazen_, istockphoto.com/Ridofranz, istockphoto.com/yongyuan, istockphoto.com/JohnnyGreig, istockphoto.com/fizkes, istockphoto.com/monkeybusinessimages.

proximity, we tend to marry someone with whom we share things in common. **Homogamy** refers to partnering with someone who is similar to you in ethnic and racial background, religious upbringing, age, education level, political ideology, socioeconomic status, and values and beliefs. For example, although my husband and I possess quite different personality traits, we are very similar in our social backgrounds and our belief systems. According to the Filter theory, this explains why our relationship works.

With greater social acceptance of gay and lesbian marriage, more and more studies are looking at the qualities that lesbians and gay men seek in romantic partners. These studies reveal that regardless of sexual orientation, most people value certain things in a mate, such as

Homogamy:
partnering with someone similar in ethnic and racial background, religious upbringing, age, education level, political ideology, socioeconomic status, and values and beliefs.

iStock.com/jjneff

When we look for romantic or marriage partners, we tend to partner with someone who is similar to us in many areas such as education, political beliefs, or religious beliefs and values.

Exogamy:

a requirement to marry outside of a particular group. In the United States, for example, we cannot marry a sibling or, in some states, a first cousin.

Endogamy:

refers to marrying within one's group, such as Muslims marrying Muslims, Catholics marrying Catholics, or Asians marrying Asians.

Heterogamy:

partners who are dissimilar in one or more dimensions, such as race, ethnicity, or religion, or dissimilar in age, political ideology, socioeconomic status, and values and beliefs.

affection and dependability. Just as with heterosexuals, homosexuals also tend to partner with someone who is similar to them, and they place importance on things such as shared interest and similarity of religious beliefs (Carpenter & Gates, 2008; Clausell & Roisman, 2009; Gates, 2013; Gotta et al., 2011; Umberson et al., 2015). Further, lesbians and gays are more likely than heterosexuals to begin relationships as friendships that develop into a love relationship and eventually a sexual relationship (Peplau & Fingerhut, 2007).

As you saw in Chapter 1, certain cultural rules and norms define who we can and cannot marry. **Exogamy** means that we must marry outside of a particular group. In the United States, for example, we cannot marry a sibling or, in some states, a first cousin. **Endogamy** is the custom of marrying within that same group, such as Muslims marrying Muslims or Asians marrying Asians. Conversely, **heterogamy** refers to partners who are different races, religions, and ethnicities. It also refers to partners of different ages. While in today's diverse society more and more people are choosing heterogamous lifelong partners, they often face difficulties. Chapter 8 explores in detail interracial and interfaith marriages.

Each of us has our own ideal of what we find physically attractive in a potential mate, and we filter potential mates based on these culturally socialized internalized standards of physical attractiveness. Unlike Evolutionary theory, Filter theory isn't necessarily as concerned with *why* or *how* we are attracted to someone as it is with the notion that we just *are*—and physical attraction is one filtering mechanism. Regardless of sexual orientation, men are more likely than women to emphasize the importance of their partner's physical attractiveness; women, regardless of sexual orientation, assign greater importance to personality characteristics (Peplau & Spalding, 2000).

The balance sheet filter refers to *reciprocity*. When all is said done and we have exhausted all propinquity, social, and physical attractiveness filters, we look at what someone can offer us that we cannot find in anyone else. Ultimately, whomever we choose must reflect a mutual, reciprocal commitment to the relationship in order for a mate to be considered "the one." Although this theory doesn't have much to do with developing a love relationship, it does help explain how and why we're attracted to one person and not another.

Now that we have looked at the various theories of how and why we select a particular mate over another, let's examine the pathway to committed relationships that may or may not result in marriage.

THE PATH TO COMMITMENT

Though the customs and rituals may vary across racial, cultural, ethnic, economic, and religious boundaries, people come together to form **pair bonds**, or couples. For example, the Surma people of a remote region of southwest Ethiopia engage in an annual courtship ritual during which hundreds of men join together to fight for the available women. To woo a potential bride, the men engage in a mock display of violence, wielding and wildly swinging large sticks.

Wodaabe nomad men of Niger participate in a males-only beauty pageant in which they parade before unmarried women who select their lovers from the parading pageant "contestants." The men spend countless hours painting elaborate patterns on their bodies in the hope of turning a young woman's eye. Although Western civilization's interpersonal attraction rituals may pale in comparison to other global mate selection customs, all serve the same purpose—to form a bond that will lead to marriage.

Courtship: Marriage Is the Goal

Although not all Americans follow the same path to marriage or committed partner relationships, when asked what causes young adults and adolescents the most stress, issues surrounding dating and mate selection were at the top of the list (Price, Hides, Cockshaw, Staneva, & Stoyanov, 2016). In a culturally, ethnically, and religiously diverse nation such as the United States, the path to commitment varies greatly. Not all of us will be in a committed relationship, nor will all of us marry. Certainly, some people are single by choice or by happenstance, and we'll discuss singlehood at length in the next chapter. Here, our purpose is to explore how couples go from being attracted to one another to committed relationships.

In 1828, Webster's Dictionary defined *courtship* as "the act of soliciting favor. The act of wooing in love. Solicitation of a woman to marriage. Civility, elegance of manners." **Courting** is a practice that grooms young adults for marriage, with socially prescribed forms of conduct that guide men and women toward matrimony (Kass, 1997). The following example better illustrates the concept of courting.

My grandmother, Neva, was born in 1904. It was she who first taught me the difference between courtship and dating when she described how she and my grandfather came to be married. Her parents were of French origin and in that culture they viewed the notion of wooing a potential mate as a true art form. On the other hand, my grandfather, George, was the son of an Irish immigrant and aspired to become a professional baseball player—not quite polished, refined, sophisticated, or a match for a French American girl. Despite the fact that his manners and etiquette were sub-par for the era, he pursued my grandmother for *eight years*. (I suspect the time would have been shorter had he shown a little more finesse!) There was nothing casual about their times together. The strict rules of the era mandated that the woman and her mother set the conditions of the interactions, and that if the man was truly serious about her, then their relationship was pursued with a view to nothing short of marriage.

Although the practices and rituals associated with couple formation have changed dramatically in Western societies over the past 60 years, there are still members of these cultures who adhere to the practices of courting. For example, in Japan there is a type of courtship called *omiai,* which is formal courting with the intention of pursuing a marriage partner. *Miai* or *omiai* means "matchmaking" or "looking at one another." Still today, about 6 percent of marriages in Japan are arranged via *omiai* (National Institute of Population and Social Security Research, 2019).

Pair bond:

a couple who is emotionally bonded to one another, which characterizes the couple's union.

Courting:

socially prescribed forms of conduct that guide or groom young men and women toward matrimony.

To some, courtship may seem outdated and quaint for contemporary society, but it is making a rebound in certain religious sectors of the United States. For example, in Islamic American cultures, premarital, one-on-one intimate relationships with the opposite sex are strictly forbidden. According to Islam, the choice of a marriage partner is considered to be life's most important decision, and it should therefore not be taken lightly or left to hormones to decide. When a young adult is ready to marry, the decision is made with his or her family's involvement (Akhtar, 2018). In Islamic cultures, the process of courtship is viewed as an assurance that the marriage will be a strong, enduring relationship because it draws on others' wisdom and guidance, not on erotic or romantic feelings of young adults (in part, from Akhtar, 2018).

In some mainstream religious denominations in the United States, the concept of courtship is seen as a response to secular dating cultures. As religious commentator and psychologist James Dobson (2005) notes, "[Young people] are being taught to go from one relationship to another. Wouldn't they then be more inclined later to bail out on a marriage partner when bored or frustrated?" Some religious contemporaries maintain that courting or courtship charts the course for a committed marital relationship with the probable husband or wife. The customs and rituals of courting help the couple navigate the complexities of physical attraction, falling in love, and committing to a lifelong partnership (Cere, 2001).

The Dating Game: Hanging Out, Hooking Up, Going Out

Dating is a relatively new concept that became increasingly popular in Western culture during the mid-20th century. Prior to today's dating rituals, courtship was the common path to marital commitment. In contemporary Western societies, **dating** is an occasion where people get together socially for any number of reasons, such as a means of relaxation and escape from everyday responsibilities ("hanging out"), pursuing a relationship to determine whether the partner is a potential spouse or a partner for a lifelong relationship ("going out"), or getting together sexually with no strings attached ("hooking up"). Today, dating can be described as an activity that encompasses various social activities between two people; during the dating period, couples may or may not assess the possibility of deepening the relationship over time (Braboy Jackson, Kleiner, Geist, & Cebulko, 2011). Dating today doesn't necessarily have rigidly defined stages or sequences that lead to a "serious" relationship; rather,

Dating:
socializing for any number of reasons, such as for relaxation and escape from everyday responsibilities or to pursue a relationship to determine whether the partner is a potential spouse or a partner for a lifelong relationship.

What is an ideal "date"? Is it getting together for dinner and drinks or hiking an out-of-the-way trail? Is it hanging out with each other or sexually hooking up? There's really no right answer because there are as many ideal "dates" as there are people! Dating serves a social purpose in that it allows people to get to know one another.

the progression of a dating relationship appears to be loosely defined by various actions of the couple, such as introducing one another to the parents and purchasing gifts for each other (Manning & Smock, 2005; Braboy Jackson et al., 2011).

There are several distinctions between *dating* and *courting*, but perhaps the primary distinction is that courtship is viewed as preparation for and anticipation of marriage. Dating, on the other hand, is considered more recreational and fun. It is a way for people to get to know each other and determine whether there are commonalities beyond their initial physical attraction that might lead them to a long-term, committed relationship such as marriage. When we go on dates, we tend to follow culturally determined dating scripts.

Dating Scripts

Script theory is one avenue that helps us understand dating practices among heterosexual couples and homosexual couples. According to **Script theory**, each of us uses scripts that help us organize the information in our environments. Scripts typically provide information about expected, stereotypical actions; because of this, they help us predict the behaviors of people and help guide our decisions about how to act and interact with others (Klinkenberg & Rose, 1994). In essence, scripts are guidelines, or an internalized "how-to" manual for social behavior. There are three different general types of scripts (Simon & Gagnon, 1986):

1. **Cultural scripts** are common guidelines that provide instructions about what behaviors and emotions are expected in certain situations. For example, is it okay to have sex with someone on the first date? To a large extent, culture dictates these behaviors and emotions, and for the most part we tend to stick to these cultural scripts.

2. **Intrapsychic scripts** are personal and individualized and represent our private wishes, hopes, desires, and dreams. These scripts may contain sexual or relational fantasies or personal expectations for another person's behavior. In these scripts, for instance, a woman may expect that her dating partner pay for everything on every date.

3. **Interpersonal scripts** are highly personalized and detailed and are a combination of a person's cultural and intrapsychic scripts. For instance, a common American cultural script for a first date includes going to a movie (Bartoli & Clark, 2006), whereas a person's intrapsychic script may specify engaging in a shared interest, such as attending an ice hockey game together. In order to have a successful date, it's important that each dating partner shares with the other what he or she believes to be an "ideal" date, so that each person' interpersonal script is followed.

If we put all of these scripts together, we come up with scripts that relate specifically to dating. These are referred to as **dating scripts**, and these models guide our dating interactions.

Heterosexual Dating Scripts

For a number of years, social scientists have examined the behaviors of dating couples. These studies are important because they help us better understand how relationships develop and are maintained. Among college students, for example, we know that dating scripts for heterosexual couples include role differentiation that is often stereotypically gender based. Past studies have revealed that the man is the initiator of the date, while the woman is the one who nurtures the conversation during the date (Levinger, 1982). Other research compared people's perceptions of an "ideal" first date (initiating the date, meeting, engaging in activities, ending a date, and concluding the date) with the experiences of the "actual" first date. All of the studies found one thing in common: Dating scripts reflected traditional gender roles, with the man being the *active* partner (the initiator and the planner) and the woman being the *reactive* partner (accepting the invitation, rejecting sexual activity; Rose & Frieze, 1989, 1993; Laner & Ventrone, 1998). But do college students still adhere to stereotypical dating scripts?

Script theory: the theory that individuals use scripts (information about expected, stereotypical actions) that help us organize the information in our environments.

Cultural scripts: common guidelines that provide instructions about what behaviors and emotions are expected in certain situations.

Intrapsychic scripts: sexual scripts that account for individual desires, fantasies, emotions, and intentions while at the same time considering the interpersonal responses of others.

Interpersonal scripts: sexual scripts that recognize how different people interact and relate to each other within specific social situations.

Dating scripts: the models that guide our dating interactions.

In a study of 182 college students, investigators looked at men's and women's dating scripts for a "typical date" (Bartoli & Clark, 2006). The study participants were given dating scenes and were asked to report what activities and events usually took place on a typical date in these scenes. Table 7.1 shows us dating scripts of first-year college students. For example, both men and women tend to initiate dates by meeting in class or at a party/bar, talking with their partner, and going to a movie and dinner. Dating conclusions included goodnight kisses or going to a partner's house for a drink or talking. Traditional gender roles were seen in that women were the sexual "gatekeepers" (they limited sexual activity) and men had higher expectations for sexual activities than women did. Overall, the study found that if the dating scenario was "typical," men and women held similar dating scripts or expectations.

Gender and Race Differences in Dating Experiences and Rituals

In a study, 90,000 racially diverse students in grades 7 to 12 were surveyed about their patterns of romance and dating; the researchers wanted to examine these patterns, both in adolescence and later in early adulthood (Harris & Udry, 2018). Nearly 40 percent of white, African American, and Hispanic males have never dated, compared to 60 percent of Asian males

Table 7.1 /// Scripted Events for a Typical Date

First Year Women's Dating Scripts	First Year Men's Dating Scripts
Initiation	**Initiation**
Talking	Talking
Meeting in Public	Meeting in Public
Shared Interest	Shared Interest
Meeting in Group	Man Picks up Date
Man Picks up Date	Call
Meet in Common Place	Casual Interaction
Casual Interaction	
Activities	**Activities**
Movies	Movies
Dinner	Dinner
Talking	Shared Interest
Shared Interest	
Outcomes	**Outcomes**
Talking	Talking
Watching TV	Go Back to the House
Go Back to the House	Kiss Goodnight
Kiss Goodnight	Go Home
Go Home	Relationship Development
Relationship Development	Take Date Home

Source: Bartoli & Clark, 2006.

who have never dated. This survey revealed that adolescent girls are more likely to date than are adolescent boys. In early adulthood, 20 percent of white males, nearly 30 percent of Black males, and about one-fourth of Hispanic males have never dated, in comparison to about 40 percent of Asian men (Harris & Udry, 2018). This large survey study also revealed that female romantic relationship status varied among races/ethnicities. For example, approximately 35 percent of white adolescents, 40 percent of African American teens, and nearly 50 percent of Latinas were not involved in a romantic relationship; among Asian adolescents, nearly 60 percent were not dating or in a romantic relationship (Harris & Udry, 2018). In early adulthood, about 18 percent of white women, 25 percent of Black women, 20 percent of Hispanic women, and about 16 percent of Asian women were not dating.

Another study sought to understand gender and race differences when it comes to dating rituals (Braboy Jackson et al., 2011). Studying 680 racially diverse college students, the researchers found the persistence of some traditional gender differences in dating rituals; these rituals tended to run along bipolar gender lines. For example, men placed high importance on sexual activity, while women placed significant importance on hanging out together, meeting the partner's family, and having the dating partner meet her family.

As Figure 7.2 shows us, racial and gender differences are evident in those dating rituals that need to take place in order to name someone as a boy/girlfriend. Although attending social activities is the most common dating ritual in all groups, for African Americans, meeting the family and having the dating partner meet his/her family is of much more significance than it is to whites (Braboy Jackson et al., 2011). White men rank sexual intimacy as a dating ritual higher than do African Americans, and Blacks rank family and gifting as more important than do whites. As you learned in Chapter 1, African Americans place tremendous importance on family relationships, and this is evident in their dating and mate selection practices.

Of course, not all dating couples are heterosexual couples. This leads to some interesting questions. For example, given that we are all socialized by our cultures to follow certain dating scripts—scripts that assume heterosexual coupling—what dating scripts do gay men and lesbian couples follow? And how do they come by them?

Figure 7.2 /// Gender and Race Differences in Dating Rituals

What Activities Mean a Person Is Your Boy/Girlfriend?

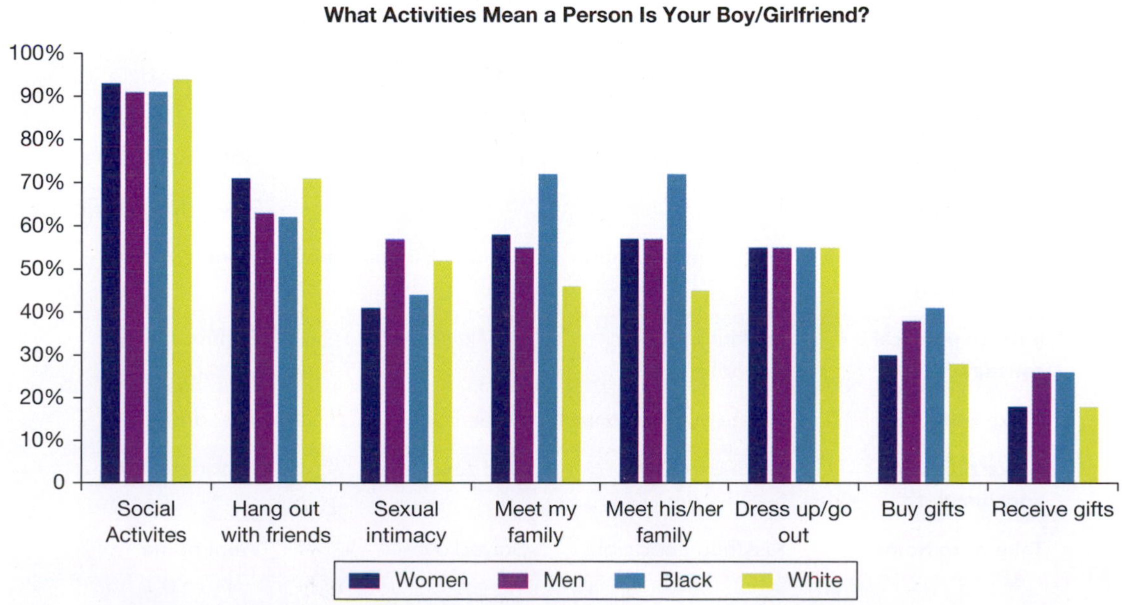

Source: Braboy Jackson, Kleiner, Geist, & Cebulko, 2011.

Same-Sex Dating Scripts

Still today, studies that address relationship initiation and formation among homosexual couples are scant. Most studies that do exist focus on the later stages of long-term relationships, such as commitment (Klinkenberg & Rose, 1994).

What we do know from earlier research is that gays and lesbians do incorporate some traditional gender roles in their dating scripts, but they also appear to have more opportunities to develop their own unique, interpersonal scripts. For example, just as with straight men, early on in relationships gay men are likely to stress the physical and sexual attraction to their dating partners over the emotional aspects (Welling, Singh, Puts, Jones & Burriss, 2013). Unique aspects of lesbian dating include feeling freed from stereotypical gender roles; indeed, few lesbians adhere to traditional gender roles in dating (Rose & Zand, 2002). Lesbian couple formation also included enhanced intimacy and friendship and a rapid pace at which lesbian couple relationships are formed (Rose & Zand, 2002). Unlike straight women, lesbians indicate emotional intimacy is a valued aspect of dating (Klinkenberg & Rose, 1994). They engage in deep levels of self-disclosure and emotional sharing on their first dates, and they are much more likely to establish a close friendship with someone before dating them (Zand & Rose, 1992).

In a study that looked at dating scripts of 96 gays and lesbians, the researchers examined hypothetical versus actual dating scripts (similar to the study that explored heterosexual dating scripts); the results are presented in Table 7.2 (Klinkenberg & Rose, 1994). The findings

Table 7.2 /// Scripts for Hypothetical and Actual First Dates for Gay Men and Lesbians

Hypothetical Date		Actual Date	
Gay Men	Lesbians	Gay Men	Lesbians
Discuss plans	Discuss plans	Discussed plans	Discussed plans
Groom/dress	Tell friends about date	Was nervous	Was nervous
Prepare (clean apartment)	Groom/dress	Groom/dress	Groom/dress
Meet date at location	Meet date at location	Picked update	Prepared (clean apartment)
Get to know by talking	Leave for another location	Left for another location	Picked up date
Talk/laugh/joke	Get to know by talking	Evaluated date	Got to know date
Go to movie/show	Talk/laugh/joke	Went to movie/show	Talked/laughed/joked
Eat/drink (nonalcohol)	Go to a movie/show	Ate/drank (nonalcohol)	Went to movie
Initiate physical contact	Eat/drink (non-alcohol)	Drank alcohol	Positive feelings
Make out	Initiate physical contact	Made out	Kissed/hugged
Make plans for another date	Make plans for another date	Had sex	Took date home
Take date home	Kiss/hug goodnight	Stayed over	Went home
	Go home	Made plans for another date	
		Went home	

Source: Klinkenberg & Rose (1994).

about initiating a date, preparing for a date, interactions with a date partner, and date closing behaviors are very interesting because they show us that the cultural/interpersonal dating scripts for same-sex partners mirror those of heterosexual partners.

In a 2017 study of 40 LGBTQ+-identified adults, the survey respondents reported that gay, lesbian, bisexual, and queer people are rejecting and "explicitly undermining" conventional heterosexual and same-sex dating scripts (Lamont, 2017). Today, people who identify as LGBTQ+ are challenging gendered behaviors in dating, romantic, and sexual relationships. The study's findings show that LGBTQ+ individuals and couples seek more egalitarian dating scripts. Although the study participants noted that their relationships cannot be totally free from the constraints of common cultural heterosexual dating scripts, they still strive to promote equal, adaptable, non-gendered dating behaviors (Lamont, 2017).

Transgender Dating Experiences

As you have seen in our study in this chapter so far, culture dictates the boundaries of dating and romance. And, as you've also learned in our examination of couple and other interpersonal relationships, in our individualistic culture our current dating traditions and norms support the idea that individuals are free to fall in love with and/or and partner with whomever they desire to. But how do these accepted cultural dating rules affect transgender individuals (Blair & Hoskin, 2018)?

In Chapter 4, we discussed the concept of cisgender identities, which refers to those people whose identity and gender expressions/experiences correspond with their birth sex; recall also that cisgenderism considers cisgender identities to be "natural and normal" (Blair & Hoskin, 2018). One body of research investigated the different patterns of acceptance or rejection of trans dating partners and explored the exclusion and marginalization of trans people from the dating world (Blair & Hoskin, 2018). Providing an extensive review of the literature, Blair and Hoskin discuss previous findings of trans' dating experiences (unless otherwise noted, additional research is as cited by Blair & Hoskin, 2018):

> *Male trans' relationship experiences:* When in a relationship, the benefits of dating include better mental health and lower levels of depression (as cited by Blair & Hoskin, 2018: Bockting, Benner, Coleman, 2009; Dargie, Blair, Pukall, & Coyle, 2014; Meier, Sharp, Michonski, Babcock, & Fitzgerald, 2013). Generally speaking, these benefits are seen more often in trans men than in trans women (Iantaffi & Bockting, 2011).

> *Female trans' relationship experiences:* Existing research suggests that trans women who are dating report feelings of anxiety more often than trans men do (Iantaffi & Bockting, 2011; Riggs, von Doussa, & Power, 2015). Although this is a new area of research, those who have studied trans dating suggest that the heightened levels of anxiety are due to trans women's concerns about "outing" themselves to a partner (Iantaffi & Bockting, 2011). Trans women are also concerned about how a dating partner will feel upon learning of her identity, and they experience anxiety about prejudice, judgment, and discrimination from potential dating partners (Riggs et al., 2015).

What is the impact on cisgender dating partners of trans women and men? Blair and Hoskin (2018) found that

- Cisgender partners sometimes experience "stigma by association" (p. 4)
- Cisgender men say that they experience psychological distress and lowered relationship quality—this may lead them to avoid dating trans women.

In their study of 958 participants, the researchers sought to better understand whether contemporary dating experiences are inclusive of trans men and trans women as being potential dating partners (Blair & Hoskin, 2018). The study participants were grouped into three categories: gay/lesbian; heterosexual/straight, and bisexual/queer/non-binary/two-spirit. Of these groups, 55 percent of bisexual/queer/non-binary/two-spirit individuals indicated they would date trans persons, and one-fourth (24 percent) of gay men and lesbian women would date trans individuals; 3 per cent of heterosexual men and women would date a trans person (Blair & Hoskin, 2018). Among all sexual and gender identities, 87 percent of the study participants excluded trans persons as potential dating partners. The authors conclude, "[Cis-normativity] shapes social attitudes and activities [and influences] the ways that trans people navigate the social world. By operating on cisnormative assumptions, [dating experiences] are ill equipped for the presence of trans people" (p. 12).

Dating Experiences of Asexual Persons

According to the Asexual Visibility & Education Network (AVEN), the most influential online community devoted to asexuality (Bogaert, 2015), an **asexual** person is an individual who does not experience sexual attraction (AVEN, 2020). Asexual people identify as straight/gay/lesbian/bi/Queer/something else; it is up to the individual to determine their sexual identity (AVEN, 2020). And, while an asexual does not experience sexual attraction to another, that's not to say that he/she lacks the capability or the desire for a romantic or emotional connection to another (AVEN, 2020). As AVEN describes, **romantic orientations** are commonly expressed in what gender someone is attracted to:

- **Heteroromantic:** romantically attracted to/desires romantic relationships with the opposite gender
- **Homoromantic:** romantically attracted to/desires romantic relationships with the same gender
- **Biromantic:** romantically attracted to/desires romantic relationships with multiple genders
- **Panromantic:** romantically attracted to/desires romantic relationships without gender being a factor
- **Aromantic:** not romantically attracted to or desiring of romantic relationships at all

It's important to understand that this list provided by AVEN is not exhaustive. There are as many romantic attraction types as there are people, and one list on AVEN includes more than 50 romantic identifications (AVEN, 2020). Given this, how does an asexual navigate the world of dating?

Although there is scant research available that helps us to better understand the experiences of asexual people, what little research that is available provides us insight. Existing bodies of work report that asexuals who desire to engage in a partner relationship have difficulties doing so (Haeffner, 2011; Van Houdenhove, Gis, T'Sjoen, & Enzlin, 2015; Dawson, McDonnell, & Scott, 2016).

The difficulties include seeking partners and forming relationships, negotiating the boundaries of what sexual intimacy is/is not, and coping with partners' feelings about being excluded from the societal norm of using sex as a way to express intimacy. One study discovered that some asexuals "gift" sex to their partners, as a way to strengthen the relationship (Dawson et al., 2016). Finally, one study that examined the "dating game" between asexuals and non-asexuals found that asexual people who desired to have a meaningful, nonsexual relationship engaged in "traditional" dating strategies, such as connecting with others at parties, bars, and night clubs (Vares, 2017).

As you can see, there is certainly no one-size-fits-all dating template in our society today. And the ways in which people meet are changing, too. Contemporary dating can take the form of more traditional dating that eventually leads to cohabitation or marriage, or it can take more casual forms, such as speed dating, online dating, and hooking up.

Speed Dating

Speed dating allows people to meet each other face to face to decide whether they share mutual interests and are interested in another, more extended date. Speed dating was established

Asexual:
an individual who does not experience sexual attraction.

Romantic orientations:
the sex or gender with which a person is likely to have a romantic relationship or fall in love.

Speed dating:
a quick face-to-face meeting that enables people to decide whether they share mutual interests and are interested in another, more extended, date.

by Rabbi Yaacov Deyo in 1999, and it is based on a Jewish tradition of supervised social gatherings of young Jewish singles. Participants meet 10 to 25 "dates" for about 4 minutes each. Its popularity quickly caught on, and now heterosexuals, homosexuals, and a variety of religious and ethnic groups are provided the opportunity to have quick one-on-one dates with a roomful of eligible singles who share common interests. What do people look for in a speed date? What ignites that initial spark of romantic attraction? One team of researchers sought to determine the answers to these questions.

In an attempt to better understand speed dating, psychologists Eli Finkel and Paul Eastwick (2009) conducted a research study to determine the "choosiness" of dating prospects. Their study involved 350 heterosexual college students; each student went on approximately 12 of the 4-minute speed dates. After each "date," the research participants rated the sexual and romantic desirability of their dates. The investigators found that women are more selective than men at speed-dating events; this finding supports previous findings (Fisman, Iyengar, Kamenica, & Simonson, 2006; Kurzban & Weeden, 2005; Todd, Penke, Fasolo, & Lenton, 2007). The researchers conclude that even in speed-dating situations, there are traditional gendered scripts at play: Who physically approached whom? Interestingly, when women approached men who were sitting, women "behaved more like men (less selective than usual) and men behaved more like women (more selective than usual)" (Finkel & Eastwick, 2009, p. 1294). What's the significance of this finding? This study shows us that the mere act of physically approaching someone who we're interested in—a gender behavior more typical of men than of women—increases sexual and romantic attraction. The research team aptly concluded, "Although Western civilization has become increasingly egalitarian over the past century, certain sexual institutions remain gendered, some in subtle, almost invisible, ways" (p. 1294).

Online Dating

The development of technology, from iPhones to iEverything-else has introduced new dynamics into the 21st-century processes of finding a date or a mate. And, Millennials have paved the way when it comes to transforming the dating industry: 12 percent of 18- to 29-year-olds indicate that they are in a relationship with a partner or a spouse that they met online, and

iStock.com/Deagreez

Instead of bars, people today often opt for online dating sites or apps to meet eligible mates. Have you ever met someone online and agreed to meet in person? What are some advantages to this contemporary way of meeting someone?

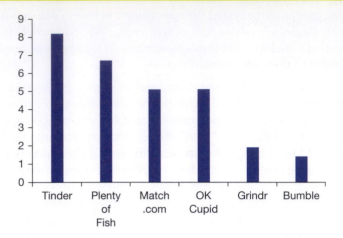

Source: Lin, M. (2019).

today there are more than 1,500 dating apps or websites whose aim is to match singles (Lin, 2019). Online connections—from Match.com, eHarmony.com, Facebook, Instagram, Twitter, Tinder, to Snapchat—provide a virtual space in which people can place personal information about themselves, blog and/or vlog and podcast daily journals of their life happenings, and upload personal photos. People can engage in synchronous communication (such as texting) or asynchronous communication (like e-mail). Today, many people Skype or Zoom (web cam) to enhance their interactions. With one online site's catchphrase, "Match. Catch. Date.," online sites generate opportunities to initially interact with someone and then move to face-to-face relationships if they desire to pursue the friendship or relationship. These electronic liaisons allow people to remain anonymous or to fully self-disclose personal information.

Today, 50 million—about 15 percent—of adults in the United States say they have or will use websites and mobile apps in the pursuit of love, sex, and romance (Lin, 2019). A $3 billion industry, online dating usage tripled between 2013 and 2015 among those between the ages of 18 and 24 (Pew Research Center, 2020). For gays and lesbians, online dating is the most popular form of dating, and it's the second most popular way to find a partner for straight couples (after meeting through friends; Lin, 2019; Paul, 2017). Figure 7.3 shows us the most popular online dating apps in the United States. Tinder is the most popular app used by 18- to 29-year-olds, and Match.com is the most popular site used by 30- to 44-year-olds.

Swipe Me off My Feet. What makes people swipe left? Or right? In a study with 393 participants that examined why people choose Tinder, the researcher found that there are reasons why potential dates swipe either right or left (LeFebvre, 2017):

Reasons for swiping right:

- Physical attraction (33 percent)
- Selective swiper (picky) (21 percent)
- Interesting/similar interests (15 percent)
- Shotgun (impulse) approach (12 percent)
- Miscellaneous (8 percent)
- Depends on mood (4 percent)
- Game (entertainment) (1.6 percent)
- Sexual hookup (1.3 percent)

Reasons for swiping left:

- Not physical attracted (30 percent)
- Picky—doesn't meet approval (28 percent)
- Not interesting (17 percent)
- Mood (went with my gut instinct) (5 percent)
- Safety (unhealthy behavior, creepers, racist) (5 percent)
- Only wants sexual hookup (1.4 percent)

But do online dating sites and apps help people meet "the one"? Although 66 percent of online dating site users have gone on a face-to-face date with someone they met through technology, still one-third of online daters have not yet met up in real life (Pew Research Center, 2020).

Even if someone doesn't find that "fish in the sea," though, research reveals some benefits to online dating, some of which challenge our existing understanding of relationship formation. For example, earlier we discussed the importance of *propinquity,* or geographic closeness, in selecting a potential mate. With online or Smartphone dating, physical proximity is de-emphasized as a necessary feature of relationship formation—individuals are free to interact with people from across the globe (Barraket & Henry-Waring, 2008).

Another benefit of Internet dating is that it frees people to meet others outside of their existing social networks (Barraket & Henry-Waring, 2008). As one 24-year-old male observed, "It elevates you out of your social circle, and you're sort of broadcast to a broad bunch of people, and if you're fairly open-ended in your profile, and not so descriptive about what you do or don't do, then you get the opportunity to meet lots of different people that you would never know" (p. 157). For some, being able to go beyond their current social network allows them the freedom to explore and express their sexuality in different ways or to experience deeper levels of self-disclosure (it's easier for some people to disclose over the Internet than face to face). For others, the increased freedom gives them the opportunity to take chances on relationships they might not venture to try in their "real" lives because if the relationship doesn't work out, they don't have to see them every day. One female noted, "I think the fact that you never have to see them again is wonderful. You know, if it's friends or work or whatever, and it doesn't work out, then you've got all the awkwardness . . . that carries into your life" (Barraket & Henry-Waring, 2008, p. 157).

Others indicate that being able to have high levels of control over the "pace and place" of electronic communication is a benefit (Barraket & Henry-Waring, 2008). What may be surprising to some people is that online dating etiquette seems to mimic offline dating norms. Traditionally gendered patterns of interaction are practiced in online dating, with male users "making the first move" in contacting their prospective partners online (Barraket & Henry-Waring, 2008).

It's Not All Fun and Games: The Dangers of Cyber-Dating. Because adolescents, young adults, and an increasing percentage of the general population believe that online dating resources are a socially acceptable outlet for meeting romantic, sexual, and love interests, most perceive these cyber activities to be favorable and safe (Flug, 2016). One study set out to determine in what ways and to what degree online dating site users perceived its use to be risky or dangerous (Couch, Liamputtong, & Pitts, 2012). The research team discovered that online daters expressed these primary concerns: online deceit; emotional vulnerability; sexually transmitted infections/pregnancy; violence; and the risks that are inherent to Internet anonymity. Interestingly, however, the users did not believe that cyber-dating was any more or less dangerous than face-to-face dating. As social worker and researcher Kyla Flug (2016) observes, "These findings seem to challenge notions that the Internet is perceived as more dangerous than traditional venues of meeting partners, like bars, and illustrates how the social acceptability of online dating has increased over the years" (p. 10).

There is an even more hazardous side to cyber-dating, however. You may be looking for love, but the person on the other end of the mouse may be looking for a quick sexual encounter or may have even more dangerous intentions (Madden & Lenhart, 2006). For example, in 2005, 17-year-old college coed Taylor Behl formed an Internet relationship with a 38-year-old man who portrayed himself on the Internet as a photographic artist. After meeting the man and having a brief sexual encounter with him, Behl tried to sever the relationship. She was murdered a short time later.

To minimize risk to a person's safety and well-being, some guidelines to Internet dating have been proposed (Starling, 2000):

1. *Practice common sense.* Don't give out personal information such as phone numbers, e-mail address, or home address. If you do decide to meet, meet in a public place.

2. *Pay attention.* Liars, exploiters, and predators abound on the Internet.

3. *Research.* Before getting too involved in an online relationship or before agreeing to meet face to face, research phone numbers, places of work, and e-mail addresses to make sure the person is who he or she says. Ask for references and *check them.*

4. *Know what you want.* Before getting too involved in an Internet relationship, make sure you know your intentions. Do you want a casual fling or a long-term friend? Make sure your intentions are made clear to your cyber-dating partner.

If approached with caution and care, Internet dating is another alternative for meeting people of like interests.

Dating Violence. **Dating violence** is the perpetration or the threat of an act of violence against a person, straight, gay, bi, trans, queer, or asexual involved in a dating or courting relationship. Violence includes any type of sexual assault (including rape) or physical violence and any form of verbal or emotional abuse. Both males and females inflict and are victims of dating violence; however, women and girls are twice as likely to be victims of coercion and violence in dating relationships than are men and boys.

Dating violence:

the perpetration or the threat of an act of violence against a person involved in a dating or courting relationship.

Not every online encounter is looking for romance or love. Some are looking for victims. When agreeing to meet someone you met online, use common sense and meet in a public place, where you are safe.

Sexual assault is the act of forcing sex on an individual who has not consented, and it happens every two minutes across North America. In 8 out of 10 instances of sexual assault, the perpetrator knows the victim (RAINN, 2020), either because they have an established relationship, are friends, or they are on a first or subsequent date. Of the rapes that occur on college campuses across the United States, up to 95 percent are carried out by someone the victim knows (RAINN, 2020).

Any sexual activity committed against the will of the victim is considered to be an act of sexual assault. The sexual act or acts *do not need to conclude with penetration* in order for the aggression to be considered rape or a sexual assault.

Protect yourself against sexual assault:

- Avoid secluded places until you fully trust a partner
- Stay sober
- Never leave your drink unattended
- Never accept open drinks (alcoholic or nonalcoholic) from people you do not know; only accept drinks in closed containers to avoid falling prey to "club drugs" such as Rohypnol and GHB
- Never spend time alone with someone who makes you feel uneasy or uncomfortable—trust your instincts! (Witmer, 2005; Russo, 2000; RAINN, 2020)

Use your voice. Say *No! Say No* loudly, clearly, and often. *NO ALWAYS MEANS NO.*

Hooking Up: Meanings, Motives, and Methods

Hooking up refers to brief physical interactions (usually sexual) with the absence of commitment or affection. As one of my students described it, "It's *awesome*—there are literally no expectations from each other, no strings attached." Still today, researchers have a difficult time coming up with a consistent definition of the term "hooking up" (Garcia et al., 2019). In an extensive review of the existing empirical information, the researchers summarize the known characteristics of hooking up (see Garcia et al., 2019):

1.   The nature of the relationship is non-committed—there are, as my student said, no expectations of a relationship following the hookup.
2.   Hooking up sexual behaviors are wide-ranging, from kissing to penetrative sex.
3.   Partners of hookups can be strangers, acquaintances, friends, or ex-partners.

Today on college campuses students are frequently opting to hook up, and college fraternities, sororities, and residence halls commonly host hooking-up parties (England & Thomas, 2007). As one social science researcher observes, "Today, almost all of America's residential college campuses are characterized by a hookup culture—large and small, private and public, secular and religious, and left- and right-leaning campuses" (Wade, 2017, p. 1). So pervasive are sexual hookups on college campuses, Wade asserts, that hooking up is part of the university/college *culture:* Not only do students have the opportunity to hook up, they are "also immersed in a culture that endorses and facilitates hookups" (Wade & Heldman, 2012, p. 128). To be certain, among straight emerging adults of both sexes, sexual hookups are the norm and are now socially acceptable—between 60 and 80 percent of North American college students have sexually hooked up (Bogle, 2007, 2008; Garcia, Reiber, Massey, & Merriwether, 2012; Stinson, 2010). This latest trend in physical attraction involves sexual encounters and includes anything from kissing, to mutual masturbation, to oral or anal sex, to sexual intercourse (Glenn & Marquardt, 2001). Figure 7.4 shows us where college students commonly hook up. As you can see, all of these hookup venues are typical of the college lifestyle.

The practice of hooking up is not as ambiguous as it might appear. Across college and university campuses hookups are shaped by culturally shared rules that include sexual behaviors without the expectation of a committed relationship. In a study of dating attitudes of college

Sexual assault:
illegal sexual contact that usually involves force upon a person without consent or is inflicted upon a person who is incapable of giving consent.

Hooking up:
physical or sexual interaction with the absence of commitment or affection.

Figure 7.4 /// Where Do College Students Hook Up?

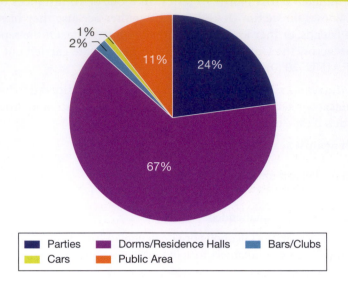

Parties — 24%
Dorms/Residence Halls — 67%
Bars/Clubs
Cars — 1%
Public Area — 11%
(2%)

Source: Paul & Hayes (2002).

women, researchers found a distinction between whites and Blacks when describing hooking up. In a study of more than 18,000 college students, white women reported almost double the hookup partners on average than do women of other races/ethnicities, and Asian men reported almost one-half of the hookup partners in comparison to their white, Black, and Hispanic counterparts; of all races and ethnicities, African American women are the least likely to engage in casual sex hookups (Spell, 2016).

College students who hook up do so for a wide variety of individual reasons. In a study of more than 700 college coeds, the investigation team found several motivations for both men and women. As the data in Figure 7.5 presents, college coeds hook up because of either

Figure 7.5 /// College Students' Motives for Casual Sex

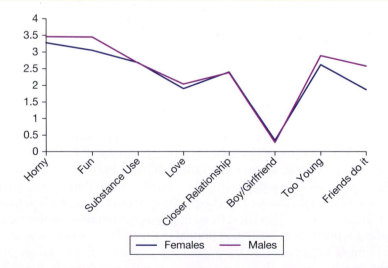

Note: Respondents were asked "To what extend do you agree that the following are reasons why you had a casual sex partner?" Responses ranged from 1= "Strongly Disagree" to 5= "Strongly Agree". Results shown in the figure represent the mean responses.

Source: Lyons, Manning, Longmore, & Giordano (2014).

conventional motivations (it's fun and physically enjoyable; it happened because of substance use; there's no emotional commitment; and it's a way to gain a friend's approval), or life course–specific motivations (transitional relationships; not ready for commitment; geographic mobility; and too young to be tied down) (Lyons, Manning, Longmore, & Giordano, 2014).

The types of relationships of those college students who hooked up varies a great deal. Casual sexual relationships and experiences manifest in different ways, from casual dating, friends with benefits, or a booty call/one night stand (Wesche, Claxton, Lefkowitz, & van Dulmen, 2018). Contrary to popular belief, college coeds generally don't hook up with people they don't know. Multiple hookups with the same person sometimes lead to an exclusive relationship. In Lyons's study, nearly 90 percent knew their most recent casual sex partner (Lyons et al., 2014). Interestingly, 10 percent of the women engaged in casual sex with a partner they had just met that day, in comparison to 13 percent of men. Not surprisingly, 65 percent of the study participants indicated that their sexual hookup partner was an ex-boyfriend or girlfriend. It's also important to note that these sexual encounters aren't "one night stands"—a sexual relationship that only lasts one night and is not repeated—more than half (61 percent) of the study participants who had casual sex with a partner have had sex with that person more than one time (Lyons et al., 2014). Earlier work, however, demonstrated that people who hook up are more likely to have concurrent sexual partners (Paik, 2010).

Regret and Risk

The last decade has given us much in the way of research results about how men and women feel after they have casual sex. Hooking up isn't always a positive experience, and as one researcher puts it, "[Hookup partners] experienced a kaleidoscope of reactions" (Garcia, Rieber, Massey, & Merriwether, 2013, p. 1):

- Embarrassment (27 percent); emotional difficulties (25 percent); loss of respect (21 percent), and ongoing difficulties with a steady partner (10 percent; Lewis, Granato, Blayney, Lostutter, & Kilmer, 2011).
- Regret following vaginal, anal, and/or oral sex (78 percent of women, 72 percent of men; Fisher, Worth, Garcia, & Meredith, 2012).
- Men reported being "sorry because I felt I used another person," while women reported "regret because I felt used" (Campbell, 2008, p. 1).

Although it's sometimes tempting to skip over the numbers when we're reading about research studies, the numbers here are worth paying attention to because they show us that at a minimum, one-fourth of college students who hook up in these various studies experienced negative emotions following the hookups. Other research is even more unsettling: Those students who experience regret, embarrassment, loss of respect, etc., also report increased symptoms associated with depression (Grello, Welsh, & Harper, 2006). A similar study found that women—not men—who had engaged in sexual intercourse during a hookup showed higher rates of mental distress (Fielder & Carey, 2010).

Sexual Risk. There are other negatives associated with hooking up. For example, in a study of nearly 1,500 college students, the investigation team found that only 46 percent reported using a condom during sex, putting the partners at risk for sexually transmitted infections and unintended pregnancy (Lewis et al., 2011). It is alarming to learn that a smaller study revealed that nearly one-half of the study participants *were not concerned* about acquiring STIs during a hookup, and almost all of them were unconcerned about getting diseases from oral sex (Downing-Matibag & Geisinger, 2009).

Alcohol Consumption. Hooking up commonly follows a lot of drinking, with men averaging five drinks before hooking up and women averaging three drinks (England & Thomas, 2007; Fielder & Carey, 2010; Lewis et al., 2011). Because alcohol lowers people's inhibitions, it plays a significant role in hooking up—nearly one-third of undergraduate students reported that their engagement in uncommitted sex was "unintentional," due to alcohol and other drugs (Garcia & Reiber, 2008).

iStock.com/gorodenkoff

Hooking up frequently occurs after a lot of drinking. College students report that drinking allows them to do things they might be too self-conscious to do while they are sober. Girls report that drinking allows them to be more sexual.

Some college students report that alcohol played a role in their going further sexually than they normally would, but they also indicated that drinking allows them to do things they might be too self-conscious to do while they're sober (England & Thomas, 2007). Girls report that drinking allows them to be more sexual.

Sexual Assault. Although certainly hooking up is becoming a college experience norm, it doesn't necessarily mean that the encounters are without danger and harm: It is not uncommon for women to report that their hooking up experiences involved being pressured or forced by a male partner to engage in unwanted sexual behaviors. Because of the alcohol involved in hooking up, as well as other drugs like marijuana and cocaine, it is not surprising that sexual assault can be an outcome. Indeed, one study found that the higher the alcohol consumption, the more forcible penetrative vaginal intercourse occurred (Owen & Fincham, 2011). Further, in a study that examined unwanted sexual behaviors among 178 college students, more than three-fourths of the female study participants indicated that their unwanted vaginal, anal, and/or oral sexual experiences (sexual assault) took place within the context of a hookup (Flack et al., 2008). These studies reveal a lot because they first show us that hooking up relationships may be sexually dangerous for women and may be ripe situations for sexual assault and rape to occur. The studies also show us that hooking up is no time to be ambiguous about expectations—partners need to be very clear about how far they're willing to go *before* the hookup encounter takes place. Even if these expectations are discussed prior to sexually hooking up, *consent*—explicit, enthusiastic, and continuous—*must be given.* To be clear: Consent. Must. Be. Given.

But given the amount of alcohol that is typically consumed prior to hooking up, set boundaries may be difficult to adhere to. Most states have laws regarding consent: A person cannot *legally* consent to sex if she/he is incapacitated due to alcohol or other substances. Consent to sex can only occur if it is free from the influence of substances and free from pressure (RAINN, 2020).

Is hooking up a negative experience in the lives of young adults? Perhaps a concern on a developmental level is that hooking up experiences do not allow adults in a transition phase of their lives to learn how to form and maintain mature, committed relationships. More often than not, long-term committed relationships do not result from hookups.

The ways in which people come together to form intimate couple bonds have changed significantly in the United States. From the years-past practice of courtship under the watchful eye of a parent to today's Internet dating, speed dating, and hooking up, couples have always found ways to be intimate with one another. Now let's look at how these relationships develop over time.

RELATIONSHIP DEVELOPMENT

The pathways to commitment are different from culture to culture. In some parts of the world today, forced marriages, child marriages, and arranged marriages are still practiced (see Chapter 8). In some of these cultures, it is the parents' responsibility—particularly the father's—to choose their child's life mate. In other industrialized, individualistic cultures, such as America, however, most couples marry for romantic love (see Chapter 6). How couples move beyond the initial physical attraction and form committed relationships is explored through two models: Knapp's Relationship Escalation Model and Duck's Relationship Filtering Model.

Knapp's Relationship Escalation Model

Mark Knapp (1984), communication studies author, studied interpersonal relationships to better determine how they develop. His work is often referred to as the Relationship Escalation Model because it describes how relationships are initially formed and how they progress over time:

- *Initiation:* The initiation into a relationship can occur in just a few seconds. This is the point at which individuals present their "public selves" by using common pleasantries and everyday greetings such as "Hi, how are you?" It is this stage in the relationship when people initially observe the traits or characteristics of another person, while they are also being judged.

- *Experimenting/Exploration.* This stage can be thought of as the information-gathering stage of a relationship. Individuals still have not spent a lot of time together, but it is at this point that they gather enough information, through casual conversation, to determine whether either party desires to continue the relationship.

- *Intensification.* As individuals spend more time together, their formal interactions give way to less formal and more spontaneous conversation. The level of self-disclosure increases, as might the level of physical contact. During this stage, the parameters of the relationship are set and individuals begin to state their levels of commitment.

- *Integrating.* This is when the two individuals become a "couple" and are identified as a couple among their friends and family. Each shares their relational identity.

- *Bonding/Intimacy.* During this stage, the couple reaches a shared level of interdependence. Knapp (1984) notes that during this relationship stage, some type of formal, official announcement is made of the couple's commitment to one another (such as an engagement or marriage).

Duck's Relationship Filtering Model

Similar to the filter model of mate selection we discussed earlier in this chapter, Stephen Duck (1985) proposed that when deciding whether to enter into or continue an interpersonal relationship—or what type of relationship—we sort information through a set of filters.

According to Duck (1985), we use different types of cues to sort interpersonal relationship information. The first filter is the **sociological or incidental cue**, which relates to the restrictions and limitations placed on our ability to meet people. These cues speak to a person's *sociological* location or position or the places where we live and work. **Preinteraction cues** provide at-a-glance information that helps us decide whether we would even consider wanting a date with a certain person. For example, someone's appearance might be physically attractive to you, and you might determine right away whether the person is your type or not.

Interaction cues allow us to make assessments about whether we want to get to know a person better. For example, most of us at some time have had a crush on someone we barely knew. Our crush may be based on physical attraction, but the attraction may end when he or she begins to talk. Through this interaction we learn more about one another. If we do find we want to spend more time with someone, we rely on **cognitive cues**, which tell us more about a person beyond a superficial, casual level. We get to know another's personality traits, beliefs,

Sociological or incidental cue:

the first filter of Stephen Duck's system, this relates to the restrictions and limitations placed on one's ability to meet people. These cues speak to one's sociological location or position or the places where one lives and works.

Preinteraction cues:

at-a-glance information that helps us decide whether we would even consider wanting a date with a certain person. Outward attractiveness would be an example of a preinteraction cue.

Interaction cues:

cues that enable us to assess whether we want to get to know a person any better. As we interact, we gain a better idea of the extent to which we may want to relate to a person.

Cognitive cues:

another's personality traits, beliefs, goals and aspirations, as well as the roles they play in life.

goals, and aspirations, as well as the roles they play in life. From these cues we determine whether any of them match with who we are and what we need or desire in a life partner. At this point, after much self-disclosure and time, we decide to try to take the relationship to a deeper level and enter into a committed partnership.

Commitment

The process of moving from a casual dating or sexual relationship to a committed relationship occurs over time. Increasingly today, young adults and older adults alike choose singlehood as a lifestyle instead of marriage or lifelong partnership. (In Chapter 8, we examine in depth the experiences of singlehood in the United States.)

Like love and intimacy, commitment is difficult to define because it can mean different things to different people. For many, commitment is the until-death-do-us-part component of a couple's relationship. It speaks to relationship longevity, stability, quality, and satisfaction. According to relationship psychologist Eli J. Finkel and his colleagues (2002), the growth of commitment in a relationship is the result of three factors:

1. Growing satisfaction with each other's ability to meet and gratify important needs
2. Decreasing reliance on friends and family to meet needs that members of a couple provide each other
3. Increasing investments in the relationship, such as time, material resources, and emotional/personal investment

When these factors are present in a relationship, it indicates that partners have made a commitment, a *long-term orientation* (Rusbult & Buunk, 1993). As a college student, for example, you may be committed to your relationships with your siblings and your parents and you may be committed to your studies at your university. Commitment involves the viewpoint that no matter the costs (such as in the social exchange perspective), a person is in it for the long haul—and that the long haul will undoubtedly involve difficulties and hardships at some (or many) points along the way. As I noted on the very first page of this textbook, the long haul is the *everything that comes with it.*

She said yes! Commonly in our society, an engagement to a love partner is a significant milestone in the relationship because it symbolizes the couple's love, dedication, and commitment to one another.

Family and social psychologist Michael P. Johnson (1991) identified three different types of commitment. First, **personal commitment** refers to the feelings, thoughts, and beliefs we have about a spouse, life mate, or significant other. This type of commitment is reflected in the sense of connection, liking, fondness, affection, tenderness, warmth, and love that couples feel for each other. Empirical research suggests that people who are committed to a spouse as a *person*—not just in terms of their commitment to the relationship—report less marital distress and fewer marital problems, as well as higher levels of marital happiness and marital satisfaction (Swenson & Trahaug, 1985). Those who exhibit personal commitment also express more love to their partners.

Second, **moral commitment** refers to each person's value and belief systems. Before committing to or ending a relationship, individuals consciously weigh what is right and what is wrong. They are guided by their value/belief/religious framework. Third, **structural commitment** refers to those commitments bound by institutions such as marriage. Although many individuals who have personal commitments also have structural commitments, having a structural commitment to the marital union does not necessarily mean that the partners are committed to one another on a personal level or that there is love or affection present in the relationship. In fact, Swenson and Trahaug's (1985) research concludes that marital happiness and marital satisfaction are lower in those couples who display only structural commitment.

Same-sex couples face unique challenges in constructing committed relationships because they have to create scripts that are different from the typical heterosexual commitment scripts (Rostosky, Riggle, Dudley, & Wright, 2006). In other words, there is no *social template* or *prototype*. In a study that explored commitment in 90 same-sex couples, the researchers found that these couples perceived relationship commitment as involving the following:

- *Investments in their partners.* Emotional and physical investment as well as investments of personal resources
- *Rewards.* Companionship, sexual satisfaction, and fulfillment
- *Costs.* Limits of personal freedom, legal constraints, and stress/conflict associated with disclosing the relationship to family and friends
- *Personal values and ideals.* Desire for sexual and emotional intimacy, communication, and overall high relationship quality

Many of these may seem similar to the relationship components found in committed heterosexual relationships, but each of these factors can have different meanings or levels of importance for same-sex couples (Rostosky et al., 2006). In addition, other factors such as moving in together, social disclosure of the relationship, and actively making plans for the future as a couple, signify relationship commitment for gay and lesbian couples (Rostosky et al., 2006).

Like love, intimacy, communication, or any other area of relational or family life, commitment is a *process* that progresses over time. As with any other area of family life, comment requires an active, practical effort from both members of the couple to ensure its success. Left unattended or ignored for too long, it will wane—and breaking up is more than likely to occur.

Breaking Up

It seems as though the people who love us the most—family, friends, or romantic partners—are the people who hurt us the most. This is because feeling hurt is almost always the result of interpersonal relationships (not the result of words or actions). The nature of relationships is that hurt is always possible because someone said or did something—or didn't say or do something. Sometimes we let the hurt stay under the surface and allow it to fester. This unresolved conflict almost always becomes the "background" of the relationship, and it's always present no matter how hard we try to make the relationship work. Other times it seems as though all we do is fight with our partner, over big things, small things, and things that don't really matter at all.

Personal commitment: the feelings, thoughts, and beliefs we have about a spouse, life mate, or significant other.

Moral commitment: each person's value and belief systems. Before committing to or ending a relationship, individuals consciously weigh what is right and what is wrong, guided by their value/belief/religious framework.

Structural commitment: commitments bound by institutions such as marriage.

There are a number of relational transgressions that cause hurt. It would be impossible to discuss all of them here because as you learned in Chapter 3 about symbolic interaction, each of us acquires and assigns different meanings to behaviors—what is hurtful to you may not be hurtful to another person. Generally speaking, however, **relational transgressions** are hurtful words or actions that communicate a devaluation of the partner or the relationship (Bachman & Guerrero, 2006). Relational transgressions include deceit, unfaithfulness, criticism, blaming, and betrayal of self-disclosure (Bachman & Guerrero, 2006). At the very least, these hurtful comments or actions may increase uncertainty about the relationship and may create temporary problems for the couple. For many, the ultimate consequence of relational transgressions is a breakup. Although some people do stay in relationships and work out even the most serious violations of trust (Roloff, Soule, & Carey, 2001), people who are deeply hurt by their partner's actions are likely to dissolve the relationship (Vangelisti & Young, 2000).

Breaking up is tough for most people, and it is associated with a number of negative physical and emotional responses, from anxiety and depression, to loneliness, to the suppression of the immune system due to stress (Davis, Shaver, & Vernon, 2003). In a study of nearly 5,300 participants (mostly in their teens and 20s), the researchers observed a range of reactions to breaking up; these are presented in Table 7.3. As the table shows us, there are two types of breakup reactions: distress and protest. **Distress reactions** include such things as physical and emotional pain, loss of interest in sex, and guilt; **protest reactions** are behaviors and feelings that attempt to reestablish the relationship, such as trying to reinvolve the ex-partner in sexual relations (Davis et al., 2003). The researchers also found that those who did not initiate the breakup felt a lost sense of identity and were more likely to jump immediately into a replacement relationship. Some also turned to alcohol and/or drugs to help them cope with the breakup.

Clearly, the end of a relationship sometimes means that we'll go through a period of mourning and loss. There appear to be three phases that follow ending a relationship, particularly in breakups that involve college students: (1) experiencing a loss, which includes emotionally processing the loss and realizing its implications; (2) pulling apart, which involves separating emotionally, physically, and symbolically from the partner; and (3) moving beyond, which encompasses not only a reduction in distress but also an ability to grow from the experience (Herbert & Popadiuk, 2008). College students in this study went from devastation ("This wasn't a breakup—it was a smash up") to coping ("I'm sad, but I'm trying to use my sadness in the most constructive ways possible; I'm letting it motivate me to do better in school and

Table 7.3 /// Distress/Protest Reactions to Breaking Up
Distress Reactions
Physical/emotional distress
Lost interest in sex
Self-blame
Guilt
Partner blame
Protest Reactions
Want/try to get back together
Sexual arousal
Anger/hostility/revenge
Physical hurt
Preoccupation
Exploration/interference

Source: Davis, Shaver, & Vernon (2003).

go to the gym"), to healing and resolution ("Breaking up is the best divorce you can have before you get married—you learn *a lot* from it").

Although there is an abundance of empirical works that address the link between cohabitation and divorce, next to no bodies of research investigate cohabitation breakups. However, in a first-of-its kind study, one group of researchers took a look at 1,295 adults (18 to 35 years old) in nonmarital relationships who experienced breakups, to assess the psychological impact and their overall life satisfaction; of these, nearly one-third had plans to marry before the breakup (Rhoades, Stanley, & Markman, 2011). This study found that couples who were cohabiting experienced greater declines in life satisfaction than couples who were not living together.

There are a number of how-to-survive-a-breakup sites on the Internet. Many of these sites contain good advice, such as taking time to examine what really happened and why; thinking through things thoroughly, but not excessively; dealing effectively with the hate phase, such as talking to friends or writing your feelings down in a journal; staying active; and making a conscious decision to let go of the hatred and realizing that harboring hate only hurts you, not your ex. If, after a breakup, you find that your sleeping and eating patterns are changing, that you can't focus, that you have low energy or are irritable, or if you feel a continued, general sense of sadness, it's best to talk to a healthcare professional on campus. Being single doesn't mean you have to be alone.

NONMARITAL COHABITATION: LIVING TOGETHER

Traditionally, the initial route to commitment for heterosexual couples has been attraction, courtship/dating, and then marriage; in recent years, however, a detour of sorts has appeared on the relationship scene—cohabitation. Increasingly in Western civilizations across the world, cohabitation is viewed as the next step following dating and preceding marriage.

Cohabitation is a term used to describe the living arrangements of unmarried, intimate partners who typically have a sexual relationship, and such relationships often resemble marriages. A cohabiting relationship can be a short-term arrangement or a long-term union with the shared economic and parenting responsibilities found in marriage (Trask & Koivunen, 2006).

Cohabitation is the prevailing living arrangement of intimates today. This type of couple relationship carries with it both advantages and disadvantages.

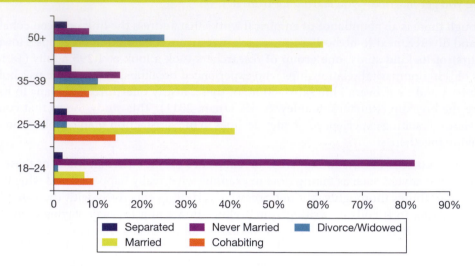

Figure 7.6 /// Adults Who Cohabit by Age Group

Legend:
- Separated
- Married
- Never Married
- Cohabiting
- Divorce/Widowed

Source: Pew Research Center (2017).

Common law marriage:

a relationship between cohabiting heterosexual partners who are not legally married; however, the couple holds themselves out as husband and wife.

A **common law marriage** is a relationship between cohabiting heterosexual partners without a legal marriage ceremony; however, the couple presents themselves as husband and wife. After the couple has been living together for a certain length of time (the time varies by state), they are considered legally wed. In Canada, common law marriage is referred to as *common-law status*.

Cohabiters can be straight or gay, never-before-married, or divorced-and-now-single. They can be young parents or 68-year-old widows and widowers (see Figure 7.6). Studying cohabitation is important to our understanding of relational and family life because this social phenomenon corresponds to a dramatic shift in the social and demographic behaviors through which intimate and sexual relationships, as well as families, are formed, organized, and dissolved (Wu, 2007).

Once considered a scandalous, uncommon alternative lifestyle, cohabiting before marriage (or instead of marriage) is now the prevailing living arrangement of intimate partners—the next step following serious dating. In fact, data show that in 2018, there were 8.5 million unmarried opposite-sex couples living together –up 29 percent since 2007 (U.S. Census Bureau, 2018). When gay couples are included in the numbers of those cohabiting, the figure increases to nearly 10 million people (The Williams Institute, 2019).

Characteristics of Cohabitation

Cohabitation has become a normal part of the lifecourse for many Americans, young and old alike. Consider the following trends of nonmarital cohabitation in the United States (Pew Research Center, 2017):

- Roughly one-half of all cohabiters are younger than 35
- Nearly one-fourth of all cohabiting adults are ages 50 and older; this number has grown by 75 percent since 2007
- 67 percent of those currently married cohabited before marriage with one or more partners

Several factors contribute to whether a person chooses to live with an intimate partner and forego the traditional path of marriage. The rates of cohabitation vary between different regions in the United States, religion, age, among races, social class, and levels of educational attainment.

Unmarried to Each Other: Is Cohabitation a Trial Marriage or Playing Commitment?

The reasons people live together vary. For example, some divorced people may be hesitant to marry again and choose instead to cohabit. Others would rather drive over a cliff than walk down the marital aisle and have a piece of paper define their relationship. The question arises, then, "Does living together before marriage serve as a trial, practice marriage?"

YES: According to cohabitation advocates and authors Dorian Solot and Marshall Miller (2004), living together before marriage serves as a trial to a marriage in the following ways:

- It provides each member of the couple time to examine why she or he desires to be together as a couple and to form clear expectations of each other and of the relationship.

- It helps couples keep reasonable expectations for each other and the relationship.

- It allows cohabiting partners to see the "real" partner. "If you don't like what you see in an unmarried significant other, you definitely won't like it in a spouse."

- Negotiating roles, finances, the sexual relationship, and property provide opportunities for conversations that help clarify the couple's expectations and help strengthen the relationship. It is a good reality check.

NO: If living together serves as a trial or a test of what the marital relationship will be like, doom lies ahead. The *cohabitation effect* is the effect that cohabitation has on first marriages, and it posits a negative relationship between premarital cohabitation and marriage. Those who cohabit before marriage and later marry commonly experience the following:

- Higher divorce rates (Institute of Family Studies, 2018)

- Difficulties in ending unhappy relationships (Institute of Family Studies, 2018)

- An erosion in the belief that marriage is permanent (Teachman, 2003)

- *Sliding into marriage effect*—those who probably would not (and should not) get married, but do so because they believe it's the next step after cohabitation (Stanley, Kline Rhoades, & Markman, 2006)

- Potential of *sunk cost*, where each additional investment into the relationship makes it that much harder to end it (Stanley et al., 2006)

- Less satisfying sexual relationships (Waite & Gallagher, 2001)

What Do You Think?

1. Is cohabitation good preparation for marriage—a good trial of marriage?

2. What are good reasons to live together before marriage? What are good reasons not to live together before marriage? Are your reasons based on your personal opinions or are they based on the research findings?

3. In your opinion, is nonmarital cohabitation a positive or a negative life experience? Support your answer.

Factors That Affect Cohabitation

When discussing issues that affect whether couples choose to cohabit, it's best to keep at the forefront our discussion in Chapter 1 about the different birth cohorts and generations in the United States because these significantly impact attitudes and beliefs about cohabitation.

- The Silent Generation (born between 1925 and 1945): This generation has been described as conservative and conformist; they are typically uncomfortable with cultural changes and nontraditional families (Taylor, 2014). It's understandable, then, if their attitudes and beliefs about cohabiting before or instead of marriage are unfavorable.

- Baby Boomers (born between 1946 and 1964): This generation grew up with war, the civil rights movement, and the feminist movement (Taylor, 2014). Baby boomers were the first to experiment with cohabitation in the 1970s. Because of their belief in controlling their own destinies (Mitchell, 2003), many boomers are in favor of cohabitation—and the rates at which couples live together instead of marrying supports this belief.

- Generation X (born between 1965 and 1980): Experiencing in the early 2000s one of the worst economic crises this country has seen since the Depression, and experiencing the explosive divorce rates of parents in the 1980s, Gen Xers saw the population of cohabiting couples grow by 25 percent in the late 1980s and early 1990s (Bumpass & Lu, 2000).

- Millennials (born between 1981 and 2000): Living with their parents for longer periods of time than previous generations, and slow to marry, Millennials have experienced the cultural normalization of cohabitation and are therefore more likely to cohabit than other generations (Pew Research Center, 2017).

Generally speaking, the data today reflect an increasing approval of premarital cohabitation and unmarried parenthood, away from favor of marriage (Institute for Family Studies, 2018). As Figure 7.7 shows us, the percentage of Americans who disapprove of cohabitation has significantly decreased since 2002. Demographers maintain that couples today believe that living together helps people avoid a divorce, which is why we are seeing this increase in cohabitation: 60 percent of women and 67 percent of men surveyed agreed that "Living together before marriage may help prevent divorce" (Institute of Family Studies, 2018; Daugherty & Copen, 2016).

Cohabitation and Religion

Nonmarital cohabitation is commoner in the Northeast than it is in the South or the Midwest. In states in which religion is a predominant part of the culture (such as the Church of Latter-Day Saints in Utah and throughout the Bible Belt, or the South and the Midwest), cohabitation rates are lower. Nearly 65 percent of those who cohabit before marriage claim no religious affiliation, whereas 93 percent of those who attend church or other religious services (temple or mosque) on a weekly basis are likely to not cohabit before marriage (Barna Research Group, 2017).

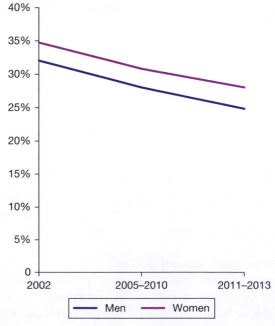

Figure 7.7 /// Percentage of Americans Aged 15–44 Who Disapprove of Cohabitation

Source: Institute for Family Studies (2019).

Those who attend church or temple frequently (weekly or more) tend to believe that living together in lieu of marriage is a bad thing for society, whereas those who attend church or temple less frequently (monthly or less) tend to look more favorably on cohabitation. Similarly, those who hold more moderate or liberal political beliefs tend to view cohabitation more favorably than those who do not (Barna Research Group, 2017).

Cohabitation and Race

Race is also a key factor in rates of cohabitation; cohabitation is especially common among lower-income minority groups such as Blacks and Hispanics (Simmons & O'Connell, 2003). In the United States, cohabitation is more prevalent among African Americans and Native Americans/Alaska Natives than whites; Asian Americans have the lowest rate of nonmarital cohabitation (U.S. Census Bureau, 2019; see Figure 7.8). One demographer notes, "The prevalence rates of cohabitation across racial groups suggest that cohabitation may have different meanings and dynamics—and therefore provide different social, psychological, and economic resources—for [different racial and ethnic groups]" (U.S. Census Bureau, 2019). The authors also suggest that among whites, cohabitation is viewed more as a trial marriage. In contrast, cohabitation appears to be more of a marriage alternative ("marriage-like") among African Americans. This is interesting to note because, as the researchers speculate, a trial marriage is more similar to relationships of dating couples, whereas "marriage-like" cohabitation relationships have dynamics more similar to married couples, including higher levels of shared social, psychological, and economic resources.

Cohabitation and Finances

Employment also plays a key role in whether a cohabiting couple eventually marries. Research focusing on marriage among cohabiters indicates that cohabiting couples who have greater economic resources are more likely to marry if they have a child while living together rather than remain simply cohabiting partners (Osborn, 2005; see Table 7.4). Research also finds that often cohabiters desire marriage, but they delay or forgo it until they become financially stable (Gibson-Davis, Edin, & McLanahan, 2005). Among Blacks, if both partners are working, they are more likely to marry; however, among white couples, if a woman is not working, the couple is less likely to wed (Manning & Jones, 2006). It is very important to note, however, that even though nonmarital cohabitation is seen among all groups, it still continues to be a trend among those who are economically disadvantaged (Smock, Manning, & Porter, 2005).

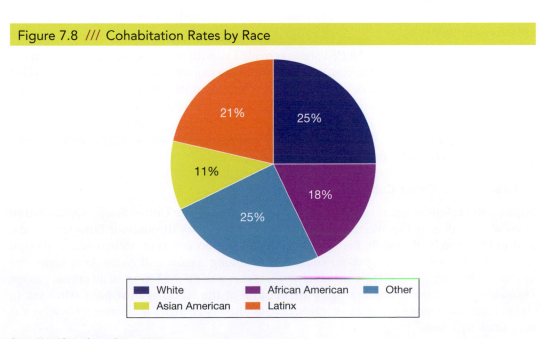

Figure 7.8 /// Cohabitation Rates by Race

- White 25%
- African American 18%
- Other 25%
- Asian American 11%
- Latinx 21%

Source: United States Census Bureau (2017).

Table 7.4 /// Percentage of Parents Who Were Married or Cohabitating at the Birth of Their First Child, by Race/Ethnicity and Sex

	Married	Cohabitating	Other
Hispanic males	52	32	16
Hispanic females	54	22	24
Black males	37	24	39
Black females	23	15	62
White males	77	12	10
White females	74	9	15

Source: National Vital Statistics Reports (2015).

Among Puerto Ricans, cohabitation unions usually begin informally, and these relationships are unlikely to be legalized through marriage (Brown, Van Hook, & Glick, 2008). However, unlike Blacks and whites who cohabit, Puerto Ricans' live-together relationships are similar to their married counterparts in terms of education, employment, and childbearing (Brown et al., 2008). In one study, most Puerto Rican women described their cohabiting relationships as a form of marriage (Brown et al., 2008).

Cohabitation Among Gay Men and Lesbians

The availability of social science data concerning cohabitation experiences of gay men and lesbians is rapidly changing, largely due to the U.S. Supreme Court ruling in 2015 that legalized gay marriage in all 50 states. Demographic characteristics reveal that gay male cohabiters are more likely to be white, are more highly educated, and are less likely to have children in their household compared to nonpartnered gay men (Black, Sanders, & Taylor, 2007). Lesbians in cohabiting relationship tend to be older (about age 39), are more likely to be white and to have been in a prior legal heterosexual marriage, more likely to have children in their household, and are more highly educated than nonpartnered lesbians (Black et al., 2007).

In 2017, Gallup polling in the United States provided us with a glimpse of the changes in living arrangements of gay and lesbian couples. While the majority of gays and lesbians polled indicated that they are single or never married, what's interesting to note is that for the first time in our nation's history, more gays and lesbians are married to their same-sex spouse than are cohabiting. Today, 10.2 percent of LGBT individuals are married to their same-sex spouse, an increase from 7.9 percent just two years ago (Gallup News, 2017). To be certain, the landscape of intimate relationships is changing.

Cohabitation in Other Cultures

Nonmarital cohabitation is not a trend that is seen only in the United States. Cohabitation is present in all over the Western world, including countries throughout Europe. In Asia, and in the Near and Middle East countries, cohabitation is a rare occurrence. Although we know essentially nothing about cohabitation among Asians and Asian Americans, the available data suggest that their cohabitation rates are among the lowest of all ethnic groups (Brown et al., 2008). These low rates are because of the taboo against premarital sex in Asian cultures. Among Islamic countries, cohabitation is virtually nonexistent because it is forbidden by Islam.

A live-together arrangement between intimate partners is the contemporary "next step" in relationship development. But are these arrangements a *substitute* for marriage or viewed among the couples as a *trial* marriage? And what reasons do couples give for cohabiting?

Why Do Couples Cohabit?

With the increasing number of years that most young adults are single, and the growing trend in cohabitation, couples report several common reasons for cohabiting. David H. Olson created the PREPARE/ENRICH Couple Program for couples who want to better prepare for marriage or enrich their existing marriages. In this program, couples complete inventories that assess their relationship types, as well as characteristics of each member's family of origin. In a survey of more than 50,000 respondents, David Olson and his colleague found these contemporary reasons that couples live together before marriage (Olson & Olson-Sigg, 2007):

- Economic advantages
- Time together
- Increased intimacy
- Less complication in dissolution of relationship if it doesn't work out
- "Testing" compatibility
- Trial marriage

Data gathered by the Pew Research Center (2007) give us further insight into why couples live together before marriage or instead of marriage. Nearly one-fourth of those survey respondents who cohabit did so to test the relationship, to make sure that the partner is the right one.

But what is cohabitation like behind the numbers? In an effort to go beyond the raw numbers, more than 100 Black, Hispanic, and white young adult cohabiters were interviewed to better understand how nonmarital cohabitation relationship begin and end, their living arrangements, and the language used to refer to their partners (Manning & Smock, 2003). The extensive, in-depth interviews reveal much about the beginnings and endings of cohabiting relationships: "In a way it did just kind of happen . . . I would come over and stay with him at night and one night led into two nights, two nights leading into three nights and then next thing you know I have clothes over there and I'm cooking dinner for him" (Black female, computer services, age 28, p. 15).

When called on to describe their relationship with their live-in, intimate partner, many cohabiters are at a loss: "It wasn't 'roommate' and I realize . . . there is no term for somebody who is in between girlfriend and wife" (white male, office worker, age 33, p. 20).

Unlike marital relationships, there is much ambiguity with cohabiting relationships. As the researchers note, there are really no defining moments that signal the beginning or end of the cohabiting arrangements (Manning & Smock, 2003). In many instances, there is a gradual transition, with most couples drifting in and out of these arrangements. The researchers contend that living together before marriage does not appear to be a substitute marriage (a long-term commitment between intimate partners that does not involve legal marriage) or a trial marriage (living together to see what marriage would be like). Cohabitation, instead, is seen as an alternative to being single.

There also appears to be ambiguity in what to call one's partner, because those who participated in the research felt that the term *unmarried partners* did not fully capture the essence of their relationships—it didn't convey how the intimate partners actually felt about one another (Manning & Smock, 2003). As one Black female concludes, "[The term *unmarried partner*] . . . to me [sounds like] just a person I'm having sex with" (p. 23).

But Does Cohabitation Work?

In certain regions of the United States, there are few more hotly or intensely debated topics in family life than the issue of whether or not couples should cohabit before marriage. Aside from whether cohabitation is a moral life choice is the issue of whether cohabitation is an advantageous or disadvantageous choice for couples. Does cohabitation work?

Advantages of Cohabitation

Our study so far has shown us that nonmarital cohabitation is an increasingly common living arrangement for intimate partners both in the United States and other cultures. Although the literature is virtually silent on the potential positive outcomes associated with cohabiting, there is some empirical evidence that suggests that couples do experience a few advantages if they cohabit before or instead of marriage:

- Couples who cohabit have more personal autonomy than those who are married (Bernhardt, 2004).
- Cohabiters have more personal freedom than those who are married (Waite & Gallagher, 2001).
- Those who live together have more individual financial freedom than married partners do (Waite & Gallagher, 2001).
- Cohabiters have greater gender equity, less-traditional gender roles, and share household chores more than married couples do (Bernhardt, 2004).
- Couples who cohabit have greater flexibility in their commitments to their relationships (Bernhardt, 2004).

Given the unique, individualized nature of intimate relationships, some might argue that these points are disadvantages, rather than advantages, of nonmarital cohabitation.

Disadvantages of Cohabitation

Although there is little information available regarding the advantages of cohabitation, the research is consistently clear regarding its disadvantages—cohabitation before marriage or in place of marriage is, by and large, a negative relationship experience:

- Cohabitation before marriage is related to higher relationship dissatisfaction and higher risk of divorce (Olson & Olson-Sigg, 2007).
- Couples who live together have the lowest level of premarital satisfaction when compared to other living arrangements (among many others, Waite & Gallagher, 2001).
- Married couples who live together before marriage have poorer communication skills in discussing problems than those couples who do not live together (Cohan & Kleinbaum, 2002).
- Cohabiting couples are less sexually committed than married couples are (Olson & Olson-Sigg, 2007).
- Cohabiting women report twice the rate of abuse that married women report. There is more verbal aggression, anger, and attempts to control the partner's feelings than exists in married relationships (Cohan & Kleinbaum, 2002). (Chapter 15 provides an in-depth look at family violence.)

Upon reviewing these aspects, you may be asking yourself, "If cohabitation is thought of as a trial marriage for some, why are such negative consequences associated with this living arrangement?" David Olson notes,

Who Determines Society's "Ideal Body" Standard—Men or Women?

Who determines society's "ideal body" standard—men or women? One researcher tried to answer this question by doing his own content analysis of *Vogue* magazine models (to assess the female standard of ideal body shape), *Playboy* centerfold models (to assess the male standard of ideal body shape), and Miss America winners (a sort of catch-all to assess both female and male standards of ideal body shape; Barber, 1998). He posed two questions:

1. Is a male's standard of women's attractiveness curvier than the female's standard?

2. Do women or men determine the "ideal body" standard?

According to Barber (1998, p. 3), "American women's standard for female bodily attractiveness differs greatly from that of men." From 1978 to 1986, the *Vogue* models bustlines were significantly smaller than the *Playboy* models' bustlines or those of the winners of the Miss America beauty pageant. In fact, the *Vogue* standard for physical attractiveness did not predict the *Playboy* or Miss America standard of the "ideal" body shape! Barber's analysis also determined that the bust-waist ratios for *Playboy* models and Miss America winners were not significantly different; in other words, the bust and the waist measurements of *Playboy* models and Miss America contestants were virtually the same. Barber subsequently concluded from this research that the female body standard, over time, has converged with the male ideal body standard—curves.

Wondering how students today would respond to Barber's research questions and findings, I posed them to my intimate relationships and marriage class. The students responded:

Source: Barber (1998).

Her Side: "I just don't get it. I mean, as women we are bombarded day after day after day with images in print and electronic media that tell us we are never thin enough. We're urged to purge, we're urged to get rid of curves—and now we find out that men actually *like* curves? If that's the case, then why is a woman in a size 14 considered to be a "plus size" model, when *most* of American women are size 14? Why do women's magazines constantly insist on pushing their impossible-to-achieve-version of 'beautiful' on us?'"

"Why do *men* get to decide the standard of beauty?!"

His Side: "But I don't think that the images in *Playboy* are fair to women, either. That magazine sends the message that all women have to be perfectly proportioned to be attractive and beautiful, and that's not true. I think if you asked most guys they would say that women are attractive and beautiful if they are *healthy*."

"Hey, don't blame the guys! Every man knows that women don't dress to please men; they dress and diet to please other women!"

Your Side: From your casual observations,

1. Do you think men or women determine the ideal body standard for women in today's society?

2. From looking at women's magazine covers, what is the woman's ideal body standard? From looking at men's magazine covers, what is the male's ideal body standard for women? Do you agree with the images that are advertised as "ideal"?

3. Do you think the ideal body standard for women will change over time?

One explanation is that while the basis for marriage is a strong ethic of commitment, cohabiting couples are much more oriented toward their own personal autonomy and are more willing to terminate the relationship. It is easy to speculate that once this *low-commitment/high autonomy pattern* of relating is learned, it becomes hard to change. Cohabitation reflects uncertainty. (Olson & Olson-Sigg, 2007)

Although it is clear from the skyrocketing increase in the numbers of those who cohabit before marriage that public opinion approves of this relational pathway, some family life specialists and researchers are not so sure this relationship course is the best route. As noted by the Australian Family Association (2008),

> The sharp rise in unmarried cohabitation is perhaps one of the most alarming trends of the . . . family this century. Living together prior to or instead of marriage may seem like a progressive approach to intimate relationships . . . [but] among other things, unmarried cohabiting couples express less commitment to an ideal of relationship permanence. [Cohabitation] is, for the most part, not a relationship with a future, but one that lasts for a period of time and then ends. [It] does not improve the choice of marital partners, nor does it offer an enriched courtship where partners can get to know each other and gain experience with matters related to marriage. Unmarried cohabitation's only advantage over marriage is that it guarantees free entry, free exit, no commitment, and no responsibility.

Despite the increasing numbers of singles today, despite the noticeable trend of couples delaying marriage for longer periods of time, and despite the increased trends in nonmarital cohabitation, most Americans still marry at least once in their lifetime.

FAMILY LIFE EDUCATION: USING REINFORCING STRATEGIES TO AID COUPLE FORMATION AND MAINTENANCE

I vividly remember when I suspected my husband was "the one" I wanted to marry (Spring Break, 1979, South Padre Island). Our relationship took a very untraditional path (for the time), from casual acquaintance, to casual dating, to more serious dating, to cohabitation (quite scandalous in the 1970s!), to engagement, to marriage. I have to wonder, however, if we were to meet each other for the first time today, would our path commitment be the same? Would we skip any steps? Would we lengthen any steps, such as the years spent in cohabitation?

As you are learning throughout our study together, helping professionals such as therapists, social workers, psychologists, CFLEs, nurses, physicians, and teachers are instrumental in promoting reinforcing strategies that assist individuals and partners in the successful formation and maintenance of their couple relationship (National Council on Family Relations, 2020). Because of the developmental transitions that occur in dating and courtship partners, as well as cohabiting partners, CFLEs and others must be aware of changing gender and sexual identity experiences, expectations, and behaviors that are prevalent in our culture. To be sure, this is no easy task: The diversity in racial and ethnic experiences, and the range of experiences of those with different sexual identities have undergone significant changes over the last two decades. So, too, have the dating and courtship behaviors of different-sex couples.

The study of interpersonal attraction and the pathways to partnering are important in our examination of marital and intimate relationships because dating, courtship, and partnering practices map out different courses to marriage and other lifelong couple relationships. Today, some looking for love still choose a traditional route to finding someone they hope to spend the rest of their life with, while others choose a present-day dot-com approach and use the Internet.

Relationally, as a society we are living in uncharted and unprecedented times. How did we move from the tradition of courting under the eye of a parent, to free-for-all, transient sexual hookups? If we look at the past 50 to 60 years, the way people develop interpersonal partnerships has undergone extraordinary changes, from parent-directed and parent-approved courtship with the intention of marriage, to speed and Internet dating, to no-strings-attached sexual hookups, and to trial sexual and economic live-together unions. We wonder what other types of changes might be in store.

"Frisky Business": Interpersonal Attraction Theories

- Evolutionary theory for mate selection purports that we choose mates solely to further our reproduction. Since every society has some form of socially approved union between men and women, sociologists and anthropologists have sought to determine the mechanisms by which men and women are attracted to one another.

- Mate selection evolutionist-based theories maintain that there are two specific biological goals—male sexual selection goals and female sexual selection goals—that must be achieved when selecting a mate. According to evolutionists, men are concerned with quantity: To impregnate as many women as possible, males must select females who are able to bear children and will select women who possess certain fertility cues, such as youth, attractiveness, body shape, and permissiveness. Women

are concerned with the quality of the children they produce and search for provider/protector cues such as intelligence, dominance, physical strength, and prowess, and ambition.

- Social Exchange theory explains what motivates individuals to act and asserts that individuals act out of self-interest in ways to maximize their rewards and minimize their costs. Although each individual in a relationship may seek personal rewards with minimal costs according to researchers Thibaut and Kelley, both individuals are mutually reliant on one another for rewarding results.

- The Filter Theory of Mate Selection suggests that individuals use a filtering mechanism (based on propinquity, homogamy, heterogamy, physical attraction, or reciprocity) that helps individuals sort out a potential mate from the vast pool of candidates, or eligible partners.

The Path to Commitment

- Courting and courtship are socially prescribed forms of conduct that guide men and women toward matrimony. Dating is an occasion where people get together socially for various reasons, such as for relaxation or to determine whether the partner is a potential spouse or lifelong partner, a lifelong relationship, or a sexual encounter with no strings attached.

- Today, hooking up—brief physical (usually sexual) interactions—are part of the college climate in the United States. There are many reasons why people choose to hook up, but there is no expectation of commitment or affection.

Relationship Development

- Knapp's Relational Model describes how relationships are initially formed and how they progress over time through the stages of initiation, experimenting/exploration, intensification, integrating, and bonding/intimacy. Duck's Relationship Filtering Model asserts that we use different types of cues or filters to sort interpersonal relationship information: sociological/incidental cues, preinteraction cues, interaction cues, and cognitive cues.

- The growth of commitment (personal, moral, or structural) in a relationship is the result of (1) growing satisfaction with each other's ability to meet and gratify important needs; (2) decreasing reliance on friends and family to meet needs that a partner provides; and (3) increasing investments in the relationship, such as time, material resources, and emotional involvement. When these are present, partners have made a commitment, or long-term orientation.

Nonmarital Cohabitation: Living Together

- *Cohabitation*—the term that is used to describe the living arrangements of unmarried, intimate partners who typically have a sexual relationship—is the prevailing living arrangement of intimate partners and the step following serious dating. Religion, age, race, social class, and levels of education all affect the rate of cohabitation among different regions in the United States.

- Public opinion suggests that cohabitation is the next logical step after serious dating, yet research consistently makes clear that cohabitation before marriage or in place of marriage is by and large a negative relationship experience. Cohabitation before marriage not only correlates with higher relationship dissatisfaction and higher risk of divorce in the event of marriage but it also carries with it an increased risk of violence against women and children.

/// **KEY TERMS**

Asexual 232	Common law marriage 246	Courting 225
Cognitive cues 241	Cost 221	Cultural scripts 227

SINGLEHOOD, COUPLING, AND MARRIAGE

LEARNING OBJECTIVES

8.1 Describe the contemporary trends and experiences of singlehood in the United States.

8.2 Summarize the social and legal dimensions of marriage and the rights and privileges associated with marriage.

8.3 Discuss why the transition to a marital relationship is difficult.

8.4 Explain the different premarital and marital couple types that contribute to marital satisfaction and happiness.

The pastor asked the young couple, "Eric and Gretchen, will you have one another, to be one flesh with you? Will you love one another, care for one another, honor one another, respect one another, and protect one another, in every situation of life? Will you prefer each other above all others and forsaking all others, be faithful as long as you both shall live?"

Gretchen and Eric nervously held each other's hands and answered the pastor's questions in unison by vowing to each other:

"Gretchen/Eric, I ask you to come with me and be my wife/husband. I promise to love you as no one else can. I will give you my strength and will accept yours in return. In happy times, or in sad times, when life is stormy or quiet. I will love you when we are together, I will love you when we are apart. From the depths of my heart I will always be open and honest with you. Your happiness will be my happiness, and my strength will be your protection, my tenderness and care will be your comfort. I will make your goals and dreams my goals and dreams. Together we will build a home where love abides. I give myself to you."

There is an indescribable joy when you witness the marriage of your own children. At each of their weddings, my husband and I sat in the surreal moment, smiling and crying from the inside out (where *did* the time go?), remarked that no bride has ever looked as beautiful as the brides before us (our new *daughters!*), and that our sons (no longer boys, but *men*) had never looked more nervous. As soon as the wedding official asked the marrying couples of their intentions toward one another and they each, in turn replied, "I do," my husband and I exchanged a knowing glance. If they only knew!

If they only knew that their promises to love one another, care for one another, respect one another, and protect one another will be tested time and time again—sometimes to the breaking point. *If they only knew* that it's not always easy to be open and honest, and that it's not always easy to be happy for their partner or share their partner's sorrow. *If they only knew*, while they today pledge that they will be "one," that oneness in purpose and goals and dreams is much easier said than done. Even though most young married couples know that their marital union will be a journey fraught with ups and downs and unexpected joys and sorrows, few know at the outset the complexities of being married. And as current divorce statistics indicate, few are adequately prepared and equipped to negotiate their new roles and to navigate these complexities.

In our examination of intimate relationships we must obviously consider marriage; however, discussing all of the nuances associated with marriage is an arduous and demanding task. To complicate matters further, the subject is greatly influenced by our own family of origin experiences—for example, Are your parents divorced or have they been married for some time? Were you raised by a single-parent mother or a single-parent father? Have you ever witnessed marital violence between your parents? Compound your family experiences of marriage with your cultural and ethnic background and your religious upbringing, and you can see how our perceptions of marriage are influenced by many factors.

Our family studies framework is an applied approach to examining marriage and marital life, and because of this integration of application and theory, the following discussion may be quite unlike other textbooks you may have read that focus on sociological and anthropological aspects of marriage. In this approach we might think of marriage as a compass to provide direction, rather than as a road map. A road map provides the details a journey can take. A compass helps you learn where you are—and which direction to take. Neither a text nor an instructor can provide a map for marital bliss, but we can become oriented and directed by some landmarks along the way.

Before we examine marriage, we will first discuss being single, which is an increasing trend among America's young adults. We will then look at marriage in a variety of contexts, such as how marriage is both a relational and legal reality, as well as the ever-evolving status of gay and lesbian marriages. We'll study the rights, privileges, and benefits of marriage, as well as the pitfalls that might trap some couples in marital dissatisfaction. Finally, we will examine the keys to a successful marriage—marital expectations.

BEING SINGLE

In Chapter 7, we looked at the contemporary trends in dating and cohabitation in the United States. As you discovered, dating and courtship are practices that typically lead to the selection of a marriage partner or a life mate. In U.S. culture, and in cultures around the world, marriage is assumed to be the next stage in a person' life following adolescence and early adulthood. But not everyone who dates necessarily has marriage on his or her mind. American culture today is seeing increasing numbers of singles, and singlehood is becoming a popular trend among the young and old as well. This trend is due, in part, to the *individualistic* nature of American society; that is, individual needs and wants, such as self-fulfillment, educational attainment, and the fulfillment of career goals, are promoted over the *collective* needs of the society (see Chapter 1). This current trend in the large and increasing numbers of singles is also partly because numbers of young adults are delaying marriage. Today, the average age at marriage for men is 29.8 years; for women it is 27.8 years (U.S. Census Bureau, 2019c). Figure 8.1 shows the average age of marriage for men and women from 1890 to 2018. As you can see, the age at which

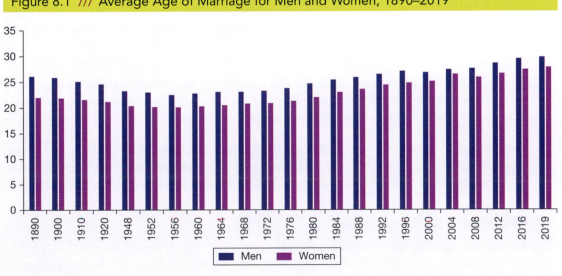

Figure 8.1 /// Average Age of Marriage for Men and Women, 1890–2019

Source: United States Census Bureau (2019).

people marry fluctuates over time. It's important to understand that these fluctuations mirror society's attitudes toward marriage and singlehood. In 1978, for instance, 59 percent of 18- to 34-year-olds were married; today, only 29 percent are married (U.S. Census Bureau, 2019b).

Historically, U.S. culture viewed singlehood as a transitional stage that preceded marriage and parenting—being single was not viewed as a lifestyle that adults purposely chose, but as a stepping stone to the eventual, expected adult roles of spouse and parent. Today, marriage still remains the normative life course for most Americans, with 90 to 95 percent of adults eventually marrying (U.S. Census Bureau, 2019b), but in contemporary society there is an increasing number of adults who are single. In 2016, for instance, there were nearly 111 million unmarried people in America age 18 and older—or about 45 percent of all U.S. residents over the age of 18 (U.S. Census Bureau, 2019a). Of these 111 million, 53 percent are women and nearly 47 percent are men. Of the households maintained in the United States, nearly 48 percent are headed by singles. By comparison, the number of households composed of married couples stood at slightly more than 61 million (U.S. Census Bureau, 2019a). These trends are quite significant, because they represent a dramatic shift in singlehood, and this raises a critical question: Will singlehood rates continue to increase as the millennial generation ages?

The experience of being single is not universal. Singles are a complex and diverse group, and there are differences in how people experience singlehood. For instance, people may be single because they have never married, because they are divorced, or because they are widowed. We'll explore the characteristics of these single types a bit later on in this discussion, but first we begin by gaining an understanding of the broad categories of singlehood.

Types of Singlehood

Sociologist Peter Stein (1981) developed a typology of singlehood. According to this classification, there are four categories of single people: voluntary temporary, voluntary permanent, involuntary temporary, and involuntary permanent (see Table 8.1).

- **Voluntary temporary singles.** Singles in this category include those who have never married, as well as those who were previously married and are now divorced or widowed. Voluntary singles are not opposed to marriage; rather, they are not currently looking for a mate because it is not a priority.

- **Voluntary permanent singles.** This category of singles includes those who have chosen deliberately to remain unmarried. The choice to remain single is stable and permanent over time. Voluntary permanent singles include never-marrieds, those who have divorced and have no intention of remarrying, cohabiting individuals, gay and lesbian couples, and certain members of the clergy, such as priests and nuns.

- **Involuntary temporary singles.** Among this category are singles who want to be married and who are actively seeking a marriage mate. This group of singles includes people who have never married, as well as those who were previously married and are now divorced or single.

- **Involuntary permanent singles.** In this category are those singles who wanted to marry but did not find a marriage mate. These singles may be never married, divorced, or widowed. Over time, they come to accept their unmarried status.

Stein's (1981) typology shows us that being single is a fluid, changeable state. In other words, there will always be people who are single for a certain period of time, and there will always be people who remain single throughout their lives—either by choice or by circumstance.

Experiencing Singlehood

As you saw in Chapter 7, for some people dating is a way to have fun, relax, and get to know other people. For others, dating or courting is a pathway for people to find a life mate (Sheehan, 2003). Most of us, at some point in our lives, will find ourselves single—whether it's because we haven't found Mr. or Ms. Right, because we just ended a relationship, or

Table 8.1 /// Using Stein's Types of Singlehood

Singlehood Type	Example
Involuntary Temporary	Vajra is 29 and has a young son, the product of a previous marriage. He is busy and doesn't get to go on dates often, but he keeps up his OKCupid profile and hopes to find his future wife online.
Voluntary Temporary	After another bad breakup, Aliyah decides to avoid getting romantically involved during her last year in college. She knows she'll eventually find the right woman, but right now her GPA matters more.
Voluntary Permanent	As an asexual aromantic person, Jordan was never interested in getting married. He lives with some other friends and is content with his family of choice.
Involuntary Permanent	Lois has been involved in children's ministry since she was young. She always assumed she'd get married and have kids of her own, but she never found the right person. At 50, after her mother has a heart attack, she gives up on marriage and moves in with her mom to take care of her.

because a spouse has died. Being single means that someone is not married; however, there are different experiences of unmarried people.

Never-Married Singles

Never-married singles are those individuals who have not married, but they may or may not live alone and they may or may not have an intimate partner. Never-married people are gay or straight, young or old, cohabiters or live-alones.

As you saw earlier, the United States is experiencing an increasing number of singles. It is important to note, however, that there are different racial/ethnic trends among never-marrieds. As Figure 8.2 shows us, nearly three-fourths of African American/Black Caribbeans are not married; this racial group has the highest percentage of not-married singles (U.S. Census Bureau, 2019a). Note also that among Native Americans/Alaska Natives the percentage of those who are married is similar to those who are unmarried. Whites experience the highest percentage of marriage, with more than two-thirds married, while Asian Americans have the lowest rate of non-married singles.

Never-married singles: individuals who have not married; they may or may not live alone or have an intimate partner.

Figure 8.2 /// Percentage of Married Adults in the United States Under Age 34, by Race

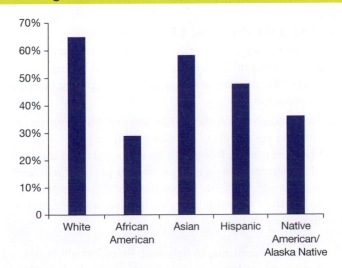

Sources: Black Demographics (2019); United States Census Bureau (2019).

Figure 8.3 /// Majority of Never-Marrieds Want to Marry Someday

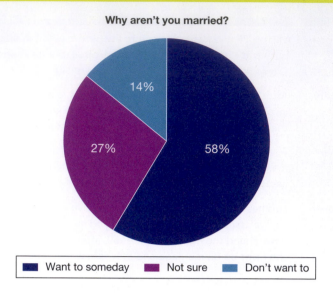

Why aren't you married?

- Want to someday — 58%
- Not sure — 27%
- Don't want to — 14%

Source: Pew Research Center (2017).

Why do we have an increasing number of singles in the United States? We've already seen that adults are choosing to marry later in life and that the share of adults cohabiting has increased significantly. Today, most never-married adults say they just haven't found the right person yet, as Figure 8.3 shows us. As the data tells, us, 58 percent of never-married singles want to get married someday, while slightly more than one-fourth aren't sure if they ever want to get married (Pew Research Center, 2017b). But this trend toward delaying marriage or forgoing marriage has also emerged over several decades because of financial forces, such as hard economic times, and social attitudes, such as those things that comprise a "fulfilling life," and adult children living at home with their parents (Pew Research Center, 2014).

Financial Woes: Student Loan Debt. Today, student loan debt is the highest it's ever been—$1.5 trillion in the United States alone (Forbes, 2019). With nearly 45 million borrowers with an average of nearly $29,000 in student loan debt, one-half of all Millennials today move back home with their parents after they graduate from college (Forbes, 2019). In a study of more than 1,000 Millennials and 1,000 Gen Z'ers, the researchers found (Friedman, 2019):

- **Student loan debt is delaying major life decisions.** Many individual, couple, and family development milestones are being delayed because of the responsibilities of carrying student loan debt, and this includes getting married and having children. For example, 21 percent indicate they are delaying marriage and 21 percent are delaying childbearing until their debt is under control.

- **Moving home isn't temporary.** College graduates aren't heading out on their own any time soon: 50 percent who are currently enrolled in college plan on moving back home after graduation; 31 percent plan on living with their parents for at least two years after college graduation; and 56 percent plan on living with their parents for at least a year. When does it become "embarrassing" to live with your parents? According to the study, at age 28. In fact, nearly one-fourth of those Millennials surveyed said they planned to live with their parents until their 30s.

If parents and other caregivers continue to help with living expenses post-college, it is financially advantageous for a young adult to remain single (Campbell, 2002).

It Doesn't Take Two. Today, fewer than one in three adults in the United States believe that a person must be married in order to live a fulfilling life (DePaulo, 2018). In a study of more than 3,000 young adults, participants were asked what the essential factors were to living a satisfying, enjoyable life. An interesting fact emerged from this research: Those surveyed indicated that the most important factor is having a rewarding job. This finding is in direct contrast to previous research that indicated the main reason people get married is for happiness (Pew Research Center, 2007). In fact, more than twice as many people revealed that a rewarding job was more rewarding and fulfilling (65 percent) than being happily married (31 percent; DePaulo, 2018). Another change in social attitudes was revealed: nearly one-half of the study participants said that *community engagement* was more essential to fulfillment than marriage or children; 40 percent said that *religious community* was more essential.

In the past, those who delayed marriage or chose singlehood were frowned on by society; after all, taking on spousal and parenting roles was expected, considered to be *the* only appropriate gender roles and as *the* next steps in aging after adolescence (Campbell, 2002). But as this study informs us, being single is more socially acceptable today than it was in the past. As DePaulo (2018) notes, "the stereotypes [of marriage and children being important to womanhood and manhood] were shattered" (p. 1). Of great significance is both women and men rated getting married and having children at the bottom of the list of importance. Table 8.2 lays out for us the study's findings. How do these results align with your beliefs about "womanhood" and "manhood"?

One Is the Loneliest Number? Social and Emotional Characteristics

The social, emotional, and health experiences of never-marrieds vary from those of other unmarried people. Overall, never-married people report high satisfaction in areas of friendship, general health, and personal economic status (Barrett, 1999; Campbell, 2002). For example, overall life satisfaction tends to be high among never-married people, and it is similar to married couples' life satisfaction (Campbell, 2002); however, some research indicates that the satisfaction and happiness of never-married singles has more to do with the fact that their social and economic needs are met than their single status (Bedard, 1992). In general, never-married people experience rich, active social lives with family and friends and enjoy relationships with dating or cohabiting partners (Barrett, 1999; Campbell, 2002).

Existing research seems to indicate that singlehood is a positive, satisfying experience for many—not a lonely, isolated one. Nevertheless, in a society that reveres marriage,

Table 8.2 /// What's Important in Becoming a Woman or a Man in Adulthood?			
Women		**Men**	
Experiences rated "extremely important"	%	Experiences rated "extremely important"	%
Financially independent from parents	62	Financially independent from parents	73
No longer living in parents' household	54	Capable of supporting a family financially	66
Capable of supporting a family financially	47	No longer living in parents' household	66
Complete formal schooling	44	Be employed full time	55
Be employed full time	34	Complete formal schooling	40
Get married	21	Get married	20
Have a child	20	Have a child	17

Source: American Family Survey (2018).

never-married people are often victims of cultural stereotypes. Unmarried women may be referred to as "spinster" or "old maids," and unmarried men may be referred to as "confirmed bachelors" (Gordon, 2003). But despite the negative stereotypes people may hold about singlehood, recent research shows us that being single may carry with it *social capital*—and this may negate widely held misconceptions about the experiences of being single.

Social capital:

an individual's pool of social resources found in his or her personal network.

Social Capital. Social capital is defined as the individual's pool of social resources found in his/her personal network (Amati, Meggiolaro, Rivellni, & Zaccarin, 2018). It's important to understand the concept of social capital because it is an essential component to *life satisfaction* and *happiness*, subjective aspects of well-being, among never-marrieds and singles.

In a study that analyzed the relationship between friendship ties and life satisfaction, the investigators found that friendships—necessary social resources—are positively related to overall life satisfaction and happiness (Amati et al., 2018). This study found three particular areas in which social capital strengthened the well-being of single individuals:

1. *Affirming an individual's sense of self.* As you learned in our discussion about intimacy in Chapter 5, all of us have a need to belong—all of us have a need to be with someone, to share with someone, to be intimate with someone. Social capital is a source of positive affirmation.

2. *Positively contributes to overall mental and physical health.* A wealth of empirical science shows us that social interactions help to decrease the effects of stress and increase our ability to cope with it (Halpren, 2005), fight infections and disease (Myers, 2000), and reinforce healthy lifestyle choices and behaviors (Putnam, 2000). The absence of social relationships increases the likelihood of negative health and psychological distress (Nguyen, Chatters, Taylor, & Mouzon, 2015).

3. *Social relationships are a necessary resource pool.* In Chapter 15 we will discuss at length the importance of resources to navigate the paths of stress and life crises, such as job loss, illness, and the death of a loved one. Here, it's imperative to note that whether we are single or married, each of us needs rich social relationships that serve to buffer the consequences of what life sometimes throws at us. Without question, when we have people in our lives we can turn to for both the big things and small things in life, we are better able to see the positives and not focus solely on the negatives (Myers, 2000).

To be sure, quality friendships are essential and necessary for health and well-being. And today, everyone from Baby Boomers to Gen Z'ers understands the richness that social capital provides.

Urban Tribes. Given that the traditional social institutions of marriage and family are presumed to provide social and emotional support, an interesting question arises when considering the increasing number of never-marrieds: Who becomes the primary institution or system of support between the years of living in a family of origin and a family of choice? With new trends comes new terminology, and to describe the phenomenon of the increasing numbers of young singles, author and social science research Evan Waters (2004) coined the term *urban tribes*.

Urban tribe:

refers to mixed-gender circles of friends (typically in their twenties or thirties) who are the primary social support system for singles.

Urban tribe refers to mixed-gender circles of friends (typically in their 20s and 30s) who are the primary social support system for singles. Similar to the peer groups portrayed in popular television shows such as *Friends, How I Met Your Mother,* and *The Big Bang Theory,* urban tribes are redefining family and commitment. Typically, urban tribes begin as a group of friends who socialize together every now and then, but over a period of five years or so, each individual within the tribe assumes a certain role, much like in a family. Similar also to families, urban tribes share rituals, such as holiday celebrations, stories and, over time, histories. As you saw in Chapter 3, shared stories and shared histories create unique group meanings, and a group history deepens the bond between family members or, in this case,

Who needs marriage? Increasing numbers of young adults today lean on their circle of friends—their urban tribes—to meet their emotional, physical, and, sometimes, sexual needs.

between tribe members. Urban tribe members feel a mutual obligation to support each other and to care for one another. As Waters (2004) observed, it appears that today these circles of friends are becoming substitutes for spouses. He believes that in our current complex society, it is these emerging support systems that let marriage wait. Because these friendships are emotionally satisfying—and sometimes sexually satisfying, as hookups are not uncommon among these urban friendships—young adults do not feel the need to rush into marriage. Is the urban tribe an emerging developmental phase in the lives of young adults?

Gay and Lesbian Never-Marrieds

Today in the United States, 12 percent of the adult population identifies as a sexual minority (gay, lesbian, bisexual, asexual, or pansexual) or identifies as something other than cisgender—a person whose sense of personal identity and gender corresponds with their birth sex (see Chapter 4). Overall, 4.5 percent of the U.S. adult population adhere to an LGBT identity, while about 91 percent of the population identify as heterosexual (Gallup Daily, 2018).

According to Pew Research Center (2013), an overwhelming 92 percent of the nation's LGBT population says that society is becoming more and more accepting of them and that they believe in the years ahead, their sexual identities will become even more widely accepted. America is also becoming more supportive of same-sex marriage

A bit later in this chapter we'll discuss the 2015 landmark civil rights case in which the Supreme Court of the United States ruled that same-sex couples have the fundamental right to marry and recognized the marriages of same-sex couples. In other words, gay, lesbian, bisexual, and transgender adults in the United States have the same right to legally marry as heterosexual couples do. Since this ruling, domestic partnerships (living together with same-sex partner) has, as expected, sharply decreased from nearly 13 percent to 6 percent, while marriages to same-sex partners has only increased by about 2 percent (Jones, 2017). As presented to us in Table 8.3, what is interesting is that LGBT never-marrieds have increased substantially, from 47 percent to nearly 56 percent. Social demographer Jeffrey Jones (2017) speculates that the reason for the seemingly low marriage rates/high never-married rates is because same-sex marriage is more common among men and older LGBT adults—the marriage rate among older adults is higher than it is among younger adults. For example, although only about 14 percent of 30- to 49-year-old LGBT Americans are married to their

Table 8.3 /// Marital Status of LGBT Americans

	Pre–Supreme Court decision	Year 2, Post–Supreme Court decision
	%	%
Married to same-sex spouse	7.9	10.2
Living with same-sex partner	12.8	6.6
Single/Never married	47.4	55.7
Living with opposite-sex partner	4.8	4.2
Married to opposite-sex spouse	14.2	13.1
Divorced	7.1	5.4
Separated	2.5	2.1
Widowed	2.8	2.2
Sample size	4,752	12,832

Source: Gallup Daily (2017).

Table 8.4 /// Total Number of Same-Sex Households in the United States in 2017, by Marital Status

	Married Couples	Unmarried Couples
Same-Sex Households	555,492	379,737
Male-Male Households	262,323	189,171
Female-Female Households	292,169	190,566

Source: Statista (2018).

same-sex spouse, more than 18 percent of those 50 and older are married. Similarly, more than three-fourths (77 percent) of LGBT persons ages 18 to 29, and 42 percent of those ages 30 to 49, indicate they are single and never married, but less than one-third of those 50 and older report that they are single/never married. Table 8.4 shows the total number of same-sex households in the United States in 2017, delineated by marital status.

What's the bottom line when considering these data trends? As Jones (2017) notes, it's simple: Same-sex marriages are becoming increasingly common, whereas same-sex domestic partnerships are becoming less common. The 2015 Supreme Court ruling allow LGBTQ persons to marry is changing the landscape of singlehood and marriage in the United States.

Divorced Singles

With about 40 percent of first marriages ending in divorce, a small percentage of America's singles are divorced men and women (U.S. Census Bureau, 2019a). Today, nearly one-fourth of singles are divorced (U.S. Census Bureau, 2019a). Figure 8.4 illustrates for us that there are gender differences seen in all couple types. A vast number of other variables, such as age and education, affect divorce rates; we will discuss these in depth in Chapter 14. For our discussion here, it is important to understand that most divorced people will experience life as a single person at least for some period of time following the end of their marriages.

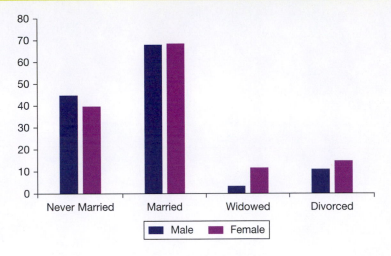

Figure 8.4 /// Marital Status of the U.S. Population, by Sex 2018 (in millions)

Source: Statista (2018).

The Widowed

Women are much more likely to outlive their husbands. There is a greater percentage of single *widows* (women) than single *widowers* (men), among all races. As you can see in Figure 8.4, there are more widows in the United States than there are widowers. This is because men are more likely than women to remarry following the death of a spouse, thus reducing the numbers of single widowers (Lemme, 2006). The experiences of widowhood are discussed in Chapter 16.

As the current trends in singlehood highlight, marriage exerts less influence over how U.S. adults experience their intimate relationships today. Despite the increasing number of singles today, and despite the noticeable trend of couples delaying marriage for longer periods of time, most Americans still marry at least once in their lifetime.

THE ACT OF MARRIAGE

In most cultures throughout the world, there is an expectation that when a person reaches adulthood (ages of adulthood vary among cultures) marriage should soon follow. In the United States alone, each month upwards of 208,000 couples wed, vowing to love, honor, and respect their chosen life mates until death parts them (Statisa, 2018a). The expectation is deeply ingrained. One-half of Americans ages 18 and older were married in 2017; this number represented an 8 percent decreases in U.S. marriages since 1990 (Pew Research Center, 2019a).

However, the social functions, purposes, and relevance of marriage are rapidly changing in contemporary society, making them less clear-cut than they have been throughout history. Early in the 21st century, Americans indicated that it was important that couples legally marry if they were going to be life partners, and these opinions were similar across races and ethnicities (see Figure 8.5).

But these attitudes are changing. For example, in a Pew Research Center survey (2014), study participants were asked to identify which of the following statements reflected their own views:

1. Society is better off if people make marriage and having children a priority.
2. Society is just as well off if people have priorities other than marriage and children.

Marriage is an important step for most couples because it provides an identity for the relationship. This identity embodies the relational and legal expectations of the relationship and the marital roles that define the relationship.

Figure 8.5 /// Importance of Legal Marriage

Percent of Americans who say that marriage is "very important" if they plan to spend the rest of their lives together

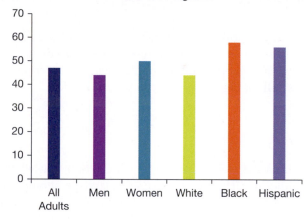

Source: Pew Research Center (2014). Public views on marriage. Retrieved April 10, 2020 form https://www.pewsocialtrends.org/2014/09/24/chapter-1-public-views-on-marriage/

The results were nearly the same: Forty-six percent of those surveyed indicated that statement 1 reflected their attitudes towards marriage, and 50 percent chose the second statement (Pew Research Center, 2014). These attitudes are in sharp contrast to those expressed by the American public just a few years earlier. Of course, there are age, race, and ethnicity differences in how people feel about the importance of marriage. These differences are shown in Figure 8.6 and 8.7.

Those of us who choose to marry have specific reasons why we decide to marry the person we do. There is a common desire, however, in our Western, individualistic culture: We tend to marry for reasons that benefit *ourselves*, rather than for reasons that benefit the *society at large*, such as found in collective cultures. Research in Western cultures has found, for

268 ■ Family Life Now

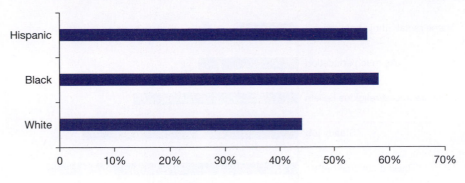

Figure 8.6 /// Importance of Marriage, by Race and Ethnicity

Percentage who say it is "very important" to them that a couple legally marries.

Source: Pew Research Center (2014).

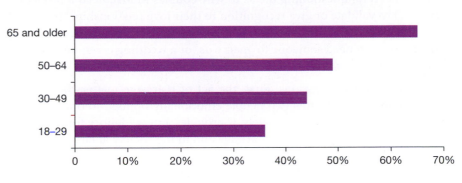

Figure 8.7 /// Importance of Marriage, by Age

Percentage who say it is "very important" to them that a couple legally marries.

Source: Pew Research Center (2014).

example, that the number one reason people cite for marrying is to enter into a lifelong partnership with someone they love (Pew Research Center, 2019a). However, this reason is not the only response to why people wed—today, people get married for reasons of commitment, companionship, having children, and other personal belief systems, such as having a relationship recognized in a religious ceremony. The Pew Research Center's (2019a) recent findings suggest that the main reasons people get married are for love (88 percent) and commitment (81 percent).

When choosing a lifelong partner, there are several factors that people consider. Overall, today's adults place greatest importance on sharing life and marriage with someone who has similar ideas and beliefs about having and raising children (Pew Research Center, 2014). Nearly one-half place a high degree of importance on having a marital partner who shares their moral and religious beliefs (Pew Research Center, 2014). Figure 8.8 illustrates the factors that adults in the United States consider to matter the most in choosing a marital partner.

The Social Dimensions of Marriage

As a family life educator, healthy sexuality coach, and a professor in the study of coupling, marriage, and the family, I've found that a semester doesn't pass without a student or two

Figure 8.8 /// What Matters Most in Choosing a Spouse?

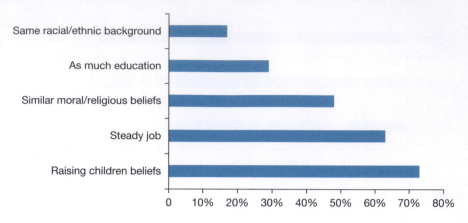

Percent of what people say is "very important" to them in choosing a spouse.

- Same racial/ethnic background
- As much education
- Similar moral/religious beliefs
- Steady job
- Raising children beliefs

(x-axis: 0, 10%, 20%, 30%, 40%, 50%, 60%, 70%, 80%)

Source: Pew Research Center (2014).

seriously (and sincerely) questioning me as to why couples in love need a piece of paper (a marriage license) to validate or give recognition to their love relationship. "If we declare our love and commitment before one another, why do we need a marriage license or a piece of paper? Why do we even need someone to 'marry us,' or a wedding ceremony? What's the big deal? *Why does marriage matter?*"

Marriage matters for several reasons. First, the act of marriage matters because it defines the couple as having a pair bond—two people emotionally bonded to one another—and it characterizes the couple's union. Ultimately, it provides a new identify for a couple and the subsequent roles they will play in their marriage and in the society at large.

From a Necessary Foundation to Deinstitutionalization

In her testimony before the U.S. Senate concerning the importance of marriage to society, Barbara Dafoe Whitehead (2004), codirector of the National Marriage Project (a nonpartisan, nonsectarian, interdisciplinary initiative located at Rutgers University), commented on the purposes of marriage. She observed that marriage, found in all types of cultures the world over, performs a number of key functions in every known society. These functions include things such as establishing family identities, regulating sexual behavior, providing and caring for children, and channeling the flow of economic resources. Whitehead's comments raise an important question: If marriage plays such a crucial role, why is this social institution undergoing such change?

Don Browning (2004), director of the Religion, Culture, and Family project at the University of Chicago, contends that marriage has undergone a shift throughout history, even as recently as during the past 30 or so years. In centuries past, both collectivist and individualistic cultures embraced **institutional marriage**, which encompasses not only the responsibilities of socializing children to the culture's norms but also adherence to the idea that marriage is sexually exclusive (monogamous) and permanent (Cherlin, 2004).

The institution of marriage is also typically associated with patriarchal authority, where the husband is acknowledged as the leader of and provider for the family. As you learned in Chapter 1, families of the past were economic partnerships—people didn't necessarily marry for romantic reasons (love), but instead, they married so they could purchase land. They then had children out of necessity, to help them cultivate and farm their crops; for some, children were nothing more than property. Today, state and federal income tax policies still benefit those couples who are married and have children. For instance, the Tax Cuts and Jobs Act of

Institutional marriage: marriage that considers socializing children to the culture's norms to be a responsibility and also includes adhering to the idea that marriage is sexually exclusive and permanent.

2017 lowered individual tax rates and boosted tax credits for families with children (Human Rights Campaign, 2018). The *marriage bonus* refers to the fact that married couples, on average, pay less in income taxes than they would pay as unmarried individuals. Consider widows and widowers: When one spouse dies, the survivor often has similar or only slightly less taxable income than the married couple did together. Because there are no options available for surviving spouses (unless they have children at home), the tax payer must file as a single taxpayer, rather than married filing a joint return. The result is a much higher tax—this is referred to as the *widow's penalty,* and it is especially difficult for those who are middle aged or retired and have limited or fixed incomes.

Thus, although marriage was once considered to be *the* social foundation responsible for the procreation and the socialization of children, as well as the structure for economic security of its members, it is being replaced today by pair bonds that meet individual needs, such as cohabitation. This change is referred to as the **deinstitutionalization of marriage** (Cherlin, 2004). To this end, Don Browning (2004) suggests that in Western, individualistic cultures such as the United States, people pursue relationships that meet their private, intimate, emotional, and sexual needs. Consequently, the notion that marriage serves an essential *social* function is rapidly losing ground.

According to Browning (2004), determining the cultural and intellectual purposes of marriage in today's culture is less definitive, and he argues that this may be the reason contemporary marital trends are on the decline and cohabitation rates are increasing. In order to better understand marriage as a social institution, Browning outlines five social dimensions of marriage:

1. **Marriage as an organizer of natural desires.** The ancient Greeks viewed the marital union as a way to organize natural sex drives of men and women and their urges to bear children. The Greeks also viewed marriage as a vehicle for ensuring that other natural, daily needs—such as safety and security needs, needs for shelter, and needs for food—were met through the division of labor that pair bonding provides. They believed that this need of meeting and sustaining natural desires and daily needs brought a man and a woman together, which, in turn, led to marriage.

2. **Marriage as a social good.** Browning's (2004) second dimension of marriage concerns its contribution to the overall good of the culture. This dimension reflects the ideas associated with collectivist cultures wherein the needs of society are put before individual needs. In this context, healthy marriages and healthy families are a vital, necessary, and essential component of a healthy, productive society. According to Browning, Martin Luther in 1522 asserted that marriage is ordained by God for the good and beneficial gain of the married couples, their children, and the culture and society in which they live. This concept is the impetus or driving force behind the concept of **covenant marriages** (see Dimension 4).

3. **Marriage is a communicative reality.** Browning (2004) asserts that marriage should not be thought of as a union in which marital lives run parallel to one another, but instead as a communicative alley—the nature of contemporary marriage is a bond: lives are meant to intersect for the purposes of mutual support and mutual comfort, or "oneness." This dimension of marriage is a relatively new occurrence in society, particularly in Western, individualistic societies where people marry for romantic love, Browning observes. Because the emphasis of marriage today is more an individualistic rather than a collectivist need, contemporary marriage places greater emphasis on the *emotional* and *communication* aspects of the marriage. According to Browning, in order to achieve equity and satisfaction in marriage, married couples must develop both communication and interpersonal relationship skills and nurture them through the life course of the marriage. As you've come to know in our study so far, helping couples and families develop these relational skills to promote family well-being is the driving force behind the science of studying families.

Should Couples Enter Into a Covenant Marriage?

With staggering divorce rates in the United States in the 1990s, lawmakers began to focus on ways to reduce the number of divorces. Social scientists had, for about two decades, gathered enough empirical evidence to know that divorce negatively impacts the health and well-being of children and also was a major driving force in the poverty rates in our country. Thinking that divorce was perhaps too easy to obtain, legislators in three U.S. states began attempts to strengthen marriages. To this end, they proposed and passed legislation in support of covenant marriages.

Because covenant marriages are supportive of marriage counseling and other ways to strengthen families, should couples be encouraged to enter into a covenant marriage rather than a civil marriage?

YES: The primary purpose of a covenant marriage is to make it more difficult for marriage partners to call it quits when things go wrong in the marriage. But does this legal pact work? According to Nock and his colleagues (2008), the difficulty of leaving a covenant marriage is having the effect the legislation intended it to have. An early study suggests that couples who enter into this marriage type are about half as likely to divorce as couples who have a traditional civil union. The researchers also discovered that over time, both husbands and wives experienced a positive growth in their marital quality (Nock et al., 2008). A recent study also found that marital satisfaction was positively affected by a covenant-type marriage (DeMaris, Sanchez, & Krivickas, 2013). It appears, then, that not only are divorces staved off, but marital satisfaction is enhanced.

Sources: DeMaris et al. (2012); Hawkins et al. (2002); Nock et al. (2008).

NO: Since the overarching goal of covenant marriage is to strengthen marriage through such things as required marital counseling in the event of trouble and requiring proof for misconduct (i.e., sexual infidelity) of a spouse, is it possible that an agreement of this type may hold spouses in an unhappy—and worse, an unsafe—marital environment? Some researchers warn that covenant marriages serve to create lengthy, ugly divorce court battles, and that such marriages make it difficult for an abused spouse to leave a violent marriage (Hawkins, Nock, Wilson, Sanchez, & Wright, 2002). There is also concern that this type of marriage tends to favor men, making women subservient to them. Some claim that covenant marriages are a veiled religious movement, a religious power grab, that seeks to bring about biblical ideals of marriage in which the woman is required to be obedient to the man (Nock et al., 2008).

Should couples enter into a covenant marriage?

What Do You Think?

1. Are the stricter criteria for divorce in a covenant marriage a good thing or a bad thing?

2. In what ways do you think a covenant marriage could strengthen a marriage? In what ways could a covenant marriage weaken a marriage? Who do you think a covenant marriage favors—the husband, the wife, or the couple? Why do you feel this way?

3. In what ways do covenant marriages potentially protect a woman from an abusive partner? In what ways might this type of marriage hold her in an unsafe marriage?

---

4. **Marriage as a sacrament and covenant.** Many people view marriage as something bound together by more than legal ties or a personal, intimate commitment to one another. The Christian, Jewish, Hindu dharma, and Islamic religions consider marriage to be divinely ordered and ordained; thus, no marriage should be entered into without much thought and consideration. The **sacrament of marriage** is deemed a sacred act. In most religions, marriage is a union between one man and one woman that can be severed only by the death of one partner. An estimated 75 percent of all first-time marriages in the United States take place in a church, temple, or mosque, and the wedding ceremonies are officiated by a pastor, minister, priest, rabbi, chaplain, or other clergy (Pew Research Center, 2016). For those couples married in a place of worship and/or by clergy, marriage is more than a legal state—it is a religious state as well.

Sacrament of marriage: marriage as a sacred act, dissolved only by the death of one partner.

Marriage as a Religious Covenant

In an effort to curb the escalating divorce rates in the United States, to date more than 20 states have actively considered implementing some form of legislation that would more adequately prepare couples for married life. The legislation would also attempt to preserve marriages through mandated divorce counseling or by delaying divorce.

The Covenant Marriage Acts, for example, adopted in Arizona, Arkansas, and Louisiana in the late 1990s, are statutes that impose additional requirements to marry or end a marriage. Couples sign a Declaration of Intent that spells out the couple's intent to obtain premarital education and/or counseling, clearly delineates the couple's commitment to preserving the marital union and/or a commitment to marriage counseling, if needed, and provides the grounds for divorce. For example, the Louisiana Marriage Covenant outlines specific provisions:

> *Signing a Covenant Marriage.* In order to enter into a covenant marriage, the couple is bound by two conditions if they wish to divorce or separate: They must agree to participate in couple and family counseling, and they must agree to separate or divorce according to the reasons specified in the state's Marriage Covenant legislation.

> *Declaration of Intent.* The Declaration of Intent is a legally binding sworn statement indicating that the couple views marriage as a lifelong commitment and union.

> *Legal Separation.* Legal separation from a spouse can take place only after the couple undergoes joint marital counseling. In addition, one or more parties must *prove* that their spouse has engaged in certain breaches of trust or dangerous behaviors, such as committing adultery, abusing drugs or alcohol, or being the perpetrator of domestic violence or sexual abuse.

> *Divorce in a Covenant Marriage.* In a covenant marriage, divorce is much more difficult to obtain than it is with traditional marriages and marriage licenses. The conditions for divorce are quite similar to those conditions that must exist in order to obtain a legal separation. Just as in the case of separation, the marital parties must participate in joint marital counseling before they are able to proceed with their intentions to divorce.

The covenant form of marriage is not exclusive to newly engaged couples; couples who are already married may file for a covenant marriage by signing a Declaration of Intent and a sworn statement and receiving marital education/counseling. Since the covenant form of marriage is a relatively new phenomenon in this country—in existence since only the late 1990s—data do not currently exist that would show whether this form of marriage results in its intended purpose of lowering divorce rates or making divorce more difficult to obtain.

5. **Marriage as a legal contract.** Whether a couple marries in a tribal ritual or in an elaborate church or temple ceremony, marriage across cultures is considered a contractual agreement between parties, whether an arrangement between the bride and groom's families where betrothal took place perhaps before the child was even born, or the conventional contractual agreement made between today's bride and groom.

Although marriage means different things to different people, Browning's (2004) discussion about marriage as a social institution helps us see that marriage is more than simply a piece of paper that legalizes a commitment or an intimate bond between two people. Marriage is an act that serves society on many levels, including health and productivity, religiously, and legally. It is perhaps the legal dimensions of marriage that distinguish it from all other forms of coupling.

The Legal Dimensions of Marriage

The way we experience intimacy, love, romance, dating/courtship, and mate selection differs depending on our regions of the world, as well as our race, ethnicity, and religious beliefs. The same factors influence how different people experience marriage.

There are a number of rights and privileges associated with marriage that gay men and lesbian partners were denied before the U.S. Supreme Court sanctioned same-sex marriages. These rights include aspects such as being allowed to care for their spouse in the hospital in situations where only "family members" are allowed.

In the United States, marriage is considered foremost as a legal contract. Although a couple's union is a private, intimate, special bond, before they say "I do" before an official, whether with much fanfare and expense or in a subdued personal setting, their union acquires a legal status. The union becomes a legally binding, contractual, state and federally regulated agreement between the two parties. For instance, marriage laws specifically delineate the boundaries of the marital union, such as restrictions on age or kinship. Although marriage laws vary from state to state, all states follow the same general legal parameters.

What the Law Requires

Every state requires couples intending to marry to receive a marriage license issued by a town, county, state, or similar authority at least one month before the wedding. When applying for a marriage license, couples must provide proof of age; the legal age to get married is 18 in the United States. If an applicant does not meet the legal age of adulthood, she or he must have notarized, written consent from both living parents or legal guardians. Additionally, marriage laws prohibit marrying close kin because it can result in devastating birth defects to offspring. Nationwide, laws mandate that siblings or half-siblings cannot marry; about half of the states will not allow first cousins to marry.

Furthermore, all individuals intending to marry must be single. There is no place in the United States where a person who is currently married can marry another person. Finally, some states require that blood tests are performed in order to discover any potential genetic disorders that might afflict future offspring; these blood tests also detect the presence of HIV/AIDS and syphilis.

Gender: Sexual Orientation and Marriage Laws

When discussing gender as it relates to marriage, biological sex is not the issue—*sexual orientation* is. At the forefront of much social, political, and religious debate for decades, lesbian, gay, bisexual, and transgender (LGBT) rights took a huge leap forward between the years of 1996 and 2015 with landmark United States Supreme Court rulings:

> *Sodomy laws struck down nationwide.* In 2003 the Court's ruling invalidated sodomy laws (laws that made oral and anal sex illegal) in Texas and 13 other states, making same-sex sexual activity legal in every U.S. state and territory.

Section 3 of the Defense of Marriage Act deemed unconstitutional. The Defense of Marriage Act (DOMA) of 1996 was a federal law that defined marriage for federal purposes as the union of one man and one woman; it allowed states to refuse to recognize same-sex marriages granted under the laws of other states.

Same-sex marriage is legal nationwide. In 2015, the United States Supreme Court struck down all state bans on same-sex marriage, thus legalizing these unions in all states. States are now required to honor out-of-state same-sex marriage licenses.

The Court's rulings appear to mirror public opinion, as support for the legalization of same-sex marriages grew significantly between 2007 and 2017. For example, in 2007, slightly more than one-half (54 percent) of Americans polled indicated that they favored the marital unions of same-sex partners; in 2017, nearly two-thirds (62 percent) of Americans said they favor same-sex marriages (Pew Research Center, 2019b). Of course, age affects opinions and support for same-sex marriages, as shown in Figure 8.9. As you can see, there are generational differences between those who say that same-sex marriage is good thing for society, a bad thing for society, or it doesn't make a difference.

So far, we have examined why marriage matters because of the number of social functions it serves. Beyond the legal responsibilities and requirements associated with the act of marriage there are certain rights, privileges, and benefits of marriage, too. These rights and benefits distinguish the marital union from any other intimate pair bond relationship, such as cohabitation. In the following section, we'll take a look at other reasons why marriage matters: the rights and privileges of marriage as well as the benefits of marriage to adults and children.

Before You Say "I Do"

In Western cultures, most people marry because they are in love. Having realistic expectations about marriage—what each partner expects of a spouse and the marital relationship—significantly affects overall marital satisfaction and happiness (Birditt, Wan, Orbuch, & Antonucci, 2017). Because each partner comes into a marriage with different family-of-origin experiences and models, couples often have different goals and expectations. By discussing these expectations before they trek down the marriage aisle, couples have a chance to align their ideas and attitudes about what marriage will—and won't—be. Discussing expectations about marriage also gives couples the opportunity to strengthen their communication skills, a key component in successful marriage (Lavner, Karney, & Bradbury, 2016).

Figure 8.9 /// Opinions About Same-Sex Marriage, by Generation

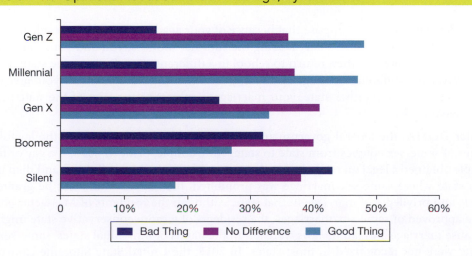

Source: Pew Research Center (2019).

Before you say "I do," there are many issues to consider. First, you should consider *why* (other than being in love) you want to get married. The aim of this discussion is for each partner to fully understand and appreciate the other's reasons for marrying. As you and your partner consider your reasons for getting married, check off each item that applies to you:

- Because it's the next logical step in our relationship
- Because I want to show my commitment to him/her
- I'm tired of being single
- I want more independence in my life
- My religion mandates marriage before we can be sexually intimate with one another
- I want security
- I'm ready to have children
- I need his/her friendship and companionship
- I'm not getting any younger
- I'm a single parent and I want two parents in my child's life

Did you and your partner come to a general agreement on the reasons why you want to marry? Are your expectations for marriage realistic in comparison to your partner's expectations? Do you see significant discrepancies in your reasons for marrying? If there are some, do you believe these are potential trouble spots in your marriage? Communication about these similarities and differences before marriage is important because poor communication is the most common reason why couples seek professional help for their marriages (Doss, Rhoades, Stanley, & Markman, 2009). In a study of 431 couples of diverse races, ethnicities, and socioeconomic backgrounds, the researchers discovered that premarital and marital communication foreshadowed later relationship satisfaction (Lavner et al., 2016). Without question, when couples communicate with each other their reasons for marrying, they can thwart potential trouble spots down the road.

The Rights and Privileges of Marriage

The U.S. government sanctions marriage and provides the boundaries of the prevailing marriage laws, but it also grants each state the ability to determine the rights, privileges, benefits, and responsibilities associated with marriage. These state-generated and state-regulated laws specifically define the privileges of marriage. These privileges may or may not be applicable in other states.

Consider the following: Suppose that because of your academic path, you reside in a different state than your "home" state. During the summer months, you and your fiancé marry in your home state and then return to school in a different state. Perhaps the state in which you marry has different marriage and family laws that the state in which you later reside. Once you move to another state, your marriage is subject to the laws of the state that you now live in.

Under DOMA, the federal government was prohibited from recognizing the lawful marriages of same-sex couples from state to state. For example, prior to 2015, if a gay or lesbian couple obtained a legal marriage license to wed in the state of Massachusetts and then moved to a state where same-sex marriage was prohibited, the couple would not be granted the rights and privileges of marriage in that state. Although the residents of Massachusetts may have approved of same-sex marriages, the residents of a more conservative state might not. Because marriage and family laws were left in the hands of individual states, same-sex marriages were not recognized in most states. In 2015, the United State Supreme Court ruled that marriage is a fundamental right guaranteed to all citizens and thus legalized same-sex marriage nationwide.

You may be asking, "So what's all the fuss about?" Several implied rights and privileges accompany marriage. The following are recognized (although perhaps at varying levels) by all states:

- The right to visit a spouse in the hospital
- The right to make medical decisions on behalf of a spouse in the event that he or she is unable to do so
- The right to joint custody of children
- The right to adopt children
- The right to privileged and confidential communication between spouses
- The right to rear children in a manner the couple deems appropriate (i.e., religious training, education, discipline)
- The right to terminate a marriage according to the laws of the state

Federal and state legislation also provide additional legal benefits to married couples. Prior to the U.S. Supreme Court's *federal* ruling in 2015 that legalized same-sex marriage, same-sex married couples were not afforded these *federal* benefits:

- Lower federal income tax rates—both heterosexual and homosexual couples are now permitted to file joint tax returns, which substantially reduces their tax debt
- Social Security and Medicare benefits
- Health insurance benefits that cover spouses
- Lower home and auto insurance rates
- Legal protection from domestic violence and abuse
- State-specific inheritance and death benefits for spouses
- The rights associated with the Federal Family Medical Leave Act
- State-specific rights afforded in instances of divorce

The Benefits of Marriage

In recent years, because of what some Americans perceive as a decline in the moral health of the family and its status in the U.S. society, there has been renewed interest in researchers' attempts to discover what accounts for successful marriage and family living. Taken as a whole, the countless empirical studies of marriage indicate that marriage is a beneficial institution across all areas of well-being—in the social and emotional areas, in the cognitive area, and in the physical areas of living.

Economic Benefits

The adage "Two can live as cheaply as one" is often true of married couples. For example, married couples often save money by filing federal and state taxes jointly, and owning one house or renting one apartment is cheaper than owning or renting two dwellings.

Professor of economics at George Washington University David Ribar (2003) cites a substantial body of research that consistently demonstrates that average annual incomes and financial assets are greater among married couple households than for unmarried adults or for nonmarried cohabiting couples. In his article, "What Do Social Scientists Know About the Benefits of Marriage?" Ribar suggests additional reasons why married people fare better economically than single adults.

- Marriage allows for **specialization**, in which each spouse can take on tasks and concentrate on those things they do well (for example, he may like to do light carpentry while she may like to do yard work).

Specialization:
the element of marriage in which each spouse can take on tasks and concentrate on those things he or she does well.

- Marriage allows for **instrumental support**, in which marital partners both boost the well-being, productivity, and career of their spouse. For example, in some families, a husband may willingly take over the lion's share of parenting, household chores, and meal preparation while his wife works as a nurse. His pitching in increases her productivity because she does not have to stop and tend to the other details of their lives. As another example, if one spouse becomes ill, the other spouse steps in and takes on the roles and responsibilities of the spouse who is ill. In both examples, the benefits to the spouses are reciprocal.

- The life commitment of marriage provides **stability**—especially for men. According to Ribar (2003), this stability allows men to mature, making them more likely to find a job and think toward the future instead of engaging in risk-taking behaviors. Marriage results in a feeling of interdependent financial responsibility to one another. Thus, married men and women are more likely to accept and maintain jobs that may not be all that personally rewarding, but are in the best interest of the couple/family in the way of economic rewards.

- Marriage provides **status**. Because many employers today are "traditional" in their beliefs, they tend to pay married men and women at a higher rate than single men and women. According to Ribar (2003), this discrimination toward unmarried men allows for great economic gain and greater economic opportunities for married men, thereby affording them and their families a certain status unmarried individuals do not have.

Health Benefits

Not only are economic resources boosted (Waite & Gallagher, 2002), but so are social and emotional support, which includes companionship and daily interaction (Perelli-Harris et al., 2018; Umberson, Crosnoe, & Reczek, 2010), as well as the benefits of social capital (Umberson & Montez, 2010). And, extensive research has found that married people are healthier than nonmarried individuals (among many, Grundy & Tomassini, 2010; Hughes & Waite, 2009; Williams, Sassler, Frech, Addo, & Cooksey, 2011; Robles, Slatcher, Trombello, & McGinn, 2014). For example, regardless of the type of partnership (heterosexual or same-sex, marriage or cohabitation), living in an intimate relationship as a couple influences positive health behaviors, such as maintaining a healthy lifestyle and making healthy choices—we strive for health not necessarily for ourselves, but for our partners (Perelli-Harris et al., 2018).

Married people have other unique benefits. As many researchers observe, the fact that marriage carries with it a legal contract signifies to the society that the marriage partners have made a strong commitment to each other (Berrington, Perelli-Harris, & Trevena, 2015; Perelli-Harris et al., 2018), a commitment that is not easily broken. As one investigative teams observes, "Marriage's 'enforceable trust' may persuade couples to work harder on their relationships, especially during stressful periods" (Perelli-Harris et al., 2018, p. 704). This seemingly results in a buffer of sorts, as this enforceable trust and legal protection that marriage brings provides individuals with a sense of security and well-being. Interestingly, study participants in Europe and Australia noted that in addition to the emotional reassurance that marital commitment carries, security for their children and the comfort of knowing they won't be alone in old age are also health benefits to marriage (Perelli-Harris et al., 2014; Perelli-Harris et al., 2018).

Children's Benefits

A substantial body of empirical evidence over the past three decades tells us that children from homes with married parents fare better in their overall health and well-being, behavior, emotions, and school success (including reading scores and math achievement) than children living in nonmarital cohabiting homes, or with formerly married parents, stepfamilies, or single-parent homes (among many, Anderson, 2014; Ehrle, Kortenkampt, & Stagner, 2003; Ginther & Pollack, 2003). Conversely, children raised in lone-parent families and families with cohabiting parents have been found, on average, to do less well across a wide range of aspects of well-being (Anderson, 2014; Mackay, 2005). Researchers also found that regarding poverty and the availability of and access to material goods, children living in nonmarital cohabiting homes, with single parents, or with foster parents or legal guardians fare worse than children who live in a home where parents are married (Lerman, 2002a,

2002b; Ryan, Claessens, & Markowitz, 2013-2014). We visit the issue of family structure and children's health and well-being at length in Chapter 11.

Note that not every married couple will end up with happy, well-adjusted children nor will all children end up in poverty because they're being raised by single parents. Research does not present an all-inclusive picture; it does, however, present indicators. And research suggests that marriage is not simply a private bond made between two people who love and care for one another; it also is a matter of great interest to federal and state governments—because *marriage matters* to adults, children, and society.

THE TRANSITION TO MARRIAGE: WHY IT'S SO TOUGH

Marriage is hard work! Although we may start our marriages vowing "I do," most married people will tell you that very soon, those words are replaced with "I won't," or "I can't," or "You do it!" or "Are you kidding?!"

The very nature of marriage requires that the relationship be continuously negotiated. While meeting the needs of their spouses, people often need to meet the needs of their children and employers. In the midst of meeting everyone's needs, many spouses forget to have their own needs met. Although everyone may have the best of intentions when they marry, sooner or later, juggling everything conspires against even the most stable couples and competes for their already-divided attention. Even without the different responsibilities and stresses that accompany marriage, newlywed couples soon find out (often before the bills for the ceremony are paid) that they must establish strategies for negotiating and navigating marital life.

Forming a New Family System

Before we discuss the transitions that are inherent in adapting to married life, let's revisit two key concepts presented in previous chapters. Recall from Chapter 1 that the Family Life Cycle is a paradigm that allows us to view the multiple entrances and exits that individuals make within the family of origin, such as young adults leaving home for college or, as it pertains to our discussion here, forming a new family of origin as young adults marry. This paradigm helps depict not only the changes in the *structure* of the family but also certain insights into *emotional transitions* and other related changes in the family status.

Along with the Family Life Cycle paradigm, consider the family systems theoretical model discussed in Chapter 3. Recall that in order to truly understand the interactions that take place in marriage and in family life, we must consider the concept of wholeness—the concept of *interconnection* that speaks to how we affect and are affected by each member of the family. Using this paradigm, we need instead to view marriage as a newly formed system (the joined couple).

The paradigm is helpful on two counts. First, it allows us to think about marriage in a broader context, beyond its traditional meaning of procreation and socialization. Specifically, it allows us to consider same-sex couples who pledge a long-term commitment to each other, and it allows us to take into account other family forms, such as stable, committed cohabiting relationships (Anderson & Sabatelli, 2007, 2011). We also use this paradigm to examine all of the components and relationship processes that make up the new subsystem (regardless of relationship type or sexual orientation). For example, consider two people from two different families of origin with two distinct experiences with marriage. These two people have distinct ways of communicating and resolving conflict. They also have two very different sets of expectations about what the relationship will provide them. Given these dissimilarities, consider what needs to be accomplished in order for the new family subsystem to be incorporated into the other existing family systems (each member of the couple's family of origin; see Figure 8.10).

By integrating the Family Life Cycle and the Family Systems theories, we have before us a working model of why the transition to marriage (and married life, for that matter) is a

Figure 8.10 /// A Newly Formed Subsystem

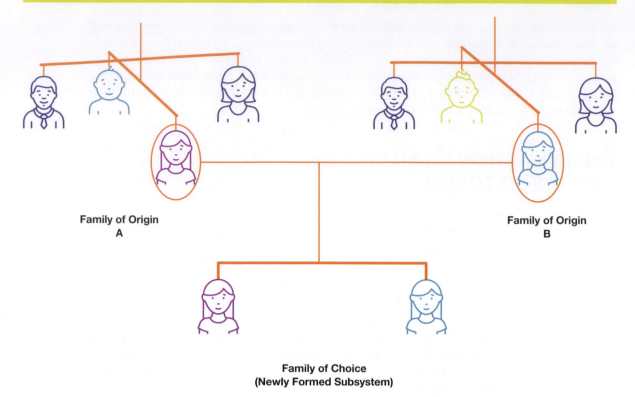

Family of Origin
A

Family of Origin
B

Family of Choice
(Newly Formed Subsystem)

Source: iStock.com/matsabe

difficult road for many young couples. As you will see in the following discussion, there are developmental tasks associated with forming a new family system. These include establishing marital roles, establishing marital boundaries, managing the house and money, and fostering a marital emotional climate.

Determining who does what in the marriage, such as who handles the money and the bills, is an important negotiation that needs to take place early in the marriage. As the couple's relationship changes over time, it's important that any established responsibilities and roles be reexamined.

Developmental Tasks in the New Family System

In Chapter 3, we discussed the family as a dynamic system that undergoes growth throughout its lifecourse. Just as an individual has experiences throughout his or her lifespan that both meet and fail to meet expectations, so, too, does a family system. For example, during the developmental phase of young adulthood, most young men and women accomplish the developmental task of learning to nurture not just themselves but also the emotional and physical needs of their friends, family, and those whom they love. At this point in lifespan development, most young men and women also experience interdependence, mutuality, and reciprocity in mature relationships. Many of them marry. These newly married couples must then navigate their way through a new phase of the Family Life Cycle as they negotiate the developmental tasks of their newly formed family. Marriage and family practitioners and researchers Stephen Anderson and Ronald Sabatelli (2007, 2011) describe the number of transitions that newly married couples must negotiate.

Establishing Marital Roles

Recall from earlier discussions that within our families of origin and within our daily lives, each of us has roles we play. When we take on a role, we take on the rules or expectations that society assigns to that role. When we join together in a marriage or other lifelong committed relationship, we tend to take on the roles society dictates. A **conjugal role** is a culturally defined, culturally assigned set of behaviors (for instance, behaviors related to housekeeping, childrearing, and work outside the home) each spouse is expected to carry out.

Conjugal role:
a culturally defined and assigned set of behaviors each marriage partner is expected to carry out.

As we grow up, our own family of origin shapes and plays a large part in the roles we will take on in our intimate relationships. For instance, imagine a woman reared in a home where the father goes to work each day while the mother stays home to care for the children, clean the house, and prepare meals. A woman raised in this environment may, from a very young age, want nothing more in her adult life than to be a mother and a wife. She would marry with a preconceived, ready set of expectations of her roles and her husband's roles; if her husband was reared in a similar background, then their expectations of marriage would initially reinforce how they felt about each other and their relationship. When marital roles (reality) match our predetermined notions (expectations), the early years of marriage may be relatively uncomplicated. But, when the reality of conjugal roles does not line up with socialized expectations, a rocky road lies ahead. For this reason, those intending to marry or make a lifelong commitment should know from the start what roles they expect their partner to fulfill and what roles they intend to fulfill in that relationship. Anderson and Sabatelli (2007, 2011) suggest that same-sex couples experience greater stress during their transition to a lifelong partnership because of ambiguity or uncertainty about conjugal roles.

Establishing Marital Boundaries

Recall from Chapter 3 that all systems must maintain boundaries in order to distinguish them from other systems and from their environment. Marriage is one of these systems. Anderson and Sabatelli (2007, 2011) explain that when people marry, they expect to be the primary recipient of their partner's loyalty and devotion. To secure this relationship, some sort of boundary structure must be put into place that incorporates family and friends each partner brings into the relationship. To establish these boundaries, couples must negotiate such things as how often they should get together for dinner or other activities with parents, friends, and other family members. They also need to discuss whether it is acceptable to discuss intimate, personal details about married life with family and friends.

With most couples, each spouse has different expectations, which often depend on how each is socialized within his or her family of origin. For instance, the wife's family may not gather for every major (and minor) holiday, and they may not disclose as much as the husband is accustomed to. The husband's family, on the other hand, may gather for meals every Sunday. If the wife has different expectations and isn't used to so much contact, this behavior may cause conflict.

Managing the House and the Money

Determining who takes on which household responsibilities is an important negotiation that should take place early in the marriage—and be revisited as the needs of the family change. According to Anderson and Sabatelli (2007, 2011), this issue boils down to three primary factors:

1. *Gender socialization.* Recall from Chapter 4 our discussion about how males and females are socialized to perform different tasks within society. Typically, spouses' ideas of what men's household tasks should be and what women do tend to fall along traditionally held beliefs (Oláh, Kotowska, & Richter, 2018). Women take care of the cleaning, cooking, and childrearing, while men take care of the lawn, taking out the trash, and household and automotive repairs. However, with the new female gender role increasingly evolving into one of economic independence (which, until quite recently, belonged solely to the male gender role), a gender rearrangement, restructuring, and reorganization of housework and childcare is taking place (Oláh et al., 2018). It's important to note, though, that some researchers contend that women do not release traditional housework responsibilities, nor do men help with more traditional female household tasks, because of a shift in their attitudes about gender; rather, it's because of the woman's greater involvement in the work force—women simply do not have the time to dedicate to cooking, cleaning, and childrearing (Anxo et al., 2011; Sayer, Bianchi, & Robinson, 2004; Craig & Mullan, 2011).

   Some research suggests that younger fathers today embrace the idea of childrearing roles that traditionally belonged to women (Smith Koslowski, 2011). Lesbian couples tend to have an equal distribution of household tasks and labor and shun traditional gendered divisions of managing the house and money (Brewster, 2017).

2. *Abilities and expertise.* Whether or not my husband would be willing to do the laundry is not important; what is important is that he is not allowed to be anywhere near the laundry room! Early in the marriage he had the best intentions and was sincere in his efforts to do this household task, but only a few ruined loads of laundry were folded before we mutually decided he did not possess the ability to perform this chore. Similarly, although I have great interest in our family's financial picture, I do not have the expertise that he does when it comes to managing the monthly budget or investments. Lesbian couples engage in the division of household and financial responsibilities according to expertise, quality of the work needed for the task, and ability (Brewster 2017).

3. *Power and control.* In many marriages, one spouse may exert more power and control than the other. In these cases, the spouse with the most power will hand over "low-status" tasks (such as cleaning out the litter box or doing the dishes) to the other partner.

Fostering a Healthy Emotional Climate

When couples marry, most expect their emotional and physical needs to be met by a spouse. But do spouses realize that they must also meet the needs of their partner? A difficult developmental task for newlywed couples is finding a balance between meeting their own needs and meeting those of their spouse. As they learn to juggle these needs, they learn to foster and maintain intimacy and love as they develop a sexual identity (this is referred to as a *sexual script)*, communication patterns, and conflict management strategies.

The magnitude of the transition into married life is far-reaching. The multiple, complex processes of marriage (intimacy, finances, sexuality, juggling the responsibilities of work and home, communication, etc.) indicate how difficult the transition to marriage is (McGoldrick & Carter, 1999).

Peer Marriages

Is there a way to make love last? According to Pepper Schwartz (1994, 2001), professor of sociology at the University of Washington, prolific author, and international speaker on relationship topics, today's couples are changing the rules about traditional marriage. Schwartz calls this increasingly popular couple type among married couples peer marriages. A **peer marriage** is one in which partners agree to shared responsibility for all aspects of marriage, from earning money to raising the children to how they spend their leisure time.

Peer marriage: a marriage in which partners agree to shared responsibility for all aspects of marriage, from earning money to raising the children to how they spend their leisure time. Equity and fairness are hallmarks of peer marriages.

Unlike traditional marriages in which the man and woman live by traditionally socialized gender behaviors (and thus, according to Schwartz, live separate but parallel lives), peer couples collaborate, not only in their love relationships but also in day-to-day household tasks, parenting, and managing family finances. According to Schwartz (1994, 2001), by "reshuffling" gender relations and behaviors, peer partners foster profound intimacy, closeness, and respect within their marriage. With peer marriages, each partner feels the relationship is fair and that it supports the emotional needs of both. Indeed, hallmarks of peer marriages are the concepts of *equity* and *fairness:* Each partner is thought to be vital to the relationship. It is this collaboration from which deep friendship and companionship grow.

There are four characteristics of peer marriages that distinguish them from traditional marriages in which men dominate decision making and women assume childrearing responsibilities (Schwartz, 1994, 2001):

1. Marriage is not always 50–50. Peer marriage partners do not believe that marriages have to have an equal split of responsibilities; instead, as Schwartz found, couples ask themselves, "What wouldn't get done if I didn't do it?"—and they do it without getting angry or resenting the other spouse for not pitching in.

2. When it comes to important decisions (such as major financial decisions or relocating for career opportunities), both partners believe the other has an equal say, an equal influence.

3. Both partners know they have equal control of the family's budget, and both partners have equal access to the family's earnings. Schwartz contends that comments such as, "I'll do that if he'll let me" or "I don't know if she'll let me" are red flags and indicate equal control is not given.

4. Each partner's work is given equal weight in the couple's life plans—one person's work isn't automatically sacrificed for the other person's. Furthermore, the person who works the fewest hours outside of the home or who earns the lesser amount isn't necessarily the one who takes on the most household tasks or childcare responsibilities.

Near peers are couples or marriage partners who believe in equality, though when children are born, or to maximize the family's finances, the male often assumes less responsibility for the children.

But if peer marriages are so wonderful, why doesn't everyone have one—or, at the very least, why doesn't every couple strive to be a peer couple? Schwartz (1994, 2001) looks at the costs and benefits. Yes, peer marriages are rewarding in that they provide a unique intimacy for couples. But there are also costs:

1. There is often little validation and social support for peer marriages. Society (family, friends, co-workers, outsiders) questions the couple's marriage role philosophy.

2. Peer couples have to redefine "successful" marriage because traditional marriage defines successful marriage along traditional male/female gender roles.

3. Other couples frequently feel resentful of peer marriages. Because peer couples tend to be dedicated to their marriage and to parenting their children, they often will not engage in spouse "put-downs" with their family and friends. This makes others feel excluded.

4. The sexual dynamics of peer marriages are quite different from those in traditional marriages. Peer couples experience much intimacy on a day-to-day basis. Schwartz (1994, 2001) contends that because of this everyday intimacy, they have to work harder to find eroticism in their relationship.

5. There is no template for peer marriages, so all of their experiences are by trial and error.

A peer marriage may or may not be right for you because the success of this type of relationship is dependent on the couple, their individual family-of-origin experiences, and their marital expectations. As with every other aspect of marital satisfaction and success, it's important that couples have a serious discussion—before they get married—about not only what they expect from each other in the marital partnership, but also what they will or hope to experience in day-to-day interactions.

The Challenges of Blending Culture, Religion, and Sexual Orientation in Marriage

Our concepts of family and marriage are undergoing many quick-paced changes. An indicator of the rapid changes occurring in the structure of marriage and other intimate pair bond relationships is the increase in heterogamous interpersonal relationships—partnering with someone who is dissimilar to you in one or more dimensions, such as race, religious background, age, or values systems and beliefs. In this section, we examine some of the changes that are giving marriage a new face and a new set of circumstances to negotiate over time.

Interracial and Interethnic Marriage

Interracial couple: romantic or marriage partners of differing races.

In an **interracial couple**, the partners are of different races and/or ethnicities. More often than not, racial differences go hand in hand with cultural and ethnic differences, so couples of different races face potential struggles on three fronts. Xuanning Fu, Heather Tora, and Jessika Kendall (2001), social science researchers from Brigham Young University, define culture as a "learned orientation of 'way of life,'" and a "social heritage that includes values, norms, [and] institutions . . . that are passed from generation to generation" (p. 47). The

Since the legalization of interracial marriages in the United States in 1967, our culture has seen a steady increase in the numbers of mixed-race relationships. One benefit of the increase in interracial marriages is that these relationships bring awareness of peoples' intolerances and open the door to conversations about race.

iStock.com/Drazen_

authors note that interracial/intercultural/interethnic marriages are also inherently accompanied by these distinct racial traditions, attitudes, and behaviors.

Historically, interracial unions were viewed as a threat to the continuation of a society because of the "racial impurity" that would result if children were produced with a racially mixed union. *Miscegenation* is a term that was coined in the mid-1800s to describe the "mixed race" offspring produced by interracial couples. In 1967, the U.S. Supreme Court ruled that miscegenation laws violated the civil rights of U.S. citizens and were unconstitutional, and for the first time in U.S. history, couples of different races were legally allowed to wed.

In the 50 years since interracial marriages became legal in the United States, the numbers of brides and grooms married to a spouse of a different race or ethnicity—often referred to as *mixed marriages*—has increased more than five times: In 1967, only 3 percent of all marriages were interracial or interethnic; today 17 percent of marriages in the U.S. are (U.S. Census Bureau, 2018b). Seven types of interracial/interethnic married-couple combinations comprise 95 percent of mixed marriages; the largest group are non-Hispanic whites who are married to Hispanics (U.S. Census Bureau, 2018b):

1. Non-Hispanic white/Hispanic

2. Non-Hispanic white/Non-Hispanic Black or African American

3. Non-Hispanic white/Non-Hispanic American Indian and Alaska Native

4. Non-Hispanic white/Non-Hispanic Asian

5. One spouse reports multiple races (both Hispanic or both Non-Hispanic)

6. Both spouses report multiple races (both Hispanic or both Non-Hispanic)

7. Hispanic (any race alone)/Non-Hispanic (any race alone excluding Non-Hispanic white alone)

When viewing these couple types, it is important to note that these statistics do not take into account ethnic groups within the same broad categories. For example, a marriage involving a person of Japanese origin and a person of Korean origin would not be considered an interracial marriage, although because of the differences in cultures, it would be an interethnic marriage.

Researchers theorize that because today's youth have grown up with an ideology that supports racial integration, they are "more color-blind than their elders when it comes to matters of the heart" (Padgett & Sikora, 2003). Recent data support this notion, as Figure 8.11

Figure 8.11 /// Opinions About Interracial Marriage, by Generation

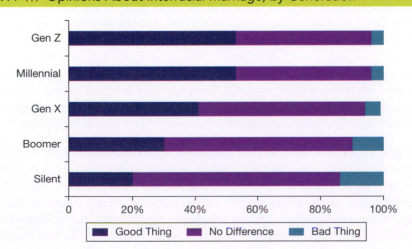

Source: Pew Research Center (2019).

presents. Not only have Millennials and Gen Z'ers been at the "vanguard of changing views on same-sex marriage" (Pew Research Center, 2019e), they also believe that people marrying outside of their race or ethnicity is a good thing for our society.

Who Intermarries?. Sociologist Zhenchao Qian (1999) believes that the increase in interracial marriages indicates a decline in racism. According to Qian, several factors affect those who intermarry:

- **Educational attainment.** According to Qian, when people share the same level of educational attainment, they are more likely to intermarry. Racial differences are evident, however. For instance, educational level isn't important to interracial couples in which one partner is white, but Black and Latinx interracial marrieds with at least a college degree are more likely to choose a spouse of a different race or ethnicity (Pew Research Center, 2019e). Interracial and interethnic marriages are more likely to occur among college-educated African American and Latinx couples, but not whites or Asians.

- **Immigration status.** Those who are born outside of the United States and then immigrate here are less likely to intermarry than those who are of different racial, ethnic, or cultural backgrounds who are born here.

- **Region of residence.** Those who live in the West or the Northeast of the United States are more likely to intermarry than those in the South or the Midwest (Pew Research Center, 2019e). Coupled with the more conservative leanings in the South and Midwest and the more liberal leanings in the Northeast and Northwest is the fact that these regions of the country have fewer minorities residing there, lessening the opportunity to meet someone of a different race. According to the Pew Research Center (2019e), nearly one-half (49 percent) of Democrats believe that marrying someone of a different race is good for society, while only slightly more than one-fourth (28 percent) of Republicans think it is a good thing; however, nearly two-thirds of Republicans believe the rise in these marriages doesn't make a big difference.

Challenges for Contemporary Interracial Couples. Interracial couples face the same marital challenges and stresses as couples of the same race, such as negotiating gender roles, communication, financial worries, and intimacy issues (Leslie & Young, 2015). Mix-raced couples, however, must deal with one significant difference: How others perceive their union (Kenney, 2002). And, each couple has their own individual stressors associated with their couple identity. Samuel Anderson (2014), a clinical social worker, ably and accurately describes this stress when he notes, "a white male and an African American female will have differing stressors than an African American male and a white female. The stressors will also differ between a white male and an African American female versus a white male and an Asian female. This is based on cultural differences, level of acceptance of interracial relationships within the racial groups, and acceptance levels within individual families" (pp. 5–6). Other research supports Anderson's ideas. Leigh Leslie and Jennifer Young (2015) of the University of Maryland found two central areas of stress for different-race marriages: Managing societal disapproval and managing the effects of racial privilege. Key to interracial couples' marital happiness, then, is the degree to which the couple receives social support for their relationship (Kenney, 2002). Even with this in mind, by and large the research evidence suggest that interracial marriage is more difficult than same-race marriage every step of the way because of the limited social support (Anderson, 2014; Leslie & Young, 2015).

To be sure, in comparison to same-race marriages, interracial unions are less likely to last three months or more (Lichter & Qian, 2004); interracial marriages are typically shorter in duration than marriages that aren't interracial (Wang, Joyner, & Kao, 2006). Fu and colleagues' (2001) examination of interracial marriages found strong evidence that racial differences have a negative effect on marital happiness. Specifically, the authors maintain that it is not the cultural differences per se that affect marital happiness. Rather, they believe the marriages appear to be affected *domestically* on two counts: cultural lifestyle and the spouses' expectations of marital life formed throughout childhood and adolescence. Kristen Goodman (1991), interfaith marriage researcher, also found that in regard to racial and ethnic differences, understanding and responding to a spouse's expectations for the marriage are key factors in overall marital happiness and satisfaction, and that similarity of cultural backgrounds affects expectations for marriage. Goodman differs from Fu and colleagues, though, in her contention that cultural differences *do* affect marital happiness. She believes that marital expectations are based on socialization to marriage that takes place through childhood. Our study so far supports her ideas.

Because we live in a largely race-based society, it is important for educators, social workers, family life practitioners, clergy, mental health professionals, and other providers of human services to understand the heritages of the families they serve, to avoid uninformed characterizations of biracial families and children. By seeking to understand the diversity among the populations we serve, we can better transcend negative attitudes and conceptualizations about intermarried spouses and their biracial children (Glass & Wallace, 1996). Biracial children form their identities through the multiple influences of family and community (recall Bronfenbrenner's Ecological Model of human development from Chapter 1), and because of this, human service providers should support them in ways that allow them to feel a sense of pride and to embrace all of their heritages (Chiong, 1998).

Interfaith Marriage

Like marriage, religion is a dominant social institution in the United States that affects every sphere of human life (Sewenet, Tessagaye, & Tadele, 2017). When people of different religious faiths marry (for example, when a Christian marries a Hindu), their union is called an **interfaith marriage**. **Intrafaith marriages** are those in which individuals adhere to the same religion but may have different beliefs or follow different traditions within that faith (such as a Baptist who marries a Presbyterian). These marriages are single dimensions of **intercultural marriage**—the marriage of two people from two different cultural backgrounds (Sewenet et al., 2018). These marriages are also sometimes referred to as *mixed religious marriages*.

Throughout history and in most societies, marrying outside of a person's religion was strictly forbidden. Although some contemporary societies no longer forbid interfaith marriages, some research indicates that marrying outside of a person's religion sometimes carries with it consequences such as being ostracized from the family and/or church community, disinheritance, or both (Ross & Ross, 2004). In contemporary America, however, with its increasingly diverse population and with a growing acceptance of others' differences, more couples are moving beyond the established social norm of marrying only within their own religion. Finding even an approximate number of those with interfaith marriages is difficult because, in many instances, one marriage partner will convert to the faith of the other partner, either before marriage or when children are born into the marriage. But according to a Pew Research Center survey (2014), it appears that about 4 in 10 Americans have a spouse who is of a different religion—about 40 percent. This is in comparison to only 19 percent of those who were married before 1960.

Today, Hindus are the least likely religious group to have partners of other faiths; in 91 percent of marriages, both parties are Hindu. About 8 in 10 Mormons (82 percent) and Muslims (79 percent) share religious beliefs with their partners (Pew Research Center, 2015). Similarly, about three-fourths of Catholics and Protestants are of similar religious faiths as their partners (Pew Research Center, 2015).

Benefits of Interfaith Marriages. Perhaps the largest benefit of interfaith marriages is that these types of marriages contribute to the awareness of multiple cultures within the United States, as well as religious tolerance (Sewenet et al., 2018). Notes one researcher of interfaith marriages, "increasing intermarriage of various groups leads to the solidarity of the groups and helps to develop positive attitudes towards the practice. This enhances tolerance and plays a significant role for nations or societies with diverse religion and ethnic groups" (Sewenet et al., 2018, p. 358).

Potential Difficulties. Despite the promise of emerging literature and evidence that, as a nation, America is beginning to embrace cultural, racial, ethnic, and religious differences of marriage

Interfaith marriage: marriage between people of different religious faiths.

Intrafaith marriages: those in which individuals adhere to the same religion but may have different beliefs or follow different traditions within that faith (such as a Baptist who marries a Presbyterian).

Intercultural marriage: the marriage of two people from different cultural backgrounds.

partners, there are potential difficulties that interfaith couples may encounter. For example, new research has found that interreligious marriages can be a potential challenge to overall family stability and functioning (for a full review, see Sewenet et al., 2018). Perhaps one of the biggest concerns about mixed-religion marriages is the potential threat it poses to the religious practices of the couple. In some couples, for instance, as religious practices increase in one spouse, the spouse of the other faith participates less and less in his or her faith of origin (Peterson, 1986).

In some cases, when couples are first in love, it is easy to gloss over religious differences. Some find that as they near the wedding ceremony, which may bring to light some immediate differences in beliefs and values, the challenge begins. One woman in a Christian-Hindu marriage provides for us a glimpse into the difficulties faced in her relationship:

> Each family wants its own religious [wedding] rite . . . what normally marks the coming together of two families can become the first sign of division . . . Would I fit into [their religious] culture? Was I willing to accept the joint family and the loss of self it entailed? How would I cope in this community? . . . Practice of my own religion was in question . . . Would I have to play down my own familiar religious celebrations? Would this [marriage] affect my religious affiliation? (Gajuwala, 2004)

As this woman illustrates, combining faiths presents yet one more challenge that a couple must explore and resolve together. Forming a new religious identity while making the joint transition to marriage may also require individual soul searching and discovery.

Strengthening Interfaith Marriages. Although the challenges are many and potentially great, there are suggestions to help interfaith couples strengthen their marital unions:

- Understand the traditions of your faith as well as those of your partner's faith (Gruzen, 1990).
- Do not try to push your spouse into converting to your faith; a noncoercive, nonmanipulative family environment is important (Gruzen, 1990).
- Be sensitive to cross-cultural issues by encouraging a relationship between the two religious communities (Mayer, 1987).
- Recognize that a spouse's religion is not just something he or she participates in; it is something that is a part of him or her (Mayer, 1987).
- Before marriage, discuss how children will be reared in a religion (Gruzen, 1990; Mayer, 1987).

Mixed-Orientation Marriages

Mixed-orientation marriage:

marriage between partners who have different sexual orientations. Also called "mixed-orientation relationship."

A **mixed-orientation marriage** is a marriage between partners who have different sexual orientations, such as a straight woman who is married to a gay man or a bisexual individual who is married to a heterosexual. Frequently, the term *mixed-orientation relationship* is used; when discussing these types of relationships, social scientists typically use the terms *MOM* and *MOR*. The exact number of mixed-orientation marriages is unknown, partly because a number of gay men and lesbians are in heterosexual marriages and have not yet come out (Kort, 2015). Additionally, in demographic research there is still ambiguity and inconsistency in the ways in which "gay" and "lesbian" are defined (Kort, 2015). Gary Gates (2017), a researcher for the U.S. Census Bureau, notes that of the 27 million American men who are currently married, nearly 2 percent identify as gay or bisexual.

The Pathways to Mixed-Orientation Marriages. Initially, mixed-orientation couples enter into marriage for the same reason most other couples do in the United States: they love each other (Zimmerman, 2013). Scant empirical evidence exists to help us better understand these unique marriages, but one researcher provides insight into the various pathways to a mixed-orientation marriage (Kort, 2015):

Conforming to Society's Expectations. As you've seen in our study so far, our society has certain expectations of men and women to marry. Gay men and lesbians may enter into heterosexual marriages to conform to cultural and familial sexuality standards. Observes Kort, "It is much easier for people to marry heterosexuality than to discover their authentic selves" (2015, p. 1). Most straight spouses marry lesbian, gay, or bisexual partners without knowing their sexual orientation.

The Gradually Gay Spouse. Women repress their homosexuality more than gay men do (Kort, 2015). While gay women tend to discover their same-sex attraction when they experience sexual and/or romantic desires for another woman, gay men usually do not label themselves as a homosexual until they fall in love with another man. So, there appears to be a gradual unfolding of sexual orientation in mixed-orientation marriages, leaving one spouse unaware.

Revealing the True Self and Identity. Almost always, there is some deception about sexual orientation status by gays, lesbians, and bisexuals in mixed-orientation marriages (Kort, 2015). When the straight spouse discovers the orientation of their partner, it is understandable that the straight spouse may experience a sense of betrayal, being cheated, or fooled, or even become enraged (Kort, 2015). Others, however, feel relieved by knowing the sexual orientation of their partner and are happy to see a person they love find their true identity. Many continue to enjoy a warm, emotional, nonsexual relationship that may or may not include sexual interactions.

Coming Out: Getting Out or Staying Put? About 80 percent of mixed-orientation marriages end in divorce (Family Equality Council, 2017). One of the complications that arises in these types of relationships is that many are hetero-emotional. While they may be *sexually* attracted to same-sex partners, they are *emotionally* oriented to, or prefer, psychological intimacy with an opposite-sex partner; often they cannot imagine their lives without their spouse (Fleisher, 2005). No different than same-orientation marriage partners, MOM/MOR partners may feel a strong friendship, love, and have a strong desire to remain committed to their marriage partner (Zimmerman, 2013).

Hetero-emotional: a person who is emotionally oriented to prefer psychological intimacy with an opposite-sex partner.

One body of research indicates that a couple's decision to stay together or divorce depends on many factors: their ages, personalities, comfort with their own sexuality and sexual identities, level of sexual openness, and the degree to which they were invested in each other (financially, emotionally, and psychologically; Fleisher, 2005). Some couples opt for a closed-loop relationship, in which the gay/lesbian/bisexual partner agrees to have only monogamous relationships outside of the marriage to avoid the risks associated with sexual promiscuity (such as sexually transmitted infections). But sometimes, even after a marriage ends, the partners are still deeply committed to one another. As Kort (2015) describes, "A gay man I know divorced his wife and married his male partner . . . but he insisted on wearing his wedding band on his right hand to honor his first marriage to his wife" (p. 6).

Closed-loop relationship: a type of relationship experienced by a heterosexual individual and a queer individual, in which the queer partner agrees to only have monogamous relationships outside of the marriage.

Regardless of the cultural or sexual orientation differences in some relationships, marriages built on love, shared interests, and mutual respect are destined to become stronger and deeper with time. Indeed, an essential protective factor in all relationships is open, empathic, frequent, and honest communication (Zimmerman, 2013). Regardless of the challenges, if couples work together, they greatly improve their chances for a long and enduring life together.

SATISFYING MARRIAGES

In preparation for writing and teaching about marriage, I did a bit of my own impromptu research; I purchased several bridal magazines to try to get a glimpse into how the media portray marriage today. Although the purpose of these magazines is, indeed, to "sell" *weddings,* there is little content that addresses how to enter *marriage.* Consider, for example, the titles of the articles dealing with marriage (what one magazine called the "Heart to Heart" section):

- "Real Love; Planning your Big Day"
- "Honeymoon How-To's"
- "The Newlywed Rulebook"—with helpful marriage tips such as "humor us while we play matchmaker for your single friends"

With the articles' emphasis on the fairytale event and the romantic getaway that follows, it is understandable how and why people today spend many months and thousands upon thousands of dollars planning for a one-day celebration of love, but not nearly the same investment in preparation for their actual *marriage.* What the magazines don't tell you is that sooner or later the honeymoon must come to an end, and when the reality of marriage kicks into full gear many couples find they are unprepared. The question then becomes, Is it really possible to plan for the perfect marriage? How can we *predict* beforehand those marriages that will be successful?

Premarital Couple Types

As early as the 1930s, social scientists and family practitioners tried to determine what factors were associated with successful marriage (Fowers, Montel, & Olson, 1996). These efforts continue today as researchers seek ways to curb the high incidence of divorce. A host of investigations into marital process repeatedly demonstrates that the quality of couples' premarital relationship is predictive of marital satisfaction and stability (Fowers & Olson, 1986; Larsen & Olson, 1989). By knowing and better understanding the factors that contribute to or detract from marital adjustment and marital satisfaction, family scientists and family practitioners are able to develop premarital educational and counseling programs to enhance couples' relationships—and ameliorate the current trends in divorce.

In studying the correlation between premarital relationships and subsequent marital outcomes, family practitioner and marriage therapist Blaine Fowers and his colleagues (1996)

There's a big difference between preparing for the wedding and preparing for marriage. Sooner or later, the couple must negotiate those things that will contribute to a happy and satisfying marriage. Spouses who have satisfying marriages report that they experience love, commitment, trust, attention, listening, partnership, openness, and a willingness to compromise.

developed typologies of premarital couples in order to assess premarital relationship quality. According to Fowers, their study suggested that when relationship difficulties were identified before marriage, high-risk couples might "reconsider their marriage plans." Fowers's typologies consist of several types of couples:

- *Vitalized couples.* These couples are characterized by high levels of overall relationship satisfaction, self-disclosing, and sharing feelings. They also have high levels of expressing affection and sexuality. They have equal roles and often emphasize religion in their marriages.
- *Harmonious couples.* These couples experience moderate levels of relationship satisfaction and have the ability to resolve conflict. They feel comfortable with their levels of self-disclosure.
- *Traditional couples.* Among these couples there is strength in decision making and planning, but there is a bit of dissatisfaction with a partner's personality and habits. There are moderate levels of relationship dissatisfaction.
- *Conflicted couples.* These couples are characterized by communication problems and difficulties in their sexual relationship. They also experience difficulties in relating to a partner's family and friends and in participating in joint activities.

In a follow-up group studied by Fowers and his colleagues (1996), conflicted couples made up almost one-half of the separated or divorced couples. Conflicted couples were also three times more likely to break off their engagements and cancel the wedding as were vitalized couples. Harmonious couples divorced or separated twice as often as traditional couples. Vitalized couples had the highest overall marital satisfaction.

Marital Couple Types

Just as researchers developed premarital typologies to better understand marital adjustment factors for the purpose of developing education programs, researchers have also developed marital couple typologies with a similar goal—to determine marital satisfaction.

Couple Types

Mary Anne Fitzpatrick, recognized as a leading scholar in family and marital communication, has done extensive research in the area of different couple types. Fitzpatrick's findings revealed that some types of married couples consistently report higher levels of marital satisfaction than other couple types. Some of the differences among couple types revolved around their levels of self-disclosure, the way they communicate their emotions and feelings to one another, the manner in which they handle conflict, and whether their expectations of the relationship are fulfilled.

Traditional couple:
a married couple who adhere to conventional beliefs about marriage. These couples are interdependent in their relationship and prefer to be less independent and self-sufficient than the other marital types.

Traditional Couples. **Traditional couple** types adhere to conventional beliefs about marriage. These couples are interdependent in their relationship and prefer to be less independent and self-sufficient than the other marital types. Traditional couples place emphasis on self-disclosing and sharing and often convey their positive feelings about each other and their relationship more than the other couple types. Although these couples tend not to be assertive, they do deal with conflict as it arises in the relationship because of the high value they place on relationship stability. Of all the couple typologies, traditional couples report the highest level of marital satisfaction (Fitzpatrick, 1988; Fitzpatrick & Best, 1979; Kelley, 1999).

Independent couple:
a married couple who value closeness, companionship, sharing, and self-disclosure (although they do not disclose quite as much as traditional couples). They are not as conventional in their beliefs as traditional couples.

Independents. Like traditional couples, **independent couple** types value closeness, companionship, sharing, and self-disclosure (although they do not disclose quite as much as traditional couples). Unlike traditionals, independent couples are not as conventional in their beliefs about marriage. Perhaps one thing that best distinguishes independents from traditional couples is their competitiveness, or the need for "one-upmanship" (outdoing the other or controlling the other). This couple typology reports lower levels of marital satisfaction than traditional couple types do.

Separate couple:

a married couple who do not share the levels of companionship of traditional or independent couple types; they tend to share fewer positive feelings about their spouse and about their relationship than the other couple types do. Individuals in this couple type are less willing to relinquish their autonomy than those in traditional and independent couple types. They report lower levels of self-disclosure and sharing, and, as a result, experience psychological distance.

Mixed couple:

a married couple with different marital types, e.g., one spouse may have the expectations and characteristics of a traditional couple whereas the other spouse may have expectations typical of an individual couple type.

Separates. Individuals in separate couple types are less willing to relinquish their autonomy than those in traditional and independent couple types. This couple type reports lower levels of self-disclosure and sharing and, as a result, experiences psychological distance. Separate couples do not share the same levels of companionship as the other two couple types, and they tend to share fewer positive feelings about their spouse and about their relationship than the other couple types do. This couple type avoids conflict. According to Fitzpatrick (1988), this couple type scores the lowest in marital satisfaction among all couple types.

Mixed. In a mixed couple type, the spouses differ in their marital types. For example, one spouse may have the expectations and characteristics of a traditional couple, whereas the other spouse may have expectations typical of an individual couple type. Overall, mixed couple types place importance on affection within the marriage and will compromise when necessary. If the mixed couple type is the common traditional/separate type, marital satisfaction is similar to that found in traditional couples.

Examining marital couple types and the correlation between couple types and marital satisfaction helps researchers predict which types of marriages are more likely to end in divorce and which are more likely to succeed. For example, researchers have found that in couple types where the man is pessimistic and has negative feelings and emotions (common in traditional and conflicted premarital types), marital satisfaction is much lower—and divorce is much higher (Gee, Scott, Castellani, & Cordova, 2002). Fowers and his colleagues (1996) perhaps best sum up the importance as they conclude,

> Divorce has become a critical social problem with serious consequences for the physical and mental well-being of spouses and children. . . . Marriage and family therapists cannot afford to focus solely on alleviating the discomfort of distressed couples or members of divorced families. It is important for us to work proactively to help couples build strong and lasting relationships. (p. 117)

And by understanding the factors and the couple types more prone to divorce, this goal is better accomplished.

Marital Satisfaction and Happiness

How do marital satisfaction and happiness change over time? In Chapter 14, we will discuss in depth the factors that are known to be associated with couples' happiness and satisfaction with their marriages and the factors that may lead to uncoupling and divorce. For our purposes here, it's necessary to know that this area of family life has been studied since the 1920s, and many decades of research since then has shown us that the quality of marriages tends to decline over time (among many, Anderson, Russell, & Schumm, 1983; Karney & Bradbury, 1997; Orbuch, House, Mero, & Webster, 1996; Sternberg, 1986). If we were to quickly sketch out a graph of the level of marital satisfaction and happiness across the lifespan of a marriage, it would look like a U-shaped curve. If we use the U-shaped curve as a guide, we can see how the lifespan of marriage follows a pattern. For example, first marriages tend to begin with peak levels of satisfaction, happiness, and positive outlooks (Karney & Bradbury, 1997). After the honeymoon, when the realities of marriage begin to set in and the euphoria associated with the wedding day and honeymoon wanes, when passionate love begins to give way to companionate love, we see levels of marital satisfaction, happiness, and positive outlooks begin to decline (Sternberg, 1986). This does not mean that one spouse is no longer in love with the other spouse; it simply means that the realities of day-to-day living make it impossible to continue with a "mountaintop" marital existence.

A particular body of research suggests that the decline in marital happiness is quite steep during the first several years of marriage, particularly during the first seven years or so (Kovacs, 1983). Similar research also found that marital satisfaction rapidly declines during the first four years of marriage; it then stabilizes for a time, then declines again steeply through the eighth year of marriage (Kurdek, 1999). One family theorist, Wesley Burr (1970), examined

Some couples are conflicted because their relationship is characterized by communication problems and an unwillingness to compromise.

couples' satisfaction with different aspects of marriage over the lifecourse and found that marital happiness, marital satisfaction, and overall marital quality are at their lowest level when children begin to arrive. These levels stay relatively low until the children enter adolescence and are "launched" (move away). One body of research (Belsky, Woodworth, & Crnic, 1996) notes that the decline in marital quality during the parenting years is due to the stressors associated with the demands on parents' time, energy, and money. Recent research tends to support prior studies, but only to a certain extent. Results from a survey of more than 700 married study participants show that, over time, marital quality tends to decline, rebounds a bit, then tapers off again—the steep upward trend is not seen as in previous research (Anderson, Doherty, & Van Ryzin, 2008).

It is important to point out, however, that most of the research about marital satisfaction is tied to the Family Life Cycle paradigm, and the research conclusions may not necessarily be representative of all families. For example, divorced couples are not included in marital satisfaction research; because of this, marital satisfaction levels go up because the curve is only representing those couples who are still married and more satisfied (Miller, 2001). In addition to the lack of inclusion of divorced families, the Family Life Cycle paradigm does not consider the variations in today's complex families, such as childless couples, single parents, and cohabiters; it also doesn't account for differences in couples' religious beliefs, remarriage, economic status, education, attitudes toward marriage, and racial and ethnic differences (Anderson et al., 2008). When taking all of these factors into consideration, recent research suggests that there are actually five different marital quality trajectories. Some couples experience high levels of marital satisfaction and maintain that over time; others start high and experience the common U-shaped decline; others start low and remain fairly steady; and others start somewhat low and further decline (Anderson et al., 2008). Many other aspects of family living, such as the couple's involvement with their extended family and physical and emotional changes in the marriage partners, are all ignored by the Family Life Cycle as potential contributors to marital satisfaction. Because of this, the Family Life Cycle alone cannot be used to explain why there are changes in marital satisfaction over the lifespan of the marriage (Miller, 2001).

At this point you might be thinking, "What's the use? If the research says we're going to be so miserable after we marry and have children, why marry—or why have children?" All hope is not lost; Burr's (1970, 1973) research revealed that as children enter adolescence, marital quality begins to climb and continues to do so as each child leaves the nest. As the couple enters late middle adulthood and late adulthood, marital quality and marital satisfaction reach levels that nearly rival the peak levels at which marriage begins.

The consistency of the research findings brings into focus what all couples, married or contemplating marriage, need to know: "Marriage is not a single life event but . . . a set of stages" (Kurdek, 1999, pp. 1283–1284). In other words, although marriage may begin with peaks of happiness, satisfaction, and positive feelings toward a spouse, these levels of marital quality *will* change. In all likelihood, the first seven or eight years of marriage *will* bring a decline in marital happiness; children *will* bring different stressors to marriages, and while they live at home, marital interaction *will* change. There are periods of parenting when marital happiness stabilizes, but overall levels of marital satisfaction typically *will not* begin to increase until the children grow older and eventually leave home. Kurdek concludes that "instances of marital distress might be mitigated by spouses' *expecting and being prepared for* 'normal' periods of decline in marital quality." Stated another way: Marriage should be entered into with realistic expectations.

Realistic Expectations

When entering into a marital relationship, perhaps wedding vows should reflect the reality of hassled, day-to-day married life rather than the idealized, traditional vows that were exchanged by the couple in the opening vignette of this chapter. In the classic 1980s movie *She's Having a Baby,* the nervous groom thinks he hears the priest reciting these vows:

> Will thou, Jefferson, have this woman to be thy wedded wife? Will thou comfort her and keep her, in sickness and in health? Will thou provide her with credit cards, and a four bedroom/two and one-half bath home with central air conditioning and professional decorating, and two weeks in the Bahamas every spring? Will thou try to remember the little things that mean so much, like flowers on your anniversary, a kind word when she's had a bad day, and an occasional "Gee honey, you look pretty today"? . . . Will thou listen to stories about kids' colds, kitchen tile . . . and checkbook covers?

Relational expectancies:

the expectations about their marriage and spouse that couples enter marriage with, which have developed throughout the course of their lives. Relational expectancies are key factors in marital satisfaction and marriage longevity.

Social Expectations model:

developed by psychologist Mary Levitt, this model illustrates how spouses' expectations of marital relationships are based on past relationship interactions with the spouse. This model also takes into account the influence of societal norms on spousal expectations.

Those who are married could add a litany of things to these "wedding vows" that speak to the *reality* of married life. We've mentioned the importance of entering a marriage with realistic expectations. But what should those expectations be? How do these expectations help a couple achieve better marital satisfaction?

If you choose to marry, what will your priorities be? Perhaps companionship or friendship? Do you anticipate a marriage with children? A marriage partner who shares your dreams and life goals? And a marriage that is united in purpose and direction?

When any couple enters into marriage, they inevitably have **relational expectancies**—key factors in marital satisfaction and longevity of their marriage. These expectations that couples have for their marriage and their spouses develop throughout the course of their lives.

Throughout this book, we have seen how our family of origin influences who we are. In the same way, our experiences with our parents' marital history and our own past relational experiences impact and influence our expectancies. Lifespan psychologist Mary Levitt (1991) developed the **Social Expectations model**, which illustrates how spouses' expectations of marital relationships are based on past relationship interactions with the spouse. This model also takes into account the influence of societal norms (such as women being caregivers and men being providers) on spousal expectations. Both factors help shape our expectancies for married life.

The degree to which relational expectancies are met or violated affects marital satisfaction. Levitt's (1991) model examines the link between expectations and marital satisfaction. Her

Taking Sides

Who Are Your Marriage Models?

We frequently carry interaction patterns and behaviors from our family of origin to our family of choice when we marry. At times, continuing these behaviors is a deliberate choice; other times, we may not want to interact in ways similar to our parents, but because these patterns are so deeply ingrained in our way of thinking, we carry them into our own marriages. When contemplating marriage, couples must consider the marriage models in their lives and how these have shaped their own attitudes and ideas about marriage.

On One Side: For the most part, the marriage models in my life have been quite positive. My parents have been married for more than 25 years, and still today they are warm and affectionate toward each other. My grandparents were married for more than 50 years before my grandma died. My parents frequently talk things over, and many times it seems as though they communicate without saying a single word to each other. Of course they've argued—quite passionately at times. But I always get the feeling that they really *enjoy* being married. Divorce? No way. Our religion really frowns on divorce . . . I have a feeling that if they had a bad marriage, they would stay married because of their religious beliefs. I've never given it much thought, but as I look across my family background, there is no divorce in the family tree. I've always wanted a marriage like my parents have. To me, theirs is an "ideal" marriage. I am concerned because I feel that my fiancé's parents' marriage is a very empty marriage and void of these things I see in my marriage models.

On the Flip Side: My parents' marriage was sometimes good, sometimes bad. I suppose this is how *all* marriages are. Unlike my fiancé's parents, my parents are more independent of one another in their marriage; they do things together, but they are just as content doing things separately from one another. And unlike her side of the family, my side of the family typically doesn't interact a lot with extended family. For example, we seldom have family reunions or celebrate holidays together with them. Yes, there is divorce in our family tree. My fiancé is concerned about this. She thinks that because it has been an acceptable way of handling marital distress in my family background (my sister recently divorced), it might be easier for me to divorce her if things don't work out. It would be fruitless for me to argue that the marriage models in my life have not influenced me. I believe that it is my *choice* whether I adopt their behaviors or not, and that I will not necessarily repeat these behaviors in my own marriage,

Your Side: In your opinion, how will this couple's marriage models influence their marriage? In reaching your decision, consider the following questions:

1. In what ways does each of these partners' marriage models differ? Specifically, what are her marriage model influences? What are his marriage model influences?

2. Do you foresee any potential marital distress ahead for this couple? Why? What areas of their marriage may have difficulty, and why did you choose these specific areas?

3. In your opinion, what things should this couple focus on before they wed?

model takes into account the fact that because we are human, expectations are set and expectations are going to be tested within a marriage. Levitt found that when (not *if*) relational expectancies are tested, one of three outcomes will occur:

1. When a spouse's *expectations are confirmed,* the relationship will remain stable. For example, everyone enters into marriage expecting a spouse to be faithful and loyal. Suppose a wife is on a business trip with an attractive, single man. The spouse's expectation is that his wife will not cheat. Once the expectation is tested and confirmed, the marriage remains stable.

2. When a spouse's *expectations are violated,* it has a negative effect on the relationship, Consider the same example of a spouse's loyalty or faithfulness. Assume that when the expectation was tested, the spouse did cheat and have an affair. This violation will destabilize the relationship.

3. When the relationship *expectations are tested* and the spouse's expectations are exceeded, the highest levels of marital satisfaction are reached.

In a study that examined Mary Fitzpatrick's (1988) couple types and relational expectancy, traditional couples had the highest level of marital satisfaction because they had the highest levels of met and exceeded relational expectations (Kelley, 1999). Conversely, separate couple types had the highest level of unmet expectations and, hence, lower marital satisfaction.

Expectations *set* versus expectations *met*—can a partner realistically meet the relational expectations that have been set? This appears to be a pivotal issue in marital satisfaction and overall relationship satisfaction.

FAMILY LIFE EDUCATION: IDENTIFYING SOCIAL AND CULTURAL INFLUENCES AFFECTING THE MARITAL EXPERIENCE

When working with individuals and families to help to promote their optimal health and well-being, it is imperative that Family Life Educators and other helping professionals understand the social and cultural influences on today's marriages (NCFR, 2019). A Family Life Educator is prepared to understand the impact of changing attitudes toward diversity in relationships, be it racial or religious differences in marital couples, gender role expectations, or the diversity that couples embrace today in forming their marital partnerships, such as with mixed-orientation marriages.

Although marriage is a universal experience and sanctioned by all societies the world over, no two couples experience marriage the same way. The marriage experience is influenced and affected by our individual experiences within our families of origin. The experience of marriage is also influenced by our racial, ethnic, cultural, and religious backgrounds. A relational process that undergoes change across time, and a relationship that has a distinct life-course of its own, marriage can be experienced as a legal contract, a social contract, a sacred act, or a covenant. Many of you will someday vow to love, honor, and cherish your partner until death parts you, and many of you will someday vow to stick by your partner for "better or worse" or in "sickness and in health," but the divorce trends in the United States indicate that these promises are much easier made than kept.

Empirical evidence indicates that marriage is tougher than most of us anticipate because of the developmental tasks associated with the transition to marital life. Spousal roles must be established and continuously negotiated; marital boundaries need to be created and maintained; along with nurturing a marital emotional climate and countless needs of children, we must also manage the house, bills, and work, as well as a multitude of other daily tasks.

Given the overscheduled nature of contemporary marriages, it is necessary for each partner to enter into the marriage with realistic expectations. The research bears out the notion that, in the end, successful marriages are those marriages in which the expectations set and the expectations met are in alignment. While reciting marriage vows, couples acknowledge from the outset that marriage will be anything but a carefree existence. Wedding promises speak to the either/ors in life—either things will be good or they will be bad; either someone will be healthy or someone will be sick; either the bills will be paid or they won't.

But as you will find when you make a lifelong commitment to another, a marital partnership is not about just the good days or the bad days. It's about all the days in between. Some days just *are*—they're not good, they're not bad, they're not great, they're not horrible. They just *are*. When the honeymoon excitement fades to the activities of daily living; when the pressures of daily living tempt us to attack one another instead of attacking the problem; and when it's easier to throw in the towel than to stick to the marital commitment, marital partners need to take a close look at their expectations and determine whether they are asking their spouse to do the impossible.

This is the point where everything we have studied in this book comes together: the experiences of family living, family communication, intimacy, love, experiences of gender, dating, and the other pathways to a committed, lifelong relationship. Each of you has unique, individual experiences within all areas of family life and will probably merge your experiences with another person whose experiences are vastly different. As you enter into a relationship and perhaps marriage, you will have to somehow negotiate and find your way to an interdependent bond that works and is satisfactory and fulfilling for you and your partner.

Hard work? Without a doubt!

Being Single

- Today, there is an increasing number of singles in the United States, and singlehood is becoming a popular trend among the young and the old alike. This contemporary trend is due to the individualistic nature of Western society that embraces pursuing individual goals, such as education, and to the number of young adults who delay marriage. The average age at which people marry fluctuates over time. Today, 90 to 95 percent of adults eventually marry.

- Peter Stein developed a typology of singlehood that comprises four categories. His model acknowledges that some people are single by choice, while others are single for the time being, or are unintentionally single. Stein's four categories of singles are voluntary temporary, voluntary permanent, involuntary temporary, and involuntary permanent.

- Never-married singles are those people who have not married; they may or may not live alone, or may or may not have an intimate partner. There are racial and ethnic differences in the experiences of singlehood. In general, the existing research seems to indicate that singlehood is a positive, satisfying experience for many.

- Urban tribes are mixed-gender circles of friends who are the primary social support system for singles. Each individual within the tribe assumes certain roles, much like in a family. Urban tribe members feel a mutual obligation to support each other and care for one another.

- Demographic surveys of gay men and lesbians indicate that between 45 and 80 percent are in a steady or long-term cohabiting relationship.

- A small percentage of America's singles are divorced men and women. Most divorced people will experience life as a single person at least for some period of time following the end of their marriages.

- An even smaller percentage of America's singles are widows and widowers, or people who have lost a spouse to death. Men are more likely than women to remarry following the death of a spouse.

The Act of Marriage

- In most cultures people are expected to marry when they reach adulthood. Although empirical evidence seems to indicate that people marry for many personal, individual reasons, marriage serves society on several levels. The act of marriage also defines the pair bond and provides a new identity for a couple and the subsequent roles they will play in their marriage and in the society at large.

- Marriage was once considered to be the social foundation responsible for the procreation and the socialization of children but is now being replaced by pair bonds that meet individual needs. This change is referred to as *the deinstitutionalization of marriage.* Browning outlined five specific dimensions of marriage: as organizer of natural desires, as a social good, as a communicative reality, as a legal contract, and as a sacrament or covenant.

- In the United States, marriage is foremost a state and federally regulated legal contract. Every slate requires a marriage license. Factors limiting marriage vary from state to state, but may include the age, kinship, or sexual orientation of couples intending to marry. The privileges that come with marriage may also vary by state.

- Marriage tends to benefit all areas of well-being. Measurable benefits include economic benefits (including higher average annual incomes and financial assets), health benefits to each partner, and children's benefits (living standards, better health, and better developmental outcomes).

- In many cultures, marriage is a sacred act, and many measures are undertaken to ensure its protection. To curb escalating divorce rates in the United States, many states have considered implementing legislation that forces couples to prepare for married life and some have adopted Marriage Covenant Acts—legally binding agreements that spell out the couple's intent to obtain premarital education and/or counseling, clearly delineate the couple's commitment to preserving the marital union, and provide the grounds for divorce.

The Transition to Marriage: Why It's So Tough

- There are often difficulties associated with the transition to married life. By using the Family Life Cycle paradigm, family life educators can track the changes in the structure of the family as well as emotional transitions and other related changes in the family status. Through the Family Systems theoretical model, researchers better understand the interactions that take place in marriage and in family life. Viewed in this light, marriage is best seen as a newly formed system of the family and of society.

- Newly married couples must negotiate the developmental tasks of their newly formed family. This includes establishing marital roles and boundaries, managing the house and the money, and fostering a healthy emotional climate,

- Concepts of family and marriage in the United States are undergoing many changes, including an increase in heterogamous interpersonal relationships. Couples in heterogamous relationships—including interracial and interfaith marriages—face difficulties in addition to the normal transitional challenges all newlyweds face.

Satisfying Marriages

- Since the 1930s, family life educators have tried to determine factors associated with successful marriage. By learning how they contribute to or detract from marital adjustment and marital satisfaction, family and social scientists and family practitioners are able to develop premarital educational and counseling programs to enhance couples' relationships.

- Researchers developed typologies of premarital couples in order to assess premarital relationship quality in order to understand the correlation between premarital relationships and subsequent marital outcomes. These premarital couple types include vitalized couples, harmonious couples, traditional couples, and conflicted couples.

- Researchers also developed marital couple typologies to determine marital satisfaction. These include traditional couple types, independent couple types, separate couple types, and the mixed couple types.

- The lifecourse of marriage typically follows a pattern: marriages begin with peak levels of satisfaction; marital satisfaction wanes when the realities of marriage set in and the couple has children; satisfaction levels stay low until the children enter adolescence and move away; and as children enter into adolescence, marital quality begins to climb and continues to do so as each child leaves the nest.

- As the couple enters late middle adulthood and late adulthood, levels of marital quality and marital satisfaction reach levels that nearly rival the peak levels at which marriage begins.

- Couples entering marriage have expectations for their marriage and their spouses that have been developed throughout the course of their lives. The Social Expectations Model illustrates how spouses' expectations are based on past relationship interactions with the spouse. This model also takes into account the influence of societal norms (such as women being caregivers and men being providers) on spousal expectations.

/// KEY TERMS

iStock.com/Vlacheslav Peretiatko

CHAPTER 9

YOU, SEX, AND YOUR SEXUALITY

LEARNING OBJECTIVES

9.1 Describe the importance of sexual scripts and how they relate to racial and ethnic groups in the United States.

9.2 Discuss the patterns of sexual arousal and desire and relate them to the experiences of adolescents and young adults.

9.3 Summarize the trends in sexually transmitted infections (STIs) today in the United States.

9.4 Explain how relationship satisfaction and marriage satisfaction relate to nonmarital sex, sex outside of the relationship, and the connection between love and sex.

9.5 Discuss the sexual difficulties people experience and the available treatments.

Though they didn't say it out loud, they both knew that after 38 years of marriage their time together would soon draw to an end. Despite the valiant war she waged, the cancer had overtaken every aspect of her being and we all knew she would not be with us when the morning came. We moved her into the family room as she requested, so she could be among her children and grandchildren, not tucked far away from them in a corner bedroom.

My father knelt beside her. Thinking he was simply bathing her (a task I had performed every day over the course of that week), I stayed in the kitchen nearby. He raised her left hand and kissed her wedding band. He began to bathe her hand, her arm, her shoulder. He stroked her hair, over and over. She was much calmer, and her breathing that had been so labored in the previous minutes seemed to become less difficult. She turned her face so they were only inches apart from one another. They did not speak; their gaze locked onto one another. His hand lingered over her shoulder, then moved toward her chest. Through her entire illness, I had never seen her shed one tear, until now. His hand did not move. I could only imagine what each of them was thinking. Were they remembering, were they longing, yearning? Were they aching in anticipation of separation? Was he trying to memorize her?

It suddenly dawned on me what was taking place just a few feet away from me. I hurriedly left the room, allowing them to be alone for the last time. To the casual observer, the scene unfolding may have appeared to be a sponge bath from a caregiver for a dying woman—but it was so much more than that. What I was witnessing was a most tender act of lovemaking.

I would only learn later in my life how much my parents' physical and emotional interactions with each other would shape my own sexuality.

The year 1977 marked the freshman year of my university experience. Abortion had been legal for about four years and was relatively easy and inexpensive to obtain; cohabitation before marriage was becoming more common; the more serious sexually transmitted infections could be treated with a dose of penicillin; the AIDS epidemic was still a few years away. But despite all the sexual freedom my generation was enjoying, *Playboy* magazine was still displayed in brown paper wrappers on magazine stands. In fact, even at colleges and universities, usually among the more open-minded communities, sex was still a controversial subject. The first human sexuality course I took at the university is a case in point. Although the course was available, it was offered in a cloud of secrecy—it was not listed in the course offerings schedules printed each semester! Students knew about it by word of mouth; parents did not. The course was wrapped in "brown paper." Today on college campuses across the country, sexuality courses are taught in filled-to-capacity rooms.

What exactly is sexuality? Too often we mistake *sex* and *sexuality* for the same thing, but they are two distinct, separate entities. While sex refers to acts associated with sexual intercourse, sociologist Ira Reiss (1989) defined sexuality as "the erotic arousal and genital responses resulting from following *sexual scripts* of that society." To better understand how we develop these sexual scripts and what influences them, in this chapter we will explore the significant cultural contributions to our sexuality and sexual experiences in adolescence and early adulthood. We'll then view sexuality through the lens of relationships—marital sexuality, extramarital sexuality, and nonmarital sexuality—as well as what happens when partners experience sexual dysfunction.

Sexuality:
the erotic arousal and genital responses resulting from following sexual scripts of a society.

At the very foundation of our sexuality are biological contributions, and as you learned in Chapter 4, the biological aspects of our sexual development and sexual maturity begin in the womb and continue until the end of our lives. Based on their extensive research and review of the sexual development literature, sex scientists and sociologists John DeLamater and William Friedrich (2002) developed a progression of benchmarks in sexual development from birth through adulthood. Although beyond the scope of our discussion here, this information is summarized in Figure 9.1 as a reminder that our sexuality is a continuous progression across the lifespan.

LEARNING SEXUALITY: CULTURAL CONTRIBUTIONS

You don't *become* sexual at a certain point in your lifespan such as in adolescence or early adulthood; more correctly, you *are continuously becoming* a sexual being. From your very earliest days of life, well into very old age, who you are as a sexual being is shaped by many interrelated factors that include biological influences, your family of origin, the different intimate relationships you may have, life experiences, and other cultural influences (such as the media, as you learned in Chapter 4). Through these influences and contributions, you also develop your *sexual identity*, your awareness of yourself as a sexual male or sexual female. Let's explore how we learn to be sexual through the influences of sexual scripts.

Sexual Scripts

If we are raised in the same culture, do we differ in how we experience the feelings, behaviors, and attitudes associated with sex? If we do, why? How do we ultimately arrive at what *sex* and *sexuality* mean to us?

John Gagnon and his colleague, William Simon, were sociologists and sexologists in the 1970s who pioneered the ideas that people learn how to be sexual as a function of being raised in a particular culture, and that sexuality is ultimately created by the culture in which we live (Gagnon & Simon, 1973). They put forth the idea of *sexual scripts* as an explanation for how we internalize—make a part of ourselves—our culture's unique expectations for sexual attitudes and behaviors.

The sexual scripting framework proposes that societal and cultural processes ultimately determine and prescribe what we perceive as "sexual" and how we behave sexually (Laumann, Gagnon, Michael, & Michaels, 1994). Sexual scripts are shared, gender-specific social and cultural expectations that guide our beliefs, attitudes, and values about sex, such as our beliefs about appropriate sexual partners, sexual behaviors, and sexual conduct (Bowleg, Lucas, & Tschann, 2004), and as some bodies of research suggest, "Heterosexual relationships

Sexual scripting framework:
the notion that societal and cultural processes ultimately determine and proscribe what we perceive as "sexual" and how we behave sexually.

Sexual scripts:
shared, gender-specific social and cultural expectations that guide our beliefs, attitudes, and values about sex, such as our beliefs about appropriate sexual partners, sexual behaviors, and sexual conduct.

Figure 9.1 /// Sexual Development Across the Lifespan

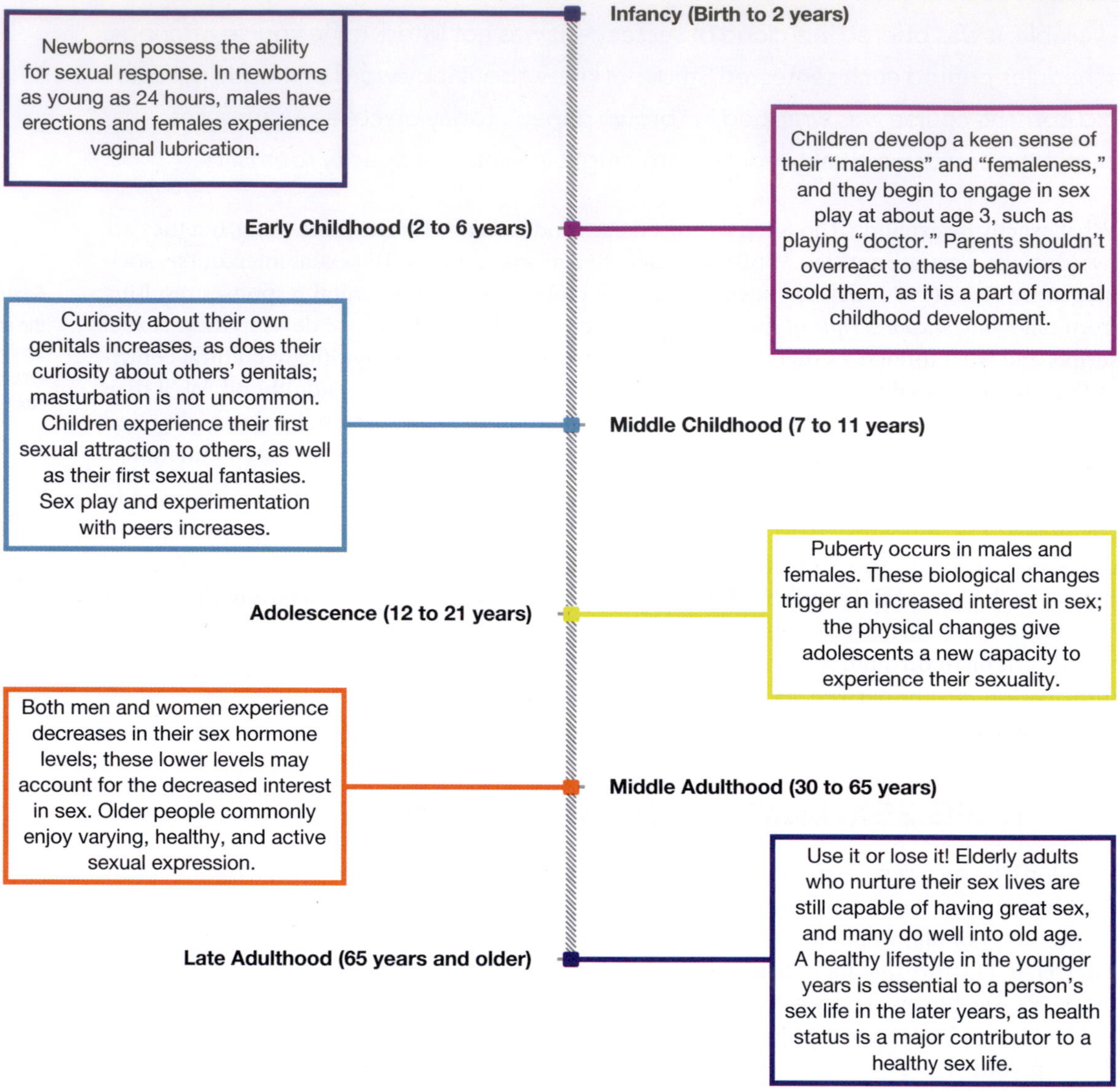

Infancy (Birth to 2 years)

Newborns possess the ability for sexual response. In newborns as young as 24 hours, males have erections and females experience vaginal lubrication.

Early Childhood (2 to 6 years)

Children develop a keen sense of their "maleness" and "femaleness," and they begin to engage in sex play at about age 3, such as playing "doctor." Parents shouldn't overreact to these behaviors or scold them, as it is a part of normal childhood development.

Curiosity about their own genitals increases, as does their curiosity about others' genitals; masturbation is not uncommon. Children experience their first sexual attraction to others, as well as their first sexual fantasies. Sex play and experimentation with peers increases.

Middle Childhood (7 to 11 years)

Adolescence (12 to 21 years)

Puberty occurs in males and females. These biological changes trigger an increased interest in sex; the physical changes give adolescents a new capacity to experience their sexuality.

Both men and women experience decreases in their sex hormone levels; these lower levels may account for the decreased interest in sex. Older people commonly enjoy varying, healthy, and active sexual expression.

Middle Adulthood (30 to 65 years)

Use it or lose it! Elderly adults who nurture their sex lives are still capable of having great sex, and many do well into old age. A healthy lifestyle in the younger years is essential to a person's sex life in the later years, as health status is a major contributor to a healthy sex life.

Late Adulthood (65 years and older)

Heterosexual:

sexual and emotional relationships between people of opposite sexes.

Homosexual:

sexual and emotional relationships with persons of the same sex.

Bisexual:

sexual and/or romantic attraction to members of both sexes.

Asexual:

an individual who does not experience sexual attraction.

are a significant stage on which men and women enact gender" (Masters, Casey, Wells, & Morrison, 2013, p. 410; Connell, 2002; Gavey, 2005; Hamilton & Armstrong, 2009). Embedded within our sexual scripts is our sexual orientation, which is the enduring emotional, romantic, sexual, or affectional attraction we feel toward others. There are four general types of sexual orientation:

- **Heterosexual**, which characterizes the sexual and emotional relationships between people of opposite sexes
- **Homosexual**, which are the sexual and emotional relationships with persons of the same sex
- **Bisexual**, which is the sexual and/or romantic attraction toward members of both sexes
- **Asexual**, which describes individuals who experience no sexual attraction to others

From the moment we are born, and throughout our entire lives, we are bombarded with parental, peer, school, spiritual, media, and other cultural messages. These messages write

As with most other aspects of a couple's relationship, how the partners experience sex and sexuality is largely determined by their sexual scripts—their culturally shaped expectations that guide their beliefs and behaviors.

our sexual scripts and ultimately prescribe our sexuality. Our sexual scripts determine, among other things (DeLamater & Hyde, 1998),

- *With whom* we can engage in sexual relations (age, relationship to self, gender)
- *How* we engage in sex (anal sex, oral sex, "legal" sexual positions)
- *How often* we engage in sexual relations (for instance, it is expected that younger couples have sex more frequently than older couples)
- *When* we have sex (timing parameters such as age at first intercourse or when the children are not present)
- *Where* we have sex (other than the bedroom)
- *Why* we have sexual relations (love, lust, anger, fun, play, boredom, jealousy)

Sexual scripts serve two primary functions. First, they provide us a framework for what is considered normative and expected sexual behavior within a given culture. For instance, in the West, the frequency of sexual intercourse in married or committed couples ranges from less than once per week to twice per week. In other societies, such as the Lepchas in the Himalayas, sexual intercourse is practiced at least once a night; the Chaga people from Tanzania engage in sexual intercourse at least three times a night (Ubillos, Paez, & Gonzalez, 2000). Second, sexual scripts provide a road map of sorts for us—they give us directions as to how we should feel, think, and act in certain sexual situations (Wiederman, 2005). And, without question, these scripts are opposites for men and women (Masters et al., 2013; Gavey, 2005). In America, for example, traditional sex scripts prescribe that females should put their own sexual desires aside in order to please their male partners, be aware of the dangers of sex and to protect themselves, and only engage in sex if they are involved in an emotionally committed relationship (Holland, Ramazanoglu, Scott, Sharpe, & Thomson, 1990; Hynie, Lyndon, Cote, & Wiener, 1998; Wiederman, 2005). Males, on the other hand, are sexually scripted to be independent, assertive, goal directed, and divorced from an emotional commitment to their sexual partner (Wiederman, 2005). Men are also scripted to be sexually skilled, to value sex over relationships, and to be "players" (Masters et al., 2013).

Specifically, the sexual scripting approach delineates three different levels of sexual scripts: (1) **cultural scenarios** that recognize influences such as our families of origin, our communities,

Cultural scenarios: sexual scripts that recognize influences such as our families of origin and our communities, mass media, educational systems, and religious beliefs.

mass media, the educational system, and religious beliefs (as shown in Chapter 1); (2) interpersonal scripts that recognize how different people interact and relate to each other within specific social situations (as seen in Chapter 7); and (3) intrapsychic scripts (intrapersonal; see Chapter 7) that account for individual desires, fantasies, emotions, and intensions while at the same time considering the interpersonal responses of others (Simon & Gagnon, 1984). All three levels of these cognitive representations of sex are important in the creation of our sexual identity and how we experience sex and sexuality, and, as with all areas of human development, these changes and development occur simultaneously with our physical and cognitive development.

Cultural Scenarios: Parents as Sexuality Educators

Most parents, sexuality educators, and even adolescents believe that parents should be the primary providers of sexuality and health education to their children (Byers et al., 2003; Ashcraft & Murray, 2017). Parents remain influential regarding their teens' decisions and attitudes about sex. Today, 70 percent of males and 78 percent of females aged 15 to 19 report that they have talked to a parent or their parents about at least one of the primary topics of sex education: how to say no to sex; methods of contraception; STIs, how/where to get birth control; how to prevent HIV infection; and how to use a condom (Gutmacher Institute, 2018).

That's not to say, however, that parents and teens are satisfied with the quality of their sexual communication, or the amount of it (Byers, Sears, & Weaver, 2008). Contemporary pre-teens and teens also turn to the Internet to search for education and information, where they can gather their information confidentially (Guilamo-Ramos et al., 2015).

Parent–Child Sexual Communication

How did you learn about sex? Did your parents have "The Talk" with you? If so, was it a well-planned, one-time, uncomfortable conversation, or was it laid back, informal, and frequent? There are several factors that play into sexual communication within a family. For example, there is a large body of science that indicates that parents will commonly provide the same level of sex education to their children that they received from their parents (for a complete review, see Byers et al., 2008). Parent–child sexual communication is also influenced by parents' perceptions of their own sexual knowledge and the comfort level they have when discussing sexual topics with their children. In fact, some studies have found that when mothers did not discuss sexual issues with their daughters it was related to their self-perceived low levels of sexual knowledge and their discomfort with the topic (Jaccard, Dittus, & Gordon, 2000; Pariera, 2016; Pariera & Brody, 2017). The mothers were not only embarrassed to approach the subject but they were also afraid that they would be asked something they didn't know the answer(s) to. On the other hand, parents who feel that they have an adequate background in sexuality education, who feel knowledgeable, and who are comfortable with sexuality topics and issues are much more likely to communicate about sex often with their children (Jaccard et al., 2000; Pariera, 2016; Pariera & Brody, 2017). Also, mothers are much more involved in the sexuality and health education of their children than fathers are; parents are also more likely to talk about sex with their adolescent daughters than they are their adolescent sons (see Pariera, 2016; Pariera & Brody, 2017; and Ritchwood, Peasant Bonner, Powell, & Taggart, 2017, for a full review).

Just Talk to Me!

There is no question: Young people *want* to have conversations with their parents about a wide range of topics related to sex, and they want these conversations to happen earlier than parents are ready for it; they also want to engage in these conversations frequently and regularly (Grossman, Jenkins, & Richer, 2018). In general, there are five components that affect parent–child sexual communication: the communication source (the parent or the child?); the communication recipient (the parent or the child?); the communication itself (what is the content?); the family context (under what circumstances did the communication take place?); and how the message is communicated (is it done to promote knowledge—or fear? (Jaccard, Dodge, & Dittus, 2002).

iStock.com/Georgijevic

What was your "sex talk" like with your parent(s) or guardian? Or are you still waiting for them to have "The Talk" with you? Although many parents are uncomfortable discussing sex with their children, parents are children's first and best sex educators.

Sandra Byers is a professor of sexuality at the University of New Brunswick, and her influential research is concentrated in the areas of sexual satisfaction, sexuality education, and sexual communication. In her work that studied nearly 4,000 parents and youth, she wanted to better understand how the sexual communication factors listed above affect sexual communication with children from Kindergarten to about Grade 8. She especially wanted to see how often parents talked to their children about 10 sexuality topics: personal safety, correct names for genitalia, puberty, reproduction, sexual coercion and assault, STDs, abstinence, birth control, sexual decision making, and sexual pleasure/enjoyment (Byers et al., 2008). In general, she and her colleagues found that the characteristics of the parent, the characteristics of the child, and the content of the communication were all associated with the quality and quantity of parent–child sexual communication. Overall, the study found that parents who were supportive of comprehensive sexuality and health education (both in the home and at school) were more likely to engage in sexual communication with their children, to engage in it more frequently, and to encourage their children to ask questions—no topic was "off limits."

Parent–child sexual communication (PCSC) is an especially important resource to improve the overall sexual health and well-being of youth and adolescents (Pariera, 2016; Ritchwood et al., 2017). In a study that sought to better understand the barriers to effective sexual communication between parents and their children/teens, parents assessed certain statements that either prompted or prohibited sexual communication. The researcher discovered that the two most significant barriers to parent–child sexual communication were "Thinking he/she doesn't want to hear what you have to say," and "Thinking he/she is too young" (Pariera, 2016). Table 9.1 shows us the reasons parents were prompted to initiate sexual communication with their children and/or adolescents. As you can see, parents didn't communicate about sex with their children because *they* felt it was time to have the conversation—rather, they waited for outside factors, such as having a child participating in a sex education program at school, to prompt them to have the conversations (Pariera, 2016). It's also interesting to see that sexual communication was rarely prompted by a healthcare provider.

This body of research also revealed that parent–child conversations about sex and sexuality haven't changed much over the past three decades, and it confirms early studies. Common

Table 9.1 /// Reasons Why Parents Are Prompted to Have Parent–Child Sexual Communication	
Measure	Percentage
My child was in a sex education program at school	18
I was prompted by a friend or family member	1
I was prompted by a healthcare provider	5
I was prompted by my child asking questions	30
I thought my child might be sexually active	13
I felt that my child had become old enough to talk about sex	33
Other	8

Source: Pariera (2016).

responses for barriers to communicating openly with youth and adolescents about sex included the following (Pariera, 2016):

- Being uncomfortable talking about sex
- Thinking the child doesn't want to hear what the parent(s) had to say
- Parents not sure they had the correct information
- Thinking that talking to the child will make him/her want to have sex
- Thinking the child is too young to learn about sex or talk about it
- Thinking that talking about sex would affect the child's behavior

What is sexual communication like between parents and their LGBTQ+ child or adolescent? As you saw in Chapter 1, many in the LGBTQ community have *chosen families* because they don't feel they have emotional support at home. How does that impact sex talk discussions with parents and their kids?

In a 2018 study of 44 parents of LGBTQ adolescents aged 13 to 17, the researchers found that parents are especially uncomfortable with the topic of sex and feel ill-prepared to educate their children about sex and dating (Newcomb et al., 2018). As one mother in the study commented, "My challenge around talking about sex is that I have no idea what sex is really like for him, especially for gay men." Another parent noted, "I don't have an opportunity to talk to other parents whose kids are LGBTQ." There are two particularly striking findings:

- Many of the gay and bisexual males *wanted* to have closer relationships with their parents and *wanted* to be able to talk about sex and dating.
- Upon coming out, parents tended to *shut down* sexual communication; when they did talk about it, the conversations were brief and focused exclusively on HIV and condom use.

As Brian Mustanski (2020), director of Institute for Sexual and Gender Minority Health, observes, "Research on family relationships is a high priority for us because it is an extremely understudied area, and because parents are asking us for advice. We need new research to give parents the right answers."

It appears that America has a way to go to confront the challenges associated with providing frank, accurate, and truthful information to their children about sex and sexuality.

Teens Are People, Too: Sources of Anxiety for Teens

Interestingly, most research focuses on the *parents'* fears, anxieties, and concerns about addressing sex and sexuality with their children and teens. But how do *teens* feel about having the conversation with their parents? What are their sources of anxiety? One study helps us better understand the teens' perspectives.

Should Abstinence Until Marriage Be the Only Sex Education?

Is it great to wait? At issue is whether such educational programs keep preteens and teens from having sex until marriage, or whether a lack of education and information serves only to put teens at greater risk for not only unwanted pregnancies but sexually transmitted infections and HIV/AIDS as well. Should abstinence until marriage be the only sex education youth and teens receive?

YES: Three million teens—one-fourth of all sexually active teens in America—have a sexually transmitted disease. In addition, teenage moms are more likely to live under the constraints of poverty because 41 percent will drop out of school Their poverty and limited education have a profound effect on *their* children, who are more likely to have lower grades, be abused, and drop out from school themselves.

But can Abstinence-Only Programs (AOP) reduce such sobering statistics? In the late 1990s, the Georgia State Board of Education requested a study be done on "Choosing the Best," an AOP adopted for use in all eighth-grade classes in Columbus, Georgia, over a period of four years. The results?

- There was a 38 percent drop in pregnancies among middle school students between 1997 and 1999.
- In other school districts that did not provide AOPs, there was a 6 percent drop in pregnancies among middle school students during the same timeframe.
- Teens who take virginity pledges—vowing that they will remain virgins until they are married—are 34 percent less likely to engage in sexual activity.

As the old axiom goes, "Abstinence is the only method proven to work every time."

NO: Sue Alford (2001), Director of Public Information Services at Advocates for Youth, believes that AOPs are dangerous to America's youth. "Federally mandated abstinence-only-until-marriage education jeopardizes the health and lives of young people," Alford argues, "by denying them information that can prevent unintended pregnancy and infection with sexually transmitted diseases, including HIV." Supporters of sex education maintain that AOPs

- Provide fear-based education that tries to scare adolescents into sexual abstinence
- Are unrealistic—adolescents will have sex; they should protect their health
- Omit critical information, such as options for birth control, including the use of condoms
- Risk alienating bisexuals, gays, lesbians, single moms, and other sexually active teens

Advocates of sex education note that although some teens claim they are virgins, accounts of mutual masturbation, oral sex, and anal sex abound among "abstaining" teens. Abstinence-based programs give one answer to a complex issue. Comprehensive Sex Education (CSE) teaches young people *how* to think through and process sexual choices, all the while providing many tools for engaging in safer activities.

What Do You Think?

1. Are Abstinence-Only Programs effective in reducing the numbers of preteens and teens who have sex before marriage?

2. Do Abstinence-Only Programs put adolescents at risk for unwanted consequences of sex, such as pregnancy and sexually transmitted infections?

3. In your opinion, what is the most effective sex education: abstinence only, birth control/prevention only, or a combination of both programs? Why did you reach this decision?

Sources: Alford (2001). Maher (2004): National Guidelines Task Force (2004).

Drs. Amie Ashcraft and Pamela Murray (2017), Department of Pediatrics at West Virginia University School of Medicine, provide us insight as to how teens feel. Their research shows us three primary areas of concern of teens when it comes to talking about sex with their parents:

- Real or perceived ignorance
- Saying too much
- Fear of difficult questions

Table 9.2 /// Sources of Anxiety for Teens When Discussing Sexuality

Real or perceived ignorance:

- Not knowing the correct language to use/sounding crude
- Not knowing the right questions to ask
- Being wrong or corrected

Saying too much:

- Revealing sexual thoughts or behaviors to the parent that might elicit criticism or punishment
- Disclosure of abuse (of self or another)

Fear of difficult questions

- Questions about current sexual behavior
- Questions about abuse
- Questions about the sexuality spectrum

Source: Adapted in part from Ashcraft & Murray (2017).

In Table 9.2, we can see that teens are just as nervous and anxious talking to their parents about sexuality as their parents are talking to them! But regardless of the jitters these conversations may cause, one fact cannot be stated strongly enough: "Conversations with parents have the potential to become the benchmarks against which teens measure other information about sexuality and serve as a buffer against early sexual activity" (Ashcraft & Murray, 2017, p. 305).

The Benefits of Talking to Kids About Sex and Sexuality

Parent–child sexual communication offers tremendous benefits to teens during a critical period of their lifespan development (Lantos et al., 2019). So far, we've already looked at teen pregnancy and birth rates, and a bit later in this chapter we'll take a look at sexually transmitted infections. Right now, it's important to know that having conversations early and often with adolescents about a wide range of sexual topics helps to reduce their sexual risk—about sexual behaviors, contraception, sexually transmitted infections, preventing pregnancy, and safer sexual alternatives, such as abstinence (Lantos et al., 2019). The benefits associated with high levels of parent–teen sexual communication are many:

- Teens are more likely to delay sexual intercourse (Commendador, 2010).
- Teens are more likely to discuss ways to prevent pregnancy and STIs (Hicks, McRee, & Eisenberg, 2013).
- Teens are more likely to use contraception, and use it in correct ways (Commendador, 2010).
- Teens are more likely to use condoms from their first sexual encounters and subsequently (Miller, Levin, Whitaker, & Xu, 1998).

Next, we need to explore the racial and ethnic differences in PCSC.

Racial/Ethnic Differences in Parent–Child Sexual Communication

Up to this point, our study has shown us that there are disparities in premarital sex, cohabitation, marriage, and childbearing by race and ethnicity. Our discussion here will shed some light on perhaps why these differences exist. Many bodies of research help us to better understand the racial and ethnic differences in parent–child sexual communication. For example, white and Black mothers have more frequent conversations with their kids and teens about sex and sexuality than Hispanic mothers do (see Lantos et. al, 2019 for a full review; Meneses, Orrell-Valente, Guendelman, Oman, & Irwin, 2006; Hutchinson, 2002).

In a study of 135 African American/Black Caribbean parent/co-parent/child triads, researchers wanted to determine what types of sexuality and health topics were discussed

Table 9.3 /// Percentage of African American/Black Caribbean Parent–Child Pairs Discussing Each Sexuality Topic

	Sons' Report of Discussion with:		Daughters' Report of Discussion with:	
	Mother	Father	Mother	Father
Risk Factor				
Alcohol	79	77	87	72
Drugs	80	77	90	75
Sexuality Education				
Puberty	71	66	88	42
Menstruation	41	25	84	31
Reproduction	67	58	75	41
Dating	63	63	79	57
What sex is	59	55	75	39
Abstinence	45	39	66	35
Sexual Risk Prevention Reduction				
Condoms	27	23	29	16
HIV AIDS	49	52	46	24

Source: Wyckoff and others (2008).

and whether parents communicated differently with their daughters than they did their sons (Wyckoff et al., 2008). Table 9.3 presents the findings of this study, and the data show us that parents of color are sexuality educators for their children. As you can see, the parents are not at all hesitant to discuss risky behaviors with their kids, such as drug and alcohol use. And although parents of color commonly and easily talk about puberty, reproduction, and dating with their children, they are a little more reluctant to converse about what sex is and abstinence and about sexual risk prevention (HIV/AIDS and the use of condoms). Contrary to the findings of the study we previously discussed that examined a predominantly white population, parent–child sexual communication with preadolescents is common among Blacks in this study. These findings are very important to our understanding of human sexuality among African Americans/Black Caribbeans because, as you will learn a bit later in this chapter, this population is at the greatest risk for acquiring sexually transmitted disease and HIV/AIDS; they are also at the greatest risk for premarital pregnancies.

Still today, little attention has been given to sexual communication among Chinese (Xiao, Li, Lin, & Jiang, 2013), and only a handful of studies have examined how this group communicates about sex (Cottrell et al., 2005; Xiao, 2012; Xiao, Li, Liu, Li, & Jiang, 2013). This is because talking about sex in public, or between people of different generations, is frowned upon in Chinese culture because of its private and sensitive nature; it is also considered to be an offensive topic (Zhang, Li, Shah, Baldwin, & Stanton, 2007; Leiber et al., 2009; Ayehu, Kassaw, & Hailu, 2016). As one group of researchers note, "[Sexual] education strategies often involve conversations with health 'experts' about condom use, safe sex, and partner communication. The gap between [communication with health experts] and the private and norm-bound nature of sex conversation is particularly challenging" (Leiber et al., 2009, p. 415). Due to this taboo, many parents today (even among Asian Americans) still believe that it is inappropriate to provide sexuality and health education/information for their children. But are these attitudes changing?

In a study of 1,319 Chinese men and women (aged 15 to 24) who reside in China, study participants were asked questions about the quality of sex communication with their parents on general topics (Zhang et al., 2007). About one-fourth of the survey respondents reported that it was easy to talk about sex with their fathers, and about one-third of them indicated it was easy to communicate with their mothers. Overall, however, the results of this study showed that parent–adolescent sex communication was less frequent in China than in Western countries, such as the United States—less than one-third of the study participants had *ever* discussed sex-related issues with their parents. But, consistent with the studies we discussed earlier and with other prior research, both male and female adolescents are more comfortable talking with their moms about sex than they are with their dads. There may be less frequent communication, but one of the most important findings of this study is that parents *are* talking to their children about sex.

A new study of 8,796 teens examined parent–teen conversations about sexual and reproductive health (SRH; Lantos et al., 2019). I've prepared Figures 9.2 and 9.3 so that you can see the contemporary gender, racial, and ethnic differences in sexual communication. The investigating team wanted to see whether there were differences in how often parents and teens talked about certain sexual topics, such as how to say no, contraception information/use, and how to use a condom.

This study revealed some very encouraging trends. First of all, communication in all content areas across all races/ethnicities improved in an approximate 10-year period. For example, in 2006 the percentage of parents talking to their male teens about any SRH topic was about 70 percent—today, it's nearly 85 percent (Lantos et al., 2019). Similarly, the percentage of Black parents talking to their male teens about any SRH topic improved from 78 percent to nearly 87 percent. The differences weren't as stark with parents talking to their female teens, and in some instances, the percentage of parents who talked to their teen daughters was less than it was 10 years prior. In 2006, for example, 82 percent of parents talked to their daughters about any SRH; today, only 79 percent do (Lantos et al., 2019). Encouragingly, however, the overall trend appears to be that parents of both daughters and sons are communicating at nearly the same levels across races and ethnicities. Because we know that parent–child and parent–teen sexual communication serves to promote better health and wellness outcomes,

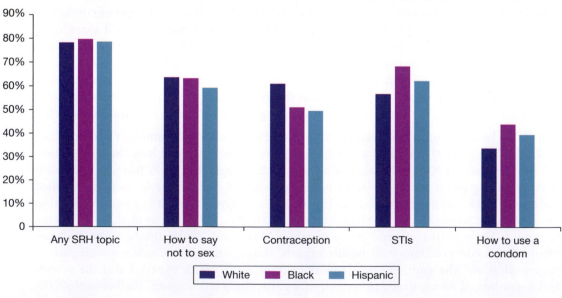

Figure 9.2 /// Percentage of U.S. Parents Who Talk to Their Daughters About Sexual and Reproductive Health, by Race and Ethnicity

Source: Lantos (2019).

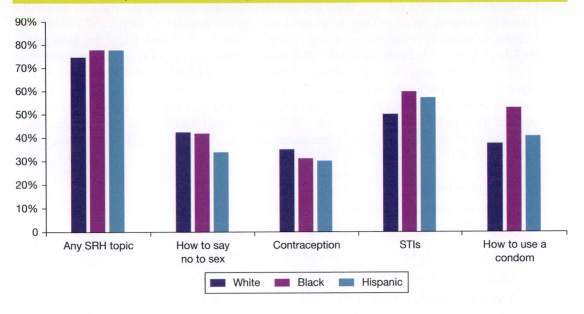

Source: Lantos and others (2019).

it is imperative that teachers, healthcare providers, clergy, social workers, and others who influence teens' behaviors encourage parents to talk to their kids about sex and sexuality.

But just what is the best way to have a conversation about sex with a child?

Sexual Communication: How to Talk to Kids About Sex

Although it does take some planning (and some courage), parents can be accurate, trustworthy, and safe sources of sex education. Planned Parenthood (2018) suggests parents do the following when talking to their kids about sex:

- *Be clear about the family's values and expectations.* It is important for parents to emphasize their faith traditions and what their values are. Parents should explain to children how their values and beliefs agree or disagree with other forms of sex education their children may be exposed to.

- *Talk about facts versus beliefs.* Parents should make sure that they present accurate, factual information, even if it challenges a personal value or religious belief they may have.

- *Don't preach.* Parents should be careful to talk *with* their children—not *at* them. They should take time to listen to their children, and find out what they think and feel about sex and sexuality,

- *Keep the conversation going.* As a popular television commercial reminds us, children have to be reminded several times a week to make their beds, brush their teeth, do their homework, or take out the trash. All too often, parents have "The Talk" with their children, rather than use "teachable moments" and casual conversations to convey information about sex.

Cultural Scenarios: Race and Ethnicity

Race and ethnicity are cultural scenarios that shape sexual scripts, and these sexual scripts in turn affect our sexual attitudes and beliefs, the types of sexual behaviors we engage in, and our sexual health practices. These cultural scripts are briefly discussed in the sections that follow.

Latinx Cultures

Because of the *marianismo* cultural mindset (see Chapter 4), Latina women are taught to assume submissive roles in their sexual relationships, allowing the men to direct the sexual encounters. In an attempt to understand Latinas' definitions of sex and sexual relationships, previous research examined young Latinas from Puerto Rico, the Dominican Republic, and Cuba (Faulkner, 2003). This body of research found that, despite influences of 21st-century culture and the increasing freedom of expression of sexuality across cultures, the study respondents indicated that they desired to be seen as sexually moral. They did not want to dress or behave in ways that suggested they were flirts but, instead, they wanted their behaviors to indicate that they were "good Latinas." In essence, this study found what is referred to as "The Commandments of Marianismo" (Hussain, Jeija, Lewis, & Sanches, 2015):

1. Do not forget a woman's place
2. Do not put your needs first
3. Do not be single, self-supporting, or independent-minded
4. Do not discuss personal problems outside the house
5. Do not wish anything but to be a housewife
6. Do not forsake tradition
7. Do not use sex for pleasure
8. Do not criticize your man
9. Do not ask for help

For many Latinas, perceived *marianismo*—and hence, sexual morality—is a significant factor that shapes their character (Hussain et al., 2015). As you can see, though, traditional characteristics of *marianismo,* and traditional studies regarding Latina sexual identity, fail to take into account the woman's sexual pleasure and satisfaction (Hall & Graham, 2012).

This *marianismo,* "good Latina" philosophy may also be why using hormonal contraception and/or using a condom is not practiced by a significant percentage of Latina women (Sastre et al., 2015). Further, *machismo* cultural values among Latino men include the role of power to decide contraceptive behavior, and *machismo* has been associated with unprotected sexual behavior and multiple sexual partners (Knipper et al., 2007; Harvey & Henderson, 2006; Hernandez, Zule, Karg, Browne, & Wechsberg, 2012).

Black Cultures

Certain populations, such as African Americans/Black Caribbeans, are in a particularly high-risk category because they tend to initiate sexual intercourse at early ages (Lindberg Maddow-Zimet, & Marcell, 2019).

On the whole, Blacks become sexually active at much younger ages; have more sexual partners over their lifetime; have more casual sexual partners; are less likely to marry or to have long-term, stable marriages; and have many more children born outside of marriage than other racial/ethnic groups do (Lindberg et al., 2019; Smith, 2006; Kinsey Institute, 2007). One study examined the sexual behaviors and attitudes of 744 Black high schoolers and found several personal and family factors that shaped their sexual scripts and were associated with the age at which they first had sex. These factors included such things as cultural perceptions of risky sexual behaviors and perceived cultural norms as to when it is "acceptable" to have sex or whether it is "okay" to have sex (Lindley, Joshi, & Vincent, 2007). To the extent that the study participants experienced parental involvement and communication, and to the extent that adolescents held the sexual attitude that it was socially acceptable to delay sexual intercourse, adolescents were more likely to delay having sex.

Researchers have also discovered that female African American study participants hold to traditional sex scripts prescribed by their culture—that is, being submissive in their heterosexual relationships (Bowleg et al., 2004; Seal, Smith, Coley, Perry, & Gamez, 2008; Hussen, Bowleg, Sangaramoorthy, & Malebranche, 2012; Bowleg et al., 2015). This prevailing cultural scenario encourages women to assume a passive role in their sexual relationships, despite the fact that this passive role may put them at greater risk for acquiring a sexually transmitted infection or HIV.

Asian Cultures

Within traditional Asian culture, sexual behaviors and expressions outside of marriage are considered to be inappropriate and a violation of their strict moral conduct; thus, modesty and restrained sexuality are highly valued. Investigations into Asian American sexuality indicate that today, adolescents and young adults express more sexually conservative beliefs, attitudes, and behaviors, and have first sexual intercourse experiences at a later age, than do those in Western cultures (Okazaki, 2002; Ahluwalia, Suzuki, & Mir, 2018; Edwards, Liu, & Dennis, 2015). Because of the taboo nature of sexuality in this culture, it is often difficult to study this racial group, but available data suggest that Asian Americans show conservatism in their sexual scripts. For instance, they hold later sexual timetables for initiating all types of sexual behavior in comparison to other ethnic groups, and they are less likely than any racial/ethnic group to have had sex as an adolescent (Okazaki, 2002). Similar patterns are seen among Asian American college students.

Native American Cultures

In all aspects of their lives, Native Americans' beliefs, attitudes, and behaviors are deeply embedded within their religious traditions that emphasize respect and reverence. But how these beliefs shape their sexual scripts is unknown because Native Americans are among the most misunderstood and understudied ethnic groups in our culture due to their relative cultural isolation (Hellerstedt, Peterson-Hickey, Rhodes, & Garwick, 2006). However, we do know from the available research that the family is the primary influence on Native Americans' sexual scripts. For instance, one body of research found that involvement with family and family support, and the family s scholastic values, were associated with safer sexual behaviors (Chewning and others, 2001). Another recent study found that the strongest influence of positive sexual scripts among Native Americans was having a father present in the home (Hellerstedt et al., 2006).

Arab American Cultures

Not all Arab Americans adhere to the Muslim faith, as you saw in Chapter 1; here, though, it is necessary to discuss Islam because these beliefs significantly influence the sexual scripts of those who practice this religion.

Within Islam, religious and cultural customs and rituals reinforce traditional gender roles wherein women raise and nurture the children and men protect and provide for the family. As a result, many Arab Americans' sexuality is strongly shaped by traditional Arab views of honor and modesty, as well as by the values of Islam (Davis & Davis, 1993). Perhaps one of the best examples of modesty is the veil, or the *hijab,* that some Muslim women wear in public. Many Arab Americans believe that the *hijab* is a religious mandate because, according to Muslim religious tenets, a woman's hair is to be covered because it's the very essence of her sensuality and sexuality (Abboud, Jemmott, & Sommers, 2015; Zahedi, 2007).

The Islamic religion is sex-positive and because of this attitude, sex and sexuality are viewed as gifts from God, or Allah; sexuality is thought to be the right of every person, and sexual pleasure is seen as an essential part of human life (Boellstorff, 2005). Virginity (relating to the presence of a hymen) is embodied in Arab American women's sexual scripts (Abboud et al., 2015). Marriage is the social institution that is believed to organize and control sexuality,

Lucas Oleniuk/Toronto Star via Getty Images

In some Islamic cultures, the hijab is a religious mandate for a woman because it covers her hair—her very essence of being a sexual person.

so this culture's sex scripts are very strict about sex outside of marriage for women (such as adultery, premarital sex, and prostitution).

Our sexual behaviors and sexual decisions are guided and directed by the society and culture in which we are raised. Although sometimes it can seem tedious (and perhaps boring) to explore the demographics and characteristics associated with different cultural groups, doing so is very important. Aside from needing to understand the general trends so you have a solid knowledge base in the formation and maintenance of sexual scripts, doing so is necessary on a relational level. As you saw in the previous chapter, interracial and interfaith relationships are on the increase in the United States and in many other Western cultures. Given that many of you may someday enter into an interracial or interfaith relationship, it is important that you understand the influences your culture has not only on *your* sexuality but also on *your partner's*. With this understanding, you can each better appreciate—and enjoy—your sexuality and your sexual relationship.

The influences of parents and other cultural factors on our sexual scripts lessen as we get older, although these influences will always be at least a part of "who" we are as a sexual person. Other important aspects of sexual scripts are the biological contributions that include sexual arousal and desire, and response.

OUR SEXUAL SELVES

The media are screaming "sex, sex, and more sex" to today's adolescents and young adults, yet she often doesn't understand or accept her body; he often feels that he doesn't measure up to her sexual expectations (or to his own)—and the act of sex becomes a proving ground. Certainly, it is clear that today's young men and women are barraged with images of sexuality at an early age, but they are not taught how their bodies respond to sexual stimulation—or why. Each semester when I teach the sexuality information in my marriage and family classes, there is never enough time to answer all the questions my students have about sex. They want to know such things as, "How important a role does the clitoris really play in my girlfriend's sexual response?" "Is it okay to have anal sex?" "Why is it that my boyfriend can become sexually excited so much quicker than I can?" and "Why is it that I can have an orgasm when I masturbate, but not when I have sex with my fiancé?"

In the following section, we'll examine human sexual response. Having a good understanding of sexual arousal and desire, and of sexual response, allows us to comprehend not only *how* our bodies work but *why* we respond the way we do. It also allows us to appreciate how and why our partners respond the way they do. Knowing and understanding our bodies increases our sexual pleasure and satisfaction as well as enhances our sexual relationships.

Sizzle and Sigh: Sexual Arousal and Desire

Do women want sex as much as men do? Are men more easily sexually aroused than women? What are sexual turn-ons for men and women? Do women get turned on by viewing erotic materials—or are they offended by such pictures or movies? What makes us sizzle, sigh, and curl our toes? These are common questions students ask, and they speak to our need as human beings to understand a relationship process that is vitally important to most couples—the act of sex.

Despite popular belief that there is a huge gap between men's and women's sexual arousal and desire, empirical evidence shows us that healthy men and women easily become sexually aroused by "[any] sexually meaningful stimulus" (Laan & Both, 2008, p. 510). Without a sexual stimulus, there is no sexual desire. You may be asking, "So what is a sexual stimulus?" The answer is simple: It depends.

For most of us, our sexual scripts are largely responsible for what sexually stimulates us. For example, what is your cultural background? Your religious background? Who were your *sex models* as you were growing up—were your parents affectionate (holding hands, patting bottoms) in front of you, or did they seldom show affection for one another in front of the children? Are you comfortable in your own skin, or do you struggle with your body image? Other than research that examines how people respond to erotic books, photos, and movies, there are no scientific studies that address what men and women find to be sexually stimulating; this is probably because the potential sex stimuli are potentially endless, given the individual nature of them. There are physical things we can do that are sexually stimulating,

What makes us sizzle and sigh and curl our toes? For most of us, our sexual scripts determine what sexually stimulates us. This is why it's so important to communicate what turns you on (and what doesn't) to your partner. And, once you have the first conversation, don't let it end there—make it a priority to keep the conversation going!

Table 9.4 /// The Phases of Sexual Response

Physician William Masters and psychologist Virginia Johnson (1966) scientifically measured human sexual response in men and women. They determined that women and men experience four distinct phases of sexual response.

The Phases of Sexual Response

- **Excitement phase**. Within the very first few seconds of this phase, a man's penis becomes erect. Women experience vaginal lubrication, which is a "sweating" on the vaginal walls.

- **Plateau phase**. Both men and women experience an increase in heart rate, blood pressure, and rate of breathing. Involuntary muscle tension occurs; this is what gives us the "toe curling" feelings of muscle intensity during sex.

- **Orgasm Phase**. This phase involves the sudden release of the muscle tension and blood engorgement that has occurred in the penis (males) and labia (females). The intensity of orgasms varies from one sex act to another and is influenced by how recent and how often intercourse or masturbation has taken place.

- **Resolution**. In both men and women, the heart rate, blood pressure, and respiration return to pre-excitement levels. The penis returns to its flaccid state. Men experience a refractory period, when they are incapable of achieving an erection. The length of the **refractory period** is directly associated with age and other factors such as health and lifestyle habits. Women do not experience refractory periods and are capable of multiple orgasms if they are effectively stimulated.

Refractory period: the period following orgasm when men are incapable of achieving an erection. The length of the refractory period is directly associated with age and other factors such as health and lifestyle habits.

such as kissing and touching, and there are also emotional turn-ons, such as having a strong body image or self-esteem. As sexual arousal begins, we begin the four phases of sexual response, which are presented in Table 9.4. But ultimately, great sex isn't just about knowing each other's hot spots. To have great sex, partners need to have great communication. Being able to tell our sexual partners what feels good and what doesn't feel good, and what works and what doesn't work, not only helps us to become better lovers but it also deepens the intimacy bonds.

Other Kinds of Sex

Sex encompasses many other behaviors besides sexual intercourse. These behaviors are termed **noncoital** and include masturbation, oral-genital sex, and anal sex.

Self-stimulation of the genitals, or **masturbation**, was damned by theologians in the past as a weakness of the flesh and a sin against nature. But by the 1990s, not only was masturbation accepted, but it became the topic of television shows, such as a popular episode of *Seinfeld* in which there was a contest among the main characters to see who could refrain from masturbating the longest and remain the "master of [his or her] domain."

In the Janus Report on Sexual Behavior (Janus & Janus, 1993), two-thirds of male respondents agreed with the survey statement, "Masturbation is a natural part of life and continues in marriage." Using data from 18- to 20-year-old college males, another body of research discovered that 67 percent of the study participants had masturbated by age 15 (Leitenberg, Detzer, & Srebnik, 1993) Sex researcher Carolyn Halpern and her colleagues (2000), in their examination of adolescent males' willingness to report masturbation, similarly found that the majority of the study participants had engaged in solitary sexual practices. Given that the data from these studies were generated via self-report mechanisms, how accurate are the numbers? As a sex therapist colleague of mine remarked, "About 95 percent of men indicate that they masturbate—and the other 5 percent lie."

Janus and Janus (1993) found that 88 percent of married women reported that they masturbated. That women masturbate is not simply a function of today's more liberating practices for female sexuality.

Noncoital: sexual activities besides sexual intercourse, such as masturbation, oral-genital sex, and anal sex.

Masturbation: sexual self-stimulation.

"I did not have sexual relations with that woman!" declared President Bill Clinton in an address to the nation on January 26, 1998, in response to Clinton's well-publicized extra-marital relationship with a 20-something White House intern. The nation was brought to polarity in opinions as the question of the decade presented itself to the American people: Is oral sex "sex"?

Cunnilingus involves the erotic oral stimulation of the woman's external sex organs; **fellatio** is the oral stimulation of the male's external sex organs. **Oral-genital sex (oral sex)** is practiced by all couple types: heterosexual, gay, lesbian, cohabiting, and bisexuals, and it is typically engaged in more by white middle-class individuals than by Black or Hispanic individuals (Leichliter, Chandra, Liddon, Fenton, & Aral, 2007). Additionally, the practice is becoming more acceptable and common among today's youth. In fact, children as young as age 11 reported engaging in oral sex (Booth, 2001). According to Dr. Jonathan Trager (2009), "They think they can participate in an intense sexual act while staying a virgin" (p. 1). College students apparently agree. In a study that focused on gender differences in beliefs held by university students about sexuality, both men and women agreed with the statement, "Oral sex is not sex" (Knox, Zusman, & McNeely, 2008).

Anal intercourse is the sexual activity of the male placing his penis into his partner's anus and rectum; **anal eroticism** can include anal intercourse, as well as oral stimulation of the anus, manually stroking the outside of the anus, and inserting one or more fingers into the anus. Stimulating the anus is very erotic for most people because it contains a vast supply of nerve endings.

Anal intercourse and anal eroticism are an integral aspect of sexual pleasure among gay men (Blumstein & Schwartz, 1983; Leichliter et al., 2007), but many people incorrectly believe that anal intercourse/stimulation/eroticism is practiced only by homosexual men. In actuality, data from a recent U.S. study of more than 12,000 men and women aged 15 to 44 reveal that nearly one-third of those surveyed indicated they had engaged in anal sex as a sexual behavior (Leichliter et al., 2007); additionally, 1 in 10 female and male adolescents have engaged in heterosexual anal sex.

As we age and experience different relationships with others, whether they are friendships, casual sexual hookups, or serious intimate relationships (that may or may not include sex), we incorporate these new experiences into our sexual scripts. Your sex scripts are not fixed by a certain age; instead, like any other process associated with intimate relationships (such as love, intimacy, and communication), sexual scripts change over time—you continually affect and are affected by your relationships and other cultural/environmental influences.

Sexuality in Adolescence and Early Adulthood

Puberty encompasses skeletal, muscular, and reproductive maturation, but we commonly tend to associate this universal developmental stage as the time when sexual maturation occurs, the time when we are "awakened" sexually. Although some children may begin masturbation as early as the first or second grade (Weinstein & Rosen, 2006), most of us become more aware of our sexuality—and desire to act on these new feelings and sensations-—during early adolescence. Figure 9.4 presents an overview of the sexual orientation of teens today. It's important to understand, however, that during the adolescent years of development, sexual attraction, behavior, and identity are not always aligned (ACT for Youth, 2018).

Adolescents and Sex: What the Numbers Say

Young people are engaging in sexual activity—and their attitudes about sexuality and sexual expression are becoming increasingly open-minded. Adolescent sex and sexuality are of great interest to social science researchers and demographers because often the behaviors put adolescents at risk for a number of health concerns, such as unwanted pregnancies, violence, and sexually transmitted diseases (O'Donnell et al., 2006).

Cunnilingus:
the erotic, oral stimulation of the woman's external sex organs.

Fellatio:
the oral stimulation of the male's external sex organs.

Oral-genital sex (oral sex):
stimulation of the genitals using the mouth or tongue.

Anal intercourse:
the sexual activity of the male placing his penis into his partner's anus.

Anal eroticism:
sexual activity that includes anal intercourse as well as oral stimulation of the anus, manually stroking the outside of the anus, and inserting one or more fingers into the anus.

Figure 9.4 /// Teen Sexual Orientation

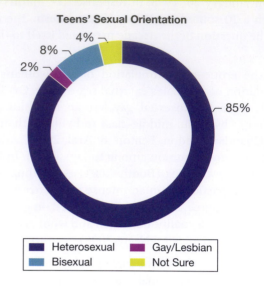

Teens' Sexual Orientation

4%
8%
2%
85%

- Heterosexual
- Bisexual
- Gay/Lesbian
- Not Sure

Source: Kann, McManus, Harries, et al. (2018).

The age at which adolescents lose their virginity has varied across time (National Campaign to Prevent Teen Pregnancy, 2018). In a study that examined the sexual histories of 500 Americans and 500 Europeans (Zava, 2018), the researchers found that except for Baby Boomers, each consecutively younger generation lost their virginity at an earlier age:

- Baby Boomers: 17.6 years old
- Generation X: 18.1 years old
- Millennials: 17.4 years old
- Generation Z: 16.2 years old

However, between 1991 and 2015, the proportion of students in the United States who have ever had sexual intercourse decreased from 66.7 percent to 40 percent; this is the lowest level of sexual behavior observed since data were first gathered in 1991 (Guttmacher, 2018). The likelihood of being sexually active increases each year a student is in school (Guttmacher, 2018):

- 20 percent of ninth graders have had sexual intercourse.
- 36 percent of 10th graders have had sexual intercourse.
- 47 percent of 11th graders have had sexual intercourse.
- 57 percent of 12th graders have had sexual intercourse.

Of course, there are gender and racial/ethnic differences in the percentages of both high school students having had sexual intercourse and those who used condoms at last intercourse.

There is an encouraging downward trend in the number of students who report having sex, and this trend is occurring across all racial and ethnic groups. These data are presented in Figure 9.5 (females) and Figure 9.6 (males). Between 2013 and 2017, the proportion of U.S. high school students who had ever had sexual intercourse declined across racial, ethnic and gender groups. As you can see, Black females had a decrease in sexual intercourse by 26 percent, while African American males had a decrease of 23 percent. Unfortunately, only a small percentage of sexually active females in 2017 had used a condom when they last had intercourse (Guttmacher, 2018):

- Black females: 24 percent
- Hispanic females: 21 percent
- White females: 12 percent

Among their male counterparts:

- Black males: 10 percent
- Hispanic males: 15 percent
- White males: 7 percent

Figure 9.5 /// Percentage of Female Students Who Have Had Sex, by Race and Ethnicity (2013 and 2017)

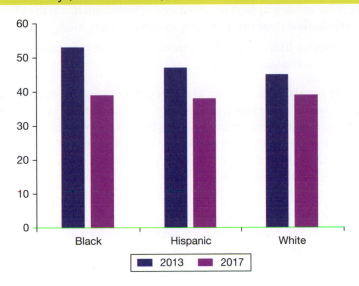

Source: Guttmacher Institute (2017).

Figure 9.6 /// Percentage of Male Students Who Have Had Sex, by Race and Ethnicity (2013 and 2017)

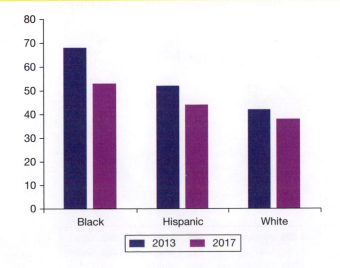

Source: Guttmacher Institute (2017).

Consequences of Adolescent Sexual Behaviors

It is quite concerning that so few students use contraception routinely. Although there are obvious consequences of sexual behaviors for any age group, such as acquiring an STI or experiencing an unwanted pregnancy, there are other consequences that also affect this age group. In a study that wanted to identify the physical, social, and emotional consequences for 275 high schoolers (all about age 14) who engaged in oral and/or vaginal sex for the first time, students reported on a number of items, such as, "I got in trouble with my parents after I had sex," "I got a bad reputation," and "I feel bad about myself (Brady & Halpern-Felsher, 2007). General findings of this study include the following:

- Students believe that oral sex is associated with fewer negative consequences than vaginal sex.
- Students who had only oral sex were less likely to feel guilty or used, feel their relationship got worse, or get in trouble with their parents.
- Girls were twice as likely as boys to report feeling bad about themselves following a sex act, and they were almost three times as likely to report feeling used.
- Boys were twice as likely to report an increase in their popularity after reporting their sexual activities to friends.

It is clear that there are significant medical and social consequences of adolescent sex, but as this study shows us, teenagers do feel that there are some positive consequences of having sex. These are somewhat concerning findings because experiencing positive outcomes, such as an increase in popularity, may encourage sexual behavior—convincing teens (particularly boys) that there is a negative side with potential life-changing outcomes may be difficult (Brady & Halpern-Felsher, 2007).

Many of you reading this text are in the developmental stage of early adulthood, and many of you may feel that you are in the "prime" of your lives with regard to your social lives and your sex lives. You are still discovering *who* you are sexually and how your sexuality coexists with your partner's. As you saw in Chapter 7, many young adults explore and experience their sexuality through dating relationships, cohabiting relationships, and hooking up.

Doing It: Sexuality in Early Adulthood

Figure 9.7 shows how college students today describe their sexual identity. What's interesting to note is that, compared to high school students, college students are much more keenly aware of their identity and ways in which to identify themselves.

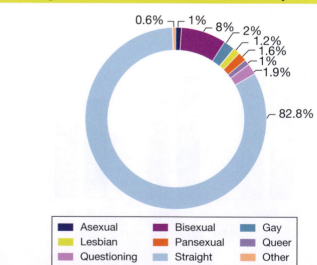

Figure 9.7 /// College Students' Sexual Orientation/Identity

0.6% — 1% — 8% — 2% — 1.2% — 1.6% — 1% — 1.9% — 82.8%

Legend:
- Asexual
- Lesbian
- Questioning
- Bisexual
- Pansexual
- Straight
- Gay
- Queer
- Other

Source: National College Health Assessment (2018).

Is everyone doing it on college campuses? The National College Health Assessment (NCHA, 2018) provides a glimpse into the sex and health behaviors of America's college students. In their recent national survey of 26,121 college students, the NCHA found that nearly 35 percent of the study participants had not had sex within the past 12 months. Table 9.5 shows the percentages of college students who had sex within the past 12 months. Table 9.6 presents the percentages of college students who had oral sex, vaginal sex, and anal sex within the past 30 days.

One study that focused on oral sex behaviors among college students revealed some very interesting findings in regard to college students' knowledge about the safety of oral sex, their knowledge about the transmission of sexually transmitted infections via oral sex, and their knowledge of what protects them against sexually transmitted infections and HIV during oral sex (Chambers, 2007). For instance, although the majority of the 2,100 research participants

Table 9.5 /// Percentage of College Students Who Had Sex in the Past 12 Months

	Male	Female	Total
College students reported within the last 12 months having:			
No sexual partner	36.6	33.5	34.6
1 sexual partner	37.8	43.7	41.6
2 sexual partners	9.2	9.4	9.3
3 sexual partners	5.8	5.3	5.4
4 or more sexual partners	10.6	8.2	9.0

Source: National College Health Assessment (2018); American College Health Association.

Table 9.6 /// Percentage of College Students Who Had Sex in the Past 30 Days

	Male	Female	Total
Oral Sex within the Past 30 Days			
Never did this sexual act	33.4	32.3	32.7
Have not done this the past 30 days	26.9	25.2	25.8
Did this one or more times	39.7	42.5	41.5
Vaginal Sex within the Past 30 Days			
Never did this sexual act	39.3	33.9	35.8
Have not done this the past 30 days	22.4	18.3	19.4
Did this one or more times	39.3	47.8	44.8
Anal Sex within the Past 30 Days			
Never did this sexual act	74.3	77.4	76.2
Have not done this the past 30 days	19.4	18.9	18.8
Did this one or more times	6.4	4.1	5.0

Source: National College Health Assessment (2018).

Alcohol and sex are a bad combination for college students, particularly college women. It's important to remember that if a woman says "no" to sexual behaviors and activities (even kissing), it *always means NO*—even if she has had something (or a lot) to drink.

iStock.com/PeskyMonkey

were aware of the risks associated with oral sex (such as acquiring an STI), women were less knowledgeable than men when it came to protecting themselves during oral sex—up to nearly three-fourths of the students were not aware of the ways to practice safe oral sex, such as males using condoms or women making dental dams from condoms.

The findings of this study give us insight into sexual behaviors of young adults. What is particularly interesting is that women give more oral sex than men do, and men indicate that they receive oral sex more than women do (Chambers, 2007). Does this mean that women use oral sex more frequently as a means to please their male sex partner? Or does this mean they are less receptive to receiving oral sex? More research is needed in this area. Also, oral sex is no longer considered to be just a prelude to sexual intercourse; instead, it is something college students participate in for the act itself. Alarmingly, nearly 51 percent of college males and 45 percent of college females surveyed did not use a method of contraception the last time they had sex, and one-fourth of the males indicated they used the withdrawal method (NCHA, 2018). Also concerning is the fact that females tend to rely on birth control pills, shots, or implants for contraception. Although these methods are effective in preventing pregnancy, they *are not* effective in preventing STIs or HIV.

Spring Break and Sex

As you saw in Chapter 7, sexual hookups on college campuses are common. But in addition to college campuses, Spring Break is a time when many emerging adults engage in either planned or unplanned sexual activity (Garcia, Reiber, Massey, & Merriwether, 2012). Make no mistake about it: Alcohol and sex are a dangerous combination for college women. In a study of 644 college women by the American Medical Association (AMA, 2006), Spring Break binge drinking lead to unsafe and unwanted sex, sexually transmitted infections, blackouts, and violence. Key findings of this relevant study reveal that among study participants,

- 83 percent drank every night while on Spring Break, or had friends who did.
- 74 percent believed that drinking is an excuse to engage in outrageous behaviors.
- 86 percent believed that these outrageous behaviors contributed to dangerous behaviors by males toward females.

- 57 percent agreed that being sexually promiscuous was a way to fit in with the crowd.
- 92 percent said that it was very easy to obtain alcohol.
- 59 percent knew friends who had sex with more than one partner during the week of Spring Break.
- 3 out of every 5 respondents had friends who had unprotected sex during Spring Break.
- 1 in 5 women regretted the sexual activity they engaged in during Spring Break.
- 12 percent felt forced to have sex.

The National College Health Assessment also tracks alcohol and drug use among college students. In 2018, slightly more than 61 percent of college students reported that they had alcoholic drinks within the last 30 days (NCHA, 2018). Relative to our discussion here, college students who drank alcohol reported experiencing a number of negative consequences and emotions, as seen in Figure 9.8. Relevant to our discussion here, you can see that a number of students engaged in risky behaviors while drinking, such as doing something they later regretted and having unprotected sex.

The combination of alcohol and sex is treacherous. The AMA (2006) notes that each spring in Cancun, Mexico, a popular Spring Break destination, there is a significant increase in the numbers of deaths, rapes, and assaults reported, and all are related to drinking. In 2005 during Spring Break in Daytona, Florida, another popular beach destination, twice as many rape cases were reported than in any other month of the year. As a matter of safety and well-being for college students, the AMA contends that universities and colleges need to change their current policies, requiring Spring Break tour promoters to restrict ads that promote cheap and free alcohol or to offer Spring Break alternatives that do not include alcohol.

You are beginning to understand that your sexuality does not develop in isolation. Throughout your lifespan, your sexual development is multifaceted, shaped, and reshaped by many interacting influences. Who you are as a sexual person and how you came to be the sexual person you are is a complex tapestry woven together from biological, developmental, and cultural influences. And who you will be as an older sexual person is no exception. We will explore many facets of sexuality development during middle and late adulthood in Chapter 16.

Figure 9.8 /// Drinking and Consequences

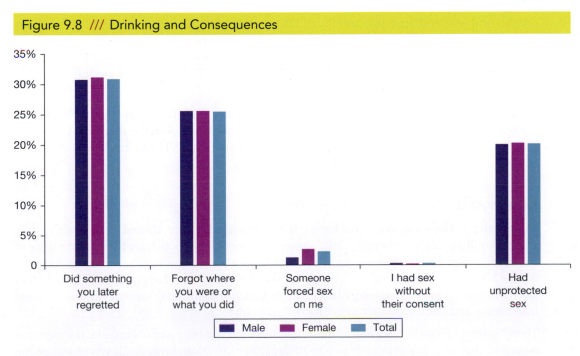

Source: National College Health Assessment (2018).

SEXUALLY TRANSMITTED INFECTIONS

Sexually transmitted infections (STI):

infectious diseases transmitted between partners through sexual contact.

Sexually transmitted infections (STIs) are diseases that are transmitted between partners through sexual contact, such as vaginal intercourse, oral sex, nonpenetrative genital contact, or anal sex, and they remain one of our nation's greatest health challenges. America today has reached an all-time high of sexually transmitted infections: nearly 2.3 million new cases were diagnosed in 2018, and 1 out of 2 sexually active persons will contract an STI (Centers for Disease Control and Prevention, 2019). Just as distressing, the U.S. is seeing a plateau in its fight against HIV (Centers for Disease Control and Prevention, 2019).

Because all of us who are sexually active are at risk, it is necessary to have an understanding of the trends, treatments, and prevention of common STIs. By gaining an understanding of STIs, young men and women can protect their sexual and reproductive health and they can better enjoy their sexuality. In addition to the burden on youth and young adults, women are also severely affected because their physiology places them at greater risk than men for the severe consequences of STIs (Centers for Disease Control, 2019).

There are two broad categories of sexually transmitted illnesses. Bacterial infections include gonorrhea, chlamydia, and syphilis. Caused by certain micro-organisms, bacterial infections can be treated with antibiotics. Viral infections include herpes, human papillomavirus (HPV), and viral hepatitis. These diseases cannot be treated with antibiotics, although there are medications that help alleviate or lessen the symptoms. Unless otherwise noted, all data trends are gathered from the Centers for Disease Control and Prevention (2019).

Gonorrhea

Gonorrhea:

the second most common sexually transmitted infection reported in the United States; sometimes referred to as *the clap* or *the drip*; it is transmitted through intercourse, oral sex, and anal sex, and it can also be transmitted from the mother to her baby during childbirth.

Sometimes referred to as the *clap* or *drip,* **gonorrhea** is the second most common STI reported in the United States. On average, more than a half a million people are diagnosed with gonorrhea each year. Racial disparities in gonorrhea rates are severe. African Americans have more than 8 times the rate of infection compared to whites: while there are 66 cases per 100,000 population among whites, there are 548 cases per 100,000 among Blacks. Native Americans/Alaska Natives have similar rates of infection, with 363 infections per 100,000 population.

Gonorrhea is caused by a bacterium that survives in the mucous membranes of the body, such as the eyes, throat, mouth, cervix, rectum, and urethra. It is transmitted through intercourse, oral sex, and anal sex, and it can also be transmitted from the mother to her baby during birth; ejaculation does not have to occur for gonorrhea to be transmitted or acquired. In most cases, there are no symptoms of gonorrhea: 80 percent of women and 10 percent of men with the STI show no symptoms. Most people do not know that they are infected; nevertheless, they are still able to infect their sex partners.

Because gonorrhea is a bacterial infection, it responds to antibiotics, such as penicillin. There is a wide range of antibiotics used today to treat gonorrhea; however, the disease is becoming more resistant to the standard treatments. Left untreated, this STI can cause pelvic inflammatory disease in women, causing infertility.

Chlamydia

Chlamydia:

the most common bacterial sexually transmitted infection reported in the United States; it is transmitted through vaginal and anal intercourse and from a mother to her baby during birth.

Chlamydia is the most common bacterial STI reported in the United States, with more than 1.7 million cases reported in 2017; however, demographers believe that the majority of chlamydia cases are unreported. As with other STIs, African Americans, American Indians/Alaska Natives, and Hispanics are disproportionately affected, and approximately one-half of all chlamydia cases occur among Blacks. The disease is transmitted through vaginal and anal intercourse and from a mother to her baby during birth.

Three-fourths of women and half of men experience no symptoms of chlamydia. If symptoms do occur, they may begin as early as 5 to 10 days after infection; however, if symptoms occur, most experience them within 1 to 3 weeks after they have become infected (Johnsen, 2005).

Chlamydia is very easy to treat with antibiotics. In fact, one treatment is given in only one dose. Commonly, the antibiotics are taken over the course of 7 days. To avoid the risk of re-infection, both partners are typically treated and are advised to be tested again after treatment before they resume sexual activity.

Syphilis

Syphilis is a bacterial infection that is spread through direct contact with a syphilis sore, which typically occurs on the external genitals, vagina, or anus. These sores can also develop on the lips, tongue, or mouth. This STI is transmitted through vaginal, oral, and anal sex, as well as from the mother to her unborn baby during birth. If a mother is untreated, her unborn baby has a 70 percent chance of being infected with syphilis during birth; more than 40 percent of babies are stillborn if the mother is untreated. The syphilis rate among Blacks is nearly 5 times higher than that of whites (rates are per 100,000):

- African Americans/Black Caribbeans: 24.2
- Hispanics: 11.8
- American Indians/Alaska Natives: 11.1
- Whites: 5.3
- Asians: 4.4

Syphilis:
a sexually transmitted bacterial infection caused by a microscopic organism; may be either congenital or acquired through sexual contact or contaminated needles.

There are three stages of syphilis:

1. During the primary stage, the first sore, or *chancre* (SHANK-ker), appears at the site of the infection. This usually occurs 10 days to 3 months after contact; the site of the infection is often internal and not visible to the eye. During this stage, there are no other symptoms.

2. About 3 to 6 weeks after the chancre appears, a rash develops over some or all of the body. This is called the secondary stage. During this stage, an infected person may also experience headaches, fever, fatigue, sore throat, and enlarged lymph nodes. These symptoms disappear without treatment.

3. Even left untreated, syphilis goes into a latent period, during which the infected person is no longer contagious. During this stage, however, about one-third will experience damage to the heart, brain, eyes, and nervous system. Untreated, this can result in mental illness and even death.

Can syphilis be treated? Yes. Even during the latent stage of the disease, patients can be treated and cured, although the damage that occurs is irreversible. The drug of choice since the 1940s is penicillin.

Herpes

Herpes is a *viral* infection. It is caused when the herpes simplex virus (HSV) enters the body. Once a virus enters the body, it has the capability of reproducing itself—it cannot be destroyed by antibiotics like bacterial infections can be. Consequently, once a person becomes infected with a viral sexually transmitted infection, he or she will have it for the rest of his or her life. When the viral infection occurs on or near the mouth, it is called *oral herpes;* when it occurs on or near the genitals, it is called *genital herpes.* Each year, nearly 1 million people are infected with genital herpes, and nationwide, at least 45 million people over the age of 12 have had genital HSV—this represents 1 out of 5 adolescents/adults. Today, about 1 in every 5 women and 1 out of 10 men has herpes.

Herpes:
a sexually transmitted infection caused by the herpes simplex virus; it is transmitted through touching and kissing and through vaginal, anal, or oral sex.

The virus is transmitted through touching and kissing, and through vaginal, anal, or oral sex. Generally, transmission occurs from an infected partner who is not aware that he or she has the virus. Most people are not aware that they are infected with genital herpes. Those that have symptoms notice the development of a herpes sore, usually within *2* weeks after the person is infected. The blister-like sores will open and "weep," and then scab over and heal in 2 to 4 weeks. It is important to note that most people with herpes will not develop these blisters, and if they do, the blisters may be so mild that they are mistaken for a bug bite or skin rash.

After the first outbreak or episode of genital herpes, most people will have four or five additional outbreaks within the first year. There is no cure for genital herpes. Usually, over a period of 5 or 6 years, the outbreaks of the sores become less frequent and weaker, gradually disappearing all together. If a person experiences more than six outbreaks in a 1-year period, there are medications that can help reduce the frequency and the symptoms of the virus. These types of treatment are called *suppressive therapy* because while they do not cure the infection, they alleviate the symptoms.

Human Papilloma Virus (HPV)

Human papillomavirus (HPV):

a common sexually transmitted infection that can lead to six different types of cancer later in life.

The **human papillomavirus (HPV)** is the most common sexually transmitted infection in the United States. Experts estimate that three out of four sexually active men and women will be infected with HPV at some point. In its more severe form, high-risk HPV can lead to certain cancers, such as cancer of the cervix, vagina, anus, and penis. Other types of the virus, low risk, can cause genital warts. This STI is spread through vaginal, oral, and anal intercourse, as well as through skin-to-skin contact, such as during sex play and body rubbing.

In most cases of HPV, there are no symptoms. The virus lives, undetected, in the skin or mucous membranes of the body. Sometimes a symptom of the virus is the appearance of genital warts, which are soft, moist, pink/flesh-colored growths found on the vulva, vagina, anus, cervix, penis, scrotum, groin, or thigh. These warts may appear anywhere from 6 weeks to 9 months after infection, or not at all. Most people learn of their infection upon visual diagnosis of a wart or cluster of warts. Women are typically diagnosed by a PAP test, which is a routine cancer-screening tool.

The human papillomavirus can be treated, but not cured. But because most of the cases of HPV are low-risk cases and go away by themselves, HPV is considered to be relatively harmless. To keep the warts from growing and multiplying, doctors have several treatment options:

- Applying chemical solutions that destroy the warts
- Removing the warts by freezing them with liquid nitrogen (cryotherapy)
- Removing the warts with surgery or lasers

There is a vaccine that is highly effective against the types of genital HPV that cause most cases of cervical cancer and genital warts. The vaccine, *Gardasil,* is given in three shots over a six-month period. It is routinely recommended for 11- and 12-year-old boys and girls and for males and females ages 13 through 26 who have not yet been vaccinated. If you are sexually active and have not yet had the vaccination, your healthcare provider on campus will be able to give you helpful information.

Viral Hepatitis

Viral hepatitis:

an inflammation of the liver causing impairments in liver function; there are three types of viral hepatitis: Hepatitis A, Hepatitis B, and Hepatitis C.

In general, **viral hepatitis** refers to inflammation of the liver, causing impairments in liver function. There are three types of viral hepatitis:

1. *Hepatitis A (HAV),* which is spread through infected fecal matter that is found in water and in food. This type of hepatitis is usually transmitted when people do not wash their hands after using the bathroom.

2. *Hepatitis B (HBV),* which is transmitted through bodily fluids during sexual contact, such as through semen, vaginal fluids, saliva, blood, and urine.

3. *Hepatitis C (HCV),* which is typically spread through illegal drug use (infected needles), and unscreened blood transfusions.

HBV is the most common type of hepatitis. Each year in the United States, 80,000 people are infected with HBV; about 1 in 20 Americans will become infected with HBV at some point during their lives. Because hepatitis is a viral infection, it cannot be treated by the use of antibiotics.

Understanding and protecting your sexual health is essential. Not only is it crucial to your overall health during your reproductive years, and to having a child or avoiding an unwanted pregnancy, but it also affects the health of the next generation—the children you may bear. But the importance of sexual health goes beyond your childbearing years. It directly contributes to your intimate relationships in many areas, including sexual fulfillment, and the physical and emotional comfort and closeness you share with your partner.

RELATIONSHIPS AND SEX

None of us simply become "sexual" once we make the transition from adolescence into early adulthood or enter into a life partnership with someone we love—our sexual selves are in a continuous state of growth and change. Yet to fully develop our sexuality and sexual potential, we need an intimate partnership because sexual expression most often occurs in the context of interpersonal relationships (Ridley, Ogolsky, Payne, Totenhagen, & Gate, 2008).

Simon Montefiore (1993), in his qualitative study of "not-thirtysomething" sex (sex in our 30s, 40s, and beyond) noted, "Many of the married couples I spoke to have fantastic sex lives—even if none of them have sex as much as they did when they were single—and are blissfully happy" (p. 66). In his study, one couple married for 10 years noted, "You won't believe this, but we simply don't have sex anymore. On holidays we do, but we really have to convince each other. We're very happy, but a real chunk of my life that used to be important to me is dead. Maybe it's the cost of being happy" (p. 69).

Not as much sex as when they were single? They don't have sex anymore? Sex only on holidays? After only 10 years of marriage? You might be thinking, "How can you have less sex and still be 'blissfully happy'?!"

Throughout the 1990s, the scientific study of interpersonal relationships intensified with an increased emphasis placed on the *relational* aspects of sexuality. As marriage is still the most socially recognizable and socially approved coupling for the expression of sexuality, we first turn our attention to marital sexuality. Yet what makes a sexually satisfying marital relationship depends on a number of factors, which we'll explore, such as sexual frequency, orgasmic response, and extramarital sexuality,

Sexual Relationship Satisfaction and Marital Satisfaction

What makes a great sex life? A rich, committed, communicative marriage? Or, does a great sex life make a great marriage? Is it possible to have a great marriage without a great sexual relationship? Is it possible to have a great sexual relationship without a caring, committed, rich marital partnership? Although researchers have attempted to find answers to these questions, it has been much like the chicken and the egg debate—which comes first, sexual satisfaction or marital satisfaction? Can these issues be disentangled?

As early as the 1960s, researchers explored the roles of sexual satisfaction, as a contributor to overall marital satisfaction. According to community health professor Kelli-Ann Lawrance and her colleague, psychologist Sandra Byers (1995), who specialize in marital and sexual

If you want a great sex life, you have to know your sexual self and those things that are important to your partner's sexual self. You can start the conversation by talking to each other about such things as, "When we have sex, I like it best when you/we _____," or "If there's one thing our sexual relationship is missing, it's _____."

iStock.com/jhorrocks

satisfaction, sexual satisfaction in long-term heterosexual relationships depends on the partners' perceptions of the relationship. These perceptions include expectations, hopes, desires, and anticipation. All of us enter into relationships with these perceptions and expectations, whether they are spoken or unspoken, realistic or unrealistic.

In a study that examined sexual practices in the United States, one body of research found that, overall, married couples are enjoying sex (Laumann et al., 1994). The majority of individuals, around 88 percent, indicated that their sexual relationships were either extremely or very physically pleasing, and these relationships tended to be high in physical affection. Of all couple types who responded to the survey, including married people, cohabitants, gays and lesbians, monogamous married couples reported the highest level of sexual satisfaction. An abundance of other research also indicates that married couples have high levels of sexual satisfaction within their marital relationships (among many others, Edwards & Booth, 1994; Haavio-Mannila & Kontula, 1997; Janus & Janus, 1993; Lawrance & Byers, 1995; Purnine, Carey, & Jorgensen, 1994). Researchers discovered that the quality of the couple's intimate communication—particularly self-disclosure—leads to greater relationship satisfaction, which, in turn, leads to greater sexual satisfaction (MacNeil & Byers, 2005).

Researchers have sought to determine how sexual scripts influence marital relationship and sexual satisfaction. Sociologist Susan Sprecher (2002) found that among women, increased relationship satisfaction leads to increased sexual satisfaction, and among men, increased sexual satisfaction leads to increased relationship satisfaction. Sprecher attributed her findings to the fact that women's sex scripts socialize them to enjoy sex only in committed, fulfilling relationships, while men's sex scripts socialize them to be motivated by sex. Other research confirmed Sprecher's ideas about sex scripts and relationship/sexual satisfaction in marriages (Byers, 2005; Vohs, Cantonese, & Baumeister, 2004).

In a rare study that sought to determine sexual and relationship satisfaction of married couples in mainland China, researchers found that Chinese men and women are moderately satisfied with their marital sexual relationships (Renaud, Byers, & Pan, 1997). The more affection and sexual behavior in the relationship, the greater the sexual and marital relationship satisfaction. These conclusions are consistent with U.S. and Canadian research where husbands' and wives' ratings of sexual satisfaction are associated with increased marital relationship satisfaction (Henderson-King & Veroff, 1994; Lawrance & Byers, 1995; Oggins, Leber, & Veroff, 1993; Schenk, Pfrang, & Rausche, 1983; Young, Young, & Luquis, 2000).

So, what makes great marital lives and great sex lives? Perhaps Hunt (1974) sums it up best: "The [partners] who have a free and intensely pleasurable sexual relationship are much more likely to be emotionally close than the husband and wife who do not, and the close marriage is more likely to involve a genuinely liberated marital sex than the distant one" (p. 232).

Sexual Frequency in Intimate Relationships

Frequency of intercourse and overall satisfaction with the marital sexual relationship have received a great deal of scientific inquiry and attention, although it's difficult to find data that address sexual frequency in different couple types. However, some research suggests that, on average, 53 percent of Americans have sex once per week, while 76 percent of Italians report having weekly sex (Face of Global Sex, 2012). By country, Mexico and Nigeria report having the most "exciting" sex lives. By way of contrast, only 10 percent of Japanese people surveyed indicated that their sex lives were exciting. According to the Kinsey Institute (2019),

- Those ages 18 to 29 have sex 112 times per year, or twice per week
- Those ages 30 to 39 have sex 86 times per year, or 1.6 times per week
- Those ages 40 to 49 have sex 69 times per year, about half the total for 18- to 29- year-olds

It's important to note that much of sexual frequency and sexual satisfaction depends on the partner status of the individual—single, partnered, or married? For example, married men and women between the ages of 25 and 49 report having sex "a few times per month to weekly"—more than their single and partnered peers. One study of 30,000 Americans found that those in committed relationships experienced greater sexual satisfaction than those who were not (Muise, Schimmack, & Impett, 2015). According to this study, relationship happiness tended to increase with frequent sex, but that finding no longer holds true even if couples have sex more than once per week.

We do know from research that age is often negatively associated with sexual frequency and sexual satisfaction. Married couples tend to have sex less frequently and to feel less sexually satisfied as they age; this finding is also true among Chinese societies (Chevret, Jaudinot, Sullivan. Marrel, & De Gendre, 2004; Mazur, Mueller, Krause, & Booth, 2002; Guo & Huang, 2005; International Society for Sexual Medicine, 2019).

Orgasmic Response

The ubiquitous orgasm. Songs have been written about it ("Oh, sweet mystery of life at last I've found you!"). Men's and women's magazines proudly boast the latest "how to" when it comes to achieving better and more frequent orgasms. Merely mentioning the word to young, inexperienced sexual couples or to those who have not had an orgasm or even to long-term couples adds pressure—she experiences the pressure to "achieve an orgasm," and he feels the pressure to "bring her" to (supposedly) ultimate sexual fulfillment.

In heterosexual encounters, women are less likely to reach orgasm than men; this delay or absence of orgasm is referred to as **anorgasmia** (Richters, de Visser, Rissel, & Smith, 2006). In a study of more than 19,000 male and female participants, ages 16 to 59, the investigators found that 69 percent of the female respondents had an orgasm during their most recent sexual encounter (such as vaginal intercourse, intercourse with manual stimulation of the clitoris, or intercourse with manual and oral stimulation of the clitoris; Richters et al., 2006). This is in comparison to 95 percent of males who had an orgasm in their most recent sexual encounter. A previous study found that nearly two-thirds of the female study participants did not experience orgasm in their recent sexual encounters (Seeber & Gorrell, 2001).

Anorgasmia: absence of orgasm.

In a study that examined orgasm frequency among lesbian ($n = 340$), bisexual ($n = 1,112$), and heterosexual women ($n = 24,102$), the researchers discovered that lesbian women experienced orgasm (86 percent) more frequently than bisexual women (66 percent) and heterosexual women (65 percent; Frederick, St. John, Garcia, & Lloyd, 2018). In this study, women who orgasmed more frequently

- Received more oral sex
- Had longer durations of sex
- Were more satisfied with their relationship
- Asked for what they wanted during sex
- Tried new sexual positions
- Expressed love during sex

Women who frequently experienced orgasm also engaged in manual genital stimulation and/or oral sex in addition to vaginal sex (Frederick et al., 2018).

Why is it that so many women have difficulties with orgasm, in comparison to men? A number of factors are known to influence orgasmic response in women, such as upbringing, attitudes, religion, anxiety, and previous sexually traumatic experiences (Davidson & Darling, 1989; Andersen & Cyranowski, 1995). Other studies have revealed other factors associated with women's orgasm experiences (Wade, Kremer & Brown, 2005; Richters et al., 2006):

- *Age.* There appears to be a "learning effect" associated with orgasm. Men and women under the age of 20 and men with less than 3 years of sexual experience are less likely to have an orgasm. Women aged 16 to 19 are least likely to have an orgasm. Older women, aged 50 to 59, are also less likely to experience an orgasm; this may be due to hormonal decreases.

- *Partner type.* Both men and women are less likely to have an orgasm if the sexual encounter was with an occasional or casual sex partner rather than a steady partner; they are more likely to have an orgasm if they have been with their partner for at least one year.

- *Sexual behavior.* Men and women are more likely to experience an orgasm if they engage in a variety of sexual behaviors during the encounter. Women are more likely to have an orgasm when oral and manual stimulation of the clitoris are added to vaginal intercourse (70 percent versus 50 percent whose only reported practice is vaginal intercourse).

- *Knowledge of the clitoris.* In general, men's knowledge about the clitoris is equivalent to women's; however, this knowledge does not translate into orgasm for women. Women's self-exploration and masturbation appear to be associated with higher rates of orgasm.

- *Partner's technique.* Hitting the "hot spots" doesn't happen without practice, practice, practice. Partners' clitoral stimulation techniques increase the likelihood that a woman will have an orgasm.

There is a prevailing North American cultural belief that orgasmic response during the sex act is the be-all and end-all of sexual response. But it is possible that sexual satisfaction and orgasmic response/consistency are two different things.

In support of this notion, sexologist Suiming Pan's (1993) study of Chinese women found that 54 percent experienced low orgasmic response, yet they felt that this was perfectly fine and acceptable. In fact, 11 percent of the women surveyed felt that their orgasmic responses were too high! While this study illustrates possible cultural differences in how women view their sexuality, it also indicates that there is a difference between *goal-oriented* sexual activity ("achieving," "reaching," "attaining" orgasmic response) and *pleasure-oriented* sexual activity ("I may not be having an orgasm, but this feels really good and I'm having a great time!").

Nonmarital Sex

Throughout this text, deliberate effort has been made to refer to sexual couples as "partners" rather than as spouse or husband and wife. This is important to point out because much of what we have previously discussed can be applied to any type of sexual dyad (a two-person sexual relationship), whether the couple is married, cohabiting, gay, lesbian, or bisexual. For example, the information concerning sexual dysfunctions and problems can be applied to all couple types. Although the overall trends may be different than for marital sexual partners, nonmarital sexual couples are, by and large, also concerned about relationship satisfaction, sexual frequency, and sexual relationships outside of their committed relationships.

Cohabiting Couples

Despite the tenfold increase in cohabiting relationships since the sexual revolution of the 1960s, surprisingly scant attention has been given to the sexual and relational aspects of this dyad type. The landmark 1983 study by Blumstein and Schwartz of American couple types is perhaps the most extensive study to date. In their research, the authors found differences in sexual expression between cohabiting and married couples. The findings suggest that cohabiting couples were more likely to have sexual intercourse more frequently than married couples (three times per week compared to once per week), and were not only more likely to have sex outside of the cohabiting relationship but were also less secretive than married couples about the outside sexual activities. In cohabitant relationships, the female was more likely to initiate sexual acts than were married women. Men in cohabiting relationships tended to be more committed to the relationship if the partner was "attractive."

In a study that examined sexual satisfaction in premarital cohabitating relationships, Sprecher (2002) found that the respondents indicated overall sexual satisfaction within the cohabiting relationship, and that sexual satisfaction was also positively correlated with relationship satisfaction, love for partner, and the level of commitment to the relationship. It's important to note, however, that relationship and sexual satisfaction studies only represent a snapshot in time. That is to say, just as with any other process in couple and family life, there are shifts—ebbs and flows—that occur over time. One researcher took this into account and found that relationship status wasn't as important as how long the couple had been together (Schröder & Schmiedeberg, 2015). In this study, the investigation team found that yes, couples *do* experience sharp declines in sexual frequency and relationship satisfaction, but these declines have more to do with changes in life (such as, pregnancy and the birth of a baby), than with age. The important, take-away message from this study is: As a couple ages, regardless of their relationship status, it is important for couples to continue to cultivate a relationship culture of communication, respect, and emotional intimacy (Schröder & Schmiedeberg, 2015).

Gay and Lesbian Couples

Information concerning sexual relationships of committed same-sex couples indicates that sexuality is quite similar to that of heterosexual couples. For instance, in one study that explored sexual satisfaction, no differences in sexual satisfaction were found among gay, lesbian, heterosexual cohabitants, and heterosexual married couples (Kurdek, 1991). As the discussion of marital relationship satisfaction revealed, overall relationship satisfaction corresponds with sexual satisfaction. Similar to Blumstein and Schwartz's study (1983), other research found that lesbian couples engage in sexual intercourse less frequently than heterosexual married women (Kurdek, 1991; Lever, 1995; Leichliter et al., 2007). Gay couples, on the other hand, have sexual intercourse more frequently than any other couple type, although as the duration of the relationship increases, sexual intercourse tends to decrease, as in the case of married heterosexual couples. According to Blumstein and Schwartz (1983), gay men exhibit the highest rate of accepted extra-relationship (nonmonogamy) sex than any other couple type.

In 2002, *The Advocate,* a magazine marketed to the gay, lesbian, bisexual, and transgender populations, conducted a poll intended to survey feelings about sexual relationships. Respondents to this nonscientific poll indicated that, overall, they are quite satisfied with their sexual relationships. For example, 88 percent of the males and 79 percent of the women noted that they are quite happy in their same-sex sexual relationships and have no intention of "converting" to heterosexuality. Of the gay/bisexual men surveyed, 22 percent indicated that for them, kissing is the most important part of sex; conversely, 16 percent of the lesbian/bisexual women indicated this to be true. For both sexes (64 percent of women and 57 percent of men) "foreplay" is considered the most important part of the sex act. When asked, "When is sex the best for you?," 67 percent of the men and 87 percent of the women indicated that "building intimacy with a single partner" makes for the best sex.

Cheating: Sex Outside the Relationship

Infidelity:

a breach of faith that occurs when there is a violation of the couple's mutually agreed rules or boundaries of a relationship.

Infidelity, or cheating, is a breach of faith that occurs when there is a violation of the couple's mutually agreed-on rules or boundaries of a relationship. Oftentimes infidelity is referred to as *extramarital affairs* or *extramarital experiences*. Extramarital experiences can occur when one marital partner ventures outside the relationship and becomes emotionally and/or sexually involved with another person. What constitutes an act of infidelity varies between and within cultures, as well as within individual relationships. Almost always, these types of extramarital experiences result in a breakdown of trust within the relationship. When one partner ventures outside the relationship without the other's knowledge or permission, it is said to be an **involuntary extramarital experience.**

Involuntary Experiences

Involuntary extramarital experience:

occurs when one partner ventures outside the relationship without the other's knowledge or permission.

As our study of intimate relationships and sex has shown us so far, intimate relationships—be they dating, cohabiting, gay/lesbian, or marriages—involve behaviors and emotions that are generally expected to be restricted to the relationship. When any behavior oversteps the expectations of exclusivity and expectations of monogamy, it is considered to be an **extra-relationship involvement (ERI)** (Banfield & McCabe, 2001). There are three types of ERI (Thompson, 1984):

Extra-relationship involvement (ERI):

any behavior that oversteps the expectations of exclusivity and monogamy in a relationship.

1. *Sexual ERI.* This type of behavior involves a wide range of behaviors, from flirting, to mutual masturbation, to oral and anal sex, to sexual intercourse.

2. *Emotional ERI.* Emotional extra relationship involvement also includes a range of behaviors and includes a close friendship (with much self-disclosure) rather than being "in love."

3. *Combination of sexual and emotional ERI.* As the term implies, in this category a person can engage in a wide variety of behaviors that encompass both emotional and sexual areas of a relationship.

Extramarital sex (EMS):

occurs when a married person has a sexual relationship (any type of sexual activity, such as mutual masturbation, or oral, anal, or vaginal sex) with someone other than his or her spouse.

Extramarital sex (EMS) occurs when a married person has a sexual relationship with anyone other than her or his spouse. Just as with ERI, there are different types of EMS (Bullough & Bullough, 1994):

1. *Clandestine.* In this type of EMS, the participating members do not believe either of their spouses if the partner is married) knows about the sexual relationship, nor do they believe their spouse(s) would approve.

2. *Ambiguous.* In these relationships, the role of the nonparticipating spouse is crucial. The nonparticipating spouse may know about the EMS but cannot prove it; the nonparticipating spouse may choose to tolerate it rather than seek divorce; the nonparticipating spouse may have at one time endorsed the EMS but later disapproved; or he or she may approve of the EMS but does not want details.

3. *Consensual.* In this type of relationship, the nonparticipating spouse both knows and approves of the EMS; each spouse may have a consensual relationship outside the boundaries oi marriage (we discuss these types of relationships in just a bit).

It is very difficult to acquire data on just how many spouses cheat on their partners, and what data are available are probably outdated. One study suggested that nearly 20 percent of married men and 13 percent of married women have been involved in ERI/EMS at least once during their marriage (Institute of Family Studies, 2019). Interestingly, women ages 18 to 29 are more likely to cheat on their married partner than men are (11 percent versus 10 percent). Across races and ethnicities, Black men are more likely to cheat (22 percent) than white men (16 percent) or Hispanic men (13 percent; Institute of Family Studies, 2019). Overall, however, this data support the decades old trend that men are more likely to cheat than women. Figure 9.9 presents the demographics of cheating in America.

Given the devastating effect cheating has on marital relationships and the difficulty in repairing marriages that have been impacted by extramarital relationships (Oppenheimer, 2007), why do people cheat on their spouses?

Why Do People Cheat?

Research has revealed a number of factors that are associated with an increased risk of engaging in ERI/EMS:

- *Gender.* Men are more likely to have extramarital relationships than women are (Atkins, Jacobson, & Baucom, 2001).

Figure 9.9 /// Cheating in America

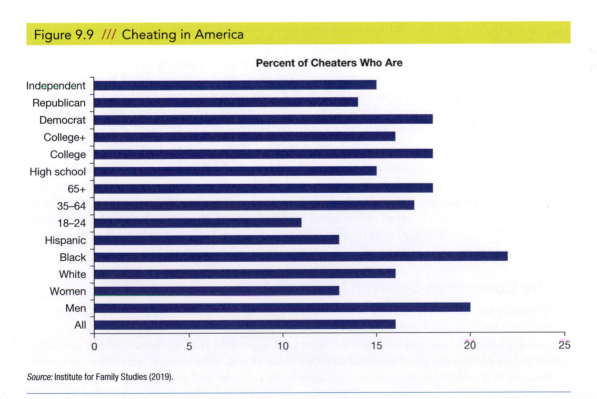

Percent of Cheaters Who Are

Source: Institute for Family Studies (2019).

- *Age.* Younger married people experience higher rates of extramarital activity than older married people (Kimuna & Kjamba, 2005).
- *Personality traits.* Some personality traits, such as narcissism and low levels of conscientiousness, are associated with cheating (Atkins et al., 2001).
- *Marital satisfaction.* Lower levels of relationship satisfaction are linked to increased rates of extramarital behaviors for both men and women (Wiederman, 1997).
- *Length of marriage.* The longer the duration of the marriage, the less likely a man or a woman is to cheat on the spouse (Liu, 2000).
- *Opportunity.* Some people have more opportunities to cheat, such as jobs that take them away from their spouses (Atkins et al., 2001).

Past research claimed that men and women have different ideas about sex and love. For instance, one study found that men believe women must be in love to have sex, whereas women think that men may have sex without being in love (Harris & Christenfeld, 1996). Other research has similarly found that women do not tend to become sexually involved in the absence of emotional commitment (love), but men can (Townsend, 1995). This research is interesting because it suggests that women may be more likely to engage in emotional ERI, whereas men are more likely to engage in EMS. This leads us to another important question that needs to be addressed: Is an Internet relationship "cheating"?

Are Internet Relationships "Cheating"?

This is a common question that my students ask. In some respects, it is a difficult question to answer because research into this ever-evolving area subsumes romantic relationships, friendships, and sexual partnerships under the general category of online relationships (McQuillen, 2003). In addition to this, it is difficult to determine the meaning people attach to these relationships—is it just for fun because an Internet user is bored? Is it for sexual pleasure/gratification? Is it "innocent" flirting?

In a study of more than 500 online users, researchers found several themes in online relationships. When it came to the question as to whether online relationships constituted extramarital affairs, views were mixed among study participants. Several indicated that they participated in Internet affairs because they were unhappy in their real-life marriages—they stressed that their pre-existing marriage problems caused them to seek an affair. Other participants noted that the online affairs were just as painful a betrayal as real-life affairs, and just as devastating. Noted one participant, "The effect on a husband when he discovers his wife has been having cyber-sex is sheer hell. I now have a deep distrust of my wife and a feeling of constant paranoia. The effects on my marriage [of her online affair] have been disastrous" (Wildermuth & Vogl-Bauer, 2007, p. 219).

Extramarital affairs, or sexual relationships outside of committed relationships, cause much emotional pain, devastation, and torment for the victimized partner and include reactions such as rage, feelings of shame, depression, overwhelming powerlessness, and abandonment, along with a prolonged disruption in daily functioning (Gordon, Baucom, & Snyder, 2004). So traumatic are the effects of extramarital affairs, marriage therapist Douglas Snyder maintains that sexual infidelity is the most difficult relationship issue to treat (Snyder, Gordon, & Baucom, 2004).

The Connection Between Love and Sex

Certainly we can love someone without experiencing sex, and certainly we can experience sex without loving the sexual partner, such as in hookups (see Chapter 7). Is there a connection between love and sex? Some researchers argue that the link between love and sex is forged by natural sex selection (Buss, 1985; Frey & Hojjat, 1998). Sex is important, of course, because it transfers genes from one generation to the next and ensures the longevity of the culture. But love is just as important as sex because it binds together family units that serve to nurture and protect the helpless, defenseless offspring; just like sex, love is a necessary mechanism to perpetuate the species. Thus, sex and love are inextricably linked to survival (Frey & Hojjat, 1998).

Some research suggests that being in love is what actually drives someone to want to have sex with his or her love object. Neuroscientist Arthur Aron and his team of anthropology and social psychology colleagues (2005) used brain scans to study the brains of 17 young men and women who were "newly" or "madly" in love. This study is particularly relevant to our discussion here because the researchers wanted to answer the historic question of whether love and sex are really the same thing. More specifically, the researchers wanted to know if the feelings we have in our early love relationships are, in actuality, just warmed-over feelings of sexual arousal. The results of the brain scans indicated that the early, intense feelings associated with passionate/romantic love have more to do with motivation and reward than with the sex drive. The researchers found that romantic love is a highly motivated, goal-oriented state—and this state is what makes us want to pursue sex with our lovers, and to protect our lovers and the relationship. According to this research, romantic love is more powerful than the human sex drive, and sex and romantic love involve quite different brain systems.

You may be wondering on a more practical level about the connection between love and sex. For instance, is sex better if we love our partner?

Is Sex Better if We Love Our Sex Partner?

Love can be an important motivational force for the participation in sexual activities (Kaestle & Tucker-Halpern, 2007; Aron et al., 2005). But is sex actually better if we love our partner?

How we experience sex, and the sense of enjoyment or satisfaction we get from sex is highly personal (Davidson, Darling, & Norton, 1995). There are, of course, a number of characteristics, behaviors, emotions, relationship background factors, and social background factors that contribute to sexual satisfaction, as our study of sexual scripts has shown us (Sprecher & McKinney, 1993). But a wide body of empirical evidence indicates that there is an association between sexual satisfaction and relationship satisfaction (among many, Bartels & Zeki, 2000; Sprecher & Regan, 2000; Christopher & Sprecher, 2000; Sprecher, 2002; Aron et al., 2005; Kaestle & Tucker-Halpern, 2007). For example, one study of 101 college-age dating couples found that men and women who are most sexually satisfied tended also to report high levels of love and commitment; couples who reported lower levels of sexual satisfaction were more likely to report lower levels of love and commitment (Sprecher, 2002).

An investigation of 6,421 young adults, ages 18 to 26, revealed that study participants who were in love reported higher levels of sexual satisfaction (Kaestle & Tucker-Halpern, 2007). For instance, study respondents who reported high levels of love for their partner and who reported that their partner felt high levels of love for them, engaged in a greater variety of sexual activities than those who reported lower levels of love. For both males and females, participating in a particular sexual activity was associated with the love pattern within the relationship. In this study, for example, males were twice as likely to have received oral sex when the partners loved each other; similarly, females were more likely to have received oral sex when the partners loved each other a lot and when she felt that her partner loved her. Also, if partners indicated they loved each other a lot, they were more likely to engage in anal sex than when neither partner loved the other a lot. Overall, the research findings supported the researchers' notion that higher levels of love are associated with greater sexual variety within the relationship, leading to higher levels of relationship satisfaction. Previous studies have also demonstrated that sexual satisfaction is positively associated with other indicators of relationship quality, including love and commitment (Waite & Joyner, 2001; Christopher & Sprecher, 2000; Sprecher & Regan, 2000; Sprecher, 2002). The research certainly tends to support the idea that sex is better if we love our sex partner.

Are There Differences in How Men and Women View Love and Sex?

Are men and women really that different when it comes to how they view love and sex? There is some evidence that it is easier for men to have sex with little or no emotional attachment or commitment to the sex partner than it is for women; it is also easier for men to have sex just for pleasure than it is for women (Buss, 1999). There is also empirical evidence that indicates men are more likely than women to want sex early on in the relationship (perhaps within hours!; Knox, Sturdivant, & Zusman, 2001). Interestingly, although men are more likely to engage in sex without an emotional attachment to their partner, they tend to express their love first and have higher levels of romantic beliefs than do women (Sharp & Ganong, 2000).

A recent study of 147 college undergraduates showed that men are significantly more likely than females to say "I love you" sooner in the relationship—but they have a sexual agenda for doing so (Brantley, Knox, & Zusman, 2002). In this study, the sociology researchers wanted to understand the timing and meaning of saying "I love you" to a new partner. Analysis of their findings showed two interesting results:

1. *Men tend to say "I love you" first.* Men reported that in relationships where both partners mutually loved each other, men disclosed their love first.

2. *Men tend to say "I love you" for sex.* If men thought that saying "I love you" would increase the chance that their partners would have sex with them, they did so.

The authors of the study suggest that men say "I love you" because their past sexual encounters reinforced that declaring their love is associated with women being more willing to have sex. The authors even go a step further and explain that males have adopted this particular sex script as a way to ensure their reproductive success with as many women as possible (see the Evolutionary theory discussion in Chapter 7). Whatever the reason, this study clearly showed that within this study sample, men used love to get sex. As the researchers note, "Students now have empirical verification that hearing 'I love you' may mean little more than 'I am saying this just so . . . you will have sex with me'" (Knox & Zusman, 2002, p, 615).

EXPERIENCING SEXUAL DIFFICULTIES

Let's face it—at some time in our relational careers, our sex parts may fail to meet our expectations or our partner's expectations. While this failure to meet expectations has often been made fun of in television and film comedies, the fact is, sexual difficulties can be emotionally agonizing and negatively affect relationships.

Sexuality is a complex process. It includes the involvement of a number of biological factors, such as the neurological, vascular, and endocrine systems, in addition to a number of societal influences, such as family of origin influences, cultural contexts, and religious beliefs (Bachmann & Phillips, 1998). It also encompasses individual influences, such as relationship quality, needs, and moods. Our sexuality is also altered as we age, or with a decline in health status. A breakdown in any one or more of these areas may lead to or directly cause sexual dysfunction (Phillips, 2000).

Sexual dysfunction:
the inability to fully enjoy sex.

Broadly speaking, **sexual dysfunction** is the inability to fully enjoy sex. Sexual dysfunction can begin early in a person's life, or it may gradually develop after a person has previously experienced satisfying and pleasurable sex. For convenience and ease of study, we'll organize our discussion into two categories: women and men.

Sexual Dysfunctions in Women

Sexual dysfunctions in women are common occurrences. In the United States, about 40 percent of women report having sexual concerns, and 12 percent report that they have ongoing distressing sexual problems (Shifren, Barbieri, & Falk, 2019). Specifically, sexual dysfunctions

iStock.com/grinvalds

include disorders that result in inadequate sexual functioning in sexual arousal and response; it also includes sexual pain, referred to as **dyspareunia**.

Dyspareunia: sexual pain experienced by women as a result of sexual dysfunction.

Having too little sexual desire is the most common sexual issue that women encounter, reported by anywhere from 10 to 51 percent of multiethnic women in sexual studies; this low level of desire is commonly accompanied by low levels of sexual excitement and infrequent orgasms in women (Mercer et al., 2003; Matthiesen & Wenn, 2004; Laumann et al., 2005; Basson, 2006; Elnashar, Ibrahim, El-Desoky, Ali, & Hasson, 2006). Rosemary Basson (2005, 2006) has extensively studied the topic of female sexual desire. In her studies, she has found several interrelated factors that are relevant to difficulties in female sexual desire:

- *Interpersonal and contextual factors.* The two strongest predictors of distress about sex are the emotional relationship with the partner and general emotional well-being. Feeling emotionally close to a partner during sexual activity and having good emotional health are correlated with higher levels of sexual desire.

- *Personal psychological factors.* Sometimes a woman's sexual desire is affected by distractions, such as daily-life distractions (bills, children, schedules, worry, anxiety) or sexual distractions (worrying about becoming pregnant, STIs, not becoming sufficiently aroused, reaching orgasm, body image, or a partner's lack of orgasm or premature ejaculation). This category also includes memories of past sexual experiences, such as rape, abuse, or negative expectations that "this time" will be just like "last time" (such as experiencing physical pain during sex).

- *Biological factors.* A number of biological factors may diminish women's sexual desire, including depression, the use of antidepressants, directly after the birth of a child, hormonal imbalances due to surgical removal of the ovaries or the aging process (menopause), and other illnesses such as diabetes, heart disease, and cancer. We discuss these illnesses, as well as the option of hormone replacement therapy (HRT), in the next chapter.

"He wants it all the time—at least three times a week!" "I hardly want it at all—only three times a week!"

A common theme runs through families today: too many demands, too many pressures, and too little time for couples to connect and feel a part of each other's lives. Often, hectic lives lead to hectic relationships, and rather than talk about hurt feelings and pent-up sexual frustrations, the couple rolls over in bed away from each other, and the hurt intensifies.

Her Side: It's not that I don't love him. I do love him, and I know he tries so hard to make me happy. It's just that I'm *so tired* all the time. With my job, the kids and all of their activities, plus all the things that need to be done around the house all the time . . . I'm just too tired to have sex. And I don't think he even notices what I do in a day, or that I even exist until he wants to have sex. Plus, I don't get a whole lot out of it. I mean, it's great for him, but I never feel like he's in it for me. He just doesn't understand that I can't get in the mood as quickly as he can, and then he gets upset because he thinks I don't need him like he needs me. It's just not worth the trouble—I'm tired of not feeling satisfied; he's tired of me pushing him away,

His Side: I try to be understanding. I mean, I know it's hard for her to have to be a "single parent" all the time with my work schedule and all. I know it's not fair for her to have to do everything for the kids and around the house, plus her job, but I wish she would understand the tremendous pressure I feel at work—and the pressure to succeed and give her the things she deserves. I feel like I give her so much! Not just material things—I'm constantly trying to surprise her with romantic things I know she likes, but she thinks I'm doing those things just so we can have sex. These things aren't just to get her in the mood. I really do want her to be happy. But when we have sex, she just seems so distant. I never know if she's enjoying it or not.

Your Side: Typical of many today, this couple's sex life is beginning to suffer the effects of too much to do, too little time. In your opinion,

1. What are three main issues that are affecting this couple?

2. If you were a couple and family therapist or counselor, what would you recommend for this couple?

Of course, it's understandable that at times we all experience low sexual desire. "Life" sometimes causes us to be too tired or just loo stressed to get in the mood. To be better able to determine if we or our partners are experiencing a sexual desire disorder, it is important to become familiar with what our "normal" levels of sexual desire are, so we can then compare this with situations that may cause us to lose interest in sex. Given time and attention, low sexual desire is often reversible.

Sexual Dysfunctions in Men

Male sexual dysfunction is one of the most common health problems that affects men, with 31 percent of men reporting they experience some type of sexual dysfunction (Cleveland Clinic, 2019). Just as with women, male sexual difficulties can be caused by physical problems, psychological problems, or a combination of both.

Erectile dysfunction:

also known as *impotence*, this condition is marked by an inability to achieve an erection.

Often referred to as *impotence*, **erectile dysfunction (ED)** is the inability of a man to develop and/or maintain a firm erection long enough to have satisfactory sex. This problem can occur at any age, and most men experience it from time to time. It is thought to be a concern if it persists over a period of 3 months (Parmet, 2004). Erectile dysfunction is the most common sexual problem for men, affecting 52 percent of the male population (Cleveland Clinic, 2019). In a study of 3,400 heterosexual and gay men, for example, the researchers found that from one-third to nearly one-half of the study participants experience ED at least occasionally (Bancroft, Carnes, Janssen, & Long, 2005). ED is most commonly associated with age, becoming more common as men age (Cleveland Clinic, 2019).

Rapid ejaculation (RE), also referred to as **premature ejaculation**, is ejaculation that occurs before, on, or shortly after penetration with minimal sexual stimulation (American Urological Association, 2018). Rapid ejaculation is the most common sexual dysfunction among men, affecting as many as 1 out of 3 men (Mayo Clinic, 2019). It's not enough to diagnose the problem because any one problem can cause a domino effect—premature ejaculation can be addressed, but aspects of the couple's relationship may yet need to be addressed, depression may need to be treated, past traumas may need to be addressed, medication may need to be prescribed, and couples may need to learn or re-learn different ways of thinking and sexual behaviors (Basson, 2005). Any sexual problem that persists for more than a few weeks is worth a visit to a healthcare provider, counselor, or sex therapist.

Rapid ejaculation (RE): ejaculation that occurs before, on, or shortly after penetration with minimal sexual stimulation.

FAMILY LIFE EDUCATION: ADVANCING HEALTHY SEXUAL WELL-BEING FROM A VALUE-RESPECTFUL POSITION

There is no question that human sexuality across the lifespan is a topic of great magnitude to Family Life Educators, therapists, social workers, psychologists, and other helping professionals. As you have seen in this chapter, sex and sexuality affect every aspect of our who we are: physiologically, psychologically, emotionally, socially, and for some, spiritually. Given the significance of sexuality to every aspect of our lives, it is of the utmost importance that CFLE's understand not only the biological aspects of human sexuality (i.e., sexual functioning, reproductive health, sexually transmitted infections), but also the social and emotional aspects of human sexuality, such as the diversity of sex and sexuality experienced by different cultures and ethnicities (NCFR, 2020). For this reason, it is imperative that CLFE's approach human sexuality from a value-respectful position, because each of us enter into a sexual relationship with our own, one-of-a-kind sexual script.

The couple portrayed in the opening page of this chapter is my mother and father. From as early as I can remember, my parents were always demonstrative in their feelings toward one another, and quite open in the expression of their sexuality—holding hands, sitting on one another's laps, patting each other on the rear end, kissing, and nuzzling each other. Their final act of intimacy, then, was simply an extension of what I had witnessed as my own sexuality grew, changed, and evolved across my lifespan. Their final act of intimacy was a reminder to me that we are born sexual and we die sexual.

Their experiences were the foundations of my sexual scripts and today contribute significantly to my own sexuality. The expression of their marital sexuality throughout their marriage was an expression of the richness of their marital union, an expression of pleasure and play, an expression of the mutual comfort and help they provided one another, an expression of the commitment to their relationship, and, in my mother's final moments, an expression of agony and separation. Their corporate sexuality was a compilation of individual development and shared experiences, and of individual and societal expectations—not unlike our own sexuality.

You see, real sex isn't about explosive, perfectly timed orgasms (every time, no less). It's not about two beautiful, perfect bodies performing in perfect, rhythmic sync. Real sex isn't about an affair where suddenly every emotional and physical need of yours is met by someone you don't even know the last name of.

Real sex is so much more than our sex-saturated society portrays. It is so much more than what the academic numbers tell us it is. Yes, frequency of sex is important to marital satisfaction; yes, orgasm consistency is related to sexual satisfaction and thus, marital satisfaction. These data are important in our overall understanding of sexuality.

But real sex also means that sometimes you don't feel like sex, and your partner understands. It means telling your partner what you want and what you need and your partner respecting those wants and needs. Real sex means the "hot spots" are there because *you* put them there: Your partner is beautiful and sexy and sensual and "hot" because that's how you see him or her—and you treat him or her that way.

Real sex means being interrupted, perhaps even at the moment of climax, because your child just threw up in the bedroom next door or the UPS truck pulled up in the driveway. And sometimes it means you can't get aroused because there are too many bills to think about or you have too much work to do. Real sex means reaching out to your partner out of anger or disappointment, exhilaration or desperation, loneliness or celebration. It means clinging helplessly to your partner as if you were on a life raft in the middle of a swollen ocean because you just received word of your father's death or your child's death. Real sex means navigating around the tubes and the innumerable stitches in her chest because the cancer wouldn't let go. It means aging and finding out that sometimes the emotional connection is just as intense as the physical connection was in earlier years. And, like the couple in the opening page of this chapter, real sex means longing for, aching for, and memorizing your terminally ill partner's body. The pain was real because the sex was real.

/// SUMMARY

Learning Sexuality: Cultural Contributions

- Sexual identity is the awareness of oneself as a sexual male or sexual female. Family of origin, family of choice, life experiences, and other cultural influences help shape sexuality.

- Societal norms and expectations dictate the gender-specific public and private expression of our sexuality and help form sexual scripts—shared, gender-specific social and cultural expectations that guide our beliefs about sex, such as our beliefs about appropriate sexual partners and sexual

behaviors. There are three levels of sexual scripts: cultural scenarios, interpersonal scripts, and intrapsychic scripts.

- Parents are their children's first and best sex educators. Parents are influential regarding their teens' decisions and attitudes about sex. Mothers are typically more involved in communicating about sex and sexual health to their children than fathers are.

- There are racial/ethnic differences in how parents communicate with their children about sex.

Our Sexual Selves

- Adolescents and young adults are besieged with images of sexuality at an early age without being taught how and why their bodies respond to sexual stimulation. Knowing and understanding our bodies not only increases our sexual pleasure and satisfaction but it also enhances our sexual relationships.

- Sex encompasses many other behaviors besides sexual intercourse. These behaviors are termed *noncoital,* and include masturbation, oral-genital sex, and anal sex.

- Research also indicates that the average age of a person's first experience with sexual intercourse is influenced by race or ethnicity.

- Recent studies show that the majority of college students are sexually active. Of concern to medical health professionals and family practitioners are the risky behaviors that often lead to unsafe or unwanted sex.

- Because Spring Break binge drinking has been shown to lead to unsafe and unwanted sex, sexually transmitted diseases, blackouts, and violence, the American Medical Association (AMA) contends that universities and colleges should stop Spring Break tour promoters from promoting alcohol, or offer Spring Break alternatives that do not include alcohol.

Sexually Transmitted Infections

- Sexually transmitted infections (STIs) are diseases that are transmitted between partners through sexual contact.

- Bacterial infections include gonorrhea, syphilis, and chlamydia. These can be treated by the use of antibiotics.

- Viral infections include herpes, human papillomavirus (HPV), and viral hepatitis. These cannot be treated by antibiotics.

Relationships and Sex

- Research has found that, overall, married couples are enjoying sex. Among several couple types (married, cohabitants, gay men, and lesbians), monogamous married couples reported the highest level or sexual satisfaction.

- Sexual satisfaction in long-term heterosexual relationships depends on the partners' perceptions—expectations, hopes, and desires—of the relationship. Additionally, sexual scripts influence marital relationship and sexual satisfaction.

- While orgasmic consistency and the ability to have an orgasm have long been used as a yardstick of sexual satisfaction, recent studies suggest that sexual satisfaction and orgasmic response/consistency are two completely different things, that there is a difference between *goal-oriented* sexual activity and *pleasure-oriented* sexual activity.

- Extramarital sexuality is a sexual relationship with someone other than a spouse; it may be clandestine, ambiguous,

or consensual. Extramarital affairs or sexual relationships outside of committed relationships cause much emotional pain for the victimized partner, and sexual infidelity is considered the most difficult relationship issue to treat. People cheat for different reasons.

- We can love someone without having sex, and we can have sex without being in love. Newer research suggests that for some, being in love is what drives someone to want to have sex.

- Couples who are in love report higher levels of sexual satisfaction in their relationships than people who are not in love.

- It's easier for men to have sex without being in love than it is for women. Some men say "I love you" as part of a sexual agenda.

Experiencing Sexual Difficulties

- Sexual dysfunction covers a wide array of sexual problems or difficulties, but can essentially be broken down into two categories; female sexual dysfunction and male sexual dysfunction. One type of female sexual dysfunction is female sexual arousal disorder, and is said to occur when

a woman cannot maintain arousal and lubrication during intercourse, is unable to reach orgasm, or has no desire for sexual intercourse. Types of male sexual dysfunction include erectile dysfunction and rapid ejaculation.

/// KEY TERMS

Anal eroticism   317

Anal intercourse   317

Anorgasmia   329

Asexual   302

Bisexual   302

Chlamydia   324

Cultural scenarios   303

Cunnilingus   317

Dyspareunia   337

Erectile dysfunction (ED)   338

Extramarital sex (EMS)   332

Extra-relationship involvement (ERI)   332

Fellatio   317

Gonorrhea   324

Herpes   325

Heterosexual   302

Homosexual   302

Human papillomavirus (HPV)   326

Infidelity   332

Involuntary extramarital experience   332

Masturbation   316

Noncoital   316

Oral-genital sex (oral sex)   317

Premature ejaculation   339

Rapid ejaculation (RE)   339

Refractory period   316

Sexual dysfunction   336

Sexual scripting framework   301

Sexual scripts   301

Sexuality   301

Sexually transmitted infections (STIs)   324

Syphilis   325

Viral hepatitis   326

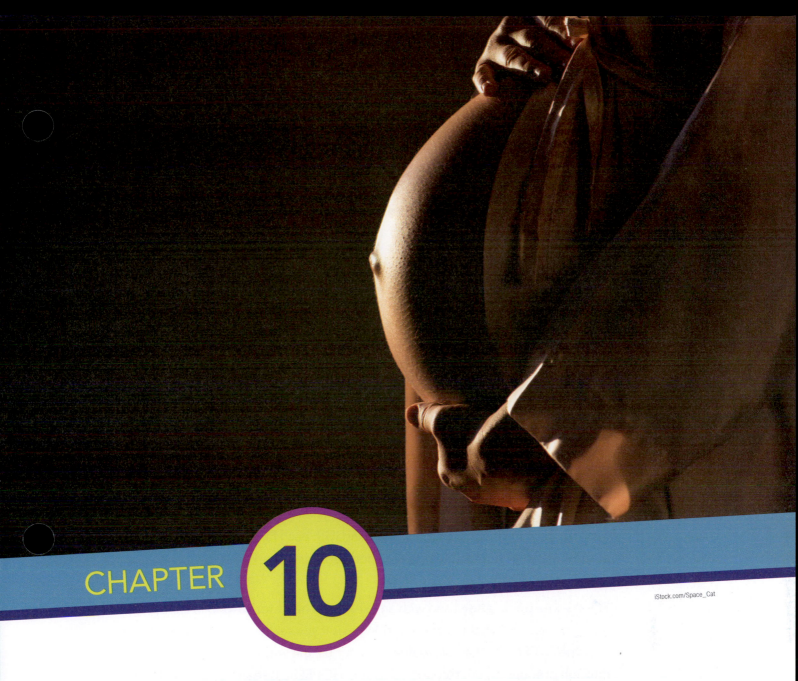

CHAPTER 10

BECOMING PARENTS: CHOICES AND CHALLENGES

LEARNING OBJECTIVES

10.1 Explain the childbearing trends in the United States, including why birth to unmarried parents is becoming more common.

10.2 Discuss why parents today choose to have children, to delay childbearing, or to remain childfree by choice.

10.3 Describe the emotional and relationship changes that occur throughout pregnancy and in the transition to parenthood.

10.4 Identify the issues associated with unexpected outcomes, including infertility, birth defects, and pregnancy loss.

10.5 Outline the processes of adoption and the experiences of LGBTQ+ individuals who adopt.

10.6 Summarize the types of contraceptives available today and describe the practice of abortion.

....

After four years of marriage, my husband and I were in a place in our lives where we decided it was time to start a family. A year and a half later, I was nowhere near being pregnant. So began the journey for answers and help in becoming parents as we began infertility testing and treatment.

At first it was difficult, the not knowing. During this time of trying, hoping, and praying, many friends around me began to start their families, too. And with each phone call to tell me of their pregnancies I found myself there again, trying to hold back my sadness and tears as I congratulated them on their happiness . . . Why me?

A year of testing and treatment began for us. Then month after month, the hope of becoming pregnant started to fade. And with each failed attempt to get pregnant with all the technology and medical assistance, I again could not stop the tears . . . Why me?

But at some point, after living with an exhausted heart for so long, a shift in our thoughts began. What is it you want? What is it you really want? The answer: To become PARENTS. Then we realized that for us, the way to become parents was not through pregnancy, but through adoption. HOPE! So began the second leg of our journey, our journey to *make a family*.

Many months went by as we went through the process of getting on the adoption list . . . selecting an agency, doing the home study, preparing our home for that someone. And then came The Wait.

Two and a half years go by, and then one October morning it happened—The CALL! "You have a son!" For years I questioned, "Why me?" But then suddenly I knew why . . . Our son was always supposed to be ours, but we just had to wait on him to get here. And oh, he was so worth the wait!

Doula:

a professional provider of labor support (emotional, physical, and informational) to women and their companions.

Pregnancy always intrigued me, and newborns always took me captive. So it did not come as a surprise to anyone who knew me when I became a childbirth educator and a **doula**—a professional provider of labor support (emotional, physical, and informational) to women and their companions. Many years and countless births later, I am still intrigued with the mystery of how a single cell zygote is knit together in the secrecy of the mother's women into a 10-trillion-celled person.

The birth of a baby is life altering. Each time a child is born, or added to a family through adoption or fostering, a family is born as well. People can grow their families in a number of ways. In this chapter, we begin our study of becoming parents by taking a look at the historical reasons people had children and how some of these influences still linger in our society today. We then get a good picture of the current childbearing trends in the United States, which include examining teen pregnancy and parenthood, as well as pathways to gay and lesbian parenting. We look at how people decide to have children and how they determine their family sizes, the emotional and relationship changes that are brought about by pregnancy, and the process of giving birth. We'll conclude our discussion by looking at ways to prevent pregnancy.

CHILDBEARING TRENDS: WHO'S HAVING BABIES?

Parents and family life are the foundations that influence a child's development and well-being from birth into early adulthood; both play instrumental roles in stimulating and shaping a child's cognitive, social, and emotional development (Solomon-Fears, 2008). Because of the tremendous influences parents and the home environment exert on a child's development, we begin our study of the pathways to parenting by gaining an understanding of the childbearing trends in the United States today: Who's having babies, and how old are America's parents?

Who Are America's Parents?

Each year, the population in the United States increased by the addition of slightly less than 4 million babies (Centers for Disease Control and Prevention, 2019a). The **crude birth rate** is the number of childbirths per 1,000 women, per year. These figures are tracked worldwide; in general, the crude birth rate in economically disadvantaged countries is higher than in more economically advantaged countries. In less economically developed countries, such as Niger, Uganda, Kenya, and Pakistan, the crude birth rate is significantly higher than in richer countries. In 2018, the crude birth rate in the United States was 11.8 (per 1,000 women); this is in comparison to 14.2 in 2007 and 24 in 1960 (National Vital Statistics Reports, 2019).

Crude birth rate: the number of childbirths per 1,000 women, per year.

The **total fertility rate** is the average number of live births per woman, in a given population, per year. The U.S. fertility rate in 2018 was 1.72, down from 1.76 in 2017 (National Vital Statistics Reports, 2019). Countries that are less economically advantaged tend to have higher fertility rates, just as they have higher crude birth rates. It is important to note, however, that fertility rates are also a reflection of a region's religious, cultural, and ethnic norms. For example, because of their collectivist cultural beliefs and their strong ties to families, Latinx cultures tend to have more children than individualistic cultures such as the United States and the United Kingdom. The one-child policy in China—a practice implemented in 1980 that mandated only one child per couple in urban areas—was a cultural norm that accounted for China's and Taiwan's low fertility rates. In 2015 this policy was relaxed; under a new policy, families today are permitted to have two children. For any given country, a fertility rate of 2.1 is considered to be the **replacement fertility rate**. As you can see, the United States is currently below this replacement rate. By tracking the crude birth rate from year to year, as well as the fertility rates, demographers are able to see certain childbearing trends, such as the age of birth mother.

Total fertility rate: the average number of live births per woman, in a given population, per year.

Replacement fertility rate: the average number of children born per woman, at which the population is exactly replaced.

What is the current teen birth rate? Are women waiting until they are older to have children? Are there more babies born to single women than there are to married women? Answers to these questions can be found by looking at birth certificate data—the registered births. How many teens are giving birth?

Trends Among Teenagers

In 2007, the Academy Award winning film *Juno* took the nation by surprise. In this film, high school junior Juno is faced with an unplanned pregnancy. Fresh, frank, and funny, this movie illustrated the social, emotional, physical, and relational struggles teens confront when they become pregnant. How many teens are giving birth?

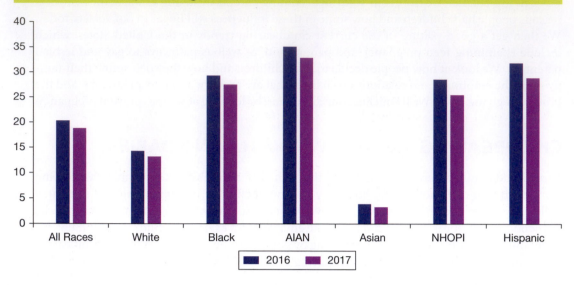

Figure 10.1 /// Birth Rates (per 1,000 Women) for Females Aged 15–19, by Race and Hispanic Origin of Mother: 2016 and 2017

Source: Centers for Disease Control and Prevention, 2017.

In 2004, the birth rates for teenaged mothers reached a historic low, with a birth rate of 41.2 births per 1,000 women aged 15 to 19 (Centers for Disease Control and Prevention, 2005). At the time, these trends were quite encouraging because in 1991 the birth rates for teen moms was nearly 62 per 1,000 women. In 2018, the birth rate for women aged 15 to 19 was 17.4 births per 1,000—an all-time low and a 55 percent decline since 2007 (National Vital Statistics Reports, 2019). It's still too early to know if this downward trend is permanent, but one thing is for certain: Today, teenaged sexual partners are either abstaining from sexual intercourse or they are practicing safer methods of sex and contraception. As you can see in Figure 10.1, the numbers of births among teen moms vary between races and ethnicities. Encouragingly, the birth rates have declined for all groups.

Trends Among Unmarried Parents

Nonmarital births are widespread, and they touch families of all different races and ethnicities, income class, religious groups, and demographic areas. In 2018, slightly more than 40 percent of all births in the United States were nonmarital births; this rate has remained relatively steady since 2014 (Centers for Disease Control and Prevention, 2019a). Births to unmarried partners can be first births or subsequent births; they can occur to a person who has never been married, as well as to divorced or widowed individuals. Further, a woman with children may have had one or more within a marriage and other births outside of marriage. And, because prior to 2016, U.S. demographers did not consider gay or lesbian partnerships to be "marriages," births to these couple were considered to be "nonmarital" births. As you learned in Chapter 1, African American/Black Caribbean families are typically formed when an unmarried mother gives birth a child; the recent data confirm that more than two-thirds (67 percent) of African American births were nonmarital births (National Vital Statistics Reports, 2017). By way of comparison, slightly more than one-half of births among American Indians/Native Alaskans were to unmarried women, and about one-fourth were to nonmarried white women (National Vital Statistics Reports, 2017).

A number of factors are associated with the unprecedented rates of births that occur outside of marriage (Solomon-Fears, 2008):

- Marriage postponement—there is an increase in the median age at first marriage
- Childfree movement—there is decreased childbearing among married couples

- Increased divorce rates
- Increased numbers of cohabiting couples
- Increased sexual activity outside of marriage
- Improper use/lack of use of contraceptive methods
- Participation in risky behaviors that often lead to sex, such as alcohol and drug use

When considering all of these factors, the trend of births to unmarried partners may very well continue and may even further increase. Certainly, these trends will continue to reshape the landscape of American family life and experiences.

Pregnancy at Different Ages

In the past, women in their 20s were thought to be at the peak of their childbearing years and have historically accounted for the most births. What are today's trends? In 2017, among women aged 20 to 24, the birth rate was 71.0—down from 85.1 in 2008 (National Vital Statistics Reports, 2018; see Figure 10.2). In contemporary America, the primary childbearing years are now a woman's early 30s. These data may reflect the overall trends of women who delay childbearing to pursue educational and professional endeavors, as well as an increase in cohabitation. Today, Millennial women account for the vast majority of births in the United States—82 percent (Pew Research Center, 2018). However, they are delaying childbearing in comparison to Generation X women. For example, while today 48 percent of Millennial women are moms, when Gen X women were the same age, 57 percent of them were already moms (Pew Research Center, 2018). These data support the idea that women are delaying childbearing today.

The United States is also seeing an increase in births among older women not traditionally thought of as in their "childbearing years." As you can see in Table 10.1, birth rates are increasing among women between the ages of 40 and 49. A bit later, we'll discuss the possible birth complications that may arise when a woman delays childbearing.

Childbearing trends evolved throughout the 20th and into the 21st centuries. As the data show, many women are delaying childbearing—perhaps due to education and career opportunities or perhaps due to relationship circumstances. Later we'll explore in depth why some women and couples delay—or defer all together—childbearing.

Now that you have a good understanding of the birth trends in the United States, let's take a more in-depth look at two groups of parents that have become an increasing focus of family and social scientists: teenage mothers and gay and lesbian parents.

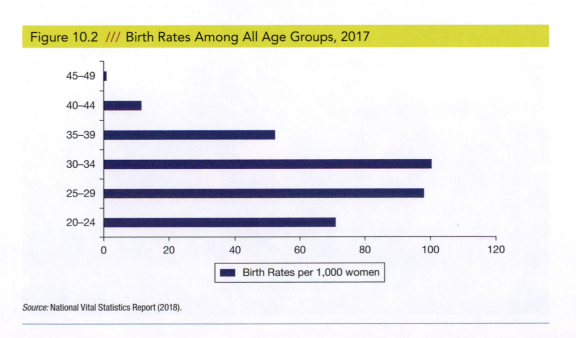

Figure 10.2 /// Birth Rates Among All Age Groups, 2017

Source: National Vital Statistics Report (2018).

Table 10.1 /// Birth Rates Among Older Women, Ages 40–49: 2010–1017

Year	Age of Mother Giving Birth	
	40–44	45–49
2010	10.2	0.7
2011	10.3	0.7
2012	10.4	0.7
2013	10.4	0.8
2014	10.6	0.8
2015	11.0	0.8
2016	11.4	0.9
2017	11.6	0.9

Source: National Vital Statistics Report (2017).

Teenage Pregnancy

During the next 12 months, more than half a million teenagers will become pregnant and nearly 195,000 will give birth (Guttmacher Institute, 2018). In spite of the recent declines in teen birth rates to U.S. adolescent girls and young women, the teen pregnancy rate in the United States is substantially higher than in other Western industrialized nations. For example, in America the teen pregnancy rate is 17.4, while Canada has a teen pregnancy rate of 12.8 (Guttmacher Institute, 2018). The Guttmacher Institute, a nonprofit organization that focuses on sexual and reproductive health research, notes that although the United States has seen substantial declines in teen pregnancy rates over the past 10 years, adolescent birth rates remain more than twice as high as those found in other countries. Figure 10.3 presents the birth rates of other Western countries.

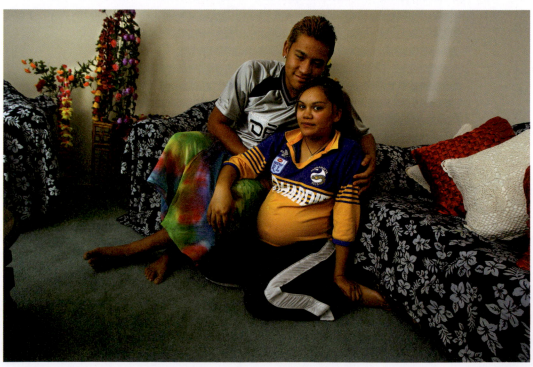

Although teenage pregnancy carries with it many medical, psychological, and developmental obstacles, with educational, informational, and emotional support young parents can overcome these difficulties.

Figure 10.3 /// Birth Rates, by Country

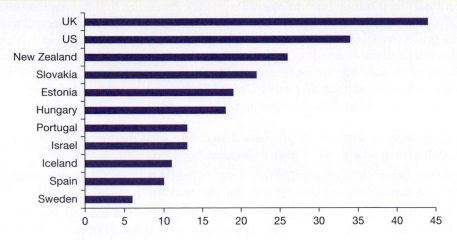

Notes: Graph shows number of births per 1,000 women aged 15–19. All estimates are for 2011 except for Slovenia (2009), and Sweden and the United States (2010).

Source: The Guttmacher Institute (2015).

In our study of intimate relationships, coupling, marriage, and family life, it is important to understand the incidence of teen pregnancy because births to teen moms are linked to a host of critical issues in our society today: poverty, overall child health and well-being, births to unmarried women, responsible fatherhood, sexuality and health concerns, education/school failure, child abuse and neglect, and other risky behaviors, such as drug and alcohol use and abuse and crime (Power to Decide, 2019). There is no doubt that teen pregnancy and childbearing carry both social and economic impacts on the teen moms and their children. Without question, teen mothers face a range of developmental risks.

Impacts of Teen Pregnancy on the Mom

Teen parents and their babies start out with many disadvantages. When the head of the family is an adolescent girl, both the teen parent and her child are at increased risk for medical, psychological, developmental, and social-emotional problems.

- *Medical/Psychological.* The medical risks for adolescent mothers and their babies are significant, especially for younger adolescent mothers (10- to 14-year-olds). Young adolescents face a higher risk of complications and death as a result of pregnancy than other women (World Health Organization, 2018). For example, the risk of dying during labor and birth is two to four times higher for women at age 17 than it is for women who have children in their 20s (Guttmacher Institute, 2004).

- *Developmental.* Research consistently shows that adolescent mothers struggle when trying to form and maintain stable interpersonal relationships and family life (see Barber, Kusunoki, Gatny, & Melendez, 2017, for a full review). Many of these teen parents continue their dependence on family members rather than shifting to more independence and autonomy (Hanson, 1992). Furthermore, the children of teenage mothers "are more likely to have lower school achievement and drop out of high school, have more health problems, be incarcerated at some time during adolescence, give birth as a teen, and face unemployment as a young adult" (Centers for Disease Control and Prevention, 2019c).

- *Socioeconomic.* More than two-thirds of all teen moms are on welfare (federal support to promote the basic physical and material well-being of people in need), and more than one-half of mothers who receive welfare today are teen moms. Teen pregnancy and birth are also significant contributors to high school dropout rates: Today, only about 50 percent of teen moms receive a high school diploma or obtain their GED (diploma equivalent) by age 22 (Centers for Disease Control and Prevention, 2019c).

Interventions for Adolescent Parents

The National Organization on Adolescent Pregnancy, Parenting, and Prevention (2008) has stated, "[Given that] all children need healthy, nurturing, stable relationships and to experience the protective factors during early childhood . . . [and] given the competing dynamics of adolescence and the demands of parenthood, it is incumbent upon families, communities, and society to provide supportive [structures] to teen parents to ensure their children grow health and safe and reach school ready to learn." To this end, a national campaign to reduce teen pregnancy should include the following:

- *Comprehensive school-based programs* designed to keep the pregnant and/or parenting adolescent in school and on track to complete her degree
- *Comprehensive family support services* designed to help parents of the pregnant and/or parenting teen to develop parenting skills and coping skills
- *Expansion of government programs* designed to improve the medical and psychosocial health and well-being of pregnant and parenting teens and their offspring. Youth-friendly contraceptive and reproduce health services should be included.
- *Comprehensive community programs* designed to enhance adolescents' parenting skills and support the unique needs of teen mothers and fathers and to provide early education for at-risk infants and children

In 2007, then-U.S. presidential candidate Senator Barack Obama (D-IL) introduced a bill to reduce teen pregnancies in minority communities. The Communities of Color Teen Pregnancy Prevention Act of 2007 sought to strengthen community-based intervention efforts for teen pregnancy services and to establish a comprehensive national database to provide culturally and linguistically sensitive information on teen pregnancy reduction. Senator Obama noted,

> Teen pregnancy can derail the plans of students with dreams of achieving professional success, and it's hitting minority communities particularly hard. Pregnancies in African American and Latino communities remain inexcusably high. We must develop innovative approaches to strengthen our community support networks and services to educate our teens about pregnancy and provide them with every chance to succeed in school and beyond. (110th Cong., 1st Sess. 1790, 2007)

HAVING CHILDREN: NOW, LATER, OR NEVER?

Do you want children? At what age did you come to your decision—have you wanted to have children/not have children for as long as you can remember, or have you only recently come to this decision, as you have acquired more relationship and life experiences? And when is the "right time" to have children?

Why Do People Want Children?

The decision to become a parent is a very complex issue because it includes a number of interrelated components. For instance, do we have a child because of the subjective value societies place on them or because of personal, intrinsic reasons—or both? Do we have children because society *expects* us to?

Since the 1970s, researchers have attempted to document the various needs that children fulfill for adults; they have also tried to better understand how adults perceive the value of children (see Hoffman & Hoffman, 1973). Over the past four decades, researchers have discovered that people most often desire to have children because of the psychological and emotional satisfaction they offer to parents, the social ties children offer as adults age, and their economic value (such as tax breaks; for a complete review, see Lawson, 2004). On the other hand, the lack of desire to become a parent has been associated with adults who place a greater importance on self-fulfillment, leisure time, relationship quality, career advancement, and greater financial freedom (Seccombe, 1991).

Two main approaches have been taken by social science researchers to understand the attitudes and motivations associated with becoming a parent: The perceived value of children and the appeal of parenthood.

The Perceived Value of Children

Most studies and theories about the motivation to become a parent center on the perspective that there are perceived rewards and costs associated with parenthood (Lawson, 2004). As you learned in Chapter 7, many of us engage in a cost-benefit analysis when we choose our life partners; we also do the same when we decide whether to have children. For example, some research suggests that one of the rewards of having children is that they meet some of our basic psychological needs (such as love and affection), and this is what motivates peoples' desires to have children (Al-Fadhli & Smith, 1996; Yamaguchi & Fergusson, 1995). Some adults may evaluate the costs (such as substantial decreases in personal time and freedom and substantial increases in financial responsibilities) and decide against having children. If prospective parents believe that the net value of having children is greater than the costs associated with having children, they will be motivated to have children (Lawson, 2004). On the other hand, if they judge that the costs outweigh the benefits, they will forgo the Mommy/Daddy track and seek other sources to meet their needs, such as turning to nieces and nephews for psychological need fulfillment not met by having their own children.

Table 10.2 shows the Perceptions of Parenting Inventory, which helps people determine the rewards and costs they associate with having children (Lawson, 2004). As you can see, this

---

Table 10.2 /// Perceptions of Parenting Inventory: Factors People Consider Before Becoming Parents

Enrichment
Caring for the child would bring me happiness.
Parenting the child would be rewarding,
My spouse/partner and I would grow closer together through the experience.
Parenting the child would make me a better person.

Isolation
I would have less time to spend doing what I enjoy.
Caring for the child would interfere with the time I want to spend with my spouse.

Commitment
Parenting the child would be a never-ending responsibility.
The child would be dependent on me.

Instrumental Costs
Raising the child would be financially expensive.
Parenting the child would be emotionally exhausting.
Caring for the child would be physically exhausting.

Continuity
I would look forward to being a grandparent in the future.
Our relationship would change over the years from parent to friend.
The child would carry on my family name.

Perceived Support
My friends and family would help me care for the child.
My family and friends would provide social support.

Source: Lawson (2004).

inventory assesses the rewards of parenting, which include *enrichment* and *continuity*, as well as the costs, which include *isolation, instrumental costs,* and *commitment.* As you look through the table, which items do you most strongly agree with? Most strongly disagree with? It's important to note that your answers may change over time. For example, you may not want to have a child at this time because of the financial and emotional costs; however, when your circumstances change, you might decide that the benefits of having children outweigh these particular costs.

The Appeal of Parenthood

Probably all of us have seen children having a temper tantrum at the grocery store or Target and go limp as a wet noodle when an exasperated parent tries to pick the child up to get him or her out of the store as fast as possible. And under our breath (or out loud), we have probably said, "I will *never* have children!" Certainly, there are times when having children doesn't seem like a very appealing thought—even after we've had them! Despite the fact that all of us have probably not wanted children at one time or another, there is some evidence that there are certain psychological factors that are related to the appeal of parenting, particularly that of early childhood experiences.

A number of studies have attempted to show that our early experiences with our parents, such as parental nurturance, discipline, and attention, are significantly related to the motivation to parent. For example, some research has demonstrated that bad memories of our childhood experiences have accounted for unique variances in why some men and women choose to have children and others do not (Gerson, 1980, 1985, 1986). These experiences underlie what is known as the **family projection process** (Bowen, 1966). This process stresses that the appeal of having children is the result of finding a way to satisfy our individual unmet needs from childhood. Stated another way, people who become parents do so because they feel that they were not given enough love, attention, or support as a child. Their own children, then, serve to enact their internalized unsatisfactory childhood experiences—parents have children to give them what they themselves never had as a child. It's important to note, however, that other research has shown that as individuals enter their 30s, they feel less dependent on childhood memories in making important life choices, such as having children (Gerson, Posner, & Morris, 1991).

Family projection process:

a theory that people who have children do so because they are trying to gain what they did not have in their own childhood, such as love and attention.

Gay Men and Lesbians: Deciding to Have Children

How do sexual minorities become parents? What are the routes available to them to build families? Although the number of planned families by gay men and lesbian women has been steadily growing in recent years, little research has been undertaken to understand the motivations of gays and lesbians to become parents (Bos, van Balen, & van den Boom 2004; Costa & Tasker, 2018; Goldberg, Gartrell, & Gates, 2014). Certainly the existing research concerning the perceived value of children and the appeal of parenthood applies to homosexual parents as well as to heterosexual parents, but some have tried to determine whether gays and lesbians have additional, different motivations to become parents.

In general, LGBTQ+ parents are more likely than opposite-sex couples to choose adoption as their preferred route to parenthood (Goldberg, Downing, & Moyer, 2012; Goldberg, Downing, & Richardson, 2009). In a recent study of 366 prospective LGBTQ+ adopters of children, the researcher wanted to determine the reasons why same-sex couples wanted children, specifically, their motivations for adoption (Costa & Tasker, 2018). The study found these overarching themes among LGBTQ parents:

- *Seeking permanency:* "We wanted a forever family" (p. 4165).
- *Altruistic/moral motivation:* Couples wanted to provide a permanent home for a child in need.
- *Individualistic/intrinsic motivation:* "I thought that sharing the adoptive experience with my trans partner would be more equitable than being the biological parent in our partnership" (p. 4168).
- *Motivated reasoning:* Although some potential parents had hoped to have a biological child, ultimately their desire for being a parent was more important than how the child came to their family.

iStock.com/Monkeybusinessimages

Sexual orientation and/ or identity have nothing to do with the quality of parenting, caregiving, nurturing, and love provided to children.

The emergence of planned gay fatherhood and lesbian motherhood is indicative of broad social change that is taking place in our society and societies around the world. Regardless of their sexual orientation, people are questioning existing parenting norms and are finding ways to create families (Berkowitz & Marsiglio, 2007). Examining the experiences of gay men and lesbians gives us an important opportunity to accept them into the parenting mainstream. In Chapter 11, we'll take an extensive look at the parenting experiences of LGBT people, as well as their experiences with the transition to parenthood.

The decision to have a child or forgo childbearing is a crucial—and irrevocable—decision that warrants careful and thoughtful attention. And, although many of you may know that you desire to have children, the timing of parenthood is also an issue that needs to be considered. Just when is the "right time" to have children in the lifespan of a couple's relationship?

Ready or Not? The "Right Time" to Have Children

You learned in Chapter 1 that families experience a common lifecourse pattern, referred to as the Family Life Cycle; for many families, this lifecourse includes having children. Within psychology and family studies/family sciences, a **life transition** (such as the decision to become a parent) is considered to be a point at which people take on new roles and obligations (Hagestad & Call, 2007). A **turning point** is a transition that entails a permanent, lasting shift in the direction of the lifecourse of a person's relationship. Often, this term is used in connection with the transition to parenthood (Hagestad & Call, 2007). **Timing** refers to the age at which a transition takes place. Thus, when considering the decision to become a parent, the timing of parenthood is given much attention because it speaks to the significance of this transition/turning point in a person's life.

Across life, the majority of individuals follow and relatively adhere to socially approved and shaped pathways, such as the "right" time to get married and the "right" time to have children. These proper times are referred to as **age-related norms**—and these norms are culturally specific. In the United States, for example, the age-related norm of a woman giving birth for the first time is 26 years old, and for fathers it's 31 (Centers for Disease Control and Prevention, 2019a). By way of comparison, in Switzerland, Japan, Spain, Italy, and South Korea, the age-related norm for women to give birth for the first time is 31. As sociologists Gunhild

Life transition:
within psychology and family studies, a point at which people take on new roles and obligations, such as becoming a parent.

Turning point:
a transition that entails a permanent, lasting shift in the direction of the lifecourse of a person's relationship.

Timing:
refers to the age at which a transition takes place.

Age-related norms:
socially approved and shaped pathways that determine the "right" time for certain life events, such as marriage or having children.

Hagestad and Vaughn Call (2007) observe, unlike men who can produce children well into old age, "biology presents a woman with nonnegotiable deadlines [for becoming pregnant]," because after a certain point in her lifespan she no longer has the ability to produce eggs (p. 1342). Thus, a woman's "window of opportunity" to become pregnant is essentially limited to her teens, 20s, and 30s. Women who pass these age norms are often subjected to informal chastising with comments such as, "Having a baby at *your* age?" (Hagestad & Call, 2007). Society also structures the sequence of life transitions. For instance, may societies condone childbearing only after a couple is married. However, as you saw earlier, a significant number of childbirths in this country are to unmarried women; it is clear the childbearing sequence is undergoing change in our society and in other Western societies, as well.

So, when is the "right" time to have children? There is no research that helps us to understand parenthood timing from a practical viewpoint, but there are a number of questions a woman, gestational parent, or a couple might ask themselves before becoming pregnant or deciding to bring a child into the relationship through adoption:

- *Do I have the parenting skills necessary to raise a child?* Parenting skills include things such as patience; being able to stay calm in the midst of turmoil; being able to control your anger; understanding how to effectively discipline a child in age-appropriate ways; being able to communicate expectations, warmth, and nurturance; and being an effective role model.

- *How strong is your relationship?* The way a couple treats each other teaches children about love, intimacy, communication, relationships, trust, and respect. Do you have a solid foundation on which to raise a family?

- *Do you and your partner have similar beliefs?* It is imperative that parents in relationships share similar beliefs about discipline, education, childcare, and what child behaviors are or are not acceptable. This is especially important if you have an interracial or interfaith relationship.

- *Where are you financially?* Not only must you be able to provide for your child's basic needs (food, shelter, clothing) but you also need to consider saving for their future education needs, as well as your own.

- *When do you want children?* Rarely does a child bring a couple closer together. Be sure to examine the true motivations for wanting a child.

As most parents will attest, children are wonderful and worth the sleep deprivation, arguments how to/not to raise them, and overdue credit card bills. But in each family, there are many personal factors involved in deciding when to have children. It's not a simple decision because having children *will* change your life. Are you up to the challenge?

Childfree by Choice

Never married, Ricky Gervais, the co-creator of the television series *The Office,* has been with his partner, Jane Fallon, for more than 30 years, and they remain childless. As Gervais said, "We never wanted to be parents, with all that entails: the loss of freedom, total dependency." The **childfree-by-choice** trend is certainly nothing new as a number of A-list celebrities, such as Oprah Winfrey, have opted to remain childfree. Even Dr. Seuss, the infamous children's book author, was childfree by choice. But the "no kids, no thanks" trend is moving beyond the borders of Hollywood and extending to mainstream USA. Today, 4 in 10 (37 percent) of adults over the age of 50 say they don't ever expect to become parents; among adults under age 50, about one-fourth say they just don't want kids (Pew Research Center, 2018).

To date, there has been sparse empirical research in family studies, sociology, or psychology that examines the motives of women and men who are voluntarily childless; however, there are a few studies that help us understand why people opt to remain childfree. For example, one body of research found that there are certain categories or groups among those who elect not to become parents. These groups include those who are certain they

Childfree-by-choice: the voluntary choice not to have children.

do not want children, those who are certain they do not want children at this point in their lives, those who are ambivalent about having children, and those who feel the decision was made for them due to health reasons or lack of a partner (Cartwright, 1999). In 2019, American politician Alexandria Ocasio-Cortez (D-NY) raised the issue of whether adults should continue to have children, given the environmental impact of doing so and given the impact of climate change. Although no empirical studies to date have addressed this topic, an online poll of *Business Insider* readers found that 38 percent of Americans aged 18 to 29 who responded to the survey believe that climate change should be considered when deciding to have children (Irfan, 2019).

The reasons people remain childfree are as many and varying as the reasons people opt to become parents. Rathus and Nevid (1992) found in their study of hundreds of couples that there are various reasons why individuals and couples opt for the no-kids track: more time with one another, freedom from the responsibility of raising children, financial freedom, able to devote more time to careers, and concerns about worldwide overpopulation. More recent research seems to confirm these findings. For example, one study posits that there is a value shift taking place in Western cultures, and because of this, people place higher priority on individualization and secularization, a disconnection from the eras-old importance placed on religious and spiritual concerns (Lesthaeghe, 2014).

Other research found that beyond individual factors ("micro" factors), social factors ("macro" factors), such as the increase in women's education levels and their participation in the job market, "compete with raising children" (Weston & Qu, 2001). Changing social values, decreasing importance of religion, access to legal abortion, and effective contraceptives also alter childbearing. These research findings indicated that those who choose to be childless do so because of their dislike of children, choice of lifestyle, lack of interest in children and parenting, or a belief that the world is too dangerous for children.

Similar to Rathus and Nevid, other studies found that financial security and job security are also factors closely linked to an individual's decision to become a parent (MacKay, 1994; McDonald, 2000; Wooden, 1999). An additional study appears to confirm the findings from prior research. Sociologist Kristin Park (2005) analyzed the motives of 23 childless men and women. Through in-depth interviews, she found that women believed parenting

iStock.com/GibsonPictures

Couples may adopt the no-kids/no-thanks track so they can pursue other endeavors, such as traveling.

would conflict with their careers and/or leisure activities. The women also indicated that they lacked a "maternal instinct" or they were generally uninterested in children. Men, more than women, believed that parenting required too many sacrifices, including great financial expense. Both men and women indicated that they felt their personalities were not suited to parenting.

Although to some it may appear that women remain childfree for selfish reasons, this is not necessarily the case. Couples must be honest when assessing whether or not to become parents. Some people feel that their lives are complete and full without children. Others choose to be childfree because of unfortunate circumstances, and in these instances, the decision can be a painful one. For example, a close friend of mine desperately desired to be a mother but because she is a genetic carrier of an always-fatal type of muscular dystrophy, she opted to remain childless. Other couples may not consciously decide not to have children—they simply fall into childlessness.

Delayed Childbearing

While some couples remain childfree by choice and other couples are childless for medical or physiological reasons that prohibit them from becoming pregnant, some couples have perhaps every intention of becoming parents but for one reason or another parenthood eludes them. As Megan, a colleague of mine, explains,

> Before we became engaged, Kale and I knew we wanted children—it was something we held in common. He comes very large family, and I come from a family with three other siblings. Our plan was to have our first child by the age of 35, but our business was really taking off and we thought we had plenty of time. We began trying to conceive at about the age of 35 or so and found out we had infertility problems. We tried fertility treatments for a few years with no success . . . so now we find ourselves in our mid-40s without children. Totally not planned. Or wanted. But even though it's not what we planned, after the grief passed for the family we had hoped for, we're very content with our lives right now.

Sociology professor Jean Veevers (1980) wanted to better understand how couples like Megan and Kale become a childless couple. This study defined four specific stages involved in delayed childbearing decision making:

1. *Postponing childbearing for a definite period of time.* Couples in this first stage intentionally delay childbearing in order to achieve certain goals they have set for themselves, such as meeting educational goals. Like Megan and Kale, perhaps they want to devote their attention to their careers or give their new business time to get established.

2. *Postponing childbearing for an indefinite period of time.* "We'll eventually get around to having children." In this stage of decision making, couples' reasons for not having children become more and more unclear and perhaps indefinable even to themselves. For whatever reasons, they feel that the timing is "just not right."

3. *Weighing the pros and cons of being parents.* During this stage of decision making, couples deliberate the costs and benefits associated with parenthood.

4. *Coming to terms with being childless.* It is at this point that couples realize they have become childless by default. Like Megan and Kale, many couples may have intended to become parents, but numerous postponements in their decision making essentially made the decision for them.

Even though subsequent infertility and significantly increased risks of negative outcomes for the baby are associated with delayed childbearing in women, there are several bodies of empirical evidence that suggest childbearing among older parents is advantageous to children. For example, University of Maryland sociology professor Steve Martin (2002) found through his review of the literature that both economic and psychosocial (social and emotional) benefits for the child are associated with delayed childbearing. He cites a number of studies that indicate that the older a woman is when she has her first child, the greater the economic benefit to both herself and her baby. Findings further indicate that women who postpone childbearing are more likely to stay in the workforce throughout retirement eligibility, and, as a result, they have distinctively higher earning potential than early child bearers. Women who postpone childbearing are also better able to find quality childcare because of their earnings. Quality childcare, in turn, increases the woman's work productivity, and her earnings potential greatly reduces "lost career time." In addition to being born into a higher income bracket, children born to older parents have better access to education opportunities. Children of older parents also suffer fewer financial consequences if their parents divorce.

Children of older parents also experience psychosocial benefits. For instance, older parents have stronger and more reliable social support networks than younger parents, providing more stability for the entire family to cope with the inevitable stressors that accompany childrearing (Martin, 2002). The quality of the mother-child relationship is higher compared to mother-child relationships of younger mothers. For example, older mothers tend to be more positive about parenting and show less anger and frustration in parenting, while older fathers tend to be very involved in their children's lives, although they are not as physically active in play as are younger fathers. Older fathers are also more likely than younger fathers to share household tasks following the birth of a baby. And finally, because they have already experienced many significant life experiences, older parents are less likely than younger parents to experience depression, loss of self-esteem, or feelings of incompetence in parenting. Martin concludes that although older parents may experience fatigue and a lack of energy, their increased maturity seems to outweigh these negative psychosocial outcomes.

Family Size: Lots of Tots?

So, you've made the decision to have children. The next question is, How many children do you desire to have? A recent Gallup Poll (2018) of 1,000 U.S. adults revealed that slightly less than one-half of those surveyed indicated that two children is the "ideal" family size; about one-fourth said that three children were ideal (see Figure 10.4). The ideal family size trends change over time and reflect cultural and societal changes. For instance, there is a sharp decline in the perceptions of ideal family size between the 1960s and 1970s. This trend may reflect the advent of the birth control pill in the 1960s, which gave women more control over their fertility; this increased control may have, in turn, shaped attitudes about ideal family size.

In many ways, the United States is considered to be a pronatalist society. **Pronatalism**, or **natalism**, is an ideology that embraces childbearing. Pronatalist attitudes and beliefs are prevalent in the United States (Watkins, 2008). For instance, when a woman or a couple gives birth to just one child and says, "no more," or when she or they decide to forgo having children altogether, sometimes people aren't sure how to respond. Is she infertile? Do they feel overwhelmed as parents? Are they selfish? **Antinatalist** countries discourage childbearing. China's previous one-child-per-family policy is an example of this.

Do parents have only so much to give to their kids? One theory maintains that some parents' resources are limited and become depleted when additional children are added to the family.

Draining Mom and Dad: The Resource Dilution Hypothesis

Parental time, energy, and resources are limited, and the **resource dilution hypothesis** contends that parents' finite resources become diluted when spread over a larger number of children (Blake, 1981). A number of studies in the 1980s and 1990s seemed to support this

Pronatalism:
an ideology that embraces childbearing.

Antinatalist:
an ideology that discourages childbearing.

Resource dilution hypothesis:
a theory that contends parents' finite resources become diluted when spread over a larger number of children.

Figure 10.4 /// Perception of "Ideal" Family Size

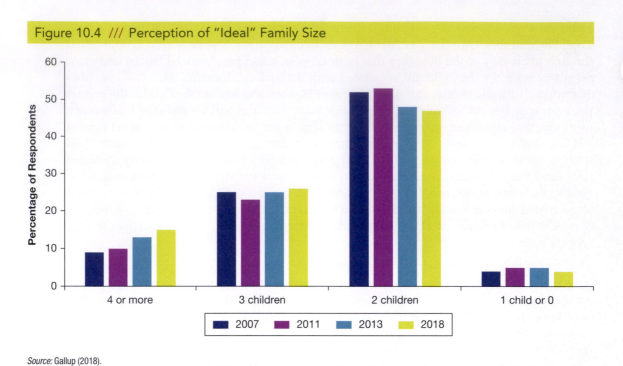

Source: Gallup (2018).

theory when the researchers discovered that a child in a large household receives less attention than a child in a smaller household, and this lack of attention later affected the educational level the child attained (see Strohschein, Gauthier, Campbell, & Kleparchuk, 2008, for a complete review). Other studies have similarly shown that maternal attention is greatest for firstborn children and less for subsequent siblings, and that mothers reduce positive interactions with their older children following the birth of another. With these results in mind, you may be thinking, "Wow, family size *does* matter—I'm only going to have one child!" But newer research may contradict these prior findings.

Researchers from Canada surveyed more than 13,000 parents and found that, because the relationship of a parent to each child is unique, effects of family size need to be studied differently than they were in the past (Strohschein et al., 2008). In their current study, the investigators looked at two different areas of parenting: positive interaction (the extent to which parents are responsive to their children's needs) and consistent parenting (the frequency with which parents set boundaries and establish standards for appropriate behavior). Using these two factors, they wanted to determine how parenting practices change when new children are added to the family system. In their long-term study, the researchers discovered that "parents do not so much *dilute* their resources when a new child is added . . . [rather,] they act to deploy their resources differently" (p. 681). This body of research indicates that instead of draining resources away from other children, as prior studies suggested, when new siblings are added to the family, parents employ a "managerial approach" to parenting—they shift, reallocate, and reorganize their resources to ensure that every family member's needs are met.

As you learned in Chapter 2, it is always important, as consumers of science and empirical studies, to keep at the forefront that all research must be considered in its full context. In this case, we need to fully consider how the "economic development, SES, increasing incomes [today]" as well as our abilities to time fertility, all play key roles in how our parenting resources are allocated across generations (Riswick & Engelen, 2018, p. 521).

Although prior evidence does suggest potential negative outcomes for children who are members of large families, "negative [outcomes] are not present in all populations, for all outcomes or in all time periods" (Riswick & Engelen, 2018, p. 521).

James Ambler/Barcroft USA/Getty Images

It's impossible to determine the "ideal" family size because it is a uniquely personal decision that is affected by many factors. Today, there is an emerging trend that needs to be addressed when discussing family size: the Quiverfull movement.

The Quiverfull Movement: "Don't You Know What Causes That?"

Large families are unusual in the United States (Arnold, 2005). Although rather common in the past, families with more than 6 children are so rare today that the Census no longer tracks these data (Hartill, 2001). But in the Quiverfull movement, parents are having as many as 20 children.

The **Quiverfull movement**, which began in the 1980s, is a pronatalist belief that is practiced among some evangelical Protestant Christian couples in the United States, as well as some Catholics and Mormons, and also has some adherents in Canada, Australia, New Zealand, and England. Forgoing all forms of birth control as a matter of principle and personal choice, a "QF" couple is motivated to have many children because of a desire to be obedient to what they believe are spiritual commands and mandates. Citing biblical passages such as "be fruitful and multiply" and "blessed is the person who has a quiver full of children," adherents to the Quiverfull movement maintain an "open willingness" to joyfully receive and not thwart however many children are bestowed upon them (Campbell, 2003).

Quiverfull movement: a fundamentalist Christian group that encourages couples to have many children because of a desire to be obedient to what they believe are commands in the Bible.

But how does religion affect a person's fertility? Some earlier research suggested that there are three conditions that produce religious effects on fertility: (1) The religion promotes norms about fertility-related behaviors, such as the use of birth control; (2) the organization is able to enforce conformity to these norms (either through social influence or through sanctions); and (3) the religion is a very important part of a person's individual identity (McQuillan, 2004). A study of 7,600 nationally representative subjects to identify what determines differences in rates of fertility among some religious groups confirms the earlier research (Hayford & Morgan, 2008). The researchers found that women for whom religion is an important facet in daily life have higher fertility intentions, compared to nonreligious women. As sociologists Jennifer McMorris and Jennifer Glass (2018) observe, "religious messages, mores [norms], and laws profoundly shape the gendered lives of men and women" (p. 433). The Pew Research Center's (2017) investigation into the relationship between religiosity and fertility supports the idea that women who practice their religious beliefs have more children than those who state they are unaffiliated with a religion. This demographic examination looked specifically at Christian and Muslim fertility:

- *Globally:* On average, women who are affiliated with religiosity have 2.5 children; those who are not have 1.6.
- *Christian:* Between 2010 and 2015, 33 percent of all births worldwide were to Christians.
- *Muslim:* Between 2010 and 2015, 31 percent of all births worldwide were to Muslims.
- *Unaffiliated:* Between 2010 and 2015, 10 percent of all births worldwide were to those unaffiliated with a religious belief or practice.

It is projected that by 2060, 36 percent of all births globally will be to Muslims, and 35 percent will be to Christians; 9 percent of births will be to the religiously unaffiliated. This information is important because it helps us to see that for some women and their partners, religious affiliation appears to impact childbearing attitudes, beliefs, and behaviors. Without question, further study needs to be undertaken to better understand this intersection of gender expectations and religion.

Although some may disagree with couples' choices to have large numbers of children, it is important to consider whether they—just as other diverse family forms—should be afforded the same social support as other families are.

BEING PREGNANT AND GIVING BIRTH

Just as with other events associated with family life, pregnancy and childbirth are processes that change over time, and the experiences encompass a number of sequential stages (conception, pregnancy, childbirth, and caring for the baby); these emotional and physical changes in the gestational parent are associated with changes in spousal well-being and marital satisfaction, and are illustrated in Figure 10.5 (Cowan & Cowan, 2000).

In the sections that follow, we'll explore the common emotional and relationship changes that occur during pregnancy and how these changes affect a couple's relationship, from conflict, to sexuality, to the early days of transitioning to parenthood and incorporating another member into the family system. Having realistic expectations when you are about to become a parent can make the transition to parenthood much smoother because there's a lot to consider—and to worry about—when a woman or a couple is expecting a baby.

Having a baby and raising it to the age of 18, for example, is a costly endeavor! Table 10.3 shows the estimated annual costs of raising a child; the data are based on a survey by the U.S. Department of Agriculture (2019) and show costs based on a family with two children, on a per-child basis. These figures to not include any estimates for sending a child to college, or any costs associated with a child who lives in the home after the age of 18 (which, as you have learned, is common today in America). Each baby brought into a family system (through birth or adoption) is anywhere from a 100-thousand-dollar to a quarter of a million–dollar investment. As soon as pregnancy is confirmed or the adoption is finalized, parents should sit down together and work out a *realistic* budget—from maternity clothes, baby gear, the baby's nursery, and medical costs associated with having a baby, to perhaps going from two incomes to one—it all adds up quickly! Talking about these anticipated changes early on helps parents better manage their finances, and it also helps reduce conflicts that arise because of money issues.

Aside from the money concerns, couples have other things they must negotiate as they start their journeys to become parents. In particular, the mother will experience emotional and physical changes that will affect the couple's relationship.

Figure 10.5 /// A Month-by-Month Guide to Pregnancy

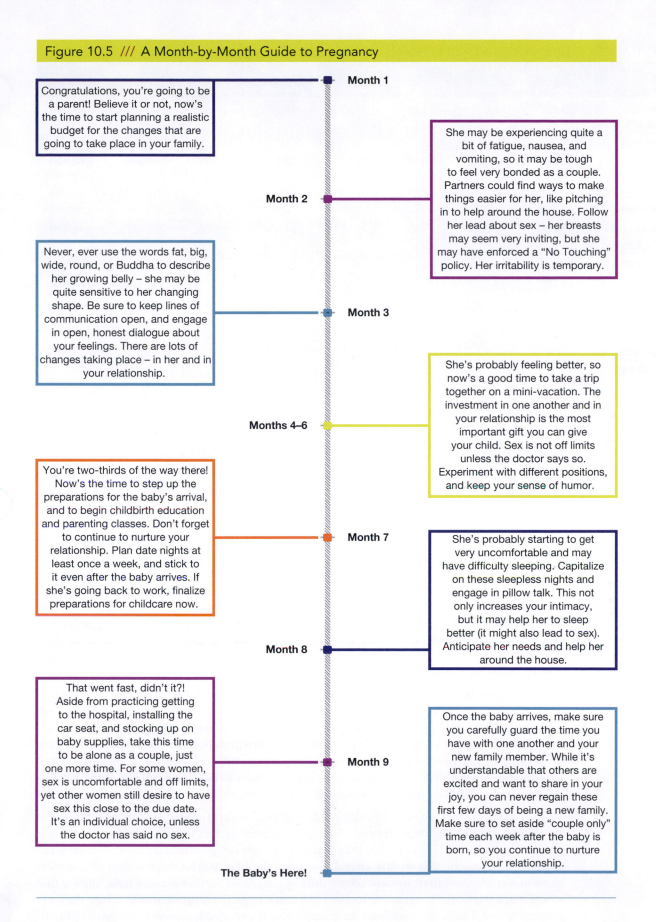

Month 1

Congratulations, you're going to be a parent! Believe it or not, now's the time to start planning a realistic budget for the changes that are going to take place in your family.

Month 2

She may be experiencing quite a bit of fatigue, nausea, and vomiting, so it may be tough to feel very bonded as a couple. Partners could find ways to make things easier for her, like pitching in to help around the house. Follow her lead about sex – her breasts may seem very inviting, but she may have enforced a "No Touching" policy. Her irritability is temporary.

Month 3

Never, ever use the words fat, big, wide, round, or Buddha to describe her growing belly – she may be quite sensitive to her changing shape. Be sure to keep lines of communication open, and engage in open, honest dialogue about your feelings. There are lots of changes taking place – in her and in your relationship.

Months 4–6

She's probably feeling better, so now's a good time to take a trip together on a mini-vacation. The investment in one another and in your relationship is the most important gift you can give your child. Sex is not off limits unless the doctor says so. Experiment with different positions, and keep your sense of humor.

Month 7

You're two-thirds of the way there! Now's the time to step up the preparations for the baby's arrival, and to begin childbirth education and parenting classes. Don't forget to continue to nurture your relationship. Plan date nights at least once a week, and stick to it even after the baby arrives. If she's going back to work, finalize preparations for childcare now.

She's probably starting to get very uncomfortable and may have difficulty sleeping. Capitalize on these sleepless nights and engage in pillow talk. This not only increases your intimacy, but it may help her to sleep better (it might also lead to sex). Anticipate her needs and help her around the house.

Month 8

Month 9

That went fast, didn't it?! Aside from practicing getting to the hospital, installing the car seat, and stocking up on baby supplies, take this time to be alone as a couple, just one more time. For some women, sex is uncomfortable and off limits, yet other women still desire to have sex this close to the due date. It's an individual choice, unless the doctor has said no sex.

Once the baby arrives, make sure you carefully guard the time you have with one another and your new family member. While it's understandable that others are excited and want to share in your joy, you can never regain these first few days of being a new family. Make sure to set aside "couple only" time each week after the baby is born, so you continue to nurture your relationship.

The Baby's Here!

Table 10.3 /// The Cost of Raising a Child to the Age of 18 (in US Dollars): 2019

	Housing	Food	Transport.	Clothing	Health	Childcare/ Education	Misc.	Total
Dual-Parent Up to $59,410 Annual Income	53,820	31,050	24,630	11,130	14,070	23,640	10,740	**169,080**
Dual-Parent Up to $102,870 Annual Income	70,560	37,620	33,900	13,500	18,990	41,100	19,230	**234,900**
Dual-Parent More Than $102,870 Annual Income	127,800	47,640	49,500	19,080	21,810	88,440	35,400	**389,670**
Single-Parent Up to $40,410 Annual Income	51,120	33,090	17,850	7,080	12840	22,980	12,450	**157,410**
Single-Parent More Than $59,410 Annual Income	105,840	48,390	40,140	10,830	22,410	72,910	33,000	**333,420**

Source: U.S. Department of Agriculture (2019).

Pregnancy: Emotional and Relationship Changes

The birth of a child is a demanding couple and family life situation, and the transition to parenthood is a very difficult adjustment for most couples (Parfitt & Ayers, 2014; Salmela-Aro, Aunola, Saisto, Halmesmaki, & Nurmi, 2006). What follows are the emotional and relationship changes associated with the stages in pregnancy (see Figure 10.5). It's important to note that this discussion is inclusive of all birthing parents. For example, transgender men and non-binary people (TGNB) who still have a functioning vagina (birth canal), ovaries, and a uterus are capable of pregnancy and childbirth, and their experiences are similar to those of cisgender females (Obedin-Maliver & Makadon, 2016; Kirczenow MacDonald, 2019). TGNB who give birth can choose whether they want to be referred to as Mom, Dad, or Parent. For the purposes of our discussion here, TGNB are referred to as the **gestational parent**—the parent who is carrying the pregnancy and giving birth.

Gestational parent: the individual who is carrying a pregnancy and gives birth.

The First Three Months

Due mostly to the hormonal changes that occur during pregnancy, in the early weeks a pregnant person's emotions are often unstable, resulting in mood swings, and it is not uncommon for her to feel depressed. Even if the pregnancy was planned and hoped for, the pregnant person may cry—often for no apparent reason. Frequently, these emotional changes are unsettling for her partner or husband, and the partner may feel inadequate or incapable of meeting her needs. It is not uncommon for both partners to be concerned about the family's finances and the additional costs associated with rearing a child.

Studies that explore couple relationships during pregnancy are rare, but in one study, the researcher found that couple relationships are more stable than unstable during pregnancy, despite the hormonal changes that take place in the woman/gestational parent (Richardson, 1981). The researcher found that, overall, women rate their relationships with their partners as more satisfactory than unsatisfactory during pregnancy. Other studies have shown that women are particularly sensitive to their partner's negative attitude/mood while they are pregnant, and these emotions from men may cause depressive symptoms in women (Buehlman, Gottman, & Katz, 1992; Notarius, Benson, Sloane, Vanzetti, & Hornyak, 1989); these depressive symptoms are thought to lead to increased levels of conflict and jealousy in the couple's relationship (Massar & Buunk, 2019; Salmela-Aro et al., 2006). Other studies have found that pregnancy can result in decreased levels of closeness and communication in couples, and this leads to increased conflict between the two (Florsheim et al., 2003).

As you learned in the previous chapter, human sexuality is reactive to our daily circumstances, and a couple's sex life changes as they encounter altered circumstances. And, certainly, pregnancy is a time of "altered" circumstances! Couples are often concerned that having sex during the early weeks of pregnancy may harm the baby or the mother, but these concerns are typically unwarranted. Unless her physician indicates otherwise, sexual activity is permissible throughout pregnancy. However, both the woman/gestational parent and her partner should remember that because of the early changes associated with pregnancy (such as breast tenderness), she may not be in the mood for any kind of touch because she is reacting to the changes in her body. Couples needs to keep in mind that the pregnant parent is not rejecting the *partner*—just the *thought of/act of sex*. It's best for a partner to follow the pregnant partner's lead about sex throughout pregnancy.

The Next Three Months

The second trimester brings changes in the woman's emotions, too. Most women/gestational parents understand that weight gain is a normal and necessary part of pregnancy, but some women—particularly those who struggle with eating disorders—may become dismayed at their ever-increasing weight. Some pregnant individuals may feel overwhelmed with the responsibilities of parenting or frustrated because their expanding abdomen prevents them from performing job tasks; some may even find that pregnancy interferes with educational or career plans. Worries about finances may affect decisions regarding whether and when to return to work after the baby's birth, and, in turn, may affect the couple's relationship. Although many pregnant people feel attractive and sexy during pregnancy, some feel awkward and unappealing. Most women, however, indicate this as a time of great sexual pleasure. A lot of partners worry that they will "hit" the baby during sexual intercourse, but this concern is unwarranted. The baby is way out of reach, tucked securely in the uterus. Some positions can be uncomfortable, though, so couples often have to get creative in finding sexual positions, such as side-lying positions. The key to sexuality in pregnancy is the same as during any other point in a couple's communication—open and honest communication. It's also important the couple continues to nurture their relationship by going out on dates together or having special nights at home with no interruptions from family and friends. The best parents are parents who make their relationship a priority and foster intimacy.

Pregnancy and the birth of a baby are emotionally demanding for both the gestational parent and the birth partner. Despite these challenges, most couples report that their relationships are stable during pregnancy.

The Last Three Months

Coupled with the physiological changes that occur as the big day nears are multiple relational and emotional changes. By the ninth month, many women feel overwhelmed and, quite frankly, tired of being pregnant! Many pregnant people (and their partners) may lose interest in sex, not only because of exhaustion but also because finding a comfortable sexual position is at times an exercise of futility and hilarity. With baby showers being given for the parents-to-be and final preparations being made in anticipation of bringing the baby home, fears, anxieties, and worries about labor and birth become very real and very intense for mothers and their partners. Women may worry that they will not be able to tolerate the pain or that they will appear foolish; the birth partners may worry that they will not be able to meet their partner's physical and emotional needs during the birth process. It is not uncommon for birth partners to worry that the expectant mother will turn to someone else for support; they worry that they will be inadequate. Sometimes a woman may feel that the baby is taking over not only her body but also her entire being. Sometimes a birth partner feels that the mother-to-be is no longer interested in him or her—that she will turn all of her attention to the baby. Financial worries may escalate during this time, as well.

Labor and Birth

Labor:
the rhythmic uterine contractions that expel a baby.

Several theories exist that explain what may trigger the onset of **labor**, the rhythmic uterine contractions that help expel the baby, but no one knows for certain why someone enters labor when she does. Does the fetus somehow transmit a hormonal signal that it is ready for birth? Does the placenta emit a signal that it can no longer sustain the growing baby? Although the exact reason may remain a mystery in medical science, the pregnant body does provide clues that the birth of a child is approaching, such as a backache and achiness in the pelvic region.

With true labor, the contractions always become longer, stronger, and closer together. Labor is divided into four stages, and each stage has one or more phases. It is during these stages that the opening to the uterus—the cervix—effaces (becomes thinner) and it dilates (opens). Before pushing can begin, the cervix must dilate to an opening of 10 centimeters or about 4 inches. Typically about the thickness of the space between your eyebrows, and about as firm as the tip of your nose, the cervix thins to about the thickness of the small piece of skin between your thumb and forefinger; by the time the baby is born, it is as soft as the inside of your cheek.

Stage 1: This stage is divided into three phases: early labor, active labor, and transition.

Early labor:
the first phase of labor in which the cervix dilates from 0 to 3 centimeters.

Active labor:
the second stage of labor, during which the cervix dilates from 4 to 7 centimeters and contractions occur every 2 to 3 minutes and last 60 to 90 seconds.

Transition:
the third stage of labor, during which contractions occur as frequently as every 90 seconds and last for 90 seconds and the cervix is dilated to 10 centimeters; at this time, pushing can begin.

- **Early labor:** The easiest and longest part of labor, in early labor the cervix dilates from 0 to 3 centimeters. In this stage, contractions may start as far as 20 minutes apart but gradually occur every 5 minutes. When contractions are 5 minutes apart, last for one minute, and this pattern continues for one hour (the 5-1-1 rule), it is time for the gestational parent to head to the birthing facility. During early labor, the uterus is about as firm as the tip of your nose.

- **Active labor:** In this stage, the cervix dilates from 4 to 7 centimeters. This is typically the most emotionally challenging part of labor for the birth-giver. Contractions occur every 2 to 3 minutes and last 60 to 90 seconds. In active labor, the uterus becomes as hard as your chin.

- **Transition:** This is the most physically and emotionally challenging phase of labor. Contractions occur as frequently as every 90 seconds and last for 90 seconds; there is seemingly no break between contractions. During transition, the uterus feels as hard as your forehead. Stage 1 is complete when the cervix is dilated to 10 centimeters, and at this time, pushing can begin.

Stage 2: Although the journey through the vagina is only about 5 inches, it may take a first-time mother about 2 hours to push her baby out. During the uterine contractions, as the mother bears down, the force of the contraction holds the baby down, helping the opening to stretch. As the intensity of the contraction lessens, the baby retreats upward. Thus, pushing is somewhat of a 3-steps-forward-2-steps-backward process. Once the baby's head is visible, the baby no longer retreats after a contraction.

Stage 3: During this stage, the placenta (the baby's life support system throughout pregnancy) is delivered. This typically occurs within 5 to 30 minutes after the delivery of the baby.

Stage 4: This stage is often overlooked by many when discussing the processes of labor and birth, but it is no less important. This stage involves the first 2 to 3 hours after birth through the first 24 months after labor and delivery. Because of the tremendous fluctuations that a woman's hormones undergo during the nine months of pregnancy, labor, and birth, it takes time for her body to return to its pre-pregnant state.

Although the hours of labor are challenging, many gestational parents and couples experience great closeness and intimacy as they work together to bring their child into the world.

Conflict and the Transition to Parenthood

The transition to parenthood is difficult for most people. In the past, researchers have concentrated on the *individual* factors that may lead to conflict in relationships during pregnancy and have ignored the importance of the *relational dynamics* of marital dissatisfaction and symptoms of depression (Salmela-Aro et al., 2006). Thus, results of such studies concluded that the changes in the couple's relationship following pregnancy and during the transition to parenthood were due to such things as a woman's/gestational parent's depressed mood, rather than due to the systems nature of their relationship (for example, see Campbell et al., 1992).

To illustrate the importance of examining the couple's relationship and not just the individual, researchers from Finland studied the experiences of 320 women and their partners through pregnancy and into the early months of parenthood (Salmela-Aro et al., 2006). They discovered that, in those couples who reported high levels of conflict, the struggles and disagreements that were present during the transition to becoming parents were already a part of the couple's relationship. In other words, depressive symptoms and marital satisfaction during pregnancy were common to the couple's relationship during pregnancy—these characteristics didn't suddenly appear as the couple became parents, as earlier studies suggested.

iStock.com/ArtMarie

Pregnancy and the birth of a baby are emotionally demanding for both the gestational parent and the birth partner. Despite these challenges, most couples report that their relationships are stable during pregnancy.

The researchers also found a decrease in marital satisfaction during the transition to parenthood among couples who reported high levels of marital satisfaction during early pregnancy. The investigators speculated that this is because pre-pregnancy "happy" couples have taken time to nurture their relationships, and that as pregnancy/parenting demands increase over time, their attention shifts from their relationship to the baby.

Other research that examined 293 Dutch couples explored relationship quality during pregnancy and the early months of pregnancy (Kluwer & Johnson, 2007). Based on the assumption that adding a new member to the family system is accompanied by drastic and dramatic changes in a couple's relationship, this study looked at conflict frequency during pregnancy and found the following:

- More frequent conflict during pregnancy was related to lower levels of relationship quality across the transition to parenthood.
- Lower levels of relationship quality during pregnancy were linked with more conflict during pregnancy.
- Frequent conflict is likely to determine declines in relationship quality during the early months of parenthood.

These findings are very important to our understanding of intimate and family life because they show us that couples' marital discord and distress stemmed from problems that *existed during pregnancy*, not necessarily because of the *transition to parenthood*. It may very well be that the first childbirth isn't what elicits marriage troubles, but instead, the troubles have always been there and are just highlighted once the baby arrives. Some couples may be more vulnerable to a difficult transition to parenthood than others (Kluwer & Johnson, 2007).

Finally, other evidence suggest that couples who do not live together, who are unhappy with their partner, or who perceive their relationship to be a negative experience, experience increased anxiety and depression during pregnancy and the early months of parenting (Figueiredo et al., 2008). All the empirical findings are important, for they suggest that *both* members of the couple need to be supported during pregnancy in order to prevent or decrease the stressors associated with the transition to parenting.

Sexual and Relationship Satisfaction After Childbirth

As a childbirth educator and sexuality professor, one of the most common questions I am asked by my students in this unit is "How soon after childbirth can we have sex?" According to the American College of Obstetricians and Gynecologists (ACOG, 2019), couples are encouraged to wait for six weeks before resuming intercourse. This waiting period allows the birth parent's body to heal after her birth and labor experiences. Primarily, it is important to wait because it gives time for the vaginal area to heal and time for the cervix to close and regain its barrier to infection. A general rule of thumb is to wait to resume sexual intercourse until after the initial postpartum checkup; at this point, couples can also discuss birth control options available to them. Nevertheless, most couples resume sexual activity when they feel comfortable doing so. A recent study indicates that although most couples resume sexual activity within six weeks of delivery, women may not experience an orgasm until about three months after delivery (Connolly, Thorp, & Pahel, 2005). As one body of research confirmed, if both partners enjoy a rich sex life throughout pregnancy, they tend to evaluate their levels of tenderness and communication higher in the first six months after delivery (von Sydow, 1999).

Generally, couples' sex lives typically undergo change after they become parents. In particular, sexual desire appears to be lower for mothers than it is for fathers in the first year after giving birth (Ahlborg, Dahlof, & Strandmark, 2000; Ahlborg, Lars-Gosta, & Hallberg, 2005). Apart from lower sexual desire, there are also physical changes in the experience of sex after childbirth. A study that examined 480 postpartum women found that more than 50 percent experienced pain during first intercourse after delivery; this pain continued somewhat for six months (Barrett et al., 2000). Another examined more than 500 women and their partners to evaluate which factors determined sexual activity and sexual relationship satisfaction one year after a first birth (Brummen, Bruinse, van de Pol, Heintz, & van der Vaart, 2006). By three months after the birth of their babies, more than 80 percent of couples had had sex; by one year after birth, about 94 percent had. The most significant finding was that there was a predictive factor for no sexual intercourse one year following birth: Women who were not sexually active when they were three months pregnant had an 11 times higher chance of not being sexually active one year after giving birth (Brummen et al., 2006).

These changes, in turn, cause stress and tension between the couple and compound the transition to assume the new roles of parents. If new parents are able to communicate openly about their sexual desires and the stressors associated with becoming parents, and if they confirm each other emotionally and sexually, they experience better adjustment—and have more sex (Ahlborg et al., 2000; Ahlborg et al., 2005). Indeed, an investigation of 820 postpartum couples found that, by the time the babies were about 6 months old, most of the parents indicated that they were "very happy" in their relationships (Ahlborg et al., 2005). Factors contributing to their relationship happiness were a strong social support network and having someone to provide relief so the couple could spend some time away from the baby. Among those who indicated that they were unhappy, factors included economic problems, having a partner who was away from home too much (which led to less emotional and physical intimacy), and frustration with the partner's lack of help or sharing responsibility.

UNEXPECTED OUTCOMES

During each of my four pregnancies, I experienced the common fears and worries about the health and well-being of my babies. I went through all of the "what ifs" I could possibly think of, yet there were admittedly some things I dared not think about, such as delivering an unhealthy, physically impaired, or physically challenged baby, or even the death of the baby. Many couples experience unexpected outcomes when they are unable to become pregnant, such as the woman in the opening vignette of this chapter. For most couples, the process of fertilization and conception works as it is supposed to. But for other couples, becoming pregnant represents grueling work and becomes a difficult and heart-wrenching challenge.

When Conception Fails: Infertility

In the United States today, approximately 6 million women, or about 10 percent of women aged 15 to 44, have an impaired ability to become pregnant (Centers for Disease Control and Prevention, 2019b). **Sterility** refers to the absolute inability to reproduce, either because the woman has no uterus or ovaries or the male has no testes or sperm production. No amount of medical intervention can help a sterile person reproduce. **Infertility** is the inability to conceive a baby after trying for a period of one year. Infertile women are also those who have no difficulties conceiving but are unable to sustain the pregnancy.

Women and Infertility

Approximately one-third of the problems associated with infertility are due to women's reproductive systems (American Society for Reproductive Medicine [ASRM], 2019). Specifically, problems with the monthly release of an ovum from the ovary (ovulation) are responsible for most female infertility. Lack of ovulation may be due to hormonal imbalances, which refers to a decline in or an absence of the hormones estrogen and progesterone, which are necessary for pregnancy. Other causes for infertility may be a pituitary gland tumor (quite rare) or lifestyle habits such as poor nutrition (as in the case of anorexia or bulimia), stress, or even intense athletic training (U.S. Department of Health and Human Services, 2003). Once a woman reaches the age of 35, her ovaries' ability to produce eggs diminishes.

Sterility:
the absolute inability to reproduce, either because the woman has no uterus or ovaries, or the male has no testes or sperm production.

Infertility:
the inability to conceive a baby after trying for a period of one year.

iStock.com/Freemixer

People who experience infertility and pregnancy loss report low life satisfaction and high levels of depression. The inability to conceive or carry a baby to full term is a life crisis for most couples.

Pelvic inflammatory disease (PID):

a disorder caused by untreated sexually transmitted infections (e.g., gonorrhea and chlamydia) that results in a fertilized ovum having difficulty reaching the uterus due to blocked or scarred fallopian tubes.

Endometriosis:

a disease characterized by the buildup or migration of uterine tissue to other parts of the body (such as the ovaries or fallopian tubes).

Azoospermia:

a type of male infertility in which no sperm cells are produced.

Oligospermia:

a type of male infertility in which few sperm cells are produced.

Even when women successfully ovulate, the fertilized ovum may have difficulty reaching the uterus due to blocked or scarred fallopian tubes. This disorder, called **pelvic inflammatory disease (PID)**, is primarily caused by untreated sexually transmitted infections. PID renders 1 in 10 women per year infertile, making it the leading cause of infertility in young women (ACOG, 2019). **Endometriosis** may also prevent the fertilized ovum from traveling through the fallopian tube to the uterus or may prevent the fertilized ovum from becoming embedded in the uterine lining.

Men and Infertility

About one-third of fertility difficulties are due to male reproductive problems (U.S. Department of Health and Human Services, 2019). Healthy, robust sperm are necessary in order for fertilization of the ovum to take place. There are two primary forms of infertility in men: **azoospermia**, which means that no sperm cells are produced, and **oligospermia**, which means that few sperms cells are produced. Sometimes these conditions are the result of a genetic disease, such as cystic fibrosis, and sometimes they are the result of poor reproductive health. To produce an adequate number of sperm cells (at least 20 million sperm per milliliter of semen), the male must be healthy and lead a healthy lifestyle.

The ASRM is an internationally recognized nonprofit medical organization that disseminates information, education, and standards in the field of reproductive health. According to the ASRM (2019), to improve fertility, men should consult with a physician about the proper vitamins and minerals that improve sperm function. In addition, men should limit alcohol intake and stop smoking, as alcohol lowers testosterone levels and smoking may cause the production of malformed, slow-moving sperm. Finally, men should keep their cool. For health sperm production, the testes must be cooler than the rest of the body—this is why nature designed the male's testicles to hang outside of the body. Males considering parenthood may want to avoid hot tubs, saunas, steam rooms, very hot baths, and placing laptop computers on their laps. And yes, men should wear boxers instead of briefs.

Treating Infertility

There are a variety of treatment options available for infertility, ranging from medication (fertility drugs to enhance ovulation) to surgery. Less invasive medical treatments include fertility drugs and donor insemination, often referred to as **artificial insemination**. In women, fertility drugs increase egg production. When fertility drugs are used, sometimes more than one egg is produced, leading to multiple births. Artificial insemination, a popular fertility treatment used by both heterosexual and homosexual couples, is the medical process in which donor sperm is placed into the woman's vagina, cervix, or uterus by a syringe. Sperm are collected (through masturbation by the donor) and stored by medical facilities called **sperm banks**; sperm can be donated by someone known to a prospective parent or can be donated anonymously. Compensation varies, but someone who donates twice per week can earn about $1500 a month; a vial of sperm from a sperm bank costs anywhere from $150 to $3,000 (Mayo Clinic, 2019). If these treatment options fail, there are other more invasive (and more costly) treatment options. Today, women have available to them various routes of **Assisted Reproductive Technology (ART)**, which are treatments that involve fertilization through the hands-on manipulation of the woman's ova and the male's sperm. To date, 17 states in the U.S. require that health insurance companies cover these medical procedures (although the extent of coverage varies state to state). Some states offer infertility insurance coverage, but it is not a state mandate that they do so.

- For infertile couples in which a woman has blocked or absent fallopian tubes, or where a man has a low sperm count, **in vitro fertilization (IVF)** is typically used to help the couple conceive. IVF is a process whereby a woman's eggs are surgically removed from her ovary and mixed with a man's sperm in a laboratory culture dish. After about 40 hours in the culture dish, the eggs are examined to see if they were fertilized, and if they were, to see if cell division is taking place. If the balls of cells appear to be growing at a normal rate, the eggs (embryos) are placed within the uterus. This process bypasses the fallopian tubes. The average cost of IVF is $12,400 per attempt (Penn Medicine, 2019).

- **Gamete intrafallopian transfer (GIFT)** involves manually manipulating the sperm and eggs, but instead of fertilizing the eggs in a dish, the unfertilized eggs and the male's sperm are placed in the woman's fallopian tubes. This is designed to foster natural fertilization within the woman's fallopian tubes. The average cost of GIFT is about $10,000 to $15,000 per attempt (ASRM, 2019).

- In **zygote intrafallopian transfer (ZIFT)**, the man's sperm fertilizes the woman's eggs in a laboratory. The fertilized eggs are placed immediately in the woman's fallopian tubes, rather than in her uterus (as in IVF), allowing the conceptus to travel naturally to the uterus and implant. The average cost of ZIFT is $10,000 per attempt (ASRM, 2019).

Surrogacy is an option when men or women may desire to have a biological child, but for medical or other reasons (as in the case of gay men or trans individuals who have undergone sex confirmation surgery) they may not be able to do so. IVF is performed, but the embryos are implanted into a **surrogate mother** who carries the pregnancy to term—the surrogate is the baby's biological mother. Upon birth, the baby is given to the biological parents. In some instances, a surrogate mother is artificially inseminated with the father's sperm. She carries the baby through delivery and gives the baby to the biological father and his partner to raise.

Since 1987, there have been 1 million babies born in the United States as a result of ART (Penn Medicine, 2019).

Traditionally, gay men have experienced barriers to becoming fathers, but with the increase of society's acceptance of gay parenting, and with the legal changes that have granted gay men the option of fatherhood, more gay men are turning to surrogacy as an option to becoming a parent (Berkowitz, 2013; Gato, Santos, & Fontaine, 2016). According to some bodies of research, gay men prefer surrogacy over adoption or fostering because it allows for genetic fatherhood; gay couples prefer surrogacy because it allows for the genetic expression of at least one of the partners (Berkowitz, 2013; Blake et al., 2017; Goldberg & Scheib, 2015; Golombok et al., 2018). IVF and surrogacy is the most common route to biological parenthood for gay men in the United States (Perkins, Boulet, Jamieson, & Kissin, 2016). Although every case is

Artificial insemination: the medical process by which donor sperm is placed by syringe into the woman's vagina, cervix, or uterus.

Sperm bank: sperm for artificial insemination procedures is retrieved from donors and stored in sperm banks.

Assisted reproductive technology (ART): treatments that involve fertilization through the manipulation of the woman's ova and the male's sperm.

In vitro fertilization (IVF): an assisted reproductive technology process whereby a woman's eggs are surgically removed from her ovary and mixed with a man's sperm in a laboratory culture dish; if the eggs are fertilized and appear to be growing at a normal rate, the embryos are placed in the uterus.

Gamete intrafallopian transfer (GIFT): an assisted reproductive technology process in which unfertilized eggs and a male's sperm are placed in a woman's fallopian tubes to foster natural fertilization.

Zygote intrafallopian transfer (ZIFT): an assisted reproductive technology process in which an egg is fertilized outside of the body and then is placed immediately in the woman's fallopian tubes, allowing the conceptus to travel naturally to the uterus and implant.

Surrogate mother: a woman who carries the fetus of another couple.

different, the cost of surrogacy ranges from $90,000 to $130,000 in the United States; India, Thailand, Russia, and Mexico only allow surrogacy to heterosexual parents.

According to the ASRM (2015), only one-fourth (24 percent) of the ART needs in the U.S. are being met, and this involuntary childlessness as the result of infertility profoundly impacts the physical, social, economic, and psychological well-being of women and men. The ASRM's ethics committee believes that the creation of a family is a basic human right, and the lack of insurance coverage for infertility—which creates treatment gaps among underserved populations—creates racial, ethnic, geographic, and economic disparities in childbearing.

The Psychological Impact of Infertility

Infertility is often distressing, frustrating, and depressing. Hoping, longing, and wishing month after month after month for a positive pregnancy test only to find out that the efforts failed again constitutes a real-life crisis for couples. The stress on finances and on the marriage or partnership can lead to a breakdown of the couple's relationship. Fortunately, many support groups and infertility counseling organizations exist to help infertile women and couples navigate through the physical and emotional challenges infertility brings. Groups such as the National Infertility Association and the International Council on Infertility Information Dissemination offer psychological, psychosocial, and informational support for those experiencing infertility.

The Physically Challenged Baby

Although we all long for a healthy baby, not all of us will have the perfect baby. Birth defects and anomalies can range from barely noticeable to life threatening to fatal. No matter how severe the defect, parents of infants with birth defects and physically challenged babies mourn the loss of the healthy child they imagined they'd deliver.

Birth defect:

a physical anomaly that is present and birth. It may be inherited or may be the result of environmental influences during pregnancy and/or birth.

A **birth defect** is a physical anomaly that is present at birth; it may be inherited, or it may be the result of environmental influences during pregnancy and/or birth (March of Dimes, 2018). Major birth defects can have serious effects on a child's health and development and may impact the functional ability of the child (Centers for Disease Control and Prevention, 2019b). Today, 1 in every 33 babies—about 3 percent of all babies—born in the U.S. has a birth defect (Centers for Disease Control and Prevention, 2019b). These defects account for 20 percent of infant deaths and are the leading cause of deaths in infants. Birth defects include the following:

- Brain/spine: 2,600 per year
- Eye: 751 per year
- Heart: 16,282 per year
- Mouth/face: 6,253 per year
- Stomach/intestine: 2,706 per year
- Muscle/bone: 17,723 per year
- Chromosome (genetic): 7,286 per year

At the Parents Encouraging Parents Conference, Roger and Ann Figard (1992, personal communication) presented the Loss and Grief Cycle for parents of physically challenged babies (see Figure 10.6). As you can see, parents don't experience the loss just one time, such as when discovering the baby has a birth defect. Rather, the loss is experienced at various ages and stages of the child's development, throughout the child's life.

Pregnancy Loss

Most pregnancies proceed without many complications. Even when complications do occur, Western medical science provides women with treatment for nearly every complication

Figure 10.6 /// Loss and Grief Cycle for Parents of Physically Challenged Children

When parents lose a child to death, or when they have a baby born with birth defects, they experience a cycle of grief and loss.

Pregnancy In pregnancy, the unknowns about the baby encourage a parent to hope and dream and fantasize about what the baby will be like.

The Fantasized, Hoped-For Child Often, the parents develop an idea or mental picture of the perfect child-to-be. This can include the sex of the child, talents, or other characteristics important to the parents.

Birth of a Challenged Child The parent is faced with the reality that the hoped-for child and the real child are not the same child.

Ideational Object Loss Unconsciously, the parent's mind recognizes the death of the dream of the hoped-for child and this moves the parent into a cycle of grief . . . letting go of the hoped-for child and accepting the real child.

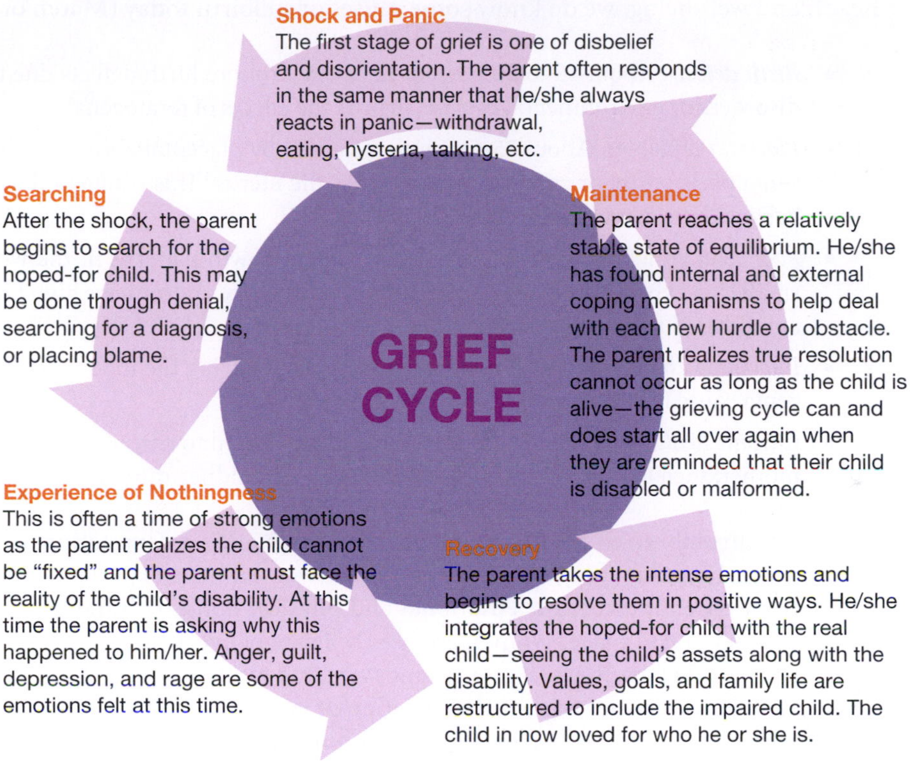

Shock and Panic
The first stage of grief is one of disbelief and disorientation. The parent often responds in the same manner that he/she always reacts in panic—withdrawal, eating, hysteria, talking, etc.

Searching
After the shock, the parent begins to search for the hoped-for child. This may be done through denial, searching for a diagnosis, or placing blame.

Maintenance
The parent reaches a relatively stable state of equilibrium. He/she has found internal and external coping mechanisms to help deal with each new hurdle or obstacle. The parent realizes true resolution cannot occur as long as the child is alive—the grieving cycle can and does start all over again when they are reminded that their child is disabled or malformed.

GRIEF CYCLE

Experience of Nothingness
This is often a time of strong emotions as the parent realizes the child cannot be "fixed" and the parent must face the reality of the child's disability. At this time the parent is asking why this happened to him/her. Anger, guilt, depression, and rage are some of the emotions felt at this time.

Recovery
The parent takes the intense emotions and begins to resolve them in positive ways. He/she integrates the hoped-for child with the real child—seeing the child's assets along with the disability. Values, goals, and family life are restructured to include the impaired child. The child in now loved for who he or she is.

Source: Roger and Ann Figard (1992), personal communication.

---

related to pregnancy. Complications can range from skin rashes, to excessive vomiting, to high blood pressure, to anemia, to vaginal bleeding or cramping, to the loss of the pregnancy.

Miscarriage

The most common reason for loss in the first month of pregnancy is miscarriage. Any loss of a fetus or embryo before the 20th week of pregnancy (the fourth month of pregnancy) is termed a spontaneous abortion or **miscarriage** (Merck Manual, 2020). Early miscarriage occurs with the loss of a fetus before the 12th week of pregnancy; late miscarriage occurs with the loss of a fetus between the 12th and 20th weeks of pregnancy. Approximately one-fourth to one-third of pregnant women experience some type of bleeding or cramping during the first 20 weeks of pregnancy; of those, about half result in pregnancy loss. About 85 percent of all miscarriages take place during the first 12 weeks of pregnancy; these pregnancy losses usually take place because of abnormalities in the embryo or fetus (Merck Manual, 2020). In two-thirds of these miscarriages, the pregnancy loss can be linked to the mother's health or lifestyle, and in one-third, no cause is known (Merck Manual, 2020). Known causes of miscarriage include abnormalities in the embryo or fetus resulting from illnesses or disorders such as diabetes, infections, injury, hypothyroidism, or from lifestyle choices such as using cocaine, especially crack (Merck Manual, 2020).

Miscarriage:

spontaneous abortion, or loss of a fetus or embryo before the 20th week of pregnancy.

Stillbirth

Stillbirth:
the death of a fetus after the 20th week of pregnancy. Stillbirth occurs approximately once in every 115 births, or about 26,000 per year.

Even though society at large may not recognize the emotional and physical impact of a pregnancy loss, the impact on the parents is life-altering. **Stillbirth** refers to the death of a fetus after the 20th week (four months) of pregnancy, and it occurs in approximately 1 in every 115 births, or about 26,000 per year (March of Dimes, 2018). Only about 14 percent of the fetuses die during the labor and birth process; the remaining 86 percent die before labor has begun (March of Dimes, 2018). In developing countries or less economically advantaged countries, the stillbirth rates are much higher because medical care is not as readily available. In up to half of all cases, tests cannot determine the cause of the stillbirth (March of Dimes, 2018). However, because of ongoing research in the United States and a commitment to children's health and well-being, we do know some causes of stillbirth today (March of Dimes, 2018):

- *Birth defects.* About 15 to 20 percent have one or more birth defects due to chromosomal disorders or environmental causes (such as the effects of teratogens).
- *Placenta problems.* About 25 percent are caused by placental abruption, in which the placenta peels partly or completely away from the uterus. This results in heavy bleeding; the baby will die from lack of oxygen.
- *Poor fetal growth.* About 40 percent have poor growth patterns in the womb and are too small to survive within the womb. Women who smoke and/or have high blood pressure are at increased risk for stillbirth.
- *Infections.* In about 10 to 25 percent, infections involving the mother, the fetus, or the placenta cause fetal death.
- *Chronic health conditions.* About 10 percent are related to chronic health conditions of the mother, such as high blood pressure, diabetes, and kidney disease.

The loss of an embryo or fetus at any stage in the pregnancy is devastating. A stillbirth is particularly crushing, however, because most often women have experienced fetal movement, and many women indicate the emotional and physical bond with the baby intensifies once fetal movement takes place. Women are keenly aware of every flutter, poke, kick, and jab the baby makes, and when the fetal movement stops, the mother becomes aware that something is wrong. When a mother reports the cessation of movement to her physician, an ultrasound is performed to detect cardiac movement, or a heartbeat. If there is no cardiac movement, the baby is no longer alive.

Some women will choose to carry the baby and let labor begin naturally; most prefer to have labor *induced*, or started by artificial methods. Although at first glance it may seem cruel to allow a woman to endure the pain of labor to deliver a stillborn baby, it is essential for the woman to preserve her capacity for future childbearing and to minimize any possible complications (ACOG, 2019). The other alternative is to have the fetus delivered by cesarean birth. As with any surgical procedure, a cesarean birth carries with it added risk to the mother's health such as complications from the anesthesia, postoperative infection, and permanent scar tissue that forms near her reproductive organs. Even though cesarean birth rates are soaring, vaginal birth is still the safest method of delivery with the shortest and least painful physical recovery.

Many women find the labor and birth experiences of stillborns to be rewarding and satisfying. Despite the fact that the woman and her partner did not receive the outcome they had hoped for, the birth process is a time of quiet reflection and recognition that the baby was, is, and will always be a significant part of their lives and in the lives of their family. Although it may seem morbid, after the birth of the baby, physicians encourage parents and family to hold, bathe, dress, cuddle, and sing to their infant to bond with the baby. Parents and families of stillborn babies are typically given several hours to bond with the baby because this bonding experience is crucial in their grieving and mourning.

In instances of stillbirth, greeting the baby also means saying good-bye. Although parting with anyone we love is devastating, parents who suffer the prenatal or postnatal loss of a baby carry the loss for the rest of their lives. Whether or not the baby ever took a breath, the life had meaning and significance to the parents and their families. The intense, overwhelming feelings of grief are simply an affirmation that the baby's life was real. Moving through the grief and mourning to a place of healing takes time. Sometimes outside resources are necessary to help parents cope with their devastating loss. In time, the loss is integrated into their marriage, their relationship, and their lives.

When the Unexpected Happens

Unexpected outcomes are just that—something we do not anticipate. When preparing for childbirth, most books and childbirth preparation classes skim over—or ignore altogether—the possibility that a baby may be born with a birth defect. But when parents have a baby born with a birth defect they are often, understandably, overwhelmed by fears and emotions. Family Life Educators, human service providers, social workers, healthcare providers, and clergy encourage parents to

- *Acknowledge their emotions.* As you learned in this chapter, expectant parents have an image of a hoped-for child. When a baby is born with birth defects, parents need time to mourn the loss of this hoped-for child. Shock, denial, and grief are common emotions.

- *Seek support.* Joining support groups or talking with someone who has had similar experiences, or seeking help from a psychologist, clergy member, or social worker is helpful for parents.

- *Seek information.* Parents should educate themselves about their child's condition. Sources of information include the baby's physician, online resources, books, the March of Dimes, the National Information Center for Children and Youth with Disabilities, and various support groups. There are also resources (state and local) that assist parents in paying for costs associated with certain birth defects. Hospital social workers can help direct parents to appropriate information resources.

- *Use a team approach.* For the most part, children born with birth defects needs a team made up of doctors, child life specialists or developmentalists, and social workers to treat them. Some children's hospitals have such teams already in place. Parents need to play an active role in their child's treatment plan.

When educating expectant parents, I encourage them to create their personalized "what if" list. What if I don't want to be a parent or I'm not ready to be a parent? What if my partner doesn't find me attractive? What if I wanted a nonmedicated birth and I have to use pain medications? What if I have a premature baby? What if my baby has birth defects? What if I can't look at my baby because of the defect? What if my baby is stillborn? What if my baby dies? While we certainly cannot anticipate every possible result associated with pregnancy and childbirth, coming to terms with the fact that sometimes the pregnancy and childbirth experience doesn't yield our desired outcomes is an essential and necessary step in becoming a parent.

ADOPTION: BY CIRCUMSTANCE OR CHOICE

Having a baby is something that seems so easy. But each year, more than 6 million couples in the United States face difficulties becoming pregnant; hundreds of others desire to become parents, but for numerous reasons they wish to adopt rather than to become pregnant. In general, there are three main types of adoption (Davenport, 2018):

1. *Domestic Infant Adoptions.* Annually, there are about 18,000 such adoptions in the United States. This type of adoption comprises only about 0.5 percent of all live births in the United States and only about 1 percent of births to single parents.

2. *International Adoptions to the U.S.:* There are roughly 20,000 international adoptions each year in the United States. The countries children are adopted from include China, Ukraine, India, Haiti, Ethiopia, Uganda, and the Philippines.

3. *Foster Care Adoptions:* Annually, about 57,000 children are adopted from foster care. On average, about one-fourth of children who enter foster care are adopted, and about one-half go back to their families. The remaining children remain in foster care.

Once a family decides to growth their family through adoption, a standard process is put into place.

The Adoption Process

Each adoption agency may have its own policies and procedures, but generally there are five steps to adoption. The process may take months, or a few years, depending on whether the couple or individual desires to adopt a newborn baby or if they are waiting for a specific race/ethnicity.

Step 1: Initial Information. To begin, each prospective adopt parent must select an agency or a private organization through which to adopt. Couples may choose to adopt domestically (from the United States) or internationally (from abroad). Many people believe that international adoptions cost far less than domestic adoptions, but this is not the case. For example, the average cost to adopt a baby within the U.S. is $38,000; the average cost to adopt a child from China is $36,000 (Davenport, 2018). Wait times also vary, depending on the country from which a couple adopts. In the United States, the average wait time is about 1 to 2 years; the average wait time for a child from China is 6 months to a year (Davenport, 2018).

Step 2: Preparation. To be eligible for adoption, prospective parents must undergo a home study. The home study helps to ensure that the child is going to be placed in a loving, caring, nurturing home. During the study, an adoption specialist social worker interviews the couple and assesses such things as their relationship stability, their feelings about and readiness for becoming parents, and aspects about their daily lives. The social worker also checks the parents' health and income status; parents undergo a background check as well. Many adoption agencies assign the parents an adoption specialist social worker who helps them through each stage of the adoption process.

Step 3: The family in waiting. After the adoptive family has successfully completed all required documentation and the home study, they are considered to be a family in waiting—they enter a waiting period of somewhat unknown length, until a match occurs that results in a successful adoptive placement. This time frame varies for every adoptive family.

Step 4: The placement. After the couple is matched with a birth mother/couple, the adoptive couple works with the specialist until the baby is born; if a birth mother is not located, adoptive parents may choose to work with the adoption specialist until an older child is found. Placement typically occurs immediately after all the paperwork is completed and filed. Perhaps one of the most intensely felt fears of adopt parents is that the birth mother will change her mind; in reality, however, very few birth mothers decide to raise their babies after initiating the adoption process, but it is their right to do so. It is very important that a birth mom is not forced into her decision by others. Women who do change their minds about relinquishing their children for adoption are typically under the age of 17, have no plans for the future, live with their parents, and have mothers who oppose the adoption (Adamec, 2004).

Step 5: It's final! After the specified time frame has passed (this varies from state to state), and all of the documentation has been completed and filed with the court, a final court hearing is held and the adoption decree is awarded to the parents.

Gay and Lesbian Adoption

Today, same-sex couples are about 4.5 times more likely than different-sex couples to rear adopted children, and the number of available children who need to be adopted far exceeds the number of heterosexual adoptive parents (Gates, 2013). The landscape of gay and lesbian adoption continues to undergo rapid change. As of this writing in 2019, rampant discrimination in adoption policies exists in the United States: Five states prohibit adoption discrimination based on sexual orientation and gender identity; 4 states prohibit discrimination based on sexual orientation only; and 41 states remain silent on the issue altogether. It's important to note that 10 states permit state-licensed child welfare agencies to refuse to place children with LGBT people and same-sex couples, if doing so goes against their religious beliefs. These states are primarily situated in the Midwest and the South (i.e., Texas, Oklahoma, Kansas, Mississippi, Alabama, and South Carolina; Movement Advancement Project, 2019).

Generally, when considering any gay/lesbian adoption, today's courts are primarily focused on the "best interest of the child," and beliefs that lesbian and gay adults are not fit parents have no empirical foundation (among many others, Anderssen, Amlie, & Ytteroy, 2002; Patterson, 2000; Perrin, 2002). As such, a person's sexual orientation should not be used as a factor in determining whether a homosexual individual or couple can adopt or foster parent a child. The American Civil Liberties Union (ACLU), a nonprofit, nonpartisan group that monitors the individual civil liberties of Americans spelled out in the Constitution, maintains that where same-sex parenting is prohibited, it is because these states adhere to "stereotypical" views that gays and lesbians are unfit to be parents.

Those opposed to the concept of same-sex adoption may believe that a female role model and a male role model are necessary in children's lives. Others claim that children who are reared by gay or lesbian parents might themselves grow up to be homosexual. Others are concern that children of gay and lesbian parents will be teased ruthlessly and relentlessly by

iStock.com/SolStock

In 2017, the U.S. Supreme Court legalized same-sex adoption in all 50 states. Prior to this landmark decision, many states had tight restrictions on same-sex couples being allowed to adopt children.

their classmates. Issues at the forefront of this discussion address gender identify and sexual orientation, as well as children's overall well-being:

- *Gender identity.* In response to whether children need both a mother and a father in order to establish a solid gender identity, studies show that few differences in gender identity exist between children reared by same-sex parents and heterosexual parents (for a review, see Bos, Kuyper, & Gartrell, 2018).

- *Sexual orientation.* Empirical studies reveal that being raised by homosexual parents does not increase the likelihood that the child will be gay or lesbian. Notes one body of research, "sexual identities (including gender identity, gender-role behavior, and sexual orientation) develop in much the same ways among children of lesbian mothers as they do among children of heterosexual parents" (American Psychological Association, 2004).

- *Children's well-being.* Having gay or lesbian parents is less an indicator of the quality of the parent–child relationship than parenting styles are. Ultimately, it is the quality of parenting, not sexual orientation, that determines how children of same-sex parents fare (Bos et al., 2018; Gartrell, Bos, & Koh, 2018; Bos, Knox, van Rijn-van Gelderen, & Gartrell, 2016).

- *Shared parenting.* Lesbian and gay parents tend to divide childcare tasks and responsibilities relatively evenly, and they report higher levels of satisfaction in their couple relationship than heterosexual couples do (Bos et al., 2004; Johnson & O'Conner, 2002; Ciano-Boyce & Shelley-Sireci, 2002).

- *Parenting.* Gay and lesbian parents possess strong parenting skills; this is reportedly due to greater levels of parent–child interaction and lower levels of physical punishment (Goldberg et al., 2014; Goldberg & Smith, 2014).

Perhaps Sara Bonkowski (2003) best sums up the experience of same-sex adoption when she explains,

> Remember that a child needs the love and support of both parents. If [parents are] gay or lesbian, in time the child will know and come to understand. Many of the concerns and worries that may be raised about homosexuality are concerns of adults; the concern of a child are much simpler. If a gay or lesbian parent forms a caring paternal or maternal bond with his or her young child, by the time the child is old enough to understand homosexuality the child will know the parent and appreciate that Mom or Dad is, in every respect, a good parent.

In other words, if states are truly making decisions in the best interest of the children, the verdict is in: Children don't care. And they thrive.

CONTRACEPTION AND ABORTION

When considering pathways to parenting, it is also important to consider methods of protection against unwanted pregnancy. The forms and methods of birth control are wide and varied, as are the effectiveness rates and complications. In general, there are three categories of contraceptives: barrier methods, hormone methods, and other methods. Deciding which method is right for you often depends on individual needs and circumstances. There are several things to think about when choosing a method. It's best to discuss the pros and cons of each method with your health care provider, as well as your partner, so you can determine which method is best for your sexual health and circumstances.

Failure rate:
a measurement for contraception that is based on the number of women who become pregnant if 100 women used the method for one year.

It's also important to consider the advantages and disadvantages of each method. The **failure rate** for each method is the number of women who become pregnant if 100 women used the method for one year. For example, approximately 85 of 100 women will become pregnant if they use no method at all; about 11 women of 100 will become pregnant using condoms (ACOG, 2019).

Contraception

Just as the name implies, **barrier contraceptive** methods provide a chemical or physical barrier between the sperm and the ovum; sperm cannot reach the egg, and fertilization is thus prevented. These methods are typically not invasive (do not interfere with a woman's menstrual cycle) and will usually not affect lifelong fertility. They are inexpensive and some are available over the counter (OTC), without a doctor's prescription. To be effective, they must be used each and every time sexual intercourse occurs. Table 10.4 presents each type of barrier contraceptive method, as well as each method's pros and cons and failure rates.

Estrogen and progesterone fluctuate throughout a woman's menstrual cycle and orchestrate the maturation and release of an ovum. **Hormone contraceptive** methods use artificial hormones (estrogen and progesterone) to prevent ovulation; due to the addition of synthetic hormones in the body, certain hormones are not released that signal the ovaries to release an egg. In addition, the increased levels of artificial estrogen mimic the estrogen levels of pregnancy; this, too, interrupts the process of ovulation. The hormones simultaneously thicken the cervical mucus, which inhibits sperm from traveling into the uterus and also reduce the buildup of the blood-rich endometrial lining, the nutrients necessary to sustain a pregnancy.

Each hormone method uses the same basic principle (the mode of delivery is usually the biggest difference), so the advantages and disadvantages of each method are similar.

Barrier contraceptive: a contraceptive method that provides a chemical or physical barrier between the sperm and the ovum.

Hormone contraceptive: methods of contraception that use artificial hormones to prevent ovulation as well as thicken the cervical mucus, which inhibits sperm from traveling into the uterus.

Table 10.4 /// Barrier Contraceptive Methods

Method	Pros	Cons	Failure Rate (rated by the FDA)
Condom	Available OTC; inexpensive; STI protection	Lack of sensitivity; interruption of "the moment"	11%
Female Condom	Available OTC; STI protection	Cumbersome; interruption of "the moment"	21%
Diaphragm	Can be inserted hours before sex; does not impede sensitivity	Available only by prescription; often messy; no STI protection	17%*
Cervical Cap	Can be used for multiple acts of sex; convenience	Available only by prescription; often messy; no STI protection	17–23%*
Cervical Shield	Can be used for multiple acts of sex; convenience	Available only by prescription; often messy; no STI protection	15%*
Contraceptive Sponge	Can be used for multiple acts of sex; available OTC	Messy (requires spermicide); possible health side effects; no STI protection	14–28%*
Intrauterine Device (IUD)	Can remain in place for 10 years; very convenient	Must be inserted by a health care professional; no STI protection	<1%
Spermicides	Inexpensive; available OTC	Messy; no STI protection; not as reliable when used alone	20–50%

*when used with spermicide

Source: ACOG (2019).

The convenience of hormonal methods makes them very desirable, but because the hormones essentially alter the body's chemistry, side effects are common. Only women use hormonal methods, which come in several forms:

- Birth control pills
- Skin patch
- Vaginal ring
- Injections
- Implant

Hormonal methods prevent pregnancy but offer no protection against STIs and HIV.

Emergency contraception (EC), also referred to as the **morning-after pill** or **Plan B**, is made of the same hormones found in birth control pills. EC is a form of backup birth control that can be taken up to several days after unprotected sexual intercourse or contraceptive failure and still prevent a pregnancy.

Many have confused EC with the "abortion pill," but EC does not cause abortion; it works by delaying or inhibiting ovulation and will not work if the woman is already pregnant. The morning-after pill is *not* an abortion pill. Abortion pills empty the uterus of an already fertilized egg, but the morning-after pill prevents pregnancy by interrupting the release of an egg. If taken within 72 hours of an "oops!" sexual experience (the condom broke or slipped off, a woman forgets to take her birth control pill, he didn't pull out in time, etc.), EC reduces the risk of pregnancy by 89 percent; the combination pill has an effectiveness rate of about 74 percent (ACOG, 2019). Although college students haven't typically been using EC, it can be obtained by seeing a health care provider on campus or in your community. EC is not intended for routine birth control methods.

Abortion and Other Methods

Many couples are faced with an unwanted pregnancy and opt to terminate the pregnancy through abortion. In 1973, the United States Supreme Court ruled that restrictive state regulation of abortion is unconstitutional. Their landmark ruling protects a pregnant woman's liberty and privacy and thus her right to choose whether or not to have an abortion. After this ruling, U.S. abortion rates peaked in 1981, with about 29 women per 1,000 obtaining legal abortions. Since 1981, however, the abortion rate in the U.S. has declined each year, reaching an historic low of 14.6 abortions per 1,000 women in 2017 (Guttmacher Institute, 2018).

There are two types of abortion: the abortion pill and the in-clinic abortion. A woman or a couple has many decisions to make when considering abortion. A decision to terminate a pregnancy is a highly personal, individual one, and for many women, the decision is an agonizing one. Depending on her circumstances and how far along she is in her pregnancy, she may decide to use a medication that ends an early pregnancy.

The Abortion Pill (Medication Abortion)

Generally speaking, the abortion pill can be used up to 63 days (nine weeks) after the first day of a woman's last menstrual period (Planned Parenthood, 2019). This nonsurgical, medication abortion involves three steps:

1. **The Abortion Pill** (Mifepristone, or RU-486): At the clinic, the health care provider gives the woman mifepristone in pill form; Methotrexate (MTX) is the injection form of this medication (the preferred procedure for up to seven weeks' gestation). The pill works by blocking the hormone progesterone; without this hormone, the lining of the uterus breaks down and pregnancy cannot continue. The woman is also given an antibiotic to prevent infection.

Should States Have the Right to Make Their Own Abortion Laws?

In 1970, an unmarried pregnant woman in Texas (given the fictitious name of Jane Roe to protect her identity) sought legal action to have the Texas anti-abortion statute overturned. She claimed that the state's abortion laws violated her constitutional right to privacy. The battle ended up in the United States Supreme Court, and in 1973, the Court ruled that state abortion laws across the nation violated women's rights to privacy. One of the most politically polarizing decisions in U.S. history, the Court's decision overturned every state law that outlawed or restricted the elective termination of a pregnancy. For more than 40 years, the Supreme Court has not been directly challenged on state abortion laws—that is, until now. As of mid-2019, 16 states have introduced, moved, or enacted legislation that would ban abortion at six weeks gestation (pregnancy). For most women, a six-week ban stops access to abortion a mere two weeks after a missed period.

Do you think states should have the right to determine their own abortion laws?

YES: Anti-abortion organizations, such as the National Right to Life campaign, contend that states should have the right to enact their own abortion legislation. They maintain that

- Representatives are elected by people in their state to set policy and make laws that reflect the people they are serving; thus, if states outlaw abortion, it is because the state's constituents desire the legislation.
- If put to a popular vote, most Americans would vote that abortion should be made illegal.
- Most abortions are for matters of convenience, not because of rape, incest, or the mother's life being endangered.

NO: Pro-choice organizations, such as Planned Parenthood, contend that every woman in every state should have the same and equal access to abortion services, should they need to or desire to terminate a pregnancy. They maintain that giving states individual control over abortion laws

- Puts the health, safety, and personal well-being of women at risk
- Makes women turn to unsafe, unsanitary methods of terminating pregnancies that put their lives in jeopardy
- Violates a woman's constitutional right to privacy and jeopardizes her right to manage her own reproductive health

What Do You Think?

1. Should the federal government or individual states determine access to abortion services?

2. In your opinion, do you expect the Supreme Court's 1973 decision to be overturned? Why or why not?

Sources: Planned Parenthood (2006), National Right to Life Campaign, "Abortion in Healthcare Bills."www.nric.org.

2. **Misoprostol:** The second pill is taken at the woman's convenience, up to three days after taking the abortion pill. This pill causes cramps and bleeding usually within a few hours of taking it. It causes the uterus to empty. It is common for a woman to have bleeding and cramping for up to four weeks after the abortion.

3. **Follow-up:** A follow-up appointment is made with the health care provider, to ensure that the abortion is complete and that the woman is well.

Women choose this option because it can be done early in the pregnancy and because it is very private. The abortion pill is safe for most women, but risks include allergic reactions, incomplete abortions, infections, and very heavy bleeding. If the abortion pill is ineffective, a woman must agree to a surgical abortion (Planned Parenthood, 2019). Abortions performed this early pose virtually no long-term risks of infertility, ectopic pregnancy, miscarriage, or birth defects (Planned Parenthood, 2019). Medical abortions are 95 to 97 percent effective.

Taking Sides

Childbearing and Intimate Partner Violence

For many women, pregnancy is not a time of joy—in fact, for more than 300,000 women each year in this nation, pregnancy is the most dangerous time of their lives because of violence they suffer from their partners. Intimate partner violence includes physical, emotional, and sexual abuse. (See also "The Crisis of Family Violence" in Chapter 15.) Murder by an intimate partner is the most common cause of death among pregnant woman (The National Domestic Violence Hotline, 2019).

Her Side: My fiancé is not violent. He's not. He's just feeling insecure about our relationship, worried that the baby is going to take up so of my time that I won't have time for him. He's very moody right now, and he does get in my face and yell a lot, but that's my fault—I'm so moody and teary right now because of all of these hormones, and he doesn't know how to react to that. He has pushed me a couple of times, and he has hit me (again, totally my fault), but that was only one time.

Source: Family Violence Prevention (2006).

He was never like this before I got pregnant, so I'm sure his moods and stuff are temporary. Once the baby gets here, he'll be fine.

His Side: This is not my fault. It's not. I may have pushed her around a couple of times, but it's only because I was drunk. And why was I drunk? Because she wanted this kid. I won't go as far as to say she deserved it, but she did keep the fight going until I just lost it. Everyone always blames the dude, but they're not living here with this emotional basket case.

Your Side: There are signs that intimate partner violence is taking place in this couple's relationship, although some of them might be subtle.

1. What evidence do you see of intimate partner violence?
2. If you were this woman's healthcare provider, what would you recommend she do?
3. Why do you believe that pregnancy is such a dangerous time for women? Why do you think that violence escalates?

In-Clinic Abortion

There are several different kinds of abortions that are performed by health care providers in medical clinics or hospitals; the type of procedure performed largely depends upon how far along the woman is in her pregnancy. **In-clinic abortions** are typically performed when a woman is in her second or third trimester (Planned Parenthood, 2019).

In-clinic abortions: a medical procedure in which suction is used to remove a pregnancy from the uterus.

During these procedures, the woman is medicated with numbing medications, pain medications, or with other types of sedation, to make her more comfortable. The uterus is emptied by aspiration (a suction device), or by D&C or D&E, the use of suction and other devices. There are risks associated with any medical procedure, and abortion is no exception. Risks for in-clinic abortions range from blood clots, injury to the cervix or other organs, to very heavy bleeding; death can occur, but this is a very rare complication.

Feelings After an Abortion

Deciding to terminate a pregnancy is difficult for many women, and it's not unusual for women to have a wide range of feelings after an abortion. It's important to understand, though, that while choosing to have an abortion is stressful, it doesn't mean that the outcome will not be positive. Little empirical evidence exists that tracks the long-term emotional, physical, and psychological consequences of abortion procedures. Some organizations, such as Planned Parenthood and the National Abortion Federation (NAF), note that immediately after the abortion it is common for women to experience anger, regret, guilt, sadness or depression, and grief—even if they know they made the right decision for themselves. All of these feelings are real and understandable (NAF, 2019). Post-abortion counseling is available from Planned Parenthood and NAF.

FAMILY LIFE EDUCATION: FOSTERING HEALTHY FAMILY FORMATION

It's been said before that you can't really understand the changes in your life that children will bring until you've actually become a parent. Our course of study together has shown us that even good changes that occur in a family system can be very challenging, and becoming parents is no exception to that. Certainly, though, there are rewards that accompany the challenges.

As with most other areas that we have examined in our study of couple and family life, family life educators' and other helping professionals' educational efforts for individuals and couples considering parenthood or who are transitioning to parenthood center on fostering healthy family formation. By promoting strong communication skills and a knowledge of typical pregnancy and childbirth changes, this preventive approach helps individuals and couples to tackle the challenges and changes that accompany the transition to parenthood.

We've covered a lot in this chapter, from gaining an understanding of the current trends in childbearing, to the factors that go into the decision to have children, to the emotional and relationship changes that take place during pregnancy, and the unexpected outcomes that unfortunately occur for some parents. We've also explored ways to protect your reproductive health by examining ways to prevent pregnancy. All of these issues are very important for a fundamental understanding of the choices and challenges people encounter as they begin their journey to parenthood—this period in a couple's relationship is a crucial time for them to enhance, nurture, and fortify their relationship so they are better equipped to handle the stressors associated with parenthood.

Expectant and adoptive parents spend many months preparing for the arrival of their baby. By the time they bring their baby home, they've probably taken birth classes, attended a few parenting classes, read articles about their newborn baby, and completed the baby's room. But even with all of this preparation, the reality is, many parents don't know just how much their day-to-day lives are about to change. The transition to parenthood is one of the greatest stressors a couple or an individual will encounter. To survive and to thrive, preparation needs to go beyond welcoming the baby home. In the next chapter, we explore the ups and downs of parenting.

/// SUMMARY

Childbearing Trends: Who's Having Babies?

- Each year, the population in the United States increased by the addition of slightly less than 4 million babies. In 2018, the crude birth rate—the number of childbirths per 1,000 per year—in the United States was 11.8. In less economically developed countries the crude birth rate is significantly higher than in richer countries.

- The U.S. fertility rate—the average number of live births per woman, in a given population, per year—in 2018 was 1.72. Countries that are less economically advantaged tend to have higher fertility rates. Fertility rates may be influenced by religious, cultural, and ethnic norms.

- Since 1991, in the United States, the rate of pregnancy among America's teens has steadily declined to a historic low in 2018. While the teen birth rates have declined for all racial and ethnic groups, the rates are still higher among African American, Hispanic, and American Indians/Alaska Natives than they are for whites.

- Childbearing by unmarried women (of all ages) reached a record high in 2014 and have since stabilized. Birth rates among women in their 30s and 40s has increased steadily from 1984 to today, perhaps reflecting the cultural trend of women who delay childbearing to establish their careers.

- Teenage mothers face a number of medical, psychological, developmental, and socioeconomic challenges. Their babies also face challenges. A number of programs exist that intervene to assist teenage parents.

- While gay men and lesbian may choose alternate routes to parenthood, such as adoption and foster parenting, their motivations to become parents are no different than are the motivations of different-sex couples.

Having Children: Now, Later, or Never?

- Most studies and theories about the desire to become parents focus on the perspective that there are perceived rewards and costs associated with parenthood; people tend to engage in a cost-benefit analysis when considering parenthood.

- The perceived value of children and the appeal of parenthood also help to determine whether an individual or couple decides to become a parent(s).

- There are few studies that examine planned families but the emergence of planned parenthood by same-sex couples is indicative of broad social change that is taking place in our society.

- Many couples struggle in determining when the "right" time to have a child is. The lifecourse of each family includes life transitions and turning points, and these influence timing; these all influence when someone decides to become a parent. Age-related norms are socially approved and shaped pathways that somewhat dictate when the "right time" to have a child is.

- Some couples prefer to remain childfree by choice, while others delay childbearing for reasons that are unique to them.

- Americans who were polled believe that the "ideal" family size is two children. However, the Quiverfull movement believes that parents should have as many children as possible, and they do not try to prevent conception. The resource dilution hypothesis maintains that parents' energy, time, and resources are drained with each subsequent child.

Being Pregnant and Giving Birth

- Children are costly endeavors!

- A number of emotional and relationship changes occur throughout the nine months of pregnancy. Human sexuality is reactive to our daily circumstances; thus, a couple's sex life undergoes many changes throughout pregnancy.

- The transition to parenthood is difficult for most people, and conflict is common among pregnant couples. Research shows that it's not the transition to parenthood per se that is stressful; rather, the struggles and disagreements that were present during the transition to becoming parents was already a part of the couple's relationship, before the baby was born.

- A couple's sex life undergoes changes after they become parents. Sexual desire appears to be lower for mothers than it is for fathers in about the first year following birth.

Unexpected Outcomes

- Infertility is the inability to conceive a about after the couple has tried for a period of one year. About one-third of the problems associated with infertility are due to women's reproductive systems; about one-third are due to men's reproductive problems.

- There are a number of medical treatments available for infertility. These include artificial insemination, in vitro fertilization, gamete intrafallopian transfer, zygote intrafallopian transfer, and surrogacy.

- Birth defects and anomalies can range from barely noticeable, to life threatening, to fatal. No matter how severe the defect, parents of infants with birth defects and physically challenged babies mourn the loss of the healthy child they imagined they'd deliver. Parents tend to follow similar patterns in dealing with the birth of a physically challenged child, articulated in The Loss and Grief Cycle for parents of physically challenged children.

- Any loss of a fetus or embryo before the 20th week of pregnancy is termed a miscarriage, and about 85 percent of all miscarriages take place within the first 12 weeks of pregnancy. Known causes included abnormalities within the embryo or fetus, resulting from illnesses to disorders such as diabetes, infections, injury, hypothyroidism, or from lifestyle choices such as using cocaine, especially crack.

- Stillbirth refers to the death of a fetus after the 20th week of pregnancy and occurs in approximately 1 in every 115 births, or about 26,000 per year. In developing countries, the stillbirth rates are much higher because medical care is not as readily available.

Adoption: By Circumstance or Choice

- Once a family decides to grow their family through adoption, a standard process unfolds that includes five steps: Initial Information, Preparation, The Family in Waiting, The Placement, and It's Final!

- Issues at the forefront of gay/lesbian adopting focus on the child's gender identity, sexual orientation, and overall well-being; shared parenting; and parenting styles.

Contraception and Abortion

- The forms and methods of birth control are wide and varied, as are the effectiveness rates and complications.

- Contraception is a personal choice and it falls within three primary categories: barrier methods, hormone methods, and other methods.

- Emergency contraception, taken within 72 hours of a pregnancy score, is nearly 90 percent effective in preventing an unwanted pregnancy.

- The two types of abortion, medication and in-clinic, terminate an unwanted pregnancy. Deciding to end a pregnancy is a stressful decision for most women.

- Evidence exists as to the short-term consequences of abortion. These include grief, depression, sadness, anger, regret, and guilt. There are support measures in place for post-abortive women.

/// KEY TERMS

Active labor   364

Age-related norms   353

Antinatalist   357

Artificial insemination   369

Assisted Reproductive Technology (ART)   369

Azoospermia   368

Barrier contraceptive   377

Birth defect   370

Childfree-by-choice   354

Crude birth rate   345

Doula   344

Early labor   364

Emergency contraception (EC)   378

Endometriosis   368

Failure rate   376

Family projection process   352

Gamete intrafallopian transfer (GIFT)   369

Gestational parent   362

Hormone contraceptive   377

In vitro fertilization (IVF)   369

In-clinic abortions   380

Infertility   367

Labor   364

Life transition   353

Miscarriage   371

Morning-after pill or Plan B   378

Natalism   357

Oligospermia   368

Pelvic inflammatory disease (PID)   368

Pronatalism   357

Quiverfull movement   359

Replacement fertility rate   345

Resource dilution hypothesis   357

Sperm bank   369

Sterility   367

Stillbirth   372

Surrogate mother   369

Timing   353

Total fertility rate   345

Transition   364

Turning point   353

Zygote intrafallopian transfer (ZIFT)   369

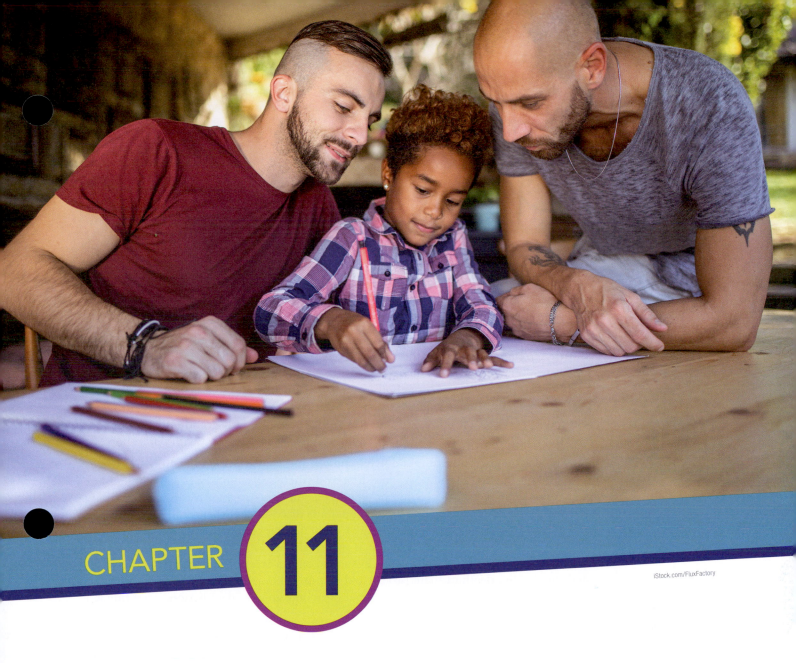

iStock.com/FluxFactory

PARENTING LIFE NOW

11.1 Understand the multiple processes associated with parenting.

11.2 Explain why the transition to parenthood is difficult for most people.

11.3 Assess the differences in trends among contemporary parents.

11.4 Describe the best practices for parenthood.

"You know, when I was nineteen, Grandpa took me on a roller coaster. Up, down. Up, down. Oh, what a ride! It was just interesting to me that a ride could make me so frightened, so scared, so sick . . . so excited and so thrilled all together. Some didn't like it. They went on the merry-go-round. That just goes around. Nothing. I like the roller coaster. You get more out of it."

The movie *Parenthood* depicts families' everyday struggles while the parents try to balance parenting responsibilities with marital roles and careers. At his wits' end with his parenting frustrations, his marriage, and his failing career, Steve Martin's character, Gil, declares that as a male in this society, unlike women, he has no choices about marriage, parenting, or work. He laments. "My whole life is have-to's." At this point, his very elderly grandmother relays her story about the roller coaster—and in doing so humorously compares it with parenthood.

Parenthood is fraught with ups and downs, choices and challenges, and elation and disappointment. For parents, a "good day" may hinge on whether a child passes a spelling test or wins a blue ribbon at the science fair, or whether a son or a daughter receives a university scholarship. A bad day may be one in which parents discover that their child is victim of a school bully. My husband and I have seen the fear on the faces of our friends as they engaged in a war for their 4-year old daughter's life as she fought (and lost) her battle with leukemia. We have seen the hopeless, helpless, and lost looks on the faces of our friends as they confronted the sudden death of their 14-year-old son in a skiing accident, and we've watched friends strive to help their adolescent daughter overcome an opioid addiction. Parenting is a daunting task—and sometimes frightening.

Across the pages of time and history, children were considered a vital, necessary segment of society because they were needed to ensure the survival of the culture or race—they were viewed as necessary economic assets for society's continuation and as the manual labor needed to bring about that continuation. Although the challenges of parenting today are vastly different from those of parenting many years ago, contemporary parents still face unique demands as they raise their children.

Children the world over represent their culture's future, and because of this, society expects parents to do a good job, to create healthy, productive citizens (Lerner, Noh, & Wilson, 2004). To be sure, having a child is a monumental task. Sometimes a pregnancy is planned; sometimes a pregnancy comes as a surprise. Either way, bringing a child into this world is perhaps the biggest decision a couple or a woman will ever make. As you saw in the previous chapters, the transition to parenthood is undeniably one of the greatest challenges a marriage or intimate relationship will encounter. In this chapter, we will explore what it means to become a mother or a father and to parent. We'll also take a look at current issues that today's parents face, such as discipline practices and child care, and juggling parenting with other responsibilities, such as household chores. As with other areas of family and intimate living, knowing what to expect about parenting and equipping ourselves with knowledge and expertise prepare and equip us to rise to the challenges.

CHANGE OVER TIME: PARENTING IS A PROCESS

For those who are to become parents, there are no words to convey the excitement they will feel the first time they hear the baby's heartbeat or hear their baby's first cries and first words. When a parent sees a baby's first smile, the sense of love, responsibility, and commitment is palpable. But the thrills move beyond infancy. Watching children grow, learn, and discover and uncover this world at every stage of their development is both entertaining and exciting (except for driver's education and dating—those fall into the "frightening and scary" category!). To watch them move from the rambunctious, rough-and-tumble years of childhood to the young men and women they become fills parents with a sense of pride, and at times apprehension, as they enter the real world on their own. But that growth from infancy to manhood or womanhood involves a tremendous process of not only individual growth and change but also growth and change in the parents and in their relationship.

Today, most parents in the United States state that being a mother or a father is central to their overall identity (Pew Research Center, 2015). Interestingly, parenting being an important contributor to identity doesn't vary much by generation. The percentages of respondents who indicated being a mother/father is important to their identity were as follows:

- Baby Boomers: 51 percent
- Millennials: 60 percent
- Gen X'ers: 58 percent

Also, 9 in 10 parents today say that being a parent is a rewarding experience for them (Pew Research Center, 2015). Of course, the age of the children influences parents' satisfaction with raising children: Those who have younger children (under age 6) are more likely to indicate that parenting is rewarding than parents who have older children. Both mothers (54 percent) and fathers (56 percent) say that at times, parenting is tiring (Pew Research Center, 2015).

In 2020, due to the COVID-19 pandemic, a significant number of working couples found themselves working from home—while simultaneously parenting. Even though parenthood has always been fraught with ups and downs, parents faced new challenges as they balanced the responsibilities of careers and parenting.

Survival needs:
food, shelter, safety, security, and love—provision of survival needs is a goal of parenting.

Socialization needs:
a goal of parenting is to meet the socialization needs of children, which encompasses ensuring they become productive, contributing members of society.

Richard Lerner and his colleagues (1995) suggest that parenting is a *process,* a course of events that evolve and change over time. As you saw in the previous chapter, the early days of parenting bring new challenges, experiences, and trials into the family system. As children grow, parents grow, too. This parenting process meets both the biological needs of the children and, at the same time, the needs of the society in which children are socialized. Indeed, two of the base goals of parenting are to meet the **survival needs** of infants, which include the provision of food, shelter, safety, security, and love, and to meet the **socialization needs** of children, which encompasses ensuring they become productive, contributing members to society. Parent educator and author Chris Theisen (2004) notes that there are eight essential parenting responsibilities:

1. Providing a safe environment
2. Providing basic needs
3. Providing self-esteem
4. Teaching children morals and values
5. Developing mutual respect
6. Providing effective and age-appropriate discipline
7. Being involved in the child's education
8. Knowing the child by communicating with him or her

Everything you have learned so far in this book about relationships now begins to come together—our intimacy patterns, the way we love, how we communicate, the way we express and feel about our gender, how we find a partner for life, and our sexual identity. All of our interpersonal relationship patterns and behaviors are learned over a period of years from our parents or family of origin. Given the sheer importance of parenting, then, there is little wonder that so much attention has been focused on this area of family life and intimate relationships. Family practitioner Virginia Satir once observed, "Parents teach in the toughest school in the world—*the school for making people.*"

Motherhood

Our study in the previous chapter showed us that in societies across the globe, women are expected to become mothers by certain culturally determined ages, and this expectation creates pressures for them to bear children. Thus, becoming a mother is considered to be a normative developmental stage for women in all cultures. In the broadest sense, **mothering** is defined as a process whereby someone performs the relational and logistical work of caring for others (Arendell, 2000). With this definition, we can see how someone—a woman or a man—could "mother" someone who is not a child, such as an aging parent or a sibling who has a disability; we can also "mother" a friend or a loved one who is in need. However, in most societies women are expected not only to be the bearers of children but also to nurture, care for, and socialize them as well—mothers are expected to "mother" the children in society (Arendell, 2000).

Mothering:
performing the relational and logistical work of caring for others.

Our study in Chapter 4 showed us that girls and boys are socialized to fulfill roles that are determined and defined by their cultures; although each society's roles are unique, motherhood is one of the few roles assigned to women that appears to be universal, and the experience of motherhood today remains a central part of many women's identities (Arendell, 2000). For example, in a study of 1,200 parents, women identified themselves as mothers more often than they identified themselves by their occupation or career or their marital status; on the other hand, fathers identified themselves by their occupation and not by their status as fathers (Rogers & White, 1998). Even though today women fill multiple roles, such as provider and caregiver to aging parents, they are also expected to simultaneously "nurture, schedule, taxi, and feed their families"—and to do it all well (Medina & Magnuson, 2009).

Because of these multiple demands and expectations, some researchers believe that the standards for "good mothering" are escalating (Douglas & Michaels, 2004, cited in Medina & Magnuson, 2009). Today, 60 percent of full-time working moms indicate that they have little free time to engage with hobbies and friends, in comparison to mothers who work part time (48 percent) and mothers who are not employed outside of the home (47 percent; Pew Research Center, 2015).

Professor of sociology and women's and gender studies Sharon Hays (1996) examined the social construction of motherhood in the latter part of the 20th century. From her scholarly works, she coined the term **intensive mothering** to reflect the mothering roles and expectations that have been evolving since the 1980s, when women flooded the workplace. **Intensive mothering ideology** is the Western cultural belief that a mother should give of herself unconditionally and focus all of her time, energy, money, love, support, and every other resource she has on raising her children. If she works outside of the home, she is expected to make up the time with her children that is "lost" at work. Furthermore, intensive mothering is expected of mothers even if a father is present in the home, if he is employed, and if they share equally in household and childrearing tasks. As this ideology shows us, the cultural expectation of mothers today is clear: The well-being of children is the responsibility of the mother, and she is to respond to their needs before those of her own or of her husband or partner. Of course, this means that women who fall short of this cultural ideal do not fit today's social construction of "good mothers" (Medina & Magnuson, 2009). In Chapter 12, we'll explore the stressors associated with mothers' multiple roles and the pressures they feel in trying to adhere to the intensive mothering standard.

The transition to motherhood is a major developmental life event for most women because it requires women to restructure their goals, behaviors, and responsibilities (Mercer, 2004). The theory of **Maternal Role Attainment (MRA)** speaks to the fluid, continual, fluctuating processes associated with becoming a mother (Rubin, 1967). According to this theory, women actually begin adopting roles associated with motherhood during their pregnancies, such as bonding emotionally with the growing fetus. While pregnant, a woman also begins to observe the behaviors of mother models she has in her environment (such as her own mother, grandmothers, and friends); as her pregnancy continues, she adopts those behaviors she believes would be ideal for her and her child, and she rejects behaviors she

Intensive mothering:
term coined by Sharon Hays to reflect the mothering roles and expectations that have been evolving since the 1980s, when women flooded the workplace.

Intensive mothering ideology:
the Western cultural belief that a mother should give herself unconditionally and focus all of her time, energy, money, love, support, and every other resource she has on raising her children.

Maternal Role Attainment (MRA):
the process by which a woman, through pregnancy and after the birth of her child, continues to construct an "ideal" image of herself as mother and adopts roles that support this ideal image.

iStock.com/Kyryl Gorlov

Nothing left to give? The Western cultural standard of intensive mothering asserts that mothers are to give of themselves unconditionally and that their children's needs should be met before their own. Do you agree or disagree with this ideology? Is this type of sacrificial mothering good for children, or not?

judges as inappropriate for herself. Through pregnancy, and after the birth of her child, she continues to construct an "ideal" image of herself as mother; she then adopts roles that support this ideal image.

There are a number of factors that influence MRA (Mercer, 1986):

- Age of the mother
- Socioeconomic background
- Social stress and support
- Temperament
- Self-concept
- Childrearing beliefs and attitudes
- Role strain
- Perception of the infant

Particularly important to MRA is the woman's relationship with her own mother. For example, one body of research demonstrated that young mothers' current relationships with their mothers were re-created in their relationships with their infants (Kretchmar & Jacobvitz, 2002). Other research found that pregnant mothers' attitudes and memories about their mothers influenced their prenatal attachment to their babies, and that young mothers' memories of how accepting or rejecting their own mothers were also influenced their ability to adopt motherhood roles (Priel & Besser, 2001; Crockenberg & Leerkes, 2003).

"Motherhood" is a developmental process that is influenced by many factors and is one that unfolds over time—the new mother affects and is affected by her child, by her spouse or partner, by her past experiences in her own childhood, and by her relationship with her mother.

Lesbian Co-Motherhood

In 2018, nearly 90,000 lesbian mothers were raising children in the United States (Goldberg & Conron, 2018). Like their heterosexual counterparts, most lesbian-mother couples were raising their biological children (68 percent), but today, lesbian couples are significantly more likely to adopt or foster children than different-sex couples (Goldberg & Conron, 2018). Do lesbian mothers attain motherhood roles differently than heterosexual mothers? A substantial body of research suggests that regardless of sexual orientation, becoming parents for the first time is challenging for most couples because of the renegotiation of roles and identities that must take place to incorporate the role of "parent" (Cao, Mills-Koonce, Wood, & Fine, 2016). But sexual minority female parents encounter additional role/identity stressors in the transition to parenthood because they are required to balance the heteronormative ideals of "mother" (Cao et al., 2016). It is indisputable that when it comes to mothering, our culture "often fails to acknowledge that there are families with other types of arrangements (Walker, 2017, p. 2).

Perhaps the greatest difference between heterosexual and lesbian motherhood is the uniqueness of the couple relationship. With heterosexual couples, each partner enters parenthood with clearly defined "mother" and "father" templates (Walker, 2017). Conversely, with same-sex mothers, the mothering role is shared—this is referred to as **lesbian co-mothering (LCM)**. Birth nurse practitioner Katherine Walker (2017) works closely with LCM couples and describes the specific challenges these mothers face:

Ambiguous Roles—Beyond the Mother/Father Binary: What is the role of the mother who does not give birth? As Walker has discovered in working with LCMs, lesbian co-mothers often find it difficult to identify with the role of mother or father. As one of her clients stated, "[When we went to our childbirth classes] I dreaded the prospect of potentially being the only woman in a group of 'dads.' It felt strange at times to be part of this group because there was

Lesbian co-mothering (LCM):

in a lesbian couple, the nonbirth parent takes an equal role in parenting, or mothering, the child.

an assumption that I would simply take on the role of a 'dad' during my partner's pregnancy [and birth experience]." Walker's research also discovered that the non-birth LCM often feels invisible and insecure due to the maternal gatekeeping of the birth LCM.

Bonding and Breastfeeding: A common fear among lesbian co-mothers is that a baby will form a stronger emotional and physical bond with the breastfeeding birth mother than with the co-mother, particularly because breastfeeding is known to enhance the development of maternal identity (Zizzo, 2009). It is not uncommon for LCMs to experience jealousy; this is also common among heterosexual fathers. Walker notes that some lesbian mothers have successfully established co-breastfeeding, or shared feeding. Other lesbian mothers enjoy non-nutritive breastfeeding, where babies suckle at the breast without receiving milk.

Emotional Support: Lack of emotional support following birth is known to increase the likelihood of postnatal depression (PND; Hatloy, 2013). Today, scant literature exists that addresses PND among lesbian co-mothers, but Walker's (2017) review of the literature suggests that LCMs are at greater risk because they do not have the cultural and community support that heterosexual couples do following the birth of a baby.

As with every other area of couple relationships and family life, it's important to understand that there is great diversity in the experiences of motherhood. As Walker (2017) concludes, "LCMs are not fathers! [In childbirth and parenting classes] LCM may not want to be grouped with fathers . . . and they may not feel like mothers yet either."

Fatherhood

Like motherhood, the social construction of fatherhood continues to change over time. Among America's first families in Colonial Williamsburg in the 17th century, for example, British immigrants brought the traditional patriarchal family structure to Virginia. The **patriarchal family structure** included the father figure, who was considered to be the authority over his entire household—wife, children, dependent kin, servants, slaves, and apprentices. This family structure served to preserve the wealth and power of the patriarch's household and the family's lineage. When fathers died, they willed their land and property to their sons, ensuring that the family's wealth remained within the family. Daughters typically inherited servants and livestock, rather than land or money. Within this family structure, fathers were all-powerful and served as the unquestioned, oftentimes uncaring, ruler (Lamb, 1987). In this era, men were charged with the responsibility of their children's moral and spiritual development, and because of this, discipline was their responsibility. The early father-child relationship was typically emotionally distant and correctional; it also lacked warmth, nurturing, and affection, because these behaviors were associated with parental indulgence that was thought to ruin the character of the children (Pleck & Pleck, 1997). Patriarchal parenting continued in the United States until the mid-18th century.

Patriarchal family structure: a family form that includes the father figure, his wife, and his children. Everyone in the family is considered to be under the authority of the patriarch, the father.

With the rise of industrialism and urbanization in Western cultures, the social construction of fatherhood began to change. As fathers moved their work into factories and away from the home, mothers' roles expanded to include moral teacher and disciplinarian (Pleck & Pleck, 1997). Historians note that the separation of the workplace from the home life created two opposing trends that are still in existence today: *father-absence* and *father-involvement* (Rotundo, 1993). Some men, for instance, withdraw emotionally, psychologically, and physically from their children because their work requires that they are absent from their families; on the other hand, the decline of patriarchy has given men "permission" to display more warmth, nurturing, and intimacy with their children, allowing them to be more involved.

Today, modern fathers tend to fall somewhere between these two opposing fatherhood types, and researchers are suggesting that a "new fatherhood" is emerging in our culture (Yogman & Garfield, 2016). **Father involvement** is defined as the time a father and his child(ren) spend together (Gauthier, Smeeding, & Furstenberg, 2004). With this new model of father involvement, fathers are expected to be both the provider of the family's needs and also actively engage in the everyday caring of their children (Barbeta & Cano, 2017). The importance of

Father involvement: the time a father and his children spend together.

fathers' involvement in the lives of their children cannot be overstated. One new body of research suggests that father involvement is essential for two primary reasons (for a complete review, see Cano, Perales, & Baxter, 2018):

1. Father involvement increases gender equality within families.
2. Father involvement is associated with positive child development.

Among contemporary parenting, involved fathering is a distinguishing feature of parents from fathers in the historical past. There are racial and ethnic differences in fathering experiences, and we'll discuss those in just a bit. Still today, however, the vast majority of mothers are more involved in the daily care and routines of their children than fathers are (Craig, 2006; Cano et al., 2018).

Whether people are discussing divorce laws in suburbia or crime rates in the inner city, the issue of fathering takes an active, often political, role in the ongoing dialogue over the status of the American family. There is a wide spectrum of thought concerning the importance of fathers in the United States. For some, fathers are merely a perk for children, adding interesting yet nonessential elements to a child's development. To others, the mere presence of a father is enough to cure all of society's ills. Politics aside, the research does seem to suggest that fathers are a valuable part of a child's healthy upbringing.

Consequences of Absent Fathers

Research shows that fatherlessness is linked to several social ills:

- Young children living without their father in the home are 10 times more likely to be extremely poor (Krumholz, 2019).
- Fatherless children are more prone to drug and alcohol abuse (Jackson, Rogers, & Sartor, 2016).

Although mothers still spend more time with their children than fathers do, today more fathers are actively involved in the nurturing and rearing of their children.

- Children from single-parent homes have more instances of physical and mental health problems than those from two-parent homes. Children without fathers are 20 times more likely to have behavioral disorders than are children with father involvement (Anderson, 2014).

- Among high school dropouts, 71 percent have no father involvement (Kruk, 2012).

- Children from single-mother families are more likely to commit crime. Those with no father involvement are 20 times more likely to end up in prison (National Center for Juvenile Justice, 2014).

- In homes where there is no father, children and adolescents are 32 times more likely to run away from home than children who have a father present (Children's Bureau, 2018).

- The suicide rate is 5 times higher among those with no father involvement (American Academy of Pediatrics, 2016).

Dads as Playmates

In one study of cognitive development in children, the intellectual and social development a child gains through the mother's verbal expressions and educational activities are also learned and reinforced through physical play with the father. Mothers do play with their kids, but children generally respond more to play with their fathers. Fathers are usually more lenient with children when it comes to exploration and adventure, which helps develop cognitive skills and encourages independence.

Decreased Behavioral Problems

As fathers take a more active role in the lives of their children, behavioral issues are positively affected. Eating meals at the table, helping with homework, working on projects together, and informal, spontaneous moments are linked to fewer behavioral issues with children. Children show greater prowess at school when both parents are actively involved, but the level of *fatherly* involvement has been shown to be a more important predictor of scholarly success.

If we use a family systems approach to understanding parenting, we can see that mothers and fathers together create a subsystem in the family—the parent subsystem. Every day, parents are faced with decisions and challenges about how to bring up their children and how to most effectively parent them. When fathers and mothers share parenting responsibilities and when they agree on parenting decisions—when they co-parent—all family members benefit.

Co-Parenting: Go Team!

How parents negotiate their childrearing beliefs and share in everyday parenting responsibilities is referred to as **co-parenting**; in essence, it is the support parents provide to one another in the raising of their children (Gable, Crnic, & Belsky, 1994). Joint parenting is important to children's well-being because it creates a home environment that fosters their growth and development. Although most research concentrates on heterosexual parents who are married or divorced, co-parenting also applies to others who are jointly raising children, such as grandparents, gay men, and lesbians.

Co-parenting can best be thought of as an alliance between parents (Gable et al., 1994). It is a significant component of parenthood because partners can turn to one another for support when they are faced with the stressors and demands of raising children. In a very real way, co-parenting is an extension of the couple's relationship, and it is just as important a process in family living as is communication, love, intimacy, or sex. That's not to say that co-parenting is easy to achieve, however. When a new baby or a child arrives on the scene, partners have to find ways to expand their interactions to include the new addition—but at the same time, they have to set limits on these interactions so as to maintain a healthy couple relationship,

Co-parenting:
sharing in everyday parenting responsibilities; the support parents provide to one another in the raising of their children.

In other words, they have to remember that their role as a couple is just as important (if not more so) as their roles of parents. This is sometimes easier said than done! In general, there are three types of co-parenting: supportive, unsupportive, and mixed (Belsky, 1990). There is a wide range in ways in which parents work to raise their children:

Supportive co-parenting. Parents directly or indirectly agree with each other by promoting the same general message to the child (such as sticking to the agreed-on curfew and not changing it without consent of the other parent). It also occurs when one parent directly asks the other for assistance with an issue that involves the child (such as helping with discipline).

Unsupportive co-parenting. This occurs when one parent subtly—or not so subtly—undermines the other parent's efforts (such as changing curfew without consulting with the other parent). It also takes place when one parent interrupts the interactions of the other parent and child (such as following a divorce), when one parent is openly critical of the other's parenting styles or parenting activity, or when a parent ignores the other parent's request for assistance with a child's needs.

Mixed co-parenting. In this type of co-parenting, one or both parents' responses are mixed—sometimes they support one another, sometimes they don't.

Co-parenting strategies are important to a child's overall development and well-being because they provide predictability and stability in family rules, practices, and discipline for children. For example, numerous studies have linked positive co-parenting to children's emotional well-being and academic success (among others, Schoppe, Mangelsdorf, & Frosch, 2001; McHale, Rao, & Krasnow, 2000). Supportive co-parenting has also been associated with older children's well-developed self-regulatory abilities (Brody, Flor, & Neubaum, 1998). Although many of the studies of co-parenting in the United States have focused on white, middle-class samples, research on urban Chinese families and Japanese families has demonstrated that both parents' involvement in daily, meaningful caregiving was linked to academic success and greater child empathy; when parents have conflict in their co-parenting, children are more likely to act out and to display anxious behaviors (McHale et al., 2000; Ogata & Miyashita, 2000).

Children receive far greater benefits if their parents work together in childrearing tasks.

Despite what family and social scientists currently understand about co-parenting, much still needs to be learned about the relationship between effective and ineffective shared parenting and its impact on children. There are also other factors that have been found to be strong predictors of children's overall well-being: parenting styles.

The Styles of Parenting

Parenting or parenthood is not a single behavior. Professor of family studies and family life educator Nancy Darling and her colleague (1993) describe parenting as multiple behaviors that, together, shape children's outcomes. Research psychologist Diana Baumrind (1991) asserts that normal parenting centers on the issue of control and that parents' primary roles are to influence, teach, and control their children. Based on her observations of parent-child interactions, Baumrind believes that there are two specific dimensions of childrearing: parental warmth or responsiveness/affection/supportiveness toward the child, and parental control or how demanding or restrictive the parents are toward their child (also referred to as *behavioral control*). In examining these two dimensions, Baumrind identifies four parenting styles, which we discuss here. Each of these parenting styles reflects different patterns of parental values, practices, and behaviors.

Uninvolved Parenting

Uninvolved parents are typically low in responsiveness, warmth, and affection, and they are low in parental control or demands (Sanders, 2008). Parents may both reject and neglect their children. Not all parents who are uninvolved are neglectful or rejecting; some are simply detached and uninterested in their children's lives. For example, some parents, although they may meet their child's basic needs (shelter, clothing, education, food), may not offer praise for a child's efforts or compliment the child's accomplishments. In essence, there are few meaningful and inclusive family interactions.

Uninvolved parents: parents who are typically low in responsiveness, warmth, and affection. They are also low in parental control or demands. Both parents reject and neglect their children.

There are a number of negative consequences of uninvolved or disengaged parenting for children and adolescent well-being (for a thorough review, see Kuppens & Ceulemans, 2018). Across all racial and ethnic groups, for example, there are reports of increased substance use and abuse, higher rates of delinquency, poorer school performance, and negative psychological well-being (Pittman & Chase-Landsdale, 2001; Samaniego & Gonzales, 1999; Steinberg, Lamborn, Darling, Mounts, & Dornbusch, 1994; Steinberg, Mounts, Lamborn, & Dornbusch 1991). Today, we know that there are certain outcomes associated with uninvolved parenting (Cherry, 2018):

- Children must learn to provide for themselves.
- Children and adolescents may become fearful of depending on others.
- Kids are often emotionally withdrawn.
- Adolescence tend to exhibit more delinquency.
- Children and adolescents experience fear, anxiety, or stress because of lack of family support.
- Adolescents are at greater risk for substance abuse.

Other research further suggests that disengaged parenting styles, when combined with families who live in dangerous or socially disorganized neighborhoods, are linked with increased adolescent delinquency in African American and Latino boys (Roche, Ensminger, & Cherlin, 2007). There was also an association of uninvolved/disengaged parenting with increased school problem behavior and depression among African American youth, particularly when mothers are not involved in their children's parenting. This evidence is clear and convincing: The stakes of uninvolved or detached parenting are profound among African Americans, particularly among adolescent males.

Permissive Parenting

Permissive parents: also referred to as *indulgent parents*, permissive parents demonstrate high levels of warmth, affection, and responsiveness toward their children, and also show adequate to high levels of parent–child communication. This parenting style does not place high demands on children, nor do parents attempt to control their children's behavior; children's behavior is mostly self-regulated.

Also referred to as *indulgent* and *careless* parents, **permissive parents** demonstrate high levels of warmth, affection, and responsiveness toward their children, and also show adequate to high levels of parent–child communication (Odame-Mensah & Gyimah, 2018). This parenting style does not place high demands on children, nor do parents attempt to control their children's behavior; children's behavior is mostly self-regulated. Baumrind (1991) refers to these parents as *lenient* and *nontraditional*. Permissive parents rarely invoke the use of punishment, and very often children are given great latitude in making decisions for their lives (Kang & Moore, 2011; Odame-Mensah & Gyimah, 2018).

Autonomy granting: permissive parents allowing their children age-appropriate independence and self-governance.

Similar to uninvolved or disengaged parenting, when parents set no boundaries and do not provide behavioral regulations, children and adolescents experience higher levels of depression, poorer school performance, poorer psychological adjustment and well-being, and greater use of substances (Pittman & Chase-Landsdale, 2001; Samaniego & Gonzales, 1999; Steinberg et al., 1994; Steinberg et al., 1991). Parents who engage in **autonomy granting** might allow their children to set their own curfews and do not monitor the children's free time (Kang & Moore, 2011). This can evolve into putting their children at risk for elevated depression; this is particularly true for Asian females and African American males (Radziszewska, Richardson, Dent, & Flay, 1996). In high-risk (low income/low education), dangerous neighborhoods and communities, permissive parenting was associated with increased adolescent delinquency, school problem behavior, and poor school performance, particularly among adolescent African American males (Roche et al., 2007).

Authoritarian Parenting

Authoritarian parents: parents who exert authority and control over their children, but without being responsive, warm, or affectionate, imposing rigid rules of behavior that must be obeyed without question. Parent–child communication is very low.

According to Baumrind (1991), **authoritarian parents** are "obedience- and status-oriented, and expect their orders to be obeyed without explanation" (p. 62). To put it another way, authoritarian parents are very demanding and controlling with their children, but at the same time not very responsive, warm, or affectionate toward their children. This type of parenting style is characterized by rigid rules of behavior, which children are expected to follow with no questions asked; it is often referred to as *punitive* parenting

Authoritarian parents typically have high demands of their children, and often these demands are not age appropriate or developmentally appropriate. When children make mistakes they are punished harshly, with little to no communication about behavioral expectations.

iStock.com/triloks

(Hosokawa & Katsura, 2019). Parent–child communication is very low, and there is no room for compromise. Power is the key player.

Across all racial and ethnic groups, this type of restrictive, punitive parenting is associated with increased emotional problems (such as anxiety), psychological problems (such as depression), and increased behavioral problems (Eamon & Mulder, 2005; Grogan-Kaylor, 2005; McLeod & Nonnemaker, 2000). When parents use corporal punishment (spanking or hitting), children and adolescents exhibit more incidences of problem behaviors; however, this is found more among whites and Latinos than it is among African Americans (Lansford, Deater-Deckard, Dodge, Bates, & Pettit, 2004). Corporal punishment also appears to be more strongly associated with behavior problems in boys than it is in girls (Grogan-Kaylor, 2005). Interestingly, punitive/restrictive parenting is associated with *increases* in depression, delinquencies, and problem behaviors for African American males who live in safe neighborhoods/communities, but it is linked with *decreases* in these maladies for Blacks who live in dangerous neighborhoods. We'll discuss the possible reasons for these findings a bit later.

Authoritative Parenting

With an authoritative parenting style, parents are responsive while demanding certain behavioral standards. This style of parenting does not use shame, withdrawal of love, or guilt (as might authoritarian parents) to control behavior. **Authoritative parents** set clear boundaries for their children's behavior, but they are flexible and will change these boundaries if the situation warrants. For example, a teen's regular curfew may be at midnight, but on prom night, she may be allowed to stay out much later. Authoritative parents are warm and responsive, and they encourage parent–child communication. Children are expected to follow the rules of the house but are still allowed to be autonomous. With this style, parents use a balance of power and reason.

Authoritative parents: parents who are responsive while expecting certain behavior of their children. Parents do not use shame, withdraw love, or impose guilt to control behavior. They set clear but flexible boundaries for their children's behavior, encourage parent–child communication, and use a balance of power and reason.

Of all of Baumrind's (1991) parenting styles, authoritative parenting provides children with a balance of control and warmth, which yields the best outcome for children's health and well-being in the areas of social competence and psychosocial development. A number of research studies consistently demonstrate that children reared by authoritative parents exhibit more social competence than do other children (Amato & Fowler, 2002; McClun & Merrell, 1998; Steinberg & Morris, 2001):

- Both boys and girls reared by authoritative parents exhibit lower levels of problem behavior across all stages of the lifespan, across all ethnic groups (Jackson, Henriksen, & Foshee, 1998; Kim, Hetherington, & Reiss, 1999).

- Children reared by authoritative parents are better able to balance the demands of conforming to others' expectations with their own needs for uniqueness and autonomy (Durbin et al., 1993; Shucksmith, Leo, Hendry, & Glendinning, 1995).

- Both boys and girls tend to perform better in school if they are reared by authoritative parents—this higher level of performance is seen from preschool throughout early adulthood (Brooks-Gunn & Markman, 2005; Chen & Kaplan, 2001).

- Effective parenting skills further the growth of children's social and communication skills, as well as their ability to concentrate on tasks and at school (Connell & Prinz, 2002; Lamb-Parker, Boak, Griffin, Ripple, & Peay, 1999).

- Authoritative parents of adolescents allow their teens to have autonomy, but they simultaneously define clear boundaries and articulate their concerns about safety and well-being (Smetana, 1995).

When parents are warm, sensitive, and responsive to their child's needs, they foster a wide range of interpersonal development in children, from the development of a healthy sense of self, to a sense of belonging and well-being, to high levels of self-esteem (Harvard Family Research Project, 2006).

Ethnic Group Differences in Parenting

Research demonstrates that race and ethnicity influence parenting styles (Hill & Tyson, 2008; Jackson-Newsom and others, 2008; Weis & Toolis, 2010). Overall, research indicates that African American parents utilize authoritarian parenting (involving more physical discipline and higher control) more than other parenting styles (Hill & Tyson, 2008; Jackson-Newsom, Buchanan, & McDonald, 2008; Weis & Toolis, 2010); however, while using the authoritarian parenting style, Black parents do have communication and warmth in their parent–child relationships (Murry, Brody, Simons, Cutrona, & Gibbons, 2008). It has been suggested that the increased use of discipline and strictness among Black American parents is a protective factor for Black youth; among African Americans, strictness is viewed as "protection, affection, compliance, and respect for authority" (McMurtry, 2013).

In a landmark, large-scale study of approximately 10,000 adolescents representing four ethnic groups (African American, white, Hispanic, and Asian American), the researchers found that the *authoritative* parenting style was the most common among white families and least common among Asian Americans; it was also more common among married biological parents than it was among single-parent or stepfamilies (Steinberg et al., 1991). The study also showed that parenting styles differ by social class. Authoritative parenting was more common among middle-class parents than among working-class parents, with the exception of Asian American parents, who demonstrated authoritarian parenting styles.

Interestingly, this study also demonstrated that there was a strong correlation between *authoritative* parenting and positive outcomes for whites and Hispanics, but Asian American and African American teens had better social and school performance outcomes when their parents used the *authoritarian* parenting style. Subsequent research has found that parenting goals, such as raising children so they will succeed in college and in their careers, are tied to parenting styles (Cheah & Rubin, 2004). Parenting goals are influenced by the parents' cultural values. For example, Asian American parents may raise their children with the authoritarian parenting style because they believe it helps to maintain their cultural identity; African American parents may do so because they are "keenly aware of the degree to which social forces such as racism may impede their children's achievement of educational, economic, and social success. . . . They [believe] that adopting an authoritarian parenting style will enhance their children's potential for success" (Boyd & Bee, 2009, p. 224). The link between this parenting style and child outcome variables such as self-control suggest that it is effective for African Americans (Broman, Reckase, & Freedman-Doan, 2006). It is important to note, however, that not *all* African American parents adopt this parenting style—parenting styles are as unique as each individual.

These studies show us that there are *culturally specific* processes that underlie parents' behaviors and communication. The reality of parenting is that it is an experience consisting of interconnected, multiple processes that are affected by the parents' race/ethnicity, cultural beliefs, income level, and living environment. Much more work needs to be done to fully understand the interplay of cultural contexts and parenting; these studies can serve as a launching pad for family life education programs and public policies to strengthen family life (Ceballo & Hurd, 2008).

Consider the interaction and relational patterns between you and your parent(s) or primary caregiver. Did these experiences allow you to feel that you were worthy of affection and love? Or instead, did your early parent–child experiences cause you to feel shame, guilt, and doubt, resulting in fear of intimacy, fear of abandonment, betrayal, and rejection in your adult relationships? As we are growing up, our parent and family interactions convey to us our worth—our purpose—as individuals, and this perception influences our ability to relate to others on an intimate level the remainder of our lifespan.

It is indisputable that the manner in which parents interact with and guide their children influences their development in more ways than are immediately visible (such as behavior and school performance). Children's abilities to love, to be loved by another, to feel secure and accepted, and to form attachment bonds with others—the very bonds that will later allow children to enter into love relationships of their own—are also shaped by their parents' parenting style.

Given the tips and downs of parenting and the inherent adjustments that must be made as a result of children's demands, given its uncertainty, given the fact that no two children are alike, and given the fact that no two people (or parent) experience parenting in the same way, is it really possible to prepare for what one developmentalist (Carter & McGoldrick, 1999) describes as "one of the most definitive stages of life"? Probably not. Nevertheless, we can address those contemporary issues that affect parenting and the stressors associated with the transition into parenthood and parenting. Although the experience of parenthood is without a doubt unpredictable, many parents, though not all, find it to be the most rewarding life experience.

FROM PARTNERS TO PARENTS: MAKING THE TRANSITION

When a new baby or child joins a couple, thus creating a new family form, all of the couple's established ways of interacting and relating, their patterns of behavior, and their marital and gender roles have to be adjusted to accommodate the addition to the family system. Whether it's baby number one or baby number seven, transitioning to life with the new family member presents challenges. In this section, we'll examine those challenges that new families face, including adjusting to their new roles, the responsibilities of bringing up baby, juggling parenting and household chores, and the day-to-day decisions parents must face, such as disciplining their children.

Motherhood and Fatherhood: Adjusting to New Family Roles

Most new parents expect a period of transition after the birth of a baby, but they tend to underestimate the demands and changes that accompany parenting. Part of new parents' disillusionment stems from the unrealistic expectations that come from cultural myths that

One of the reasons the transition to parenthood is so difficult for most is that established roles and responsibilities have to change to accommodate the new role of parent.

paint an idyllic picture of parenting (Lazarus & Rossouw, 2015; Delmore-Ko, Pancer, Hunsberger, & Pratt, 2000; Lawrence, Nylen, & Cobb, 2007). Although there are special, tender, and precious times when parenting seems idyllic, there are more times that dispel these myths, such as when the baby cries through the night, fusses all day, or won't touch his or her food but enjoys eating the pet's food. There is always something to attend to. And it is the new parents' responsibility to learn how to care for, nurture, and love the baby. Meanwhile, parents still have to figure out who they are in their new roles and who their spouse is in their new family system. No longer is the couple simply "husband" and "wife"—they are also a mother or a father and all that goes along with this redefined, multifaceted position. Suddenly, the mom or dad becomes a child development specialist, behavior expert, communications director, therapist, financial wizard/estate planner, nurse, head of safety and health administration, dispute and arbitration authority, labor boss, teacher, sex educator, spiritual advisor, and funeral director/grief counselor (to date, my family has buried two dogs, three cats, three hamsters, one bunny, one squirrel, and about 100 goldfish).

To understand the transition and stressors associated with bringing a baby or a child into the family, we need to recall our study of Family Systems theory from Chapter 3. Remember that the family can be likened to a mobile—any time we add or take away a member from the mobile (the family system) an imbalance is temporarily created (see Figure 11.1). This imbalance is felt and experienced as stress and conflict. Even though bringing home a new baby or adopting a child is a joyous occasion for most couples, the happy nature of the event doesn't minimize the fact that a new subsystem has been added to the family system, calling for a shifting of family roles, family balance, and family boundaries; all of these factors are what account for the stressful transition when baby makes three (or four, or five, or . . .).

Figure 11.1 /// Revisiting Virginia Satir's Mobile From Chapter 3

In general, research has looked at the transition to parenthood in two different ways. In the first, new parents are seen as making an abrupt shift that results in persistent change, and this transition to parenthood is thought to cause negative changes in a couple's relationship dynamics (Lawrence, Rothman, Cobb, Rothman, & Bradbury 2008). The second predominant perspective views the transition to parenthood as a significant—yet temporary—stage in a couple's marriage and family development. According to this paradigm, the changes associated with new parenting roles are anticipated, short-lived, and small in magnitude, normative changes, and different couple types adapt to these challenges in varying ways (Lawrence et al., 2008). Over many years, research into the changes associated with parenthood, be it through birth, adoption, or the formation of stepfamilies, has centered on four primary areas (for a comprehensive review, see Ceballo et al., 2004):

1. *Psychological well-being.* Among biological parents, the transition to parenthood has been associated with increased levels of depression for both mothers and fathers, and these in turn affect marital satisfaction. Because of the stressors associated with adopting a child (such as the drawn-out adoption process and perhaps prolonged periods of infertility), the transition to parenthood for adoptive parents is typically associated with overall positive quality of life and high marital satisfaction. Among stepfamilies who are gaining a stepchild, the transition to step-parenthood has been associated with increased levels of depression.

2. *Marital quality.* Following the birth of a child, marital relationships are often characterized by negative interactions, declines in marital satisfaction and sexual intimacy, increased levels of conflict, and drops in leisure time spent as a couple. Most research, however, indicates that these declines persist for only about one year, and that they are modest. In a majority of the studies, parents indicated that the rewards of parenting outweighed the initial negative experiences. Adoptive parents may experience these same declines, but to a lesser extent than biological parents do; creating a stepfamily with children creates a difficult transition for most couples.

3. *Family relations and social support.* For some families, the birth of a child enhances family relationships, and oftentimes relatives help new parents adjust to their roles of mother and father by providing practical and emotional support; some parents experience higher levels of depression and distress if their extended family does not offer such support. Among adoptive parents, studies to date show that the emotional and practical support from family members exceeded their expectations, and this support was related to positive family experiences.

4. *Roles.* After the birth or adoption of a child, roles significantly change for mothers and fathers. Some research suggests that adults indicate that the "parent" role is greater than the "partner" role. Among men, the "worker" role remains stable, but women report sharp declines in that role and relate more to the "mother" role.

As you can see, for several decades family life educators and family practitioners have characterized the transition to parenthood as a challenging, and often difficult, lifecourse stage where couples are faced with unanticipated realities of limited time, energy, and resources. But as emerging research shows us, if prospective parents hold realistic expectations going into parenting, becoming parents is less stressful to them and to their relationship (Harwood, McLean, & Durkin, 2007). Of course, just when parents believe they have figured out the ins and outs of parenting, the child passes into a new phase of growth and development (with its own uncharted territory) or another baby is added to the family.

Theories of Child Development

There are several theories that seek to explain and understand child development. In general, there are four theories of child development—psychoanalytic, learning, cognitive, and

Table 11.1 /// Ages and Stages of Child Development

Age	Cognitive Stage	Social and Emotional Stage
0–1	Cries to signal needs; vocalizes, babbles, coos; says first words; interested in picture books	Recognizes family members; shows anxiety when separated from parents; fearful of strangers; likes to be tickled and touched; wants parents in sight
1–2	Has vocabulary of 8 to 20 words; identifies objects in books; makes animal sounds	Can play alone with toys; likes to be read to; will comfort others in distress; enjoys pretend play; shows affection
2	Uses 2- to 3-word sentences; sings; names toys, animals, people; enjoys stories and rhymes; enjoys simple make-believe	Possessive of parents' attention; can show beginning of independence; shy around/ doesn't share with others
3	Uses 5- to 8-word sentences; listens actively to stories/songs; pretends to read; names colors; counts to 2 or 3	Seeks adult attention; helps with chores; engages in solitary play, but with others nearby; doesn't share; likes to laugh and be silly
4	Is imaginative, loves to make believe; uses complex sentences; counts to 10 or higher; understands categories (small, big, tall); very inquisitive and curious	Likes to engage in cooperative play with others; shares; cooperates; obeys simple instructions; loves to love others
5	Uses complex sentences of 10 or more words; enjoys storytelling, tracing, drawing, writing, coloring; counts; has good attention span; can memorize	Seeks adults' approval; embarrassed by own mistakes; understands relationships among people; likes to give to others; shares and takes turns; enjoys playing with friends
6–8	Reads; understands time of day and days of week; increased attention span; problem-solving capabilities increase; begins logical thinking	Friends become very important; wants to do everything well; easily hurt by criticism; still self-centered, but begins to see others' points of view; gender-centric
9–11	Reads; daydreams about future; logic becomes solidified; begins abstract thinking; begins to think about justice and ethics	Friendships become very important, consuming as much as 40 percent of their time; empathy toward others continues
12–14	Engages in abstract thought; able to think about hypothetical situations; able to think about the future	More mature friendships; friendship groups become larger and now include friends of opposite sex; embarrassed by parents

Psychoanalytic theory: the theory of personality development in children developed by Sigmund Freud.

Psychosexual stages: in Sigmund Freud's view, development takes place through a series of psychosexual stages, in which sensual energy or satisfaction is focused on one particular part of the body.

Oral stage: the psychosexual stage from birth to about age 1 when the focus of sensual energy is the mouth and the tongue; the emphasis for personality development is thus centered on breastfeeding.

Anal stage: the psychosexual stage from ages 1 to 3, during which the focus of the sensual energy is associated with toilet training, particularly with respect to the anus.

Phallic stage: the psychosexual stage from ages 3 to 6, during which children are intensely interested in the physical differences between men and women.

socio-cultural. Each theory offers its own unique contribution to our understanding of how and why children develop the way that they do. (See also Table 11.1.)

Psychoanalytic Theories

The "grandfather of psychology," Sigmund Freud (1856–1939), developed his **psychoanalytic theory**, which focused on the personality development of children. In his view, development takes place through a series of **psychosexual stages**, in which sensual energy or satisfaction is focused on one particular part of the body. For example, during the **oral stage** (from birth to about age 1), the focus of sensual energy is the mouth and the tongue; the emphasis for personality development is thus centered on breastfeeding. In the **anal stage** (ages 1 to 3), the focus of the sensual energy is associated with potty training, particularly with respect to the anus, in the **phallic stage** (ages 3 to 6), Freud believed children were intensely interested in the physical differences between men and women. He also maintained that the focus of the sensual energy during this stage was the genitals, and believed that children engaged in self-stimulation of their genitals to derive pleasure. In the latency stage (ages 7 to 11), according to psychoanalytic theory, the sensual energies subside for a time, and during the final, or genital stage (ages 12 and beyond), people developed mature sexual interests in the opposite sex. The experiences through these stages—particularly through age 5—shaped a child's personality for an entire lifetime. Freud's psychoanalytic theory also emphasized the role of the unconscious and held that most of people's actions, behaviors, and emotions are the result of these drives that lie below a person's level of awareness.

Erik Erikson (1902–1994) developed his own psychoanalytic theory based on Freud's original work. (We learned about Erikson's theory in Chapter 5.) Unlike Freud's theory, Erikson developed eight stages that spanned a person's entire lifetime. He also believed that, although early childhood experiences are crucial in shaping a person's personality, later events in life could alter the influence of the earlier experiences.

Learning Theories

In general, learning theories emphasize the role of the environment—such as the home, school, community, and peers—in shaping a child's development. In other words, all behavior is learned from environmental influences. According to learning theories, parents play a significant role in who their children ultimately become. There are several learning theorists.

B. F. Skinner (1904–1990) believed that children learn behaviors through a series of rewards and punishments, and this series is called operant conditioning. Rewards reinforce behavior, and increase the likelihood that the behavior will occur again. For example, if a child is praised for making his bed, it is likely that he will repeat that behavior. If, on the other hand, a child is criticized because he didn't do a good job or make his bed perfectly, it is not likely that he will repeat the behavior. Punishments decrease the likelihood that a behavior will be repeated. According to Skinner, operant conditioning is the way that parents guide, shape, and mold the behaviors they desire of their children.

John B. Watson (1878–1958) promoted his theory of classical conditioning, which proposes that people make associations between two events. For example, babies open their mouths and smack their lips when their parent puts them in a highchair, or when their parent opens the jar of baby food. Conditioning (opening their mouths or smacking their lips) has taken place because the babies make the association between one event (being put in a high-chair) and the other event (hearing their food source being opened). Similarly, some children (and college students!) cringe, become panicked, or get sick to their stomachs when an exam is handed out.

Have you ever been told that you sound just like your mother or father? Or that one of your behaviors is just like that of your mother or father, or another family member? Albert Bandura's (1923–) Social Learning theory focused on how children acquire behaviors. He believed that the acquisition of behaviors and personality traits are the result of observing others, and that we then imitate the behaviors we observe. For example, parents model certain gender roles, their children observe these modeled behaviors, and they subsequently acquire the same or similar behaviors. As Bandura (1986) once noted, "Of the many cues that influence behavior, at any point in time, none is more common than the actions of others" (p. 206).

Cognitive Theories

Cognitive theories focus on how children think and how they understand their world. The focus of childhood development is not centered on personality development but on children's thinking and reasoning. A 4-year-old will comprehend and reason about his parents' divorce differently than will his 10-year-old brother; a 10-year-old will comprehend and reason about his parents' divorce differently than will his 15-year-old sister. Jean Piaget (1896–1980) advanced the most widely recognized cognitive development theory, which consists of four sequential stages.

Latency stage: the psychosexual stage from about ages 7 to 11, during which the sensual energies subside for a time.

Genital stage: the psychosexual stage beginning at puberty (age 12), when people develop mature sexual interests.

Operant conditioning: B. F. Skinner's theory that children learn behaviors as a result of a series of rewards and punishments.

Punishment: something that decreases the likelihood that a behavior will be repeated.

Classical conditioning: John B. Watson's theory that people make associations between two events. For example, babies open their mouths and smack their lips when their parent puts them in a highchair or when their parent opens the jar of baby food.

Cognitive theories: theories that focus on how children think and how they understand their world.

Piaget maintained that as children progressed from stage to Stage, they applied their current thinking and reasoning capabilities to new experiences. Unlike behaviorist theorists, who believed that children were passive learners, Piaget believed that children actively seek to understand their environment.

Sociocultural Theories

Sociocultural theories:
theories maintaining that children's development does not occur by stages but through direct interaction with culture, which shapes their values, goals, and expectations.

Unlike the previously mentioned theories that stated that children proceed from one stage of development through the next, **sociocultural theories** propose that children do not progress through any stages. Instead, children's development is thought to occur as a result of direct interaction with their culture—that the values, goals, and expectations of their culture significantly shape and mold them. Thus, "development" means different things to different children in different cultures; what is considered developmentally appropriate for a child in one culture may not be considered so in another culture. The pioneer of Sociocultural theory is Russian-born psychologist Lev Vygotsky (1896–1934), who believed that parents are children's primary teachers. According to Vygotsky, parents who are sensitive to their child's development can sense when the child is ready to learn new tasks and skills, and they engage their children in different activities to help their child develop these new skills. For example, whether it is a Mayan mother teaching her daughter to make tortillas or an American mother teaching her son to measure flour and sugar to make cookies, each parent is teaching her child new skills—and cultural values at the same time.

Studying children and their development is a fascinating field of study. Each theory has a different explanation of how and why children develop the way they do, but each one helps us belter understand the complexities of children's development.

Bringing Up Baby (or Babies)

Historically—*and still today*—much of the responsibility for caregiving and childrearing rests on the mother's shoulders, a pattern seen in industrialized and non-industrialized societies alike. Traditional gender roles in Western culture are based on the belief that mothers (or women in general) have an innate ability that allows them to nurture and care for infants and children better than men do. From diapers to discipline, from empty bottles to emotional support, from daycare to dating dilemmas, mothers seem to be the predominant advisors and guides. They are also the ones doing the laundry, the cleaning, the grocery shopping, and the daily scheduling. In many households, mothers put in twice as much lime as fathers when it comes to childrearing (among many, Bianchi, 2000; Cohen, 1993; Deutsch, Lozy, & Saxon, 1993; McBride & Mills, 1993; Pleck, 1997).

Even couples who have an egalitarian (equal) relationship (see Chapter 8) prior to the arrival of a baby tend to fall back into traditional roles once the new baby arrives. Sociologist and researcher of women's issues, Melissa Milkie and her associates (Milkie, Bianchi, Mattingly, & Robinson 2002) examined 234 married couples about their attitudes toward conjugal roles (see Chapter 8) and childrearing. They found that although the parents asserted that both should be equally responsible and equally involved in parenting, caregiving, and childrearing, mothers consistently reported higher levels of involvement for themselves than did their husbands. In particular, mothers expressed significantly higher levels of involvement in the areas of child discipline and providing emotional support for their children. Fathers perceived their involvement in parenting (discipline, emotional support, play, monitoring, caregiving) at much higher levels than the mothers reported, resulting in what the researchers term an **ideal–actual gap**. When mothers viewed the fathers' parenting involvement as less-than-ideal (not equal to their own involvement), their relationships were found to have higher levels of stress. When women felt that discrepancies existed between their roles as disciplinarians and those same roles of their husbands—when they felt they were more involved than their husbands—they reported higher levels of dissatisfaction due to perceived unfairness. Similarly, child and adolescent psychologist and childrearing expert Ron Taffel (1994) discovered that although his study

Ideal–actual gap:
the difference between the parenting tasks that are reported and the parent's actual performance.

participants reported a fairly equal divide over childrearing tasks, when lists were compared the division was more along the lines of the woman doing about four times more than her husband.

Studies such as these speak to a broader point: Despite the efforts in the twentieth and twenty-first centuries to more actively involve fathers in child care and childrearing, we cannot escape the ways we have been socialized. Several research studies investigating the division of family work and parental responsibilities showed that women's socialization—and the inherent cultural notion that she will always be the better parent—makes it difficult for the mother to relinquish her traditional role (for a comprehensive review, see Baxter, Hewitt, & Haynes, 2008). This is described as **maternal gatekeeping**.

Women and men today may anticipate and expect their parenting involvement to be equal, but socialization and established ways of thinking make it very easy to fall into traditional gender roles once the first baby arrives. Suddenly, this egalitarian relationship no longer exists, challenging pre-set expectations, raising stress levels, and giving rise to feelings of unfairness. As a result, conflict ensues and marital satisfaction plummets.

Juggling Parenting and Household Chores

During the 1990s, more than 200 research articles addressed the many nuances of the division of household labor. Couples may marry with the intent to share household chores just as they intend to share childrearing. But when children enter into the family system, these intentions often do not become reality. Often, discrepancies between who does what becomes a source of recurring conflict. With the majority of mothers today working at least 30 hours a week outside the home, the expectation that they are still responsible for the lion's share of running the household and performing household tasks can become a source of resentment. Sociologist Arlie Hochschild (1989) referred to this burden of taking on the duel responsibilities of wage-earner and housekeeper as the second shift.

During this second shift, women spend three times as much time performing household tasks as men do, consuming 32 hours compared to men's 10 hours (Coltrane, 2000). These tasks include house cleaning, meal preparation, grocery shopping, cleanup after meals, and laundry (Blair & Lichter, 1991). Coltrane (2000) refers to these essential tasks as **routine housework**

Maternal gatekeeping: when a woman's socialization—and the inherent cultural notion that she will always be the better parent—makes it difficult for her to relinquish her traditional roles.

Routine housework: house cleaning, meal preparation, grocery shopping, cleaning up after meals, and laundry.

iStock.com/FluxFactory

In today's heterosexual-partner families, women still tend to do the lion's share of the work around the house.

but maintains that "this family work or social reproductive labor is just as important to the maintenance of society as the productive work that occurs in the formal market economy" (p. 1209), and that these tasks keep the household, the family, and society going. Coltrane cites numerous studies that indicate that, for the most part, neither women nor men enjoy performing routine household chores. They tend to find occasional residual tasks, such as bill paying, yard work, and chauffeuring children to be more flexible in nature and more enjoyable to carry out.

Like parenting roles, the division of household duties tends to fall along traditional gender roles once a child is born, even if such tasks were previously handled fairly equally (Baxter et al., 2008). For example, in a study of 2,231 married and cohabiting new parents, the researchers found that the birth of a first child resulted in a dramatic increase in women's housework time—about six additional hours a week on average; having additional children continued to increase women's time on household chores. There was no corresponding change in men's housework hours after the arrival of a child (Baxter et al., 2008). Another excellent example of this happened in my own marital relationship when 1 was very seriously ill and bedridden for several weeks. I saw the disarray the upstairs was in—I couldn't even bring myself to imagine what the downstairs looked like. In discussing my concerns with my husband, he said to me, "You have your way of doing things and I have my way of doing things. My way may not be just like yours, but it still gets the job done. You have to give me permission to do things my way." I conceded and agreed that as long as the kids were being fed, their homework was being done, and they got to school on time wearing clean underwear, then other things could temporarily slide. (Although I did add, "But my way is still the better way!")

Coltrane (2000) identifies several factors that contribute to the division of household chores:

- *Women's employment.* When there are two wage earners in the family, these couples tend to share household tasks more than those couples where only one spouse works.
- *Men's employment.* Men who work fewer hours outside the home tend to pitch in more around the house and with childrearing responsibilities.
- *Earnings.* Women who earn more money benefit from more shared divisions of household tasks.
- *Education.* In households in which one or both spouses have high education levels (a college degree or a postgraduate degree), women tend to perform fewer household tasks and are more likely to hire outside help to render services such as house cleaning. Men with high education levels tend to engage in more household labor.
- *Presence of children.* When children enter the marriage (and change the family dynamic), household labor is less frequently shared evenly between the marital partners, and the woman assumes the majority of housework, along with the responsibilities of childrearing.

Although gender appears to be an important factor that dictates generally who does what housework and how often, the research does seem to indicate that the division of labor along traditional gender roles is slowly giving way to changing roles of men and women in contemporary society. This is a "ray of hope" for those who struggle with balancing marital and parenting roles, because, as Coltrane (2000) concludes, "We now know that when men perform more of the routine household work, employed women feel that the division of labor is fairer, are less depressed, and enjoy higher levels of marital satisfaction" (p. 1226).

The challenges of childrearing go far beyond the stereotypical jokes about changing diapers and getting up in the middle of the night. Childrearing not only demands a realignment of roles within a family but it also insists that parents learn how to avoid the potential who-does-what-around-the-house conflicts that may arise. It requires that parents learn how to juggle careers and parenting responsibilities while remaining attentive to the emotional needs of partners and maintaining a strong marriage. Challenging? You bet.

TODAY'S PARENTS

What makes a father? What makes a mother? What makes a "parent"? Just as the challenges associated with parenting have changed over the past 20 years, so have the faces of today's parents (U.S. Census Bureau, 2018b):

- Nearly 51 million children live with two parents.
- 17 million children live with their single-parent mother.
- 3 million children live with their single-parent father.

Whether a baby is born because of an unintended adolescent or nonmarital pregnancy, an intended marital or nonmarital pregnancy, or by choice (such as with adoption, gay and lesbian parenting, or parenting by grandparents), the shifting boundaries of parenthood in contemporary society are evident,

Single Parents

Single parenthood is not a new phenomenon. Throughout history, widows and widowers have reared children alone. But since 1970, the proportion of households made up of married couples with children has decreased while the proportion of households with single parents has increased. According to U.S. Census Bureau demographers (2018c), approximately 35 percent of families in the United States are single-parent families. Figure 11.2 shows us the distribution of single-parent experiences, by race. In Chapter 1, we saw the racial and ethnic differences among single parents, and in our study throughout this textbook we discovered that there are a number of reasons why the United States is seeing increasing numbers of single parents, such as women getting married later in life, the growth in divorce rates, and an increasing acceptance by society of unmarried childbearing.

Single-Family Models

Along with the shift in demographic and societal trends, the way researchers are viewing single parenting is changing, too. Throughout the past three decades, two models of single-parent families have been used predominately.

Figure 11.2 /// Children in Single-Parent Families, by Race: 2010–2014

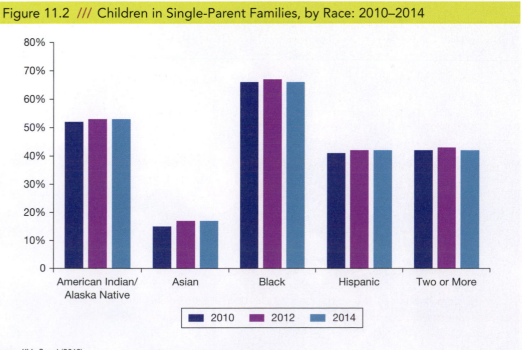

Source: Kids Count (2018).

Family Deficit Model. The **Family Deficit Model** dates back to the 1970s, when single-parent families were far less common than they are today. This model promoted the idea that single-parent households were negative experiences for children for the sole reason that the *family structure was not nuclear* (Marsh, 1990). With the base assumption that one-parent families are not the ideal family situation for children, much of the research yielded while using this theory supported this basic assumption (Donahoo, 2004).

Risk and Protective Factor Model. Unlike the Family Deficit Model, which assumes at the outset that the only "ideal" family structure is the traditional nuclear family, the **Risk and Protective Factor Model** does not assume at its base that single-parent families are out of the norm (Seifer, Sameroff, Baldwin, & Baldwin, 1992). This model assumes that *every* family form has strengths, or protective factors. According to Seifer and his colleagues, *protective factors* are those factors that positively influence children and lessen the influence and/or impact of any existing risk factors. *Risk factors* are, in essence, the weaknesses in the family system that can have a potentially negative impact on families and children. For example, a family member's employment status, mental health, poverty, educational level, mother's age at first birth, or number of siblings are all factors. Depending on which factors come into play, when risk factors outweigh protective factors, the result most likely will be a negative experience for children; conversely, when protective factors outweigh risk factors, the result will most likely be a positive family experience for children. Although single parenting can be a risk factor for children's overall well-being, it is not *the sole predictor* of negative outcomes as suggested by the Family Deficit Model.

Women as Single Parents. As of 2018, 1 in 4 children under the age of 18—slightly more than 16 million children—living in single-parent mother household (U.S. Census Bureau, 2018b). And, of the nearly 11 million single parents, more than 80 percent are mothers. Census Bureau demographers estimate that one-half of the women rearing children by themselves have never been married, and nearly 30 percent are divorced. More than one-third of these families live below the poverty line, and 30 percent are food insecure; about 13 percent rely on food pantries to feed their families (U.S. Census Bureau, 2018a). Divorced single mothers seem to fare better economically than do never-married single mothers, but single mothers on average make $41,000 per year, while married couples earn approximately $90,000 per year. Racial differences among single mothers reveal different outcomes. White single mothers are more likely to be divorced, whereas African American single mothers are more likely to have never been married.

Today, men make up a large share of single parents. Just as with single mothers, single dads have to balance work with parenting, and finding time to take care of themselves.

iStock.com/NoSystem images

Men as Single Parents. According to Census Bureau data, of the single-parent families in America today, about 2 million are headed by men; about 44 percent of the single-parent fathers are divorced, 19 percent were separated from their spouse, and about one-third have never married (U.S. Census Bureau, 2018a). Though these family forms are increasing in number, very little research exists to shed more light on the unique characteristics of these families. Kirk Bloir (2005) asserts that more fathers are rearing children by themselves as a result of four social factors:

1. Current divorce laws and "gender-neutral criteria" for rearing children have made it easier for fathers to gain custody of their children following divorce than in years past.

2. To allow themselves the opportunity to pursue career or personal goals, mothers may choose to grant the father custody of the children.

3. Divorce courts have a more favorable view of the role of fathers in childrearing, resulting in an increase in joint custody arrangements following divorce.

4. There has been an increase in fathers' willingness to take a more active role in parenting than in years past.

Bloir (2005) also notes characteristics that differentiate single fathers from single mothers. These include:

- Single fathers are less likely to live at or below the poverty line (although they tend to be poorer than married fathers).
- They are more likely to be employed.
- They tend to be younger than married fathers, but older than single mothers.
- Single fathers do not have as many children as married fathers, but have more than single mothers.
- They are more likely to live with other relatives in the household.
- Very few single fathers receive child support from the mother, whereas many mothers receive child support from fathers.
- Single fathers tend to suffer more from work–family role conflicts such as being late, child care, missing work, leaving early, or work-related travel concerns than married fathers or single mothers.

Just as single fathers are evidence of parenthood in transition, grandparents raising their grandchildren, and gays and lesbians desiring to form a family by choice are also changing the face of today's families.

Grandparents as Parents: A Growing Phenomenon

Today, about 3 percent of children live apart from their parents, and of those, nearly two-thirds are being raised by grandparents (U.S. Census Bureau, 2018a). It is estimated that nearly 3 million grandparents live with their grandchildren and are responsible for raising their grandchildren (United States Census Bureau, 2018a). Referred to as **kinship care**, grandparents provide a living environment for their grandchildren for a number of reasons, but particularly because the parents struggle with substance abuse, mental illness, economic hardship, divorce, domestic violence, and incarceration (Raphel, 2008). Most of these living arrangements are informal, private, and voluntary—the court system and/or the social welfare system are typically not involved in these arrangements. Parents commonly retain legal custody and can make decisions regarding their children, although in some cases the grandparents share legal custody. Although not common, some grandparents adopt the grandchildren, and the rights of the parents are legally terminated.

Kinship care:
a situation in which grandparents provide a living environment for their grandchildren.

The role of grandparents as parents is classified into four categories (Reynolds, Wright, & Beale, 2003):

1. *Limited caretaking.* Grandparents have limited contact with their grandchildren, and parents have primary responsibility.

2. *Participatory caretaking.* In these situations, grandparents are engaged and involved in their grandchildren's lives, such as taking an active interest in the children's education and their activities. Care may be provided for grandchildren while the parents are at work, but parents have primary responsibility for them.

3. *Voluntary caretaking.* Grandparents assume the parental role and responsibilities for raising their grandchildren. Although situations vary, typically these types of caregivers assume the role of grandparents as parents to make sure their grandchildren are in a safe, stable environment in the absence of their parents.

4. *Involuntary caretaking.* These grandparents are full-time caregivers of their grandchildren, and most often they have little to no warning; many times, it is not the grandparents' preference—the situation was more or less thrust on them. These types of arrangements are often difficult for children because of the unexpected shift in environments and caregivers.

Many grandparents welcome the opportunity to care for their grandchildren, but others experience financial, social, and emotional intrusions, as well as an increase in health problems. As one body of research suggests, for many grandparents the role of second parenthood limits their independence and their personal development in mid- to later adulthood (Glass & Hunneycutt, 2002). However, other research suggests that there are rewards, such as getting a chance to raise a child differently, to nurture family relationships, and to receive love and companionship from their grandchildren (Burton, Dilworth-Anderson, & Merriwether-deVries, 1995).

Grandparents raising their grandchildren is a growing phenomenon in the United States, and much more study needs to be done so family practitioners understand the unique needs of the grandparents and the children they are parenting. With this knowledge, human service providers, such as teachers, social workers, ministers, and mental health workers can begin to successfully implement parenting classes and other resources for caregiving grandparents in order to equip them with the necessary skills to best raise their grandchildren.

Gay and Lesbian Parents

Until recently, the majority of gay and lesbian parents were people who entered into a heterosexual relationship and had children prior to coming out of the closet. However, many same-sex couples today are entering into planned parenthood through adoption, surrogacy, or fertilization techniques, as Chapter 10 showed us. Today, between 2 million and nearly 4 million children have an LGBTQ parent or parents; many children are raised by a single LGBTQ parent, or by a different-sex couple where one parent is bisexual (Family Equality Council, 2017). LGBTQ individuals and same-sex couples are much more likely than heterosexual couples to adopt or foster a child—same-sex couples are 6 times more likely to foster a child, and at least 4 times more likely to adopt (Family Equality Council, 2017).

Despite the increasing number of gay and lesbian parents, research demonstrates that some heterosexual adults hold negative attitudes toward them as parents. For instance, some people are concerned that gay male parents are more likely to sexually abuse their children than straight parents are. Research shows, however, that gay men are no more likely to do so than heterosexual men are, and that girls are at far greater risk to be abused by their heterosexual fathers than their gay fathers (Jenny, Roesler, & Poyer, 1994). Gay and lesbian parents are also more likely to be well-educated and affluent, in comparison to heterosexual parents (Patterson, 1996). Other benefits have been documented for children of lesbian parents: They learn respect, empathy, and acceptance of diversity, and are more assertive in challenging traditional gender roles in their relationships (Allen, 1997; Savin-Williams & Esterberg, 2000). More recent research indicates that there are few differences between adolescents living with same-sex parents and those living with heterosexual parents (Wainright & Patterson, 2006). For instance, in this study the investigators looked at the responses of 44 junior high and high schoolers who lived with their same-sex parents who were matched with a similar group of adolescents who lived with their opposite-sex parents. The study revealed that there were no significant differences in the teens' psychological well-being (self-esteem and anxiety), school outcomes (grades and trouble in school), or family relationships (parental warmth and care).

Although much more research needs to take place in this area of family living, to date the empirical evidence seems to indicate that children of gay and lesbian parents do not experience physical, emotional, psychological, or developmental disadvantages. As with any child, it appears to the be *quality of the parent–child relationship* that is the most important to a child's health and well-being—*not* the parents' sexual orientations or their genders (Wainright & Patterson, 2006).

How Do Children Learn About Their Racial/Ethnic Identity?

As our earlier discussion about parenting styles showed us, there are racial/ethnic differences in the strategies parents employ to raise their children. Emerging research is beginning to shed even more light on these differences, especially in the distinct parenting challenges with which people of color are faced.

African American/Black Caribbeans, Hispanics, Native Americans, Asian Americans, and Arab Americans in this country often experience racism. **Racism** is a belief system which holds that race accounts for differences in human character and/or ability; it results in discrimination and prejudice based on someone's race or ethnic background. Because of the historical disparaging and marginalizing views of people of color, and because of historical racial barriers in equal opportunities, racial and ethnic minority parents are faced with the challenges of insulating their children from the negative consequences of racism. They deal with these challenges by teaching their children how to "navigate and negotiate" the racism terrain through a process referred to as racial/ethnic socialization (Coard, Foy-Watson, Zimmer, & Wallace, 2007). And today, many adults have negative feelings about racial relations in the United States, as Figure 11.3 shows us.

Racism: a belief system that holds that race accounts for differences in human character and/or ability; it results in discrimination and prejudice based on someone's race or ethnic background.

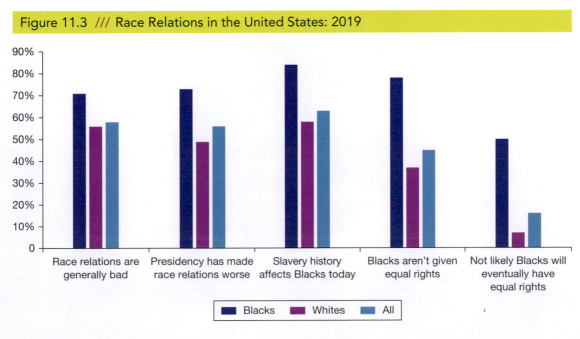

Figure 11.3 /// Race Relations in the United States: 2019

Source: Pew Research Center (2019).

Furthermore, most Americans across all racial and ethnic groups say that today, more and more people in the United States express racist and/or racially insensitive views, as illustrated in Figures 11.4 and 11.5 (Pew Research Center, 2019).

Racial/ethnic socialization is the way in which families teach children about the social meanings of their race/ethnicity: What does it mean to "be" Black, Hispanic, Asian, Native American, or of Arab descent? Oftentimes, this socialization also includes teaching children the consequences of ethnicity and race, such as racism (Brown, Tanner-Smith, Lesane-Brown, & Ezell, 2007). Throughout the socialization process, which is presented in Figure 11.6, children learn

Racial/ethnic socialization:

the way in which families teach children about the social meanings of their race/ethnicity.

Figure 11.4 /// How Common Is It for People to Express Racist Views?

Since Trump was elected, it has become _____ for people to express racist or racially insensitive views.

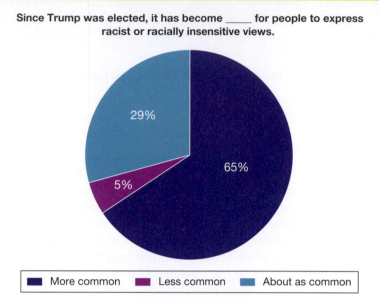

Legend: More common | Less common | About as common

65% / 5% / 29%

Source: Pew Research Center (2019)

Figure 11.5 /// How Acceptable Is It for People to Express Racist Views?

Since Trump was elected, it has become _____ for people to express racist or racially insensitive views.

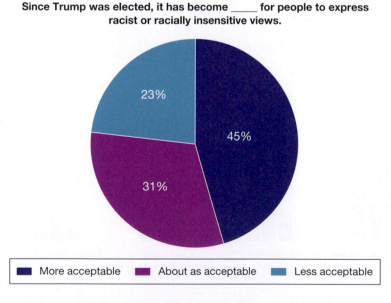

Legend: More acceptable | About as acceptable | Less acceptable

45% / 31% / 23%

Source: Pew Research Center (2019)

Racial/ethnic socialization is a process that unfolds across a number of years. How are children taught to "be" their race/ethnicity and what are the social meanings attached to being a member of a racial or ethnic group?

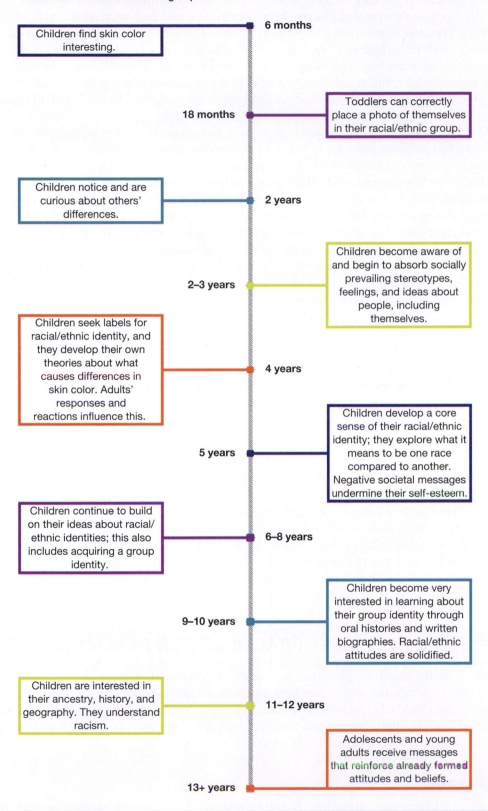

Children find skin color interesting. — **6 months**

18 months — Toddlers can correctly place a photo of themselves in their racial/ethnic group.

Children notice and are curious about others' differences. — **2 years**

2–3 years — Children become aware of and begin to absorb socially prevailing stereotypes, feelings, and ideas about people, including themselves.

Children seek labels for racial/ethnic identity, and they develop their own theories about what causes differences in skin color. Adults' responses and reactions influence this. — **4 years**

5 years — Children develop a core sense of their racial/ethnic identity; they explore what it means to be one race compared to another. Negative societal messages undermine their self-esteem.

Children continue to build on their ideas about racial/ethnic identities; this also includes acquiring a group identity. — **6–8 years**

9–10 years — Children become very interested in learning about their group identity through oral histories and written biographies. Racial/ethnic attitudes are solidified.

Children are interested in their ancestry, history, and geography. They understand racism. — **11–12 years**

13+ years — Adolescents and young adults receive messages that reinforce already formed attitudes and beliefs.

about the similarities and differences between races/ethnicities, as well as prejudice and discrimination that some people face. Through intergenerational discussions (which often include story-telling of ancestors' histories), conversations with parents, observations, and modeling, cultural knowledge is transmitted and children learn to "perform" race (Brown et al., 2007). Racial socialization not only teaches children the values and norms associated with their race/ethnicity, but it also shapes attitudes that help them to cope with race-related barriers (Coard et al., 2007). Typically, many white parents don't place importance on discussing racial or ethnic differences with their children (Brown et al., 2007). But given that racism and racial insensitivity appears to be increasing in prevalence in the United States, teaching children to be empathic about race, ethnicity, and racial identity is of critical importance (Markus & Moya, 2010). As African American former school principal and student advocate Paul Richards (2018) notes,

> Empathy is a critical disposition to possess in today's context. Developing cultural empathy can come from exploring the practice of arranged marriages, or the central importance of family hierarchy in certain cultures, or what it is like to have dark skin in a white environment. There are countless examples that are appropriate [to educate children about]. The exploration should culminate in the [child] developing a strong sense of his or her own ethnic identity, and how this identity is interdependent with how other people and society view it. It is with this cultural toolkit that our youth will be ready to thrive in the global world.

Racial/ethnic socialization practices have been linked to a number of positive outcomes in minority children and adolescents, as shown here. For a comprehensive review of the literature, see Coard and colleagues (2007), Hughes and colleagues (2006), and Huynh and Fuligni (2010).

- *Well-developed racial identity.* Children embrace racial and ethnic pride, history, and cultural traditions.
- *Heightened self-esteem.* Children's and adolescents' self-esteem is sensitive to the racial/ethnic messages they receive from their parents. Children who are taught to "blend" with mainstream culture have lower levels of self-esteem because they in some ways deny their heritage.
- *Higher academic functioning.* Positive ethnic identity and high self-esteem are associated with better academic outcomes and higher levels of motivation among children and adolescents.
- *Decreased levels of depression and anger.* The practice of cultural socialization is protective against racial discrimination because children and adolescents develop coping and problem-solving strategies to help buffer racism and deal with prejudice.

Racial/ethnic socialization among minority families is an emerging field of family and social science studies. It is a very complex issue and we have much to learn about the multiple processes associated with this type of socialization, as well as how what children are taught about race influences their lives.

PARENTING 101: BEST PRACTICES FOR PARENTING

There's no doubt about it—parenting is a tough job. Although children do not come with instruction manuals, there are some best practices parents can use to help them bring up their children effectively and lovingly. Some parents are "naturals" and seem to be born with these skills, while others learn along the way. And, for many parents, some situations that arise force them to gain a new skill—in a hurry!

Be a Leader

It's been said before that values, beliefs, and behaviors aren't *taught* by parents, but that they are *caught* by children. That is to say, children aren't taught the differences between right and wrong, to be moral, to be responsible, and to be kind and sensitive toward others—more accurately, they mimic the behaviors of their parents: Children are honest because parents stress and model honesty, children are forgiving because their parents value forgiveness, children are open in their communication because their parents embrace openness, and so forth (Olson, 2004). Parents who are leaders have goals for their family, and they communicate these goals through their values and their beliefs. For example, is promoting the greater good of society important to a family? If so, parents could model this behavior to their children by volunteering at soup kitchens or homeless shelters or by exposing their children to the needs of others and encouraging them to serve on mission trips to inner cities or to impoverished areas. These behaviors reflect those they want their kids to emulate. In short, parents who are leaders don't tell their children what to value and what to believe—they show them through words and actions (Olson, 2004). Finally, being a leader also means being an effective communicator—it means talking *with* children, not *at* them.

Be a Teacher

Parents are their children's first and best educators. Every skill you have today—from walking to talking to writing to driving to using your debit card—was learned, and these skills were probably learned from your parents.

Effective parents take an active role in their children's education, both formal and informal. They provide a rich environment at home, and they willingly engage in their children's schooling, attending parent–teacher conferences, volunteering to be field trip sponsors, helping gather insects for bug collections, going to ball games and sporting events. They give praise when praise is due, but equally important, they know that sometimes the best kind of education comes from the school of hard knocks—they don't rescue their children from consequences when homework is forgotten or trumpets are left on the bus. They're not quick to find solutions for all of their kids' problems, but instead they allow the child to find her or his own successful ways to deal with a problem or a difficulty, while providing a safety net of unconditional love just in case the solution doesn't work.

Parenting is the toughest job in the world—they're in the business of growing people! Although the realities of parenting can mean rough seas ahead, many parents find that the rewards of having children far outweigh the difficulties.

Should Parents Spank Their Children?

Good parents sometimes struggle to maintain the balance between *effective* discipline and *appropriate* response. Then comes the question: Should we spank our kids? Is it ever appropriate to spank a child?

YES: All experts agree that child abuse is wrong. Just what constitutes abuse and where the line between abuse and spanking is crossed are still up for debate. Robert Larzelere, a professor of human development at Oklahoma State University, and his colleague maintain that *how* parents use spanking is more important than *whether* they use it (Larzelere & Kuhn, 2005).

- **Spanking is not abuse.** All rational people are outraged when a child is abused, and we should do all we can to prevent such behavior,

- **Spanking is effective if it is appropriately used.** Mild spanking (a couple of swats on the child's bottom) should be an option to parents who wish to shape the behavior of their children. To be appropriate, spanking should never be done when a parent is angry and should be used in conjunction with other disciplinary tools (time-outs, grounding, etc.).

- **Spanking is not harmful.** When studies separate mild spanking from abusive contact, the results show time and again that appropriately administered spanking is not harmful, especially among children between the ages of 2 and 6.

NO: In 2002, U.S. researcher Elizabeth Gershoff published one of the most thorough reviews to date of spanking research, analyzing 82 studies that covered 62 years of data. Her review found that spanking is linked to a wide range of negative outcomes for children:

- **Children are adversely affected.** Frequent spanking is regularly associated with delinquent children who are prone to cheating, violence, and destructive behavior.

Sources: Larzelere & Kuhn (2005). Gershoff (2002).

- **Spanking fosters low self-esteem.** Some insist that spanking should be administered appropriately with love and not out of anger, but spanking always contributes to lowered self-esteem.

- **There are effective alternatives**. Parents can employ behavioral techniques and other tools to modify the behavior of their children.

The American Academy of Pediatrics (AAP) is an organization of 67,000 primary care pediatricians, pediatric medical subspecialists, and pediatric surgical specialists dedicated to the health, safety, and well-being of infants, children, adolescents, and young adults (AAP, 2020). In 2018, the Academy released a policy statement regarding the use of spanking when raising children. A policy statement is an organizational principal that guides the child healthcare system to improve the health of all children (AAP, 2018). Due to mounting empirical evidence that "spanking increases aggression in young children in the long run and is ineffective in teaching a child responsibility and self-control," and "[spanking] may cause harm to the child by affecting normal brain development," the Academy issued a call to ban this parenting practice:

Parents, other caregivers, and adults interacting with children and adolescents should not use corporal punishment (including hitting and spanking), either in anger or as a punishment for or consequence of misbehavior, nor should they use any disciplinary strategy, including verbal abuse, that causes shame or humiliation.

What Do You Think?

1. Were you spanked as a child? How do you remember it making you feel then? How do you feel about it now?

2. Is physical force ever appropriate for adults? When or why not?

3. Will you employ spanking when disciplining your own children? If so, how do you think it should be done? If not. what alternatives will you use?

Being a teacher also requires that parents understand how children develop emotionally, psychologically, cognitively, and biologically. As teachers of children, skilled parents help them build on existing skills, and provide direction when it is needed—they know just how far to push them without frustrating or discouraging them. Skill by skill, ability by ability, children learn their way to maturity.

Be a Disciplinarian—But Be Patient

It's tough work to grow people, and being patient is perhaps the greatest parenting skill of all. Children learn by trial and error, and this means too-many-to-count messes and mishaps. Children can be frustrating, and often it is difficult for parents to discipline them in love, and not out of anger.

For many parents, the word *discipline* refers to some type of punishment, such as spanking a child or having the child sit in "time out" for a period of time. Though the type of child discipline parents use is a highly personal decision adults must make, there is no disputing that there is value in instructing children through disciplinary techniques. However, when correcting children, parents must make sure that their intention is to stop the unwanted behavior—not to *harm* the child because a parent is angry. The overall quality of the parent-child relationship is crucial for healthy discipline, and research shows that parental nurturance is the most critical aspect of this relationship (Chamberlain & Patterson, 1995).

To enhance a child's moral and behavioral development, psychologists and developmentalists note that children's responses to discipline are more effective when parents *consistently* communicate love toward the child. This is accomplished by (Chamberlain & Patterson, 1995)

- Positive involvement
- Using verbal and nonverbal expressions of love, concern, pride, and gratitude
- Praising and encouraging appropriate behavior
- Using calm responses to problem behaviors, disobedience, and conflict

Proactive discipline involves using techniques that encourage appropriate behavior and that discourage inappropriate behaviors from occurring. For example, "catch them being good" is an aspect of this type of discipline. With this technique, parents praise children for good behavior (such as not insisting on getting a new toy during the trip to Walmart). As one researcher noted, "Every time a parent misses an opportunity to catch a child being good, they miss a chance to teach that child appropriate behavior" (Christophersen, 1988).

Although discipline is tough and can cause conflict between parents, successful parents balance patience and love with setting necessary limits and boundaries. In this way, they avoid becoming permissive parents.

Proactive discipline: using techniques that encourage appropriate behavior and that discourage inappropriate behaviors.

Be a Realist

Often, as adults we have unrealistic expectations for our children. These typically come from our own childhood and family of origin—when we become parents, we turn to the expectations our own parents had for us (Hudson, 2009). Similarly, we may have childhood needs or desires that were unmet by our parents, and we then strive to ensure that our children have these things, whether they want them or not!

Unrealistic expectations of our children may also originate from cultural viewpoints of how children are "supposed" to behave, and too frequently parents have a tough time letting go of what other people think. For example, when you see a child having a temper tantrum in the store, do you instantly assume the child is misbehaving and that the parent should be able to control the child? Or do you recognize that the tantrum is a way the child is asserting his or her independence, or that he or she is in need of a nap? Although most of us would acknowledge that these kinds of tantrums are normal behaviors for young children, why we do cringe and get embarrassed when it happens to *us?* The answer is simple—we're worried that someone may judge us to be an ineffective parent.

When raising children, it's important to examine our expectations. As parent educator Mimi Hudson (2009) notes, "Where did the expectations come from? What is their purpose?

Don't Call Me Mr. Mom!

In contemporary America, more and more fathers are staying at home full time with their children, while their wives head off to work each day. How do wives and husbands really feel about stay-at-home dads?

Her Side: It's hard to put into words how I feel about me working full time and him staying home with the kids. I always wanted to be able to stay home with them, but truthfully, I make more money than my husband does. We both agree that we don't want our kids spending their days in day care, so the only logical option was for him to stay at home. I have mixed feelings—in some ways I feel relieved and happy that he gets to care for them and watch them grow. How many dads are given this opportunity? But on the other hand, it saddens me that I'm not the one that is home. Often, I feel guilty and frustrated, and I regret our decision. I don't like it that we have just abandoned our traditional roles. Doesn't he feel the need to provide for us? How will this ultimately affect him? I think the biggest thing in our favor is that we have a shared goal: We want what's best for our kids, and for us, that means one of us staying home with them.

His Side: I'm not saying that the transition has been an easy one. But what we have found is that instead of ditching the roles we had before, we've had to expand them. And let me tell you, that doesn't happen overnight. We've had to be very open and honest with each other, and we've had to make sure we discuss what our expectations are of each other. The biggest problem so far? She's had a really hard time of letting me do things my way—she tends to want to micromanage the house, the kids, the bills. Plus, there aren't really any role models out there for dads like me, and there's not a lot of social support for people in our situation. Sometimes that makes me feel like I'm not supporting my family, that I'm failing them or letting them down. That's my biggest frustration with our situation.

Your Side: In considering the recent trends of stay-at-home dads in America, do you think these couples face greater challenges than traditional couples? In your answer to this question, consider the following:

1. What are the specific role challenges for this couple?

2. In cases of stay-at-home dads, who do you think makes the most sacrifices: moms or dads? On what do you base your decision?

3. In your own life, would you consider being a stay-at-home dad or having your spouse or partner be a stay-at-home dad? Why or why not?

Whose needs are they based on—mine or my child's? And, do these expectations fit with my child's temperament, age, and developmental stage? Expectations are powerful motivators—but as parents we must be careful not to damage the parent–child relationship by setting unrealistic expectations."

When it comes to successful parenting, our job as adults is to nourish an unconditional, strong, safe, nurturing relationship with our children. No matter what, we need to consistently convey the message that our kids are great—just the way they are.

FAMILY LIFE EDUCATION: GUIDING AND INFLUENCING A CHILD'S DEVELOPMENT

Family practitioners, social workers, psychologists, couples and family therapists, and family life educators have a critical role in educating parents, not only about the rights and responsibilities that come along with parenting, but also about various parenting styles and best parenting practices to promote the healthy development of infants, children, adolescents, and young adults (NCFR, 2020). It's also important that parents are guided in gaining an understanding their child's development across the lifespan, as well as the changing nature of parenthood across the family's lifespan.

Carter and McGoldrick (1999) echo the sentiments illustrated in the opening words of this chapter and shed some light on why parenting is, at once, frightening and exciting at the same time:

> Once there is a child, life will never be the same again, for better and for worse. It is certainly true that most parents fall passionately in love with their new babies and consider them fascinating, delightful, and unique additions to the family. However, the roller coaster of the early months and years still comes as a shock to almost all new parents: sleep deprivation, shredded schedules, endless chores, worry about the baby's development or one's own competence, and the need for ceaseless diligence. This sudden threat of chaos puts enormous stress on new parents and on their relationship. (p. 249)

Whether or not to have a child is perhaps one of life's most difficult decisions. Although most individuals and couples know the decision carries with it life-altering implications, most underestimate how significantly marital relationships are affected after a child is born.

How we parent our children significantly impacts *who* they become. In addition, the changing landscape of "who" can parent—married couples, single mothers, single fathers, grandparents, and gay and lesbian parents—further requires that today's family professional fully recognizes the responsibility associated with parenthood. It follows then that in studying marriage, family, and other intimate relationships, it is important to gain an understanding of those factors and stressors associated with childrearing—what accounts for the "roller coaster" ride.

Parenting is a choice for most, and there are many factors to weigh when deciding whether or not to have children. Couples must consider how this will affect their lifestyle and their needs, and they must realize that family roles have to be realigned to make room for baby. They need to understand that the family system *will* be out of balance for a while, and that the strains associated with household tasks *are inevitable*. The responsibilities of parenthood *will* restrict the couple's freedom and marital satisfaction *will* change (more than likely, it *will decline*).

These are the realities of parenting. If you choose to have children, you will be tired. You may find you have quite a bit of month left at the end of the money. At least in the early years, there will be many times when you must place your own needs aside in order to meet the needs of your children. You will be pulled in more directions than you thought possible. And you will make mistakes.

But those drawbacks, difficulties, snags, and snares associated with parenting and (hose things that can potentially affect marital satisfaction, many of these negative outcomes can be greatly reduced—if not entirely eliminated—by becoming aware of and understanding the realities of parenthood (Belsky & Pensky, 1988).

And remember—parenting isn't about the destination, it's about the journey. Enjoy the ride!

/// SUMMARY

Parenting Is a Process: Change Over Time

- Parenting is a process that addresses the biological, emotional, and socialization needs of children while it addresses the needs of the society in which children are raised.

- Women are expected to become mothers by certain culturally determined ages.

- Mothering is the process of performing the logistical aspects of caring for someone, as well as tending to and nurturing the relationship.

- Intensive mothering reflects today's mothers who simultaneously manage several roles, including their roles in the workplace. The intensive mothering ideology promotes the notion that women should give their sacrificial all to their children. Maternal Role Attainment (MRA) speaks to how women assume the "mother" role overtime.

- Lesbian co-mothers often experience ambiguous roles, because there is no social template for two mothers in a family system. It is inaccurate to assume that one lesbian parent will take on the "mother" role, while the other lesbian parent takes on the "father" role.

- In eras past, the patriarchal family structure embraced the father as the headship and authority over the family. This was done to ensure that land and money were inherited by his children.

- Today, there are two opposing forces that fathers contend with: father-absence and father-involvement. Contemporary fathers tend to fall somewhere in the middle of these polar opposite types.

- Co-parenting is an alliance that parents form to best raise and support their children. There are three types of co-parenting: supportive, unsupportive, and mixed. It is vitally important that parents co-parent because this parenting strategy provides predictability and stability for children.

The Styles of Parenting

- Regarding two important childrearing dimensions—parental warmth/responsiveness/affection and parental control—research psychologist Diana Baumrind constructed four parenting styles: uninvolved parenting, permissive parenting, authoritarian parenting, and authoritative parenting.

- Of all of Baumrind's parenting styles, authoritative parenting yields the best outcome for children's health and well-being in the areas of social competence and psychosocial development.

- Uninvolved parenting and permissive parenting yield negative outcomes for children, such as increased rates of substance use, higher rates of delinquency, poorer school performance, and negative psychological well-being.

- Authoritarian parents are very demanding and controlling, and this parenting style is associated with increased emotional and behavioral problems in children.

From Partners to Parents: Making the Transition

- When a new baby joins a couple, a new family form is created. All of the couple's established ways of interacting and relating, their patterns of behavior, and their marital/gender roles must be adjusted to accommodate the addition to the family system.

- In general, the changes associated with parenthood affect four primary areas in the couple's life: their psychological well-being, their marital quality, their family relations and social support, and their roles.

- There are a number of theories that explore child development. These include psychoanalytic theories, learning theories, cognitive theories, and sociocultural theories.

- In industrialized and nonindustrialized societies alike, the mother bears most of the responsibility for caregiving and childrearing. Even couples who have an egalitarian relationship tend to fall back into traditional roles once the new baby arrives.

- Research has shown that when mothers view the fathers' parenting involvement as less-than-ideal (not equal to their own involvement), their relationships have higher levels of stress. When women feel that discrepancies exist between their roles as disciplinarians and those same roles of their husbands (more involved than their husbands), they report higher levels of dissatisfaction due to perceived unfairness.

- Working women are still often expected to do the majority of housekeeping tasks. Sociologist Arlie Hochschild referred to this burden of taking on the dual responsibilities of wage-earner and housekeeper as "the second shift."

Today's Parents

- The boundaries of parenthood in contemporary society are currently shifting, evidenced by an increase in childbearing/childrearing through nonmarital pregnancies, parenting by grandparents, and gay men and lesbian parents.

- As parenting demographics shift, the way in which researchers study parenting shifts, too. Throughout the past three decades, two models of single-parent families have been used predominately. The family Deficit Model promotes the idea that single-parent households were negative experiences for children for the sole reason that the family structure was not nuclear. Alternatively, the Risk and Protective Factor Model assumes that every family form has strengths, or protective factors, which lessen the influence risk factors. Although single parenting can be a risk factor for children's overall well-being, it is not the sole predictor of negative outcomes as suggested by the Family Deficit Model.

- Single fathers are rearing children by themselves as a result of four social factors: current divorce laws and "gender-neutral criteria"; mothers granting the fathers custody of the children so that the mothers may pursue career or personal goals; divorce courts' more favorable view of the role of fathers in childrearing; and an increase in fathers' willingness to take a more active role in parenting than in years past.

- Increasingly, more and more LGBTQ individuals and couples are becoming parents. Research suggests that the quality of the parent–child relationship is more important to a child's health and well-being that having parents that are opposite-sexed.

Parenting 101: Best Practices for Parenting

- There are a number of skills parents need to be effective parents.

- Parents should model the values and beliefs they hope to instill in their children.

- Skilled parents teach with patience and provide rich learning opportunities for their children, both formally and informally.

- Racial/ethnic socialization is the process by which parents transmit messages to their children about the significance and meaning of race and ethnicity. This socialization is associated with a number of positive outcomes for minority children.

- Discipline is a necessary part of parenting, and parents should know that there are a number of effective parenting techniques that serve to develop children's moral development.

- It is essential that parents have realistic expectations when it comes to parenting.

/// KEY TERMS

Anal stage   402

Authoritarian parents   396

Authoritative parents   397

Autonomy granting   396

Co-parenting   393

Classical conditioning   403

Cognitive theories   403

Family Deficit Model   408

Father involvement   391

Genital stage   403

Ideal–actual gap   404

Intensive mothering   389

Intensive mothering ideology   389

Kinship care   409

Latency stage   403

Lesbian co-mothering (LCM)   390

Maternal gatekeeping   405

Maternal Role Attainment (MRA)   389

Mixed co-parenting   394

Mothering   388

Operant conditioning   403

Oral stage   402

Patriarchal family structure   391

Permissive parents   396

Phallic stage   402

Proactive discipline   417

Psychoanalytic theory   402

Psychosexual stages   402

Punishments   403

Racial/ethnic socialization   412

Racism   411

Risk and Protective Factor Model   408

Routine housework   405

Socialization needs   388

Sociocultural theories   404

Supportive co-parenting   394

Survival needs   388

Uninvolved parents   395

Unsupportive co-parenting   394

iStock.com/zeljkosantrac

CHAPTER **12**

FAMILY LIFE AND WORK: A BALANCING ACT

LEARNING OBJECTIVES

12.1 Describe the history of dual-earner couples in the United States and the current landscape of working couples.

12.2 Summarize the effects of working couples on family well-being.

12.3 Identify the challenges that dual-earner couples confront.

12.4 Discuss government policies for U.S. working families.

12.5 Explain how differing attitudes toward money affect a couple's relationship.

A friend of mine recently confided in me that he was frustrated, angry, and disheartened about the direction his life, marriage, and parenting were taking. As the conversation continued, it was clear that work and money issues were significantly impacting his overall life and marital satisfaction. He shared,

> I know my life stopped being my life a long time ago. When you get married and have kids, that's part of the deal, I know that. But when you're sitting there and you're figuring out, "Okay, can we afford to have a kid? Can we afford to buy a house? A second car?" you work it out, and it all looks good on paper. On your little worksheet.
>
> But there's nowhere on the worksheet for the other stuff. There's no entry for "Daughter needs therapy." Or, "Mom's really sick; fly home three or four times in one month." Or, "Wife goes through cancer scare." There's *always something* and we never get a chance to breathe. And you look up and, like, 20 years have passed and this is how you've lived. Not hand-to-mouth anymore, like when we were a young couple, but never really a chance to get any momentum going. And it just wears on me. I mean, my wife doesn't know this, but this is the stuff that rocks me out of sleep at two in the morning, you know, a couple of times a week at least, and you just lay there, thinking about everything that has to get done. And so I'm tired all day, and then I act like a jerk because I'm tired and THAT upsets my wife and then something else happens and it's just this big pile of angst that never goes away. And at the bottom of that pile, it's always about money. I mean, dig into any issue, and there it is. Money.

Today, work and family play major roles in the lives of adults. Most Americans come face to face on a daily basis with the demands and challenges of trying to balance work and family life—far too often, there are negative effects when work responsibilities spill over into family life. Married and intimate life brings with it things we can't predict or plan for: Spouses get sick, parents get sick, children need medical care, and money becomes the focus of our every thought. Other things happen that also cause financial worry. For example, the global financial crisis that began in the latter part of 2008 with the failures of large financial institutions in the United States rapidly evolved into a crisis for many Americans—adults experienced job losses by the hundreds of thousands, cars were repossessed, families were forced into bankruptcy, and an unprecedented number of homes were lost because families couldn't afford to pay their house payments. What does a family do in these situations? And what happens to their relationships when they experience such stressors?

Research indicates that money is a major source of relationship concerns for couples today and that there are potentially serious implications for couples when money issues crop up (Papp, Cummings, & Goeke-Morey, 2009; Dew, 2007). One recent study found that the larger a couple's debt, the more likely they are to say money is the thing they fight most about (Ramsey Solutions, 2018). For these reasons, in this chapter we will begin our study of work and family by looking at the landscape of dual-earner couples, including the demands faced by military families when a loved one is deployed to Iraq or Afghanistan, as well as the challenges single parents encounter when they try to balance work and family. We'll then shift our attention to the types of strain and stress families face when they try to juggle work with family life. To best equip you with tools for your own intimate and family relationships, we'll conclude by exploring the skills that effective working families use in their daily lives and how best to manage your money.

WORKING FAMILIES: THE TRANSFORMATION OF AMERICAN HOMES

Economic stability and the ability of families to meet their daily needs is an important measure of family health and well-being (Allegretto, 2005; Hardie & Lucas, 2010; Killewald, 2016; Lewin, 2005). The socioeconomic status (SES) of a family is the government's measure of the family's relative economic and social ranking within a community (Krieger, 2001). Measures of SES typically include the adults' occupation, education level, community/group associations, and income. Other measures may include location of residence and certain home amenities such as a television, computer, telephone, books, and so forth. *Attained SES* refers to the parents' socioeconomic status, and *SES of origin* is the term used when describing a child's family's SES (Krieger, 2001).

Socioeconomic status (SES): the government's measure of a family's relative economic and social ranking within a community.

We learned in Chapter 1 that as our nation moved into the second half of the 20th century, a number of sociocultural, economic, and political changes occurred that changed the face of families in the United States. These changes include lowered birth rates and delays in marriage, women's abilities to control their fertility through contraceptives, the legalization of abortion in 1973 and the adoption of no-fault divorce laws, and Civil Rights legislation in 1965 that banned discrimination. All of the factors worked in tandem not only to change how we experience family life but also to change America's workforce, as many of these social and cultural factors propelled women into the workplace.

Women Enter the Workforce

The 1960s ushered in many changes that helped to shape our conceptions and experiences of women in the workplace today. A new-wave feminist movement, referred to as Women's Liberation, put forth the idea that women suffered oppression in patriarchal, male-dominated cultures such as the United States. Equality in the job place and economic equality were primary goals of feminist organizations (such as the National Organization for Women) throughout the 1960s and 1970s. This was referred to as gender equality, and in 1964 a last-minute addition to Civil Rights legislation mandated that discrimination based on a person's gender was illegal.

Women's Liberation: a feminist movement that put forth the idea that women suffered oppression in patriarchal, male-dominated cultures such as those in the United States.

This is not to say, however, that women have achieved equality. In the ensuing decades since the passage of the Civil Rights Act, women continue to fight against bias, prejudice, discrimination, and sexual harassment as they attempt to break down barriers and stereotypes, and as they enter occupations traditionally held by males. The term *glass ceiling* (see Chapter 4) refers to discrimination against women in the workplace, specifically in situations where advancement in an organization is stopped because of occupational sexism, or beliefs that the male gender is more capable of certain work-related tasks and professions than women are. Types of glass ceiling barriers include different pay for comparable work, sexual discrimination in the workplace, and lack of family-friendly work policies (Thomas-Hunt & Phillips, 2004). For example, in 2009, the U.S. Census Bureau estimated that women make 77.6 cents for every dollar that men make (Institute for Women's Policy Research, 2008). This disparity in earnings is referred to as the *gender wage gap*. We discussed the various aspects of the

Gender equality: equality between men and women in the job place and economic equality.

Occupational sexism: belief that the male gender is more capable of certain work-related tasks and professions than women are.

Signed by President Kennedy in 1963, the Equal Pay Act mandates equal pay for equal work by forbidding employers from paying men and women different wages or benefits for doing jobs that require the same skills and responsibilities. Fifty-seven years later, wages are still not equal.

gender wage gap in Chapter 4; here, it's important to know that the gap isn't closing—in fact, it has remained relatively stable the past 15 years (Pew Research Center, 2019a). In 2018, women earned only 85 percent of what men earned. On average, it takes a woman an extra 39 days of work to earn what men do (Pew Research Center 2019).

Although a large portion of the wage gap can be explained by such things as education, occupation, and skills and experience, it is necessary to account for the fact that wage discrimination may be at play. **Wage discrimination** is the discrimination shown in the payment of wages, salaries, and earnings to minority groups. More often than not, the targets of wage discrimination are people of color (both men and women) and white women. When wage discrimination takes place, the employee earns less for the same job with the same performance levels and responsibilities as white males. In a recent survey, about 4 in 10 working women (roughly 42 percent) said they have been the victims of gender wage discrimination; in comparison, only about 5 percent of men have reported the same type of discrimination (Pew Research Center, 2019a). Figure 12.1 illustrates for us the various ways in which they experienced gender discrimination at work.

Wage discrimination: the discrimination shown in the payment of wages, salaries, and earnings to minority groups.

Figure 12.1 /// Discrimination in the Work Place

Percent of Employed Adults Who Have Reported Having These Experiences at Work Because of Their Gender

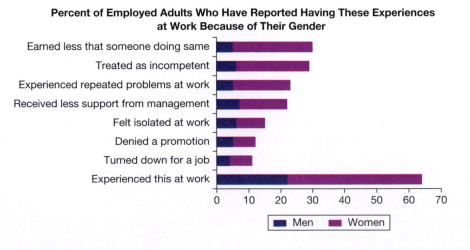

Source: Pew Research Center (2019).

Identifying and challenging wage discrimination in the workplace has been an uphill battle, despite the passage of the Equal Pay Act of 1963. For example, in 2004 the case known as *Dukes v. Wal-Mart* became the largest class action lawsuit in history—approximately 1.5 million women were parties to the lawsuit, and they claimed that they received less pay and promotion opportunities than their male coworkers. Additionally, in what is now a historic case, Lilly Ledbetter, a former employee of the Goodyear Tire and Rubber Company, sued the company to receive back pay and damages. After her retirement from the company, she discovered that for years she was paid at significantly lower rates in comparison to her male counterparts. Although she was awarded back pay from a lower court, the U.S. Supreme Court overturned the lower court's decision in 2007. However, in 2009, in his first week in office, President Barack Obama signed into law the Lilly Ledbetter Fair Pay Act. This law removes the legal obstacles for women seeking equal pay in the workforce, and it is also a tool to combat workplace discrimination in all forms. As President Obama observed at the signing of the law,

> Ultimately, equal pay isn't just an economic issue for millions of Americans and their families, it's a question of who we are—and whether we're truly living up to our fundamental ideals; whether we'll do our part, as generations before us, to ensure those words put on paper some 200 years ago really mean something—to breathe new life into them with a more enlightened understanding that is appropriate for our time. That is what Lilly Ledbetter challenged us to do. (The White House, Office of the Press Secretary, 2009)

When comparing women with other women in the workforce, the earnings gap is widened even further when race and ethnicity are added to the picture. As you discovered in Chapter 4, the concept of *intersectionality* looks at the ways in which the interaction of sex, race, and ethnicity form barriers to people in society (U.S. Census Bureau, 2019e)—in this case, the intersection creates barriers to equal pay and wages in the workplace. The data in Table 12.1 show us that women of all racial and ethnic groups earn less than men of the same group; they also earn less than men overall (Institute for Women's Policy Research, 2019). To help you to better understand the significance of the differences, if a man makes $48,000 per year, a white woman in the same job doing the same tasks with the same skills and abilities would make $39,120; a Black woman would make $31,344; a Latino woman would make slightly more than $29,500; and an Asian woman would make $44,880.

Deborah Chalfie, senior counsel of the National Women's Law Center, observes, "One of the problems that women and women of color face in the workforce is that female-dominated and jobs dominated by women of color are undervalued and underpaid" (Sullivan, 2009, p. 1). That is to say, women tend to be concentrated in certain occupational categories—this is referred to as the **pink-collar phenomenon**. For example, in 2018, 55 percent of the entire workforce was made up of pink-collar workers in "traditionally female" jobs: health care, child

Pink-collar phenomenon: the tendency for women to be concentrated in certain occupational categories.

Table 12.1 /// Gender Earnings Ratio by Race and Ethnicity		
Racial/Ethnic Background	Female earnings as % of male earnings of same group	Female earnings as % of white male earnings
All Races/Ethnicities	81.1	N/A
White	81.5	81.5
Black	89.0	65.3
Hispanic	85.7	61.6
Asian	75.5	93.5

Source: Institute for Women's Policy Research (2019).

care, education, customer service, sales, and administrative positions (U.S. Bureau of Labor Statistics, 2019). And, frequently, these jobs are rated as deserving less pay than more "masculine" occupations.

This shift from one-earner families to dual-earner families has not only advanced women's opportunities in society but it also dramatically changed the face of American families and how they experience family living today.

A PORTRAIT OF CONTEMPORARY DUAL-EARNER COUPLES

Dual-earner couples:
couples in which both spouses are actively engaged in the workforce.

Dual-earner couples is defined as marriages or relationships in which both partners work. Workforce participation varies among dual-earner couples. For example, two-thirds (66 percent) of married couples in the United States today are dual-earners, whereas in about one-fourth of couples only the male works, and in 5 percent only the female is employed (Pew Research Center, 2019a). In many such couples, one partner works full time while the other partner works part time; in other families, both partners work full time. Many factors influence labor force participation and earnings among dual-earner couples, such as education level, urban living, unemployment, and discrimination. There are also racial and ethnic differences in dual-earner couples.

White couples are highly involved in the workforce, and only Asian couples are more likely to be involved in the workforce than whites. One reason for white couples' high participation in the workforce is that they tend to have higher levels of education, which are strongly associated with higher levels of employment. As a result, whites generally earn more than Black and Hispanic men and women, even within the same occupation (U.S. Census Bureau, 2019d). The median annual income of white families and these higher earnings are associated with enhanced marital quality among whites (we discuss marital quality later in the chapter; Amato, Johnson, Booth, & Rogers, 2003; Bianchi, Sayer, Milkie, & Robinson, 2012; Killewald, 2016).

Blue-collar workers:
individuals holding jobs in the service sector, such as sales, office, production, and transportation.

White-collar professional occupations:
professional occupations such as attorneys, bankers, and doctors.

Educational attainment is a key factor in employment and earnings for Black couples. African American/Black Caribbean men are the least likely to be employed among each of the ethnic groups, whereas Black women are the most likely to be employed. In fact, African American/Black Caribbean men are more than twice as likely to be unemployed than whites. Both Black men and women are typically **blue-collar workers**, which means they are highly represented in the service sector (such as sales, office, production, and transportation); as a result, their earnings are generally lower than those employed in **white-collar professional occupations** (such as attorneys, bankers, and doctors; U.S. Bureau of Labor Statistics, 2018). Of all racial and ethnic groups in the United States, African American/Black Caribbean families suffer one of the highest levels of unemployment and poverty and the lowest median family income—slightly more than $40,000 annually (U.S. Census Bureau, 2018a).

Asian men and women are more likely than any of the other ethnic groups to be employed in professional positions (U.S. Bureau of Labor Statistics, 2019). Low divorce rates, high education levels, a strong work ethic, self-sufficiency, familism, and high participation in the labor force have led to the "model minority" status for many Asian couples (Taylor, 2002). With an annual income of over $80,000 per year, Asian American families have the highest median household income of all racial groups in the United States (U.S. Census Bureau, 2019b). This is perhaps because Asian Americans have the highest educational qualifications of all ethnic groups in the United States—more than one-half of all Asian American adults have attained at least a bachelor's degree (U.S. Census Bureau, 2019b).

Influenced by Confucian ideology, Asian households are typically patriarchal with well-defined roles (Choi, Yeun Kim, Noh, Lee, & Takeuchi, 2018). Their cultural traditions and roles tend to provide them with order and stability between work life and family life. Additionally, their collectivist perspective has led to a willingness on the part of many

Asian Americans to sacrifice personal needs in order for their families and employees to be successful (Fong, 2002; Choi et al., 2018).

Hispanic couples are similar to Asian couples in that they tend to be patriarchal, familistic, and traditional in their views of men's and women's work roles (Constante, Marchand, Cross, & Rivas-Drake, 2019). Hispanic men are generally highly employed, while Hispanic women tend to have lower employment rates than each of the other ethnic groups (U.S. Bureau of Labor Statistics, 2019). Although Hispanic couples are becoming more educated and, therefore, more represented in professional occupations, they are less likely to have completed high school than each of the other ethnic groups; as a result, they are still highly employed in the service sector, resulting in lower earnings than those employed as professionals (U.S. Bureau of Labor Statistics, 2019).

One of the poorest ethnic groups in America today, Latinx families earn, on average, about $50,000 per year (U.S. Census Bureau, 2019c). It's important to keep in mind that many Hispanic immigrants may have successful businesses in other countries or professional degrees from other countries, but because of the language barrier when they arrive in the United States, they are unable to secure high-paying jobs. Many immigrants today also face discrimination in the workplace; for example, it is not uncommon in California for field workers to earn as little as $10,000 per year for full-time work—about $800 per month (National Farm Worker Ministry, 2019). Furthermore, the transnational (families who are divided because they live in different countries) and bi-national (families whose legal citizenship is mixed) status of many Hispanic families has challenged their ability to manage work and family roles (Baca Zinn & Pok, 2002). In the United States, Hispanic children are at least twice as likely to live in poverty as their non-Hispanic counterparts (Child Trends, 2019).

Arab American couples are typically patriarchal and traditional—men are often the family's providers, and women are homemakers and raise the children (Aboulhassan & Brumley, 2018). Arab American men and women tend to be highly educated and are, therefore, well represented in the professional labor force, with higher earnings than the national average. In the United States, Arab Americans' educational attainment levels are similar to the general public, with 31 percent having graduated from college; 11 percent have a postgraduate degree (Pew Research Center, 2017b). Today, more than two-thirds of Arab American adults are in the labor force and are employed in a wide array of occupations (Arab American Institute, 2019). Their median annual income is about $60,000.

Limited education, high unemployment, divorce, single-mother families, and substance abuse rates have contributed to labor force participation among Native Americans that is varied and sporadic. (U.S. Census Bureau, 2019a). Although nearly 80 percent of this population has at least a high school diploma, the median household income of single-race Native American and Alaska Native households is slightly over $39,000. This compares with $58,000 for the nation as a whole.

In recent years, families in the United States have been challenged in new ways as service men and women have been

Craig F. Walker/The Denver Post via Getty Images

Military families face the same day-to-day struggles and stressors that all working couples face, but they also face unique situations when they are deployed overseas for months at a time.

deployed overseas due to military engagements in Iraq and Afghanistan. The challenges are many, and all affect the portrait of wage earners in America.

Service Men and Women

The United States military, which consists of the Army, Navy, Air Force, Coast Guard, and Marines, deployed nearly 200,000 men and women; about 15 percent of the U.S. Armed Forces are deployed each year to regions around the world (Pew Research Center, 2017a). Military families deal with stressors that are common to all families, such as parenting concerns, child care, juggling work with family, and career decisions, but they are also subject to unique stressors because of the separation from family members (van der Wal, Gorter, Reinjnen, Geuze, & Vermetten, 2019).

Preparing for Deployment

Until recently, most military personnel had a period of one to two years between deployments. These days, however, deployments can often occur in quick succession or tours of duty are extended for prolonged periods of time. For example, during the Gulf War in the early 1990s, single parents and dual-career couples were mobilized so quickly that these families had only a few hours to find child care for their children—both immediate child care and extended child care while the parent(s) was deployed overseas in a combat zone (Drummet, Coleman, & Cable, 2003). Army personnel are deployed more frequently than any other branch; their deployments are often 12 months, followed by a few months at home, and then 12 months deployed again (Congressional Research Service, 2019).

Alongside frequent moves, financial worries are of particular concern to deployed military families (Military Family Advisory Network, 2019). What makes the financial picture much worse for so many military families today is that anywhere from 40 percent (Air Force) to 60 percent (Marines) of soldiers are 18 to 24 years of age (Council on Foreign Relations, 2019). Because of this, young couples have not yet learned effective money management skills, and this puts them at significantly higher risk for money troubles during deployment.

Financial Difficulties for Deployed Families

Today, there are increasing incidents of burgeoning financial difficulties among service families because separations due to deployment often catch families financially unprepared. In a survey of more than 5,600 service men and women, nearly two-thirds said they didn't have enough savings to cover three months of living expenses (Bushatz, 2018). Furthermore, paying for mental health care was cited as the major barrier to getting help for those suffering with mental health problems, such as Post Traumatic Stress Disorder (PTSD), and nearly 80 percent said that military moves cause high financial burdens and stress. Over one-fourth of all service members have more than $10,000 in credit card debt, and, sadly, food insecurity issues were also uncovered in this study, with about 22,000 active-duty troops using food stamps (Bushatz, 2018).

The bottom line? "Military families described [many] financial burdens: They're going into debt to pay for moving expenses, unable to find child care, unwilling to move forward in their education, forgoing necessary health care, and feeling the mental and physical effects of financial stress" (Bushatz, 2018).

Among family practitioners who work with military families to improve their financial well-being, current programs are used that focus on financial situations that are unique to the military. Financial programs for military personnel, such as *Money Sense* and *Financial Fitness,* are preventive educational programs that provide information to service members and their spouses/significant others about ways to manage their financial resources. These types of curricula, especially tailored to the needs of military men and women, teach money management skills and include such things as learning how to budget, keep financial records, develop healthy spending habits, establish realistic savings habits, and manage credit card debt. Research demonstrates that financial education as a part of deployment readiness reduces the frequency of families' money problems (Varcoe, Empter, & Lee, 2002).

There are, of course, numerous other issues military families face, and we'll explore those a bit later in this chapter when we look at what it takes for all families to juggle work and family life. Here, it's important to recognize the unique financial situations military families experience, and that family life educators and other family practitioners can provide invaluable resources to these families to assist them during these stressful work-related situations.

Single Parents in the Workforce

There is great diversity among single-parent, or lone parent, households. For example, households headed by single parents include impoverished, never-married ethnic minority women or teenaged mothers, wealthy never-married women who have adopted or borne a child, widows and widowers, and women and men who find themselves single after a marital breakup (Gottfried & Gottfried, 1994; Richter & Lemola, 2017). Today,

- About one-half of all single mothers have never married
- 29 percent are divorced
- 21 percent are separated from their spouse or are widowed (U.S. Census Bureau, 2019f)

Additionally, many families instantly become single-parent families when a spouse is called to war or when a spouse dies in military service.

Regardless of its makeup, each single-parent family has its own unique starting point and its own unique developmental history (Anderson & Sabatelli, 2011). Because mothers with children comprise the largest segment of single-parent households—80 percent of single-parent families are headed by single mothers—our discussion begins with looking at work/money issues and challenges faced by single women who are parenting (U.S. Census Bureau, 2018b).

Single-Parent Mothers

A large majority of single women with children of all ages work outside the home in the paid labor force. Employment rates among single female mothers have significantly increased since the 1990s, when 44 percent of single mothers worked; in 2018, slightly more than two-thirds of single moms worked outside the home, more than the share of married mothers who also worked outside the home (U.S. Census Bureau, 2018b). Less than a quarter (22 percent) of single moms receive unemployment benefits. On average, single mothers earn about $42,000 per year (U.S. Census Bureau, 2017).

As you can see from the information in Figure 12.2, there are a number of factors that affect the economic well-being of women and their children. According to the American Community Survey (ACS) from the U.S. Census Bureau (2017), a significant number of all households with children headed by mothers live in poverty. Figure 12.3 shows us, two-fifths of all single-mother families live in economic despair. American Indian/Alaska Natives fare worse than any other group, with a poverty rate of 46 percent. Importantly, any spousal support, child support, or public assistance (welfare) the woman receives typically does not come close to offsetting the differences in income between single-mother parents and married parents. Only one-third of single mothers today receive child support from the child's father, and if a mother does receive support, it is only about $400 a month (Kids Count Data, 2017; Congressional Research Service, 2016).

A study sponsored by the Congressional Caucus on Women's Issues (2005) revealed that "single mothers find themselves on a downward slide in their struggle to establish secure and solid footing in the workforce" (Corbett, 2005, p. 2). Other key data from the report reveal that

- Single mothers are "poor" or "near poor," despite the fact that they work, many of them full time.
- Those who are employed work in low-paying jobs; more often than not, these jobs do not include benefits such as health insurance.

Figure 12.2 /// Single Mothers' Characteristics

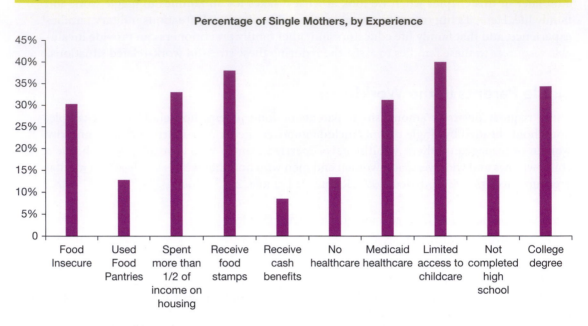

Percentage of Single Mothers, by Experience

Sources: USDA, 2017; HUD, 2018; U.S. Census Bureau, 2016.

Figure 12.3 /// Percentage of Children in Poverty, by Family Structure and Race

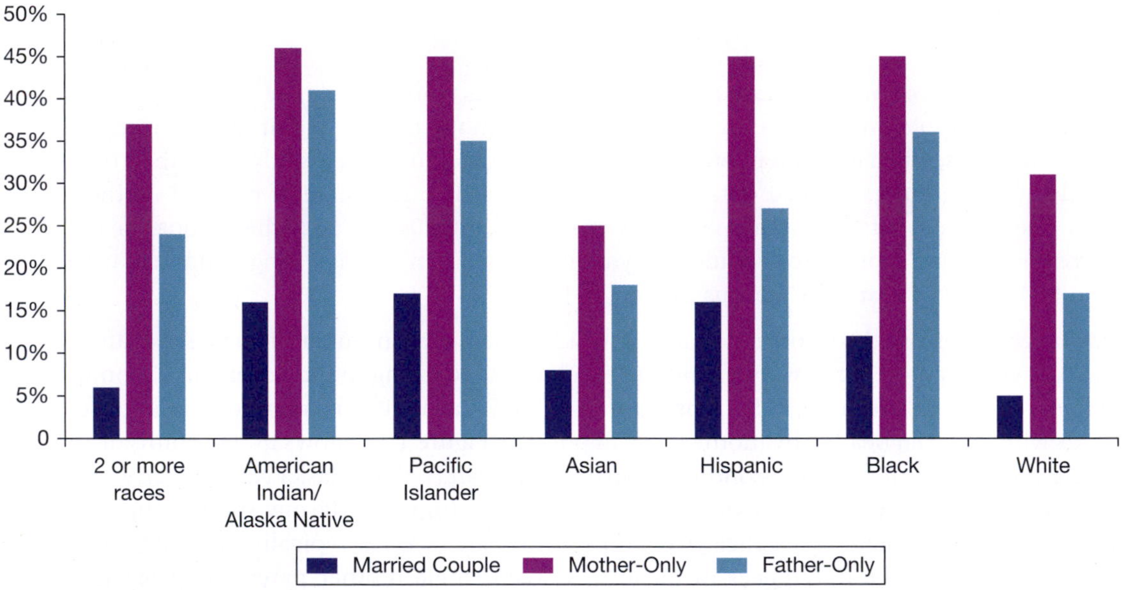

■ Married Couple   ■ Mother-Only   ■ Father-Only

Source: American Community Survey (ACS), 2017.

Not much has changed since this study was undertaken. In 2017, the poverty rate for children under age 18 was highest among those who lived in households with a parent or parents who did not complete high school; these findings are shown in Figure 12.4. For example, among African Americans, poverty was highest for those children whose parent(s) didn't complete high school (68 percent), and substantially lower among those children who have a parent who completed a college degree (8 percent). Regardless of race or ethnicity, the less education a child's parent has, the more likely the child is to live in poverty.

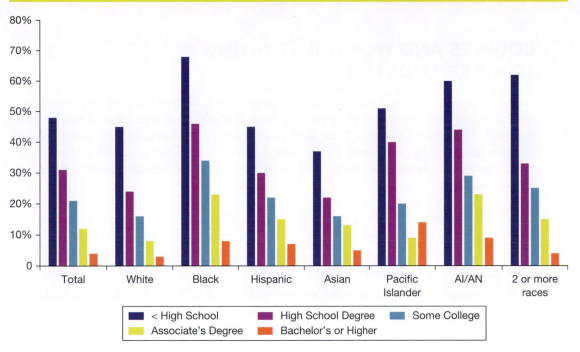

Figure 12.4 /// Percentage of Children Under Age 18 in Families Living in Poverty, by Race and Parent's Highest Level of Educational Attainment

Legend:
- < High School
- High School Degree
- Some College
- Associate's Degree
- Bachelor's or Higher

Source: American Community Survey (2017).

As the Congressional Caucus on Women's Issues (2005) notes, local, state, and federal policy makers must begin to develop programs that better serve single mothers. Women's access to educational training, job training, and support programs that provide skills such as life management and work readiness will contribute to women's successes in the workforce—and consequently, parenting.

Single-Parent Fathers

There is an abundance of literature about single mothers, their income levels, their education attainment, and their occupation status, but virtually none exists about single fathers as household heads. That's not to say, however, that there are not increased numbers of single-dad households. Although most single parents are females, the proportion of families headed by single fathers is increasing in the United States, as well as in many other developed countries. Today, about 1 of every 5 custodial parents is the father (about 20 percent; U.S. Census Bureau, 2018b).

Family and social scientists attribute the increased number of single-father households to a variety of reasons. For instance, more judges are awarding custody to fathers in divorce cases, more women are opting to pursue careers rather than seek custody of their children in divorce cases, and today more fathers are seeking joint custody arrangements (this arrangement reduces their monthly child support payments). Still, single-father households constitute only a small percentage of the overall picture of single-parent homes. Poverty rates are higher among single-father households than they are among married-couple households.

For children, family structure affects every aspect of their development and well-being. As recent economic downturns in the United States and the mushrooming student loan debt continue to squeeze parents and families, millions more children will suffer without sufficient economic resources. There is no doubt about it: A family's economic well-being and health are crucial to successful family living and overall development. A bit later we'll take a look at the government's role in shaping and implementing family policies and how these policies influence couple, marital, and family life. Today, a significant number of American families are struggling just to make ends meet.

COUPLES AND WORK: JUST TRYING TO MAKE ENDS MEET

Basic budgets:

the amount of money families need to manage at the most basic level; it must cover costs associated with housing, food, transportation, child care, health care, clothing, personal care items, school materials, and taxes.

Economic stability and the ability of families to meet their daily needs is an important measure of family well-being (Allegretto, 2005). **Basic budgets,** or the amount of money families need to manage at the most basic level, must cover costs associated with housing, food, transportation, child care, health care, clothing, personal care items, school materials, and taxes. However, a significant number of Americans today have difficulty meeting their family's economic needs.

- The average U.S. employee works 2,080 hours each year; this figure represents a 38-hour increase (nearly a full week) since 1990 (U.S. Bureau of Labor Statistics, 2018).
- There are nearly 75 million women in the workforce today, about 47 percent of all U.S. workers (U.S. Department of Labor, 2017).
- 70 percent of mothers with children under the age of 18 are in the workforce, with more than three-fourths employed full-time (U.S. Department of Labor, 2017).
- At least one parent is employed in 91 percent of families with children (U.S. Bureau of Labor Statistics, 2019).
- Three-fourths of adults who care for their aging, ill, or disabled parents are also working at a paying job during their caregiving experience (AARP, 2019).

Depending on where you live in the United States, the annual salary you need to support your family can vary significantly. For example, if you and your partner have two children and live in New York or California, you will need at least $88,000 a year to make ends meet (U.S. Bureau of Labor Statistics, 2019). If you live in Kansas or Tennessee, you can get by on about $55,000 or $60,000. When determining a family's financial needs, factors such as food, housing, child care, health care, utilities, and food costs are included. Housing costs typically consume the major portion of the family's income. Table 12.2 provides a quick, at-a-glance look at housing costs around the country. As you can see, it's no surprise that in many parts of the United States, families must be supported by two incomes.

Dual-Earner Couples and Family Well-Being

Job status:

refers to a type or kind of job that offers some kind of prestige in an organization or community.

Job complexity:

occurs when jobs are challenging and stimulating at the same time.

Job autonomy:

occurs when employees are allowed a high degree of independence and self-direction.

For both men and women, job status, job complexity, job autonomy, and the number of hours worked are some of the important variables that influence child and family well-being (Perry-Jenkins, Repetti, & Crouter, 2001). **Job status** refers to a type of job that offers some kind of prestige in an organization or community (such as managers or executive officers). **Job complexity** occurs when jobs are at the same time challenging and stimulating, and **job autonomy** happens when employees are allowed a high degree of independence and self-direction. Maureen Perry-Jenkins and her colleagues' (2001) decade review of couples who juggle work with family revealed that when fathers' and mothers' jobs have a high degree of complexity and autonomy, they are more apt to create a positive home environment and show greater warmth in parenting. Job complexity and autonomy are also linked with child outcomes such as enhanced verbal and reading skills and decreases in problem behaviors.

Interestingly, most studies about couples and work focus on the well-being of the *couple,* not well-being at the *family* level (Behnke & MacDermid, 2004). But because of the systems nature of family living—when one family member struggles, all others are affected—it is

Table 12.2 /// Selected Housing and Food Costs for a Family of Four in the United States

State	Income needed before income taxes	Estimated annual housing costs	Estimated annual food costs
Arkansas	$59,000	$5,585	$8,822
California	$81,056	$19,875	$10,529
Connecticut	$74,216	$15,670	$10,245
Florida	$66,057	$13,239	$8,822
Georgia	$63,209	$10,932	$8,882
Illinois	$69,760	$12,564	$9,012
Kentucky	$64,017	$8,872	$8,822
Louisiana	$61.643	$10,261	$8,822
Massachusetts	$75,418	$17,721	$10,245
Minnesota	$68,948	$11,607	$9,012
Missouri	$62,943	$9,597	$9,012
Nevada	$67,137	$11,581	$10,529
New Jersey	$75,884	$17,409	$10,245
Oregon	$72,312	$13,166	$10,529
South Carolina	$59,902	$10,168	$8,822
Texas	$61,501	$11,880	$8,822
Virginia	$72,223	$14,900	$8,822
West Virginia	$72,673	$16,321	$10,529

Source: U.S. Bureau of Labor Statistics (2019).

essential that we gain an understanding of how work affects the lives of families. Generally speaking, **family well-being** includes the following (Behnke & MacDermid, 2004):

- Psychological health, such as low levels of depression and anxiety and high levels of life satisfaction
- High levels of self-esteem, sense of power, and internal locus of control
- Good physical health
- Low behavior/conduct problems, such as alcohol abuse
- Good social support, such as friendships and contact with extended family
- High marital quality
- High marital stability
- Good parent–child relationships

If a family member is struggling at work, or if work conditions are not conducive to a quality family life, then every family member eventually suffers—a family member's occupational well-being is directly related to a good, healthy, comfortable state for the family. Given the importance of family health and functioning in our lives, it is essential to have an awareness and understanding of the interrelated nature of the workplace and the home. Toward the end

Family well-being:

psychological health; high levels of self-esteem, sense of power, and internal locus of control; good physical health; low behavior/conduct problems; good social support; high marital quality and stability; and good parent–child relationships.

Although there are a number of challenges associated with dual-career couples, such as increased stress on personal lives and role conflict, many couples experience an increase in equality in the relationship.

of this chapter, we'll explore at length those factors necessary for couples to balance work life with family life to promote the family's health and well-being.

Money and Power

Couple and family therapist Dr. Assaei Romanelli (2019) stresses that money and power are almost always at play if a couple is experiencing relationship difficulties. Romanelli describes the dynamic that occurs when one partner in the relationship earns more money than the other; he refers to this couple type as $$$ and $. Notes Romanelli,

> The dynamic often manifests as follows: The $$$ partner implicitly and semi-consciously expects $ partner to compensate for their diminished income by investing extra time in the relationship, the house, the cooking. Or the kids. The $ partner is grateful for the extra income their partner makes, but the financial dependence can generate feelings of guilt, which motivates them to constantly show the $$$ partner how essential they are. Ultimately, both partners act out their frustrations with mutual contempt, criticism, defensiveness, and stonewalling . . . which eventually lead to the relationship ending. (p. 1)

Romanelli offers suggestions for couples who have a discrepancy in their earnings—and thus, a power differential:

- **Know your worth:** The $-partner is valuable, whether it's because he/she is covering their own expenses through their employment or because they contribute to the couple's and family's well-being in other, nonquantifiable ways. Romanelli encourages couples to openly discuss their feelings of worth with each other and to encourage partners who feel guilty for not pulling their financial weight.

- **Say it out loud:** Money and power is a topic that couples rarely discuss, so it is important that couples give each other the time and space to share their experiences. It is equally important for each partner to listen and to validate the other's feelings.

- **Renegotiate the power differential:** Once couples have validated each other's worth, and the importance of each partner to the relationship and to the family, couples can slowly begin to renegotiate financial agreements or boundaries that have already been established. This *takes time* because it challenges the existing balance of the family system.

By taking time to clarify the financial power dynamic in a relationship, couples can confront head-on any issues this differential poses, rather than ignoring it and allowing it to become a potent, powerful point of resentment in the relationship.

Work Hours and Family Life: Shift Work

Researchers and family practitioners are interested not only in the total number of work hours that couples put in each week but they're also interested in how those hours are structured throughout the week (Grosswald, 2004). In many dual-earner families today, one partner works on a schedule that is different from the typical 8:00 to 5:00 schedule. **Shift work** can mean that a partner works nonstandard hours, such as working from 6:00 in the morning until 2:00 in the afternoon, or it could mean working a schedule other than the typical work week (Monday through Friday in the United States; Grosswald, 2004). For example, contemporary couples may have a partner who works 12-hours shifts, four times a week, which are common shifts for nurses, emergency personnel, and firefighters.

Shift work: working nonstandard hours or working a schedule other than the typical Monday to Friday work week.

A number of advantages and disadvantages are associated with shift work schedules. Potential positive effects of these work schedules include such things as working fewer days each week, having more family time, and getting more time to be away from the job (for a complete review, see Loudoun, 2008).

However, there are negative impacts of shift work on families. For example, although shift workers may physically have more time to be with their families than standard-shift workers do, researchers believe the *quality* of these interactions is significantly less (White, 2018). This is because of the fatigue that intensifies throughout the shift week—some research has revealed that after a shift worker comes home from work and sleeps, he or she has less than two hours a day to attend to family duties, do household tasks, and prepare for the next work day. One law firm noted that the proportion of divorce cases it has dealt with that involved shift workers increased from 7 percent to 35 percent from 2014 to 2017 (Rudgard, 2017). So common are marital breakups with shift workers, some now refer to them as *shift work divorces* (Rudgard, 2017). Other studies have demonstrated that shift work significantly impacts family relationships (for a full review, see Davis, Crouter, & McHale, 2006):

- *Parental involvement.* There is a "mismatch" in parents' shift schedules and time for children. Overall, studies show that shift workers spend less time with their children than standard, daytime workers do.
- *Marital conflict.* Sometimes, high stress and work demands associated with shift work lead to increased levels of marital conflict. As one divorce attorney noted, shift work marriages "effectively mean living under the same roof but leading separate lives" (Rudgard, 2017).

With the evolving global economy and the increase in shift work within different industries, much more needs to be understood about the effects of nonstandard work hours on family life. As some family practitioners note, these types of hours make it difficult for parents to create routines, rituals, and family activities—the very things that help to knit family members together and provide the foundation for family closeness (Davis et al., 2006).

Student Loan Debt: Credit Hostages

Today, few things impact couple and family life as significantly as student loan debt (Robb, Chatterjee, Porto, & Cude, 2018). So extensive is the debt in the United States, the topic is becoming central in policy concerns (Robb et al., 2018), and took center stage as a primary

Many who carry student loan debt report that they feel they are drowning, sinking, or being crushed by their student loans. Do you own student loan debt? How do you feel when you think about repaying the loans?

concern of U.S. adults in the 2020 presidential election. In 2020, 44 million student loan borrowers owed a total of 1.5 trillion dollars (Pew Foundation, 2020). As one borrower said, "I'm a credit hostage" (Proctor, 2020).

Student loan debt is money that is owed on a loan that was taken out by a student to pay for educational expenses, and currently more than one *trillion* dollars are owed. In 2019, 15 percent of all adults in the United States carried student loan debt (Pew Research Center, 2019b); more than one-third of all adults ages 18 to 29 have student loan debt. And this debt is taking its toll on marriages and families. A recent survey of nearly 1400 adults who owe student loan debt found the following (Proctor, 2020):

- *Interfering with dating:* One in eight survey respondents indicated that dating has been affected by their student loan debt because potential partners to not want to "marry" significant debt.

- *Delaying marriage:* More than one-fourth of borrowers are delaying marriage until they are in a better financial position.

- *Delaying childbearing:* Fifty-one percent indicated that although they desire to start a family, they feel they must delay having children until their student loan debt is paid down or off. One in three have opted to delay having children or forgo having children due to student loan debt.

- *Relationship stress:* Nearly 60 percent of those surveyed said that student loan debt is a significant source of stress and conflict in the marital relationship.

- *Divorce:* Slightly more than 20 percent of student loan borrowers in this study indicated that they would divorce their marriage partner if it would result in a lower student loan payment.

There is also a great deal of psychological and emotional pain that borrowers feel due to the "weight of the debt" (Lockert, 2019). In a study of 829 student loan borrowers, the research revealed that student loan debt is linked to depression and suicidal thoughts (Lockert, 2019):

- *Anxiety:* Ninety percent of borrowers experience "life-impeding" anxiety due to student loan debt.
- *Depression:* More than one-half of the borrowers surveyed noted that they experience depression due to their unpaid student loans.
- *Suicidal thoughts:* One in 15 student loan borrowers has considered suicide. When survey respondents who knew someone who had committed suicide were asked whether they thought it was because of student loans, 1 in 11 answered "yes."

What makes this type of debt so different from home mortgages or credit card debt? As one survey respondent said, "If you want to have a good life, you get an education. It *has* to be college. There's an unspoken promise that if you follow this plan, the golden doors will open, everything will be fine" (Lockert, 2019). Another borrower succinctly said, "There is a [prevailing] feeling of hopelessness—you feel like you'll never recover."

Although student loan forgiveness programs and lower payment programs exist, annually only about 1 percent of those who apply are accepted into these programs (Lockert, 2019). As the researcher observes, when an individual or a couple have student loan debt, there is uncertainty about how to pay back the debt, and borrowers also have significantly more pressure to find a high-paying job that accommodates large student loan payments. Finally, the inability to live life as planned creates anxiety and depression among those who are repaying student loan debt. In short, "Student loan debt [causes problems in relationships] because it impacts overall economic stability and flexibility for young Americans at a critical point in the life cycle" (Robb et al., 2018, p. 51). Something needs to give.

The Demands of Overtime

Organizations typically define overtime as the hours a person works beyond her or his normal 40-hour per week schedule (Baird & Beccia, 1980). Working overtime often leads us to feel overworked, burned out—and just plain cranky. But given the systems nature of family living, it's important to keep in mind that these feelings of "enough is enough!" not only influence working moms and dads but they also impact their families.

Decades of research have shown that long work hours increase workers' perceptions that their jobs interfere with their emotional states, and these, in turn, increase marital tension between spouses (for a complete review, see Crouter, Bumpus, Head, & McHale, 2001). Other studies have demonstrated that when fathers are pressured or stressed at work, they tend to have more conflict with their adolescent children (Crouter, 1995). Finally, research has revealed that wives' overtime work (46+ hours per week) decreases marital interaction and happiness and increases the potential of divorce (Amato et al., 2003).

Working overtime can be successfully managed in the short term, but for many couples it is challenging to manage and balance their family relationships over the long haul due to the limited amount of time they can spend with one another. That's not to say, however, that families can't make it work. As one family practitioner observed, quality time in great quantity is a staple of creating strong family relationships (Defrain, 2000).

Coping With Unemployment: It's Not About the Money

Hopelessness. Anger. Hurt. Depression. Apprehension. Powerlessness. Fear. Helplessness. Worry. Anxiety. Feeling worthless. Nervousness. Feeling useless. Losing a job or not being able to find a job is more than losing an income—for many people, being jobless carries with it severe emotional and psychological distress, as well as a loss of self-esteem, self-confidence, and professional identity (Hiswals and others, 2017). Without question: Job loss and financial hardship rank among the most severe stressor that individuals and families can encounter, and for many this constitutes living in active trauma (Hiswals, Marttila, Malstam, & Marcassa, 2017). In 2018, 4.3 million people were unemployed, and the proportion of families with an unemployed person was slightly more than 5 percent (U.S. Bureau of Labor Statistics, 2019).

Unemployment is a traumatic situation for families to deal with, and aside from the obvious financial constraints it puts on a family, there are a number of other negative impacts on the family's emotional and physical health (Furstenberg, 1974; Hanisch, 1999; Hiswals et al., 2017; Voydanoff, 1983):

- Family instability
- Decreased family interactions
- Increased levels of family violence
- Increased mental hospital admissions
- Loss of social capital
- Individual and family isolation

In a study that sought to better understand unemployed individuals' experiences and their perceptions of self and family, study participants revealed the pain they were experiencing when they noted,

> *I belong to nothing. When you have a job, you belong to something. You're included in something. But now I'm not that. Now I'm just something being tossed around somewhere.*

> *Work means security, the feeling that you are safe, that you have a role in life. Now you are not.*

> *You are affected all the time. Your entire life is affected.* (Hiswals et al., 2017, p. 995)

As you can see, it's not just about money, or loss of money. It's about the *everything else that comes with it*, as we discussed in Chapter 1. So, when you look at the unemployment rates among races and ethnicities in the United States (Figure 12.5), I encourage you to look beyond the numbers and the percentages and see not just the financial pain, but also the emotional and psychological pain. The truth about unemployment and job loss is, it hurts.

Previous research suggests that being married and having children seems to buffer against the negative impacts of unemployment for women but tends to have the reverse effect

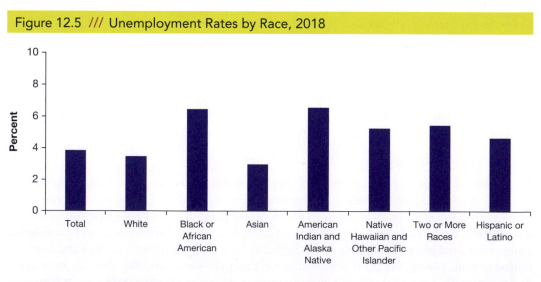

Figure 12.5 /// Unemployment Rates by Race, 2018

Source: U.S. Bureau of Labor Statistics (2019).

for men (Artazcoz, Benach, Borrell, & Cortes, 2004). This may be because when married women are unemployed, frequently they still have their basic economic needs met by their husbands; periods of job loss also lessen the multiple demands on women and allow them greater involvement in family life. The risks of poor mental health for men may be higher than it is for women because of the pressures of traditional patriarchal gender roles that dictate that men are to protect and provide for their families. Certainly, job loss may make them feel that they are not living up to their prescribed role of breadwinner. And, because men are traditionally less involved in the care and nurturing of children, the researchers speculated that these activities can't successfully replace their jobs, as they do with women.

In many ways, the stress associated with unemployment is similar to other transitions some families have to weather, such as divorce, acquiring a disability, or losing a home—and it can be as disrupting to a family's balance and health. But research has shown that people can cope well with unemployment and maintain mental health and well-being if they employ certain strategies. If faced with the loss of a job, healthy families should

- Allow themselves to grieve, to feel anger, and be depressed or anxious
- Adopt the attitude. "We're a strong family. We *can* bounce back from this setback!"
- Maintain consistent daily and weekly routines that provide structure and stability for the family
- Seek emotional support from friends, relatives, and neighbors
- Assess personal strengths, skills, and values. Often, new directions emerge after doing so
- If signs of depression emerge, immediately seek counseling either from a professional source or from a pastor, priest, or rabbi
- Communicate often and honestly with family members (Fetsch, 2009)

Unemployment is often a traumatic situation for families to deal with. But if couples tackle the problem as a team and remain supportive of one another, they can take steps that promote their adaptability and emotional closeness—they can "struggle well."

Opting Out: Stay-at-Home Moms

Some mothers have decided that staying at home with their children is how they can best balance personal, partner, and family needs with their partner's work responsibilities. These mothers have opted out of the workforce and choose instead to stay at home and nurture their children; this is referred to **household work**. Of the millions of mothers in the U.S. today, it is estimated that nearly 30 percent stay at home and do not participate in the paid workforce (Pew Research Center, 2018).

The fact that household work is still a critical component of a successful home for dual-earner couples has led some economists to try to place a value on household work. The **opportunity cost method** asks the question, "What would a person be paid in wage labor for one hour of household work?" Because what people earn in wage labor varies, this method can tend to skew the real value of household work. An alternative method is the **market alternative cost method**, which estimates the value of household labor by looking at what it would cost in the current market to pay someone to do the household labor the mother performs, such as preparing three meals a day, doing the laundry, caring for the children, and taking care of the home. For example, a group that tracks salaries and wages conducted a recent survey of stay-at-home moms and found if paid, stay-at-home moms would earn $162,581 annually (Salary.com, 2018). They also discovered that a stay-at-home mom works 97 hours per week, spending 13 hours as a day care provider/teacher to her children; nearly 4 hours as "household CEO"; almost 8 hours as a psychologist; 14 hours as

Household work:
the work associated with staying at home in order to nurture one's children.

Opportunity cost method:
attempts to value household work by asking "What would a person be paid in wage labor for one hour of household work?"

Market alternative cost method:
estimates the value of household labor by looking at what it would cost in the current market to pay someone to do the household labor the mother performs.

Today, more and more dads are leaving the workforce and are staying home to raise the kids and to care for household tasks.

a chef; 15 hours as a housekeeper; almost 7 hours as a laundress; about 9 hours as a computer operator; and nearly 11 hours as a facilities keeper. And they sleep about 6 hours per night.

Senior vice president of Salary.com Bill Coleman noted that this study "is an eye opener for many people when they see the real market value of the work moms perform." Of course, moms aren't the only ones who opt to stay at home and care for the children and the home. Today, an increasing number of fathers are doing the same.

Leaving the Workforce: Stay-at-Home Dads

Stay-at-home dads:

fathers who have remained out of the labor force for at least one year primarily so they can care for their children while their wives or partners work outside of the home.

A growing number of men have decided to stay at home. **Stay-at-home dads** are those who have remained out of the labor force for at least one year primarily so they can care for their children while their wives work outside of the home. In 2018, 17 percent of all stay-at-home parents were fathers (Pew Research Center, 2018). For most of these dads, the wife has the better, higher-paying job and the couple believes that it is in the best interest of the family if the father stays home while the wife works. This is a good example of how each individual and every family must make a choice that is good, better, or best for them in order to balance work and family successfully. As you can see in Table 12.3, there are both gender and racial/ethnic differences in parents who do not work outside the home.

In today's economic environment, there appear to be three social circumstances that are contributing to the increasing numbers of dads who stay home to care for their children. First, among married fathers, the family's economic considerations make it more appealing for him to stay home than they do for her to do so. Second, today's increased divorce rates have resulted in some fathers becoming their children's primary caregiver; because some fathers have economic security, they may opt to stay at home and care for their children, rather than place the children in child care. Finally, a number of stay-at-home dads today are gay men whose husbands or partners work outside of the home, while they care for the children and assume household tasks. The prevalence of dads staying at home and opting out of the paid workforce will likely increase as this movement continues and as social acceptance becomes more widespread and attitudes change.

Table 12.3 /// Characteristics of Stay-at-Home Parents

Characteristic	% of stay-at-home dads who aren't working . . .		% of stay-at-home moms who aren't working . . .	
	In order to care for home/family	For some other reason	In order to care for home/family	For some other reason
White	49	51	49	48
African American	15	19	7	23
Latinx	21	20	32	20
Asian/Pacific Islander	11	7	32	20
Married w/ working spouse	61	42	77	35
Married w/ non-working spouse	15	27	5	11
Cohabiting	15	15	7	10
Single	9	16	11	43
At least one child <5	44	29	50	31

Source: Pew Research Center (2018).

THE BALANCING ACT: JUGGLING FAMILY LIFE AND WORK

"Come on, we're late!" "Let's *go!*" "Do you have your (backpack, briefcase, trumpet, book report, science project)?" "Where are my car keys?" Balancing work and family is nothing new. Since the women's movement in the 1960s and the surging flood of women into the workplace the past few decades, working families across the United States engage in similar morning rituals in their dash to get the kids off to school and parents off to work.

After the birth or the adoption of a child, dual-earner families must make numerous adjustments to accommodate the schedules and needs of both spouses and the children. Unlike the traditional homemaker/breadwinner family configurations found in the 1950s, once a baby arrives, contemporary couples must not only incorporate sleepless nights into their daily lives but they must also find a way to juggle the responsibilities, stressors, and struggles associated with managing the multiple roles of mother/father, employee, and wife/husband.

Conflicting Demands: Heartstrings Versus Purse Strings

Sometimes our obligations to our jobs come into direct conflict with the needs of our families. When we take on (or have assigned to us) many roles simultaneously—for example, when the family role demands are incompatible with or conflict with the stresses from the work role—**interrole conflict** occurs (Hammer & Thompson, 2003). Such conflict can result in increased work absenteeism, intentions to leave the work force, decreased job satisfaction, decreased family satisfaction, decreased life satisfaction, negative mental and physical

Interrole conflict: conflict that occurs when we take on (or have assigned to us) many roles simultaneously.

health, strain associated with dependent care responsibilities (both child care and elder care), and increased interpersonal conflict or divorce.

Something's Gotta Give: Work–Family Conflict

Work–family conflict falls into three specific areas and is bi-directional—the conflict goes both ways (Greenhaus & Beutell, 1985):

Time-based conflict:

takes place when demands from the work domain and the family domain vie for a parent's time and attention.

Strain-based conflict:

occurs when the demands in one domain make it difficult to perform effectively in another domain.

Family and Medical Leave Act (FMLA):

under the FMLA, federal and state employees and those who work for employers with 50 or more employees are able to take up to 12 weeks of unpaid leave to care for an ill child, parent, or spouse, or for one's own serious illness without fear of losing their job, benefits, or status.

Behavior-based conflict:

occurs when incompatibilities exist between the demands of the work role and the demands of the family role.

1. **Time-based conflict** takes place when demands from the work domain and the family domain vie for a parent's time and attention. This is the most common type of role conflict found in working families. For instance, a meeting that runs late at work might make one parent late for coaching a son's soccer game. A last-minute business call might make another parent late for a parent–teacher conference.

2. **Strain-based conflict** occurs when the demands in one domain make it difficult to carry out effective role performance in another domain. For example, consider a mother who finds it difficult to concentrate on her job or complete her job tasks on time because she is also caring for her elderly ill father.

   In recognition of the multiple roles with which most American families must now cope, in 1993, the federal government enacted the **Family and Medical Leave Act (FMLA)**. Under the FMLA, federal and state employees and those who work for employers with 50 or more employees are able to take up to 12 weeks of unpaid leave in order to care for an ill child, parent, or spouse, or for one's own serious illness, without fear of losing their job, benefits, or status. Unpaid leave can also be taken for the birth or adoption of a child or when placing a child for adoption or foster care. Both working men and women are protected by this legislation.

3. **Behavior-based conflict** occurs when incompatibilities exist between the demands of the work role and the demands of the family role. For example, on the job, police officers may need to be aggressive, forceful, emotionally detached, and uncompromising. Airline pilots need to be task oriented, detail oriented, hard driving, and single-minded in their purpose. Although these behavior traits may help these professionals be successful in their careers, bringing home these same behaviors to family life may not settle well with the spouse and the children.

Something's gotta give. Often, the demands of work conflict with the needs of our partners and families. In what ways can couples better balance the demands of family and career? Would you ever consider a career that pays less so you can spend more time with your family? Why or why not?

Thomas Trutschel/Photothek via Getty Images

Family life is a balancing act. Deciding who will work, who will care for the children, when and how to coordinate schedules, and determining who will transport the children to and from events and activities undoubtedly leads to role conflicts. Commonly, the partner with more flexibility in work schedules is called on to "pick up the slack" when it comes to trying to balance work and family. Often, though, this leads to frustration and a feeling of being "used" and "unappreciated." Consider, for example, a mother who is frequently frustrated with her husband after the birth of their first child. Because they both work full time, she feels that he should shoulder more of the childrearing responsibilities. Sleep deprivation for both partners is a daily reality and, unfortunately, can result in a cycle of escalating conflict: He feels she should appreciate his efforts more and she believes that she shouldn't have to express appreciation because he was just doing his duty as a father. Good communication and a willingness to avoid criticism, contempt, defensiveness, and stonewalling are important keys to negotiating work–family role conflicts effectively (Gottman, 1994), When conflicts do arise, learning to calm down, speak without causing defensiveness, and to validate our partner can help us reduce the possibility that these conflicts will harm the successful balancing of our work and family relationships (see also Gottman, 1999).

Work–Family Spillover/Crossover

Research psychologist Patricia Roehling and her colleague, professor and sociologist Phyllis Moen (2003), conclude that dual-earner couples are vulnerable to work–family conflict, as well as **work–family spillover/crossover**, which occurs when a spouse brings the emotional events and tensions of one environment to the other. This spillover/crossover can occur from family to work; for example, if a parent has an argument with a teenager before leaving for work, it can lead to poor concentration at work. In the case of work-to-family conflict, a "bad day at the office" for either parent may end up being a bad day for everyone else at home. Work–family spillover/crossover can also have positive individual and family outcomes. Roehling and Moen note that good relationships at home energize people, which in turn improves a person's productivity at work; a great day at work can translate to a great day for everyone else at home. The researchers also note that much scientific study shows that couples who combine work, married life, and family report

Work–family spillover/ crossover: occurs when a spouse carries the emotional events and tensions of one environment to the other.

- Levels of well-being are higher for both men and women.
- Women experience less anxiety and depression.
- Women report better physical health and higher self-esteem.
- Husbands are more involved with the children.
- Children have a stronger network of social support and social relationships.
- Two wages allow the couple to more adequately provide for their children.
- Marital satisfaction is high when the woman's employment is consistent with the husband's and wife's gender role beliefs.

Current economic trends indicate that dual-career marriages are here to stay, but there are things couples can do to better handle the challenges associated with juggling work and family. In addition to promoting the physical well-being and the health of the children through shared caregiving, and in addition to ensuring the economic survival of the family, parents are also charged with the tremendous responsibility of fostering their children's optimal growth.

Balancing It All

When our lives are in balance, life just seems better, doesn't it? When it comes to work and family, **balance** can be thought of as the positive psychological state we achieve through regularly meeting our own, others', and work-related needs. It is the state of equilibrium we feel when these needs—and their accompanying responsibilities—are fulfilled to improve our own well-being and the well-being of those we love (Harris, 2008).

Balance: in terms of work and family, the positive psychological state we achieve through regularly meeting our own, others', and work-related needs.

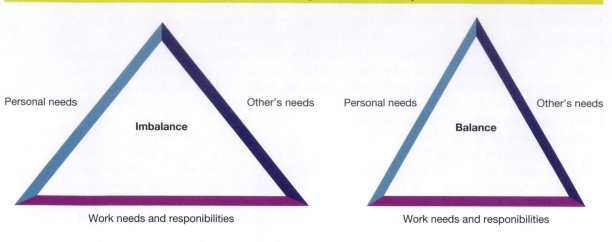

Figure 12.6 /// The Triangular Theory of Balancing Work and Family

Personal needs · **Imbalance** · Other's needs

Work needs and responibilities

Personal needs · **Balance** · Other's needs

Work needs and responibilities

Source: Annotated from ©V.W Harris (2008).

Perhaps we can think about balance in another way by using the triangular theory of balancing work and family, presented in Figure 12.6 (Harris, 2008). This theory maintains that the interaction of our personal needs, others' needs, and work responsibilities creates ever-changing situations that cause either balance or imbalance in a family. Individuals can choose and change how their needs and responsibilities interact to create greater balance in their relationships and improve subsequent happiness and well-being. In other words, we have a choice in how we attempt to balance our work and family relationships while, at the same time, try to meet our own personal needs. When we are out of balance in any of the three areas (personal needs, others' needs, and work needs/responsibilities), we intuitively sense that a change needs to occur; how we approach these changes makes all the difference in how happy and satisfied we are in our relationships. Other research recently demonstrated that family health and **family cohesion**—the extent to which family members feel emotionally close and bonded to one another—are influenced by how well working couples are able to integrate the demands of work and family life (Stevens, Kiger, & Riley, 2006). One of the biggest challenges working couples face is who is going to do the tasks necessary to keep the house running, and when.

Family cohesion:
the extent to which family members feel emotionally close and bonded to one another.

Who Does What and When? Dividing Household Chores

Couples may marry with the intent to share household chores just as they intend to share childrearing. But when children enter into the family system, these intentions often do not become reality. Discrepancies between who does what often become a source of recurring conflict. With the majority of mothers today working at least 30 hours a week outside the home, the expectation that they are still responsible for the lion's share of running the household and performing household tasks can become a source of resentment. Sociologist Arlie Hochschild (1989) referred to this burden of taking on the dual responsibilities of wage-earner and housekeeper as the **second shift**.

Second shift:
sociologist Arlie Hochschild's (1989) term for the burden of the dual responsibilities of wage earner and housekeeper.

During this second shift, women spend three times as much time performing household tasks as men do, spending 32 hours compared to men's 10 hours (Coltrane, 2000). These tasks include house cleaning, meal preparation, grocery shopping, cleanup after meals, and laundry (Blair & Lichter, 1991). Coltrane (2000) refers to these essential tasks as "routine housework" but maintains that "this family work or social reproductive labor is just as important to the maintenance of society as the productive work that occurs in the formal market economy" (p. 1209), and that these tasks keep the household, the family, and society going. The author cites numerous studies that indicate that, for the most part, neither women nor men enjoy performing routine household chores. They tend to find occasional **residual tasks**, such as bill paying, yard work, and chauffeuring children, to be more flexible in nature and more enjoyable to carry out.

Residual tasks: household tasks such as bill paying, yard work, and chauffeuring children.

Like parenting roles, the division of household duties tends to fall along traditional gender roles once a child is born, even if such tasks were previously handled fairly equally (Baxter, 1993).

Coltrane (2000) identifies several factors that contribute to the division of household chores. These factors include women's employment (the more hours a woman works outside the home, the more men share in household tasks); men's employment (men who work fewer hours outside the home tend to pitch in more around the house and with childrearing); earnings (women who earn more hire someone to perform household chores); education (men with higher education levels tend to engage in more household labor); and the presence of children (when children enter the picture, women assume the majority of housework).

Although gender appears to be an important factor that dictates generally who does what housework and how often, the research does seem to indicate that the division of labor along traditional gender roles is slowly giving way to changing roles of men and women in contemporary society. This is a "ray of hope" for those who struggle with balancing marital and parenting roles, because, as Coltrane (2000) concludes, "We now know that when men perform more of the routine household work, employed women feel that the division of labor is fairer, are less depressed, and enjoy higher levels of marital satisfaction" (p. 1226).

Child Care

In 1940, only 10 percent of children in the United States lived in a home in which the mother worked outside the home. By 2019, more than 11 million children under the age of 5 were in some form of child care in the United States (Child Care Aware, 2019). And care for children doesn't come cheap. There is great variation in child care costs across the country, but on average parents spend anywhere from $9,800 per year for infant care in Missouri, to $15,000 in New York, to $16,000 in California (Child Care Aware, 2019). The cost of care for a child under the age of 2 ranges from about $6,500 at the low end to nearly $12,000, and the range for child care for a 4-year-old is about the same.

Marvin Joseph/The Washington Post via Getty Images

Although child care is a common family experience, today many families with young children face child care challenges, such as finding quality child care at affordable costs. A significant number of parents today are leaving the workforce because of child care challenges.

With both parents working, parents must weigh options regarding child care. Some spouses try to work different shifts so that their children spend less time in a child care setting. Consequently, the parents have less time to spend together developing and nurturing their own relationship. Other families have extended family members who are willing to provide child care. When this option is available, many parents view it as a way for children to receive loving care with trusted family members at a reduced cost. A third option is a child care center or preschool. Today, many parents are opting for **shared care**, a child care arrangement in which parents share a babysitter or nanny.

In 2016, the Facebook company announced a multi-million dollar expansion that included several on-site services, such as a bicycle repair shop and doggy day care. Unfortunately, they left child care off the list (Trautner, 2016). As of 2016, only about 7 percent of U.S. companies offered on-site day care to its employees (Trautner, 2016). According to Michigan State University, there are advantages and disadvantages to having day care in the workplace:

Advantages:

- *Productivity is increased:* Workers report increased concentration and productivity.
- *Attraction/retention of employees:* 90 percent of those surveyed indicated that on-site day care was a deciding factor in returning to work after the birth of a baby.
- *Convenience:* On-site care allows parents to check on their children throughout the day and minimizes commute time as there is no drop off/pick up of children. Many parents also enjoy eating lunch with their children; breastfeeding mothers are able to feed their infants during the work day.
- *High morale:* Employees who use on-site day care report that they feel valued and appreciated as an employee because an emphasis is placed on their children's well-being.

Disadvantages:

- *High cost:* On-site day care and child care may be even more expensive than other child care facilities.
- *Distracted parent:* Some companies report that having a child so close is sometimes distracting for a parent.
- *Lower productivity:* In some instances, having a child close by impacted work productivity because of a parent's frequent visits to the child care facility.

Whether parents choose a private day care provider, a child care center or facility, or on-site care, three things matter the most: (1) high quality; (2) reliability; and (3) convenience (Trautner, 2016).

Making Work for Families

Work and family are central to our lives, but finding ways to balance the two is not always easy. How important is it for people to manage work so that they can still enjoy marriage, children, and recreation?

Many corporations are finding out that it is *very* important—so important that some employers are finding ways to provide workers with tools and benefits aiding family life and living. Lancaster Laboratories, a company specializing in laboratory services for the environmental and pharmaceutical industry, was one of the first in a wave of companies to offer family-friendly benefits for employees (Powers, 2004).

In the mid-1980s, executives at Lancaster Laboratories noticed a continuing theme in the needs assessments of its employees, 60 percent of whom were women: When women were absent from work, it was typically due to problems with day care. With the number of employees at Lancaster who currently had a family or planned on having one in the near future, the $50 million company knew it had to find a way to retain its workers and to reduce absenteeism (Powers, 2004).

Is Day Care Harmful to a Child's Development?

Over the past 20 to 30 years, much intense empirical research has focused on the effects of day care on children's health, development, and overall well-being. Although researchers have found that parents are the first and most important influence on their child's development, nonparental care also affects children's health and well-being. Is day care harmful to a child's development? Researchers disagree.

YES: A number of studies indicate that there are negative developmental effects associated with children who spend their days in paid child care settings:

- When mothers return to work shortly after giving birth, their children may exhibit slower emotional development. As the child enters adolescence, the delay in emotional development manifests in lower educational attainments (Ermisch & Francesconi, 2002).

- Children who are in child care outside of the home from infancy tend to be less compliant and more aggressive. Children who experience 10 or more hours per week of nonparental child care are more likely to experience behavioral problems than those children who are cared for by their parents at home (Belsky, 2001).

- Children who receive extensive and early child care receive the lowest teacher and parental ratings for peer relationships, compliance, work habits, and emotional health by age 8 (Vandell & Corsaniti, 1990).

- Long hours in the day care setting and couples with stressful parent–child interactions at home are associated with angry, aggressive preschool children (Early Child Care Research Network, 2003).

NO: Whether or not children suffer negative effects from their day care or child care experiences depends largely on the relationship with their parents and the parents' ability to provide sensitive, nurturing, intimate, and patient care at home. The day care experience can have positive influences on a child's development and well-being:

- Day care and child care settings allow children the increased opportunity for peer interaction and to learn rules of getting along with others and social interaction (Hartup & Moore, 1990).

- Nearly all children benefit from some level of cognitive enrichment from day care and child care experiences (Lamb, 2000).

- Quality day care/child care providers and smaller child care groups or classes lead to improved cognitive skills (McCartney & Haas, 2002).

- Low-income children who are given access to early childhood education and quality day care/child care programs have higher reading and math grades from elementary school to adulthood, are more likely to go to college, are older when their first child is born, have enhanced language skills, and have higher educational employment and educational status compared to those children who did not participate in the program (Campbell, Ramey, Pungello, Sparling, & Miller-Johnson, 2002).

What Do You Think?

1. Do you think day care is beneficial or harmful to a child's development? What is the basis for your decision?

2. What is the parents' role in ensuring children experience positive, beneficial outcomes from the day care experience?

In August 1986, Lancaster Laboratories Child Care Center opened its doors. The first-of-its-kind on-site day care had 29 openings, which were quickly filled. Parents soon took advantage of day care just a few feet away from their job site. Today, the child care center serves 161 children from infancy to school age and even offers summer day care and kindergarten programs.

The programs are great for working parents, but aside from a spot on *Working Mother's* "Top 100 Companies for Working Mothers" list for 11 years, is it beneficial for employers? Human resources executives at Lancaster Laboratories seem to think so. Turnover remains at around

8 percent companywide, employees skip fewer days of work, and 96 percent of new mothers return to their posts in three months.

Creative benefits programs today are not just for working parents. Taking a job with a company used to mean the standard insurance/company car/401(k) package. But today, more and more companies are offering extras such as on-site fitness centers, concert and sporting event tickets, concierge services, and flex scheduling (Powers, 2004). Employers are seeing great value in making sure their employees balance good living and hard working (Powers, 2004). Having happy workers means keeping a healthy bottom line.

Ten Strategies for Family and Work Balance

Although money doesn't buy happiness, it can definitely provide opportunities for more comfortable daily living and better educational opportunities, health care, family vacations, marriage getaways, and other leisure activities. It can also reduce many of the stressors and strains that those who lack economic advantage inevitably endure (Dyk, 2004). Although the demands of balancing work and family can sometimes be draining on a family, research suggests that most employed women and men believe that there are strong benefits to combining work and family and that the benefits far outweigh the costs (Barnett & Rivers, 1996). Though it takes some effort, it is possible for families to successfully blend and manage these two most important domains in their lives.

In a study that examined the work/family lives of 47 married couples who appear to successfully manage both spheres, the data revealed that these couples structured their lives around 10 major strategies (Haddock, Zimmerman, Ziemba, & Current, 2001). We discuss these in the sections that follow.

Value Family. Dual-earner couples who make their relationship and their children a priority experience greater satisfaction and well-being in their family relationships (Eyre & Eyre, 2008). Through words and actions, couples who do well at balancing work and family work hard to keep their family as their number one priority, and all of their decisions reflect this priority. Couples can proactively create opportunities for family time and couple time, and during these times they can create family rituals and routines—special family times—that are unique to them. Above all, couples need to remember to nurture their relationship: *Strong couples make stronger parents!* Successful couples also emphasize family happiness and well-being over professional responsibilities.

Strive for Partnership. Stressing equality and partnership in the marital relationship is critical to working couples' success. Certainly there are varying degrees of equality among couples, and although there is no doubt that some situations call for greater degrees of partnership than others, partners who possess an overall high degree of equality fare better than those who do not. There appear to be three principal areas where equality is a must: the division of household labor, making decisions together as a couple, and having a "team" mentality. As one partner noted, "If I win and she loses, then we both lose. If she wins and I lose, then we both lose. [This belief] has probably made all the difference . . . because you just can't live your life trying to always win. The couple will lose, period."

Derive Meaning From Work. Even if it's not always possible to love their jobs, couples who are successful at balancing work and family note that being able to derive meaning out of what they do is important. For these couples, experiencing enjoyment and purpose in their jobs brings energy, enthusiasm, and excitement to their lives; it also seems to buffer them against work-related fatigue and burnout.

Maintain Work Boundaries. If couples are able to keep their families as their top priority, it's easier for them to maintain clear—and immovable—boundaries between their home life and their work life. As researchers note, couples who are committed to not allowing work to dictate the pace of their lives are better able to compartmentalize their lives and prevent overlap between their personal and professional lives. As one study participant said, "I think the biggest [strategy] is: When you're at home, you're at home; and when you're at work, you're at work. There's not the crossover. You don't get to think about work unless there's a huge problem."

Be Focused and Productive at Work. Many couples talked about the importance of being productive while at work. They observed that even though they set boundaries, their employers tended to better support their commitment to family if they were efficient while they were on the job.

Prioritize Family Fun. You gotta have fun! Successful working families make a point to enjoy a lot of fun time together as a family. Not only is family fun a way to relax and de-stress, it's also a way that families build emotional connections and create family rituals. Family time together doesn't have to be a costly trip to Disneyworld—it can be an every-Friday-night board game or movie and popcorn night, a spontaneous bike ride on a Saturday, or a quick toss of the Frisbee in the backyard. Of course, a sense of humor goes a long way in buffering the stressors associated with the demands of balancing work and family. Successful families strive to make laughter and humor the general atmosphere in the family.

Take Pride in Dual Earning. Although the reality of family life for many today means that both partners are in the paid labor force, some women today still feel that there are negative societal messages about them working instead of staying home with the children. Couples who successfully balance work and home life adopt the attitude that dual earning is positive for every member of their family, and they refuse to accept negative comments from family or friends. Overall, these couples do not struggle with feelings of guilt, and they don't fret over not spending every spare minute with their children—if they had to sit down to pay the bills, they did so in lieu of playing with the kids. As one parent noted, "I think it's a big benefit for [my son] to have a working mom. . . . He's going to grow up understanding that women and men share equally in what's going on, and he's growing up expecting that he's going to share what happens in [his house.]"

Live Simply. A number of successful couples have learned to simplify their lives. For example, rather than allowing their children to be involved in as many activities as they wanted to, parents limit each child to one or two activities that they really enjoy doing. Limiting activities in this way

Families who are effective at juggling work and family life know that having fun when they're not at work is essential to their health and well-being. A little laughter goes a long way!

helps minimize the chaos of family living. Couples also note the importance of controlling their finances and living within their budgets as a way to simplify their lives. They also find creative time-saving strategies that make family life more efficient and less complicated. For example, one family helps their children line up their clothes for the entire week; this minimizes the "Where's my other Nike?" and "Where'd you put my belt?" last-minute disorder and confusion in the mornings.

Learn to Say "No." Keeping a clear sense of priorities helps couples make decisions that are in the best interest of their marriage, children, families, and careers. Successful couples don't allow the pace of their lives to dictate their schedules—their schedules dictate the pace. As one husband noted, "I view it as my choice. I have control over what I'm going to do. Rather than, 'This schedule is driving me crazy this week!' I remind myself, 'If it's crazy, then I need to make some other choices—I need to say no.'" Couples who balance family life and work well also note the importance of consistent and frequent communication so they can stay on top of their priorities and always keep the big picture in mind; this keeps them from getting off track by focusing on things that aren't important.

Value Time. Couples realize that their time together and time with their families is a valuable commodity and a resource to be spent with great care. They are protective of their family time and seldom allow others or other things to get in the way of the time they've carved out for each other. They carefully determine how their time will be best utilized. Couples also find ways to do things together, such as learning to play golf, so that when their kids are grown they have shared interests.

All too often, families struggle with work/family balance, and frequently these difficulties can begin to erode the couple's relationship. These adaptive strategies, individualized to each family's needs, can significantly help couples' abilities to become active participants in creating a successful balance of family and work. The government has also created family policies that help undergird working families.

POLICIES FOR WORKING FAMILIES

Recall from Chapter 1 that of particular interest to Bronfenbrenner were the social forces that have impact on people and their families, such as being able to afford adequate housing, access to affordable health care and quality child care, access to quality education, being able to work, or living in or above poverty. Broadly speaking, *family policy* refers to governmental goals and/or programs that seek to support and strengthen families. These programs focus on current social factors that often face contemporary families, such as work, health, education, or the community. Family policies address, for example,

- School readiness and literacy
- After-school programs aimed at keeping children safe
- Parenting and childrearing
- Child care
- Care of the elderly
- Substance abuse/use awareness programs geared toward youth
- Equal housing opportunities

The Government's Role

Today, federal, state, and local agencies promote social policies that relate to families and communities. The mission of these agencies is to create and distribute research-based educational programs and policies that support families. Centers for family policy are especially crucial today because more and more frequently the welfare and the care of families is moving from the federal to the state level. Thus, family policies seek to strengthen families through research, education, and civic involvement. In the section that follows, we examine social forces that affect today's working families and the family policies that exist to offer assistance: poverty, health/health care, and social welfare.

Poverty

What does it mean to be poor or to live in poverty? Defining poverty is difficult because it is a complex social issue and because there are different degrees of poverty. Nevertheless, knowing about poverty in the United States is important, for those affected by poverty are at risk for hunger, disease, and increased mortality rates. Additionally, poverty among children is associated with lower cognitive abilities and difficulty in school, impaired health and development, and other risks such as increased exposure to environmental toxins, poor nutrition, parental substance abuse, and trauma/abuse (Webster & Bishaw, 2007).

The **poverty rate** reflects the percentage of people with incomes below the federal government's published **poverty line**. The poverty lines are issued each year by the United States Department of Health and Human Services (HHS). The poverty line varies by the number of people in a given household; Table 12.4 presents for us the poverty lines in 2019. It is necessary to be knowledgeable of poverty trends because these are an indicator of a nation's well-being and, in large part, shape many governmental policies. Figure 12.7 shows us

Poverty rate: the percentage of people with incomes below the published poverty line.

Poverty line: the estimated minimum income necessary for a family to meet basic needs, such as food, shelter, clothing, and other essentials.

Table 12.4 /// 2019 Poverty Guidelines for the United States	
Persons in family/household	Poverty guideline
1	$12,490
2	$16,910
3	$21,330
4	$25,750
5	$30,170
6	$34,590
7	$39,010
8	$43,430

Source: U.S. Department of Health & Human Services (2019).

Figure 12.7 /// Children in Poverty, by Race: 2018

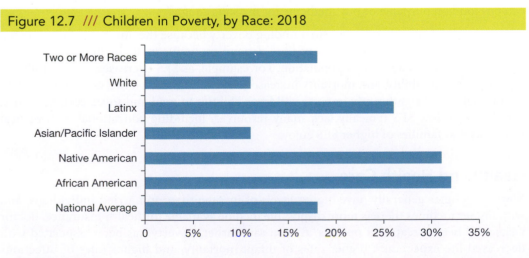

Source: Kids Count (2019).

The outbreak of the COVID-19 virus in 2020 caused widespread, devastating job losses for nearly 45 percent of Americans. Among lower income families, more than one-half suffered job loss and economic hardship. More people were unemployed than during the Great Depression. It is unknown how or whether these families can recover from this blow.

percentages of children who live in poverty and household poverty rates for different racial/ethnic groups in the United States. When comparing poverty rates by race and ethnicity, African Americans and Native Americans/Alaska Natives had the highest percentage of poverty (33 percent) across all ethnic groups, whereas whites had the lowest poverty rates (11 percent). As you have seen in our study so far, female-headed households are particularly vulnerable to poverty—the high rate of female headship among American Indian/Alaskan Native, Hispanic, and African American/Black Caribbean families is the reason so many children and youth in this country are poor. Roughly 18 percent of America's children live in poverty (Kids Count, 2019).

Working poor:

people who are working but who continue to remain below the poverty threshold for their family size.

The term **working poor** refers to people who are working but who continue to remain below the poverty line for their family size. High gas prices, food prices, and health care costs often require the working poor to choose between using their income for food or for paying bills, such as their mortgage or rent. As a young married student of mine noted, "Every month is a struggle to make ends meet. I often skip meals for myself or skip taking my medicine so I can put food on our table or buy medicine for my son's cough."

We need to know about the issues surrounding poverty because the numbers of those living in poverty—and, thus, their quality of life—depend on how equally or unequally income is distributed across a society's population. For example, as SES decreases, physical illness, mental illness, disability, and mortality increase (Hayen, Lincoln, Moore, & Thomas, 2002). Additionally, SES significantly impacts children's abilities to read and to succeed in school. Families with low SES typically lack many resources, including educational and medical resources that families of higher SES enjoy.

Health and Health Care

Married couples generally have higher levels of income than unmarried individuals, and with higher incomes there is more disposable income available for health insurance, doctor visits, and better treatment options. As you saw earlier, poverty has been associated with decreased life expectancy, higher rates of infant mortality, and higher rates of infectious diseases, disability, and mortality. These afflictions can be caused by some combination of factors, including the inability to afford doctor visits or necessary medical treatment and working at jobs that expose individuals to environmental risks and physical danger.

As of 2019, 13.7 percent of U.S. adults aged 18 to 64 were without health insurance (Gallup National Health and Well-Being Index, 2019). In addition, about 40 percent of Americans reported skipping a recommended medical test or treatment because of costs, and 44 percent said they didn't seek medical care when they were sick because they couldn't afford it (West Health Institute, 2019).

In March 2010, the comprehensive health care reform law—the Affordable Care Act (ACA)— was enacted in the United States. The law had three primary goals (HealthCare.gov, 2019):

1. Make affordable health insurance available to more people.
2. Expand the Medicaid program to cover all adults with incomes below the federal poverty level.
3. Support innovative medical care delivery methods that lower the cost of health care.

Prior to ACA legislation, nearly 20 percent of U.S. citizens were uninsured; that number decreased nearly by one-half, to 10.9 percent in 2016 (West Health Institute, 2019). In 2016, however, the new Trump administration voiced its dissatisfaction with the ACA and made a number of changes that significantly impacted Americans' abilities to participate in ACA:

- *Limited support for open enrollment in benefits* by cutting in half the time consumers had to sign up for the program
- *Eliminated cost-sharing subsidies* that reimbursed insurers for reducing their deductibles and out-of-pocket expenses
- *Gave individual states more power and control over Medicaid programs.* States can now, for example, implement work requirements for recipients.
- *Weakened the birth control mandate* by giving employers more freedom to withhold coverage for birth control for religious reasons

The primary effect of these changes? The cost of coverage for individuals has grown substantially: 7 million Americans have lost their health care insurance because of these changes (Commonwealth Fund Commission, 2018).

In contrast, there are many other industrialized nations that provide **universal health care**, or guaranteed access to medical treatment for all citizens without regard to their ability to pay. Examples include Germany and Japan, who have a higher overall health status than the United States, while they spend half as much as the United States as a percentage of gross national product (Commonwealth Fund Commission, 2018). Because there is no universal health coverage in the United States, socioeconomic status is a primary determinant of the ability to access appropriate health care and attain the highest level of health. Further, those in poverty are restricted to care provided by Medicaid (government-assisted health care), which may limit their treatment options, and those working poor who have no insurance or who are underinsured risk bankruptcy in the face of even moderate health procedures.

Universal health care: guaranteed access to quality medical treatment, for all citizens, without regard to their ability to pay.

Social Welfare

In 1964, President Lyndon B. Johnson delivered a message to Congress that became known as the War on Poverty. In this address, he acknowledged the impact of poverty on families throughout the United States. To fight poverty, President Johnson proposed federal legislation that would require federal and state resources to fund a number of social programs and social policies, all in an effort to improve the living quality of the poor. Today, these programs are often referred to as **social welfare**. By highlighting poverty and making it a national concern, numerous welfare programs were established, all of which exist today:

Social welfare: a group of government or private assistant programs designed to ensure the well-being of the nation's disadvantage groups (impoverished, ill, elderly).

- *Head Start.* This federal program focuses on educating and assisting preschool children of low-income families so they are better prepared for school.
- *Medicare.* This national health care insurance program provides medical benefits for people over the age of 65. People with certain disabilities or major health problems are also eligible for Medicare benefits, regardless of their age.
- *Medicaid.* Medicaid is a federally funded medical benefits program for those who live below the poverty level.
- *Food stamps.* Food stamps are coupons issued by the state welfare agency to low-income people or families for the purchase of certain grocery items.
- *Housing assistance.* Housing assistance is available to low- to moderate-income families to assist them in finding safe and affordable housing.

President Johnson's programs worked to reduce poverty and improve life for poor Americans. However, over time, the established welfare policies created an environment of irresponsibility, and even family pathology, in which reliance on welfare was passed from generation to generation (Bailey & Duquette, 2014). In short, fewer impoverished able-bodied people elected to work, and instead they became dependent on governmental assistance.

In 1996, President Clinton signed into law the Welfare and Medicaid Reform Act of 1996, and today needy families receive what is known as Temporary Assistance for Needy Families (TANF). Although governmental assistance is still provided to low-income families, it is limited to a maximum of five years. Today, assistance is more restrictive, requiring that heads of households work and receive job training and job education. These changes in the social welfare policy provide families the help that they need but are designed to limit assistance so the recipients become less dependent on the government.

But given the severity of the economic crisis in the United States, those at the poverty level aren't the only ones struggling to keep their heads above water. Today, a significant number of American couples are drowning in debt—and it's affecting nearly every aspect of their family and relational lives.

MARRIAGE AND MONEY

Most couples undergo some degree of financial culture shock when they begin to merge their finances. According to family financial expert Alena Johnson (2008), spending styles are directly related to financial personality styles, and these personality styles develop as a result of past experiences with money. *Was money readily available or pretty tight growing up in your home?* and *What do you like to spend money on?* and *What kinds of things have you saved money for in the past?* are just a few of the questions that help us identify whether we are a spender or a saver, a worrier about or an avoider of money issues, and a risk-inclined or risk-averse financial personality type (see also Mellan, 1994). For example, complete this sentence: If I had a lot more money, I would _____. Would you pay off your student loans? Or would you go to Vegas? In most cases, when our financial personality is not in sync with our partner's conflict occurs.

Interestingly, it is common that one partner possesses a dominant financial personality, and this personality overrides the other partner's. In some cases, the dominant partner is able to persuade the more submissive partner to become more like his or her own financial personality profile (Johnson, 2008). What often happens, though, is that the submissive partner becomes even more entrenched in his or her own financial personality style. According to Johnson, this "can create an opposite spending style." When this happens, conflict over money is sure to occur.

Johnson (2008) also asserts that financial issues are usually more of a catalyst to revealing underlying, hidden, or deeper couple issues than the actual financial problems are themselves.

In other words, couples may fight about finances, but often the financial issues are symptomatic of a couple's communication, intimacy, loyalty, or commitment problems. And often money is an emotional issue.

Money as an Emotional Issue

Whether a person is rich or poor, middle class or low income, money is intricately connected with emotion. Have you ever

- worried yourself sick over a bill you couldn't pay?
- felt fantastic because you loaned your friend in need some money to get by until payday?
- splurged on something and felt excited—until the reality of the cost hit you and then you became upset for spending that much?

There is no question that each of us has felt an array of emotions when it comes to money: The lack of it can cause stress and strain, while the abundance of money can engender feelings of security and opportunity (Dyk, 2004).

People spend money when they are sad, happy, angry, excited, content, or depressed, and often they spend it *because* they are sad, happy, angry, excited, content, or depressed. Indeed, the media are very aware of the close connection between emotion and spending money, and millions of dollars are spent each year to exploit this connection. Their attempts to speak to who we are or who we would like to be, to get us to interact emotionally with their promotional advertisements, and to eventually convince us to purchase their products are their primary goals. For example, think about the latest movie you went to see, the last restaurant you ate at, or the newest technology toy you purchased. Can you pinpoint where you learned about it, what caused you to identify with it, and why you eventually chose to purchase it?

Many of us indulge in spending (or as I refer to it, *retail therapy)* to cope with stress, cure the blues, diffuse feelings of anger or frustration, ease boredom, or soothe ourselves after a bad day. Although an occasional little pick-me-up is probably therapeutic to some extent, it's important not to underestimate how these impulsive purchases can create or perpetuate financial problems. Unfortunately, our emotional connection with money can lead to unmanageable debt.

Dealing With Debt

Household debt is at an all-time high. In 2018, consumer debt (credit card debt, student loans, and auto loans) reached $14 trillion—almost double the rate from 2004. Collectively, Americans owe more than one-fourth of their monthly income to debt, and they spend 10 percent of their monthly income on car loans, credit card debt, and student loans (Statista, 2019).

Debt is a significant topic when discussing families and work; money problems and economic hardship can lead to financial ruin, bankruptcy, the breakup of relationships, and eventual divorce. Today, nearly 45 percent of Americans carry credit card debt, and more than two-thirds owe on installment loans (such as auto loans; Statista, 2019). Two previous studies revealed that couples cited financial and economic problems as the fifth and sixth leading causes of their divorces (Johnson, Backlund, Sorlie, & Loveless, 2000; Schramm, Marshall, Harris, & George, 2003). A recent study also found that financial matters significantly affect overall marital satisfaction and quality of life (for a complete review, see Baisden, Fox, & Bartholomae, 2018).

Among newlyweds' top relationship concerns were debt brought into marriage and financial decision making (Schramm, Marshall, Harris, & Lee, 2005). Another study of newly married couples found that consumer debt greatly inhibited these couples' attempts to form their new family system (Dew, 2008). Because of their high debt, couples have difficulty finding time together because they work longer hours in attempts to pay down their debt.

These findings are important to our understanding of family life and work. They provide insight for family practitioners who work with premarital couples, such as those who provide premarital education; through educational programs, these practitioners can sensitize couples to debt issues prior to their marriages. If couples learn about debt prior to marriage,

- They may decide to postpone their wedding until their debt is paid down or is paid off.
- They may decide to marry, but with the understanding that paying off their debt will yield higher levels of relationship satisfaction.
- They may decide not to acquire credit cards and incur debt because they know that such debt creates declines in marital happiness.
- They are better able to construct effective plans to pay down their debt and to minimize conflict while doing so. (Dew, 2008)

Of course, beyond learning about debt and its consequences, couples should take efforts to learn about financial management strategies, such as learning how to budget so that debt isn't a necessary way of life (Dew, 2008). Understanding money and its significance to married life is perhaps one of the ways in which young couples can best prepare for marriage.

Saving for the future also takes discipline and planning. There are several principles that people intent on saving might want to consider:

1. Is this expenditure really necessary? (Or is it possible to get the same personal effect without using money or using less of it?)
2. Is this expenditure contributing to my wealth or taking from it?
3. Is this an impulse purchase or a planned purchase?
4. Am I being pressured to make an expenditure I'm not certain about? (Evans, 2004)

All couples need to talk about money and its significance to their relationships. The best time to talk about it is all the time! Topics such as acquiring and managing debt, goal setting, distinguishing between wants and needs, and establishing and maintaining a monthly budget are just a few of the issues couples should address on a regular basis. How healthy are your money matters?

FAMILY LIFE EDUCATION: UNDERSTANDING AND ASSISTING FAMILIES' DECISIONS

A key role of the family life educator or family scientist is to assist and aid families as they make decisions about allocating their resources to meet individual family members' and family goals (National Council on Family Relations, 2020). All too often, though, when people think of "resources," they think in terms of money, income, or personal assets—and neglect to consider the human side of resources, such as personal, familial, professional, and community resources. *All* of these are important to help individuals, couples, and families to navigate the complexities of making ends meet.

Today, balancing the demands of work and family life is a challenging—but necessary—task for a significant number of American families. In this chapter, we spent some time looking at the differences in work experiences among various racial and ethnic groups, as well as the differing configurations (such as married or single parents) of working families. Although a number of trends were presented, it's important to have an understanding of these trends because they give us a real picture of what's happening in our economic lives today, what a lot of families are up against, and what their day-to-day struggles are. Given the interrelated nature of family living, it's easy to see how what goes on at work can significantly impact a family's well-being, functioning, and overall health.

Taking Sides

Is Love Enough to Overcome Financial Incompatibility?

Republican and Democrat. Dog lover and cat lover. Mountains and beach. Catholic and Muslim. A lot of people with opposite likes and beliefs are happy and content in their relationships. But can couples with polar opposite financial habits merge their spending and find a way to make it all work? Can love overcome financial incompatibility?

One Side: Okay, here's the deal, the way I look at things. My parents are an upper-class family, and I admit I've been a bit spoiled my whole life. I had the privilege of going to private schools, I graduated from college without any student loan debt, and my parents bought me a car for my college graduation gift. I got my first credit card when I was in high school, and I admit that they have always paid the balance for me every month. I guess I'm not that worried about when we get married because, first of all, it's not like she or her parents are going to help with the wedding or anything—yes, it's going to be lavish, but my parents are paying for it, so we won't have any debt from that. Also, my parents have said that they'll always be there to help us, so I'm not even worried about when we get married—money has never been anything to me, and I think that's the way things will continue after we get married.

The Other Side: I grew up on a farm in a rural area. Money was always tight. Always. We never went without, but I never remember a time when my mom bought name brands at the grocery store—she always bought the generic brands to save money, and for as long as I can remember, she clipped coupons out of the newspaper to help "find pennies" wherever she could. I'm worried because I don't think my fiancée has a realistic picture of what finances and household expenses really are. . . . To her, when she spends, it's like spending Monopoly money because she's never had to earn it or even touch it! It always just appears in her bank account, like it's magic or something. I've tried to talk to her about it; I want us to both be aware of our spending beliefs and styles. I *want* to have a financial plan in place before we're married. I *want* each of us to have a good understanding of personal finance. I *want* to establish a realistic spending plan. But I don't think it's possible. I love her to death, but I'm wondering if there's such a thing as financial incompatibility? Will it always be *the* issue we're struggling with in our marriage? I don't earn what her dad does—and I don't think I'll ever make that kind of money.

Your Side: Good communication is the key to any lasting relationship, and communicating about money is no exception. Given this couple's differences in their experiences with money,

1. Do you believe that compatibility in this area is too important to ignore?

2. If you were friends with this couple, or if you were working with them as their financial planner, how would you best advise them? Would you suggest they have joint bank accounts and credit cards or separate ones? Why?

3. Will their marriage work? Why or why not?

Managing complex, multifaceted work/family roles is also a reality for many Americans today. There are a number of ways in which families can ease the stress and strain associated with work, such as keeping their families a priority, managing time more effectively, and carving out time for one another. But today it's just as important to have realistic expectations about trying to balance work and family life. There will be times when things won't get done around the house—the carpet will be in desperate need of vacuuming, children will be able to drive their Hot Wheels cars through the dust on the furniture and become excited about the "road" they created, and sometimes it will just be easier to put dirty dishes in the dishwasher with the clean ones, and wash them all—again. There will be times when couples yell and fight and scream at one another because they're so overworked and overwhelmed, and they're just plain tired. That's the reality of balancing work and family. Much like a circus act when the performer is trying to keep a number of plates spinning in the air at the same time, sometimes in work and family life we can't keep all the plates going. And certainly today, money constraints due to the economic crisis make matters worse—as the man noted in the opening vignette of this chapter, money seems to be at the base of all of his worries and anxieties.

Can combining work and family really work today? We learned a number of strategies that families who effectively balance the two employ. But above all, it's necessary to keep in mind that we can't possibly control everything. If families keep a sense of humor about the neglected housework, if they're willing to revise plans and schedules as necessary to accommodate everyone's needs, and if they communicate often, they can minimize the stressors associated with work and family. Learning to let go of things that won't really matter in the long run is fairly easy to do. When confronted with work/family stressors, ask yourself: Is this going to make a difference in five years? If not, let it go and focus on the things that *will* make a difference a few years from now.

/// SUMMARY

Working Families: The Transformation of American Homes

- An important measure of family health and well-being is economic stability and the ability of families to meet their daily needs. The socioeconomic status of a family is the government's measure of the family's relative economic and social ranking within a community.

- Although gender equality has been the law of the land in the United States since the passing of the Civil Rights Act, women have continued to fight against bias, prejudice, discrimination, and sexual harassment in the workplace.

- There is also a disparity among women's earnings when viewed across the ethnic spectrum.

- Dual-earner couples are defined as marriages or relationships in which both partners work. Workforce participation among couples is influenced by factors such as education level, urban living, ethnicity, unemployment, and discrimination.

- Military families must not only deal with stressors that are common to all families but they must also navigate stressors associated with separation from family members. Responding to the deleterious effects of short-notice deployment, the military has revamped their pre-deployment support programs to better prepare families for these stressors, including helping military families improve their financial planning and well-being.

- Just as each single-parent family has its own unique starting point and its own unique developmental history, each type of single-parent family has a unique demographic presence in the workforce of the United States.

Couples and Work: Just Trying to Make Ends Meet

- Economic stability is an important measure of family well-being, and research indicates that a significant number of Americans today have difficulty meeting their family's economic needs.

- The way work hours are structured throughout the week greatly influences personal and family well-being. Working overtime is an additional stressor that resonates strongly throughout all family systems.

- Job loss and financial hardship rank among the more severe stressors that families can encounter, and aside from the financial constraints it puts on a family, there are multiple negative impacts on the family's emotional and physical health.

- Some mothers opt out of the workforce and choose instead to stay at home and nurture their children. This sort of household work is often a critical component of a successful home for dual-earner couples. Additionally, a growing number of men have decided to stay at home so they can care for their children while their wives work outside the home.

The Balancing Act: Juggling Family Life and Work

- After the birth or the adoption of a child, dual-earner couples often struggle to find a way to juggle the responsibilities associated with managing the multiple roles of mother/father, employee, and wife/husband.

- This juggling act often creates stressors such as interrole conflict, time-based conflict, strain-based conflict, or behavior-based conflict. In recognition of the multiple roles with which most U.S. families must now cope, the federal government enacted the Family and Medical Leave Act.

- Dual-earner couples are vulnerable to work–family conflict, as well as work–family spillover/crossover (when a spouse brings the emotional events and tensions of one environment to the other).

- Balance is the positive psychological state we achieve through regularly meeting our own, others', and work-related needs. Family health and family cohesion is greatly influenced by how well working couples are able to find balance between the demands of work and family life.

- Although couples may marry with the intent to share household chores and childrearing, discrepancies between who does what often becomes a source of recurring conflict.

- Although the assignment of parenting duties and household chores is influenced by factors such as wage earnings and education, it often simply falls along traditional gender roles.

Policies for Working Families

- Although understanding the full scope of poverty is difficult, the effects of poverty are so profound—particularly on children—that it is important to learn all we can.

- *Family policy* refers to governmental goals and/or programs that support and strengthen families through research, education, and civic involvement that centers on current social factors that often face contemporary families, such as work, health, education, or the community.

- Because poverty and lack of insurance has such an impact on the health of a population, many industrialized nations

Marriage and Money

- A couple's spending styles are directly related to financial personality styles, and these personality styles develop through past experiences with money. If a couple's individual financial personalities are not in sync, conflict can occur.

- No matter what income level, money is intricately connected with emotion.

- Household debt is at an all-time high, and debt is a significant topic when discussing families and work, because

The majority of mothers today work at least 30 hours a week outside the home, and the burden of taking on the dual responsibilities of wage earner and housekeeper can become a source of resentment.

- Contemporary parents must weigh options regarding child care, whether it's rearranging work schedules, having extended family provide child care, or opting to use a child care center or preschool. Yet another option is shared care—a child care arrangement in which parents share a babysitter or nanny.

- Although the demands of balancing work and family can sometimes be draining on a family, research indicates that families who successfully juggle work and family obligations tend to employ similar strategies.

provide universal health care or guaranteed access to medical treatment. Because there is no universal health coverage in the United States, socioeconomic status is a primary determinant of the ability to access appropriate health care.

- To improve the living quality of the poor in the United States, numerous social welfare programs have been established, such as Head Start, Medicare, Medicaid, and Temporary Assistance for Needy Families.

money problems and economic hardship can lead to financial ruin, filing for bankruptcy, the breakup of relationships, and eventual divorce.

- Understanding money and its significance to married life is one of the ways in which young couples can best prepare for marriage, and through premarital educational programs, family practitioners attempt to teach couples about debt issues so they can better plan for the future.

/// KEY TERMS

Balance   445

Basic budgets   434

Behavior-based conflict   444

Blue-collar workers   428

Dual-earner couples   428

Family and Medical Leave Act (FMLA)   444

Family cohesion   446

Family well-being   435

Gender equality   425

Household work   441

Interrole conflict   443

Job autonomy   434

Job complexity   434

Job status   434

Market alternative cost method   441

Occupational sexism   425

Opportunity cost method   441

Pink-collar phenomenon   427

Poverty line   453

Poverty rate   453

Residual tasks   447

CHAPTER 13

UNCOUPLING: RELATIONSHIP DETERIORATION AND DIVORCE

LEARNING OBJECTIVES

13.1 List the predictors of divorce and the social and cultural influences of divorce in the United States.

13.2 Describe the processes that lead to the dissolution of a relationship or marriage.

13.3 Explain the process of legally ending a marriage.

13.4 Evaluate the ways in which couples can avoid divorce and the options available to them for help.

....

My parents were married for almost 24 years when their marriage—and our lives—seemed to start coming apart. To this day I don't know what caused their marriage to end. The change in the family's atmosphere wasn't sudden, it wasn't drastic . . . it was very gradual. But there was a change.

My dad worked for a trucking company and had long working hours. I think at some point, Mom felt like she was a single parent. I remember one argument where my mom threw some of my dad's clothes down the steps and yelled, "If all you want is a roommate instead of a wife, go back to college. Go back to your buddies!" I saw the look of hurt on Dad's face. He just turned away and walked out of the house. After that episode, their arguments became more and more frequent, and more and more volatile. It seemed as though they couldn't be in the same room without putting each other down or saying hurtful things to one another.

I remember when Mom and Dad sat us all down to tell us that they were going to get a divorce. It didn't surprise me—in some ways I felt that they had already divorced one another, but just continued to live in the same house. But the arguing didn't stop after the divorce. Instead of arguing about Dad never being home and always working, the arguments turned to who got what furniture, about money, and about who "got" us kids. Instead of arguing in the home we once shared, they argued in the driveway when Dad came to pick us up. Not too long ago my mom died from leukemia, and the most tragic part of her death is that I don't think she and Dad ever found closure. I don't think they ever found a way to put the divorce behind them and grow beyond the destruction and the hurt they caused one another—and us.

How is it that couples who once vowed to love one another until death parted them, who vowed to stick together through thick and thin, end up with such disdain for one another? With the frequently (albeit inaccurate) reported divorce rates hovering between 40 and 50 percent in the United States, it is little wonder that many people today believe that to "love and cherish" one another until they are parted by death is unrealistic and unlikely. Like any other family process, marital separation and/or divorce do not happen overnight, but happen over time, through a series of changes and transitions within the marriage relationship, as the opening vignette illustrates. Because each marital relationship has its own set of unique circumstances, there is no universal, one-size-fits-all pathway to uncoupling or to marital dissolution. Nor is there is a single cause for marital or relationship distress.

No relationship is immune to problems. This chapter offers a perspective on relationship deterioration and uncoupling, describing current divorce trends and factors that may predict the likelihood of divorce. It's important that you understand that couple type—heterosexual, gay, lesbian, cohabiting—doesn't matter. Regardless the couple formation, the uncoupling process is by and large the same. And the hurt is no less significant. We'll focus our attention on the multidimensional processes that contribute to marital breakdown and/or uncoupling. By doing this, you will gain a firm understanding of those factors that put couples most at risk to divorce. Because of the uniqueness of each couple's intimate relationships, it is impossible to say that there is a way to breakup-proof or divorce-proof relationships. But having this knowledge base certainly better equips us to recognize difficulties that lead to divorce—and to avoid them. In Chapter 14 we'll turn our attention to the outcomes of divorce, such as emotionally rebounding after a marriage ends, as well as the processes involved with rebuilding individual and family life after divorce.

UNCOUPLING

Divorce is not a new social phenomenon—its occurrence throughout history is well documented. From biblical days, when a male spouse could simply utter the words "I divorce thee" to his wife if he was dissatisfied, to today's current climate of no-fault divorce (a divorce in which neither spouse is legally required to blame the other for the breakdown of the marriage), **divorce** involves socially and culturally sanctioned methods that legally terminate the marriage. Today, every 13 seconds there is a divorce in America (U.S. Census Bureau, 2018). There are about 9 divorces in the time it takes for a couple to recite their wedding vows (2 minutes; U.S. Census Bureau, 2018).

Divorce:
socially sanctioned actions to legally terminate marriage.

To get a sense of divorce in the United States, in the following section we will discuss the current trends in marital disruption/termination.

Today's Divorce Trends

So, what *is* the accurate picture of divorce in the United States? Determining a precise statistic for the number of annual divorces in the United States is difficult because some states, including California, Colorado, Indiana, and Louisiana, do not record these figures. The best we can do, therefore, is look at the available **raw numbers**, or the actual number of those who marry and divorce. For example, in the year 2017, slightly more than 2 million people wed while nearly 800,000 couples divorced (U.S. Census Bureau, 2018). Using these figures, it appears that about one-third—36 percent—of these marriages ended in divorce; however, this figure is inaccurate because the people who were *divorced* in that year are not necessarily the same people who were *married* in that year.

Raw numbers:
actual numbers, not derived percentages or statistics; e.g., the actual number of people who marry and divorce.

For a more accurate picture of the divorce rate, we can look at different age cohorts to see who is more likely to divorce. In general, divorce is more common among younger couples, with most divorces concentrated among individuals ages 24 to 44 years (National Health Statistics Reports, 2018). For example, the latest available data from the National Center for Health Statistics reports that the likelihood for divorce is highest for men between the ages of 20 and 24, nearly 40 percent of whom are getting divorces. This is in contrast to men aged 35 to 39, who have the lowest rate, about 6 percent. Similarly, the likelihood for divorce is highest for women aged 20 to 24, with nearly a 37 percent divorce rate; about 5 percent of women aged 35 to 39 divorce (National Health Statistics Reports, 2018).

Although using age cohorts to determine divorce rates docs not provide an entirely accurate picture of divorce rates in the United States, we can see that as the percentage of aging adults increases proportionately, the number of divorces decreases. Thus, to get a more accurate understanding of the number of those divorcing, most countries use the crude divorce rate. The **crude divorce rate** is the number of divorces that occur per 1,000 population. The crude divorce rate allows us to compare trends over time, and it takes into account the size of the population we are studying. To view the crude divorce rates in the United States since 2000, refer to Figure 13.1. This figure allows us to observe fluctuations and variations—the rise and

Crude divorce rate:
the number of divorces per 1,000 population, per year.

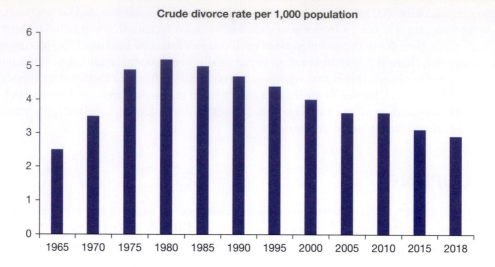

Figure 13.1 /// Crude Divorce Rates in the United States, 1965–2018

Crude divorce rate per 1,000 population

fall—in the numbers marrying and divorcing. As you can see, the divorce rate has begun to level off; currently, the divorce rate is at its lowest rate since 1975 (before the no-fault divorce legislation) and is approaching the divorce rate in 1965.

Predictors of Divorce: Are Some Couples More Prone to Divorce Than Others?

Correlates of divorce:
social and socioeconomic characteristics that affect the longevity of a marriage and the probability that a marriage will end in divorce.

In Chapter 3 we learned about the different premarital and marital couple types (identified by Drs. John and Julie Gottman through their marital stability research) who may be prone to divorce. But although decades of empirical research have yet to isolate and determine precisely who will divorce and who will not, scientific study has identified **correlates of divorce**—certain social and socioeconomic characteristics that affect the longevity of a marriage and the probability that a marriage will end in divorce. These characteristics do not *cause* divorce, but their presence has been found to *strongly correlate* with those who do divorce.

Researchers have found that an individual's social and demographic characteristics, as well as certain lifecourse circumstances at the time of marriage are significant predictors of divorce; these make some couples more prone to divorce than others. These predictors include the couple's age, premarital pregnancy, parental separation, whether or not the couple cohabits before marriage, religiosity of the couple, and the socioeconomic background of the couple.

Age at Marriage

The age of the partners when they marry has been found to be the most consistent predictor of divorce (Bramlett & Mosher, 2001; Heaton, 2002; Oropesa & Landale, 2004; Raley & Bumpass, 2003). For instance, research has revealed that nearly one-half (48 percent) of those who marry before age 18 divorce (U.S. Census Bureau, 2018). Furthermore, 60 percent of those who marry between the ages of 20 and 25 will end in divorce. Men who are at least five years older or five years younger than their spouses are also more likely to divorce (Heaton, Albrecht, & Martin, 1985; Heaton, 2002; National Health Statistics Reports, 2018; U.S. Census Bureau, 2018). In comparison, only about one-fourth of those who get married after the age of 25 get divorced (Heaton, 2002; National Health Statistics Reports, 2018; U.S. Census Bureau, 2018).

What's the ideal age to get married? The relationship between age at marriage and divorce are correlated—the older you are, the lower your chances are to divorce.

For teenagers in particular, it appears that lack of marital preparation, poor marital role performance, and lack of life coping skills contribute to marital breakup (Amalo & Previti, 2004; Booth & Edwards, 1985; Hetherington, 2003). Emotional immaturity may also contribute to increased divorce rates among teens. Referred to as the **maturity effect**, young teenagers often have unrealistic expectations about marriage, and they are also more likely than those in their 20s to misjudge their mate's qualities and characteristics (Lehrer, 2006). Additionally, research that examined divorce among whites, African Americans, and Hispanic women found that marrying in the teens is a **destabilizing effect**, or a factor/factors that disrupts the stability of a marital relationship (Phillips & Sweeney, 2005).

Maturity effect: the higher likelihood of teenagers to have unrealistic expectations about marriage and to misjudge their mate's qualities and characteristics.

Destabilizing effect: a factor that disrupts the stability of a marital relationship; these are individual to each couple.

Premarital Pregnancy

The correlation between premarital childbearing and subsequent marital dissolution has long been established. Historically, those who experience premarital pregnancy or premarital childbearing (either as an unmarried teenager or young adult, or as a cohabiting couple) had greater incidences of marital dissolution than those who do not have children prior to marriage, both in the United States and nations abroad (Heaton, 2002; Teachman, 2002; Phillips & Sweeney, 2005). These findings suggested that the timing of childbearing had a significant influence on marital stability; today other data suggest that a premarital pregnancy or birth increased the likelihood of divorce by as much as 24 percent (U.S. Census Bureau, 2018). However, this trend may be reversing.

Kelly Musick is a professor and member of the Council on Contemporary Families, which is a nonprofit, nonpartisan organization that provides the American public with the latest research concerning U.S. families and best family living practices. Dr. Musick and her colleagues analyzed data collected by the National Survey of Family Growth (NSFT); they examined the 2,656 married and cohabiting study participants' responses to survey questions. In looking at data gathered from cohabiting couples who had their first child between 1985 and 1995, they found what research at that time suggested—those who had a child outside of marriage were more likely to divorce than the second group (Council on Contemporary Families, 2015). In the first group, those who lived together and had a baby before they married were more than 60 percent more likely to divorce than those couples who married and then had children. The researchers then examined survey responses of those cohabiting couples who had a child between 1997 and 2010 and found that they were far less likely to file for a divorce than those couples in the first group (those cohabiting between 1987 and 1995). Even though the two groups were similar (both groups were cohabiters, both had children before marriage) why is it that the latter group experienced lower divorce rates than the first group? Perhaps it's a change in our social attitudes and expectations. Dr. Musick provides us with insight when she observes,

> There is less social pressure now to marry [before having children]. Couples are establishing their relationships and maybe considering marriage, but not worrying to much about marriage before starting a family. Living together has become a common part of the family landscape in the U.S., and many advanced industrialized countries. There is less pressure nowadays to marry and more leeway in how to organize family living. (Council on Contemporary Families, 2015)

In short, Musick and her colleagues believe that there are three interacting social forces that have led to the reduction in the divorce rate among those who experience pre-marital pregnancies:

- A shift in attitudes toward various couple, family, and interpersonal relationship structures
- Socioeconomic factors, such as increasing higher education levels among those who cohabit
- The declining importance of marriage being essential to parenthood

In essence, the research indicates that today, relationship success depends more on economic stability. Musick concludes, "Marriage is less a silver bullet than it is an outcome of a whole set of factors linked to stability and security that help parents stay together" (Council on Contemporary Families, 2015).

Parental Separation

Research has demonstrated that those who experience the end of their parents' marriage are more likely to divorce than those whose parents do not divorce (among many others, Hetherington, 2003; Kapinus, 2004, 2005). Many social scientists refer to this phenomenon as **intergenerational transmission** of divorce. The **socialization hypothesis** further explains this by putting forward the notion that because children of divorce have less experience with successful marital role models, their inability to adequately cope with the difficulties of marital living puts them at greater risk for divorce (Amato, 1996; Amato & DeBoer, 2001; Teachman, 2002). Other researchers suggest that divorce is a learned behavior in that the experience of parental divorce may reduce an individual's expectations for the longevity of his or her relationship or perhaps promote acceptance of marital dissolution (Axinn & Thornton, 1996; Thornton, 1991).

Because children and adolescents spend a great deal of time casually observing their parents' marriage, it is understandable their attitudes about marriage can be shaped by these experiences. For instance, in a study of more than 400 children who experienced the divorce of their parents, the researcher found that girls tend to adopt more pro-divorce attitudes than boys do (Kapinus, 2004). Another study by the same investigator revealed that young adults who feel that their parents should divorce appear to hold more positive views of divorce (Kapinus, 2005). These studies help lend insight into how parents' marital quality facilitates the intergenerational transmission of attitudes.

Premarital Cohabitation

We discussed premarital cohabitation at length in Chapter 7, and we learned about the ways in which breaking up psychologically impacts cohabiters. Here, we examine cohabitation as a predictor of divorce.

Intergenerational transmission:

research suggests that those who experience the end of their parents' marriage are more likely to divorce than those whose parents do not divorce. Many social scientists refer to this phenomenon as *intergenerational transmission of divorce*.

Socialization hypothesis:

the hypothesis that because children of divorce have less experience with successful marital role models, they are less able to cope with their own marital difficulties and are thus at greater risk for divorce.

Happily ever after? Unfortunately, those who cohabit before marriage experience lower relationship satisfaction and quality.

Today many couples view cohabitation as a trial marriage of sorts. Does this mean that couples who live together before marriage are less likely to divorce? The short answer is *no*. Despite the fact that premarital cohabitation allows the couple to rehearse marital roles, these couples divorce *more frequently* than those who do not live together before marriage (Heaton 2002; Perelli-Harris et al., 2018; Rosenfeld & Roesler, 2018). In fact, in the United States, just over 50 percent of cohabiting relationships dissolve within five years, and cohabitation is not a stable family type (Andersson, Thomson, & Duntava, 2017; Milan, 2000; Musick and Michelmore, 2016; Perelli-Harris et al., 2018). Researchers have repeated similar findings in other developed countries such as Australia, Britain, Canada, Germany, and Sweden, where it's been found that cohabiters are more likely to dissolve the unions than are married couples (for a review, see Galezewska, 2016). In general, cohabitation is linked to lower relationship quality (Wiik, Keizer, & Lappegård, 2012). One new body of research found that cohabiting before marriage *does* help couples better navigate the transition to marriage and reduce the risk of divorce, but only in the short-term (very early on in the marriage, in the first year); after the first year, there appear to be no benefits to cohabitation and its effect on marital stability (Rosenfeld & Roesler, 2018).

Researchers attribute the high risk of divorce among couples who cohabit before marriage to lesser commitment—although about 90 percent of cohabiters plan to marry, only about 50 percent actually do (Rosenfeld & Roesler, 2018; U.S. Census Bureau, 2018). Furthermore, cohabiters have higher levels of marital expectations (Rosenfeld & Roesler, 2018). Because living together prior to marriage is thought to be a trial marriage and a time to work out differences, cohabiters have higher expectations of relationship quality when they actually marry.

Religiosity

Religion and religiosity are other relevant factors in predicting who is most at risk to divorce. **Religiosity** refers to the religious beliefs a couple holds. Those couples who do not have a religious preference or who do not hold strong religious beliefs have higher divorce rates than those couples who do. Figure 13.2 shows us the marital status of those who adhere to different religions. As you can see, for all religious groups, the divorce rate is less than 15 percent (Pew Research Center, 2018).

Religiosity: an individual's preference for religious expression.

Figure 13.2 /// Religiosity and Marital Status, 2018

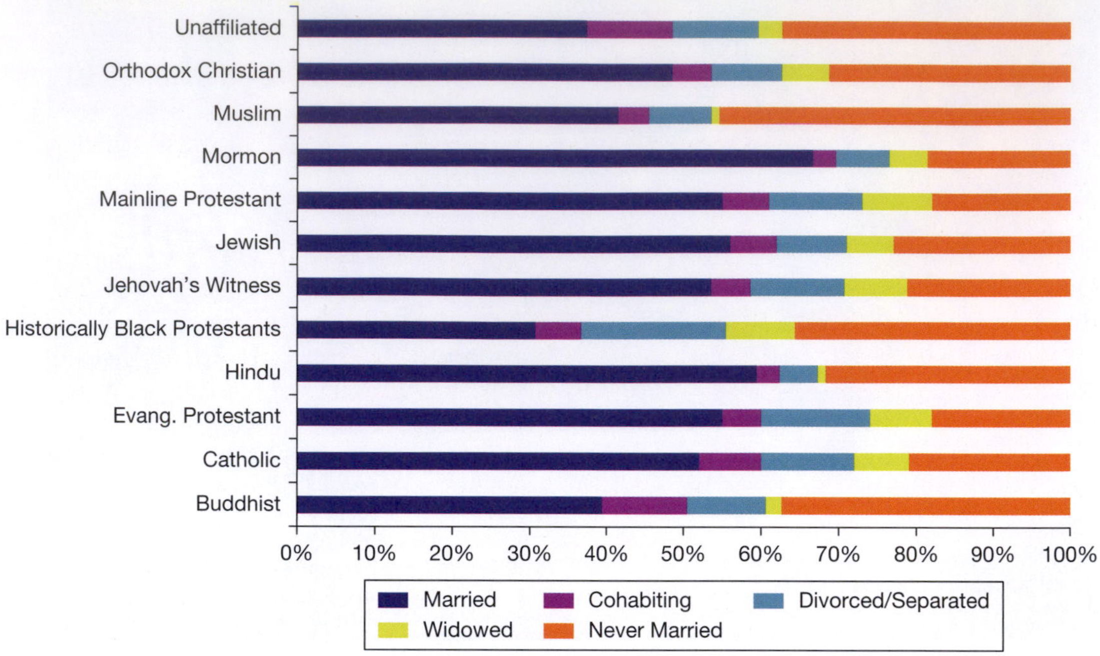

Source: Pew Research Center (2018).

A number of researchers in the United States have found that spouses who share religiosity in their marriage have higher levels of marital happiness and are at a lower risk for divorce (among many, Treas & Giesen, 2000; Brown, Orbuch, & Bauermeister, 2008). In one study that examined religious beliefs and marital stability among white and African American couples in the United States, the researchers discovered that, although Blacks were more likely than whites to have lower incomes, longer periods of cohabitation prior to marriage, more premarital births, and divorced parents (all predictors of divorce), religiosity was predictive of marital stability (Brown et al., 2008). Also, the more frequently Black and white wives attended religious services, the less likely the couple was to divorce.

Socioeconomic Background

Substantial bodies of empirical evidence suggest that the risk of divorce is much greater among those from lower socioeconomic backgrounds and among those with lower levels of educational attainment (Greenstein, 1995; South, 1995; Teachman & Polonko, 1990; White & Rogers, 2000). This may be because those from lower socioeconomic backgrounds are more likely to marry at young ages (Kiernan, 1986). As we learned in the previous chapter, there are a significant number of stressors associated with household finances; thus, increased rates of divorce among those from lower SES backgrounds may also be due to the difficulties associated with living from paycheck to paycheck (White, 1991).

Social and Cultural Causes of Divorce

The reasons couples cite for divorce are many: abuse, financial difficulties, sex and sexuality difficulties, alcohol or other substance use or abuse, heightened conflict, one or both spouses feeling that their needs have not been met or fulfilled by the other spouse, adultery, "falling out of love," and irreconcilable differences. Gathering information describing precise reasons couples dissolve their marriages is difficult because these data are not collected from state to state.

According to sociologist Anne-Marie Ambert (2005), the reasons for marital discontentment that may eventually result in marital dissolution are culture specific. Ambert suggests that a couple's social and cultural backgrounds provide a framework for the dissolution of marriage. For example, in cultures where there is an emphasis on individualism and individual gratification, such as in Western, individualistic societies, couples divorce because they are unhappy, "fall out of love," have sexual problems or communication problems, or have what they perceive as irreconcilable differences. On the other hand, in collectivist societies, where marriage is thought necessary to promote the well-being of the community, divorce on the basis of unhappiness would be considered thoughtless and trivial.

Still, the *reasons* people divorce are not the same as the *causes* of divorce. According to Ambert (2005), a number of interrelated cultural factors have contributed to the rise of divorce in the United States and other Western countries. For example, as the significance of religion in Western cultures lessened throughout the 19th century, divorce rates began to slowly rise. Ambert contends that because religion is increasingly absent in the institution of marriage, marriage has undergone a shift from a covenant (formal religious or spiritual) union to a union of individual choice. This desacralization of marriage has been a significant factor in Western societies' accepting a temporary nature of marriage, as opposed to a "'til death do us part" concept of marriage.

Covenant:
a religious or spiritual agreement.

Desacralization of marriage:
the societal shift from marriage as a binding religious union to a union of individual choice.

The sociocultural trends of the desacralization of marriage have led to more liberal divorce laws, such as the no-fault divorce laws in the 1970s. Since that time, divorce rates have increased and remain relatively high; since these laws were passed, many couples tend to view the institution of marriage with less significance and turn to divorce as an easy way out of a troubled relationship. Ambert (2005) maintains that divorce legislation perpetuates a "normalization" of divorce in society, making it socially and culturally accepted.

As we discussed in our study of dating and mate selection in Chapter 7, Western cultures have become increasingly individualistic over the past two centuries. As a result, the institution of marriage emphasizes *individuals'* needs and wants rather than the *mutual* responsibilities of each partner in the marital relationship. According to Ambert (2005), marriage is based on rights rather than duties. This emphasis on individual fulfillment increases demands on the marriage.

Sociologist Frank Furstenberg (1994) agrees with Ambert (2005) when he notes that divorce patterns in the United States and other Western societies are directly related to the high value that Americans place on autonomy and independence, rather than on commitment to family. Although many couples manage to maintain mutual respect while satisfying individual needs, that mutual support is sometimes sacrificed for individual fulfillment. Simons and his colleagues (1996) note, "If the reason for marriage is mutual love and support, it is difficult for people to justify staying in a relationship where this is no longer present" (p. 219).

Because of the trends toward the secularization of marriage and the subsequent changes in divorce legislation, along with the increase of individualism, Western cultures have developed lower levels of tolerance when marriages do not meet individual expectations for fulfillment, contentment, happiness, and companionship. Ambert (2005) concludes that because couples today expect more from their partners and are unwilling to tolerate mutual sacrifices and challenges that accompany marital life, these unrealistic expectations contribute to the sociocultural factors that have given rise to divorce rates over the past half century.

One body of research sheds additional light on the role of cultural forces on divorce trends. These very powerful and complex forces are interrelated and include the following (Fine & Fine, 1994):

- Changes in popular opinion concerning divorce
- Lawmakers' desires to make divorce laws more consistent with the behaviors of those seeking divorce (such as, did the spouse really have an affair, or was this story fabricated in order to facilitate divorce?)

Sometimes the day-to-day pile-up of stressors, such as those associated with coursework when the couple is in college, can take its toll on marital satisfaction.

- Changes in the acceptance of divorce among religious denominations
- Recognition of the impact of special groups, such as fathers' rights and women's rights
- Desire among helping professionals (therapists, counselors, pastors, priests, social workers, family life educators) to make the processes of divorce less harmful and adversarial

As the divorce rate reaches new historic lows, today more Americans than ever before believe that divorce is morally acceptable; 73 percent of Americans polled say that divorce is morally acceptable today, up 14 percent since 2001 (Gallup, 2017). Table 13.1 presents for us peoples' attitudes about the moral acceptability of divorce, by their marital status. As you can see, across all categories, divorce acceptance has grown in U.S. culture (Gallup, 2017).

Although the research identifies many reasons people seek divorce, it is more difficult to specify which reasons best reflect current divorce trends. Are the trends seen in divorce over the past 50 years or so due to changes in Western cultural values, as Ambert (2005) asserts? Or do the trends relate to changes in divorce laws, such as the no-fault divorce legislation of the 1970s? It is difficult to determine whether the changes seen in divorce trends are due to legislative efforts that drive the changes in cultural values or whether the cultural values push changes in divorce laws.

Table 13.1 /// Moral Acceptability of Divorce, by Marital Status				
Marital Status	2001–2001	2005–2009	2010–2014	2015–2017
	%	%	%	%
Married	60	62	66	70
Never married (Includes cohabitation)	70	76	73	76
Divorced/Separated	73	72	73	73

Source: Gallup (2017).

Whatever the role of cultural forces, the no-fault divorce legislation "clearly contributed to changed perceptions of marriage and divorce. As opposed to the belief that marriage is a life-time commitment that involves continuing responsibilities of each spouse to the other, the perception that marriage is a contract between equals that can be terminated at will by one spouse has become increasingly popular" (Fine & Fine, 1994, p. 261).

Racial and Ethnic Differences in Divorce

Are there racial and ethnic differences that make some couples more prone to divorce than others? African American couples are 1.5 to 2 times as likely to end their marriages than whites and Hispanics are; they also experience less marital stability (29 percent) than do whites (54 percent; Raley, Durden, & Wildsmith, 2004; Sweeney & Phillips, 2004; Bulanda & Brown, 2007; Raley, Sweeney, & Wondra, 2015). But what accounts for this trend?

To better understand the racial and ethnic differences in the experiences of divorce, we first need to re-visit the concept of intersectionality, introduced in Chapter 4. As you'll recall, *intersectionality* refers to the various interlocking strata—class, race, ethnicity, age, gender, social orientation—and how these differences intersect to create oppression and inequality in society (Crenshaw, 1989). In this case, we need to consider how socio-economic class, race, ethnicity, and gender intersect and how these intersections create oppression for some and privilege for others. Our study so far has shown us that there are racial and ethnic differences in the formation of couples and marital relationships, as well as childbearing experiences. We've also come to know that these differences are, in large part, due to the cultural shift in attitudes about family formation (Raley et al., 2015). So, as we move forward in our discussion here, it's important to keep at the forefront what we know about the correlates, or *predictors*, of divorce: premarital pregnancy, age at marriage, parental separation/divorce, premarital cohabitation, and socioeconomic forces. When we consider all of these factors together, and *interlock* them with race and ethnicity, we can begin to get a clear understanding as to why some races and ethnicities divorce more than others.

When trying to determine what puts some couples at greater risk to divorce than others, researchers have distinguished between *structural* factors and *cultural* factors.

Structural Factors

Structural factors refer to the family's finances and its economic status; understandably, these factors are integral to the formation and maintenance of marriages and all types of other intimate relationships (Bulanda & Brown, 2007). For example, researchers have attributed poor marital quality/satisfaction (and thus, higher divorce rates) among couples to economic stability, which includes such things as employment, annual income, and educational attainment (Trent & South, 2003). Additionally, many men believe that they are not ready for marriage until they have established financial independence and stability (Smock, 2004).

Structural factors: a family's finances and economic status; these factors are integral to the formation and maintenance of marriages and other intimate relationships.

Today, the economic disadvantages and financial burdens faced by Hispanics and Blacks are great (Bulanda & Brown, 2007). As we saw in the previous chapter, when couples deal with economic stressors and instability, the quality and the stability of their marriages suffer (White & Rogers, 2000). Although Blacks and Hispanics have similar economic and educational disadvantages, it appears that the economic circumstances are particularly uncertain and insecure for Blacks, and that these factors are very closely tied to their marital quality. In a study that examined marital quality and divorce among 6,231 whites, Blacks, and Hispanics, the researchers discovered that, in comparison to whites, when Blacks are economically disadvantaged they exhibit lower marital happiness, lower levels of marital interaction, and higher levels of conflict; they also perceive their marriages to be more unstable than whites and Hispanics do (Bulanda & Brown, 2007). Although the economic picture for Blacks and Hispanics is bleak, and although people from lower socioeconomic backgrounds are at a

Especially among Black and Latinx couples, marital quality and stability suffer due to economic stressors associated with low incomes.

greater risk for divorce, this factor alone does not account for the divorce trends seen among these cohorts (Bulanda & Brown, 2007). Instead, it appears that certain cultural factors are more responsible than economic factors for the differences in divorce trends among African Americans and Hispanics.

Cultural Factors

Cultural factors:

in terms of divorce, this refers to whether the couple embraces an individualistic or collectivist social identity.

Cultural factors refer to whether the couple embraces an individualistic or collectivist social identity. In earlier chapters, you discovered that among all races and ethnicities, African Americans are the least likely to marry, are the mostly likely to cohabit before and instead of marriage, and are the most likely to have children outside of marriage. African American couples are also more likely to have parents who divorced than other races and ethnicities (Teachman, 2002). As you've just seen, all of these cultural factors make African American couples more divorce-prone and explain, to a large extent, why this racial group has a higher percentage of divorces than whites and Hispanics.

Interestingly, despite being more educationally and economically disadvantaged than African Americans, Hispanics tend to have relatively high levels of marital satisfaction and marital quality (Bulanda & Brown, 2007). Their economic picture does not seem to negatively impact their marriages (Raley et al., 2004; Phillips & Sweeney, 2005). Certain cultural factors appear to minimize Hispanic couples' risk of divorce.

Paradox of Mexican American nuptiality:

the phenomenon in which divorce rates among Mexican Americans are lower than among Blacks, despite the fact that Mexican Americans are more educationally and economically disadvantaged.

For instance, as our study of marriage and intimate relationships has shown, family, or *familism,* is central to the lives of Hispanics. They are also a pro-marriage culture because of their religious beliefs, and they socialize their children to value marriage and family. As we have also learned, Hispanic cultures are collectivist cultures, wherein the needs of the culture are valued over individualistic needs. The high value Hispanics place on family partly explains why divorce rates among Hispanics are lower than among Blacks, despite the fact that Hispanics are more educationally and economically disadvantaged (Umaña-Taylor & Fine, 2003). This phenomenon is referred to as the **paradox of Mexican American nuptiality**—their collectivist orientation may buffer against their disadvantaged economic situation, and help preserve their marital quality and stability (Oropesa & Gorman, 2000).

These research findings are interesting because they appear to support Ambert's (2005) belief that collectivist cultures have lower divorce rates than individualistic cultures. The Catholic religion is central in the lives of Hispanic families (Umana-Taylor & Fine, 2003), and as you have just seen, religion and religiosity also minimize divorce risk. What all of these studies tell us is that the combined cultural factors such as familism, a collectivist identity, and religiosity all work together to make these families less likely to divorce.

Recent events in the United States have put another group at greater risk to the experiences of divorce: service men and women. Prior to deployments to Iraq and Afghanistan, rates of marital dissolution were lower than the national average, around 2.1 for Army personnel, and about 3.0 among enlisted members in other branches of the military; this is in comparison to current national divorce rates of 2.9 (Teachman & Tedrow, 2008; U.S. Census Bureau, 2018). Now, the strains of deployment on service men and women are evident.

Divorce and Military Service

In the previous chapter, we discovered that military personnel today face significant stressors, many of which are related to longer and more frequent deployments than service men and women have experienced in the past. In just the last few years, the divorce rate among enlisted members has significantly increased. In 2018, the U.S. Department of Defense noted that the military divorce rates continued to climb to unprecedented rates:

- *Army:* 8.0 percent
- *Air Force:* 14.6 percent
- *Navy:* 12.5 percent
- *Marine Corps:* 8.0 percent

There are also gender differences in divorces among military personnel. In 2018, 2.6 of male service members experienced divorce, in comparison to 6.3 percent of female troops (U.S. Department of Defense, 2018). Historically, divorce rates for women serving in the military are twice that of men; marriages between civilian husbands and military wives have the highest rate of divorce (U.S. Department of Defense, 2018).

The stressors associated with family living among those who have careers in the military are many, and most of these unprecedented strains are associated with deployment to the wars overseas: Spouses are left to be single parents to children and to take care of everything at home, finances are affected, marriages are disrupted, mental health is at risk, and often households are run differently when the military member is home than when he or she is away. Reintegration after deployment is also stressful. The U.S. Department of Defense (2018) notes that families with the least successful reintegration are those who were not ready for deployment, had low communication with their partner and/or family at home while deployed, and who were not comfortable financially. Of course, those who return with combat-related injuries or are suffering the psychological impacts of military conflict do not integrate as well as those soldiers who do not have these issues to contend with.

Can anything be done to preserve and to better protect these marriages? Although it is too early to determine the effectiveness of programs, all branches of the U.S. military have established and implemented support programs to help ease the family stressors associated with deployment. The goal of each of these programs is to help families navigate the difficult transitions and situations.

Sometimes, love turns sour to the point that ending the marriage appears to be the only solution to the turmoil and the angst. In Chapter 8 we discussed many marriage stressors that may ultimately culminate in the termination of the marital relationship. Divorce, however, is not simply a matter of signing a piece of paper; it is just as multifaceted and complex as the marriage it ultimately dissolves.

A couple's relationship typically doesn't end because of one big problem. More often than not, the couple's relationship gradually deteriorates over time.

iStock.com/Martins

EMOTIONALLY ENDING THE MARRIAGE/COUPLE

Many researchers have studied the processes involved in relationship deterioration and relationship end (for example, Knapp, 1978; Phillips & Wood, 1983; Wood, 1982), but one researcher in particular put forth a model of relationship deterioration that recognizes the processes involved in ending a marital relationship.

Processes of Relationship Decline

Psychologist Steven Duck's (1982, 1984) model of relationship deterioration emphasizes both *intrapersonal dynamics,* which focus on the individual's intellectual and emotional roles in the relationship, and *interpersonal dynamics,* which focus on how spouses or relational partners interact. As you read about the process of relationship decline/deterioration, recall our discussion in Chapter 3 about how the couple and/or the family is a system of inter-related parts (members), or subsystems. When we view relationships through this lens, it doesn't matter who the "subsystems" are—Duck's model can easily be applied to opposite-sex marriages and cohabiting relationships, same-sex marriages and cohabiting relationships, or polyamorous relationships. Rather than focus on the end of a relationship as simply a process of a decline in intimacy (or the **de-escalation of intimacy**), Duck's model notes five phases of breakdown in the couple's relationship.

1. *Dyadic breakdown.* The **dyadic breakdown phase** refers to the breakdown of the couple's established relational patterns. During this first phase of decline, couples cannot identify precisely what is wrong with the relationship, yet they begin to sense that something is not right. Frequent disruptions—caused by these increased responsibilities such as childrearing and careers—in the everyday interactions between spouses eventually lead to dissatisfaction. The dissatisfaction eventually threatens the longevity of the relationship.

2. *Intrapsychic phase.* According to Duck, the second phase of relationship deterioration is the **intrapsychic phase**, or *individual cognition,* which refers to the point at which couples begin to focus on those aspects of the relationship with

De-escalation of intimacy:

a decline in intimacy.

Dyadic breakdown phase:

the period during which a couple's established pattern or relationship breaks down.

Intrapsychic phase:

according to Stephen Duck, the second phase of relationship deterioration, also called *individual cognition,* when a couple begins to focus on aspects of the relationship with which they are dissatisfied or disappointed.

which they are dissatisfied or disappointed. Importantly, these feelings of distress are *rarely* mutual. The feelings of discontent are initially experienced as nagging thoughts that ebb and flow in strength, or may begin as feelings of depression (Anderson & Sabatelli, 2011).

During this phase of decline, conflict may escalate and one or both partners may begin to blame and criticize the other. Constance Ahrons (1999), one of the nation's leading researchers in the field of divorce and remarriage, describes this as a phase in which couples "collect evidence" in order to justify leaving or ending the marriage. Duck (1992) notes similar findings when he observes that during this phase of relationship turmoil, couples adopt negative, pessimistic, or distrustful attitudes about their spouses or the marital relationship in general. He describes the attitude as one of "brooding." In the beginning, spouses may keep their brooding to themselves as they may think of possible solutions or resolutions to the problem. At some point during this phase, however, the spouses can no longer keep the brooding to themselves and they begin to talk to others about the problems they are experiencing within their marriage. Duck contends that when spouses begin to complain to others about their dissatisfaction with their marriage, it is perhaps in an effort to test the waters, to see how their friends might react if they bring up the possibility of terminating the relationship. Sadly, children are often brought into the middle of the conflict and asked to choose sides (Ahrons, 1999).

3. *Dyadic phase.* According to Duck, the **dyadic phase** occurs when couples discuss their dissatisfaction with their marriage and attempt to find either a resolution or decide to end the relationship. Not all couples enter into discussions, however. Some simply become emotionally divorced, emotionally withdrawing from one another or from their marriage (Bowen, 1978). Others may choose to remain in a marriage with high levels of conflict, distress, and dissatisfaction.

Dyadic phase:

according to Stephen Duck, the dyadic phase occurs when couples discuss their dissatisfaction with their marriage and attempt either to find a resolution or to end the relationship.

In some instances, couples may intend to work together to solve the difficulties, yet in the end, they may determine that the marriage cannot be salvaged, as in the following scenario. As the husband explains,

> For me, it began with the deaths of my wife's father, and then my father about a year apart. Confrontation with the early deaths of parents led me to evaluate my own life, In the process, old issues surfaced that had to be dealt with—in retrospect, I don't think I did a very good job at it. There was depression, increasing conflict with my wife as I withdrew more and more, and failed attempts at counseling. We tried, but nothing worked. The question still remains today—did we try hard enough? (Welch, 2004)

Sometimes, unlike the husband above, spouses never communicate their marital dissatisfaction. Duck (1984, 1992) later modified his model to acknowledge that not only do some spouses not always communicate their dissatisfactions and disappointments with one another, but many may even make arrangements to leave the relationship without discussing the decision with their spouse. Many partners simply leave the relationship because it is too difficult to openly communicate about the relationship problems (Metts, Cupach, & Bejlovec, 1989).

Social phase:

according to Stephen Duck, the public disclosure of a couple's decision to terminate the marriage.

Family metacognition:

the phase in marriage deterioration in which the spouses begin to openly share with others the problems in their marriage and the possibility that it may come to an end.

4. *Social phase.* Once a couple decides that the relationship will be terminated, they then decide, either individually or jointly, how they will disclose the news of their breakup to family and friends. According to Duck, this public announcement constitutes the **social phase** of relationship deterioration. Ahrons (1994) refers to this transition as **family metacognition**, the phase in which the spouses begin to openly share with others the problems in their marriage and the possibility that it may come to an end. This is a time of much insecurity and imbalance within

the family system, particularly for the spouse who did not initiate the divorce, as well as for the children (Lauer & Lauer, 1991; Sprenkle & Cyrus, 1983). During this time of destabilization, husbands and wives often begin to shift their roles to that of co-divorced parents and ex-spouses, even though they may not have made arrangements for one spouse to leave the family home or begin formal separation proceedings (Anderson & Sabatelli, 2011).

Eventually the news of the breakup circulates among family and friends. During this phase of relationship end, the soon-to-be-divorced partners begin to provide either their joint account or individual account of what led to the deterioration of their marriage, which, according to Duck, is rarely the absolute truth! This process is termed **account making**. At this point in the process, spouses openly criticize their partners (Duck, 1992) or disparage them to the point where family and friends often conclude that the end of the marriage is for the best (La Gapia, 1982). Once the news of the imminent divorce is made public, the final stage of relationship decline begins.

> **Account making:**
>
> the process in which couples share with family and friends their individual accounts of what led to the deterioration of their marriage.

5. *Grave dressing.* Whenever we lose someone we love, we need a proper way to say goodbye. According to Duck (1992), the "death" of a marriage is no exception. In the **grave dressing phase** of relationship end, the couple must come to terms with the breakup of the marriage. This part of the process is similar to dealing with the death of a loved one, as couples who divorce begin to piece together a rational explanation that explains why the marriage "died." According to Duck, the grave dressing extends the account making that couples engaged in during the social phase of relationship deterioration. But more importantly, grave dressing allows the dissolved couple to cope with the feelings that so often accompany divorce, such as depression, loneliness, guilt, remorse, confusion, and grief. Duck contends that the grave dressing phase completes the multifaceted process of relationship deterioration.

> **Grave dressing phase:**
>
> a divorcing couple comes to terms with the breakup of the marriage and they begin to piece together a rational, logical explanation that explains why the marriage "died."

At this point, the many facets of the breaking up or divorce process begin. As this section illustrates, relationship deterioration involves much more than a reversal or loss of intimacy in the relationship. It initially begins with one or both partners experiencing feelings of dissatisfaction or unease about something that is occurring in the marital relationship; this leads to an eventual breakdown in the interaction patterns in the marriage. The partners may discuss their difficulties and attempt to resolve their problems or move toward dissolving the marriage if they feel the marriage is beyond repair. During the final stages of relationship deterioration, couples make public among their various social networks their intent to end the marriage, and eventually grieve the loss of the relationship, giving it some sense of finality.

The Transition to Uncoupling and Divorce

Divorce seldom occurs because of a single, isolated event (such as an episode of marital infidelity), but instead involves a series of gradual transitions to relationship or marital end. According to Ahrons (1994), the decision to divorce, the announcement of the impending divorce to family and friends, and the couple's separation are the "most grueling disruptions" that occur during the transition to divorce (p. 77). She explains, "These first three turbulent transitions—the decision, the announcement, the separation—form the core of the **emotional divorce**" (p. 116). Following the decision during the intrapsychic or individual cognition phase (as discussed earlier), and the announcement during the social phase or the family metacognition phase (also discussed earlier), at some point, the couple decides to separate.

> **Emotional divorce:**
>
> emotionally withdrawing from a marriage partner or from the marriage.

"Separating" does not necessarily mean the same thing to every couple. To some, it may mean a cooling-off period; to others, it is the first step on the way to the divorce attorneys.

iStock.com/simarik

The separation period is a time of great disruption in the family system, and it is marked by much ambiguity in spousal and parental roles.

Whatever the assigned meaning, the **separation period** is a time marked by a disruption in the norms of family relationships—**normlessness**—and ambiguity, in which spousal and parental roles may become unclear. As a result, the future of the family seems uncertain. Because there are no clear-cut rules about how couples should separate, many are faced with unfamiliar, ambivalent, and conflicting feelings. The angst felt by separating couples has much to do with the type of separation they experience (Ahrons, 1994).

Separation period: a period marked by a disruption in the norms of family relationships. To some, it may mean a cooling off period; to others, it may mean the first step on the way to the divorce attorneys.

Normlessness: a disruption in the norms of family relationships.

Disorderly Separation

A disorderly separation is characterized by its abruptness and is usually not the result of careful consideration. Consider the relationship of Allison and Patrick, the parents of four grown children. On the way home from their anniversary celebration with family and friends, Patrick unexpectedly announced to his wife of 28 years that he was in love with a colleague from work and that he wanted out of the marriage—immediately. This sudden announcement set the stage for a tumultuous, turbulent, and chaotic separation. Not only did it signal a sudden halt to a long-term relationship but it also launched the family into an immediate crisis that threatened the family dynamic. Ahrons (1994) notes that abrupt departures such as these create feelings of rejection, abandonment, confusion, helplessness, uncertainty, and rage. And, unfortunately, existing coping skills are seldom sufficient to aid in navigating this new crisis.

Orderly Separation

Now consider the relationship of Shauna and Tony, the parents of three school-aged children. Over a period of about two years, Shauna became increasingly unhappy in her marriage. Although she and Tony both willingly entered marriage counseling in hopes of saving their marriage, it became obvious to both of them that their marriage could not be salvaged. Before they told their children, Shauna and Tony spent several weeks discussing how to end their marriage. As part of this process, they discussed how, what, and when they would tell their children, their family, and their friends; how, what, and when they would divide their marital property; how their roles as parents and providers would change; and how they would continue to be divorced co-parents. As Shauna notes, "Our approach to this was that we were not getting divorced *from* one another, but that we were getting divorced *to* one another. We wanted to put as much thought and planning into our separation and divorce as we did into our marriage." As Ahrons (1994) observes, even though a separation may be orderly, it is still painful. In the case of Shauna and Tony, they noted that even though the planning did not prevent devastation and emotional hurt for them and their children, it allowed them to rebound much more quickly when the actual separation and divorce took place. Ahrons concludes that despite the fact that pain is unavoidable in any instance of marital breakup, when a separation is orderly, "at least the family [makes] the active choice to heal" (p. 112).

LEGALLY ENDING THE MARRIAGE: THE FORMAL DIVORCE

Making the transition from married life to divorced life is not an easy process. We've discussed the difficulty of making the emotional transition, but the legal processes that must take place to formalize and finalize the divorce can further compound this stressful experience. Once the decision to divorce has been made, there is much to decide: child custody, community property settlement, child support, and spousal support.

Family law:

policies and regulations to protect the rights and well-being of all family members and ensure that married or divorced couples fulfill their obligations to each other and to their children. Specific family laws vary from state to state.

In the United States, **family law** establishes policies and regulations to ensure that married or divorced couples fulfill their obligations to each other and to their children. Although specific family laws vary from state to state, these laws were enacted to protect the rights and well-being of all family members. There are contractual obligations of marital parties according to family laws. These marriage laws ensure that

- Each spouse financially supports one another, as is their obligation.
- After the death of a spouse, the deceased spouse's property must be shared with his or her spouse. In most states the minimum is one-third of the estate.
- Each spouse shares equal responsibility in all debts that are incurred while married.
- State property laws are void if spouses negotiate pre- or postnuptial agreements. Pre- or postnuptial agreements are legally binding agreements between spouses regarding the distribution of assets after divorce or the death of one or both spouses. (Ventura & Reed, 1998)

Like marriage laws, family laws that govern formal separation and divorce proceedings are also intended to ensure that ex-spouses' and children's rights are protected. Although these laws do not lessen the emotional toll families endure post divorce, they do provide a framework for the legal aspects of marital dissolution.

Community Property Settlement

If couples have not discussed it prior to the legal proceedings, dividing marital property and assets—and even debt—is a daunting task, particularly so if the marriage has been long. When dividing assets and debt, a number of types of property must be negotiated:

- *Marital property.* Assets owned by both spouses or acquired jointly during the marriage
- *Separate property.* Assets owned individually, such as a piece of heirloom jewelry owned by one spouse
- *Tangible property.* Property or assets that have physical substance, such as homes, cars, boats, furniture, jewelry, and pets
- *Intangible property.* Property or assets that have no physical substance but have inherent value, such as retirement benefits, bank certificates, or stocks

Once these assets are determined, a dollar value must be assigned to each asset. Depending on the amount and value of the property, divorcing couples may be able to do this on their own (although they will require an attorney to finalize the distribution) or they may need to acquire the help of various appraisers (professional property valuators).

Each state has specific legal guidelines for dividing marital assets and debt. Family laws guiding property division take into account the following:

- *Current and future earnings.* Judges often award a larger share of marital property to the spouse who earns the least and who has the lower earnings potential.

- *Current standard of living.* Judges often distribute the marital property and assets so that neither spouse suffers a dramatic decline in the lifestyle to which he or she had become accustomed. Nevertheless, women's lifestyles are more negatively impacted than men's are.

- *Individual contributions to the marriage.* Judges consider the unique contributions each spouse has brought to the marriage, whether an economic contribution or a less tangible contribution such as being a full-time parent or managing the household chores.

- *The length of the marriage.* The longer couples are married, the more difficult it is to determine separate property.

- *Age and health.* Spouses who are older or who are in poorer mental or physical health are usually awarded a larger share of marital property than healthier spouses. (Ventura & Reed, 1998)

Other factors that come into play when determining a property settlement include whether the divorcing couple lives in an *equitable distribution* state, wherein spouses receive their fair share of the marital property ("fair share" meaning whatever the judge determines!) or in a *community property state,* where there is a strict 50/50 split. Currently, only nine states are community property states; Puerto Rico allows property to be owned as community property also. Figure 13.3 illustrates which states are equitable distribution states and which

Figure 13.3 /// Community Property and Equitable Distribution States

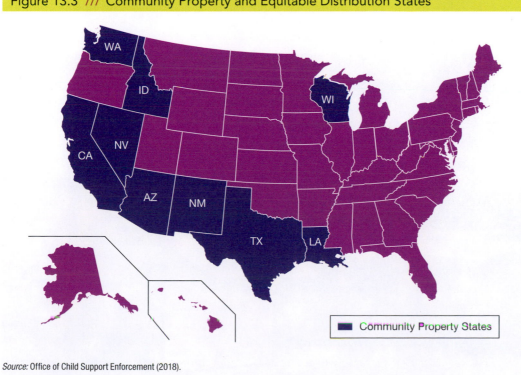

■ Community Property States

Source: Office of Child Support Enforcement (2018).

are community property states. When couples are dividing community property and trying to reach a properly settlement, they should keep in mind their personal goals and financial needs for life after divorce (Ventura & Reed, 1998).

Spousal Support

Historically, spousal support was absolutely essential. Because ex-wives were typically less educated than their husbands, had fewer employment opportunities, and had fewer job skills, women had very little means of supporting themselves and their children. To compensate, ex-husbands were responsible for paying **alimony** to their ex-spouses. Alimony, today more commonly referred to as **spousal support**, is a monetary payment, typically paid monthly, that one spouse pays to the other spouse during and after the divorce proceedings. A great misconception is that spousal support payments are mandatory by law. Not so! Family court judges determine whether or not alimony is to be paid, and their decisions are legally binding.

Spousal support payments are predicated on the assumption that most men and women can provide for themselves following divorce; thus, today's support payments are considered to be *rehabilitative* alimony payments, which are short-term in nature, rather than *permanent* alimony payments. Rehabilitative payments are based on such things as the length of the marriage, the number of children, and the needs of each ex-spouse (Ventura & Reed, 1998).

Divorce attorneys, family court judges, and divorce mediators help negotiate spousal support settlements. It is sometimes possible for a spouse to opt for a lump-sum alimony payment, rather than monthly payments. Spousal support can also be modified if spouses' circumstances change.

Child Support

Whether the parents are married or divorced, spouses have an obligation to provide for their children under 18 years old. Just as with spousal support payments following divorce, **child support** payments are typically paid out as fixed, monthly payments. They may be paid by one or the other spouse, or ex-spouses may split the costs associated with raising children,

iStock.com/AntonioGuillem

typically until the children reach their early 20s. The amount assigned to one or both spouses is determined largely by the custody arrangements, and though the child support guidelines (mathematical formulas) vary from state to state, these guidelines are typically percentages of the parents' income. Because of state-to-state variances in the mathematical formula, it is difficult to determine what an "average" monthly child support payment might be. For example, in Texas, child support awards are based on a percentage of the parents' gross income, or the income before federal, state, and local income taxes are deducted. The court will generally follow these guidelines unless the parents agree to a different payment amount (Office of Child Support Enforcement [OCSE], 2018):

- 20 percent for 1 child
- 25 percent for 2 children
- 30 percent for 3 children
- 35 percent for 4 children
- 40 percent for 5 children
- not less than 40 percent for 6 children

Special rules apply in cases of split or joint custody or multiple children in different households. In addition, if the family court believes that the paying parent is not making as much money as he or she could (given the individual's past employment history or education level), the payment can be based on *earning potential,* the income the parent could potentially earn. This monthly payment is just for the "basics." If children require special education, have medical costs that exceed health insurance benefits, or are involved in extracurricular activities, parents are expected to share these costs equally.

How Much Child Support Is Paid Annually?

According to the OCSE (2018), a division of the federal government that tracks child support payments, there are 13.4 million custodial single parents in the United States; one-half receive some type of formal or informal child support. Annually nearly $34 billion in child support payments are collected and distributed—an average of $3,500 per *year*, per *custodial parent* (U.S. Census Bureau, 2018).

Child support payments are collected in a variety of ways, including withholding wages, intercepting unemployment compensation, and intercepting federal income tax returns (U.S. Census Bureau, 2018). Custodial parents may also receive other types of noncash support from their ex-partners. These types of support can include material things, such as clothing and diapers, food, or paying costs associated with health care. The types of noncash support are presented in Table 13.2.

Table 13.2 /// Noncash Support Received by Custodial Parents: 2015	
Noncash Support Received	%
Pay for child care or summer camps	12.5
Pay for medical expenses	20.0
Food or groceries	33.1
Clothes, diapers, shoes, etc.	45.0
Birthday, holiday, other gifts	57.7
At least one type of support	61.3

Source: Grall, T. (2018)

Does Everyone Pay?

Just because a family court issues a judgment does not mean that spouses pay the court-mandated amount. Some spouses may view child support payments as nothing more than spousal support in disguise. The spouses believe the money will go to support the ex-spouse's lifestyle, and not toward raising the children. Some ex-spouses feel that the amount designated for child support is too great and they subsequently pay an amount they feel is "fair." Conversely, custodial parents often feel that the amount awarded is too low, and may go back to family court, sometimes repeatedly, to request modification of the initial decision. Sometimes this is done out of anger or revenge; other times the request is made out of genuine need.

No matter the reason people do not pay child support, as of 2018, non-custodial parents owed a staggering $114 billion in past due child support (OCSE, 2018). One-half of noncustodial parents who owe back child support owe less than $10,000, but 15 percent owe more than $40,000.

As you will see in Chapter 14, the economic hardship of the noncustodial parent forces many divorced parents onto public assistance from the federal government.

Child Custody

Perhaps one of the most grueling aspects associated with divorce is determining child custody arrangements. **Custody** refers to who is responsible for the children's financial, physical, and emotional well-being (Ahrons, 1994). **Legal custody** refers to which parent has the right to make decisions about how the child is reared, such as decisions concerning education or religion. It is common today for parents to be awarded **shared legal custody**, which means that both parents have an equal say in the child's upbringing. Family laws provide several custody options for divorced co-parents.

Joint Custody

Parents who have **joint custody** of their children share in the decision making regarding their children. They may also share the physical custody of their children. This type of arrangement helps ensure that children receive the benefits of having both parents actively involved in their lives. There are three types of joint custody:

- *Joint legal custody.* Both parents share equally in decisions in childrearing, but the child resides primarily with one parent.
- *Joint physical custody.* Children spend close to equal time with each parent but one parent has primary legal custody.
- *Joint legal and physical custody.* Both parents share equally in decisions and physical custody.

Physical Custody

When a parent is granted **physical custody**, he or she is granted the legal right to have the child live primarily with him or her, making this parent the *custodial parent*. The *noncustodial parent* is granted the right to have child visitations on a schedule determined by the parents, or by the courts if the co-parents cannot agree. About 4 of every 5 custodial parents are mothers, while 1 of every 5 are fathers (U.S. Census Bureau, 2018).

Sole Custody

Just as the term implies, **sole custody** means that one parent is the primary parent—legally, physically, or both legally and physically. This type of custody arrangement was historically awarded to mothers because courts assumed they were the more nurturing parent, but today, more states have moved away from this arrangement because it tends to significantly minimize and limit the role of one parent. Even in the event that sole legal and physical custody is awarded to one parent, the other parent is often awarded visitation rights; however, if one parent is deemed unfit for reasons such as substance or alcohol abuse, or physical, sexual,

---

Custody:

refers to who is responsible for the children's financial, physical, and emotional well-being.

Legal custody:

refers to which parent has the right to make decisions about how the child is reared, such as decisions concerning education or religion.

Shared legal custody:

an arrangement in which both parents have an equal say in a child's upbringing.

Joint custody:

an arrangement in which parents share in the decision making regarding their children. They may also share the physical custody of their children.

Physical custody:

the legal right to have a child live primarily with one parent, who becomes the custodial parent.

Sole custody:

an arrangement in which one parent is the primary parent—legally, physically, or both legally and physically.

No-Fault Divorce Laws: Is It Time for a Change?

Mark and Jan have been married for 13 years. If you ask Mark, that's long enough. Is Mark having an affair? No. Is Jan no longer a fit mother to their three children? Of course not, Mark insists, she's a great mom. Jan will tell you she loves Mark and very much wants to preserve their marriage. Mark's reason? "I'm ready for a change. I'm just not in love with her anymore."

Ever since no-fault divorce became the norm in the 1970s and 1980s, experts have debated its merits and faults. Have no-fault laws hurt marriage? Is it time for a change?

YES: According to opponents of no-fault divorce, divorce is too often seen as the best solution to a bad situation long before other options can be explored. According to no-fault divorce opponents, the problems with the legislation are many:

- **Divorce doesn't promise fulfillment**. Adults who were once in an unhappy marriage but are now divorced are no more likely to be happy and fulfilled than their counterparts who remained in a difficult marriage to work things out (Powell, 2005).

- **Divorce is rarely the decision of both partners**. Rather than promoting individual freedom within relationships, no-fault divorce enables one partner to impose his or her will over the other.

- **Divorce is a consequence to be avoided**. Many studies suggest that divorce leads to poorer health and shorter life expectancy (Powell, 2005).

Sources: Powell (2005); Krauth (2005).

NO: Divorce, fault or no-fault, is never a pleasant time for a couple and their children. Advocates of no-fault divorce legislation maintain that no-fault divorce legislation benefits each party of the divorce—including children—in the following ways:

- **It allows for cleaner divorce proceedings**. Current no-fault statutes allow for the dissolution of a marriage without one partner or the other being forced to make a legal case against the other for proof of irreconcilability.

- **It benefits children**. Children's post-divorce adjustment relies more on the visibility of their parents' conflict, post-divorce involvement with both parents in childrearing, and economic circumstances than on the divorce itself (Krauth, 2005).

- **It provides equity in divorce settlements**. Divorce legislation protects women and children and helps ensure that they receive equal and fair settlements as well as post-divorce support.

What Do You Think?

1. How easy do you think divorce should be? Is divorce something to be avoided or embraced? Why?

2. What kinds of incentives/disincentives should state governments include in their marriage laws? Should the government be involved in divorce matters? Why or why not?

or emotional abuse or neglect, he or she may only be awarded supervised visitation. In that event, the court requires supervision of the noncustodial parent's visitation by a third party, such as the custodial parent or a representative of a public or private supervisory agency. In extreme cases when a parent is determined by the court to pose a threat to the children, the parent may be denied all parental rights.

Bird's Nest

This is an alternative to some of the more common custody arrangements just discussed. The bird's nest custody arrangement is joint legal and physical custody with a bit of a twist: Rather than have the children move between two different homes, the parents take turns going back and forth to their separate homes. This way, the children are able to remain in the family home. The core distinction of this arrangement is that each parent maintains a separate residence where they reside when it's not their turn to live in the "bird's nest." Sometimes one parent leaves right away when the other parent arrives; sometimes the family shares a family dinner together or another activity. This is typically the most expensive type of child custody arrangement because parents need to maintain three different residences—the bird's nest and each parent's separate residence.

Divorce Mediation

Navigating through the legal processes of divorce can be an intimidating and overwhelming task, even in the best of circumstances. That ex-spouses are often hurt and angry only compounds the complexities associated with terminating a marriage. **Divorce mediation** is a process that helps ex-spouses resolve child support, child custody, and property settlements for themselves and for their children, rather than having a judge determine these issues for them. With the help of a **divorce mediator**, who is an objective third party to the divorce, the divorcing couple determines the terms of their divorce settlement, such as child support and visitation rights and schedules for the parent who does not receive custody. During the mediation process, a host of other parenting issues can also be settled, including who pays for health insurance benefits or/and dental care, and even who pays for dance lessons and music lessons. The only issue that is off limits to divorce mediators is family violence because of its potential volatility.

To come to a settlement that is acceptable to both parties, divorce mediators first ask the ex-spouses to present the things they want in a divorce settlement. Then, using a structured format, the mediator helps the ex-partners find options and solutions to their disputes, He or she also guides ex-partners to a mutually agreed-on divorce settlement.

Does divorce mediation work? Overall, yes. Although both parties need to commit to the process for it to be successful, the clear winners in a mediated parenting agreement and divorce settlement are the children. By helping parents come to an agreement that is in the best interest of their children, mediation often reduces the emotions that accompany the divorce process, and it frequently reduces (or eliminates altogether) the need to go to court. There are fees associated with divorce mediation, which vary from mediator to mediator, but in most cases divorce mediation reduces the costs associated with divorce because it reduces court costs and other expenses associated with prolonged divorce settlements.

Ending a marriage causes strife and turmoil for all the parties involved. It is difficult for hurting, angry people to be effective parents. It is difficult for hurting, angry ex-spouses to be effective divorced partners. And too often, children are caught in the middle. As Ahrons (1994) concludes, "The interests of the children must come first . . . [and] they must feel as protected and secure as possible" (p. 175).

A Good Divorce: Is There Such a Thing?

The real issues in divorce aren't about child support payments, sharing parenting, and winning in court. Almost always, the real issues in divorce are hostility, rejection, pain, and depression, all leading to a conflict and more pain. The divorce often becomes a weapon of destruction for spouses to use against each other. By structuring problem solving in the divorce process, couples can avoid compounding the problems.

Divorce attorney Ed Sherman (2003) helps spouses legally end their marriage while they find ways to heal existing emotional wounds caused by the failed relationship. To keep the divorce as conflict-free as possible, he advises his clients as follows:

- **Get reliable legal information and advice**. Many couples can avoid the court process if they work toward mutual agreements that are in the best interests of their children and of themselves.
- **Prepare your case**. Each party should prepare the facts of his or her own case and gather the necessary information and the supporting documents before consulting a divorce attorney.

- **Prepare yourself**. Couples need to separate *legal* divorce issues from *real* divorce issues and keep them separate throughout the divorce process. Entangling the two only prolongs the legal process.

- **Decide what you really want**. Is the settlement you want about your children's well-being, security, and peace of mind? Or is it about revenge, getting even, and getting every cent the other spouse has?

- **Don't make decisions until your emotions have leveled off**. Don't react—respond.

Not all marriages will survive. Not all marriages *should* survive. But a great many marriages *can* survive if both partners are committed to working on the underlying problems that precipitated the hurt and conflict, and the issues that led them to the divorce option.

AVOIDING DIVORCE: GETTING A MARRIAGE BACK ON TRACK

Saving a marriage is not an easy task. It can take weeks, months, or even years, but if couples are willing to put work into the relationship, there is a wide range of resources available to them today. Couple and family therapy or counseling are the most effective ways to help couples work through their difficulties, to help them increase their marital satisfaction and happiness, and to stop a divorce that seemed inevitable.

Couples in distress do not seek counseling: Only about 37 percent of divorcing couples report seeking any type of professional help for their marriage (Doss, Rhoades, Stanley, & Markman, 2009). Those who do go to counseling or therapy experience marriage problems for about six years before they turn to professionals for help. A number of couples attend marriage workshops and retreats, refer to self-help relationship books, or turn to the Internet before they turn to marriage counseling or therapy, despite the seriousness of their relationship troubles. It's important for couples to know that although self-help books can provide meaningful information, therapy/counseling helps couples work together to settle issues without adding to the frustration, anger, and disappointment that are common among divorcing couples.

Where to Find Help for Troubled Marriages/Relationships

Couple and family therapists (CFTs) are mental health professionals who are trained and licensed to diagnose and treat a number of issues, including marital problems. The marriage and family therapy discipline is based on substantial bodies of empirical research that show family problems and marital problems are best treated within the context of relationships. To this end, CFTs use Family Systems theory to understand a couple's interaction and relational patterns. Introduced in Chapter 3, this is the theory we have used to understand the multitude of family processes we have studied together so far. Using what is referred to as solution-focused treatments, a CFT works with the couple to help them understand their marital problems as they exist now, and they focus on solutions and actions that help to resolve the problems. For example, in therapy sessions the couple and the CFT will explore the couple's roles, rules, and stages of their family's development. (Refer to Chapter 1 for a refresher on the lifecourse of families.) They will also determine the couple's interaction patterns (such as their communication skills and the ways in which they handle conflict), and find ways to improve on these. Sometimes one or both members of the couple will have a problem, such as depression or an addiction to alcohol or other substances. These problems, too, are addressed within the context of the couple's relationship because in the practice of marriage and family therapy, the unit of treatment is not the *person*—it is the relationships in which the person interacts on a daily basis.

When a marriage is on the verge of divorce, can it really be saved? Today, couples look to couple/marriage family therapists to help them overcome their troubles.

Commonly, a couple's therapy will concentrate on various aspects of the relationship, such as communication, mutual respect, building trust, improving family balance, and honesty. In essence, marriage and family therapy can best be thought of as a skills-building process where couples develop or build on skills necessary for a successful marriage. Throughout this text, we have focused on strengthening a number of these skills, such as understanding the processes associated with intimacy, love, gender roles, communication, conflict resolution, and sexuality.

Healing Couple Relationships

Today, more and more couples are realizing that couple or marriage therapy/counseling is an effective tool to enhance their relationship and to promote a healthy, lifelong marriage. Unfortunately, many couples wait until their problems seem insurmountable before they seek help. But with a trained therapist who can help them identify the issues that are affecting their relationship, couples are finding that it *is* possible to bring a marriage back from the brink of divorce. As family life educator Dr. Vic Harris (2009), associate professor of family studies at the University of Florida, observes, "Most relationships get stuck at some point and they need a little help (or sometimes a lot of help) to get unstuck. One of the best ways couples can [help themselves] is to overcome the stigma sometimes associated with seeking couples or marital therapy. Couples [should be] proactive and seek therapy early—before the relationship falls apart." Harris suggests a number of ways for couples to take the first steps toward healing their relationships:

- *Understand contexts and environments.* When struggling, it helps if couples can identify the settings or contexts in which the problems originate. Are the problems stemming from *personal* contexts, such as the degree of love a person experienced in his or her family of origin, or do the problems originate because of *relationship* contexts, such as chronically unresolved stress or conflict, or financial problems?

- *Understand individual traits.* Individual traits include such things as 'personality, attitudes, and skills. For example, some people handle stress differently than others, and some people exhibit extreme anger while others hold their feelings inside.

When a Marriage Is on the Verge of Divorce, Can It Be Saved?

When a couple is hurting and experiencing relationship difficulties, marital therapy can often help them mend their broken relationship. Today, couples look to marriage and family therapists to help them overcome their troubles from difficulties with emotional affection, communication problems, infidelity, high conflict levels, or concerns about separation or divorce (Doss et al., 2009). But when a marriage is on the verge of divorce, can it really be saved?

One Side: The weight of this entire marriage is on me. I am the primary breadwinner; I pay all the bills; I am responsible for cleaning the house, taking care of the kids, the cars, the dogs; I'm responsible for planning every holiday, for everyone's health . . . I can't talk about anything because as soon as I do I feel like I'm just shut down, shut out. I've read books and tried all sorts of things, but I feel like I'm trying all alone. Can this marriage ever work if *I* am the only one who wants to work on things? At this point, I'm not even sure I *want* it to work . . . it's just one more thing *I* have to do.

The Other Side: I have been very unhappy for a long time, and now I see that my spouse is unhappy and depressed. In all honesty, I have been taking out my unhappiness on my partner—it's like I want my spouse to feel as miserable as I do all the

time, and I think deep down that's why I haven't even tried to lift a finger to help out—I *wanted* there to be hurt. I *wanted* there to be pain. This may be hard to believe, but I still want to give us a chance; I really do still love my spouse. I'm willing to do anything to make this work. Both of our parents are divorced, and we promised each other a long time ago that we would never do that to our kids. And here we are. I'm willing to go to counseling or whatever it takes to turn this marriage around, to get it back where it used to be. But at this point, I'm not sure anyone can help us. I never thought my partner would want to leave, but now that there's one foot out of the door thinking about it, I realize I did the pushing away and the pushing out.

Your Side: Looking at this couple's situation,

1. Do you believe there is hope for this couple's marriage? Why or why not?

2. Saving a marriage is not just about preventing a divorce but about rebuilding a relationship of trust, respect, and happiness. If you were this couple's counselor, what three things would you suggest they do first to take steps toward reconciliation?

3. Do you think that current divorce laws should mandate marriage counseling for all couples who are considering divorce? What would be the benefits of such legislation? The downfalls?

- *Understand couple traits.* Couples can improve their troubled state by working to improve their cohesion (emotional closeness), control (increase give-and-take), and consensus (the level of agreement on issues).

- *Change yourself first.* Often when a couple is experiencing great distress, it's easy for them to focus on the problems with their spouse, and not on things they perhaps need to work on themselves. Harris provides three principles that can help a person who is considering divorce: (1) change his or her own behavior first, (2) change his or her attitude about the relationship/spouse, and (3) change his or her heart.

When we get married, the possibility of separation or divorce is probably the furthest thing from our minds. But as our study this term has showed us, there are a number of normative and non-normative stressors, as well as the challenges of living day to day, that can take their toll on even the strongest of couples. Sadly, marriages often take the brunt of the stress. If a marriage is in trouble, couples should never feel embarrassed about seeking help from a professional. Getting a marriage back on track is tough work, but the potential outcome makes it an avenue definitely worth exploring.

FAMILY LIFE EDUCATION: EDUCATING AND ASSISTING FAMILIES THROUGH TRANSITION AND CHANGE

Certainly, divorce is not a new social phenomenon, and as the divorce trends indicated, the United States has seen divorce rates fluctuate throughout its history. What remains unclear is whether the trends seen in divorce rates over the past 50 years or so are due to changing cultural values that, in turn, influence changes in divorce legislation, or whether the legislative efforts have been responsible for changes in cultural values.

The National Council on Family Relations (NCFR, 2020) has several goals for certified family life educators and other helping professionals who work with families:

- Teaching and modeling coping strategies for parents and children to assist them during a difficult transition time
- Providing parents and children with a sense of hope that they will be able to move forward with their lives
- Fostering healthy parent–child relationships
- Establishing and enhancing co-parent relationships
- Normalizing family change and surrounding families with community understanding and support
- Teaching and modeling skills and knowledge to assist families in adjusting to financial, psychological, legal, and social changes

The opening story of this chapter illustrates the gradual, progressive deterioration of the marriage of the parents of one of my students. In real life, *every* family fights. In real marriages, *every* couple has arguments and disagreements, and *every* couple will at one time or another have a verbal exchange that hurts one or the other partner.

The breakdown and subsequent termination of a marital relationship is not necessarily a result of the de-escalation of intimacy, but is instead, as Duck (1982, 1984) and Ahrons (1994) described, a process of dissatisfaction with a couple's relational patterns. This dissatisfaction, left unattended, eventually reaches a point at which marital partners emotionally divorce from one another long before the legal divorce takes place. When the divorce proceedings do begin, the transition from married family life to divorced family life is very difficult for parents and their children. As the author of the opening vignette described, "The arguments turned to who got what furniture, about money, and who 'got' us kids." Indeed, once the decision to divorce was made, the spouses then entered into the long-term legal process of divorce and had to come to agreement on issues such as community property settlement, child support, and child custody.

Despite our most blue-ribbon efforts, there are some relationships that we cannot prevent from coming unraveled—we cannot always prevent divorce. I leave the concluding comments to the student who wrote the opening story of this chapter:

> If I could title this paper the title would be "The Deception of the Gradual." You see, the changes that took place in our family took place slowly and gradually, bit by bit. And as each change occurred, my parents became comfortable and complacent with the changes. Rather than try to actively do something about what was happening, they let it go on, slowly but surely, letting the conflict and discontent progress to the point where there was no turning back. They let it progress to the point where there were too many hurt feelings, too many words hurled at one another to ever take back and start over. Gradual, ever so gradual. The deception of the gradual . . .

Uncoupling

- Uncoupling and the factors that lead to it are complex. Because each marital relationship has its own set of unique circumstances, there is no universal, one-size-fits-all pathway to uncoupling or to marital dissolution.

- Divorce involves socially sanctioned methods that legally terminate the marriage. Because some states do not record annual divorce statistics, the best way to determine the number of annual divorces in the United States is to look at the crude divorce rate—the number of divorces that occur per 1,000 population.

- Correlates of divorce are certain social and socioeconomic characteristics that affect the longevity of a marriage and the probability that a marriage will end in divorce. These predictors include the couple's age, premarital pregnancy, parental separation, whether the couple cohabits before marriage, religiosity of the couple, and the socioeconomic background of the couple.

- Reasons for marital discontentment that may eventually result in marital dissolution tend to be culture-specific in cultures where there is an emphasis on individualism and individual gratification, couples divorce because they are unhappy or because of what they perceive as irreconcilable differences. In collectivist societies, where marriage is thought necessary to promote the health of the community, divorce on the basis of unhappiness is considered thoughtless and trivial.

- The reasons people divorce are not the same as the causes of divorce, and there are interrelated cultural factors that contribute to the rise of divorce in the United States and other Western countries. These factors include the desacralization of marriage, the liberalization of divorce laws, the trend toward individualism, unrealistic expectations, and other cultural forces, such as the legislation that created no-fault divorce.

- Racial and ethnic differences make some couples more likely to divorce. Economic factors and education influence higher divorce rates, but cultural factors have even more impact, especially among African Americans and Hispanics. Although many Hispanic families face great economic difficulties, cultural factors such as familism, a collectivist identity, and religiosity all work together to make divorce less likely. This is known as the paradox of Mexican American nuptiality.

- Service men and women experience higher-than-average rates of divorce, and women in the service experience twice the divorce rates as men in the service. Researchers believe the increase in divorce rates is due to the stressors associated with deployment to Iraq and Afghanistan.

Emotionally Ending the Marriage

- Divorce is not an isolated event in a family's life; rather, it involves a series of transitions that include both emotional and legal processes.

- Psychologist Steven Duck's model of relationship deterioration describes five phases of breakdown in the couple's relationship; the dyadic breakdown, the intrapsychic phase, the dyadic phase, the social phase, and the grave dressing phase.

- Divorce seldom occurs because of a single event; instead, it involves a series of transitions, which include the decision, the announcement, and the separation. These transitions form the core of the emotional divorce.

- The separation period tends to be a time of disruption in the norms of family relationships and a time of ambiguity in which spousal and parental roles may become unclear.

- The anxiety felt by separating couples depends on what type of separation they experience: orderly separation, characterized by planning (though still painful), or disorderly separation, characterized by abruptness and usually not the result of careful consideration.

Legally Ending the Marriage: The Formal Divorce

- After the emotional transition to divorce takes place, the legal processes that take place to formalize, and finalize, the divorce often intensify this stressful experience.

- In the United States, family law establishes policies and regulations to ensure that married or divorced couples fulfill their obligations to each other and to their children, and that ex-spouses' and children's rights are protected.

- Dividing marital property and assets can be a difficult task. When dividing assets and debt, marital property, separate property, tangible property, and intangible property all must be negotiated. Family laws guiding property division consider current and future earnings, current standards of living, individual contributions to the marriage, the length of the marriage, and the age and health of each ex-spouse.

- Spousal support payments are considered as short-term rehabilitative alimony payments, and are based on the needs and resources of each ex-spouse, the value of the property received in the settlement, the length of the marriage, the physical and emotional health of each spouse, and the number of children present in the home, among other factors.

- Whether married or divorced, parents have an obligation to provide for their children under age 18, child support payments may be made by either spouse. Ex-spouses may split the costs associated with raising children, typically until the children reach their early 20s. The amount assigned to one or both spouses is determined by the custody arrangements.

- Custody refers to who is responsible for the children's financial, physical, and emotional well-being. A parent who has legal custody has the right to make decisions about how the child is reared, such as decisions concerning education or religion. With shared legal custody, both parents have an equal say in the child's upbringing. Family laws provide several custody options for divorced co-parents, including joint custody, physical custody, sole custody, and the bird's nest custody option.

- Divorce mediation helps ex-spouses resolve child support, child custody, and property settlements for themselves and for their children, rather than having a judge determine these issues for them. Mediation often reduces the anger and hurt that accompany the divorce process, and reduces or eliminates the need to go to court.

Avoiding Divorce: Getting a Marriage Back on Track

- Marriage and family therapy are effective ways that help couples work through their marital difficulties. However, only slightly more than one-third of couples in trouble seek any type of professional help for their marriages.

- Couple and family therapists (CFTs) are trained and licensed professionals who treat a number of family and marital issues. Using the Family Systems theory, a CFT explores the couple's relational and interaction patterns with solution-focused goals in mind.

- There are a number of ways for couples to take steps toward healing their relationships. These include understanding the contexts and environments in which the problems originated, understanding individual and couple traits, and being willing to change oneself first.

/// KEY TERMS

CHAPTER 14

REBUILDING: FAMILY LIFE FOLLOWING COUPLE DISSOLUTION AND DIVORCE

LEARNING OBJECTIVES

14.1 Describe the transitions to post-divorce that people experience.

14.2 Assess the effects of divorce on children and adults.

14.3 Discuss the challenges single parents face following divorce.

14.4 Summarize the transitions to repartnering and stepfamily living that children and adults experience.

I fell for it every time when I was younger. Every time my brothers asked, "Do you wanna play 52 pick-up?" I zealously jumped at the chance to "play cards" with them. I felt grown up and proud that I was included in their card game. It wasn't until I was 5 or 6 that I realized the game of 52 pick-up was only a game for them because they had a lot of fun watching me pick up 52 cards that were scattered all over the floor!

When my parents divorced, and then when each of them remarried, a recurring thought I had was, "This is just like 52 pick-up." Our lives were a mess of scattered pieces, flipped upside down. Just like the cards in the game, our lives were disorganized and thrown all over the place. And someone had to pick them up and reorganize them again. It took time, but we all did eventually get all the pieces picked up, and got everything back in order—not in the same order, a different order. But it works for us.

When parents go through a divorce, the entire family system is thrown into turmoil, with each family member feeling the disturbance in different ways. For those who are divorcing, the ramifications weigh heavily as family life undergoes reconstruction. The transitions associated with divorce, as outlined in the previous chapter, include

1. *The decision* to terminate the marriage
2. *The announcement* to children, family, and friends that the relationship is beyond repair and will be ending
3. *The separation,* which, whether orderly or disorderly, ultimately results in a period of time marked by multiple disruptions in the "normal" way of family living
4. *The formal divorce,* a period of time during which grueling decisions relating to the division of property, spousal support, child support, and child custody must be made (Ahrons, 1994; Duck, 1982)

The events leading up to the family court's decree finalizing the divorce involves changes in all aspects of family life. Not only do spouses lose their marriage, they also are at risk of losing important networks of social support (McPherson, Brashears, & Smith-Lovin, 2006), and they experience decreased psychological, emotional, and physical well-being (Sbarra, 2015). At this point in your study of couple and family life, you should have a clearer understanding of why divorce is ranked as one of the most stressful life events a family can experience, second only to the death of a loved one. You should also have a clearer understanding of how family stress and family crisis can affect the emotional and physical well-being of family members. Divorce is deeply intertwined with those areas of family crisis and stress (see Chapter 15).

Beyond the challenges, demands, and stressors associated with divorce, there is a final transition that must be traversed that we haven't yet discussed—the *aftermath* of divorce. It is during this transition that families re-establish their identities. Well after the decision to divorce is made public to family and friends, well after the separation takes place, and well after the legal divorce is finalized, the reconstruction continues. Just as there is no universal pathway to uncoupling, there is no universal pathway to rebuilding following divorce. In this chapter, we will discuss the transitions and the ways in which families rebuild their new lives. Different families' structures bring them certain challenges, which we will explore in the context of binuclear families, single-parent families, and remarriage and stepfamilies.

THE AFTERMATH OF DIVORCE: TRANSITIONS

Just as the opening student comments illustrate, divorce ultimately results in a complex mix-up of existing family relationships. The transition of status from married to divorced often leads to upheaval and disorganization within the family system. To cope with these changes, families must take on the central task associated with the aftermath of divorce—the reorganization of the family. This requires reconstructing the single nuclear family into a binuclear family, a process that creates two family systems from one family of origin.

The Binuclear Family

The term **binuclear family** refers to the separate, distinct households that form after marital separation or divorce. This dramatic change in family life reverberates throughout the entire family system, and this turn of events often brings the entire family to new levels of stress and crisis. The two subsystems that have been formed—the maternal (mother) and the paternal (father)—are now the child's family of origin. This restructuring from one central family into two accounts for much of the upheaval and confusion associated with divorce.

Constance Ahrons is a therapist and an internationally recognized lecturer and top professional in the area of divorce. Based on their landmark research, she and her colleague, therapist Roy Rodgers (1987), believe that the major goal of family reorganization centers on establishing healthy patterns of relating within *all* areas of family life. This transformation involves replacing old patterns of interrelating with new patterns, and replacing existing family boundaries with new ones. *Over time, these changes help to redefine the family into a*

Binuclear family: the separate, distinct households that form after marital separation or divorce.

The experiences associated with divorce are so disrupting to families that divorce is ranked as one of the most stressful life events a family can encounter. The aftermath of divorce must be navigated well so that families can successfully rebuild themselves.

binuclear family. As the former spouses navigate this rocky transition, they must find a way to establish their independence while continuing to fulfill their obligations to their children, their families, their friends, and their careers (Ahrons & Rodgers, 1987). According to anthropologist Paul Bohannan (1971), the co-parental divorce is the most painful, difficult, and complex aspect of the divorce. To better understand co-parenting in the aftermath of divorce, it helps to understand former spouse relationships.

Former Spouse Relationships

Despite the frequency of divorce in today's family life, the ongoing relationship between divorced partners is often marked by bitterness, anger, hurt, and hostility. Former spouse relationships are especially important to consider because the relationship between ex-spouses lays the groundwork and sets the emotional climate for the newly defined binuclear family (Ahrons & Rodgers, 1987). Research characterizes five former spouse relationship styles (Ahrons & Rodgers, 1987; Gold, 1991):

- *Perfect Pals*. These are divorced partners who remain friends after they divorce, and they try to accommodate their ex-partner's needs so that they can better focus on parenting. In most cases, these ex-spouses have joint legal custody of their children.

- *Cooperative Colleagues*. Following divorce, a considerable number of ex-spouses are able to cooperate as parents, but they do not feel that they are friends as do Perfect Pals. Even though they may still have disagreements and differences of opinion regarding childrearing and financial issues, they work diligently to keep the conflicts to a minimum so their children will not experience any additional trauma.

- *Angry Associates*. Anger is an integral part of this type of post-divorce relationship. Not only is the divorce experience marked with long, heated battles over property, custody, visitation, and other matters, the fighting continues for many years following the divorce. Effective co-parenting is not a goal of these divorced partners; consequently, children of Angry Associates are all too often caught in the middle of their parents' battles.

- *Fiery Foes*. These divorced couples are incapable of co-parenting. The anger is so intense that they will not allow the other lo parent—the other parent represents the enemy. These divorces are marked by significant litigation, with the legal battles continuing for several years following the divorce, and children become pawns in their parents' ongoing battles.

- *Dissolved Duos*. After the divorce, these couples break off all contact with one another. In some instances, one partner (typically the man) literally "disappears," and thus leaves the mother with the entire burden and responsibility of reorganizing and redefining the family.

Primary divorce stressors:
provisions such as custody arrangements, visitation, and child support.

Secondary divorce stressors:
the "fallout" associated with divorce, including depression and greater risks for health problems.

By any definition, the dissolution of a marriage is a stressful life event. There is no question that **primary divorce stressors**, such as custody arrangements, visitation, and child support, are demanding and that they exert a number of strains on the entire family. **Secondary divorce stressors** are those things that occur following the divorce. In essence, secondary stressors are the "fallout" associated with divorce. For example, hundreds of studies have revealed that divorced individuals experience more depression, are less happy, and are at greater risks for health problems than married individuals are (for a complete review, see Stephenson & DeLongis, 2018). But are there differences between how women and men experience divorce? Is there such a thing as his-and-her divorces?

Divorced Moms

Divorced women—particularly those who have children—face a number of negative, life-altering experiences following divorce (for a detailed review, see Leopold, 2018):

- Health declines (Shor, Roelfs, Bugyi, & Schwartz, 2012)
- Taking on bad health and lifestyle habits (Umberson, 1992)

- Increased mortality (Bernsten & Kravdal, 2012; Sbarra, Law, & Portley, 2011)
- Greater decline in satisfaction with family life (Leopold & Kalmijn, 2016)
- Greater feelings of loneliness (Dykstra & Fokkema, 2007)
- Social isolation (Dykstra & Fokkema, 2007)

In addition, they must contend with role overload when they assume the roles of both mother and father to their children. As you saw in Chapters 12 and 13, these financial limitations directly influence things such as housing, food, clothing, transportation, medical care, child care, and the opportunities for recreational and/or leisure activities (Lynch & Kaplan, 2000).

Such difficulties not only have immediate negative impacts on women and their children but they may also have cumulative impacts on the single mother. First, the ongoing stressful conditions associated with divorce exert negative health effects on a person, causing such things as a lowered ability to fight infections and an increased risk to cancer (Wickrama, Lorenze, Conger, & Elder, 2006). Second, the stressors and strains associated with divorce also affect emotional health, and oftentimes mothers experience increased levels of depression, anxiety, stress, self-doubt, and pessimism about the future. For example, after a divorce, mothers tend to stay angrier longer and are less likely to forgive than fathers (Hetherington & Kelly, 2002; Bonach, Sales, & Koeske, 2005). Furthermore, the adverse social conditions associated with divorced single motherhood expose mothers to disadvantaged social positions that include such things as long work weeks and single-handed parenting and child care—that mothers are often solely responsible for their children's well-being is especially difficult for divorced moms (Wickrama et al., 2006; Braver, Shapiro, & Goodman, 2006).

In addition to these findings, research reveals another disturbing finding: The demands of single motherhood following divorce are so great that it appears to substantially increase the probability of alcohol abuse in mothers of young children (Williams & Dunne-Bryant, 2006). In a study of nearly 5,000 post-divorce women, the investigators found that among parents of preschool children, women reported greater consumption of alcohol than men did. The researchers attach some caution to these findings because they did not assess the mothers' and fathers' *pre-divorce* levels of alcohol use. However, they speculate that an increase in mothers' drinking may be the result of social drinking (such as attending more clubs or bars

Divorced moms often struggle with role overload because they typically assume the roles of both mother and father to their children.

following their divorces) or the result of a decline in social support; feeling alone, the women turn to alcohol. Because of the ramification of these findings for children's well-being, family and social scientists need to explore whether mothers are at greater risk of abusing alcohol following divorce.

Divorced Dads

While mothers' difficulties following divorce are commonly due to financial worries and single-handed parenting, divorced dads' greatest stressors are associated with the decreased contact they have with their children (Braver et al., 2006). A number of studies show that fathers are more depressed, stressed, and disheartened than mothers after divorce because of their inability to be with their children, and because they miss their children so much (Baum, 2006; Bokker, Farley, & Denny, 2005; Stone, 2007; Hallman & Deinhart, 2007). Often, the father doesn't have control over how often he sees his children, because frequent contact with the children may be impeded or altogether prohibited by his former wife who continues to carry hostile, angry, or bitter feelings toward her ex-husband. For example, about one-third of divorced mothers move the kids 400 to 500 miles away from their fathers within the first two years following divorce; this drastically reduces the amount of time fathers can spend with their children (Bailey & Zvonkovic, 2003; Kelly, 2007). Other research also suggests that custodial moms discourage children's contact with their fathers by denying access to the children, by engaging in conflicts or confrontations at the time of picking up the children, and by cutting into the time fathers have with their kids by not having them ready when the father arrives to pick them up (Lehr & MacMillan, 2001; Leite & McKenry, 2002). Many times, fathers will reduce or greatly avoid contact with their children in an effort to keep away from the ongoing conflict with their former wives (Hetherington & Kelly, 2002). In addition, some mothers act as **gatekeepers** of their children, but too frequently mothers not only guard the gate—they lock it. A number of studies show that many mothers acknowledge that they deny visitation, make it difficult for fathers to see their children, and that they do not intend to share parenting with the father (Cookston, Braver, Griffin, deLusé, & Miles, 2007; Markham, Ganong, & Coleman, 2007; Henley & Pasley, 2006; Criddle & Scott, 2005). Children's involvement with their fathers following divorce is important to their development. Studies show that children who experience a warm post-divorce relationship with their fathers have higher self-esteem, fewer behavioral problems, and better social, academic, and cognitive skills (Hetherington, 1991; Anderson, 2014). This appears to be especially true for African American children (McLanahan & Sandefur, 1994). Fathers' involvement in the lives of their children matters, because children without fathers are more likely to drop out of high school, become dependent on alcohol or other substances, become delinquent, run away from home, end up in prison, or commit suicide (Parke & Brott, 1999; Finley, 2003; Anderson, 2014).

Unfortunately, however, divorce often brings with it significant changes in the ways in which fathers parent, particularly the noncustodial father. For example, post-divorce noncustodial fathers are more likely to be permissive in their parenting and take on a recreational, companion role rather than the role of disciplinarian (Furstenberg & Cherlin, 1991). This phenomenon of fathers taking on the "friend" role following divorce is so common that some have labeled noncustodial fathers as "Disneyland Dads." Although these fathers are happy to entertain their children, fathers who do not have custody tend to be less sensitive to their children's emotional needs and are less supportive of them in times of crisis and stress (Stewart, 1999). Other research findings suggest that children have a more difficult time trusting their father following divorce, than they do their mothers (King, 2002), and adolescents rate their fathers as less caring post-divorce (Dunlop, Bermingham, & Burns, 2001).

This inability to effectively parent may, in turn, contribute to the amount of contact a father seeks to have with his children following divorce. For instance, some research suggests that many newly divorced dads feel overwhelmed with their new parenting role because their experiences with their children before divorce were most often limited to day-to-day tasks

Gatekeepers: divorced mothers who deny visitation, make it difficult for fathers to see their children, and intend not to share parenting with the fathers of their children.

and responsibilities (Pleck, 1997). Because of this lack of parenting skills, many fathers take on the "friend" role. Others may completely withdraw from their children rather than risk being inadequate.

Each year, more than 1 million children experience the divorce of their parents (U.S. Census Bureau, 2018). Understandably, over the past several decades, much attention has been given to the effects of divorce on children, as divorce is one of the most common stressors experienced by today's children (Anderson, 2014; Haimi & Lerner, 2016; Sbarra, 2015; Stephenson & DeLongis, 2018).

The Psychological Impact of Divorce on Men and Women

In an effort to educate physicians about the effects of divorce on men's and women's psychological health, researcher and physician Basem Abbas Al Ubaidi (2017) put forth a five-stage model that describes the psychological and emotional stages of divorce. In this model, the author distinguishes between the **initiator** (the spouse who initiates the divorce proceedings) and the **receiver** (the spouse on the receiving end of the partner's intent to dissolve the marriage). Unlike other models that describe the processes of divorce, this model is particularly interesting because it describes how the helping professional, such as a certified family life educator (CFLE) can help the couple to prepare early on for their post-divorce relationship:

Initiator: the spouse who commences divorce proceedings.

Receiver: the spouse who is on the receiving end of the partner's intent to dissolve the marriage.

> **Stage 1. Blaming the spouse and disillusionment of one party:** The couple places blame on one another for past, present, and future relationship problems. The *initiator* experiences feelings of dissatisfaction, anger, anxiety, depression, guilt, and negative self-image. The *receiver* experiences helplessness, lack of control, fear of the unknown, and shock. During this time, the couple and family therapist's (CFT) role or the CFLE's role is to help foster a sense of control in the divorcing couple and to neutralize the couple's fears. The counselor can also help the couple to prepare themselves and their children for the upcoming physical separation.
>
> **Stage 2. Mourning the loss and expressing dissatisfaction:** In this stage, both partners experience feelings of grief and experience intense preoccupation with the situation. Each partner also has difficulty concentrating; it's not uncommon to see a deterioration of the parenting

iStock.com/AleksandarNakic

The greatest stressor divorced fathers face is the lack of contact with their children. This decreased involvement with children often leads to fathers taking on the role of friend, rather than parent, when they are with their children.

role. The counselor or CFLE can assist the couple by helping them through the grieving process and by redirecting the couple's energy to short-term, necessary tasks.

Stage 3. Anger and Resentment: The anger and resentment can stem from past and present "wrongs" that occurred in the marriage, and this is typically the stage in which both partners experience roller coaster emotions. But it's important for the CFLE to help couples to understand that the anger is stemming from the fears and uncertainty about the future. The receiver typically experiences more fear, anger, and resentment than the initiator does. A therapist or CFLE can help to redirect the anger to constructive tasks, such as improving the couple's communication and long-term problem-solving skills to prepare them for co-parenting post-divorce.

Stage 4. Being Single and Moving Ahead With the Divorce: The initiator tries out new experiences of independency and singlehood. It is during this time that emotional distance between the spouses is the greatest. The helping professional's role in this stage is to help the divorcing couple focus not on the losses associated with divorce, but on the potential that moving forward can bring.

Stage 5. New Beginnings: Here, both the initiator and the receiver have accepted the end of the marriage on their own timeframe and begin to settle into the "new normal." The couple negotiates a fair divorce settlement and child custody arrangements. The therapist or CFLE can help couples get to this stage by encouraging them to focus on their own emotional health and that of their children, rather than on the problems of the past.

There is no question that divorce is intensely painful for most people. However, it's important to remember that most people cope well with the stressors associated with divorce, and resiliency is the most common response (Sbarra, 2015). In the section that follows, we'll take a closer look at how divorce affects children and adolescents.

HOW DIVORCE AFFECTS CHILDREN AND ADOLESCENTS

A substantive body of research shows that divorce has detrimental impacts on both short- and long-term adjustment in children and adolescents. As one researcher notes, "Divorce [diminishes] a child's future competence in all areas of life, including family relationships, education, emotional well-being, and future earning power" (Anderson, 2014). Without question, divorce impacts children's mental health and various behaviors (Haimi & Lerner, 2016). In a landmark work in 1991, Amato and Keith examined the results of 92 studies (involving 13,000 children of divorce); the overwhelming results indicated that children of divorce are "less well" than children who had not experienced the divorce of their parents. In general, it was found that children were affected in these ways:

- More difficulties in school
- More behavioral problems
- More negative self-concept
- More social problems with their peers
- More difficulties getting along with their parents (for a complete review, see Haimi & Lerner, 2016)

With 67 percent of second marriages ending in divorce, and nearly three-fourths of third marriages ending in divorce (U.S. Census Bureau, 2018), is there a cumulative effect of divorce on children? Table 14.1 shows us the factors that may contribute to children's post-divorce outcomes.

Of course, in some instances divorce is beneficial to children, such as when there is physical, sexual, or emotional violence, but in most instances, divorce has some negative effects on

Table 14.1 /// How Are Children Affected?	
Loss of Parent(s)	Divorce brings the loss of a parent, and with this loss brings emotional, physical, and financial losses.
Economic Loss	Single-parent families, particularly mothers, often experience near-poverty or poverty levels of financial constraints.
Emotional Security Loss	Divorced mothers and fathers are less emotionally available to their children. Children also experience the loss of grandparent relationships.
Lower Coping	Parents experience a reduction in their abilities to cope because of the many new demands.
Parent's Lack of Skills and Knowledge	The competence of the parents regarding post-divorce living and parents has a significant impact on children's outcomes.
Parental Conflict	The level of conflict to which children are exposed has a tremendous impact on the well-being of children.

Sources: Anderson (2014); Haimi & Lerner (2016).

children (Wallerstein & Lewis, 2004; Hetherington, 2003; Kelly & Emery, 2003; Cartwright, 2006; Haimi & Lerner, 2016). Because divorce is a social norm in our culture, how do children respond today to their parent's divorce?

The Negative Effects of Divorce

An abundance of empirical research concludes that children who experience their parents' divorce are at increased risk for certain difficulties. Post-divorce effects on children and adolescents are broken down into three areas: acting out, emotional problems, and problems in school (Shaw & Ingoldsby, 1999). Children **externalize** difficulties through their behavior when they grapple with the inner turmoil, confusion, anger, and hurt they feel in the aftermath of their parents' divorce. Commonly known as **acting out**, children and adolescents externalize their feelings about the divorce, typically through aggressive misbehaviors, non-compliance, disobedience, delinquency, increased absences from school, and increased aggressiveness (Amato, 2010; Fincham, 2002; Hetherington & Kelly, 2002; Stanley & Fincham, 2002). Children of divorce are also more likely to become teenage parents and leave home earlier (Hetherington, 2003). It is not surprising that boys exhibit externalizing behaviors more frequently than girls. This may be due to boys' increased vulnerability to stressor experiences in general (Shaw, 1993). This also explains why boys experience greater post-divorce adjustment difficulties than girls do (Fincham, 2002).

Internalizing difficulties results in emotional problems such as worry, feelings of unhappiness, anxiety, depression, distress, guilt, and poor self-concept. When compared with children whose parents' marriages are intact, children of divorced families have been shown to have a lower concept of self, as well as a lower sense of well-being, and they also have less problem-solving skills (Gohm, Oishi, Darlington, & Diener, 1998; Parish & Wigle, 1985; Hetherington, 2003). Additionally, children of divorced parents report lower levels of intimacy with parents and friends and experience interpersonal relationship problems, including difficulty in trusting others (Fincham, 2002; King, 2002; Stanley & Fincham, 2002; Hetherington, 2003). The correlation between divorce and internalizing problems is especially high for girls (Fincham, 2002; Stanley & Fincham, 2002; Furstenberg & Allison, 1989).

In general, children who experience their parents' separation or divorce have more difficulties in the classroom and performing academically than children who have not had similar experiences (Carlson, 1995). In fact, children from established households headed by one

Externalize:
to direct outward and generate discomfort and conflict in the surrounding environment.

Acting out:
a post-divorce behavior in which children and adolescents externalize their feelings about the divorce, typically through aggressive misbehaviors, noncompliance, disobedience, delinquency, increased absences from school, and increased aggressiveness.

Internalizing:
to direct inward and generate distress in the individual; internalizing difficulties result in emotional problems such as worry, feelings of unhappiness, anxiety, depression, distress, guilt, and poor self-concept.

Gary Friedmann/Los Angeles Times via Getty Images

Children who are struggling with the breakup of their parents' marriage may exhibit external behaviors, such as rebellion, smoking or drinking, and skipping school. These behaviors are referred to as *acting out*.

parent or children who live in an established stepfamily perform better academically than those children who have recently experienced their parents' divorce.

Why is this so? To a large extent, the reasons children whose parents are divorcing demonstrate poor academic performance are intrinsically tied to the internalization problems encountered by children of divorced families. The emotional aspects of divorce, such as anxiety, depression, guilt, and possibly aggression, affect the children's ability to concentrate in school, negatively affecting their ability to meet scholastic expectations (Dacey & Travers, 2002). This emotional toll may also affect children's ability to interact socially with teachers and peers.

Shaw and Ingoldsby (1999) point to a body of research that speaks to the fact that children of divorced families often experience a subsequently lower socioeconomic status (SES), which has consistently been linked to poor school achievement. This tends to be the case especially among those children who reside in single-parent families that have little interaction with the other parent. Although some children experience great resilience after family dissolution, a significantly large number of children are not as fortunate.

Children's and Adolescents' Adaptation

In terms of those aspects that determine how children and adolescents adjust to family reorganization and redefinition, empirical evidence strongly suggests that it is not the divorce per se that ultimately influences post-divorce adaptation; rather, there appear to be mediating family process variables that account for children's responses to divorce. Shaw and Ingoldsby (1999) outline the interrelated family factors that affect children's and adolescents' long-term adjustment to divorce.

Separation From an Attachment Figure

Recall from Chapter 6 that emotional attachment between a child and a caregiver is critical to a child's development. Central to the concept of attachment is the idea that as a result of this initial attachment, children develop a sense of security and trust, allowing for optimal development. When a child experiences the loss of a primary attachment figure, such as in the case of divorce, it may trigger difficulties in interpersonal relationships, including friendships and love relationships (Hannum & Dvorak, 2004; Hinderlie & Kenny, 2002; McIntyre, Heron, McIntyre, Burton, & Engler, 2003). Research has shown us the common reactions children have to divorce, by age group (Broadwell, 2019):

- **Infants:** Infants may react to their parents' distress by losing their appetites, changing their sleep patterns, or exhibiting changes in other routines, such as being fussy during play time. Parents should try to maintain a daily routine, and relate physically and emotionally to the infant.

- **Toddlers:** Toddlers may react to the absence of the parent by crying more and becoming clingy. They may have trouble eating and sleeping, and they may regress to behaviors they had as infants, such as thumb sucking or needing diapers. Parents should reassure their toddler that they will always love her or him. Regular contact with both parents is essential.

- **Preschoolers:** Preschoolers are often called the "forgotten mourners." They know something is wrong and they grieve the loss of the absent parent, but they do not know how to put their feelings into words, They often blame themselves for their parents' breakup. Parents should reassure them that the children did nothing to cause the divorce, and that they will always be loved. Regular contact with both parents is essential.

- **School-Aged:** Children at this age understand that their parents don't love each other and that they can't live together. Children may fantasize about ways to reunite their parents. They feel a tremendous sense of loss and rejection, and they worry a lot about the future, about who will care for them and what will happen if their remaining parent dies. They may have physical symptoms such as headaches and stomach aches, and they may have problems sleeping. They may show signs of depression, such as withdrawing from friends and activities. Parents need to be good listeners and reassure children that the divorce is not the children's fault. They need to have predictable contact with the absent parent.

- **Preteens and Adolescents:** Although children of this age understand the permanence of divorce, they don't like it, and they don't readily accept it. It is not uncommon for children of this age to act out and become rebellious. Parents need to talk about the adolescent's feelings and concerns, not about the problems the parents are having with their ex-spouses. Parents need to make sure the child's responsibilities are age appropriate and not so demanding that they have to grow up too soon.

Haimi and Lerner (2016) recognize that it is difficult to determine conclusively whether these relationship difficulties are due to the separation from the parent, or whether the problems are due to the multifaceted, multidimensional family processes associated with divorce and the resulting family reorganization.

Children's and Adolescents' Reactions to Parents Dating

Dating following divorce is common. For example, in a study of 1,700 divorced women in the United States, 78 percent of the women surveyed indicated that they starting thinking about dating before their divorces were finalized, and 65 percent began dating within the first year following divorce (Worthy, 2019). In a study of 1,220 divorced individuals, the researcher discovered that men repartner sooner than do women; within three to five years post-divorce, 40 percent of men were with another partner (Leopold, 2018). According to family scientists, there are certain age-specific reactions that children have to their parents dating post divorce (Anderson-Burdine & Armstrong, 2014):

Early Childhood: Common fears include the safety of the mother, whether she will return from the date, that the dating partner will be scary, and that the parents will never get back together.

Middle Childhood: Children see themselves as a part of their parent ("we" and "us"), so they see themselves as dating the partner, as well; they view the parent's dating partner in a personally beneficial or non-beneficial way (i.e., "What material things can the partner give to me? What fun things will the partner let me do?").

Adolescents: Teens become easily annoyed at their parents; the parent's dating relationship can reignite the teen's relationship struggles; the parenting role boundaries are often altered due to the new dating activities.

The researchers suggest that when parents begin dating again after divorce, they should be honest with their children about what their intentions are with the dating partner; parents should also accept that the child will be affected, at least initially, by the dating relationship. The researchers also note that it's important for the parent to introduce the topic of dating again before introducing the dating partner to the children/teens. Most important, it is imperative that a parent does not place the emotional burden of dating on the child or put the child in the role of the supporter.

The Passage of Time

Is it true that time heals all wounds? The effects of **temporal influences**, such as the passage of time and the child's age at the time of divorce, may play a role in children's long-term adjustment to their parents' divorce, although there is conflicting evidence. For example, Shaw and Ingoldsby (1999) observe, "As time passes, many of the stressors associated with divorce are lessened in intensity as adults and children adapt to new living situations" (p. 350). Other research offers conflicting findings.

Psychologist Judith Wallerstein devoted more than two decades to studying the effects of divorce on children. In her landmark longitudinal study in the early 1970s of 131 children from dissolved families, she found that one-half to two-thirds of the children in her study carried with them feelings of vulnerability and fear, and she noted that for children of divorce, growing up was harder every step of the way than it was for children whose parents did not divorce (Wallerstein & Kelly, 1980). In *The Unexpected Legacy of Divorce* (2000), Wallerstein, Lewis, and Blakeslee discuss a research finding that materialized some 30 years after her research had begun—that children carried with them these same feelings of vulnerability and fear well into adulthood. Notes Wallerstein, "When children of divorce become adults, they are badly frightened that their relationships will fail, just like the most important relationship in their parents' lives failed. Their decisions about whether or not to marry are shadowed by the experience of growing up in a home where their parents could not hold it together" (p. 8).

Another body of research appears to confirm Wallerstein's findings. Using data gathered from life-story interviews of 40 young adults aged 19 to 29, the researcher discovered that although a majority of the study participants were positive about their parents' divorces, the majority also considered that they were currently experiencing negative effects related to their parents' separations (Cartwright, 2006). One study participant discussed her hesitancy to enter relationships:

> I've never really had any boyfriend from 14 onwards. . . . I don't [know] whether that's a reflection of me and not wanting to because of my parents breaking up. I kind of almost think, I've almost got a bad way of thinking. Like, I don't want to start something if I know it's going to be a waste of time, where it's not going to ever go anywhere, cuz then it's wasting my time, I kind of don't ever open up to anyone, so I think [their divorce] affected me. (p. 132)

Is Divorce Hazardous to a Person's Health?

The federal government has made it standard practice to warn us of impending danger, from tobacco to sugar. But what if you were to learn that there was something as hazardous to your health as a pack-a-day Marlboro habit? Would you consider this important information?

We have discussed the emotional impact, financial issues, and more—but what about physical health? What kind of impact does uncoupling have on our bodies? According to research (DiIulio, 1997):

- Becoming single shortens a person s lifespan by 7 years.
- Married men and women are half as likely as divorced men to die prematurely from heart disease.
- Divorced or separated adults are 4.5 times more likely to become addicted to alcohol than are those who are married.
- The risk of becoming seriously ill is 12 times greater for divorced and separated adults than it is for married adults.
- People going through a divorce or separation are at double the risk for being involved in an accident.

In the left margin:

Temporal influences: the passage of time that may mitigate the effects of divorce.

Interestingly, results such as these cross all racial and ethnic lines. Couples in Europe and Asia share similar statistics. Advantages like economic stability and emotional support, found commonly in marriages, result in benefits such as better diet, safer living environments, fewer hours spent at work, and more hours spent on leisure activities.

People have only so much stress reserve, and indeed, experiencing a divorce is one of the greatest stressors an individual and a family can endure. To help minimize stress, therapists suggest:

- Set realistic goals and priorities—family reorganization takes time.
- Talk about your feelings with someone you trust, and cry when you need to.
- Eliminate blame, criticism, "should have," "could have," and "would have" from your vocabulary—none of these changes the situation.
- Exercise and get plenty of rest.
- Let others help.

The Relationship Between the Custodial Parent and the Child

Without question, the greatest change to which children and adolescents need to adapt post-divorce is their relationship with their parents. These changes are so significant that researchers have coined the phrase **diminished parenting** to describe this new relationship that takes place during the first few years following divorce. Today, an estimated 13.6 million custodial parents live with 22.4 million children under the age of 21—more than one-fourth of all children under the age of 21 in the United States live with a custodial parent, while the other parent lives somewhere else (Grall, 2018). In 2018, 8 of every 10 custodial parents were mothers (80 percent), and nearly 20 percent were fathers (16 percent). The racial and ethnic differences in custodial and noncustodial parenting are presented in Figure 14.1.

Research has revealed changes in the custodial parent's (most typically the mother) behavior, such as less frequent displays of showing affection, particularly to boys, and less nurturing behavior (Amato, 2010). One body of research shows that the conflict between the custodial parent and the children increases, and the ability to communicate with the children declines (Amato & Rezac, 1994). This study is of particular note because the

Diminished parenting: the new relationship between parents and children in the first few years following a divorce.

Figure 14.1 /// Percentage of Children in Custodial Families, by Race: 2018

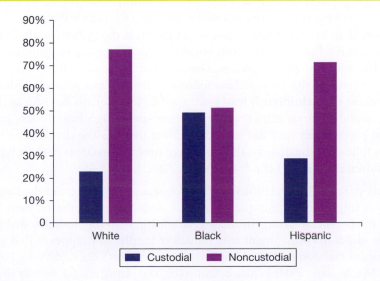

Source: Grall, T. (2018).

Studies have shown that children who experience close relationships with their parents following the divorce are provided a cushion against the negative side-effects of divorce.

iStock.com/georgeclerk

researchers studied more than 12,000 children in all types of single-parent homes. During the first year or so following divorce, many children assume more household responsibilities and often exhibit greater independence. Meanwhile, the custodial parent's parenting becomes more negative and less consistent. Some custodial mothers may become permissive in their parenting style and emotionally dependent on their children. But there are any number of family process variables (such as economic difficulties or support, the mother's emotional state, her extended family and social support) that contribute to disturbances in parenting.

The Relationship Between the Noncustodial Parent and the Child

One of the single greatest adjustments required for family reorganization into a binuclear family is that of incorporating a noncustodial parent into the family dynamics. In the United States, it is more than likely that the nonresident parent is the father (Grall, 2018). The success or failure of this adjustment depends largely on the frequency of visitation the noncustodial parent has with his or her children. One third of today's children—33 percent—have no contact or visitation with their fathers following divorce, but nearly one-fourth of nonresident fathers see their children at least once a week (U.S. Census Bureau, 2018). For those who do have visitation arrangements, the children spend significantly less time with the nonresidential parent than they did with that parent prior to the divorce. As the length of time increases following the divorce, the amount of time nonresident parents typically spend with their children decreases (Lehr & MacMillan, 2001).

But as with any parent–child relationship, the frequency of contact and the length of visitations are not as important as the quality of the interactions and the relationship between the child and the parent. A strong, intimate relationship with the noncustodial parent, then, bodes well for children's adjustment to a binuclear family, as it appears that good parent-child relationships cushion and shield against the adverse effects of divorce (Davis & Friel, 2001; Lehr & MacMillan, 2001; White & Gilbreth, 2001; Institute for Family Studies, 2019). One study indicated that as children of divorce became adults, 62 percent of those studied noted that their relationships with their fathers improved or stayed the same over the 20 years since their parents' divorce (Ahrons & Tanner, 2003).

Co-Parenting in Binuclear Families

It has been said that it is difficult for suffering parents to be effective parents. Divorced parents understandably have many adjustments of their own to make following the dissolution of their marriage, such as adjusting to custody arrangements and binuclear family parenting, financial support, and relocation, but these do not lessen the parents' responsibilities in assuring the needs of their children are met.

Regardless of the custodial arrangements, the parents' post-divorce relationship—such as those detailed in Ahrons and Rodgers's couple relationship types—greatly influences how they fulfill their parental functions. One study supports this. For example, data drawn from the binuclear family study, a study that followed the lives of 98 pairs of spouses and their children for 20 years, revealed that more than half of the participants indicated that their parents got along fairly well, now that the children were grown (Ahrons, 2007). Further, one-half of those surveyed reported that their parents were now Cooperative Colleagues, and another 10 percent believed their parents were Perfect Pals. Only 22 percent indicated that their parents were still Angry Associates or Fiery Foes. Several factors affect parenting following divorce:

- *Parents' education level.* Parents with higher education levels lend to engage in higher levels of co-parenting than do parents with lower education levels (Cooksey & Craig, 1998).

- *Income level.* Parents in higher SES brackets tend to co-parent more effectively than do parents in lower income brackets (Arditti, 1999).

- *Duration of the marriage.* Couples who were married longer are more likely to engage in more cooperative post-divorce parenting (Ahrons & Rodgers, 1987).

- *Time elapsed since the divorce.* If other variables, such as higher education levels and higher SES levels are present, divorced couples are more apt to effectively co-parent over time as "wounds begin to heal" (Furstenberg & Cherlin, 1991).

- *Remarriage of one or both spouses.* Remarriage often negatively impacts former spouses' ability to co-parent (Ahrons & Rodgers, 1987).

- *Who initiated the divorce.* Most commonly, the spouse who initiates the divorce is the more cooperative co-parent (Duran-Aydingtug, 1995).

- *The legal process of divorce.* If the divorce process involved hostility and conflict or was difficult and protracted, the father tends to be less involved with his children (Madden-Derdich & Arditti, 1999).

Although more parents share joint custody of their children following divorce than in past decades, as you saw earlier, significantly more children live with their mothers following divorce than with their fathers (Grall, 2018). This distinction is important because family study researchers have determined that there are considerable differences between mothers and fathers and how they fulfill their parental duties and functions following divorce—for example, the majority of custodial mothers carry out their parenting responsibilities in the same way they parented before they divorced (Baum, 2003). And although some fathers also continue to parent in the same way as before they divorced, other fathers' parental involvement increases, and as we saw earlier, others' involvement decreases.

For the past several decades, social norms dictated that because mothers are the more "nurturing" parent, they should be awarded custody of the children following divorce. Yet because recent scientific studies have revealed that children fare belter when both parents are involved in their growing up, legal and social policies have changed to accommodate the needs of the children. Family courts today are more likely than in the past to award joint custody (Emery, 1994).

Should Parents Stay Together for the Sake of the Kids?

Divorce is an icon of the American family experience. Even those who reach adulthood with an intact family have witnessed its effects on others in their circle of close relationships. To use a cliché, "What about the children?"

Should parents, for the children's sake, keep their dissolving marriages together?

YES: According to Judith Wallerstein (1991), children do not need healthy, happy, and affirmed parents as much as they need their parents to stay together. With the exceptions of abuse and severe dysfunction, Wallerstein contends that a terrible marriage is better than a great divorce.

- **Divorce restricts dual parenting.** In many broken marriages today, the noncustodial parent (usually the father) becomes increasingly absent. Joint custody rarely occurs.

- **Children are not as adversely affected by marital stress.** It is often claimed that it is better for children for their parents to divorce than for them to be in a household of stress and discord. Evidence seems to suggest otherwise. Wallerstein's findings suggest that 90 percent of children felt more content pre-divorce than afterward.

NO: Mavis Hetherington (2003), psychology professor at the University of Virginia and authority on divorce, states that although there is a pronounced relationship between divorce and childhood behavioral disorders, more than 75 percent of children who have gone through divorce are eventually able to reason through their new lives and develop into normal, well-adjusted adults.

Hetherington asserts:

- **Family dysfunction, not divorce, is the real culprit.** Typically, couples do not split over behaviors and traits acquired by their mates in the last weeks preceding the breakup. The dysfunction present at the time of the divorce is often an amplified image of the dysfunction that has been present in the marriage all along.

- **Situational complications are to blame.** Often, a child's post-split development hinges on the environmental complications. Healthy adjustment is very likely, so far as the children receive social support and adequate financial resources. Parental remarriage is also a strong help in maintaining a healthy recovery in children and adolescents.

What Do You Think?

1. Can you think of people who, although products of divorce, have successfully adjusted to life and have lived up to society's expectations of "success"? Describe them.

2. Can you think of people who experienced parental divorce and as a result have struggled to maintain normalcy in their daily living? Describe them.

3. Compare the people you described in questions 1 and 2. What are the factors that may have contributed to their respective outcomes?

Source: Hetherington (2003): Wallerstein (1991).

Living, Loving, and Parenting in Post-Divorce Families

Decades of research indicate that, by and large, the picture of divorce for children isn't usually bright or optimistic. Emerging findings, however, show that Americans are finding newer and better ways to "live, love, and parent" in a divorce-saturated society. Hetherington and Kelly (2002) found, after studying 1,400 families, that the multiple processes of divorce can result in healing and ultimate fulfillment. Their research addresses past research findings:

- *Divorce only has two outcomes: Win or lose.* Hetherington and Kelly (2002) maintain that there are a number of different ways that people adjust to divorce. The process of divorce does *not* produce only winners or losers. Each of these patterns of adjusting are not permanent, and will change over time.

- *Children always lose out after a divorce.* Divorce is not a rosy experience for children, but *over time* children demonstrate their resiliency to their parents' divorce.
- *The pathways following divorce are fixed and unchanging.* According to the researchers, the effects of divorce are not irrevocable. A negative experience can be offset by later positive experiences.
- *Men are the big winners in divorce.* Although women experience greater economic losses following divorce, overall they do better emotionally following divorce than do men. Even though women frequently fall into poverty following divorce, this trend is changing as women become better educated, and as federal and state agencies become stricter about enforcing child support payments.
- *The absence of a father is the greatest risk to children.* Indeed, fathers matter. But it's not the mere *presence* of a father that makes a difference. The researchers discovered that involved, supportive mothers can counter the adverse effects of a father's absence.

Divorce presents many disruptions in children's and adolescents' lives. Some of these changes require coping and adaptation beyond their years, and clearly put the child at risk for short- and long-term developmental, academic, and interpersonal problems. The interconnected family and environmental variables influencing a youth's adjustment and adaptation to divorce point to the need for effective parenting and co-parenting when establishing a binuclear family. Reorganizing and redefining a family from one nuclear family into a binuclear family is a multifaceted transition that requires tremendous efforts of both parents to assure the best interests of the children are met. Former spouse relationships that promote collaborative, cooperative shared parenting foster positive parent–child relationships that benefit both the parents and the children. The divorce transition still involves many challenges, particularly for single mothers. In the next section, we'll explore the difficulties faced by single mothers.

CHALLENGES FOR SINGLE PARENTS

Households headed by single parents include impoverished, never-married ethnic minority women or teenaged mothers, gay and lesbian parents whose unions are not legally recognized, never-married women who have adopted or borne a child, widows and widowers, and women and men who find themselves single after a marital breakup (Gottfried & Gottfried, 1994). Additionally, many families instantly became single-parent families when a spouse is called to war or when a spouse dies in combat.

Regardless of its makeup, each single-parent family has its own unique starting point and its own unique developmental history (Anderson & Sabatelli, 2011). Because mothers with children comprise the largest segment of single-parent households, our discussion will center on the issues and challenges faced by single mothers.

As you have learned, family structure is a crucial determinant for the health and well-being of children and adults alike. Although the majority of children who are brought up in single-parent homes fare well, there are risks associated with single-parent living. Children from single-parent homes are twice as likely to repeat a grade in school and/or to drop out of high school, and they are at much greater risk of being unemployed (McLanahan & Sandefur; 1994; Hetherington, 2003). And although every family structure is prone to its fair share of problems, single mothers face issues that magnify the stress of raising children, Anderson and Sabatelli (2011) identify the most significant challenges that face single-parent mothers following divorce: changes in financial status, changes in residence, changes in boundaries for children, changes in the emotional environment, and post-divorce dating.

Changes in Household Finances

Another interrelated family factor that affects children's and adolescents' long-term adjustment to divorce is the state of family economics before and after divorce. Economic hardship

iStock.com/Geber86

Post-divorce economic hardship is a harsh reality for many women because less than half receive the child support owed them. The *feminization of poverty* is a concept that depicts the increase in poverty in divorced women.

Feminization of poverty:
the phenomenon in which women experience poverty rates that are disproportionately high in comparison to men.

is a post-divorce reality for many families, particularly for women—less than half (43 percent) receive the full child support they are owed (Grall, 2018). Recall from Chapter 13 that part of the legal terms of a divorce is determining child support due the custodial parent. Even if the noncustodial parent (usually the father) faithfully pays child support, however, the amount is rarely sufficient to meet the living expenses of the mother and children. In 2018, for example, 30 percent of single mothers live below the poverty line, while only 17 percent of solo fathers do; this is in comparison to 8 percent of married couples (Pew Research Center, 2018). The **feminization of poverty** refers to the experience in which women experience poverty rates that are disproportionately high in comparison to men (McLanahan & Kelly, 2006). And, it appears that women suffer more from divorce than men do, especially in disproportionate declines in household income (De Vaus, Gray, Qu, & Stanton, 2015; Leopold, 2018). Further, women are at a greater risk of losing their homes following divorce (Dewilde, 2018).

The economic toll of divorce often translates into still more adjustments for children (Amato, 2000; Grall, 2018). These adjustments may require enduring potentially poorer quality of parenting as the custodial parent must take on more work, and coping with the effects of financial pressures and strains on the family. Although some children are more fortunate and are able to remain living in the family home, the financial pressures may mean that they need to make other sacrifices such as forgoing music lessons and/or sports lessons in order to make ends meet.

When economic hardship afflicts single-parent households, other challenges arise for families already struggling to reorganize and redefine themselves following divorce. Because of the interrelated nature of family living, economic hardship then affects every other aspect of family life, including the challenges newly divorced families face.

Changes in Residence

A common expression in the realm of family life education is that divorce brings with it "new everythings"—a new family structure, a new way of interacting with parents, and perhaps at some point, a new family if one or both parents remarry. In many cases, these transitions include relocating to a new home. Unless the move is within the same neighborhood, a move to a new home introduces other "new everythings," for it also brings new neighborhoods, new peers, new schools, and new teachers.

Divorced single parents often find that because of the radical changes in their finances, they are no longer able to live in their pre-divorce home (Kelly & Emery, 2003). Quite frequently, in an effort to lessen the strain on the family budget that comes with transitioning to single-parent living, divorced women find that they are forced to sell their homes. Additionally, this transition involves not just an economic rebalancing but also an emotional rebalancing (Anderson & Sabatelli, 2011). When recently divorced single parents then move to a different neighborhood and into a less expensive home, they and their children are faced with the harsh reality of a new beginning that redefines the family system (Kelly & Emery, 2003). Perhaps Trisch, a divorced woman who is selling her home and moving forward, sums it up best:

> Goodbye to the home that I spent endless afternoons and weekends looking for—making sure it met all of the rigid requirements. I'll probably never find another house like that again. It was so much more than a house—it represented an achievement of a goal, a new beginning of the beginning. And now I've lost it all. Goodbye to the home we were making. Goodbye to the tulips planted in the fall but that we never saw together in the spring when it came time for them to bloom. (cited in Fisher & Alberti, 2000, p. 106)

Changes in Boundaries

Central to the challenges of post-divorce parenting is the issue of reworking parenting roles. And as Anderson and Sabatelli (2011) note, even for those parents who are willing, strongly desiring of, and firmly committed to parenting cooperatively, divorce is always accompanied by greater separateness and autonomy, along with a decline in interdependence—and this change in the relationship between parents and children adds to the other everyday, ordinary stresses associated with parenting.

In essence, the re-establishment of parenting roles ensures that what was once shared by both parents is now covered independently by each parent. Tasks associated with establishing new parental roles following divorce include the following (Graham, 2005):

- Forming new relationships with children that do not include ongoing input, support, and the collaboration from the other parent. Even in the best of circumstances where both parents are actively involved in the children's lives, one parent is still absent from the home.
- Creating a working business relationship with the former spouse that ensures successful completion of childrearing tasks, such as helping children with homework, taking them to after-school activities, or taking them to doctor or dentist appointments.
- Establishing methods of discipline that do not rely on the other parent's input or aid.
- Developing a parenting plan. The parenting plan outlines the rights, and responsibilities of each parent and establishes an appropriate working relationship between the parents (for issues regarding the children's health, education, and well-being).
- Communicating clearly and accurately to the other parent those things that are taking place in the child's life. At the forefront of such communication are the child's emotional stability and the protection of the child's best interests. Making these the priority of communication minimizes the children's exposure to ongoing parental conflict and minimizes the temptation to drag the child into the parents' battles.

It is beyond question that the exit of one member from the family system disrupts the balance of the entire system. However, if proper care and attention are given to the re-establishment of parental roles following divorce, over time the family will re-establish itself and find a new reorganized balance.

Changes in the Emotional Environment

There is no other way to state it: Divorce hurts! Managing the emotional climate of the binuclear family is just as important as managing finances and new parenting roles.

Single mothers' ability to become sole administrator of the home hinges on their ability to manage the emotional climate of their newly defined single-parent homes. In other words, the mother must assume all authority and responsibility, as well as provide love, understanding, and support. Although many single mothers rely on their former spouses, day care providers, or the children's grandparents to assist them, many others decide that if they are the custodial parent, they should have complete authority in whatever decisions are made (Anderson & Sabatelli, 2011; Graham, 2004). This shift in authority allows single mothers to separate from former spouses and gain autonomy. Without this authority, boundaries may not be clear and, all too often children, former spouses, and/or grandparents may undermine the mother's efforts and render her ineffective—thus ensuring that inconsistent, dysfunctional parenting roles are established.

According to Anderson and Sabatelli (2011), fathers also have difficulties in managing the emotional tasks of the post-divorce family. Divorced fathers tend to struggle with managing the emotional climate of the home because of a frequent inability to maintain a sense of home and family, even if he is the noncustodial parent. Typically, when the father is the non-resident parent, he experiences these feelings of loss and he may feel that he has lost control and influence over his children (Kruk, 1991). Fathers will often experience an even greater sense of loss and powerlessness if there remain high levels of conflict between the father and his former wife, if his ex-spouse limits his visitations to his children (in order to exert control over him or punish him), or if the custodial and visitation agreements are not strictly adhered to (Wallerstein, 1998).

Dating

When women and men experience being single after they divorce, many feel a mix of positive and negative emotions. Some choose to date because they simply do not like being alone. In fact, for some individuals, being single is particularly difficult if they never learned how to live as a single before their marriage, perhaps moving straight from their parents' homes to their marital homes (Fisher & Alberti, 2000). But many may find their newfound status to be liberating—a time to invest in themselves. As one newly divorced man explains,

> I've become aware that living as a single person is an affirmation of strength and self—not an embarrassing admission of failure. I'm more relaxed in the company of others. Postmarital guilt, self-doubts, and questions like "Will I ever love again?" are greatly diminished. I am happy as a single person—something I had not thought possible before, (p. 235)

Most people, however, are not disenchanted with marriage and are not content to remain single following their divorce. Indeed, it is not unusual for many men and women to rush into dating following their marital separation or divorce. For many of these individuals, dating helps them fill the void of their loss with a new, more intense love (Ahrons, 1994). The way men and women handle postmarital romance differs, however. According to Anderson and Sabatelli (2007),

- Post-divorce men initiate dating relationships sooner than do post-divorce women.
- Following divorce, men rely more on their dating partners for intimacy and support than do women.
- Women have stronger, more intimate social support networks than do men and turn to these rather than to a dating partner for intimacy and support.

- Men have greater financial resources to pursue a new partner.
- The demands of single parenting and economic pressures leave women with less energy to pursue a dating relationship.

There are further reasons why newly divorced individuals choose whether or not to date. Some may delay dating to protect themselves from being hurt; others may delay dating in an attempt to gain independence and autonomy; and still others may rush into dating and courtship in an effort to quickly remarry. Beyond not wanting to be "alone," some of these individuals may want to quickly re-establish "normalcy," or find supportive relationships that will help them redefine their identities. While the reasons for dating following divorce are complex and varied, creating new relationships helps restructure an individual's social network in a way that more closely meets the individual's changing needs (Anderson & Sabatelli, 2011).

Not all dating relationships end with another trip down the aisle, but about 64 percent of men and 52 percent of divorced women remarry (Pew Research Center, 2018), and today, nearly 4 million children in the United States live in a stepparent home (U.S. Census Bureau, 2018). In America, more than 40 percent of adults have at least one step-relative (U.S. Census Bureau, 2018).

There are a number of transitions associated with repartnering following divorce. Perhaps the greatest difficulty of repartnering is subsequent relationship stability. As one researcher notes, "[Repartnering] can help improve the well-being of adults and children, [but] it appears that the challenges of divorce are rarely overcome completely (Jensen, Shafer, Guo, & Larson, 2015).

Helping Kids Cope With Divorce

There is no concrete formula or recipe that guarantees that children will come out of divorce unscathed, but there are things that divorcing parents can do to help reduce the impact of their decision to end their marriage on their children (Mayo Clinic, 2004):

iStock.com/Sisoje

Men are sooner to date following divorce than women are. This may be because they have greater financial freedom and because they commonly do not have physical custody of the children.

How to Tell Them. Child psychologists and family therapists recommend that, if possible, spouses should be together when they tell their children about their divorce.

- Parents should reaffirm their love and commitment to their children, and assure them they will always take care of them.
- Parents should assure children that they are not responsible for the divorce.
- Parents should speak honestly and simply, but they should leave out all the ugly details.

Keep the Kids Out of the Fight. How ex-spouses act toward each other and toward the children impacts children s adjustment.

- Children should never be forced to side with one parent over the other; they are not pawns or weapons to be used to hurt the other parent,
- Children should never be used as messengers, and parents should never speak badly about the other parent to the children.
- Child support issues should never be talked about in front of children.

Don't Spoil Them. Although it's tempting to spoil children or to lavish them with gifts to help absolve some of the guilt parents feel, child psychologists believe this only makes children feel more insecure.

- Don't relax the household rules or boundaries, and they should be similar for both parents.
- Kids and adolescents need stable routines and stable boundaries, even though they will push the limits.

Put the Children First. Angry, hurting, vengeful ex-spouses can make angry, hurting, vengeful parents. Even though it is understandable that ex-spouses want little interaction with each other, parents need to make co-parenting work for the sake of the children.

- Work on parenting goals together for the well-being of the children.
- Custody arrangements should be centered on what the children need, not what the parents need or want.

TRANSITIONS TO REPARTNERING

Although remarriages are common today, there remains a stereotypical view that these marriages are not as functional as "traditional" marriages (Ganong & Coleman, 2004). To better understand the transitions associated with forming a new family system following divorce, in the following section we'll examine the stages of the remarriage experience, remarriage stability, and the many characteristics of stepfamilies today.

Remarriage

Today in the United States, 4 out of 10 new marriages involve remarriage (Pew Research Center, 2018). As you can see in Figure 14.2, 40 percent of all marriages in the U.S. are remarriages, either for one spouse or for both spouses. The data in Figure 14.3 present for us the percentage of those who remarry, by age group. Overall, whites are more likely to remarry than are other races:

- Whites: 60 percent
- Hispanic: 51 percent
- Black: 48 percent
- Asian: 46 percent

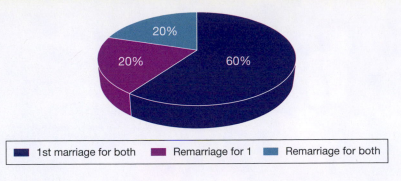

1st marriage for both ■   Remarriage for 1 ■   Remarriage for both

Source: Pew Research Center (2018).

Figure 14.3 /// Percentage of Previously Married Individuals Who Remarried, by Age

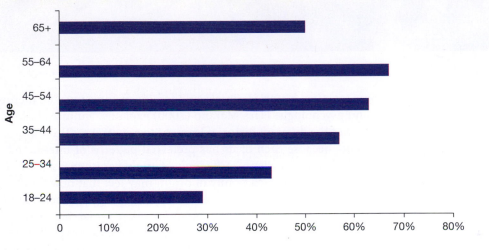

Source: Pew Research Center (2014).

Transitioning to a new family structure involves a developmental process, just as with any other change encountered throughout the life cycle of the family. As you know, with the dissolution of the nuclear family system because of divorce, two separate family forms emerge, creating a binuclear family. When either one or both of the former spouses choose to remarry, a stepfamily is formed. Like many of the family processes we have discussed throughout this text, remarriage is also a process of different developmental stages: early remarriage, middle remarriage, and late remarriage.

Early Remarriage

Psychologist Patricia Papernow (1984, 1993) has addressed the patterns commonly seen in the family life cycle development of remarried and stepfamilies. **Remarriage** refers to instances when either one or both of the spouses have been previously married. As its name implies, **early remarriage** refers to the early stages of the new relationship, and brings with it not only the developmental difficulties of a traditional marriage, but also carries with it difficulties unique to stepfamilies. When one or both of the married partners bring children from a previous relationship into the new marital relationship, the newly merged family is referred to as a stepfamily.

Remarriage:
a marriage in which one or both spouses have been previously married.

Early remarriage:
the early stages of the new relationship, when the developmental difficulties of a traditional marriage occur, along with difficulties unique to stepfamilies.

Today, 40 percent of all marriages in the United States are remarriages. When spouses remarry, a stepfamily is formed.

When two families come together, histories, rituals, and family customs must be merged. As noted family scientist and psychologist Hara Marano (2000) explains, "culture clash" is built into any marriage because of the different histories brought to a marriage. This culture clash within a new family occurs because each of us has preferred patterns of interacting along with shared memories and shared histories—*each family of origin has its own shared identity.* When families merge, members from each family of origin may feel that new family members are intruding into their family, and in a very real sense, intruding into their identity. As Papernow points out, however, this is the starting point for every remarried or stepfamily. A lack of shared patterns of interacting and a lack of shared histories are expected and normal at this stage of remarriage. Because newly formed stepfamilies lack shared experiences, the two families interact primarily with their biological parents, siblings, grandparents, and other extended family members during the early remarriage stage (Anderson & Sabatelli, 2011). These interaction patterns may last for up to two to three years after remarriage or the formation of a stepfamily; thus, one of the central developmental tasks of remarriage is to allow time for the newly merged family system to grow and share new experiences together.

Middle Remarriage

Middle remarriage: the middle stage of a remarriage, which takes most families about three to five years to complete, when the family becomes a more cohesive system and functions less along strictly biological lines.

During the **middle remarriage** stage of development, which takes most families about three to five years to complete, the family becomes a more cohesive system and functions less along strictly biological lines. In order to successfully transition to this stage of remarried family life, the family needs to restructure family boundaries and identity-family members' roles (Anderson & Sabatelli, 2011):

- Ensure that each family member's needs, expectations, and feelings are considered equally. This is accomplished through honest communication and shared empathy.
- Compromise between "old" and "new" ways of doing things such as homework or celebrating holidays. "Out with the old, in with the new" doesn't apply when it comes to remarried families.
- Clarify family boundaries and expectations with regard to the noncustodial parent, biological relatives, and step-relatives.

If the family makes this successful transition, the family will emerge as not only a more cohesive system with unambiguous boundaries but also as a family with a shared purpose and a shared family identity (Papernow, 1984).

Late Remarriage

During **late remarriage**—approximately 6 to 10 (or more) years after the remarriage—the family's boundaries and roles are restructured to the point there is a greater deal of "authenticity" in interactions and shared intimacy within the family system (Anderson & Sabatelli, 2011). If family members are flexible and successful in realigning their boundaries to accommodate the realities of remarried and/or stepfamily living, then closer, warmer, more endearing relationships are likely to form among stepfamily members. This doesn't mean that family living is sunshine and roses all of the time. As with any family, there will be times of conflict, anger, and hurt feelings. There will be times when one family member feels excluded or when another family member feels awkward including a nonbiological family member in decision making or family rituals. In some remarried families, members may simply agree to accept more distant, less involved relationships with one another (Anderson & Sabatelli, 2011). To be a successful remarried family not only requires a realization from the married partners that "there's a history of something that came before" (Marano, 2000) it also requires the belief that trust and understanding will grow as families share experiences over time.

Remarriage Stability

In the case of remarriage, practice does not make perfect. In comparison to first marriages, remarriages have, for several decades, consistently demonstrated higher rates of divorce (for a complete review of the literature, see Jensen et al., 2015). **Relationship stability** is defined by clinical social worker Todd Jensen (University of North Carolina Chapel Hill) as "the perceptions and behaviors associated with the dissolution of a marriage or committed relationship" (Jensen et al., 2015). In other words, these factors are indicators of a couple's proneness to divorce. And today, one indicator of divorce proneness is remarriage. Indeed, marital instability is more marked among remarried couples than it is in one-marriage couples (Amato, 2010; Sweeney, 2010). Why is the future of remarriage so grim?

There are several reasons. For example, as we just discussed, when couples embark on a second marriage, they often do not have a firm understanding of their identity as a stepfamily, or what it means to merge two families (Gerlach, 2005). Many remarrying partners enter into a second marriage with unrealistic expectations and without a sound understanding of the complexities of stepfamily life. As a result, these couples lack the necessary coping skills to traverse many transitions as they rebuild their lives together. According to Peter Gerlach, a social worker and board member of the Stepfamily Association of America, remarried families also face greater differences than once-married families in the emotional, legal, social, and financial environments of their families. Gerlach explains that there are as many as 60 significant ways a second marriage differs from a first-marriage environment.

Other research suggests that instability in subsequent marriages is the result of a breakdown in the commitment, cohesion, and communication in first marriages (Ihinger-Tallman & Pasley, 1987). For example, some couples use divorce to resolve marital conflict, and others experience deep emotional wounds following divorce. These situations often result in partners who have difficulty making another commitment. Other couples have difficulties establishing cohesion, or the emotional ties that bind families together, because of the lack of a shared family history. Finally, unless remarrying couples address communication problems— near the top of the list of reasons why people seek divorce—they run the risk of carrying the same problems into a subsequent marriage.

According to Gerlach (2005), the essence of remarriage is not really different from first marriages: "The relationship objectives are the same—to lovingly help each other fulfill a set of core personal needs over time . . . while each partner evolves as a unique individual in a

Late remarriage: six to ten (or more) years after the remarriage, when the family's boundaries and roles are restructured to the point there is a greater deal of "authenticity" in interactions and shared intimacy within the family system.

Relationship stability: the perceptions and behaviors associated with the dissolution of a marriage or committed relationship.

changing world. The shared [goals] needed to grow and keep a healthy, satisfying love relationship are the same in both cases." The key to establishing a successful subsequent marriage and family system is a joint commitment from both partners. This will help ensure that all members of the newly formed family system are met. Today, it is important to understand that stepfamilies are not one-size-fits-all in their characteristics.

Stepfamilies Today

Stepfamilies are very common in today's world, but there used to be negative undertones associated with the term *stepfamily,* such as the "evil" stepmother who is cruel to her stepchildren, so often portrayed in children's storybooks. Due to the increasing incidence of stepfamilies, there have been attempts over the years to soften the terminology and to use other terms that do not carry the negative connotation, such as "integrated family," "complicated family form," "merged family," or "reconstituted" or "combined family." The alternative term with which most of us are familiar is **blended families**. The Stepfamily Association of America (SAA, 2009), however, disagrees with the use of this term, pointing out that when two family systems join together, they do not "blend." Notes the SAA, "A stepfamily does not *recreate* a first family (or, blend into something entirely new with all prior connections severed and the former existence obliterated)." Thus, according to the SAA, to "blend" a family would mean that children and spouses in stepfamilies must lose their identity, their individuality, and their active attachment to the absent parent, to the former first family. All other family forms are defined by the relationship that exists between the parent and child, such as foster, adoptive, single-parent, or biological. The SAA holds, then, that it is more accurate and preferred to use the term *stepfamily.* They also assert that implying that two distinct family systems can fold into one sets the new family structure up for unrealistic expectations and "doom" (SAA, 2009).

Stepfamily Types

The presence of children from a previous marriage defines a stepfamily, but the composition of stepfamilies differs. In some instances, members of a stepfamily may or may not live full time within the stepfamily household; in many cases, children are members of *two* stepfamily households. Table 14.2 summarizes the different types of stepfamilies, each defined by the

Blended families: alternative term for stepfamilies.

When two families merge, it is common for each side to feel that the other is intruding into their family. These feelings often compound the interactions of stepfamilies and significantly contribute to why it takes stepfamilies two to three years to adjust to stepfamily living.

Table 14.2 /// Types of Stepfamilies

Biological mother/stepfather	The household consists of the mother's biological children and her stepchildren (the children of the stepfather).
Biological father/stepmother	The household consists of the father's biological children and his stepchildren (the children of the stepmother).
Complex stepfamily	Both partners have children from previous relationships or marriage, although the children may reside in different households.
Joint biological-stepfamily	The couple has at least one biological child that is the product of both married parents, and at least one biological child of either parent (meaning the other parent would be the stepparent).

Source: Stepfamily Association of America (2009).

parent–child relationship. Also, in stepfamilies, children are described in different ways. For example, *siblings* share the same two biological parents, while *stepsiblings* are not biologically related, but have parents who are married to one another. A *mutual child* is the child (or children) who is born to the remarried couple. Some researchers refer to this as the "cement" child, as they are thought to cement the relationship.

Stepfamily Characteristics

Many students often mistakenly assume that stepfamilies are no different than first families since there are two parents in the home who share in the everyday tasks of rearing children. Although on the surface it may appear that there are not significant differences, the complex combination of roles and relationships makes stepfamily living very different from a nuclear family's, as Table 14.3 shows us. Certain characteristics distinguish stepfamilies from first families (Parziale & Parziale, 2002).

The stepfamily is born of loss. Every stepfamily has one thing in common: they have all faced loss (Wallerstein & Kelly, 1980). Unlike first marriages, a stepfamily is typically born of loss—of a parent or family through death, through divorce, or through desertion. And because divorce is frequently accompanied by relocation, the members of a stepfamily may also be mourning the loss of other family members (such as a grandmother or grandfather, a favorite aunt or uncle), previous friends, their former home or school, their former neighborhood, or their dreams. The grief is exacerbated during holidays, birthdays, school events, and other special family times. According to the SAA (2009), adults and children each grieve over certain specific losses associated with divorce. For example, adults typically grieve over the loss of a partner and the loss of the marital relationship, while children grieve the loss of a parent and stability.

The family boundaries and roles are ambiguous. The frequent entrances and exits of family members from the various stepfamily households, such as stepchildren/stepsiblings leaving for visitations or coming for visitations, may lead to indistinct or blurred boundaries. This ambiguity creates confusion and uncertainty as to who is "in" the family and who is not, and causes doubt about family affiliations. Further, the roles in stepfamilies have no clear, traditionally understood labels, no clear definitions, and no clear expectations (Parziale & Parziale, 2002). In a biological family, the role of Mom or Dad is typically well understood by the family, the community, and society. In a stepfamily, however, there is no how-to manual or job description for the roles of "stepparent" or "stepchild," and these roles are not clearly defined by society. Additionally, there are different roles depending on the composition of the stepfamily structure (such as biological mother, biological father, etc.). Further compounding the complexity of stepparenting relationships and heightening the ambiguity is that there is no legal relationship between stepparents and stepchildren: Stepparents cannot authorize emergency medical care, access the child's academic records, or sign legal documents relating to the child.

Table 14.3 /// The Ways That Stepfamilies and Nuclear Families Differ

Structural Factor	Typical Stepfamily	Typical Nuclear Family
Number of co-parenting homes	Usually homes linked by legal documents, emotions, finances, genes and ancestry, shared history, responsibilities, and memories	Usually one home
Grandparents (living and dead)	Usually six or eight or more	Usually four
Physical and legal child custody	Sole, joint, or split; usually subject to legal decree(s) and often legally contested	Shared; no legal suits or decrees
Spouses' parenting values and styles (e.g., child discipline)	Preformed before remarrying and cohabiting; often needs compromising	Evolved together over years; differences are usually less stressful
Caregivers' legal parenting rights and responsibilities regarding minor kids' school/ health/ custody/etc. (varies by state)	Fewer and less clear rights (stepparents and step-grandparents); responsibilities more confusing; a legal parenting agreement may exist, which excludes any stepparents	More and clearer rights (bio-parents and bio-grandparents); responsibilities far clearer; no legal documents to enforce or litigate
Last names	Re-wedded bio-mom's names may differ from their kids' names: without adoption, stepsibs have different last names	Adults and kids usually all have the same last name, so less chance of identity and loyalty (priority) confusions
Family-member loyalty, bonding, and cohesion	Initially, pseudo or little among merging families; may or may not improve with time; much more fragile	Generally much stronger throughout the family life cycle; they usually transcend traumas

Source: Adapted from Gerlach (2005).

There is a disparity of individual, marital, and family life cycles. When two family systems form a stepfamily, an obstacle that all family members face is the fact that they do not share a common history, common traditions, or common life experiences. Compounding these differences is that fact that there will be children with varying developmental needs. It is also quite likely that there will be differences in parenting styles, career aspirations, finances, retirement goals, and lifestyles. As Parziale and Parziale (2002) note, when developmental phases among family members are crossed, individual family members' needs may be out of sync with those of other family members, which adds to the stressors associated with role ambiguity.

There are several loyalty conflicts. Because children have strong emotional ties to their biological parents, their loyalty to the biological parents remains strong. The most common loyalty conflict involves the stepparent whenever children feel that their relationship with their biological parent(s) is threatened as a result of the stepparent joining the family system (Parziale & Parziale, 2002). Another common loyalty conflict exists among siblings. For example, what happens if one sibling *likes* the new stepparent and other siblings *do not*? Is it okay to "love" the new stepparent? Because of these types of loyalty conflicts, the cohesion of the stepfamily is seldom at the same level as the first family's.

Stepfamilies experience more stress than nuclear families. Unlike first families, stepfamilies sometimes face years of instability due to the inherent multiple changes. The first two years are often quite turbulent; it may take as long as eight years for the family to reorganize and adjust. All too often, stepparents and children are immediately thrust into conflicting multiple roles. Stepparents walk into a parenting role before emotional or attachment ties with the children have been established; meanwhile, children are expected to instantly love Mom or Dad's new spouse and to get along with their new stepsiblings. All of these changes and expectations are sources of great stress for all involved. Is it any wonder that stepfamily formation and stepfamily life is so challenging?

Stepfamily Challenges

It takes a long time for stepfamily members to get used to the new roles each are being assigned, as well as the new relationships and boundaries intrinsic to new stepfamilies. Because of the inherent "relational overload" that accompanies the numerous and complex steprelationships, stepfamilies face many more challenges than do those in first-time families (Parziale & Parziale, 2002).

Common Challenges for Adults

Even though remarriage is rapidly becoming the most common family form in the United States (Bramlett & Mosher, 2001), it still carries with it a stigma of sorts. In general, first-time marriages receive substantially more emotional and physical support from family and friends, as well as from their place of worship. When adults remarry, they inherit new responsibilities and obligations to their new family. These additional responsibilities may cause added strain, and may include the following:

- *Financial difficulties.* Financial strain is common in stepfamilies as stepfathers and step-mothers alike may be under a court order to pay child and/or spousal support to their former families (Mason, Fine, & Carnochan, 2001; Manning, Stewart, & Smock, 2003).

- *Adjusting to new parenting roles.* Stepping immediately into the role of stepparent is difficult because it requires learning how to share parenting. Stepparents find that they must change existing parenting techniques, developing new techniques that fit the new family—and developing a new role with the children (Bray, 1999). Because children of divorce experience higher rates of emotional, behavioral, and academic problems than do children of never-divorced families, stepparents have a formidable task as they try to establish a sense of normalcy (Coleman, Ganong, & Fine, 2000).

- *Establishing discipline.* Exerting authority' and discipline are two of the biggest obstacles associated with stepparenting. The SAA (2009) recommends that stepparents initially adopt a "friend" role with their stepchildren, rather than role of instant parent. Giving children time to get to know a new stepparent affords the stepfamily the opportunity to begin to build a shared history. Reassuring children that the stepparent is not trying to replace the child's biological parent also helps to ease the transition (Coleman et al., 2000).

- *Bonding as a couple.* It is essential that the couple take time to nurture one another and their relationship. This requires finding time to spend time alone together in order to affirm each other and to demonstrate affection (Kheshgi-Genovese & Genovese, 1997).

- *Grieving past losses.* Most divorce adults are wounded in some way and frequently experience guilt, shame, fear, distrust, and a feeling of failure. Even if the individual is the one who initiated the divorce, he or she may experience deep feelings of loss—the loss of dreams, the loss of goals, the loss of security, or the loss of a fairytale type of love. The sense of loss is one of the most difficult obstacles to overcome.

Common Challenges for Children

Children enter into a stepfamily with a history of loss that is beyond their control. They tend to respond to this transition with feelings of helplessness and anger. Too often, parents mistakenly assume that because children are young, they are oblivious to the changes that surround them, or they believe that because children are young, they will quickly "bounce back." As we have seen throughout this chapter, a child's ability to bounce back is largely dependent on how they are pa rented during the turbulent processes of transition—not only by their biological parents but also by their stepparents. To help children thrive as they transition to stepfamily living, adults must understand the common challenges children face as they enter into this new family system:

- *Loss of power and control.* Children lose more than a parent when their nuclear family dissolves; because they have no choice in how the events unfold, they frequently feel a loss of power and control. This sense of powerlessness can be overwhelming for a child. To help children heal, it is imperative that they be given control over some aspect of their new life. For example, when children are allowed to make small decisions, such as how to spend their allowance or devising new stepfamily rules, this contributes to their feelings of control and minimizes their feelings of helplessness (Kalter, Alpern, Spence, & Plunkett, 1984; Robson, Cook, & Gilliland, 1995).

- *Guilt.* Children often blame themselves for their parents' divorce. They may believe that they were "bad" or "naughty" and that their behavior drove the other parent away; they may believe that they are too "unlovable" or that they are too "expensive" for the parent to care for them; in the case of a deceased parent, they may have "wished" their parent was dead at some point in time. It is crucial that parents engage in honest communication with their children throughout the many processes of divorce and convey to the children that divorce or death is *never* the fault of the child. It is also of the utmost importance that parents assure their children that their parents love them under any circumstances (Warshak, 2000).

- *Loyalty conflicts.* When a parent remarries, children often feel that if they become close to the new stepparent or if they "love" the stepparent, they are unfaithful and disloyal to their biological parent—they feel they have betrayed that parent. If divorced parents continue arguing in front of their children or use the children as pawns in the divorce process, this heightens these loyalty struggles. Thus, the rejection of a new stepparent or a new home may be more a reflection of their fear of abandoning their biological parent rather than dislike for the stepparent. It is vital that both parents and stepparents assure (again and again!) the children that it is possible to love many people at the same time and that having a relationship with a stepparent in no way means that they love their biological parent any less (Kheshgi-Genovese & Genovese, 1997).

- *Anger.* It is normal for children to feel angry toward their parents following divorce and during the formation of a stepfamily. The anger may be due to the sense of powerlessness and lack of control they have in the situation, and it may be directed toward a parent who visits infrequently or fails to follow through on promises. The anger may also be a response lo a move from the family home, neighborhood, or school. However the child's anger is expressed, it is essential that parents and stepparents reassure the children that it is normal to feel angry, and to feel whatever they have been feeling (Kelly & Emery, 2003; Strohschein, 2005).

Because stepfamilies are structurally and emotionally different from first families, both adults and children have difficulty adjusting and adapting to the changes swept in by divorce (Seymour, Francis, & Steffens, 1995). For adults, adjustment centers on their ability to maintain a close relationship with their new spouse. Children's ability to adapt is largely dependent on how sensitive parents and stepparents are to children's feelings and behaviors. "A little understanding [is] the right foundation for the beginning of a strong stepfamily relationship" (Seymour et al., 1995).

Successful Stepfamily Living

With all the added stressors and tensions so commonly experienced in stepfamily life, newly formed families may wonder if it is possible for family life to be high in happiness and satisfaction. Marriage and family therapists Emily Visher and John Visher (1993) provide key characteristics of those families who successfully adapt to the multifaceted changes associated with divorce and remarriage.

- *They develop realistic expectations.* All members within the stepfamily understand that it will never be the same as the first family. They also understand that love and care do not develop instantly; these develop slowly, over time, as the family builds its own history, rituals, and traditions through shared experiences.

- *They allow time for mourning.* Adults and children come to understand that they need time to mourn the loss of the family they once had. By allowing open, honest communication, and by sharing feelings of anger, fear, and guilt, the family begins healing.

- *Remarried couples nurture a strong relationship.* Adults take time to nurture their relationship and pay close attention to their needs as a couple. It is difficult to be effective parents and stepparents when couples suffer in their own relationships.

- *They accept that becoming a stepparent takes time.* Although biological parents have time to evolve into their parenting roles, stepparents are instantly thrust into their roles. When stepparents do not force togetherness with their stepchildren, their relationships with their stepchildren have a better chance of thriving.

- *Stepparents slowly develop the role of disciplinarian.* Not only does intimacy take time to be earned, so does the role of authoritarian. Discipline works better if the biological parent takes the lead until the relationship between the stepparent and stepchild is stronger (Shoup Olsen, 1997). In successful stepfamilies, stepparents are able to vary their roles, particularly if they have biological children of their own (taking the lead parenting role with their own children but stepping aside to allow the parent and co-parent of stepchildren to discipline their children).

- *They develop a stepfamily history.* For successful stepfamily living, flexibility is key! It is necessary to give each other permission to do things differently than they did in their first family, from establishing a new homework schedule, to doing household chores, to establishing new (and perhaps different) birthday and holiday rituals and traditions. Over time, as families share experiences, they weave together their own unique family history—and thus strengthen family ties.

- *They work cooperatively with the absent parent.* Stepparents learn to make arrangements far in advance of events and visitations to ensure collaborative shared parenting. Stepfamilies who have flexible family boundaries that allow for multiple exits and entrances into and from the family system tend to experience more cooperative parenting, such as is common with African American and Hispanic families. Whether or not residual angry, hostile, or bitter feelings exist, communication is essential.

Those who are successful in transitioning their multiple family systems into a cohesive stepfamily system know that, just as with divorce, remarriage involves multiple, simultaneous processes and is accompanied by common struggles faced by both children and adults.

FAMILY LIFE EDUCATION: PROTECTING CHILDREN'S AND ADULTS' WELL-BEING

Divorce hurts. And the transitions that take place in life after divorce are no less emotionally confusing or painful than is the process of divorce. As noted by the student in the opening of this chapter, divorce is a broken experience that requires time for family members to pick up all of the pieces, to reassemble, and to reorganize their lives. Feelings of despair, disappointment, and helplessness are not uncommon, as it takes years for family members to develop a new orientation to post-divorce life.

Taking Sides

The Reality of Remarriage

Many people mistakenly assume that a marriage is a marriage is a marriage. But when couples remarry, they need to understand that their second or subsequent marriages will be vastly different from their first marriage. As you learned in this chapter, first marriages differ from subsequent marriages in a number of ways. Is it any wonder that divorce rates are higher among remarriages than they are among first marriages? Does the following couple have realistic expectations about their remarriage?

Her Side: Experience counts! I know the mistakes I made the first time around, and I vowed never to repeat those mistakes. A family is a family. I don't think that his children with his first wife will come between us, and I don't think that my kids will come between us. We both *knew* what we were getting into when we started dating each other. My teenage daughter is having a little difficulty accepting him as her stepfather, but I believe that time heals all wounds and that she'll eventually come around. I think my expectations are realistic. I know it will take time, but I think eventually we will all settle into a good pattern of relating to each other. If I were being honest, I'd have to say I'm more worried about his ex-wife coming between us than I am about his kids visiting us every weekend.

His Side: My concerns are the polar opposite of her concerns. I don't think my ex-wife will be as big a problem as the kids will be. I don't think she's being realistic about merging our two families. I know she wants it to work, and I know that she believes that if she is warm and honest and caring that my kids will respect her and love her—but it won't be as *automatic* as I think she expects it to be. Yes, time heals all wounds. But during that *time* is when the conflicts, the problems with loyalty, learning to parent different children, and learning to emotionally connect with every family member happens. I'm not saying we can't do it, or that we shouldn't do it. . . . I'm just saying that I think we have a rougher road ahead of us than either of us can imagine.

Your Side: Making a go of any marriage is tough work, but it's even tougher to make remarriages work. In considering the couple's comments,

1. What strengths does this couple possess that will help better navigate the transitions to remarried life? What are the couple's realistic expectations?

2. In your opinion, what are the primary unrealistic expectations of this couple? What can be done to help them forge new role expectations, new rules, and goals for a life together as a stepfamily?

Given the psychological distress that divorce and relationship end brings to couples and their families, the role helping professionals play post-divorce is crucial to the well-being of children and adults (Beckmeyer, Krejnik, McCray, Markham, & Troilo, 2018). Family processes such as coparenting cooperation, ex-spouses' communication, and the realignment of boundaries are known to encourage optimal post-divorce psychological health in children (ages 4 to 9), and youth (ages 10 to 18). Understanding and identifying how former spouses' post-divorce ongoing relationship impacts children and youth is a key role of CFLEs. According to family life practitioner Johnathan Beckmeyer (2018), when working with post-divorce families, CFLEs should:

- Create and implement age appropriate education programs.
- Focus on aspects of the former spousal relationship, such as coparenting and communication.
- Help partners transition from spouses to partners in childrearing.
- Establish new communication and relationship boundaries.
- Establish identities independent and separate from former spouses.

The transition to life following divorce involves many processes, which involve emotional, economic, parental, and legal ramifications. For children and adolescents whose parents divorce, there are many negative outcomes. There are also many variables associated with post-divorce outcomes, such as being separated from an important attachment figure, the relationship between the parents and their children, the family's economics, and whether one or both parents remarry. The most critical factor in determining outcomes, however, is the parents' ability to effectively co-parent or share parenting.

Although adapting to single-parent life is difficult for mothers, fathers, and children, the most dramatic changes in family life and family structure come about when parents remarry and form stepfamilies. Despite the fact that popular television shows often portray first families and remarried families as similar entities, the differences between the two are vast. Not only does the family structure vary, but so too do their histories, their experiences, and family members' roles. Becoming a stepfamily requires unique tasks for both adults and children— accepting these changes does not happen overnight, but requires years to fully integrate as a family system. Realistic expectations—recognizing that the stepfamily will never be the same as the first family and that love and care do not develop instantly—is the foundation on which strong, successful stepfamilies are built and fostered.

Is there family life after divorce? This is a question that I've posed to many of my students taking my course. I often ask my students to draw a "picture" of divorce. Quite often, students draw a "broken" or "split" home of sorts, with the children residing with the mother while the father lives in another home. In many of these drawings, students draw tears or expressions of sadness on family members' faces. But one drawing in particular captured my attention. It was an illustration of a mature tree that had split, as if it had been struck by lightning or had been destroyed during a storm. In the midst of the split tree trunk was just a hint of new growth—a sprig of bright green, spring-like growth. That drawing captured the essence of divorce and remarriage, the transitions to stepfamily living. When a marriage breaks down and the nuclear family dissolves, the family feels as though it was struck by lightning or twisted apart by a storm. Left wounded, battered, broken, and damaged, many families feel that the family will never recover. Yet, slowly over time, new growth takes place—a new structure grows from the old.

/// SUMMARY

The Aftermath of Divorce: Transitions

- Just as there is no universal pathway to uncoupling, there is no universal pathway to rebuilding following divorce.

- *Binuclear family* refers to the separate, distinct households that form after marital separation or divorce. Two subsystems—maternal and paternal—are now the child's family of origin, and this restructuring from one central family unit into two accounts for much of the upheaval and confusion associated with divorce.

- The relationship between ex-spouses during their marriage sets the emotional climate for the newly defined binuclear family.

- There are five former spouse relationship styles: Perfect Pals, Cooperative Colleagues, Angry Associates, Fiery Foes, and Dissolved Duos.

- Divorced women often face financial difficulties, and these have cumulative impacts on her and her children because the financial limitations influence housing, food, clothing, transportation, medical care, child care, and the opportunities for recreation and/or leisure. Divorced moms are also at greater risk to abuse alcohol.

- Divorced dads' stressors are associated with the decreased contact they have with their children.

- Although parents have many adjustments to make following the dissolution of their marriage, these do not lessen the parents' responsibilities to meet the needs of their children. In addition to the parents' post-divorce relationship, parents' education level, income level, the duration of the marriage, the time elapsed since the divorce, whether or not one or both spouses remarry, who initiated the divorce, and whether the legal process of divorce was hostile or cooperative all affect their parenting.

- Mothers and fathers differ considerably in how they fulfill their parental duties and functions following divorce. Although most custodial mothers carry out their parenting responsibilities in the same way they did before they divorced, custodial fathers are more likely to parent differently. Additionally, post-divorce noncustodial fathers are more likely to be more permissive in their parenting and take on a "friend" role following divorce,

perhaps due to many fathers' lack of parenting skills or lack of understanding of child development.

How Divorce Affects Children and Adolescents

- Although divorce is sometimes beneficial to children, children of divorce are at increased risk for emotional difficulties, which they may externalize by "acting out," or internalize as anxiety, depression, and poor self-concept. Children who experience their parents' separation or divorce also have more difficulties in the classroom and performing academically than children who have not had similar experiences.

- The interrelated family factors that affect children' sand adolescents' long-term adjustment to divorce include the separation of the child from an attachment figure, the

passage of time, the age of the child when the divorce takes place, the relationship the child has with each parent post-divorce, whether or not one or both parents remarry after divorce, and the economic status of the binuclear family post-divorce.

- Although mothers have been awarded custody of the children following divorce for the past several decades, recent scientific studies have revealed that children fare better when both parents are involved in their growing up. Now legal and social policies have changed and family courts today are more likely to award joint custody.

Challenges for Single Parents

- Whether headed solely by mothers or solely by fathers, single-parent households are becoming more common and more diverse.

- Single-parent mothers face many significant challenges following divorce, including changes in financial status, residence, setting boundaries for children, and emotional environment, along with post-divorce dating.

- Recently divorced single women often find that they are forced to sell their homes and relocate to a more affordable home. Unless the move is within the same neighborhood, a move to a new home introduces other "new everythings" as well as the stressors that come with them.

- Since the interdependence divorced parents once had with each other no longer exists, they have to re-establish their parenting roles to ensure that what was once shared by both parents is now covered independently by each parent.

- Managing the emotional climate of the binuclear family is just as important as managing finances and new parenting roles. Single mothers' ability to become sole administrator of

the home hinges on their ability to assume all authority and responsibility, as well as provide love, understanding, and support. Divorced fathers tend to struggle with managing the emotional climate of the home because of their frequent inability to maintain a sense of home and family.

- After divorce, men and women often experience being single with a mix of positive and negative emotions. Some may struggle with loneliness and a lack of normalcy; others many may find their newfound status liberating.

- Men and women handle postmarital dating differently. Post-divorce men tend to initiate dating relationships sooner, are more apt to redefine their identity through another love relationship, experience lesser degrees of work and role strain, and may date sooner after divorce, Post-divorce women redefine their identity through independence and autonomy, turn to social support networks for intimacy and support, and have less energy to pursue a dating relationship due to the demands of single parenting and economic pressures.

Transitions to Repartnering

- When either one or both of the former spouses choose to remarry, a stepfamily is formed. The United States has the highest remarriage rate in the world, and stepfamilies are rapidly becoming the most common family structure.

- Remarriage may be run as a process of early, middle, and late developmental stages.

- Because members of a stepfamily bring into the newly formed family system their own unique, intimate histories, a central developmental task is to allow time for the newly merged family system to grow and share new experiences together. Additionally, the family's boundaries and roles must be restructured.

- Many people use the alternative term *blended families* to refer to stepfamilies, but the Stepfamily Association of America (SAA) disagrees with this term and points out that to "blend" a family would mean that children and spouses in stepfamilies must lose their identity, their individuality, and their active attachment to the absent parent, to the former first family. Thus, the SAA prefers the term *stepfamily*.

- The complex combination of roles and relationships makes stepfamily living very different from that of a nuclear family. First, all stepfamilies are born of loss, and the children are members of two [or more] households. Because of the difference in the individual, marital, and family life cycles of the various family members, the family boundaries and roles tend to be ambiguous. Second, there tend to be several loyalty conflicts. Finally, compounded by the fact that society promotes a widespread negative connotation of stepfamilies, stepfamilies tend to experience more stress than nuclear families.

- It can take four years or more for a stepfamily to feel like an integrated family, and upward of two years for children to be friendly to their new stepparent and stepsiblings. For adults, adjustment centers on their ability to maintain a close relationship with their new spouse. Children's ability

to adapt is largely dependent on how sensitive parents and stepparents are to their feelings and behaviors.

- Parents who successfully adapt to the changes associated with divorce and remarriage develop realistic expectations, allow the family time for mourning the loss of the family they once had, take time to nurture their relationship and pay close attention to their needs as a couple, accept that becoming a stepparent takes time, slowly develop their roles as disciplinarians, develop a unique stepfamily history, and work cooperatively with the absent parent.

/// KEY TERMS

Acting out   501

Binuclear family   495

Blended families   518

Diminished parenting   505

Early remarriage   515

Externalize   501

Feminization of poverty   510

Gatekeepers   498

Initiator   499

Internalizing   501

Late remarriage   517

Middle remarriage   516

Primary divorce stressors   496

Receiver   499

Relationship stability   517

Remarriage   515

Secondary divorce stressors   496

Temporal influences   504

CHAPTER 15

FAMILY CHANGE: STRESS, CRISIS, AND TRANSITION

LEARNING OBJECTIVES

15.1 Describe the ways in which normative and non-normative family processes and experience create individual and family stress.

15.2 List the factors that lead to family crisis and explain how resilience can be a protective factor.

15.3 Describe strategies for coping and maintaining family resilience.

15.4 Explain the multifaceted aspects of family violence.

It was a typically bitter-cold, grey-blue day in January. The snow on the ground looked particularly bright with ice crystals blanketing the snow. "Diamonds," I said out loud. She didn't look over at me, but looking at nothing in particular out of her car window she nodded her head in agreement. I patted her knee. "Mom, let's not worry until we know the test results, okay?" A few hours later, traveling down the same highway and looking at the same snow-covered prairie, I heard myself thinking, "It's just a dream . . . I'll wake up tomorrow and all this will be just a horrible dream . . . there's no way she has terminal cancer, she's only 56 . . . this is all just a dream."

It was a typically bitter-cold, grey-blue day in December. The wind had a particular bite to it and there were snow crystals swirling in the air. "Maybe we'll get our first snow tonight?" he said out loud. I didn't look over at him, but I nodded silently in agreement. He put his arm around my shoulder, "Let's not worry about this until we hear what the doctor says, okay?" A few hours later, traveling down the highway in the first snowstorm of the winter, I heard myself thinking, "It's just a dream . . . I'll wake up tomorrow and all this will be just a horrible dream . . . there's no way I have cancer . . . I'm only 37, I have four small sons to raise, what will they do without me? . . . this is all just a dream."

This is all just a dream . . .

No one can predict what tomorrow or the months and years ahead will bring for any given family. The very nature of the family life process involves countless complexities, and along with it, inevitable change. When I lost my mother to breast cancer, I didn't know that the same crisis would confront me, my husband, and my children just two years later.

At this point in our study of marriage and the family, we have discussed that there are expected, or normative, changes that take place throughout the family life cycle. Some of these changes are considered "vulnerability points," such as getting married; starting a sexual relationship; having a baby; parenting a teenager (or four!); juggling dual careers, financial commitments and over-commitments; and caring for aging parents. Non-normative life events, or things we cannot predict or anticipate, or things that are not commonly experienced by most families, also bring much disruption to family living. These would include life events such as a child being diagnosed with cancer, unemployment, experiencing a natural disaster, mothers fighting in combat, or a teenager becoming pregnant.

Most people know and accept this fact of inevitable change in family life, so why is it that some families stay intact during times of change and crisis (even if they're hanging on only by a thread), while other families totally unravel in response to the slightest hint of change? While some families experience life's expected events—and even the unexpected events—and circumstances as bumps in the road, other families are derailed and destabilized during stressful times and times of crisis.

My own experiences with cancer and the near loss of my own life was, without question, a personal life-altering experience. It was also life altering for every member of my family. As difficult as those years were, however, we came through it deeply enriched with a stronger sense of "who" we were as a family.

As we examine the family crisis studies throughout the following pages, we will discover that some families bind together during times of uncertainty, and other families do not "struggle well." For many families today, the pile-up of day-to-day stressors, change, and transition ultimately gives way to crisis—and signals the beginning of the end for the family. In the section that follows, we'll explore how stress affects family development and how it tends to change family roles and family rules. We'll then look at different types of family stress and crises, including the unique crisis of family violence. Finally, we'll examine the different ways families cope with and adapt to change.

FAMILY CHANGE

Family life never stays the same because *families always change*. Marriage and family therapist David Olson and his colleagues (Olson, Russell, & Sprenkel, 1983) delineate three specific types of stress that families experience: family development stress, psychological stress (stress within the individual), and family stress and crisis.

Family Development Stress

As early as World War I and the Great Depression in the early part of the 20th century, social and family scientists focused on how stress affects people and what techniques and strategies people use to cope with the stressors associated with significant personal challenges, such as experiencing the death of a loved one, or social, global, and economic events such as war or the Depression.

There is no way to arrive at a generic, one-size-fits-all definition of *stress*, but the author of the *Encyclopedia of Stress* describes stress as any stimulus that "affects the body in complex ways" and "evokes complex reactions in the various systems of the body" (McGuigan, 1999, p. 216). Along these same lines, anything that elicits a physiological and/or psychological

iStock.com/Halfpoint

Anticipated and joyous life events, such as the birth of a baby, can nonetheless be stressful experiences.

response—a stress response—to any stimuli is termed a **stressor**. The stressor can either be "good stress" or "positive stress" or "productive stress" (termed **eustress**), or "bad stress" or "negative stress" or "harmful stress" (termed **distress**). Stressors are considered to be either **acute**, meaning that they last a relatively short period of time, or **chronic**, indicating that the stressor is usually longer in duration. Most common stressors fall within four primary categories: personal, social/family, work (school), and environmental (Cordon, 1997). These categories of stress allow us to use the assumption that different people can experience the same event and not necessarily be affected in the same way (Pearlin, 1982). Any number of things can cause "stress" to an individual or family—for instance, what is "stressful" to one family, such as planning a wedding, may be "challenging" or "exciting" to another family. Stress can be experienced as a physiological or mental response to certain stimuli, or it can be experienced as a result of certain life events.

Just as an individual grows up and faces stressors of life and stressors associated with developmental tasks, so too does the family. As you saw in Chapter 1, Evelyn Duvall's (1977) classic work viewed families as dynamic systems that are in constant growth-motion, and she asserted that the best way to understand families is to understand the human development phases of the individual, as well as to get a grasp on the stages of development a family experiences. As the many tasks in Duvall's work illustrate, building and maintaining a family is hard work. Many of the transitions throughout the lifecourse of the family cause stress; sometimes this stress is experienced as a **family crisis**. As David Olson and his colleagues (1983) point out, using a family development framework allows us to see that families always change, and as a family system grows and changes, there is a call for the family to reorganize itself and to adapt and adjust to the changes. Specifically, according to Olson and others, family reorganization and adaptation involve the following characteristics.

Changes in Structure

The structure of the family is dynamic and must therefore adapt to the ongoing entrances and exits within the family system. Family stress theorist Pauline Boss (2017) notes that stress is often the result of family members being added to or subtracted from the family system, and the stress will remain until the structure is reorganized. Babies are born. Adolescents grow up and leave the home. Young adults marry and have children of their own. Parents age and may require care. Spouses may die. And sometimes, children may die. All of these changes require reorganization in the family's structure—in their family mobile.

Changes in Family Roles

As the family structure changes, family roles change. Over the course of your life, for example, your roles will likely change from being a son or a daughter, to being part of a couple, perhaps to being mother or father, to being caregiver for your aging parents, mother-in-law or father-in-law, and perhaps grandparent. Boss (2017) points out that changing family roles perpetuate changes in previously established family boundaries. Like family structures, family boundaries are in a continuous state of change and growth.

Changes in Family Rules

As roles change, the rules of communication among family members also change. For instance, perhaps you found that as you grew from childhood to adolescence to young adult, you assumed more autonomy and independence. Your individual growth demands that, along with the change in family structure and family roles, your parents must now allow you to be a young adult. This requires that previously established rules give way to new rules that accommodate your newfound independence.

Understanding what is required of families to reorganize and adapt to change and transition is at the heart of family stress theories. Yet, before we get into the fundamentals of family stress and crisis, it is necessary to recall from our discussion about the nature of a family as a system (see Chapter 3) some of the assumptions of Family Systems theory and apply them to the family crisis context:

- *The family is a system of interrelated components.* A "family" is not a whole entity, but rather a whole composed of interconnected parts. When examining family stress and crisis, then, we need to consider how we relate to and interact with others in interdependent relationships. Thus, if we experience psychological stress or distress in our own daily lives, we will most likely transfer this stress to our families. Similarly, if we experience psychological stress in our own development, we will most likely transfer this stress to our families as well. This helps explain why the *entire family* experiences the stress and/or crisis.

- *Family members affect and are affected by each other.* What happens to one family member eventually affects (or happens to) others within the family system. Recall from Chapter 3 Virginia Satir's concept of the "hanging mobile," which illustrates the delicate balance among components that make up a family. Whether the disruption is a normative life event or non-normative, such events have an impact on every member of the family system.

- *Each family must be viewed as a whole.* Because we affect and are affected by each member in our family, others outside of our family cannot fully understand the nature of a stressful event or a crisis without knowing more about our family of origin.

- *Each family's goal is to maintain homeostasis or balance.* As a family undergoes change, the disruption in balance can result in stress or crisis. Whenever a family is thrown off balance as a result of normative or non-normative disruptions, either from within or outside the family, the system will do whatever it takes to bring it back to balance. Sometimes a family may erupt in arguments and disagreements, escalating family conflict. To restore equilibrium, families will often employ previously established interactions and behaviors. All too often, families find that attempts to restore equilibrium through conflict are ill suited to aid them through the change the family is experiencing.

Duvall's (1977) family development framework (see Table 15.1) helps us to see the changes and transitions associated with family living, and it also enables us to more fully understand that the *entire family system* experiences the ripple effects of the stressor(s).

Table 15.1 /// The Family Life Cycle and Associated Developmental Tasks

Family Life Cycle Stage	Developmental Task
Married Couple	• Establish and maintain effective communication patterns • Establish and maintain mutually satisfying intimacy levels and marital relationship • Establish and maintain a mutually satisfying sexual relationship
Childbearing and Preschool-Age Children	• Adjust income to include new family member and the associated costs of child care • Realign marital roles to include the role of parents • Allow for changes in emotional and physical needs
School-Age Children	• Establish and maintain effective family communication systems/patterns • Find ways to enjoy privacy as a couple • Support children's educational achievement
Teenagers	• Renegotiate parental roles to include more adult/almost adult communication/interaction with teens • Establish balance of allowing teens freedom to become independent with mature responsibility • Maintain financial security and anticipation of costs associated with postsecondary education

(Continued)

Table 15.1 /// (Continued)

Family Life Cycle Stage	Developmental Task
Launching Young Adults	• Release young adults into the world (college, the military, marriage, the workforce) while still maintaining a home to which they can *occasionally* return • Adjust marital relationship to return to a two-member family system
Middle-Aged Parents	• Rebuild the pre-child intimacy levels in the marital relationship • Assure financial security for later years • Accept multiple entrances and exits from family system (children leaving, children marrying and becoming parents)
Later-in-Life Families	• Adjust to retirement life • Adjust to aging • Cope with inevitable death of spouse and acknowledge one's own impending end of life

Source: Adapted from Duvall (1977).

Stress doesn't simply affect our mood or temperament; it also impacts our physical and mental health and overall well-being. In the following section, we explore response-based stress, the type of stress people experience at an individual level. We'll then examine event-based stress, the types of individual stress people experience within the context of family living.

Response-Based Stress

Whether we are experiencing eustress or distress, or chronic stress or acute stress, the demands on the human body are the same (Selye, 1982). Physician Hans Selye (1985) developed the three-stage **General Adaptation Syndrome** to describe the physiological responses to eustress and distress (see Figure 15.1). Because stress can result from any number of sources and stimuli, Selye primarily focuses on the internal processes of stress. Understanding the effects of stress on individuals is important because most of us live our daily lives within the context of our family—and because of the nature of family as interconnecting members of a whole, our individual stress will ultimately be felt within the family.

In the first stage of stress response, *alarm reaction,* the brain perceives the stressor and immediately signals the body to deal with it by neurological and physiological means. The body is innately programmed to react to the imminent threat. Because of our inborn **fight or flight** tendency—either to fight the stressor or run away from it—our normal slate of homeostasis, or balance, in the mind and body is upset. The body responds by producing increased levels of corticosteroids (giving us that sense of "nervousness" and/or "anxiousness" when we perceive a stressor) and by increasing the metabolism (giving us that sense of anxious, "extra" energy).

During the second stage, the *stage of resistance,* the body continues to battle the stressor and remains in a continued state of elevated arousal. Because the immune system has remained on "high alert" for a prolonged period, it begins to weaken, placing the individual at a greater risk of becoming ill. For example, have you ever noticed that during finals week a great number of students in class or in the residence halls are coughing or sneezing, or have a runny nose, a sore throat, mono, or the flu? With a continuous state of arousal, such as the stress of preparing for finals, students' immune systems become weakened, putting them at a greater risk of becoming ill. If the stress continues, a person will enter stage three, *exhaustion.*

General Adaptation syndrome:

physician Hans Selye (1985) developed the three-stage General Adaptation syndrome to describe the physiological responses to eustress and distress. The stages are alarm reaction, stage of resistance, and exhaustion.

Fight or flight:

the instinctive physiological response to a threatening situation, which readies one either to fight or to run away.

Figure 15.1 /// Stages of Selye's General Adaptation Syndrome

The General Adaptation Syndrome describes the physical reactions we experience to eustress and distress.

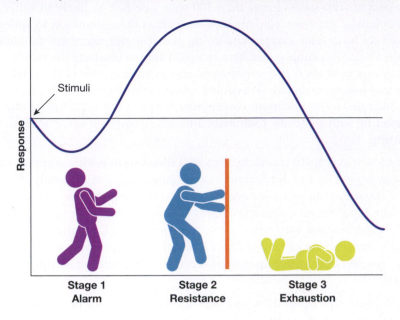

Source: iStock.com/cherstva.

During this stage, the body has depleted every resource it has; often this results in long-term illnesses. People under too much stress may also experience such things as worry, stomach problems, frequent headaches, and the inability to sleep or to eat.

As professor of community health John Romas and preventive medicine physician Manoj Sharma (2000) point out, though, psychological stress is not isolated to an individual's experience or perception; in order to fully understand an individual's response to stress, situational contexts in which the stress occurs, referred to as *event-based stress,* must also be taken into consideration.

Event-Based Stress

Any change, whether experienced at the individual level or the family level, can result in the physiological and psychological side effects of stress. Indeed, we all experience daily hassles, such as traffic, that can cause stress. A **life change event**, however, is typically an event that is forever life altering and that requires significant social and psychological adjustment (Wheaton, 1994).

Social Readjustment Rating Scale

To help us better understand the range of life change events and the impact they have on our health, physicians T. H. Holmes and R. H. Rahe (1967) studied 5,000 medical patient records in order to determine whether certain situational or life events (such as divorce, changing schools, or trouble with the in-laws) created enough stress to cause patients to experience stressors that eventually led to physical illness. To make this determination, these researchers created the **Social Readjustment Rating Scale (SRRS)**, which identified associations between life events and life transitions and the impact of those events and transitions on individual physical health and well-being. They assigned numerical values to a range of life events, from the most severe to the least severe, such as the death of a spouse to changes in sleeping and eating habits.

Life change event:

typically, a life-altering event that requires significant social and psychological adjustment.

Social Readjustment Rating Scale (SRRS):

a scale identifying associations between life events and life transitions and the impact of those events and transitions on individual physical health and well-being.

In their classic, landmark study, Holmes and Rahe (1967) found that higher scores indicated anywhere from nearly a 40 percent chance to nearly an 80 percent chance of becoming ill within the next year. Scores above 300 in the study were linked to heart attacks, diabetes, and depression; people with scores lower than 300 were one-half as likely to suffer from these illnesses. People who experienced daily hassles, such as those common to college students, were more likely to develop coughs and colds. But it is not necessary to come to a total "score" on the SRRS. It is simply used here as a guideline to illustrate the multitude of stressors present in our individual and family lives, and as an indicator of the relative impact of stressful life and situational events. We could probably add items to this list that the researchers did not include to make it more contemporary and more reflective of our lives today, such as cohabiting with someone, roommate difficulties, working while going to school, and single parenting.

As Romas and Sharma (2000) conclude, the SRRS allows us to see life events as stressors that have potential impact on the development of an individual and/or family. Very few major life events or situational stressors (or even individual stressors) are experienced in isolation; they are usually experienced within the context of family living. For example, if one member of the family experiences a very stressful event, a ripple effect reverberates throughout the entire family system, causing a temporary or long-term disruption in the balance of the family. As one of my students once commented succinctly, "Something is really yanking on our family mobile!"

Family stress:
the result of an imbalance between the demands an event places on a family and that family's ability or inability to meet them.

If we view stress in this light, then, our definition of stress can be broadened to include the family and **family stress**, which is the result of an imbalance between the demands an event places on a family and that family's ability—or inability—to meet them. Duvall (1977) describes family stress as "any situation for which the usual patterns of family living are inadequate." Although the demands brought on by family developmental changes or transitions are stressors, many families learn to cope with them. Other families, however, have a more difficult time adjusting. Some families "struggle well" and adapt to life's uncertainties, while other families unravel.

Young Families and Stress Management

Consider Bryan and Misty, who have been married for almost 14 years and have four children under the age of 9. To them, life is very good. That's not to say, however, that there aren't challenges. Bryan works a full-time career as a campus chaplain, and Misty home-schools all of their children. The house needs repairs, the laundry needs washing, the bills need to be paid, the kids need time, and Bryan and Misty need . . . each other.

Stress takes its toll on all families, particularly young families. School competes with parenting competes with work competes with . . . and on it goes. Young families need to be intentional when dealing with stress ("Managing Stress in Young Families," 2008):

Financial:

- *Plan ahead for all spending activities.* Set aside a place in your budget for leisure and rest. Extravagance is not necessary—a simple trip to the zoo or a "date night" twice a month may do wonders for young couples and families.

- *Live within your means.* Spend no more than you earn, save no less than what you are able. Simplicity may be more elegant than you think.

Time:

- *Set priorities.* Decide for your family a "pecking order" for time consumption. For example, when work activities and family needs conflict, make decisions based on the principles you and your spouse set ahead of time.

- *Keep "organized" activities to a minimum.* As children enter school, more and more activities compete against family time. Soccer, play practice, recitals, and the like can wear families down. Extracurricular activities are a wonderful tool for socialization of your children, but they will never take the place of quality family time.

- *Make reservations for romance.* Children are affected by the level of emotional intimacy shared by their parents. Make time for special times of togetherness, be they date nights on a regular basis or even one hour of quiet time together after the kids go to bed.

Relationships:

- *Make friends.* Get to know some new neighbors. Invite someone over to dinner. Offer to babysit a friend's children for a night in exchange for another night when they can watch yours.

- *Connect with extended family.* E-mail and cell phones make it easier than ever to connect (or perhaps re-connect) with family and friends you haven't seen in a while.

Transactional Model of Stress

The **Transactional Model of Stress** is also called the *interactional model* of stress. Rather than focusing on the physiological/psychological effects, as the General Adaptation Syndrome does, or emphasizing specific life change events in the environment, as the SRRS does, other stress theorists instead consider stress to be the result of an interaction between the person and his or her environment (Antonovsky, 1979; Lazarus, 1966, 1984). More important, these bodies of research suggest that it doesn't matter *what* event causes the stress; what matters is the *meaning* we attach to the stressor (recall the Symbolic Interaction framework from Chapter 3). In other words, when we are exposed to a stressor, how do we *perceive* it? What *meaning* do we assign to it? How is the stimulus or stressor *interpreted*? What cultural and ethnic factors contribute to how we interpret our stressors?

According to the Transactional Model of Stress, the impact of the stressor is wholly dependent on our perception and appraisal of the stressor (Cohen, 1984; Lazarus & Cohen, 1977). Karen Glanz, a researcher for social and behavioral medicine, and her colleagues (Glanz, Rimer, & Lewis, 2002) provide the three key concepts of the Transactional Model of Stress and Coping:

- *Primary appraisal.* When a stressor occurs, we instinctively evaluate and assess the significance of it. The questions that come to mind include, Is it a challenge? If so, then we probably have the personal and family resources needed to overcome it successfully. Is it a threat? If so, then our personal and family resources may not be sufficient to meet the demands of the stressor. Is it potentially life altering? Is it beyond our control? Is it anticipated? Is it manageable? Is it of little consequence? If so, we can ignore it.

- *Secondary appraisal.* In this appraisal of the stressor, we first assess how controllable the stressor is and then decide which resources we are going to use to enable us to cope. This is the "What can I do?" appraisal. **External locus of control** refers to the perception that we cannot control what happens in some aspects of our lives. For example, consider an alcoholic who blames her alcoholism on the fact that her abusive father was an alcoholic and her grandmother was an alcoholic as well. She may believe that she was predestined to a life of alcohol abuse. This woman perceives her circumstances as beyond her control. She blames her alcoholism, or her stressor, as external to her own behaviors. On the other hand, an **internal locus of control** refers to the perception that we are, to a large extent, in control of our destiny. For instance, if this same woman were to break the cycle of alcoholism in her family, seek treatment, and abstain from alcohol, she would have the ability to control her lifestyle. Research shows that people who possess an internal locus of control cope more effectively and efficiently with individual and family stress and family crisis (Bogenschultz, 2005; Gamm, Nussbaum, & Biesecker, 2004; Murray, Malcarne, & Goggin, 2003).

- *Coping efforts.* The coping efforts refer to those methods and strategies individuals and families use to bring order to, normalize, or regulate the stressor. Some individuals and families use **problem management** strategies. These strategies are aimed at directly

Transactional Model of Stress:
according to this model, stress is the result of an interaction between the person and his or her environment.

External locus of control:
refers to the perception that we cannot control what happens in some aspects of our lives.

Internal locus of control:
refers to the perception that we are, to a large extent, in control of our destiny.

Problem management:
management strategies aimed at directly attacking the stressor or changing the stressor.

Emotional regulation:
strategies designed to help individuals and families change their perception, interpretation, and the meaning of the stressor.

Meaning-based coping:
employing deliberate strategies to produce positive emotion, such as arming oneself with information about one's illness and treatment in order to remain optimistic.

attacking the stressor or changing the stressor. **Emotional regulation** strategies help individuals and families change their perception, interpretation, and the meaning of the stressor. In my own situation, for example, my husband and I chose to view my illness as a challenge, something that we would overcome together, instead of perceiving it as something that could ultimately take my life. We used **meaning-based coping** strategies, which are those coping techniques that produce positive emotion. By equipping ourselves with as much information about my illness and treatment plan as we could, we were choosing to remain optimistic (Glanz et al., 2002).

Ultimately, the coping efforts that individuals and families use largely determine the outcome of the stressor. If a stressor is perceived as being insurmountable, the stressor may lead to a personal and familial crisis. On the other hand, if the stressor is experienced as a temporary bump in the road on the relational journey, the outcome may be less detrimental.

FAMILY CRISIS

While it is a certainty that families grow, change, and experience many transitions, whether the family experiences these changes and transitions as family *stress* or family *crisis* largely depends on whether the family has the ability to adapt to these changes in the family environment.

Recall that in cases of family stress, there is an imbalance between the stressor(s) placed on the family and their ability to meet the demands of the stressor(s). If the family adapts to meet these demands, they will weather this significant, but temporary, period of family stress. If, however, they cannot make the adjustments necessary to cope with these inevitable changes, reorganizations, and disruptions, the stressors may develop into a family crisis. There are four categories of family stress, and each stressor places different demands on the family system. Family stress is said to occur when the demands of the stressor(s) outweigh the family's ability to meet those demands. The four categories of family stress are dismemberment, demoralization, accession, and demoralization plus dismemberment or accession (Duvall & Hill, 1960):

Dismemberment family crisis depicts the separation or isolation of an individual from the rest of his or her family. This includes hospitalization, loss of a child, loss of a spouse, being orphaned, and physical separation (military, work, etc.).

Demoralization family crisis describes crises that tend to bring disgrace or embarrassment to a family system, such as alcoholism, substance use/abuse, crime, and delinquency. This also includes infidelity, nonsupport from a divorced spouse, and ongoing conflict or discord in the family system.

Accession family crisis is when turbulence occurs due to the addition of a family member, such as with the pregnancy or birth of a child, adoption, fostering, relatives moving in, a parent remarries (creating a stepfamily system), the reunion after a separation.

Demoralization plus dismemberment or accession occurs when a family is thought to be demoralized because of "embarrassing" stressors, such as the imprisonment or the suicide of a family member, or for some families, an out-of-marriage birth.

Like family stress situations, when a family crisis occurs, family members must use their problem-solving and coping skills to navigate the situation until balance is restored. Typically, however, because a crisis is almost always unexpected, families find themselves in unfamiliar territory, and their established repertoire of problem-solving strategies is not effective. This shortage of coping and problem-solving skills increases fear, anger, guilt, and anxiety—and these feelings lead to an increased state of turbulence or family crisis (Moos, 1987). The following foundational theoretical models will shed light on the "how" and "why" some families experience change as stress, while others experience it as crisis.

A family crisis is naturally stressful. When a family experiences a crisis, the crisis demands a change or changes in the family's established, day-to-day roles and routines. Family life educators and other family practitioners are essential helpers in times of crisis for individuals and families.

iStock.com/gorodenkoff

The ABCs of Family Crisis: The Family Crisis Model

For decades, family researchers and social scientists have been intrigued with why some families who face a given stressor, such as the death of a spouse or child or the serious illness or injury of a close family member, seem to adjust while others who face the same stressor do not. To examine this difference, family therapist Rueben Hill (1949) conducted research to understand the stressors that families experienced during times of war. From his early work that examined war separation and reunion, Hill put forth the **ABC-X Family Crisis Model**, still considered a major contribution to the area of family stress and family vulnerability research. Hill's model explains why families vary in the way they adapt and adjust to change, transition, and stress. Hill's ABC-X model views a family crisis situation as a combination of various factors: *A* factors are the initial crisis-causing events; *B* factors are the resources a family has at its disposal to meet the demands of the crisis; *C* factors are the meanings families ascribe to the event; and *X* factors are the outcomes of the event, the results of whether or not a family copes effectively with the crisis event. Figure 15.2 illustrates Hill's (1958) interactive ABC-X Family Crisis Model.

ABC-X family crisis model:

Reuben Hill's model that views a family crisis situation as a combination of various factors.

Figure 15.2 /// Hill's Interactive ABC-X Family Crisis Model

Why do some families adapt and adjust to stress, and other families have difficulty doing so? The ABC-X model helps us understand the variances in family coping.

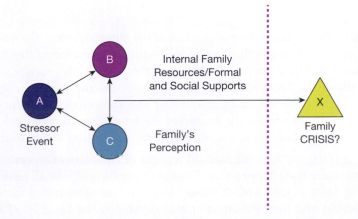

The A Factor

The *A factor* is the event that initially causes the stress. This stressor can be a normative development in the family life cycle, such as the birth of a child or the marriage of an adult child. It can also be a non-normative event, such as the early death of a spouse, job loss, or winning the lottery. It is important to note that *A* factors can fall anywhere along the continuum of expected family developmental tasks noted earlier in this chapter, from individual developmental tasks to catastrophic life events. *A* factors are *family-specific:* What one family perceives as a stressor or vulnerability, another family may not. Whatever the stressor, because of the interconnecting nature of the family, it provokes change within the *entire* family system—changes in such aspects as family boundaries, family roles, family communication, or family processes (Burr, 1973). When the change is significant, the stressor induces a disturbance in the family's routine way of functioning. According to Hill (1958), then, it isn't just the nature of the stressor event that influences the depth of a person's reaction to the stressor. Whether "stress" becomes a "crisis" depends on the amount of disruption the stressor causes in the family system. The *A* factor then interacts with the *B* factor.

The B Factor

The *B factor* refers to the number of family resources that will help the family meet the demands of the stressor or crisis. Some families possess particular strengths within the family system, such as effective communication skills and problem-solving or coping strategies. Other families are weaker in these areas. Some families have access to extended family and community resources. To illustrate, consider a family in which a parent has a serious illness. Sometimes family and friends may pitch in and prepare meals for the family for a period of weeks or months to get them through the most critical period. This community may also arrange for rides for the children to and from school, take in the children after school, and provide comfort to the individual who is ill as well as the spouse who is taking care of the house, the expenses, and the children. Having friends and family "pitching in" minimizes the disruption—and, in turn, the vulnerability—a family may experience during a parent's illness. Hill (1958) theorized that the *A* and *B* factors then interact with the *C* factor.

The C Factor

The *C factor* refers to the definition the family assigns to the change, transition, stressor, or disruption. *This is why* A *factors are said to be family specific;* whether a family experiences a stressor as a crisis depends on their *perception* or *interpretation* of the event. According to Hill (1958), the amount of change (such as changes in family boundaries, family roles, family rules, communication, and routine) that occurs and induces stress influences the severity of the crisis; thus, the family's vulnerability depends on how the family perceives these changes. Factors that come into play include how families answer questions such as, Are the changes serious? Are they minor? Are they short term? Ultimately, the definition the family assigns to the stressor event produces the *X* factor.

The X Factor

The *X factor* can be thought of as the end product of the initiating event, the family's resources to cope with it, and the meaning they assign to it—the combination of the *A, B,* and *C* factors. The *X* factor could be a momentary bump in the family's life journey, or it could be a life-altering family crisis. Recall that each person processes and perceives stress in unique ways. Families operate with the same uniqueness and subjectivity, and the outcome—the *X* factor—is wholly dependent on the resources the family has to meet life's challenges, in tandem with their perception of the stressor or the definition they assign to the challenge.

At one time or another, we have all reached a point of complete exasperation and uttered the words, "If *one more thing* happens," or "This is the *last straw!*" We all have felt the effects of **pile-up**. Using Hill's (1958) ABC-X Model as the foundation, noted family researchers Hamilton McCubbin and Joan Patterson (1982) developed the **Double ABC-X Model** to

The Double ABC-X model helps us understand the effects of pile-up stressors.

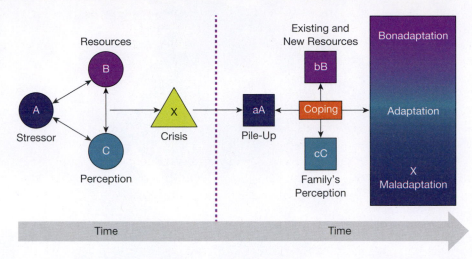

understand the effects of the accumulation, or pile-up, of stressors and strains and how families adapt to them. Pile-up can result from either a single stressor that coincides with life events/changes, multiple stressors, or multiple stressors that coincide with life events/changes. Regardless of the nature of the pile-up, this model recognizes that the effects of prior stresses and strains are exacerbated and intensified when another stressor is added into the mix. Figure 15.3 illustrates the Double ABC-X Model.

We have now established that the stressors, or the life changes, aren't necessarily the key elements that lead to crisis. More important is the family's ability to make the necessary adaptations and adjustments in the family system to accommodate the change. When the appropriate adjustments are made, not only are families able to add to their repertoire of problem-solving and coping skills, but stressors and life crises can actually propel both individuals and families to develop more intimate, satisfying levels of functioning. Nevertheless, in order to achieve those intimate levels of functioning—in order to survive a family crisis—the family must learn to complete a standard set of adaptive tasks demanded by life's many transitions, changes, and stressors.

Family Adaptive Tasks

Professor of psychiatry and behavioral sciences Rudolf Moos and research health scientist Jeanne Schaefer (1987) created a framework to help guide students of family life as well as professionals in the field of family studies to understand and appreciate those adaptive tasks and adjustments that families need to successfully navigate normative and non-normative life transitions and changes. Families facing change encounter five major adaptive tasks they must perform in order to successfully adjust:

1. *Establish the meaning and understand the personal significance of the situation.* When a stressor is introduced into the family system, the family as a collective system tries to make sense of what is happening. Charles Darwin once noted that "human beings cannot adapt to their environment alone; they are *interdependent* and must make collective efforts to survive." Sometimes the stressor is of such great magnitude, such as discovering that a spouse is having an extramarital affair or learning that parents are divorcing, that common initial reactions may include numbness, shock, confusion, and disbelief. A family member or members

Although easier said than done, sustaining and maintaining family ties and other relationships during times of stress and crisis is essential in helping people to weather the storm. Although it's tempting to isolate from others, struggling well often requires the help of others.

iStock.com/FG Trade

confronting a stressor may also have a keen sense that there is no reality or past experience on which they can draw to handle this stressful event. As disbelief gives way to reality, the life event becomes clearer and the family attempts to "wrap their minds around it," to cognitively grasp what is unfolding, Eventually, the family must acknowledge the reality of the circumstances; at this point, individual family members and the family as a collective system assign significance to the situation. As Moos and Schaefer (1987) explain, it is important to understand that major life events are not "singular" in nature. Finding out that a spouse or an intimate partner has been cheating, for example, potentially involves other stressors, such as the realization that the marriage or the relationship is in trouble, the possibility of divorce, and contemplating the losses associated with a marital dissolution. The potential for this type of "domino" effect exists for many life changes. Consequently, establishing the meaning of transition and change is an ongoing process.

2. *Confront reality and respond to the requirements of the external situation.* Stressor events demand our attention: A loved one who dies must be buried and his or her personal items sorted through; a family who experiences violence must cope with not only the trauma of the physical violence but also the need to realign family roles and rules. Moos and Schaefer's (1987) point is that sometimes, in the midst of the confusion and shock associated with life change and crisis, families must still cope with the immediate needs of the situation.

3. *Sustain relationships with family members and friends as well as with other individuals who may be helpful in resolving the crisis and aftermath.* This is perhaps not as easy as it may seem. Many times people who experience change and crisis turn inward, becoming private in their grief as a result of their experiences. Whether a family opens up to other extended family members or friends depends on their cultural and ethnic backgrounds, as some cultures and ethnicities are more open and willing to share than are others. Culture and society are the sculptors that shape what events a particular family perceives as stressful (Pearlin, 1982), and culture also dictates which coping strategies and problem-solving skills are appropriate and acceptable to use (Cordon, 1997). Moos and Schaefer (1987) suggest that these interpersonal relationships often "help individuals obtain

information necessary to make wise decisions, find emotional support for them, and secure reassurance about the problems they face" (p. 12).

4. *Preserve a reasonable emotional balance by managing distressful feelings in response to the situation.* Life transitions and change are often accompanied by powerful, sometimes overwhelming, emotions. According to Moos and Schaefer (1987), the feelings of anger, guilt, self-blame, resentment, fear, anxiety, worry, hopelessness, and helplessness may be overpowering. Being able to maintain some level of emotional balance is necessary in order for a family to adapt to the change and maintain a sense of hope, even when that hope is temporarily overshadowed by the circumstances.

5. *Preserve a satisfactory self-image and maintain a sense of competence and mastery.* It is important to maintain a sense of confidence in the family's ability to adapt to, adjust to, and overcome life's challenges; the family must have a sense of an internal locus of control. When families are able to recognize that *all* families face struggles and challenges, with sufficient support networks and time, *all* families can successfully navigate change.

No family is immune from stress, change, and transition. Perhaps now you have a better understanding of why some families weather the storms of crisis and change and come out stronger, and why other families can experience similar situations and circumstances only to become weaker or dissolve altogether. You should now understand how the family's perception of the event and the ability of family members to face it head on, while making the necessary adjustments within the family system, help push the family toward adaptation. When lines of communication remain open among family members and friends, and when these individuals are able to simultaneously accept help and yet do what they can for themselves, they are able to avoid crisis and manage stress. According to family sociologist Ronald L. Pitzer (2004),

> In every life crisis [and change] there is danger and opportunity . . . a turning point for better or worse. Things will never be quite the same again. They may not necessarily be worse; perhaps they will be better, but they will definitely be different. Though not entirely masters of our fate, neither are we prisoners.

FAMILY COPING AND RESILIENCE

Finding a way to cope with the pile-up of daily stressors and transcending profound life crises is possible. Yet, to overcome the stresses and crises many families experience, family members must have an awareness of those behaviors that promote coping and resiliency to help lessen the influence and impact of a quickly changing, demanding, difficult life circumstance.

Family Coping

A family's ability to cope effectively in the face of adversity and change increases if the family possesses a variety of coping strategies. By using personal, family, and community resources, families are better able to make the necessary adaptations to reduce the impact of stressors. Rudolf Moos and Jeanne Schaefer (1987) provide an overview of the major types of family coping skills that families tend to use in times of change and crisis.

Appraisal-Focused Coping

With **appraisal-focused coping**, families try to understand why the crisis occurred and to find meaning in the circumstances that caused the crisis. Skills needed include the ability to analyze the situation logically and to prepare mentally for certain events to unfold. **Cognitive redefinition** occurs when families attempt to reframe the life event or stressor in ways that are

Appraisal-focused coping:

a coping style that attempts to understand why the crisis occurred and to find meaning in the circumstances. Skills needed include the ability to logically analyze the situation and mentally prepare for certain events to unfold.

Cognitive redefinition:

occurs when families attempt to reframe the life event or stressor in ways that are seen as more favorable.

Family Life Now

Should Women Fight in Combat?

As you take a stroll through the tents and barracks of soldiers deployed in Afghanistan, Iraq, and Kuwait, you will notice the signs of a new era in the American family: Moms in combat. Should women be allowed to serve in combative military roles?

YES: Today, there are more than 200,000 women serving in the United States military. That's roughly 15 percent of the U.S. armed forces. Beginning with the first woman who fired a missile in combat over Iraq in 1999, women are here to stay on the front lines and should be allowed to fight if they so desire:

- *Societal factors encouraging female participation in combat.* An integration of women into the military is merely a reflection of current society. Gender segregation is not as prevalent today. Women are waiting longer to wed. It is illegal to discriminate against women in civilian society. All of these factors make gender integration in the military a given.

- *The changing face of war.* War today is less *Braveheart* and more *Matrix*: computer technology, miniaturization, and other new tactics make war less brawn and more brain. Women are not fighting bayonet to bayonet.

- *Lack of recruits.* Recruiters are having more and more difficulty finding men to fill jobs as mechanics, analysts, and engineers, necessitating the use of more women in these and other roles.

NO: Motherhood is crucial to healthy children and the United States. Therefore, the military should not purposely place young women, especially mothers, in harm's way.

Sources: Carlson (2003); Rivers (2003).

- *It's against common understanding.* The protection of motherhood and of children is one of the oldest ideas in humanity; some argue that it is instinctual.

- *Children need moms at home.* In the event of a child losing a mother, of course the best person to fill the motherly role is a healthy and loving father; however, the two are not interchangeable. Children especially need their mothers up through age 3. Separation due to military deployment, often lasting several months to a year or longer, increases the risks these children face in their development.

- *The United States is unique in enlisting women.* Taking the brutality and insensitivity of the Soviet military and the totalitarian notions of the Ba'athist Iraqi army into consideration, neither of these nations allow women into combat. Even Sweden and other egalitarian European nations will not let women serve in combat roles The United States is at the cutting edge when it comes to socially damaging military policies.

What Do You Think?

1. How might the presence of women affect the job of the American military, or does it?

2. Imagine you are a single mother about to deploy into military action. How might you feel about your son or daughter not being with you for a year or more?

3. Discuss what unique values and skills women might bring to the battlefield. Can you think of ways that having women fighting for our country would be valuable?

Cognitive avoidance:

the attempt to deny the seriousness of a particular situation or events.

Denial:

see **Cognitive avoidance.**

Problem-focused coping:

a coping strategy that allows the family to confront the reality of the crisis head-on by seeking and obtaining information about the crisis.

more favorable. If a spouse loses a job, for example, a family might reframe the situation by saying, "Well, at least she has her health." This type of coping mechanism appears to take the "sting" out of the reality/threat of the situation. **Cognitive avoidance** or **denial** is an attempt to deny the seriousness of the situation, saying, for example, "He isn't cheating on me—I'm sure there is a reasonable explanation for why they were together."

Problem-Focused Coping

The **problem-focused coping** strategy allows the family to confront the reality of the crisis head on by seeking and obtaining information about the crisis, thereby allowing family members to regain a sense of control over their situation. Families who lose a child to a violent act, for example, might petition lawmakers to create legislation to protect other children

In an attempt to cope with the tragic murder of her son, Trayvon Martin's mother, Sybrina Fulton, ran for public office. This type of coping strategy following a tragedy is known as *problem-focused coping*.

from similar acts of violence, as does Mothers Against Drunk Driving (MADD). In cases such as these, families seek the support from the community as well from family members. Problem-solving actions are concrete, tangible ways of meeting the demands of the crisis that provide a sense of competence and that bolster the family's esteem.

Emotion-Focused Coping

Family crises often evoke a wide range of feelings and emotions. In many cases, these feelings and emotions are so new that just experiencing them produces fear and anxiety. To manage their feelings, families might develop **emotion-focused coping** skills or capacities to maintain hope. One coping strategy families develop is **progressive desensitization**, in which family members gradually allow themselves increasing exposure to the varying aspects of the stressor. This was evidenced after the attacks of September 11, 2001, when family members of those who lost their lives in the Twin Towers ventured to "Ground Zero." **Emotional discharge**, another coping skill, is just what the term implies—venting! Emotional discharge entails venting anger, frustration, confusion, disappointment, hatred, and despair in response to tragic or sudden and unexpected news. While some families tend to vent their emotions, other families use humor. All of these strategies have one goal—to reduce the tension produced by the stressor event. **Resigned acceptance** occurs when the family ultimately accepts the situation and recognizes that nothing will change the course their family life has taken.

Couple and Family Therapy

Over several decades, stress and coping in couples and families has received wide attention from family scientists, psychologists, social workers, researchers, couple and family therapists, and other family practitioners (Bodenmann, 2010). For good reason—as you have seen so far in our study together, even everyday stressors such as job and work strain, the challenges associated with parenting, role conflict, and financial constraints can have a negative impact on a couple's relationship quality and satisfaction. Today, couples do not need to struggle alone and in isolation. With the guidance of a qualified mental health professional, such as a marriage and family therapist, family members can learn to identify the specific behaviors that affect their relationship and other relationships within the family. They can also learn new, healthier ways of relating to each other, how to effectively resolve conflict,

Emotion-focused coping: a type of stress management used to help a person tolerate, reduce, or eliminate negative emotions that occur due to a stressful event.

Progressive desensitization: occurs when family members gradually allow themselves increasing exposure to the varying aspects of the stressor.

Emotional discharge: the act of giving vent to or expressing anger, frustration, confusion, disappointment, hatred, and despair in response to tragic or sudden/unexpected news.

Resigned acceptance: the ultimate acceptance of circumstances, as when family members recognize that nothing will change the course their family life has taken.

and how to communicate in ways that serve to promote the well-being of the couple's relationship as well as the family's (American Association for Marriage and Family Therapists [AAMFT], 2020).

Because of the systems nature of relationships and family life, marriage and family therapists (MFT) and couple and family therapists (CFT) do not focus on an individual person (even if it is an individual who is seeking treatment); rather, therapy focuses on the interrelated relationships in which the person is embedded, and the treatment plan is focused on the long-term, overall health of the couple and/or their family (AAMFT, 2020). Therapists focus on a wide range of problems, such as anxiety, addictions, child-parent relationships, anxiety, post-traumatic stress disorder (PTSD), depression, and children's conduct disorders. Treatment is brief (about 12 sessions on average), and it is solution-focused. As the term implies, the **solution-focused therapy model** focuses on the default solution patterns individuals, couples, or families, are using, not talking about the problem(s) over and over. The aim of therapy, then, is for the clients and the therapist to find alternative problem-solving approaches that work (AAMFT, 2020).

Family Resilience

Family resilience refers to a family's ability to function in a healthy fashion during times of change, stress, adversity, crisis, and transition. Successful adaptation to periods of family stress and crisis involves resilience and a certain "hardiness" that allows the family to "withstand and rebound from disruptive life changes" (Walsh, 2003, p. 1). Often, a crisis serves as a wake-up call to the family. Confronted with a crisis, family members often reevaluate their priorities and tend to invest more deeply in meaningful relationships and life pursuits. The crisis may even serve as a time of personal and relational growth, as the newfound personal exploration that accompanies crises can often help family members "discover or develop new insights and abilities . . . through weathering a crisis together, relationships [can be] enriched and more loving than they might otherwise have been" (Walsh, 2003, p. 3).

Key Family Resilience Processes

Family resilience is reinforced by numerous family resilience processes that help guide families through the times of change and challenge. These processes also help foster a speedier recovery and help family members create deeper interpersonal relationships following the stressor or crisis event (Cowan, Cowan, & Schultz, 1996). By drawing from these family resiliency resources, the family system can "rally in times of crisis, buffer stress, reduce the risk of dysfunction, and support optimal adaptation—emerge stronger and more resourceful in meeting future challenges" (Walsh, 2003, p. 3). Professor of psychiatry and co-director of the University of Chicago's Center for Family Health Froma Walsh (2003) refers to a number of empirical family stress/crisis research findings and delineates the key processes in family resilience.

Family Belief System and Spirituality

A family's belief system has a powerful effect in how a stressor, such as the loss of a job, or a tragedy, such as the death of a child, is viewed. The belief system informs the meaning the family assigns to the event. It also determines whether a family has a shared meaning or a shared reality. Walsh (2003) refers to empirical research, which suggests that family belief systems help families organize their family processes and their approaches to family crisis and change; this, in turn, fosters resiliency by promoting problem solving, healing, and growth.

In addition, medical studies consistently offer evidence that spiritual beliefs and the practice of faith, prayer, and other spiritual rituals not only help families frame their life changes and challenges with shared meaning and purpose but they also give meaning to situations that are "beyond ourselves." For example, we may be able to tap into resources to help empower us to leave an abusive relationship, but some of life's challenges are beyond us. Walsh (2003)

Solution-focused therapy model:

a type of therapy that focuses on a person's present and future circumstances and goals, not on past experiences.

Family resilience:

a family's ability to function in a healthy fashion during times of change, stress, adversity, crisis, and transition.

iStock.com/RyanJLane

For many people, a spiritual belief system helps them cope in times of crisis. Research indicates that spirituality helps families to be more resilient to the effects of change or crisis.

further notes that cultural, ethnic, and religious beliefs and traditions help families find strength, comfort, and guidance and ultimately facilitate passage through life's transitions.

Making Meaning of Adversity

As we discussed earlier, the meaning a family attaches to family change and challenge greatly influences how families cope with and adapt to the life event. Families who approach change as a *shared challenge,* as opposed to an individual's problem, have an enhanced ability to overcome adversity. Walsh (2003) notes that highly functioning and healthy functioning families understand that becoming a family entails continuous growth and motion across the family's life cycle. The family researcher notes,

> A family life-cycle orientation helps [family] members see disruptive transitions as *milestones* in their shared life passage. By normalizing and contextualizing distress, family members can enlarge their perspective to see their reactions and difficulties as understandable. . . . The tendency for blame [and] shame is reduced in viewing their complicated feelings and dilemmas as "normal," common, and *expectable* among families facing similar predicaments. [italics added]

Highly functioning families also have a positive view of life. Even in the midst of the grimmest circumstances, these families remain optimistic and maintain a positive outlook rather than prematurely giving up and giving in. This "can-do" spirit promotes shared confidence and encouragement, bolsters courage and determination, and fuels shared initiative and perseverance—all hallmarks of family resilience (Walsh, 2003).

Flexibility

Walsh (2003) refers to flexibility in this family process as the ability to "bounce forward," or to change whatever needs to be changed in the family system in order to accommodate new challenges. This reorganization of the family system allows families to reconstruct and recalibrate what is "normal" and allows members to adjust their interactions and behaviors to fit the current conditions into the family's daily life. Flexibility and adaptability are key factors in family resilience.

Communication

In determining those factors that foster family resiliency, Walsh (2003) posits that the family communication processes of bringing clarity to the situation, encouraging open emotional expression by all family members, and promoting collaborative problem solving are each key elements. For example, *delivering clear messages* removes any ambiguity that might exist; this, in turn, helps to facilitate the meaning the family assigns to the situation and also promotes informed decision making and problem solving. Walsh notes that allowing *open emotional expression* promotes a family climate of trust, empathy, and tolerance. Further, when family members cannot or are not allowed to be open with their feelings, self-destructive behaviors may result. *Collaborative problem solving* helps facilitate "bouncing forward." Families who share in decision making and conflict resolution promote resiliency by setting clear goals and by taking the necessary steps toward meeting those goals.

Walsh's (2003) work presents for us an empirically based resiliency framework that enables us to see the importance of fostering a strong, healthy family system that helps families navigate the normative and non-normative twists and turns that naturally accompany family life and intimate relationships. This framework is based on the basic family system premise that takes into account the interconnections that exist between family members and the idea that key family processes influence adaptation and adjustment for each family member. Furthermore, the resiliency framework supports families' efforts to "work well, play well, and love well." According to Walsh, understanding the importance of a shared perception of the situation, shared hope, shared resources, and a shared commitment to struggle together may ultimately result in personal growth and surprisingly deep levels of intimacy. "In bouncing forward . . . each family must find its own pathways through adversity, fitting their situation, their cultural orientation, and their personal strengths and resources. Families build on small successes and use failures as learning experiences" (p. 15).

THE CRISIS OF FAMILY VIOLENCE

Divorce. Poverty. Suicide. Illness. Sexual violence. Mental illness. Family separation because of war. Bankruptcy. Foreclosure. Job loss. Families today are experiencing a wide variety of changes, transitions, and challenges and are often called on to confront simultaneous challenges. Entire chapters could be written about dealing with each of these family crises, but an increasingly widespread social problem in the United States demands our attention: family violence. Today, in the United States alone, more than 30,000 women will find refuge in a domestic violence shelter as the result of having been severely abused by their male intimate partner; between 3 and 10 million children will witness violence taking place in their homes (U.S. Bureau of Justice Statistics, 2019).

In this section, we'll take a close look at the number of family members who were battered in the United States over a five-year period. It is important to keep in mind that behind the numbers are countless lives that are, undeniably, forever changed because of the violence committed against them. We begin by considering the following experience of a college student (Welch, 2004).

Melanie is a 20-year-old university sophomore. She carries a pretty full class load, she juggles her academic load with her job responsibilities, and she tries to find time to be with her fiancé, friends, and family. She dreads finals week. But Melanie lives with past childhood experiences that make her day-to-day college life tougher to handle than that of many students. From the age of 10, her stepfather repeatedly sexually assaulted her. She recalls,

> When I was in fourth grade, my step-dad one morning before work and after my mom had already left for work sexually molested me at least 30 or 40 times. [In my 7th-grade year] it was at least once or twice a week during that time period. . . . It was always after my mom went to bed . . . he came into my room and then. . . .

Flashbacks still haunt me . . . where I wake up in the middle of the night, curled up in a ball because I'm scared and I can still, after all these years, feel him on my skin . . . it's like, you wake up and you know he's in the room with you. . . . Even though I'm in college now, there are some nights I can't sleep, and I'm still absolutely terrified of someone who is dead.

I'm engaged and my wedding is less than a month away. [Aside from the normal fears of getting married] I also have to deal with, if Danny holds me a certain way, or touches me a certain way, I remember something that Alan did to me. . . . It's so unfair that Alan stole that part away from Danny, that there are some things that Danny can't do with me because Alan did them to me. 1 am absolutely terrified because of what happened to me when I was 10 and then when I was 14. Things like this stay with you.

The effects are long lasting.

Domestic Violence

Violence that takes place in the home is a prevalent, multifaceted social ailment in the United States. Contributing to these assaults are individual factors, such as family of origin patterns, psychopathology, mental illness, and genetic causes; community factors, such as poverty, educational levels, absent or inaccessible family services; and cultural factors, such as media influences.

Domestic violence, or family violence, is violence perpetrated against family members by an offender who is related to the victim either biologically or legally, such as by marriage or through adoption (U.S. Department of Justice, 2018). Although most people think of family violence as something that takes place between intimate partners and children, the people who carry out family violence—the **batterer**—include current or former spouses, parents or adoptive parents, legal guardians or foster parents, biological or adopted children, current or former stepchildren, a sibling, grandchildren, grandparents, in-laws, or other relatives, such as aunts, uncles, nephews, and nieces.

Domestic violence: violence perpetrated against family members by a person who is related to the victim either biologically or legally, such as by marriage or through adoption.

Batterer: a person who commits domestic violence.

Robert Daemmrich Photography Inc/Corbis via Getty Images

In the United States today, nearly 20 people every minute suffer at the hands of a batterer.

Domestic violence is an umbrella term that encompasses any behavior designed to intentionally inflict emotional, sexual, or physical harm. Acts of domestic or family violence may result in harming children, intimate partners (spouse, cohabiting partner, gay or lesbian partner), and/or elderly family members. There are three broad categories of domestic violence:

- **Physical violence** includes such acts as hitting, punching, pushing, slapping, biting, or throwing something at the victim.
- **Emotional violence** includes such acts as controlling the amount of contact a family member has with family and friends, name-calling, constant criticism, threats to leave the partner or throw him or her out, displays of intense jealousy/accusations that one is being unfaithful, controlling the spending and distribution of money, excessive rule-making, and threats of physical or sexual harm.
- **Sexual violence** includes marital rape (unwanted, forcible sex by a person's marital partner), battering rape (rape along with other acts of physical violence), and forced sexual acts (such as forced oral or anal sex).

Demographers measure family violence in two ways: through survey interviews with the victims and through statistics gathered by police. The National Intimate Partner and Sexual Violence Survey (NIPSVS), a division of the U.S. Centers for Disease Control and Prevention, collects lifetime and past-year information about people's experiences with rape, physical violence, and stalking. Our figures here present some of their 2018 findings.

The Battered

Although no one is immune from abuse, there are specific factors that place some at greater risk for experiencing violence than others; for example, women who have less education (especially women who do not attend college), who come from lower socioeconomic status, or who are single parents or young teenage parents are more likely to be victims of violence. Also, women who have witnessed a parent being battered are at higher risk of being victims themselves. Generally, women who have low self-esteem, feel a sense of inferiority, are passive, or believe that they are responsible for the batterer's actions are more likely to be abused. When violence is perpetrated against a partner, it is referred to as **intimate partner violence (IPV)**.

No gender or racial/ethnic group is immune from family violence, as the data in Figure 15.4 illustrate. Although women (5.4 per 1,000 population) are victimized more frequently than men, about 7 percent of all acts of IPV are perpetrated against men by women (National Center for Victims of Crime, 2018). In addition, intimate partner violence and family violence cross every socioeconomic and educational level and every family type, including married, single-parent, gay, straight, and cohabiting families.

Gender-Based Violence. Gays, lesbians, bisexuals, and transgender people experience higher rates of violence than heterosexuals, as Figure 15.5 shows us. Violence against LGBTQ people includes rape, emotional or psychological violence, physical violence, or stalking by an intimate partner. **Gender-based violence (GBV)** is broadly defined as violence perpetrated against an individual because of their gender/gender identity (Leddy et al., 2019). It's important to understand that GBV is *any* harm that is done to another person against that person's will, and this harm results from power imbalances and inequalities (Wirtz, Poteat, Mannat, & Glass, 2020). In a publication that sought to highlight GBV and to determine why GBV is tolerated still today, Elisabeth Duban observes, "GBV is rooted in gender norms regarding masculinity, including the need to assert control or power, enforce roles or prevent, discourage, or punish behavior considered unacceptable because it does not conform to socially constructed norms" (Duban, 2018, p. 8).

Globally, it is estimated that 1 in 3 women experience some form of GBV—most often from an intimate partner (Leddy et al., 2019); however, this estimate almost always refers to the experiences of cisgender, heterosexual women (Wirtz et al., 2020). Marginalized women, such as transgender women, experience higher rates of gender-based violence

---

Physical violence:
violence that includes such acts as hitting, punching, pushing, slapping, biting, or throwing something at the victim.

Emotional violence:
violence that includes such acts as controlling the amount of contact a family member has with family and friends, namecalling, constant criticism.

Sexual violence:
violence that is sexual in nature, including marital rape, battering rape, and forced sexual acts.

Intimate partner violence (IPV):
violence perpetrated against a relationship partner.

Gender-based violence (GBV):
violence perpetrated against an individual because of their gender/ gender identity.

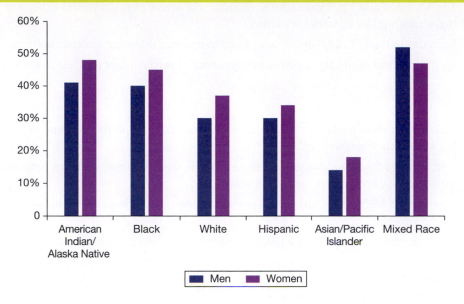

Figure 15.4 /// Intimate Partner Violence by Race, Ethnicity, and Sex

Source: National Center for Victims of Crime (2018).

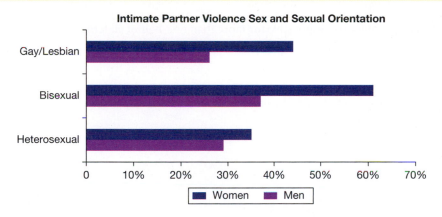

Figure 15.5 /// Rape, Physical Violence, and/or Stalking by an Intimate Partner by Sex and Sexual Orientation

Source: National Center for Victims of Crime (2018)

(Leddy et al., 2019), and they are targeted because of their gender nonconformity or gender expression (Wirtz et al., 2020).

In the United States, one in four women and one in nine men suffers physical and/or emotional violence at the hands of an intimate partner—nearly 20 people every minute (U.S. Department of Justice, 2018). The statistics regarding violence perpetrated at the hands of an intimate partner or a family member are staggering and include the following (National Center for Victims of Crime, 2018; U.S. Department of Justice, 2018):

Domestic Violence

- Women aged 18 to 24 are most commonly abused by an intimate partner
- 1 in 3 women, and 1 in 4 men have experienced slapping, shoving, pushing, and other forms of physical violence by an intimate partner

- 1 in 10 women have been raped by an intimate partner
- 1 in 4 women and 1 in 7 men have been victims of severe physical violence (beating, burning, strangling) by an intimate partner
- Each day in the U.S., 20,000 calls are placed to national domestic violence hotlines
- Only one-third injured by intimate partners receive medical care for their injuries

Dating Violence/Teen Violence

- 1 in 4 teen girls in a relationship report being pressured into performing oral sex or having sex against their wishes
- 1 in 3 high school students experience either physical or sexual violence perpetrated by someone they are dating or going out with
- 9 percent of high school girls and 7 percent of high school boys report being a victim of dating violence
- Hispanic girls report the highest proportion of physical dating violence, as seen in Figure 15.6

Domestic Murders

- Each year, nearly 2,000 women in the United States are killed by their intimate partners
- IPV is the second leading cause of death among pregnant women in the United States (second only to car accidents)
- Pregnancy is a time of increased risk—most pregnant women who experience violence have been abused before, but pregnancy increased the frequency and severity of attacks by intimate partners
- Intimate partners are responsible for more than one-half of all female homicides each year and 5 percent of all male homicides

Figure 15.6 /// Percentage of Students in Grades 9–12 Reporting Dating Violence, by Race

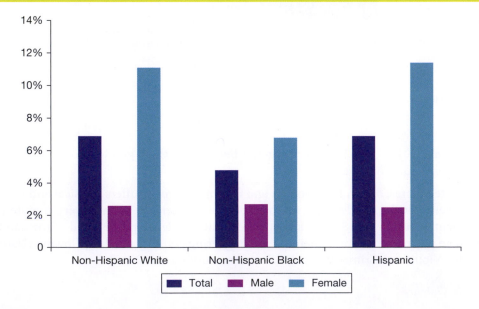

Source: CDC (2018).

Violence Against Children. **Child maltreatment** is any act, intentional or not, that results in harm to a child, the threat of harm, or the potential for harm (U.S. Centers for Disease Control and Prevention [CDC], 2020b). There are four types of child maltreatment:

Child maltreatment: any act, intentional or not, that results in harm to a child, the threat of harm, or the potential for harm.

1. *Physical abuse:* Generally defined as "any nonaccidental physical injury to the child" (Child Welfare Information Gateway, 2019). These injuries are usually caused by a parent or person in a position of responsibility, power, or trust (CDC, 2020b).

2. *Emotional abuse:* The failure to provide a supportive environment for the child (CDC, 2020b) that results in "injury to the psychological capacity or emotional stability of the child" (Child Welfare Information Gateway, 2019). Emotional abuse is typically evidenced by anxiety, depression, withdrawal, or aggressive behavior.

3. *Sexual abuse:* The involvement of a child in any sexual behavior or activity that the child is unable to give informed consent to and is against the laws of society (CDC, 2020b). All states in the U.S. include sexual abuse in their definitions of child abuse (Child Welfare Information Gateway, 2019). Human trafficking is currently a crime in only 15 states in the U.S.

4. *Neglect:* The failure of parents or caregivers to provide for the holistic well-being and development of the child, including safe living conditions, education, medical care, and education; this includes the failure to properly supervise a child (CDC, 2020b).

Today,

- More than one-fourth (27 percent) of victims of child maltreatment are younger than 3 years.
- Physical abuse is the leading cause of death in infants under 4 years of age.
- Each year, 4 million children experience some type of maltreatment by a parent/caregiver; sadly, these numbers are believed to be vastly underreported.

Figure 15.7 shows us the racial and ethnic differences in children who are abused each year.

Figure 15.7 /// Victims of Child Abuse by Race and Ethnicity

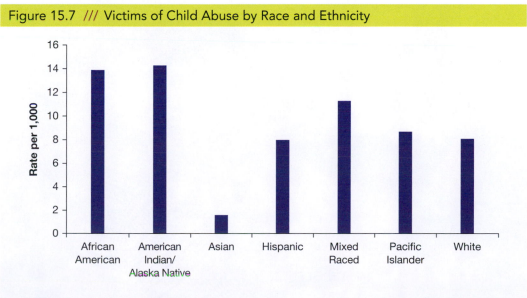

Source: U.S. Department of Health and Human Services (2018).

Adverse childhood experiences (ACEs): experiences that occur during childhood (ages 0 to 17) and are potentially traumatic, life-altering events.

Adverse Childhood Experiences (ACEs). Adverse childhood experiences (ACEs) occur during childhood (ages 0 to 17) and are potentially traumatic, life-altering events. ACEs may include witnessing violence in the home, neighborhood, or community; being a victim of child maltreatment; having parents/caregivers who misuse or abuse substances; having parents/caregivers or other family members who have mental health problems and instability; or being separated from a parent or parents due to parental imprisonment (CDC, 2020a). ACEs are traumatic to children and adolescents because they have a strong probability to undermine their sense of safety and stability; ACEs also affect emotional bonding with parents or caregivers (CDC, 2020a). Early adversity has a number of potential life-long impacts (CDC, 2019):

- *Injury:* Traumatic brain injury
- *Mental health:* Depression, anxiety, suicide, PTSD
- *Maternal health:* Unintended pregnancy, pregnancy complications, fetal death
- *Infectious disease:* STDs, HIV
- *Chronic disease:* Cancer, diabetes
- *Risky behaviors:* Unsafe sex, alcohol and drug use/misuse
- *Opportunities:* Education, opportunities, income

There is hope, though! There are a number of protective factors that help children and adolescents more effectively cope with stressful, traumatic events, and that can lessen the long-term effects of ACEs. These protective factors include healthy relationships with parents; a stable, predictable home environment; and having families and communities that help to cultivate a sense of purpose and meaning (CDC, 2019).

Indeed, these trends are alarming, and it's distressing that the United States is not successful in addressing the violence perpetrated against women, children, and sexual minorities. But *why* do people batter? What are the characteristics of those who abuse their family members or intimate partners? We'll examine these questions in the following section.

The Batterer

As the statistics reveal, men are more likely to abuse a family member more than are women. Those who abuse their partners or their children share some common characteristics;

Perpetrators of domestic violence are driven by the need for power and control. It is almost never a situation of an argument that went too far or got "out of hand."

iStock.com/South_agency

Table 15.2 /// Signs of an Abusive Partner

Everyone has a right not to be abused in a relationship. *Abuse is not inevitable,* and there are ways to minimize your risk of encountering abuse in your relationships. Following are signs that you may be in an abusive relationship. Pay attention to these signs—they don't go away; they don't get better. If he promises it will never happen again, just remember: IT WILL.

- **Overly protective mannerisms.** Your boyfriend berates your friends and tries to keep you from seeing them. He repeatedly asks for detailed descriptions of who you were with, where you went, and why you were with them.

- **Problems with anger.** Trivial and mundane things set him off. He has random and erratic mood swings, putting you at the mercy of his emotional states.

- **Rigidity and belligerence.** Instead of a balanced view of relationship roles, he insists on defining the relationship in his terms, and his terms only. He ignores your needs and forges ahead with his desires.

- **Highly critical.** He is always making comments about your appearance. Healthy relationships are affirming relationships.

Source: National Coalition Against Domestic Violence (2020).

for example, most batterers have low self-esteem and tend to blame everyone else for their behavior. They are also typically extremely jealous and often use sex as their weapon of aggression and ultimate instrument of control. Although violence is the way they express their anger or frustration, they underestimate or even deny that their behaviors are "really that violent" or harmful. Batterers have the need to control and dominate, and they become master manipulators—they can manipulate their partner's weaknesses and strengths.

There is a common misconception that family violence results from an argument that "got out of hand," or that a partner "flew out of control," then escalated into physical blows. Most often, this is not the case—the batterer doesn't just lose control. Rather, domestic and intimate partner violence are patterns of behavior in which the abuser exerts power over the victim.

Another common misconception is that alcohol use or substance abuse are almost always associated with acts of family violence. Today, it is estimated that in America, England, and Wales, only about one-half (55 percent) of victims believed that their partners had been drinking prior to the physical or sexual assault (World Health Organization, 2018).

Although on the surface, domestic violence appears to be acts of physical, emotional, or sexual aggression against a victim, the central issues in family violence are not the acts of aggression at all. Rather, the central issues of domestic violence are *power, control,* and *domination*—and are commonly perpetuated by the strongest against the weakest (McGoldrick, Broken Nose, & Potenza, 1999). And batterers use a lot of strategies to control and dominate their partners: verbal abuse, isolation, controlling the finances, reproductive coercion (such as mandating whether birth control can or will be used), or sabotaging birth control so a partner gets pregnant. The important message here is this: *Rarely* is violence a one-time incident. Instead, domestic and intimate partner violence are patterns of behaviors that are consistently repeated over time, and over time, they instill great fear in the partner victim. Table 15.2 presents information to help people determine whether they are in an abusive relationship.

The Domestic Abuse Intervention Project (2020) created a tool that helps to describe the many ways in which an abusive partner uses *power* and *control* to manipulate a relationship. Although physical battering and sexual assaults (or the threats to commit them) are common abusive behaviors, other forms of abusive actions often contribute to the overall pattern of abuse:

- intimidation
- emotional abuse

- isolation
- minimizing, denying, and bullying
- using children against the woman (such as threatening to take the children away)
- male privilege
- economic abuse
- coercion and threats

These behaviors are not commonly identified as "abusive" by some women, but they contribute to the larger system of abuse and are often used to reinforce the physical and/or sexual abusive behaviors by the batterer. These behaviors send the clear message that a physical or sexual assault can be just around the corner.

As you can see, abusive and battering men use a whole host of tactics, ranging from degrading and humiliating comments to physical hits, punches, and kicks; false imprisonment; various forms of sexual abuse; threats and intimidation; economic exploitation; and murder to control and dominate.

Other researchers identify three categories of means that batterers use to control and dominate (Dalton & Schneider, 2001):

- *The ruler and the ruled.* Batterers often set stringent, unreasonable rules at home while also exerting extreme control in every facet of family life. For example, a husband might dictate which route the spouse must use when driving to the grocery store or taking the children to school. Any violation of the rules results in subsequent punishment.

- *Internalizing the rules.* Over lime, batterers need to use less and less overt methods of control and can rely on more subtle forms of control due to a *generalized climate of abuse*. This change is a result of the spouse and the children internalizing which behaviors result in abuse. Family members learn to suppress themselves in order to ensure the batterer is not "set off." For example, a mother may put the children to bed early so they are not present when the batterer comes home from work, or a woman may not voice her opinion—even over a trivial issue, such as where she would like to eat dinner—for fear of being hit.

- *Rules enforced by punishment.* According to Dalton and Schneider (2001), batterers "cement" their enforcement of the rules through the use of fear, emotional abuse, and social isolation. Batterers maintain an environment of control and fear through humiliation, criticism, financial abuse, sexual abuse, and emotional abuse. By cutting victims off from family and friends, a batterer's domination is enhanced. Furthermore, victims cannot leave if they do not have access to economic resources. As a wife battered for 17 years recounts, "When he wasn't hitting me, he was reminding me that he could. He was reminding me and getting me ready. Like the cat playing with the bird, letting it live a bit longer before he killed it" (p. 72).

The Cycle of Violence

Cycle of Violence model:

a model illustrating the three phases of violence commonly seen in abusive relationships: the tension-building phase, the acute battering or violent act, and the respite (nonviolent) phase.

In 1979, a professor of psychological studies and victim advocate for battered women, Lenore Walker, pioneered research that resulted in her **Cycle of Violence model**. In her research, she examined the lives of battered women and found that two-thirds of the 1,600 study respondents recounted similar patterns of intimate partner abuse. Not every abusive relationship experiences every phase of this cycle every time, but Walker's research shows how abusive relationships are cyclical in nature.

The Cycle of Violence, shown in Figure 15.8, illustrates three phases of violence commonly seen in abusive relationships: the *tension-building* phase, the *acute battering* or violent act, and the *respite* (nonviolent) phase.

Figure 15.8 /// Lenore Walker's Cycle of Violence

The Cycle of Violence, created by Lenore Walker, illustrates the three phases of violence in abusive relationships: tension-building, acute battering, and the respite phase.

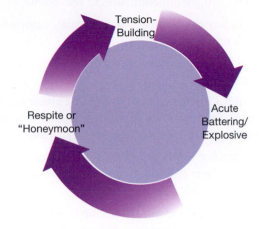

Source: Walker (1979).

Tension Building

In this phase, the victim senses that an explosive, violent incident is about to take place. The batterer begins to isolate his partner, threaten her, slap her, pinch her, belittle her, destroy her property, and withdraw affection. As the victim begins to feel tension and fear, her fear builds, and in response, she tries to keep her partner calm and happy by being agreeable, nurturing, and kind. At this point, some women begin to withdraw from or isolate themselves from their family and friends. All of her efforts have one goal: to keep the batterer from becoming violent. According to Walker (1979), the psychological anguish that accompanies this phase is the worst aspect of relationship violence. In fact, the psychological anguish may become so unbearable that many women antagonize or provoke the batterer in order to "just get it over with."

Acute Battering Incident

Savage. Destructive. Out of control. Brutal. This is how Walker (1979) describes the next phase of the Cycle of Violence. During this phase, the violence from the tension-building phase escalates into an acute battering incident during which the violence can become deadly. Along with degrading, humiliating verbal abuse, the batterer severely beats his partner, either by hitting, punching, and kicking or by using a weapon. He may even rape her. The battered woman cannot control when the episode will end. According to Walker, the victim usually does not fight back because she realizes doing so may only make it worse. Sometimes the victim may call the police, but typically she does not do so until several days after the incident. If she attempts to leave, she is at a greater risk of being killed by her partner.

Respite

This phase is often called the loving phase or the "honeymoon" or "flower" phase. Walker (1979) terms this as a time of "illusion of bliss." During this time, the abuser apologizes profusely. He may cry, beg for forgiveness, and vow that he will never harm the victim again. He will often give her gifts to express his regret and lavish her with attention and love. In fact, this may provide an answer to a common question: Why does she stay? Perhaps she stays because she has a sense of renewed hope that things are getting better. Research has identified eight reasons why women typically stay in abusive relationships (Cravens, Whiting, & Aamar, 2015; Whiting, 2016):

1. Distorted thoughts: Over time, emotional control and physical pain is traumatizing, and this leads to everything from confusion to self-blame.

2. Damaged self-worth: Repeated abuse causes mental, emotional, and physical damage to a person's sense of self.

3. Fear: The continued threat of harm—spoken or unspoken, acted upon or not acted upon—is powerful.

4. Hoping to change him: "I believed I could love the abuse out of him" (Institute of Family Studies, 2016). Some women's commitments to their marriages or other internal values systems make it difficult for them to leave.

5. Children: Women sacrifice their own safety for the children. Some women say they stay because they want their children to have a father; others say they stay so *they* will be the one who is abused, not the children.

6. Past family experiences: Many women describe how past experiences of violence in their childhood betrayed their sense of what a healthy relationship is.

7. Financial constraints: From having no income, to losing jobs because of their abuser's control, to having a partner accrue thousands of dollars in credit card debt in her name, to having no family, often women have financial limitations that prevent them from leaving.

8. Isolation: It is common for abusers to emotionally and physically separate their victim from family, friends, co-workers, and sometimes, society at large.

If a victim has filed charges against her abuser, her renewed sense of hope might cause her to drop the legal charges or to cancel appointments with mental health counselors or victims' advocates because she really believes he will change for good this time. Her renewed sense of hope leads her to believe that the violence won't happen again. *But it will.* Table 15.3 offers resources for battered women and their children. I encourage you to snap a photo of this table on your phone so you always have access to it.

Child Sexual Abuse

Child sexual abuse (CSA):
a form of child abuse that involves sexual activity with a minor (a child under the age of 18).

Some of the content in this section may cause distress to some readers. If you have been affected by child sexual abuse and are distressed, please skip this section.

Every nine minutes in the United States Child Protective Services confirms a claim of child sexual abuse. **Child sexual abuse (CSA)** is a form of child abuse that involves sexual activity

Table 15.3 /// Resources for Women and Children
The following resources are available for more information about relationships, violence, and safety and leaving abusive relationships
• Office on Women's Health Helpline: 800-994-9662
• National Coalition of Anti-Violence Programs: 212-714-1141
• Domestic Violence Hotline: 800-799-SAFE
• National Sexual Assault Hotline: 800-656-HOPE
• Victim Connect Resource Center: 855-484-2846

Source: Smith, S.G., Chen, J., Basile, K.C., Gilbert, L.K., Merrick, M.T., Patel, N., Walling, M., & Jain, A. (2017). The National Intimate Partner and Sexual Violence Survey (NISVS): 2010-2012 State Report. Atlanta, GA: National Center for Injury Prevention and Control.

with a minor (a child under the age of 18; RAINN, 2019). Today, two-thirds of CSA victims are aged 12 to 17 and one-third are under the age of 12 (U.S. Department of Health & Human Services, 2018a). Each year in America, 1 in 9 girls and 1 in 53 boys under the age of 18 experience sexual abuse at the hands of an adult (U.S. Department of Health & Human Services, 2018a). In our culture today, girls between the ages of 16 and 19 are *4 times* more likely than the general population to be victims or rape, attempted rape, or sexual assault (U.S. Department of Health & Human Services, 2018a). *A child cannot consent to any form of sexual activity.* Thus, *all* sexual behaviors with a child are crimes.

Characteristics of Child Sexual Abuse

Physical contact between a child and a perpetrator is not necessary for an act to be CSA. Child sexual abuse includes the following:

- Exhibitionism (exposing genitals to a minor child)
- Fondling
- Intercourse
- Masturbation in the presence of a minor
- Obscene phone calls, text messages
- Producing, owning, or sharing pornographic images of children
- Sexual harassment (RAINN, 2018)

It's important to understand that CSA is rarely perpetrated by a stranger: 93 percent of victims under the age of 18 know their abuser (RAINN, 2018). It's also important to note that the abuser does not have to be an adult—any person (including siblings, peers, minor neighbors) who takes advantage of a child's vulnerability is an abuser. As with batterers and perpetrators of domestic and intimate partner violence, child sexual abusers use their position of power, control, and domination to coerce or intimidate the child. There are several warning signs that a child is being sexually abused. I've presented these in Table 15.4.

Table 15.4 /// The Warning Signs of Child Sexual Abuse

Physical Signs

- Bleeding, bruises, swelling in the genital area
- Bloody, torn, or stained underpants
- Difficulty walking or sitting
- Frequent urinary or yeast infections
- Pain, itching, burning in genital area
- Genital discharge

Behavioral Signs

- Develops fears
- Depression
- Difficulties in school (absences, drops in grades)
- Inappropriate sexual knowledge or behaviors
- Nightmares
- Bed-wetting
- Self-harm
- Ducks away from physical contact
- Regressive behaviors, such as thumb-sucking or wetting pants
- Using words that are "too adult" for their age

Source: RAINN (2018).

The Lasting Effects of Child Sexual Abuse: "It Never Stops Shaping You"

The effects of child sexual abuse are potentially life long and include later physical, psychological, and behavioral consequences (Okur, Pereda, Van Der Knaap, & Bogaerts, 2018; Vrolijk-Bosschaart, Brillesliper-Kater, Benninga, Lindauer, & Teeuw, 2018). Because of the differences in our individual development, families of origin, and other lifecourse experiences, outcomes are, understandably, not the same for every victim. However, a very large body of scientific evidence helps us to appreciate the many consequences of child sexual abuse. As one survivor stated, "It never stops shaping you."

Physical Health Consequences. There are a number of physical health consequences of CSA, including immediate injuries, such as bleeding, tearing, and bruising of young genitalia and rectal tissue, as well as the threat of sexually transmitted infections (ACOG, 2019). Child sexual abuse and trauma also impact the development of the child's brain, which leads to differences in both structure and function; these alterations in the development of the brain have lifelong consequences for the child's mental health and well-being, which we will discuss in just a bit (Edwards, 2018). Child sexual abuse has also been linked to *future* health problems, including the following:

- Diabetes
- Poor nutrition, malnutrition
- Heart attack
- High blood pressure
- Bowel disease
- Migraine headaches
- Chronic lung disease
- Chronic fatigue syndrome
- Cancer (Widom, Czaia, Bentley, & Johnson, 2012; Monnat & Chandler, 2015; Afifi et al., 2016)

Clergy sexual abuse survivor Alexa MacPherson, 42, holds up a photograph of herself as a 7 year old child during a press conference regarding the death of Cardinal Bernard Law. MacPherson says she was sexually abused by Father Peter Canchong in Dorchester from the time she was 3 or 4 years old until she was 9. The press conference was organized by attorney Mitchell Garabedian, who played a key role in battling for victims and unmasking Law's practice of secretly circulating predatory priests around Greater Boston parishes.

Boston Globe via Getty

What is the link between these later-in-life physical difficulties and child sexual abuse? Some researchers have found that those who experience CSA are more likely to use and abuse alcohol and other substances; they are also more likely to smoke cigarettes, have a poor diet, and be morbidly obese (Felitti and others, 1998; De Bellis, 2002; Hart & Rubia, 2012; Putnam, 2003). These subsequent lifestyle habits and choices—perhaps used as coping mechanisms and self-medicating techniques due to the violence perpetrated against them as children—lead to down-the-road negative health consequences.

Psychological Consequences. CSA causes a number of immediate and long-term psychological consequences (for a complete review of the current literature, see Edwards, 2018). In the immediate wake of the violence, children experience isolation, fear, and distrust (National Scientific Council on the Developing Child, 2014). Substantive bodies of research show us that when children are victims of sexual abuse, children experience

- *Diminished cognitive skills.* Due to the disruptions in brain development and the subsequent alterations in the anatomy and function of the brain, CSA victims experience difficulties in working memory, learning, and paying attention (Bick & Nelson, 2016).

- *Attachment difficulties.* As you learned in Chapter 6, in the early years of life children develop the ability to emotionally attach to others, and these attachment bonds promote the ability to trust others. Victims of CSA are more likely to develop attachment disorders (see Chapter 6), and these disorders negatively affect a child's ability to form positive peer and social relationships and impact their ability to form intimate and love relationships later in life (Doyle & Cicchetti, 2017).

- *Poorer mental and emotional health.* There is no question that CSA creates risk factors for developing depression, anxiety, and suicidal thoughts, both immediately and later in life (Choi, DiNitto, Marti, & Choi, 2017).

Behavioral Consequences. All behavior is a form of communication, and children who are victims of CSA often exhibit behavioral difficulties. For the school-age child, behavioral difficulties can be displayed as outbursts of anger, inability to get along with peers, and difficulties in attention or staying on task/track (National Scientific Council on the Developing Child, 2014). When the

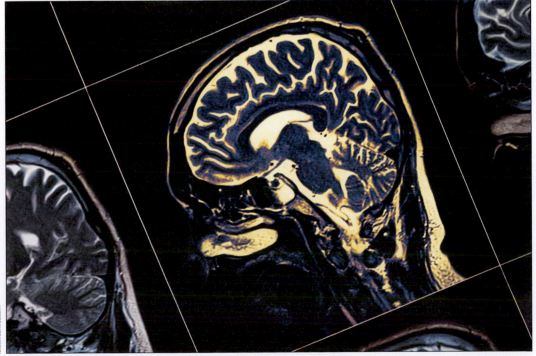

iStock.com/sudok1

Frequent, strong, and ongoing stress, such as in the case of child sexual abuse, is referred to as *toxic stress*. This prolonged exposure to stress creates a toxic coating of sorts on the child's brain, causing long-lasting damage to the child's brain and overall development. These changes impact a child's mental health.

victim either ages into adolescence, or is an adolescent at the time of the assault(s), they commonly experience the following:

- *Risky sexual behaviors.* Risky sexual behaviors include early onset of sexual behaviors, greater number of sexual partners, infrequent use of contraception, and transactional sex (sex exchanged for money, gifts, drugs, etc.).
- *Alcohol and drug use.* Adolescent and adult survivors of CSA are at a significantly greater risk to use and abuse alcohol and other substances than people who are not victims.
- *Juvenile delinquency and/or adult criminality.* Victims of CSA and other types of child abuse are more likely to develop antisocial behaviors than those who are not victims. (Choi et al., 2017; Child Welfare Information Gateway, 2019)

Keeping Our Kids Safe

There is no question that child sexual abuse is devastating, both in the immediate aftermath and in its long-lasting consequences. Despite its prevalence in our society, there are things we can do, together as a community of human service providers who care, to prevent CSA and minimize its effects. First, there are a number of online resources that provide a wealth of information, such as Information Gateway's "Preventing Child Abuse & Neglect" and "Responding to Child Abuse & Neglect." We can also stem the effects of abuse by utilizing the many known *protective factors* we have (Child Welfare Information Gateway, 2019), most of which we have discussed in our study together throughout this textbook:

- Parenting knowledge, competencies, and education
- Child nurturing and the importance of the healthy development of attachment
- Knowledge of child development
- Knowledge of the development of intimacy across the lifespan and healthy relational skills
- Knowledge of the social and emotional development of children
- Knowledge of the development of relationships
- Understanding of the importance of peers and healthy peer relationships
- Parent or caregiver well-being
- Strong communication skills
- Stable family environments and living situations
- Positive community involvement
- Strong local, state, and federal policies that support the family's well-being

Equipped with this knowledge, we *can* work together to build a stronger, safer society for our children and our children's children.

FAMILY LIFE EDUCATION: PROVIDING KNOWLEDGE AND SKILLS

Stress and crisis are inevitable experiences in couple and family life. As we've discussed throughout our time together in our study of intimate and family relationships, it's not a question of *whether* partners and family members will experience difficulties—it's a question of *when.* Family life educators, therapists, social workers, and family practitioners and scientists, with their knowledge of family strengths and weaknesses and how family members relate to each other, are valuable resources to today's families because they have the knowledge necessary to help individuals and families acquire the necessary skills to traverse these inevitabilities.

Life is filled with irony, isn't it? When writing the third edition of this text, as I prepared to put the "finishing touches" on this chapter, I was suddenly plunged into the depths of grief and despair. My husband of 37 years was killed in an auto accident. As we both left the house to run separate

Are There Gender Differences in the Experiences of Stress?

College—homework, exams, relationship trials and triumphs, finances, trying to figure out future careers. Is it any wonder that college is considered to be one of the most trying, stressful developmental phases in a person's lifetime (Ross, Niebling, Bradley, & Heckert, 1999)? Over the past 10 years, researchers have sought to better understand gender differences in the sources of stress among college students. Female students tend to be affected most by financial pressures, exam pressures, failing an exam, being rejected by someone, and relationship breakups (Frazier & Schauben, 1994). Males, on the other hand, have a greater number of stressors related to changes in their sleeping and eating habits, heavier workloads, increased and new responsibilities, and breaking up with a girlfriend (Ross et al., 1999). Both genders' experiences of stress are related to their self-esteem and overall health status (Hudd et al., 2000). But there's one more key player in how men and women respond to stress: sex hormones.

Her Side: Estrogen appears to heighten the effects of the stress hormone oxytocin. Because of this, women tend to feel the effects of stress more than men. This isn't to say, however, that they react more strongly; to the contrary! Because of the way women are socialized (for instance, to be nurturing and relational), women "tend" to their stress by "befriending" other people. The "tend and befriend" tactic—turning to family and friends, talking to them, venting to them—appears to help women work through their stress in healthy, productive ways. They may stress out more often and get upset more frequently than men do, but they work through it much more quickly.

His Side: Testosterone appears to buffer the effects of the stress hormone oxytocin. Because of this, men are somewhat immune to minor or day-to-day stressors. In cases of extreme stress, men are more apt to respond aggressively. Men, therefore, "fight" their stressors through aggression, or they ignore them by means of withdrawal or bottling up of emotions, by "flight." This "fight or flight" tactic appears to work against men. They may stress out less often than women, and ignore minor daily hassles better than women, but when bigger stressors hit, all of the pent-up frustrations are released.

Your Side: Think about your experiences with stress.

1. Do you believe that women and men are affected by different stressors, as the research suggests? Do your stressors fall in the categories that the research documents? How might they differ?

2. What is your reaction to the notion that estrogen and testosterone affect the feelings and reactions to stress?

Source: Taylor and others (2000).

errands, we kissed each other goodbye in the driveway, as we always did when we parted. I made it home from my errand. He did not. In an instant, I lost everything I knew to be true and solid. I lost my best buddy. My lover. My partner in all. The father of my children. The grandfather of my grandchildren. In essence, I lost everything that I study and teach about for a living. I didn't know that the quick kiss in the driveway would be the last time I ever kissed this man that I have loved since high school. And, just as if someone had plunged my head into water without warning, I emerged from this tragedy gasping for air, sputtering, disoriented. And scared.

Many times, I have said, "I can't do this." And many times, I have said, "I don't want to do this without him." I've watched my sons and their wives deal with indescribable agony. And for the first time as their mother, I can't make the pain go away. I can't make things better. As I write this, my heart is in a million pieces. And I don't know how it will ever be put back together. The stark reality is this: My happily ever after is gone.

But the stark truth is this: As difficult as it will be, we will find a way to be a family without him. It will hurt. It will be hard. It will sometimes seem impossible. As our family system tries to find a new balance without this vitally important, necessary, so loved person, we will struggle. We will argue. We will cry. We will love. We'll hurt each other. And we'll hurt some more. And somehow, we'll find our way along this uncharted, jagged path. And I *know* we'll be stronger, together. Why am I so certain we'll be okay and healthy and thriving as a family on the other side of this? Because I trust the *science of the family*. I trust in everything I have taught you in our study together.

There are many predictable "vulnerability points" throughout the lifecourse of a family: Marriages begin; couples experience stress over finances, sex, in-laws, and day care; babies are born; kids get ear infections and sometimes get hurt and need stitches; adolescents grow up, move out, fall in love, get married—and the cycle begins all over again. When the pressures associated with daily life in this quick-paced culture accompany these normative developmental changes, it is no wonder that families experience the pile-up effect of these stressors. And sometimes, people we love are taken from us.

Many of us wish we didn't have to confront some of life's daily challenges, but these day-to-day events actually serve an important function. Just as we put money in the bank to have it available in times of need, our "routine" stressors allow our families to build coping strategies for when we need them. Normative changes, transitions, and stressors strengthen our resiliency. They help develop the identity of "who" the family is. They allow us to hone our coping skills, our communication skills, and our relational skills. With each life change, we add to this "bank account" of coping. As a result, when (not *if*) the inevitable life-altering event happens, we have resources on which to draw to help us make it through. The reality of family living is that change—sometimes agonizingly painful—is inevitable. As Duvall (1971) puts it, "Strong families are not without their problems, but they use their resources to weather the storms that strike every family from time to time" (p. 516).

And that is how my family will continue to "be" a family without my husband's presence. Like all families who find the capacity to cope, we will confront the reality of his death and respond to the tasks at hand. We will make the necessary choices that fit with our cultural and religious beliefs. We will continue to sustain the strong family and kinship ties that bound us together before this tragedy. We will rely on family and friends and accept help where and when it is needed, yet at the same time, we will do what we can for ourselves. And, over time, the balance lost in our forever-changed family system will eventually find itself again.

Different . . . and that's okay.

/// SUMMARY

Family Change

- Family life never stays the same because families always change.

- Stress is best viewed as the result of stimuli that evoke physiological and/or psychological responses, and anything that elicits these stress responses is a stressor. The stressor can either be eustress (positive stress) or distress (negative stress), and most fall within four primary categories: personal, social/family, work/school, and environmental.

- Like individuals, families face stress too. Family stress often occurs during lifecourse transitions, and sometimes this stress is experienced as a family crisis. As family systems confront stress, grow, and change, they must adjust to these changes, which involves making changes in family structure, making changes in family roles, and making changes in family rules.

- David Olson and colleagues outline three types of stress that families experience; family development stress,

psychological stress (stress within the individual), and family stress and crisis.

- To fully understand the fundamentals of family stress and crisis and why the entire family system experiences the ripple effects of the stressor(s), it is necessary to view the family as a system and apply elements of Family Systems theory.

- The General Adaptation Syndrome model describes three stages of physiological responses to eustress and distress: alarm reaction, stage of resistance, and exhaustion,

- A life change event is typically life altering, requiring significant social and psychological adjustment. The Social Readjustment Rating Scale Identifies associations between life events and life transitions, and the impact of these events and transitions on individual physical health and well-being. Few life change events are experienced in isolation; they often affect the entire family.

- Family stress is the result of an imbalance between the demands an event places on a family, and that family's ability or inability to meet them.

- The Transactional Model of Stress reflects the interaction between a person and his or her environment. Whatever event causes the stress, the impact of the stressor is wholly dependent on our perception and appraisal of the stressor. The model includes three key concepts: *Primary appraisal*, when people instinctively evaluate and assess the significance of the event; *secondary appraisal*, when people assess how controllable the stressor is and then decide which resources they will use to cope. External locus of control refers to the perception that we cannot control what happens in some aspects of our lives, while internal locus of control refers to the perception that we are in control of our destiny. Finally, *coping efforts* are those strategies individuals and families use to bring order to and regulate the stressor.

Family Crisis

- Whether a family experiences changes and transitions as family *stress* or family crisis depends largely on whether the family has the ability to adapt to these changes in the family environment.

- Typically, there are four types of family crises: *dismemberment,* the separation or isolation of an individual from the rest of his or her family; *demoralization,* crises that tend to bring disgrace to a family system; *accession*, when turbulence occurs due to the addition of a family member; and *demoralization plus dismemberment or accession,* when a family is thought to be demoralized because of embarrassing stressors.

- The ABC-X Family Crisis Model explains why families vary in the way they adapt and adjust to change, transition, and stress. This model views a family crisis situation as a combination of various factors: *A* factors are the initial crisis-causing events; *B* factors are the resources a family has at its disposal to meet the demands of the crisis; *C* factors are the meanings families ascribe to the event; and *X* factors are the outcomes of the event, the results of whether or not a family copes effectively with the crisis event. The Double ABC-X Model aims to identify the effects of the pile-up of stressors and how families adapt to them.

- There are adaptive tasks that families facing change must encounter. To successfully adjust, families must establish the meaning and understand the personal significance of the situation; confront reality and respond to the requirements of the external situation; sustain relationships with family members and friends as well as with other individuals who may be helpful in resolving the crisis and aftermath; preserve a reasonable emotional balance by managing distressful feelings in response to the situation; and preserve a satisfactory self-image and maintain a sense of competence and mastery.

Family Coping and Resilience

- By using personal, family, and community resources, families are better able to cope with stressors. The major types of family coping skills used in times of change and crisis are *appraisal-focused coping,* when families try to understand why the crisis occurred and to find meaning in the circumstances that caused the crisis; *problem-focused coping* allows the family to confront the reality of the crisis by obtaining information about the crisis; and *emotion-focused coping,* when families develop the capacity to maintain hope.

- Family resilience refers to a family's ability to function in a healthy fashion during times of change, stress, adversity, crisis, and transition. Confronted with a crisis, resilient families often reevaluate their priorities and may invest more deeply in meaningful relationships as a result.

- Family resilience is reinforced by numerous family resilience processes that help guide families through the times of change and challenge: the family belief system, the ability to make meaning of adversity, having a positive outlook, and the presence of spirituality, flexibility, connectedness, and family communication skills.

The Crisis of Family Violence

- Domestic violence—violence perpetrated against family members by a person who is related to the victim either biologically or legally—crosses every socioeconomic and educational level, and every family type. Family of origin patterns, psychopathology, mental illness, and genetic causes; poverty, educational levels, absent or inaccessible family services; and cultural factors, such as media influences, all may contribute to domestic violence.

- There are three broad categories of domestic violence: *physical violence,* such as hitting, punching, or slapping; *emotional violence*—for example, controlling the amount of contact a family member has with family and friends, and showing intense displays of jealousy, or threats of physical or sexual harm; and *sexual violence,* which includes marital rape, battering rape, and forced sexual acts.

- Women with less education, of lower socioeconomic status, and who are single parents or young teenage parents are more likely to be victims of violence. Generally, women with low self-esteem, who are passive, or believe that they are responsible for the batterer's actions, are more likely to be abused.

- Batterers share some common characteristics, such as low self-esteem, the tendency to blame others for their behavior, a propensity for extreme jealousy, and the frequent use of sex as their weapon of aggression and their instrument of control. Batterers also tend to deny that their behaviors are harmful, and because they have the need to control and dominate, they become master manipulators.

- Most often, violence appears to have no trigger. At the root of domestic violence is the need for control and domination.

- The **Power and Control Wheel** depicts behaviors that batterers use to control and dominate their intimate partners and/or children, and shows that abusive and battering men use many tactics, including degrading and humiliating comments, physical attacks, imprisonment, various forms of sexual abuse, threats and intimidations, economic exploitation, and murder.

- The tactics batterers frequently use fall into three categories: the *Ruler and the Ruled,* wherein batterers set unreasonable rules at home while also exerting extreme control in every facet of family life; *Internalizing the Rules,* which describes how, over time, batterers need to use less overt methods

of control, and can rely on more subtle forms of control due to a generalized climate of abuse; and *Rules Enforced by Punishment,* which is when batterers "cement" their enforcement of the rules through the use of fear, emotional abuse, and social isolation.

- Lenore Walker's Cycle of Violence model shows how abusive relationships are cyclical in nature, and describes three phases of violence commonly seen in abusive relationships: the *tension-building phase,* in which the victim senses that a violent incident is about to take place; the *acute battering,* when the violence from the tension-building phase escalates into a violent battering incident; and the *nonviolent respite phase,* when the abuser apologizes profusely, begs for forgiveness, and may vow that he will never harm her again.

- *Child sexual abuse (CSA)* is a type of violence perpetrated against minor children (children under the age of 18); it is a form of child abuse that involves sexual activity.

- There are both immediate and long-term consequences of CSA. These include physical, psychological, and behavioral consequences.

Power and Control Wheel: a model depicting behaviors batterers use to control and dominate their intimate partners and/or children.

/// KEY TERMS

iStock.com/FatCamera

CHAPTER 16

FAMILY LIFE AND AGING

LEARNING OBJECTIVES

16.1 Summarize the landscape and trends of aging in contemporary America.

16.2 Explain how experiences of the Family Life Cycle and marriage change throughout aging.

16.3 Discuss the distinguishing characteristics of intergenerational ties in later life.

16.4 Describe the challenges faced by caregivers.

16.5 Relate death and dying experiences to changes in the Family Life Cycle.

....

It was years ago, very early on a bitterly cold winter morning. My mother had been ill for some time and we were on our way to a cancer specialist, several hours' drive away. I helped her into the car and after she was situated I fastened her seatbelt. And then it happened.

Suddenly, for the first time, I noticed that she appeared so weak, and at that moment I knew: *She* needed me. This woman, the very pillar of strength who fought (and beat) cancer twice before, who single-handedly had raised her four children while her husband fought in the Vietnam war, this woman who had supported, encouraged, guided, and taught us, appeared so small and fragile and helpless beneath the blankets. Fighting back tears, I tucked the blanket around her legs, thinking, *"When did this happen? When did I become the parent and she the child?"*

Over the next few weeks she died by inches. I cared for her every day . . . bathing her, feeding her, loving her. The stress was indescribable—I left my home every morning at 7:30, as soon as I got my children off to school, cared for her all day, got home in time to get the kids from school, work on homework with them, feed them, bathe them, tuck them into bed. . . . This was our routine for about 6 weeks, until she died. Although it was the most difficult thing I had ever done in my life, my relationship with my parents deepened to a level we had never experienced before. . . . In that situation, you're forced to talk about things you would otherwise never talk about.

My mother held me when I was first born, weak and unable, and I held her at the end, weak and unable. Together, we had traveled the arc of life. I didn't think my heart could ever be as broken as it was in the months that followed her death. And then, unexpectedly, my husband died.

Baby Boomers:

people who were born between 1946 and 1964.

Life expectancy:

based on statistical averages, the age at which adults are expected to die is anywhere from 68 to 80, depending on a person's race and gender.

Our nation is moving into an unprecedented time in its history: By the year 2030, 1 in every 5 people (roughly 20 percent of the population) will be over the age of 65 living in the United States—more than ever before (U.S. Census Bureau, 2018a). What accounts for this surge in the aging population? Baby Boomers are getting older. **Baby Boomers** are those people who were born between 1946 and 1964. During this time in American history, the birth rates rose sharply because of the economic prosperity following World War II. The first Baby Boomers turned 65 years old in 2011. Is this country prepared for its aging population?

This entire generation, accustomed to living in a "youthful culture," is growing old. But do they know how? After the age of 40 or so, is it really downhill until we die? One hundred years ago, few people made it past the age of 70—the average **life expectancy** was 47. Today, the average

Figure 16.1 /// The Racial Gap in Life Expectancy

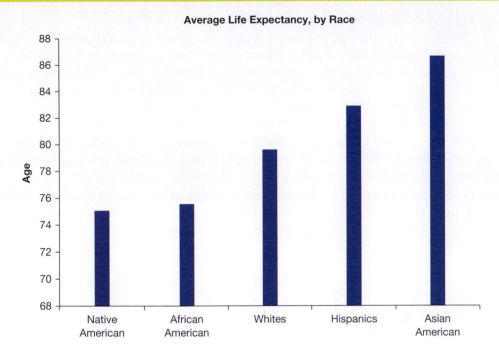

Average Life Expectancy, by Race

Source: Centers for Disease Control and Prevention (2018b).

life expectancy is about 79, depending on a person's race and gender (Centers for Disease Control and Prevention, 2018a). White females are expected to live to the age of 81, and African American women have a life expectancy of 76 (Kochanke, Murphy, Xu, & Arias, 2019). Figure 16.1 illustrates death rates by race and ethnicity. As you can see, there is a racial gap in life expectancy. How will the aging live out the years that have been added to their lifespan?

In this chapter, we'll examine the demographics of America's aging. We'll also discuss the developmental forces involved in aging, such as the biological changes that take place, and family development through aging, including the aged's sexuality experiences and grandparenting. Finally, we'll look at the changes associated with aging lifestyles, such as retirement and caregiving.

AGING AND THE AGED

Understanding the aging population is important in our study of marriage, family, and intimate relationships because the increasing numbers of this population are challenging U.S. policy makers, healthcare providers, health and life insurance companies, businesses, and families (He, Sangupta, Velkoff, & DeBarros, 2005). How will the nation meet the needs of the increasing numbers of the aging and the aged? How will families care for their aging loved ones?

America is turning gray. One hundred years ago, there were significantly more young people than older Americans. Looking further into the future, from the years 2018 to 2060, the senior population is expected to more than double, from 46 million to nearly 98 million; by 2060, it is expected that one-fourth of the entire U.S. population will be 65 and older (Centers for Disease Control and Prevention, 2018b).

The Portrait of Age in the United States

In the nearly two decades that spanned 1990 to 2019, Baby Boomers represented the most expansive generation of any before it.

- *Older population.* In 2020, there will be slightly more than 40 million older adults (those aged 65 and older) in the United States, representing slightly more than 13 percent of its population. The median age of the elderly today is 75 years of age.

- *Diversity.* Within the U.S. population, there is great diversity among older adults; today, 9 percent of the racial and ethnic minority populations are elderly, in comparison to 19 percent of whites (U.S. Department of Health and Human Services, 2018). Compared with African American and white older adults, Hispanic Americans are experiencing significantly larger increases. For example, by the year 2050, according to the U.S. Census Bureau (2018a), the percentage of older Hispanic Americans will nearly double.

- *Education.* In 2009, about 20 percent of those age 65 and over had a college degree. The U.S. Census Bureau (2018b) projects that by the year 2030, as Baby Boomers age, 85 percent will have graduated from high school, and 75 percent will have a college degree.

- *Centenarians.* There were more than 72,000 centenarians (those aged 100 or more) in 2017. By 2050, it is projected that there will be close to 1 million people in the United States over the age of 100. More than 80 percent of centenarians today are women, and the majority live in metropolitan areas.

To be sure, the face of America is changing! As you can see, there are gender, racial, and ethnic differences in the life expectancies of people. What are the forces that influence their aging? Why do some people age well, and others do not?

Developmental Forces in Aging

Gerontologists:
scientists who study aging.

Lifespan perspective:
emphasizes that human beings are in a constant, continuous state of growth from the cradle to the grave.

Multiple forces influence and affect how people age. **Gerontologists**, who are scientists who study aging, along with family sociologists, developmentalists, and family life educators, have developed perspectives that help them analyze these influences. The **lifespan perspective** of development emphasizes that from the cradle to the grave, human beings are in a constant, continuous state of growth-motion. This perspective posits that simply because we age does not mean that we completed our intrapersonal and interpersonal developmental tasks and growth. In applying the lifespan perspective, those who study aging are interested in answering the larger question: Why and how do we age the way we do?

By 2050, it is projected that there will be close to 1 million people in the United States over the age of 100. Would you like to live to 100—or beyond? Why or why not?

Mark Rightmire/MediaNews Group/Orange County Register via Getty Images

One ongoing controversy is the **nature vs. nurture debate**: Are the influences of aging determined by nature (your inborn, hereditary characteristics such as genetic influences) or by nurture (your environmental, experiential, societal, and cultural experiences across your lifespan)? For many years, most social scientists who studied aging focused on the nature side of the argument—that is, they believed that the influences of aging are biologically driven and as such, not much could be done to prevent certain, inevitable outcomes. Today, however, those who study human development and the aging process argue that aging is a process of *both* nature *and* nurture and that the two forces interact to create a unique individual. In particular, there are four interactive forces of development:

1. *Biological forces.* These refer to all genetic and health-related factors. For example, is a person genetically predisposed to getting cancer? Also included in this area of development are lifestyle choices such as diet, exercise, smoking, and alcohol consumption. Race and ethnic differences are also included because some races are more predisposed for certain illnesses such as high blood pressure and diabetes.

2. *Psychological forces.* These refer to all cognitive, emotional, and perceptual factors. Among the aging, things such as cognitive impairment due to certain diseases, and memory loss and retention are considered.

3. *Sociocultural forces.* These include cultural, ethnic, societal, relational, and interpersonal factors. In this area of development, family scientists consider employment, living arrangements, marital status, parenting and grandparenting, and caregiving.

4. *Lifecycle forces.* All of these forces interact and combine to create a person's unique, individual developmental experiences.

As you have seen, there are certain expected life-course events as well as those that we do not expect or anticipate. Paul Baltes, a psychologist who specializes in aging, and his research associates (Baltes, Lindenberger, & Staudinger, 1998) identify three varying sets of interacting life-course influences: normative age-graded influences, normative history-graded influences, and non-normative influences.

Normative age-graded influences are developmental changes that are caused by biological, psychological, and sociocultural forces. These age-graded influences are typically highly correlated to person's chronological age, such as the start of menstruation, puberty growth spurts, menopause, hearing loss, vision loss, or the loss of memory skills. These biological developmental changes are significant because they often signal major transitions in people's lives. For example, a teenager who begins menstruating is now capable of bearing children; a woman who begins menopause can no longer bear children. In many cultures, there are rituals or rites of passage that mark progression into different stages of life, and these events correspond to certain ages. Among Israeli women, for instance, menopause is marked with a *croning ceremony*. This rite of passage is celebrated at the age of 50, and during this ceremony aging women are recognized as the embodiment of wisdom, healing, and teaching. Within this culture, crones are the ones who care for the dying and are the "spiritual midwives," the "knowers of all mysteries" (Alpert, 1991).

Every culture establishes norms associated with the timing of the events. This is the culture's **social clock**, and it includes rites of passage, such as graduating from high school or college, getting married, or retiring—all by a socially and culturally accepted age.

Normative history-graded influences are events or conditions that people in a given culture or society experience simultaneously. The history-related events may be *biological* in nature, such as the AIDS epidemic in Africa; *psychological* in nature, such as racism in this country that resulted in the Civil Rights Movement of the 1960s; or *sociocultural*, such as the Great Depression of the 1930s or the sexual revolution that took place throughout the 1960s and the 1970s. It is these history-graded influences that sometimes give certain generations their nicknames, such as those who grew up during the Great Depression era, the Baby Boomers, or Generation X (those born after 1965). The impact and effect of history-graded influences is great. For

Nature vs. nurture debate:
the ongoing debate between those people who feel the influences of aging are determined by nature (your inborn, hereditary characteristics such as genetic influences) and those who believe they are determined by nurture (your environmental, experiential, societal, and cultural experiences across your lifespan).

Normative age-graded influences:
developmental changes caused by biological, psychological, and sociocultural forces.

Social clock:
culturally established norms associated with the timing of events. The social clock includes rites of passage, such as graduating from high school or college, getting married, or retiring—all by a socially and culturally accepted age.

Normative history-graded influences:
events or conditions that people in a given culture or society experience simultaneously.

example, most people in the United States remember where they were when they learned of the terrorist attacks on September 11, 2001. For many Americans, the destruction and devastation caused by the terrorist attacks will remain etched on our memories for quite some time.

Non-normative influences are things that most people do not experience—these influences are uncommon, rare, or unanticipated events. Some non-normative influences may be favorable, such as gaining a large, unexpected inheritance from a long-lost uncle, but most often these events are not favorable and cause disruption in individual and family life. Although we expect that we will have to experience the death of our parents, for example, we do not expect that this will occur while we are in college. Similarly, we might expect that we ourselves will experience a serious illness as we enter mid- or later life, but we do not anticipate that we will experience a life-threatening illness in our teens or 20s—or that our children will at any point in their childhood. As we discussed in Chapter 15, such non-normative events are experienced as crises.

As you learned in Chapter 1, *we do not develop in isolation.* Throughout our lifespan, our development is multifaceted, shaped and reshaped by many interacting influences. Who we are and how we came to be the persons we are is a complex tapestry woven together from biological, psychological, social, and cultural influences. And how we age is no exception.

What Is Aging?

Most of us have heard the cliché, "You're as young as you feel!" But are we? Although I may feel as though I'm 25 or 30 in spirit, my uncooperative knees and my need for bifocal eyeglasses tell me that my 20s and 30s are history! So how do we characterize the aging process? Is it a pattern of intricate, genetically timed biological changes? Or is aging a mindset? Aging is not a uniform process for all; certainly, there are universal aging processes, but individual coping and adaptation to lifecourse experiences all affect how we age (Crosnoe & Elder, 2002).

Primary Aging

Primary aging: basic biological processes that are genetically programmed to occur over time.

To better understand the aging process, it is necessary to examine biological, age-related declines. Researchers, gerontologists, and developmentalists alike distinguish between primary aging and secondary aging. **Primary aging** refers to the basic biological processes that

Age isn't just a number—it's an attitude! Does aging mean we have to be "old"?

are genetically programmed and that take place with the passage of time (Cavanaugh & Blanchard-Fields, 2002). These aging processes represent the core aspects of aging (Cavanaugh & Blanchard-Fields, 2002):

- **Primary aging: Biological changes associated with aging.** These changes are genetically programmed and take place over time, and all of the changes are irreversible. Eventually, the biological changes lead to death. Death by primary aging factors is referred to as "death by natural causes."

- **Age-related anatomical and functional changes.** These include changes in the immune system and the ability to fight infection or disease, changes in vision and hearing, changes in the function of joints, and changes in memory retention.

- **Progressive changes.** Starting at about age 30, we begin to lose brain neurons. By the age of 50, our brain size is reduced to 97 percent, and by the age of 70, our brain size is reduced to about 92 percent.

- **Inevitable changes.** This category includes declines in sensory functions. Hearing, vision, taste, and balance become less acute. Reaction times become slower because the speed of nerve impulses slows.

- **Universally experienced changes.** Regardless of society or culture, all primary aging changes are experienced by everyone.

According to biologist Leonard Hayflick (1994), every species in the animal kingdom has a maximum lifespan. For humans, it appears to be about 110 to 120 years. According to Hayflick, each species has a genetically programmed time limit because at a certain point in time, cells lose their ability to replicate. This time limit, known as the **Hayflick limit**, is what accounts for the aging process and life expectancy. Hayflick proposed that there are three cellular factors that cause aging: the diminished capacity to adapt to stressors, a reduction in the speed of performance, and an increased susceptibility to disease (Hayflick, 1994). It appears, then, that there is little a person can do to prevent the inevitability of aging. Are there things we can do, however, to help us slow the aging process?

Secondary Aging

Although the characteristics associated with primary aging cannot be delayed inevitably, to a very large extent we have control over age-related declines that are associated with **secondary aging**—physiological declines that are the result of environmental and behavioral influences that significantly impact how we age. Among other things, secondary aging is influenced by lifestyle choices such as smoking, poor nutrition, lack of exercise, sun exposure, alcohol and/ or substance use, and sexual behaviors.

It is often difficult to determine whether the declines associated with aging are due to primary or secondary influences. For example, smoking, which is associated with secondary age-related declines, accelerates the deterioration of the cardiovascular and respiratory systems. Yet it is sometimes difficult to determine whether it is the primary aging influences, such as being more susceptible to disease, or the behavior that causes the greater likelihood that an aged person will develop cancer. The easiest way, then, to determine whether physical deterioration is related to primary or secondary causes is to keep in mind that, as developmental psychologist Barbara Lemme (2011) observed, "primary aging is generally identifiable by its inevitability, universality, and irreversibility, while secondary aging appears only among a part of the population, is related to extrinsic factors such as behavior and socioeconomic status, and may . . . be prevented or perhaps reversed."

Ageism

Ageism refers to the stereotypical attitudes people hold about the aging and the elderly. People who are **ageist** have a fixed and negative mindset about older people. As a result of these attitudes, the aging population is often subjected to bias and unfair treatment.

Hayflick limit:
according to Leonard Hayflick, each species has a genetically programmed time limit because at a certain point in time, cells lose their ability to replicate. The Hayflick limit accounts for the aging process and life expectancy.

Secondary aging:
physiological declines that are the result of environmental and behavioral influences, which significantly affect how we age.

Ageism:
stereotypical altitudes toward the aging and elderly.

The biggest problem associated with ageism is that it limits the things people can accomplish, and it denies them the respect and freedom that all people deserve (Lemme, 2011). Ageism may lead to unfair housing, unfair employment, and unfair educational opportunities. For example, a woman with 20 years of administrative office experience may be turned down for a job, or she may be denied a promotion over a younger employee with less experience. Ageism can also interfere with proper medical diagnoses, such as in instances of depression or anxiety in the aging and the elderly; too often these mental diagnoses are misinterpreted or diagnosed as physical conditions and are subsequently either mistreated or left untreated (Lemme, 2011).

Although there are, indeed, losses associated with aging, there are also many inherent gains. For instance, in a study completed by the National Council on Aging (NCOA), nearly one-half of the older Americans surveyed considered themselves to be middle-aged or young. Only about 15 percent of those age 75 or older consider themselves to be "old" (NCOA, 2015).

So what does it mean to age successfully? In a biological sense, it might mean that as a person ages there is a minimal level of decline in physiological, cognitive, and social and emotional functioning. But for our purposes here, we must consider which life experiences allow some people to age more successfully than others—how do they manage their later years in life? With this in mind, we turn our attention to the effects of aging with regard to family relationships and family living in middle and old age.

MARRIAGE EXPERIENCES THROUGH AGING

As life expectancies increase, so do issues concerning later-life family living because as we age we experience a number of transitions, challenges, losses, and gains—in our health, and in our family relationships and lifestyles. Relationships are essential in later age because stable, intimate relationships throughout the life cycle protect us against various biological losses associated with aging and buffers us against the loss of social roles (Kulik, 1999; Lemon, Bengston, & Peterson, 1972; Lowenthal & Haven, 1968). In fact, today middle-aged and older Americans cite a loving family as a reason for having a positive outlook on life (NCOA, 2015). In the following section, we'll explore family development among the aging, including marital satisfaction among aging couples, sexuality, and experiences with parenting and grandparenting.

The Marriage Relationship: Marital Satisfaction

When we view families from a developmental perspective, we can see the relatively predictable changes associated with family living (see Chapter 1). The Family Life Cycle model not only helps to define a family's current developmental stage but it also helps us to understand the organization of the family system, how it changes over time, and the significance and importance of these changes for each individual within the family system (Lemme, 2011). Just as individuals are in a constant state of growth-motion and must accomplish certain developmental tasks, families, too, must navigate the developmental tasks associated with the aging family. As Table 16.1 illustrates, a family spends about 25 to 30+ years from the time the last child leaves home, a period known as the **empty nest**, through retirement, until the death of both spouses. Indeed, the middle and later years of family life make up at least half of the family life cycle. As the family moves through time, many changes take place and responsibilities change. Relationships with others are a key aspect of adulthood and aging (Cavanaugh & Blanchard-Fields, 2002).

Have you ever wondered how couples stay married for 40, 50, or 60 years? With all of the changes across individual and family life cycles; with all of the challenges, transitions, and crises families confront; and with all of the environmental and non-normative events that can occur, what is the secret to marital success? As you have seen through our study, marital satisfaction and happiness ebb and flow throughout the family life cycle and are affected

Empty nest:
the home with no children after children have grown and left.

Table 16.1 /// Family Life Cycle by Length of Time in Each of the Eight Stages

Stage	Length of time
Married couple without children	2 years
Childbearing families (oldest child is up to 30 months)	2.5 years
Families with preschool children (oldest child is 30 months-6 years)	3.5 years
Families with schoolchildren (oldest child is 6-13 years)	7 years
Families with teenagers (oldest child is 13-20 years)	7 years
Families launch young adults (children leave home)	8 years
Middle-aged parents (empty nest to retirement)	15+ years
Aging family members (retirement to death of both spouses)	10–15+ years

Source: Based on Duvall, Evelyn Millis & Miller, Brent C. *Marriages and Family Development* 6/E © 1985. Published by Allyn and Bacon, Boston, MA.

by events such as childbirth and the launching of a child into early adulthood. As married couples age, their relationship continues to undergo changes, influencing their relationship quality. According to social psychologists Benjamin Karney and Thomas Bradbury (1995), marriages that are strong in reciprocity and interdependence remain high in intimacy and closeness and continue to thrive through old age. On the other hand, marriages that demonstrate lower levels of interdependence and reciprocity are characterized by higher levels of stress and conflict during this phase of family development.

Researchers identify some specific characteristics that speak directly to the differences in relational quality between middle-aged and older married couples. For instance, two bodies of research discovered that as couples age, there are fewer sources of marital conflict and there is greater potential for pleasure than in middle adulthood (Carstensen, Gottman, & Levenson, 1995; Levenson, Carstensen, & Gottman, 1993). They also found that as couples

iStock.com/Dean Mitchell

Couples who experience high levels of intimacy and interdependence in their marriages typically have high levels of marital satisfaction as they age. Overall, older couples tend to be more positive in their communication and emotions.

age, there are fewer gender differences in those things each spouse finds pleasurable. Overall, researchers found couples to have more positive emotions. In comparison to younger couples, older couples tend to use more affectionate, positive language during times of conflict, and tend to be less emotionally negative toward their spouse. It should be noted, however, that if a couple is unhappy during the earlier years of their marriage, becoming older does not mean that they will suddenly find happiness! Younger, unhappy couples eventually age to become older, unhappy couples.

It's also important to understand that both physical and mental health in middle-aged and older adults impacts marital satisfaction. For example, bodies of research evidence indicate that when physical health becomes burdened, marital satisfaction declines (Choi, Yorgason, & Johnson, 2016; Iveniuk, Waite, McClintock, & Teidt, 2014). But, for couple relationships to be advantageous to middle-aged and older adults, the relationships need to be of high quality (Hung, Wright Voss, Bounsanga, Graff, & Birmingham, 2019).

In middle-aged couples, sources of conflict tend to center on childrearing, money issues, communication, sex, and in-laws, whereas in older couples (age 65 and older), sources of conflict include communication, what the couple does for recreation, money issues, sex, and adult children (Levenson et al., 1993). In general, older couples report less upset in response to conflict, disagreements, and quarrels—but that doesn't mean they experience conflict less often than younger couples (Akiyama, Antonucci, Takahashi, & Langfahl, 2003; Birditt, Fingerman, & Almeida, 2005; Smith et al., 2009). Furthermore, older couples tend to interpret their spouses' behaviors, words, and actions more positively than younger couples do (Story et al., 2007). The bottom line? As couples age, they continue to experience conflict and disagreements in their relationships, but they choose to interpret and respond to the conflict in less negative ways than they did when they were younger. As I read these research articles, this question was raised in my mind: In what ways would younger couples' relationship and marital satisfaction increase if they adopted these same interpretation/response behaviors? It appears as though there is a lot we can learn from older couples who have navigated the relationship path ahead of us.

Overall, the majority of middle-aged adults are happy with their lives and their relationships (Lachman, Teshale, & Agrigoroaei, 2015). When distress does exist, it is typically associated with such things as divorce, job loss or declining health (Wethington, 2000; Lachman et al., 2015). In midlife, things that bring couples pleasure include memories of past good times, children and grandchildren, spending time with friends, and vacations. Older couples enjoy the same things, except children and grandchildren are at the top of their list (Levenson et al., 1993).

The Sexual Relationship

Current knowledge suggests that sexual functioning and frequency decline with age and that sex decreases in importance over time; these declines are largely associated with the physical changes and health declines that occur during aging (Lindau et al., 2007). Despite these declines, however, throughout adulthood and into later adulthood sexual activity plays an important role in intimate relationships. In fact, according to the NCOA (1998a, 1998b), "an active sex life appears to be as normal a part of aging as retirement and having grandchildren." A 2018 survey of middle-aged and the elderly's sexual attitudes and behaviors, conducted by the American Association of Retired People (AARP, 2018), reveals that sexual activity is important in older peoples' lives—and that it is pleasurable (see Figure 16.2). Research also shows that sex is still an important and positive aspect in the lives of 70-year-olds, even if sexual dysfunctions are present (Bechman, Waem, Gustafson, & Skoog, 2008).

Many of the health-related problems people commonly experience as they get older cause concern for older adults with regard to sexual activity. For instance, following a heart attack, men and women are often concerned that the physical demands of the sex act may place additional stress on their hearts; consequently, they avoid sexual activity. What are the keys to a great sex life later in life?

Figure 16.2 /// Sex and Sexuality in Older Adults

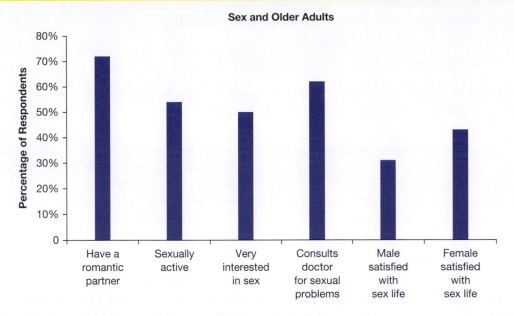

Sex and Older Adults

Note: N = 1,060.

Source: National Poll on Healthy Aging (AARP, University of Michigan, 2018).

iStock.com/blackCAT

Contrary to popular belief, older adults enjoy rich, satisfying, pleasurable sex lives. Essential to later-life sexuality is a healthy lifestyle that includes good nutrition, exercise, and stress reduction.

According to a recent study about health status, sexual activity, and sexual satisfaction among older adults, there is a complex interaction between health, lifestyle, and relationship factors that affect a couple's sex life in late age (Erens et al., 2019). Throughout the Family Life Cycle, a healthy lifestyle is key to enjoying satisfying sexual relations. Indeed, what is good for a person's overall health is also good for their sexual health. Thus, to improve or maintain overall health throughout the lifecycle, adults should do the following (Erens et al., 2019):

- Eat a nutritious, well balanced diet.
- Stop smoking!

- Consume alcohol only in moderation.
- Engage in regular exercise, which lowers blood pressure (and thereby helps with erection health), helps control weight, and improves lung capacity.
- Receive regular medical check-ups.
- Reduce stress (stress and anxiety decrease sexual arousal).

With good health, and equipped with a sound knowledge and realistic expectations about sexuality through aging, sexual fulfillment later in life is a healthy, positive, and attainable goal.

Clearly, older Americans are sexually active. But how do they rate the quality of their sexual experiences? Is sex better when we age? Worse? The same as when we are younger? How people experience their sexuality involves a complex interaction between mind, body, and emotions. As people get older, age-related changes (associated with both primary and secondary aging) influence the physical and psychological aspects of their sex life.

Gray Divorce

As Baby Boomers reach old age, divorce rates are rising among older couples. **Gray divorce** is the term used for people aged 50 and older who divorce after 20+ years of marriage. Figures 16.3 and 16.4 depict the martial status of those over the age of 65. As you can see, more men than women are married, and more women remain widows and do not remarry after the death of their husbands—nearly three-fourths of women over age 85 are widows, whereas only about one-third of men are (U.S. Census Bureau, 2018b). The experience of separation and divorce in later life is similar to separation and divorce experienced earlier in the lifespan: there are psychological, social, and financial consequences of divorce for both younger and older adults. However, divorce in middle and later ages carries with it special characteristics and stressors unique to older adults. Unlike younger adults who divorce, older people (particularly over age 50) were brought up in an era when marriage was considered to be a 'til-death-do-us-part commitment and divorce was less acceptable. Because of long-held beliefs and values, divorce later in life contributes to the stressors associated with marital breakup.

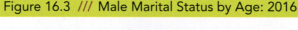

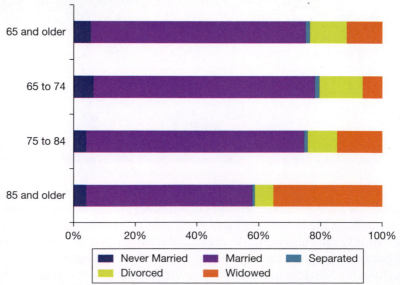

Figure 16.3 /// Male Marital Status by Age: 2016

Source: United States Census Bureau (2018).

Figure 16.4 /// Female Marital Status by Age: 2016

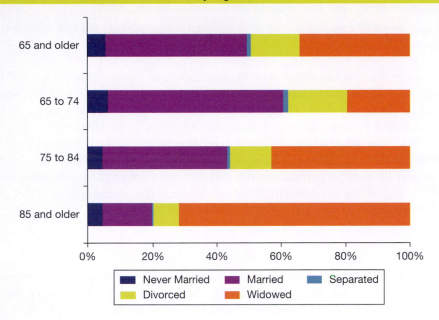

Source: United States Census Bureau (2018).

More Traumatic

Because of the longer commitment and investment into each other's lives, divorce later in life is more traumatic and is comparable to spousal bereavement following the death of a spouse (Stack & Scourfield, 2015; Daly, MacNeela, & Sarma, 2018; Uhlenberg, Cooney, & Boyd, 1990). Divorcing couples face losing longtime friendships and other social networks, further distinguishing later-in-life divorce from divorce earlier in the lifecourse (Gerstel, 2003). Because older women obtain much of their identity and self-worth from their roles of wife and mother, divorce is even more traumatic.

Greater Financial Burdens

Although the financial responsibilities associated with rearing children decrease over time, divorce in mid- and later life may limit the amount of support parents can provide to their children, particularly in areas such as college tuition or other areas of assistance (such as helping with a down payment for a home; Pasley, 1998). Because some older women lack education, skills, and employment experiences that affect their ability to either re-enter the paid labor force or to move up the ladder in their current positions, women who divorce in later life have significantly more limitations in their range of options following divorce than do younger women. Furthermore, retirement benefits, healthcare benefits, and Social Security benefits may also be negatively affected by divorce in later life.

Significant Impacts on Parent–Child Relationships

When parents of adult children divorce, adult children often experience negative reactions, making life difficult for them socially, psychologically, and emotionally (Schwartzhoff, 2013). Adult children commonly experience the following (for a review, see Schwartzhoff, 2013):

- Feeling responsible for the divorce
- Feelings of anger and confusion (particularly in the case of adultery)
- Feelings that they need to take either the mom's side or the dad's side
- Less emotional support and nurturing from their fathers (Fagan & Churchill, 2012)
- Difficulty in coping with their own adult relationships (Fagan & Churchill, 2012)

- Difficulty in finding a mate and creating lasting relationships (Anisman-Reiner, 2007)
- Anxiety, mistrust, and fear of the future (Anisman-Reiner, 2007)
- Higher levels of depression than adult children whose parents did not divorce (Uphold-Carrier & Utz, 2011)

The divorced parents' relationship with their children is significantly affected. Although issues such as child support and visitation do not affect the parent–child relationship as they do when younger parents divorce, there is less contact between parents and young adult children after parental divorce in later life (Aquilino, 1994; Furstenberg, Hoffman, & Shrestha, 1995). The father–child relationship tends to be particularly vulnerable, while the relationship between the mother and the children appears to remain intact (Cooney, 1994). Divorce in later life may be particularly difficult as it can weaken the kinship ties and intergenerational ties that are so important to successful aging (Furstenberg et al., 1995; Pasley & Ihinger-Tallman, 1994).

Remarriage

Current trends indicate that older adults are less likely to remarry following divorce or the death of a spouse than are younger adults. Yet, when older adults do remarry, they face a unique set of obstacles. For instance, grown children are more likely to accept their parents' remarriage, while the aging adults' peers are less accepting (Vinick, 1978, 1986). Grown stepchildren, however, are frequently concerned about inheritance issues, which may influence their feelings about a parent's remarriage.

The marital relationship of remarried older adults differs as well. A study by professor of child and family studies Kay Pasley and her colleagues (1994) found that remarried older adults reported less frequent negative types of conflict, such as arguing, shouting, sulking, or brooding; and less frequent occurrences of abusive physical behavior, such as slapping or hitting. The researchers assert that the infrequent instances of negative conflict contribute to increased levels of marital happiness and satisfaction. In a similar study, aging psychologists Ruth Bograd and Bernard Spilka (1996) examined self-disclosure and its relationship to marital satisfaction in midlife (ages 30 to 40) and late life (ages 60 to 75) remarriages among 125 couples. Their overall findings suggest that couples who remarried in midlife appear to develop more effective communication and interaction patterns that were missing in their first marriages. As a result, these newly developed communication skills contribute to higher levels of marital satisfaction.

As Baby Boomers begin to age and as the population of older age cohorts continues to grow, increasing attention will be given to the significance of the marital relationship throughout the later years in the lifecourse. What is known is that most long-term marriages are rich and rewarding, both emotionally and sexually.

INTERGENERATIONAL TIES

Intergenerational ties:
the relationships between family members across multiple generations.

Intergenerational ties refer to the relationships between family members across multiple generations, and these relationships are indeed important to the aging population. Women over the age of 65, for example, are three times more likely to be widowed than men (He et al., 2005). Figures 16.3 and 16.4 show us the percentages of widows and widowers from the age of 65. Thus, as adults grow older through later adulthood, their interpersonal relationships across generations become increasingly important because these intergenerational ties provide the foundation for intimacy throughout the aging process (Fingerman, 2001).

In everyday language, the term *generation* describes people who were born during the relatively same time period (such as the "Baby Boomer" generation). When discussing intergenerational relationships, however, the term *generation* is used to describe family members who are "on the same rung of the family ladder," or who are related to one another either biologically or through adoption. Most intergenerational relationships are offshoots of the parent–child relationship, although biological ties are not a necessary prerequisite in order for someone to experience a sense of family, kinship, and intimacy (Fingerman, 2001). For example, sometimes after many years with a stepmother or stepfather, the "step" aspect of the relationship becomes less significant and the relationship becomes as meaningful as those between biological parents and their children.

Similarly, older African American adults frequently do not distinguish "kin" along biological lines; for instance, it is common for nieces, nephews, godchildren, or even younger adults who are not blood or otherwise related to fill the role of an adult child for older African American males (Johnson, 1999). Fictive kin are people who are not biologically related to someone, but who fulfill a family role. Among African American families, fictive kin are important sources of emotional support, as well as support in meeting the elderly's needs (MacRae, 1992). As African Americans age, they tend to enjoy warmer relationships with their brothers, sisters, children, and fictive kin than white aging Americans do (MacRae, 1992). Aging Hispanic and Asian families also experience extended kin and fictive kin relationships more often than white families do. Importantly, later in the developmental lifecourse, intimacy "may exist between individuals who *define themselves* as parent and offspring" (Fingerman, 2001, p. 23, italics added). Of the many different and varying interpersonal intimate relationships we form throughout our lives, none is as important to some people as the relationship between parent and child.

Parenting: Are We There Yet?

Some parents look forward to launching their children, while others do so with much trepidation and doubt. Still others do not successfully manage the transition to an empty nest— the home with no children—well at all. As parents begin to empty the nest, there are changes that occur in the family system and common struggles that most couples encounter:

- **Change in roles/loss of roles.** When children leave, it's not uncommon for parents to feel a void once their parenting rote is diminished or lost. Some parents try to fill this void with volunteer or other activities. Parents also need to shift to the role of parent of *adult* children.

- **Marital issues.** Raising children requires so much time, energy, and attention that sometimes children are a diversion that keeps parents from working on problems in their marriage. When children leave the nest, the diversion is no longer there. Parents need to reexamine their goals as a couple as they enter the second half of their marriage.

- **Career change**. Frequently, emptying the nest coincides with changes in one or both parents' careers. While men may be thinking of early retirement, women who entered the workforce later because of childrearing responsibilities may be just reaching a peak in their careers.

- **Caregiving shifts.** Typically, as children leave the home, parents find that their own parents need more care and attention. Caregiving responsibilities don't lessen—they simply shift to a different generation.

- **Relationships with children**. For many parents, accepting their children as adults is difficult; other parents accept that their children are adults and require less advice and support. What is more important to midlife parents, however, is *how* children leave the nest: Are the parents and children on good terms?

As you can see, significant changes take place in the family members' roles, as well as in the relationships with the now-grown children. While marriage and family courses emphasize the earlier years of parenting and the significance of the parent–child relationship during the early years, preschool years, and school years of a child's life, too often much is left unsaid about the importance of the parent–adult child relationship.

When a child enters into early adolescence, an important turning point is reached in the parent–child relationship. It is during this phase of development that parents and children alike establish intimacy levels that will, to a very large extent, define their subsequent *parent–adult child* relationship. This developmental stage of the family life cycle brings important questions to the forefront, such as: How do adolescent children affect the well-being of their parents? Because children come of age during this period of family development and eventually leave the nest (and perhaps return to the nest again and again), what impact does this have on midlife parents?

In many families, children's entry into adolescence coincides with the parents' transition to midlife. As young adolescents strive for increased independence and autonomy, they often begin to challenge their parents' authority. Meanwhile, parents are encountering their own developmental tasks associated with midlife, such as caring for their aging parents and preparing for retirement. These normative lifecourse events introduce many challenges into the family system, as parents are forced to play simultaneous roles as caretaker and parent. But typically, marital satisfaction and stability increase as children enter into their adolescent years (Swensen, Eskew, & Kohlhepp, 1981; Veroff, Douvan, & Kulka, 1981; Wu & Penning, 1997). This increase is likely because conflicts over childrearing issues decline.

It is also during these middle years of the family life cycle that parents and children begin to renegotiate their relationship, and parents begin to reflect on their parenting experiences, and "accept their life choices, relate to their children, and adjust to 'how [the children] have turned out" (Lemme, 2011). These reflections about their success or failure as parents greatly affect the parents' purpose in life, their self-acceptance, and thus their well-being.

The Parent–Adult Child Relationship in Late Adulthood

As parents age and begin to experience physiological and cognitive changes, their roles within the family change, also. The parent–adult child relationship is central to the lives of the elderly: Aside from having their adult children there to provide care when needed, having warm and close relationships with their children provide aging parents a sense of well-being (Pinquart & Soerensen, 2000). According to aging developmentalist Karen Fingerman (2001), four

Adults' relationships with their parents are affected by their gender, geographic distance, their parents' marital status, and their culture.

iStock.com/Halfpoint

primary factors influence intimacy between older adults and their adult children: gender, geographic distance, a parent's marital status, and culture.

1. *Gender.* Gender plays a significant role in the intimacy levels of the elderly and their grown children. Women, for example, tend to express greater emotional intensity than do men in their intergenerational ties (Fingerman, 2001; Troll & Fingerman, 1996). Subsequently, elderly mothers and their adult daughters and daughters-in-law experience greater intimacy than do fathers and sons.

2. *Geographic distance.* One national survey indicated that 63 percent of elderly parents see at least one of their children weekly (Crimmins & Ingegneri, 1990). Of the 11,000 senior citizen respondents in the national study, only 20 percent noted that they see their children once per month (or less).

3. *Parent's marital status.* The older parent's marital status also influences the quality of intimacy between elderly parents and their children. Widowed or single older people (particularly women) frequently turn to their grown children or grandchildren for companionship and emotional support.

4. *Culture.* Culture and ethnicity are key determinants in how intergenerational relationships develop and how intimacy is fostered within these relationships. In the United States, for example, involvement in the aging parent's daily life is not supported by American culture, whereas in Japan and other Asian cultures such involvement is a dominant belief. These cultural differences may explain in part the discrepancies seen in the research as it relates to the impact of adult-child involvement in aging parents' lives, such as in India and among Mexican Americans. But clearly, although the "intimacy parents and offspring share in late life does not involve the close sense of oneness they could derive from a romantic partner" (Fingerman, 2001, p. 31), older adults take pleasure in these intergenerational ties.

Today, some of the most enjoyable, enriching intergenerational relationships the aging experience are with their grandchildren.

Becoming a Grandparent

I admit it—I love being a grandma, or Emaw, to my five grandchildren! I confess that I am the type of grandparent who is armed and ready with photos and videos on my phone, ready to spring them on unsuspecting victims, including you, as you can see in the photo. I love being a grandma so much, I often quip that if I had known grandparenting was this much fun, I would have skipped parenting altogether and jumped right into this phase.

Becoming a grandparent is an exciting time for most people (Somary & Stricker, 1998). As adults enter their middle years, they begin to take on several new roles, such as in-law, grandparent, and caregiver to their aging parents. In the United States, some parents become grandparents in their 30s (Szinovacz, 1998), but typically most do so while in their 40s (about one-third), and about one-half of women become grandparents while in their 50s. And, as you saw in Chapter 11, today a significant number of grandparents assume the parenting role. Figure 16.5 provides a snapshot of the percentage of grandparents who are responsible for their grandchildren. In the United States, nearly 3 million children receive their daily care from their grandparents (Wiltz, 2016). These types of families are referred to as **grandfamilies** (Dunn & Wamsley, 2018).

Grandfamilies: families in which the grandparents are responsible for their grandchildren.

Overall, the experience of grandparenting appears to be immensely satisfying; to be sure, 92 percent of survey respondents in one study expressed high levels of satisfaction with their grandparenting role (Kaufman & Elder, 2003; Segatto & Di Filippo, 2003). Studies have shown that grandparents wish to see their grandchildren on a frequent basis, and these relationships have positive outcomes on grandchildren's development (Adkins, 1999). Of course, there are many different ways that people grandparent.

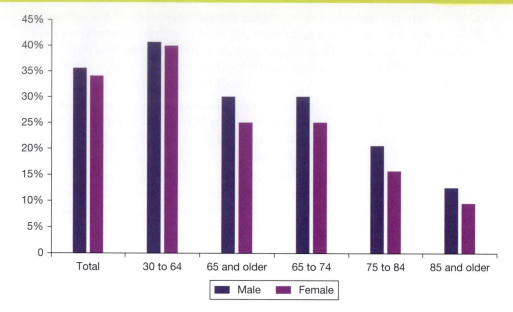

Figure 16.5 /// Grandparents Who Were Caregivers for Their Grandchildren, by Age: 2016

Note: Graph shows the percentage of grandparents living in households with one or more own grandchildren under age 18 who were responsible for their coresident grandchildren.

Source: United States Census Bureau (2018).

Formal grandparenting:

a style of grandparenting in which grandparents see their role along common, traditional lines.

Companionate relationship:

companionate grandparents enjoy warm, loving, and nurturing relationships with their grandchildren, though they may be happy to send them home when it is time.

Kelly Welch

Styles of Grandparenting

Just as there are different parenting styles, there are different styles of grandparenting. In a classic study by a pioneer in the study of aging, Bernice Neugarten and her colleague K. K. Weinstein (1964) identified five primary styles of grandparenting: formal, fun seeker, remote, involved, and dispenser of wisdom.

In the **formal grandparenting** role, grandparents see their role along common, traditional lines. These grandparents babysit every now and then and indulge their grandchildren on occasion, but when it comes to childrearing and discipline, they play a "hands-off role; they are content to leave that aspect of parenting to the parents. About one-third of the grandparents practiced this grandparenting style. One study surveyed a representative sample of grandparents and found that more than one-half of their research participants had a **companionate relationship** with their grandchildren (Cherlin & Furstenberg, 1986). Similar to the formal relationship, companionate grandparents enjoy warm, loving, and nurturing relationships with their grandkids, although they are happy to send them home when it is time!

Another common style of grandparenting is the **fun seeker**. These grandparents have a relationship with their grandchildren that is characterized by an informal, spontaneous playfulness. On the other hand, the distant grandparent has little or no contact with grandchildren and is only involved on occasional holidays or birthdays. This grandparenting style is defined as a **remote relationship**.

As you know, many grandparents today assume the role of parent and are *surrogate* parents; this grandpa renting style is described as an **involved relationship**. Overall, African Americans, Asian Americans, Italian Americans, and Hispanic Americans are more likely to be actively involved in their grandchildren's lives than are whites because the sense of family is a core value among these cultures (Dunn & Wamsley, 2018). Finally, the **dispenser of wisdom** grandparent offers information and advice to their grandchildren— often whether it is asked for or not.

To be sure, there are many changes that lake place in family relationships as people age. Central to the lives of the aging are intergenerational relationships, whether they are with biological kin or with fictive kin. As you learned in Chapter 11, many couples today are forgoing parenting altogether; given the significance of intergenerational relationships in later life, it will be interesting to see the impact of childlessness on couples in the future.

As individuals and couples near the later years in life, there are other substantial changes that must be navigated. In the section that follows, we'll explore other factors associated with aging, including retirement and family caregiving.

FAMILY CHANGES TOWARD THE END OF LIFE

Throughout this text, we have discussed how marital and intimate relationship development and family development involve multiple processes that unfold over the life of the relationship. To fully understand family development, we must take into account the cultural and social contexts in which the family evolves and understand that each transition or milestone has both positive and negative ramifications.

So far in this chapter we've discussed how marriages and other family relationships change as men and women age and enter the later years of their lifespans. But a discussion about family life through the maturing years would not be complete without examining other significant life transitions that also have significant impact on a person's later years. These are the changes that take place within a family's day-to-day living. External factors affect the daily lives of aging adults and their families, including retirement and caregiving.

Retirement and Leisure

Contemporary themes of aging research focus on the successful adaptation to the later years by viewing aging as a series of multiple, interrelated processes (Crosnoe & Elder, 2002). Beyond the biological and physiological changes that people experience as they age are external factors that determine how people's later years will progress. If we consider "aging" as a holistic experience that involves changes not just in people's bodies but also in their marital and other interpersonal relationships, as well as in their ability to use their leisure time in productive and meaningful ways, we can reassess our view of the aging process. Let's expand our definition of aging, then, to an even broader view; that is, "successful aging" is a *pattern* of well-being and adaptation to the challenges of middle adulthood and later life (Rowe & Kahn, 1990). With this definition in mind, we consider later-in-life changes that significantly affect the later years in the lifecourse: retirement and family caregiving.

Retirement as a Developmental Process

Retirement is not an isolated event but a developmental process requiring several adjustments and adaptations. It is also considered a life stage because it spans many years of middle

Fun seeker:
a grandparent whose relationship with their grandchildren is characterized by an informal, spontaneous playfulness.

Remote relationship:
the distant grandparent who has little or no contact with grandchildren and is only involved on occasional holidays or birthdays.

Involved relationship:
the grandparent who assumes the role of parent and is involved in the everyday rearing of their grandchildren.

Dispenser of wisdom:
the grandparent who offers information and advice to their grandchildren.

and late adulthood. Most of us will spend anywhere from 5 to more than 20 years in the retirement stage of life. Some researchers refer to retirement as *the encore stage* or a *third age* comprised of "an on-going engagement with meaningful activities" (Moen & Flood, 2013, p. 206). Although many adults diligently plan for financial security by the time they retire, such as preparing a financial portfolio, all too often they neglect their "psychological" portfolio and do not prepare themselves for the psychological aspects of retirement (American Psychological Association, 2005).

To address the transitional processes associated with permanently exiting the workforce, gerontologist Robert Atchley (2000) identified six phases associated with the processes of retirement as the result of numerous research studies. Atchley's phases provide a general framework of the steps associated with retirement, but keep in mind that retirement is experienced on an individual level that is influenced by a person's culture. Indeed, every phase identified by Atchley will not be experienced by everyone. The phases do provide a framework, however, with which to understand the multiple transitions necessary to navigate this normative change in the lifecourse. Figure 16.6 presents the six phases of retirement. As you can see, the retirement process typically unfolds gradually, from someone slowly disengaging from the workplace (sometimes this is referred to as *phased retirement*) to reorienting to establishing a daily routine that does not involve going to work. This stage in the lifespan ends when a person's health begins to decline and she or he can no longer live independently, or when a person's spouse or partner becomes dependent on the other for care. The important thing to keep in mind about retirement is that it is a unique experience for each person. How do relationships fare when someone retires?

Marital Life After Retirement

A substantive body of research concludes that because social relationships and acquaintances that originate in the workplace dissolve after retirement (Bosse, Aldwin, Levinson, Workman-Daniels, & Ekerdt, 1990), pensioners tend to place greater emphasis on family life and will gain support, love, and friendship from these family relationships (Kulik, 1999). Because retirement is such a significant marker of transition and adaptation for the retiree and his or her family, one body of research examined the impacts of a number of factors on the lives of male retirees. In a sample of 137 men on the verge of retirement and a sample of 211 men who had already retired, empirical investigation revealed some significant findings among the two groups (Kulik, 1999).

Life orientation:

the emphasis pre-retirees or retirees place on various aspects of life, such as family life and economic security.

First, both groups of men attached greater importance to their marriages than they did to their own health status, but there were significant differences between the two groups of men in their life orientation. **Life orientation** refers to the emphasis pre-retirees or retirees place on various aspects of life, such as family life and economic security. For instance, pre-retired men focused more on the economic factors, such as career, finances, and material possessions than did retired men. Retired men attached greater significance to their marital and family relationships than did the pre-retired men.

Second, there were also significant differences between the two groups' attitudes regarding gender role behaviors, particularly with respect to household labor. Retired husbands expressed more conservative, traditional values about gender roles than did pre-retired men. In both groups, husbands of working women expressed more liberal views regarding gender role behaviors than did the men whose wives did not work outside the home. Interestingly, gender role behaviors, such as the division of household labor, present in the early years of the marital relationship, are apparently central issues in marital interaction and family living in the later years of life, too.

Third, Kulik's (1999) research also looked at marital intimacy in the later years of life and found three distinct types of intimacy: *reciprocity,* in which both spouses confide in one another and self-disclose; *nonreciprocity,* in which one spouse confides and shares, but the other spouse has a confidant outside of the marriage; and *segregative,* in which neither spouse shares with the other, but instead shares with someone outside the marriage. The research revealed that among

Figure 16.6 /// The Phases of Retirement

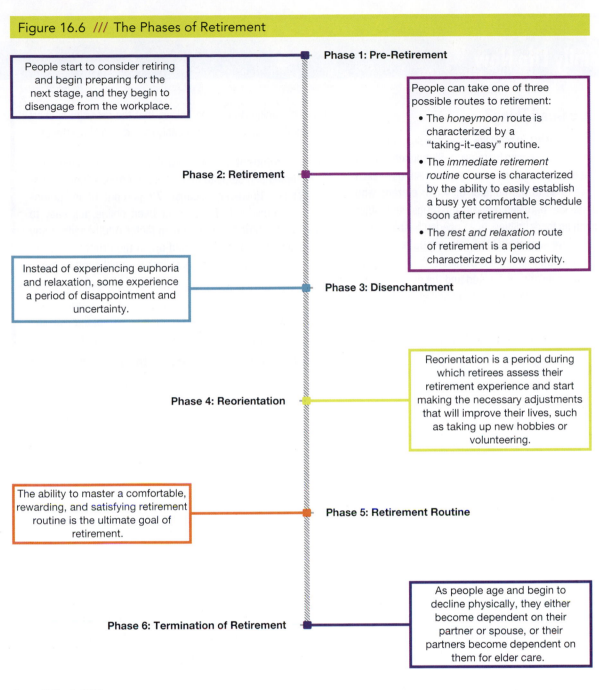

Phase 1: Pre-Retirement

People start to consider retiring and begin preparing for the next stage, and they begin to disengage from the workplace.

Phase 2: Retirement

People can take one of three possible routes to retirement:

- The *honeymoon* route is characterized by a "taking-it-easy" routine.
- The *immediate retirement routine* course is characterized by the ability to easily establish a busy yet comfortable schedule soon after retirement.
- The *rest and relaxation* route of retirement is a period characterized by low activity.

Phase 3: Disenchantment

Instead of experiencing euphoria and relaxation, some experience a period of disappointment and uncertainty.

Phase 4: Reorientation

Reorientation is a period during which retirees assess their retirement experience and start making the necessary adjustments that will improve their lives, such as taking up new hobbies or volunteering.

Phase 5: Retirement Routine

The ability to master a comfortable, rewarding, and satisfying retirement routine is the ultimate goal of retirement.

Phase 6: Termination of Retirement

As people age and begin to decline physically, they either become dependent on their partner or spouse, or their partners become dependent on them for elder care.

Source: Atchley, R. (2001).

the study participants, reciprocity is the most commonly expressed type of intimacy (approximately 70 percent), and nonreciprocity is the least common type (11 percent). A recent review of a vast body of contemporary literature indicates that overall, men have more positive attitudes about retirement than women do (for a complete review, see Hyde et al., 2018).

As you have come to know throughout our study together, there are gendered experiences across the lifespan. Although there is a wealth of empirical studies that examine men's retirement experiences, to date far less research has explored how gender affects well-being in retirement; because of this lack of research, the role gender plays in women's psychological well-being in retirement is unclear (Kubicek, Korunka, Raymo, & Hoonakker, 2011). However, in one study, 778 retired women were asked, "How long did it take you to get used to retirement?" and "How difficult has it been for you to adjust to retirement?" Women

Is Medicare a Good Thing?

As people gain extra years in their life expectancies, the costs to help them stay alive are also increasing. Skyrocketing drug bills costing the elderly hundreds—or even thousands—each month have given rise to the number of senior citizens who may have to decide between life-saving drugs and other necessities, such as food, utilities, even needed hospital care. Aged Americans have support in Medicare, a federally administered system of health insurance available to people over the age of 65. The legislation is passed and the coverage is in place, but not all of America's aged are satisfied. Is Medicare a good thing?

YES: Medicare is an answer to years of support and positioning by aging advocates. The process of obtaining Medicare is involved but nonetheless worth doing. Once enrolled, seniors save money, and that is the bottom line.

- **Seniors support it.** Trained senior volunteers, in testimony before the U.S. Senate Special Committee on Aging, stated that Medicare saves money and is not overly confusing.

- **Personal interaction is necessary**. Most seniors find that if they take time to visit with the many experts who have volunteered to walk them through enrollment, their anxiety over the "confusing" elements of Medicare is relieved.

- **People already enrolled support it overwhelmingly.** Those asked said that the time and effort required to review the various coverage plans was more than worth it. The bottom line? Medicare does what it sets out to do: It saves seniors money.

Sources: Friedman (2006); Ganz (2006).

NO: Some aging Americans believe that the program is short on benefits, long on cost, and deeply rooted in political rhetoric.

- **Enrollment is too complicated.** The government has taken steps to make enrollment easy and accessible. However, because 72 percent of its potential customers have never been online, it's easy to understand the intimidation factor. Additionally, many seniors may be confused about the drugs they take, which makes phone enrollment a challenge as well.

- **Medicare is overpriced.** Research from the Congressional Budget Office estimates that the program will cost about $800 billion more than estimated over the next 10 years because of complications in enrollment

- **Private companies are on the take.** The current Medicare bill as drafted ensures that private insurance companies are the ones primarily administrating (and profiting from) Medicare. Doing so establishes higher drug prices and adds confusion to Medicare administration.

What Do You Think?

1. How important is drug coverage for U.S. seniors? Do you think we, as taxpayers, are responsible for covering these costs? Why or why not?

2. In what ways does the inclusion of private health insurers help or complicate prescription drug benefits?

3. It is said that seniors are having to go without drugs due to economics. Discuss the role and responsibility of government in this dilemma. What about drug companies? What about personal responsibility?

---

reported that they had more difficulties adjusting to retirement than men did; the researchers posited that these post-retirement adjustment difficulties were due to the loss of social connections in the workplace (van Solinge & Henkens, 2008). Interestingly, using the same sample of women and asking similar questions, Damman, Henkens, and Kalmijn (2013) found that women's post-retirement dissatisfaction and adjustment aren't necessarily about loss of identity and loss of social contacts at work; instead, post-working life adjustment has more to do with the *loss of a previous role*, rather than *adjustment to the current role*.

In summary, certain aspects of marital life are characterized by change as men and women approach and enter their retirement years. It appears that both pre-retired men and retired men alike find their marital lives to be enjoyable and positive, although retired men report higher degrees of marital satisfaction. As men and women approach retirement and enter retirement, their families and family life become central to their lives (Kulik, 1999).

Family Caregiving

Many people hold the common misconception that elderly people who can no longer "do" for themselves reside in a long-term care facility, such as a retirement home or a nursing home. On the contrary: For every one person who resides in a healthcare facility, there are at least two who live out their remaining years with the help of family caregivers (He et al., 2005). A caregiver—sometimes referred to as an informal caregiver—is an unpaid individual who is involved in assisting others with daily living (Family Caregiver Alliance, 2018). These family members provide the lion's share of medical and personal health assistance, in addition to emotional, spiritual, and financial support. In the United States, today (Family Caregiver Alliance, 2018):

Caregiver: an unpaid individual who is involved in assisting others with daily living.

- About 34 million Americans provide unpaid care to an adult age 50 or older.
- About 16 million adult family caregivers care for someone with dementia or Alzheimer's disease.
- Annually, the value of services provided by informal caregivers is estimated at $470 billion.

Today's longer lifespans present a new challenge to spouses and adult children alike because providing care for aging spouses and parents extends the caregiving career by a number of years. In most cases, caregiving is not isolated to a single period in the family life cycle, but instead exists throughout the entire family life cycle. The caregiving career consists of the years that caregivers tend to dependent children, aging parents, and eventually, dependent husbands or wives (Brody, 1985). By the latter part of the human life cycle, it is often the spouse who provides the necessary help or assistance for her or his aging partner (Zarit, Birkel, & Malonebeach, 1989), If the spouse cannot provide the necessary care, the burden shifts to the adult children—most typically to the adult daughters (Lemme, 2011).

Caregiving career: the years caregivers commit to tending to dependent children, aging parents, and eventually, dependent spouses.

Characteristics of Caregivers

There is great variability among caregivers and their experiences. Race, ethnicity, socioeconomic status, education level, marital status, and personality characteristics affect both the caregiver and the person receiving the care. In most cases, family members work together to decide who will help with what in providing various caregiving tasks (Ingersoll-Dayton, Neal, Ha, & Hammer, 2003). Research has shown that people who have launched all of their children, are not working outside of the home, and are not married are more likely to provide care for aging parents (Brody & Schoonover, 1986). According to the Family Caregiver Alliance (2018), there are other general characteristics of caregivers. For example, the caregiving landscape is dominated by women, making daughters and daughters-in-law the most common caregiver: three-fourths of all informal caregivers are female, and spend at least 50 percent more time providing care than males do. Male caregivers are less likely to provide personal care to their loved ones, compared to female caregivers. However, among spousal caregivers over the age of 75, both men and women provide equal amounts of care (Family Caregiver Alliance, 2018). Table 16.2 presents for us the types of caregiving tasks older family members provide for their loved ones, and Figure 16.7 shows us how many hours caregivers dedicate to caregiving.

Developmentalists Denise Boyd and Helen Bee (2009) offer two suggestions. One factor may be that women experience greater emotional closeness to their parents, and consequently they feel a greater need to care for them as they age. Another factor may be related to the ways in which women are socialized. As you learned in Chapter 4, women are typically socialized to be the nurturing parent to their own children; they simply transfer their nurturing to their aging parents.

Table 16.2 /// Caregiving Tasks

On average, caregivers spend:

- *13 days* each month on tasks such as shopping, food preparation, housekeeping, laundry, transportation, giving medication
- *6 days* per month on feeding, dressing, grooming, bathing, and other assistance
- *13 hours per month* researching care and services

Those who provide complex care:

- *46 percent* of time on nursing tasks (dressing wounds, giving medications)
- *96 percent* help with activities of daily (dressing and undressing, toileting, feeding, etc.)
- *75 percent* help with housekeeping tasks

Significant decision-making regarding:

- *66 percent* monitor the care recipient's care and adjusting care
- *63 percent* communicate with healthcare professionals on behalf of the care recipient
- *50 percent* act as advocate for the care recipient

Source: Family Caregiver Alliance (2018).

Figure 16.7 /// Number of Hours Dedicated to Caregiving by Age of Family Caregiver

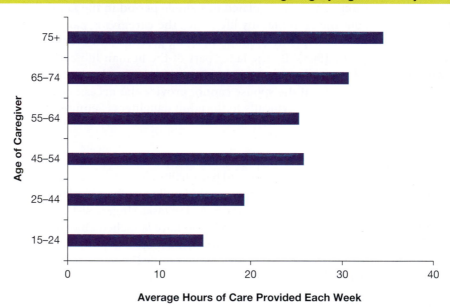

Average Hours of Care Provided Each Week

Source: Family Caregiver Alliance (2018).

Caregiver burden:
the physical and emotional wear and tear on caregivers.

Caregiving responsibilities exert physical and emotional wear and tear on caregivers. This is called **caregiver burden**.

Stressors Associated With Caregiving

Providing care for aging loved ones is a stressful experience, both for the caregiver and for the entire family system. So stressful is caring for an aging loved one that depression rates for caregivers is between 30 and 50 percent (Lemme, 2011). The more stressful aspects of caregiving include (NCOA, 2005)

- *Transformation of a cherished relationship.* For many caregivers, it is difficult when an interdependent relationship is transformed to a dependent relationship. When the caregiver is a spouse, the caregiving role becomes the overarching aspect of the marital relationship.
- *Problematic physical behaviors.* Because the caregiver is responsible for helping a loved one with dressing, bathing, toileting, and communicating, many caregivers feel a great deal of stress from these perpetual responsibilities.
- *Cognitive impairments.* When caregivers are taking care of a cognitively impaired spouse or parent, such as those with dementia or Alzheimer's disease, emotional distress is felt greatly by both patient and caregiver.

A number of stressors and rewards are commonly reported by adult child caregivers. Psychologist Mary Ann Parris Stephens and several colleagues undertook numerous studies to determine the types of stressors caregivers experience when caring for a loved one (among many others, Stephens, Townsend, Martire, & Druley, 2001; Stephens & Franks, 1999; Stephens, Franks, & Atienza, 1997). The stressors include the following:

- Receiving complaints and criticisms from parents
- Uncooperative or demanding parents
- Agitated parents
- Forgetful or unresponsive parents
- Helping with personal care needs
- Managing a parent's financial or legal affairs
- Receiving little help from family or friends

Although caregiving is often difficult and demanding, it also provides many rewards. Stephens's multiple research studies show many rewards:

- Knowing the parent is well cared for
- Spending quality time with a parent
- Enjoying the parent's affection and appreciation
- Seeing a parent derive pleasure from small things
- Seeing a parent calm and content
- Experiencing a closer relationship with a parent

The stressors are not isolated to individual caregivers, however. As we have discussed throughout this text, any life event—anticipated or not—produces ripple effects that reverberate throughout the entire family system. When a parent or family member becomes a caregiver tor a spouse or elderly parent, not only does it cause stress and strain on the caregiver, but these also radiate throughout the entire family system and, in turn, affect the family's balance. This stress causes increased family tensions, reduced time families have to spend together, role conflict and role strain, changes in individual and family lifestyles, and financial strain (Lemme, 2011). And according to Lemme, the tensions created by family caregiving can exacerbate previously existing strengths or weaknesses in the family system.

The Sandwich Generation

Being in the middle of two generations—parenting adolescents or younger children while at the same time caring for aging parents—is known as the **sandwich generation**, and it presents many challenges to middle-aged adults, as the opening vignette illustrates for us. As Boyd and Bee (2009) observe, being squeezed between two generations is perhaps one

Sandwich generation: adults who are parenting adolescents or younger children while at the same time caring for aging parents.

Gordon Chibroski/Portland Press Herald via Getty Images

Today, a significant number of middle-aged adults are pulled in two directions as they provide care for their children and their elderly parents. While there are a number of stressors associated with being a part of the sandwich generation, can you think of any possible benefits or rewards?

of the greatest distinguishing features of families today compared to the family decades ago. Note the authors,

> In middle adulthood . . . the family role involves not only giving assistance in both directions in the generational chain, but also shouldering the primary responsibility for maintaining affectional bonds. These responsibilities produce what is sometimes called the midlife "squeeze," and those being squeezed form the sandwich generation. (p. 433)

When the tables turn and middle-aged adults begin to parent their parents, they are suddenly taking on conflicting roles. In negotiating these competing roles, many of these adults experience losses associated with providing care to their aging parent. Understanding these losses are key in understanding and coping with the feelings associated with parenting parents (Conway & Conway, 2000).

Parents' Losses and Needs. As parents age and lose their independence, their children notice other gradual losses along the way. In addition to losing their financial stability, for example, aging parents also lose what was once an important social network, an important source of identity. As their aging friends begin to die, their social identity is further eroded. With the loss of their social network, losses associated with physical decline become that much more pronounced. With their vision, hearing, mobility, memory, strength, and independence in jeopardy, many older adults feel that they will lose their usefulness and their worth, Therefore, it is essential that aging parents are shown that they have continued dignity, and that they are still valued and useful to society. Older parents may also need to have their business needs met, such as helping them pay bills and care for their property. While caring for the parents, adult children also have needs and experience losses, too.

Adult Children's Losses and Needs. The caregiver—the adult child—experiences losses, too. As we have discussed, middle-aged adults lose their time and freedom and take on a number of additional stressors that may affect their own personal health and intimate relationships. As they devote increasing amounts of time to their parents' needs, adult children are leaving less time to spend with their own spouses and children, or to furthering their careers. By and large, parents have been backups throughout life, providing for their children's every need. Thus, when they age, "not only are they weakening physically and shrinking physically in size, [they also] shrink in their capacity to help" (Conway & Conway, 2000). As we observe the gradual deterioration and decline in our parents, we realize (often quite suddenly, as in my experience) that our parents are mortal—and that death is an eventuality.

It is important to understand, then, that when adult children assume the role of caregiver for their aging parents, new needs and family challenges emerge (Conway & Conway, 2000). Being the "squeeze" generation often means that in the process of meeting the needs of two generations, the adult children's personal needs are squeezed out and forgotten. Consequently, it is important for sandwiched caregivers to nurture their marital and other intimate relationships by making time to spend with one another (Conway & Conway, 2000). It's also imperative that adult-children caregivers guard their own mental, emotional, and physical health. This may include learning coping techniques that help buffer the stress associated with caregiving, and doing things that nourish mental health and the physical body. Finally, middle-aged children caring for their parents need to be realistic. A parent may sometimes require "tough love," just as parenting a child does. It is necessary to balance being rational with sensitivity and compassion.

Managing the dual roles of parenting two generations simultaneously brings a variety of conflicting feelings. Bui if family members understand the legitimate needs of the family members and can make the adaptations and adjustments necessary to meet those needs, then parenting parents while parenting children can be a deeply rich and rewarding life experience. Yet there is one more lifecourse event with which family members must cope: death.

DYING AND DEATH EXPERIENCES

Are you afraid of dying? When you think about people in your life who have died, which words would you use to describe your feelings? Would you avoid talking with someone who is dying?

It is difficult to think about death, especially the death of a family member. But death is as much a part of our life cycle development as is birth. None of us is immune to the gut-wrenching heartache and the feelings of despair that accompany losing someone we love. Death is not isolated to the later years in life; people lose friends, boyfriends, girlfriends, sexual partners, intimate cohabiting partners, fiancés, children, and young spouses to death at every point in the life cycle of family development. Because dying in old age is an expected lifecourse event, we study it here.

There is a seemingly endless list of topics associated with death and dying: the biomedical approach to death, the nature and meaning of death, suicide, murder, war, terrorism, euthanasia, the right to die, death in childhood, the funeral. All of these topics are worthy of study and discussion. But because acknowledging, accepting, and understanding death is important for the dying person as well as those the person is leaving behind, in this section we will examine the topics that are significant to the end of life: dying as a transition from life, the grief process, and losing a spouse in old age.

Dying: The Transition From Life

About three days before my mother died, she was somewhere between "life" and "death." She was alert, yet distant. What struck me the most was the intensity of her labor—the intensity of her death-work. About 48 hours before she took her final breath, I crawled into bed with her and cuddled with her. I wasn't sure 1 could ask the question that was burning in my heart to ask her. But I decided that throughout my entire life she encouraged her children to ask her anything, so I did. "What's it like to die?" I asked. She didn't answer right away, but I knew she heard me so 1 didn't pose the question again. After a while, she closed her eyes and gasping for each breath she said, "You know honey . . . I thought it was hard work to bring you children into this world . . . but it is much harder to leave this world . . . you ask me what it's like to die . . . it's hard work . . . it's hard work."

Dying is but one of the countless transitions we make throughout our lifespan. Some transitions are hoped for and are long awaited; others, like death, are anticipated yet not necessarily

Whether the trajectory to the end of life is sudden or a lengthy, hard-fought battle against disease, coping with the death and loss of someone we love presents many challenges to us, both on the individual and family levels. And, as Robert Kastenbaum reminds us, because no two people have the same relationship experiences, a person's transition from life is very much dependent on the quality of the relationships with loved ones.

iStock.com/KatarzynaBialasiewicz

welcome. What makes the transition from life to death so compelling? Robert Kastenbaum (2007), the author of the landmark text in death research and death education, explains some of the complexities of this transition:

> The transition from life is unique because the separation is so complete. However, the dying process does have aspects in common with other types of transitions: There are interactions that can either be upsetting or comforting, communications that can either inform or confuse, and self-evaluations that can either undermine or strengthen one's sense of identity. The transition from life is unique for every individual, [because] no two people bring the same thoughts, feelings, accomplishments, and illness-related experiences. Furthermore, no two people have the same set of human relationships. The quality of life during the final illness depends much on the quality of the individual's relationships with others and the availability of those who are most capable of providing comfort and support. (p. 115)

Dying

When does "dying" begin? From the moment of birth? Is aging equivalent to dying? According to Kastenbaum (2007), dying does not necessarily begin as a biological or physiological process, but rather begins as a psychosocial event. In other words, *we* construct our personal conceptions of "dying" throughout our lifecourse, a definition drawn from our individual life experiences.

As death appears imminent, the medical community, the family, and friends adjust their mindset from preventing death to helping a loved one make the transition from life to death, For some, this can become a highly anxious time. The fear of death—whether our own death or the death of a loved one—can lead to death anxiety. **Death anxiety** refers to the tension, feelings of distress, and apprehension associated with discussions and thoughts of death (Kastenbaum, 2007). When death is an inevitability, individuals may attempt to avoid the painful tension associated with death anxiety by responding with denial, which rejects key features of the reality of the dying or death experience. So accustomed are people to suppressing their death anxieties and fears, Kastenbaum observes, empirical studies that attempt to measure death anxiety are of little use.

Death anxiety: tension, feelings of distress, and apprehension associated with discussions and thoughts of death.

Pathways to Death

Kastenbaum (2007) explains that all dying processes take time and all take a unique shape; however, there are three trajectories or pathways to death. These trajectories each have unique characteristics in how the dying are cared for.

The **lingering trajectory** of death is one in which the transition from life to death takes an extended period of time, such as with some types of cancer, diabetes, or other progressive illnesses or diseases. Caregivers do what they can to keep the patient or loved one comfortable, but recognize that they have done all that they can to preserve life. At this point in the process, it is quite unusual to see "dramatic rescue scenes" as the person inches closer to death. Kastenbaum (2007) notes that it is rare that a patient on a lingering pathway to death has much control over the management of his or her condition. In fact, "the slowly dying person seldom speaks of final things to family and friends—or to anybody" (p. 124). Sometimes it is difficult for family members to accept the finality of their loved one's condition and their imminent death. Conversely, sometimes family members become impatient when a loved one lingers well beyond expectations because they need time to organize their emotions. According to Kastenbaum, the lingering trajectory is advantageous in that it allows both the dying person and the family time to get used to the idea of dying, work out any unresolved conflicts, and engage in meaningful life review.

While the lingering trajectory allows the dying person as well as family and friends a chance to prepare for the impending death, this is not the case with the **expected quick trajectory**, typically associated with an acute crisis or illness, such as a heart attack or vehicle accident. These types of events demand quick action to save a life. In expected quick trajectories of death, time is the critical factor. There are several types of expected quick trajectories:

- *Pointed.* The ill person may or may not be saved, and thus is exposed to any number of very high-risk procedures in an attempt to save the life.

- *Danger period.* The ill person may or may not be conscious. The family vigilantly waits by the bedside as the family member lingers between life and death, waiting for the danger period to subside (the danger period can last from several hours to several days).

- *Crisis.* The ill person is not in immediate danger of dying but still runs the risk of dying suddenly, such as with an acute case of pneumonia.

- *Will probably die.* Nothing can be done to preserve the life of the ill person. Medical staff keep the person as comfortable as possible as family members wait for the death to occur.

The **unexpected quick trajectory** has the elements of time pressure and surprise. For example, a young girl may be admitted to the hospital for a routine case of pneumonia, but within days her case worsens drastically, and she dies in a week. In these cases, there is typically not enough time to save the life of the injured or ill person. Since their rapid decline in health is usually unexpected, there is no time allowed for friends and family to plan or to prepare themselves emotionally. This pathway to death is surrounded with resounding cries of confusion, sadness, and a sense of helplessness as family members wonder, "What's happening?" "What should we do?" and "What *can* we do?"

When an elderly loved one becomes ill and begins to die, any one of the aforementioned trajectories can be the pathway to death. Although many elderly patients die from lengthy terminal illnesses such as advanced cancers, progressive heart disease or diabetes, dementia or Alzheimer's disease, or Parkinson's disease, not all elderly people die from lengthy, prolonged illnesses. Ageism and stereotypes may cause us to forget that some elderly people live active, vibrant lives and may die as the result of a skiing accident, a fall, or a car accident. For example, a former nontraditional student of mine was 86 years old and was completing her first college degree at the time of her death. "Miss Mary" survived heart attacks and the amputation of her leg due to diabetes, yet she was killed suddenly in a car accident in which she was not the driver.

Lingering trajectory:
a term that describes a lengthy transition from life to death, such as occurs with some types of cancer, diabetes, or other progressive illnesses or diseases.

Expected quick trajectory:
a transition from life to death typically associated with an acute crisis or illness, such as a heart attack or vehicle accident. These types of events demand quick action to save a life.

Unexpected quick trajectory:
a rapid transition from life to death with elements of time pressure and surprise, when there is typically not enough time to save the life of the injured or ill person and there is no time allowed for friends and family to plan or to prepare themselves emotionally.

As dying people and their families follow different pathways toward death, those who are left take different pathways as they mourn the loss of someone they loved. Each of us responds to the death of a loved one in different ways.

Responses to Loss

There is no singular, universal, "right" way to transition to the death of someone we love.

Most of us are uncomfortable around death, and some of us are uncomfortable talking about death. Think about it:

- Talking about death or thinking about death makes me feel . . .
- What frightens me most about death is . . .
- What intrigues me most about death is . . .
- Sometimes, I worry that I will die too soon. This makes me feel . . .
- The following people in my life have died . . .
- To die is to . . .

Did any of these statements make you feel uncomfortable? Uneasy? In large part, our responses to death are determined by our cultural and ethnic backgrounds. In American culture, often death is far removed from us: We die in hospitals, not in our family homes as in eras past; we have funeral directors and mortuaries prepare our loved one for burial and take care of the funeral services: at funeral services the family members are often curtained off in a private area.

Mourning refers to the culturally prescribed expressions of the thoughts and feelings of a **bereaved person**—someone who suffers the loss of a loved one. In essence, mourning refers to how people display their grief. Most rituals associated with death are deeply rooted in the culture's religious beliefs. For instance, among the Hmong, an ethnic group from the mountainous regions of southern China, the response to death is very elaborate and complex and includes a number of people to assure the deceased person's passage to the next life. With this death experience, those who serve as guides to the spirit world include coffin makers, warriors, food servers, drummers, and counselors to the dead. With Middle Eastern Muslim families, it is commonplace for women to be extreme in their expressions of sadness (screaming, pulling their hair) at the time of death and at the funeral and to mourn the loss for a period of at least one year (Sharifzadeh, 1997). Among Latinx families, death brings family members together, even though they may have been geographically or emotionally separated; the death experience strengthens family values and family ties (Cavanaugh & Blanchard-Fields, 2002).

Despite the culturally specific ways in which we grieve, there are death-related experiences that are common to people and cultures throughout the world. Every culture expresses bereavement and grief. We are said to be bereaved when someone we love or someone we are close to dies. According to Kastenbaum (2007), "Bereavement conveys the idea of a tearing-apart, forcible separation that results in the loss of something we once had" (p. 350). **Bereavement** is active—it refers to a person's specific, unique reactions following the news that a loved one has died. People can mourn and grieve over the loss of any number of things (such as the end of a marriage or intimate relationship or the loss of a job), but bereavement is experienced only by people who lose someone to death.

Grief is a response to the painful, forcible separation that takes place when we are faced with death. Grief can be expressed in many physiological forms: a feeling of tightness in the throat, shortness of breath, a need for sighing, an empty feeling in the abdomen, muscular weakness, tension, inability to sleep, changes in appetite, absent-mindedness or difficulty in concentrating, failures of memory, and the tendency to do the same things over and over. In addition to its physiological manifestations, grief is also characterized by three emotional and cognitive stages (Hooyman & Kiyak, 2002):

Mourning:
culturally prescribed expressions of the thoughts, feelings, and behaviors of a bereaved person.

Bereaved person:
someone who suffers the loss of a loved one.

Bereavement:
a person's specific, unique reactions following the news that a loved one has died.

Grief:
physical and emotional responses to the painful, forcible separation that takes place when we are faced with death.

1. *Initial phase.* Initial responses to death include shock, numbness, and disbelief, followed by overwhelming sorrow. Elderly spouses and caregivers can become ill quickly following the death of an intimate partner or family member.

2. *Intermediate phase.* People idealize the deceased. Widows and widowers tend to regret every wrongdoing or misspoken word in their relationship. Some become angry at the deceased or displace their anger onto other family members or healthcare providers. The bereaved may experience anguish, disorganization, and despair, and may feel they have lost the motivation to carry on.

3. *Final phase.* Recovery and reorganization occur but may take several years. Because the elderly may have diminished coping skills and lack the physical capacity required to do their "grief work," grieving may be a much more complex experience.

As Kastenbaum (2007) notes, grief affects every sphere of one's life. There are many different types of loss and grief (such as the death of a friend, the death of a parent, and the death of a child), and all require coping and rebuilding. As you learned in Chapter 15, the death of a spouse, however, is thought to be the greatest stressor one can experience. More women than men experience the death of a spouse because women's average life expectancy is longer than that of men.

Grief experiences also differ between widows and widowers. Older spouses lend to grieve for 30 months or more following the death of a spouse (Thompson, Itzen, & Abendstern, 1991), while younger widows and widowers mourn for significantly shorter periods of time. On the other hand, younger mourners tend to express more intense grief reactions than do older spouses. This may be partly because older adults anticipate, at least to some degree, that they will eventually lose a spouse to death.

Gender differences are also seen in how men and women respond as bereaved spouses. In general, men experience deeper levels of depression than do women. This may be attributable to women's larger social support networks (Diamond, Lund, & Caserta, 1987). Men, on the other hand, experience greater social isolation and loneliness following the death of a spouse. Some research suggests that this may be partly because men long for the emotional support they received from their wives. Since women have larger social support networks and thus can receive emotional support from sources other than a spouse, they tend to fare better than men following the death of their marriage partner (Bradsher, 1997). This difference in social support may account for the discrepancies observed between men and women's grieving.

According to one body of research, another difference in mental health may relate to the stresses and strains associated with the caregiving role for an ill or dependent spouse (Wilcox, 2003). Many women indicate that because they no longer experience the stress of caring for their ill husband, their mental health is stronger after his death.

FAMILY LIFE EDUCATION: REMOVING BARRIERS AND ASSISTING IN TRANSITIONS

Based on the knowledge of the physical, emotional, cognitive, social, and unique differences that people in interpersonal relationships can experience, and on the knowledge about the ebbs and flows of transitions in the Family Life Cycle, the family life educator and other family practitioners are equipped to help those couples and families in later life, and to remove barriers that prevent them from attaining their relationship and family goals.

As we near the end of our study of family, intimate, and marital relationships, it is only fitting that we consider the last phase or chapter of life—aging and death. Miss Mabel, 108 years old, provides insight and experience that brings closure to our study (Welch, 2004):

> That is probably the worst part about aging—losing the people you love. Oh, I've grown accustomed to my vision and to my hearing. I've grown accustomed to having troubles when I stand . . . I've lost my husband and my children, and even two

of my grandchildren. And you know, no matter how long you live, no matter how many people die, you never become accustomed to death. I miss them all. But death is a part of living. The sadness we encounter when a loved one dies is all related to the happiness we have when they are alive. You can't have one without the other. We lose. We mourn. We pick ourselves back up. And we go on. But you still miss them every day, you still think of them every day.

Nearly 40 years ago, when I took those first steps down the marital aisle on my father's arm, I promised my dad that I would accept the "everythings" that marriage would bring. Young and naïve, all I could see before me was my soon-to-be-husband. I couldn't possibly begin to image the "everythings" that would come with marital and family life. I never knew true joy until I held each of my newborn sons . . . and I never knew true brokenness until I laid my hand on my husband's casket, knowing I would never see his gray-blue eyes again, would never hold him again, and would never hear him say my name again.

My students often ask me, "Knowing the ending of your love story, would you do it all over again?"

My answer is as unique to me as your answer would be to you. But I do know this: Great love carries with it great rewards and great risks. Beautiful and terrible things. And now, after our study together, you're equipped to tackle the everything.

/// SUMMARY

Aging and the Aged

- Baby Boomers—people who were born between 1946 and 1964—are getting older and life expectancies are increasing. The increasing number of this population challenges U.S. policy makers, healthcare providers, health and life insurance companies, businesses, and families.

- Gerontologists, family sociologists, developmentalists, and family life educators have developed perspectives that help them analyze the various influences on aging. One such model is the lifespan perspective of development, which emphasizes that just because one is older does not mean that one has completed one's intrapersonal and interpersonal developmental growth.

- For many years, most social scientists who studied aging focused on the biologically driven forces of aging. But today, social scientists believe that aging is a process of four interactive forces of development—biological forces, psychological forces, sociocultural forces, and life-cycle forces—and that all of the forces interact and combine to create a person's unique, individual developmental experiences. Furthermore, there are three varying sets of interacting lifecourse influences: normative age-graded influences, normative history-graded influences, and non-normative influences.

- *Primary aging* refers to the basic biological processes that take place over time. *Secondary aging* refers to physiological declines that are the result of environmental and behavioral influences.

- *Ageism* refers to the stereotypical attitudes people hold about the aging and the elderly.

Marriage Experiences Through Aging

- Just as individuals must accomplish certain developmental tasks, families, too, must navigate the developmental tasks associated with the aging family.

- Maintaining stable intimate relationships throughout the life cycle protects against biological losses associated with aging and buffers against the loss of social roles. Marriages that are strong in reciprocity remain high in intimacy, while marriages that demonstrate lower levels of interdependence are prone to higher levels of stress and conflict.

- As couples age, there are often fewer sources of marital conflict and greater potential for marital satisfaction. Couples tend to find more pleasures in common in later marriage and to have more positive emotions.

- Sexual activity plays an active role in intimate relationships into later adulthood. While men's and women's desire for more frequent sex may differ, an active sex life is important to marital satisfaction in later life. Nearly three-fourths of sexually active older men and women said that they are as sexually satisfied or even more satisfied than they were in their 40s.

- With good health, and with sound knowledge and realistic expectations about sexuality through aging, sexual fulfillment later in life is a healthy, positive, and attainable goal.

- The experience of separation and divorce in later life is similar to that experienced earlier in the lifespan, but divorce in middle and later ages carries with it special characteristics and stressors unique to older adults. Because of long-held beliefs and values, divorce later in life contributes to the stressors associated with marital breakup.

- Remarried older adults experience less frequent negative types of conflict, and less frequent occurrences of abusive physical behavior than remarried younger couples. Consequently, remarried older adults experience increased levels of marital happiness and satisfaction. Additionally, couples remarried in midlife appear to develop more effective communication and interaction patterns that were missing in their first marriages. These contribute to higher levels of marital satisfaction.

Intergenerational Ties

- As adults grow older through later adulthood, their interpersonal relationships across generations, or intergenerational ties, become increasingly important because they provide the foundation for intimacy throughout the aging process.

- In many families, children's entry into adolescence coincides with the parents' transition to midlife. While young adolescents strive for independence and challenge their parents' authority, the parents are encountering their own midlife developmental tasks such as caring for aging parents and preparing for retirement. These normative lifecourse events challenge the family system.

- Because most disagreements between parents and teens are commonly over insignificant matters, parents' marital satisfaction tends to increase as their children enter adolescence.

- During the middle years of the family life cycle, parents and children begin to renegotiate their relationship, and parents begin to reflect on their success or failure as parents. These reflections greatly affect the parents' purpose in life, self-acceptance, and thus their well-being.

- Midlife couples commonly encounter struggles such as changing or losing roles, dealing with marital issues that often surface after the nest is emptied, changing careers, shifting their caregiving to a different generation, and maintaining strong relationships with their children who are adults themselves and require less advice and support.

- The parent–adult child relationship is central to the lives of the elderly. Four primary factors influence intimacy between older adults and their adult children: gender, geographic distance, parents' marital status, and culture,

- For many adults in their middle years, the experience of grandparenting is immensely satisfying. Grandparenting styles may be categorized as formal, fun-seeking, distant, surrogate, and dispenser of wisdom.

Family Changes Toward the End of Life

- "Successful aging" is a pattern of well-being and adaptation to the challenges of middle adulthood and later life.

- *Life orientation* refers to the emphasis pre-retirees or retirees place on various aspects of life, such as family life and economic security. Because social relationships and acquaintances that originate in the workplace dissolve after retirement, retirees tend to place greater emphasis on family life.

- Research indicates there are three distinct types of marital intimacy in the later years of life: *reciprocity,* in which both spouses confide in one another and self-disclose; *nonreciprocity,* in which one spouse confides and shares, but the other spouse has a confidant outside of the marriage; and *segregative,* in which neither spouse shares with the other, but instead with someone outside the marriage.

- Contrary to popular belief, most older people don't reside in healthcare facilities, but live out their remaining years with the help of family caregivers. The *caregiving career* consists of those years that caregivers tend to dependent children, aging parents, and eventually, dependent husbands or wives.

- In most cases, family members work together to decide who will help with what in providing various caregiving tasks. People who have launched all of their children, are not working outside of the home, and are not married are more likely to provide care for aging parents. Daughters and daughters-in-law are the most common caregivers.

- *Caregiver burden* refers to the physical and emotional wear and tear caregiving responsibilities exert on the caregivers.

- The *sandwich generation* refers to those parents who are in the middle of two generations—parenting adolescent or younger children while caring for aging parents.

Dying and Death Experiences

- When death is an inevitability, individuals may attempt to avoid the painful tension associated with death anxiety by responding with denial. Additionally, they may experience death anxiety—the tension, feelings of distress, and apprehension associated with discussions and thoughts of death.

- There are three trajectories or pathways to death, each with its unique characteristics in how the dying are cared for: The *lingering trajectory* describes the transition from life to death over an extended period of time; the *expected quick trajectory* is typically associated with an acute crisis or illness; and the *unexpected quick trajectory* applies when there is typically not enough time to save the life of the injured or ill person. Since the rapid decline in health is usually unexpected in an unexpected quick trajectory, there is no time allowed for friends and family to plan or to prepare themselves emotionally.

- Responses to death are largely determined by one's cultural and ethnic background but there are death-related experiences common to people and cultures throughout the world. Every culture expresses bereavement and grief. *Mourning* refers to the culturally prescribed expressions of the thoughts and feelings of a bereaved person—someone who suffers the loss of a loved one. *Grief* is a response to the painful separation that takes place when we are faced with death, and is expressed physiologically, emotionally, and cognitively.

/// KEY TERMS

GLOSSARY

A factor: in Reuben Hill's ABC-X Family Crisis Model, these are the initial crisis-causing events.

ABC-X family crisis model: Reuben Hill's model that views a family crisis situation as a combination of various factors.

Account making: the process in which couples share with family and friends their individual accounts of what led to the deterioration of their marriage.

Acting out: a post-divorce behavior in which children and adolescents externalize their feelings about the divorce, typically through aggressive misbehaviors, noncompliance, disobedience, delinquency, increased absences from school, and increased aggressiveness.

Active labor: the second stage of labor, during which the cervix dilates from 4 to 7 centimeters and contractions occur every 2 to 3 minutes and last 60 to 90 seconds.

Active listening: when we actively listen, we become connected to another person so we not only hear what they are saying but understand what they are feeling.

Acute: lasting a relatively short time. See also **Chronic.**

Adverse childhood experiences (ACEs): experiences that occur during childhood (ages 0 to 17) and are potentially traumatic, life-altering events.

Agape: self-sacrificing, spiritual love that looks out for the interests and well-being of others; a selfless, enduring, other-centered type of love that provides intrinsic satisfaction with no reciprocity expected or demanded.

Agape love: a love type that provides intrinsic satisfaction, with no reciprocity expected or demanded. Inherent to agape love is patience, kindness, and permanence.

Ageism: stereotypical altitudes toward the aging and elderly.

Ageist: ageists make predetermined, negative assumptions about older people.

Age-related norms: socially approved and shaped pathways that determine the "right" time for certain life events, such as marriage or having children.

Alimony: money typically paid monthly by one spouse to the other during and after the divorce proceedings.

Altruistic love: an unselfish, giving kind of love. Most of us do not feel the need to reciprocate altruistic love because the rewards are intrinsic. See also **Intrinsic rewards.**

Anal eroticism: sexual activity that includes anal intercourse as well as oral stimulation of the anus, manually stroking the outside of the anus, and inserting one or more fingers into the anus.

Anal intercourse: the sexual activity of the male placing his penis into his partner's anus.

Anal stage: the psychosexual stage from ages 1 to 3, during which the focus of the sensual energy is associated with toilet training, particularly with respect to the anus. See also **Psychosexual stages.**

Androgens: the group of masculinizing sex hormones.

Androgyny: without assigned gender value; when a person possesses traits, behaviors, or characteristics typically associated with the opposite gender.

Anorgasmia: absence of orgasm.

Antinatalist: an ideology that discourages childbearing.

Anxious/ambivalent attachment types: insecurity is the hallmark of this attachment type. Fearing for the partner's love, anxious/ambivalent adults cling to the partner and push for commitment—often pushing the partner away.

Appraisal-focused coping: a coping style that attempts to understand why the crisis occurred and to find meaning in the circumstances. Skills needed include the ability to logically analyze the situation and mentally prepare for certain events to unfold.

Artificial insemination: the medical process by which donor sperm is placed by syringe into the woman's vagina, cervix, or uterus.

Asexual: an individual who does not experience sexual attraction.

Assisted reproductive technology (ART): treatments that involve fertilization through the manipulation of the woman's ova and the male's sperm.

Attachment theory: John Bowlby's Attachment theory describes enduring patterns of interpersonal relationships from cradle to grave. With the premise that all newborns must be nurtured in order to survive, Bowlby observed that they form a type of bond—an attachment—with their caregivers. From this close affectional and emotional bond, children derive a sense of security, a trusting sense that the world is a safe place to be.

Attachment: an emotional or affectional bond that binds the child to a parent or primary caregiver.

Authoritarian parents: parents who exert authority and control over their children, but without being responsive, warm, or affectionate, imposing rigid rules of behavior that must be obeyed without question. Parent–child communication is very low.

Authoritative parents: parents who are responsive while expecting certain behavior of their children. Parents do not use shame, withdraw love, or impose guilt to control behavior. They set clear but flexible boundaries for their children's behavior, encourage parent–child communication, and use a balance of power and reason.

Autonomy: one's desire to self-rule, or one's will.

Autonomy granting: permissive parents allowing their children age-appropriate independence and self-governance.

Avoidant attachment types: avoidant adults show discomfort with intimacy and are hesitant to trust others. Avoidant types report that they seldom find "real" love.

Azoospermia: a type of male infertility in which no sperm cells are produced.

B factor: in Reuben Hill's ABC-X Family Crisis Model, B factors are the resources a family has at its disposal to meet the demands of the crisis.

Baby Boomers: people who were born between 1946 and 1964.

Balance: in terms of work and family, the positive psychological state we achieve through regularly meeting our own, others', and work-related needs.

Barrier contraceptive: a contraceptive method that provides a chemical or physical barrier between the sperm and the ovum.

Basic budgets: the amount of money families need to manage at the most basic level; it must cover costs associated with housing, food, transportation, child care, health care, clothing, personal care items, school materials, and taxes.

Batterer: a person who commits domestic violence.

601

Beginning of the crowd: still same-sex in nature, peer groups toward the end of sixth grade/beginning of seventh grade begin to shift to crowds that consist of 10 or more core members. Crowd activities (dances, ball games, etc.) provide preadolescents the chance to "practice" interacting with the opposite sex.

Behavior-based conflict: occurs when incompatibilities exist between the demands of the work role and the demands of the family role.

Bereaved person: someone who suffers the loss of a loved one.

Bereavement: a person's specific, unique reactions following the news that a loved one has died.

Binuclear family: the separate, distinct households that form after marital separation or divorce.

Bipolar gender: see **Gender polarization.**

Birth defect: a physical anomaly that is present and birth. It may be inherited or may be the result of environmental influences during pregnancy and/or birth.

Bisexual: sexual and/or romantic attraction to members of both sexes.

Blended families: alternative term for stepfamilies.

Blue-collar workers: individuals holding jobs in the service sector, such as sales, office, production, and transportation.

Boundary: every system has some type of border, or boundary, between it and its environment. In a family, boundaries serve the purpose of affecting the flow of information within the system. They are essential because they are what separate us from our environment or from other family members.

Breakup costs: emotional and financial costs of a breakup, and the search cost necessary to find another love.

Breakup risk: a relationship cost that includes determining the lover's future overall benefit with the individual, the lover's future net benefit with another lover, and the lover's current breakup costs. If these costs are considered high, the risk of being "dumped" is relatively low.

C factor: in Reuben Hill's ABC-X Family Crisis Model, C factors are the meanings families ascribe to the event.

Caregiver: an unpaid individual who is involved in assisting others with daily living.

Caregiver burden: the physical and emotional wear and tear on caregivers.

Caregiving career: the years caregivers commit to tending to dependent children, aging parents, and eventually, dependent spouses.

Case study: the study of either a single person or a small group of people.

Cenogamy: a form of marriage often referred to as "group marriage," in which every man and woman is married to each other at the same time.

Certified Family Life Educator (CFLE): a person who has demonstrated knowledge (gained through work experience and college coursework) in the following content areas: families in society, family dynamics, human growth and development, human sexuality, interpersonal relationships, family resource management, parent education, family law and public policy, and ethics.

Child maltreatment: any act, intentional or not, that results in harm to a child, the threat of harm, or the potential for harm.

Child sexual abuse (CSA): a form of child abuse that involves sexual activity with a minor (a child under the age of 18).

Child support: money, typically paid monthly, by a spouse for the costs associated with raising children under 18 years old.

Childfree: people who deliberately choose not to have children.

Childfree-by-choice: the voluntary choice not to have children.

Childless: couples may consider themselves childless if they are unable to conceive or bear children of their own or adopt children.

Chlamydia: the most common bacterial sexually transmitted infection reported in the United States; it is transmitted through vaginal and anal intercourse and from a mother to her baby during birth.

Chosen family: a type of informal family structure that is common among LGBTQ+ communities and is based on nonbiological kinship bonds.

Chronic: long-lasting. See also **Acute.**

Chronosystem: the changes that happen over time, accounting for the collective historical precursors of current social attitudes (discrimination, definition of marriage, etc.).

Circumplex Model of Marital and Family Systems: this model was created to address family cohesion, adaptability, and communication, providing the means to assess a family's level of functioning and health. According to David Olson's model, families who exhibit balance function more sufficiently and effectively over time than families who are more out of balance.

Cisgender: a person whose gender identity and birth sex are in alignment.

Civil union: see **Social union.**

Classical conditioning: John B. Watson's theory that people make associations between two events. For example, babies open their mouths and smack their lips when their parent puts them in a highchair or when their parent opens the jar of baby food.

Closed boundaries: forming one end of the boundary spectrum, closed boundaries prevent information from coming in or going out. See also **Open boundaries.**

Closed-loop relationship: a type of relationship experienced by a heterosexual individual and a queer individual, in which the queer partner agrees to only have monogamous relationships outside of the marriage.

Cognitive avoidance: the attempt to deny the seriousness of a particular situation or events.

Cognitive cues: another's personality traits, beliefs, goals and aspirations, as well as the roles they play in life.

Cognitive Development theory: this theory holds that before social and environmental forces can influence a child's concept of gender, the child must first gain a certain awareness or understanding about gender.

Cognitive redefinition: occurs when families attempt to reframe the life event or stressor in ways that are seen as more favorable.

Cognitive theories: theories that focus on how children think and how they understand their world.

Cohabiting: unmarried partners who live together in a single household.

Collectivist cultures: cultures that define their identity in terms of the relationships individuals hold with others, which takes priority over individual needs; group membership is important.

Commitment: refers to loving another person as a conscious act of will—it is a deliberate choice. Commitment can thus be thought of as the cognitive component in a love relationship.

Common law marriage: a relationship between cohabiting heterosexual partners who are not legally married; however, the couple holds themselves out as husband and wife.

Communication: the process of making and sharing meanings.

Communication rules: rules that govern what family members can and cannot discuss or share and how they are to interact with their own family members.

Companionate love: deep, tender, mature, affectionate attachment bonds shared between two people; companionate love may or may not include feelings of physical arousal.

Companionate relationship: companionate grandparents enjoy warm, loving, and nurturing relationships with their grandchildren, though they may be happy to send them home when it is time.

Conceptualization: the process by which the researcher specifically denotes or indicates all of the concepts—or constructs—under investigation.

Conditional forgiveness: the type of forgiveness used when people want relational repair, but they want to make it very clear that repeating certain behaviors will not be tolerated.

Confidence gap: the phenomenon in which men and women have different confidence levels in their academic abilities—men tend to have more confidence in their academic abilities than women.

Confirming messages or responses: types of communication characterized by recognition of the other person, relevant dialogue, and acceptance; all of these show a willingness to be involved in the relationship.

Conflict theory: similar to Structural Functionalism, Conflict theory concentrates primarily on social structures and their interrelationships. Like the functionalist view, this theory supports the notion that society has some bearing on and to some degree shapes individual behavior. It differs in its basic theme that human beings are prone to conflict.

Confounding (or rival) variables: variables that are unrelated, unconnected, or not pertinent to the variables under investigation that can skew or affect the results of the study.

Conjugal role: a culturally defined and assigned set of behaviors each marriage partner is expected to carry out.

Construct: a concept referring to intangibles in the inquiry.

Constructive conflict: conflict that serves to build relationships and to foster loyalty, commitment, and intimacy.

Consummate love: considered by Sternberg to be total, whole, absolute, and all-inclusive, consummate love combines all three elements of love—intimacy, commitment, and passion.

Contact hypothesis: the idea that negative stereotypes (prejudices) about other groups exist because of the lack of contact and interaction between groups.

Contexts: areas of individual and family development that play a role in the relationship between people and their environments. These multiple environments surround individuals from birth; a person is in constant interaction with these different contexts. See also **Ecological Model, Ecosystem.**

Control group: in an experiment, the subjects in this group are treated exactly the same as those in the experimental group, except they are not exposed to the independent variable.

Convenience sample: a sample whose elements are selected based on convenience.

Co-parenting: sharing in everyday parenting responsibilities; the support parents provide to one another in the raising of their children.

Correlates of divorce: social and socioeconomic characteristics that affect the longevity of a marriage and the probability that a marriage will end in divorce.

Cost: a missed opportunity or exchanged resources that results in loss or punishment and increases the likelihood or probability that a person will *not* take part in a given behavior. See also **Social Exchange theory.**

Courting: socially prescribed forms of conduct that guide or groom young men and women toward matrimony.

Covenant: a religious or spiritual agreement.

Covenant marriages: a legally distinct kind of marriage in Arizona, Arkansas, and Louisiana, in which the marrying spouses agree to obtain counseling should marriage difficulties arise; these marriages have limited grounds for divorce.

Cross-sex friendships (CSFs): friendships between different-sex peers.

Crowd disintegration: as adolescents mature into adulthood and take on adult responsibilities, such as a job, and as they become involved in serious intimate relationships, crowd-type friendship groups begin to disintegrate. Often the support of friends is replaced by an intimate partner with whom young adults now share and disclose.

Crowd in transition: during the end of junior high and throughout high school, peer groups are seen as in transition. Smaller cliques are formed within the larger crowd.

Crude birth rate: the number of childbirths per 1,000 women, per year.

Crude divorce rate: the number of divorces per 1,000 population, per year.

Cultural factors: in terms of divorce, this refers to whether the couple embraces an individualistic or collectivist social identity.

Cultural scenarios: sexual scripts that recognize influences such as our families of origin and our communities, mass media, educational systems, and religious beliefs.

Cultural scripts: common guidelines that provide instructions about what behaviors and emotions are expected in certain situations.

Cunnilingus: the erotic, oral stimulation of the woman's external sex organs.

Custody: refers to who is responsible for the children's financial, physical, and emotional well-being.

Cyber-stalking: online stalking. See also **Stalking.**

Cycle of Violence model: a model illustrating the three phases of violence commonly seen in abusive relationships: the tension-building phase, the acute battering or violent act, and the respite (nonviolent) phase.

Data churning: also known as "fishing," this refers to the practice of devising the purposes of the research or formulating a research hypothesis after the data are gathered and analyzed.

Dating: socializing for any number of reasons, such as for relaxation and escape from everyday responsibilities or to pursue a relationship to determine whether the partner is a potential spouse or a partner for a lifelong relationship.

Dating scripts: the models that guide our dating interactions.

Dating violence: the perpetration or the threat of an act of violence against a person involved in a dating or courting relationship.

Dealing-with-problems focus: education for family living that focused on problems of sexuality, gender roles, marriage, and other social issues.

Death anxiety: tension, feelings of distress, and apprehension associated with discussions and thoughts of death.

Decode: to interpret unspoken exchanges.

De-escalation of intimacy: a decline in intimacy.

Defense of Marriage Act (DOMA): a law signed by President Bill Clinton confirming that marriage is a legal union of one man and one woman as husband and wife.

Deinstitutionalization of marriage: the idea that marriage is no longer a sacred institution because society has evolved to include other ways in which to couple and procreate.

Denial: see **Cognitive avoidance.**

Dependent love: love between an adult and an infant or child, wherein the adult meets and gratifies the needs of the infant or child without expectation of anything in return.

Desacralization of marriage: the societal shift from marriage as a binding religious union to a union of individual choice.

Destabilizing effect: a factor that disrupts the stability of a marital relationship; these are individual to each couple.

Destructive conflict: destructive conflict can be either overt, which refers to obvious conflict, or covert, which is more subtle, but nonetheless hurtful. Whether it is overt or covert, destructive conflict is unhelpful and, at its very worst, deadly (as in the case of physical violence that escalates).

Developing-family-potentials focus: family life education that aims to build on positive aspects of family life and the family's potential to enhance personal life and family living by promoting goals ranging from building on family strengths to developing healthy, fulfilling, and responsible interpersonal relationships.

Developmental tasks: developmental tasks entail achieving certain biological, physical, cognitive/intellectual, social, emotional, and spiritual tasks across the lifecourse.

Diminished parenting: the new relationship between parents and children in the first few years following a divorce.

Direct forgiveness: family members or intimate partners clearly, plainly, and directly tell the offender that she or he is forgiven.

Disorders of sex development (DSD): a mismatch between a person's genetic sex and the appearance of their genitals.

Dispenser of wisdom: the grandparent who offers information and advice to their grandchildren.

Distress: a stressor that is "bad stress," "negative stress," or "harmful stress."

Distress reactions: reactions to a breakup that include such things as physical and emotional pain, loss of interest in sex, and guilt.

Diverse: people's differences in age, gender, race, ethnicity, cultures, sexual orientation, and religion.

Diversity: the broad spectrum of demographic and philosophical differences among groups within a culture.

Divorce: socially sanctioned actions to legally terminate marriage.

Divorce mediation: the process involving an objective third party who helps ex-spouses resolve child support, child custody, and property settlements for themselves and for their children, rather than having a judge determine these issues for them.

Divorce mediator: an objective third party to the divorce who aids the divorcing couple in determining the terms of their divorce settlement, such as child support and visitation rights and schedules for the parent who does not receive custody.

Domestic violence: violence perpetrated against family members by a person who is related to the victim either biologically or legally, such as by marriage or through adoption.

Double ABC-X Model: using Reuben Hill's ABC-X Model as the foundation, family researchers developed the Double ABC-X Model to better understand the effects of the accumulation, or pile-up, of stressors and strains and how families adapt to them.

Doula: a professional provider of labor support (emotional, physical, and informational) to women and their companions.

Dual-earner couples: couples in which both spouses are actively engaged in the workforce.

Dyadic breakdown phase: the period during which a couple's established pattern or relationship breaks down.

Dyadic phase: according to Stephen Duck, the dyadic phase occurs when couples discuss their dissatisfaction with their marriage and attempt either to find a resolution or to end the relationship.

Dyspareunia: sexual pain experienced by women as a result of sexual dysfunction.

Early labor: the first phase of labor in which the cervix dilates from 0 to 3 centimeters.

Early remarriage: the early stages of the new relationship, when the developmental difficulties of a traditional marriage occur, along with difficulties unique to stepfamilies.

Ecological Model: a theory developed by Russian-born Uri Bronfenbrenner that explains the multiple influences that affect individuals' and families' development over their lifetimes. The central concept is that people develop in a variety of interacting contexts.

Ecosystem: areas of individual and family development that play a role in the relationship between people and their environments. See also **Contexts, Ecological Model.**

Eight Stages of Man: Erik Erikson's theory that social and emotional development is a lifelong process that takes place in eight stages.

Elopement: secret marriages between love partners that take place without parental approval and/or knowledge.

Emergency contraception (EC): made of the same hormones found in birth control pills, EC prevents pregnancy by interrupting the release of an egg.

Emotional attachment: feelings that promote a sense of closeness, bonding with one another, and connection.

Emotional communication: the physical gestures and movements that convey our emotions. See also **Nonverbal communication.**

Emotional discharge: the act of giving vent to or expressing anger, frustration, confusion, disappointment, hatred, and despair in response to tragic or sudden/unexpected news.

Emotional divorce: emotionally withdrawing from a marriage partner or from the marriage.

Emotional needs: self-esteem, social and spiritual needs, and safety.

Emotional regulation: strategies designed to help individuals and families change their perception, interpretation, and the meaning of the stressor.

Emotional safety: the high degree of trust required to self-disclose.

Emotional violence: violence that includes such acts as controlling the amount of contact a family member has with family and friends, name-calling, constant criticism.

Emotion-focused coping: a type of stress management used to help a person tolerate, reduce, or eliminate negative emotions that occur due to a stressful event.

Empathy: the capacity to understand another's circumstances or situation and the ability to feel or express emotional concern for another person.

Empty love: this type of love is void of passion and intimacy. Commitment is the only element in the relationship.

Empty nest: the home with no children after children have grown and left.

Endogamy: refers to marrying within one's group, such as Muslims marrying Muslims, Catholics marrying Catholics, or Asians marrying Asians.

Endometriosis: a disease characterized by the buildup or migration of uterine tissue to other parts of the body (such as the ovaries or fallopian tubes).

Entertainment needs: social aspects of day-to-day living and family life (hobbies, interests, etc.).

Equal Rights Amendment (ERA): proposed amendment to the U.S. Constitution to prohibit sex discrimination. The amendment was passed by Congress in 1972, but as of 2020, only 38 states had ratified the ERA.

Erectile dysfunction (ED): also known as *impotence,* this condition is marked by an inability to achieve an erection.

Eros: sensual or sexual love.

Erotic lovers: people who are passionate and romantic and seek out passionately expressive lovers.

Estrogen: the feminizing hormone.

Ethics: in social science research, the rules and standards that govern researchers' conduct as they examine human behaviors, feelings, and attitudes.

Eustress: a stressor that is "good stress," "positive stress," or "productive stress."

Evolutionary theory: the theory that we choose mates for the sole purpose of ensuring reproductive success—and thus the success of the species and society.

Exogamy: a requirement to marry outside of a particular group. In the United States, for example, we cannot marry a sibling or, in some states, a first cousin.

Exosystem: the fabrics of society in which policies are made and influenced that ultimately have an impact on the elements of the microsystem and the individual.

Expected quick trajectory: a transition from life to death typically associated with an acute crisis or illness, such as a heart attack or vehicle accident. These types of events demand quick action to save a life.

Experimental design: used to determine causal relationships among variables. In this mode, researchers control or hold constant certain variables being studied in order to determine which variable is effecting the change in the other variable.

Experimental group: in an experiment, the subjects in this group are exposed to the independent variable.

Expressive roles: these roles, described by Talcott Parsons, were given to the female as a compliment to the male. The wife-mother was the people-oriented mate responsible for enhancing emotional relationships among members of the family.

Expressive schemas: patterns of behavior associated with femininity that have an interpersonal or relational orientation.

Extended family: a family unit in which two or more generations of close family relatives live together in one household.

External locus of control: refers to the perception that we cannot control what happens in some aspects of our lives.

Externalize: to direct outward and generate discomfort and conflict in the surrounding environment. See also **Acting out.**

Extramarital sex (EMS): occurs when a married person has a sexual relationship (any type of sexual activity, such as mutual masturbation, or oral, anal, or vaginal sex) with someone other than his or her spouse.

Extra-relationship involvement (ERI): any behavior that oversteps the expectations of exclusivity and monogamy in a relationship.

Failure rate: a measurement for contraception that is based on the number of women who become pregnant if 100 women used the method for one year.

Family: two or more people related by birth, marriage, or adoption residing in the same housing unit.

Family and Medical Leave Act (FMLA): under the FMLA, federal and state employees and those who work for employers with 50 or more employees are able to take up to 12 weeks of unpaid leave to care for an ill child, parent, or spouse, or for one's own serious illness without fear of losing their job, benefits, or status.

Family cohesion: the extent to which family members feel emotionally close and bonded to one another.

Family crisis: a situation that upsets the normal functioning of the family and requires a new set of responses to the stressor.

Family Deficit Model: promoted the idea that single-parent households were negative experiences for children for the sole reason that the family structure was not nuclear.

Family law: policies and regulations to protect the rights and well-being of all family members and ensure that married or divorced couples fulfill their obligations to each other and to their children. Specific family laws vary from state to state.

Family life cycle: the life cycle consisting of multiple entrances and exits from the family of origin.

Family life education: borrowing and adapting theoretical frameworks from the fields of sociology and psychology, this perspective provides organized, programmatic education to help families cope with change.

Family meetings: formal or informal regular family discussions that provide structure and organization to the family system and allow for meaningful conversation.

Family metacognition: the phase in marriage deterioration in which the spouses begin to openly share with others the problems in their marriage and the possibility that it may come to an end.

Family of origin: the family into which we are born or brought by adoption.

Family of procreation: the family unit that is formed when we marry and produce children.

Family projection process: a theory that people who have children do so because they are trying to gain what they did not have in their own childhood, such as love and attention.

Family resilience: a family's ability to function in a healthy fashion during times of change, stress, adversity, crisis, and transition.

Family stress: the result of an imbalance between the demands an event places on a family and that family's ability or inability to meet them.

Family system: the family is a living, ever-changing, dynamic system that consists of various individuals and their interconnected, intergenerational patterns of interactions. In this context a system's primary function is to bring together and arrange the various interrelated parts into a whole, organized entity.

Family Systems theory (FST): developed by Murray Bowen, this theory views a family as a whole entity consisting of interconnected parts seeking to maintain balance.

Family values: usually refers to a society's paradigm or viewpoint that expects its members to adhere to perceived proper social roles, such as marrying and having children, remaining monogamous and faithful to the marriage partner, and opposing same-sex relationships, marriages, and parenting by gay or lesbian partners.

Family well-being: psychological health; high levels of self-esteem, sense of power, and internal locus of control; good physical health; low behavior/conduct problems; good social support; high marital quality and stability; and good parent–child relationships.

Father involvement: the time a father and his children spend together.

Fatuous: a descriptive term referring to infatuation-based relationships.

Fatuous love: combining passion and commitment, fatuous love relationships result in a sprint toward cohabitation or marriage. Because the relationship lacks intimacy and the time necessary for intimacy to grow and develop, and because passion will fade sooner or later, the only element remaining is commitment.

Fellatio: the oral stimulation of the male's external sex organs.

Femininity: the qualities, behaviors, and attitudes that are deemed by a particular culture to be ideally appropriate for girls and women; most often associated with nurturing and life-giving attributes such as kindness, gentleness, and patience.

Feminist theory: a theory that embraces the conflict approach to understanding and analyzing the roles of women in terms of marriage and family in perpetuating inequalities in male/female relationships.

Feminization of poverty: the phenomenon in which women experience poverty rates that are disproportionately high in comparison to men.

Fertility cues: physical traits associated with fertility, such as youth and curves in women.

Fictive kin: people who are not biologically related but who fulfill a family role.

Field research: observational research taking place in a natural setting, such as at the family's own home or a playground, instead of at a clinic.

Fight or flight: the instinctive physiological response to a threatening situation, which readies one either to fight or to run away.

Filter Theory of Mate Selection: this theory suggests that individuals use a filtering mechanism that helps them sort out a potential mate from the vast pool of candidates.

Forgiveness: a deliberate process that transforms a strong desire for revenge into a positive response.

Formal grandparenting: a style of grandparenting in which grandparents see their role along common, traditional lines.

Framework: a systematic structure for classifying families, their behaviors, or their experiences.

Fully developed crowd: a group of opposite-sex cliques; the same-sex friendship affiliations from elementary school and early years of junior high are no longer dominant.

Fun seeker: a grandparent whose relationship with their grandchildren is characterized by an informal, spontaneous playfulness.

Functional communication: communication that addresses only the ins and outs of daily life, leaving one feeling as though something is lacking in one's family connections.

Gamete intrafallopian transfer (GIFT): an assisted reproductive technology process in which unfertilized eggs and a male's sperm are placed in a woman's fallopian tubes to foster natural fertilization.

Gatekeepers: divorced mothers who deny visitation, make it difficult for fathers to see their children, and intend not to share parenting with the fathers of their children.

Gender: encompasses characteristics such as gender role, gender identity, gender presentation, and gender stereotypes.

Gender-based violence (GBV): violence perpetrated against an individual because of their gender/gender identity.

Gender binary: the classification of gender into two distinct, opposite, and disconnected forms of masculine and feminine, whether by social system or cultural belief.

Gender constancy: between kindergarten and about second grade, children understand that acting like a girl if you are a boy doesn't make you a girl, and acting like a boy if you are a girl doesn't make you a boy. Children realize that sex is a permanent attribute.

Gender dysphoria: the distress a person feels because their sex assigned at birth is in conflict with the gender with which they identify.

Gender equality: equality between men and women in the job place and economic equality.

Gender expression: external manifestations of gender, expressed through a person's name, pronouns, clothing, behavior, voice, and/or body characteristics.

Gender fluid: see **Gender nonconforming.**

Gender identity: our intuitive sense of our gender.

Gender inequality: the obvious or hidden disparities or discrimination in opportunities or advancements among individuals, based solely on a person's gender.

Gender nonconforming: umbrella term that describes people who have gender expressions that don't conform to a society's traditional gender norms.

Gender polarization: a model in which cultural viewpoints almost always emphasize the differences between men and women.

Gender role development: the process whereby children acquire behaviors, attitudes, interests, and emotional reactions that are culturally appropriate for members of their sex.

Gender roles: the explicitly expressed and implicitly implied behaviors, feelings, attributes, and traits that society expects of the male or the female.

Gender schemas: the ways in which we internalize and incorporate specific gendered behaviors and expectations.

Gender socialization: the specific messages and practices we receive from our culture concerning the nature of being a male or a female, of being feminine or masculine.

Gender stability: between the ages of 4 and 6, children reach the realization that their gender will always be the same—that they were a boy or a girl as a baby and will be a boy or a girl when they grow up.

Gender typing: the process of developing the behaviors, thoughts, and emotions associated with a particular gender.

General Adaptation syndrome: physician Hans Selye (1985) developed the three-stage General Adaptation syndrome to describe the physiological responses to eustress and distress. The stages are alarm reaction, stage of resistance, and exhaustion.

General fertility rate: the ratio of the number of live births per 1,000 women of childbearing age.

General System theory (GST): encompassing areas of study from economics to biology to the intricacies of family life, this theory constitutes a world view or a paradigm that keeps at the forefront the notion that objects do not exist in isolation, but instead are interconnected to parts of a larger whole.

Genital stage: the psychosexual stage beginning at puberty (age 12), when people develop mature sexual interests. See also **Psychosexual stages.**

Genogram: a diagram with various figures that illustrate relationships between family members.

Gerontologists: scientists who study aging.

Gestational parent: the individual who is carrying a pregnancy and gives birth.

Glass ceiling: refers to discrimination against women in the workplace, specifically in situations where advancement in an organization is stopped because of occupational sexism.

Gonorrhea: the second most common sexually transmitted infection reported in the United States; sometimes referred to as *the clap* or *the drip;* it is transmitted through intercourse, oral sex, and anal sex, and it can also be transmitted from the mother to her baby during childbirth.

Grandfamilies: families in which the grandparents are responsible for their grandchildren.

Grave dressing phase: a divorcing couple comes to terms with the breakup of the marriage and they begin to piece together a rational, logical explanation that explains why the marriage "died."

Gray divorce: a term used for people aged 50 and older who divorce after 20+ years of marriage.

Grief: physical and emotional responses to the painful, forcible separation that takes place when we are faced with death.

Group context: the couple's social network of family, peers, and community.

Gunnysacking: this refers to a spouse or a family member who holds in resentment, hurt, anger, frustration, and bitter feelings until that "last straw," when the spouse or family member unloads all of the pent-up feelings in the midst of an argument.

Hayflick limit: according to Leonard Hayflick, each species has a genetically programmed time limit because at a certain point in time, cells lose their ability to replicate. The Hayflick limit accounts for the aging process and life expectancy.

Hegemonic masculinity: each culture's ideal, dominant standard of masculinity for which men are to aim.

Herpes: a sexually transmitted infection caused by the herpes simplex virus; it is transmitted through touching and kissing and through vaginal, anal, or oral sex.

Hetero-emotional: a person who is emotionally oriented to prefer psychological intimacy with an opposite-sex partner.

Heterogamy: partners who are dissimilar in one or more dimensions, such as race, ethnicity, or religion, or dissimilar in age, political ideology, socioeconomic status, and values and beliefs.

Heterosexual: sexual and emotional relationships between people of opposite sexes.

Homeostasis: when an infection enters the body, various systems work together to bring it back into balance or homeostasis. The same holds true for a family system when it experiences any departure from its usual state of balance (normal).

Homogamy: partnering with someone similar in ethnic and racial background, religious upbringing, age, education level, political ideology, socioeconomic status, and values and beliefs.

Homosexual: sexual and emotional relationships with persons of the same sex.

Homosocial play: children's preference for same-sex playmates; occurs from age 3 to age 11 or 12.

Hooking up: physical or sexual interaction with the absence of commitment or affection.

Hormone contraceptive: methods of contraception that use artificial hormones to prevent ovulation as well as thicken the cervical mucus, which inhibits sperm from traveling into the uterus.

Household: all people who occupy a housing unit, regardless of relationship.

Household work: the work associated with staying at home in order to nurture one's children.

Human papillomavirus (HPV): a common sexually transmitted infection that can lead to six different types of cancer later in life.

Hypotheses testing: based on evidence gathered, a researcher can either reject a hypothesis or fail to reject a hypothesis.

Hypothesis: a speculative statement about a variable or the relationship between variables in a study.

Ideal–actual gap: the difference between the parenting tasks that are reported and the parent's actual performance.

Identity: an individual's sense of who she or he is.

Immediate context: factors influencing a couple's interaction, such as the physical setting, the couple's mood, and the couple's reason for talking.

Immigrants: foreign-born people who have been granted the right to permanently live and work in the United States.

In-clinic abortions: a medical procedure in which suction is used to remove a pregnancy from the uterus.

In vitro fertilization (IVF): an assisted reproductive technology process whereby a woman's eggs are surgically removed from her ovary and mixed with a man's sperm in a laboratory culture dish; if the eggs are fertilized and appear to be growing at a normal rate, the embryos are placed in the uterus.

Incompetent suitors: stalkers who have poor social and emotional skills and have difficulty expressing themselves.

Independent couple: a married couple who value closeness, companionship, sharing, and self-disclosure (although they do not disclose quite as much as traditional couples). They are not as conventional in their beliefs as traditional couples.

Indirect forgiveness: family members or intimate partners communicate this type of forgiveness by nonverbal displays (such as a hug, a smile, or eye contact) and by acting as though the transgression never happened,

Individualistic cultures: culture in which individual goals are more important than the goals of the group. Individuals define their identity or sense of self by way of personal attributes (wealth, social status, education level, marital status, etc.).

Individuation: the process of forming an identity separate from one's family of origin.

Infatuated love: this type of love consists of passion only; "Hollywood" marriages are made of this, but not long-term marriages.

Infatuation: an intense, extravagant, and often short-lived passion for another person, often confused with love.

Infertility: the inability to conceive a baby after trying for a period of one year.

Infidelity: a breach of faith that occurs when there is a violation of the couple's mutually agreed rules or boundaries of a relationship.

Informal caregiver: see **Caregiver**.

Initiator: the spouse who commences divorce proceedings.

Institutional marriage: marriage that considers socializing children to the culture's norms to be a responsibility and also includes adhering to the idea that marriage is sexually exclusive and permanent.

Institutional Review Boards (IRBs): research review committees established by academic and other research institutions that review and approve research plans for scholars and researchers and ensure the ethical treatment of research subjects.

Instrumental roles: an element of Parsons's Structural-Functionalist theory, instrumental roles were assigned to the male husband-father who, as the task-oriented mate, was assigned responsibility for being primary breadwinner and protector against imbalance or disequilibrium in the family.

Instrumental schemas: patterns associated with masculinity that focus on task-oriented behaviors and "getting the job done."

Instrumental support: the element of marriage in which husband and wife boost each other's well-being, productivity, and career.

Intensive mothering: term coined by Sharon Hays to reflect the mothering roles and expectations that have been evolving since the 1980s, when women flooded the workplace.

Intensive mothering ideology: the Western cultural belief that a mother should give herself unconditionally and focus all of her time, energy, money, love, support, and every other resource she has on raising her children.

Interaction cues: cues that enable us to assess whether we want to get to know a person any better. As we interact, we gain a better idea of the extent to which we may want to relate to a person.

Intercultural marriage: the marriage of two people from different cultural backgrounds.

Interdependent love: the ability for people to be dependent and have someone depend on them. Interdependent love is expressed between emotionally mature adults who recognize that love is a give-and-take process.

Interfaith marriage: marriage between people of different religious faiths.

Intergenerational approach to family therapy: an approach seeking to understand the transmission of relational behaviors from one generation to the next.

Intergenerational Family theory: the theory that patterns of relational functioning (including intimacy) are passed down from generation to generation.

Intergenerational ties: the relationships between family members across multiple generations.

Intergenerational transmission: research suggests that those who experience the end of their parents' marriage are more likely to divorce than those whose parents do not divorce. Many social scientists refer to this phenomenon as *intergenerational transmission of divorce*.

Internal locus of control: refers to the perception that we are, to a large extent, in control of our destiny.

Internalizing: to direct inward and generate distress in the individual; internalizing difficulties result in emotional problems such as worry, feelings of unhappiness, anxiety, depression, distress, guilt, and poor self-concept.

Interpersonal attraction: the attraction between people that leads to the development of platonic (friendly, nonsexual) or romantic (sexual) relationships.

Interpersonal scripts: sexual scripts that recognize how different people interact and relate to each other within specific social situations.

Interracial couple: romantic or marriage partners of differing races.

Interrole conflict: conflict that occurs when we take on (or have assigned to us) many roles simultaneously.

Intersex: an individual whose genitalia are ambiguous or indistinguishable.

Intersectionality: the interconnected nature of social categorizations—such as race, class, and gender—regarded as creating overlapping and interdependent systems of discrimination or disadvantage.

Intimacy: loving relationships characterized by feelings of closeness, connectedness, and bondedness.

Intimacy seekers: stalkers who want to establish an intimate, loving relationship with their victim.

Intimacy status: the commitment to and depth of a relationship.

Intimate: a person capable of experiencing closeness and forming a deep and enduring emotional attachment to another.

Intimate partner violence (IPV): violence perpetrated against a relationship partner.

Intrafaith marriages: those in which individuals adhere to the same religion but may have different beliefs or follow different traditions within that faith (such as a Baptist who marries a Presbyterian).

Intrapsychic phase: according to Stephen Duck, the second phase of relationship deterioration, also called *individual cognition*, when a couple begins to focus on aspects of the relationship with which they are dissatisfied or disappointed.

Intrapsychic scripts: sexual scripts that account for individual desires, fantasies, emotions, and intentions while at the same time considering the interpersonal responses of others.

Intrinsic rewards: rewards that are pleasurable in and of themselves, such as joy, satisfaction, contentment, pleasure, gratification.

Involuntary extramarital experience: occurs when one partner ventures outside the relationship without the other's knowledge or permission.

Involved relationship: the grandparent who assumes the role of parent and is involved in the everyday rearing of their grandchildren.

Isolates: people who are socially withdrawn with no apparent need for social or close personal interactions.

Jealousy: an emotional reaction to the perception that a valued relationship is threatened because of a third party.

Job autonomy: occurs when employees are allowed a high degree of independence and self-direction.

Job complexity: occurs when jobs are challenging and stimulating at the same time.

Job status: refers to a type or kind of job that offers some kind of prestige in an organization or community.

Joint custody: an arrangement in which parents share in the decision making regarding their children. They may also share the physical custody of their children.

Kinship care: a situation in which grandparents provide a living environment for their grandchildren.

Labor: the rhythmic uterine contractions that expel a baby.

Late remarriage: six to ten (or more) years after the remarriage, when the family's boundaries and roles are restructured to the point there is a greater deal of "authenticity" in interactions and shared intimacy within the family system.

Latency stage: the psychosexual stage from about ages 7 to 11, during which the sensual energies subside for a time. See also **Psychosexual stages**.

Latinx: people of Latin American origin or descent. The term is used as a gender-neutral alternative to Latino or Latina.

Learning theory: the theory that traits and behaviors are not inborn, but learned.

Legal custody: refers to which parent has the right to make decisions about how the child is reared, such as decisions concerning education or religion.

Lesbian co-mothering (LCM): in a lesbian couple, the nonbirth parent takes an equal role in parenting, or mothering, the child.

Life change event: typically, a life-altering event that requires significant social and psychological adjustment.

Life expectancy: based on statistical averages, the age at which adults are expected to die is anywhere from 68 to 80, depending on a person's race and gender.

Life orientation: the emphasis pre-retirees or retirees place on various aspects of life, such as family life and economic security.

Life transition: within psychology and family studies, a point at which people take on new roles and obligations, such as becoming a parent.

Lifespan perspective: emphasizes that human beings are in a constant, continuous state of growth from the cradle to the grave.

Liking: intimacy is the sole element in the relationship and is the stuff that great, long-lasting friendships are made of. There is typically no passion or commitment.

Lingering trajectory: a term that describes a lengthy transition from life to death, such as occurs with some types of cancer, diabetes, or other progressive illnesses or diseases.

Literature review: a comprehensive search of existing research studies related to a particular topic of inquiry.

Love Economic model: Chau Vuong's Love Economic model is based on the primary assumptions that people are rational decision makers and, as a result, are able to tally up both the benefits and costs of falling in love and being in love. Vuong further contends that "sex and commitment are the only differences between friendship and love."

Love maps: a mental blueprint of the "ideal" love relationship, which is shaped by our experiences with love in infancy and early childhood and by our parents' and primary caregivers' attitudes toward love and sexuality.

Love stories: our unique, personal experiences with love.

Ludic lovers: people who don't care as much about commitment as they do about playing the sport or the game of love.

Ludus: love that is playful, flirtatious, carefree, and casual.

Machismo: the attitude, common in Latin American cultures, that men are superior to women and that men are socially and physically dominant.

Macrosystem: the set of overarching cultural values and beliefs that affect individual development by establishing either implicit or explicit rules about what is or is not acceptable behavior in a society.

Maintenance costs: emotional costs and time costs involved in finding the right person.

Manic lovers: jealousy, envy, protectiveness, and exclusivity are the hallmark traits of manic lovers. Manic love is frenzied, agitated, hectic, and chaotic all at the same time.

Marianismo: the belief among Latin American cultures that women are semi-divine and are morally superior to and spiritually stronger than men.

Market alternative cost method: estimates the value of household labor by looking at what it would cost in the current market to pay someone to do the household labor the mother performs.

Masculine Gender Roles Stress theory (MGRS): this theory maintains that there are stressors that may result from a man's fear that he is not measuring up to or meeting societal expectations for masculinity.

Masculinity: a socially/culturally constructed set of beliefs, values, and opinions that shape manly character or manliness.

Masturbation: sexual self-stimulation.

Matching hypothesis: the premise that most of us want a socially desirable person regardless of our own degree of social desirability.

Maternal gatekeeping: when a woman's socialization—and the inherent cultural notion that she will always be the better parent—makes it difficult for her to relinquish her traditional roles.

Materialistic needs: the primary needs required for survival and happiness, including food, water, shelter, and transportation.

Maternal Role Attainment (MRA): the process by which a woman, through pregnancy and after the birth of her child, continues to construct an "ideal" image of herself as mother and adopts roles that support this ideal image.

Maturity effect: the higher likelihood of teenagers to have unrealistic expectations about marriage and to misjudge their mate's qualities and characteristics.

Meaning-based coping: employing deliberate strategies to produce positive emotion, such as arming oneself with information about one's illness and treatment in order to remain optimistic.

Meanings: in the context of family communication, the definition we assign to verbal and nonverbal interactions.

Men's studies: research and study of male/female inequality (conflict, antagonism, and tension) from the male perspective.

Merger status: when intimate partners in a relationship experience an equal balance of power or merger.

Mesosystem: the ecosystem that shares all of the elements that are present in the microsystem but focuses on the interaction between the various elements rather than on the individual.

Message: the obvious meaning of a communication.

Meta message: the underlying context in which a communication takes place.

Microsystem: the developmental context nearest the individual and representing those interactions to which people are directly exposed. The elements composing this ecosystem are the individuals, groups, and agencies that have the earliest and most immediate influences on the individual.

Middle remarriage: the middle stage of a remarriage, which takes most families about three to five years to complete, when the family becomes a more cohesive system and functions less along strictly biological lines.

Miscarriage: spontaneous abortion, or loss of a fetus or embryo before the 20th week of pregnancy.

Mixed co-parenting: a type of co-parenting in which one or both parents' responses are mixed—sometimes they support one another, sometimes they don't.

Mixed couple: a married couple with different marital types, e.g., one spouse may have the expectations and characteristics of a traditional couple whereas the other spouse may have expectations typical of an individual couple type.

Mixed-orientation marriage: marriage between partners who have different sexual orientations. Also called "mixed-orientation relationship."

Monogamism: the belief that monogamy is the only true morally and socially appropriate type of marriage or love relationship.

Monogamy: a dyadic (two-person) form of marriage that involves the practice of having only one sexual partner.

Moral commitment: each person's value and belief systems. Before committing to or ending a relationship, individuals consciously weigh what is right and what is wrong, guided by their value/belief/religious framework.

Morning-after pill: see **Emergency contraception**.

Mothering: performing the relational and logistical work of caring for others.

Mourning: culturally prescribed expressions of the thoughts, feelings, and behaviors of a bereaved person.

Mutual dependency: a couple's reliance on one another for need fulfillment, such as socially and sexually.

Narcissistic entitlement: a sense of being entitled to, or deserving, only the good things in life; a pride-related barrier to forgiveness.

Natalism: an ideology that embraces childbearing.

Native American/Alaska Native: the aboriginal peoples of the United States and their descendants, who maintain tribal affiliation or community attachment.

Natural selection: the process by which nature selects the best adapted varieties of species to survive and reproduce.

Nature: the influences of biology.

Nature vs. nurture debate: the ongoing debate between those people who feel the influences of aging are determined by nature (your inborn, hereditary characteristics such as genetic influences) and those who believe they are determined by nurture (your environmental, experiential, societal, and cultural experiences across your lifespan).

Need for affiliation: the universal and innate drive to have relationships in our lives.

Never-married singles: individuals who have not married; they may or may not live alone or have an intimate partner.

Nonbinary (NB): a term used to describe persons who don't fall into either/or categories of male/female.

Noncoital: sexual activities besides sexual intercourse, such as masturbation, oral-genital sex, and anal sex.

Nonfamily household: a householder living alone, such as a widow, or a householder sharing the home with people to whom she/he is not related, such as a widow sharing her home with two friends.

Nonlove: the absence of intimacy, commitment, and passion. Nonlove may exist in a relationship where physical, emotional, or sexual violence is present.

Non-normative life events: life events not occurring at the typical, more common points in a person's lifespan. For example, a pregnancy is considered non-normative if it occurs during adolescence.

Nonprobability samples: nonrandom samples used when the use of probability samples is impossible.

Nonregulated couples: couples who have a difficult time bouncing back from arguments and disputes because the manner in which they handle the conflict only compounds the issues at hand.

Nonrelational messages: issues or topics concerning things outside of the relationship.

Nonverbal communication: communication via facial expressions, motions of the body, eye contact, patterns of touch, expressive movements, hand gestures, the spatial arrangements in the physical environment, and emotions that occurs with or without the spoken word. See also **Emotional communication**.

Normative age-graded influences: developmental changes caused by biological, psychological, and sociocultural forces.

Normative history-graded influences: events or conditions that people in a given culture or society experience simultaneously.

Normative life events: life events that are relatively predictable across the lifespan.

Normlessness: a disruption in the norms of family relationships.

Nuclear family: a father, a mother, and their biological or adopted children.

Nurture: environmental influences.

Nurturing communication: interactions that convey intimacy, caring, recognition, and validation of family members.

Observational research method: a type of research method wherein an observation is systematically planned and data are gathered and recorded systematically.

Occupational sexism: belief that the male gender is more capable of certain work-related tasks and professions than women are.

Off-time events: see **Non-normative life events.**

Oligospermia: a type of male infertility in which few sperm cells are produced.

On-time events: see **Normative life events.**

Open boundaries: boundaries where the transfer of information is so unobstructed that family members within the systems lose their identities. See also **Closed boundaries.**

Operant conditioning: B. F. Skinner's theory that children learn behaviors as a result of a series of rewards and punishments.

Operational definitions: created by researchers at the outset of research to describe or characterize the constructs (concepts) that are being studied.

Opportunity cost method: attempts to value household work by asking "What would a person be paid in wage labor for one hour of household work?"

Oral-genital sex (oral sex): stimulation of the genitals using the mouth or tongue.

Oral stage: the psychosexual stage from birth to about age 1 when the focus of sensual energy is the mouth and the tongue; the emphasis for personality development is thus centered on breastfeeding. See also **Psychosexual stages.**

Pair bond: a couple who is emotionally bonded to one another, which characterizes the couple's union.

Paradox of Mexican American nuptiality: the phenomenon in which divorce rates among Mexican Americans are lower than among Blacks, despite the fact that Mexican Americans are more educationally and economically disadvantaged.

Passion: the physical attraction and romantic feelings that initially draw us to another person.

Passionate love: a wildly powerful emotion experienced as intense longing for the selected love object, along with profound sexual arousal and confused feelings.

Patriarchal family structure: a family form that includes the father figure, his wife, and his children. Everyone in the family is considered to be under the authority of the patriarch, the father.

Peer marriage: a marriage in which partners agree to shared responsibility for all aspects of marriage, from earning money to raising the children to how they spend their leisure time. Equity and fairness are hallmarks of peer marriages.

Pelvic inflammatory disease (PID): a disorder caused by untreated sexually transmitted infections (e.g., gonorrhea and chlamydia) that results in a fertilized ovum having difficulty reaching the uterus due to blocked or scarred fallopian tubes.

Permissive parents: also referred to as *indulgent parents,* permissive parents demonstrate high levels of warmth, affection, and responsiveness toward their children, and also show adequate to high levels of parent-child communication. This parenting style does not place high demands on children, nor do parents attempt to control their children's behavior; children's behavior is mostly self-regulated.

Personal commitment: the feelings, thoughts, and beliefs we have about a spouse, life mate, or significant other.

Personal context: factors specific to each member of the couple, such as personality traits and the attitudes and beliefs about the overall status of the relationship; emotional reactions to intimacy; willingness to self-disclose; and each partner's intimacy needs, goals, and motives.

Personality need fulfilment: an established pattern of mutual exchanges of support, sympathy, and decision making. Each person also satisfies his or her partner's deeper emotional and sexual needs.

Phallic stage: the psychosexual stage from ages 3 to 6, during which children are intensely interested in the physical differences between men and women. See also **Psychosexual stages.**

Philos: brotherly love, used to describe the affectionate feelings shared between friends and family.

Physical custody: the legal right to have a child live primarily with one parent, who becomes the custodial parent.

Physical violence: violence that includes such acts as hitting, punching, pushing, slapping, biting, or throwing something at the victim.

Pile-up: the accumulation of stressors that can result from either a single stressor that coincides with life events/changes, multiple stressors, or multiple stressors that coincide with life events/changes.

Pink-collar phenomenon: the tendency for women to be concentrated in certain occupational categories.

Plan B: see **Emergency contraception.**

Polyamory: the practice of intimate relationships with more than one partner with all partners' consent.

Polyandry: the practice of a woman having multiple husbands at the same time.

Polygamy: the practice of having more than one marriage partner.

Polygyny: the practice of a man having multiple wives at the same time.

Pool of candidates: eligible relationship partners.

Population: the entire group of people who share a common experience or characteristic under academic examination.

Poverty line: the estimated minimum income necessary for a family to meet basic needs, such as food, shelter, clothing, and other essentials.

Poverty rate: the percentage of people with incomes below the published poverty line.

Power and Control Wheel: a model depicting behaviors batterers use to control and dominate their intimate partners and/or children.

Pragma love: practicality and logic guide the pragmatic lover; the costs and benefits associated with love are carefully weighed and considered before entering into a relationship.

Pre-crowd stage: from about kindergarten through fifth grade, isolated same-sex peer groups exist in the form of cliques, or small groups, of four to nine members. Spontaneous shared activities provide the opportunity to relate personally.

Predatory stalkers: stalkers who spy on the victim in order to plan a sexual attack.

Preinteraction cues: at-a-glance information that helps us decide whether we would even consider wanting a date with a certain person. Outward attractiveness would be an example of a preinteraction cue.

Preintimates: individuals who are capable of intimacy, and may even desire it, but lack the ability to make the commitment necessary to sustain long-term relationships.

Premature ejaculation: see **Rapid ejaculation.**

Preventing-the-problems focus: family life educator Richard Kerckhoff maintained that families faced with radical societal changes only need to be shown how to do the correct things to prevent family problems.

Primary aging: basic biological processes that are genetically programmed to occur over time.

Primary divorce stressors: provisions such as custody arrangements, visitation, and child support.

Proactive discipline: using techniques that encourage appropriate behavior and that discourage inappropriate behaviors.

Probability sample: a random sample in which each person has the same likelihood (probability) of being selected for the study.

Problem-focused coping: a coping strategy that allows the family to confront the reality of the crisis head-on by seeking and obtaining information about the crisis.

Problem management: management strategies aimed at directly attacking the stressor or changing the stressor.

Progressive desensitization: occurs when family members gradually allow themselves increasing exposure to the varying aspects of the stressor.

Pronatalism: an ideology that embraces childbearing.

Propinquity: geographical closeness.

Protector/provider cues: the cues women tend to look for in a mate, such as intelligence, physical strength, and ambition.

Protest reactions: behaviors and feelings that attempt to reestablish a relationship, such as trying to reinvolve the ex-partner in sexual relations.

Prototype: a model. Researcher Beverly Fehr asked her study sample to free write various features or attributes they assigned to "love." The list provided a prototype of love.

Pseudointimate: a person or relationship that appears to be intimate but lacks depth.

Psychoanalytic theory: the theory of personality development in children developed by Sigmund Freud.

Psychosexual stages: in Sigmund Freud's view, development takes place through a series of psychosexual stages, in which sensual energy or satisfaction is focused on one particular part of the body. See also **anal stage, genital stage, latency stage, oral stage, phallic stage.**

Psychosocial: the social and emotional aspects of development.

Psychosocial development: the social and emotional development of an individual.

Punishment: something that decreases the likelihood that a behavior will be repeated. See also **Operant conditioning.**

Qualitative research: a form of research that involves detailed verbal or written descriptions of characteristics under investigation.

Quantitative research: a form of research that uses statistical methods to count and measure outcomes from a study.

Quiverfull movement: a fundamentalist Christian group that encourages couples to have many children because of a desire to be obedient to what they believe are commands in the Bible.

Racial/ethnic socialization: the way in which families teach children about the social meanings of their race/ethnicity.

Racism: a belief system that holds that race accounts for differences in human character and/or ability; it results in discrimination and prejudice based on someone's race or ethnic background.

Rapid ejaculation (RE): ejaculation that occurs before, on, or shortly after penetration with minimal sexual stimulation.

Rapport: a connection or bond we feel with another person.

Raw numbers: actual numbers, not derived percentages or statistics; e.g., the actual number of people who marry and divorce.

Receiver: the spouse who is on the receiving end of the partner's intent to dissolve the marriage.

Reflective listening: a form of active listening in which we pay close attention to a person's verbal and emotional messages and respectfully acknowledge their perspective.

Refractory period: the period following orgasm when men are incapable of achieving an erection. The length of the refractory period is directly associated with age and other factors such as health and lifestyle habits.

Reframe: to view the issue from another perspective.

Regulated couples: regulated couples use communication patterns and interpersonal behaviors that promote closeness and intimacy, such as using more positive comments than negative comments during times of tension.

Reiss's Wheel Theory of Love: sociologist Ira Reiss described love as a developmental process that unfolds over time, with four stages: rapport, self-revelation, mutual dependency, and personality need fulfillment. Similar to a rolling wheel, these stages of love may be experienced many times and, in turn, deepen the love bonds between partners.

Rejected stalkers: stalkers who want to reverse, correct, or avenge rejection of their affections, infatuation, or love.

Rejection costs: include rejection sensitivity (anxiety, lowered self-esteem), immunity to rejection (frequency of past rejections), and the emotional cost of the rejection.

Relational context: characteristics of the relationship and how the couple defines it. Factors such as companionship, trust, commitment level, intimacy needs, and type of conflict.

Relational culture: a framework of understandings—a private, unique, distinct language—that couples construct in private.

Relational expectancies: the expectations about their marriage and spouse that couples enter marriage with, which have developed throughout the course of their lives. Relational expectancies are key factors in marital satisfaction and marriage longevity.

Relational messages: messages that have something to do with the partner or relationship.

Relational transgressions: hurtful words or actions that communicate a devaluation of the partner or the relationship.

Relationship stability: the perceptions and behaviors associated with the dissolution of a marriage or committed relationship.

Religiosity: an individual's preference for religious expression.

Remarriage: a marriage in which one or both spouses have been previously married.

Remote relationship: the distant grandparent who has little or no contact with grandchildren and is only involved on occasional holidays or birthdays.

Replacement fertility rate: the average number of children born per woman, at which the population is exactly replaced.

Representativeness: the degree to which the characteristics of the population are represented by the sample.

Research: to study the family thoroughly using the process of scholarly or scientific inquiry.

Research integrity: the relationship between researchers and the truth in reporting their findings.

Research question: the research question, or research hypothesis, is the core of any valid project and takes into account a clear understanding of the problem to be addressed and a clear vision of the objective. With these addressed, the answer to this question is presented clearly and concisely.

Resentful stalkers: stalkers who are out for vengeance because they believe they were wronged by their victim.

Residual tasks: household tasks such as bill paying, yard work, and chauffeuring children.

Resigned acceptance: the ultimate acceptance of circumstances, as when family members recognize that nothing will change the course their family life has taken.

Resource dilution hypothesis: a theory that contends parents' finite resources become diluted when spread over a larger number of children.

Response bias: when using human beings as subjects, this is the risk whereby subjects' past and current experiences may affect their responses. This is a flaw that may occur when researchers rely on individuals' self-reports.

Response rate: the percentage of study subjects who respond to the survey.

Responsiveness: the verbal and/or nonverbal behavior that conveys support and affection to a partner.

Retroactive jealousy: a type of jealousy that occurs when a romantic partner is bothered by their partner's past romantic or sexual relationships.

Rewards: the benefits (the payback, profit, or compensations) exchanged in a social relationship to reinforce behavior and increase the likelihood that the behavior will occur again. Offered consistently, relationship rewards such as nurture, appreciation, trust, and making/seeing the other person happy develop a strong sense of liking in a relationship. Essentially, whatever attributes a person has on her or his love prototype list are her or his perceived rewards in the relationship.

Risk and Protective Factor Model: assumes that every family form has protective factors, which positively influence children, and risk factors, which have a potentially negative impact on families and children; the overall experience of the children is determined by whether the protective factors outweigh the risk factors or vice versa.

Role: a key concept in Symbolic Interaction theory is that of role, or a "system of meanings." A woman may simultaneously have the role of wife, mother, sister, daughter, aunt, and so forth. She will take on the role of actor and follow the rules—the expectations—assigned to that role.

Romantic infatuation: a type of infatuation that is often referred to as *romantic love.* Defined in the *American Heritage Dictionary* as "a foolish, unreasoning, or extravagant passion or attraction," and "an object of extravagant short-lived passion," romantic infatuation involves a complicated, often overpowering, blend of emotion and sexuality.

Romantic love: intimacy and passion comprise romantic love. Because of the accompanying physical and/or sexual attraction and arousal, it is a more intense form of love than liking.

Romantic orientations: the sex or gender with which a person is likely to have a romantic relationship or fall in love.

Routine housework: house cleaning, meal preparation, grocery shopping, cleaning up after meals, and laundry.

Sacrament of marriage: marriage as a sacred act, dissolved only by the death of one partner.

Sample: a group of people from whom researchers collect survey responses.

Sample size: the value (number, weight, etc.) of the sample. Sample size affects the degree to which the sample is considered to be representative.

Sandwich generation: adults who are parenting adolescents or younger children while at the same time caring for aging parents.

Scapegoating: an example of displacement, scapegoating occurs when anger and hostility are directed at one family member in particular who always bears the brunt of everyone's frustration.

Scientific method: the process by which researchers formulate questions concerning social and individual phenomena and seek out answers.

Script theory: the theory that individuals use scripts (information about expected, stereotypical actions) that help us organize the information in our environments.

Search costs: include our attractiveness, or our ability to attract potential partners, along with social networking skills.

Second shift: sociologist Arlie Hochschild's (1989) term for the burden of the dual responsibilities of wage earner and housekeeper.

Secondary aging: physiological declines that are the result of environmental and behavioral influences, which significantly affect how we age.

Secondary divorce stressors: the "fallout" associated with divorce, including depression and greater risks for health problems.

Secure attachment types: secure adults, like securely attached infants, have little difficulty seeking or maintaining closeness with another. They don't fear being abandoned or losing their partner.

Self-disclosure: voluntarily sharing things with someone else that are personal or private to us.

Self-revelation: when we feel comfortable in another person's presence, we feel more comfortable self-disclosing our personal hopes, dreams, fears, and goals. See also **Self-disclosure**.

Self-righteousness: the inability to see one's own potential for doing wrong or hurting another person; a pride-related barrier to forgiveness.

Separate couple: a married couple who do not share the levels of companionship of traditional or independent couple types; they tend to share fewer positive feelings about their spouse and about their relationship than the other couple types do. Individuals in this couple type are less willing to relinquish their autonomy than those in traditional and independent couple types. They report lower levels of self-disclosure and sharing, and, as a result, experience psychological distance.

Separation period: a period marked by a disruption in the norms of family relationships. To some, it may mean a cooling off period; to others, it may mean the first step on the way to the divorce attorneys.

Sex: biological traits that distinguish males from females, such as the internal and external reproductive anatomy, chromosomes, hormones, and other physiological characteristics.

Sex confirmation surgery (SCS): the surgical alteration to the body that transforms a person's gender from male to female or female to male.

Sex hormones: hormones that direct sexual differentiation in the womb and continue to influence sexual maturation through puberty.

Sex reassignment surgery (SRS): see **Sex confirmation surgery (SCS)**.

Sexism: a prejudice or discrimination based on biological sex; a belief system that assumes a hierarchy of human worth based on the social construction of the differences between the sexes; an ideology of male supremacy, superiority, authority, and beliefs/behaviors that support and sustain this ideology.

Sexual assault: illegal sexual contact that usually involves force upon a person without consent or is inflicted upon a person who is incapable of giving consent.

Sexual differentiation: the prenatal physiological and anatomical differentiation into male and female.

Sexual dysfunction: the inability to fully enjoy sex.

Sexual harassment: any unwelcome sexual or physical conduct by a person of either gender, directed to a person of either gender.

Sexual orientation: the focus of a person's erotic desires or fantasies, or a person's affectionate or romantic feelings toward a particular gender.

Sexual preference: the term used by people who believe that sexuality is fluid and is more a matter of choice than of biology.

Sexual scripting framework: the notion that societal and cultural processes ultimately determine and proscribe what we perceive as "sexual" and how we behave sexually.

Sexual scripts: shared, gender-specific social and cultural expectations that guide our beliefs, attitudes, and values about sex, such as our beliefs about appropriate sexual partners, sexual behaviors, and sexual conduct.

Sexual selection: a form of natural selection that happens in two ways: (1) Members of one sex compete among themselves for opportunities to mate, thereby "out-reproducing" other competitors; and (2) a sex chooses to mate with a specific, more preferable person.

Sexual violence: violence that is sexual in nature, including marital rape, battering rape, and forced sexual acts.

Sexuality: the erotic arousal and genital responses resulting from following sexual scripts of a society.

Sexually transmitted infections (STI): infectious diseases transmitted between partners through sexual contact.

Shared care: a child care arrangement in which parents share a babysitter or nanny.

Shared legal custody: an arrangement in which both parents have an equal say in a child's upbringing.

Shift work: working nonstandard hours or working a schedule other than the typical Monday to Friday work week.

Simple infatuation: physical attraction that is often accompanied by emotion-filled daydreams and fantasies about someone, perhaps an actor or actress, a pop star or singing idol, or even a teacher.

Single-parent family: families with only one parent, as a result of the choice of the parent or of circumstance such as divorce, the death of a spouse, or unmarried parenthood.

Social capital: an individual's pool of social resources found in his or her personal network.

Social clock: culturally established norms associated with the timing of events. The social clock includes rites of passage, such as graduating from high school or college, getting married, or retiring—all by a socially and culturally accepted age.

Social ecology: the perspective that recognizes that individual family members' experiences, as well as outside social factors and policies, significantly affect the quality and the nature of their relationships.

Social Exchange theory: this theory centers on the exchange of people's material or symbolic resources, asserting that individuals act out of self-interest to capitalize on the resources they possess.

Social Expectations model: developed by psychologist Mary Levitt, this model illustrates how spouses' expectations of marital relationships are based on past relationship interactions with the spouse. This model also takes into account the influence of societal norms on spousal expectations.

Social identity: whether the goals of a society/culture emphasize the advancement of the group's interests or individual interests. See also **Collectivist cultures, Individualist cultures.**

Social Learning theory (SET): Albert Bandura's (1925–present) theory that children acquire behaviors and personality traits by observing others. An offshoot of the traditional Behaviorism theory, this theory addresses the roles of reward and punishment, and it goes a step further to include an individual's realm of cognition—the role of observation—in the process of learning.

Social phase: according to Stephen Duck, the public disclosure of a couple's decision to terminate the marriage.

Social Readjustment Rating Scale (SRRS): a scale identifying associations between life events and life transitions and the impact of those events and transitions on individual physical health and well-being.

Social science research: the scholarly discipline used to examine human society and relationships.

Social union: a legal relationship between two people that provides legal protections to the couple at the state level.

Social welfare: a group of government or private assistant programs designed to ensure the well-being of the nation's disadvantage groups (impoverished, ill, elderly).

Socialization hypothesis: the hypothesis that because children of divorce have less experience with successful marital role models, they are less able to cope with their own marital difficulties and are thus at greater risk for divorce.

Socialization needs: a goal of parenting is to meet the socialization needs of children, which encompasses ensuring they become productive, contributing members of society.

Sociocultural context: the norms, beliefs, and ideals of the culture and subcultures in which couples live and relate.

Sociocultural theories: theories maintaining that children's development does not occur by stages but through direct interaction with culture, which shapes their values, goals, and expectations.

Socioeconomic status (SES): the government's measure of a family's relative economic and social ranking within a community.

Sociological or incidental cue: the first filter of Stephen Duck's system, this relates to the restrictions and limitations placed on one's ability to meet people. These cues speak to one's sociological location or position or the places where one lives and works.

Sole custody: an arrangement in which one parent is the primary parent—legally, physically, or both legally and physically.

Solution-focused therapy model: a type of therapy that focuses on a person's present and future circumstances and goals, not on past experiences.

Specialization: the element of marriage in which each spouse can take on tasks and concentrate on those things he or she does well.

Speed dating: a quick face-to-face meeting that enables people to decide whether they share mutual interests and are interested in another, more extended, date.

Sperm bank: sperm for artificial insemination procedures is retrieved from donors and stored in sperm banks.

Spousal support: see **Alimony.**

Stability: the stability provided by marriage allows men to mature, making them more likely to find a job and think toward the future instead of engaging in risk-taking behaviors such as drug and alcohol abuse. Married men and women are also more likely to accept and maintain jobs that may not be as personally rewarding, but are in the couple/family's best economic interests.

Stalking: the obsessive following, observing, or contacting of another person, or the obsessive attempt to engage in any of these activities.

Status: employers tend to pay married men and women at a higher rate than single men and women. This discrimination toward unmarried men allows for great economic gain and greater economic opportunities for married men, thereby affording them and their families a certain status unmarried individuals do not have.

Stay-at-home dads: fathers who have remained out of the labor force for at least one year primarily so they can care for their children while their wives or partners work outside of the home.

Stepfamily: a family formed when, after death or divorce, a parent marries again. A stepfamily is also formed when a never-married person marries someone who has children.

Stereotyped relationships: relationships in which an individual has a number of casual relationships that are devoid of commitment.

Sterility: the absolute inability to reproduce, either because the woman has no uterus or ovaries, or the male has no testes or sperm production.

Stillbirth: the death of a fetus after the 20th week of pregnancy. Stillbirth occurs approximately once in every 115 births, or about 26,000 per year.

Stonewalling: takes place when communication between marital partners completely shuts down. Either one or both spouses distance themselves by refusing to communicate, ignoring each other, and becoming remote.

Storge: friendship love, or a type of affectionate love between companions.

Storgic lovers: people who typically come to love each other over time, as opposed to the instantaneous type of love found with eros lovers.

Strain-based conflict: occurs when the demands in one domain make it difficult to perform effectively in another domain.

Stressor: anything that elicits a physiological and/or psychological response to any stimuli.

Structural commitment: commitments bound by institutions such as marriage.

Structural factors: a family's finances and economic status; these factors are integral to the formation and maintenance of marriages and other intimate relationships.

Structural-Functionalist theory: this theory, introduced by Talcott Parsons, maintains that gender-based role specialization is a necessary function in order to promote family (and, hence, societal) equilibrium.

Structures: patterns of role arrangement within a society.

Subsystems: the relational patterns and interactions among the separate individuals within a family.

Supportive co-parenting: parents who directly or indirectly agree by promoting the same general message to the child, or when one parent directly asks the other for assistance with an issue that involves the child.

Surrogate mother: a woman who carries the fetus of another couple.

Survey: a structured questionnaire comprising a list of questions.

Survival needs: food, shelter, safety, security, and love—provision of survival needs is a goal of parenting.

Symbolic Interaction theory: this approach to examining family life and family communication assumes that human behavior is a continuous dialogue in which people watch the behaviors of other people and then react to these behaviors.

Symbols: in an attempt to share meanings, each culture uses symbols, or codes. Some symbols are universal behaviors, such as the kiss, which represents affection, love, or a greeting.

Syphilis: a sexually transmitted bacterial infection caused by a microscopic organism; may be either congenital or acquired through sexual contact or contaminated needles.

System: according to Rosenblatt, it means to "piece together" or to connect one entity to another.

Temporal influences: the passage of time that may mitigate the effects of divorce.

Testosterone: the masculinizing hormone produced by the testicles.

Theory: a general principle that is used to understand or to explain certain events or family experiences.

Time-based conflict: takes place when demands from the work domain and the family domain vie for a parent's time and attention.

Timing: refers to the age at which a transition takes place.

Total fertility rate: the average number of live births per woman, in a given population, per year.

Traditional couple: a married couple who adhere to conventional beliefs about marriage. These couples are interdependent in their relationship and prefer to be less independent and self-sufficient than the other marital types.

Transactional: the dynamic process whereby our exchanges with others simultaneously affect and are affected by our intimate relations.

Transactional Model of Stress: according to this model, stress is the result of an interaction between the person and his or her environment.

Transgender: an umbrella term for people whose gender identity and/or gender expression differs from their assigned sex at birth.

Transition: the third stage of labor, during which contractions occur as frequently as every 90 seconds and last for 90 seconds and the cervix is dilated to 10 centimeters; at this time, pushing can begin.

Transsexual: an older term for someone who has permanently changed or seeks to change their body through medical interventions because their identity is opposite to the sex they were assigned at birth.

Triangular Theory of Love: Robert Sternberg's theory conceptualizes eight different types of love relationships. These relationships take into account that each individual will experience many types of love throughout life.

Trouble talk: talking about emotional and relationship problems.

Turning point: a transition that entails a permanent, lasting shift in the direction of the lifecourse of a person's relationship.

Unexpected quick trajectory: a rapid transition from life to death with elements of time pressure and surprise, when there is typically not enough time to save the life of the injured or ill person and there is no time allowed for friends and family to plan or to prepare themselves emotionally.

Uninvolved parents: parents who are typically low in responsiveness, warmth, and affection. They are also low in parental control or demands. Both parents reject and neglect their children.

Universal health care: guaranteed access to quality medical treatment, for all citizens, without regard to their ability to pay.

Unsupportive co-parenting: one parent undermines the other parent's efforts, interrupts the interactions of the other parent and child, is openly critical of the other's parenting styles or parenting activity, or ignores the other parent's request for assistance with a child's needs.

Urban tribe: refers to mixed-gender circles of friends (typically in their twenties or thirties) who are the primary social support system for singles.

Validity: the extent to which a researcher is able to provide an empirical definition that reflects the true meaning of the construct being considered.

Variable: a characteristic that is measured in a study. The value of the characteristic varies among the people or group being studied, hence the name.

Verbal communication: refers to exchanges of thoughts, messages, or information through the spoken word.

Violence Against Women Act of 1994 (VAWA): federal law signed by President Bill Clinton in 1994 to provided more than $1.6 billion for financial restitution to women who were victims of violent crimes. The Act expired in 2019. As of 2020, although it was passed in the House of Representatives, the VAWA is stalled by the U.S. Senate.

Viral hepatitis: an inflammation of the liver causing impairments in liver function; there are three types of viral hepatitis: Hepatitis A, Hepatitis B, and Hepatitis C.

Wage discrimination: the discrimination shown in the payment of wages, salaries, and earnings to minority groups.

Wage gap: the inequality between men's and women's wages in the United States.

White-collar professional occupations: professional occupations such as attorneys, bankers, and doctors.

Women's Liberation: a feminist movement that put forth the idea that women suffered oppression in patriarchal, male-dominated cultures such as those in the United States.

Work–family spillover/crossover: occurs when a spouse carries the emotional events and tensions of one environment to the other.

Working poor: people who are working but who continue to remain below the poverty threshold for their family size.

X factor: in Reuben Hill's ABC-X Family Crisis Model, X factors are the outcomes of the event, the results of whether or not a family copes effectively with the crisis event.

XX sex chromosome: this chromosome combination results in a "female" genetic blueprint for the developing embryo.

XY sex chromosome: this chromosome combination results in a "male" genetic blueprint for the developing embryo.

Zygote intrafallopian transfer (ZIFT): an assisted reproductive technology process in which an egg is fertilized outside of the body and then is placed immediately in the woman's fallopian tubes, allowing the conceptus to travel naturally to the uterus and implant.

/// CHAPTER 1

Alberts, M. (2002). The ecological model of human development: The foundation for a family policy perspective. *The University of Minnesota Children, Youth, and Family Consortium.* Retrieved from http://www.cyfc.umn.edu/publications/connettion/pubs/05summer/0l-foundationfamilypolicy.html

Anderson, J. (2014). The impact of family structure on the health of children: Effects of divorce. *Linacre Quarterly,* 81(4), 378–387.

Arab American Institute. (2019). Who are Arab Americans? Retrieved May 26, 2019 from http://www.aaiusa.org

Arcus, M. (1993). *Handbook of family life education.* Thousand Oaks, CA: SAGE.

Arcus, M. E., Schvaneveldt, J. D., & Moss, J.J. (1993). The nature of family life education. In M. E. Arcus, J. D. Schvaneveldt, and J. J. Moss (Eds.), *Handbook of family life education: Foundations of family life education* (Vol. 1). Newbury Park, CA: SAGE.

Banerjee, M. (2019). More than one-third of American kids have lived in extended family households. Retrieved May 23, 2019, from www.phys.org/news/2018-01-one-third-american-kids-family-households.html

Banks, J. A., & McGee-Banks, C. A. (2002). *Multicultural education: Issues and perspectives* (4th ed.). New York: Wiley.

Barbour, C., Barbour, N. H., & Scully, P.A. (2005). *Families, schools, and communities: Building partnerships for educating children.* Upper Saddle River, NJ: Pearson.

Ben David, M. (2006). From a woman's place: The case for polygamy. Retrieved from www.polygamy.com/practical/From-A-Woman-Place.htm

Boellstorff, T. (2005). Between religion and desire: Being Muslim and gay in Indonesia. *American Anthropologist* 107(4), 575–585.

Bouhdiba, A. (2001). Sexuality in Islam. San Francisco: Saqi Books.

Bronfenbrenner, U. (1979). *The ecology of human development: Experiments by nature and design.* Cambridge, MA: Harvard University Press.

Carlson, J., & Dermer, S. B. (2017). The SAGE encyclopedia of marriage, family, and couples counseling. Thousand Oaks, CA: SAGE.

Carranza, M. A., Gouveia, L., Cogua, J., & Ondracek-Sayers, K. (2002). The integration of the Hispanic/Latino immigrant workforce: Final project report. *Task Force on the Productive Integration of the Immigrant Workforce Population.* Retrieved from http://lri.unl.edu/HLIWSREPORTfinal.pdf

Castañeda, D. M. (1993) The meaning of romantic love among Mexican-Americans. *Journal of Social Behavior and Personality,* 8(2), 257–272.

Chapman, S. (2004). Practical aspects of polygamy: The benefits polygamy has for women and the controls it places on men. Retrieved from www.polygamy.com/Practical-Aspects-of-Polygamy.html

Child Trends. (2018a). Births to unmarried women. Retrieved May 13, 2019 from www.childtrends.org/indicators/births-to-unmarried-women

Child Trends. (2018b). Immigrant children. Retrieved May 11, 2019 from www.childtrends.org/indicators/immigrant-children

Cilluffo, A., & Cohn, D. (2019). Six demographic trends shaping the U.S. and the world in 2019. Retrieved May 23, 2019 from www.pewresearch.org/fact-tank/2019/04/11/6-demographic-trends-shaping-the-u-s-and-the-world-in-2019/

Conger, R. D., & Conger, K. J. (2002). Resilience in midwestern families: Selected findings from the first decade of a prospective, longitudinal study. *Journal of Marriage and Family,* 64, 361–373.

Constante, K., Marchand, A. D., Cross, F. L., & Rivas-Drake, D. (2019). Understanding the promotive role of familism in the link between ethnic-racial identity and Latino youth school engagement. *Journal of Latinx Psychology,* 7(3), 230–244.

Coontz, S. (1992). *The way we never were: American families and the nostalgia trap.* New York: Basic Books.

Coontz, S. (1999). *American families: A multicultural reader.* New York: Routledge.

Czaplewski, M. J., & Jorgensen, S. R. (1993). The professionalization of family life education. In M. E. Arcus, J. D. Schvaneveldt, and J. J. Moss (Eds.), *Handbook of family life education: Foundations of family life education* (pp. 51–75). Newbury Park, CA: SAGE.

Darling, C. A. (1987). Family life education. In M. B. Sussman and S. K. Steinmetz (Eds.), *Handbook of marriage and the family* (pp. 815–833). New York: Plenum.

David, M. B. (2005). From a woman's place: The case for polygamy. Retrieved from www.polygamy.com/practical/From-A-Woman-Place.htm

Davis, D. A., & Davis, S. S. (1993). Sexual values in a Moroccan town. In W. J. Lonner and R. S. Malpass (Eds.), *Psychology and culture* (pp. 225–230). Boston: Allyn & Bacon.

DeFrain, J. (2018). The state of the American family: The paradox of how families and family values are changing while staying the same. *RUDN Journal of Sociology,* 18, 73–87.

Dimock, M. (2019). Defining generations: Where Millennials end and Gen Z begins. Retrieved April 17, 2020 from https://www.pewresearch.org/fact-tank/2019/01/17/where-millennials-end-and-generation-z-begins/

Dion, K. L., & Dion, K. K. (1993). Individualistic and collectivistic perspectives on gender and the cultural context of love and intimacy. *Journal of Social Issues,* 49, 53–69.

Dutton, M. A. (1998, March/April). Cultural issues in trauma treatment. *Centering Newsletter,* 3(2).

Fernandez-Dols, J. M. (1999). Facial expression and emotion: A situationist view. In P. Philippot, R. S. Feldman, & E. J. Coats (Eds.), *The social context of nonverbal behavior* (2nd ed.; vol. 1; pp. 242–261). Cambridge: Cambridge University Press.

Fleming, W. C. (2007). Getting past our myths and stereotypes about Native Americans. *The Educational Digest,* 72(7), 51–58.

Fong, T. P. (2002). *The contemporary Asian American experience: Beyond the model minority* (2nd ed.). Upper Saddle River, NJ: Prentice Hall.

Gaille, B. (2017). 21 noteworthy statistics of blended families. Retrieved March 12, 2019 from https://brandongaille.com/20-noteworthy-statistics-of-blended-families/

Girls Not Brides. (2020). Child marriage around the world. Retrieved from https://www.girlsnotbrides.org/where-does-it-happen/

Goldberg Jones. (2018, August). *Breaking down divorce stats by generation.* Retrieved March 15, 2019 from www.goldbergjones-wa.com/divorce/divorce-by-generation/

Goldstein, M. C. (1987/2002). When brothers share a wife. *Natural History,* 96(3), 109–112.

Hadfield, K., & Ungar, M. (2018). Family resilience: Emerging trends in theory and practice. *Journal of Family Social Work,* 21(2), 81–84.

Hellerstedt, W. L., Peterson-Hickey, M., Rhodes, K. L., & Garwick, A. (2006). Environmental, social, and personal correlates of having ever had sexual intercourse among American Indian youths. *American Journal of Public Health,* 96(12), 2228–2234.

Huitt, W. (2003). A systems model of human behavior. *Educational Psychology Interactive.* Valdosta, GA: Valdosta State University.

Hull, K. (2018). Conventional and cutting-edge: Definitions of family in LGBT communities. *Sexuality Research and Social Policy,* 1–13.

Institut National de la Statistique. (2013). Enquête démographique et de santé et à indicateurs multiples du Niger 2012. Retrieved from https://www.dhsprogram.com/pubs/pdf/FR277/FR277.pdf

Institute of Family Studies. (2019). Cohabitation is pervasive. Retrieved May 10, 2019 from www.ifstudies.org/blog/cohabitation-is-pervasive

Johnson, T., Kulesa, P., Cho, Y., & Shavitt, S. (2005). The relation between culture and response styles: Evidence from 19 countries. *Journal of Cross-Cultural Psychology,* 36, 264–277.

Kerckhoff, R. K. (1964). Family life education in America. In H. T. Christensen (Ed.), *Handbook of marriage and the family* (pp. 881–911). Chicago: Rand McNally.

Kids Count Data Center. (2019a). Children in single-parent families by race in the United States. Retrieved May 24, 2019 from https://datacenter.kidscount.org

Kids Count Data Center. (2019b). Children who live in two-parent families, by race ethnicity in the United States. Retrieved May 24, 2019 from https://datacenter.kidscount.org

Kupperbusch, C, Matstumoto, D., Kooken, K., Loewinger. S., Uchida, H., Wilson-Cohn, C., & Yrizarry, N. (1999). Cultural influences on nonverbal expressions of emotion. In P. Philippot, R. S. Feldman, and E. J. Coats (Eds.), *The social context of nonverbal behavior* (2nd ed.; vol. 1; pp. 17–44). Cambridge: Cambridge University Press.

Makes Marks, L. F. (2007). Great mysteries: Native North American religions and participatory visions. *Revision*, 29(3), 29–37.

McWilliams, P. (1998). *Ain't nobody's business if you do: The absurdity of consensual crimes in a free country*. Los Angeles, CA: Prelude Press.

Ministry of Health and Family Welfare. (2016). India fact sheet. Retrieved from https://dhsprogram.com/pubs/pdf/OF31/India_National_FactSheet.pdf

Mitchell, V. (2008). Choosing family: Meaning and membership in the lesbian family of choice. *Journal of Lesbian Studies*, 12(2–3), 301–313.

Myers, D. G. (2008). *Social psychology* (9th ed.). New York: McGraw-Hill.

National Council on Family Relations. (2019). Strengthening families. Retrieved April 17, 2020 from http://www.ncfr.org

National Issues Forum. (1996). Retrieved from http://www.pbs.org/new-shour/forum/january96/fishkin_l-19.html

Neto, F. (2007). Forgiveness, personality and gratitude. *Personality and Individual Differences*, 43, 2313–2323.

Niemiec, R., Sikorski, M., & Walberg, H. (1999). Designing school volunteer programs. *NASSP Bulletin*, 83, 114–116.

Nord, W., & Haynes, C. (1998). *Taking religion seriously across the curriculum*. Alexandria, VA: Association for Supervision and Curriculum Development.

Pew Research Center. (2017a). Number of Muslims in the U.S. *continues to grow*. Retrieved May 23, 2019 from https://www.pewforum.org/2017/07/26/demographic-portrait-of-muslim-americans/pf_2017-06-26_muslimamericans-01new-12/

Pew Research Center. (2017b). Religion and public life. Retrieved May 23, 2019 from https://www.pewforum.org/2017/07/26/demographic-portrait-of-muslim-americans/pf_2017-06-26_muslimamericans-01new-02/

Pew Research Center. (2018a). About one-third of US children are living with an unmarried parent. Retrieved May 25, 2019 from www.pewresearch.org/fact-tank/2018/04/27/about-one-third-of-u-s-children-are-living-with-an-unmarried-parent.

Pew Research Center. (2018b). They're waiting longer, but U.S. women today more likely to have children than a decade ago. Retrieved May 13, 2019 from www.pewsocialtrends.org/2018/01/18/theyre-waiting-longer-but-u-s-women-today-more-likely-to-have-children-than-a-decade-age

Pew Research Center. (2018c). A record 64 million Americans live in multigenerational households. Retrieved May 13, 2019 from https://www.pewresearch.org/fact-tank/2018/04/05/a-record-64-million-americans-live-in-multigenerational-households/

Pew Research Center. (2019). Is U.S. fertility at an all-time low? Two of three measure point to yes. Retrieved May 13, 2019 from www.pewresearch.org/fact-tank/2018/05/22/u-s-fertility-rate-explained

Popenoe, D., & Whitehead, B. D. (2002). Why men won't commit: Exploring young men's attitudes about sex, dating, and marriage. *The National Marriage Project, Rutgers University*. Retrieved from www.marriage.rutgers.edu

Popenoe, D., & Whitehead, B. D. (2005). *The state of our unions*. New Brunswick, NJ: National Marriage Project.

Read, J. G. (2003), The sources of gender role attitudes among Christian and Muslim Arab-American women. *Sociology of Religion*, 64(2), 207–223.

Saad, F. M. (2002, July). Marriage in Africa: Islam versus culture. Paper presented to the Woman's World Congress, Makrere University, Kampala. Retrieved from www.makerere.ac.ug/womenstudies/full-papcrsySAAD.htm

Smith, W, M., Jr. (1968). Family life education—Who needs it? *The Family Coordinator*, 17, 55–61.

Solot, D., & Miller, M. (2004). Affirmation of family diversity. *Alternatives to Marriage Project*. Retrieved from www.unmarried.org/family.html

St. Vil, N. M., McDonald, K. B., & Cross-Barnet, C. (2018). A qualitative study of Black married couples' relationships with their extended family networks. *Families in Society: The Journal of Contemporary Social Services*, 99(1), 56–66.

Stack, P. F. (1998, September 20). Globally, polygamy is commonplace. *The Salt Lake Tribune*.

Starkweather, K., & Hames, R. (2012). A survey of non-classical polyandry. *Human Nature*, 23(2), 149–172.

Stein, G. L., Cavanaugh, A. M., Castro-Schilo, L., Mejia, Y., & Plunkett, S. W. (2019). Making my family proud: The unique contribution of familism pride to the psychological adjustment of Latinx emerging adults. *Cultural Diversity and Ethnic Minority Psychology*, 25(2), 188–198.

Taylor, R. L. (2000). Diversity within African American families. In D. H. Demo, K. R. Allen, & M.A. Fine (Eds.), *Handbook of family diversity* (pp. 232–251). New York: Oxford.

Taylor, T. S. (2005, January 19). When a marriage can't make room for daddy. *Chicago Tribune*. Retrieved from http://www.turnonyourinnerlight.com/ChicagoTribune01192005.htm

Triandis, H., & Suh, E. (2002). Cultural influences on personality. *Annual Review of Psychology*. 53, 133–160.

U.S. Census Bureau. (2018a). Black (African American) history month. Retrieved May 24, 2019 from www.census.gov

U.S. Census Bureau. (2018b). Household income by race and Hispanic origin: 1957 to 2017. Retrieved May 11, 2019 from www.census.gov/content/dam/Census/library/visualizations/2018/demo/p60-263/figure1.pdf

U.S. Census Bureau. (2019a). American Indian and Alaska Native heritage month. Retrieved May 24, 2019 from www.census.gov/newsroom/facts-for-features/2017/aian-month.html

U.S. Census Bureau. (2019b). America's family and living arrangements. *Current population survey (CPS)*. Retrieved May 13, 2019 from www.census.gov/data/tables/2017/demo/families/cps-2017.htm

U.S. Census Bureau. (2019c). Census Information Centers (CIC): Asian American data links. Retrieved May 24, 2019 from www.census.gov/about/partners/cic/resources/data-links/asian.html

U.S. Census Bureau. (2019d). Characteristics of same-sex couple households: 2005 to present. Retrieved May 10, 2019 from www.census.gov/data/tables/time-series/demo/same-sex-couples/ssc-house-characteristics.html

U.S. Census Bureau. (2019e). Current Population Survey (CPS): Subject definitions. Retrieved March 10, 2019 from www.census.gov/programs-surveys/cps/technical-documentation/subject-definitions.html#household

U.S. Census Bureau. (2019f). Selected population profile in the United States: 2018 American Community Survey 1-year estimates. Retrieved May 25, 2019 from www.census.gov/programs-surveys/acs

Vespa, J., Armstrong, D. M., & Medina, L. (2018). Demographic turning points for the United States: Population projections for 2020 to 2060. Current Population Reports, P25-1144. Washington, DC: U.S. Census Bureau.

Weiss, H. B. (1990). Beyond parens patriae: Building policies and programs to care for our own and others' children. *Children and Youth Services Review*, 12, 269–284.

Zahedi, A. (2007). Contested meanings of the veil and political ideologies of Iranian regimes. *Journal of Middle East Women's Studies*, 3(3), 75–99.

Zong, J., Batalova, J., and Burrows, M. (2019). Frequently requested statistics on immigrants and immigration in the United States. Retrieved May 25, 2019, from www.migrationpolicy.org/article/frequently-requested-statistics-immigrants-and-immigration-united-states

/// CHAPTER 2

Agresti, A., & Finlay, B. (2008), *Statistical methods for the social sciences* (4th ed.). Boston: Pearson Prentice Hall.

American Academy of Pediatrics, Committee on Psychosocial Aspects of Child and Family Health. (2002). Coparent or second parent adoption by same-sex parents. *Pediatrics*, 109, 339–240.

American Men's Studies Association. (2020). Advancing the critical study of men and masculinities. Retrieved April 17, 2020 from https://mensstudies.org/

Babbie, E. R. (2016). *The practice of social research* (14th ed.). Boston: Cengage.

Baiocco, R., Carone, N., Ioverno, S., & Lingiardi, V. (2019). Same-sex and different-sex parent families in Italy. *Journal of Developmental & Behavioral Pediatrics*, 39(7), 555–563.

Baiocco, R., Santamaria, F., Ioverno, S., Fontanesi, L., Baumgartner, E., Laghi, F., & Lingiardi, V. (2015). Lesbian mother families and gay father families in Italy: Family functioning, dyadic satisfaction, and child well-being. *Sexuality Research and Social Policy, A Journal of the SRC*, 12(3), 202–212.

Behson, S., Holmes, E. K., Hill, E. J., & Robbins, N. L. (2018). Fatherhood, work, and family across the globe: A review and research agenda. In K. M. Shockley, W. Shen, & R. C. Johnson (Eds.), *The Cambridge handbook of the global work–family interface* (pp. 614–628). London: Cambridge University Press. https://doi.org/10.1017/9781108235556.033

Bernardes, J. (2000). *Family studies: An introduction*. London: Routledge.

Bos, H. M., Know, J. R., vanRijn-van Gelderen, L., & Gartrell, N. K. (2016). Same-sex and different-sex parent households and child health outcomes: Findings from the National Survey of Children's Health. *Journal of Developmental and Behavioral Pediatrics*, 37(3), 179–187.

Boss, P. G., Doherty, W. J., LaRossa, R., Schumm, W. R., & Steinmetz, S. K. (1993). *Sourcebook of family theories and methods: A contextual approach*. New York: Plenum.

Cabrera, N. J., Volling, B. L., & Barr, R. (2018). Fathers are parents, too! Widening the lens on parenting for children's development. *Child Development Perspectives*, 12(3), 152–157. https://doi.org/10.1111/cdep.12275

Carter, B., & McGoldrick, M. (1999). *The expanded family life cycle: Individual, family, and social perspectives* (3rd ed.). Boston: Allyn & Bacon.

Carter, B., & McGoldrick, M. (2005). *The expanded family life cycle: Individual, family, and social perspectives* (4th ed.). Boston: Allyn & Bacon.

Coston, B. M., & Kimmel, M. (2012). White men as the new victims: Reverse discrimination cases and the Men's Rights Movement. *Nevada Law Journal*, 13, 368–385.

Davis, S. E. (2018). Objectification, sexualization, and misrepresentation: Social media and the college experience. *Social Media + Society*, July-September, 1–9.

Dillman, D. A. (1999). *Mail and Internet surveys: The tailored design method*. New York: Wiley.

Doan, L., & Quadlin, N. (2018). Partner characteristics and perceptions of responsibility for housework and child care. *Journal of Marriage and Family*, 81(1), 145–163.

Emmons, B., & Morcarski, R. (2014). She poses, he performs: A visual content analysis of male and female professional athlete Facebook profile photos. *Visual Communication Quarterly*, 21(3), 125–137.

Farr, R. H. (2017). Does parental sexual orientation matter? A longitudinal follow-up of adoptive families with school-age children. *Developmental Psychology*, 53(2), 252–264.

Fowers, B. J., & Olson, D. H. (1993), ENRICH marital satisfaction scale: A brief research and clinical tool. *Journal of Family Psychology*, 7(2), 176–185.

Fox, R. C., Lidz, V., & Bershady, H. L. (2005). *After Parsons: A theory of social action for the twenty-first century*. New York: Russell Sage Foundation.

Gartrell, N., Bos, M. W. B., Peyser, H., Deck, A., & Rodas, C. (2012). Adolescents with lesbian mothers describe their own lives. *Journal of Homosexuality*, 59(9), 1211–1229.

Golombok, S. (1983). Children in lesbian and single-parent households: Psychosexual and psychiatric appraisal. *Journal of Child Psychology*, 24(4), 551–572.

Golombok, S. (1999). Lesbian and gay families. In A. Bainham, S. Day Sclater, and M. Richards (Eds.), *What is a parent?* Oxford: Hart.

Guvensel, K., Dixon, A., Chang, C., & Dew, C. (2017). The relationship among gender role conflict, normative male alexithymia, men's friendship discords with other men, and psychological well-being. *The Journal of Men's Studies*, 26(1), 56–76.

Kamp, C. M., Dush, M. G., Taylor, R., & Kroger, A. (2008). Marital happiness and psychological well-being across the life course. *Family Relations*, 57, 211–226.

Kidder, L. H. (1981). *Selltiz, Wrightsman, and Cook's research methods in social relations*. New York: Holt, Rinehart, and Winston.

Laughlin, J. (2005). Men's studies and fatherhood. Retrieved from www.akamaiuniversity.us/MensStudies

Lengermann, P. M., & Brantley, J. N. (1988). Feminist theory. In G. Ritzer (Ed.), *Sociological theory* (pp. 400–443). New York: Knopf.

Maney, D. L. (2016). Perils and pitfalls of reporting sex differences. *Philosophical Transactions of the Royal Society B*, 371, 16–88.

Manzi, F. (2019). Are the processes underlying discrimination the same for women and men? A critical review of congruity models of gender discrimination. *Frontiers in Psychology*, 10, 489.

Marthouse, M. (2015). Defining meninism. Retrieved April 17, 2020 from https://themeninismmovement.wordpress.com/author/jmarthouse/

McCready, S., Harland, K., & Beattie, K. (2006, January). Violent victims? Young men as perpetrators and victims of violent crime. Centre for Men's Studies, Research Update No. 1. Retrieved from www.incore.ulst.ac.uk/about/specialist/cyms/CYMS_rul.pdf

National Academy of Sciences. (1995). *Research ethics*. Washington, DC: National Academy of Sciences Press.

National Council on Family Relationships. (2020). Understanding families: Research and practice. Retrieved from https://www.ncfr.org/membership

Neighbour, R. H. (1985). The family life cycle. *Journal of the Royal Society of Medicine*, 78(Suppl 8), 11–15.

Parsons, T. (1951). *The social system*. Glencoe, IL: Free Press.

Pearson, K. (1911). *The grammar of science* (3rd ed.). London: Adam and Charles Black.

Pedhazur, E. J., & Schmelkin, L. P. (1991). *Measurement, design, and analysis: An integrated approach*. Hillsdale, NJ: Erlbaum.

Pimple, K. D. (2001). *Six domains of research ethics*. Bloomington: Indiana University Poynter Center for the Study of Ethics and American Institutions.

Pitts, J. R. (1964). The structural functional approach. In E. T. Christensen (Ed.), *Handbook of marriage and the family*. Chicago: Rand McNally.

Schumm, W. R., Bell, B. D., & Gade, P. A. (2000). Effects of a military overseas peacekeeping deployment on marital quality, satisfaction, and stability. *Psychological Reports*, 87, 815–821.

Schwartz, M. A., & Scott, B. M. (2003). *Marriages and families: Diversity and change* (4th ed.). Upper Saddle River, NJ: Prentice Hall.

Smith, S. (1995). Family theory and multicultural family studies. In B. B. Ingoldsby and S. Smith (Eds.), *Families in multicultural perspective* (pp. 5–35). New York: Guilford.

U.S. Bureau of Labor Statistics. (2019). Women had higher median earnings than men in relatively few occupations in 2018. Retrieved April 17, 2020, from https://www.bls.gov/opub/ted/2019/women-had-higher-median-earnings-than-men-in-relatively-few-occupations-in-2018.htm

White, J. M., Klein, D. M., & Martin, T. F. (2014). *Family theories: An introduction* (4th ed.). Thousand Oaks, CA: SAGE.

Williams Institute. (2018). How many same-sex couples in the US are raising children? Retrieved from https://williamsinstitute.law.ucla.edu/publications/same-sex-parents-us/

Young, M., & Schieman, S. (2017). Scaling back and finding flexibility: Gender differences in parents' strategies to manage work-family conflict. *Journal of Marriage and Family*, 80(1), 99–118.

/// CHAPTER 3

Adetunji, R. R., & Sze, K. (2012). Understanding non-verbal communication across cultures: A symbolic interactionism approach. International Conference on Communication and Media, 2012, Penang, Malaysia, 103, November 2012. Retrieved March 28, 2020 from https://papers.ssrn.com/sol3/papers.cfm?abstract_id=2178486

Akechi, H., Senju, A., Uibo, H., Kikuchi, Y., Hasegawa, T., & Hietanen, J. K. (2013). Attention to eye contact in the West and East: Autonomic responses and evaluative ratings. *PLoS ONE*, 8(3): e59312. doi:10.1371/journal.pone.0059312

American Psychological Association. (2005). Controlling anger— before it controls you. Retrieved from www.apa.org/pubinfo/anger.html

Anderson, S. A., & Sabatelli, R. M. (2011). Family interaction: A multigenerational developmental perspective (5th ed.). Boston: Pearson.

Bagarozzi, D. A., & Anderson, S. A. (1989). *Personal, marital, and family myths: Theoretical formulations and clinical strategies*. New York: Norton.

Baumeister, R. (2002). Humility, egotism, forgiveness, and the victim role. Retrieved from www.forgiving.org.htm

Bippus, A. M. (2000). Humor usage in comforting messages: Factors predicting outcomes. Western *Journal of Communication*. 64, 359–384.

Blumer, H. (1969). Symbolic interaction. Englewood Cliffs, NJ: Prentice Hall.

Boss, P. G., Doherty, W. J., LaRossa, R., Schumm, W. R., & Steinmetz, S. K. (1993). *Sourcebook of family theories and methods: A contextual approach*. New York: Plenum.

Braithwaite, S.R., Mitchell, C.M., Selby, E.A., & Fincham, F.D. (2016). Trait forgiveness and enduring vulnerabilities neuroticism and catastrophizing influence relationship satisfaction via less forgiveness. *Personality and Individual Differences*, 94, 237–246.

Burleson, B. R. (1992). Taking communication seriously. *Communication Monographs*, 59, 79–86.

Burleson, B. R., & Denton, W. H. (1997). The relationship between communication skill and marital satisfaction: Some moderating effects. *Journal of Marriage and Family*, 9(4), 884–902.

Canary, D. J., Cody, M. J., & Manusov, V. (2000). *Interpersonal communication: A goals-based approach* (2nd ed.). New York: Bedford/St. Martin's Press.

Carton, J. S., Kessler, E. A., & Pape, C. L (1999). Nonverbal decoding skills and relationship well-being in adults. *Communication Monographs*, 69(1), 33–51.

Christensen, A., & Shenk, J. L. (1991). Communication, conflict, and psychological distance in nondistressed, clinic, and divorcing couples. *Journal of Consulting and Clinical Psychology*, 59, 458–463.

Coleman, M., & Ganong, L. H. (Eds.). (2003). *Handbook of contemporary families: Considering the past, contemplating the future*. Thousand Oaks, CA: SAGE.

David, P., & Stafford, L. (2015). A relational approach to religion and spirituality in marriage: The role of couples' religious communication in marital satisfaction. *Journal of Family Issues*, 36(2), 232–249.

Edwards, R., & Hamilton, M. A. (2004). You need to understand my gender role: An empirical test of Tannen's model of gender and communication. *Sex Roles*, 50, 491–504.

Entezar, R. K., Othman, N., Kosnin, A. B. M., & Panah, A. G. (2011). Relation between emotional intelligence and forgiveness and marital satisfaction. *International Journal of Fundamental Psychology Social Science*, 1, 21–25.

Exline, J. J., Baumeister, R. F., Bushman, B. J., Campbell, W. K., & Finkel, E. J. (2004). Too proud to let go: Narcissistic entitlement as a barrier to forgiveness, *Journal of Personality and Social Psychology*, 87, 894–912.

Fincham, F. D., Beach, S. R H., & Davila, J. (2004). Forgiveness and conflict resolution in marriage. *Journal of Family Psychology*, 18, 72–81.

Fincham, F. D., Hall, J. H., & Beach, S. R. H. (2006). Forgiveness in marriage: Current status and future directions. *Family Relations*, 55, 415–427.

Fincham, F. D., & May, R. W. (2019). Self-forgiveness and well-being: Does divine forgiveness matter? *Journal of Positive Psychology*, 14(6), 854–859.

Galvin, K. M., Braithwaite, D. O., Schrodt, P., & Bylund, C. L. (2019). *Family communication: Cohesion and change*. New York: Routledge.

Gottman, J. M. (1994a). *What predicts divorce? The relationship between marital process and marital outcomes*. Hillsdale, NJ: Erlbaum.

Gottman, J. M. (1994b). *Why marriages succeed or fail*. New York: Simon & Schuster.

Gottman, J. M. (1999). *The marriage clinic: A scientifically based marital therapy*. New York: Norton.

Gottman, J. M., Markham, J. J., & Notarius, C. I. (1977). The topography of marital conflict: A sequential analysis of verbal and nonverbal behavior. *Journal of Marriage and the Family*. 39, 461–477.

Gottman, J. M., & Porterfield, A. (1981). Communicative competence in the nonverbal behavior of married couples. *Journal of Marriage and the Family*, 43, 817–824.

Gottman, J. M., Ryan, K. D., Carrere, S., & Erlye, A. M. (2002). Toward a scientifically based marital therapy. In H. A. Liddle, D. A. Santisteban, R. F. Levant, and J. H. Bray (Eds.), *Family psychology: Science-based interventions* (pp. 147–174). Washington, DC: American Psychological Association.

Halgunseth, L. (2003). Language brokering: Positive developmental outcomes. In M. Coleman & L. Ganong (Eds.), *Points & counterpoints: Controversial relationship and family issues in the 21st century: An anthology* (pp. 154–156). New York: Roxbury.

Hall, J. A., & Matsumoto, D. (2004). Gender differences in judgments of multiple emotions from facial expressions. *Emotion*, 4(2), 201–206.

He, Q, Zhong, M., Tong, W., Lan, J., Li, X., et al. (2018). Forgiveness, marital quality, and marital stability in the early years of Chinese marriage: An actor-partner interdependence mediation model. *Frontiers in Psychology*, 9(1510), 1–11.

Hidalgo Tenorio, E. (2016). Genderlect. In N. Naples, R. C. Hoogland, M. Wickramasinghe, & A. Wong (Eds.), *The Wiley-Blackwell encyclopedia of gender and sexuality studies*. Malden, MA and Oxford: Wiley-Blackwell.

Hook, J. N., Davis, D. E., Owen, J., Worthington, E. L., Jr., & Utsey, S. O. (2013). Cultural humility: Measuring openness to culturally diverse clients. *Journal of Counseling Psychology*, 60(3), 353–366.

Hook, J. N., Worthington, E. L., & Utsey, S. O. (2009). Collectivism, forgiveness, and social harmony. *The Counseling Psychologist*, 37(6), 821–847.

Ictech, B. (2018). Smartphones and face-to-face interaction: Digital cross-talk during encounters in everyday life. *Symbolic Interaction*, 42(1), 27–45.

Kachadourian, L. K., Fincham, F. D., & Davila, J. (2004). Attitudinal ambivalence, rumination, and forgiveness of partner transgressions in marriage. *Personality and Social Psychology Bulletin*, 31, 334–342.

Kato, T. (2016). Effects of partner forgiveness on romantic break-ups in dating relationships: A longitudinal study. *Personality and Individual Differences*, 95, 185–189.

Kelley, D. (1998). The communication of forgiveness. *Communication Studies*, 49, 255–271.

Kellogg, T. (1990). *Broken toys, broken dreams: Understanding and healing boundaries, codependence, compulsion, and family relationships*. Amherst, MA: BRAT.

Kids Count. (2018). The number of bilingual kids in America continues to rise. Retrieved June 30, 2018 from https://datacenter.kidscount.org/updates/show/184-the-number-of-bilingual-kids-in-america-continues-to-rise

Knutson, J., Enright, R., & Garbers, B. (2008). Validating the developmental pathway of forgiveness. *Journal of Counseling and Development*, 86(2), 193–199.

Koerner, A. F., & Fitzpatrick, M. A. (2002a). Nonverbal communication and marital adjustment and satisfaction: The role of decoding relationship relevant and relationship irrelevant affect. *Communication Monographs*, 69, 33–51.

Koerner, A. F., & Fitzpatrick, M. A. (2002b). Toward a theory of family communication. *Communication Theory*, 12, 70–91.

Lindgren, H. G. (1998). Listening with your heart as well as your words. *NebGuide 92–1092*. Lincoln: University of Nebraska Cooperative Extension.

Lindlof, T. R., & Taylor, B. C. (2002). *Qualitative communication research methods* (2nd ed.). Thousand Oaks, CA: SAGE.

Luskin, F. (2003). *Forgive for good: A proven prescription for health and happiness*. San Francisco: Harper.

MacGeorge, E. L, Graves, A. R., Feng, B., & Gillihan, S. J. (2004). The myth of gender cultures: Similarities outweigh differences in men's and women's provision of and responses to supportive communication. *Sex Roles: A Journal of Sex Research*, 50(3–4), 143–175.

Maio, G. R., Thomas, G., Fincham, F. D., & Carnelley, K. B. (2008). Unraveling the role of forgiveness in family relationships. *Journal of Personality and Social Psychology*, 94(2), 307–319.

Markman, H. J. (1984). The longitudinal study of couples' interaction: Implications for understanding and predicting the development of marital distress. In K. Hahlweg & N. S. Jacobson (Eds.), *Marital interaction: Analysis and modification* (pp. 253–281). New York: Guilford.

McNulty, J. K. (2008). Forgiveness in marriage: Putting the benefits into context. *Journal of Family Psychology*, 22(1), 171–175.

Mead, G. H. (1934). *Mind, self, and society* (C. Morris, Introduction and Ed.). Chicago: University of Chicago Press.

Merchant, K. (2012). How men and women differ: Gender differences in communication Styles, influence tactics, and leadership styles. CMC Senior Theses. Paper 513. Retrieved March 29, 2020, from http://scholarship.claremont.edu/cmc_theses/513

Merolla, A. J. (2008). Communicating forgiveness in friendships and dating relationships. *Communication Studies*, 59(2), 114–130.

Michaud, S. L. & Warner, R. M. (1997). Gender differences in self-reported response in troubles talk. *Sex Roles: A Journal of Sex Research*. 37, 527–540.

Moir, A., & Jessel, D. (1991). *Brain sex: The real difference between men and women*. New York: Doubleday.

Natenshon, H. (1999). *A day center for adolescents with eating disorders within Southern Health*. Paper presented to the Butterfly-Southern Health Rating Disorder Conference.

National Council on Family Relations (NCFR). (2019). Strengthening families. Retrieved from www.ncfr.org

Nichols, M. P., & Schwartz, R. C. (2009). *The essentials of family therapy* (4th ed.). Boston: Allyn & Bacon.

Noller, P. (1993). Gender and emotional communication in marriage; Different cultures or differential social power? *Journal of Language and Social Psychology*, 12, 132–152.

O'Donohue, W., & Crouch, J. L (1996). Marital therapy and gender-linked factors in communication. *Journal of Marital and Family Therapy*, 22, 87–101.

O'Keeffe, G. S., & Clarke-Pearson, K. (2011). The impact of social media on children, adolescents, and families. *Pediatrics*, 127(4), 800–804.

Okun, B. F. (2002). *Effective helping: Interviewing and counseling techniques* (6th ed.). Monterey, CA; Brooks/Cole.

Olson, D. H., Sprenkel, D. H., & Russell, C. S. (1979). Circumplex model of marital and family systems: Cohesion and adaptability dimensions, family types, and clinical applications. *Family Process*, 18, 3–28.

Omarzu, J. (2000). A disclosure model: Determining how and when individuals will self-disclose. *Personality and Social Psychology Review*, 4(2), 174–185.

Pew Research Center. (2016). Americans increasingly use smartphones for more than voice calls, texting. Retrieved from https://www.pewresearch.org/internet/ft_01-27-16_smartphoneactivities_640/

Pew Research Center. (2018). Teens, social media, and technology. Retrieved March 28, 2020 from https://www.pewresearch.org/internet/2018/05/31/teens-social-media-technology-2018/

Pew Research Center. (2019). 8 facts about American dads. Retrieved June 30, 2019 from https://www.pewresearch.org/fact-tank/2019/06/12/fathers-day-facts/

Phoon, A. (2017). Social media and its start influences on society. *Journal of First-Year Writing*, 1(1). Retrieved March 28, 2020, from https://scholarworks.bgsu.edu

Povenmire-Kirk, T. C., Bethune, L. K., Alverson, C. Y., & Guttman Kahn, L. (2015). A journey, not a destination: Developing cultural competence in secondary transition. *Teaching Exceptional Children*, 47, 319–328.

Procentese, F., Gatti, F., & Di Napoli, I. (2019). Families and social media use: The role of parents' perceptions about social media impact on family systems in the relationship between family collective efficacy and open communication. *International Journal of Environmental Research and Public Health*, 16(24), 5006, 1–38.

Richardson, B. (2012). Cultural awareness to help while serving Native veterans. *Office of Rural Health*. Retrieved March 28, 2020 from https://www.ruralhealth.va.gov/docs/webinars/richardson-cultural-sensitivity-062712.pdf

Rosenblatt, P. C. (1994). *Metaphors of family systems theory: Toward new constructions*. New York: Guilford.

Rusbult, C. (2002). Betrayal, forgiveness, and reconciliation in close relationships. Retrieved from www.forgiving.org.htm

Sabatelli, R. M. (1988). Exploring relationship satisfaction: A social exchange perspective on the interdependence between theory, research, and practice. *Family Relations*, 37, 217–222.

Senecal, S., Murad, N., & Hess, U. (2003). Do you know what I feel? Predictors and judgments of each other's emotional reactions to emotion-eliciting situations. *Sex Roles*, 48(1/2), 21–37.

Shadish, W. (1993). Effects of family and marital psychotherapies: A meta-analysis. *Journal of Consulting and Clinical Psychology*, 61(6), 992–1002.

Sieburg, E. (1973). *Interpersonal confirmation: A paradigm for conceptualization and measurement*. Paper presented to the International Communication Association, Montreal, Quebec. ERIC Reproduction Service: ERIC Item: ED 098 634 1975.

Silberman, S. (1995). The relationships among love, marital satisfaction, and duration of marriage. Unpublished dissertation, Arizona State University, Tempe, AZ.

Sorokowska, A., Sorokowski, P., Hilpert, P., Cantarera, K., Frackowiak, T., Ahmadi, K. . . . Pierce, J. D. (2017). Preferred interpersonal distances: A global comparison. *Journal of Cross-Cultural Psychology*, 48(4), 577–592.

Stanley, S. (2017). Reasons people give for divorce. *Institute for Family Studies*. Retrieved June 29, 2019 from https://ifstudies.org/blog/reasons-people-give-for-divorce

Tannen, D. (1990). *You just don't understand: Women and men in conversation*. New York: William Morrow.

Thompson, L. Y., Snyder, C. R., Hoffman, L., Michael, S. T., Rasmussen, H. N., Billings, L. S., et al. (2005). Dispositional forgiveness of self, others, and situations. *Journal of Personality*. 73, 313–359.

Torres, M. N. (1993. July). Cultural sensitivity. *ADVANCE for Nurse Practitioners*, 16–18.

Tschann, J. (1988). Self-disclosure in adult friendship: Gender and marital status differences. *Journal of Social and Personal Relationships*, 5, 65–81.

Turner, L. H., & West, R. (2006). *Perspectives on family communication* (3rd ed.). Boston: McGraw-Hill.

Umaña-Taylor, A. J., & Fine, M. A. (2003). Predicting commitment to wed among Hispanic and Anglo partners. *Journal of Marriage and Family*, 65, 117–139.

Wade, N. G., Bailey, D. C., & Shaffer, P. (2005). Helping clients heal: Does forgiveness make a difference? *Professional Psychology: Research and Practice*, 36(6), 634–641.

West, R. L., & Turner, L. H. (2018). *Introducing communication theory: Analysis and application* (6th ed.). New York: McGraw Hill Education.

White, J. M., Klein, D. M., & Martin, T. F. (2014). *Family theories: An introduction* (4th ed.). Thousand Oaks, CA: SAGE.

Worthington, E. L. (2006). *Forgiveness and reconciliation: Theory and application*. Abingdon, UK: Routledge.

Worthington, E. L., & Scherer, M. (2004). Forgiveness is an emotion-focused coping strategy that can reduce health risks and promote health resilience: Theory, review, and hypotheses. *Psychology & Health*, 19(3), 385–405.

Worthington, E. L., Witvliet, C. V. O., Pietrini, P., & Miller, A. J. (2007). Forgiveness, health, and well-being: A review of evidence for emotional versus decisional forgiveness, dispositional forgivingness, and reduced unforgiveness. *Journal of Behavioral Medicine*, 30, 291–302.

Younger, J. W., Piferi, R. L., Jobe, R. L., & Lawler, J. A. (2004). Dimensions of forgiveness: The views of laypersons. *Journal of Social and Personal Relationships*, 21, 837–855.

/// CHAPTER 4

Afable-Munsuz, A., & Brindis, C. D. (2006), Acculturation and the sexual reproductive health of Latino youth in the United States: A literature review. *Perspectives on Sexual and Reproductive Health*, 38(4), 208–220.

Albrecht, M. M. (2016). *Masculinity in contemporary quality television*. New York: Routledge.

Alice Paul Institute. (2018). ERA. Retrieved May 9, 2020 from https://www.equalrightsamendment.org/faq

Bancroft, J. (2009). *Human sexuality and its problems* (3rd ed.). London: Elsevier.

Banda, J, (2004, March). Africa News Service.

Bandura, A. (1977). *Social learning theory*. Englewood Cliffs, NJ: Prentice Hall.

Bandura, A. (1986). *Social foundations of thought and action: A social cognitive theory*. Englewood Cliffs, NJ: Prentice Hall.

Belanger, J. (2020). Why won't the Senate pass the Violence Against Women Act? Retrieved May 9, 2020 from https://giffords.org/blog/2020/04/why-wont-the-senate-pass-the-violence-against-women-act/

Belansky, E. S., & Boggiano, A. K. (1994). Predicting helping behaviors: The role of gender and instrumental/expressive self-schemata. *Sex Roles: A Journal of Research*, 30(9), 647–662.

Bem, S. L. (1974). The measurement of psychological androgyny. *Journal of Consulting and Clinical Psychology*, 42(2), 155–162.

Bem, S. L. (1981). Gender schema theory: A cognitive account of sex typing. *Psychological Review*, 88, 354–364.

Bem, S. (1993). *The lenses of gender: Transforming the debate on sexual inequality*. New Haven, CT: Yale University Press.

Bem, S. (1998). *An unconventional family*. New Haven, CT: Yale University Press.

Bi, L., & D'Agostino, F. (2004). The doctrine of filial piety: A philosophical analysis of the concealment case. *Journal of Chinese Philosophy*, 31(4), 451–167.

Bland, J. (1998). About gender: Social learning theory. Retrieved from www.gender.org.uk/about/02psycho/22_socln.htm

Bleidorn, W., Arslan, R. C., Denissen, J. J. A., Rentfrow, P. J., Gebauer, J. E., Potter, J., & Gosling, S. D. (2016). Age and gender differences in self-esteem—A cross-cultural window. *Journal of Personality and Social Psychology,* 111(3), 396–410.

Bosson, J. K., Vandello, J. A., Michniewicz, K. S., & Lenes, J. G. (2012). American men's and women's beliefs about gender discrimination: For men, it's not quite a zero-sum game. *Psychology Faculty Publications.* 1162. Retrieved from https://scholarcommons.usf.edu/psy_facpub/116

Boyd, D., & Bee, H. (2015). *Lifespan development* (7th ed.) New York: Pearson Education.

Boyse, C. (2008). Media trends tracked. Retrieved July 13, 2009 from http://www.tvb.org/rcentral/MediaTrendsTrack/tvbasics/09TimeViewingPersons.asp

Buckley, T. R, & Carter, R. T. (2005). Black adolescent girls: Do gender role and racial identity impact their self-esteem? *Sex Roles,* 53(9–10), 647–661.

Bussey, K., & Bandura, A. (1984). Influence and gender constancy and social power on sex-linked modeling. *Journal of Personality and Social Psychology,* 47, 1292–1302.

Bussey, K., & Bandura, A. (1999). Social cognitive theory of gender development and differentiation. *Psychological Review,* 106, 676–713.

Cahill, B. & Adams, E. (1997). An exploratory study of early childhood teachers' attitudes toward gender roles. *Sex Roles: A Journal of Research,* 36(7/8), 517–530.

Campaign for a Commercial-Free Childhood (CCFC). (2019). Marketing to children overview. Retrieved June 6, 2019, from https://commercialfreechildhood.org/resource/marketing-children-overview

Campenni, C. E. (1999). Gender stereotyping of children's toys: A comparison of parents and nonparents. *Sex Roles,* 40, 121–138.

Canales, G. (2000). Gender as subculture: The first division of multicultural diversity. In I. Cuellar & F. A. Paniagua (Eds.), *Handbook of multicultural mental health: Assessment and treatment of diverse populations* (pp. 63–77). New York: Academic Press.

Carver, P. R., Yunger, J. L., & Perry, D. G. (2003). Gender identity and adjustment in middle childhood. *Sex Rotes: A Journal of Research,* 49, 95–110.

Chafetz S. (1975). Masculine/feminine or human?? An overview of the sociology of sex roles. *Contemporary Sociology,* 4(3), 230–231.

Chandler, D. (2005). Television and gender roles. Retrieved from www.aber.ac.uk/media/Modules/TF33120/gendertv

Chowdhury, R., & Baset, Z. A. (2018). *Men and feminism in India.* London: Routledge.

Collins, P. H. (2004). *Black sexual politics: African Americans, gender and the new racism.* New York: Routledge.

Connell, R. W. (1987). *Gender and power: Society, the person, and sexual politics.* Stanford, CA: Stanford University Press.

Coyne, S., Ward, M. L., Kroff, S. L., & Davis, E. J. (2019). Contributions of mainstream sexual media exposure to sexual attitudes, perceived peer norms, and sexual behavior: A meta-analysis. *Journal of Adolescent Health,* 64(4), 430–436.

Crawford, M., & Unger, R. (2000). *Women and gender: A feminist psychology* (3rd ed.). Boston: McGraw-Hill.

Danon, L.M. (2018). Comparing contemporary medical treatment practices aimed at intersex/DSD bodies in Israel and Germany. *Sociology of Health & Illness,* 41(1). doi:https://doi.org/10.1111/1467-9566.12812

Dasgupta, R. K., & Gokulsing, M. (2013). *Masculinity and its challenges in India: Essays on changing perceptions.* Jefferson, NC: McFarland.

Dinella, L. M., Claps, J. M., & Lewandowski, G. W. (2017). Princesses, princes, and superheroes: Children's gender cognitions and fictional characters. *Journal of Genetic Psychology,* 178(5), 262–280.

Drydakis, N., Sidiropoulou, K., Patnaik, S., Selmanovic, S., & Bozani, V. (2017). Masculine vs feminine personality traits and women's employment outcomes in Britain: A field experiment. Discussion Paper Series, IZA DP No. 11179, November. Retrieved May 3, 2020 from http://ftp.iza.org/dp11179.pdf

Eisler, R. M., & Skidmore, J. R. (1987). Masculine gender role stress: Scale development and component factors in the appraisal of stressful situations. *Behavior Modification,* 11, 123–136.

Equal Employment Opportunity Commission. (2004). Federal sexual harassment policy. Retrieved March, 2019 from www.eeoc.gov/facts/fs-sex.html

ERA Coalition. (2016). Equal future. Retrieved May 9, 2020 from http://www.eracoalition.org/

Eskridge, W. N., & Hunter, N. D. (1997). *Sexuality, gender, and the law.* Westbury, NY: Foundation Press.

Faulkner, S. (2003). Good girl or flirt girl: Latinas' definitions of sex and sexual relationships. *Hispanic Journal of Behavioral Sciences,* 25(2), 174–200.

Franken, M. W. (1983). Sex role expectations in children's vocational aspirations and perceptions of occupations. *Psychology of Women Quarterly,* 8, 59–68.

Gallagher, K. E., & Parrott, D. J. (2011). What accounts for men's hostile attitudes toward women? The influence of hegemonic male role norms and masculine gender role stress. *Violence Against Women,* 17(5), 568–583.

Geary, D. C. (1998). Male, female: The evolution of human sex differences. *Current Directions in Psychological Science,* 8, 115–120.

Gilligan, C. (1982). *In a different voice: Psychological theory and women's development.* Cambridge, MA: Harvard University Press.

Gilmore, D. (1990). *Manhood in the making: Cultural concepts of masculinity.* New Haven, CT: Yale University Press.

Goldberg, A. E., Kashy, D. A., & Smith, J. Z. (2012). Gender-typed play behavior in early childhood: Adopted children with lesbian, gay, and heterosexual parents. *Sex Roles,* 67(9–10), 503–515.

Goldberg, H. (1976). *The hazards of being male: Surviving the myth of masculine privilege.* New York: Nash.

Golombok, S., Perry, B., Burson, A., Murray, C., Mooney-Somers, J., et al. (2003). Children with lesbian parents: A community study. *Developmental Psychology,* 39(1), 20–33.

Gough, H. G. (1957). *Manual for the California Psychological Inventory.* Palo Alto, CA: Consulting Psychologists Press.

Graydon, S. (2003). *Made you look: How advertising works and why you should know.* Vancouver, BC: Annick.

Greenberg, D., Najle, M., Jackson, N., Bola, O., & Jones, R. P. (2019) American's growing support for transgender rights. *PRRI.* Retrieved April 2, 2020 from https://www.prri.org/research/americas-growing-support-for-transgender-rights/

Hager, B., & Jenkins, C. (2016). Americans by 94% overwhelmingly support the Equal Rights Amendment (ERA). Retrieved May 9, 2020 from http://www.eracoalition.org/wp-content/uploads/2019/09/ERA-Polling-Press-Release-1.pdf

Hall, N. M., & Pichon, L. C. (2014). Gender roles, sociosexuality, and sexual behavior among US Black women. *Health Psychology and Behavioral Medicine,* 2(1), 171–182.

Harris III, F., Palmer, T., & Struve, L. E. (2011). "Cool posing" on campus: A qualitative study of masculinities and gender expression among Black men at a private research institution. *The Journal of Negro Education,* 80(1), 47–62.

Haymon, B. S. (2018). The Taliban's legacy in Afghanistan has plundered women's basic rights. Retrieved April 18, 2020 from https://www.independent.co.uk/voices/taliban-afghanistan-latest-womens-human-rights-unhcr-ashraf-ghani-kabul-asia-a8380396.html

Hegewisch, A. (2018). The gender wage gap: 2017 earnings differences by gender, race, and ethnicity. Retrieved June 2, 2019 from https://iwpr.org/publications/gender-wage-gap-2017/

Helwig, A. A. (1998). Gender-role stereotyping: Testing theory with a longitudinal sample. *Sex Roles: A Journal of Research,* 35(5), 403–423.

Hesse-Biber, S. N., & Carter, G. L. (2005). *Working women in America.* New York: Oxford University Press.

Hines, M. (2015). Gendered development. In M. E. Lamb & R. M. Lerner (Eds.), *Handbook of child psychology and developmental science: Socioemotional processes* (pp. 842–887). Hoboken, NJ: John Wiley & Sons.

Howard, J. A., & Hollander, J, A. (1997). *Gendered situations, gendered selves: A gender lens on social psychology.* Newbury Park, CA: SAGE.

Hsin, A. (2018). Hegemonic gender norms and the gender gap in achievement: The case of Asian Americans. *Sociological Science,* 5, 752–774.

Human Rights Campaign. (2019). Sexual orientation and gender identity terminology and definitions. Retrieved June 2, 2019 from www.hrc.org/resources/sexual-orientation-and-gender-identity-terminology-and-definitions

Huston, A. C. (1983). Sex typing. In P. H. Mussen & E. M. Hetherington (Eds.), *Handbook of child psychology: Socialization personality and social behavior.* New York: Wiley.

Intersex Campaign for Equality. (2019). Raising an intersex child: "This is your body. There's nothing to be ashamed of." Retrieved May 8, 2020 from https://www.intersexequality.com/category/articles/

Intersex Society of North America. (2019). How common is intersex? Retrieved June 3, 2019 from http://www.isna.org/faq/frequency

Jandt, F., & Hundley, H. (2007). Intercultural dimensions of communicating masculinities. *Journal of Men's Studies*, 15(2), 216–231.

Jardine, S. A., & Dallalfar, A. (2012). Sex and gender roles: Examining gender dynamics in the context of African American families. *Journal of Pedagogy, Pluralism, and Practice*, 4(4), 17–26.

Jhally, S. (2002). *Wrestling and manhood: Gender, race, and class in professional wrestling*. Northhampton, MA: Media Education Foundation.

Kirsch, A. C., & Murnen, S. K. (2015). "Hot" girls and "cool dudes": Examining the prevalence of the heterosexual script in American children's television media. *Psychology of Popular Media Culture*, 4(1), 18–30.

Landén, M., Wålinder, J., Hambert, G., & Lundström, B. (1998). Factors predictive of regret in sex reassignment. *Acta Psychiatrica Scandinavica*, 97, 284–289.

Leaper, C. (2015). Gender and social-cognitive development. In L. S. Liben, U. Müller, & R. M. Lerner (Eds.), *Handbook of child psychology and developmental science: Cognitive processes* (pp. 806–853). Hoboken, NJ: John Wiley & Sons.

Levant, R., Richmond, K., Cook, S., House, A. T., & Aupont, M. (2007). The Femininity Ideology Scale: Factor, structure, reliability, convergent and discriminate validity, and social contextual variation. *Sex Roles*, 57, 373–383.

Liben, L. S., & Bigler, R. (2017). Understanding and undermining the development of gender dichotomies: The legacy of Sandra Lipsitz Bem. *Sex Roles*, 76(9–10), 544–555.

Lundberg, T., Donasen, I., Hegarty, P., & Roen, K. (2019). Moving intersex/DSD rights and care forward: Lay understandings of common dilemmas. *Journal of Social and Political Psychology*, 7(1), 354–377.

Macdonald, H. (2003). Magazine advertising and gender: Representations of gender in magazine advertising. Retrieved April 18, 2020 from www.mediacd.org.uk/posted_documcnts/MagazineAdverts.htm

Mackinnon, C. A. (2001). *Sex equality*. New York: Foundation Press.

Malhotra, A. (2002). *Gender, caste, and religious identities: Restructuring class in colonial Punjab*. New York: Oxford University Press.

Manzi, F. (2019). Are the processes underlying discrimination the same for women and men? A critical review of congruity models of gender discrimination. *Frontiers in Psychology*, 10(469). doi:10.3389/fpsyg.2019.00469

Martin, C. L., & Ruble, D. N. (2013). Patterns of gender development. *Annual Review of Psychology*, 61, 353–381.

McCreary, D. R., Newcomb, M. D., & Sadava, S. W. (1998). The relationship between masculine gender role stress and psychological adjustment: A question of construct validity? *Sex Roles*, 39, 81–95.

McCune, J. Q. (2014). *Sexual discretion: Black masculinity and the politics of passing*. Chicago, IL: University of Chicago Press.

Media Watch. (2008). Retrieved July 13, 2009 from http://citizenmediawatch.com/index.php/2008/10/

Mmari, K., Blum, R. W., Atnafou, R., Chilet, E., de Meyer, S., El-Gibaly, O., . . . Zuo, X. (2017). Exploration of gender norms and socialization among early adolescents: The use of qualitative methods for the Global Early Adolescent Study. *Journal of Adolescent Health*, 61, S12–S18.

Monllos, K. (2017). Men appear in ads 4 times more than women, according to research revealed at Cannes. *JWT and the Geena Davis Institute on Gender in Media*. Retrieved June 6, 2019 from www.adweek.com/brand-marketing/men-appear-in-ads-4-times-more-than-women-according-to-research-revealed-at-cannes/

Muehlenhard, C. L., Peterson, Z. D., Karwoski, L., Bryan, T. S., & Lee, R. S. (2003). Gender and sexuality: An introduction to the special issue. *Journal of Sex Research*, 40(1), 1–4.

Murnen, S. K., Greenfield, C., Younger, A., & Hope, B. (2016). Boys act and girls appear: A content analysis of gender stereotypes associated with characters in children's popular culture. *Sex Roles*, 74, 78–91.

Nanda, S. (1990). *Neither man nor woman: The Hijras of India*. Belmont, CA: Wadsworth.

National Center for Transgender Equality. (2018). Understanding non-binary people: How to be respectful and supportive. Retrieved April 18, 2020 from https://transequality.org/issues/resources/understanding-non-binary-people-how-to-be-respectful-and-supportive

National Institutes of Health. (2019). Klinefelter's Syndrome. Retrieved June 2, 2019 from www.ghr.nlm.nih.gov/condition/klinefelter-syndrome

National Transgender Advocacy Coalition. (2019). Retrieved April 18, 2020 from https://www.transgendermap.com/politics/activism/national-transgender-advocacy-coalition/

Nelson, J. N. (1978). Age and sex differences in the development of children's occupational reasoning. *Journal of Vocational Behavior*, 13, 287–297.

Nguyen, T. H. (2014). *A view from the bottom: Asian American masculinity and representation*. Durham, NC: Duke University Press.

Nielson Media. (2019). How teens use media. Retrieved April 18, 2020 from https://www.nielsen.com/wp-content/uploads/sites/3/2019/04/How-Teens-Use-Media.pdf

Noland, C. (2006). Listening to the sound of silence: Gender roles and communication about sex in Puerto Rico. *Sex Roles*, 55(5–6), 283–294.

O'Keefe, E. S. C., & Hyde, J. S. (1983), The development of occupational sex-role stereotypes: The effects of gender stability and age. *Sex Roles*, 9, 481–492.

Oldstone-Moore, J. (2002). *Confucianism: Origins, beliefs, practices, holy texts, sacred place*. New York: Oxford University Press.

Oxford Learner's Dictionary. (2019). People in society: Gender identity. Retrieved April 18, 2020 from https://www.oxfordlearnersdictionaries.com/us/definition/english/non-binary

Patterson, C. J. (2004). Lesbian and gay parents and their children: Summary of research findings. *In Lesbian and gay parenting: A resource for psychologists*. Washington, DC: American Psychological Association.

Perry, D. G., & Bussey, K. (1984). *Social development*. Englewood Cliffs, NJ: Prentice Hall.

Petersen, J., & Hide, J. S. (2014). Gender-related academic and occupational interests and goals. *Advances in Child Development and Behavior*, 47, 43–76.

Pew Research Center. (2017). Gender discrimination comes in many forms for today's working women. Retrieved April 1, 2020 from https://www.pewresearch.org/fact-tank/2017/12/14/gender-discrimination-comes-in-many-forms-for-todays-working-women/

Phuong-Mai, N., Terlouw, C., & Pilot, A. (2005). Cooperative learning vs. Confucian heritage culture's collectivism: Confrontation to reveal some cultural conflicts and mismatch. *Asia Europe Journal*, 3(3), 403–419.

Pinel, J. P. (1997). *Biopsychology* (3rd ed.). Boston; Allyn & Bacon.

Powers-Barker, P. (2020). How do you support LGBTQ+ families in community work? *National Council on Family Relations Network*, 33(1). Retrieved April 3, 2020 from ncfr.org

Public Religion Research Institute. (2019). Americans increasingly support transgender rights. Retrieved April 1, 2020 from https://www.prri.org/press-release/survey-americans-increasingly-support-transgender-rights/

Richmond, K., Levant, R., Smalley, B., & Cook, S. (2015). The Femininity Ideology Scale (FIS): Dimensions and its relationship to anxiety and feminine gender role stress. *Women's Health*, 55(3), 263–79.

Rosenblum, K. E., & Travis, T-M. C. (2003). *The meaning of difference: American constructions of race, sex and gender, social class, and sexual orientation*. Boston: McGraw-Hill.

Rutledge, K. (2000). Social learning theory. Retrieved from http://teachnet.edb.Utexas.edu/~lynda_abbott/Social.html

Saewyc, E. (2017). A global perspective on gender roles and identity. *Journal of Adolescent Health*, 61(4), S1–S2.

Sax, L. J. (2008). *The gender gap in college: Maximizing the developmental potential of women and men*. San Francisco; Jossey-Bass.

Segura, D. A., & Pierce, J. L. (1993, Autumn). Chicana/o family structure and gender personality: Chodorow, familism, and psychoanalytic sociology revisited. Signs.

Sharifi, S., & Adamou, L. (2018). Taliban threaten 70% of Afghanistan, BBC finds. BBC.com. Retrieved May 8, 2020 from https://www.bbc.com/news/world-asia-42863116

Singh, D. (2001). *Myself Mona Ahmed*. Zurich, Switzerland: Scalo.

Skelton, C., & Hall, E. (2001). The development of gender roles in young children. Retrieved from www.eoc.org.uk/research.html

Stacey, J., & Biblarz, T. J. (2001). (How) Does sexual orientation of parents matter? *American Sociological Review*, 65, 159–183.

Suarez-Orozco, C., & Qin, D. B. (2006). Gendered perspectives in psychology: Immigrant origin youth. *International Migration Review*, 40(1), 165–198.

Sue, D. W., & Sue, D. (2003). Counseling the culturally different: Theory and practice (2nd ed.). New York: Wiley.

Swabb, D. F., Gooren, L. J., & Hofman, M. A. (1992). The human hypothalamus in relation to gender and sexual orientation. *Progress in Brain Research*, 93, 205–219.

Swartout, K. M., Parrott, D. J., Cohn, A. M., Hagman, B. T., & Gallagher, K. E. (2015). Development of the Abbreviated Masculine Gender Role Stress Scale. *Psychological Assessment*, 27(2), 489–500.

Trekels, J., & Eggermont, S. (2018). "I can/should look like a media figure": The association between direct and indirect media exposure and teens' sexualizing appearance behaviors. *Journal of Sex Research*, 55(3), 320–333.

Turner Syndrome Society. (2019). About Turner Syndrome. Retrieved May 8, 2020 from https://www.turnersyndrome.org/about-turnersyndrome

Villarruel, A. M., & Rodriguez, D. (2003). Beyond stereotypes: Promoting safer sex behaviors among Latino adolescents. *Journal of Obstetric, Gynecologic, and Neonatal Nursing*, 32(2), 258–263.

Violence Against Women Reauthorization Act of 2019, H.R. 1585, 116th Cong. (2019–2020).

Wester, S. R., Vogel, D. L, Wei, M., & McLain, R. (2006). African American men, gender role conflict, and psychological distress: The role of racial identity. *Journal of Counseling and Development*, 84, 419–429.

White, J. (2003, Sept./Oct.). Sex and gender confusion: Our sense of being manly or womanly. Indian Life.

Williams, J. E., & Best, D. L. (1990). *Measuring sex stereotypes: A multination study*. Newbury Park, CA: SAGE.

Witt, S. (1997). Parental influence on children's socialization to gender roles. *Adolescence*, 32, 253–258.

Wood, E., Desmarais, S., & Gugula, S. (2002). The impact of parenting experience on gender stereotyped toy play of children. *Sex Roles*, 47, 39–49.

Yim, J. Y., & Mahalingam, R. (2006). Culture, masculinity, and psychological well-being in Punjab, India. *Sex Roles*, 55, 715–724.

/// CHAPTER 5

Allport, G. W. (1958). *The nature of prejudice*. Garden City, NY: Doubleday.

American Psychological Association. (2005). Controlling anger— before it controls you. Retrieved from www.apa.org/pubinfo/anger.html

Ashton-James, C. E., Kushlev, K., & Dunn, E. W. (2013). Parents reap what they sow: Child- centrism and parental well-being. *Social Psychological and Personality Science*, 4, 635–642.

Atwater, E. (1992). Peers. *Adolescence*, 3, 151–153.

Aykutoğlu, B., & Uysal, A. (2017). The relationship between intimacy change and passion: A dyadic diary study. *Frontiers in Psychology*, 8, Article ID 2257. Retrieved June 30, 2019 from http://dx.doi.org/10.3389/fpsyg.2017.02257

Bank, B. J., & Hansford, S. L. (2000), Gender and friendship: Whey are men's best same-sex friendships less intimate and supportive? *Journal of Social and Personal Relationships*, 7, 63–78.

Barbor, C. (2001, Jan/Feb). Finding real love. *Psychology Today*.

Basow, S. A., & Rubenfeld, K. (2003). Troubles talk. *Sex Roles: A Journal of Research*, 48(3/4), 183–188.

Berndt, T. S., & Savin-Williams, R. C. (1990). Friendship and peer relations. In S. S. Feldman & G. R. Elliot (Eds.), *At the threshold* (pp. 277–307). Cambridge, MA: Harvard University Press.

Berscheid, E. (1985). Interpersonal attraction. In G. Lindzey & E. Aronson (Eds.), *Handbook of social psychology* (3rd ed.; vol. 2; pp. 413–484). New York: Random House.

Bleske-Rechek, A. L., & Buss, D. M. (2001). Opposite-sex friendship; Sex differences and similarities in initiation, selection, and dissolution. *Personality and Social Psychology Bulletin*, 27, 1310–1323.

Bloom, C., & Bloom, L. (2011). Who comes first, the kids or the marriage? Retrieved June 30, 2019 from https://www.psychologytoday.com/us/blog/stronger-the-broken-places/201111/who-comes-first-the-kids-or-the-marriage

Brooks, R. (2002). Transitional friends? Young people's strategies to manage and maintain their friendships during a period of repositioning. *Journal of Youth Studies*, 5, 449–467.

Burleson, B. R. (2003). The experience and effects of emotional support: What the study of cultural and gender differences can tell us about close relationships, emotion, and interpersonal communication. *Journal of Social and Personal Relationships*, 10, 1–23.

Burney, M. A. (2002). *Codependence: The dance of wounded souls*. Cambria, CA: Joy to You & Me Enterprises.

Cardillo, M. (2005). Intimate relationships: Personality development through interaction during early life. Retrieved from www.personalityresearch.org/papers/cardillo

Carlson, J., & Sperry, L. (Eds.). (1999). *The intimate couple*. New York: Routledge/Taylor & Francis.

Chen, G. M. (1995). Differences in self-disclosure patterns among Americans versus Chinese: A comparative study. *Journal of Cross-Cultural Psychology*, 26, 84–91.

Clinebell, H. J., & Clinebell, C. H. (1970). *The intimate marriage*. New York: Harper & Row.

Code, D. (2009). *To raise happy kids, put your marriage first*. Spring Valley, NY: Crossroad.

Dolich, C. (2005), Male-female sex differences in cross-sex and same-sex adolescent friendships. Retrieved from http://students.haverford.edu/cdolich/final%20paper.htm

Duncan, G. J., Boisjoly, J., I.evy, D. M., Kremer, M., & Eccles, J. (2003). Empathy or antipathy? *The consequences of racially and socially diverse peers on attitudes and behaviors*. Working Paper Series. Chicago, IL: Joint Center for Policy Research.

Dunphy, D. C. (1963). The social structure of urban adolescent peer groups. *Sociometry*, 26, 230–246.

Erber, R., & Erber, M. W. (2001). *Intimate relationships: Issues, theories, and research* (2nd ed.). Boston: Allyn & Bacon.

Erikson, E. H. (1963). *Childhood and society* (2nd ed.). New York: Norton.

Erikson, E. H. (1986). *Vital involvement of old age*. New York: Norton.

Fernandez-Dols, J. M. (1999). Facial expression and emotion: A situationist view. In P. Philippot, R. S, Feldman, and E. J. Coats (Eds.), *The social context of nonverbal behavior* (2nd ed.; vol. 1; pp. 242–261). Cambridge: Cambridge University Press.

Firestone, R., & Catlett, J. (2000). *Fear of intimacy*. Santa Barbara, CA: Glendon.

Firestone. R. W., & Firestone, L. (2004). Methods for overcoming the fear of intimacy. In D. J. Mashek & A. P. Aron (Eds.), *Handbook of closeness and intimacy* (pp. 375–395). Mahwah, NJ: Erlbaum.

Fischer, M. J. (2008). Does campus diversity promote friendship diversity? A look at interracial friendships in college. *Social Science Quarterly*, 89(3), 631–655.

Galupo, M. P. (2007). Women's close friendships across sexual orientation: An analysis of lesbian-heterosexual and bisexual-heterosexual women's friendships. *Sex Roles*, 56, 473–482.

Galupo, M. P. (2009). Cross-category friendship patterns: Comparison of heterosexual and sexual minority adults. *Journal of Social and Personal Relationships*, 26, 811–831.

Galupo, M. P., Bauerband, L. A., Gonzalez, K. A., Hagen, D. B., Hether, S. D., & Krum, T. E. (2014). Transgender friendship experiences: Benefits and barriers of friendships across gender identity and sexual orientation. *Feminism & Psychology*, 24(2), 193–215.

Galvin, K. M., Braithwaite, D. O., & Bylund, C. L. (2014). *Family communication: Cohesion and change* (9th ed.). New York: Pearson Education.

German, K. (2002). Effects of intimacy on adult development. Retrieved from www.oberlin.edu/faculty/darling

The Glendon Association. (2005). Parent-child relationships. Retrieved from http://64.82.2.174/glendon_compass.html

Gordon, L. H. (2001). Intimacy: The art of working out your relationships. In R. Manis (Ed.), *The marriage and family workbook: An interactive reader, text, and workbook* (pp. 101–110). Boston: Allyn & Bacon.

Hassebrauck, M., & Fehr, B. (2002). Dimensions of relationship quality. *Personal Relationships*, 9, 253–270.

Hatfield, E., & Rapson, R. (1993). Historical and cross-cultural perspectives on passionate love and sexual desire. *Annual Review of Sex Research*, 4, 67–97.

Heath, C. (1999). The unbearable Bradness of being: Further on down Brad Pitt's ramble-on road. *Rolling Stone*. Retrieved May 22, 2020 from http://ah-bp.tripod.com/rs-oct99.html

Heine, S. J. (2001). Self as cultural product: An examination of East Asian and North American selves. *Journal of Personality*, 69, 881–906.

Heller, P., & Wood, B. (1998). The process of intimacy: Similarity, understanding, and gender. *Journal of Marital and Family Therapy*, 24(3), 273–288.

Heller, P., & Wood, B. (2000). The influence of religious and ethnic differences on marital intimacy: Intermarriage versus intramarriage. *Journal of Marital and Family Therapy*, 26(2), 241–252.

Hines, S. (2007). *TransForming gender: Transgender practices of identity, intimacy, and care*. Bristol, UK: Policy Press.

Hook, M. K., Gerstein, L. H., Detterich, L., & Gridley, B. (2003). How close are we? Measuring intimacy and examining gender differences. *Journal of Counseling and Development*, 81(4), 462–472.

Huebner, A. (2000, March). Adolescent growth and development. *Virginia Cooperative Extension Publication Number* 350–850.

Johnson, F. L., & Airies, E. J. (1983). Conversational patterns among same-sex pairs of late-adolescent close friends. *The Journal of Genetic Psychology*, 142, 225–238.

Johnson, T., Kulesa, P., Cho, Y., & Shavitt, S. (2005). The relation between culture and response styles: Evidence from 19 countries. *Journal of Cross-Cultural Psychology*, 36, 264–277.

Kirby, J. S., Baucom, D. H., & Peterman, M. A. (2005). An investigation of unmet intimacy needs in marital relationships. *Journal of Marital and Family Therapy*, 31(4), 313–325.

Kupperbusch, C., Matstumoto, D., Kooken, K., Loewinger. S., Uchida, H., Wilson-Cohn, C., & Yrizarry, N. (1999). Cultural influences on nonverbal expressions of emotion. In P. Philippot, R. S. Feldman, & E. J. Coats (Eds.), *The social context of nonverbal behavior* (2nd ed.; vol. 1; pp. 17–44). Cambridge: Cambridge University Press.

Kuttler, A. F., LaGreca, A. M., & Prinstein, M. J. (1999). Friendship qualities and social-emotional functioning of adolescents with close, cross-sex friendships. *Journal of Adolescent Research*, 9(3), 339–366.

Laurenceau, J. P., Barrett, L. F., & Rovine, M. J. (2005). The Interpersonal Process Model of Intimacy in Marriage: A daily-diary and multilevel modeling approach. *Journal of Family Psychology*, 19(2), 314–323.

Lawson, D., & Brossart, F. (2001). Intergenerational transmission: Individuation and intimacy across three generations. *Family Process*, 40, 429–442.

Lempers, J. D., & Clark-Lempers, D. S. (1993). A functional comparison of same-sex and opposite-sex friendships during adolescence. *Journal of Adolescent Research*, 8(1), 89–108.

Lenton, A. P., & Webber, L. (2006). Cross-sex friendships: Who has more? *Sex Roles: A Journal of Research*, 54, 809–820.

Mackey, R., Diemer, M., & O'Brien, A. (2000). Psychological intimacy in the lasting relationships of heterosexual and same-gender couples. *Sex Roles: A Journal of Research*, 43(4), 201–227.

Maleki, M. (2000). Intimacy difficulties. Retrieved from www.class.utoronto.ca/pamphlets/intimacy.htm

Marshall, T. C. (2008). Cultural differences in intimacy: The influence of gender-role ideology and individualism-collectivism. *Journal of Social and Personal Relationships*, 25(1), 143–168.

McAdams, D. P. (1989). *Intimacy: The need to be close*. New York: Doubleday.

Mendelson, M. J., & Kay, A. C. (2003). Positive feelings in friendship: Does imbalance in the relationship matter? *Journal of Social and Personal Relationships*, 20, 101–116.

Miller, L. C., Berg, J. H., & Archer, R. L. (1983). Openers: Individuals who elicit intimate self-disclosure. *Journal of Personality and Social Psychology*, 44, 1234–1244.

Miller, R. S., & Lefcourt, H. M. (1982). The assessment of intimacy. *Journal of Personality Assessment*, 46, 514–518.

Monsour, M. (2002). *Women and men as friends: Relationships across the lifespan in the 21st century*. Mahwah, NJ: Erlbaum.

Morgan, E., & Kuykendall, C. (2000). Spiritual intimacy. *Marriage Partnership*, 17(2), 60.

Myers, D. G. (2005). *Psychology* (8th ed.). New York: Worth.

National Council on Family Relations. (2020). Understanding families: Research and practice. Retrieved April 18, 2020 from https://www.ncfr.org/membership

Openshaw, D. K. (1999). Resiliency. In C. A. Smith (Ed.), *The encyclopedia of parenting*. Westport, CT: Greenwood.

Openshaw, D. K. (2004). The psychosocial development of adolescence: Intimacy. Retrieved from www.usu.edu/openshaw

Orlofsky, J. L., Marcia, J. E., & Lesser, I. M. (1973). Ego identity status and the intimacy versus isolation crisis of young adulthood. *Journal of Personality and Social Psychology*, 27, 211–219.

Oswald, D. L., & Clark, E. M. (2003). Best friends forever? High school best friendships and the transition to college, *Journal of Social and Personal Relationships*, 10, 187–196.

Paul, E. L., & White, K. M. (1990, Summer). The development of intimate relationships during late adolescence. *Adolescence*, 375–400.

Pettigrew, T. F., & Tropp, L. R. (2006). A meta-analytic test of intergroup contact theory. *Journal of Personality and Social Psychology*, 90(5), 751–783.

Peven, D. A., & Shulman, B. H. (1999). The issue of intimacy in marriage. In J. Carlson & L. Sperry (Eds.), *The intimate couple* (pp. 276–283). New York: Bruner/Mazel.

Pew Research Center. (2018). Teens, friendships, and online groups. Retrieved June 30, 2019 from https://www.pewinternet.org/2018/11/28/teens-friendships-and-online-groups/

Prager, K. J. (1999). The multi-layered context of intimacy. In J. Carlson & L. Sperry (Eds.), *The intimate couple*. New York: Bruner/Mazel.

Prager, K. J., & Buhrmester, D. (1998). Intimacy and need fulfillment in couple relationships. *Journal of Social and Personal Relationships*, 15(4), 435–469.

Prince, D. W., & Hoppe, M. H. (2000). Getting the message: How to feel your way with other cultures. *Leadership in Action*, 20(2), 1–4.

Quillian, L., & Campbell, M. E. (2003). Beyond Black and white: The present and future of multiracial friendship segregation. *American Sociological Review*, 68, 540–566.

Reeder, H. M. (2003). The effect of gender role orientation on same- and cross-sex friendship formation. *Sex Roles: A Journal of Research*, 49, 143–152.

Rubin, L. (1986). On men and friendship. *Psychoanalytic Review*, 73, 165–181.

Rybak, A., & McAndrew, F. T. (2006). How do we decide whom our friends are? Defining levels of friendship in Poland and the United States. *The Journal of Social Psychology*, 146(2), 147–163.

Sacerdote, B., & Marmaros, D. (2005). How do friendships form? *NBER* Working Paper W11530. Retrieved from www.ssrn.com/abstract=776569

Schneller, D. P., & Arditti, J. A. (2004). After the break-up: Interpreting divorce and rethinking intimacy. *Journal of Divorce and Remarriage*, 42, 1–37.

Sjoberg, D. L. (2002). How the family environment affects intimacy. Retrieved from www.oberlin.edu/faculty/ndarling/adini.htm#sjoberg

Tannen, D. (1990). *You just don't understand: Women and men in conversation*. New York: William Morrow.

Thorne, B. (1986). Girls and boys together . . . but mostly apart: Gender arrangements in elementary schools. In W. W. Hartup & Z. Rubin (Eds.), *Relationships and development* (pp. 167–184). Hillsdale, NJ: Erlbaum.

Timmermann, G. M. (1991). A concept analysis of intimacy. *Issues of Mental Health Nursing*, 12(1), 19–30.

Triandis, H., & Suh, E. (2002). Cultural influences on personality. *Annual Review of Psychology*, 53, 133–160.

Triscoli, C., Croy, I., Olausson, H., & Sailer, U. (2017). Touch between romantic partners: Being stroked is more pleasant than stroking and decelerates heart rate. *Physiology & Behavior*, 177, 169–175.

Ubando, M. (2016). Gender differences in intimacy, emotional expressivity, and relationship satisfaction. *Pepperdine Journal of Communication Research*, 4, Article 13.

van Lankveld, J., Jacobs, N., Thewissen, V., Dewitte, M., & Verboon, P. (2018). The associations of intimacy and sexuality in daily life. *Journal of Social and Personal Relationships*, 35(4), 557–576.

Waring, E. M. (1984). The measurement of marital intimacy. *Journal of Marital and Family Therapy*, 10, 185–192.

Weiss, R. (1969). The fund of sociability. *Transaction*, 6(9), 36–43.

West, L., Anderson, J., & Duck, S. (1996). Crossing the barriers to friendships between men and women. In J. T. Wood (Ed.), *Gendered relationships* (pp. 111–127). Mountain View, CA: Mayfield.

Whitbourne, S. K., & Weinstock, C. (1979). *Adult development: The differentiation of experience*. New York: Holt, Rinehart & Winston.

Yau, J. C. & Reich, S. M. (2018). Are the qualities of adolescents' offline friendships present in digital interactions? *Adolescent Research Review*, 3, 339–355.

Yoo, H., Bartle-Haring, S., Day, R. D., & Gangamma, R. (2013). Couple communication, emotional and sexual intimacy, and relationship satisfaction. *Journal of Sex & Marital Therapy*, 40(4), 275–293.

Aaron, A., Fisher, H. E., Mashek, D. J., Strong, G., Hai-Fang, L., & Brown. L. L. (2005). Reward, motivation, and emotion systems associated with early-stage intense romantic love, *Journal of Neurophysiology*, 94(1), 327–337.

Ainsworth, M. D. S., Blehar, M. C., Waters, E., & Wall, S. (1978). *Patterns of attachment: A psychological study of the strange situation*. Hillsdale, NJ: Erlbaum.

Allen, J., & Land, D. (1999). Attachment in adolescence. In J. Cassidy & P. Shaver (Eds.), *Handbook of attachment* (pp. 319–335). New York: Guilford.

Ballard, J. (2020). Millennials are less likely to want a monogamous relationship. *YouGov*. Retrieved April 18, 2020 from https://today.yougov.com/topics/relationships/articles-reports/2020/01/31/millennials-monogamy-poly-poll-survey-data

Bartholomew, K. (1990). Avoidance of intimacy: An attachment perspective. *Journal of Social and Personal Relationships*, 7, 147–178.

Beall, A. E., & Sternberg, R. J. (1995). The social construction of love. *Journal of Social and Personal Relationships*, 12, 417–438.

Benoit, D., & Parker, K. C. H. (1994). Stability and transmission of attachment across three generations. *Child Development*, 65, 1444–1456.

Bevan, J. L. (2013). *The communication of jealousy*. New York: Peter Lang.

Bowen, M. (1974). Toward the differentiation of self in one's family of origin. In F. Andres & J. Lorio (Eds.), *Georgetown family symposium*. Washington, DC: Georgetown University Medical Center, Department of Psychiatry.

Bowlby, J. (1969–1980). *Attachment and loss: Attachment* (Vols. 1–3). New York: Basic Books.

Bowlby, J. (1988). *A secure base*. London: Routledge.

Brem, S. S. (1992). *Intimate relationships*. New York: McGraw-Hill.

Brunning, L. (2016). The distinctiveness of polyamory. *Journal of Applied Philosophy*, 35(3), 16–26.

Collins, W. A., Welsh, D. P., & Furman, W. (2009). Adolescent romantic relationships. *Annual Review of Psychology*, 60, 631–652.

Crittenden, P. M., Partridge, M. F., & Claussen, A. H. (1991). Family patterns of relationship in normative and dysfunctional families. *Development and Psychopathology*, 3, 491–512.

Dainton, M., & Stokes, A. (2015). College students' romantic relationships on Facebook: Linking the gratification for maintenance to Facebook maintenance activity and the experience of jealousy. *Communication Quarterly*, 63(4), 365–383. doi:10.1080/01463373.2015.1058283

Davies, M. F. (2001). Socially desirable responding and impression management in the endorsement of love styles. *Journal of Psychology*, 135(5), 562–570.

DeSteno, D. (2004, May). *New perspectives on jealousy: An integrative view of the most social of social emotions*. Paper presented at the meeting of the American Psychological Society, Chicago.

DeSteno, D., Valdesolo, P., & Bartlett, M. Y. (2006). Jealousy and the threatened self: Getting to the heart of the green-eyed monster. *Journal of Personality and Social Psychology*, 91(4), 626–641.

Dion, K. L., & Dion, K. K. (1993). Individualistic and collectivistic perspectives on gender and the cultural context of love and intimacy. *Journal of Social Issues*, 49, 53–69.

Elliot, A. J., & Reis, H. T. (2003). Attachment and exploration in adulthood. *Journal of Personality and Social Psychology*, 85, 317–331.

Feeney, J. A., & Noller, P. (1991). Attachment style and verbal descriptions of romantic partners. *Journal of Social and Personal Relationships*, 8(2), 187–215.

Fehr, B. (1988). Prototype analysis of the concepts of love and commitment. *Journal of Personality and Social Psychology*, 55, 557–579.

Field, T. (1996). Attachment and separation in young children. *Annual Review of Psychology*, 47, 541–562.

Fisher, H. E. (2004). *Why we love: The nature and chemistry of romantic love*. New York: Henry Holt.

Fox, J., Osborn, J., Warber, K. M. (2014). Relational dialectics and social networking sites: The role of Facebook in romantic relationship escalation, maintenance, conflict, and dissolution. *Computers in Human Behavior*, 35, 527–534.

Frampton, J. R., & Fox, J. (2018). Social media's role in romantic partners' retroactive jealousy: Social comparison, uncertainty, and information seeking. *Social Media & Society*, 4(3), 1–12.

Furukawa, T., Yokouchi, T., Hirai, T., Kitamura, T., & Takahashi, K. (1999), Parental loss in childhood and social support in adulthood among psychiatric patients. *Journal of Psychiatric Research*, 22, 165–169.

Geiger, B. (1996). Fathers as primary caregivers. Westport, CT: Greenwood.

Grunebaum, H. (2003). Thinking about romantic/erotic love. In M. Coleman & L. Ganong (Eds.), *Points and counterpoints* (pp. 88–91). Los Angeles: Roxbury.

Harley, W. F. (2001). *His needs, her needs: Building an affair-proof marriage*. Grand Rapids, MI: Fleming H. Revell.

Hatfield, E. (1988). Passionate and companionate love. In R. L. Sternberg & M. L. Barns (Eds.), *The psychology of love* (pp. 191–217). New Haven, CT: Yale University Press.

Hatfield, E., Brinton, C., & Cornelius, J. (1989). Passionate love and anxiety in young adolescents. *Motivation and Emotion*, 13, 271–289.

Hatfield, E., & Rapson, R. (1987). Passionate love. New directions in research. In W. H. Jones & D. Perlman (Eds.), *Advances in interpersonal relations* (pp. 109–139). Greenwich, CT: JAI Press.

Hatfield, E., & Rapson, R. (1993). Historical and cross-cultural perspectives on passionate love and sexual desire. *Annual Review of Sex Research*, 4, 67–97.

Hatfield, E., & Rapson, R. L. (1998). Emotional contagion and the communication of emotion. In M. T. Palmer & G. A. Barnett (Eds.), *Progress in Communication Sciences*, 14, 73–89.

Hatfield, E., & Rapson, R. L. (2007). *Passionate love and sexual desire: Multidisciplinary perspectives*. In J. P. Forgas (Ed.), Personal relationships: Cognitive, affective, and motivational processes. Tenth Symposium of Social Psychology, Sydney, Australia.

Hatfield, E., & Sprecher, S. (1986). Measuring passionate love in intimate relations. *Journal of Adolescence*, 9, 383–410.

Hawkins, A. J., & Van Den Berghe, B. (2017). The new math of consensual nonmonogamy. *National Review*. Retrieved July 1, 2019 from https://www.nationalreview.com/2017/12/consensual-non-monogamy-bad-math/

Hazan, C., & Shaver, P. (1987). Romantic love conceptualized as an attachment process. *Journal of Personality and Social Psychology*, 52, 511–524.

Hendrick, C., & Hendrick, S. S. (1989). Research on love: Does it measure up? *Journal of Personality and Social Psychology*, 56, 784–794.

Hendrick, S., & Hendrick, C. (1983). *Liking, loving, and relating*. Monterey, CA: Brooks/Cole.

Hendrick, S., & Hendrick, C. (1992). *Romantic love*. Newbury Park, CA: SAGE.

Howe, D., Brandon, M., Hinings, D., & Schofiled, G. (1999). *Attachment theory, child maltreatment, and family support*. Mahwah, NJ: Erlbaum.

Hunt, M. M. (1994). The natural history of love. New York: Funk and Wagnalls.

Keenan, J. (2013). Marry me. And me: The case for polyamory. *And while we're at it, let's privatize marriage*. Retrieved July 1, 2019 from https://slate.com/human-interest/2013/06/polyamory-should-be-legal-its-consensual-and-fine-for-children.html

Kim, J., & Hatfield, E. (2004). Love types and subjective well-being. *Social Behavior and Personality: An International Journal*, 32, 173–182.

Klaus, M. H., Kennell, J. H., & Klaus, P. H. (1995). *Bonding: Building the foundations of secure attachment and independence*. Boston: Addison-Wesley.

Klesse, C. (2011). Notions of love in polyamory—Elements in a discourse on multiple loving. *Laboratorium*, 3(2), 4–25.

Klesse, C. (2016). Polyamory and its "others": Contesting the terms of non-monogamy. *Sexualities*, 9(5), 565–583.

Knox, D., Breed, R., & Zusman, M. (2007). College men and jealousy. *College Student Journal*, 41(2), 494–499.

Landis, D., & O'Shea, W. A. (2000). Cross-cultural aspects of passionate love: An individual differences analysis. *Journal of Cross-Cultural Psychology*, 31, 752–777.

Lee, J. A. (1973). *The color of love: An exploration of the ways of loving*. Don Mills, ON: New Press.

Luhmann, N. (1986). *Love as passion: The codification of intimacy*. Cambridge, MA: Harvard University Press.

Lundqvist, L. O. (2006). A Swedish adaptation of the Emotional Contagion Scale: Factor structure and psychometric properties. *Scandinavian Journal of Psychology*, 47, 263–272.

Main, M., & Hesse, E. (1990). Parents' unresolved traumatic experiences are related to infant disorganized attachment status: Is frightened and/or frightening parental behavior the linking mechanism? In M. T. Greenberg,

D. Cicchetti, & E. M. Cummings (Eds.), *Attachment in the preschool years: Theory, research, and intervention* (pp. 161–182). Chicago: University of Chicago Press.

Markeiwicz, D., Doyle, A. B., & Brendgen, M. (2001). The quality of adolescents' friendships: Associations with mothers' interpersonal relationships, attachments to parents and friends, and prosocial behaviors. *Journal of Adolescence*, 24, 429–445.

Marsden, M. (2007). Love and elopement in northern Pakistan. *Journal of the Royal Anthropological Institute*, 13(1), 91–108.

Marshall, T. C., Bejanyan, K., Di Castro, G., & Lee, R. A. (2013). Attachment styles as predictors of Facebook-related jealousy and surveillance in romantic relationships. *Personal Relationships*, 20, 1–22.

Masters, R. (2011). *Transformation through intimacy: The journey toward awakened monogamy*. Berkeley, CA: North Atlantic Books.

Medora, N. P., Larson, J. H., Hortacsu, N., & Dave, P. (2002). Perceived attitudes towards romanticism: A cross-cultural study of American, Asian-India, and Turkish young adults. *Journal of Comparative Family Studies*, 33, 155–179.

Mitchell, M. E., Barhtolomew, K., & Cobb, R. J. (2013). Need fulfillment in polyamorous relationships. *Journal of Sex Research*, 1–11.

Money, J. (2003). *Mate selection across cultures*. Newbury Park, CA: SAGE.

Mullen, P. E., Pathe, M., & Purcell, R. (2000). *Stalkers and their victims*. Cambridge, MA: Cambridge University Press.

Neto, F. (1993). Love styles and self-representations. *Personality and Individual Differences*, 14, 795–803.

Neto, F. (1994). Love styles among Portuguese students. *Journal of Psychology*, 128, 613–616.

Neto, F. (2001). Love styles of three generations of women. *Marriage & Family Review*, 33(4), 19–30.

Neto, F., Mullet, E., Deschamps, J., Barros, J., Benvinido, R., Camino, L., . . . Machado, M. (2000). Attitudes toward love. *Journal of Cross-Cultural Psychology*, 31(5), 626–636.

Nichols, M. P., & Schwartz, R. C. (2004). *Family therapy: Concepts and methods* (6th ed.). Boston: Allyn & Bacon.

Oxford Dictionary. (2019). Polyamory. Retrieved April 18, 2020 from https://www.oxfordlearnersdictionaries.com/us/definition/english/polyamory

Penke, L., & Asendorph, J. B. (2008). Beyond global sociosexual orientations: A more differentiated look at sociosexuality and its effects on courtship and romantic relationships. *Journal of Personality and Social Psychology*, 95(5), 1113–1135.

Pickover, S. (2002). Breaking the cycle: A clinical example of disrupting an insecure attachment system. *Journal of Mental Health Counseling*, 24, 358–367.

Reiss, I. L. (1960, May). Toward a sociology of the heterosexual love relationship. *Marriage and Family Living*, 22, 139–145.

Reiss, I. L. (1971). *The family system in America*. New York: Holt, Rinehart, & Winston.

Rice, P. F. (1993). *Intimate relationships, marriage, and families*. Mountain View, CA: Mayfield.

Rubel, A. N., & Bogaert, A. F. (2014). Consensual nonmonogamy: Psychological well-being and relationship quality correlates. *The Journal of Sex Research*, 52(9), 961–982.

Rubin, Z. (1973). *Liking and loving: An invitation to social psychology*. New York: Holt, Rinehart, & Winston.

Russell, E. B., & Harton, H. C. (2005). The "other factors": Using individual and relationship characteristics to predict sexual and emotional jealousy. *Current Psychology: Developmental, Learning, Personality, Social*, 24(4), 242–257.

Sagarin, B. J. D., Becker, V., Guadango, R. E., Nicastle, L. D., & Millevoi, A. (2003). Sex differences (and similarities) in jealousy. *Evolution and Human Behavior*, 24, 17–23.

Sanger, M. (1914, March). The woman rebel. *The Aim*, 1(1).

Seepersad, S., Choi, M-K., & Shin, N. (2008). How does culture influence the degree of romantic loneliness and closeness? *The Journal of Psychology*, 142(2), 209–217.

Seiffge-Krenke, I. (1993). Close friendship and imaginary companions in adolescence. In B. Laursen (Ed.), *Close friendships in adolescence (pp. 73–87)*. San Francisco: Jossey-Bass.

Selzer, R. (1978). *Mortal lessons: Notes on the art of surgery* (pp. 45–46). Baltimore, MD: Johns Hopkins University Press.

Sheff, E. A. (2015). Five disadvantages of polyamory. Retrieved July 1, 2019 from https://www.psychologytoday.com/us/blog/the-polyamorists-next-door/201509/five-disadvantages-polyamory

Sheff, E. A. (2016). *When someone you love is polyamorous: Understanding poly people and relationships*. Portland, OR: Thorntree Press.

Shernoff, M. (2006). Negotiated nonmonogamy and male couples. *Family Process*, 45(4), 407–418.

Silverman, J. S. (2003). Fallacies about love and marriage. In M. Coleman & L. Ganong (Eds.), *Points and counterpoints* (pp. 91–93). Los Angeles: Roxbury.

Sorgen, C. (2008). All about jealousy. Retrieved November 6, 2008 from www.medicinenet.com

Sprecher, S., Sullivan, Q., & Hatfield, E. (1994). Mate selection preferences: Gender differences examined in a national sample. *Journal of Personality and Social Psychology*, 66, 1074–1080.

Sternberg, R. J. (1986). A triangular theory of love. *Psychological Review*, 93, 119–135.

Sternberg, R. J. (1988). *The psychology of love*. New Haven, CT: Yale University Press.

Tokunaga, R. (2011). Social networking site or social surveillance site? Understanding the use of interpersonal electronic surveillance in romantic relationships. *Computers in Human Behavior*, 27, 705–713.

U.S. Department of Justice. (2003). Intimate partner homicide. *National Institute of Justice Journal, 250*. Retrieved April 18, 2020 from https://www.ncjrs.gov/pdffiles1/jr000250.pdf

U.S. Department of Justice. (2018). Stalking Resource Center: Stalking fact sheet. Retrieved July 1, 2019 from https://victimsofcrime.org/docs/default-source/src/stalking-fact-sheet-2015_eng.pdf

van Ijzendoorn, M. H. (1995). Adult attachment representations, parental responsiveness, and infant attachment: A meta-analysis on the predictive validity of the Adult Attachment Interview. *Psychological Bulletin*, 117, 387–403.

Vuong, C. (2003). *The soulmate manifesto: Uniting all soulmate believers in an effort to solve dating*. San Francisco: Aluran.

Weiss, R. S. (1982). Attachment in adult life. In C. M. Parkes & J. Stevenson-Hinde (Eds.), *The place of attachment in human behavior* (pp. 171–184). New York: Basic Books.

White, G. L. (1981). A model of romantic jealousy. *Motivation and Emotion, 5*, 295–310.

Wood, M., & Stichman, A. (2018). Stalking on the college campus: The influence of suitable target and guardianship variables on victimization comparing male and female students. *Victims & Offenders*, 13(4), 47–503.

/// CHAPTER 7

Akhtar, R. C. (2018). Modern traditions in Muslim marriage practices: Exploring English narratives. *Oxford Journal of Law and Religion*, 7(3), 427–454.

Arnocky, S., Pearson, M., & Vaillancourt, T. (2015). Health, anticipated partner infidelity, and jealousy in men and women. *Evolutionary Psychology*, 13, 1–10. doi:10.1177/1474704915593666

Arnocky, S., Perilloux, C., Cloud, J. M., Bird, B. M., & Thomas, K. (2016). Envy mediates the link between social comparison and appearance enhancement in women. *Evolutionary Psychological Science*, 2, 71–83.

Arnocky, S., Ribout, A., Mirza, R., & Knack, J. M. (2014). Perceived mate availability influences intrasexual competition, jealousy and mate guarding behavior. *Journal of Evolutionary Psychology*, 12, 45–64. doi:10.1556/JEP.12.2014.1

Arnocky, S., Sunderani, S., Miller, J., & Vaillancourt, T. (2012). Jealousy mediates the relationship between attractiveness comparison and females' indirect aggression. *Personal Relationships*, 19, 290–303. doi:10.1111/j.1475-6811.2011.01362.x

Arnocky, S., & Vaillancourt, T. (2017). Sexual competition among women: A review of the theory and supporting evidence. In M. L. Fisher (Ed.), *The Oxford handbook of women and competition* (pp. 25–39). New York, NY: Oxford University Press. doi:10.1093/oxfordhb/9780199376377.013.3

Arnocky, S., Woodruff, N. W., & Schmitt, D. P. (2016). Men's sociosexuality is sensitive to changes in mate availability. *Personal Relationships*, 23, 172–181. doi:10.1111/pere.12118

Asexual Visibility & Education Network. (2020). About asexuality. Retrieved March 31, 2020 from https://www.asexuality.org

Australian Family Association. (2008). Retrieved July 20, 2008 from https://family.org.au/

Bachman, G. F., & Guerrero, L. K. (2006). Relational quality and communicative responses following hurtful events in dating relationships: An expectancy violations analysis. *Journal of Social and Personal Relationships*, 23(6), 943–963.

Barber, N. (1998). Secular changes in standards of bodily attractiveness in American women: Different masculine and feminine ideals. *Journal of Psychology*, 132(1), 87–95.

BARNA Research Group. (2017). Majority of Americans now believe in cohabitation. Retrieved December 29, 2017 from www.barna.com/research/majority-of-americans-now-believe-in-cohabitation/

Barraket, J., & Henry-Waring, M. S. (2008). Getting it on(line). *Journal of Sociology*, 44(2), 149–165.

Bartoli, A. M., & Clark, M. D. (2006). The dating game: Similarities and differences in dating scripts among college students. *Sexuality and Culture*, 10(4), 54–80.

Bernhardt, E. (2004). Cohabitation and marriage among young adults in Sweden: Attitudes, expectations, and plans. *Scandinavian Population Studies*, 13, 157–170.

Black, D., Sanders, S., & Taylor, L. (2007). The economics of lesbian and gay families. *Journal of Economic Perspectives*, 21(2), 53–70.

Blair, K. L., & Hoskin, R. A. (2018). Transgender exclusion from the world of dating: Patterns of acceptance and rejection of hypothetical trans dating partners as a function of sexual and gender identity. *Journal of Social and Personal Relationships*. https://doi.org/10.1177/0265407518779139

Bockting, W., Benner, A., & Coleman, E. (2009). Gay and bisexual identity development among female-to-male transsexuals in North America: Emergence of a transgender sexuality. *Archives of Sexual Behaviors*, 38, 688–701.

Bogaert, A. F. (2015). Asexuality: What it is and why it matters. *The Journal of Sex Research*, 52(4), 362–379.

Bogle, K. A. (2007). The shift from dating to hooking up in college: What scholars have missed. *Sociology Compass*, 1(2), 775–788.

Bogle, K. A. (2008). *Hooking up: Sex, dating, and relationships on campus*. New York: New York University Press.

Boss, P. G., Doherty, W. J., LaRossa, R., Schuram, W. R., & Steinmetz, S. K. (1993). *Sourcebook of family theories and methods: A contextual approach*. New York: Plenum.

Braboy Jackson, P., Kleiner, S., Geist, C., & Cebulko, K. (2011). Conventions of courtship: Gender and race differences in the significance of dating rituals. *Journal of Family Issues*, 32, 629–652.

Brown, S. L., Van Hook, J., & Glick, J. E. (2008). Generational differences in cohabitation and marriage in the U.S. *Population Research and Policy Review*, 27(5), 531–550.

Bumpass, L., & Lu, H. H. (2000). Trends in cohabitation and implications for children's family contexts in the United States. *Population Studies*, 54, 29–41.

Buss, D. M., & Shackelford, T. K. (2008). Attractive women want it all: Good genes, economic investment, parenting proclivities, and emotional commitment. *Evolutionary Psychology*, 6, 134–146. doi:10.1177/147470490800600116

Campbell, A. (2008). The morning after the night before: Affective reactions to one-night stands among mated and unmated women and men. *Human Nature*, 19, 157–173.

Carpenter, C., & Gates. G. J. (2008). Gay and lesbian partnership: Evidence from California. *Demography*, 45(3), 573–590.

Cere, D. (2001, Spring). Courtship today: The view from academia. *Public Interest*, 53.

Child Trends. (2015). Births to unmarried women: Indicators on children and youth. Retrieved May 22, 2020 from https://www.childtrends.org/wp-content/uploads/2015/03/75_Births_to_Unmarried_Women.pdf

Clausell, E., & Roisman, G. I. (2009). Outness, Big Five personality traits, and same-sex relationship quality. *Journal of Social and Personal Relationships*, 26, 211–226.

Cohan, C. I., & Kleinbaum, S. (2002). Toward a greater understanding of the cohabitation effect: Premarital cohabitation and marital communication. *Journal of Marriage and Family*, 64, 180–192.

Couch, D., Liamputtong, P., & Pitts, M. (2012). What are the real and perceived risks and dangers of online dating? Perspectives from online daters. *Health, Risk, & Society*, 14(7–8), 697–714.

Dargie, E., Blair, K. L., Pukall, C. F., & Coyle, S. M. (2014). Somewhere under the rainbow: Exploring the identities and experiences of trans persons. The Canadian Journal of Human Sexuality, 23, 60–74.

Darwin, C. (1871). *The descent of man and selection in relation to sex*. London: Murray.

Daugherty, J., & Copen, C. (2016). Trends in attitudes about marriage, childbearing, and sexual behavior: United States, 2002, 2006–2010, and 2011–2013. *National Health Statistics Reports*, 92, March 17.

Davis, D., Shaver, P. R., & Vernon, M. L. (2003). Physical, emotional, and behavioral reactions to breaking up: The roles of gender, age, emotional involvement, and attachment style. *Personality and Social Psychology Bulletin*, 29(7), 871–884.

Dawson, M., McDonnell, L., & Scott, S. (2016). Negotiating the boundaries of intimacy: The personal lives of asexual people. *The Sociological Review*, 64, 349–365.

Dixson, A. F. (2009). *Sexual selection and the origins of human mating systems*. New York: Oxford University Press.

Dobson, J. (2005). Courtship is an alternative to the dating model. Retrieved from www.uexpress.com/focusonthefamily/index.html

Downing-Matibag, T., & Geisinger, B. (2009). Hooking up and sexual risk taking among college students: A health belief model perspective. *Qualitative Health Research*, 19, 1196–1209.

Duck, S. W. (1985). Social and personal relationships. In M. L. Knapp & G. R. Miller (Eds.), *Handbook of interpersonal communication* (pp. 665–686). Beverly Hills, CA: SAGE.

Edlund, J. E., & Sagarin, B. J. (2010). Mate value and mate preferences: An investigation into decisions made with and without constraints. *Personality and Individual Differences*, 49, 835–839. doi:10.1016/j.paid.2010.07.004

England, P., & Thomas, R. (2007). The decline of the date and the rise of the college hook up. In A. Skolnick and J. Skolnick (Eds.), *Family in transition* (14th ed.). Boston: Allyn & Bacon.

Erber, R., & Erber, M. W. (2001). *Intimate relationships: Issues, theories, and research* (2nd ed.). Boston: Allyn & Bacon.

Fernandez, D. (2002). Sexual attraction among humans. Retrieved from http://serendip.brynmawr.edu/biology/bl03/f02/web1/dfernandez.html

Fielder, R. L., & Carey, M. P. (2010). Predictors and consequences of sexual "hookups" among college students: A short-term prospective study. *Archives of Sexual Behavior*, 39(5), 1105–1119.

Finkel, E. J., & Eastwick, P. W. (2009). Arbitrary social norms influence sex differences in romantic selectivity. *Psychological Science*, 20(10), 1290–1295.

Finkel, E. J., Rusbult, C. E., Kumashiro, M., & Hannon, P. A. (2002). Dealing with betrayal in close relationships: Does commitment promote forgiveness? *Journal of Personality and Social Psychology*, 82(6), 956–974.

Fisher, M. L., Worth, K., Garcia, J. R., & Meredith, T. (2012). Feelings of regret following uncommitted sexual encounters in Canadian university students. *Culture, Health & Sexuality*, 14, 45–57.

Fishman, R., Iyengar, S. S., Kamenica, E., & Simonson, I. (2006). Gender differences in mate selection: Evidence from a speed dating experiment. *Quarterly Journal of Economics*, 121, 673– 697.

Flack, W. F., Caron, M. L., Leinen, S. J., Breitenbach, K. G., Barger, A. M. et. al (2008). "The red zone": Temporal risk for unwanted sex among college students. *Journal of Interpersonal Violence*, 23, 1177–1196.

Flug, K. C. (2016). Swipe right? Young people and online dating in the digital age. *Master of Social Work and Clinical Research Papers*. Retrieved April 1, 2020 from https://sophia.stkate.edu/msw_papers/578/

Gallup News. (2017). In U.S., 10.2% of LGBT adults now married to same-sex spouse. Retrieved April 1, 2020 from https://news.gallup.com/poll/212702/lgbt-adults-married-sex-spouse.aspx

Garcia, J. R., & Reiber, C. (2008). Hook-up behavior: A biopsychosocial perspective. *Journal of Social, Evolutionary, and Cultural Psychology*, 2(4), 192–208.

Garcia, J. R., Reiber, B. C., Massey, S. G., & Merriwether, A. M. (2012). Sexual hookup culture: A review. *Review of General Psychology*, 16(2), 161–176.

Garcia, J. R., Rieber, C., Massey, S. G., & Merriwether, A. M. (2013). Sexual hook-up culture. *American Psychological Association*, 44(2), 1–60.

Garcia, T. A., Litt, D. M., Davis, K. C., Norris, J., Kaysen, D., & Lewis, M. A. (2019). Growing up, hooking up, and drinking: A review of uncommitted sexual behavior and its association with alcohol use and related consequences among adolescents and young adults in the United States. *Frontiers in Psychology*, 10. doi:10.3389/fpsyg.2019.01872

Gates, G. J. (2013). *LGBT parenting in the United States*. Los Angeles: The Williams Institute.

Gibson-Davis, C. M., Edin, K. J., & McLanahan, S. (2005). High hopes but even higher expectations: The retreat from marriage among low-income couples. *Journal of Marriage and Family*, 67(5), 1301–1312.

Gilks, W. P., Abbott, J. K., & Morrow, E. H. (2014). Sex differences in disease genetics: Evidence, evolution, and detection. *Trends in Genetics*, 30(10), 453–464.

Glenn, N., & Marquardt, E. (2001). Hooking up, hanging out, and hoping for Mr. Right: College women on dating and mating today. *Institute for American Values*. Retrieved from www.americanvalues.org/Hooking_Up.pdf

Gotta, G., Green, R., Rothblum, E., Solomon, S., Balsam, K., & Schwartz, P. (2011). Heterosexual, lesbian, and gay male relationships: A comparison of couples in 1975 and 2000. *Family Process*, 50, 353–376.

Grello, C. M., Welsh, D. P., & Harper, M. S. (2006). No strings attached: The nature of casual sex in college students. *Journal of Sex Research*, 43(3), 255–267.

Haefner, C. (2011). Asexual scripts: A grounded theory inquiry into the intrapsychic scripts asexuals use to negotiate romantic relationships (unpublished doctoral dissertation). Institute of Transpersonal Psychology, Palo Alto, CA.

Harris, K. M., & Udry, J. R. (2018). *National Longitudinal Study of Adolescent to Adult Health (Add Health), 1994–2008*. Chapel Hill, NC: Carolina Population Center, University of North Carolina-Chapel Hill. https://doi.org/10.3886/ICPSR21600.v21

Herbert, S., & Popadiuk, N. (2008). University students' experiences of nonmarital breakups: A grounded theory. *Journal of College Student Development*, 49(1), 1–14.

Iantaffi, A., & Bockting, W. O. (2011). Views from both sides of the bridge? Gender, sexual legitimacy and transgender people's experiences of relationships. *Culture, Health and Sexuality*, 13, 355–370.

Institute for Family Studies. (2016). Acceptance of divorce falling, tolerance for cohabitation rising. Retrieved June 12, 2019 from https://ifstudies.org/blog/acceptance-of-divorce-falling-tolerance-of-cohabitation-rising

Institute for Family Studies. (2018). Cohabitation is pervasive. Retrieved June 12, 2019 from https://ifstudies.org/blog/cohabitation-is-pervasive

Janicke, T., & Morrow, E. H. (2019). Sexual selection. *Evolution, Medicine, and Public Health*, 2019(1), 36.

Johnson, M. P. (1991). Commitment to personal relationships. *Advances in Personal Relationships*, 3, 117–143.

Kass, L. R. (1997). The end of courtship. *Public Interest*, 126, 39–64.

Klinkenberg, D., & Rose, S. (1994). Dating scripts of gay men and lesbians. *Journal of Homosexuality*, 26(4), 23–35.

Knapp, M. (1984). *Interpersonal communication and human relationships*. Boston: Allyn & Bacon.

Kurzban, R., & Weeden, J. (2005). Hurrydate: Mate preferences in action. *Evolution and Human Behavior*, 26, 227–244.

Lamont, E. (2017). "We can write the scripts ourselves": Queer challenges to heteronormative courtship practices. *Gender & Society*, 31(3), 624–646.

Laner, M. R., & Ventrone, N. A. (1998). Egalitarian daters/traditionalist dates. *Journal of Family Issues*, 19(4), 468–477.

LeFebvre, L. E. (2017). Swiping me off my feet: Explicating relationship initiation on Tinder. *Journal of Social and Personal Relationships*, 35(9), 1205–1229.

Levinger, G. (1982, August). A systems perspective on the development of close relationships. Presented at the Annual American Psychological Association Meeting, Washington, DC.

Lewis, M., Granato, H., Blayney, J., Lostutter, T., & Kilmer, J. (2011). Predictors of hooking up: Sexual behaviors and emotional reactions among U.S. college students. *Archives of Sexual Behavior*, 41, 1219–1229.

Lin, M. (2019). Online dating industry: Business of love. Retrieved April 18, 2020 from https://www.toptal.com/finance/business-model-consultants/online-dating-industry

Lyons, H. A., Manning, W. D., Longmore, M. A., & Giordano, P. (2014). Young adult casual sexual behavior: Life-course-specific motivations and consequences. *Social Perspective*, 57(1), 79–101.

Madden, M., & Lenhart, A. (2006). *Online dating*. Washington, DC: Pew Internet & American Life Project.

Manning, W. D., & Brown, S. L. (2003). Children's economic well-being in cohabiting parent families: An update and extension. Working paper series 03–05. Bowling Green, OH: Bowling Green State University Center for Family and Demographic Research. Retrieved from www.bgsu.eciu/organizations/cfdr/research/pdf/2003/2003_05.pdf

Manning, W. D., & Jones, A. J. (2006, March 30–April 1). *Cohabitation and marital dissolution*. Paper presented at the annual meeting of the Population Association of America, Los Angeles.

Manning, W. D., & Smock, P. J. (2003, May 3). *Measuring and modeling cohabitation: New perspectives from quantitative data*. Paper presented to the Population Association of America.

Manning, W. D., & Smock, P. J. (2005). Measuring and modeling cohabitation: New perspectives from qualitative data. *Journal of Marriage and Family*, 67(4), 989–1002.

Manning, W. D., Smock, P. J. & Fettro, M. N. (2019). Cohabitation and marital expectations among single millennials in the U.S. *Population Research and Policy Review*, 38(3), 327–246.

Meier, S. C., Sharp, C., Michonski, J., Babcock, J. C., & Fitzgerald, K. (2013). Romantic relationships of female-to-male trans men: A descriptive study. *International Journal of Transgenderism*, 14, 75–85.

Mitchell, S. (2003). *American generations: Who they are, how they live, what they think*. Ithaca, NY: New Strategist.

Morrow, E. H. (2015). The evolution of sex differences in disease. *Biology of Sex Differences*, 6(5). doi:10.1186/s13293-015-0023-0

National Council on Family Relations. (2020). Understanding families: Research and practice. Retrieved April 18, 2020 from https://www.ncfr.org/membership

National Institute of Population and Social Security Research. (2019). *Population statistics of Japan: 2017*. Retrieved May 22, 2020 from http://www.ipss.go.jp/p-info/e/psj2017/PSJ2017.asp

Needham, L. B. (1999). An investigation of exceptions to patterns of mate selection in evolutionary theory among resource dependent and independent females. Retrieved from http://mutans.astate.edu/dcSine/Guidc/Mate_selection.html

Ngo, N. T. (2019). What historical ideals of women's shapes teach us about women's self-perception and body decisions today. *AMA Journal of Ethics* 21(10), E879–901. doi:10.1001/amajethics.2019.879.

Olson, D. H., & Olson-Sigg, A. (2007). Overview of cohabitation research. Retrieved May 22, 2020, from www.prepare-enrich.com

Osborn, C. (2005). Marriage following the birth of a child among cohabiting and visiting parents. *Journal of Marriage and Family*, 67(1), 14–26.

Owen, J., & Fincham, F. D. (2011). Young adults' emotional reactions after hooking up encounters. *Archives of Sexual Behavior*, 40(2), 321–330.

Paik, A. (2010). "Hookups," dating, and relationship quality: Does the type of sexual involvement matter? *Social Science Research*, 39(5), 739–753.

Paul, E. L., & Hayes, K. A. (2002). The casualties of "casual" sex: A qualitative exploration of the phenomenology of college students' hookups. *Journal of Social and Personal Relationships*, 19, 639–661.

Paul, K. (2017). How online dating affects divorce rates. Retrieved May 22, 2020 from https://www.marketwatch.com/story/what-online-dating-could-do-to-divorce-rates-2017-10-16

Peplau, L. A., & Fingerhut, A. D. (2007). The close relationships of lesbians and gay men. *Annual Reviews of Psychology*, 58, 405–424.

Peplau, L. A., & Spalding, L. R. (2000). The close relationships of lesbians, gay men, and bisexuals. In C. Hendrick & S. S. Hendrick (Eds.), *Close relationships: A sourcebook* (pp. 111–124). Thousand Oaks, CA: SAGE.

Pew Research Center. (2007). Purpose of marriage. Retrieved from www.pewsocialtrends.org/pubs/?chartid=447

Pew Research Center. (2017). Number of U.S. adults cohabiting with a partner continues to rise, especially among those 50 and older. Retrieved June 10, 2019 from https://www.pewresearch.org/fact-tank/2017/04/06/number-of-u-s-adults-cohabiting-with-a-partner-continues-to-rise-especially-among-those-50-and-older/

Pew Research Center. (2020). 10 facts about Americans and online dating. Retrieved April 19, 2020 from https://www.pewresearch.org/fact-tank/2020/02/06/10-facts-about-americans-and-online-dating/

Poorani, A. (2012). Who determines the ideal body? A summary of research findings on body image. *New Media & Mass Communication*, 2, 1–13. Retrieved March 31, 2020 from http://citeseerx.ist.psu.edu

Price, M., Hides, L., Cockshaw, W., Staneva, A. A., & Stoyanov, S. R. (2016). Young love: Romantic concerns and associated mental health issues among adolescent help-seekers. *Behavioral Science*, 6(2), 9.

RAINN. (2020). The legal role of consent. Retrieved March 31, 2020 from https://www.rainn.org/articles/legal-role-consent

Rhoades, G. K., Stanley, S. M., & Markman, H. J. (2011). Should I stay or should I go? Predicting dating relationship stability from 4 aspects of commitment. *Journal of Family Psychology*, 24(5), 543–550.

Riggs, D. W., von Doussa, H., & Power, J. (2015). The family and romantic relationships of trans and gender-diverse Australians: An exploratory survey. *Sexual and Relationship Therapy*, 30, 243–255.

Roloff, M. E., Soule, K. P., & Carey, C. M. (2001). Reasons for remaining in a relationship and responses to relational transgressions. *Journal of Social and Personal Relationships*, 18, 362–385.

Rose, S., & Frieze, I. H. (1989). Young singles' scripts for a first date. *Gender and Society*, 3, 258–268.

Rose, S., & Frieze, I. H. (1993). Young singles' contemporary dating scripts. *Sex Roles*, 28, 499–509.

Rose, S. M., & Zand, D. (2002). Lesbian dating and courtship from young adulthood to midlife. *Journal of Lesbian Studies*, 6(1), 85–109.

Rostosky, S. S., Riggle, E. D. B., Dudley, M. G., & Wright, M. L. (2006). Commitment in same-sex relationships: A qualitative analysis of couples' conversations. *Journal of Homosexuality*, 51(3), 199–223.

Rusbult, C. E., & Buunk, B. P. (1993). Commitment processes in close relationships: Interdependence analysis. *Journal of Social and Personal Relationships*, 10, 175–204.

Russo, L. (2000). Date rape: A hidden crime. *Australian Institute of Criminology*, ISSN 0817-8542, Number 157.

Schmitt, D. P., & Buss, D. M. (2001). Human mate poaching: Tactics and temptations for infiltrating existing mateships. *Journal of Personality and Social Psychology*, 80, 894–917.

Schmitt, D. P., Shackelfor, T., Duntley, J., Tooke, W. & Buss, D. M. (2001). The desire for sexual variety as a tool for understanding basic human mating strategies. *Personal Relationships*, 8, 425–455.

Simmons, T., & O'Connell, M. (2003). Married-couple and unmarried-partner households: 2000. United States Census Bureau report. Retrieved from www.landview.census.gov/prod/2003pubs/censr-5.pdf

Simon, W., & Gagnon, G. (1986). Sexual scripts: Permanence and change. *Archives of Sexual Behavior*, 15, 97–120.

Singh, D. (2002). Female mate value at a glance: Relationship of waist-to-hip ratio to health, fecundity, and attractiveness. *Neuroendocrinology Letters Special Issue*, 23, 81–91.

Singh, D. (2004). Mating strategies of young women: Role of physical attractiveness. *Journal of Sex Research*, 41(1), 43–54.

Smock, W., Manning, W., & Porter, M. (2005). Everything's there except money: How money shapes decisions to marry among cohabitors. *Journal of Marriage and Family*, 67(3), 680–696.

Solot, D., & Miller, M. (2004). Affirmation of family diversity. *Alternatives to Marriage Project*. Retrieved October 20, 2004 from www.unmarried.org/family.html

Spell, S. A. (2016). Not just Black and white: How race/ethnicity and gender intersect in hookup culture. *Sociology of Race and Ethnicity*. doi:10.1177/2332649216658296

Sprecher, S. (1998). Social exchange theories and sexuality. *The Journal of Sex Research*, 35(1), 32–44.

Stanley, S. M., Kline Rhoades, G., & Markman, H. J. (2006). Sliding versus deciding: Inertia and the premarital cohabitation effect. *Family Relations*, 55, 499–509.

Starling, K. (2000, February). The joys and dangers of love on the internet. *Ebony*.

Stinson, R. D. (2010). Hooking up in young adulthood: A review of factors influencing the sexual behavior of college students. *Journal of College Student Psychotherapy*, 24, 98–155.

Swenson, C. H., & Trahaug, G. (1985). Commitment in the long-term marriage relationship. *Journal of Marriage and the Family*, 47(4), 939–945.

Taylor, P. (2014). *The next America and the looming generational showdown*. New York: Public Affairs.

Teachman, J. D. (2003). Premarital sex, premarital cohabitation, and the risk of subsequent marital dissolution among women. *Journal of Marriage and Family*, 65(2), 444–455.

Thibaut, J. W., & Kelley, H. H. (1959). *The social psychology of groups*. New York: John Wiley.

Todd, P. M., Penke, L., Fasolo, B., & Lenton, A. P. (2007). Different cognitive processes underlie human mate choices and mate preferences. *Proceedings of the National Academy of Sciences*, 104, 15011–15016.

Tooman, C. (1970, April). It goes to bed with you, no matter what you are. *Marriage*, 28–31.

Townsend, J. M., & Wasserman, T. (1998). Sexual attractiveness: Sex differences in assessment and criteria. *Evolution and Human Behavior*, 19, 171–191.

Trask, B. S., & Koivunen, J. M. (2006). Trends in marriage and cohabitation in culturally diverse families. In B. S. Trask & R. Hamon (Eds.), *Cultural diversity and families: Expanding perspectives* (pp. 121–136). Thousand Oaks, CA: SAGE.

Umberson, D., Thomeer, M. B., Kroeger, R. A., Lodge, A. C., & Xu, M. (2015). Challenges and opportunities for research on same-sex relationships. *Journal of Marriage and Family*, 77(1), 96–111.

U.S. Census Bureau. (2018). For young adults, cohabitation is up, marriage is down. Retrieved June 13, 2019 from https://www.census.gov/library/stories/2018/11/cohabitaiton-is-up-marriage-is-down-for-young-adults.html

U.S. Census Bureau. (2019). Cohabitation over the last 20 years: Measuring and understanding the changing demographics of unmarried partners, 1996–2017. Retrieved March 31, 2020 from https://www.census.gov/library/working-papers/2019/demo/SEHSD-WP2019-10.html

Van Houdenhove, E., Gis, L., T'Sjoen, G., & Enzlin, P. (2015). Stories about asexuality: A qualitative study on asexual women. *Journal of Marital and Sex Therapy*, 41(3), 262–281.

Vangelisti, A. L., & Young, S. L. (2000). When words hurt: The effects of perceived intentionality on interpersonal relationships. *Journal of Social and Personal Relationships*, 17, 393–424.

Vares, T. (2017). "My [asexuality] is playing hell with my dating life." Romantic identified asexuals negotiate the dating game. *Sexualities*, 21(2). doi:10.1177/1363460717716400

Wade, L. (2017). *American hookup: The new culture of sex on campus*. New York: W.W. Norton.

Wade, L., & Heldman, C. (2012). Hooking up and opting out: Negotiating sex in the first year of college. In L. Carpenter & J. DeLamater (Eds.), *Sex for life: From virginity to Viagra, how sexuality changes throughout our lives* (pp.128–145). New York: New York University Press.

Wade, L., Kremer, E., & Brown, J. (2005). The incidental orgasm: The presence of clitoral knowledge and the absence of orgasm for women. *Women and Health*, 42(1), 117–138.

Waite, L., & Gallagher, M. (2001). *The case for marriage: Why married people are happier, healthier, and better off financially*. New York: Random House.

Welling, L. L., Singh, K., Puts, D. A., Jones, B. C., & Burriss, R. P. (2013). Self-reported sexual desire in homosexual men and women predicts preferences for sexually dimorphic facial cues. *Archives of Sexual Behavior*, 42(5), 785–791.

Wesche, R., Claxton, S. E., Lefkowitz, E. S., & van Dulmen, M. H. M. (2018). Evaluations and future plans after casual sexual experiences: Differences across partner type. *Journal of Sex Research*, 55(9), 1180–1191.

White, J. M., & Klein, D. M. (2008). *Family theories: An introduction* (3rd ed.). Thousand Oaks, CA: SAGE.

Williams Institute. (2019). Same-sex couple data and demographics. Retrieved April 1, 2020 from https://williamsinstitute.law.ucla.edu/visualization/lgbt-stats/

Witmer, D. (2005). Dating violence. Retrieved from www.parentingteens.about.com/es/daterape

Wu, Z. (2007, October 23). *Shacked up; A demographic profile of non-marital cohabitation*. Paper presented to the Breakfast on the Hill Seminar Series, Ottawa, Ontario.

Zand, D., & Rose, S. (1992). Establishing lesbian relationships. Unpublished manuscript, University of Missouri, St. Louis.

Zuk, M. (2009). The sicker sex. *PLOS Pathogens*. https://doi.org/10.1371/journal.ppat.1000267

/// CHAPTER 8

Amati, V., Meggiolaro, S., Rivellini, G., & Zaccarin, S. (2018). Social relations and life satisfaction: The role of friends. *Genus*, 74(1), 7. doi:10.1186/s41118-018-0032-z

American Adoptions. (2009). The steps to adoption. Retrieved August 1, 2009 from www.americanadoptions.com.

American Family Survey. (2019). *What Americans think about marriage and family*, 2018. Retrieved June 16, 2019 from www.desertnews.com/american-family-survey/2018

Anderson, J. (2014). The impact of family structure on the health of children: Effects of divorce. *Linacre Quarterly*, 81(4), 378–387.

Anderson, J. R., Doherty, W. J., & Van Ryzin, M. J. (2008, July 17–30). *Developmental trajectories of marital happiness: Predictors and outcomes*. Paper presented at the International Association for Relationship Research Conference, Providence, RI.

Anderson, S. A., Russell, S. R., & Schumm, W. R. (1983). Perceived marital quality and family life-cycle categories: A further analysis. *Journal of Marriage and the Family*, 45, 127–139.

Anderson, S. A., & Sabatelli, R. M. (2007). *Family interaction: A multi-generational developmental perspective* (4th ed.). New York: Pearson.

Anderson, S. A., & Sabatelli, R. M. (2011). *Family interaction: A multi-generational developmental perspective* (5th ed.). New York: Pearson.

Anxo, D., Mencarini, L., Pailhé, A., Solaz, A., Tanturri, M. L., & Flood, L. (2011) Gender differences in time use over the life course in France, Italy, Sweden, and the US. *Feminist Economics*, 17(3), 159–195.

Barrett, A. (1999). Social support and life satisfaction among the never married. *Research on Aging*, 21(1), 46–72.

Bedard, M. E. (1992). *Breaking with tradition: Diversity, conflict, and change in contemporary families*. Dix Hills, NY: General Hall.

Belsky, J., Woodworth, S., & Crnic, K. (1996). Trouble in the second year: Three questions about family interaction. *Child Development*, 67, 556–578.

Berrington, A., Perelli-Harris, B., & Trevena, P. (2015). Commitment and the changing sequence of cohabitation, childbearing, and marriage: Insights from qualitative research in the UK. *Demographic Research*, 33(12), 327–262.

Birditt, K. S., Wan, W. H., Orbuch, T. L., & Antonucci, T. C. (2017). The development of marital tension: Implications for divorce among married couples. *Developmental psychology*, 53(10), 1995–2006.

Black Demographics. (2019). Black marriage in America. Retrieved May 26, 2020 from https://blackdemographics.com/households/marriage-in-black-america/

Brewster, M. E. (2017). Lesbian women and household labor division: A systematic review of scholarly research from 2000 to 2015. *Journal of Lesbian Studies*, 21(1), 47–69.

Browning, D. (2004). Why marry? Retrieved from www.equalityinmarriage.org/bmwhy.html

Burr, W. R. (1970). Satisfaction with various aspects of marriage over the life cycle: A random middle-class sample. *Journal of Marriage and the Family*, 32, 29–37.

Burr, W. R. (1973). *Theory construction and the sociology of the family*. New York: Wiley.

Campbell, K. (2002, February 14). Today's courtship: White teeth, root beer, and e-mail? *Christian Science Monitor*, 1–4.

Carter, B., & McGoldrick, M. (1999). The expanded family life cycle: Individual, family, and social perspectives (3rd ed.). Boston: Allyn & Bacon.

Cherlin, A. J. (2004). The deinstitutionalization of American marriage. *Journal of Marriage and Family*, 66(4), 848–861.

Chiong, J. A. (1998). Racial categorization of multiracial children in schools. Westport, CT: Bergin & Garvey.

Craig, L., & Mullan, K. (2011). How mothers and fathers share childcare: A cross-national time-use comparison. *American Sociological Review*, 76(6), 834–861.

DeMaris, A., Sanchez, L. A., & Krivickas, K. (2013). Developmental patterns in marital satisfaction: Another look at covenant marriage. *Journal of Marriage and Family*, 74(5), 989–1004.

DePaulo, B. (2018). Marriage: Is it possible that Americans just aren't that into it? *Psychology Today*. Retrieved June 15, 2019 from https://www.psychologytoday.com/ca/blog/living-single/201812/no-need-marry-have-kids-be-fulfilled-new-survey

Doss, B. D., Rhoades, G. K., Stanley, S. M., & Markman, J. J. (2009). Marital therapy, retreats, and books: The who, what, when, and why of relationship help-seeking. *Journal of Marital and Family Therapy*, 35(1), 18–29.

Ehrle, J., Kortenkamp, K., & Stagner, M. (2003). Family structure and outcomes for children of long-term welfare recipients. Unpublished manuscript. Washington, DC: Urban Institute.

Family Equality Council. (2017). LGBT divorce equality. Retrieved May 26, 2020 from https://www.familyequality.org/2019/04/02/podcast-lgbtq-divorce-equality/

Fitzpatrick, M. A. (1988). Between husbands & wives: Communication in marriage. *SAGE series in interpersonal communication*, Vol. 7. Thousand Oaks, CA: SAGE.

Fitzpatrick, M. A., & Best, P. (1979). Dyadic adjustment in relational types: Consensus, cohesion, affectional expression, and satisfaction in enduring relationships. *Communication Monographs*, 46, 167–178.

Fleisher, J. (2005). Living two lives: Married to a man and in love with a woman. Los Angeles: Alyson.

Forbes. (2019). Student loan debt. Retrieved June 16, 2019 from www.forbes.com/sites/zackfriedman/2019/02/25/student-laon-debt-statistics-2019/#12513f21133f

Fowers, B. J., Montel, K. H., & Olson, D. H. (1996). Predicting marital success for premarital couple types based on PREPARE. *Journal of Marital and Family Therapy*, 22(1), 103–119.

Fowers, B. J., & Olson, D. H. (1986). Predicting marital success with PREPARE: A predictive validity study. *Journal of Marital and Family Therapy*, 12, 403–413.

Friedman, Z. (2019). 50% of millennials are moving back home with their parents after college. Retrieved June 16, 2019 from www.forbes.com/sites/zackfriedman/2019/06/06/millennials-move-back-home-college/

Fu, X., Tora, H., & Kendall, J. (2001). Marital happiness and interracial marriage: A study in a multi-ethnic community in Hawaii. *Journal of Comparative Family Studies*, 32(1), 47–60.

Gajuwala, A. L. (2004). The challenge of being different: A Christian-Hindu marriage. Retrieved from www.interchurchfamilies.org/joumal/98sul4.htm

Gallup Daily. (2017). In U.S., more adults identifying as LGBT. Retrieved April 20, 2020 from https://news.gallup.com/poll/201731/lgbt-identification-rises.aspx

Gallup Daily. (2018). In U.S., estimate of LGBT population rises to 4.5 percent. Retrieved April 2020 from https://news.gallup.com/poll/234863/estimate-lgbt-population-rises.aspx

Gates, G. (2017). LBBTQ data collection amid social and demographic shifts of the US LGBT community. *American Journal of Public Health*, 107(8), 1220–1222.

Gee, C. B., Scott, R. L., Castellani, A. M., & Cordova, J. V. (2002). Predicting 2-year marital satisfaction from partners' discussion of the marriage check-up. *Journal of Marriage and Family*, 28(4), 399–407.

Ginther, D., & Pollack, R. (2003, April). *Does family structure affect children's educational outcomes?* Working Paper No. 29628. Cambridge, MA: National Bureau of Economic Research.

Glass, R. D., & Wallace, K. R. (1996). Challenging race and racism. In M. P. P. Root (Ed.), *The multicultural experience: Racial borders as the new frontier* (pp. 341–358). Thousand Oaks, CA: SAGE.

Goodman, K. L. (1991). Racial and religious intermarriage. Unpublished work. Church of Latter Day Saints (LDS) Research Information Division.

Gordon, D. (2003). *Female sexual arousal disorder. The Gale Encyclopedia of Medicine* (2nd ed.). Farmington Hills, MI: Gale Group.

Grundy, E. M. D., & Tomassini, C. (2010). Marital history, health and mortality among older men and women in England and Wales. *BMC Public Health*, 10, 554.

Gruzen, L. (1990). *Raising your Jewish/Christian child*. New York: Newmarket Press.

Halpren, D. (2005). *Social capital*. Cambridge: Polity Press.

Hawkins, A., Nock, S., Wilson, J., Sanchez, L., & Wright, J. (2002). Attitudes about covenant marriage and divorce: Policy implications from a three-state comparison. *Family Relations*, 61, 166–175.

Hughes, M. E., & Waite, L. J. (2009). Marital biography and health at mid-life. *Journal of Health and Social Behavior*, 50(3), 344–358.

Human Rights Campaign. (2018). HRC 2018 annual report. Retrieved April 20, 2020 from https://issuu.com/humanrightscampaign/docs/hrc-annual-report-2018

Jones, J. M. (2017). In U.S., 10.2% of LGBT adults now married to same-sex spouse. *Social & Policy Issues*, June 22, 2017. Retrieved June 18, 2019 from www.news.gallup.com/poll/212702/lgbt-adlts-married-sex-spouse.aspx

Karney, B. R., & Bradbury. T. N. (1997). Neuroticism, marital interaction, and the trajectory of marital satisfaction. *Journal of Personality and Social Psychology*, 72, 1075–1092.

Kelley, D. L. (1999). Relational expectancy fulfillment as an explanatory variable for distinguishing couple types. *Human Communication Research*, 25(3), 420–442.

Kenney, K. R. (2002). Counseling interracial couples and multiracial individuals: Applying a multicultural counseling competency framework. *Counseling and Human Development*, 35(14), 1–13.

Kort, J. (2015). Mixed-orientation marriages. *GLBTQ Encyclopedia*. Retrieved June 18, 2019 from http://www.glbtqarchive.com/ssh/mixed_orientation_marriages_S.pdf

Kovacs, L. (1983). A conceptualization of marital development. *Family Therapy*, 3, 183–210.

Kurdek, L. A. (1999). The nature and predictors of the trajectory of change in marital quality for husbands and wives over the first 10 years of marriage. *Developmental Psychology*, 35(5), 1283–1296.

Larsen, A. S., & Olson, D. H. (1989). Predicting marital satisfaction using PREPARE: A replication study. *Journal of Marital and Family Therapy*, 15, 311–322.

Lavner, J. A., Karney, B. R., & Bradbury, T. N. (2016). Does couples' communication predict marital satisfaction, or does marital satisfaction predict communication? *Journal of Marriage and Family*, 78(3), 680–694.

Lemme, B. (2006). *Development in adulthood* (4th ed.) Boston: Pearson Education.

Lerman, R. A. (2002a, July). *How do marriage, cohabitation, and single parenthood affect the marital hardships of families with children?* Washington, DC: Urban Institute.

Lerman, R. A. (2002b, July). *Impact of marital status and parental presence on the material hardship of families with children.* Washington, DC: Urban Institute.

Leslie, L. A., & Young, J. L. (2015). Interracial couples in therapy: Common themes and issues. *Journal of Social Issues*, 71(4), 788–803.

Levitt, M. (1991). Attachment and close relationships: A lifespan perspective. In J. L. Gewirtz & W. F. Kurtines (Eds.), *Intersections with attachment* (pp. 183–206). Hillsdale, NJ: Erlbaum.

Lichter, D. T., & Qian, Z. (2004). *Marriage and family in a multiracial society.* New York and Washington, DC: Russell Sage Foundation and Population Reference Bureau.

Mackay, R. (2005). The impact of family structure and family change on child outcomes: A personal reading of the research literature. *Social Policy Journal of New Zealand*, 24, 111–131.

Mayer, E. (1987). *Love and tradition: Marriage between Jews and Christians.* New York: Schocken Books.

McGoldrick, M., & Carter, B. (1999). Remarried families. In B. Carter & M. McGoldrick (Eds.), *The expanded family life cycle* (3rd ed.; pp. 417–435). New York: Guilford.

Miller, R. B. (2001). Do children make a marriage unhappy? *Marriage and Families.* Retrieved from http://marriagcandfamiiies.byu.edu/issues/2001/April/children.aspx

Myers, D. G. (2000). The funds, friends, and faith of happy people. *American Psychologist*, 55(1), 56–67.

National Council on Family Relations. (2019). Strengthening families. Retrieved April 17, 2020 from http://www.ncfr.org

Nguyen, A. W., Chatters, L. M., Taylor, R. J., & Mouzon, D. M. (2015). Social support from family and friends and subjective well-being of older African Americans. *Journal of Happiness Studies.* doi:10.1007/s10902-015-9626-8

Nock, S. L., Sanchez, L. A., & Wright, J. D. (2008). *Covenant marriage: The movement to reclaim tradition in marriage.* Chicago, IL: Rutgers University Press.

Oláh L. S., Kotowska, I. E., & Richter, R. (2018) The new roles of men and women and implications for families and societies. In G. Doblhammer & J. Gumà (Eds.), *A demographic perspective on gender, family and health in Europe.* New York: Springer.

Orbuch, T. L, House, J. S. Mero, R. P., & Webster, P. S. (1996). Marital quality over the life course. *Social Psychology Quarterly*, 59, 162–171.

Padgett, T., & Sikora, F. (2003, May). Color-blind love: Once considered taboo, interracial marriages are now on the rise—even in some unexpected places. *Time.*

Perelli-Harris, B., Hoherz, S., Addo, F., Lappagard, T., Evans, A., Sassier, S., & Styrc, M. (2018). Do marriage and cohabitation provide benefits to health in mid-life? The role of childhood selection mechanisms and partnership characteristics across countries. *Population Research Policy Review*, 37(5), 703–728.

Perelli-Harris, B., Mynarska, M., Berrington, A., Berghammer, C. Evans, A. Isupova, O., . . . Vignoli, D. (2014). Towards a new understanding of cohabitation: Insights from focus group research across Europe and Australia. *Demographic Research*, 31(34), 1043–1078.

Peterson, L. R. (1986). Interfaith marriages and religious commitment among Catholics. *Journal of Marriage and Family*, 48, 725–735.

Pew Research Center. (2007). Purpose of marriage. Retrieved from www.pewsocialtrends.org/pubs/?chartid=447

Pew Research Center. (2013). The global divide on homosexuality: Greater acceptance in more secular and affluent countries. Retrieved March 28, 2020 from https://www.pewresearch.org/global/2013/06/04/the-global-divide-on-homosexuality/

Pew Research Center. (2014). Public views on marriage. Retrieved April 10, 2020 from https://www.pewsocialtrends.org/2014/09/24/chapter-1-public-views-on-marriage/

Pew Research Center. (2015). Interfaith marriage is common in U.S., particularly among the recently wed. Retrieved March 28, 2020 from https://www.pewresearch.org/fact-tank/2015/06/02/interfaith-marriage/

Pew Research Center. (2016). Shared religious beliefs in marriage are important to some, but not all married Americans. Retrieved April 19, 2020 from https://www.pewresearch.org/fact-tank/2016/10/27/shared-religious-beliefs-in-marriage-important-to-some-but-not-all-married-americans/

Pew Research Center. (2017a). As U.S. marriage rate hovers at 50%, education gap in marital status widens. Retrieved June 18, 2019 from https://www.pewresearch.org/fact-tank/2017/09/14/as-u-s-marriage-rate-hovers-at-50-education-gap-in-marital-status-widens/

Pew Research Center. (2017b). The share of Americans living without a partner has increased, especially among young adults. Retrieved March 28, 2020 from https://www.pewresearch.org/fact-tank/2017/10/11/the-share-of-americans-living-without-a-partner-has-increased-especially-among-young-adults/

Pew Research Center. (2019a). 8 facts about love and marriage in America. Retrieved April 10, 2020 from https://www.pewresearch.org/fact-tank/2019/02/13/8-facts-about-love-and-marriage/

Pew Research Center. (2019b). 5 facts about same-sex marriage. Retrieved April 10, 2020 from https://www.pewresearch.org/fact-tank/2019/06/24/same-sex-marriage/

Pew Research Center. (2019c). Key findings on marriage and cohabitation in the U.S. Retrieved April 10, 2020 from https://www.pewresearch.org/fact-tank/2019/11/06/key-findings-on-marriage-and-cohabitation-in-the-u-s/

Pew Research Center. (2019d). Marriage and cohabitation in the United States. Retrieved April 10, 2020 from https://www.pewsocialtrends.org/2019/11/06/marriage-and-cohabitation-in-the-u-s/

Pew Research Center. (2019e). Trends and patterns in intermarriage. Retrieved March 28, 2020 from https://www.pewsocialtrends.org/2017/05/18/1-trends-and-patterns-in-intermarriage/

Putnam, R. D. (2000). *Bowling alone: The collapse and revival of American community.* New York: Simon and Schuster.

Qian, Z. (1999). Who intermarries? Education, nativity, region, and interracial marriage. 1980 and 1990. *Journal of Comparative Family Studies*, 30, 579–586.

Ribar, D. C. (2003). What do social scientists know about the benefits of marriage? *A review of quantitative methodologies* (pp. 1–79). Washington, DC: George Washington University Department of Economics.

Robels, T. F., Slatcher, R. B., Trombello, J. M., & McGinn, M. M. (2014). Marital quality and health: A meta-analytic review. *Psychological Bulletin*, 140(1). doi:10.1037/a0031859

Ross, D. S., & Ross, R. R. (2004). Interfaith weddings: An introduction. Retrieved from www.love-Lrack.com/cc/cc_f_one_rabbirev.html

Ryan, R., Claessens, A., & Markowitz, A. J. (2013/2014). Family structure and children's behavior. *Focus*, 30(2), 11–14.

Sayer, L., Bianchi, S. M., & Robinson, J. P. (2004). Are parents investing less in children? Trends in mothers' and fathers' time with children. *American Journal of Sociology*, 110(1), 1–43.

Schwartz, P. (1994). *Peer marriage: How love between equals really works*. New York: Free Press.

Schwartz, P. (2001). Peer marriage: What does it take to create a truly egalitarian relationship? In A. S. Skolnick & J. H. Skolnick (Eds.), *Families in transition* (11th ed.; pp. 182–190). New York: Pearson.

Sewenet, A. M., Tessagaye, F. M., & Tadele, G. (2017). Interreligious marriage: Social and religious perspectives. *Imperial Journal of Interdisciplinary Research*, 3(6), 355–362.

Sheehan, C. L. (2003). Marriage and families (2nd ed). Boston: Allyn & Bacon.

Smith Koslowski, A. (2011). Working fathers in Europe: Earning and caring. *European Sociological Review*, 27(2), 230–245.

Statista. (2018a). *Marital status of the US population by sex*, 2018. Retrieved June 16, 2019 from https://www.statista.com/statistics/242030/marital-status-of-the-us-population-by-sex/

Statista. (2018b). Number of US same-sex households in 2017, by marital status. Retrieved June 16, 2019 from https://www.statista.com/statistics/325106/total-number-of-same-sex-households-in-the-us/

Stein, P. (1981). *Single life: Unmarried adults in social context*. New York: St. Martin's Press.

Sternberg, R. J. (1986). A triangular theory of love. *Psychological Review*, 93, 119–135.

Umberson, D., Crosnoe, R., & Reczek, C. (2010). Social relationships and health behaviors across the life course. *Annual Review of Sociology*, 36, 139–157.

Umberson, D., & Montez, J. K. (2010). Social relationships and health: A flashpoint for health policy. *Journal of Health and Social Behavior*, 51, S54–S66.

U.S. Census Bureau. (2017a). Hispanic single and married. Retrieved June 16, 2019 from www.factfinder.census.gov/faces/tableservices/jsf/pages/producview.xhtml

U.S. Census Bureau. (2017b). Unmarried singles. Retrieved June 16, 2019 from www.census.gov/newsroom/facts-for-features/2017/single-americans-week.html

U.S. Census Bureau. (2018a). Percent married 18–24. Retrieved June 16, 2019 from www.census.gov/library/visualizations/2018/comm/percent-married.html

U.S. Census Bureau. (2018b). U.S. Census Bureau releases 2018 families and living arrangements tables. Retrieved April 20, 2020 from https://www.census.gov/newsroom/press-releases/2018/families.html

U.S. Census Bureau. (2019a). *America's families and living arrangements: 2019*. Retrieved April 20, 2020 from https://www.census.gov/data/tables/2019/demo/families/cps-2019.html

U.S. Census Bureau. (2019b). Historical marital status tables. Retrieved June 16, 2019 from www.census.gov/data/tables/time-series/demo/families/marital.html

U.S. Census Bureau. (2019c). Median age at first marriage: 1890 to present. Retrieved April 20, 2020 from https://www.census.gov/content/dam/Census/library/visualizations/time-series/demo/families-and-households/ms-2.pdf

Waite, L., & Gallagher, M. (2002). *The case for marriage*. New York: Doubleday.

Wang, H., Joyner, K., & Kao, G. (2006). Stability of interracial and intraracial romantic relationships among adolescents. *Social Science Research*, 35(2), 435–453.

Waters, E. (2004). Urban tribes: Are friends the new family? New York: Bloomsbury.

Whitehead, B. (2004. April 4). Testimony before the United States Senate Committee on Health Education, Labor and Pensions Subcommittee on Children and Families. U.S. Senate, 28 April.

Williams, K., Sassler, S., Frech, A., Addo, F., & Cooksey, E. (2011). Nonmarital childbearing, union history, and women's health at midlife. *American Sociological Review*, 76(3), 465–486.

Zimmerman, K. J. (2013). Maintaining commitment in long-lasting mixed-orientation relationships: Gay men married to straight women. *Unpublished dissertation, Iowa State University*. Retrieved June 28, 2019 from https://lib.dr.iastate.edu/

/// CHAPTER 9

Abboud, S., Jemmott, L. S. & Sommers, M. S. (2015). "We are Arabs." The embodiment of virginity through Arab and Arab American women's lived experiences. *Sexuality & Culture*, 19(4), 715–736.

ACT for Youth. (2018). Youth statistics: Sexual health. Retrieved July 8, 2019 from http://actforyouth.net/adolescence/demographics/sexual_health.cfm

Ahluwalia, M., Suzuki, L., & Mir, M. (2018). Dating, partnerships, and arranged marriages. *In Asian American Psychology: Current Perspectives* (pp. 273–294). Mahwah, NJ: Lawrence Earlbaum Associates.

Alford, S. (2001), Transitions. Rights. Respect. *Responsibility*. Retrieved from www.advocatesforyouth.org

American College Health Association. (2020). Reference group executive summary: Fall 2019. Retrieved May 27, 2020 from https://www.acha.org/documents/ncha/NCHA-III_Fall_2019_Reference_Group_Executive_Summary.pdf

American Medical Association. (2006). Sex and intoxication more common among women on spring break, according to AMA poll. Retrieved April 21, 2020 from https://www.rwjf.org/en/library/articles-and-news/2006/03/sex-and-intoxication-more-common-among-women-on-spring-break-acc.html

American Urological Association. (2018). Management of premature ejaculation. Retrieved May 27, 2020 from https://www.auanet.org/guidelines/premature-ejaculation-guideline

Andersen, B. L., & Cyranowski, J. M. (1995). Women's sexuality: Behaviors, responses, and individual differences. *Journal of Consulting and Clinical Psychology*, 63, 891–906.

Aron, A., Fisher, H. E., Mashek, D. J., Strong, G., Hai-Fang, L., & Brown, L. L. (2005). Reward, motivation, and emotion systems associated with early-stage intense romantic love. *Journal of Neurophysiology*, 94(1), 327–337.

Ashcraft, A., & Murray, P. J. (2017). Talking to parents about adolescent sexuality. *Pediatric Clinicians of North America*, 64(2), 305–320.

Atkins, D. C., Jacobson, N. S., & Baucom, D. H. (2001). Understanding infidelity: Correlates in a national random sample. *Journal of Family Psychology*, 15, 735–749.

Ayehu, A., Kassaw, T., & Hailu, G. (2016). Young people's parental discussion about sexual and reproductive health issues and its associated factors in Awabel Woreda, Northwest Ethiopia. *Reproductive Health*, 13(19). doi:10.1186/s12978-016-0143-y

Bachmann, G. A., & Phillips, N. A. (1998). Sexual dysfunction. In J. F. Steege & D. A. Metzger (Eds.), *Chronic pelvic pain: An integrated approach* (pp. 77–90). Philadelphia: Saunders.

Bancroft, J., Carnes, J., Janssen, E., & Long, J. S. (2005). Erectile and ejaculatory problems in gay and heterosexual men. *Archives of Sexual Behavior*, 24, 285–297.

Banfield, S., & McCabe, M. P. (2001). Extra relationship involvement among women: Are they different from men? *Archives of Sexual Behavior*, 30(2), 119–143.

Bartels, A., & Zeki, S. (2000). The neural basis of romantic love, *Neuroreport*, 11(17), 3829–3834.

Basson, R. (2005). Women's sexual dysfunction: Revised and expanded definitions. *Canadian Medical Association Journal*, 172(10), 1327–1333.

Basson, R. (2006). Sexual desire and arousal disorders in women. *New England Journal of Medicine*, 354(14), 1497–1506.

Blumstein, P., & Schwartz, P. (1983). *American couples*. New York: William Morrow.

Boellstorff, T. (2005). Between religion and desire: Being Muslim and gay in Indonesia. *American Anthropologist* 107(4), 575–585.

Boislard, M., van de Bongardt, D., & Blais, M. (2016). Sexuality (and lack thereof) in adolescence and early adulthood: A review of the literature. *Behavioral Sciences*, 6(1), 8.

Booth, S. (2001, Nov. 1). Oral report: Are girls having oral sex to please the guys? *Teen People*, 4, 145.

Bowleg, L., Burkholder, G. J., Noar, S. M., Teti, M., Malebranche, D. J., & Tschann, J. M. (2015). Sexual scripts and sexual risk behaviors among Black heterosexual men: Development of the Sexual Scripts Scale. *Archives of Sexual Behavior*, 44(3), 639–654.

Bowleg, L., Lucas, K. J., & Tschann, J. M. (2004). The ball was always in his court: An exploratory analysis of relationship scripts, sexual scripts, and condom use among African American women. *Psychology of Women Quarterly*, 28(1), 70–82.

Brady, S. S., & Halpern-Felsher, B. L. (2007). Adolescents' reported consequences of having oral sex versus vaginal sex. *Pediatrics*, 119(2), 229–237.

Brantley, A., Knox, D., & Zusman, M. E. (2002). When and why gender differences in saying "I love you" among college students. *College Student Journal*, 36(4), 614–616.

Bullough, V. L., & Bullough, B. (1994). *Human sexuality: An encyclopedia*. New York: Garland.

Buss, D. (1985). Human mate selection. *American Scientist*, 73, 47–51.

Buss, D. (1999). Evolutionary psychology. *The new science of the mind*. Boston: Allyn & Bacon.

Byers, E. S. (2005). Relationship satisfaction and sexual satisfaction: A longitudinal study of individuals in long-term relationships. *The Journal of Sex Research*, 42,113–118.

Byers, S. E., Sears, H. A., Voyer, S. D., Thurlow, T. L., Cohen, J. N., & Weaver, A. D. (2003). An adolescent perspective on sexual health education at school and at home: I. High school students. *Canadian Journal of Human Sexuality*, 12, 1–17.

Byers, S. E., Sears, H. A., & Weaver, A. D. (2008). Parents' reports of sexual communication with children in kindergarten to grade 8. *Journal of Marriage and Family*, 70, 86–96.

Centers for Disease Control and Prevention. (2018). Reproductive health: Teen pregnancy. Retrieved April 21, 2020 from https://www.cdc.gov/teenpregnancy/about/index.htm

Centers for Disease Control and Prevention. (2019). Sexually transmitted diseases. Retrieved July 8, 2019 from https://www.cdc.gov/std/stats/default.htm

Chambers, W. C. (2007). Oral sex: Varied behaviors and perceptions in a college population. *The Journal of Sex Research*. 44(1), 28–42.

Chevret, M., Jaudinot, E., Sullivan, K., Marrel, A., & De Gendre, A. S. (2004). Quality of sexual life and satisfaction in female partners of men with ED: Psychometric validation of the index of sexual life (ISL) questionnaire, *Journal of Sex & Marital Therapy*, 30, 141–155.

Chewning, B., Douglas, J., Kokotailo, P. K., LaCourt, J., St. Clair, D., & Wilson, D. (2001). Protective factors associated with American Indian adolescents' safer sexual patterns. *Maternal and Child Health journal*, 5(4), 273–280.

Christopher, F. S., & Sprecher, S. (2000). Sexuality in marriage, dating, and other relationships: A decade review. *Journal of Marriage and the Family*, 62(4), 999–1017.

Cleveland Clinic. (2019). Erectile dysfunction. Retrieved July 9, 2019 from http://www.clevelandclinicmeded.com/medicalpubs/diseasemanagement/endocrinology/erectile-dysfunction/

Commendador, K. A. (2010). Parental influences on adolescent decision making and contraceptive use. *Pediatric Nursing*, 36, 147–156.

Connell, C. M., & Prinz, R. J. (2002). The impact of childcare and parent-child interactions on school readiness and social skill development for low-income African American children. *Journal of School Psychology*, 40(2), 177–193.

Connell, R. W. (2002). *Gender*. Malden, MA: Blackwell.

Cottrell, L., Li, X., Stanton, B., Harris, C., D'Alessandri, D., Sun, Z., . . . & Zhang, H. (2005). Perceptions regarding preventive sexual practices and communication with sexual partners among Chinese college students. *Preventive Medicine*, 40(2), 189–196.

Davidson, J. K., Sr., & Darling, C. A. (1989). Self-perceived differences in the female orgasmic response. *Family Practice Research Journal*, 8, 75–84.

Davidson, J., Darling, C. A., & Norton, L. X. (1995). Religiosity and the sexuality of women: Sexual behavior and sexual satisfaction revisited. *Journal of Sex Research*, 32, 235–243.

Davis, D. A., & Davis, S. S. (1993). Sexual values in a Moroccan town. In W. J. Lonner & R. S. Malpass (Eds.), *Psychology and culture* (pp. 225–230). Boston: Allyn & Bacon.

DeLamater, J. D., & Friedrich, W. N. (2002). Human sexual development. *The Journal of Sex Research*, 39(1), 10–15.

DeLamater, J. D., & Hyde, J. S. (1998). Essential versus social constructionism in the study of human sexuality. *The Journal of Sex Research*, 35, 10–18.

Edwards, C. P., Liu, W., & Dennis, J. (2015). Chinese parents' perspectives on adolescent sexuality education. *Faculty Publications, Department of Child, Youth, and Family Studies*, 107. Retrieved May 27, 2020 from http://digitalcommons.unl.edu/famconfacpub/107

Edwards, J. N., & Booth, A. (1994). Sexuality, marriage, and well-being: The middle years. In A. S. Rossi (Ed.), *Sexuality across the life course* (pp. 233–259). Chicago: University of Chicago Press.

Elnashar, A. M., Ibrahim, M. E., El-Desoky, M. M., Ali, O. M., & Hassan, M. (2006). Female sexual dysfunction in lower Egypt. *British Journal of Obstetrics & Gynecology*, 114, 201–206.

Face of Global Sex. (2012). Sexual frequency and satisfaction. Retrieved July 9, 2019 from https://www.drfelix.co.uk/how-were-having-sex-from-chile-to-china/

Faulkner, S. (2003). Good girl or flirt girl: Latinas' definitions of sex and sexual relationships. *Hispanic Journal of Behavioral Sciences*, 25(2), 174–200.

Frederick, D. A., St. John, H. K., Garcia, J. R., & Lloyd, E. A. (2018). Differences in orgasm frequency among gay, lesbian, bisexual, and heterosexual men and women in a U.S. national sample. *Archives of Sexual Behavior*, 47(1), 273–288.

Frey, K., & Hojjat, M. (1998). Are love styles related to sexual styles? *The Journal of Sex Research*, 35(3), 265–271.

Gagnon, J. H., & Simon, W. (1973). *Sexual conduct: The social sources of human sexuality*. Chicago: Aldine.

Garcia, J. R., Reiber, C., Massey, S. G., & Merriwether, A. M. (2012). Sexual hookup culture: A review. *Review of General Psychology*, 16(2), 161–176.

Gavey, N. (2005). Just sex? *The cultural scaffolding of rape*. New York: Routledge.

Gordon, K.C., Baucom, D. H., & Snyder, D. K. (2004). An integrative intervention for promoting recovery from extramarital affairs. *Journal of Marital and Family Therapy*, 30, 213–232.

Grossman, J. M., Jenkins, L. J., & Richer, A. M. (2018). Parents' perspectives on family sexuality communication from middle school to high school. *International Journal of Environmental Research and Public Health*, 15(1), 107.

Guilamo-Ramos, V., Lee, J. J., Kantor, L. M., Levine, D. S., Baum, S., & Johnsen, J. (2015). Potential for using online and mobile education with parents and adolescents to impact sexual and reproductive health. *Prevention Science*, 16(1), 53–60.

Guo, B., & Huang, J. (2005). Marital and sexual satisfaction in Chinese families: Exploring the moderating effects. *Journal of Sex & Marital Therapy*, 31, 21–29.

Guttmacher Institute. (2018). Sexual behavior and contraceptive us among U.S. high school students, 2013–2017. Retrieved July 8, 2019 from https://www.guttmacher.org/report/sexual-behavior-contraceptive-condom-use-us-high-school-students-2013-2017

Haavio-Mannila, E., & Kontula, O. (1997). Correlates of increased sexual satisfaction. *Archives of Sexual Behavior*, 26, 399–419.

Hall, S. K., & Graham, C. A. (2012). The cultural context of sexual pleasure and problems: Psychotherapy with diverse clients. New York: Routledge.

Halpern, C., Udry, J. R., & Suchindran, C. (2000). Adolescent males' willingness to report masturbation. *The Journal of Sex Research*, 37(4), 327–332.

Hamilton, L., & Armstrong, E. A. (2009). Gendered sexuality in young adulthood: Double binds and flawed options. *Gender & Sexuality*, 23(5), 589–616.

Harris, C. R., & Christenfeld, N. (1996). Gender, jealousy, and reason. *Psychological Science*, 7, 364–366.

Harvey, S. M., & Henderson, J. T. (2006). Correlates of condom use intentions and behaviors among a community-based sample of Latino men in Los Angeles. *Journal of Urban Health*, 83(4), 558–574.

Hellerstedt, W. L., Peterson-Hickey, M., Rhodes, K. L., & Garwick, A. (2006). Environmental, social, and personal correlates of having ever had sexual intercourse among American Indian youths. *American Journal of Public Health*, 96(12), 2228–2234.

Henderson-King, D. H., & Veroff, J. (1994). Sexual satisfaction and marital well-being in the first years of marriages. *Journal of Social and Personal Relationships*, 11, 509–534.

Hernandez, A. M., Zule, W. A., Karg, R. S., Browne, F. A., & Wechsberg, W. M. (2012). Factors that influence HIV risk among Hispanic female immigrants and their implications for HIV prevention interventions. *International Journal of Family Medicine*, 2, 1–11.

Hicks, M. S., McRee, A. L., & Eisenberg, M. E. (2013). Teens talking with their partners about sex: The role of parent communication. *American Journal of Sex Education*, 8, 1–1.

Holland, J., Ramazanoglu, C., Scott, S., Sharpe, S., & Thomson, R. (1990). Sex, gender, and power: Young women's sexuality in the shadow of AIDS. *Sociology of Health and Illness*, 12(3), 336–350.

Hunt, M. (1974). Sexual behavior in the 1970s. Chicago: Playboy Press.

Hussain, K. M., Jeija, S. G., Lewis, F., & Sanches, B. (2015). Unveiling sexual identity in the face of marianismo. *Journal of Feminist Family Therapy*, 27(2), 72–92.

Hussen, S. A., Bowleg, L., Sangaramoorthy, T., Malebranche, D. J. (2012). Parents, peers and pornography: The influence of formative sexual scripts on adult HIV sexual risk behavior among Black men in the USA. *Culture Healthy & Sexuality*, 14(8), 863–877.

Hutchinson, M. K. (2002). The influence of sexual risk communication between parents and daughters on sexual risk behaviors. *Family Relations*, 51, 238–247.

Hynie, M., Lyndon, J. E., Cote, S., & Wiener, S. (1998). Relational sexual scripts and women's condom use: The importance of internalized norms. *Journal of Sex Research*, 35(4), 370–380.

Institute for Family Studies. (2019). Who cheats more? *The demographics of infidelity in America*. Retrieved July 7, 2019 from https://ifstudies.org/blog/who-cheats-more-the-demographics-of-cheating-in-america

International Society for Sexual Medicine. (2019a). Premature ejaculation: Guidelines. Retrieved April 21, 2020 from https://emedicine.medscape.com/article/435884-guidelines

International Society for Sexual Medicine. (2019b). What is the "normal" frequency of sex? Retrieved July 8, 2019 from https://www.issm.info/sexual-health-qa/what-is-the-normal-frequency-of-sex/

Jaccard, J., Dittus, P. J., & Gordon, V. V. (2000). Parent-teen communication about premarital sex: Factors associated with the extent of communication. *Journal of Adolescent Research*, 15, 187–208.

Jaccard, J., Dodge. T., & Dittus, P. (2002). Parent-adolescent communication about sex and birth control: A conceptual framework. In S. S. Feldman and D. A. Rosenthal (Eds.), *Talking sexuality: Parent-adolescent communication* (pp. 9–41). San Francisco: Jossey-Bass.

Janus, S. S., & Janus, C. L. (1993). *The Janus report on sexual behavior*. New York: Wiley.

Johnsen, J. (2005). Sexually transmitted infections: The facts. *Planned Parenthood*. Retrieved from www.plannedparenthoud.org/pp2/portal/files/portal/medicalinfo/sliypub-sti-facts-l.xml

Kaestle, C. E., & Tucker Halpern, C. (2007). What's love got to do with it? Sexual behaviors of opposite-sex couples through emerging adulthood. *Perspectives on Sexual and Reproductive Health*, 39(3), 134–141.

Kann, L., McManus, T., Harris, W. A., et al. (2018). Youth Risk Behavior Surveillance—United States, 2017. *MMWR Surveillance Summaries*, 67(8), 1–114.

Kimuna, S, R., & Kjamba, Y. K. (2005). Wealth and extramarital sex among men in Gambia. *International Family Planning Perspectives*, 31, 83–89.

Kinsey Institute. (2007). HIV/AIDS by race. Retrieved from www.indiana.edu/~kinsey

Kinsey Institute. (2019). Sex in relationships. Retrieved May 27, 2020 from https://kinseyinstitute.org/research/faq.php

Knox. D., Sturdivant, L., & Zusman, M. E. (2001). College student attitudes toward sexual intimacy. *College Student Journal*, 35, 241–243.

Knox, D., & Zusman, M. E. (2002). When and why gender differences in saying "I love you" among college students. *College Student Journal*, 36, 614–615.

Knox, D., Zusman, M., & McNeely, A. (2008). University student beliefs about sex: Men vs. women. *College Student Journal* 42(1), 181–186.

Knipper, E., Rhodes, S. D., Lindstrom, K., Bloom, F. R., Leichliter, J. S., & Montano, J. (2007). Condom use among heterosexual immigrant Latino men in the Southeastern United States. *AIDS Education & Prevention*, 19(5), 436–447.

Kurdek, L. A. (1991). Sexuality in homosexual and heterosexual couples. In K. McKinney & S. Sprecher (Eds.), *Sexuality in close relationships* (pp. 177–191). Hillsdale, NJ: Erlbaum.

Laan, E., & Both, S. (2008). What makes women experience desire? *Feminism & Psychology*, 18(4), 505–514.

Lantos, H., Manlove, J., Wildsmith, E., Faccio, B., Guzman, L., & Moore, K. A. (2019). Parent- teen communication about sexual and reproductive health: Cohort differences by race/ethnicity and nativity. *International Journal of Environmental Research and Public Health*, 16, 1–15.

Laumann, E. O., Gagnon, J. H., Michael, R, T., & Michaels, S. (1994), The social organization of sexuality: Sexual practices in the United States. Chicago: University of Chicago Press.

Laumann, E. O., Nicolosi, A., Classer, D. B., et al. (2005) Sexual problems among women and men aged 40—80: Prevalence and correlates identified in the Global Study of Sexual Attitudes and Behaviors. *International Journal of Impotency Research*, 17, 39–57.

Lawrance, K., & Byers, E. S. (1995). Sexual satisfaction in long-term heterosexual relationships: The interpersonal exchange model of sexual satisfaction. *Personal Relationships*, 2, 267–285.

Leiber, E., Chin, D., Li, L., Rotheram-Borus, J. J., Detls, R., et al. (2009). Sociocultural contexts and communication about sex in China: Informing HIV/STD prevention programs. *AIDS Education & Prevention*, 21(5), 415–429.

Leichliter, J. S., Chandra, A., Kiddon, N., Fenton, K. A., & Aral, S. O. (2007). Prevalence and correlates of heterosexual anal and oral sex in adolescents and adults in the United States. *The Journal of Infectious Diseases*, 196, 1852–1859.

Leitenberg, H., Detzer, M. J., & Srebnik, P. (1993). Gender differences in masturbation and the relation of masturbation experiences in preadolescence and/or early adolescence to sexual behavior and sexual adjustment in young adulthood. *Archives of Sexual Behavior*, 22, 87–98.

Lever, J. (1995, August 22). Lesbian sex survey. *The Advocate*, 21–30.

Lindberg, L. D., Maddow-Zimet, I., & Marcell, A. V. (2019). Prevalence of sexual initiation before age 13 years among male adolescents and young adults in the United States. *JAMA Pediatrics*, 173(6), 553–560.

Lindley, L. L., Joshi, P., & Vincent, M. L. (2007, November 3-7). *Personal and family factors associated with virginity among African American male and female high school students*. Paper presented at the 135th American Public Health Association Annual Meeting, San Diego, CA.

Liu, C. (2000). A theory of marital sexual life. *Journal of Marriage and Family*, 62, 363–374.

MacNeil., S., & Byers, E. S. (2005). Dyadic assessment of sexual self-disclosure and sexual satisfaction. *Journal of Personal and Social Relationships*, 22, 193–205.

Maher, B. (2004). Abstinence until marriage: The best message for teens. *The Family Research Council*. Retrieved from www.frc.org

Masters, T. N., Casey, E., Wells, E. Z., & Morrison, D. M. (2013). Sexual scripts among young heterosexually active men and women: Continuity and change. *Journal of Sex Research*, 50(5), 409–420.

Masters, W. H., & Johnson, V. E. (1966). *Human sexual response*. Boston: Little, Brown.

Matthiesen, S., & Wenn, H. M. (2004). Summary of the recommendations on sexual development in females. *Journal of Sexual Medicine*, 1, 24–34.

Mayo Clinic. (2019). Premature ejaculation. Retrieved July 9, 2019 from https://www.mayoclinic.org/diseases-conditions/premature-ejaculation/symptoms-causes/syc-20354900

Mazur, A., Mueller, U., Krause, W., & Booth, A. (2002). Causes of sexual decline in aging men: Germany and America. *International Journal of Impotence Research*, 14, 101–106.

McQuillen, J. S. (2003). The influence of technology on the initiation of interpersonal relationships. *Education*, 123, 616–623.

Meneses, L. M., Orrell-Valente, J. K., Guendelman, S. R., Oman, D., & Irwin, C. E. (2006). Racial/ethnic differences in mother-daughter communication about sex. *Journal of Adolescent Health*, 39, 128–131.

Mercer, C. H., Fenton, K. A., Johnson, A. M., et al. (2003). Sexual function problems and help seeking behaviour in Britain: National probability sample survey. *British Medical Journal*, 327, 4267.

Miller, K. S., Levin, M. L., Whitaker, D. J., & Xu, X. (1998). Patterns of condom use among adolescents: The impact of mother-adolescent communication. *American Journal of Public Health*, 88, 1542–1544.

Montefiore, S. S. (1993, March/April). Let the games begin: Sex and the not-thirtysomethings. *Psychology Today*, 26(2), 66–72.

Muise, A., Schimmack, U., & Impett, E. A. (2015). Sexual frequency predicts greater well-being, but more is not always better. *Social Psychology & Personality Science*, 7(4), 295–302.

Mustanski, B. (2020). Health and development of LGBTQ youth and the application of new media and technology to sexual health promotion and HIV prevention. *Institute for Sexual and Gender Minority Health and Wellbeing*. Retrieved March 23, 2020 from https://isgmh.northwestern.edu/people/faculty/

National Campaign to Prevent Teen Pregnancy. (2018). What research says about abstinence-only education. Retrieved May 27, 2020 from https://powertodecide.org/sexual-health/your-sexual-health/articles-about-healthy-sex-life/what-research-says-about

National College Health Assessment. (2018). Spring 2018 reference group executive summary. Retrieved July 9, 2019 from https://www.acha.org/documents/ncha/NCHA-II_Fall_2018_Reference_Group_Executive_Summary.pdf

National Council on Family Relations. (2020). Family life education content areas: Content and practice guidelines. Retrieved April 21, 2020 from https://www.ncfr.org/sites/default/files/fle_content_and_practice_guidelines_2015_0.pdf

Newcomb, M. E., LaSala, M. C., Bouris, A., Mustanski, B., Prado, G., Schrager, S. M., & Huebner, D. M. (2019). The influence of families on LGBTQ youth health: A call to action for innovation in research and intervention development. *LGBT Health*,6(4), 139–145.

O'Donnell, L., Steuve, A., Wilson-Simmons, R., Dash, K., Agronick, G., & Jean Baptiste, V. (2006). Heterosexual risk behaviors among urban young adolescents. *The Journal of Early Adolescence*, 26(87), 87–109.

Oggins, J., Leber, D., & Veroff, J. (1993). Race and gender differences in Black and white newlyweds' perception of sexual and marital relations. *The Journal of Sex Research*, 30, 152–160.

Okazaki, S. (2002). Influences of culture on Asian Americans' sexuality. *Journal of Sex Research*, 39, 34–41.

Oppenheimer, M. (2007). Recovering from an extramarital relationship from a non-systemic approach. *American Journal of Psychotherapy*, 61(2), 181–191.

Pan, S. (1993). Chinese wives: Psychological and behavioral factors underlying their orgasm frequency. Unpublished manuscript. Bejing: Renmin University.

Pariera, K. (2016). Barriers and prompts to parent-child sexual communication. *Journal of Family Communication*. doi:10.1080/15267431.2016.1181068

Pariera, K., & Brody, E. (2017). Talk more about it: Emerging adults' attitudes about how and when parents should talk about sex. *Sexuality Research and Social Policy: Journal of NSRC*. doi:10.1007/s13178-017-0314-9

Parmet, S. (2004, June 23–30). Male sexual dysfunction. *JAMA*, 291(24). Retrieved from http://jama.ama-assn.org/cgi/conctenl/full/291/24/3076

Phillips, N. A. (2000). Female sexual dysfunction: Evaluation and treatment. *American Family Physician*, 62, 127–136.

Planned Parenthood. (2018). Talking to kids about sex: Tips for parents and caregivers. Retrieved April 21, 2020 from https://www.plannedparenthood.org/planned-parenthood-st-louis-region-southwest-missouri/blog/talking-to-your-kids-about-sex-tips-for-parents-and-caregivers

Purnine, D. M., Carey, M. P., fir Jorgensen, R. S. (1994). Gender differences regarding preferences for specific heterosexual practices. *Journal of Sex and Marital Therapy*, 20, 271–287.

Reiss, I. L. (1989). Society and sexuality: A sociological explanation. In K. McKinney & S. Sprecher (Eds.), *Human sexuality. The societal and interpersonal context* (pp. 3–29). Norwood, NJ: Ablex.

Renaud, C., Byers, E. S., & Pan, S. (1997). Sexual and relationship satisfaction in mainland China. *The Journal of Sex Research*, 34(4), 399–411.

Richters, J., de Visser, R., Rissel, C., & Smith, A. (2006). Sexual practices at last heterosexual encounter and occurrence of orgasm in a national survey. *Journal of Sex Research*, 43(3), 217–226.

Ridley, C., Ogolsky, B., Payne, P., Totenhagen, C., & Cate, R. (2008). Sexual expression: Its emotional context in heterosexual, gay, and lesbian couples. *The Journal of Sex Research*, 45(3), 305–315.

Ritchwood, T., Peasant Bonner, C., Powell, T. W., & Taggart, T. (2017). Predictors of caregiver communication about reproductive and sexual health and sensitive sex topics. *Journal of Family Issues*. doi:10.1177/0192513X17741920

Sastre, F., De La Rosa, M., Ibanez, G. E., Whitt, E., Martin, S. S., & O'Connell, J. (2015). Condom use preferences among Latinos in Miami-Dade: Emerging themes concerning men's and women's culturally-ascribed attitudes and behaviours. *Culture, Health, & Sexuality*, 17(6), 667–681.

Schenk, J., Pfrang, H., & Rausche, A. (1983). Personality traits versus the quality of the marital relationship as the determinant of marital sexuality. *Archives of Sexual Behavior*, 12(1), 31–42.

Schröder, J., & Schmiedeberg, C. (2015). Effects of relationship duration, cohabitation, and marriage on the frequency of intercourse in couples: Findings from German panel data. *Social Science Research*, 52, 72–82.

Seal, D. W., Smith, M., Coley, B., Perry, J., & Gamez, M. (2008). Urban heterosexual couples' sexual scripts for three shared sexual experiences. *Sex Roles*, 58, 626–638.

Seeber, M., & Gorrell, C. (2001). The science of orgasm: Sex and your psyche. *Psychology Today*, 34(6), 48–59.

SEICUS National Guidelines Task Force. (2020). The guidelines for comprehensive sexuality education. Retrieved May 27, 2020 from https://siecus.org/resources/the-guidelines/

Sharp, E, A., & Ganong, L. H. (2000). Raising awareness about marital expectations: An unrealistic belief change by integrative teaching? *Family Relations*, 49, 71–76.

Shifren, J. L., Barbieri, R. L., & Falk, S. J. (2019). Overview of sexual dysfunction in women: Management. Retrieved July 9, 2019 from https://www.uptodate.com/contents/overview-of-sexual-dysfunction-in-women-management

Simon, W., & Gagnon, J. H. (1984). Sexual scripts. *Society*, 22, 53–60.

Smith, T. W. (2006). American sexual behavior: Trends, socio-demographic differences, and risk behavior. GSS Topical Report No. 25. Chicago: National Opinion Research Center. Retrieved from www.norc.org.

Snyder, D. K., Gordon, K. C., & Baucom, D. H. (2004). Treating affair couples: Extending the written disclosure paradigm to relationship trauma. *Clinical Psychology: Science and Practice*, 11(2), 155–159.

Sprecher, S. (2002). Sexual satisfaction in premarital relationships: Associations with satisfaction, love, commitment, and stability. *The Journal of Sex Research*, 39(13), 190–197.

Sprecher, S., & McKinney, K. (1993). *Sexuality*. Newbury Park, CA: SAGE.

Sprecher, S., & Regan, P. (2000). Sexuality in a relational context. In C. Hendrick & S. S. Hendrick (Eds.), *Close relationships: A sourcebook* (pp. 217–227). Thousand Oaks, CA: SAGE.

Thompson, A. (1984). Emotional and sexual components of extramarital relations. *Journal of Marriage and the Family*, 46, 35–42.

Townsend, J. (1995). Sex without emotional involvement: An evolutionary interpretation of sex differences. *Archives of Sexual Behavior*, 24, 173–2005.

Trager, J. (2009). STDs and oral sex. *Sexual Health Communication*. Retrieved from http://www.healthcentral.com/sexual-health/safesex-270837-5.html

Ubillos, S., Paez, D., & Gonzalez, J. L. (2000). Culture and sexual behavior. *Psiothema*, 12, 70–82.

Vohs, D., Cantonese, K. R., & Baumeister, R. F. (2004). Sex in "his" versus "her" relationships. In J. H. Harvey, A. Wenzel, & S. Sprecher (Eds.), *Handbook of sexuality in close relationships* (pp. 455–474). Mahwah, NJ: Erlbaum.

Wade, L., Kremer, E., & Brown, J. (2005). The incidental orgasm: The presence of clitoral knowledge and the absence of orgasm for women. *Women and Health*, 42(1), 117–138.

Waite, L., & Joyner, K. (2001). Emotional satisfaction and physical pleasure in sexual unions: Time horizon, sexual behavior, and sexual exclusivity. *Journal of Marriage and Family*. 63, 247–264.

Weinstein, E., & Rosen, E. (2006). *Teaching about human sexuality and family: A skills-based approach*. Belmont, CA: Wadsworth.

Wiederman, M. W. (1997). Extramarital sex: Prevalence and correlates in a national survey. *Journal of Sex Research*, 34, 167–174.

Wiederman, M. W. (2005). The gendered nature of sexual scripts. *The Family Journal: Counseling and Therapy for Couples and Families*, 13(4), 496–502.

Wildermuth, S. M., & Vogl-Bauer, S. (2007). We met on the net: Exploring the perceptions of online romantic relationship participants. *Southern Communication Journal*, 72(3), 211–227.

Wyckoff, S. C., Miller, K. S., Forehand, R., Bau, J. J., Fasula, A., Long, N., & Armistead, L. (2008). Patterns of sexuality communication between preadolescents and their mothers and fathers. *Journal of Child and Family Studies*, 17, 649–662.

Xiao, Z. W. (2012). Correlates of condom use among Chinese college students in Hunan Province. *AIDS Education & Prevention*, 24(5), 469–482.

Xiao, Z., Li, X., Lin, D., & Jiang, S. (2013). Sexual communication, safer sex self-efficacy, and condom use among young Chines migrants in Beijing, China. *International Society for AIDS Education*, 25(6), 480–494.

Xiao, Z. W., Li, X., Liu, Y., Li, S., & Jiang, S. (2013). Sexual communication and condom use among Chinese men who have sex with men in Beijing. *Psychology, Health, & Medicine*, 18(1), 98–106.

Young, M., Young, D., & Luquis, T. (2000). Sexual satisfaction among married women. *American Journal of Health Studies*, 16(2), 73–84.

Zahedi, A. (2007). Contested meanings of the veil and political ideologies of Iranian regimes, *Journal of Middle East Women's Studies*, 3(3), 75–99.

Zava. (2018). Sexual journeys. Retrieved May 27, 2020 from https://www.zavamed.com/uk/sexual-journeys.html

Zhang, L., Li, X., Shah, I. H., Baldwin, W., & Stanton, B. (2007). Parent-adolescent sex communication in China. *The European Journal of Contraception and Reproductive Health Care*, 12(2), 138–147.

/// CHAPTER 10

Adamec, C. (2004). *The complete idiot's guide to adoption*. New York: Penguin.

Ahlborg, T., Dahlof, L. G., & Hallberg, L. R. (2005). Quality of intimate and sexual relationship in first-time parents six months after delivery. *Journal of Sex Research*, 42(2), 167–174.

Ahlborg, T., Dahlof, L. G., & Strandmark, M. (2000). First-time parents' sexual relationships. *Scandinavian Journal of Sexology*, 3, 127–139.

Al-Fadhli, H. M., & Smith, J. C. (1996). Assessing the impact of violence on motivation for parenthood among Blacks and whites. *Journal of Negro Education*, 65(4), 424–433.

American College of Obstetricians and Gynecologists. (2019). Pelvic inflammatory disease. Retrieved June 22, 2019 from https://www.acog.org/Patients/FAQs/Pelvic-Inflammatory-Disease-PID

American Psychological Association. (2004). Sexual orientation, parents, and children. Retrieved June 22, 2019, from https://www.apa.org/about/policy/parenting

American Society for Reproductive Medicine. (2015). Disparities in access to effective treatment for infertility in the United States: An ethics committee opinion. *Fertility and Sterility*, September, 1–7.

American Society for Reproductive Medicine. (2019). Female infertility. Retrieved May 6, 2020 from https://www.asrm.org/topics/topics-index/female-infertility/

Anderssen, N., Amlie, C., & Ytteroy, E. A. (2002). Outcomes for children with lesbian or gay parents: A review of studies from 1978 to 2000. *Scandinavian Journal of Psychology*, 43, 335–351.

Arnold, L. B. (2005). Don't you know what causes that? Advice, celebration, and justification in a large families bulletin board. *Communication Studies*, 56(4), 331–351.

Barber, J. S., Kusunoki, Y., Gatny, H., & Melendez, R. (2017). The relationship context of young pregnancies. *Law Inequality*, 35(2), 175.

Barrett, G., Pendry, E., Peacock, J., Victor, C., Thakar, R., & Manyonda, I. (2000). Women's sexual health after childbirth. *British Journal of Obstetrics and Gynecology*, 107, 186–195.

Berkowitz, D. (2013). Gay men and surrogacy. In A. Goldberg & K. R. Allen (Eds.), *LGBT-parent families: Innovations in research and implications for practice* (pp. 71–85). New York: Springer.

Berkowitz, D., & Marsiglio, W. (2007). Gay men: Negotiating procreative, father, and family identities. *Journal of Marriage and Family*, 69(2), 366–381.

Blake, J. (1981). Family size and the quality of children. *Demography*, 18, 421–442.

Blake, L., Carone, N., Raffanello, E., Slutsky, J., Ehrhardt, A. A., & Golombok, S. (2017). Gay fathers' motivations for and feelings about surrogacy as a path to parenthood. *Human Reproduction*, 32(4), 860–867.

Bonkowski, S. (2003). Gay and lesbian parenting. *Family Law Advisor*. Retrieved from www.divorcenet.com/il/ilart-15a.html

Bos, H. M. W., Knox, J. R., van Rijn-van Gelderern, L., & Gartrell, N. K. (2016). Same-sex and different-sex parent households and child health outcomes: Findings from the National Survey of Children's Health. *Journal of Developmental and Behavioral Pediatrics*, 37(3), 179–187.

Bos, H. M. W., Kuyper, L., & Gartrell, N. K. (2018). A population-based comparison of female and male same-sex and different-sex parent households. *Family Process*, 57(1), 148–164.

Bos, H. M. W., van Balen, F., & van den Boom, D. C. (2004). Experience of parenthood, couple relationship, social support, and child-rearing goals in planned lesbian mother families. *Journal of Child Psychology and Psychiatry*, 45, 755–764.

Bowen, M. (1966). The use of family theory in clinical practice. *Comprehensive Psychology*, 7, 345–374.

Brummen, H. J., Bruinse, H. W., van de Pol, G., Heintz. A. P. M., & van der Vaart, C. H. (2006). Which factors determine the sexual function 1 year after childbirth? *British Journal of Gynecology*, 113, 914–918.

Buehlman, K. T., Gottman, J. M., & Katz, L. F. (1992). How a couple views their past predicts their future: Predicting divorce from an oral history interview. *Journal of Family Psychology*, 5, 295–318.

Cartwright, R. (1999, Autumn). Childless or childfree? *Journal of Fertility Counseling*.

Campbell, N. (2003). *Be fruitful and multiply*. San Antonio, TX: Vision Forum.

Campbell, S. B., Cohn, J. F., Flanagan, C., Popper, S., et.al. (1992). Course and correlates of postpartum depression during the transition to parenthood. *Development and Psychopathology*, 4, 29–47.

Centers for Disease Control and Prevention. (2005). Births: Preliminary data for 2004. National Vital Statistics Report, 54(8). Retrieved March 20, 2006 from www.cdc.gov/nchs/data/nvsr/nvsr54/nvsr54_08.pdf

Centers for Disease Control and Prevention. (2018). Births in the United States: 2017. NCHS Data Brief, 318. Retrieved from https://www.cdc.gov/nchs/products/databriefs/db318.htm

Centers for Disease Control and Prevention. (2019a). Births: Final data for 2018. National Vital Statistics Report, 68(13). Retrieved June 1, 2020 from https://www.cdc.gov/nchs/data/nvsr/nvsr68/nvsr68_13-508.pdf

Centers for Disease Control and Prevention. (2019b). National population-based estimates for major birth defects, 2010–2014. *Birth Defects Research*, 111(18), 1420–1435.

Centers for Disease Control and Prevention. (2019c). Reproductive health: Teen pregnancy. Retrieved June 1, 2020 from https://www.cdc.gov/teenpregnancy/about/index.htm

Ciano-Boyce, C., & Shelley-Sireci, L. (2002). Who is Mommy tonight? Lesbian parenting issues. *Journal of Homosexuality*, 43, 1–13.

Connolly, A., Thorp, J., & Pahel, L. (2005). Effects of pregnancy and childbirth on postpartum sexual function: A longitudinal prospective study. *International Urogynecological Journal of Pelvic Floor Dysfunction*. Retrieved from www.ncibi.nlm.nih.gov/

Costa, P. A., & Tasker, F. (2018). We wanted a forever family: Altruistic, individualistic, and motivated reasoning motivations for adoption among LGBTQ individuals. *Journal of Family Issues*, 39(18), 4156–4178.

Cowan, C. P., & Cowan, P. A. (2000). *When partners become parents: The big life change for couples*. Mahwah, NJ: Erlbaum.

Davenport, D. (2018). *Adoption is the United States: 2018*. Retrieved June 22, 2019, from https://creatingafamily.org/adoption-category/adoption-blog/adoption-cost-length-time/

Figueiredo, B., Field, T., Diego, M., Hernandez, R. M., Deeds, O., & Ascenio, A. (2008). Partner relationships during the transition to parenthood. *Journal of Reproductive and Infant Psychology*, 26(2), 99–107.

Florsheim, P., Emi, S., McCann, C., Matthew, W., Ritsuko, F., & Trina, S., et al. (2003). The transition to parenthood among young African American and Latino couples: Relational predictors of risk for parental dysfunction. *Journal of Family Psychology*, 17, 65–79.

Gallup. (2018). Americans, in theory, think larger families are ideal. Retrieved June 22, 2019, from https://news.gallup.com/poll/236696/americans-theory-think-larger-families-ideal.aspx

Gartrell, N., Bos, H., & Koh, A. (2018). Mental health of young adults with lesbian parents. *The Williams Institute School of Law*. Retrieved June 22, 2019, from https://williamsinstitute.law.ucla.edu/research/mental-health-kids-lesbian-parents/

Gates, G. J. (2013). *LGBT parenting in the United States*. Los Angeles: The Williams Institute.

Gato, J., Santos, S., & Fontaine, A. M. (2016). To have or not to have children? That is the question. Factors influence parental decisions among lesbians and gay men. *Sexuality Research and Social Policy*, 14(3), 310–323.

Gerson, M. J. (1980). The lure of motherhood. *Psychology of Women Quarterly*, 5(2), 207–218.

Gerson, M. J. (1985). *Hard choices: How women decide about work, career, and motherhood*. Berkeley: University of California Press.

Gerson, M. J. (1986). The prospect of parenthood for women and men. *Psychology of Women Quarterly*, 10, 49–62.

Gerson, M. J., Posner, J. A., & Morris, A. M. (1991). The wish for a child in couples eager, disinterested, and conflicted about having children. *The American Journal of Family Therapy*, 19(4), 334–343.

Gianino, M. (2008). Adaptation and transformation: The transition to adoptive parenthood for gay male couples. Journal of GLBT Family Studies, 4, 205–243.

Goldberg, A. E., Downing, J. B., & Moyer, A. M. (2012). Why parenthood, and why now? Gay men's motivations for pursuing parenthood. *Family Relations*, 61, 157–174.

Goldberg, A. E., Downing, J. B., & Richardson, H. B. (2009). The transition from infertility to adoption: Perceptions of lesbian and heterosexual couples. *Journal of Social and Personal Relationships*, 29, 938–963.

Goldberg, A. E., Gartrell, N., & Gates, G. J. (2014). Research report on LGB-parent families. Retrieved June 1, 2020 from https://williamsinstitute.law.ucla.edu/publications/report-lgb-parent-families/

Goldberg, A. E., & Scheib, J. E. (2015). Why donor insemination and not adoption? Narratives of female-partnered and single mothers. *Family Relations*, 64(5), 726–742.

Goldberg, A. E., & Smith, J. Z. (2014). Preschool selection considerations and experiences of school mistreatment among lesbian, gay, and heterosexual adoptive parents. *Early Childhood Research Quarterly*, 29, 64–75.

Golombok, S., Blake, L., Slutsky, J., Raffanello, E., Roman, G. D., & Ehrhardt, A. (2018). Parenting and the adjustment of children born to gay fathers through surrogacy. *Child Development*, 89(4), 1223–1233.

The Guttmacher Institute. (2004). *U.S. teenage pregnancy statistics: Overall trends, trends by race and ethnicity, and state-by-state information.* Washington, DC: Author.

The Guttmacher Institute. (2015). Adolescent Pregnancy and Its Outcomes Across Countries. Retrieved from https://www.guttmacher.org/fact-sheet/adolescent-pregnancy-and-its-outcomes-across-countries

The Guttmacher Institute. (2018). U.S. pregnancy and births. Retrieved June 22, 2019, from https://www.guttmacher.org/news-release/2017/us-rates-pregnancy-birth-and-abortion-among-adolescents-and-young-adults-continue

Hagestad, G, O., & Call, V. R. A. (2007). Pathways to childlessness: A life course perspective. *Journal of Family Issues*, 28(10), 1338–1361.

Hanson, S. L. (1992). Involving families in programs for pregnant teens: Consequences for teens and their families. Family Relations, 41, 303–311.

Hartill, L. (2001). Life with a supersized family. *The Christian Science Monitor*. Retrieved from www.csmonitor.com/200l/0910/pl5sl-lifp.html

Hayford, S. R., & Morgan, S. P. (2008). Religiosity and fertility in the United States: The role of fertility intentions. *Social Forces*, 86(3), 1163–1189.

Hoffman, L. W., & Hoffman, M. L. (1973). The value of children to parents. In J. T. Fawcett (Ed.), *Psychological perspectives on population* (pp. 19–76). New York: Basic Books.

Irfan, U. (2019). We need to talk about the ethics of having children in a warming world. Vox.com. Retrieved March 26, 2020 from https://www.vox.com/2019/3/11/18256166/climate-change-having-kids

Johnson, S. M., & O'Connor, E. (2002). The gay baby boom: The psychology of gay parenthood. New York: New York University Press.

Kirczenow MacDonald, T. (2019). Lactation care for transgender and non-binary patients: Empowering clients and avoiding aversives. *Journal of Human Lactation*, 35(2), 223–226.

Kluwer, E. S., & Johnson, M. D. (2007). Conflict frequency and relationship quality across the transition to parenthood. *Journal of Marriage and Family*, 69, 1089–1106.

Lawson, K. (2004). Development and psychometric properties of the Perceptions of Parenting Inventory. *The Journal of Psychology*, 138(5), 433–455.

Lesthaeghe, R. (2014). The fertility transition in Sub-Saharan Africa into the 21st century. *PSC Research Report*, No. 14-823.

MacKay, H. (1994). *DINKs*. Lindfield, NSW: MacKay.

March of Dimes. (2018). March of Dimes global report on birth defects. Retrieved March 26, 2020 from https://www.marchofdimes.org/mission/march-of-dimes-global-report-on-birth-defects.aspx

Martin, S. P. (2002). *Delayed marriage and childbearing: Implications and measurement of diverging trends in family timing*. College Park: University of Maryland Department of Sociology and Maryland Population Research Center.

Massar, K., & Buunk, A.P. (2019). Expecting and competing? Jealous responses among pregnant and nonpregnant women. *Evolutionary Psychology*, 17(1). https://doi.org/10.1177/1474704919833344

Mayo Clinic. (2019). Sperm donation. Retrieved June 22, 2019, from https://www.mayoclinic.org/tests-procedures/sperm-donation/about/pac-20395032

McDonald, P. F. (2000). Low fertility in Australia: Evidence, causes, and policy responses. *People and Place*, 8(2), 6–21.

McMorris, J., & Glass, J. (2018). Contemporary approaches to gender and religion. In: B. Risman, C. Froyum, & W. Scarborough, W. (Eds.), *Handbook of the sociology of gender*. New York: Springer, Cham.

McQuillan, K. (2004). When does religion influence fertility? *Population and Development Review*, 30(1), 25–56.

Merck Manual, Professional Version. (2020). Spontaneous abortions. Retrieved June 1, 2020 from https://www.merckmanuals.com/professional/gynecology-and-obstetrics/abnormalities-of-pregnancy/spontaneous-abortion

Movement Advancement Project. (2019). Foster and adoption laws. Retrieved June 22, 2019, from https://www.familyequality.org/resources/foster-and-adoption-laws

National Abortion Federation. (2019). What to expect after the abortion. Retrieved June 22, 2019, from https://prochoice.org/think-youre-pregnant/what-should-i-expect-after-the-abortion/

The National Domestic Violence Hotline. (2019). Staying physically, emotionally, and financially safe during pregnancy. Retrieved June 23, 2019 from https://www.thehotline.org/2015/07/02/staying-physically-emotionally-and-financially-safe-during-pregnancy/

National Organization on Adolescent Pregnancy, Parenting, and Prevention. (2008). Healthy Teen Network. Retrieved January 1, 2009 from www.healthyteennetwork.org

National Right to Life Campaign. (2019). The state of abortion in the United States. Retrieved March 10, 2020 from https://www.nrlc.org/

National Vital Statistics Reports (2017). Pregnancy and childbirth demographics. *National Vital Statistics Reports*, 67(8), 1–49.

National Vital Statistics Reports. (2018). Births: Final data for 2016. *National Vital Statistics Report*, 67(1).

National Vital Statistics Reports. (2019). Births: Provisional data for 2018. Vital Statistics Rapid Release; no 7. Hyattsville, MD: National Center for Health Statistics.

Notarius, C. I., Benson, P. R., Sloane, D., Vanzetti, N. A., & Hornyak, L, M. (1989). Exploring the interface between perception and behavior: An analysis of marital interaction in distressed and nondistressed couples. *Behavioral Assessment*, 11, 39–64.

Obedin-Maliver, J., Makadon, H. J. (2016). Transgender men and pregnancy. *Obstetric Medicine*, 9(1), 4–8.

Parfitt, Y., & Ayers, S. (2014). Transition to parenthood and mental health in first-time parents. *Infant Mental Health Journal*, 35(3), 263–273.

Park, K. (2005). Choosing childlessness; Weber's typology of action and motives of the voluntarily childless. *Sociological Inquiry*, 75(3), 372–402.

Patterson, C. (2000). Family relationships of lesbians and gay men. *Journal of Marriage and Family*, 62, 1052–1069.

Patterson, C. J. (2004). Lesbian and gay parents and their children: Summary of research findings. *In Lesbian and gay parenting: A resource for psychologists*. Washington, DC: American Psychological Association.

Penn Medicine. (2019). IVF by the numbers. Retrieved June 22, 2019, from https://www.pennmedicine.org/updates/blogs/fertility-blog/2018/march/ivf-by-the-numbers

Perkins K. M., Boulet S. L., Jamieson D. J., & Kissin D. M. (2016). National Assisted Reproductive Technology Surveillance System (NASS) Group. Trends and outcomes of gestational surrogacy in the United States. *Fertility and Sterility*, 106(2), 435–442.

Perrin, E. C. (2002). *Sexual orientation in child and adolescent health care*. New York: Kluwer Academic/Plenum.

Pew Research Center. (2017). The changing global religious landscape. Retrieved March 26, 2020 from https://www.pewforum.org/2017/04/05/the-changing-global-religious-landscape/pf_17-04-05_projectionsupdate_birthsdeaths640px/

Pew Research Center. (2018a). Most parents and non-parents don't expect to have kids in the future. Retrieved June 22, 2019 from https://www.pewresearch.org/fact-tank/2018/12/12/most-parents-and-many-non-parents-dont-expect-to-have-kids-in-the-future/

Pew Research Center. (2018b). More than a million Millennials are becoming moms each year. Retrieved June 22, 2019, from https://www.pewresearch.org/fact-tank/2018/05/04/more-than-a-million-millennials-are-becoming-moms-each-year/

Planned Parenthood. (2019). We are Planned Parenthood: Annual 2018–019 report. Retrieved March 10, 2020 from https://www.plannedparenthood.org/uploads/filer_public/2e/da/2eda3f50-82aa-4ddb-acce-c2854c4ea80b/2018-2019_annual_report.pdf

Power to Decide: The Campaign to Prevent Unplanned Pregnancy. (2019). Unplanned pregnancy: National data. Retrieved June 1, 2020 from https://powertodecide.org/what-we-do/information/national-state-data/national

Rathus, S. A., & Nevid, J. S. (1992). Adjustment and growth: The challenges of life (5th ed.). Fort Worth, TX: Harcourt Brace Jovanovich.

Richardson, P. (1981). Women's perceptions of their important dyadic relationships during pregnancy. Journal of Maternal and Child Nursing, 10(3), 159–174.

Riswick, T., & Engelen, T. (2018). Siblings and life transitions: Investigating the resource dilution hypothesis across historical contexts and outcomes. The History of the Family, 23(4), 521–532.

Salmela-Aro, K., Aunola, K., Saisto, T., Halmesmaki, E., & Nurmi, J. E. (2006). Couples share similar changes in depressive symptoms and marital satisfaction anticipating the birth of a child. Journal of Social and Personal Relationships, 23(5), 781–803.

Seccombe, K. (1991). Assessing the costs and benefits of children: Gender comparisons among childfree husbands and wives. Journal of Marriage and the Family, 53, 191–202.

Solomon-Fears, C. (2008). Nonmarital childbearing: Trends, reasons, and public policy interventions. CRS Report for Congress, Order Code Rl.34756. Retrieved from http://ftp.fas.org/sgp/crs/misc/RL347S6.pdf

Strohschein, L., Gauthier, A. H., Campbell, R., & Kleparchuk, C. (2008). Parenting as a dynamic process: A test of the resource dilution hypothesis theory. Journal of Marriage and Family, 70, 670–683.

U.S. Centers for Disease Control and Prevention. (2018). Reproductive health: Teen pregnancy. Retrieved June 22, 2019, from https://www.cdc.gov/teenpregnancy/about/index.htm

U.S. Center for Disease Control and Prevention. (2019). Births and natality. Retrieved June 22, 2019, from https://www.cdc.gov/nchs/fastats/births.htm

U.S. Department of Agriculture. (2019). The cost of raising a child. Retrieved June 1, 2020 from https://www.usda.gov/media/blog/2017/01/13/cost-raising-child

U.S. Department of Health and Human Services. (2003). Researchers identify a possible cause of infertility in some women with endometriosis. National Institute of Child Health and Human Development, June 17, 2003. Retrieved from http://www.nichd.nih.gov/news/releascs/infertility.cfm

U.S. Department of Health and Human Services. (2019). Male infertility. Retrieved June 22, 2019, from https://www.hhs.gov/opa/reproductive-health/fact-sheets/male-infertility/index.html

Veevers, J. E. (1980). Childless by choice. Toronto: Butterworth.

von Sydow, K. (1999). Sexuality during pregnancy and after childbirth: A metacontent analysis of 59 studies. Journal of Psychosomatic Research, 47, 27–49.

Watkins, E. S. (2008). Conceiving the future: Pronatalism, reproduction, and the family in the United States, 1890–1938. Journal of Interdisciplinary History, 39(1), 144–145.

Weston, R., & Qu, L. (2001, Autumn). Men's and women's reasons for not having children. Family Matters.

Wooden, M. (1999). Job insecurity and job instability: Getting the facts straight. BCA Papers, 1(1), 14–18.

World Health Organization. (2018). Maternal mortality. Retrieved June 22, 2019, from https://www.who.int/news-room/fact-sheets/detail/maternal-mortality

Yamaguchi, K., & Fergusson, L. R. (1995). The stopping and spacing of childbirths and their birth history predictors: Rational choice theory and event history analysis. American Sociological Review, 60, 272–289.

/// CHAPTER 11

Allen. K. R. (1997). Lesbian and gay families. In T. Arendell (Ed.), Contemporary parenting: Challenges and issues. New York: SAGE.

Amato, P. R., & Fowler, F. (2002). Parenting practices, child adjustment, and family diversity. Journal of Marriage and Family, 64(3), 703-716.

American Academy of Pediatrics. (2016). Suicide and suicide attempts in adolescence. Pediatrics, 138(1), e20161420.

American Academy of Pediatrics (2018). AAP says spanking harms children. Retrieved March 5, 2020, from https://services.aap.org/en/news-room/news-releases/aap/2018/aap-says-spanking-harms-children/

American Academy of Pediatrics (2020). About the AAP. Retrieved from https://services.aap.org/en/about-the-aap/

Anderson, J. (2014). The impact of family structure on the health of children: Effects of divorce. Linacre Quarterly, 81(4), 378–387.

Arendell, T. (2000). Conceiving and investigating motherhood: The decade's scholarship. Journal of Marriage and the Family, 62, 1192–1207.

Bandura, A. (1986). Social foundations of thought and action: A social cognitive theory. Englewood Cliffs, NJ: Prentice Hall.

Barbeta, M., & Cano, T. (2017). Toward a new model of fatherhood? Discourses on paternal involvement in urban Spain. Revista Española de Investigaciones Sociológicas, 159, 13–30.

Baumrind, D. (1991), The influence of parenting style on adolescent competence and substance use. Journal of Early Adolescence, 11(1), 56–95.

Baxter, J., Hewitt, B., & Haynes, M. (2008). Life course transitions and housework: Marriage, parenthood, and time on housework. Journal of Marriage and Family, 70, 259–272.

Belsky, J. (1990). Children and marriage. In F. Fincham & T. Bradbury (Eds.), The psychology of marriage: Basic issues and applications (pp. 172–200). New York: Guilford.

Belsky, J., & Pensky, E. (1988). Marital change across the transition to parenthood. Marriage and Family Review, 12, 133–156.

Bianchi, S. M. (2000). Maternal employment and time with children: Dramatic change or surprising continuity? Demography, 37, 401–414.

Blair, S. L., & Lichter, D. (1991). Measuring the division of household labor: Gender segregation of housework among American couples. Journal of Family Issues, 12, 91–113.

Bloir, K. (2005), Single, custodial fathers. OSU Extension fact-sheet, Family and Consumer Sciences. Columbus: Ohio State University.

Boyd, D., & Bee, H. (2009). Lifespan development (5th ed.). Boston: Allyn & Bacon.

Brody, G., Flor, D., & Neubaum, E. (1998). Coparenting processes and child competence among rural African-American families. In M. Lewis & C. Feiring (Eds.), Families, risk, and competence. Mahwah, NJ: Erlbaum.

Broman, C. L., Reckase, M. D., & Freedman-Doan, C. R. (2006). The role of parenting in drug use among Black, Latino, and white adolescents, Journal of Ethnicity in Substance Use, 5(1), 39–50.

Brooks-Gunn, J., & Markman, L. B. (2005). The contribution of parenting to ethnic and racial gaps in school readiness. Future of Children, 15(1), 139–168.

Brown, T. N., Tanner-Smith, E. E., Lesane-Brown, C. L., & Ezell, M. E. (2007). Child, parent, and situational correlates of familial ethnic/race socialization. Journal of Marriage and Family, 69(1), 14–26.

Burton, L., Dilworth-Anderson, P., & Merriwether-de-Vries, C. (1995). Context of surrogate parenting among contemporary grandparents. Marriage and Family Review, 20, 349–366.

Cano, T., Perales, F., & Baxter, J. (2018). A matter of time: Father involvement and child cognitive outcomes. Journal of Marriage and Family, 81(1), 1–22.

Cao, H. I., Mills-Koonce, W. R., Wood, C., & Fine, M. A. (2016). Identity transformation during the transition to parenthood among same-sex couples: An ecological, stress-strategy-adaptation perspective. Journal of Family and Theory Review, 8(1), 30–59.

Carter, B., & McGoldrick, M. (1999). The expanded family life cycle: Individual, family, and social perspectives (3rd ed.). Boston: Allyn & Bacon.

Ceballo, R., & Hurd, N. (2008). Neighborhood context, SES, and parenting: Including a focus on acculturation among Latina mothers. Applied Developmental Science, 12(4), 176–180.

Chamberlain, P., & Patterson, G. R. (1995). Discipline and child compliance in parenting. In M. H. Mornstein (Ed.), *Handbook of parenting. Vol 4: Applied and practical parenting*. Mahwah, NJ: Erlbaum.

Cheah, C. S. L, & Rubin, K. H. (2004). Comparison of European American and mainland Chinese mothers' responses to aggression and social withdrawal in preschoolers. *International journal of Behavioral Development*, 28,83–94.

Chen, A., & Kaplan, H. B., (2001). Intergenerational transmission of constructive parenting, *Journal of Marriage and Family*, 63(1), 17–31.

Cherry, K. (2018). What is uninvolved parenting? *Developmental Psychology*. Retrieved July 12, 2019 from https://www.verywellmind.com/what-is-uninvolved-parenting-2794958

Children's Bureau. (2018). A father's impact on child development. Retrieved June 1, 2020 from https://www.all4kids.org/news/blog/a-fathers-impact-on-child-development/

Christophersen, E. R. (1988). *Little people: Guidelines for common sense child rearing* (3rd ed.). Kansas City, MO: Westport.

Coard, S. I., Foy-Watson. S., Zimmer, C., & Wallace, A. (2007). Considering culturally relevant parenting practices in intervention development and adaptation: A randomized controlled trial of the Black Parenting Strengths and Strategies (BPSS) Program. *The Counseling Psychologist*, 35(6), 797–820.

Cohen, T. F. (1993). What do fathers provide? Reconsidering the economic and nurturant dimensions of men as parents. In J. C. Hood (Ed.), *Men, work, and family (pp. 1–22)*. Newbury Park, CA: SAGE.

Coltrane, S. (2000). Research on household labor: Modeling and measuring the social embeddedness of routine family work. *Journal of Marriage and the Family*, 62, 1208–1233.

Connell, C. M., & Prinz, R. J. (2002). The impact of childcare and parent-child interactions on school readiness and social skill development for low-income African American children. *Journal of School Psychology*, 40(2), 177–193.

Craig, L. (2006). Do fathers care mean father's share? *Gender & Society*, 20, 259–291.

Crockenberg, S. C., & Leerkes, E. M. (2003). Parental acceptance, postpartum depression, and maternal sensitivity: Mediating and moderating processes. *Journal of Family Psychology*, 17, 80–93.

Darling, N., & Steinberg, L. (1993). Parenting style as context: An integrative model. *Psychological Bulletin*, 1(13), 487–496.

Delmore-Ko, P., Pancer, S. M., Hunsberger, P., & Pratt, M. (2000). Becoming a parent: The relation between prenatal expectations and postnatal experience. *Journal of Family Psychology*, 14, 625–640.

Deutsch, F. M., Lozy, J. L., & Saxon, S. E. (1993). Taking credit: Couples' reports of contributions to childcare. *Journal of Family Issues*, 14, 421–437.

Donahoo, S. (2004). Single parenting and children's academic achievement. Retrieved from http://library.adoption.com/pring.php

Durbin, M., DiClemente, R., Siegel, D., Krasnovsky, F., Lazarus, N., & Camacho, T. (1993). Factors associated with multiple sex partners among junior high school students. *Journa1 of Adolescent Health Care*, 14, 202–207.

Eamon, M. K., & Mulder, C. (2005). Predicting antisocial behavior among Latino young adolescents: An ecological systems analysis. *American Journal of Orthopsychiatry*, 75, 117–127.

Family Equality Council. (2017). LGBTQ family fact sheet. Retrieved July 12, 2019 from https://www2.census.gov/cac/nac/meetings/2017-11/LGBTQ-families-factsheet.pdf

Gable, S., Crnic, K., & Belsky, J. (1994). Coparenting within the family system: Influences on children's development. *Family Relations*, 43, 380–386.

Gauthier, A. H., Smeeding, T. M., & Furstenberg, F. F. (2004). Are parents investing less time in children? Trends in selected industrialized countries. *Population and Development Review*, 30(4), 647–671.

Gershoff, E. T. (2002). Parental corporal punishment and associated child behaviors and experiences: A meta-analytic and theoretical review. *Psychological Bulletin*, 128(4), 539–579.

Gilliam, J. E., & Coleman, M. C. (1981). Who influences IEP committee decisions? *Exceptional Children*, 47, 642–644.

Glass, J. C., & Hunneycutt, T. L. (2002). Grandparents parenting grandchildren: Extent of situation issues involved and educational implications. *Educational Gerontology*, 28(2), 139–161.

Goldberg, S. K., & Conron, K. J. (2018). How many same-sex couples in the U.S. are raising children? *The Williams Institute*. Retrieved March 2, 2020, from https://williamsinstitute.law.ucla.edu/research/parenting/how-many-same-sex-parents-us/

Grogan-Kaylor, A. (2005). Corporal punishment and the growth trajectory of children's antisocial behavior. *Child Maltreatment*. 10, 283–292.

Harvard Family Research Project. (2006). Family involvement makes a difference in school success. Retrieved from http://www.hfrp.org/

Harwood, K., McLean, N., & Durkin, K. (2007). First-time mothers' expectations of parenthood: What happens when optimistic expectations are not matched by later experiences? *Developmental Psychology*, 43(1), 1–12.

Hatloy I. (2013). *Understanding postnatal depression*. London: Mind.

Hays, S. (1996). *The cultural contradictions of motherhood*. New Haven, CT: Yale University Press.

Hill, N. E., & Tyson, D. F. (2008). Excavating culture: Ethnicity and context as predictors of parenting behavior. *Applied Developmental Science*, 12(4), 188–197.

Hochschild, A. (1989). *The second shift*. New York: Avon.

Hosokawa, R., & Katsura, T. (2019). Role of parenting style in children's behavioral problems through the transition from preschool to elementary school according to gender in Japan. *International Journal of Environmental Research and Public Health*, 16(1), 21.

Hudson, M. (2009). Realistic expectations for great parenting. *Community Programs, Family Services of the North Shore*. Retrieved from www .familyservices.bc.ca

Hughes, D., Rodriguez, J., Smith, E. P., Johnson, D. J., Stevenson, H. C., & Spicer, P. (2006). Parents' ethnic-racial socialization practices: A review of research and directions for future study. *Developmental Psychology*, 42(5), 747–770.

Huynh, V. W., & Fuligni, A. J. (2010). Discrimination hurts: The academic, psychological, and physical well-being of adolescents. *Journal of Research on Adolescence*, 20(4), 916–941.

Jackson, C., Henriksen, L., & Foshee, V. A. (1998). The authoritative parenting index: Predicting health risk behaviors among children and adolescents. *Health Education Behavior*, 25(3), 319–37.

Jackson, K. M., Rogers, M. L., & Sartor, C. E. (2016). Parental divorce and initiation of alcohol use in early adolescence. *Psychology of Addictive Behaviors*, 30(4), 450–461.

Jackson-Newsom, J., Buchanan, C. M., & McDonald, R. M. (2008). Parenting and perceived maternal warmth in European American and Black American adolescents. *Journal of Marriage and Family*, 70, 62–75.

Jenny, C., Roesler, T. A., & Poyer, K. L. (1994). Are children at risk for sexual abuse by homosexuals? *Pediatrics*, 94, 41–44.

Kang, Y., & Moore, J. (2011). Parenting style and adolescents' school performance in mainland China. *US-China Education Review*, 1, 133–138.

Kids Count (2017). Children in single-parent families in the United States. Retrieved July 12, 2019 from https://datacenter.kidscount.org/data/tables/106-children-in-single-parent-families

Kids Count. (2018). Children in single-parent families in the U.S. Retrieved May 7, 2020 from https://datacenter.kidscount.org/data/tables/106-children-in-single-parent-families

Kim, J. E., Hetherington, E. M., & Reiss, D. (1999). Associations among family relationships, antisocial peers, and adolescents' externalizing behaviors: Gender and family type differences. *Child Development*, 70, 1209–1230.

Kretchmar, M. D., & Jacobvitz, D. B. (2002). Observing mother-child relationships across generations: Boundary patterns, attachment, and the transmission of caregiving. *Family Process*, 41, 351–374.

Kruk, E. (2012). The vital importance of parental presence in children's lives. Retrieved June 1, 2020 from http://www.psychologytoday.com/blog/co-parenting-after-divorce/201205/father-absence-father-deficit-father-hunger

Krumholz, W. (2019). Family breakdown and America's welfare system. *Institute for Family Studies*. Retrieved June 1, 2020 from https://ifstudies.org/blog/family-breakdown-and-americas-welfare-system

Kuppens, S., & Ceulemans, E. (2018). Parenting styles: A closer look at a well-known concept. *Journal of Child and Family Studies*, 28, 168–181.

Lamb, M. E. (1987). *The father's role: Cross-cultural perspectives*. Hillsdale, NJ: Erlbaum.

Lamb-Parker, F., Boak, A. Y., Griffin, K. W., Ripple, C., & Peay, L. (1999). Parent-child relationship, home learning environment, and school readiness. *School Psychology Review*, 28, 413–125.

Lansford, J. E., Dealer-Deckard, K., Dodge, K. A. Bates, J. E., & Pettit, G. S. (2004), Ethnic differences in the link between psychical discipline and alter adolescent externalizing behaviors. *Journal of Child Psychology and Psychiatry*, 45, 801–812.

Larzelere, R. E., & Kuhn, B. R. (2005). Comparing child outcomes of physical punishment and alternative disciplinary tactics: A meta-analysis. *Clinical Child and Family Psychology Review*, 8(1), 1–37.

Lawrence, E., Nylen, K., & Cobb, R. J. (2007). Prenatal expectations and marital satisfaction over the transition to parenthood. *Journal of Family Psychology*, 21, 155–164.

Lawrence, R., Rothman, A. D., Cobb, R. J., Rothman, M, T., & Bradbury, T. N. (2008). Marital satisfaction across the transition to parenthood. *Journal of Family Psychology*, 22(1), 41–50.

Lazarus, K., & Rossouw, P. J. (2015). Mothers' expectations of parenthood: The impact of prenatal expectations on self-esteem, depression, anxiety, and stress post birth. *International Journal of Neuropsychotherapy*, 3(2), 102–123.

Lerner, R. M. (1995). *American's youth in crisis: Challenges and options for programs and policies.* Thousand Oaks, CA: SAGE.

Lerner, R. M., Castellino, D. R., Terry, P. A., Villarruel, F. A., & McKinney, M. H. (1995). A developmental contextual perspective on parenting. In M. H. Bornstein (Ed.), *Handbook of parenting: Biology and ecology of parenting* (vol. 2; pp. 285–309). Hillsdale, NJ: Erlbaum.

Lerner, R. M., Noh, E. R., & Wilson, C. (2004). The parenting of adolescents and adolescents as parents: A developmental contextual perspective. Retrieved from https://parenthood.library.wisc.edu/Lerner/Lerner.html

Markus, H.R., & Moya, P.M.L. (2010). *Doing race: 21 essays for the 21st century.* New York: Norton & Company.

Marsh, H. W. (1990). Two-parent, stepparent, and single-parent families: Changes in achievement, attitudes, and behaviors during the last two years of high school. *Journal of Educational Psychology*, 82(2), 327–340.

McBride, B. A., & Mills, G. (1993). A comparison of mother and father involvement with their preschool age children. *Early Childhood Research Quarterly*, 8, 457–477.

McClun, I. A., & Merrell, K. W. (1998). Relationship of perceived parenting styles, locus of control orientation, and self-concept among junior high age students. *Psychology in the Schools*, 35(4), 381–390.

McHale, J., Rao, N., & Krasnow, A. (2000). Constructing family climates: Chinese mothers' reports of their coparenting behavior and preschoolers' adaptation. International *Journal of Behavioral Development*, 24, 111–118.

McLeod, J. D., & Nonnemaker, J. M. (2000). Poverty and child emotional and behavioral problems; Racial/ethnic differences in processes and effects. *Journal of Health and Social Behavior*, 41, 137–161.

McMurtry, S.L. (2013). Parenting style differences in Black American and white American young adults. Abstract of a dissertation submitted to the graduate school of The University of Southern Mississippi in partial fulfillment of the requirements for the degree of doctor of philosophy. Retrieved July 12, 2019 from https://pdfs.semanticscholar.org/7cd2/a716fa0ef624284c496b9387a350154214ec.pdf

Medina, S., & Magnuson, S. (2009). Motherhood in the 21st century: Implications for counselors (Practice & Theory). *Journal of Counseling and Development*, 87(1), 90–98.

Mercer, R. T. (1986). *First-time motherhood: Experiences from teens to forties.* New York: Springer.

Mercer, R. T. (2004). Becoming a mother versus maternal role attainment. *Journal of Nursing Scholarship*, 36(3), 226–232.

Milkie, M. A., Bianchi, S. M., Mattingly, M. J., & Robinson, J. P. (2002). Gendered division of childrearing: Ideals, realities, and the relationship to parental well-being. *Sex Roles: A Journal of Research*, 21–39.

Murry, V. M., Brody, G. H., Simons, R, L., Cutrona, C. E., & Gibbons, F. X. (2008). Disentangling ethnicity and context as predictors of parenting within rural African American families. *Applied Developmental Science*, 12(4), 202–210.

National Center for Juvenile Justice. (2014). Juvenile offenders and victims: 2014 national report. Retrieved June 1, 2020 from https://www.ojjdp.gov/ojstatbb/nr2014/downloads/NR2014.pdf

National Council on Family Relations. (2020). Understanding families: Research and practice. Retrieved April 18, 2020 from https://www.ncfr.org/membership

Odame-Mensah, S., & Gyimah, E. (2018). The role of permissive and neglectful parenting style in determining the academic performance of adolescents in the senior high schools in the Birim Municipality. *Journal of Education and Practice*, 9(4), 73.

Ogata, K., & Miyashita, K. (2000). Exploring links between father's participation in family chores, child's empathy, family function, and father's identity development. *Japanese Journal of Family Psychology*, 14, 15–27.

Olson, T. (2004). Don't die with your helmet on. Retrieved from www.dontdiewithyourhelmeton

Patterson, C. J. (1996). Lesbian mothers and their children: Findings from the Bay area Families Study. In J. Laird & R. J. Green (Eds.), *Lesbians and gays in couples and families: A handbook for therapists* (pp. 420–437). San Francisco: Jossey-Bass.

Pew Research Center. (2015). Parenting approaches and concerns. Retrieved July 12, 2019 from https://www.pewsocialtrends.org/2015/12/17/3-parenting-approaches-and-concerns/

Pew Research Center. (2019). Blacks are far more likely than whites to say that discrimination is a major obstacle for Black people. Retrieved July 12, 2019 from https://www.pewsocialtrends.org/2019/04/09/race-in-america-2019/psdt_04-09-19_race-00-04/

Pittman, L. D., & Chase-Lansdale, P. L. (2001), African American adolescent girls in impoverished communities: Parenting style and adolescent outcomes. *Journal of Research on Adolescence*, 11, 199–224.

Pleck, E. H., & Pleck, J. H. (1997). Fatherhood ideals in the United States: Historical dimensions. In M. Lamb (Ed.), *The roles of the father in child development.* New York: Wiley.

Pleck, J. H. (1997). Paternal involvement: Levels, sources, and consequences. In M. E. Lamb (Ed.), *The role of the father in child development* (pp. 66–103). New York: Wiley.

Priel, B., & Besser, A. (2001). Bridging the gap between attachment and object relations theories: A study of the transition to motherhood. *British Journal of Medical Psychology*, 74, 85–100.

Radziszewska, B., Richardson. J. L., Dent, C. W., & Flay, B. R. (1996). Parenting style and adolescent depressive symptoms, smoking, and academic achievement: Ethnic, gender, and SES differences. *Journal of Behavioral Medicine*, 19, 289–305.

Raphel, S. (2008). Kinship care and the situation for grandparents. *Journal of Childhood and Adolescent Psychiatric Nursing*, 21(2), 118–120.

Reynolds, G. P., Wright, J. V., & Beale, B. (2003). The roles of grandparents in educating today's children. *Journal of Instructional Psychology*, 30(4), 316–325.

Richards, P. (2018). Teaching 'race" in our schools is more important than ever. Retrieved May 7, 2020 from https://drpaulrichards.wordpress.com/2018/02/

Roche, K. M., Ensmingcr, M. E., & Cherlin, A. J. (2007). Variations in parenting and adolescent outcomes among African American and Latino families living in low-income, urban areas. *Journal of Family Issues*, 28(7), 882–909.

Rogers, S. J., & White, L., K., (1998). Satisfaction with parenting: The role of marital happiness, family structure, and parents' gender. *Journal of Marriage and the Family*, 60(2), 293–308.

Rotundo, E. A. (1993). American motherhood. New York: Basic Books.

Rubin, R. (1967). Attainment of the maternal role. Part I. *Nursing Research*, 16, 237–245.

Samaniego, R. Y., & Gonzales, N. A. (1999). Multiple mediators of the effects of acculturation status on delinquency for Mexican American adolescents. *American Journal of Community Psychology*, 27, 189–210.

Sanders, R.M. (2008). Triple P-positive parenting program as a public health approach to strengthening parenting. *Journal of Family Psychology*, 22(3), 506–517.

Satir, V. (1972). *People making.* Palo Alto, CA: Science & Behavior.

Savin-Williams, R. C., & Esterberg. E. G. (2000). Lesbian, gay, and bisexual families. In D. H. Dmo, K. R. Allen, & M. A. Fine (Eds.), *Handbook of family diversity.* New York: Oxford University Press.

Schoppe, S. J., Mangelsdorf, S. C., & Frosch, C. (2001). Coparenting, family process, and family structure: Implications for preschoolers' externalizing behavior problems. *Journal of Family Psychology*, 15, 526–545.

Seifer, R., Sameroff, A. J., Baldwin, C. P., & Baldwin, A. (1992). Child and family factors that ameliorate risk between 4 and 13 years of age. *Journal of American Academy of Child and Adolescent Psychiatry*, 31(4), 893–903.

Shucksmith, J., Leo, B., Hendry, L. B., & Glendinning, A. (1995). Models of parenting: Implications for adolescent well-being within different types of family contexts. *Journal of Adolescence*. 18, 253–270.

Smetana, J. G. (1995). Parenting styles and conceptions of parental authority during adolescence. *Child Development*, 66, 299–316.

Steinberg, L., Lamborn, S. D., Darling, N., Mounts, N. S., & Dornbusch, S. M. (1994). Over-time changes in adjustment and competence among adolescents from authoritative, authoritarian, indulgent, and neglectful families. *Child Development*, 65, 754–770.

Steinberg, L., & Morris, A. S. (2001). Adolescent development. *Annual Review of Psychology*, 52, 83–110.

Steinberg, L., Mounts, N., Lamborn, S., & Dornbusch, S. (1991). Authoritative parenting and adolescent adjustment across various ecological niches. *Journal of Research on Adolescence*, 1, 19–36.

Taffel, R. (1994). *Why parents disagree: How men and women parent differently and how we can work together*. New York: William Morrow.

Theisen, C. (2004). The parent coach plan: Eight parenting responsibilities. Retrieved March 26, 2006 from www.parentcoachplan.com

U.S. Census Bureau (2018a). Family groups: 2018 (Table FG10). America's families and living arrangements. Retrieved July 12, 2019 from https://www.census.gov/data/tables/2018/demo/families/cps-2018.html

U.S. Census Bureau (2018b). Household relationship and living arrangements of children under 18 years, by age and sex: 2018 (Table C2). America's families and living arrangements. Retrieved July 12, 2019 from https://www.census.gov/data/tables/2018/demo/families/cps-2018.html

U.S. Census Bureau (2018c). One-parent unmarried family groups with own children under 18 (Table FG6). America's families and living arrangements. Retrieved July 12, 2019 from https://www.census.gov/data/tables/2018/demo/families/cps-2018.html

Wainright, J. L., & Patterson, C. J, (2006). Delinquency, victimization, and substance use among adolescents with female same-sex parents. *Journal of Family Psychology*. 20, 526–530.

Walker, K. (2017). What issues do lesbian co-mothers face in their transition to parenthood? *Perspective*, 34, 1–7.

Weis, R., & Toolis, E. E. (2010). Parenting across cultural contexts in the USA: Assessing parenting behavior in an ethnically socioeconomically diverse sample. *Early Child Development & Care*, 180(7), 849–867.

Yogman, M., & Garfield, C. F. (2016). Fathers' roles in the care and development of their children: The role of pediatricians. *Pediatrics*, 138(1). https://doi.org/10.1542/peds.2016-1128

Zizzo, G. (2009). Lesbian families and the negotiation of maternal identity through the unconventional use of breast milk. *Journal of Gay Lesbian Issues*, 5(2), 96–109.

/// CHAPTER 12

AARP (2019). Understanding the impact of family caregiving on work. Retrieved from https://www.aarp.org/content/dam/aarp/research/public_policy_institute/ltc/2012/understanding-impact-family-caregiving-work-AARP-ppi-ltc.pdf

Aboulhassan, S., & Brumley, K. M. (2018). Carrying the burden of a culture: Bargaining with patriarchy and the gendered reputation of Arab American women. *Journal of Family Issues*, 40(5), 637–661.

Allegretto, S. (2005, September 1). Basic family budgets: Working families' incomes often fail to meet living expenses around the U.S. Economic Policy Institute Briefing Paper #165. Retrieved from www.epi.org/coinent.cfm/bpl65 [2005, October 5].

Amato, P. R., Johnson, D. R., Booth, A., & Rogers, S. J. (2003). Continuity and change in marital quality between 1980 and 2000. *Journal of Marriage and the Family*, 65(1), 1–22.

American Community Survey. (2019). *Father's day:* 2018. Retrieved June 18, 2019 from https://www.census.gov/newsroom/stories/2018/fathers-day.html

Anderson, S. A., & Sabatelli, R. M. (2011). *Family interaction: A multigenerational developmental perspective* (5th ed.). Boston: Pearson.

Arab American Institute. (2019). Education. Retrieved March 9, 2020 from https://www.aaiusa.org/education

Artazcoz, L., Benach, J., Borrell, C., & Cortes, I. (2004). Unemployment and mental health: Understanding the interactions among gender, family roles, and social class. *American Journal of Public Health*, 94(1), 82–88.

Baca Zinn, M., & Pok, A. Y. (2002). Tradition and transition in Mexican-origin families. In R. L. Taylor (Ed.), *Minority families in the United States: A multicultural perspective* (3rd ed.; pp. 79–100). Upper Saddle River, NJ: Prentice Hall.

Bailey, M. J., & Duquette, N. J. (2014). How Johnson fought the war on poverty: The economics and politics of funding at the Office of Economic Opportunity. *Journal of Economic History*, 72(2), 351–388.

Baird, L. S., & Beccia, P. J. (1980). The potential misuse of overtime. *Personnel Psychology*, 33, 557–565.

Baisden, E. D., Fox, J. J., & Bartholomae, S. (2018). Financial management and marital quality: A phenomenological inquiry. *Journal of Financial Therapy*, 9(1), 1–27.

Barnett, R. C., & Rivers, C. (1996). *She works, he works: How two-income families are happy, healthy, and thriving*. Cambridge, MA: Harvard University Press.

Baxter, J. (1993). Work at home: The domestic division of labour. Queensland, Australia: University of Queensland Press.

Behnke, A. O., & MacDermid, S. M. (2004). Family well-being. Retrieved from http://wfnetwork.bc.edu/encyclopedia_entry.php

Belsky, J. (2001). Developmental risks (still) associated with early childcare. *Journal of Child Psychology and Psychiatry and Allied Disciplines*, 42, 845–859.

Bianchi, S. M., Sayer, L. C., Milkie, M. A., & Robinson, J. P. (2012). Housework: Who did, does or will do it, and how much does it matter? *Social Forces*, 91(1), 55–63.

Blair, S. L., & Lichter, D. (1991). Measuring the division of household labor: Gender segregation of housework among American couples. *Journal of Family Issues*, 12, 91–113.

Bushatz, A. (2018). Report shows finances as a top concern for troops, families. Retrieved June 18, 2019, from https://www.military.com/daily-news/2018/03/01/report-shows-finances-top-concern-troops-families.html

Campbell, F. A., Ramey, C. T., Pungello, E. P., Sparling, J., & Miller-Johnson, S. (2002). Early childhood education: Young adult outcomes from the Abecedarian Project. *Applied Developmental Science*, 6, 42–57.

Child Care Aware. (2019). Mapping the gap: Examining child care supply and demand across the country. Retrieved April 22, 2020 from https://www.childcareaware.org/our-issues/research/mappingthegap/

Child Trends. (2019). Children in poverty. Retrieved June 19, 2019 from https://www.childtrends.org/indicators/children-in-poverty

Choi, Y., Yeun Kim, T., Noh, S., Lee, J., & Takeuchi, D. (2018). Culture and family process: Measures of familism for Filipino and Korean American parents. *Family Processes*, 57(4), 1029–1048.

Coltrane, S. (2000). Research on household labor: Modeling and measuring the social embeddedness of routine family work. *Journal of Marriage and the Family*, 62, 1208–1233.

Commonwealth Fund Commission. (2018). State regulation of coverage options outside of the Affordable Care Act: Limiting the risk to the individual market. Retrieved April 22, 2020 from https://www.commonwealthfund.org/publications/fund-reports/2018/mar/state-regulation-coverage-options-outside-affordable-care-act

Commonwealth Fund Commission. (2020). New survey finds Americans suffering health coverage insecurity along with job losses. Retrieved April 22, 2020 from https://www.commonwealthfund.org/blog/2020/new-survey-finds-americans-suffering-health-coverage-insecurity-job-losses

Congressional Caucus on Women's Issues. (2005). Chutes & ladders: The search for solid ground for women in the workforce. Retrieved from http://www.womenwork.org/policy/chutes.htm

Congressional Research Services. (2019). Army deployments. Retrieved June 18, 2019 from https://fas.org/sgp/crs/natsec/R42738.pdf

Constante, K., Marchand, A. D., Cross, F. L., & Rivas-Drake, D. (2019). Understanding the promotive role of familism in the link between ethnic-racial identity and Latino youth social engagement. *Journal of Latinx Psychology*, 7(3), 230–244.

Corbett, M. (2005). U.S. households led by single mothers and displaced homemakers on the rise. *Women's Work*. Retrieved February 7, 2009 from www.womenwork.org

Council on Foreign Relations. (2019). Demographics of the U.S. *military*. Retrieved June 17, 2019 from www.cfr.org/article/demographics-us-military

Crouter, A. C. (1995). Processes linking families and work: Implications for behavior and developing in both settings. In R. D. Parke & S. Kellam (Eds.),

Exploring family relationships with other social contexts (pp. 55–79). Hillsdale, NJ: Erlbaum.

Crouter, A. C., Bumpus, M. F., Head, M. R., & McHale, S. M. (2001). Implications of overwork and overload for the quality of men's family relationships. *Journal of Marriage and Family*, 63(2), 404–416.

Davis, K. K., Crouter, A. C., & McHale, S. M. (2006). Implications of shift work for parent-adolescent relationships in dual-earner families. *Family Relations*, 55, 450–460.

Defrain, J. (2000). Creating a strong family: Qualities of strong families. Lincoln: University of Nebraska Cooperative Extension, Institute of Agriculture and Natural Resources.

Dew, J. (2007). Two sides of the same coin? The differing roles of assets and consumer debt in marriage. *Journal of Family and Economic Issues*, 28, 89–104.

Dew, J. (2008). Debt change and marital satisfaction change in recently married couples. *Family Relations*, 57, 60–71.

Drummet, A. R., Coleman, M., & Cable, S. (2003). Military families under stress: Implications for family life education. *Family Relations*, 52, 279–287.

Dyk, P. H. (2004). Complexity of family life among the low-income and working poor: Introduction to the special issue. *Family Relations*, 53(2), 122–126.

Early Child Care Research Network. (2003). Does amount of time spent in child care predict socioemotional adjustment during the transition to kindergarten? *Child Development*, 74, 976–1005.

Ermisch, J., & Francesconi, M. (2002). The effect of parents' employment on children's education attainment. ISER Working Paper No. 2002-21. University of Essex. Retrieved October 17, 2005 from www.socserv2 .mcmaster.ca/sedap/p/Ermise.pdf

Evans, R. P. (2004). *The five lessons a millionaire taught me*. Salt Lake City, UT: Aurcadia Press.

Eyre, R., & Eyre, L. (2008, February, 29). *Balancing work and family*. Logan: Utah State University.

Fetsch, R. (2009). Suggestion for maintaining mental health during employment transitions. *Colorado State University, Human Development & Family Studies*. Retrieved February 8, 2009 from www.ext.colostate.edu

Fong, T. P. (2002). *The contemporary Asian American experience: Beyond the model minority* (2nd ed.). Upper Saddle River, NJ: Prentice Hall.

Furstenberg, F. F. (1974). Work experience and family life. In J. O'Toole (Ed.), *Work and the quality of life*. Cambridge, MA: MIT Press.

Gallup National Health and Well-Being Index. (2019). U.S. wellbeing declines halted in 2019. Retrieved April 22, 2020 from https://news.gallup.com/ poll/266978/wellbeing-declines-halted-2019.aspx

Gottfried, A. E., & Gottfried, A. W. (1994). *Redefining families: Implications for children's development*. New York: Plenum.

Gottman, J. M. (1994). *Why marriages succeed or fail*. New York: Simon & Schuster.

Gottman, J. M. (1999). *The marriage clinic: A scientifically based marital therapy*. New York: Norton.

Greenhaus, J. H., & Beutell, N. J. (1985). Sources of conflict between work and family roles. *Academy of Management Review*, 10, 76–88.

Grosswald, B. (2004). The effects of shift work on family satisfaction. *Families in Society*, 85(3), 413–423.

Gutter, M., & Copur, Z. (2014). The relationship between financial issues for marital relationship. *International Journal of Arts and Sciences*, 7, 683–698.

Haddock, S. A., Zimmerman, T. S., Ziemba, S. J., & Current, L. R. (2001). Ten adaptive strategies for family and work balance: Advice from successful families. *Journal of Marital and Family Therapy*, 27(4), 445–458.

Hammer, L., & Thompson, C. (2003). Work-family role conflict. *Sloan work and family encyclopedia*. Retrieved from www.bc.edu/bc_org/avp/wfnetwork/rft/ wfpedia/wfpWFRCent.html

Hanisch, K. A. (1999). Job loss and unemployment research from 1994 to 1998: A review of and recommendations for research and intervention. *Journal of Vocational Behavior*, 55, 188–220.

Hardie, J. H., & Lucas, A. (2010). Economic factors and relationship quality among young couples: Comparing cohabitation and marriage. *Journal of Marriage and Family*, 72(5), 1141–1154.

Harris, V. W. (2008). The triangular theory of balancing work and family. Unpublished manuscript, Utah State University, Logan.

Hartup, W. W., & Moore, S. G. (1990). Early peer relations: Developmental significance and prognostic implications. *Early Childhood Research Quarterly*, 59(1), 1–17.

Hayen, A., Lincoln, D., Moore, H., & Thomas M. (2002). Trends in potentially avoidable mortality in NSW. *NSW Public Health Bulletin*, 13(11/12), 226–236.

HealthCare.gov. (2019). Affordable Care Act. Retrieved June 19, 2019 from www .healthcare.gov/glossary/affordable-care-act/

Hiswals, A. S., Marttila, A., Malstam, E., & Marcassa, G. (2017). Experiences of unemployment and well-being after job loss during economic recession: Results of a qualitative study in east central Sweden. *Journal of Public Health Research*, 6(3), 995. doi:10.4081/jphr.2017.995

Hoschild, A. (1989). *The second shift*. New York: Avon.

HUD. (2018). Strong families initiative. Retrieved March 12, 2020 from https:// www.hud.gov/strongfamilies

Institute for Women's Policy Research. (2008). The gender wage gap: 2007. Publication IWPR No. C350. Retrieved from www.iwpr.org/femstats/ wocdata.htm

Institute for Women's Policy Research. (2019). Median weekly earnings and gender earnings ratio for full-time workers. Retrieved June 17, 2019 from https://iwpr.org/publications/gender-wage-gap-2018/

Johnson, A. (2008, October). *Financial first aid*. Paper presented at the Family Consumer Science Agent In-Service, St. George, UT.

Johnson, N. J., Backlund, E., Sorlie, P. D., & Loveless, C. A. (2000): Marital status and mortality: The National Longitudinal Mortality Study. *Annual of Epidemiology*, 10, 224–238.

Kids Count. (2019). Children in poverty by race and ethnicity in the United States. Retrieved from https://datacenter.kidscount.org/.

Killewald, A. (2016). Money, work, and marital stability: Assessing change in the gendered determinants of divorce. *American Sociological Review*, 81(4), 696–719.

Krieger, N. (2001). Critical perspectives on racial and ethnic differences in health and later life. *The National Academic Press, Committee on Population*. Retrieved from www.darwin.nap.edu/books/0309092116.html

Lamb, M. E. (2000). The effects of quality of care on child development. *Applied Developmental Science*, 4(3), 112–115.

Lewin, A. C. (2005). The effect of economic stability on family stability among welfare recipients. *Evaluation Review*, 29(30), 223–240.

Lockert, M. (2019). Mental health survey: 1 in 15 high student debt borrowers considered suicide. *Student Loan Planner*. Retrieved February 28, 2020 from www.studentloanplanner.com/mental-health-awareness-survey/

Loudoun, R. (2008). Balancing shiftwork and life outside work: Do 12-hour shifts make a difference? Applied Ergonomics, 39, 572–579.

McCartney, K., & Haas, M. (2002). Better caregiving training, smaller childcare classes lead to improved cognitive and social skills in children. Cambridge, MA: Harvard Graduate School of Education. Retrieved from www.gse .harvard.edu/news/fealures/mccartncy05052002.html

Mellan, O. (1994). *Money harmony*. New York: Walker and Company.

Military Family Advisory Network. (2019). 2019 military family survey. Retrieved March 9, 2020 from https://militaryfamilyadvisorynetwork.org/survey/

National Council on Family Relations. (2020). Understanding families: Research and practice. Retrieved May 10, 2020 from https://www.ncfr.org/ membership

National Farm Worker Ministry. (2019). Immigration reform. Retrieved April 22, 2020 from http://nfwm.org/current-campaigns/immigration-reform-2/

Papp, L. M., Cummings, E. M., & Goeke-Morey, M. C. (2009). For richer, for poorer: Money as a topic of marital conflict in the home. Family Relations, 58, 91–103.

Perry-Jenkins, M., Repetti, R. L., & Crouter, A. C. (2001). Work and family in the 1990s. In R. Milardo (Ed.), *Understanding families into the new millennium: A decade in review* (pp. 200–217). Lawrence, KS: NCFR and Alliance Communications Group.

Pew Foundation. (2020). Law will ease access to affordable student loan repayment if implemented effectively. Retrieved March 15, 2020 from https://www.pewtrusts.org/en/research-and-analysis/articles/2020/03/02/ law-will-ease-access-to-affordable-student-loan-repayment-if- implemented-effectively

Pew Research Center. (2017a). U.S. active-duty military presence overseas is at its smallest in decades. Retrieved June 17, 2019 from https://www. pewresearch.org/fact-tank/2017/08/22/u-s-active-duty-military-presence- overseas-is-at-its-smallest-in-decades/

Pew Research Center. (2017b). U.S. Muslims concerned about their place in society. Retrieved June 17, 2019 from https://www.pewforum.org/2017/07/26/findings-from-pew-research-centers-2017-survey-of-us-muslims/

Pew Research Center. (2018). Stay at home moms and dads account for about one in five U.S. Parents. Retrieved from https://www.pewresearch.org/fact-tank/2018/09/24/stay-at-home-moms-and-dads-account-for-about-one-in-five-u-s-parents/

Pew Research Center. (2019a). The narrowing, but persistent, gender gap in pay. Retrieved April 22, 2020 from https://www.pewresearch.org/fact-tank/2019/03/22/gender-pay-gap-facts/

Pew Research Center. (2019b). Student loan system presents repayment challenges. Retrieved February 28, 2020 from pewtrusts.org/en/research_and_analysis/reports/2019/11/student-loan-system-presents-repayment-challenges/

Powers, V. (2004). T & D. In K. R. Gilbert (Ed.), *Annual editions: The family*, 06/07. New York: McGraw-Hill.

Proctor, C. (2020). Refinancing your students loans with SoFi could save you money—and even help you get a better mortgage rate. Retrieved March 14, 2020 from https://www.businessinsider.com/personal-finance/sofi-student-loan-refinancing-review-and-how-it-works

Ramsey Solutions. (2018). Money ruining marriages in America: A Ramsey Solutions study. Retrieved June 17, 2019 from https://www.daveramsey.com/pr/money-ruining-marriages-in-america

Richter, D., & Lemola, S. (2017). Growing up with a single mother and life satisfaction in adulthood: A test of mediating and moderating factors. *PLOS One*, 12(6). doi:10.1371/journal.pone.0179639

Robb, C. A., Chatterjee, S., Porto, N., & Cude, B. J. (2018). The influence of student loan debt on financial satisfaction. *Journal of Family and Economic Issues*, 40, 51–73.

Roehling, P. V., & Moen, P. (2003). Dual-earner couples. *Sloan Work and Family Encyclopedia*. Retrieved from www.bc.edu/bc_org/avp/wfnetwork/rft/wfpedia/wfpDECent.html

Romanelli, A. (2019). Let's talk about money in our intimate relationships: 3 steps to clarify the financial power dynamic in your relationship. Psychology Today, August, 2019. Retrieved February 29, 2020, from psychologytoday.com/us/blog/the-other-side-relationships.

Rudgard, O. (2017). Shift work. Retrieved June 18, 2019 from https://www.telegraph.co.uk/news/2017/09/02/shift-work-infidelity-ending-marriages/

Salary.com (2018). Moms: We know you're worth it. Retrieved April 22, 2020 from https://www.salary.com/articles/stay-at-home-mom/

Schramm, D. G., Marshall, J. P., Harris, V. W., & George, A. (2003). *Marriage in Utah: 2003 baseline statewide survey on marriage and divorce*. Salt Lake City: Utah Department of Workforce Services.

Schramm, D. G., Marshall, J. P., Harris, V. W., & Lee, T. R. (2005). After "I do": The newlywed transition. *Marriage and Family Review*, 38, 45–67.

Statista. (2019a). Families with debt in the United States. Retrieved June 19, 2019 from https://www.statista.com/statistics/247874/amount-of-family-debt-distributed-by-type-of-debt/

Statista. (2019b). Total amount provided in student loans in the United States from 1998/99 to 2019/19. Retrieved April 22, 2020 from https://www.statista.com/statistics/235367/student-loans-in-the-us/

Stevens, D. P., Kiger, G., & Riley, P. J. (2006). His, hers, our ours? Work-to-family spillover, crossover, and family cohesion. *The Social Science Journal*, 43, 425–436.

Sullivan, M. (2009). Wage gap is wider for women of color. *Women's Policy Research*. Retrieved from www.iwpr.org

Taylor, K. (2002). Minority families in the United States: A multicultural perspective. Upper Saddle River, NJ: Prentice Hall.

Thomas-Hunt, M., & Phillips, K. W. (2004). When what you know is not enough: Expertise and gender dynamics in task groups. *Personality and Social Psychology Bulletin*, 30(12), 1585–1598.

Trautner, T. (2016). Child care in the workplace: The advantages and disadvantages to offering child care at the parent's place of work. *Michigan State University Extension*. Retrieved February 25, 2020 from www.canr.msu.edu/news/child_care_in_the_workplace

U.S. Bureau of Labor Statistics. (2019a). Employment characteristics of families summary. Retrieved June 19, 2019 from www.bls.gov/news/release/famee.nr0.htm

U.S. Bureau of Labor Statistics. (2019b). Labor force characteristics by race and ethnicity, 2018. Retrieved September 14, 2020 from https://www.bls.gov/opub/reports/race-and-ethnicity/2018/home.htm

U.S. Census Bureau. (2016). Mother's Day: May 8, 2016. America's family and living arrangements. Retrieved March 12, 2020 from https://www.census.gov/newsroom/facts-for-features/2016/cb16-ff09.html

U.S. Census Bureau. (2017). *Income and poverty in the United States* 2017. Retrieved June 18, 2019 from https://www.census.gov/programs-surveys/sipp/publications/tables/hsehld-char.html

U.S. Census Bureau. (2018a). Black (African American) history month. Retrieved May 24, 2019 from www.census.gov/search-results.html

U.S. Census Bureau. (2018b). Household relationship and living arrangements of children under 18 years, by age and sex: 2018. Retrieved June 18, 2019 from https://www.census.gov/data/tables/2016/demo/families/cps-2016.html

U.S. Census Bureau. (2018c). Poverty status, food stamp receipt, and public assistance for children under 18 years by selected characteristics: 2018. Retrieved June 18, 2019 from https://www.census.gov/data/tables/2018/demo/families/cps-2018.html

U.S. Census Bureau. (2019a). American Indian and Alaska Native heritage month: November 2019. Retrieved April 22, 2020 from https://www.census.gov/newsroom/facts-for-features/2019/aian-month.html

U.S. Census Bureau. (2019b). Asian-American and Pacific Islander heritage month: May 2019. Retrieved April 22, 2020 from https://www.census.gov/newsroom/facts-for-features/2019/asian-american-pacific-islander.html

U.S. Census Bureau. (2019c). Hispanic heritage month 2019. Retrieved April 22, 2020 from https://www.census.gov/newsroom/facts-for-features/2019/hispanic-heritage-month.html

U.S. Census Bureau. (2019d). Households by labor force status of members. Retrieved June 18, 2019 from https://www.census.gov/programs-surveys/sipp/publications/tables/hsehld-char.html

U.S. Census Bureau. (2019e). The intersectionality of sex, race, and Hispanic origin in the STEM workplace. Retrieved April 22, 2020 from https://www.census.gov/library/working-papers/2019/demo/SEHSD-WP2018-27.html

U.S. Census Bureau. (2019f). One-parent unmarried family groups with own children under 18. Retrieved June 18, 2019 from https://www.census.gov/programs-surveys/sipp/publications/tables/hsehld-char.html

U.S. Department of Agriculture. (2017). Household food security in the United States, 2017. Retrieved June 18, 2019 from https://www.ers.usda.gov/webdocs/publications/90029/ap-079.pdf

U.S. Department of Health and Human Services. (2019). U.S. federal poverty guidelines. Retrieved June 19, 2019 from www.aspe.hhs.gov/2019-poverty-guidelines

U.S. Department of Labor. (2017). 12 stats about working women. Retrieved June 18, 2019, from www.blog.dol.gov/2017/03/01/12-stats-about-working-women

van der Wal, S. J., Gorter, R., Reinjnen, A. L., Geuze, E., & Vermetten, E. (2019). Cohort profile: The Prospective Research in Stress-Related Military Operations (PRISMO) study in the Dutch Armed Forces. *British Medical Journal*, 9(3), e026670.

Vandell, D. L., & Corsaniti, M. A. (1990). Childcare and the family; Complex contributors to child development. In K. McCartney (Ed.), *Childcare and maternal employment*. San Francisco: Jossey-Bass.

Varcoe, K. P., Empter, N., & Lee, N. (2002). Working with military audiences to improve financial well-being. *JFCS* (94)1, 33–34.

Voydanoff, P. (1983). Unemployment: Family strategies for adaptation. In C. R. Figley & H. I. McCubbin (Eds.), *Stress and the family, II—Coping with catastrophe* (pp. 90–102). New York: Brunner/Mazel.

Webster, B. H., Jr., & Bishaw, A. (2007). Income, earnings, and poverty data from the 2006 American Community Survey. U.S. Census Bureau, American Community Survey Reports, ACS-08. Washington, DC: U.S. Government Printing Office. Retrieved from http://www.census.gov/prod/2007pubs/acs-08.pdf

West Health Institute. (2019). Americans' views of healthcare costs, coverage, and policy. Retrieved June 19, 2019 from http://www.norc.org/

White, D. M. (2018). Shift work and relationships. Retrieved June 18, 2019 from www.psychcentral.com/lib/shift-work-and-relationships/

The White House, Office of the Press Secretary. (2009). Remarks of President Barack Obama on the Lilly Ledbetter Fair Pay Restoration Act bill signing. Retrieved March 22, 2020 from https://obamawhitehouse.archives.gov/the-press-office/remarks-president-barack-obama-lilly-ledbetter-fair-pay-restoration-act-bill-signin

/// CHAPTER 13

Ahrons, C. (1994). *The good divorce: Keeping your family together when your marriage comes apart*. New York: HarperCollins.

Ahrons, C. (1999). Divorce: An unscheduled family transition. In B. Carter & M. McGoldrick (Eds.), *The expanded family life cycle: Individual, family, and social perspectives* (3rd ed.; pp. 381–398). Boston: Allyn & Bacon.

Amato, P. (1996). Explaining the intergenerational transmission of divorce. *Journal of Marriage and the Family*, 58, 628–640.

Amato, P., & DeBoer, D. B. (2001), The transmission of marital instability across generations: Relationship skills or commitment to marriage? *Journal of Marriage and Family*, 63, 1038–1051.

Amato, P., & Previti, D. (2004). People's reasons for divorcing: Gender, social class, the life course, and adjustment. *Journal of Family Issues*, 24, 602–606.

Ambert, A. (2005). *Divorce: Facts, causes and consequences*. Ottawa, ON: Vanier Institute of the Family. Retrieved from www.vifamily.ca/library/cft/divorce.html

Anderson, S. A., & Sabatelli, R. M. (2011). Family interaction: A multigenerational developmental perspective (5th ed). New York: Pearson Education.

Andersson, G., Thomson, E., & Duntava, A. (2017). Life-table representations of family dynamics in the 21st century. *Demographic Research*, 37(35), 1081–1230.

Axinn, W., & Thornton, A. (1996). The influence of parent's marital dissolutions on children's attitudes toward family formation. *Demography*, 33, 66–81.

Booth, A., & Edwards, J. (1985). Age at marriage and marital stability. *Journal of Marriage and the Family*, 47, 67–75.

Bowen, M. (1978). *Family therapy in clinical practice*. New York: Jason Aronson.

Bramlett, M. D., & Mosher, W. D. (2001). *First marriage dissolution, divorce, and remarriage: United States. Vital and Health Statistics*, 323. Hyattsville, MD: National Center for Health Statistics.

Brown, E., Orbuch, T. L, & Bauermeister, J. A. (2008). Religiosity and marital stability among Black American and white American couples. *Family Relations*, 57, 186–197.

Bulanda, J. R., & Brown, S. L. (2007). Race-ethnic differences in marital quality and divorce. *Social Science Research*, 36, 945–967.

Council on Contemporary Families. (2015). Cohabitation, marriage, and committed relationships. Retrieved July 4, 2019 from https://contemporaryfamilies.org/experts/kelly-musick-mpa-phd/

Crenshaw, K. (1989). Demarginalizing the intersection of race and sex: A Black feminist critique of antidiscrimination doctrine, feminist theory and antiracist politics. *University of Chicago Legal Forum*, 139–167.

Doss, B. D., Rhoades, G. K., Stanley, S. M., & Markman, H. J. (2009). Marital therapy, retreats, and books: The who, what, when, and why of relationship help-seeking. *Journal of Marital and Family Therapy*, 35(1), 18–29.

Duck, S. W. (1982). A topography of relationship disengagement an dissolution. In S. W. Duck (Ed.), *Personal relationships, 4: Dissolving personal relationships* (pp. 1–30). New York: Academic Press.

Duck, S. W. (1984). A perspective on the repair of personal relationships: Repair of what? When? In S. W. Duck (Ed.), *Personal relationships, 5: Repairing personal relationships*. London: Academic Press.

Duck, S. W. (1992). *Human relationships* (2nd ed.). Newbury Park, CA: SAGE.

Fine, M. A., & Fine, D. R. (1994). An examination and evaluation of recent changes in divorce laws in five Western countries: The critical role of values. *Journal of Marriage and the Family*, 56(2), 249–263.

Furstenberg, F. F. (1994). History and current status of divorce in the United States. *The Future of Children*, 4, 29–43.

Galezewska, P. (2016). Repartnering after divorce and separation in Europe and the United States. (PhD thesis, Department of Social Statistics and Demography, University of Southampton, Southampton, UK).

Gallup. (2017). U.S. divorce rate dips, but moral acceptability hits high. Retrieved July 3, 2019 from https://news.gallup.com/poll/213677/divorce-rate-dips-moral-acceptability-hits-new-high.aspx

Grall, T. (2018). Custodial mothers and fathers and their child support. *Current Population Reports, P60-262*. Washington, DC: U.S. Census Bureau.

Greenstein, T. N. (1995). Gender ideology, marital disruption, and the employment of married women. *Journal of Marriage and the Family*, 57, 31–42.

Harris, V. W. (2009). Preparation for marriage: 10 things you'll wish you knew. *Utah Council on Family Relations*. Retrieved from www.usu.edu/fchd/htm/

Heaton, T. B. (2002). Factors contributing to increased marital stability in the United States. *Journal of Family Issues*, 23(3), 392–109.

Heaton, T. B., Albrecht, S. L., & Martin, T. K. (1985). The timing of divorce. *Journal of Marriage and the Family*, 47, 631–639.

Hetherington, E. M. (2003). Intimate pathways: Changing patterns in close personal relationships across time. *Family Relations*, 52, 318–331.

Kapinus, C. A. (2004). The effect of parents' attitudes toward divorce on offspring's attitudes: Gender and parental divorce as mediating factors. *Journal of Family Issues*, 25, 112–135.

Kapinus, C. A. (2005). The effect of parental marital quality on young adults' attitudes toward divorce. *Sociological Perspectives*, 48(3), 319–335.

Kiernan, K. E. (1986). Teenage marriage and marital breakdown: A longitudinal study. *Population Studies*, 40(1), 35–54.

Knapp, M. (1978). *Social intercourse: From greeting to goodbye*. Boston: Allyn & Bacon.

Krauth, L. D. (2005). The contentious debate about no-fault divorce: Who is most at risk? In E. Schroeder (Ed.), *Taking sides: Clashing views on controversial issues in family and personal relationships* (pp. 238–242). Dubuque, IA: McGraw-Hill.

La Gapia, J. J. (1982). Rituals of disengagement. In S. W. Duck (Ed.), *Personal relationships, 4: Dissolving personal relationships*. London: Academic Press.

Lauer, R. H., & Lauer, J. C. (1991). The long-term relational consequences of problematic family backgrounds. *Family Relations*, 40, 286–290.

Lehrer, E. L. (2006). Religion and high school graduation: A comparative analysis of patterns for white and Black young women. *Review of Economics of the Household*, 4(3), 277–293.

Metts, S., Cupach, W., & Bejlovec, R. A. (1989). "I love you too much to ever start liking you": Redefining romantic relationships. *Journal of Social and Personal Relationships*, 6, 259–274.

Milan, A. (2000). One hundred years of families. *Canadian Social Trends*, 56, 1–13.

Musick, K., & Michelmore, K. (2016). Cross-national comparisons of union stability in cohabiting and married families with children. Paper presented at the Annual Meeting of the Population Association of America, Washington DC. Retrieved July 4, 2019 from http://www.cpc.cornell.edu/html/research/WP_musick_michelmore_demog_102116.pdf

National Council on Family Relations. (2020). CFLE in context: National Family Resiliency Center. Retrieved March 20, 2020 from https://www.ncfr.org/resources/career-resources/practice/career-profiles/

National Health Statistics Reports. (2018). A demographic, attitudinal, and behavioral profile of cohabiting adults in the United States, 2011–2015. Retrieved July 4, 2019 from https://www.cdc.gov/nchs/data/nhsr/nhsr111.pdf

National Vital Statistics Reports. (2019). Marriage and divorce. Retrieved May 8, 2020 from https://www.cdc.gov/nchs/data/dvs/national-marriage-divorce-rates-00-18.pdf

National Vital Statistics Reports. (2020). Marriage rates in the United States: 1900–2018. Retrieved May 8, 2020 from https://www.cdc.gov/nchs/data/hestat/marriage_rate_2018/marriage_rate_2018.htm

Office of Child Support Enforcement. (2018). Who owes the child support debt? Retrieved July 7, 2019 from https://www.acf.hhs.gov/css/ocsedatablog/2017/09/who-owes-the-child-support-debt

Oropesa, R. S., & Gorman, B. K. (2000). Ethnicity, immigration, and beliefs about marriage as a "tie that binds." In L. J. Waile, C. Bachrach, M. Hindin, E. Thomson, & A. Thornton (Eds.), *The ties that bind: Perspectives on marriage and cohabitation* (pp. 188–211). New York: Aldine de Gruyter.

Oropesa, R. S., & Landale, N. S. (2004). The future of marriage and Hispanics. *Journal of Marriage and Family*, 66, 901–920.

Perelli-Harris, B., Hoherz, S., Addo, F., Lappegard, T., Evans, A., et al. (2018). Do marriage and cohabitation provide benefits to health in mid-life? The role of childhood selection mechanisms and partnership characteristics across countries. *Population Research and Policy Review*, 37(5), 703–728.

Pew Research Center. (2018). Marital status by religious group. Retrieved July 3, 2019 from https://www.pewforum.org/religious-landscape-study/marital-status/

Phillips, G. M., & Wood, J. T. (1983). Communication and human relationships: The study of interpersonal communication. New York: Macmillian.

Phillips, J. A., & Sweeney, M. M. (2005). Premarital cohabitation and marital disruption among white, Black, and Mexican American women. *Journal of Marriage and Family*, 67(2), 296–314.

Powell, D. (2005). Divorce-on-demand: Forget about gay marriage—What about the state of regular marriage? In E. Schroeder (Ed.), *Taking sides: Clashing views on controversial issues in family and personal relationships* (pp. 243–246). Dubuque, IA: McGraw-Hill.

Raley, R. K., & Bumpass, L. (2003). The topography of the divorce plateau: Levels and trends in union stability in the United States after 1980. *Demographic Research*, 8, 245–259.

Raley, R. K., Durden, T. E., & Wildsmith, E. (2004). Understanding Mexican-American marriage patterns using a life-course approach. *Social Science Quarterly*, 85, 872–890.

Raley, R. K., Sweeney, M. M., & Wondra, D. (2015). The growing racial and ethnic divide in U.S. marriage patterns. *Future Child*, 25(2), 89–109.

Raley, R. K., & Wildsmith, E. (2004). Cohabitation and children's family instability. *Journal of Marriage and Family*, 66(1), 210–219.

Rosenfeld, M.J., & Roesler, K. (2018). Cohabitation experience and cohabitation's association with marital dissolution. *Journal of Marriage and Family*, 81(1). doi:doi.org/10.1111/jomf.12530

Sherman, E. (2003). *Divorce solutions: How to make any divorce better*. Santa Cruz, CA: Nolo Press Occidental.

Simons, R. L., et al. (Eds.). (1996). *Understanding differences between divorced and intact families*. Thousand Oaks, CA: SAGE.

Smock, P. J. (2004). The wax and wane of marriage: Prospects for marriage in the 21st century. *Journal of Marriage and Family*, 66, 966–973.

South, S. (1995). Do you need to shop around? Age at marriage, spousal alternatives, and marital dissolution. *Journal of Family Issues*, 16, 432–449.

Sprenkle, D. H., & Cyrus, C. (1983). Abandonment: The sudden stress of divorce. In C. R. Rigley & H. I. McCubbin (Eds.), *Stress and the family: Coping with catastrophe* (vol. 2; pp. 53–75). New York: Bruner/Mazel.

Sweeney, M. M., & Phillips, J. A. (2004). Understanding racial differences in marital disruption: Recent trends and explanations. *Journal of Marriage and Family*, 66, 239–250.

Teachman, J. D. (2002). Childhood living arrangements and the intergenerational transmission of divorce. *Journal of Marriage and the Family*, 64, 717–729.

Teachman, J. D., & Polonko, K. (1990). Cohabitation and marital stability. *Social Forces*, 69, 207–220.

Teachman, J. D., & Tedrow, D. (2008). Divorce, race, and military service: More than equal pay and equal opportunity. *Journal of Marriage and Family*, 70, 1030–1044.

Thornton, A. (1991). Influence of the marital history of parents on the marital and cohabitational experiences of children. *American Journal of Sociology*, 96, 868–894.

Treas, J., & Giesen, D. (2000). Sexual infidelity among married and cohabiting Americans, *Journal of Marriage and the Family*, 64, 48–60.

Trent, K., & South, S. J. (2003). Spousal alternatives and marital relations. *Journal of Family Issues*, 24, 787–810.

Umaña-Taylor, A. J., & Fine, M. A. (2003). Predicting commitment to wed among Hispanic and Anglo partners. *Journal of Marriage and Family*, 65, 117–139.

U.S. Census Bureau. (2018). America's families and living arrangements. Retrieved July 3, 2019 from https://www.census.gov/data/tables/2018/demo/families/cps-2018.html

U.S. Department of Defense. (2018). By the numbers: The female force in the defense department. Retrieved June 1, 2020 from https://dod.defense.gov/news/special-reports/Womens-History/

Ventura, J., & Reed, M. (1998). *Divorce for dummies*. New York: Wiley.

Welch, K. J. (2004). *Development: Journey through childhood and adolescence*. Boston: Allyn & Bacon.

White, L. (1991). Divorce over the life course: The role of marital happiness. *Journal of Family Issues*, 12, 5–21.

White, L., & Rogers, S. J. (2000). Economic circumstances and family outcomes: A review of the 1990s. *Journal of Marriage and Family*, 52, 904–912.

Wiik, K. A., Keizer, R., & Lappegård, T. (2012). Relationship quality in marital and cohabiting unions across Europe. *Journal of Marriage and Family*, 74(3), 389–398.

Wood, J. T. (1982). Communication and relational culture: Bases for the study of human relationships. *Communication Quarterly*, 30, 75–84.

/// CHAPTER 14

Ahrons, C. (1994). *The good divorce: Keeping your family together when your marriage comes apart*. New York: HarperCollins.

Ahrons, C. (2007). *We're still family: What grown children have to say about their parents' divorce*. New York: HarperCollins.

Ahrons, C., & Rodgers, R. H. (1987). *Divorced families: Meeting the challenge of divorce and remarriage*. New York: Norton.

Ahrons, C., & Tanner, J. L. (2003). Adult children and their fathers: Relationship changes 20 years after parental divorce. *Family Relations*, 52, 340–351.

Al Ubaidi, B. A. (2017). The psychological and emotional stages of divorce. *Journal of Family Medicine and Disease Prevention*, 3(3), 1–4.

Amato, P. R. (2010). Research on divorce: Continuing trends and new developments. *Journal of Marriage and Family*, 72, 650–666.

Amato, P. R., & Keith, B. (1991). Parental divorce and the well-being of children: A meta-analysis. *Psychological Bulletin*, 110, 26–46.

Amato, P. R., & Rezac, S. (1994). Contact with nonresident parents, interparental conflict, and children's behavior. *Journal of Family Issues*, 15, 191–207.

Anderson, J. (2014). The impact of family structure on the health of children: Effects of divorce. *Linacre Quarterly*, 81(4), 378–387.

Anderson, S. A., & Sabatelli, R. M. (2007). *Family interaction: A multigenerational developmental perspective* (4th ed.). Boston: Allyn & Bacon.

Anderson, S. A., & Sabatelli, R. M. (2011). *Family interaction: A multigenerational developmental perspective* (5th ed). New York: Pearson Education.

Anderson-Burdine, A., & Armstrong, J. (2014). An in depth look at heterosexual single parent dating and effects on children. *Texas Women's University*. Retrieved March 21, 2019 from https://twu-ir.tdl.org

Arditti, J. (1999). Rethinking relationships between divorced mothers and their children: Capitalizing on family strengths. *Family Relations*, 48(2), 109–119.

Bailey, S., & Zvonkovic, A. (2003). Parenting after divorce. *Journal of Divorce and Remarriage*, 39(3/4), 59–80.

Baum, N. (2003). Divorce process variables and the co-parental relationship and parental role fulfillment of divorced parents: Family and couple research. *Family Process*, 42, 117–131.

Baum, N. (2006). Post-divorce paternal disengagement. *Journal of Marriage and Family Therapy*, 32, 245–254.

Beckmeyer, J. J., Krejnik, S., McCray, J., Markham, M. S., & Troilo, J. (2018, November). *Former spousal relationships and children's post-divorce well-being*. Paper presented at the National Council on Family Relations Annual Conference. San Diego, California.

Bernsten, K. N., & Kravdal, O. (2012). The relationship between mortality and time since divorce, widowhood or remarriage in Norway. *Social Science & Medicine*, 75, 2267–2274.

Bohannan, P. (1971). *Divorce and after*. New York: Doubleday.

Bokker, P., Farley, R., & Denny, G. (2005). Emotional well-being among recently divorced fathers. *Journal of Divorce and Remarriage*, 41, 157–172.

Bonach, K., Sales, E., & Koeske, G. (2005). Gender differences in co-parenting quality. *Journal of Divorce and Remarriage*, 42, 1–28.

Bramlett, M. D., & Mosher, W. D. (2002). *First marriage dissolution, divorce, and remarriage: United States. Vital and Health Statistics*, 323. Hyattsville, MD: National Center for Health Statistics.

Braver, S., Shapiro, J. R., & Goodman, M. R. (2006). Consequences of divorce for parents. In M. A. Fine & J. H. Harvey (Eds.), *Handbook of divorce and relationship dissolution* (pp. 313–337). Mahwah, NJ: Erlbaum.

Bray, J. H. (1999). From marriage to remarriage and beyond. In E. M. Hetherington (Ed.), *Coping with divorce, single parenting, and remarriage* (pp. 253–271). Mahwah, NJ: Erlbaum.

Broadwell, L. (2019). Age-by-age guide on the effects of divorce on children. Retrieved July 10, 2019 from https://www.parents.com/parenting/divorce/coping/age-by-age-guide-to-what- children-understand-about-divorce/

Carlson, C. (1995). Working with single-parent and stepfamily systems. In A. Thomas & J. Grimes (Eds.), *Best practices in school psychology* (3rd ed.; pp. 1097–1110). Washington, DC: National Association of School Psychologists.

Cartwright, C. (2006). You want to know how it affected me? Young adults' perceptions of the impact of parental divorce. *Journal of Divorce and Remarriage*, 44(3/4), 125–143.

Coleman, M., Ganong, L. H., & Fine, M. (2000). Reinvestigating remarriage: Another decade of progress. *Journal of Marriage and the Family*, 62, 1288–1307.

Cooksey, E., & Craig, P. (1998). Parenting from a distance: The effects of parental characteristics on contact between non-residential fathers and their children. *Demography*, 35(2), 187–200.

Cookston, J. T., Braver, S. L., Griffin, W., deLuse, S. R., & Miles, J. C. (2007). Effects of the Dads for Life intervention on interparental conflict and co-parenting in the two years after divorce. *Family Process*, 46(1), 123–137.

Criddle, M., & Scott, M. (2005). Mandatory divorce education and post-divorce parental conflict. *Journal of Divorce and Remarriage*, 62, 99–111.

Dacey, J., & Travers, J. (2002). *Human development across the lifespan* (5th ed.). Boston: McGraw-Hill.

Davis, E. C., & Friel, L. V. (2001). Adolescent sexuality: Disentangling the effects of family structure and family contexts. *Journal of Marriage and Family*, 63(3), 669–681.

De Vaus, D., Gray, M., Qu, L., & Stanton, D. (2015). *The economic consequences of divorce in six OECD countries (Research Report No. 31)*. Melbourne: Australian Institute of Family Studies.

Dewilde, C. (2008). Divorce and the housing movements of owner-occupiers: A European comparison. *Housing Studies*, 23, 809–832.

Dilulio, J. J. (1997, April 7). Deadly divorce: Divorce can be hazardous to your health. *National Review*. Retrieved April 6, 2006 from www.findarticles.com

Duck, S. W. (1982). A topography of relationship disengagement an dissolution, In S. W. Duck (Ed.), *Personal relationships, 4: Dissolving personal relationships* (pp. 1–30). New York: Academic Press.

Dunlop, R., Bermingham, S., & Burns, A. (2001). Parent-child relations and adolescent self-image following divorce: A 10-year study. *Journal of Youth and Adolescence*, 30(2), 117–134.

Duran-Aydingtug, C. (1995). Former spouse interaction: Normative guidelines and actual behavior. *Journal of Divorce and Remarriage*, 22, 147–161.

Dykstra, P.A., & Fokkema, T. (2007). Social and emotional loneliness among divorced and married men and women: Comparing the deficit and cognitive perspectives. *Basic and Applied Social Psychology*, 29, 1–12.

Emery, R. E. (1994). *Renegotiating family relationships: Divorce, child custody, and mediation*. New York: Guilford Press.

Fincham, F. D. (2002). Divorce. In N. J. Salkind (Ed.), *Child development: Macmillan psychology reference series*. Farmington Hills, MI: Macmillan.

Finley, G. E. (2003). Father-child relationships following divorce. In J. R. Miller, R. M. Lerner, L. B. Schiamberg, & P. M. Anderson (Eds.), *Encyclopedia of human ecology* (vol. 1; pp. 291–293). Santa Barbara, CA: ABC-CLIO.

Fisher, B., & Alberti, R. (2000). *Rebuilding: When your relationship ends* (3rd ed.). Atascadero, CA: Impact.

Furstenberg, F. F., & Allison, P. D. (1989). How marital dissolution affects children: Variations by age and sex. *Developmental Psychology*, 25, 540–549.

Furstenberg, F. F., & Cherlin, A. J. (1991). *Divided families: What happens to children when parents part*. Cambridge, MA: Harvard University Press.

Ganong, L., & Coleman, M. (2004). *Stepfamily relationships: Development, dynamics, and interventions*. New York: Kluwer Academic/Plenum.

Gerlach, P. (2005). Forge a healthy remarriage. Retrieved April 8, 2005 from http://sfhelp.org/01/bonding.htm

Gohm, C. L., Oishi, S., Darlington, J., & Diener, E. (1998). Culture, parental conflict, parental marital status, and the subjective well-being of young adults. *Journal of Marriage and the Family*, 60, 314–319.

Gold, L. (1991). *Between love and hate: A guide to civilized divorce*. New York: Plenum.

Gottfried, A. E., & Gottfried, A. W. (1994). *Redefining families: Implications for children's development*. New York: Plenum.

Graham, L. (2005). *Resource guide for parenting after divorce*. Manhattan, KS: Riley County District Court, State of Kansas.

Grall, T. (2018). *Custodial mothers and fathers and their child support: 2015. Current Population Reports, P60-262*, Washington, DC: U.S. Census Bureau.

Haimi, M., & Lerner, A. (2016). The impact of parental separation and divorce on the health status of children, and the ways to improve it. *Journal of Clinical and Medical Genomics*, 4, 137.

Hallman, J., Dienhart, A., & Beaton, J. (2007). A qualitative analysis of fathers' experiences of parental time after separation and divorce. *Fathering: A Journal of Theory, Research, and Practice About Men As Fathers*, 5, 4–24.

Hannum, J. W., & Dvorak, D. M. (2004). Effects of family conflict, divorce, and attachment patterns on the psychological distress and social adjustment of college freshmen. *Journal of College Student Development*, 45(1), 27–42.

Henley, K., & Pasley, K. (2006). Coparenting following divorce. In M. Fine and J. Harvey (Eds.), *Handbook of divorce* (pp. 24–262). Mahwah, NJ: Erlbaum.

Hetherington, E. M. (1991). The role of individual differences and family relationships in children's coping with divorce and remarriage. In P. A. Cowan & E. M. Hetherington (Eds.), *Family transitions* (pp. 165–194). Hillsdale, NJ: Erlbaum.

Hetherington, E. M. (2003). Intimate pathways: Changing patterns in close personal relationships across time. *Family Relations*, 52, 318–331.

Hetherington, E. M., & Kelly, J. (2002). *For better or worse: Divorce reconsidered*. New York: Norton.

Hinderlie, H. H., & Kenny, M. (2002). Attachment, social support, and college adjustment among Black students at predominantly white universities. *Journal of College Student Development*, 43, 327–340.

Ihinger-Tallman, M., & Pasley, K. (1987). *Remarriage*. Beverly Hills, CA: SAGE.

Institute for Family Studies. (2019). The adult children of divorce find their voice. Retrieved June 1, 2020 from https://ifstudies.org/blog/the-adult-children-of-divorce-find-their-voice

Jensen, T. M., Shafer, K., Guo, S., & Larson, J. H. (2015). Differences in relationship stability between individuals in first and second marriages: A propensity score analysis. *Journal of Family Issues*, 38(3), 1–27.

Kalter, N., Alpern, D., Spence, R., & Plunkett, J. W. (1984). Locus of control in children of divorce. *Journal of Personality Assessment*, 48(4), 410–414.

Kelly, J. B. (2007). Children's living arrangements following divorce. *Family Process*, 46, 35–52.

Kelly, J. B., & Emery, R. E. (2003). Children's adjustment following divorce: Risk and resiliency perspectives. *Family Relations*, 52(4), 352–362.

Kheshgi-Genovese, Z., & Genovese, T. A. (1997). Developing the spousal relationship within stepfamilies. *Families in Society*, 78(3), 255–264.

King, V. (2002). Parental divorce and interpersonal trust in adult offspring. *Journal of Marriage and Family*, 64(3), 642–656.

Kruk, E. (1991). Discontinuity between pre-and post-divorce father-child relationships: New evidence regarding paternal disengagement. *Journal of Divorce and Remarriage*, 16(3/4), 195–227.

Lehr, R., & MacMillan, P. (2001). The psychological and emotional impact of divorce: The noncustodial fathers' perspective. *Families in Society* 82(4), 373–382.

Leite, R. W., & McKenry, P. C. (2002). Aspects of father status and post-divorce father involvement with children. *Journal of Family Issues*, 23, 601–623.

Leopold, T. (2018). Gender differences in the consequences of divorce: A study of multiple outcomes. *Demography*, 55(3), 769–797.

Leopold, T., & Kalmijn, M. (2016). Is divorce more painful when couples have children? Evidence from long-term panel data on multiple domains of well-being. *Demography*, 53, 1717–1742.

Lynch, J., & Kaplan, G. (2000). Socioeconomic position. In L. F. Berkman & I. Kawachi (Eds.), *Social epidemiology* (pp. 13–35). New York: Oxford University Press.

Madden-Derdich, D., & Arditti, J. (1999). The ties that bind: Attachment between former spouses. *Family Relations*, 48(3), 243–249.

Manning, W. D., Steward, S. D., & Smock, P. J. (2003). The complexity of fathers' parenting responsibilities and involvement with nonresident children. *Journal of Family Issues*, 24(5), 645–667.

Marano, H. (2000, March/April). Divorced? Don't even think of remarrying until you read this. *Psychology Today*, 33(2), 57–62.

Markham, M., Ganong, L., & Coleman, M. (2007). Mothers' cooperation in coparental relationships. *Family Relations*, 56, 369–377.

Mason, M. A., Fine, M. A., & Carnochan, S. (2001). Family law in the new millennium: For whose families? *Journal of Family Issues*, 22(7), 859–881.

Mayo Clinic. (2004). Divorce: Helping your child cope with the breakup. *Children's Health*. Retrieved April 11, 2006 from www.mayoclinic.com/health/divorce/HO000055

McIntyre, A., Heron, R. L., McIntyre, M. D., Burton, S. J., & Engler, J. N. (2003). College students from families of divorce: Keys to their resilience. *Journal of Applied Developmental Psychology*, 24, 17–31.

McLanahan, S. S., & Kelly, E. L. (2006). The feminization of poverty. *Handbook of the Sociology of Gender*, 127–145.

McLanahan, S. S., & Sandefur, G. (1994). *Growing up with a single parent: What hurts, what helps*. Cambridge, MA: Harvard University Press.

McPherson, M., Brashears, M. E., & Smith-Lovin, L. (2006). Social isolation in America: Changes in core discussion networks over two decades. *American Sociological Review*, 71(3), 353–375.

Papernow, P. L. (1984). The stepfamily cycle: An experiential model for stepfamily development. *Family Relations*, 33, 355–363.

Papernow, P. L. (1993). *Becoming a stepfamily: Patterns of development in remarried families*. San Francisco: Jossey-Bass.

Parish, T. S., & Wigle, S. E. (1985). A longitudinal study of the impact of parental divorce on adolescents' evaluations of self and parents. *Adolescence*, 20(77), 239–244.

Parke, R. D., & Brott, A. A. (1999). *Throwaway dads: They myths and barriers that keep men from being the fathers they want to be*. Boston: Houghton Mifflin.

Parziale, J., & Parziale, J. B. (2002). *The journey: A traveling guide to Christian stepfamilies*. Tuscon, AZ: InStep Ministries.

Pew Research Center. (2014). The demographics of remarriage. Retrieved July 10, 2019 from https://www.pewsocialtrends.org/2014/11/14/chapter-2-the-demographics-of-remarriage/

Pew Research Center. (2018). The changing profile of unmarried parents. Retrieved July 10, 2019 from https://www.pewsocialtrends.org/2018/04/25/the-changing-profile-of-unmarried-parents/

Pleck, J. H. (1997). Paternal involvement: Levels, sources, and consequences. In M. E. Lamb (Ed.), *The role of the father in child development* (pp. 66–103). New York: Wiley.

Robson, M., Cook, P., & Gilliland, J. (1995). Helping children manage stress. *British Education Research Journal*, 21(2), 165–174.

Sbarra, D. A. (2015). Divorce and health: Current trends and future directions. *Psychosomatic Medicine*, 77(3), 227–236.

Sbarra, D. A., Law, R. W., & Portley, R. M. (2011). Divorce and death: A meta-analysis and research agenda for clinical, social, and health psychology. *Perspectives on Psychological Science*, 6, 454–474.

Seymour, T., Francis, C., & Steffens, P. (1995). *Supporting stepfamilies: What do the children feel? NF 95-223*. Lincoln: University of Nebraska Cooperative Extension.

Shaw, D. S. (1993). Parental functioning and children's adjustment in families of divorce: A prospective study. *Journal of Abnormal Child Psychology*, 21(1), 119–143.

Shaw, D. S., & Ingoldsby, E. M. (1999). Children of divorce. In R. T. Ammerman, C. G. Last, & M. Hersen (Eds.), *Handbook of prescriptive treatments for children and adolescents* (2nd ed.; pp. 346–363). Boston: Allyn & Bacon.

Shor, E., Roelfs, D. J., Bugyi, P., & Schwartz, J. E. (2012). Meta-analysis of marital dissolution and mortality: Reevaluating the intersection of gender and age. *Social Science & Medicine*, 75, 46–59.

Shoup Olsen, C. (1997). *Stepping stones for stepfamilies. MF 2238*. Manhattan, KS: Kansas State University Cooperative Extension.

Stanley, S. M., & Fincham, F. D. (2002). The effects of divorce on children. *Couples Research and Therapy Newsletter*, 8(1), 7–10.

Stepfamily Association of America. (2009). What is a stepfamily? Retrieved April 8, 2009 from www.saafamilies.org/faqs/fats.htm

Stephenson, E., & Delongis, A. (2018). A 20-year prospective study of marital separation and divorce in stepfamilies: Appraisals of family stress as predictors. *Journal of Social and Personal Relationships*, 36(6), 1600–1618.

Stewart, S. D. (1999). Disneyland dads, Disneyland moms? How nonresident parents spend time with their children. *Journal of Family Issues*, 20, 539–556.

Stone, G. (2007). Father post-divorce well-being. *Journal of Divorce and Remarriage*, 41, 139–150.

Strohschein, L. (2005). Parental divorce and child mental health trajectories. *Journal of Marriage and Family*, 67(5), 1286–1300.

Sweeney, M. (2010). Remarriage and stepfamilies: Strategic sites for family scholarship in the 21st century. *Journal of Marriage and Family*, 72, 667–684.

Umberson, D. (1992). Gender, marital status, and the social control of health behavior. *Social Science & Medicine*, 34, 907–917.

U.S. Census Bureau. (2018). National Stepfamily Day: September 16, 2018. Retrieved July 10, 2019 from https://www.census.gov/newsroom/stories/2018/stepfamily.html

Visher, E. B., & Visher, J. S. (1993). *Stepfamilies: Myths and realities*. New York: Citadel Press.

Wallerstein, J. S. (1991). The long-term effects of divorce on children: A review. *Journal of the American Academy of Child and Adolescent Psychiatry*, 30, 349–360.

Wallerstein, J. S. (1998). Children of divorce: A society in search of policy. In M. A. Mason, A. Skolnick, & S. D. Sugarman (Eds.), *All our families: New policies for a new century* (pp. 66–94). New York: Oxford University Press.

Wallerstein, J., & Kelly, J. (1980). *Surviving the break-up: How children actually cope with divorce*. New York: Basic Books.

Wallerstein, J. S., & Lewis, M. (2004). The unexpected legacy of divorce: Report of a 25-year study. *Psychoanalytic Psychology*, 21, 353–370.

Wallerstein, J. S., Lewis, J. M., & Blakeslee, S. (2000). *The unexpected legacy of divorce: A 25-year landmark study*. New York: Hyperion.

Warshak, R. (2000). Remarriage as a trigger of parental alienation syndrome. *American Journal of Family Therapy*, 28(3), 229–241.

White, L., & Gilbreth, J. G. (2001). When children have two fathers: Effects of relationships with stepfathers and noncustodial fathers on adolescent outcomes. *Journal of Marriage and Family*, 63, 155–167.

Wickrama, K. A. S., Lorenze, F. O., Conger, R. D., & Elder, G. H. (2006). Changes in family financial circumstances and the physical health of married and recently divorced mothers. *Social Science and Medicine*, 63, 123–136.

Williams, K., & Dunne-Bryant, A. (2006). Divorce and adult psychological well-being: Clarifying the role of gender and child age. *Journal of Marriage and Family*, 64, 254–268.

Worthy. (2019). Jumping in: Dating after divorce in 2019. Retrieved March 21, 2019 from https://www.worthy.com/blog/knowledge-center/insights/study-on-dating-after-divorce-in-2019/

/// CHAPTER 15

ACOG. (2019). Sexual assault. Committee on Health Care for Underserved Women. Retrieved July 14, 2019 from https://www.acog.org/Clinical-Guidance-and-Publications/Committee-Opinions/Committee-on-Health-Care-for-Underserved-Women/Sexual-Assault

Afifi, T. O., MacMillan, H. L., Boylem, M., Cheung, K., Taillieu, T., Turner, S., & Sareen, J. (2016). Child abuse and physical health in adulthood. *Health Reports*, 27(3), 10–18.

American Association for Marriage and Family Therapists. (2020). Policy on social and family policies. Retrieved April 22, 2020 from https://www.aamft.org/About_AAMFT/Position_On_Couples.aspx

Antonovsky, A. (1979). Health, stress, and coping. San Francisco: Jossey-Bass.

Bick, J., & Nelson, C. A. (2016). Early adverse experiences and the developing brain. *Neuropsychopharmacology*, 41, 177–196.

Bodenmann, G. (2010). New themes in couple therapy: The role of stress, coping, and social support. In K. Hahlweg, M. Grawe-Gerber, & D. H. Baucom (Eds.), *Enhancing couples: The shape of couple therapy to come* (pp. 142–156). Boston, MA: Hogrefe.

Bogenschultz, M. P. (2005). Specialized 12-step programs and 12-step facilitation for the dually diagnosed. *Journal of Community and Mental Health*, 41(1), 7–20.

Boss, P. E. (2017). *Family stress management: A contextual approach* (3rd ed.). Thousand Oaks, CA: SAGE.

Burr, W. R. (1973). *Theory construction and the sociology of the family*. New York: Wiley.

Carlson, A. (2003). Mothers at war: The American way? (Aired April 25, 2003, CNN). Transcript retrieved April 1, 2006, from www.wnd.com

Centers for Disease Control and Prevention. (2018). *Youth Risk Behavior Survey, United States 2017*. "TABLE 38: Percentage of high school students who experienced sexual dating violence," by sex, race/ethnicity, grade, sexual identity, and sex of sexual contacts." Retrieved from https://www.cdc.gov/healthyyouth/data/yrbs/2017_tables/contribute_to_violence.htm#t38_down.

Child Welfare Information Gateway. (2019). *Long-term consequences of child abuse and neglect*. Washington, DC: U.S. Department of Health and Human Services, Administration for Children and Families, Children's Bureau.

Choi, N. G., DiNitto, D. M., Marti, C. N., & Choi, B. Y. (2017). Association of adverse childhood experiences with lifetime mental and substance use disorders among men and women aged 50+ years. *International Psychogeriatrics, 29*, 359–372. doi:10.1017/S1041610216001800

Cohen, F. (1984). Coping. In J. D. Matarazzo, S. M. Weiss, J. A. Herd, N. E. Miller, & S. M. Weiss (Eds.), *Behavioral health: A handbook of health enhancement and disease prevention*. New York: Wiley.

Cordon, I. M. (1997). Stress. Retrieved from www.csun.edu/~vcpsy00h/students/stress.htm

Cowan, P., Cowan, C. P., & Schulz, M. (1996). Thinking about risk and resilience in families. In E. M. Hetherington & E. Blechman (Eds.), *Stress, coping, and resiliency in children and families* (pp. 1–38). Mahwah, NJ: Erlbaum.

Cravens, J. D., Whiting, J. B., & Aamar, R. O. (2015). Why I stayed/left: An analysis of voices of intimate partner violence on social media. *Contemporary Family Therapy: An International Journal, 37*(4), 372–385.

Dalton, C., & Schneider, E. M. (2001). *Battered women and the law*. New York: Foundation Press.

De Bellis, M. D. (2002) Developmental traumatology: A contributory mechanism for alcohol and substance use disorders. *Psychoneuroendocrinology, 27*, 155–170.

Domestic Abuse Intervention Project. (2020). What is the Duluth model? Retrieved from https://www.theduluthmodel.org/

Doyle, C., & Cicchetti, D. (2017). From the cradle to the grave: The effect of adverse caregiving environments on attachment and relationships throughout the lifespan. *Clinical Psychology: Science and Practice, 24*(2), 203–217.

Duban, E. (2018). Preventing and addressing sexual and gender-based violence in places of deprivation of liberty. Retrieved March 9, 2020 from https://www.osce.org/odihr/427448

Duvall, E. M. (1971). *Family development* (4th ed.). Philadelphia: Lippincott.

Duvall, E. M. (1977). *Marriage and family development* (5th ed.). Philadelphia: Lippincott.

Duvall, E. M., & Hill, R. (1960). *Being married*. New York: Association Press.

Edwards, D. (2018). Childhood sexual abuse and brain development: A discussion of associated structural changes and negative psychological outcomes. *Child Abuse Review, 27*(3), 198–208.

Felitti, V. J., Anda, R. F., Nordenberg, D., Williamson, D. F., et al. (1998). Relationship of childhood abuse and household dysfunction to many of the leading causes of death in adults. The Adverse Childhood Experiences (ACE) Study. *American Journal of Preventive Medicine, 14*, 245–258.

Frazier, A. P., & Schauben, J. L. (1994). Stressful life events and psychological adjustment among female college students. *Measurement and Evaluation in Counseling and Development, 27*(1), 1–12.

Gamm, J. L., Nussbaum, R. L., & Biesecker, B. B. (2004). Genetics and alcoholism among at-risk relatives I: Perceptions of cause, risk, and control. *American Journal of Medicine and Genetics, 128*(2), 144–150.

Glanz, K., Rimer, B. K., & Lewis, F. M. (2002). *Health behavior and health education: Theory, research, and practice*. San Francisco: Wiley & Sons.

Hart, H., & Rubia, K. (2012). Neuroimaging of child abuse: A critical review. *Frontiers in Human Neuroscience, 6*, 52.

Hill, R. (1949). *Families under stress*. New York: Harper.

Hill, R. (1958). Generic features of families under stress. *Social Casework, 49*, 139–150.

Holmes, T. H., & Rahe, R. H. (1967), The social readjustment rating scale. *Journal of Psychometric Research, 11*, 213–218.

Hudd, S. S., Dumlao, J., Erdmann-Sager, D., Murray, D., Phan, E., Soukas, N., & Yokozuka, N. (2000). Stress at college: Effects on health habits, health status, and self-esteem. *College Student Journal, 34*(2), 1–9.

Institute of Family Studies. (2016). Eight reasons why women stay in abusive relationships. Retrieved April 2, 2020 from https://ifstudies.org/blog/eight-reasons-women-stay-in-abusive-relationships

Lazarus, R. S. (1966). *Psychological stress and the coping process*. New York: McGraw-Hill.

Lazarus, R. S. (1984). Puzzles in the study of daily hassles. *Journal of Behavioral Medicine, 7*, 375–389.

Lazarus, R. S., & Cohen, J. B. (1977). Environmental stress. In I. Altman & J. F. Wohlwill (Eds.), *Human behavior and environment* (vol. 2). New York: Plenum.

Leddy, A. M., Weiss, E., Yam, E., et al. (2019). Gender-based violence and engagement in biomedical HIV preventions, care and treatment: A scoping review. *BMC Public Health, 19*, 897.

Managing stress in young families. (2008). Iowa State University Extension. Retrieved from https://store.extension.iastate.edu/product/5166.

McCubbin, H. I., & Patterson, J. M. (1982). Family adaptation to crisis. In H. I. McCubbin, M. B. Sussman, & J. M. Patterson (Eds.), *Family stress, coping, and social support*. Springfield, IL: Thomas.

McGoldrick, M., Broken Nose, M. A., & Potenza, M. (1999). Violence and the family life cycle. In B. Carter & M. McGoldrick (Eds.), *The expanded family life cycle: Individual, family, and social perspectives* (pp. 470–491). Boston: Allyn & Bacon.

McGuigan, F. J. (1999). *Encyclopedia of stress*. Boston: Allyn & Bacon.

Monnat, S. M., & Chandler, R. F. (2015). Long-term physical health consequences of adverse childhood experiences. *The Sociological Quarterly, 56*, 723–752.

Moos, R. H. (1987). *Life transitions and crises: A conceptual overview*. New York: Plenum Press.

Moos, R. H., & Schaefer, J. A. (1987). Life transitions and crises: A conceptual overview. In R. H. Moos (Ed.), *Coping with life crises: An integrated approach* (pp. 3–28). New York: Plenum Press.

Murray, M. A., Malcarne, V. L., & Goggin, K. (2003). Alcohol-related God/higher power control beliefs, locus of control, and recovery within the Alcoholics Anonymous paradigm. *Alcoholic Treatment Quarterly, 21*(3), 23–39.

National Center for Victims of Crime. (2018). Intimate partner violence. Retrieved July 14, 2019 from https://ovc.ncjrs.gov/ncvrw2018/info_flyers/fact_sheets/2018NCVRW_IPV_508_QC.pdf

National Coalition Against Domestic Violence. (2020). What is domestic violence? Retrieved May 10, 2020 from https://ncadv.org/learn-more

National Scientific Council on the Developing Child. (2014). Excessive stress disrupts the architecture of the developing brain (Working paper 3). Retrieved from https://developingchild.harvard.edu/resources/wp3/

Okur, P., Pereda, N., Van Der Knaap, L. M., & Bogaerts S. (2018). Attributions of blame among victims of child sexual abuse: Findings from a community sample. *Journal of Child Sexual Abuse 28*(3), 301–317. doi:10.1080/10538712.2018.1546249

Olson. D. H., Russell, C. S., & Sprenkel, D. H. (1983). Circumplex model of marital and family systems: VI. Theoretical update. *Family Process, 22*, 69–83.

Pearlin, L. I. (1982). The social contexts of stress. In L. Goldberger & S. Brenitz (Eds.), *Handbook of stress: Theoretical and clinical aspects*. New York: Free Press.

Pitzer, R. L. (2004). Change, crisis, and loss in our lives. Retrieved from www.extension.mn.edu/distribution/familydevelopmenl/DE2455.html

Putnam, F. W. (2003). Ten-year research update review: Child sexual abuse. *Journal of the American Academy of Child and Adolescent Psychiatry, 42*, 269–278.

RAINN. (2019). Child sexual abuse: Children and statistics. Retrieved July 13, 2019 from https://www.rainn.org/statistics/children-and-teens

Rivers, C. (2003). Critics aside, military moms are here to stay. *WeNews*. Retrieved April 1, 2006 from www.womensnews.org

Romas, J. A., & Sharma, M. (2000). Practical stress management (2nd ed.). Boston: Allyn & Bacon.

Ross, E. S., Niebling, C. B., Bradley, C., & Heckert, M. T. (1999). Sources of stress among college students. *College Student Journal, 33*(2), 1–5.

Selye, H. (1982). History and present status of stress concept. In L Goldberger & S. Breznit (Eds.), *Handbook of stress: Theoretical and clinical aspects* (pp. 7–17). New York: Free Press.

Selye, H. (1985). History and present status of the stress concept. In A. Monat & R. S. Lazarus (Eds.), *Stress and coping* (2nd ed.). New York: Columbia University.

Smith, S. G., Chen, J., Basile, K. C., Gilbert, L. K., Merrick, M. T., Patel, N., . . . Jain, A. (2017). *The National Intimate Partner and Sexual Violence Survey (NISVS): 2010–2012 State Report*. Atlanta, GA: National Center for Injury Prevention and Control.

Taylor, S. E., Klein, L. C., Lewis, B. P., Grunewald, T. L., Gurung, R. A., & Updegraff, J. A. (2000). Biobehavioral responses to stress in females: Tend-and-befriend, not fight-or-flight. *Psychological Review, 107*, 411–429.

U.S. Bureau of Justice Statistics. (2019). Criminal victimization: 2018. Retrieved April 2, 2020 from https://www.bjs.gov/index.cfm

U.S. Centers for Disease Control and Prevention. (2018). The National Intimate Partner and Sexual Violence Survey: Intimate partner violence. Retrieved April 2, 2020 from https://www.cdc.gov/violenceprevention/intimatepartnerviolence/index.html

U.S. Centers for Disease Control and Prevention. (2019). Adverse childhood experiences (ACES) Retrieved April 2, 2020 from https://www.cdc.gov/violenceprevention/childabuseandneglect/acestudy/index.html

U.S. Centers for Disease Control and Prevention. (2020a). Preventing adverse childhood experiences. Retrieved March 9, 2020 from https://www.cdc.gov/violenceprevention/childabuseandneglect/aces/fastfact.html

U.S. Centers for Disease Control and Prevention. (2020b). Preventing child abuse and neglect: What are child abuse and neglect? Retrieved March 9, 2020 from https://www.cdc.gov/violenceprevention/childabuseandneglect/fastfact.html

U.S. Department of Health and Human Services. (2018a). Child maltreatment. Retrieved July 13, 2019 from https://www.acf.hhs.gov/sites/default/files/cb/cm2017.pdf

U.S. Department of Health and Human Services. (2018b). Toxic stress. Retrieved from https://www.acf.hhs.gov/traumatoolkit/toxic-stress

U.S. Department of Justice. (2018). Domestic violence. Retrieved April 22, 2020 from https://www.justice.gov/ovw/domestic-violence

Vrolijk-Bosschart, T. F., Brillesliper-Kater, S. N., Benninga, M. A., Lindauer, R. J. L., & Teeuw, A. H. (2018). Clinical practice: Recognizing child sexual abuse—what makes it so difficult? *European Journal of Pediatrics*, 177(9), 1343–1350.

Walker, L. E. (1979). *The battered woman*. New York: Harper & Row.

Walsh, F. (2003). Family resilience: A framework for clinical practice. *Family Process*, 42, 1–18.

Welch, K. J. (2004). Development: Journey of a lifetime. Boston: Allyn & Bacon.

Wheaton, B. (1994). Sampling the stress universe. In W. R. Avison & I. H. Gotlib (Eds.), *Stress and mental health: Contemporary issues and prospects for the future*. New York: Plenum Press.

Whiting, J. (2016). Eight reasons women stay in abusive relationships. Retrieved March 10, 2020 from https://ifstudies.org/blog/eight-reasons-women-stay-in-abusive-relationships

Widom, C. S., Czaia, S. J., Bentley, T., & Johnson, M. S. (2012). A prospective investigation of physical health outcomes in abused and neglected children: New findings from a 30-year follow-up. *American Journal of Public Health*, 102(6), 1135–1144.

Wirtz, A. L., Poteat, T. C., Mannat, M., & Glass, N. (2020). Gender-based violence against transgender people in the United States: A call for research and programming. *Trauma, Violence, and Abuse*, 21(2), 227–241.

World Health Organization. (2018). Intimate partner violence and alcohol. Retrieved July 14, 2019 from https://www.who.int/violence_injury_prevention/violence/world_report/factsheets/fs_intimate.pdf

/// CHAPTER 16

AARP. (2018). Two-thirds of older adults are interested in sex, poll says. Retrieved July 13, 2019 from https://www.aarp.org/health/healthy-living/info-2018/older-sex-sexual-health-survey.html

Adkins, V. (1999). Grandparents as a national asset: A brief note. *Activities, Adaptation, and Aging*, 24, 13–18.

Akiyama, H., Antonucci, T., Takahashi, K., & Langfahl, E. S. (2003). Negative interactions in close relationships across the lifespan. *Journal of Gerontology Series B: Psychological Sciences and Social Science*, 58, 70–79.

Alpert, R. T. (1991). Our lives are the text: Exploring Jewish women's rituals. *Bridges*, 2(1), 66–80.

American Psychological Association. (2005). Controlling anger— before it controls you. Retrieved from www.apa.org/pubinfo/anger.html

Anisman-Reiner, V. (2007). Adult children of divorce. Retrieved July 13, 2019 from http://suite101.com/article/adult-children-of-divorce-a19930

Aquilino, W. S. (1994). Later life parental divorce and widowhood: Impact on young adults' assessment of parent-child relations. *Journal of Marriage and the Family*, 56, 908–922.

Atchley. R. C. (2000). *Social forces and aging* (9th ed.). Belmont, CA: Wadsworth.

Baltes, P. B., Lindenberger, U., & Staudinger, U. M. (1998). Lifespan theory in developmental psychology. In R. M. Lerned (Ed.), *Handbook of child psychology: Vol 1. Theoretical models of human development* (5th ed.; pp. 1029–1143). New York: Wiley.

Bechman, N., Waem, M., Gustafson, D., & Skoog, I. (2008). Secular trends in self-reported sexual activity and satisfaction in Swedish 70 year olds: Cross sectional survey of four populations, 1971–2001. *BMJ*. doi:10.1136/bmj.a279

Birditt, K. S., Fingerman, K., & Almeida, D. (2005). Age differences in exposure and reactions to interpersonal tensions: A daily diary study. Psychology Aging, 20, 330–340.

Bograd, R., & Spilka, B. (1996). Self-disclosure and marital satisfaction in mid-life and late-life remarriages. *International Journal of Aging and Human Development*, 42(3), 161–172.

Bosse, R., Aldwin, C. M., Levinson, M. R., Workman-Daniels, K., & Ekerdt, D. J. (1990). Differences in social support among retirees and workers: Findings from the normative aging study. *Psychology of Aging*, 5, 41–47.

Boyd, D., & Bee, H. (2009). Lifespan development (5th ed.). Boston: Allyn & Bacon.

Bradsher, J. E. (1997). Older women and widowhood. In J. M. Coyle (Ed.), *Handbook on women and aging* (pp. 418–429). Westport, CT: Praeger.

Brody, E. (1985). Parent care as a normative family stress. *The Gerontologist*, 25, 19–29.

Brody, E., & Schoonover. C. (1986). Patterns of parent care when adult daughters work and when they do not. *The Gerontologist*, 26, 372–381.

Carstensen, L. L., Gottman, J. M., & Levenson, R. W. (1995). Emotional behavior in long-term marriage. *Psychology and Aging*, 10, 140–149.

Cavanaugh, J. C., & Blanchard-Fields, F. (2002). *Adult development and aging* (4th ed.). Belmont, CA: Wadsworth.

Centers for Disease Control and Prevention. (2018). *Mortality in the United States*, 2017. Retrieved July 12, 2019 from https://www.cdc.gov/nchs/products/databriefs/db328.htm

Centers for Disease Control and Prevention. (2020). Minority health: Minority health determines the health of the nation. Retrieved March 22, 2020 from https://www.cdc.gov/minorityhealth/

Cherlin, A. J., & Furstenberg, F. F. (1986). *The new American grandparent*. New York: Basic Books.

Choi, H., Yorgason, J. B., & Johnson, D. R. (2016). Marital quality and health in middle and later adulthood: Dyadic associations. *The Journals of Gerontology: Series B*, 71(1), 154–164.

Conway, J., & Conway, S. (2000). Parenting your parents. Retrieved from www.midlife.com

Cooney, T. M. (1994), Young adults' relations with parents: The influence of recent parental divorce. *Journal of Marriage and the Family*, 56, 45–56.

Crimmins, E. M., & Ingegneri, D. G. (1990). Interaction and living arrangements of older parents and their children. *Research on Aging*, 12, 3–35.

Crosnoe, R., & Elder, G. H. (2002). Successful adaptation in the later years: A lifecourse approach to aging. *Social Psychology Quarterly*, 65(4), 309–328.

Daly, S. C., MacNeela, P., & Sarma, K. M. (2018). The female spouse: A process of separation when a husband 'comes out' as gay. *PLoS One*, 13(8). doi:0.1371/journal.pone.0203472

Damman, M., Henkens, K., & Kalmijn, M. (2013). Late-career work disengagement: The roles of retirement and career experiences. *The Journals of Gerontology*, 68(3), 445–463.

Damman, M., Henkens, K., & Kalmijn, M. (2015). Missing work after retirement: The role of life histories in the retirement adjustment process. *The Gerontologist*, 55(5), 802–813.

Diamond, M., Lund, D. A., & Caserta, M. S. (1987). The role of social support in the first two years of bereavement in an elderly sample. *The Gerontologist*, 27, 599–604.

Dunn, B., & Wamsley, B. (2018). Grandfamilies: Characteristics and needs of grandparents raising grandchildren. Retrieved July 13, 2019 from https://joe.org/joe/2018september/rb2.php

Erens, B., Mitchell, K. R., Gibson, L., Datta, J., Lewis, R., Field, N., & Wellings, K. (2019). Health status, sexual activity and satisfaction among older people in Britain: A mixed methods study. *PloS One*, 14(3), e0213835. https://doi.org/10.1371/journal.pone.0213835

Fagan, P., & Churchill, A. (2012). The effects of divorce on children. *Marriage & Religion Institute*, 1–48.

Family Caregiver Alliance. (2018). Caregiver statistics: Demographics. Retrieved July 13, 2019 from https://www.caregiver.org/caregiver-statistics-demographics

Fingerman, K. L. (2001). A distant closeness: Intimacy between parents and their children in later life. *Generations*, 25(2), 26–33.

Friedman, S. (2006). Don't blame Medicare for Part D's problem. Retrieved from www.newsday.com

Furstenberg, F. F., Hoffman, S. D., & Shrestha, L. (1995). The effect of divorce on intergenerational transfers: New evidence. *Demography*, 32, 319–333.

Ganz, M. (2006). Plan D doesn't stand for disaster. *Seattle PI*. Retrieved from http://seattlepi.com

Gerstel, N. (2003). Divorce. In W. Outhwaite (Ed.), *The Blackwell dictionary of twentieth century social thought*. Oxford: Basil Blackwell.

Hayflick, L. (1994). How and why we age. New York: Ballantine Books.

He, W., Sangupta, M., Velkoff, V. A., & DeBarros, K. S. (2005). 65+ in the United States: 2005. United States Census Bureau Current Population Reports (pp 23–209). Retrieved April 2006 from www.census.gov/prod/2006pubs/p23-209.pdf

Hooyman, N., & Kiyak, H. A. (2002). *Social gerontology: A multidisciplinary perspective* (6th ed.). Boston: Allyn & Bacon.

Hung, M., Wright Voss, M., Bounsanga, J., Graff, T., & Birmingham, W. (2019). Assessing spousal support and health in an aging population: Support and strain amidst changing social dynamics. *Social Work in Health Care*, 1–23. doi:10.1080/00981389.2019.1569577

Hyde, M., Cheshire-Allen, M., Damman, M., Henkens, K., Platts, L., Pritchard, K., & Reed, C. (2018). The experience of the transition to retirement: Rapid evidence review. *Centre for Aging Better*. Retrieved March 11, 2020 from https://www.ageing-better.org.uk/sites/default/files/2018-12/Transition-to-retirement.pdf

Ingersoll-Dayton, B., Neal, M., Ha, J., & Hammer, J. (2003). Collaboration among siblings providing care for older parents. *Journal of Gerontological Social Work*, 40, 51–66.

Iveniuk, J., Waite, L. J., McClintock, M. K., & Teidt, A. D. (2014). Marital conflict in older couples: Positivity, personality, and health. *Journal of Marriage and Family*, 76(1), 130–144.

Johnson, C. (1999). Fictive kin among oldest old African Americans in the San Francisco Bay Area. Journal of Gerontology: Psychological Sciences, 54B, S368–S375.

Karney, B. R., & Bradbury, T. N. (1995). The longitudinal course of marital quality and stability: A review of theory, method, and research. *Psychological Bulletin*. 118, 3–34.

Kastenbaum, R. J. (2007). *Death, society, and human experience* (9th ed). Boston: Pearson Education.

Kaufman, G., & Elder, G. (2003). Grandparenting and age identity. *Journal of Aging Studies*, 17, 269–282.

Kochanke, K. D., Murphy, S. L., Xu, J., & Arias, E. (2019). Deaths: Final data for 2017. *National Vital Statistics Reports*, 68(9). Hyattsville, MD: National Center for Health Statistics.

Kubicek, B., Korunka, C., Raymo, J. M., & Hoonakker, P. (2011). Psychological well-being in retirement: The effects of personal and gendered contextual resources. *Journal of Occupational Health Psychology*, 16(2), 230–246.

Kulik, L. (1999). Continuity and discontinuity in marital life after retirement: Life orientations, gender role ideology, intimacy, and satisfaction. *The Journal of Contemporary Human Services*, 8(3), 286–294.

Lachman, M. E., Teshale, S., & Agrigoroaei, S. (2015). Midlife as a pivotal period in the life course: Balancing growth and decline at the crossroads of youth and old age. *International Journal of Behavioral Development*, 39(1), 20–31.

Lemme, B. H. (2011). *Development in adulthood* (4th ed.). New York: Pearson Education.

Lemon, B. W., Bengston, V. L, & Peterson. J. A. (1972). An exploration of the activity theory of aging: Activity types and life satisfaction among in-movers to a retirement community. *Journal of Gerontology*, 27, 511–523.

Levenson, R. W., Carstensen, L. L., & Gottman, J. M. (1993). Long-term marriage: Age, gender, and satisfaction. *Psychology and Aging*, 8, 301–313.

Lindau, S. T., Schumm, L. P., Laumann, E. O., Levinson, W., O'Muircheartaigh, C. A., & Waite, I. J. (2007). A study of sexuality and health among older adults in the United States. *New England Journal of Medicine*, 357, 762–774.

Lowenthal, M. F., & Haven, C. (1968). Interaction and adaptation; Intimacy as a critical variable. *American Sociological Review*, 33(20), 20–30.

MacRae, H. (1992). Fictive kin as a component of the social networks of older people. *Research on Aging*, 14, 226–247.

Moen, P. (2013). Constrained choices: The shifting institutional contexts of aging and the life course. In L. J. Waite & T. J. Plewes (Eds.), *New directions in the sociology of aging* (pp. 175–216). Washington, DC: National Academies Press.

Moen, P., & Flood, S. (2013). Limited engagements? Women's and men's work/volunteer time in the encore life course stage. *Social Problems*, 60(2), 206–233.

National Council on Aging. (1998a). Healthy sexuality and vital aging. Retrieved February, 2005 from www.ncoa.org/index

National Council on Aging. (1998b). Sex after 60: A natural part of life. Retrieved February, 2005 from www.ncoa.org/index

National Council on Aging. (2005). Caregiver research: The latest news. Retrieved August 12, 2009 from www.ncoa.org/

National Council on Aging. (2015). The 2015 United States of Aging Survey: National findings. Retrieved March 19, 2020 from https://www.ncoa.org/wp-content/uploads/USA15-National-Fact-Sheet-Final.pdf

Neugarten, B. L., & Weinstein, K. K. (1964). The changing American grandparent. *Journal of Marriage and the Family*, 26, 299–304.

Pasley, K. (1998). Divorce: Remarriage in later adulthood. *Stepfamily Association of America*. Retrieved April 30, 2005 from www.saafamilies.org/faqs/findings/7.htm

Pasley, K., & Ihinger-Tallman, M. (1994). *Stepparenting: Issues in theory, research, & practice*. Westport, CT: Greenwood.

Pinquart, M., & Soerensen, S. (2000). Influences of socioeconomic status, social network, and competence on subjective well-being in later life: A meta-analysis. *Psychology and Aging*, 15, 187–224.

Rowe, J., & Kahn, R. (1998). *Successful aging*. New York: Random House.

Schwartzhoff, K. (2013). Later life divorce and the adult child. Master of Social Work Clinical Research Papers School of Social Work, University of St. Thomas. Retrieved July 13, 2019 from https://sophia.stkate.edu

Segatto, B., & Di Filippo, L. (2003). Relationship and emotions in couples in the retirement and/or empty nest phase. *Eta Evolutiva*, 74(1), 5–20.

Sharifzadeh, V. S. (1997). Families with Middle Eastern roots. In E. W. Lynch & M. J. Hanson (Eds.), *Developing cross-cultural competence: A guide for working with children and families* (pp. 441–482). Baltimore, MD: Paul H. Brookes.

Smith, T. W., Berg, C. A., Florsheim, P., Uchino, B. N., Pearce, G., et al. (2009). Conflict and collaboration in middle-aged and older couples: Age differences in agency and communication during marital interaction. *Psychology and Aging*, 24(2), 259–273.

Somary, K., & Stricker, G. (1998). Becoming a grandparent: A longitudinal study of expectations and early experiences as a function of sex and lineage. The Gerontologist, 38, 53–61.

Stack, S., & Scourfield, J. (2015). Recency of divorce, depression, and suicide risk. *Journal of Family Issues*, 36(6), 695–715.

Stephens, M. A. P., & Franks, M. M. (1999). Intergenerational relationships in later-life families: Adult daughters and sons as caregivers to aging parents. In J. C. Cavanaugh & S. K. Whitbourne (Eds.), *Gerontology: An interdisciplinary perspective* (pp. 329–354). New York: Oxford University Press.

Stephens, M. A. P., Franks, M. M., & Atienza, A. A. (1997). Where two roles intersect: Spillover between parent care and employment. *Psychology and Aging*, 12, 30–37.

Stephens, M. A. P., Townsend, A. L., Martire, L. M., & Druley, J. A. (2001). Balancing parent care with other roles: Inter-role conflict of adult daughter caregivers. *Journal of Gerontology: Psychological Sciences*, 56B, P24–P34.

Story, T. N., Berg, C. A., Smith, T. W., Beveridge, R., Henry, N. J. M., & Pearce, G. (2007). Age, marital satisfaction, and optimism as predictors of positive sentiment override in middle-aged and older married couples. *Psychology and Aging*, 22, 719–727.

Swensen, C. H., Eskew, R. W., & Kohlhepp, K. A. (1981). Stage of family life cycle, ego development, and the marriage relationship. *Journal of Marriage and Family*, 43, 841–853.

Szinovacz, M. E. (1998). Grandparents today: A demographic profile. *The Gerontologist*, 38, 37–52.

Thompson, P., Itzin, C., & Abendstern, M. (1991). *I don't feel old: The experience of later life*. New York: Oxford University Press.

Troll, L., & Fingerman, K. L. (1996). Parent/child bonds in adulthood. In C. Malestesta-Magai & S. McFadden (Eds.), *Handbook of emotion, adult development and aging*. Orlando, FL: Academic Press.

Uhlenberg, P., Cooney, T. M., & Boyd, R. (1990). Divorce for women after midlife. *Journal of Gerontology: Social Sciences*, 45, S3–S11.

Uphold-Carrier, H., & Utz, R. (2012). Parental divorce among young adult children: A long-term quantitative analysis of mental health and family solidarity. *Journal of Divorce & Remarriage*, 53, 247–266.

U.S. Census Bureau. (2018a). Older people projected to outnumber children for first time in U.S. history. *Number CB18-41*. Retrieved July 13, 2019 from https://www.census.gov/newsroom/press-releases/2018/cb18-41-population-projections.html

U.S. Census Bureau. (2018b). The population 65 years and older in the United States: 2016. American Community Survey Reports. Retrieved July 12, 2019 from https://www.census.gov/content/dam/Census/library/publications/2018/acs/ACS-38.pdf

U.S. Department of Health and Human Services. (2018). 2017 profile of older Americans. Retrieved July 12, 2019 from https://acl.gov/sites/default/files/Aging%20and%20Disability%20in%20America/2017OlderAmericansProfile.pdf

Van Solinge, H., & Henkens, K. (2005). Couples' adjustment to retirement: A multi-actor panel study. *Journal of Gerontology: Social Sciences*, 60B, S11–S20.

Veroff, J., Douvan, E., & Kulka, R. A. (1981). *The inner American: A self-portrait from 1957 to 1976*. New York: Basic Books.

Vinick, B. H. (1978). Remarriage in old age. *Journal of Geriatric Psychiatry*, 11(1), 75–77.

Vinick, B. H. (1986). Difficult task: Caring for an invalid wife. *Medical Aspects of Human Sexuality*, 20, 141–145.

Welch, K. (2004). *Development: Journey through childhood and adolescence*. Boston: Allyn & Bacon.

Wethington, E. (2000). Expecting stress: Americans and the "midlife crisis." *Motivation and Emotion*, 24, 85–103.

White, T. M., Townsend, A. L., & Stephens, M. A. P. (2000). Comparisons of African American and white women in the parent care role. *The Gerontologist*, 40, 718–728.

Wilcox, S. (2003). The effects of widowhood on physical and mental health, health behaviors, and health outcomes: The women's health initiative. *Health Psychology*, 22(5), 1–9.

Wiltz, T. (2016, November 2). Why more grandparents are raising children. Retrieved from http://www.pewtrusts.org/en/research-and-analysis/blogs/stateline/2016/11/02/why- more-grandparents-are-raising-children

Wu, Z., & Penning, M. J. (1997). Marital instability after midlife. *Journal of Family Issues*, 18(5), 459–478.

Zarit, S. H., Birkel, R. C., & Malonebeach, E. (1989). Spouses as caregivers: Stresses and interventions. In M. Z. Goldstein (Ed.), *Family involvement in the treatment of the frail elderly*. Washington, DC: American Psychiatric Association.

Autonomy, 164
  granting, 396
  and intimacy, 156
Avoidant attachment types, 202
Axinn, W., 468
Ayehu, A., 309
Ayers, S., 362
Aykutoğlu, B., 152
Azoospermia, 368

B factor, 540
Babbie, E. R., 38, 42, 44, 45
Baby Boomers, 7, 568
  cohabitation, 247–248
Baby/babies, 404–405
Baca Zinn, M., 429
Bachman, G. F., 244
Bachmann, G. A., 336
Bacon, 205, 575
Bagarozzi, D. A., 95
Bailey, M. J., 456
Bailey, S., 498
Baiocco, R., 56
Baird, L. S., 439
Baisden, E. D., 457
Balance, 445
  maintenance of, 74
Ballard, J., 208
Baltes, P. B., 571
Bancroft, J., 112, 339
Banda, J., 126, 127
Bandura, A., 121, 126, 134–137, 141
Banerjee, M., 11
Banfield, S., 332
Bank, B. J., 165
Banks, J. A., 9
Barber, J. S., 349
Barber, N., 253
Barbeta, M., 391
Barbor, C., 175
Barbour, C., 8, 11
Barnett, R. C., 450
Barraket, J., 235
Barrett, A., 263
Barrett, G., 367
Barrier contraceptive, 377
Bartels, A., 335
Bartholomew, K., 202
Bartoli, A. M., 227, 228
Baset, Z. A., 123
Basic budgets, 434
Battered, 550
Batterers, 549, 554–556
Baumeister, R., 104
Baumrind, D., 396, 397
Baxter, J., 405, 406, 447
Beall, A. E., 182, 184
Beccia, P. J., 439
Bechman, N., 576
Beckmeyer, J. J., 524
Bedard, M. E., 263
Bee, H., 589, 591
Behavioral androgyny, 133
Behavior-based conflict, 444
Behnke, A. O., 434, 435
Belanger, J., 145
Belansky, E. S., 131
Belsky, J., 394, 419

Bem, S., 127, 141
Bem, S. L., 121, 131
Ben David, M., 6
Benoit, D., 202
Bereaved person, 596
Bereavement, 596
Berkowitz, D., 353
Bernardes, J., 55
Berndt, T. S., 164
Bernhardt, E., 252
Bernsten, K. N., 497
Berrington, A., 278
Berscheid, E., 157
Besser, A., 390
Best, D. L., 122
Best, P., 291
Beutell, N. J., 444
Bevan, J. L., 193
Bi, L., 126
Bianchi, S. M., 428
Biblarz, T. J., 138
Bick, J., 561
Bigler, R., 120
Binuclear families, 495–496
  co-parenting in, 507
Bippus, A. M., 86
Bipolar gender, 120
Birditt, K. S., 275, 576
Bird's Nest custody, 485–486
Birth defect, 370
Birth rates
  among all age groups, 2017, 348
  among older women, ages 40–49: 2010–1017, 348
  by Country 2018, 349
Bisexual, 302
Bishaw, A., 453
Black Demographics, 261
Black, D., 250
Black cultures, 312–313
Black masculinities, 122
Blair, K. L., 231, 232, 405, 446
Blair, S. L., 405
Blake, J., 357
Blake, L., 369
Blanchard-Fields, F., 573, 574, 596
Bland, J., 134
Bleidorn, W., 130
Bleske-Rechek, 166
Bloir, K., 409
Bloom, C., 169
Blue-collar workers, 428
Blumer, H., 80, 82
Blumstein, P., 317, 331, 332
Bockting, W., 231
Bockting, W. O., 231
Bodenmann, G., 545
Boellstorff, T., 22, 313
Bogaert, A. F., 209, 232
Bogenschultz, M. P., 537
Boggiano, A. K., 131
Bogle, K. A., 237
Bograd, R., 580
Bohannan, P., 496
Bokker, P., 498
Bonach, K., 497
Bonding/intimacy, 241
Bonkowski, S., 376

Booth, A., 328, 467
Booth, S., 317
Bos, H. M. W., 376
Boss, P. E., 532
Boss, P. G., 54, 55, 71, 74, 75, 79, 221
Bosse, R., 586
Bosson, J. K., 131
Both, S., 315
Bouhdiba, A., 22
Boundaries, 73
  establishment of, 73–74
  types of, 73, 74
Bowen, M., 352
Bowlby, J., 201, 202
Bowleg, L., 301, 313
Boyd, D., 398, 579, 589, 591
"Boyfriend" Loophole, 145
Boyse, C., 144
Braboy Jackson, P., 226, 227, 229
Bradbury, T. N., 292, 575
Brady, S. S., 320
Bramlett, M. D., 466, 521
Brantley, A., 336
Brantley, J. N., 58
Braver, S., 497, 498
Bray, J. H., 521
Breaking up, 243–245
  distress/protest reactions, 244
Breakup costs, 212
Breakup risk, 212
Brem, S. S., 194
Brewster, M. E., 282
Bridge years, 171
Brindis, C. D., 123
Broadwell, L., 502
Brody, E., 304, 589
Brody, G., 394
Broman, C. L., 398
Bronfenbrenner, U., 26, 29
Brooks, R., 163
Brooks-Gunn, J., 397
Brossart, F., 174
Brott, A. A., 498
Brown, E., 250, 470
Brown, S. L., 250, 412, 414, 470, 473, 474
Brown, T. N., 412, 414, 473, 474
Browning, D., 270, 271, 273
Brumley, K. M., 429
Brummen, H. J., 367
Brunning, L., 209
Buckley, T. R., 126
Buehlman, K. T., 362
Buhrmester, D., 161
Bulanda, J. R., 473, 474
Bullough, B., 332
Bullough, V. L., 332
Bumpass, L., 248, 466
Burleson, B. R., 165
Burney, M. A., 175
Burr, W. R., 292, 293
Burton, L., 410
Bushatz, A., 430
Buss, D., 334
Buss, D. M., 219
Bussey, K., 121, 126, 134, 136, 137, 141
Buunk, A. P., 363
Buunk, B. P., 242
Byers, E. S., 327, 328, 329